Junos Security

Junos Security

Rob Cameron, Brad Woodberg, Patricio Giecco, Tim Eberhard, and James Quinn

O'REILLY®

Beijing • Cambridge • Farnham • Köln • Sebastopol • Taipei • Tokyo

Junos Security
by Rob Cameron, Brad Woodberg, Patricio Giecco, Tim Eberhard, and James Quinn

Printed in the United States of America.

Published by O'Reilly Media, Inc., 1005 Gravenstein Highway North, Sebastopol, CA 95472.

O'Reilly books may be purchased for educational, business, or sales promotional use. Online editions are also available for most titles (*http://my.safaribooksonline.com*). For more information, contact our corporate/institutional sales department: (800) 998-9938 or *corporate@oreilly.com*.

Editor: Mike Loukides
Development Editor: Patrick Ames
Production Editor: Teresa Elsey
Copyeditor: Audrey Doyle
Production Services: Newgen North America, Inc.
Indexer: John Bickelhaupt
Cover Designer: Karen Montgomery
Interior Designer: David Futato
Illustrator: Robert Romano

Printing History:
August 2010: First Edition.

ISBN: 978-1-449-38171-4

[M]

1281709621

Table of Contents

Foreword

In early 2004, when I was the product manager for Firewall VPN systems at NetScreen Technologies, I remember saying to a coworker, "Juniper Networks should acquire us. It just makes sense. They could take advantage of our security expertise, and we could get access to their great routing technologies. And they've got some great chassis technology that we could take advantage of in our next-generation security systems ... It would be a real win-win."

Little did I realize that discussions of the pending acquisition were already well underway. Within months, the acquisition of NetScreen Technologies by Juniper Networks was completed, and the combined teams were forging ahead on a plan to build a *next-generation* security system worthy of the pedigree of the two companies: NetScreen's award-winning, high-performance security systems and Juniper Networks' market-leading, high-performance carrier-class routers.

But in order to combine these technologies in an optimal manner, it was crucial to understand the environments into which these systems would be deployed. And we did exactly that. We went into the field and worked, and listened, and polled and tested, until we felt confident in our ability to deliver high levels of security, massive performance and scale, rock-solid high availability, and the robustness of the best carrier-class routing systems. The result of these efforts was the *Juniper Networks SRX Series Services Gateways*.

Having worked with hundreds of network designers, administrators, and operators over the intervening years, it's become apparent to me that no two networks are the same. There's truth to the saying, "Networks are like snowflakes; every one is different." Even comparing the network requirements and deployments of two similar companies (such as mid-sized manufacturing companies) consistently illustrates to me how differently various equipment and technologies can be deployed. So when I'm out in the field, the ever-present question remains: how do you build a successful, secure, high-performance network without following some vendor's cookie-cutter methodology? And my unswerving answer over the many years has never changed: by understanding the requirements of the network—capacity, performance, traffic types, and interconnects—and by understanding the equipment to be deployed, even if that takes some level of testing and qualification. In other words, you have to work at understanding what you really need, and what fits, and I think this book will help you to do that.

You also really need to follow best practices to ensure that the network deployment is successful. Any scale of network design and implementation is *not* an easy task, but to understand what is required and what equipment and technologies are available to satisfy those requirements, a methodical, carefully managed design process must be followed to ensure complete success. It's worth the time invested because following established best practices will secure your network. That's why in this book, from basic introduction, to policy management, to NAT, IPS, and much more, the authors strive to explain not only how these products work, but also how to get the most from them in various network deployments using best practices.

Junos Security discusses and clarifies the practical side of planning, configuring, deploying, and managing these advanced state-of-the-art Junos® security systems in real, actual networks. The authors have drawn upon their many man-years of experience deploying thousands of security systems in networks around the world, in industries as diverse as financial services and manufacturing, to the largest wireless carrier networks in the world. It's been a time-intensive, hard-fought battle to document what they know, and what they do, but having worked alongside them, and having read what they have written, I can tell you that you are in for a delightful surprise. This book rocks.

—Glen Gibson
Product Line Manager, High Performance Security Systems, Juniper Networks
July 2010

Preface

Juniper Networks built the SRX Series as an answer to the network and security challenges of today that would be ready to scale and adapt to the inevitably larger and more complex demands of tomorrow. Security remains a huge and still growing challenge for any organization grappling with modern communication networks. Whether it is the explosion in traffic (good *and* bad), the growing complexity of data centers and cloud computing, or the menacing evolution of threats to that infrastructure, the days of the simple firewall are over. Something radically new was needed, and the SRX is leading the charge into a more secure future.

Junos Security is your guide to this brighter future. It readily answers the questions you have, will have, or may even hope to have. The SRX is one awesome beast that is up to matching your challenges whether they are firewalling, routing, NAT, deep inspection, encryption, or the mitigation of nearly any form of network attack.

How do you write about such a thing? Once upon a time, there were firewall books, or routing books, or even data center deployment books. But today, this one book is here to illuminate the elaborate hybrid workings of this next-gen networking marvel. Add to that the fact that the SRX platform has multiple models across two quite distinct device classes covering everything from the smallest networks in the world to the very largest, along with the huge and legendary heritage of the Junos operating system, and you have more than enough material to fill many volumes of books.

Writing a book of this magnitude was no easy task to undertake. In fact, it took five of the best SRX engineers in the world to accomplish it, collaborating for almost a year. Together they have many times more man-years of experience working with the SRX than the device has even existed, so they bring a real-world approach in this book that you can take away to your own work immediately.

Ultimately, this book is about Junos and the SRX, and how to deploy, configure, and maintain your Juniper Networks investment with the goal of protecting and efficiently operating your network. Enjoy!

This Book's Assumptions About You

We, the authors, are assuming a certain level of knowledge from you, the reader. Sorry, but if you are not familiar with any of the following assumptions, this book will occasionally veer over your head. Please read this carefully.

First, Chapter 1's overview of the SRX platform has no assumptions; it's meant for all audiences and includes basic information that you can read right now. From Chapter 1 onward, the book will assume that you followed the documentation, got the SRX out of its shipping box or pallet, installed it in its rack or location, and made the necessary network and power connections. This book also assumes that you know how to operate networking equipment using a command-line interface (CLI).

Chapters 2 and 3 will help familiarize you with the Junos operating system. If you are migrating from an IOS-driven firewall, or from the former ScreenOS product line, these chapters are probably critical review, because all of the other chapters assume that you can follow the Junos CLI examples and tutorials at an intermediate level of expertise.

The Junos documentation suite is a great place to start if you need help with Junos. It's thorough, well written, and free (*http://www.juniper.net/techpubs*). There are also booklets available at Juniper, the *Day One* series, that are brief, to the point, and meant to get you up and running in one day (*http://www.juniper.net/dayone*), and they cover a variety of topics, including the SRX, the Junos CLI, and more.

We are also assuming you are familiar with and have a general working knowledge of:

OSI model and networking concepts
: This includes Layers 1 through 7, switching, routing, applications, the client-to-server model, and so on.

Firewall and security concepts
: A high-level understanding of firewall and security concepts is helpful. We will go into detail about best practices and how these can be implemented on the SRX.

Routing
: This includes basic knowledge of routing protocols and dynamic routing principles.

Point-to-point links
: These network segments are often thought of as WAN links in that they do not contain any end users. Often these links are used to connect routers together in disparate geographical areas. Possible encapsulations used on these links include ATM, Frame Relay, PPP, and HDLC.

IP addressing and subnetting
: Hosts using IP to communicate with each other use 32-bit addresses. Humans often use a dotted decimal format to represent this address. This address notation includes a network portion and a host portion which is normally displayed as 192.168.1.1/24.

TCP and UDP
: These Layer 4 protocols define methods for communicating between hosts. TCP provides for connection-oriented communications while UDP uses a connectionless paradigm. Other benefits of using TCP include flow control, windowing/buffering, and explicit acknowledgments.

ICMP
: This protocol is used by network engineers to troubleshoot and operate networks as it is the core protocol used by the ping and traceroute (on some platforms) programs. In addition, ICMP is used to signal error and other messages between hosts in an IP-based network.

What's In This Book?

This book was written to be the definitive and most complete source of information for working with the SRX platforms. It is divided into 13 chapters. Each chapter is written by one of the authors from our authoring pool of five. While we tried to review each other's work, you'll be able to tell different voices in the writing styles, and we hope that this is generally refreshing rather than a hindrance.

Here is a detailed accounting of what's in this book:

Chapter 1, *Introduction to the SRX*
: The SRX is Juniper Networks' next-generation services platform. The devices combine the advanced Junos operating system with the existing security offerings on a high-speed feature-rich platform. This chapter is designed to give you an understanding of the physical devices as well as their architecture. Then it walks you through common deployment scenarios and use cases. The enriching explanation provides a clear vision into the platforms and strategies that are available when using the SRX platforms.

Chapter 2, *What Makes Junos So Special?*
: Junos is one of the industry's most well-respected network operating systems. Over its 10-plus-year history, Junos has grown into a feature-rich platform. Because Junos and its capabilities are so large, it's important to build a strong base of knowledge of what Junos is all about. In this chapter, the design of the Junos operating system, its fundamental concepts, and its history are discussed. Also, for readers who are coming from other platforms, a comparison between other major firewall platforms is drawn to Junos on the SRX.

Chapter 3, *Hands-On Junos*
: Using Junos requires the use of hands on a keyboard. This chapter gets you hands-on with Junos. The CLI is the premier management tool for the SRX, and it's best to learn the fundamentals of how it works. The goal of this chapter is to provide you with a basic understanding of how to get around the CLI. It covers the use of

operational mode, configuration mode, and some of the more advanced options of the system.

Chapter 4, *Security Policy*
: This chapter provides an in-depth overview of the security policies on the SRX platform, and how they are handled in the flow process. It details how to configure interfaces, zones, address books, and applications, and how those items tie into security policies. It also covers customizing security policies to fit your network, some best practices and gotchas to watch out for, and how to tie in policy schedulers as well as inline authentication to improve the overall security model of the network.

Chapter 5, *Network Address Translation*
: This chapter covers the Network Address Translation (NAT) features of the SRX. It dives into hands-on configuration of source, destination, and static NAT, illustrates operational troubleshooting, and vividly draws out real-world examples of organizations grappling with IPv4 address exhaustion, network integration, and distributing services load in the data center.

Chapter 6, *IPsec VPN*
: Securing remote networks and hosts is a core tenet of contemporary networking. IPsec VPNs enable this secure communication to happen and are a core functionality of the SRX platform. This chapter covers the ins and outs of IPsec VPNs—from a fundamental perspective for newcomers, all the way through configuration, diagnostics, and troubleshooting so that all network administrators will have the tools they need to manage a VPN implementation on the SRX platform.

Chapter 7, *High-Performance Attack Mitigation*
: Threats of denial-of-service (DoS) and distributed denial-of-service (DDoS) attacks on everyday networks are increasing, so it's critical to protect both the network and the network's users from these attacks. This chapter covers Juniper's built-in features, such as screens, firewall filters, and self-protection mechanisms, to protect the network and the SRX from attacks. Included are best-practice tips to harden and lock down the SRX.

Chapter 8, *Intrusion Prevention*
: Intrusion Detection and Prevention (IDP) is one of the most powerful tools in a network administrator's arsenal to protect the network infrastructure at large against both client-to-server and server-to-client attacks. The SRX consolidates the power of the Intrusion Prevention System (IPS) and stateful firewalls/VPNs into a single platform. This chapter not only explains how to configure the SRX to leverage the IPS services, but also goes in-depth into IPS concepts, deployment strategies, and how to customize your IPS deployment to suit your organization's needs.

Chapter 9, *Unified Threat Management*
: At the top of the protocol stack, application layer traffic imposes some challenges on network devices trying to inspect it. The UTM feature set supported on branch

SRX Series devices was designed to overcome some of these challenges, allowing administrators to protect the network against malicious content by using a variety of inspection techniques. This chapter explains how to configure and monitor the different application layer inspection features available on the SRX platforms.

Chapter 10, *High Availability*
: Failure is not an option in today's real-time always-on expectation of information accessibility. Networks and the services they provide must always be available. This chapter explains all of the capabilities for high availability (HA) on the SRX. It walks you through the capabilities of the HA infrastructure and some sample design topologies. Then it takes you through setting up a cluster and all of its configuration options. By the end of the chapter, you will be well versed in the SRX and how to utilize HA within your network.

Chapter 11, *Routing*
: This chapter covers the gamut of Junos IP routing technology for the SRX in an extraordinarily concise space. It digs into real-world configuration, troubleshooting, and case study deployment examples. It explores the building blocks of static and dynamic IP routing integration and then walks you through the process of connecting the SRX to the global Internet, before going a step beyond the usual and covering the more advanced virtualization and traffic engineering topics of routing instances and filter-based forwarding.

Chapter 12, *Transparent Mode*
: Transparent mode is an extremely powerful mechanism to ease the deployment of firewalls and IPS into networks by relieving the burdens of network re-architectures or dealing with complex routing environments. This chapter goes in-depth to cover all of the concepts, deployment best practices, and configuration of transparent mode so that your deployment goes smoothly and successfully.

Chapter 13, *SRX Management*
: Managing modern networks, from small to large, requires not only an understanding of how the network works, but also an understanding of the management protocols used to communicate to the devices. This chapter introduces the different protocols and mechanisms that are central to the management and automation of SRX devices.

Juniper Networks Technical Certification Program (JNTCP)

This book doubles as a study guide for the JNTCP security certification tracks. Use it to prepare and study for the security certification exams. For the most current information on Juniper Networks' security certification tracks, visit the JNTCP website at *http://www.juniper.net/certification*.

Topology for This Book

Figure P-1 displays the topology for *Junos Security* that appears beginning in Chapter 3.

The topology for this book was designed to blend the deployment scenarios of four of the most common types of networks: branch deployment, enterprise data center, campus backbone, and service provider. This architecture enables us to examine how each deployment challenge can be met with the different SRX platforms, and how all of the features of the SRX platform can be leveraged to accomplish this goal. The network consists of both branch devices and the data center SRX platforms to accomplish the goals of the network administrator.

Conventions Used in This Book

The following typographical conventions are used in this book:

Italic
: Indicates new terms, URLs, email addresses, filenames, file extensions, pathnames, directories, and Unix utilities

`Constant width`
: Indicates commands, options, switches, variables, attributes, keys, functions, types, classes, namespaces, methods, modules, properties, parameters, values, objects, events, event handlers, XML tags, HTML tags, macros, the contents of files, or the output from commands

`Constant width bold`
: Shows commands or other text that should be typed literally by the user

`Constant width italic`
: Shows text that should be replaced with user-supplied values

This icon signifies a tip, suggestion, or general note.

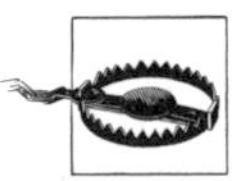

This icon indicates a warning or caution.

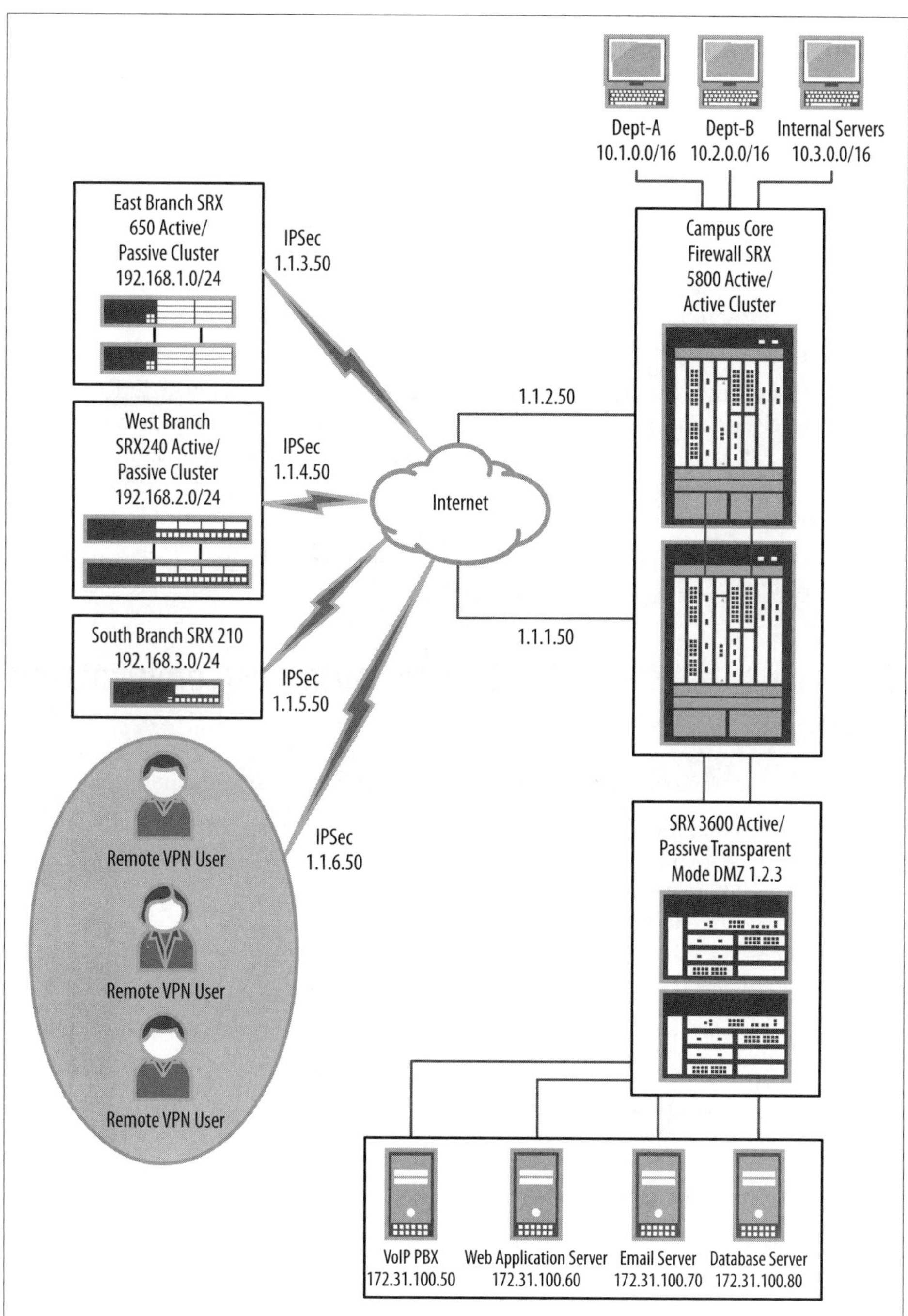

Figure P-1. This book's topology

Using Code Examples

This book is here to help you get your job done. In general, you may use the code in this book in your own configuration and documentation. You do not need to contact us for permission unless you're reproducing a significant portion of the material. For example, deploying a network based on actual configurations from this book does not require permission. Selling or distributing a CD-ROM of examples from this book does require permission. Answering a question by citing this book and quoting example code does not require permission. Incorporating a significant amount of sample configurations or operational output from this book into your product's documentation does require permission.

We appreciate, but do not require, attribution. An attribution usually includes the title, author, publisher, and ISBN. For example: "*Junos Security*, by Rob Cameron, Brad Woodberg, Patricio Giecco, Tim Eberhard, and James Quinn. Copyright 2010, Rob Cameron, Brad Woodberg, Patricio Giecco, Tim Eberhard, and James Quinn, 978-1-449-38171-4."

If you feel your use of code examples falls outside fair use or the permission given here, feel free to contact us at *permissions@oreilly.com*.

We'd Like to Hear from You/How to Contact Us/Comments and Questions

Please address comments and questions concerning this book to the publisher:

O'Reilly Media, Inc.
1005 Gravenstein Highway North
Sebastopol, CA 95472
(800) 998-9938 (in the United States or Canada)
(707) 829-0515 (international or local)
(707) 829-0104 (fax)

We have a web page for this book, where we list errata, examples, and any additional information. You can access this page at:

http://oreilly.com/catalog/9781449381714

or:

http://cubednetworks.com

To comment or ask technical questions about this book, send email to:

bookquestions@oreilly.com

For more information about our books, conferences, Resource Centers, and the O'Reilly Network, see our website at:

http://www.oreilly.com

Safari® Books Online

Safari Books Online

Safari Books Online is an on-demand digital library that lets you easily search more than 7,500 technology and creative reference books and videos to find the answers you need quickly.

With a subscription, you can read any page and watch any video from our library online. Read books on your cell phone and mobile devices. Access new titles before they are available for print, and get exclusive access to manuscripts in development and post feedback for the authors. Copy and paste code samples, organize your favorites, download chapters, bookmark key sections, create notes, print out pages, and benefit from tons of other time-saving features.

O'Reilly Media has uploaded this book to the Safari Books Online service. To have full digital access to this book and others on similar topics from O'Reilly and other publishers, sign up for free at *http://my.safaribooksonline.com*.

About the Tech Reviewers

Barny Sanchez (JNCIE FW/VPN #1, JNCIS-SSL, JNCIS-ER, JNCIS-M, JNCIS-SEC, JNCIA-IDP, JNCIA-AC, JNCIA-EX, JNCIA-WX, JNCIA-DX, JCNA, JNCI) holds a bachelor's degree in information systems security from Westwood College, completed advanced studies in electronics engineering at the Instituto Tecnologico de Costa Rica, and is currently pursuing a master's degree in information assurance and security at Capella University. He is a consulting engineer at Juniper Networks, specializing in security products and solutions. Prior to this role, he worked as a senior systems engineer supporting Juniper Networks' strategic partners, and before that, he spent more than two years as a senior instructor, teaching most of Juniper's products. Before joining Juniper, he held management positions at different technical support organizations for Intel Corporation and Cisco Systems, as well as spent several years designing and implementing multivendor networks for customers around the globe.

Vairavan Subramanian holds a bachelor's degree in computer engineering from the University of Madras and a master's degree in electrical and computer engineering from Carnegie Mellon University. He is currently a technical marketing engineer at Juniper Networks. Prior to this role, he spent four years in the design and development of the SRX Series of products. His interests lie in network infrastructure and security.

Acknowledgments

We five authors generally agreed on few things, except for the many people who came together to help us create this book. We acknowledge most of our peers, our editors, and our advisors over the many, many months it took to write this book. After what must be hundreds of emails, conference calls, lunches, dinners, and late-night writing sessions, we gratefully acknowledge our coworkers who picked up our slack, our editors who picked up words and made them into intelligible sentences, and our families who picked up our spirits and told us to go get it done.

First, we must thank Patrick Ames, Juniper Networks' editor-in-chief for its technical book program. He taught us many things, and like a coach, he pestered us until we resigned ourselves to finish the book. Our copy editor at O'Reilly, Audrey Doyle, was the second person to read this whole book and she made it easier for all subsequent readers to understand the chapters. Thank you, Audrey! To our technical reviewers, Barny Sanchez and Vairavan Subramanian, thank you for your volunteer efforts and many to-the-point comments and suggestions. The others at O'Reilly, Mike Loukides, Marlowe Shaeffer, Robert Romano, Sumita Mukherji, Teresa Elsey, and countless others, helped to create a book that really reflects on the next-generation technology of the SRX. Thank you all.

We would also like to thank Juniper Networks, the employer of four of the five authors, which has been solidly behind this writing project and supplied many of the resources, not to mention expertise, that have made the book such a success; Glen Gibson, not only for volunteering to write the wonderful Foreword introducing the SRX, but also for his years of cheerful persistence and good humor in persuading Juniper and the world that it needed a big honking firewall; and all of Juniper's brilliant development teams for creating the fantastic and wicked fast gear that we are so proud to be presenting to the world in this book.

From Rob Cameron

I am extremely appreciative of all of those people who have supported my efforts through the creation of this tome of knowledge. First and foremost, I would like to thank my wife, Katie, for the many nights that she had to endure my constant banging on the keyboard to write this book. Her support, love, respect, and admiration fueled each word that I wrote and helped energize me for my next projects. I would like to also thank all of the coauthors for helping realize my dream of completing an O'Reilly book. Without their help, this would not have been possible to achieve. After reading 70-plus O'Reilly books, it's nice to finally write one.

Many people at Juniper have helped to enable me to work with such an amazing product as the SRX. To Gregory Lebovitz, Brian Lazear, Douglas Murray, and Lior Cohen: without you challenging me, I wouldn't have expanded my horizons. Lastly, I want to thank an important team of people who I worked with on a very inspirational SRX deployment. Kevin Dineen, Steve Bryk, Joe Merchak, and Geoff Peterson, you brought to me one of my greatest design challenges. It was a rewarding and fun experience to work with you.

From Tim Eberhard

I would like to thank all of the friends and family who have supported me and my workaholic ways over the years. I'd like to thank my coworkers and mentors at both Sprint and Clearwire for teaching me, and for putting up with my personality. It wasn't always easy, but it was fun, most of the time. I'd like to give a big thanks to my coauthors, editors, peers, and friends at Juniper for their support in writing this book and their assistance on the various networks that I've worked on during my career. Finally and most importantly, I have to thank my fantastic wife, Elizabeth. She is my everything. Without her support as my partner over the years, none of this would have ever been possible.

From Patricio Giecco

I would like to thank my wife, Professor Nancy Lape, who has been challenged with the difficult task of dealing with her bad-tempered husband. She, in turn, would like to thank the fantastic Branch Solutions Business Unit team at Juniper. Without them, my anger would invariably have ended up directed toward her. I would also like to thank my parents, Isabel and Alberto, and my siblings, Adrian and Paula, who, following the trend, also thank Nancy for taking me with her to the United States.

From Glen Gibson

I would like to interrupt for a moment and extend my heartfelt thanks to the hundreds of people who have worked so hard to develop and support the SRX family of products. Without them, the SRX never would have seen the light of day. It's amazing what a couple hundred of your closest friends can do when you all envision the future.

From James Quinn

I am grateful to everyone who has taken the time to share in my life. I have been extraordinarily lucky in my friends—personal, professional, and in between. You're the ones who make this life worthwhile. I'm thankful to all the folks at Juniper and O'Reilly. They are class acts and the best in our business. My coauthors, Tim, Rob, Brad, and Patricio, and our excellent editor, Patrick Ames, are gems cut from the rough. It is only because they believed in this book that it is now in your hands. Thank you all.

And last, I'd like to thank my mom, Judith Quinn, whose sudden death came just seven days after we had sat together with the last of my writing for this book. In one person, she gave me more than I could ever deserve. Her mind was vivid, awake, and engaged with the world. She found the beauty in life, and she made life beautiful. She shaped me in careful and thoughtful ways that I can only hope one day to comprehend when I have my own children. Her love was the single greatest miracle of my life.

All that is good in me is because of her.

From Brad Woodberg

I would like to personally thank all of the people in my life who have inspired, taught, and helped me get to this moment today. Above all, I would like to thank my lovely wife, Tarah, whose support and encouragement make all of my aspirations possible, and who also puts up with all of my hobbies and nerdy endeavors. Next, I would like to thank my family and friends, most notably my parents, Bonnie and Larry, whose dedication and patience in raising me far outpace any technical effort I have ever made. Finally, I would like to thank everyone at Juniper and O'Reilly for making this project not only possible, but also a success: my manager, Rob Cameron, who is a continuous source of inspiration and knowledge; Patrick Ames, whose efforts to make this project a success cannot be overstated; the whole Juniper development team, who are absolutely brilliant and whose help was invaluable; and everyone involved in this book, who worked together as a team on their own time to make this possible!

CHAPTER 1

Introduction to the SRX

Firewalls are a staple of almost every network in the world. The firewall protects nearly every network-based transaction that occurs, and even the end user understands its metaphoric name, meant to imply keeping out the bad stuff. But firewalls have had to change. Whether it's the growth of networks or the growth of network usage, they have had to move beyond the simple devices that only require protection from inbound connections. A firewall now has to transcend its own title, the one end users are so familiar with, into a whole new type of device and service. This new class of device is a *services gateway*. And it needs to provide much more than just a firewall—it needs to look deeper into the packet and use the contained data in new ways that are advantageous to the network for which it is deployed. Can you tell if an egg is good or not by just looking at its shell? And once you break it open, isn't it best to use all of its contents? *Deep inspection* from a services gateway is the new firewall of the future.

Deep inspection isn't a new concept, nor is it something that Juniper Networks invented. What Juniper did do, however, is start from the ground up to solve the technical problems of peering deeply. With the Juniper Networks SRX Series Services Gateways, Juniper built a new platform to answer today's problems while scaling the platform's features to solve the anticipated problems of tomorrow. It's a huge challenge, especially with the rapid growth of enterprise networks. How do you not only solve the needs of your network today, but also anticipate the needs for tomorrow?

Juniper spent an enormous amount of effort to create a platform that can grow over time. The scalability is built into the features, performance, and multifunction capability of the SRX Series. This chapter introduces what solutions the SRX Series can provide for your organization today, while detailing its architecture to help you anticipate and solve your problems of tomorrow.

Evolving into the SRX

The predecessors to the SRX Series products are the legacy ScreenOS products. They really raised the bar when they were introduced to the market, first by NetScreen and then by Juniper Networks. Many features might be remembered as notable, but the most important was the migration of a split firewall software and operating system (OS) model. Firewalls at the time of their introduction consisted of a base OS and then firewall software loaded on top. This was flexible for the organization, since it could choose the underlying OS it was comfortable with, but when any sort of troubleshooting occurred, it led to all sorts of finger-pointing among vendors. ScreenOS provided an appliance-based approach by combining the underling OS and the features it provided.

The integrated approach of ScreenOS transformed the market. Today, most vendors have migrated to an appliance-based firewall model, but it has been more than 10 years since the founding of NetScreen Technologies and its ScreenOS approach. So, when Juniper began to plan for a totally new approach to firewall products, it did not have to look far to see its next-generation choice for an operating system: Junos became the base for the new product line called the SRX Series.

ScreenOS to Junos

Juniper Networks' flagship operating system is Junos. The Junos operating system has been a mainstay of Juniper and it runs on the majority of its products. Junos was created in the mid-1990s as an offshoot of the FreeBSD Unix-like operating system. The goal was to provide a robust core OS that could control the underlying chassis hardware. At that time, FreeBSD was a great choice on which to base Junos, because it provided all of the important components, including storage support, a memory controller, a kernel, and a task scheduler. The BSD license also allowed anyone to modify the source code without having to return the new code. This allowed Juniper to modify the code as it saw fit.

Junos has evolved greatly from its initial days as a spin-off of BSD. It contains millions of lines of code and an extremely strong feature set. You can learn more details about Junos in Chapter 2.

The ScreenOS operating system aged gracefully over time, but it hit some important limits that prevented it from being the choice for the next-generation SRX Series products. First, ScreenOS cannot separate the running of tasks from the kernel. All processes effectively run with the same privileges. Because of this, if any part of ScreenOS were to crash or fail, the entire OS would end up crashing or failing. Second, the modular architecture of Junos allows for the addition of new services, since this was the initial intention of Junos and the history of its release train. ScreenOS could not compare.

Finally, there's a concept called *One Junos*. Junos is one system, designed to completely rethink the way the network works. Its operating system helps to reduce the amount of time and effort required to plan, deploy, and operate network infrastructure. The one release train provides stable delivery of new functionality in a time-tested cadence.

And its one modular software architecture provides highly available and scalable software that keeps up with changing needs. As you will see in this book, Junos opened up enormous possibilities and network functionality from one device.

Inherited ScreenOS features

Although the next-generation SRX Series devices were destined to use the well-developed and long-running Junos operating system, that didn't mean the familiar features of ScreenOS were going away. For example, ScreenOS introduced the concept of *zones* to the firewall world. A zone is a logical entity that interfaces are bound to, and zones are used in security policy creation, allowing the specification of an ingress and egress zone in the security policy. Creating ingress and egress zones means the specified traffic can only pass in a specific direction. It also increases the overall speed of policy lookup, and since multiple zones are always used in a firewall, it separates the overall firewall rule base into many subsets of zone groupings. We cover zones further in Chapter 4.

The virtual router (VR) is an example of another important feature developed in ScreenOS and embraced by the new generation of SRX Series products. A VR allows for the creation of multiple routing tables inside the same device, providing the administrator with the ability to segregate traffic and virtualize the firewall.

Table 1-1 elaborates on the list of popular ScreenOS features that were added to Junos for the SRX Series. Although some of the features do not have a one-to-one naming parity, the functionality of these features is generally replicated on the Junos platform.

Table 1-1. Screen OS-to-Junos major feature comparisons

Feature	ScreenOS	Junos
Zones	Yes	Yes
Virtual routers (VRs)	VRs	Yes as routing instances
Screens	Yes	Yes
Deep packet inspection	Yes	Yes as full intrusion prevention
Network Address Translation (NAT)	Yes as NAT objects	Yes as NAT policies
Unified Threat Management (UTM)	Yes	Yes
IPsec virtual private network (VPN)	Yes	Yes
Dynamic routing	Yes	Yes
High availability (HA)	NetScreen Redundancy Protocol (NSRP)	Chassis cluster

Device management

Junos has evolved since it was first deployed in service provider networks. Over the years, many lessons were learned regarding how to best use the device running the OS. These practices have been integrated into the SRX Series and are shared throughout this book, specifically in how to use the command-line interface (CLI).

For the most part, Junos users traditionally tend to utilize the CLI for managing the platform. As strange as it may sound, even very large organizations use the CLI to manage their devices. The CLI was designed to be easy to utilize and navigate through, and once you are familiar with it, even large configurations are completely manageable through a simple terminal window. Throughout this book, we will show you various ways to navigate and configure the SRX Series products using the CLI.

In Junos, the CLI extends beyond just a simple set of commands. The CLI is actually implemented as an Extensible Markup Language (XML) interface to the operating system. This XML interface is called Junoscript and is even implemented as an open standard called NETCONF. Third-party applications can integrate with Junoscript or a user may even use it on the device. Juniper Networks provides extensive training and documentation covering this feature; an example is its Day One Automation Series (see *http://www.juniper.net/dayone*).

Sometimes, getting started with such a rich platform is a daunting task, if only because thousands of commands can be used in the Junos operating system. To ease this task and get started quickly, the SRX Series of products provides a web interface called J-Web. The J-Web tool is automatically installed on the SRX Series (on some other Junos platforms it is an optional package), and it is enabled by default. The interface is intuitive and covers most of the important tasks for configuring a device. We will cover both J-Web and the CLI in more depth in Chapter 2.

For large networks with many devices, we all know mass efficiency is required. It may be feasible to use the CLI, but it's hard to beat a policy-driven management system. Juniper provides two tools to accomplish efficient management. The first tool is called Network and Security Manager (NSM). This is the legacy tool that you can use to manage networks. It was originally designed to manage ScreenOS products, and over time, it evolved to manage most of Juniper's products. However, the architecture of the product is getting old, and it's becoming difficult to implement new features. Although it is still a viable platform for management, just like the evolution of ScreenOS to Junos, a newly architected platform is available.

This new platform is called Junos Space, and it is designed from the ground up to be a modular platform that can integrate easily with a multitude of devices, and even other management systems. The goal for Junos Space is to allow for the simplified provisioning of a network.

To provide this simplified provisioning, three important things must be accomplished:

- Integrate with a heterogeneous network environment.
- Integrate with many different types of management platforms.
- Provide this within an easy-to-use web interface.

By accomplishing these tasks, Junos Space will take network management to a new level of productivity and efficiency for an organization.

At the time of this writing, Junos Space was still being finalized. Nonetheless, readers of this book will learn about the capabilities of the SRX Series using the Junos CLI from the ground up, and will be ready to apply it within Junos Space anytime they deem appropriate.

The SRX Series Platform

The SRX Series hardware platform is a next-generation departure from the previous ScreenOS platforms, built from the ground up to provide scalable services. Now, the question that begs to be answered is: what exactly is a service?

A *service* is an action or actions that are applied to the network traffic passing through the SRX Series of products. Two examples of services are stateful firewalling and intrusion prevention.

The ScreenOS products were designed primarily to provide three services: stateful firewalling, NAT, and VPN. When ScreenOS was originally designed, these were the core value propositions for a firewall in a network. In today's network, these services are still important, but they need to be provided on a larger scale since the number of Internet Protocol (IP) devices in a network has grown significantly, and each of them relies on the Internet for access to information they need in order to run. Since the SRX is going to be processing this traffic, it is critical that it provides as many services as possible on the traffic in one single pass.

Built for Services

So, the SRX provides services on the passing traffic, but it must also provide *scalable services*. This is an important concept to review. *Scale* is the ability to provide the appropriate level of processing based on the required workload, and it's a concept that is often lost when judging firewalls because you have to think about the actual processing capability of a device and how it works. Although all devices have a maximum compute capability, or the maximum level at which they can process information, it's very important to understand how a firewall processes this load. This allows the administrator to better judge how the device scales under such load.

Scaling under load is based on the services a device is attempting to provide and the scale it needs to achieve. The traditional device required to do all this is either a branch device, or the new, high-end data center firewall. A *branch firewall* needs to provide a plethora of services at a performance level typical of the available WAN speeds. These services include the traditional stateful firewall, VPN, and NAT, as well as more security-focused services such as UTM and intrusion prevention.

A *data center firewall*, on the other hand, needs to provide highly scalable performance. When a firewall is placed in the core of a data center it cannot impede the performance of the entire network. Each transaction in the data center contains a considerable amount of value to the organization, and any packet loss or delay can cause financial implications. A data center firewall requires extreme stateful firewall speeds, a high session capacity, and very fast new sessions per second.

In response to these varied requirements, Juniper Networks created two product lines: the branch SRX Series and the data center SRX Series. Each is targeted at its specific market segments and the network needs of the device in those segments.

SRX Series Common Features: Junos

No matter which SRX Series platform you use, or plan to use, each has a common core. It's the One Junos discussed earlier.

One of the most powerful aspects of the Junos operating system is that only a single source code train, or pool of source code, is used to build a release of the network software. This provides great efficiency when it comes to integrating features and providing quality assurance testing. As new products such as those in the SRX Series are created, it is easier to take previous features, such as the Junos implementation of routing, and bring them to the new platform.

The same idea is implemented across the SRX Series. Where it makes sense, common features and code are shared. There are challenges to this mantra, such as the implementation of features in what is known as the Packet Forwarding Engine (PFE). That's because this is the location that actually processes the packets and provides services on the network traffic. The PFE in each SRX Series platform typically contains different components, creating the largest barrier for feature parity across the platforms. But as stated before, the products are designed to meet the needs of the deployment, using Junos to provide commonality.

Deployment Solutions

Networking products are created to solve problems and increase efficiencies. Before diving into the products that comprise the SRX Series, let's look at some of the problems these products solve in the two central locations in which they are deployed:

- The *branch SRX Series products* are designed for small to large office locations consisting of anywhere from a few individuals to hundreds of employees, representing either a small, single device requirement or a reasonably sized infrastructure. In these locations, the firewall is typically deployed at the edge of the network, separating the users from the Internet.
- The *data center SRX Series products* are Juniper's flagship high-end firewalls. These products are targeted at the data center and the service provider. They are designed

to provide services to scale. Data center and service provider deployments are as differentiated as branch locations.

Let's look at examples of various deployments and what type of services the SRX Series products provide. We will look at the small branch first, then larger branches, data centers, service providers, and mobile carriers, and finally all the way up (literally) to cloud networks.

Small Branch

A small branch location is defined as a network with no more than a dozen hosts. Typically, a small branch has a few servers or, most often, connects to a larger office. The requirements for a firewall device are to provide not only connectivity to an Internet source, or larger office connection, but also connectivity to all of the devices in the office. The branch firewall also needs to provide switching, and in some cases, wireless connectivity, to the network.

Figure 1-1 depicts a small branch location. Here a Juniper Networks SRX210 Services Gateway is utilized. It enables several hosts to the SRX210 and connects to an upstream device that provides Internet connectivity. In this deployment, the device consolidates a firewall, switch, and DSL router.

The small-location deployment keeps the footprint to one small device, and keeps branch management to one device—if the device were to fail, it's simple to replace and get the branch up and running using a backup of the current configuration. Finally, you should note that all of the network hosts are directly connected to the branch.

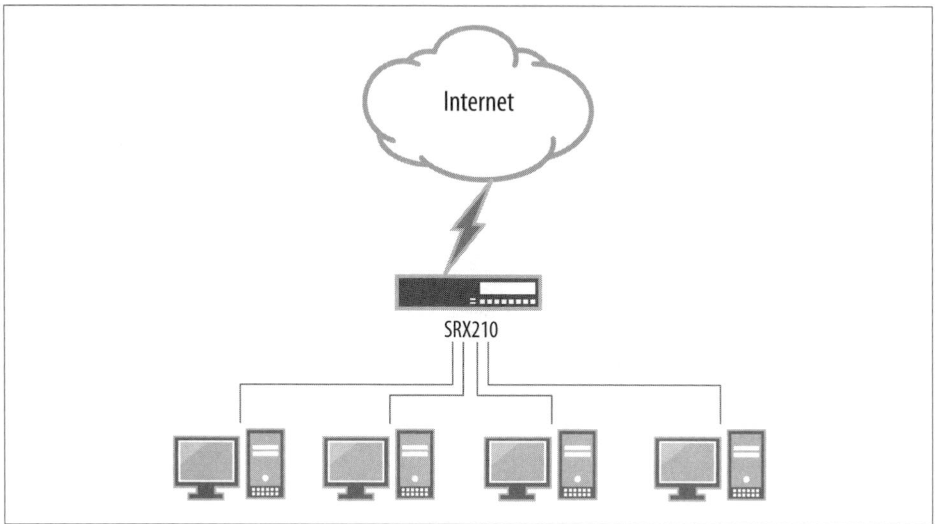

Figure 1-1. An example of a small branch network

Medium Branch

In medium to large branch offices, the network has to provide more to the location because there are 20 or more users—our network example contains about 50 client devices—so here the solution is the Juniper Networks SRX240 Services Gateway branch device. Figure 1-2 shows the deployment of the SRX240 placed at the Internet edge. It utilizes a WAN port to connect directly to the Internet service provider (ISP). For this medium branch, it contains several services and Internet-accessible services.

Note that the servers are connected directly to the SRX240 to provide maximum performance and security. Since this branch provides email and web-hosting services to the Internet, security must be provided. Not only can the SRX240 provide stateful firewalling, but it can also offer intrusion protection services (IPS) for the web and email services, including antivirus services for the email. The branch can be supported by a mix of both wired and wireless connections.

The SRX240 has sixteen 1-gigabit ports which can accommodate the four branch office servers and provide coverage for the client's two Juniper Networks AX411 Wireless LAN Access Points, adequately covering the large office area. The AX411 access points are easy to deploy since they connect directly to the Power over Ethernet (PoE) network ports on the SRX240. This leaves ten 1-gigabit Ethernet ports that can be used to accommodate any other client systems that need high-speed access to the servers.

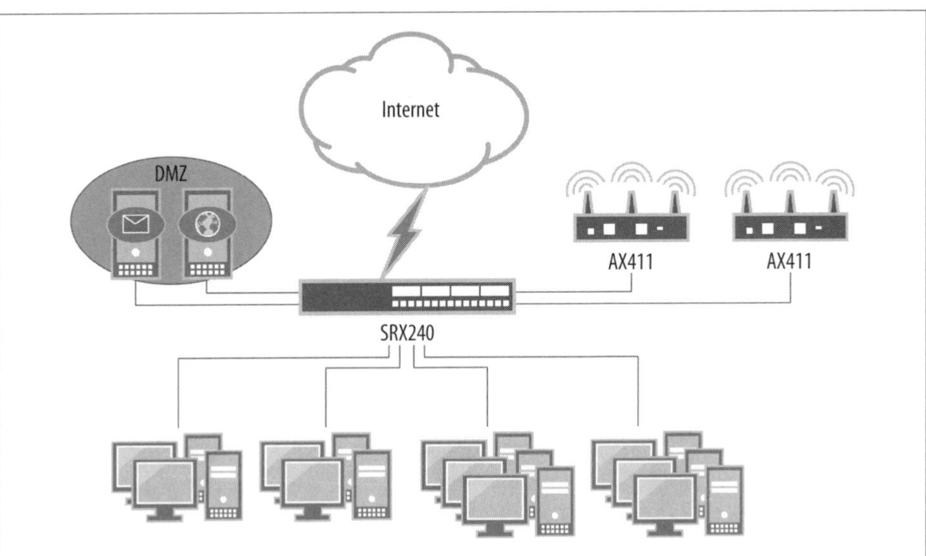

Figure 1-2. An example of a medium branch network

Large Branch

The last branch deployment to review is the large branch. For our example, the large branch has 250 clients. This network requires significantly more equipment than was used in the preceding branch examples. Note that for this network, the Juniper Networks EX Series Ethernet Switches were reutilized to provide client access to the network. Figure 1-3 depicts our large branch topology.

Our example branch network needs to provide Ethernet access for 250 clients, so to realistically depict this, six groupings of two EX4200 switches are deployed. Each switch provides 48 tri-speed Ethernet ports. To simplify management, all of the switches are connected using Juniper's virtual chassis technology.

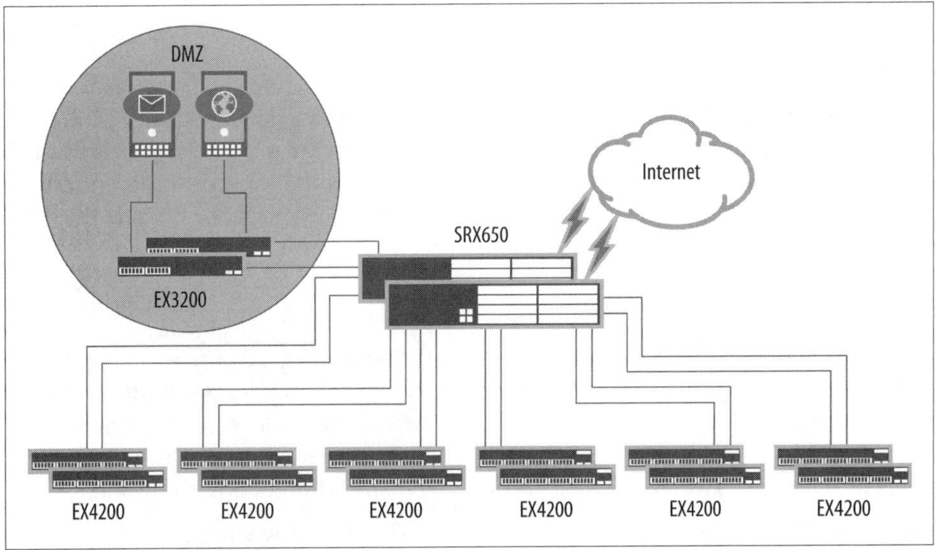

Figure 1-3. An example of a large branch network

For more details on how the EX Series switches and the virtual chassis technology operates, as well as how the EX switches can be deployed and serve various enterprise networks, see *Junos Enterprise Switching (http://oreilly.com/catalog/9780596153984/)* by Harry Reynolds and Doug Marschke (O'Reilly).

The SRX Series platform of choice for the large branch is the Juniper Networks SRX650 Services Gateway. The SRX650 is the largest of the branch SRX Series products and its performance capabilities actually exceed those of the branch, allowing for future adoption of features in the branch. Just as was done in the previous deployment, the local servers will sit off of an arm of the SRX650, but note that in this deployment, HA was utilized, so the servers must sit off of their own switch (here the Juniper Networks EX3200 switch).

The HA deployment of the SRX650 products means two devices are used, allowing the second SRX650 to take over in the event of a failure on the primary device. The SRX650 HA model provides an extreme amount of flexibility for deploying a firewall, and we detail its capabilities in Chapter 9.

Data Center

What truly is a data center has blurred in recent times. The traditional concept of a data center is a physical location that contains servers that provide services to clients. The data center does not contain client hosts (a few machines here and there to administer the servers don't count), or clear bounds of ingress and egress to the network. Ingress points may be Internet or WAN connections, but each type of ingress point requires different levels of security.

The new data center of today seems to be any network that contains services, and these networks may even span multiple physical locations. In the past, a data center and its tiers were limited to a single physical location because there were some underlying technologies that were hard to stretch. But today it's much easier to provide the same Layer 2 network across two or more physical locations, thus expanding the possibilities of creating a data center. With the popularization of MPLS and virtual private LAN service (VPLS) technologies, data centers can be built in new and creative ways.

The traditional data center design consists of a two- or three-tier switching model. Figure 1-4 shows both a two-tier and a three-tier switching design. Both are fundamentally the same, except that between the two is the addition of the aggregation switching tier. The aggregation tier compensates for the lack of port density at the core (only in the largest switched networks should a distribution tier be required).

Note that the edge tier is unchanged in both models. This is where the servers connect into the network, and the number of edge switches (and their configuration) is driven by the density of the servers. Most progressively designed data centers are using virtualization technologies which allow multiple servers to run on the same bit of hardware, reducing the overall footprint, energy consumption, and rack space.

Neither this book nor this chapter is designed to be a comprehensive primer on data centers. Design considerations for a data center are enormous and can easily comprise several volumes of text. The point here is to give a little familiarity to the next few deployment scenarios and to show how the various SRX Series platforms scale to the needs of those deployments.

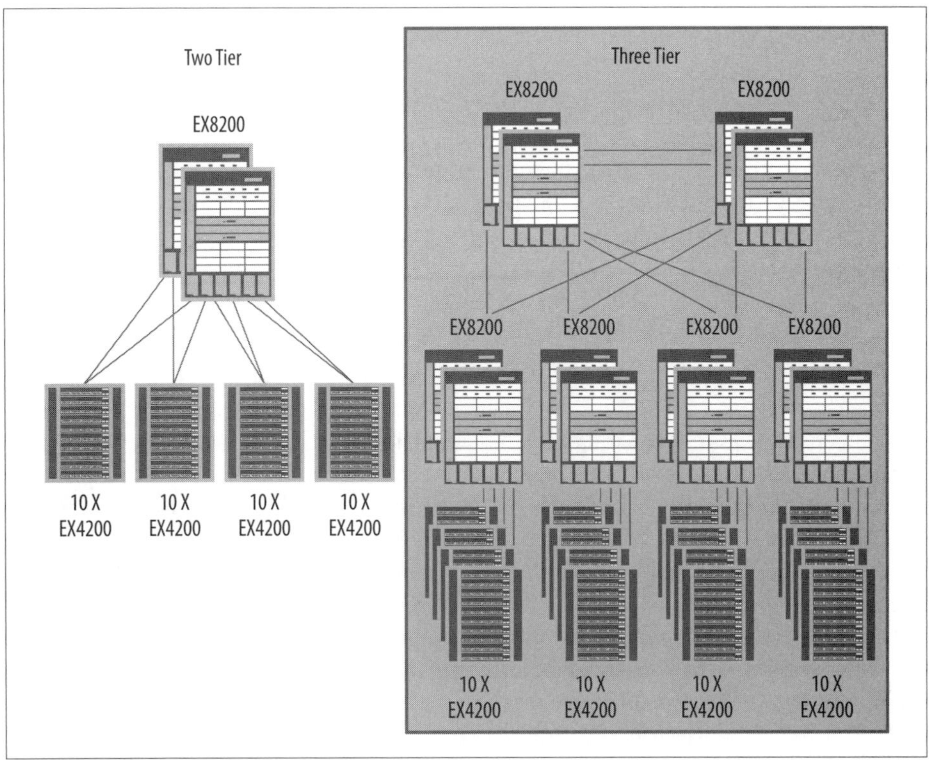

Figure 1-4. Two- and three-tier switching design

Data Center Edge

As discussed in the previous section, a data center needs to have an ingress point to allow clients to access the data center's services. The most common service is ingress Internet traffic, and as you can imagine, the ingress point is a very important area to secure. This area needs to allow access to the servers, yet in a limited and secure fashion, and because the data center services are typically high-profile, they may be the target of denial-of-service (DoS), distributed denial-of-service (DDoS), and botnet attacks. It is a fact of network life that must be taken into consideration when building a data center network.

An SRX Series product deployed at the edge of the network must handle all of these tasks, as well as handle the transactional load of the servers. Most connections into applications for a data center are quick to be created and torn down, and during the connection, only a small amount of data is sent. An example of this is accessing a web application. Many small components are actually delivered to the web browser on the client, and most of them are delivered asynchronously, so the components may not be returned in the order they were accessed. This leads to many small data exchanges or transactions, which differs greatly from the model of large continual streams of data transfer.

Figure 1-5 illustrates where the SRX Series would be deployed in our example topology. The products of choice are the Juniper Networks SRX3000 line, because they can meet the needs identified in the preceding paragraph. Figure 1-5 might look familiar to you as it is part of what we discussed regarding the data center tier in Figure 1-4. The data center is modeled after that two-tier design, with the edge being placed at the top of the diagram. The SRX3000 line of products do not have WAN interfaces, so upstream routers are used. The WAN routers consolidate the various network connections and then connect to the SRX3000 products. For connecting into the data center itself, the SRX3000 line uses its 10-gigabit Ethernet to connect to the data center core and WAN routers.

A data center relies on availability—all systems must be deployed to ensure that there is no single point of failure. This includes the SRX Series. The SRX3000 line provides a robust set of HA features. In Figure 1-5, both SRX3000 line products are deployed in what is traditionally called an *active/active* deployment. This means both firewalls can pass traffic simultaneously. When a product in the SRX3000 line operates in a cluster, the two boxes operate as though they are one unit. This simplifies HA deployment because management operations are reduced. Also, traffic can enter and exit any port on either chassis. This model is flexible compared to the traditional model of forcing traffic to only go through an active member.

Data Center Services Tier

The data center core is the network's epicenter for all server communications, and most connections in a data center flow through it. A firewall at the data center core needs to maintain many concurrent sessions. Although servers may maintain long-lived connections, they are more likely to have connectivity bursts that last a short period of time. This, coupled with the density of running systems, increases the required number of concurrent connections, but at the rate of new connections per second. If a firewall fails to create sessions quickly enough, or falls behind in allowing the creation of new sessions, transactions are lost.

For this example, the Juniper Networks SRX5800 Services Gateway is a platform that can meet these needs. The SRX5800 is the largest member of the SRX5000 line, and is well suited for the data center environment. It can meet the scaling needs of today as well as those of tomorrow. Placing a firewall inside the data center core is always challenging, and typically the overall needs of the data center dictate the placement of the firewall. However, there is a perfect location for the deployment of our SRX5800, as shown in Figure 1-6, which builds upon the example shown as part of the two-tier data center in Figure 1-4.

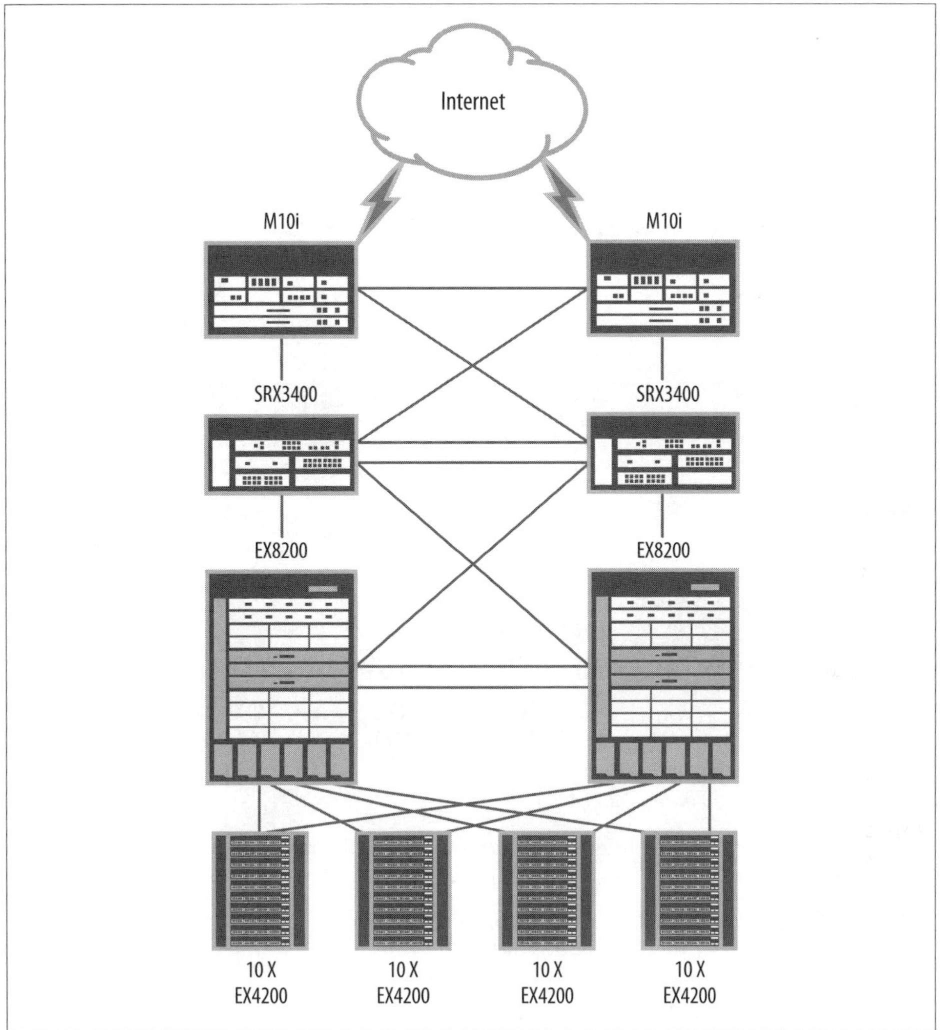

Figure 1-5. The data center edge with the SRX3000 line

This location in the data center network is called the *services tier*, and it is where services are provided to the data center servers on the network traffic. This includes services provided by the SRX5800, such as stateful firewalling, IPS, Application Denial of Service (AppDoS) prevention, and server load balancing. This allows the creation of a pool of resources that can be shared among the various servers. It is also possible to deploy multiple firewalls and distribute the load across all of them, but that increases complexity and management costs. The trend over the past five years has been to move toward consolidation for all the financial and managerial reasons you can imagine.

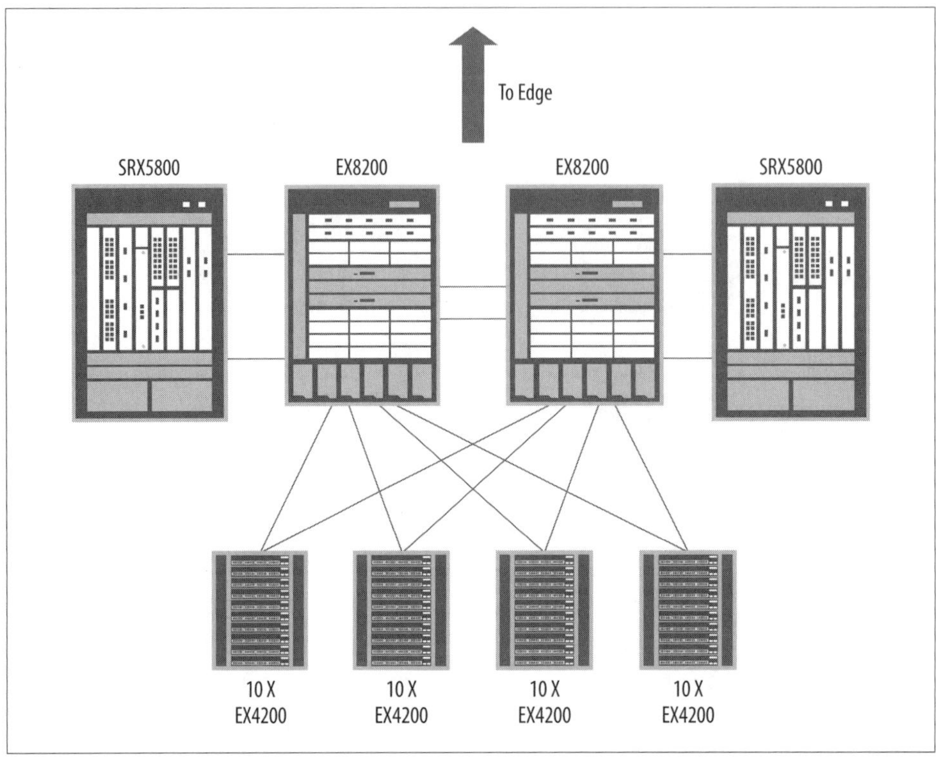

Figure 1-6. An SRX5800 in the data center core

In the data center core, AppDoS and IPS are two key services to include in the data center services tier design. The AppDoS feature allows the SRX5800 to look for attack patterns unlike other security products. AppDoS looks for DoS and DDoS patterns against a server, the application context (such as the URL), and connection rates from individual clients. By combining and triangulating the knowledge of these three items, the newer style of botnet attacks can finally be stopped.

A separate SRX Series specialty is IPS. The IPS feature differs from AppDoS as it looks for specific attacks through the streams of data. When an attack is identified, it's possible to block, log, or ignore the threat. Since all of the connections to the critical servers will pass through the SRX5800, adding the additional protection of the IPS technology provides a great deal of value, not to mention additional security for the services tier.

Service Provider

Although most administrators are more likely to use the services of a service provider than they are to run one, looking at the use case of a service provider can be quite interesting. Providing connectivity to millions of hosts in a highly available and scalable method is an extremely tough proposition. Accomplishing this task requires a Herculean effort of thousands of people. Extending a service provider network to include stateful security is just as difficult. Traditionally, a service provider processes traffic in a *stateless* manner, meaning that each packet is treated independently of any other. Although scaling stateless packet processing isn't inexpensive, or simple by any means, it does require less computing power than *stateful* processing.

In a stateful processing device, each packet is matched as part of a new or existing flow. Each packet must be processed to ensure that it is part of an existing session, or a new session must be created. All of the fields of each packet must be validated to ensure that they correctly match the values of the existing flow. For example, in TCP, this would include TCP sequencing numbers and TCP session state. Scaling a device to do this is, well, extremely challenging.

A firewall can be placed in many locations in a service provider's network. Here we'll discuss two specific examples: in the first the firewall provides a managed service, and in the second the service provider protects its own services.

Starting with the managed service provider (MSP) environment, Figure 1-7 shows a common MSP deployment. On the left, several customers are shown, and depending on the service provider environment, this may be several dozen to several thousand (for the purposes of explanation only a handful are needed). The connections from these customers are aggregated to a Layer 2 and Layer 3 routing switch, in this case a Juniper Networks MX960 3D Universal Edge Router. Then the MX Series router connects to an SRX5800. The SRX5800 is logically broken down into smaller firewalls for each customer so that each customer gains the services of a firewall while the provider consolidates all of these "devices" into a single hardware unit. The service provider can minimize its operational costs and maximize the density of customers on a single device.

Our second scenario for service providers involves protecting the services that they provide. Although a service provider provides access to other networks, such as the Internet, it also has its own hosted services. These include, but are not limited to, Domain Name System (DNS), email, and web hosting. Because these services are public, it's important for the service provider to ensure their availability, as any lack of availability can become a front-page story or at least cause a flurry of angry customers. For these services, firewalls are typically deployed, as shown in our example topology in Figure 1-8.

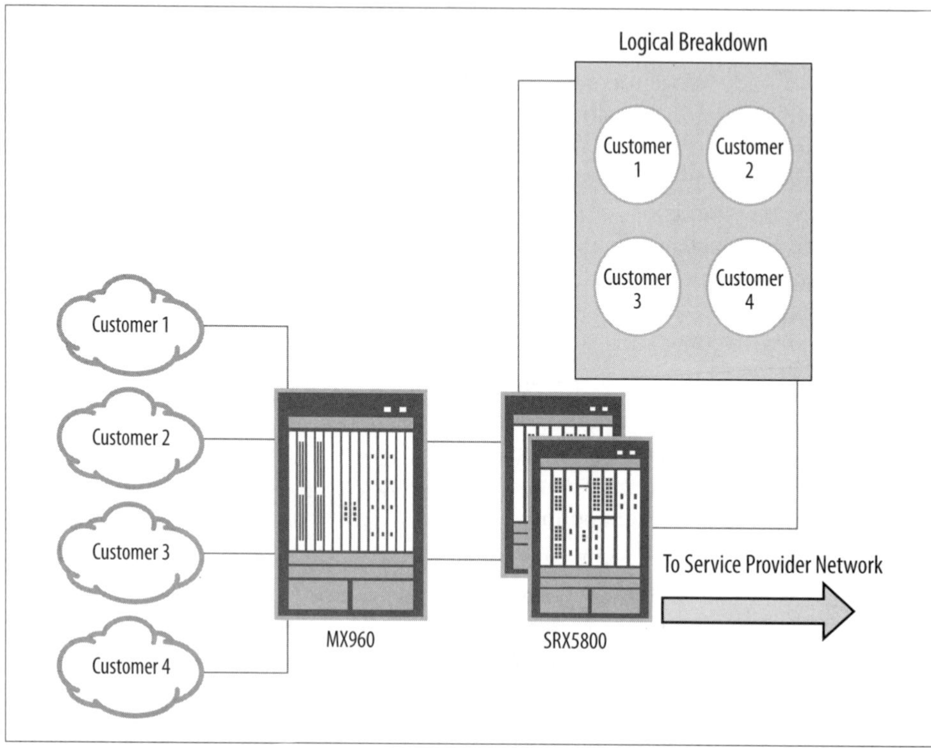

Figure 1-7. MSP SRX5800 deployment

Several attack vectors are available to service providers' public services, including DoS, DDoS, and service exploits. They are all the critical types of attacks that the provider needs to be aware of and defend. The data center SRX products can protect against both DDoS and the traditional DoS attack. In the case of a traditional DoS attack, the *screen* feature can be utilized.

A screen is a mechanism that is used to stop more simplistic attacks such as SYN and UDP floods (note that although these types of attacks are "simple" in nature, they can quickly overrun a server or even a firewall). Screens allow the administrator of an SRX Series product to set up specific thresholds for TCP and UDP sessions. Once these thresholds have been exceeded, protection mechanisms are enacted to minimize the threat of these attacks. We will discuss the screen feature in detail in Chapter 6.

Mobile Carriers

The phones of today are more than the computers of yesterday; they are fully fledged modern computers in a hand-held format, and almost all of a person's daily tasks can be performed through them. Although a small screen doesn't lend itself to managing 1,000-line spreadsheets, the devices can easily handle the job of sharing information

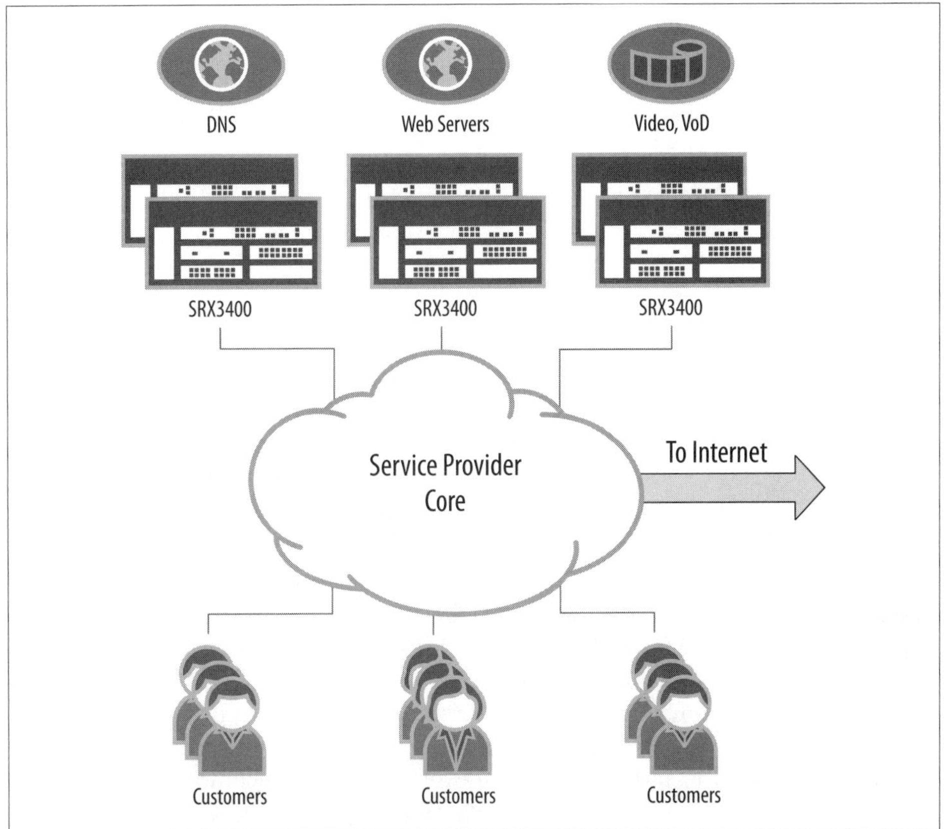

Figure 1-8. Service provider public services

through email or web browsing. More and more people who would typically not use the Internet are now accessing the Internet through these mobile devices, which means that access to the public network is advancing in staggering demographic numbers.

This explosion of usage has brought a new challenge to mobile operators: how to provide a resilient data network to every person in the world. Such a mobile network, when broken down into smaller, easy-to-manage areas, provides a perfect example of how an SRX Series firewall can be utilized to secure such a network.

For mobile carrier networks, an SRX5800 is the right choice, for a few specific reasons: its high session capacity and its high connections-per-second rate. In the network locations where this device is placed, connection rates can quickly vary from a few thousand to several hundred thousand. A quick flood of new emails or everyone scrambling to see a breaking news event can strain any well-designed network. And as mentioned in the preceding service provider example, it's difficult to provide firewall services in a carrier network.

Figure 1-9 shows a simplified example of a mobile operator network. It's simplified in order to focus more on the firewalls and less on the many layers of the wireless carrier's network. For the purposes of this discussion, the way in which IP traffic is tunneled to the firewalls isn't relevant.

In Figure 1-9, the handsets are depicted on the far left, and their radio connections, or cell connections, are terminated into the provider's network. Then, at the edge of the provider's network, when the actual data requests are terminated, the IP-based packet is ready for transport to the Internet, or to the provider's services.

An SRX5800 at the location depicted in Figure 1-9 is designed to protect the carrier's network, ensuring that its infrastructure is secure. By protecting the network, it ensures that its availability and the service that customers spend money on each month continues. If the protection of the handsets is the responsibility of the handset provider in conjunction with the carrier, the same goes for the cellular or 3G Internet services that can be utilized by consumers using cellular or 3G modems. These devices allow users to access the Internet directly from anywhere in a carrier's wireless coverage network—these computers need to employ personal firewalls for the best possible protection.

For any service provider, mobile carriers included, the provided services need to be available to the consumers. As shown in Figure 1-9, the SRX5800 devices are deployed in a highly available design. If one SRX5800 experiences a hardware failure, the second SRX5800 can completely take over for the primary. Of course, this failover is transparent to the end user for uninterrupted service and network uptime that reaches to the five, six, or even seven 9s, or 99.99999% of the time. As competitive as the mobile market is these days, the mobile carrier's networks need to be a competitive advantage.

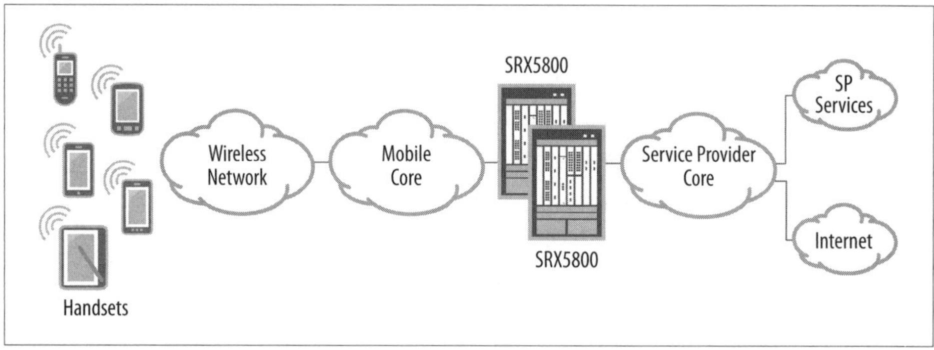

Figure 1-9. The SRX5800 in a mobile carrier network

Cloud Networks

It seems like cloud computing is on everyone's mind today. The idea of providing any service to anyone at any time to any scale with complete resilience is a dream that is becoming a reality for many organizations. Both cloud computing vendors and large enterprises are providing their own private clouds.

Although each cloud network has its own specific design needs, the SRX Series can and should play an important role.

That's because a cloud network must scale in many directions to really be a cloud. It must scale in the number of running operating systems it can provide. It must scale in the number of physical servers that can run these operating systems. And it must scale in the available number of networking ports that the network provides to the servers. The SRX Series must be able to scale to secure all of this traffic, and in some cases, it must be able to be bypassed for other services. Figure 1-10 depicts this scale in a sample cloud network that is meant to merely show the various components and how they might scale.

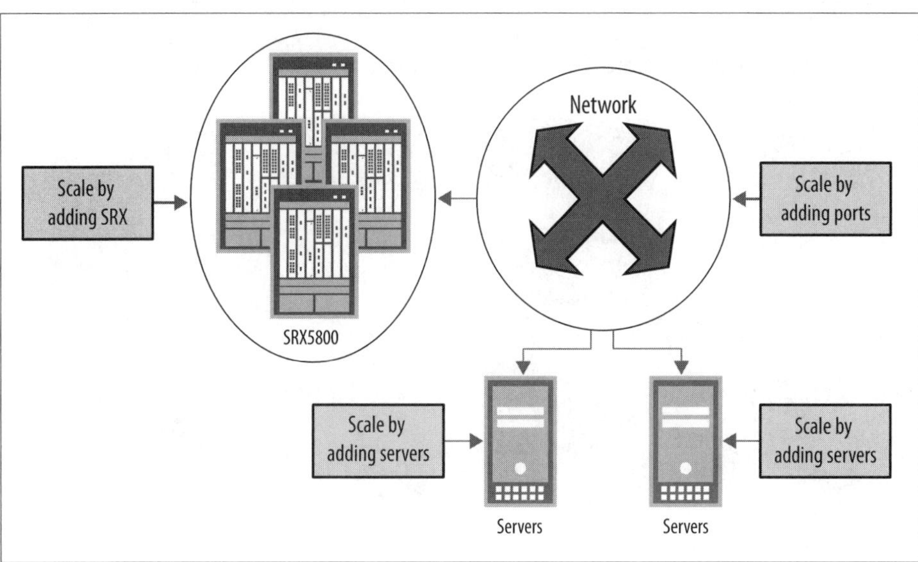

Figure 1-10. Cloud computing scaling

The logical items are easier to scale than the physical items, meaning it's easy to make 10 copies of an operating system run congruently, since they are easily instantiated, but the challenge is in ensuring that enough processing power can be provided by the servers since they are a physical entity and it takes time to get more of them installed. The same goes for the network. A network in a cloud environment will be divided into many virtual LANs (VLANs) and many routing domains. It is simple to provide more VLANs in the network, but it is hard to ensure that the network has the capacity to handle the needs of the servers. The same goes for the SRX Series firewalls.

For the SRX Series in particular, the needs of the cloud computing environment must be well planned. As we discussed in regard to service providers, the demands of a stateful device are enormous when processing large amounts of traffic. Since the SRX Series device is one of the few stateful devices in the cloud network, it needs to be deployed to scale. As Figure 1-10 shows, the SRX5800 is chosen for this environment because it can be deployed in many different configurations based on the needs of the deployment. (The scaling capabilities of the SRX5800 are discussed in detail in "SRX5000" on page 61.)

Because of the dynamic nature of cloud computing, infrastructure provisioning of services must be done seamlessly. This goes for every component in the network, including the servers, the network, and the firewalls. Juniper Networks provides several options for managing all of its devices, as shown in Figure 1-11, which illustrates the management paradigm for the devices.

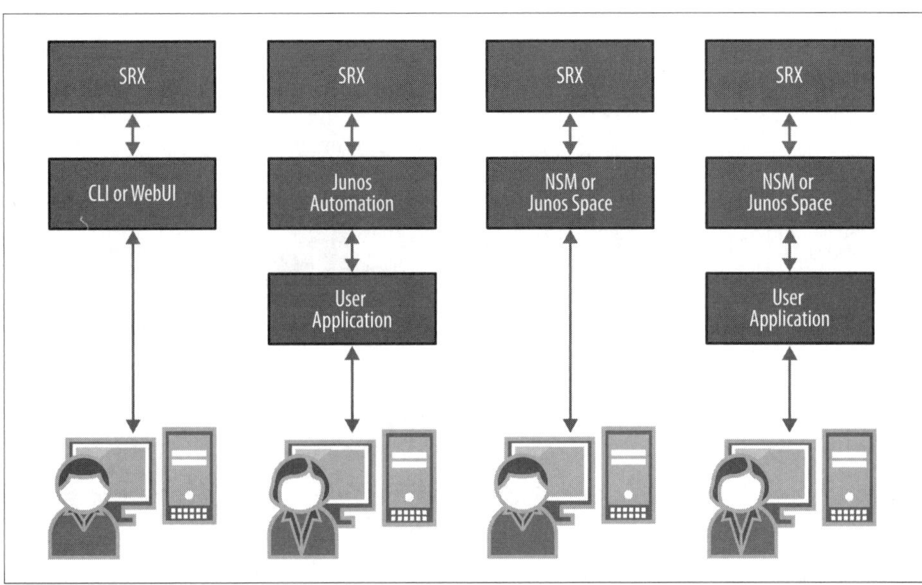

Figure 1-11. Juniper Networks management paradigm

Just as the provisioning model scales for the needs of any organization, so does the cloud computing model. On the far left, direct hands-on or user device management is shown. This is the device management done by an administrator through the CLI or web management system (J-Web). The next example is the command of the device by way of its native API (either Junos automation or NETCONF, both of which we will discuss in Chapter 2), where either a client or a script would need to act as the controller that would use the API to provision the device.

The remaining management examples are similar to the first two examples of the provisioning model, except they utilize a central management console provided by Juniper Networks. Model three shows a user interacting with the default client provided by the Juniper Networks Network and Security Manager (NSM) or Junos Space. In this case, the NSM uses the native API to talk to the devices.

Lastly, in management option six is the most layered and scalable approach. It shows a custom-written application controlling the NSM directly with its own API, and then controlling the devices with its own API.

Although this approach seems highly layered, it provides many advantages in an environment where scaling is required. First, it allows for the creation of a custom application to provide network-wide provisioning in a case where a single management product is not available to manage all of the devices on the network. Second, the native Juniper application is developed specifically around the Juniper devices, thus taking advantage of the inherent health checks and services without having to integrate them.

The Junos Enterprise Services Reference Network

To simplify the SRX Series learning process, this book consistently uses a single topology which contains a number of SRX Series devices and covers all of the scenarios, many of the tutorials, and all of the case studies in the book. A single reference network allows the reader to follow along and only have to reference one network map.

This book's reference network is primarily focused on branch topologies since the majority of readers have access to those units. For readers who are interested in or are using the data center SRX products, these are discussed as well, but the larger devices are not the focus for most of the scenarios. Where differences exist, they will be noted.

Figure 1-12 shows this book's reference network. The network consists of three branch deployments, two data center firewall deployments, and remote VPN users. Five of the topologies represent HA clusters with only a single location that specifies a non-HA deployment. The Internet is the network that provides connectivity between all of the SRX Series deployments. Although the reference network is not the perfect "real-world" network, it does provide the perfect topology to cover all of the features in the SRX Series.

Although three of the locations are called *branches*, they could also represent standalone offices without a relationship to any other location.

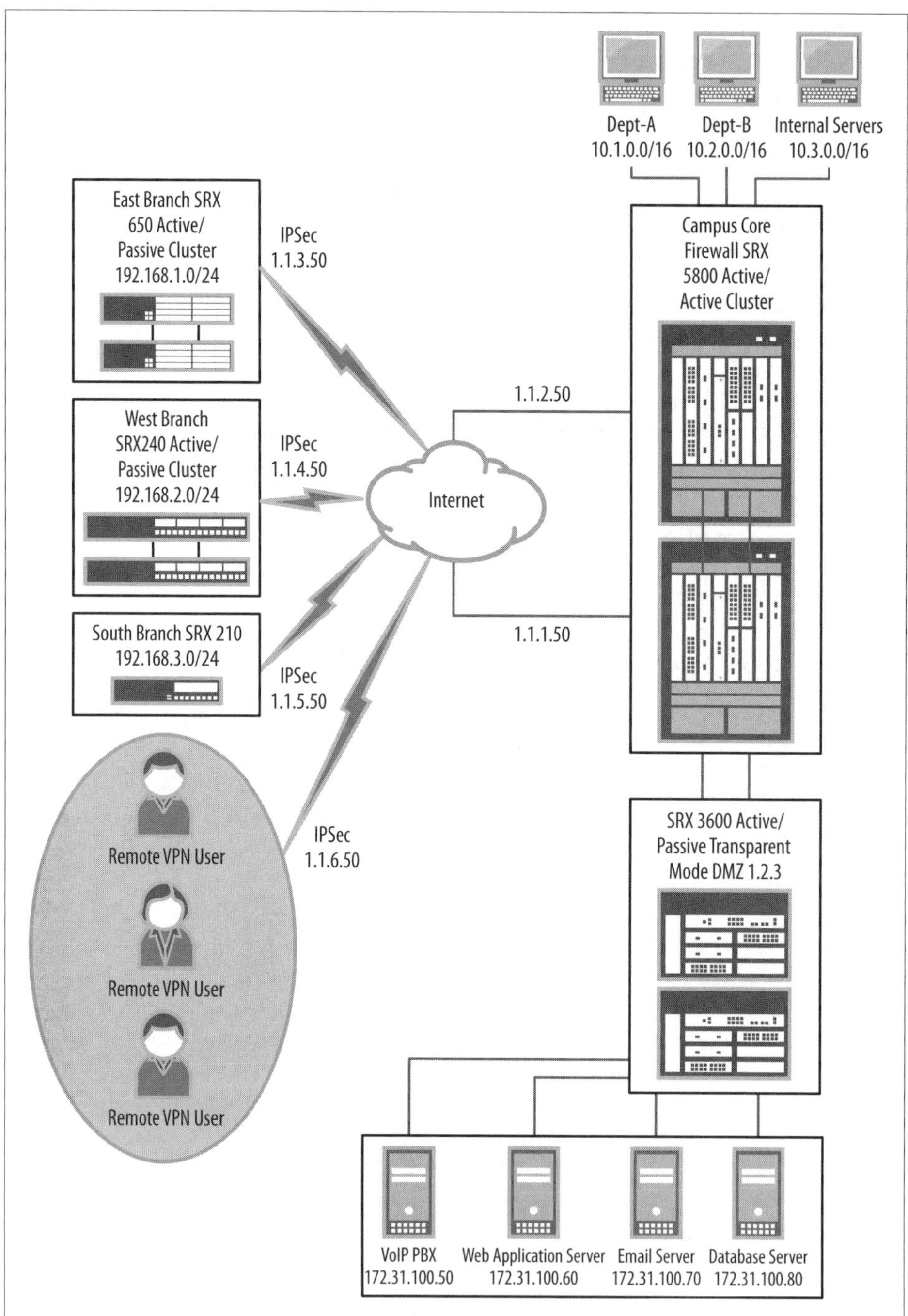

Figure 1-12. Reference network

The first location to review is the South Branch location. The South Branch location is a typical small branch, utilizing a single SRX210 device. This device is a small, low-cost appliance that can provide a wide range of features for a location with 2 to 10 users and perhaps a wireless access point, as shown in the close-up view in Figure 1-13. The remote users at this location can access both the Internet and other locations over an IPsec VPN connection. Security is provided by using a combination of stateful firewalling, IPS, and UTM. The hosts on the branch network can talk to each other over the local switch on the SRX210 or over the optional wireless AX411 access point.

The West Branch, shown in Figure 1-14, is a larger remote branch location. The West Branch location utilizes two SRX240 firewalls. These firewalls are larger in capacity than the SRX210 devices in terms of ports, throughput, and concurrent sessions. They are designed for a network with more than 10 users or where greater throughputs are needed. Because this branch has more local users, HA is required to prevent loss of productivity due to loss of access to the Internet or the corporate network.

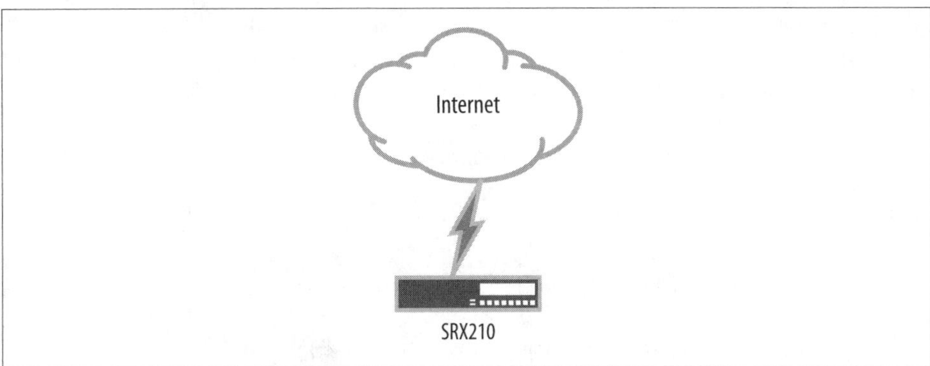

Figure 1-13. South Branch reference network

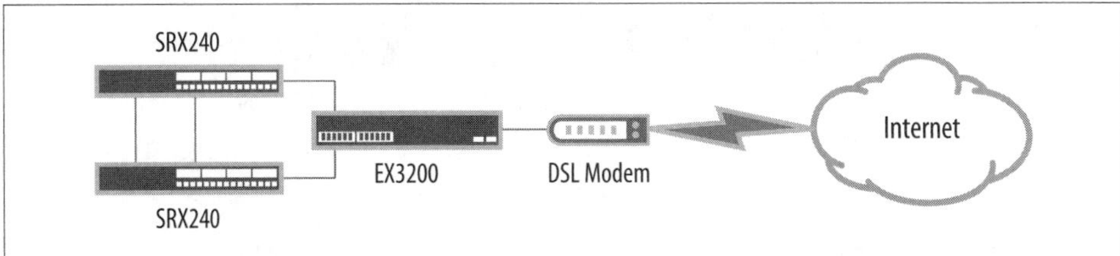

Figure 1-14. West Branch reference network

The East Branch location uses the largest branch firewall, the SRX650. This deployment represents both a large branch and a typical office environment where support for hundreds of users and several gigabits per second of throughput is needed. The detailed view of the East Branch is shown in Figure 1-15. This deployment, much like that of the West Branch, utilizes HA. Just as with the other branch SRX Series devices, the SRX650 devices can also use IPS, UTM, stateful firewalling, NAT, and many other

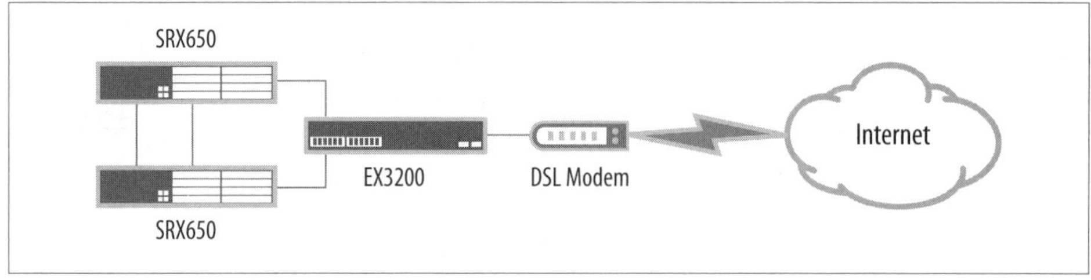

Figure 1-15. East Branch reference network

security features. The SRX650 provides the highest possible throughput for these features compared to any other *branch* product line.

Deployment of the campus core firewalls of our reference network will be our first exploration into the high-end or data center SRX Series devices. These are the largest firewalls of the Juniper Networks firewall product line (at the time of this book's publication). The deployment uses SRX5800 products, and more than 98% of the data center SRX Series firewalls sold are deployed in a highly available deployment, as represented here. These firewalls secure the largest network in the reference design, and Figure 1-16 illustrates a detailed view of the campus core.

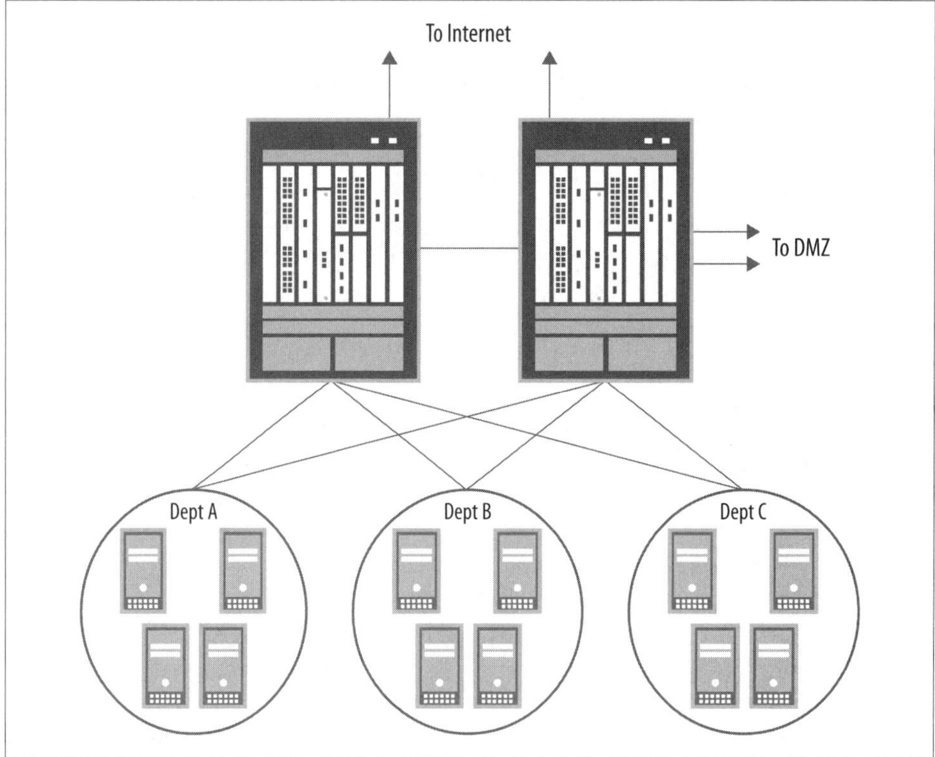

Figure 1-16. Campus core detailed view

Our campus core example network shows three networks; in a "real-world" deployment this could be hundreds or thousands of networks, but to show the fundamentals of the design and to fit on the printed page, only three are used: Department-A, Department-B, and the Internal Servers networks. These are separated by the SRX5800 HA cluster. Each network has a simple switch to allow multiple hosts to talk to each other. Off the campus core firewalls is a DMZ or demilitarized zone SRX Series firewall cluster, as shown in Figure 1-17.

The DMZ SRX Series devices' firewall deployment uses an SRX3600 firewall cluster. The SRX3600 firewalls are perfect for providing interface density with high capacity and performance. In the DMZ network, several important servers are deployed. These servers provide critical services to the network and need to be secured to ensure service continuity.

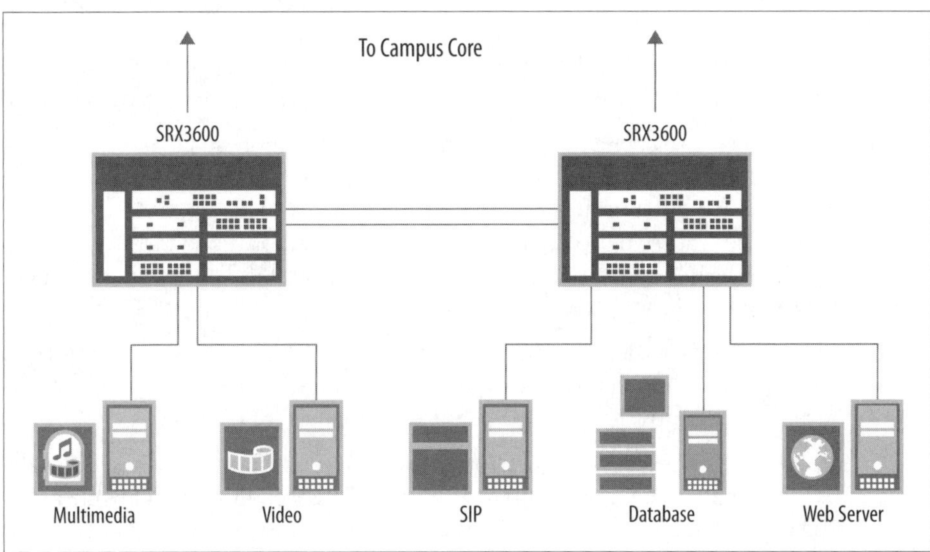

Figure 1-17. DMZ firewalls detailed view

This DMZ deployment is unique compared to the other network deployments because it is the only one that highlights *transparent mode* deployment, which allows the firewall to act as a bridge. Instead of routing packets like a Layer 3 firewall would, it routes packets to a destination host using its Media Access Control (MAC) address. This allows the firewall to act as a transparent device, hence the term.

Finally, you might note that the remote VPN users are an example use case of two different types of IPsec access to the SRX Series firewalls. The first is the dynamic VPN client, which is a dynamically downloaded client that allows client VPN access into the branch networks. The second client type highlighted is a third-party client, which is not provided by Juniper but is recommended when a customer wants to utilize a standalone software client. We will cover both use cases in Chapter 5.

The reference network contains the most common deployments for the SRX Series products, allowing you to see the full breadth of topologies within which the SRX Series is deployed. The depicted topologies show all the features of the SRX Series in ways in which actual customers use the products. The authors of this book intend for real administrators to sit down and understand how the SRX Series is used and learn how to configure it. We have seen the majority of SRX Series deployments in the world and boiled them down to our reference network.

SRX Series Product Lines

So far, this chapter has focused on SRX Series examples and concepts more than anything, and hopefully this approach has allowed you to readily identify the SRX Series products and their typical uses. For the remainder of the chapter, we will take a deep dive into the products so that you can link the specific features of each to a realistic view of its capabilities. We will begin with what is common to the entire SRX Series, and then, as before, we'll divide the product line into *branch* and *data center* categories.

Before the deep dive into each SRX Series product, we must note that each SRX Series platform has a core set of features that are shared across the other platforms. And some of the platforms have different features that are not shared. This might lead to some confusion, because feature parity is not the same across all of the platforms, but the two product lines were designed with different purposes and the underlying architectures vary between the branch and the data center.

The branch SRX Series was designed for small and wide needs, meaning that the devices offer a wide set of features that can solve a variety of problems. This does not mean performance is poor, but rather that the products provide a lot of features.

The data center SRX Series was designed for scale and speed. This means these firewalls can scale from a smaller deployment up to huge performance numbers, all while keeping performance metrics to scale linearly. So, when configuring the modular data center SRX Series device, the designer is able to easily determine how much hardware is required. Over time, product-line-specific features are likely to merge between the two platforms, as shown in Figure 1-18, which is a diagram of that merging model.

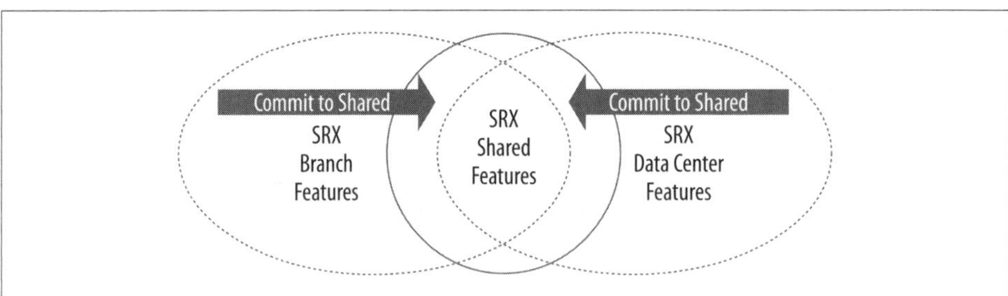

Figure 1-18. SRX Series feature merging model

Branch SRX Series

The majority of SRX Series firewalls sold and deployed are from within the branch SRX Series, designed primarily for average firewall deployment. A branch SRX Series product can be identified by its three-digit product number. The first digit represents the series and the last two digits specify the specific model number. The number is used simply to identify the product, and doesn't represent performance or the number of ports, or have any other special meaning.

When a branch product is deployed in a small office, as either a remote office location or a company's main firewall, it needs to provide many different features to secure the network and its users. This means it has to be a jack-of-all-trades, and in many cases, it is an organization's sole source of security.

Branch-Specific Features

Minimizing the number of pieces of network equipment is important in a remote or small office location, as that reduces the need to maintain several different types of equipment, their troubleshooting, and of course, their cost. One key to all of this consolidation is the network switch, and all of the branch SRX Series products provide full switching support. This includes support for spanning tree and line rate blind switching. Table 1-2 is a matrix of the possible number of supported interfaces per platform.

Table 1-2. Branch port matrix

	SRX100	SRX210	SRX240	SRX650
10/100	8	6	0	0
10/100/1000	0	2	20	52
10/100/1000 PoE	0	4	16	48

As of Junos 10.2, the data center SRX Series firewalls do not support blind switching. Although the goal is to provide this feature in the future, it is more cost-effective to utilize a Juniper Networks EX Series Ethernet Switch to provide line rate switching and then create an aggregate link back to a data center SRX Series product to provide secure routing between VLANs. In the future, Juniper may add this feature to its data center SRX Series products.

In most branch locations, SRX Series products are deployed as the only source of security. Because of this, some of the services that are typically distributed can be consolidated into the SRX, such as antivirus. Antivirus is a feature that the branch SRX Series can offer to its local network when applied to the following protocols: Simple Mail Transfer Protocol (SMTP), Post Office Protocol 3 (POP3), Internet Message Access Protocol (IMAP), Hyper Text Transfer Protocol (HTTP), and File Transfer

Protocol (FTP). The SRX Series scans for viruses silently as the data is passed through the network, allowing it to stop viruses on the protocols where viruses are most commonly found.

The data center SRX Series does not support the antivirus feature as of Junos 10.2. In organizations that deploy a data center SRX Series product, the antivirus feature set is typically decentralized for increased security as well as enabling antivirus scanning while maintaining the required performance for a data center. A bigger focus for security is utilizing IPS to secure connections into servers in a data center. This is a more common requirement than antivirus. The IPS feature is supported on both the high-end and branch SRX Series product lines.

Antispam is another UTM feature set that aids in consolidation of services on the branch SRX Series. Today it's reported that almost 95% of the email in the world is spam. And this affects productivity. In addition, although some messages are harmless, offering general-use products, others contain vulgar images, sexual overtures, or illicit offers. These messages can be offensive, a general nuisance, and a distraction.

The antispam technology included on the SRX Series can prevent such spam from being received, and it removes the need to use antispam software on another server.

Much like antivirus, the data center SRX Series does not provide antispam services. In data center locations where mail services are intended for thousands of users, a larger solution is needed, one that is distributed on mail proxies or on the mail servers.

Controlling access to what a user can or can't see on the Internet is called *universal resource locator* (URL) *filtering*. URL filtering allows the administrator to limit what categories of websites can be accessed. Sites that contain pornographic material may seem like the most logical to block, but other types of sites are common too, such as social networking sites that can be time sinks for employees. There are also a class of sites that company policy blocks or temporarily allows access to—for instance, during lunch hour. In any case, all of this is possible on the branch SRX Series products.

For the data center SRX Series product line, URL filtering is not currently integrated. In many large data centers where servers are protected, URL filtering is not needed or is delegated to other products.

Because *branch* tends to mean small locations all over the world, these branches typically require access to the local LAN for desktop maintenance or to securely access other resources. To provide a low-cost and effective solution, Juniper has introduced the *dynamic VPN client*. This IPsec client allows for dynamic access to the branch without any preinstalled software on the client station, a very helpful feature to have in the branch so that remote access is simple to set up and requires very little maintenance.

Dynamic VPN is not available on the data center SRX devices. Juniper Networks recommends the use of its SA Series SSL VPN Appliances, allowing for the scaling of tens of thousands of users while providing a rich set of features that go beyond just network access.

When the need for cost-saving consolidation is strong in certain branch scenarios, adding wireless, both cellular and WiFi, can provide interesting challenges. Part of the challenge concerns consolidating these capabilities into a device while not providing radio frequency (RF) interference; the other part concerns providing a device that can be centrally placed and still receive or send enough wireless power to provide value.

All electronic devices give off some sort of RF interference, and all electronic devices state this clearly on their packaging and/or labels. Although this may be minor interference in the big scheme of things, it can also be extremely detrimental to wireless technologies such as cellular Internet access or WiFi—therefore, extreme care is required when integrating these features into any product. Some of the branch SRX Series products have the capability to attach a cellular Internet card or USB dongle directly to them, which can make sense in some small branch locations because typically, cellular signals are fairly strong throughout most buildings.

But what if the device is placed in the basement where it's not very effective at receiving these cellular signals? Because of this and other office scenarios, Juniper Networks provides a product that can be placed anywhere and is both powered and managed by the SRX Series: the Juniper Networks CX111 Cellular Broadband Data Bridge and CX411 Cellular Broadband Data Bridge.

The same challenge carries over for WiFi. If an SRX Series product is placed in a back room or basement, an integrated WiFi access point may not be very relevant, so Juniper took the same approach and provides an external access point (AP) called the AX411 Wireless LAN Access Point. This AP is managed and powered by any of the branch SRX Series products.

As you might guess, although the wireless features are very compelling for the branch, they aren't very useful in a data center. Juniper has abstained from bringing wireless features to the data center SRX Series products, but because the two products contain the same codebase, it's easy to port the feature to the data center SRX Series if the relevance for the feature makes its case.

The first Junos products for the enterprise market were the Juniper Networks J Series Services Routers and the first iteration of the J Series was a packet-based device. This means the device acts on each packet individually without any concern for the next packet—typical of how a traditional router operates. Over time, Juniper moved the J Series products toward the capabilities of a flow-based device, and this is where the SRX Series devices evolved from.

Although a flow-based device has many merits, it's unwise to move away from being able to provide packet services, so the SRX Series can run in packet mode as well as flow. It's even possible to run both modes simultaneously! This allows the SRX Series to act as traditional packet-based routers and to run advanced services such as MPLS.

MPLS as a technology is not new—carrier networks have been using it for years. Many enterprise networks have used MPLS, but typically it has been done transparently to the enterprise. Now, with the SRX Series, the enterprise has a low-cost solution, so it can create its own MPLS network, bringing the power back to the enterprise from the service providers, and saving money on MPLS as a managed service. On the flip side, it allows the service providers to offer a low-cost service that can provide security and MPLS in a single platform.

The last feature common to the branch SRX Series products is their ability to utilize many types of WAN interfaces. We will detail these interface types as we drill down into each SRX Series platform.

The data center SRX Series products, as of Junos 10.2, only utilize Ethernet interfaces. These are the most common interfaces used in the locations where these products are deployed, and where a data center SRX Series product is deployed they are typically paired with a Juniper Networks MX Series 3D Universal Edge Router, which can provide WAN interfaces.

SRX100

The SRX100, as of Junos 10.2, is the only product in the SRX100 line (if you remember from the SRX numbering scheme, the 1 is the series number and the 00 is the product number inside that series). The SRX100 Services Gateway is shown in Figure 1-19, and it is a fixed form factor, meaning no additional modules or changes can be made to the product after it is purchased. As you can see in the figure, the SRX100 has a total of eight 10/100 Ethernet ports, and perhaps more difficult to see, but clearly onboard, are a serial console port and a USB port.

The eight Ethernet ports can be configured in many different ways. They may be configured in the traditional manner, in which each port has a single IP address, or they can be configured in any combination as an Ethernet switch. The same switching capabilities of the EX Series switches have been combined into the SRX100 so that the SRX100 not only supports line rate blind switching but also supports several variants

Figure 1-19. The SRX100

of the spanning tree protocols; therefore, if the network is expanded in the future, an errant configuration won't lead to a network loop. The SRX100 can also provide a default gateway on its local switch by using a VLAN interface, as well as a Dynamic Host Configuration Protocol (DHCP) server.

Although the SRX100 is a small, desktop-sized device, it's also a high-performing platform. It certainly stands out by providing up to 650 Mbps of throughput. This may seem like an exorbitant amount of throughput for a branch platform, but it's warranted where security is needed between two local network devices. For such a WAN connection, 650 Mbps is far more than what would be needed in a location that would use this type of device, but small offices have a way of growing.

Speaking of performance, the SRX100 supports high rates of VPN, IPS, and antivirus as well if the need to use these features arises in locations where the SRX100 is deployed. The SRX100 also supports a session ramp-up rate of 2,000 new connections per second (CPS), or the number of new TCP-based sessions that can be created per second. UDP sessions are also supported, but this new-session-per-second metric is rated with TCP since it takes three times the number of packets per second to process than it would UDP to set up a session (see Table 1-3).

Table 1-3. SRX100 capacities

Type	Capacity	
CPS	2,000	
Maximum firewall throughput	650 Mbps	
Maximum IPS throughput	60 Mbps	
Maximum VPN throughput	65 Mbps	
Maximum antivirus throughput	25 Mbps	
Maximum concurrent sessions	16K (512 MB of RAM)	32K (1 GB of RAM)
Maximum firewall policies	384	
Maximum concurrent users	Unlimited	

Although 2,000 new connections per second seems like overkill, it isn't. Many applications today are written in such a way that they may attempt to grab 100 or more data streams simultaneously. If the local firewall device is unable to handle this rate of new connections, these applications may fail to complete their transactions, leading to user complaints and, ultimately, the cost or loss of time in troubleshooting the network.

Also, because users may require many concurrent sessions, the SRX100 can support up to 32,000 sessions. A *session* is a current connection that is monitored between two peers, and can be of the more common protocols of TCP and UDP, or of other protocols such as Encapsulating Security Payload (ESP) or Generic Route Encapsulation (GRE).

The SRX100 has two separate memory options: low-memory and high-memory versions. They don't require a change of hardware, but simply the addition of a license key to activate access to the additional memory. The base memory version uses 512 MB of memory and the high-memory version uses 1 GB of memory. When the license key is added, and after a reboot, the new SRX Series flow daemon is brought online. The new flow daemon is designed to access the entire 1 GB of memory.

Activating the 1 GB of memory does more than just enable twice the number of sessions; it is required to utilize UTM. If any of the UTM features are activated, the total number of sessions are cut back to the number of low-memory sessions. Reducing the number of sessions allows the UTM processes to run. The administrator can choose whether sessions or the UTM features are the more important option.

The SRX100 can be placed in one of four different options. The default placement is on any flat surface. The other three require additional hardware to be ordered: vertically on a desktop, in a network equipment rack, or mounted on a wall. The wall mount kit can accommodate a single SRX100, and the rack mount kit can accommodate up to two SRX100 units in a single rack unit.

SRX200

The SRX200 line is the next step up in the branch SRX Series. The goal of the SRX200 line is to provide modular solutions to branch environments. This modularity comes through the use of various interface modules that allow the SRX200 line to connect to a variety of media types such as T1. Furthermore, the modules can be shared among all of the devices in the line.

The first device in the line is the SRX210. It is similar to the SRX100, except that it has additional expansion capabilities and extended throughput. The SRX210 has eight Ethernet ports, like the SRX100 does, but it also includes two 10/100/100 tri-speed Ethernet ports, allowing high-speed devices such as switches or servers to be connected. In addition, the SRX210 can be optionally ordered with built-in PoE ports. If this option is selected, the first four ports on the device can provide up to 15.4W of power to devices, be they VoIP phones or Juniper's AX and CX wireless devices.

Figure 1-20 shows the SRX210. Note in the top right the large slot where the mini-PIM is inserted. The front panel includes the eight Ethernet ports. Similar to the SRX100, the SRX210 includes a serial console port and, in this case, two USB ports. The eight Ethernet ports can be used (just like the SRX100) to provide line rate blind switching and/or a traditional Layer 3 interface.

The rear of the box contains a surprise. In the rear left, as depicted in Figure 1-21, an express card slot is shown. This express card slot can utilize 3G or cellular modem cards to provide access to the Internet, which is useful for dial backup or the new concept of a *zero-day branch*. In the past, when an organization wanted to roll out branches rapidly, it required the provisioning of a private circuit or a form of Internet access. It may take weeks or months to get this service installed. With the use of a 3G card, a branch can be installed the same day, allowing organizations and operations to move quickly to reach new markets or emergency locations. Once a permanent circuit is deployed, the 3G card can be used for dial backup or moved to a new location.

Figure 1-20. The front of the SRX210

Figure 1-21. The back of the SRX210

The performance of the SRX210 is within the range of the SRX100, but it is a higher level of performance than the SRX100 across all of its various capabilities. As you can see in Table 1-4, the overall throughput increased from 650 Mbps on the SRX100 to

750 Mbps on the SRX210. The same goes for the IPS, VPN, and antivirus throughputs. They each increased by about 10% over the SRX100. A significant change is the fact that the total number of sessions doubles, for both the low-memory and high-memory versions. That is a significant advantage in addition to the modularity of the platform.

Table 1-4. SRX210 capacities

Type	Capacity	
CPS	2,000	
Maximum firewall throughput	750 Mbps	
Maximum IPS throughput	80 Mbps	
Maximum VPN throughput	75 Mbps	
Maximum antivirus throughput	30 Mbps	
Maximum concurrent sessions	32K (512 MB of RAM)	64K (1 GB of RAM)
Maximum firewall policies	512	
Maximum concurrent users	Unlimited	

The SRX210 consists of three hardware models: the base memory model, the high-memory model, and the PoE with high-memory model (it isn't possible to purchase a base memory model and PoE). Unlike the SRX100, the memory models are actually fixed and cannot be upgraded with a license key, so when planning for a rollout with the SRX210, it's best to plan ahead in terms of what you think the device will need. The SRX210 also has a few hardware accessories: it can be ordered with a desktop stand, a rack mount kit, or a wall mount kit. The rack mount kit can accommodate one SRX210 in a single rack unit.

The SRX240 is the first departure from the small desktop form factor, as it is designed to be mounted in a single rack unit. It also can be placed on the top of a desk and is about the size of a pizza box. The SRX240, unlike the other members of the SRX200 line, includes sixteen 10/100/1000 Ethernet ports, but like the other two platforms, line rate switching can be achieved between all of the ports that are configured in the same VLAN. It's also possible to configure interfaces as a standard Layer 3 interface, and each interface can also contain multiple subinterfaces. Each subinterface is on its own separate VLAN. This is a capability that is shared across all of the SRX product lines, but it's typically used on the SRX240 since the SRX240 is deployed on larger networks.

Figure 1-22 shows the SRX240, and you should be able to see the sixteen 10/100/1000 Ethernet ports across the bottom front of the device. There's the standard fare of one serial console port and two USB ports, and on the top of the front panel of the SRX240 are the four mini-PIM slots. These slots can be used for any combination of supported mini-PIM cards.

Figure 1-22. The SRX240

The performance of the SRX240 is double that of the other platforms. It's designed for mid-range to large branch location and can handle more than eight times the connections per second, for up to 9,000 CPS. Not only is this good for outbound traffic, but it is also great for hosting small to medium-size services behind the device—including web, DNS, and email services, which are typical services for a branch network. The throughput for the device is enough for a small network, as it can secure more than 1 gigabit per second of traffic. This actually allows several servers to sit behind it and for the traffic to them from both the internal and external networks to be secured. The device can also provide for some high IPS throughput, which is great for inspecting traffic as it goes through the device from untrusted hosts.

Again, Table 1-5 shows that the total number of sessions on the device has doubled from the lower models. The maximum rate of 128,000 sessions is considerably large for most networks. Just as you saw on the SRX210, the SRX240 provides three different hardware models: the base memory model that includes 512 MB of memory (it's unable to run UTM and runs with half the number of sessions); the high-memory version which has twice the amount of memory on the device (it's able to run UTM with an additional license); and the high-memory with PoE model that can provide PoE to all 16 of its built-in Ethernet ports.

Table 1-5. SRX240 capacities

Type	Capacity	
CPS	9,000	
Maximum firewall throughput	1.5 Gbps	
Maximum IPS throughput	250 Mbps	
Maximum VPN throughput	250 Mbps	
Maximum antivirus throughput	85 Mbps	
Maximum concurrent sessions	64K (512 MB of RAM)	128K (1 GB of RAM)
Maximum firewall policies	4,096	
Maximum concurrent users	Unlimited	

Interface modules for the SRX200 line

The SRX200 Series Services Gateways currently support six different types of mini-PIMs, as shown in Table 1-6. On the SRX240 these can be mixed and matched to support any combination that the administrator chooses, offering great flexibility if there is a need to have several different types of WAN interfaces. The administrator can also add up to a total of four SFP mini-PIM modules on the SRX240, giving it a total of 20 gigabit Ethernet ports. The SFP ports can be either a fiber optic connection or a copper twisted pair link. The SRX210 can only accept one card at a time, so there isn't a capability to mix and match cards, although as stated, the SRX210 can accept any of the cards. Though the SRX210 is not capable of inspecting gigabit speeds of traffic, a fiber connection may be required in the event that a long haul fiber is used to connect the SRX210 to the network.

Table 1-6. Mini-PIMs

Type	Description
ADSL	1-port ADSL2+ mini-PIM supporting ADSL/ADSL2/ADSL2+ Annex A
ADSL	1-port ADSL2+ mini-PIM supporting ADSL/ADSL2/ADSL2+ Annex B
G.SHDSL	8-wire (4-pair) G.SHDSL mini-PIM
Serial	1-port Sync Serial mini-PIM
SFP	1-port SFP mini-PIM
T1/E1	1-port T1/E1 mini-PIM

The ADSL cards support all of the modern standards for DSL and work with most major carriers. The G.SHDSL standard is much newer than the older ADSL, and it is a higher-speed version of DSL that is provided over traditional twisted pair lines. Among the three types of cards, all common forms of ADSL are available to the SRX200 line.

The SRX200 line also supports the use of the tried-and-true serial port connection. This allows for connection to an external serial port and is the least commonly used interface card. A more commonly used interface card is the T1/E1 card, which is typical for WAN connection to the SRX200 line. Although a T1/E1 connection may be slow by today's standards, compared to the average home broadband connection, it is still commonly used in remote branch offices.

SRX600

The SRX600 line is the most different from the others in the branch SRX Series. This line is extremely modular and offers very high performance for a device that is categorized as a branch solution.

The only model in the SRX600 line (at the time of this writing) is the SRX650. The SRX650 comes with four onboard 10/100/1000 ports. All the remaining components are modules. The base system comes with the chassis and a component called the *Services and Routing Engine* or SRE. The SRE provides the processing and management capabilities for the platform. It has the same architecture as the other branch platforms, but this time the component for processing is modular.

Figure 1-23 shows the front of the SRX650 chassis, and the four onboard 10/100/1000 ports are found on the front left. The other items to notice are the eight modular slots, which are different here than in the other SRX platforms. Here the eight slots are called *G-PIM slots*, but it is also possible to utilize another card type called an *X-PIM* which utilizes multiple G-PIM slots.

On the back of the SRX650 is where the SRE is placed. There are two slots that fit the SRE into the chassis, but note that as of the Junos 10.2 release, only the bottom slot can be used. In the future, the SRX650 may support a new double-height SRE, or even multiple SREs. On the SRE there are several ports: first the standard serial console port and then a secondary serial auxiliary port, shown in the product illustration in Figure 1-24. Also, the SRE has two USB ports.

Figure 1-23. The front of the SRX650

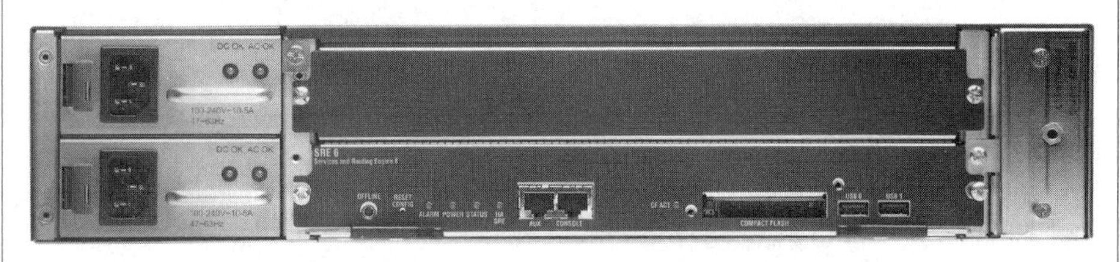

Figure 1-24. The back of the SRX650

New to this model is the inclusion of a secondary compact flash port. This port allows for expanded storage for logs or software images. The SRX650 also supports up to two power supplies for redundancy.

The crown jewel feature of the SRX650 is its performance capabilities. The SRX650 is more than enough for most branch office locations, allowing for growth in the branch office. As shown in Table 1-7, it can provide up to 30,000 new connections per second, which is ample for a fair bit of servers that can be hosted behind the firewall. It also accounts for a large number of users that can be hosted behind the SRX. The total number of concurrent sessions is four times higher than on the SRX240, with a maximum of 500,000 sessions. Only 250,000 sessions are available when UTM is enabled; the other available memory is shifted for the UTM features to utilize.

Table 1-7. SRX650 capacities

Type	Capacity
CPS	30,000
Maximum firewall throughput	7 Gbps
Maximum IPS throughput	1.5 Gbps
Maximum VPN throughput	1.5 Gbps
Maximum antivirus throughput	350 Mbps
Maximum concurrent sessions	512K (2 GB of RAM)
Maximum firewall policies	8,192
Maximum concurrent users	Unlimited

The SRX650 can provide more than enough throughput on the device, and it can provide local switching as well. The maximum total throughput is 7 gigabits per second. This represents a fair bit of secure inspection of traffic in this platform. Also, for the available UTM services it provides, it is extremely fast. IPS performance exceeds 1 gigabit as well as VPN. The lowest performing value is the inline antivirus, and although 350 Mbps is far lower than the maximum throughput, it is very fast considering the amount of inspection that is needed to scan files for viruses.

Interface modules for the SRX600 line

The SRX650 has lots of different interface options that are not available on any other platform today. This makes the SRX650 fairly unique as a platform compared to the rest of the branch SRX Series. The SRX650 can use two different types of modules: the G-PIM and the X-PIM. The G-PIM occupies only one of the possible eight slots, whereas an X-PIM takes a minimum of two slots, and some X-PIMs take a maximum of four slots. Table 1-8 lists the different interface cards.

Table 1-8. SRX600 interface matrix

Type	Description	Slots
Dual T1/E1	Dual T1/E1, two ports with integrated CSU/DSU – G-PIM. Single G-PIM slot.	1
Quad T1/E1	Quad T1/E1, four ports with integrated CSU/DSU – G-PIM. Single G-PIM slot.	1
16-port 10/100/1000	Ethernet switch 16-port 10/100/1000-baseT X-PIM.	2
16-port 10/100/1000 PoE	Ethernet switch 16-port 10/100/1000-baseT X-PIM with PoE.	2
24-port 10/100/1000 plus four SFP ports	Ethernet Switch 24-port 10/100/1000-baseT X-PIM. Includes four SFP slots.	4
24-port 10/100/1000 PoE plus four SFP ports	PoE Ethernet switch 24-port 10/100/1000-baseT X-PIM. Includes four SFP slots.	4

Two different types of G-PIM cards provide T1/E1 ports. One provides two T1/E1 ports and the other provides a total of four ports. These cards can go in any of the slots on the SRX650 chassis, up to the maximum of eight slots.

The next type of card is the dual-slot X-PIM. These cards provide sixteen 10/100/1000 ports and come in the PoE or non-PoE variety. Using this card takes up two of the eight slots. They can only be installed in the right side of the chassis, with a maximum of two cards in the chassis.

The third type of card is the quad-slot X-PIM. This card has twenty-four 10/100/1000 ports and four SFP ports and comes in a PoE and non-PoE version. The SFP ports can use either fiber or twisted-pair SFP transceivers. Figure 1-25 shows the possible locations of each type of card.

Local switching can be achieved at line rate for ports on the same card, meaning that on each card, switching must be done on *that* card to achieve line rate. It is not possible to configure switching across cards. All traffic that passes between cards must be inspected by the firewall, and the throughput is limited to the firewall's maximum inspection. Administrators who deploy the SRX should be aware of this limitation.

AX411

The AX411 Wireless LAN Access Point is not an SRX device, but more of an accessory to the branch SRX Series product line. The AX411 cannot operate on its own without an SRX Series appliance. To use the AX411 device, simply plug it into an SRX device that has DHCP enabled and an AX411 license installed. The access point will get an IP address from the SRX and register with the device, and the configuration for the AX411 will be pushed down from the SRX to the AX411. Then queries can be sent from the SRX to the AX411 to get status on the device and its associated clients. Firmware updates and remote reboots are also handled by the SRX product.

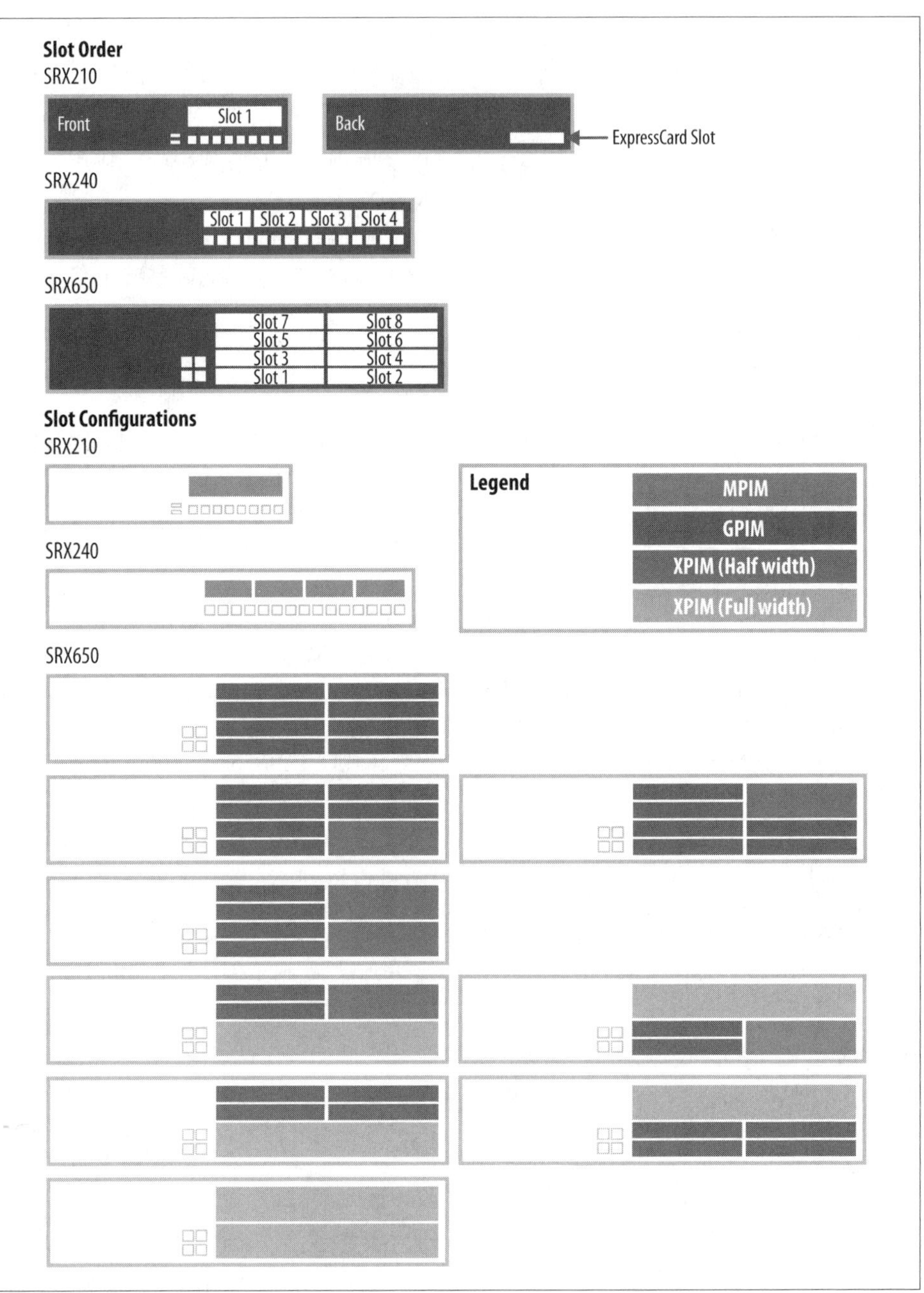

Figure 1-25. SRX650 PIM card diagram

The AX411 is designed to be placed wherever it's needed: on a desktop, mounted on a wall, or inside a drop ceiling. As shown in Figure 1-26, the AX411 has three antennas and one Ethernet port. It also has a console port, which is not user-accessible.

Figure 1-26. The AX411 WLAN Access Point

The AX411 has impressive wireless capabilities, as it supports 802.11a/b/g/n wireless networking. The three antennas provide multiple input-multiple output (MIMO) for maximum throughput. The device features two separate radios, one at the 2.4 GHz range and the other at the 5 GHz range. For the small branch, it meets all of the requirements of an access point. The AX411 is not meant to provide wireless access for a large campus network, so administrators should not expect to be able to deploy dozens of AX411 products in conjunction; the AX411 is not designed for this purpose.

Each SRX device in the branch SRX Series is only capable of managing a limited number of AX411 appliances, and Table 1-9 shows the number of access points per platform that can be managed. The SRX100 can manage up to two AX411 devices. From there, each platform doubles the total number of access points that can be managed, going all the way up to 16 access points on the SRX650.

Table 1-9. Access points per platform

Platform	Number of access points
SRX100	2
SRX210	4
SRX240	8
SRX650	16

CX111

The CX111 Cellular Broadband Data Bridge (see Figure 1-27) can be used in conjunction with the branch SRX Series products. The CX111 is designed to accept a 3G (or cellular) modem and then provide access to the Internet via a wireless carrier. The CX111 supports about 40 different manufacturers of these wireless cards and up to three USB wireless cards and one express card. Access to the various wireless providers can be always-on or dial-on-demand.

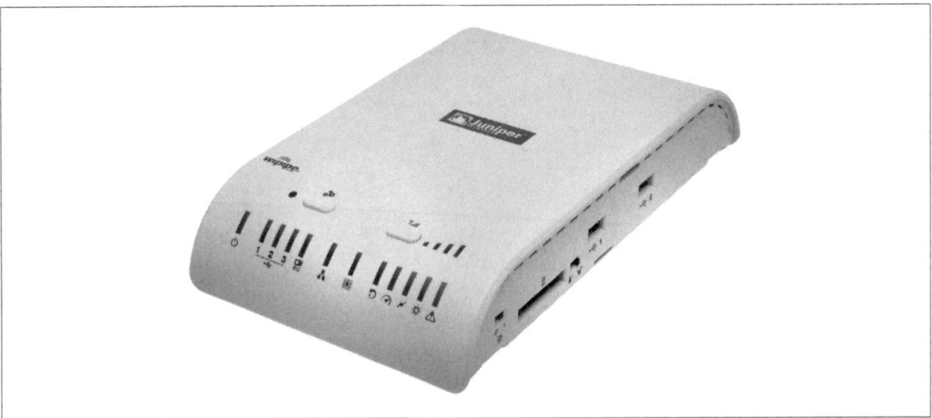

Figure 1-27. The CX111

There aren't any specific hooks between the CX111 bridge and the SRX products. The CX111 can be utilized in combination with any branch product to act as a wireless bridge. The biggest benefit is that the CX111 can be placed anywhere that a wireless signal can be best reached, so the CX111 can be powered by using PoE or a separate power supply. This way, the SRX device can be placed in a back closet or under a counter, and the CX111 can be placed by a window.

Branch SRX Series Hardware Overview

Although the branch SRX Series varies greatly in terms of form factors and capabilities, the underlying hardware architecture remains the same. Figure 1-28 may be highly simplified, but it is meant to illustrate how the platforms have a common architecture. It also provides a certain clarity to how the data center SRX Series looks when compared to the branch SRX Series.

In the center of the diagram is the shared compute resource or processor. This processor is specifically designed for processing network traffic and is intended for scaling and to provide parallel processing. With parallel processing, more than one task can be executed at a time. In this case, parallel processing is achieved by having multiple hardware cores running separate threads of execution. See "Parallel Processing" on page 43.

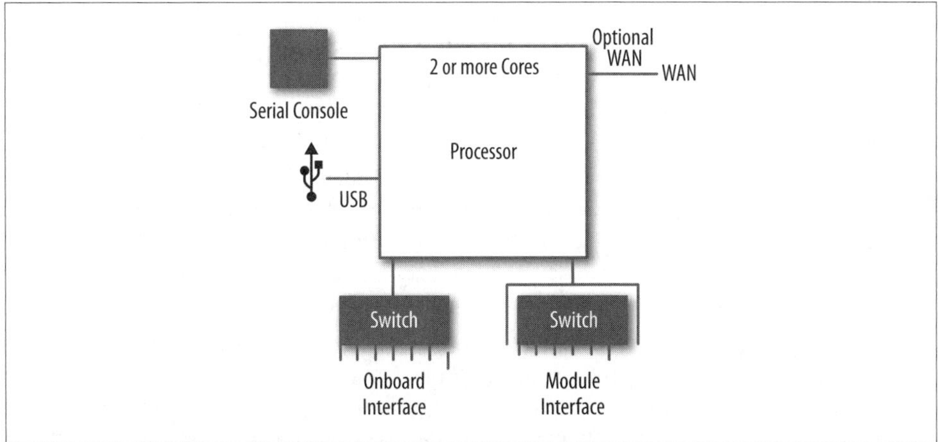

Figure 1-28. Branch SRX Series hardware overview

Connected off of this processor are the serial console and the USB ports. This allows the user to access the running system directly off of the serial console and any attached storage off of the USB ports.

Lastly in the overview are the interfaces. The interfaces connect off of the processor, and all of the onboard ports from each platform are connected as a local Ethernet switch. This is the same for all of the SRX products. Each WAN card is treated as a separate link back to the processor, and in the case of the SRX650, each Ethernet card is its own switch and then connects back to the processor. Although oversimplified, this should provide a simple understanding of what is happening inside the sheet metal.

Parallel Processing

The majority of the SRX products utilize dense processors. These processors have multiple cores, or the capability to run multiple simultaneous threads. Since there are many terms floating around, a little cleanup is in order. A *process* is an instance of a running program. It has its own memory space. On a CPU, only a single process can run at any given time.

A process can contain one or more *threads of execution*. A thread is a series of tasks that are being run in the CPU within. To scale processing, tasks are broken up into individual threads. Much like when a user uses a GUI, all of the elements seem to work simultaneously, even though the computer may run only one at a time.

To utilize all of the processor capabilities, a process would need to run multiple *threads* or *spawn off* child processes. When a process spawns off a child process, the child process is born and receives a copy of the parent's process memory. At this point, if the parent process adds or removes anything from its memory, only the parent process is aware of it. The child process is running as its own atomic unit. If the parent process wants to notify the child process of a change, it has to use interprocess communication to send data.

Sending data across processes is slow in terms of processing. Scaling this level of communication and messaging can also be difficult. There are many good use cases for this, such as scaling a web server. A web server may run many processes to serve multiple clients. The processes may need to communicate, but the speed at which they communicate may be within several milliseconds. This is completely reasonable, as other processes, such as running a script or serving an image, will be slower.

In a firewall, the interprocess communication model is best avoided because adding several milliseconds to process traffic may not be acceptable. Of course, it depends on the device. Although in a branch device several additional milliseconds of latency may be fine, in the data center this must be avoided at all costs.

The SRX Series utilizes the thread methods for processing firewall flow data. The thread model uses a single process, but utilizes multiple threads. Each thread is run on a processor core or individual hardware thread. All of the threads can execute simultaneously and process network traffic very quickly. By being part of a process, they can all share the same memory space. This allows threads to work on the same streams of information without having to pass information between them. This reduces latency and increases traffic processing efficiency.

Although this may seem like the best thing since sliced bread, it's very difficult to do. The application must be programmed to be *thread-safe*. Since all of the memory is shared, several conditions can occur where the process will crash, lock, or run infinitely without processing data. Avoiding these conditions has been one of the biggest challenges in programming over the past 40 years, and although there are several ways to solve the problem, it requires a huge amount of planning and expertise.

Licensing

The branch SRX Series supports numerous built-in features, including firewalling, routing, VPN, and NAT. However, some of the features require licensing to activate. This section is meant to clarify the licensing portion of the SRX products. Table 1-10 breaks out all of the possible licenses by vendor, description, and terms.

In regard to Table 1-10, please note the following:

- You can purchase a single license for all of the UTM features, including the antivirus, antispam, intrusion protection, and web filtering features.
- Dynamic VPN is sold as a per-seat license which counts the number of active users utilizing the features. This feature is only supported on the SRX100, SRX210, and SRX240.
- The SRX650 can support the ability to act as a BGP route reflector. This is effectively a route server that can share routes to other BGP hosts. This is licensed as a separate feature and is only applicable to the SRX650.
- To manage an AX411 access point a license is required. Two licenses are included with the purchase of the AX411; additional licenses can be purchased separately.

Table 1-10. Licensing options

Type	Vendor	Description	Terms
Antivirus	Juniper-Kaspersky	Antivirus updates	1-, 3-, or 5-year
Antispam	Juniper-Sophos	Antispam updates	1-, 3-, or 5-year
Intrusion protection	Juniper	Attack updates	1-, 3-, or 5-year
Web filtering	Websense	Category updates	1-, 3-, or 5-year
Combined set	All of the above	All of the above	1-, 3-, or 5-year
Dynamic VPN client	Juniper	Concurrent users for dynamic VPN	5, 10, 25, or 50 users, permanent
		SRX100, SRX210, and SRX240 only	
BGP router reflector	Juniper	Route reflector capability, SRX650 only	Permanent
AX411 access point	Juniper	License to run AX411	Included with access point

Branch Summary

The branch SRX Series product line is extremely well rounded. In fact, it is the most fully featured, lowest-cost Junos platform that Juniper Networks offers. (This is great news for anyone who wants to learn how to use Junos and build a small lab.)

The branch SRX Series has both flow and packet modes, allowing anyone to test flow-based firewalling and packet-based routing. It features the same routing protocol support as all Junos-based devices, from Border Gateway Protocol (BGP) to Intermediate System-to-Intermediate System (IS-IS). It has the majority of the EX Series switching features with the same configuration set. Most importantly for study, it also supports MPLS and VPLS. No other router platform supports these features at such an attractive price point.

In terms of the hardware in the branch SRX Series, the underlying device is fairly simple. It does not utilize any of the routing application-specific integrated circuits (ASICs) from the high-end routers or data center SRX Series products. Some behaviors on these features may vary across platforms, so it is not feasible to try to make a sub-$1,000 platform and have the exact same silicon as a million-dollar device. Those behaviors are noted in the documentation and throughout this book where applicable.

The branch SRX Series product line is the most accessible platform for a majority of this book's readers. And because of its lower cost, there will be many more branch SRX Series products in the field.

Where differences exist between these SRX platforms, they will be noted so that you can learn these discrepancies and take them to the field, but note that many features are shared, so there will not be large differences across platforms. Zones and firewall policies remain the same across platforms, so you will see few differences when this book delves into this material.

Data Center SRX Series

The data center SRX Series product line is designed to be scalable and fast for data center environments where high performance is required. Unlike the branch products, the data center SRX Series devices are highly modular—a case in point is the base chassis for any of the products, which does not provide any processing power to process traffic because the devices are designed to scale in performance as cards are added. (It also reduces the total amount of investment that is required for an initial deployment.)

There are two lines of products in the data center SRX Series: the SRX3000 line and the SRX5000 line. Each uses almost identical components, which is great because any testing done on one platform can carry over to the other. It's also easier to have feature parity between the two product lines since the data center SRX Series has specific ASICs and processors that cannot be shared unless they exist on both platforms. Where differences do exist, trust that they will be noted.

The SRX3000 line is the smaller of the two, designed for small to medium-size data centers and Internet edge applications. The SRX5000 line is the largest services gateway that Juniper offers. It is designed for medium to very large data centers and it can scale from a moderate to an extreme performance level.

Both platforms are open for flexible configuration, allowing the network architect to essentially create a device for his own needs. Since processing and interfaces are both modular, it's possible to create a customized device such as one with more IPS with high inspection and lower throughput. Here, the administrator would add fewer interface cards but more processing cards, allowing only a relatively small amount of traffic to enter the device but providing an extreme amount of inspection. Alternatively, the administrator can create a data center SRX with many physical interfaces but limited processors for inspection. All of this is possible with the data center SRX Series.

Data Center SRX-Specific Features

The data center SRX Series products are built to meet the specific needs of today's data centers. They share certain features that require the same underlying hardware to work as well as the need for such features—it's important to be focused on meeting the needs of the platform.

The first such feature is transparent mode. Transparent mode is the ability for the firewall to act as a transparent bridge. As a transparent bridge, the firewall routes packets by destination MAC address. Firewall policies are still enforced, as would be expected. The benefit of such a transparent firewall feature is that the firewall can easily be placed anywhere in the network.

As of Junos 10.2, transparent mode is not available for the branch SRX Series products.

In the data center, IPS is extremely important in securing services, and the data center SRX Series devices have several features for IPS that are currently not available for the branch SRX Series devices. *Inline tap mode* is one such feature for the data-center-specific SRX platform, allowing the SRX to copy any off sessions as they go through the device. The SRX will continue to process the traffic in Intrusion Detection and Prevention (IDP), as well as passing the traffic out of the SRX, but now it will alert (or log) when an attack is detected, reducing the risk of encountering a false positive and dropping legitimate traffic.

Because most data centers have a large amount of hardware at their disposal, most have the capability to decrypt SSL traffic for inspection. On the SRX, the organization's private SSL key can be loaded and the SRX can then decrypt the SSL traffic in real time and inspect for attacks. This provides an additional layer of security by eliminating attacks that could simply slip through in encrypted streams.

The branch SRX Series products do not have SSL decryption capability, mostly because of the horsepower needed to drive it.

Another specific feature that is common to the data center SRX Series is that they can be configured in what is known as *dedicated mode*. The data center SRX Series firewalls have dense and powerful processors, allowing flexibility in terms of how they can be configured. And much like adding additional processing cards, the SRX processors themselves can be tuned. Dedicated mode allows the SRX processing to be focused on IDP, and the overall throughput for IDP increases, as do the maximum session counts.

Because the branch SRX Series products utilize different processors, it is not possible to tune them for dedicated mode.

Another specific data center feature of note is the AppDoS feature. When the SRX is deployed in a data center it is designed to protect servers, and one of the most common attacks of the modern Internet era is the DDoS attack. It is extremely difficult to detect and stop these types of attacks, but using IDP technology it's possible to set thresholds and secure against these attacks. The AppDoS feature uses a series of thresholds to detects attacks and then stop only the attacking clients and not the valid devices.

Because the branch SRX Series isn't focused on protecting services, the AppDoS feature was not made available for that platform (as of Junos 10.2).

We cover many of these features, and others, throughout this book in various chapters and sections. Use the index at the end of the book as a useful cross-reference to these and other data center SRX Series features.

SPC

The element that provides all of the processing on the SRX Series is called the *Services Processing Card* (SPC). An SPC contains one or more *Services Processing Units* (SPUs). The SPU is the processor that handles all of the services on the data center SRX Series firewalls, from firewalling, NAT, and VPN to session setup and anything else the firewall does.

Each SPU provides extreme multiprocessing and can run 32 parallel tasks simultaneously. A task is run as a separate hardware thread (see "Parallel Processing" on page 43 for an explanation of hardware threads). This equates to an extreme amount of parallelism. An SPC can operate in four modes: full central point, small central point, half central point, and full flow. SPUs that operate in both central point and flow mode are said to be in *combo mode*. Based on the mode, the number of hardware threads will be divided differently.

The SPU can operate in up to four different distributions of threads, which breaks down to two different functions that it can provide: the central point and the flow processor. The central point (CP) is designed as the master session controller. The CP maintains a table for all of the sessions that are active on the SRX—if a packet is ever received on the SRX that is not matched as part of an existing session, it is sent to the CP. The CP can then check against its session table and see if there is an existing session that matches it. (We will discuss the new session setup process in more detail shortly, once all of the required components are explained.)

The CP has three different settings so that users can scale the SRX appropriately. The CP is used as part of the new session setup process or new CPS. The process is distributed across multiple components in the system. It would not make sense to dedicate a processor to provide maximum CPS if there were not enough of the other components to provide this. So, to provide a balanced performance, the CP is *automatically* tuned to provide CPS capabilities to the rest of the platform. The extra hardware threads that are remaining go back into processing network traffic. At any one time, *only one* processor is acting as the CP, hence the term *central point*.

The remaining SPUs in the SRX are dedicated to process traffic for services. These processors are distributed to traffic as part of the new session setup process. Because each SPU eventually reaches a finite amount of processing, as does any computing device, an SPU will share any available computing power it has among the services. If additional processing power is required, more SPUs can be added. Adding more SPUs provides near-linear scaling for performance, so if a feature is turned on that cuts the required performance in half, simply adding another SPU will bring performance back to where it was.

The SPU's linear scaling makes it easier to plan a network. If needed, a minimal number of SPUs can be purchased upfront, and then, over time, additional SPUs can be added to grow with the needs of the data center. To give you an indication of the processing capabilities per SPU, Table 1-11 shows off the horsepower available.

Table 1-11. SPU processing capabilities

Item	Capability
Packets per second	1,100,000
New CPS	50,000
Firewall throughput	10 Gbps
IPS throughput	2.5 Gbps
VPN throughput	2.5 Gbps

Each SPC in the SRX5000 line has two SPUs and each SPC in the SRX3000 line has a single SPU. As more processing cards are added, the SRX gains the additional capabilities listed in Table 1-11, so when additional services such as logging and NAT are turned on and the capacity per processor decreases slightly, additional processors can be added to offset the performance lost by adding new services.

NPU

The NPU or *Network Processing Unit* is similar in concept to the SPU, whereby the NPU resides on either an input/output card (IOC) or its own Network Processing Card (NPC) based on the SRX platform type (in the SRX5000 line the NPU sits on the IOC and in the SRX3000 line it is on a separate card).

When traffic enters an interface card it has to pass through an NPU before it can be sent on for processing. The physical interfaces and NPCs sit on the same interface card, so each interface or interface module has its own NPU. In the SRX3000 line, each interface card is bound to one of the NPUs in the chassis, so when the SRX3000 line appliances boot, each interface is bound to an NPU in a round-robin fashion until each interface has an NPU. It is also possible to manually bind the interfaces to the NPUs through this configuration.

The biggest difference in the design of the SRX3000 and SRX5000 lines' usage of NPUs concerns providing a lower-cost platform to the customer. Separating the physical interfaces from the NPU reduces the overall cost of the cards.

The NPU is used as a part of the session setup process to balance packets as they enter the system. The NPU takes each packet and balances it to the correct SPU that is handling that session. In the event that there is not a matching session on the NPU, it forwards the packet to the CP to figure out what to do with it.

Each NPU can process about 6.5 million packets per second inbound and about 16 million packets outbound. This applies across the entire data center SRX Series platform. The method the NPU uses to match a packet to a session is based on matching the packet to its wing table; a *wing* is half of a session and one part of the bidirectional flow. Figure 1-29 depicts an explanation of a wing in relation to a flow.

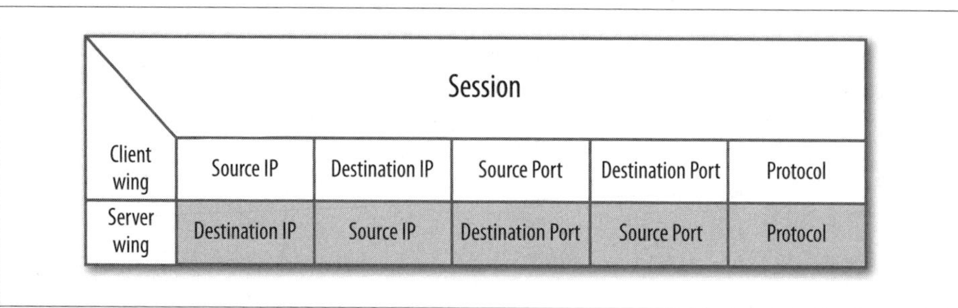

Figure 1-29. Sessions and wings

The card to which the NPU is assigned determines how much memory it will have to store wings (some cards have more memory, since there are fewer components on them). Table 1-12 lists the number of wings per NPU. Each wing has a five-minute keepalive. If five minutes pass and a packet matching the wing hasn't passed, the wing is deleted.

Table 1-12. Number of wings per NPU

Card type	NPUs per card	Wings per NPU
4x10G SRX5000	4	2 million
40x1G SRX5000	4	2 million
Flex I/O SRX5000	2	4 million
NPC SRX3000	1	4 million

It is possible that the wing table on a single SPU can fill up, and it is a possibility in the SRX5000 line since the total number of sessions exceeds the total number of possible wings on a single NPU. To get around this, Juniper introduced a feature called *NPU bundling* in Junos 9.6, allowing two or more NPUs to be bundled together. The first NPU is used as a load balancer to balance packets to the other NPUs, and then the remaining NPUs in the bundle are able to process packets. This benefits not only the total number of wings, but also the maximum number of ingress packets per second.

NPUs can be bundled on or across cards with up to 16 NPUs to be used in a single bundle, and up to eight different bundles can be created.

The NPU also provides other functions, such as a majority of the screening functions. A screen is an intrusion detection function. These functions typically relate to single packet matching or counting specific packet types. Examples of this are matching land attacks or counting the rate of TCP SYN packets. The NPU also provides some QoS functions.

Data Center SRX Series Session Setup

We discussed pieces of the session setup process in the preceding two sections, so here let's put the entire puzzle together. It's an important topic to discuss, since it is key to how the SRX balances traffic across its chassis. Figure 1-30 shows the setup we will use for our explanation.

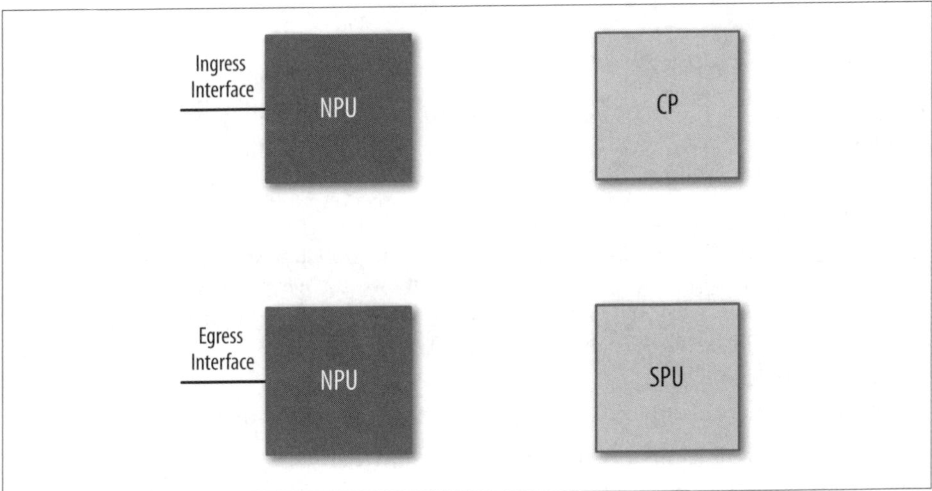

Figure 1-30. Hardware setup

Figure 1-30 depicts two NPUs: one NPU will be used for ingress traffic and the other will be used for egress traffic. The figure also shows the CP. For this example, the processor handling the CP function will be dedicated to that purpose. The last component shown is the flow SPU, which will be used to process the traffic flow.

Figure 1-31 shows the initial packet coming into the SRX. For this explanation, a TCP session will be created. This packet is first sent to the ingress NPU, where the ingress NPU checks against its existing wings. Since there are no existing wings, the NPU then must forward the packet to the CP, where the CP checks against its master session table to see if the packet matches an existing flow. Since this is the first packet into the SRX, and no sessions exist, the CP recognizes this as a potential new session.

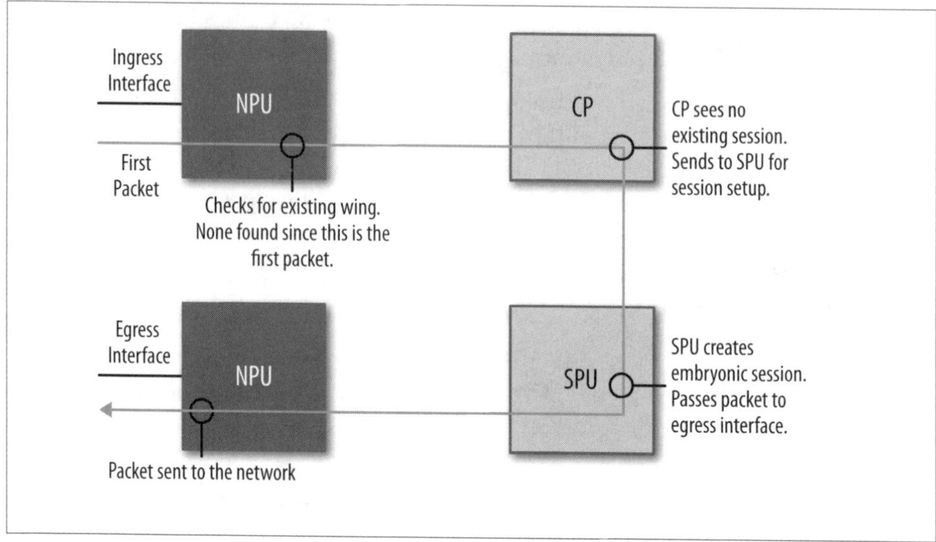

Figure 1-31. The first packet

The packet is then sent to one of the flow SPUs in the system using the weighted round-robin algorithm.

> Each SPU is weighted. A full SPU is given a weight of 100, a combo-mode SPU is given a weight of 60 if it's a majority flow and a small CP, and a half-CP and half-flow SPU is given a weight of 50. This way, when the CP is distributing new sessions, the sessions are evenly distributed across the processors.

In Figure 1-31 there is only a single SPU, so the packet is sent there.

The SPU does a basic sanity check on the packet and then sets up an embryonic session. This session lasts for up to 20 seconds. The CP is notified of this embryonic session. The remaining SYN-ACK and ACK packets must be received before the session will be fully established. Before the session is completely established, the NPUs will forward the SYN-ACK and ACK packets to the CP and the CP then must forward them to the correct SPU, which it does here because the SPU has the embryonic session in its session table.

In Figure 1-32, the session has been established. The three steps in the three-way handshake have completed. Once the SPU has seen the final ACK packet, it completes the session establishment in the box, first sending a message to the CP to turn the embryonic session into a complete session, and then starting the session timer at the full timeout for the protocol. Next, the SPU notifies the ingress NPU. Once the ingress NPU receives a message, it installs a wing. This wing identifies this session and then specifies which SPU is responsible for the session. When the ACK packet that validated the

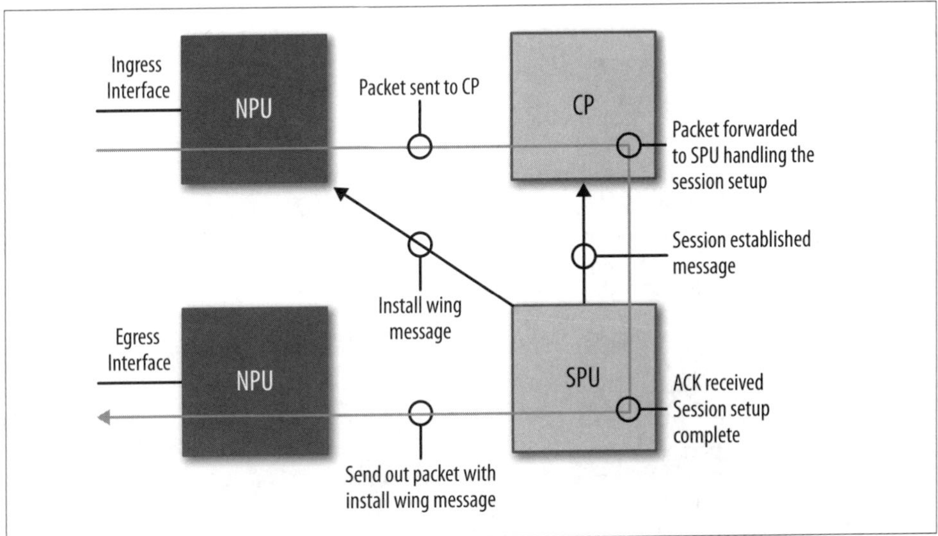

Figure 1-32. Session established

establishment of the session is sent out of the SRX, a message is tacked onto it. The egress NPU interprets this message and then installs the wing into its local cache, which is similar to the ingress wing except that some elements are reversed. This wing is matching the destination talking to the source (see Figure 1-29 for a representation of the wing).

Now that the session is established the data portion of the session begins, as shown in Figure 1-33 where a data packet is sent and received by the NPU. The NPU checks its local wing table and sees that it has a match, and then forwards the packet to the SPU. The SPU then validates the packet, matching the packet against the session table to ensure that it is the next expected packet in the data flow. The SPU then forwards the packet out the egress NPU. (The egress NPU does not check the packet against its wing table; a packet is only checked upon ingress to the NPU.) When the egress NPU receives a return packet, it is being sent from the destination back to the source. This packet is matched against its local wing table and then processed through the system as was just done for the first data packet.

Lastly, when the session has completed its purpose, the client will start to end the session. In this case, a four-way FIN close is used. The sender starts the process and the four closing packets are treated the same as packets for the existing session. What happens next is important, as shown in Figure 1-34. Once the SPU has processed the closing process, it shuts down the session on the SRX, sending a message to the ingress and egress NPUs to delete their wings. The SPU also sends a close message to the CP. The CP and SPU wait about eight seconds to complete the session close to ensure that everything was closed properly.

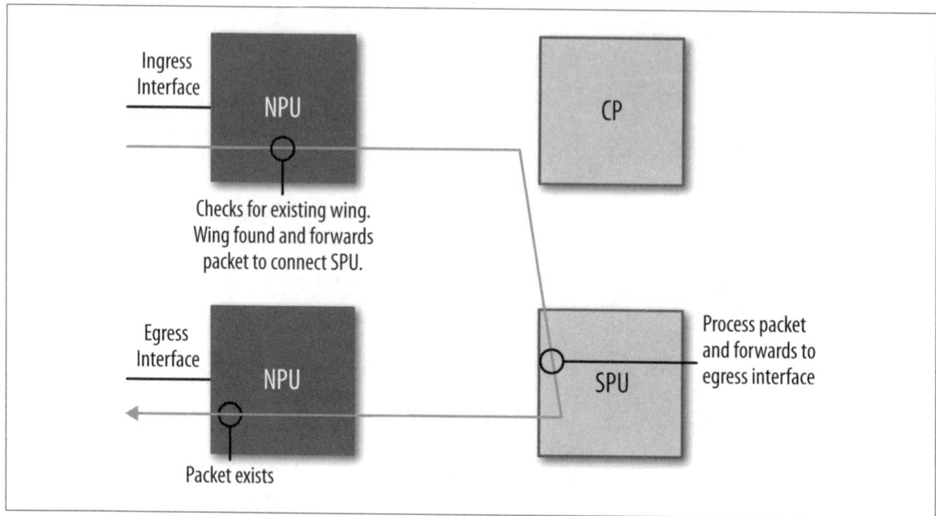

Figure 1-33. Existing session

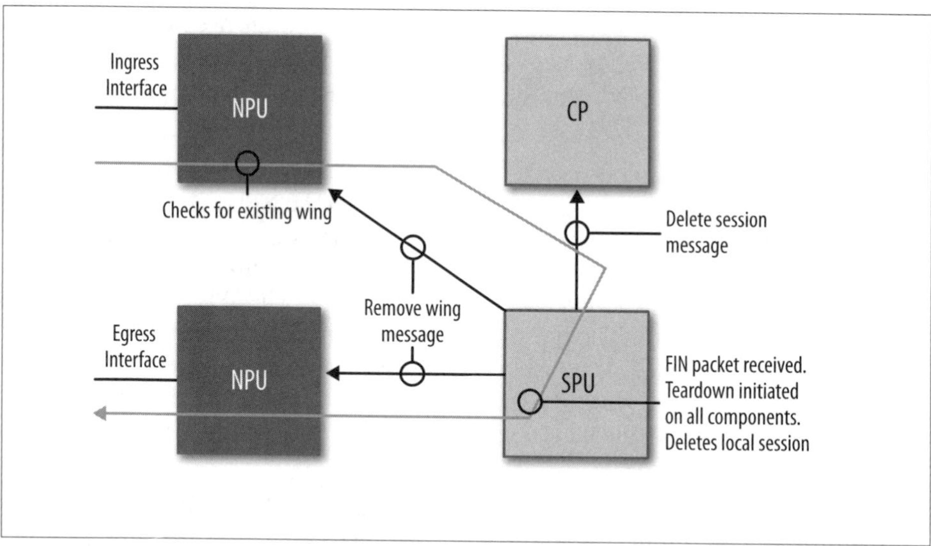

Figure 1-34. Session teardown

Although this seems like a complex process, it also allows the SRX to scale. As more and more SPUs and NPUs are added into the system, this defined process allows the SRX to balance traffic across the available resources. Over time, session distribution is almost always nearly even across all of the processors, a fact proven across many SRX customer deployments. Some have had concerns that a single processor would be overwhelmed by all of the sessions, but that has not happened and cannot happen using this balancing mechanism. In the future, if needed, Juniper could implement a least-connections model or least-utilization model for balancing traffic, but it has not had to as of Junos 10.2.

Data Center SRX Series Hardware Overview

So far we've talked about the components of the data center SRX Series, so let's start putting the components into the chassis. The data center SRX Series consists of two different lines and four different products. Although they all utilize the same fundamental components, they are designed to scale performance for where they are going to be deployed. And that isn't easy. The challenge is that a single processor can only be so fast and it can only have so many simultaneous threads of execution. To truly scale to increased performance within a single device, a series of processors and balancing mechanisms must be utilized.

Since the initial design goal of the SRX was to do all of this scaling in a single product, and allow customers to choose how they wanted (and how much) to scale the device, it should be clear that the SPUs and the NPUs are the points to scale (especially if you just finished reading the preceding section).

The NPUs allow traffic to come into the SRX, and the SPUs allow for traffic processing. Adding NPUs allows for more packets to get into the device, and adding SPUs allows for linear scaling. Of course, each platform needs to get packets into the device, which is done by using interface cards, and each section on the data center SRX Series will discuss the interface modules available per platform.

What Is Performance?

A very hot firewall topic centers on performance. Is performance the maximum throughput? Is it based on the Internet Mix (IMIX) standard? What does performance really mean? Although the answers to these questions vary among people and organizations, let's dive to find some common ground.

The first item to examine is the throughput of the firewall. At first, it would seem like an equitable item by which to compare devices, but there is no standard regarding what packet size should be used when testing a firewall. Throughput is the result of the packet rate multiplied by the packet size. When a vendor typically tests, it does so with the maximum-sized frame for an Ethernet network, typically 1,514 bytes. If the vendor tests with packets, it is doing the testing without the Ethernet header, but it only makes sense to count the Ethernet header since it has to go into the device so that the packet can ride on top of it.

There is a 20-byte gap between packets, consisting of an 8-byte preamble and a minimum of 12 bytes of packet gap. So, when testing a firewall, this is added to the overall throughput. This additional 20 bytes is not a matter of cheating, but it has to be counted since it takes up space on the wire. Add these 20 bytes to the 1,514-byte packet and it becomes 1,534 bytes. And at the end of the packet is a 4-byte CRC, making the packet 1,538 bytes.

Now, again, this may seem insignificant, but it is often overlooked when a customer looks at the performance of a firewall. It's often thought that if 1 Gbps of data is being transferred on the wire, that is actually 1 gigabit of data per second. In fact, for every 1,538 bytes on the wire frame, only 1,460 bytes of it can be data.

Let's also consider performance definitions when using TCP. For TCP to be a reliable protocol, it has to send acknowledgments after it receives a certain amount of data. By default, this is one ACK packet for every four full data packets. So, if the data rate is at millions of packets per second, that's lots of empty packets that the device has to process that do not contain any data. So, when thinking about throughput with TCP, there is a greater chance to get less-than-expected throughput.

Sometimes using large packets is good because it shows the maximum possible throughput of the device, and it's good to know the total capacity of the device. But then the question comes up: how will the device perform in a real-world network? The best way to determine the average packet size on a network is to use analysis tools or look at switch-packet counters. One number that is often thrown around is the *IMIX* number. The IMIX average packet size is 386 bytes, which was determined based on the average packet size on the Internet back in 2001. A lot has changed since then, but it is still common for vendors and customers to refer to this number.

At the root of all of these performance numbers is the actual packet rate that can go through a device, which is the maximum number of packets per second that a device can handle. To test this, an engineer would generate 64-byte packets, being the smallest possible valid packet size, and then, based on the determined packet rate multiplied by the maximum packet size, the total maximum throughput could be calculated. So, it's always best to ask a firewall vendor how to achieve the maximum possible rates on its device.

This is so important because any network device can only process so many packets per second. Think of this as the number of workloads per second that the device can compute. Any network device is nothing more than a computer, and for each packet that it receives, it needs to execute a series of tasks on it. The longer it takes to execute these tasks, the higher the latency. The more operations it has to process, the fewer packets it can process. A firewall has to validate that it has the correct attributes and that the packet is in state, and if it matches an existing session it has to name a few of those operations it has to perform. To put that in simple terms, this is how a firewall device operates. So, firewall customers should come to the purchasing table with all of the correct data from their network and then work with the vendor to best determine the capabilities of the vendor's platform.

Before leaving this sidebar, in regard to throughput testing let's talk briefly about the concept of the *jumbo frame*. A jumbo frame is a frame that is larger than the standard 1,514-byte frame, typically around 9,000 bytes. It is used more commonly in supercomputer environments and not on a common LAN, but it's actually good for a vendor to test using jumbo frames. It allows the vendor to demonstrate the maximum throughput of the device by reducing the number of packets the device has to process by nearly a factor of six, and just focus on the maximum throughput. One point to be aware of is when vendors state that throughput is tested with jumbo frames. This may hint at a limitation in terms of its packet rate.

CPS is another topic that is often discussed, because for each new TCP connection created, three packets must be processed. This is just to establish the session, which is magnitudes more difficult than passing packets from an existing session, because a firewall has many more things to check when establishing a session. When looking at a firewall and its maximum CPS rate, think about that rate and multiply it by three. That is the maximum number of packets the device can process for establishing sessions.

And the other side of the new session CPS is the *sustained* CPS rate, or how many sessions can be opened and closed per second. This metric isn't often discussed, perhaps because it is much more intensive. It requires the processing of up to nine packets per session per second. Three packets are required to open the session, another for the data, another for acknowledgment of the data, and then up to four packets to close the session. That is a total of nine packets times the total sustained CPS. It's a tough number for a product to sustain.

A network architect who can think about a firewall device like this holds a lot of powerful questions when talking to the vendor. These are the core concepts when talking about performance on a flow-based device. And it's information that will be helpful for the rest of chapter as we look individually at the capabilities of the data center SRX Series firewalls.

SRX3000

The SRX3000 line is the smaller of the two data center SRX Series lines. It is designed for the Internet edge, or small to medium-size data center environments. The SRX3000 products are extremely modular. The base chassis comes with a route engine (RE), a switch fabric board (SFB), and the minimum required power supplies. The RE is a computer that runs the management functions for the chassis, controlling and activating the other components in the device. All configuration management is also done from the RE.

The reason it is called a *route engine* is because it runs the routing protocols on it, and on other Junos device platforms such as the M Series, T Series, and MX Series, the RE is, of course, a major part of the device. However, although SRX devices do have excellent routing support, most customers do not use this feature extensively.

The SFB contains several important components for the system: the data plane fabric, the control plane Ethernet network, and built-in Ethernet data ports. The SFB has eight 10/100/1000 ports and four SFPs. It also has a USB port that connects into the RE and a serial console port. All products in the SRX3000 line contain the SFB. In fact, the SRX3000 is the only data center line that contains built-in ports (the SRX5000 line is truly modular, as it contains no built-in I/O ports). The SFB also contains an out-of-band network management port, which is not connected to the data plane: the preferred way to manage the SRX3000 line.

The SRX3400 is the base product in the SRX3000 line. It has seven FPC or *flexible PIC concentrator* slots (a PIC is a *physical interface card*, with four slots in the front of the chassis and three in the rear). The slots enable network architects to mix and match the cards, allowing them to decide how the firewall is to be configured. The three types of cards that the SRX3400 can use are interface cards, NPCs, and SPCs, and Table 1-13 lists the minimum and maximum number of cards per chassis by type.

Table 1-13. SRX3400 FPC numbers

Type	Minimum	Maximum	Install location
I/O card	0	4	Front slots
SPC	1	4	Any
NPC	1	2	Rear three

The SRX3400 is three rack units high and a full 25.5 inches deep. That's the full depth of a standard four-post rack. Figure 1-35 shows the front and back of the SRX3400 in which the SFB can be seen as the wide card that is in the top front of the chassis on the left, the FPC slots in both the front and rear of the chassis, and the two slots in the rear of the chassis for the REs. As of Junos 10.2, only one RE is supported in the left slot.

Figure 1-35. The front and back of the SRX3400

Performance on the SRX3400 is impressive, and Table 1-14 lists the maximum performance. The SRX3400 is a modular platform which includes the use of four SPCs, two NPCs, and one IOC. So, it's no wonder that the SRX3400 can provide up to 175,000 new connections per second, even though this is a huge number and may dwarf the performance of the branch series. The average customer may not need such rates on a continuous basis, but it's great to have the horsepower in the event that traffic begins to flood through the device.

The SRX3400 can pass a maximum of 20 Gbps of firewall throughput. This limitation comes from two components: the maximum number of NPCs, and interfaces, which limits the overall throughout. As discussed before, each NPC can take a maximum number of 6.5 million packets per second inbound, and in the maximum throughput configuration, one interface card and the onboard interfaces are used. With a total of 20 Gbps ingress, it isn't possible to get more traffic into the box.

Table 1-14. SRX3400 capacities

Type	Capacity
CPS	175,000
Maximum firewall throughput	20 Gbps
Maximum IPS throughput	6 Gbps
Maximum VPN throughput	6 Gbps
Maximum concurrent sessions	2.25 million
Maximum firewall policies	40,000
Maximum concurrent users	Unlimited

As shown in Table 1-14, the SRX3400 can also provide several other services, such as both IPS and VPN up to 6 Gbps. Each number is mutually exclusive (each SPU has a limited amount of computing power). The SRX3400 can also have a maximum of 2.25 million sessions as of Junos 10.2. In today's growing environment, a single host can demand dozens of sessions at a time, so 2.25 million sessions may not be a high enough number, especially for larger-scale environments.

If more performance is required, it's common to move up to the SRX3600. This platform is nearly identical to the SRX3400, except that it adds more capacity by increasing the total number of FPC slots in the chassis. The SRX3600 has a total of 14 FPC slots, doubling the capacity of the SRX3400. This does make the chassis' height increase to five rack units (the depth remains the same). Table 1-15 lists the minimum and maximum number of cards by type per chassis.

Table 1-15. SRX3600 FPC numbers

Type	Minimum	Maximum	Install location
I/O card	0	6	Front slots
SPC	1	7	Any
NPC	1	3	Last rear three

As mentioned, the SRX3600 chassis is nearly identical to the SRX3400, except for the additional FPC slots. But two other items are different between the two chassis, as you can see in Figure 1-36, where the SRX3600 has an additional card slot above the SFB. Although it currently does not provide any additional functionality, a double-height SFB could be placed in that location in the future. And in the rear of the chassis, the number of power supplies has doubled to four, to support the chassis' additional power needs. A minimum of two power supplies are required to power the chassis, but to provide full redundancy, all four should be utilized.

Figure 1-36. The SRX3600

Table 1-16 lists the maximum performance of the SRX3600. These numbers are tested with a configuration of two 10G I/O cards, three NPCs, and seven SPCs. This configuration provides additional throughput. The firewall capabilities rise to a maximum of 30 Gbps, primarily because of the inclusion of an additional interface module and NPC. The VPN and IPS numbers also rise to 10 Gbps, while the CPS and session maximums remain the same. The SRX3000 line utilizes a combo-mode CP processor, where half of the processor is dedicated to processing traffic and the other to setup sessions. The SRX5000 line has the capability of providing a full CP processor.

Table 1-16. SRX3600 capacities

Type	Capacity
CPS	175,000
Maximum firewall throughput	30 Gbps
Maximum IPS throughput	10 Gbps
Maximum VPN throughput	10 Gbps

Type	Capacity
Maximum concurrent sessions	2.25 million
Maximum firewall policies	40,000
Maximum concurrent users	Unlimited

IOC modules

In addition to the built-in SFP interface ports, you can use three additional types of interface modules with the SRX3000 line, and Table 1-17 lists them by type. Each interface module is oversubscribed, with the goal of providing port density rather than line rate cards. The capacity and oversubscription ratings are also listed.

Table 1-17. SRX3000 I/O module summary

Type	Description
10/100/1000 copper	16-port 10/100/1000 copper with 1.6:1 oversubscription
1G SFP	16-port SPF with 1.6:1 oversubscription
10G XFP	2 × 10G XFP with 2:1 oversubscription

Table 1-17 lists two types of 1G interface card, and both contain 16 1G interface slots. The media type is the only difference between the modules, and one has 16 1G 10/100/1000 copper interfaces and the other contains 16 SFP ports. The benefit of the 16 SFP interfaces is that a mix of fiber and copper interfaces can be used as opposed to the fixed-copper-only card. Both of the cards are oversubscribed to a ratio of 1.6:1.

The remaining card listed in Table 1-17 is a 2 × 10G XFP card. This card provides two 10G interfaces and is oversubscribed by a ratio of 2:1. Although the card is oversubscribed by two times, the port density is its greatest value because providing more ports allows for additional connectivity into the network. Most customers will not require all of the ports on the device to operate at line rate speeds, and if more are required, the SRX5000 line can provide these capabilities.

Each module has a 10G full duplex connection into the fabric. This means 10 gigabits of traffic per second can enter and exit the module simultaneously, providing a total of 20 gigabits of traffic per second that could traverse the card at the same time.

SRX5000

The SRX5000 line of firewalls are the *big iron* in the SRX Series, true in both size and capacity. The SRX5000 line provides maximum modularity in the number of interface cards and SPCs the device can utilize, for a "build your own services gateway" approach while allowing for expansion over time.

The SRX5000 line currently comes in two different models: the SRX5600 and the SRX5800. Fundamentally, both platforms are the same. They share the same major components, except for the chassis and how many slots are available, dictating the performance of these two platforms.

The first device to review is the SRX5600. This chassis is the smaller of the two, containing a total of eight slots. The bottom two slots are for the switch control boards (SCBs), an important component in the SRX5000 line as they contain three key items: a slot to place the RE; the switch fabric for the device; and one of the control plane networks.

The RE in the SRX5000 line is the same concept as in the SRX3000 line, providing all of the chassis and configuration management functions. It also runs the processes that run the routing protocols (if the user chooses to configure them). The RE is required to run the chassis and it has a serial port, an auxiliary console port, a USB port, and an out-of-band management Ethernet port. The USB port can be used for loading new firmware on the device, while the out-of-band Ethernet port is the suggested port for managing the SRX.

The switch fabric is used to connect the interface cards and the SPCs together, and all traffic that passes through the switch fabric is considered to be part of the data plane. The control plane network provides the connectivity between all of the components in the chassis. This gigabit Ethernet network is used for the RE to talk to all of the line cards. It also allows for management traffic to come back to the RE from the data plane. And if the RE was to send traffic, it goes from the control plane and is inserted into the data plane.

Only one SCB is required to run the SRX5600; a second SCB can be used for redundancy. (Note that if just one SCB is utilized, unfortunately the remaining slot cannot be used for an interface card or an SPC.) The SRX5600 can utilize up to two REs, one to manage the SRX and the other to create dual control links in HA.

On the front of the SRX5600, as shown in Figure 1-37, is what is called a *craft port*. This is the series of buttons that are labeled on the top front of the chassis, allowing you to enable and disable the individual cards. The SRX5600, unlike the SRX5800, can use 120v power which may be beneficial in environments where 220v power is not available, or without rewiring certain locations. The SRX5600 is eight rack units tall and 23.8 inches deep.

The SRX5000 line is quite flexible in its configuration, with each chassis requiring a minimum of one interface module and one SPC. Traffic must be able to enter the device and be processed; hence these two cards are required. The remaining slots in the chassis are the network administrator's choice. This offers several important options.

The SRX5000 line has a relatively low barrier of entry because just a chassis and a few interface cards are required. In fact, choosing between the SRX5600 and the SRX5800 comes down to space, power, and long-term expansion.

Figure 1-37. The SRX5600

For space considerations, the SRX5600 is physically half the size of the SRX5800, a significant fact considering that these devices are often deployed in pairs, and that two SRX5800s take up two-thirds of a physical rack. In terms of power, the SRX5600 can run on 110v, while the SRX5800 needs 220v.

The last significant option between the SRX5600 and the SRX5800 data center devices is their long-term expansion capabilities. Table 1-18 lists the FPC slot capacities in the SRX5600. As stated, the minimum is two cards, one interface card and one SPC, leaving four slots that can be mixed and matched among cards. Because of the high-end fabric in the SRX5600, placement of the cards versus their performance is irrelevant. This means the cards can be placed in any slots and the throughput is the same, which is important to note since in some vendors' products, maximum throughput will drop when attempting to go across the back plane.

Table 1-18. SRX5600 FPC numbers

Type	Minimum	Maximum	Install location
FPC slots used	1 (SCB)	8	All slots are FPCs
I/O card	1	5	Any
SPC	1	5	Any
SCB	1	2	Bottom slots

In the SRX5800, the requirements are similar. One interface card and one SPC are required for the minimum configuration, and the 10 remaining slots can be used for any additional combination of cards. Even if the initial deployment only requires the minimum number of cards, it still makes sense to look at the SRX5800 chassis. It's always a great idea to get investment protection out of the purchase. Table 1-19 lists the FPC capacity numbers for the SRX5800.

Table 1-19. SRX5800 FPC numbers

Type	Minimum	Maximum	Install location
FPC slots used	2 (SCBs)	14	All slots are FPCs
I/O card	1	11	Any
SPC	1	11	Any
SCB	2	3	Center slots

The SRX5800 has a total of 14 slots, and in this chassis, the two center slots must contain SCBs, which doubles the capacity of the chassis. Since it has twice the number of slots, it needs two times the fabric. Even though two fabric cards are utilized, there isn't a performance limitation for going between any of the ports or cards on the fabric (this is important to remember, as some chassis-based products do have this limitation). Optionally, a third SCB can be used, allowing for redundancy in case one of the other two SCBs fails.

Figure 1-38 illustrates the SRX5800. The chassis is similar to the SRX5600, except the cards are positioned perpendicular to the ground, which allows for front-to-back cooling and a higher density of cards within a 19-inch rack. At the top of the chassis, the same craft interface can be seen. The two fan trays for the chassis are front-accessible above and below the FPCs.

In the rear of the chassis there are four power supply slots. In an AC electrical deployment, three power supplies are required, with the fourth for redundancy. In a DC power deployment, the redundancy is 2+2, or two active supplies and two supplies for redundancy. Check with the latest hardware manuals for the most up-to-date information.

The performance metrics for the SRX5000 line are very impressive, as listed in Table 1-20. The CPS rate maxes out at 350,000, which is the maximum number of

Figure 1-38. The SRX5800

packets per second that can be processed by the central point processor. This is three per CPS multiplied by 350,000, or 1.05 million packets per second, and subsequently is about the maximum number of packets per second per SPU. Although this many connections per second is not required for most environments, at a mobile services provider, a large data center, or a full cloud network—or any environment where there are tens of thousands of servers and hundreds of thousands of inbound clients—this rate of connections per second may be just right.

Table 1-20. SRX5000 line capacities

Type	SRX5600 capacity	SRX5800 capacity
CPS	350,000	350,000
Maximum firewall throughput	60 Gbps	120 Gbps
Maximum IPS throughput	15 Gbps	30 Gbps
Maximum VPN throughput	15 Gbps	30 Gbps
Maximum concurrent sessions	9 million	10 million
Maximum firewall policies	80,000	80,000
Maximum concurrent users	Unlimited	Unlimited

For the various throughput numbers shown in Table 1-20, each metric is doubled from the SRX5600 to the SRX5800, so the maximum firewall throughput number is 60 Gbps on the SRX5600 and 120 Gbps on the SRX5800. This number is achieved utilizing HTTP large gets to create large stateful packet transfers; the number could be larger if UDP streams are used, but that is less valuable to customers, so the stateful HTTP numbers are utilized. The IPS and VPN throughputs follow the same patterns. These numbers are 15 Gbps and 30 Gbps for each of these service types on the SRX5600 and SRX5800, respectively.

The IPS throughput numbers are achieved using the older, NSS 4.2.1 testing standard. Note that this is not the same test that is used to test the maximum firewall throughput. The NSS test accounts for about half of the possible throughput of the large HTTP transfers, so if a similar test were done with IPS, about double the amount of throughput would be achieved.

These performance numbers were achieved using two interface cards and four SPCs on the SRX5600. On the SRX5800, four interface cards and eight SPCs were used. As discussed throughout this section, it's possible to mix and match modules on the SRX platforms, so if additional processing is required, more SPCs can be added. Table 1-21 lists several examples of this "more is merrier" theme.

Table 1-21. Example SRX5800 line configurations

Example network	IOCs	SPCs	Goal
Mobile provider	1	6	Max sessions and CPS
Financial network	2	10	Max PPS
Data center IPS	1	11	Maximum IPS inspection
Maximum connectivity	8 flex IOCs	4	64 10G interfaces for customer connectivity

A full matrix and example use cases for the modular data center SRX Series could fill an entire chapter in a how-to data center book. Table 1-21 highlights only a few, the first for a mobile provider. A mobile provider needs to have the highest number of sessions and the highest possible CPS, which could be achieved with six SPCs. In most environments, the total throughput for a mobile provider is low, so a single IOC should provide enough throughput.

In a financial network, the packets-per-second rate, or PPS, is the most important metric. To provide these rates, two SPCs are used, each configured using NPU bundling to allow for 10 Gbps ingress of small 64-byte packets. The 10 SPCs are used to provide packet processing and security for these small packets.

In a data center environment, an SRX may be deployed for IPS capabilities only, so here the SRX would need only one IOC to have traffic come into the SRX. The remaining 11 slots would be used to provide IPS processing, allowing for a total of 45 Gbps IPS inspection in a single SRX. That is an incredible amount of inspection in a single chassis.

The last example in Table 1-21 is for maximum connectivity. This example offers 64 10G Ethernet ports. These ports are oversubscribed at a ratio of 4:1, but again the idea here is connectivity. The remaining four slots are dedicated to SPCs. Although the number of SPCs is low, this configuration still provides up to 70 Gbps of firewall throughput. Each 10G port could use 1.1 Gbps of throughput simultaneously.

IOC modules

The SRX5000 line has three types of IOCs, two of which provide line rate throughput while the remaining is oversubscribed. Figure 1-39 illustrates an example of the interface complex of the SRX5000 line. The image on the left is the PHY, or physical chip, that handles the physical media. Next is the NPU or network processor. And the last component is the fabric chip. Together, these components make up the interface complex. Each complex can provide 10 gigabits per second in both ingress and egress directions, representing 20 gigabits per second full duplex of throughput.

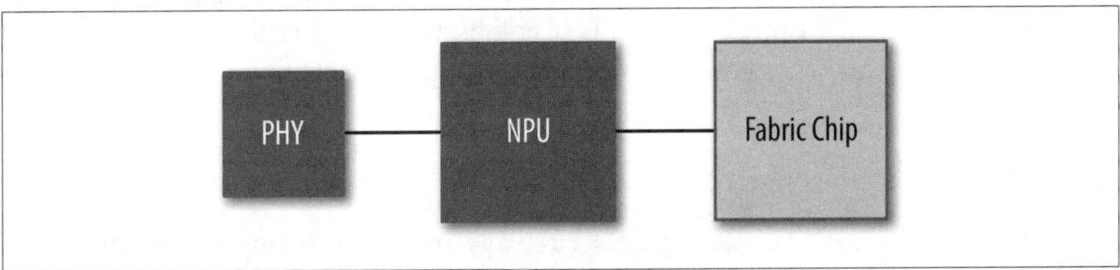

Figure 1-39. Interface complex of the SRX5000 line

Each type of card has a different number of interface complexes on it, with Table 1-22 listing the number of interface complexes per I/O type. Each complex is directly connected to the fabric, meaning there's no benefit to passing traffic between the complexes on the same card. It's a huge advantage of the SRX product line because you can place any cards you add anywhere you want in the chassis.

Table 1-22. Complexes per line card type

Type	Complexes
4 × 10G	4
40 × 1G	4
Flex IOC	2

The most popular IOC for the SRX is the four-port 10 gigabit card. The 10 gigabit ports utilize the XFP optical transceivers. Each 10G port has its own complex providing 20 Gbps full duplex of throughput, which puts the maximum ingress on a 4 × 10G IOC at 40 Gbps and the maximum egress at 40 Gbps.

The second card listed in Table 1-22 is the 41 gigabit SFP IOC. This blade has four complexes, just as the four-port 10 gigabit card has, but instead of four 10G ports, it has 10 1G ports. The blade offers the same 40 Gbps ingress and 40 Gbps egress metrics of the four-port 10 gigabit card, but this card also supports the ability to mix both copper and fiber SFPs.

The last card in Table 1-22 is the modular or Flex IOC. This card has two complexes on it, with each complex connected to a modular slot. The modular slot can utilize one of three different cards:

- The first card is a 16-port 10/100/1000 card. It has 16 tri-speed copper Ethernet ports. Because it has 16 1G ports and the complex it is connected to can only pass 10 Gbps in either direction, this card is oversubscribed by a ratio of 1.6:1.
- Similar to the first card is the 16-port SFP card. The difference here is that instead of copper ports, the ports utilize SFPs and the SFPs allow the use of either fiber or copper transceivers. This card is ideal for environments that need a mix of fiber and copper 1G ports.
- The last card is the dense four-port 10G card. It has four 10-gigabit ports. Each port is still an XFP port. This card is oversubscribed by a ratio of 4:1 and is ideal for environments where connectivity is more important than line rate throughput.

Summary

Juniper Networks' SRX Series Services Gateways are the company's next-generation firewall offerings. Juniper brings the Junos operating system onto the SRX, enabling carrier-class reliability. This chapter introduced a multitude of platforms, features, and concepts; the rest of the book will complete your knowledge in all of the areas that have been introduced here. The majority of the features are shared across the platforms, so as you read through the rest of the book, you will be learning a skill set that you can apply to small hand-sized firewalls as well as larger devices. Your journey through the material may seem great, but your reward will be great as well. The concepts in this book apply not only to the SRX, but to all of the products in the Junos product line.

Chapter Review Questions

1. Which of the SRX platforms can use WAN interfaces?
2. What are the Ethernet switching restrictions on the branch SRX Series?
3. What is the true cutoff limit for using a branch device in a branch and not using it in a larger environment such as a data center?
4. The SRX5000 line seems to have "too much" performance. Is such a device needed?
5. What is the biggest differentiator between the branch SRX Series and data center SRX Series platforms?
6. Which SRX platforms support the UTM feature set?

7. Why can't the data center SRX Series manage the AX411 Wireless LAN Access Point?
8. For how long a term can you purchase a license for a Junos feature?
9. What does a Services Processing Card do?
10. What is the benefit of the distributed processing model on the data center SRX Series?

Chapter Review Answers

1. The SRX210, SRX240, and SRX650 can use WAN interfaces. These are part of the branch SRX Series. As they are placed in a branch, they are more likely to be exposed to non-Ethernet interfaces and need to accommodate various media types.
2. Ethernet switching can only be done across the same card. It is not possible to switch across multiple line cards. The branch SRX Series devices use a switching chip on each of their interface modules. Switched traffic must stay local to the card. It is possible to go across cards, but that traffic will be processed by the firewall.
3. It's possible to place a branch device in any location. The biggest cutoff typically is the number of concurrent sessions. When you are unable to create new sessions there isn't much the firewall can do with new traffic besides drop it. The second biggest limit is throughput. If the firewall can create the session but not push the traffic, it doesn't do any good. If a branch SRX Series product can meet both of these needs, it may be the right solution for you.
4. The SRX5800 can provide an unprecedented amount of throughput and interface density. Although this device may seem like overkill, in many networks it's barely enough. Mobile carriers constantly drive for additional session capacity. In data center networks, customers want more throughput. It's not the correct device for everyone, but in the correct network, it's just what is needed.
5. The data center SRX Series devices allow the administrator to increase performance by adding more processing. All of the branch devices have fixed processing.
6. As of Junos 10.2, only the branch SRX Series devices support UTM. The focus was for a single small device to handle all of the security features for the branch. In the data center, items such as antispam are handled by dedicated servers. In the future, the feature may be added to the product.
7. It doesn't make sense for the data center SRX Series to manage the AX411 because of the typical deployment location for the product. Although it is technically possible, it is not a feature that many people would want to use, and hence Juniper didn't enable this.
8. The maximum length a Juniper license can be purchased for is five years.
9. A Services Processing Card on the data center SRX Series enables the processing of traffic for all services. All of the services available on the SRX, such as IDP, VPN,

and NAT, are processed by the same card. There is no need to add additional cards for each type of service.

10. The distributed processing model of the data center SRX Series allows the device to scale to an unprecedented degree. Each component in the processing of a flow optimizes the processing capabilities to allow you to add more than a dozen processors to the chassis, with equal distribution of sessions across all of the cards.

CHAPTER 2

What Makes Junos So Special?

Back when Juniper Networks set out to create the world's best routers, it needed to design a new hardware platform to handle extremely fast router speeds. The hardware architecture included line cards that contained a series of application-specific integrated circuits (ASICs), processors, and interfaces, with each card designed to act as a client within the chassis. The main component that could control these line cards, the *route engine*, was also created, and it is the hardware component that runs Junos.

Although this may not seem like such a big deal, it is; it was a huge advancement in the state of router technology in the 1990s and it still is today. This design creates the clear physical separation of the control and data planes; separating these two elements allows the components to operate at their full capacity without interrupting each other. The data plane can pass traffic at 100% of capacity while leaving the route engine (RE) to calculate routes and manage the device. It's at the heart of enabling extremely fast router speeds.

Just as the forwarding and control planes were once intertwined, so, too, was the control and data plane software. All processes operated in kernel space and very little prioritization was done. With Junos, the network operating system game changed. Having a separate RE allowed for the running of a more robust underlying operating system, and Junos, unlike previous network operating systems, enabled the restarting of processes, separate user and kernel spaces, and an easier way to maintain modular design. Again, it is a logical design today, but it was a game-changer back then.

This chapter is a primer for any administrator trying to understand what all the Junos hoopla is about. It examines the foundations of Junos and how it works, and then provides comparisons for those of you coming from other platforms such as ScreenOS or IOS. It is not meant to be an extensive guide on Junos—if you need such a guide, try the Day One booklets at *http://www.juniper.net/dayone* or the thorough documentation at *http://www.juniper.net/techpubs*. We, the authors, consider learning Junos to be a personal adventure.

And for all of you Junos router or switching heads who might be reading this excursion into Junos security, even after years of use there is always something new to learn, something new you can do. Besides, any Junos knowledge you gain on the SRX Series Services Gateway can easily be transferred to any other Junos platform.

OS Basics

The Junos operating system is unlike most firewall operating systems of the past. This operating system is of a more modern design. It contains the characteristics of a server and/or desktop operating system. Most firewall appliances and routers of the past used a single OS image that contained what was known as a *real-time operating system*. ScreenOS, Juniper's original firewall platform, is an example of this, and these simpler operating systems are great when the OS only needs to run a few different tasks. By the way, all of the tasks in the operating system run in kernel mode, and if any of the tasks crash, the whole system will come to a halt, as there is no process separation.

Kernel Space Versus User Space

The kernel of an operating system is no different from any other binary application that can run on a system. The kernel, as an application, is designed to be the core of the operating system. It handles specific system calls such as accessing hardware, or scheduling which processes can run and for how long. All of these tasks occur within what is known as *kernel space*. Tasks that exist in kernel space have a higher priority on the system. If something bad happens in the kernel, typically a kernel panic will occur, bringing down the entire system.

The benefit of execution in kernel space is speed. Any task done by the kernel is given the highest possible priority on the processor—that's why many early networking devices had everything run in kernel space. And frankly, if a device is simple enough, process separation isn't needed. However, when process separation isn't used, it leaves the system more exposed to crashes. The more tasks a kernel has to take on, the more that can potentially go wrong.

In most modern operating systems, user processes are separated from the kernel. This includes Junos, or any Unix-like system such as an operating system. User tasks run, and are scheduled, by the kernel as well as by memory allocation or other user-task access to hardware. If the user task crashes, the system continues to run, as it does not affect the kernel.

When Junos was created, the fact that it featured process separation was quite a revolution. Most networking devices at the time were plagued with crashes due to simple issues with Simple Network Management Protocol (SNMP) or routing protocols and the typical design at the time as a single processor providing both forwarding and management of the platform. Based on Juniper's design which separated the routing and control planes, these tasks were divided onto multiple processors. This way, the control plane would focus on controlling the device and the data plane would focus on forwarding the device. Again, with this hardware separation, if the control plane or data plane were to run into an issue, it would allow the remaining component to continue to run.

The founding engineers also came up with a new programming methodology for the product, using FreeBSD as its base. At the time, Cisco Systems' IOS software was extremely fragmented—for each Cisco hardware product there were several versions of IOS, each with dozens of releases. It was (and still is) a major effort to determine what features are in each release, and what release should be run on which device. This issue was well known among the founding engineers (several were from Cisco Systems), and they set out to correct in Junos what they saw as deficient in IOS.

FreeBSD

The Junos operating system is a derivative of the FreeBSD operating system. FreeBSD is a descendant of BSD, or Berkeley Unix (*BSD* stands for *Berkeley Software Distribution*). This operating system was created at the University of California, Berkeley, in 1977, by Bill Joy. The original BSD was a branch off of the original AT&T Unix operating system. It also contained one of the initial deployments of the TCP/IP protocol suite which made BSD one of the most popular operating systems on the Internet at the time. The TCP/IP implementation in BSD is called *Berkeley sockets*, and today it is still the fundamental standard for the TCP/IP implementation on modern operating systems.

In 1992, AT&T filed a lawsuit against the company Berkeley Software Designs for the inclusion of its source code in the BSDi fork of the BSD operating system (the BSDi software release was one of two versions of BSD that ran on the '386 architecture at the time). Because of the lawsuit, BSD development between 1992 and 1994 was slowed, and during this slowdown BSD momentum went to another kernel; eventually, another operating system was born, known as Linux. Linus Torvalds has said that if BSD were available on the '386 architecture, he most likely would not have created Linux.

The issue at hand with the lawsuit was the BSD license and the inclusion of the AT&T copyrighted software. The BSD license was extremely permissive and allowed users to do what they wanted with the software as long as they displayed the BSD license. In 1994, the lawsuit was settled, allowing for the release of 4.4BSD. This release came in two forms: 4.4BSD-Lite and 4.4BSD-Encumbered. The 4.4BSD-Lite release contained no AT&T source code. The final release of the original BSD OS was 4.4BSD-Lite2, from which FreeBSD was born.

FreeBSD started off as a compilation of software from the 386BSD fork and software from the Free Software Foundation (FSF). However, after the lawsuit hit BSD, FreeBSD was reengineered from 4.4BSD-Lite. The goal of FreeBSD is to provide an operating system free from any restrictions, to allow users to take the OS and its source code and use it as they see fit. Users can modify and use the code without having to share it—this is a key reason that Juniper and other enterprises, such as Apple, chose to use

FreeBSD as the core of their operating systems, because anyone can take it and develop it without constraints.

When Juniper started to create its first product, the M40e Multiservice Edge Router, it needed an OS. As the device's heavy lifting was done on the data plane, all of the data traffic processing was done on the Internet Processor (IP or I-Chip). But to allow users to manage and run dynamic routing protocols, an OS needed to run on the separate control plane. Because Juniper was more focused on the routing side of the house and less on creating hard disk drivers and other OS basics, FreeBSD was chosen as the base OS. It allowed Juniper to use this already existing and robust OS without restraints, and frankly, since Juniper was founded in Silicon Valley, the OS was very familiar to most of the computer and networking engineers in the area.

Today most organizations choose Linux as their base OS, often because their developers are familiar with the Linux environment. When Juniper chose BSD as its base OS, Linux was still extremely new and was not as robust as BSD. Also, Linux has a very different licensing model, and Juniper was interested in crafting BSD to meet the needs of its router—it wasn't designing a server, but an OS to run processes relating to system control and management. To accomplish this, kernel modification is required, and under the BSD license, the kernel can be modified freely. In Linux, there are licensing challenges to accomplish this; if the source code is modified, the modifications must be shared back with the community. Although this is done by design so that new features can be shared with the community, it doesn't quite protect a company's intellectual property.

Over the 10-plus years that Juniper has been making Junos, it has been heavily modifying it from its BSD past, but Juniper continues to utilize advancements in FreeBSD within Junos, as this chapter will attempt to point out, including the porting of BSD's symmetric multiprocessing (SMP) capabilities into the Junos kernel.

Process Separation

One of the key features of Junos is the process separation of the OS. Because of its design, and the fact that it is a FreeBSD derivative, Junos allows for the separation of tasks into various processes. For example, the routing daemon is its own process, called routing protocol daemon (RPD). Figure 2-1 illustrates an example of Junos process separation.

The challenge for a router or any network device is that it must remain operational. The device must be able to pass traffic at all times without service interruption, and because of this tolerance, a router or network device needs to be very robust. When Junos was brought to market this was not the case—a common reason routers of the time crashed wasn't due to forwarding traffic, but rather to routing protocols, SNMP, or other services performed by the router. A mishandled SNMP query, or an unrecognized bit in a protocol packet, often crashed routers, since they didn't have process

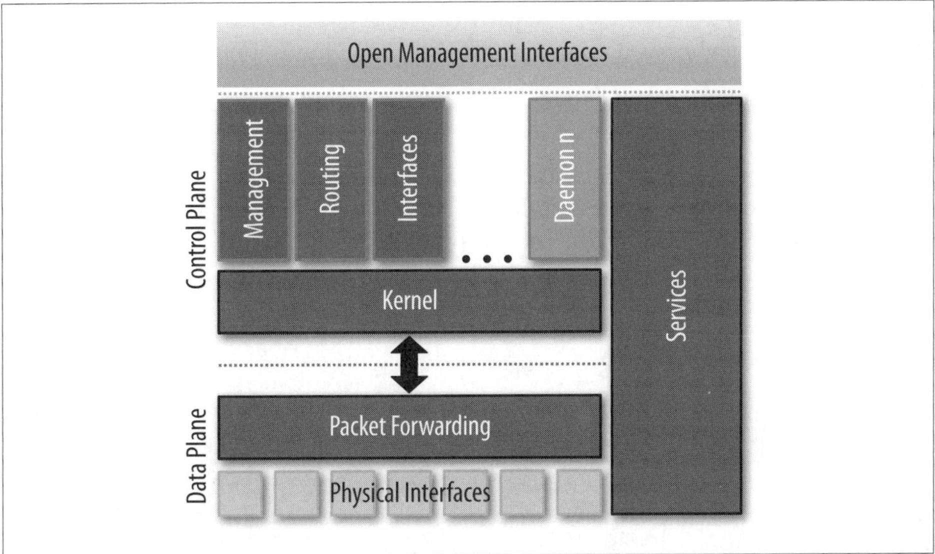

Figure 2-1. Junos process separation

separation. In the case of Junos, if a process were to crash, it would *core dump* and another instance of the process would start in its place.

A core dump is the current memory space for a process at the time it crashed. Dumping this information allows a developer to look into what caused the process to crash. It is called a core dump instead of a memory dump because memory used to consist of magnetic cores.

This is applicable to every service that is provided on the Junos control plane. It's also possible for a user to restart a process if needed. Process separation provides assurance that the administrator has total control over the system. Again, since Junos is a Unix-like OS, all of the power that comes in a Unix-like operating system also comes inside Junos.

Development Model

When Juniper Networks set out to create Junos, it wanted to break the mold of the incumbent in the router market space, and the incumbent was Cisco Systems. Cisco's IOS software has a very fragmented development model, with each Cisco device having several active versions and each version having several feature releases. This matrix of releases was the result of Cisco's driving attempt to make its customers happy, and quick releases to solve hot issues for customers or add new features as quickly as possible. The intentions were right, but the result was a messy codebase and a lot of confusion. When the engineers at Juniper were deciding how to develop their software, they came up with what would later be called the One Junos model.

The One Junos model is threefold: one OS, one release, and one architecture (see Figure 2-2).

One OS means one OS is developed across all of the available platforms. It's a powerful statement, but it is often contested. Ideally, all Junos devices are built from a single codebase; this means from a copy of the Junos source tree a working build for any product can be made. There are some points of argument around this, as we will discuss shortly.

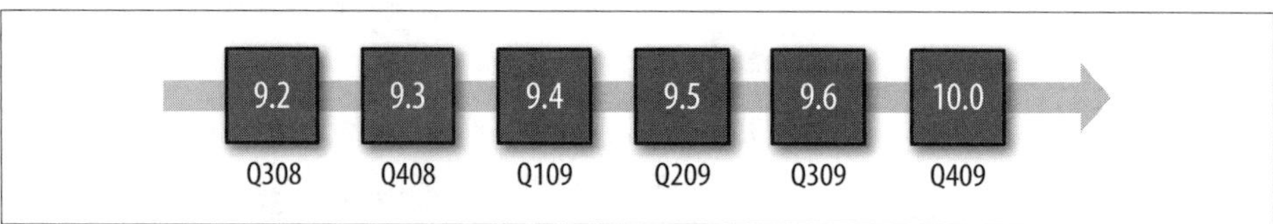

Figure 2-2. Junos release model

One release refers to the standard release cycle of Junos, which provides a predictable delivery date for software so that customers can understand when a release is going to come out and plan accordingly. Junos is released quarterly, in the middle of the month that falls in the middle of the quarter. It has been delivered consistently for more than 10 years, and is often delivered early. And when the release comes out, it is for all Junos platforms at the same time.

The Junos Release Train

Each Junos release has the following naming scheme: *MAJ.MIN(T)R.B*. This breaks down into MAJ for major release, MIN for minor release, R for release number, and B for build. T stands for the type of release, which can be R for release, which is the typical Junos release; B for beta; or S for service release. Each new release starts as an R1 and then continues throughout the release's life cycle. The number of R releases depends on the life cycle of a release.

The first three releases in a calendar year are supported for nine months after they are released. This means that new R releases providing bug fixes will be provided as needed. There are at least three releases per release. The last release in a year, which comes out in November, is supported for three years after the release comes out. At the end of the support cycle for a release, no new patches will come out for that release. If a user attempts to call in for support, the customer service organization will take calls for an end-of-support release; however, no new patches or updates will be offered for an end-of-support release. The customer will be requested to upgrade to a newer release if a bug is identified.

Adding New Features

The Junos operating system is a shared codebase across all product lines. This means that if a feature is added into the codebase, it allows any product to inherit the feature, as shown in Figure 2-3.

Using Figure 2-3, let's consider a few examples of how this works. The first example is an extension to Border Gateway Protocol (BGP), which would start on the M Series Multiservice Edge Routers, T Series Core Routers, and MX Series 3D Universal Edge Routers in Junos 10.0R1. In Junos, new features are added only in an initial R1 release. When a new feature is developed, the feature is typically available only in the originating platform; then, at the next R1 release, other platforms are allowed to utilize the feature. This lag is for performing quality assurance (QA): each platform utilizing a feature must go through a complete feature testing cycle before it can be included in the product.

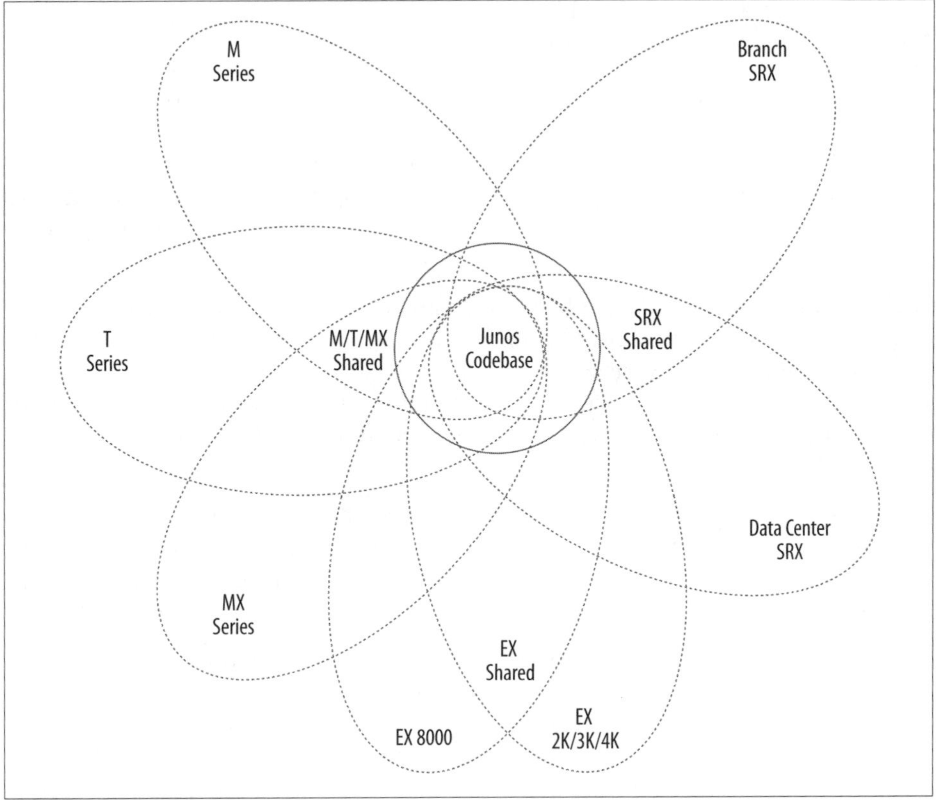

Figure 2-3. Feature migration example

Another example is importing a common feature into a product. Here there are two aspects to consider. The first is whether it is a control plane feature or not, because fundamentally, all features that run on the RE or control plane can run on any other device's control plane. The restrictions are processing, memory, and need. Some branch SRX Series products, for example, contain VoIP features that run on the control plane. This feature is not available on the MX Series simply because it doesn't make any sense for the control plane on an MX Series router to be a voice gateway; it is outside the scope of the product. If the MX Series router were to offer such a feature, it would need to be much more scalable than just running the feature on the control plane.

The second aspect to consider is whether the data plane is capable of performing the feature. This aspect is discussed in more detail in the next section, but the diagram in Figure 2-3 shows Junos using what is called the *one architecture approach*. All of the code is written in such a way that the underpinnings of the hardware are hidden from the developers. This means that when a feature is written, the development of it is platform-agnostic, which makes it easier to get features running on products that have different data planes.

Data Plane

Each Junos product series can have radically different data planes. For example, MX Series routers and the data center SRX Series, although sharing a majority of the hardware, work very differently inside the box because the packet flow is processed differently in the hardware, and even some additional hardware is called into use. The goal for Junos is to present a common configuration and interface to the two different devices where possible.

Each product series has specific targets and markets in mind when they are developed, so the data plane hardware may be different. As we discussed, the MX Series router and data center SRX Series devices share all of the hardware between the two devices, but the difference is that the SRX is a 100% flow-based device. This means all traffic processed in the SRX is looked at and inspected on a flow-based level. The entire stream of data is looked at and each packet is related to each other.

In the case of the MX, it is, by default, a packet-based device, and it optionally can use Multiservices DPCs (MS-DPCs, which are the same thing as SPCs on the data center SRX Series). An MX is designed to be an Ethernet services router and the SRX is a services gateway. Both use the same hardware, yet in fundamentally different ways.

Because the hardware on the platforms is different, the underling software driving the data plane must be different. This has been the same development model that has existed for Junos since the very beginning. To make it easy for developers, Juniper uses the one architecture model to provide an abstraction layer above the hardware. This way, the platform engineers can write code that drives the features for the specific platform when new chipsets and processors come out without disrupting the actual implementation of the feature in its abstracted layer.

Junos Is Junos Except When It's Junos

Since its launch, Junos has migrated from running on just the M40e Multiservice Edge Router to running on well over a dozen platforms. This has brought criticism about whether Junos is still the pure software that Juniper promotes it to be; if there is only one Junos, why are there so many releases to download? To address these concerns, consider the following.

Remember first that many of these platforms' control planes and data plane processors run on completely different CPUs and processors than other devices. The branch SRX Series control plane runs on a MIPS64 processor, the SRX5000 line of services gateways runs on Intel, and the SRX3000 line runs on the PowerPC processor. Each of these is very different from the other. The original source code is the same, but it is compiled into different builds to suit the platform.

Junos could do what Microsoft Windows does to cover the differences in underlying hardware: provide a single multigigabyte DVD or USB image to allow customers to load each release from a single Junos. This would be fairly impractical for devices with limited compact flash, however, and the majority of the room would be wasted on packages that the platform would not need. (Besides, who wants to insert a DVD into their switch to upgrade the software?)

Remember, too, that the data plane on the majority of the platforms is different. The branch SRX Series and data center SRX Series products share a majority of the underlying code, but they run it on very different processors. A branch SRX Series device has only one or two processors, whereas a data center SRX Series device can have upward of 50. This is very different, requiring the code to be built in different ways, even though the flow features come from the same codebase. It is in Juniper's best interest to maintain the smallest possible codebase. The smaller the codebase, the easier it is to implement new features and the quicker it is to resolve bugs.

Finally, Junos is one of the few software development models that provides regular software releases on a driven schedule. This is an extremely hard feat to accomplish, but it is done with the customer in mind. It is done to provide a consistent stream of new features, a consistent support model around releases, and an easy-to-understand model for customers to determine which release to run and what they will get out of that release. Some customers choose to be bleeding-edge, others choose to run as far behind as possible. Either way, it's all about providing customers a choice for what is best for them.

Coming from Other Products

For most people, Junos is not their first adventure in working with a network operating system. Because of this, some assistance is needed when transitioning to the product. To become an expert in a product is not to just be able to configure a few items, but to know how a product is going to react in nearly any situation. It's a skill that takes years to master, and since versions change and new hardware is launched, the job is never complete.

Because of this, there is always a concern when switching to a new platform. "Will I lose all of my knowledge? Has all of this gone to waste?" This is something that goes beyond the love of a product; it goes to the individuals' careers and their ability to support their families. Taking on a new product is a challenge, and there is always a new learning curve.

The important part to focus on is the difference between the old product and the new product. For the most part, routing protocols are the same across all devices. The commands will be different, but the underlying concepts are the same. It's important not to lose sight of the fact that many skills can be carried over from other products into Junos.

This section is dedicated to looking at three major firewall platforms and what can be taken from them when moving into Junos. It also discusses major differences between the platforms and how to migrate knowledge between them. In some cases, there will not be a parallel comparison between the platforms, but the important features will be noted.

ScreenOS

The ScreenOS platform comes from NetScreen Technologies. It was designed as an ASIC-based firewall running a custom operating system. ScreenOS at the time was revolutionary for including an ASIC to speed up traffic processing and for including the concept of security zones. A *security zone* is a logical construct that contains one or more interfaces, and zones are used to create a direction between two different areas of the network. Traditionally, up until this time, policies were created only by using IP addresses and ports. By breaking up policies into these contexts, NetScreen provided for a simplified management infrastructure.

Because ScreenOS was the previous (acquired)-generation security product from Juniper Networks, the SRX Series and its Junos operating system are looked at as the next-generation version of ScreenOS. For some, there is mild confusion when transitioning between the two platforms. ScreenOS and Junos share some similarities with respect to concepts, but it tends to end there.

The ScreenOS operating system runs a very simplistic "real-time" operating system. All processes and tasks run in kernel space. There is no separation of processes within ScreenOS, so if any one component were to fail, the entire operating system can crash, and because the OS is required for session setup, the entire device is lost. The benefit of the design of the ScreenOS software is that everything can happen very quickly, since it is executed directly in the kernel.

But the major cons of the design outweigh its advantages. The real reason for the design of the OS was because, at its inception, processors and memory were not as capable as they are today. Making a cost-effective appliance with a small footprint was just not possible on the hardware of the time. Besides, most of the heavy lifting was done by the ASIC, which was really the gem of the ScreenOS platform's design.

ScreenOS originally focused on the command-line interface (CLI) as its primary management interface, but later introduced a simple web UI to manage the device that entered the CLI commands on behalf of the user. The CLI had similarities to Cisco's IOS in its usage, which is understandable, since IOS was the most popular network operating system on the market and it made sense to follow its lead.

ScreenOS provides the traditional operational mode and configuration mode that most network operating systems provide. Operational mode allows users to retrieve information and configuration mode allows users to modify the device's configuration. All changes in configuration mode are made effective immediately.

ScreenOS changed the firewall market because of its appliance design, fast performance, and ease of use. It also utilized stateful firewall technology, which at the time was a major advancement. The more popular products of the time were proxy-based firewall solutions, very few of which are popular today. Other major firewall products at the time were not as easy to use, nor did they offer the performance that ScreenOS did. Many firewall products required an underlying OS, such as Solaris, HP-UX, and even Windows NT 4.0. ScreenOS allowed the administrator to take the appliance out of the box and literally be ready to go in minutes.

Because of ScreenOS's ease of use and its long existence in the marketplace, its usage has become extremely popular around the world. Because the SRX is also from Juniper Networks, there is an expectation that it would be a descendant of ScreenOS, but rather, the SRX products use the Junos operating system. Junos is vastly different from ScreenOS, as it is of a modern OS design and extremely modular. The next chapter talks in depth about how to use Junos; the remainder of this chapter is dedicated to assist users who are coming from ScreenOS and how to ease into using Junos.

One of the most beloved features of ScreenOS was the web UI. This helped administrators use the platform right away, because they did not need to know how to use the product. Underlying ScreenOS is a complete command-line-driven interface, and the web UI simply created the appropriate CLI commands for the user.

Junos operates in a similar manner, as all the configuration elements are primarily handled in the CLI. On top of this, devices run a web management tool called J-Web. The J-Web interface allows users to manage Junos in a similar manner. The biggest difference is that Junos was originally designed as a CLI-driven operating system, and many tools and options are provided inside the Junos command line that simply are not available in any other network operating system. Because of this flexibility, most Junos users tend to lean toward using the CLI. This may seem like a strange concept at first, but it is something that rings true with Junos. Either way, both the CLI and J-Web are available.

If you are coming from ScreenOS, there are a few items that will typically get in your way of getting started.

First, configuring something on Junos requires more commands than it would on ScreenOS, due to the hierarchy-based configuration of Junos. An example of this is a security policy. In ScreenOS, you can configure a security policy in a single command. In Junos, it takes two commands, because Junos needs a match and then a stanza, showing the device what to match in the policy and then what to do if a match is made. Because these commands are in two different stanzas, two commands are required.

The Junos configuration is designed to be extremely flexible and not to change once a stanza is added into a release, which means the configuration needs to be extremely extensible. Due to its extensibility, the commands require extra commands to add configuration. To compensate for this, Junos allows users to enter the command hierarchy much like they would when changing a directory. Once users are inside a hierarchy, they only need to enter local commands. This reduces the number of words that users need to enter per command (we will cover this in more depth in Chapter 3).

Both systems use the `set` command to enter information into the configuration. In ScreenOS, the `get` command is used to display operational information, and Junos uses the `show` command, similar to IOS.

Another quirk from the ScreenOS user's point of view is the size of the Junos operating system installation file. Junos is a full-fledged operating system with a BSD core, so the release file includes all of the various daemons, libraries, and utilities. The ScreenOS image is a single binary file, and since ScreenOS does not have process separation, everything runs quite compactly. The stability gained when using Junos is well worth the additional size of the file.

Both Junos and ScreenOS can be managed side by side using the Network and Security Manager (NSM) tool. NSM provides an abstraction that can be shared across both platforms. Users who currently utilize NSM will get a similar experience across both ScreenOS and Junos.

IOS and PIX OS

The Internetwork Operating System (IOS) was often considered the gold standard for network operating systems, and it is why ScreenOS shares many similarities with IOS. IOS is the primary OS for the majority of Cisco's devices, though several new devices, such as the Nexus series switches and the CRS product lines, use newer-style operating systems.

IOS uses a simple model of commands. The command line can operate in two modes: operational and configuration. In operational mode, the `show` command displays operational information. The administrator can then enter configuration mode and enter configuration commands. Unlike ScreenOS and Junos, the command is simply entered without the need for using `set`. Most Cisco administrators utilize the command line for administration on these devices.

Moving to Junos from an IOS device has the same challenges as moving from ScreenOS. Most users who migrate between platforms are overwhelmed by the more detailed command set in Junos. As mentioned earlier in this chapter, although this is challenging at first, it ends up becoming a benefit because so many other types of devices run Junos and they have the same command sets.

The majority of users who migrate from a Cisco firewall product to Junos will migrate from a Cisco PIX or ASA platform, which, effectively, share the same operating system. Originally, the PIX operating system ran much like IOS with all executions running in kernel mode, which is the same design as ScreenOS and other network operating systems of the time. Later versions of PIX OS, such as 8.0 and later, run a Linux kernel for the OS, and a combination of some of the older PIX OS technologies.

Both the old and new versions of PIX OS share a similar command-line infrastructure. The OS utilizes the traditional operational mode and configuration mode design for device management. Since Cisco purchased the company Network Translation, it has moved the CLI to be more IOS-like, easing administrators' transition between the two platforms.

A strength of the PIX platform is the included GUI tool called the PIX Device Manager (PDM). The PDM is a Java-based tool that allows for full administration of the device as well as built-in troubleshooting. This tool is extremely strong and allows for nearly anyone to jump into the platform. For those who rely on this tool solely to manage the device, migrating to Junos may be more difficult, as J-Web does not provide a one-to-one feature set.

Again, if you are one of these users, be sure to read Chapter 3 before jumping into the big Junos pool.

Check Point

The Check Point firewall was one of the largest game changers in firewall history. It came along at a time when most people believed a firewall was nothing more than a piece of wood inside a wall. Check Point led the stateful firewall revolution and competed with proxy firewalls. Check Point came out with the concept of a stateful firewall and this has become the industry standard over proxy firewalls. As the industry requires ever-faster performance, the market has become increasingly comfortable with stateful technologies.

The Check Point firewall is a software solution. It has the flexibility of not being tied to a specific hardware platform. Originally, Check Point was very popular on Solaris, HP-UX, and Microsoft Windows NT 4.0. Over time, it became cumbersome to patch the various base operating systems and, in the event of a disaster, rebuild them. In response to this, several vendors began to come out with appliance-based systems that could run Check Point. The appliances ran an easy-to-manage operating system and often provided an on-box web UI to manage the device. Today, Check Point offers its own OS, Secure Platform, which is Linux-based and can be run on any x86 hardware as well as on the company's own series of appliances.

The premier technology for Check Point is its management platform. The Windows-based GUI has set the bar for management on any network device. The GUI allows for configuration, log viewing, reporting, and real-time monitoring. The GUI is often the most compelling reason to use Check Point. And because of this, Check Point can be one of the most difficult firewalls from which to migrate.

The Check Point software system does provide a command line, but it is only used in certain situations. The majority of the configurations are done through the GUI tool base. Because Junos is command-line-driven, it can be very shocking to migrate over to Junos. There are two solutions to the migration. The NSM tool is the legacy management option for all of the Juniper Networks products, and it provides a single console to manage all of the various devices that are manufactured by Juniper.

The next-generation tool that will slowly replace NSM is called *Junos Space*. The Junos Space software is a modular system that is designed to manage all of Juniper's devices. The difference between Junos Space and NSM is that Junos Space provides a greater abstraction from the configuration. We will discuss the capabilities of the two platforms in Chapter 13, along with Junos automation.

Although moving from a GUI-based world to the Junos platform that is CLI-driven can seem like quite a feat, it is actually empowering. Trust us. All of the authors of this book have done it, and we are all now firm believers. The advanced capabilities of Junos expose administrators to a larger space of products and technologies that can help them, in turn, to expand their careers. Today, someone administering an SRX device can easily move over to a switch or even the largest routers in the world. This book will help you learn Junos, and learn the SRX well through Junos, if you want to make a true investment in time and learning.

Summary

The Junos operating system is an advanced modern operating system that is designed for both today's and tomorrow's needs. The thought put into the structure of Junos provides a robust implementation that allows for the addition of new features without compromising stability. In this chapter, we discussed the basics of the Junos operating system because to learn an operating system, sometimes you just have to touch its various capabilities. We wanted to provide you with an understanding of what makes Junos tick and how to migrate, as we all did, to what we think is a superior platform running a superior operating system.

In the next chapter, you'll get a hands-on crash course in Junos. To supplement that knowledge, you may want to check out the many online training tools designed to teach users about Junos. You may want to start with Junos Central, at *http://junos.juniper.net/*. Also, some free Day One Junos booklets might help (*http://www.juniper.net/dayone*). Finally, check out the O'Reilly series, Juniper Networks Technical Library, at *http://www.juniper.net/books*. A new O'Reilly book titled *Junos Fundamentals: The JNCIA* (scheduled for publication in November 2010) covers Junos for first-time users.

By the way, since Junos has new releases coming out every quarter, new features, capabilities, and even products are always on the horizon. It's best to check online for the latest on Junos at *http://juniper.net*.

Chapter Review Questions

1. What is an OS kernel?
2. What OS is Junos based upon?
3. What are the names of the two planes in the Junos operating system?
4. What is the benefit of separating processes?
5. How many Junos releases are there in a year?
6. How many software trains are there in Junos?
7. What is the only release that contains new features?
8. Why are there different builds of Junos for each release?
9. What is the primary method for managing Junos?
10. Can features created on one Junos device be shared with another Junos device?

Chapter Review Answers

1. An operating system's kernel is responsible for managing the system. It controls access to the hardware and the scheduling of running tasks.
2. Junos is derived from the FreeBSD operating system. This was done because FreeBSD contained all of the basics, such as hardware support, process separation, and a robust kernel. Its license also allowed for Juniper to utilize the code without paying royalties.
3. The two planes in the Junos operating system are the control plane and the data plane. The control plane is responsible for managing the system and running routing protocols. The data plane processes network traffic.
4. Separating processes out of the kernel allows the processes to be managed individually. In the event that a process crashes, the rest of the system will continue to run and will not be affected while that process restarts.
5. There are four Junos releases per year. One release is provided in the middle month of each quarter.

6. Junos is built on only a single train of software. Each device uses the same source codebase to build its image.
7. Each R1 release of software contains new features. The remaining R1 releases only contain bug fixes.
8. Each Junos platform contains different data plane chipsets and often different control plane processor types. Because the binary images are different, a separate release is needed. Also, some platforms may have features that others don't, based upon the deployment location of the platform.
9. Junos is primarily a command-line-managed device. All of the configuration is stored in the command line. Tools such as J-Web, NSM, and Junos Space allow for management through a GUI interface if the administrator desires to use them.
10. Since the source codebase is shared among all of the platforms, it's possible to enable features developed on one platform to be used on another. Junos is written with a single architecture, meaning that the underlying hardware is abstracted from the actual feature code. Features are enabled as needed based upon the deployment of the device.

CHAPTER 3

Hands-On Junos

This chapter is designed as a jumpstart for users who are getting into Junos for the first time. It is by no means meant to be a complete primer on Junos and all of its various features; rather, it is intended to provide administrators who are new to Junos with enough tools to get started on the SRX Series—and hopefully provide long-time Junos users with a few new tips that are specific to the SRX.

If you're coming from another network operating system such as IOS or ScreenOS, this chapter will get you started in Junos.

Introduction

The command-line interface (CLI) is the premier way to manage the Junos platform, and for the majority of its existence, the CLI has been the only way to manage Junos. Lately, Juniper Networks has created an abundance of great tools designed to enable customers to manage the platform via other management tools, including Junos Space, the Network and Security Manager (NMS), and Junos automation techniques. We will discuss these and other management tools in other chapters of this book. This chapter provides a tour of the Junos CLI, and how to jump right in.

Why promote the CLI? First, no matter which tool you use to manage Junos, the tool will *always* be represented in the CLI. So, it's important to have an understanding of the CLI, configuration output, and how the CLI works. This will give you a better understanding of what is going on inside the Junos device, no matter which management method you decide to use.

Second, for years the CLI has been the management tool of choice among the world's largest service providers, because they have learned that the CLI contains many built-in tools and tricks to assist in configuration management. Remember that Junos is a Unix-line operating system, and Unix is the master of text processing, which means these tools are used well here. Administrators who are familiar with using shells and pipes (|) will quickly see how Junos contains these same tricks. For those without this experience, it's the perfect time to learn. Learn the Junos CLI, and it becomes a trip through Unix, programming, and pure access to the network.

Junos provides administrators with so many levels of access to configure and monitor their devices. Even the default configuration for Junos is extremely deep and provides administrators with a great deal of control regarding how they want traffic to operate as it passes through a device. This can be thought of as *programming the network*.

There is a good side and a bad side to this level of depth. The bad side is that it can put users too far away from being able to use the product. In fact, starting off with Junos has proven to be a bit too daunting for some beginning users; fortunately, Juniper Networks has listened to this and responded by providing more clarified documentation, books, and management tools such as J-Web and Junos Space.

The good news is that once administrators get their minds wrapped around Junos, using it opens new doors. Since Junos runs on several different platforms, it allows administrators to use their acquired knowledge across any Junos platform, whether it is a router, switch, firewall, or something else. As your Unix skill set expands, you will have full access to the underpinnings of Junos, allowing you access to a complete understanding of how the system works. It also opens up users to learning programming, whether via Junos automation or by working with the Junos SDK. There's a vast difference between configuring your devices and programming the network, and by learning Junos via the CLI, you'll be closer to the latter, or at least to understanding how it can be done.

Driving the Command Line

You can connect into the Junos CLI in numerous ways. You can access the device via a serial port, Telnet, or secure shell (SSH). When users connect to the Junos device they are placed into the CLI by default. The CLI for Junos is a custom shell that is built into the device.

A shell is a command-line interpreter that accepts commands from the user and then executes specific tasks based on the commands. The CLI is a custom-written shell designed to allow very effective interactive access to monitoring and configuring Junos. The name of the binary is called *cli* and it is stored in the */usr/sbin* directory on the device.

Because Junos is based on BSD, its most powerful administrative user is named *root*. The root user is the only default user on a Junos device. When logging in as root the user is given access to the BSD side of Junos. This allows unlimited access to the filesystem, configuration files, and binaries.

To learn more about how the FreeBSD side of Junos works, please reference *The Complete FreeBSD: Documentation from the Source (http://oreilly.com/catalog/9780596005160/)* by Greg Lehey (O'Reilly). The book is considered a masterpiece and provides amazing detail regarding the underpinnings of FreeBSD.

The root user has access to all of this because the root user is placed into what is known as the C shell or *csh*. This is the default shell of FreeBSD. There are times when using csh is helpful in administering the device, but typically csh is for advanced users.

The root user can access the Junos CLI by executing the command `cli`. This will give the root user access to all of the Junos functions of the system. The CLI binary, much like other Unix shells, provides the user with many built-in features, such as command-line completion, help, and output redirection, all of which are included in this chapter's overview. All users other than root will have their shell access default to the CLI instead of csh, and later in this chapter we will discuss some of the secrets of what CLI access has to offer.

Operational Mode

When you first log in to the system you are presented with the CLI.

The initial mode that you see in the CLI is what is called *operational mode*. This mode provides you with access to run operational commands that enable the display of the state and status of the device. It is in this mode that most users identify what is happening on the device, and perform troubleshooting, as opposed to configuration. The commands in operational mode fall into one of several categories, as listed in Table 3-1.

Table 3-1. Operational command classification

Type	Commands	Description
View/change state	`show`, `clear`, `monitor`	Provides information about the current status of components in the system. Also allows the user to reset the state of some system components.
Configuration	`configure`, `save`, `set`, `load`	Allows access to and manipulation of configuration elements of the system.
Diagnostics	`ping`, `mtrace`, `traceroute`, `test`, `restart`, `op`, `start`	Diagnostic commands that provide device and network accessibility testing of the system.
Documentation	`help`	Provides access to all of the Junos documentation right from the command line.
Remote administration	`ssh`, `telnet`	Allows the user to connect to other remote systems.

This diverse command set offers you a venerable tool chest to work with on the Junos device. Throughout this chapter, and indeed this entire book, we will use these commands in correlation with real working examples for actual on-box troubleshooting and monitoring.

Variable Length Output

Most elements in Junos allow for several levels of informational output to be displayed, allowing you to choose what you want to see and how you want to see it. A perfect example of this is the output for interfaces on a device; in this scenario, many stats are associated with each interface, and if only one command output was available, it would require a literal cruise through the ocean of information to get the information you needed.

Because of the depth of information that can be provided per command, Junos comes with four levels of depth, as highlighted in Table 3-2.

Table 3-2. Output command options

Command	Description
`terse`	Shows the smallest amount of information for the command; for example, showing the output as a list of elements
`brief`	Shows each output element plus some additional details regarding each element
`detail`	Shows the majority of the information about each known element
`extensive`	Shows all known information on each displayed element

Although this may seem like too many options for displaying output, it places you in control, with the ability to choose the right amount of information at the right time. Throughout this book, you'll find that the CLI is designed to be the single source management solution for the SRX Series, and such flexibility is the key to providing the right amount of information when you need it.

Passing Through the Pipe

In Unix, there is a concept called *standard streams*. A stream is a channel that allows for the input or output of data. It's a fundamental concept that has been used in Unix-like operating systems since their inception. The idea is that there are three basic streams: standard input, standard output, and standard error. The groundbreaking concept that Unix provided was the fact that each of these is abstracted from its actual source. For example, output could be sent back to the command line, or to a file, and the implementation would be the same. This abstraction is very powerful, as the input/output (I/O) streams could be sent in the same manner, no matter what type of source or destination was involved.

This still applies in the case of Junos. You can use the special pipe or pipeline character (|) at the end of any Junos command, allowing you to redirect the standard output or output from any command to one of several other commands. These commands can manipulate the output, limit the output, and even redirect the output to a file. We will show various examples of the use of | throughout this chapter and throughout this book.

Seeking Immediate Help

Documentation has always been a big part of any computing system, but providing documentation to the end user at the command line gives Unix an advantage, for the user does not have to look through various paper manuals to identify commands and options. Since Unix, and Unix-like operating systems, including Junos, are primarily command-line-driven, and there tend to be many commands, users need a simple method to look up information right from their access terminal. In 1971, Ken Thompson and Dennis Richie wrote the original manpages for the Unix operating system. These were single-page documents that could be accessed directly from the command line, giving users a complete level of documentation at their fingertips.

Manpages stem from the `man` command used to access them, and they document several aspects of a Unix system. They provide documentation for each command, system call, C language library function, and several other topics. Because Unix contained so much information, and it was accessed from a single command line, this simplified method of accessing the information was heralded.

When Junos was launched, the Internet was still small, compared to today. Users often needed access to documentation for Junos and had a few different places to turn. They could access the Junos documentation online, on CD-ROM, in printed manuals, or right from the command line. Junos documentation is written in the DocBook format. This format allows for simple cross-format publication from a single source. This provides more consistency across the documentation, as well as simple distribution. Junos command-line documentation was, and still is, popular due to its quick accessibility and level of depth.

You can access the `help` command from either operational mode or configuration mode. The `help` command contains a few options. The `help reference` command shows a summary for a specific configuration statement. The `help topic` command provides information on a topic. Here is an example of each:

```
root@SRX210-A> help reference security screen-security
                               screen (Security)


   Syntax


  screen {


            ids-option screen-name {
```

```
                                    alarm-without-drop;

                                                    icmp {

                                                       flood {
                                                  threshold number ;

                                                       }

                                                  fragment;

                                                       ip-sweep {
                                                  threshold number ;

                                                       }
--snip--

root@SRX210-A> help topic firewall filter term
                    Configuring Firewall Filter Terms

   Each firewall filter consists of one or more terms. To configure a term,
   include the term statement at the [edit firewall family family-name filter
   filter-name] hierarchy level:

   [edit firewall family family-name filter filter-name]

   term term-name {
           ...match-conditions ...
           ...actions

   }

   For IPv4 traffic, configure the filter terms at the [edit firewall family
--snip--
```

In this example, the reference and topic options are shown. Each provides a different level of information on topics. Since there are so many available commands, it's also possible to search through the commands using the `help apropos` command. This command allows you to search through the text in all of the statement names and help strings. So, if you were looking for a command, `help apropos` would provide information around those specific topics quite easily:

```
root@SRX210-A> help apropos flow
clear security flow
    Clear flow information
clear services dynamic-flow-capture
    Clear dynamic flow capture information
clear services flow-collector
    Clear services flow collector information
clear services flows
    Remove established flows from flow table
show interfaces flow-statistics
    Show security flow counters and errors
show route protocol <protocol> flow
    Locally defined flow route
```

```
show route flow
    Show flow routing information
--snip--
```

In this example, all of the commands that match the `flow` option are shown (the output was trimmed for length). It's very helpful in terms of finding that one specific command you're looking for to accomplish a particular task.

On the screen, or in logs, you may encounter various strange messages. Often you may want to look up what a log means. You can do this using the `help syslog` command. This command can show you what the message means and the variables that are within the command:

```
root@SRX210-A> help syslog | match LINK
CHASSISD_FASIC_HSL_LINK_ERROR    chassisd detected F-chip link error
CHASSISD_FCHIP_HSR_INIT_LINK_ERR High-speed receiver (HSR) link initialization
CHASSISD_FCHIP_HST_INIT_LINK_ERR High-speed transmitter (HST) link
CHASSISD_FCHIP_LINK_ERROR        chassisd detected F-chip link error
CHASSISD_MULTILINK_BUNDLES_ERROR chassisd could not create link bundles for PIC
COSD_MULTILINK_CLASS_CONFLICT    Multilink class configuration exceeded limit
RPD_ISIS_LSPCKSUM                IS-IS link-state packet failed checksum tests
RPD_ISIS_OVERLOAD                IS-IS link-state database is full
RPD_LMP_RESOURCE_NO_LINK         rpd could not find TE link for resource
RPD_LMP_TE_LINK                  TE-link operation failed
RPD_LMP_TE_LINK_INDEX            rpd could not allocate TE-link index
RPD_RSVP_BYPASS_DOWN             RSVP link-protection bypass was terminated
RPD_RSVP_BYPASS_UP               RSVP link-protection bypass was established
SNMP_TRAP_LINK_DOWN              linkDown trap was sent
SNMP_TRAP_LINK_UP                linkUp trap was sent
VRRPD_LINK_LOCAL_ADD_MISMATCH    Link local address was incorrect

root@SRX210-A> help syslog SNMP_TRAP_LINK_DOWN
Name:          SNMP_TRAP_LINK_DOWN
Message:       ifIndex <snmp-interface-index>, ifAdminStatus <admin-status>,
               ifOperStatus <operational-status>, ifName <interface-name>
Help:          linkDown trap was sent
Description:   The SNMP agent process (snmpd) generated a linkDown trap because
               the indicated interface changed state to 'down'.
Type:          Event: This message reports an event, not an error
Severity:      warning
Facility:      LOG_DAEMON

root@SRX210-A>
```

In this example, the user is looking for the `SNMP_TRAP_LINK_DOWN` message. Since there are so many different types of syslog messages, the `| match LINK` option is used. This filters through all of the syslog messages and finds ones that contain the word *link*. Then the command `help syslog SNMP_TRAP_LINK_DOWN` is used to display the information on the log message.

When attempting to use commands in either operational or configuration mode, you can use the ? prompt to ask the command line what the next possible options are. You can do this after every command and it is extremely useful. It can guide you through the command hierarchy and then right to the command you need:

```
root@SRX210-A> show interfaces ?
Possible completions:
  <[Enter]>            Execute this command
  <interface-name>     Name of physical or logical interface
  ge-0/0/0
  ge-0/0/0.0
--snip--
root@SRX210-A> show interfaces ge-0/0/0 ?
Possible completions:
  <[Enter]>            Execute this command
  brief                Display brief output
  descriptions         Display interface description strings
  detail               Display detailed output
  extensive            Display extensive output
  media                Display media information
  routing-instance     Name of routing instance
  snmp-index           SNMP index of interface
  statistics           Display statistics and detailed output
  switch-port          Front end port number (0..15)
  terse                Display terse output
  |                    Pipe through a command
root@SRX210-A> show interfaces ge-0/0/0 brief
Physical interface: ge-0/0/0, Enabled, Physical link is Down
  Link-level type: Ethernet, MTU: 1514, Speed: 1000mbps, Loopback: Disabled,
  Source filtering: Disabled, Flow control: Enabled, Auto-negotiation: Enabled,
  Remote fault: Online
  Device flags   : Present Running Down
  Interface flags: Hardware-Down SNMP-Traps Internal: 0x0
  Link flags     : None

  Logical interface ge-0/0/0.0
    Flags: Device-Down SNMP-Traps Encapsulation: ENET2
    Security: Zone: untrust
    Allowed host-inbound traffic : dhcp tftp

root@SRX210-A>
```

Each command in Junos can provide tab or space completion. As you are typing commands, the appropriate or approximate command is automatically chosen for you. In many Unix shells, the Tab key is often used for completion, and you can use it here as well. However, the space bar completion in Junos is nice, because each command and its options have spaces between them. So, as you are typing the command it is being completed for you:

```
root@SRX210-A> sho<space>int<space>ter<space> #becomes

root@SRX210-A> show interfaces terse
Interface               Admin Link Proto    Local                 Remote
ge-0/0/0                up    down
ge-0/0/0.0              up    down
--snip--

root@SRX210-A>
```

Configuration Mode

The other mode in which to operate the Junos CLI is *configuration mode*. In configuration mode, you can make configuration changes to the device. Configuration mode is extremely versatile in the methods it allows you to use. Junos was designed to manage configurations comprising thousands of lines directly from the CLI, so in today's world of GUIs, this may seem like a Herculean task, but it's why the most common way to manage configuration is through the CLI.

To enter configuration mode from operational mode, you simply use the command `configure`. You will know you are in configuration mode because the prompt will end with `#` (instead of `>`, which indicates operational mode). As an alternative, you can use the hidden command `edit`, which is allowed because it is also used heavily throughout configuration mode.

There are actually several types of configuration modes. Each mode provides you with a different level of access into the configuration.

The default mode is *shared mode*. This means the configuration you are editing is shared among all of the other users on the device. When the configuration is finally made active, *all* of the users' changes will be made active.

You can also request *exclusive access* to the configuration by using the command `configure exclusive`. This means only that user can gain access to the configuration, and no one else can edit it. You can gain exclusive access only when no other users have an active configuration.

Alternatively, you can request a *private configuration*. This gives you a configuration that will not show other users' changes. If you choose to apply this configuration, it will not reflect any other changes made by others, but if another user makes a configuration change and applies it before the private configuration is applied, the previous changes will be lost.

No matter which way you request the configuration, you gain access to what is known as a *candidate configuration*. The candidate configuration is a copy of the currently running configuration. It's a scratch pad that you can use to modify the configuration. With Junos, *the configuration is not applied until it is actually committed*. This differs from other operating systems, where the configuration is applied immediately. We will discuss this commit model in more detail in the next section of this chapter.

Configuration mode is based on a hierarchical model. It allows you to step through the configuration in a fashion similar to filesystem directories on your laptop, as shown in Figure 3-1.

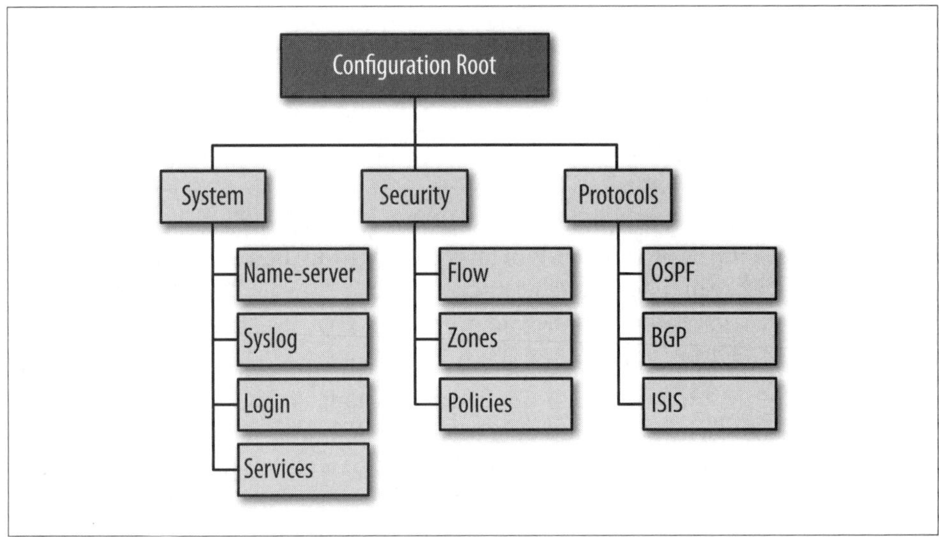

Figure 3-1. Configuration hierarchy example

This hierarchy allows you to enter and exit various areas of the configuration. It provides the benefits of restricting the scope of the command space and the size of the configuration that needs to be viewed. Here's an example:

```
root@SRX210-A# set security zones security-zone Tester interfaces ge-0/0/0
###Very long command

[edit]
root@SRX210-A# edit security zones security-zone Tester
###entering the security zones security-zone Tester hierarchy
[edit security zones security-zone Tester]
root@SRX210-A# set interfaces ge-0/0/0
###short command
[edit security zones security-zone Tester]
root@SRX210-A# show
interfaces {
    ge-0/0/0.0;
}
###running the show command displays only the local configuration.
```

In Junos configuration mode, instead of using `cd` to change directories and move through the hierarchy, you can use the `edit` command. As shown in the previous CLI example, you would use the command and then specify where in the hierarchy you want to be placed. From that position in the hierarchy, all commands are prefaced with the position in the hierarchy. So, instead of typing **set security zones security-zone Tester interfaces ge-0/0/0**, you simply type **set interfaces ge-0/0/0** and the rest of the command is assumed, due to the position in the configuration tree. This is a great feature for reducing command length and simplifying management.

Another Junos trick comes into play when viewing the configuration. When you issue the `show` command to view the configuration, you will only see what is under that hierarchy. Although this restricts the current view of the configuration, it provides you with a clear view of exactly what you want to see, and it's a huge advantage when you are editing large security policies or routing configurations.

Once you are inside a hierarchy, you can easily go up or down it. To go farther into the hierarchy you can use the `edit next-step` command, and it will take you into the next step of the configuration. Transversely, you can use the `up` command to go one step up in the configuration. Lastly, the `top` command takes you to the top of the configuration tree. Here's a sample:

```
[edit]
root@SRX210-A# edit system services ssh

[edit system services ssh]
root@SRX210-A# show
root-login allow;

[edit system services ssh]
root@SRX210-A# up

[edit system services]
root@SRX210-A# show
ssh {
    root-login allow;
}
telnet;
web-management {
    http {
        interface vlan.0;
    }
    https {
        system-generated-certificate;
        interface vlan.0;
    }
}

[edit system services]
root@SRX210-A# edit web-management http

[edit system services web-management http]
root@SRX210-A# show
interface vlan.0;
```

```
[edit system services web-management http]
root@SRX210-A# top

[edit]
root@SRX210-A#
```

You add and remove configuration changes using the `set` and `delete` commands. The `set` command *adds* the command to the configuration hierarchy. The `delete` command *removes* the command from the configuration hierarchy. Of course, the final changes to the configuration are not made active to the device until the configuration is committed. When deleting parts of the configuration it's possible to delete entire stanzas. For example, if you use the command `delete interfaces`, the entire `interfaces` stanza, no matter how long it is, will be deleted. This is much better than having to delete each line individually. It's also possible to use the `wildcard delete` command, which allows you to delete certain sections under a stanza while leaving the others intact:

```
[edit]
root@SRX210-A# wildcard delete interfaces ge-*
  matched: ge-0/0/0
Delete 1 objects? [yes,no] (no)
```

Here, only the interfaces starting with `ge-` will be deleted and the rest will be left as is. Note that Junos also asks you to confirm whether the deletion is OK. It's possible to use regular expression patterns to match the configuration, with the great advantage that you can remove only specific parts of the configuration.

Another common task is the need to rename a part of the configuration—for example, a security policy, where you want to change the policy's name because the function has changed. In other systems, you might be forced to delete the policy and then add it back into the configuration, but you can save time and reduce mistakes by copying the data to a file and then importing it, as shown in the following output:

```
[edit security policies from-zone trust to-zone untrust]
root@SRX210-A# rename policy trust-to-untrust to policy allow-outbound

[edit security policies from-zone trust to-zone untrust]
root@SRX210-A# show
policy allow-outbound {
    match {
        source-address any;
        destination-address any;
        application any;
    }
    then {
        permit;
    }
}

[edit security policies from-zone trust to-zone untrust]
root@SRX210-A#
```

You can also manipulate the configuration by using `pattern matching replace` throughout the configuration; this is a helpful procedure when migrating configurations to new interface cards. The action is simple to do, but its effects are profound:

```
[edit]
root@SRX210-A# replace pattern ge-0/0/1 with ge-5/0/0
```

This command replaces all of the entries of `ge-0/0/1` with `ge-5/0/0` in the configuration so that you don't have to find them all. A similar feature called `copy` takes one configuration stanza and duplicates it to another one:

```
[edit]
root@SRX210-A# copy interfaces ge-0/0/0 to ge-0/0/2
```

Here, all of the statements under `ge-0/0/0` are replicated under `ge-0/0/2`. This prevents you from having to type out each element by hand, or copy and paste it back into a terminal.

You can view the configuration with the `show` command, which displays the current configuration relative to your position in the hierarchy. Much like when using the `edit` or `set` command, the `show` command also lets you display a specific area in the configuration:

```
[edit]
root@SRX210-A# show
## Last changed: 2010-08-08 06:55:57 UTC
version 10.2R1.9;
system {
    host-name SRX210-A;
    root-authentication {
        encrypted-password "$1$o4rMECKV$mhN/bfMti9JnhQHtfhSka/"; ## SECRET-DATA
    }
    name-server {
        208.67.222.222;
        208.67.220.220;
    }

[edit]
root@SRX210-A# show security
nat {
    source {
        rule-set 1 {
            from zone A;
            to zone B;
            rule 1 {
                match {
                    source-address 0.0.0.0/0;
                }
--snip--

[edit]
root@SRX210-A# show security | display set
set security nat source rule-set 1 from zone A
set security nat source rule-set 1 to zone B
```

```
set security nat source rule-set 1 rule 1 source-address 0.0.0.0/0
--snip--

[edit]
root@SRX210-A#
```

The default method to display a configuration is to show it as a hierarchy. The configuration is displayed using brackets to show blocks of the configuration and semicolons to display the end of a statement. This is akin to C code. Displaying it in this manner makes the configuration easy to follow, but it is different from the commands that are entered to actually apply the configuration. Because of this, Junos offers the ability to modify the output with the `| display` option. The most commonly used option is `set`, which displays the list of configuration elements as `set` statements, as you saw in the previous output. These are the exact commands that you would type into the CLI to configure the device. Note that there are several other display options, and we will discuss them throughout this chapter.

Often, you may want to run operational commands inside configuration mode, perhaps to see what is already configured or to check the status of something on the device. This is possible to do by invoking the `run` command, which you can run when you need to commit the configuration to make it active. Switching between operational and configuration modes would be very tough to do while maintaining an effective workflow without the use of the `run` command:

```
[edit]
root@SRX210-A# run show interfaces terse
Interface               Admin Link Proto    Local                 Remote
ge-0/0/0                up    down
ge-0/0/0.0              up    down
gr-0/0/0                up    up
ip-0/0/0                up    up
lsq-0/0/0               up    up
lt-0/0/0                up    up
mt-0/0/0                up    up
```

Commit Model

Junos offers a flexible model for you to decide when a new configuration should be active, and it's called the *commit model*. The concept comes from revision control systems which are used for software version control, whereby you edit the configuration (as shown previously) and then, once the configuration is complete, you commit it to the system. Upon commit, several things happen.

First, the configuration is validated by using a commit check. A commit check reviews the configuration for any syntax errors or disallowed statements. It's a sanity check to ensure that a bad configuration is not installed. It's also possible to issue a commit check manually by using the `commit check` command. If an error is encountered, Junos responds and specifies where the error occurs and what the error is.

```
[edit]
root@SRX210-A# set interfaces fe-2/0/3.0 family inet filter input bad-filter

[edit]
root@SRX210-A# commit
[edit interfaces fe-2/0/3 unit 0 family inet]
  'filter'
    Referenced filter 'bad-filter' is not defined
error: configuration check-out failed

[edit]
root@SRX210-A#
```

In the preceding output, a commit error is highlighted. The configuration was attempting to reference a firewall filter that did not exist and the commit check provided an error which prevented the configuration from being installed. The hierarchy in which the error occurred was returned to the user, `[edit interfaces fe-2/0/3 unit 0 family inet]`, so it is easy to track down from where the error was issued. In some cases, a warning is thrown instead that is similar to the error warning, but allows the configuration to be committed because the configuration will still work and will not cause a major episode.

When a configuration is committed a few other steps are applied, too. Junos groups enable you to create a configuration part, and then apply it to the configuration. You can do this as a single element or across multiple elements. During the configuration commit, the group elements are rolled into the configuration as it is being prepared to be committed.

Another feature in Junos is the commit script. A commit script allows you to validate and modify the configuration according to your rules as to what will throw an error or a warning in the configuration—for example, if one of your devices were to accidentally delete all of the interfaces in the configuration. Although this is a perfectly legal option in Junos, it might take the other administrators by surprise when the network goes down.

Lastly, once the configuration is ready to be committed, it is broken down into the various daemons and systems within the device that accept the configuration. Some items, such as the BGP configuration, go off to the RPD process, while the firewall policy is pushed to NSD on the control plane, and then pushed down to the data plane. The statements in the configuration are broken out into stanzas not only to facilitate device configuration, but also to enable Junos to easily break the configuration apart and then push it to the various daemons that are responsible for processing it.

When a configuration is committed to the device, only the delta is actually committed. This means the change between the existing configuration and the changes made by the administrator are applied. Here's an example:

```
[edit]
root@SRX210-A# show | compare
[edit interfaces fe-2/0/3]
```

```
+    unit 0 {
+        family inet {
+            filter {
+                input bad-filter;
+            }
+        }
+    }

[edit]
root@SRX210-A#
```

Here, the administrator used the `show` command to display the current configuration and then redirected the command's output using the pipe character (|) to the compare operation. This is the same type of capability that is used on revision control for software. The output of the `show | compare` command is the same as the Unix `diff` command. It is using a plus sign, +, to show the lines that were added to the configuration; if lines were removed, a minus sign, -, would be used.

```
[edit]
root@SRX210-A# show | compare
[edit system]
-  host-name SRX210-A;

[edit]
root@SRX210-A#
```

Because only the differential is committed, it is less intensive on the system, and less disruptive. In some cases, you might have configurations that are several hundred thousand lines long, and if it were completely committed it would have a major impact on the system. Sometimes a complete recommit of the configuration is required, and in those instances, you can use the hidden command called `commit full` when you need to force the entire configuration back down to the device. This command is also useful in cases where the committed configuration is not being correctly read or the device is not acting right. However, use it with caution, as it may impact the device and potentially cause an outage for the duration of the commit.

Each time a user commits a configuration the previous version is archived. These archived configurations are versioned and kept for future comparison and even rollback. Depending on the Junos platform, it will keep anywhere from 5 to 50 archived configurations. Let's use a query to see the archival configs:

```
[edit]
root@SRX210-A# rollback ?
Possible completions:
  <[Enter]>            Execute this command
  0                    2010-05-05 14:16:22 UTC by root via cli
  1                    2010-05-01 04:26:34 UTC by root via cli
  2                    2010-04-30 07:03:28 UTC by root via cli
  3                    2010-04-30 06:25:59 UTC by root via cli
  4                    2010-04-30 06:14:46 UTC by root via cli
  5                    2010-04-30 06:10:34 UTC by root via cli
  |                    Pipe through a command
```

```
root@SRX210-A# rollback 4
load complete

[edit]
root@SRX210-A# show | compare
[edit system]
+  host-name SRX210-SUPER;
[edit system services]
-     ssh;

[edit]
root@SRX210-A#
```

In the preceding output, rollback version 4 is loaded as the candidate configuration. Then, as was done before, the loaded rollback configuration is piped to compare and perform a `diff` between the loaded configuration and the running configuration. The output shows that in this case the loaded configuration's hostname was `SRX210-SUPER`, and if the configuration were to be committed it would overwrite the current hostname. Also, the line `set system services ssh` would be deleted, as noted by the - symbol.

It's also possible to compare the current configuration against a rollback configuration or even a configuration file:

```
[edit]
root@SRX210-A# show | compare rollback 4
[edit system]
+  host-name SRX210-SUPER;
[edit system services]
-     ssh;

[edit]
root@SRX210-A#

[edit]
root@SRX210-A# show | compare old-configuration.txt
[edit system]
+  host-name SRX210-GOOD-OLD-CONFIG;
[edit system services]
+     ssh;

[edit]
root@SRX210-A#
```

At any time when you're working with the configuration it's possible to discard all of your changes and move back to the original candidate configuration. To do this, use the `rollback 0` command from configuration mode. This is helpful when you want to move back to the original configuration without having to delete all of the changes.

By default, when an administrator commits a configuration it is done at the time the command is executed. But it's also possible to schedule a commit. Scheduling the configuration for commit is useful if you need several different devices to be activated at the same time. Your commit can be scheduled for one minute into the future or even days in advance. At a minimum, the hour and minute need to be specified using the format *hh*:*mm* with *h* being the hour and *m* being the minute. The full syntax of the time is *yyyy-mm-dd hh*:*mm*[:*ss*] with seconds and the date being optional:

```
[edit]
root@SRX210-A# commit at ?
Possible completions:
  <at>                 Time at which to activate configuration changes
[edit]
root@SRX210-A# commit at 2010-08-08 18:30:00
```

If you need to clear the pending commit for whatever reason, use the following operational command:

```
root@SRX210-A> clear system commit
warning: discarding uncommitted changes
Pending commit cleared

{primary:node0}
root@SRX210-A>
```

When a commit is issued it is logged to the messages logfile as well as the commit log. This logs the user who committed the configuration and the time at which it was committed, and is a great tool when you need to track which user modified the configuration and when. But when you want to track specific information about a change, such as the reason for the change or the change control number, it's possible in Junos to add a comment to a commit:

```
[edit]
root@SRX210-A# commit comment "Finished big changes"
configuration check succeeds

commit complete

[edit]
root@SRX210-A# exit
Exiting configuration mode

syntax error, expecting <command>.
root@SRX210-A> show system commit
0   2010-05-05 16:10:48 UTC by rcameron via cli
    Finished big changes
1   2010-05-05 14:16:22 UTC by root via cli
2   2010-05-01 04:26:34 UTC by dburt via cli
3   2010-04-30 07:03:28 UTC by root via cli
4   2010-04-30 06:25:59 UTC by bwoodberg via cli
5   2010-04-30 06:14:46 UTC by root via cli

root@SRX210-A>
```

In this example, the `commit` command was run, and then the `comment` flag along with a string encapsulated in double quotes was added. The string can contain up to 512 characters, allowing for almost chatty comments to be used when committing a configuration. To show the commit log you use the operational command `show system commit`, which will show the last commits based on the total that are supported on the platform. Here, a Juniper Networks SRX210 Services Gateway was used, so the device's maximum of six is shown.

When your commit is issued in configuration mode, you will remain in configuration mode after the new configuration is applied. Often, the administrator would rather exit configuration mode after committing the configuration, so if this is your preference, you can exit and commit in one step, instead of making the commit exit a two-step process:

```
[edit]
root@SRX210-A# set system host-name SRX210-TEST

[edit]
root@SRX210-A# commit and-quit
commit complete
Exiting configuration mode

root@SRX210-TEST>
```

The only additional item you need to add at the end of the `commit` command is `and-quit`. Upon completion of a successful commit, you'll be returned to operational mode, as noted by the different prompt.

The crown jewel of the commit feature is `commit confirmed`. This feature allows the administrator to commit a configuration and then force the validation that the commit worked as expected. By default, a typical commit takes effect, and if you accidentally modify the configuration in such a way that it causes a negative effect on the device, the change will be permanent until the correct configuration is applied. This may cause an outage, and may even disconnect you from the device.

To prevent the unfortunate accident of an outage, `commit confirmed` forces you to commit twice. The first commit applies the configuration to the device and the second commit validates that you are satisfied with the changes. If a second commit is not issued the configuration is automatically rolled back to the previous release, a safeguard for when you might get disconnected from the terminal due to a configuration error; the device will reset itself to the previous configuration, restoring your access.

```
root@SRX210-TEST> edit
Entering configuration mode
The configuration has been changed but not committed

[edit]
root@SRX210-TEST# set system host-name SRX210-A

[edit]
root@SRX210-TEST# commit confirmed ?
```

```
Possible completions:
  <[Enter]>            Execute this command
  <timeout>            Number of minutes until automatic rollback (1..65535)
  and-quit             Quit configuration mode if commit succeeds
  comment              Message to write to commit log
  |                    Pipe through a command
[edit]
root@SRX210-TEST# commit confirmed
commit confirmed will be automatically rolled back in 10 minutes unless confirmed
commit complete

# commit confirmed will be rolled back in 10 minutes
[edit]
root@SRX210-A# commit
commit complete

[edit]
root@SRX210-A#
```

By default, `commit confirmed` has a 10-minute rollback window; the configuration will be automatically rolled back after 10 minutes if you don't commit for a second time within the 10 minutes. It's possible to change the timer and set it from between 1 and 65,535 minutes. You can also issue a comment and/or quit after the first commit.

The Junos commit model provides a robust method for applying configurations to a Junos device, including a versioning model that keeps several copies of the configuration to allow for a history of configuration changes and the ability to roll back to them if needed. Using `commit confirmed` enables you to roll back the configuration automatically in case there is an issue with the device. These and many other CLI features are the result of feedback regarding users' experiences with other network operating systems; the Junos engineers used that feedback to create the robust Junos operating system as it exists today.

Restarting Processes

Restarting a process in Junos allows the device to refresh its configuration or fix the process if it is stuck. Typically, you do not need to restart a process; however, in some circumstances you may need to restart a process, such as when the process is stuck at 100% utilization, which is sometimes caused when Junos tracing options are set to show *every* debug message. Restarting processes only applies to the control plane, not the data plane.

To look at the currently running processes, use the `show system processes` command. This command utilizes the underlying `ps` or "process status" BSD command. There are several variants of the command, but perhaps the most interesting is `show system processes extensive`, as shown here:

```
root@SRX210-A> show system processes extensive

last pid: 27309;  load averages: 1.02, 1.03, 1.01  up 22+05:42:10 14:18:22
```

```
127 processes: 16 running, 100 sleeping, 11 waiting

Mem: 147M Active, 89M Inact, 532M Wired, 148M Cache, 112M Buf, 55M Free
Swap:


  PID USERNAME THR PRI NICE   SIZE    RES STATE  C   TIME   WCPU COMMAND
 1060 root       4  76    0   491M 49700K select 0 611.7H 96.19% flowd_octeon_hm
   22 root       1 171   52     0K    16K RUN    0 430.4H 81.20% idle: cpu0
   24 root       1 -20 -139     0K    16K RUN    0 744:02  0.00% swi7: clock
    5 root       1 -84    0     0K    16K rtfifo 0 213:09  0.00% rtfifo_kern_recv
   23 root       1 -40 -159     0K    16K WAIT   0  74:50  0.00% swi2: net
 1092 root       1  76    0 12256K  5856K select 0  44:42  0.00% utmd
 1065 root       1  76    0  4220K  1788K select 0  42:31  0.00% license-check
 1077 root       1  76    0 14172K  4872K select 0  40:37  0.00% l2ald
 1047 root       1  76    0  2612K  1228K select 0  24:54  0.00% bslockd
 1099 root       1  76    0 15420K  9236K select 0  22:35  0.00% snmpd
   45 root       1 -16    0     0K    16K psleep 0  22:31  0.00% vmkmemdaemon
 1051 root       1  76    0  7064K  3356K select 0  18:41  0.00% alarmd
 1112 root       1   4    0     0K    16K peer_s 0  17:33  0.00% peer proxy
   26 root       1 -16    0     0K    16K -      0  13:31  0.00% yarrow
 1076 root       1   4    0 38152K 19512K kqread 0  12:44  0.00% rpd
 1057 root       1  76    0 13776K  4644K select 0  12:12  0.00% pfed
 1094 root       2  76    0 10144K  4332K select 0  11:48  0.00% wland
 1050 root       1  76    0 28088K 13656K select 0  11:15  0.00% chassisd
 1100 root       1  76    0 25172K  8948K select 0   9:42  0.00% dcd
```

Here you can see the status of all the current processes. Ideally, you would want to look for all processes that have a high CPU utilization and are stuck, except for the flowd process on the branch SRX Series platform, as it runs on one or more cores in a tight loop (a *tight loop* means the process is constantly running and ready to process packets). A process that may have issues is chassisd, as you can see in this example.

Now the process will be restarted. The command name may not tie to the process name exactly, but it represents the name of the process. In the case of chassisd, it is called `chassis-control`:

```
root@SRX210-A> restart chassis-control ?
Possible completions:
  <[Enter]>            Execute this command
  gracefully           Gracefully restart the process
  immediately          Immediately restart (SIGKILL) the process
  soft                 Soft reset (SIGHUP) the process
  |                    Pipe through a command
{primary:node0}
root@SRX210-A> restart chassis-control gracefully
Chassis control process started, pid 27310

{primary:node0}
root@SRX210-A>
```

Most processes allow for three separate options when restarting: gracefully, immediately, and soft. A *graceful restart* tells the process to complete its current task, and then restart (this is also the default option if one is not specified). A *soft restart* tells the process to restart after it has completed its tasks and its child process has done the same. An *immediate restart* stops the process immediately and starts a new process in its place; you should use this option only if a process is stuck at a high level of utilization. (That's why implementing an immediate restart is also known as *killing a process*.)

Killing a process or restarting a process can affect your running platform. These effects vary based on the process, but if chassisd is killed, the control plane can lose communication with the chassis. So, when restarting processes, it's best to ensure the outcome of the event. For the most part, the process will gracefully restart and things will continue to work well. That's the benefit of having process separation: being able to restart individual processes without impacting the rest of the running system.

Junos Automation

Junos can have all of its output displayed in XML. XML is used to describe data. For instance, when you read "1234 Easy Street" it's easy to determine that this is the street address of a house. Now there isn't anything that tells you that it is an address, but it's simply assumed because it's a format that you are familiar with. To a computer there are no assumptions. Although it's possible for a computer to try to determine what that text means, there are better ways to do it.

One of these methods uses XML. By using XML, you create the encapsulation of data between XML tags, and the tags that surround the data specify its meaning:

```
<address>
    <first-name>Juniper</first-name>
    <last-name>Networks</last-name>
    <house-number>1194</house-number>
    <street-name>North Mathilda</street-name>
    <city>Sunnyvale</city>
    <state>CA</state>
    <zip-code>94089</zip-code>
</address>
```

Here a client can read in the data and have context for what each piece of data represents. The same capabilities are available in Junos:

```
root@SRX210-A> show version
Hostname: SRX210-A
Model: srx210h
JUNOS Software Release [10.2B1.9]

root@SRX210-A> show version | display xml
<rpc-reply xmlns:junos="http://xml.juniper.net/junos/10.2B1/junos">
    <software-information>
        <host-name>SRX210-A</host-name>
        <product-model>srx210h</product-model>
        <product-name>srx210h</product-name>
        <jsr/>
        <package-information>
            <name>junos</name>
```

```
            <comment>JUNOS Software Release [10.2B1.9]</comment>
        </package-information>
    </software-information>
    <cli>
        <banner></banner>
    </cli>
</rpc-reply>

root@SRX210-A>
```

Here, the same command is executed twice. The first time is the typical Junos command and output, and the second shows the output as XML. To do this the command `show version | display xml` is used and the `| display xml` modifier transforms the output to XML. The output doesn't look like it has much value to humans, but computers eat it up. The XML can be parsed by off-the-box scripts to provide analysis. And Junos uses these XML capabilities in several ways and provides several ways to utilize it. Two remote APIs can be used to connect and talk to the device: Junoscript and NETCONF. On-box Junos automation can also be used.

Junos automation is accomplished via a series of tools that enable you to customize Junos in very powerful ways. It's something that all users of Junos should take advantage of, and we discuss it in this book to help you automate SRX functions. We will cover Junos automation in detail in Chapter 13.

Junos Configuration Essentials

Logging in to a command line for the first time can be a daunting task. You stare into a black-and-white terminal, and a seemingly infinite combination of commands are staring back—it can be extremely difficult. All users of Junos or Unix start out this way, and soon enough they become nimble on the CLI.

This section is one of two that will show you some of the basic techniques you can use if you're starting out on the Junos command line with your SRX device.

The first thing you need to do is begin to configure the device. All Junos devices come with some base configurations. In this section, we will ignore the base configurations and instead discuss the important base configuration elements. This should help you to understand how to get the device up and running with base configuration settings.

System Settings

When you configure a Junos device many options are used system-wide. These system-wide options are set in the `system` stanza. Several dozen configuration settings are in the `system` stanza, and here we'll cover the most important ones that you need to configure for a typical Junos deployment.

For further information on these and other configuration options, please review the Junos CLI tech doc references (*http://www.juniper.net/tech pubs*) or the free Day One booklets (*http://www.juniper.net/dayone*).

Before you can commit a configuration, the root user must have an authentication method configured. When a Junos device ships the root password is empty. The administrator can log in as root (the only default user that's configured) without a password. Upon the *first commit on the device* one of the authentication methods must be configured.

```
[edit system]
root@SRX210-A# set root-authentication ?
Possible completions:
+ apply-groups         Groups from which to inherit configuration data
+ apply-groups-except  Don't inherit configuration data from these groups
  encrypted-password   Encrypted password string
  load-key-file        File (URL) containing one or more ssh keys
  plain-text-password  Prompt for plain text password (autoencrypted)
> ssh-dsa              Secure shell (ssh) DSA public key string
> ssh-rsa              Secure shell (ssh) RSA public key string
[edit system]
root@SRX210-A# set root-authentication plain-text-password
New password:
Retype new password:

[edit system]
root@SRX210-A#
```

As you can see, you can use four different methods to authenticate the root user. Plain-text password is the most common. This is the normal, hand-typed password and is the example shown in the preceding output. The administrator must hand-type the password and then confirm it. The password is stored in the configuration as an MD5 password with a salt. This means it's not possible to reverse the password just by seeing it, and because it has a salt, it is extremely hard to determine the password.

The alternate methods for the root password are all about using SSH keys. When you use an SSH key a password is not used to authenticate the user. This is more secure, as the user has ownership of his private key and it is not sent over the network for authentication. In Junos, the user's public key must be loaded on the system. You can do this in one of three ways: as a DSA key, as an RSA key, or by loading the key from a file.

No matter which way you choose to set up root authentication, it is suggested that you always utilize a nonroot user for administration. Junos is designed to handle multiple user accounts and determining permissions per user based upon groups. The root user has the ultimate permissions into the system, and users logging on as root can choose to do whatever they wish. Individual user accounts enable better tracking of what each user is doing on the device. Junos tracks each user's commands and configuration commits, and identifies who changed what. So, it is considered a best practice to always use an alternate user account instead of root.

When creating a new user account you need to select a few properties for the new account:

```
[edit system]
root@SRX210-A# set login user ?
Possible completions:
+ apply-groups         Groups from which to inherit configuration data
+ apply-groups-except  Don't inherit configuration data from these groups
> authentication       Authentication method
  class                Login class
  full-name            Full name
  uid                  User identifier (uid) (100..64000)
[edit system]
root@SRX210-A# set login user rcameron class ?
Possible completions:
  <class>              Login class
  operator             permissions [ clear network reset trace view ]
  read-only            permissions [ view ]
  super-user           permissions [ all ]
  unauthorized         permissions [ none ]

[edit system]
root@SRX210-A# set login user rcameron class super-user

[edit system]
root@SRX210-A# set login user rcameron authentication plain-text-password
New password:
Retype new password:

[edit system]
root@SRX210-A#
```

The minimum items for a user are a username, a class (or group), and an authentication method. The available authentication methods are the same as those covered for the root user. In this example, the common plain-text password was chosen. One item that may not be obvious is *class*. A class is the same concept as a user group. It provides the user access to issue specific commands and modes. In this example, the super-user class was chosen and this class gives the user access to all possible commands and modes. The various prebuilt classes are a small example of what is possible for classes. It is possible to build custom classes that can restrict a user to run a specific command or view only specific portions of the configuration. You can find further details regarding classes in the Junos documentation suite for your SRX model and platform.

You can remotely access a Junos device in many different ways, all of which are done through the `system services` stanza. In this stanza, all of the various services are configured. Depending on the device type, different services may be configured. If only one service needs to be configured, it should be SSH, because SSH is the best way to access the CLI remotely.

The service allows for encrypted transport of data, key-based authentication, and even the ability to transfer files. Most Unix-like clients contain a built-in client using the OpenSSH software package. For Windows users, a plethora of SSH clients can be used. Several of them are free, and some are available as commercial packages. Even devices such as the Apple iPhone and iPad have very viable SSH clients.

Enabling SSH is simple, as it requires only a single command and just a few options:

```
[edit system services]
root@SRX210-A# set ssh ?
Possible completions:
  <[Enter]>            Execute this command
+ apply-groups         Groups from which to inherit configuration data
+ apply-groups-except  Don't inherit configuration data from these groups
  connection-limit     Maximum number of allowed connections (1..3)
+ protocol-version     Specify ssh protocol versions supported
  rate-limit           Maximum number of connections per minute (1..3)
  root-login           Configure root access via ssh
  |                    Pipe through a command
[edit system services]
root@SRX210-A# set ssh

[edit system services]
root@SRX210-A#
```

The single command `set system services ssh` enables the SSH service. You also can specify whether the root user can authenticate, whether to rate-limit the number of connections per minute, the maximum number of concurrent connections, and the protocol version. It's best to *disallow* SSH authentication for root so that unauthorized attempts to log in as root are not allowed. Also, *limiting* the rate at connections per minute ensures that someone cannot attempt to use a brute force attack to access the system.

A Junos device can use name resolution to convert Domain Name System (DNS) names to IP addresses. This is useful when using ping, SSH, and Telnet commands from the device. Configuring a name server is simple, and it is done under the `system` stanza. If a name server is not configured, name resolution will not be possible. Here's an example:

```
[edit system]
root@SRX210-A# set name-server 208.67.222.222

name-server {
    208.67.222.222;
    208.67.220.220;
}
--snip-

[edit system]
root@SRX210-A#
```

Each device should have a unique hostname. This is useful for identifying the device on the command line. Providing a unique hostname can also help prevent an accidental configuration change on the wrong device in the network. Configuring the hostname is simple and it takes only one command:

```
[edit system]
root@SRX210-A# set host-name JunosBook

[edit system]
root@SRX210-A# show
host-name JunosBook;
--snip--

[edit system]
root@SRX210-A#
```

Interfaces

A networking device without interfaces isn't much of a networking device. Since a Junos device is always in the network, and most of the time it is in the path of the network, it is critical to understand interface configuration.

Some Junos interface concepts might seem foreign to administrators who are migrating from other operating systems. Remember that the Junos CLI is designed to be extensible and scalable, and once an element is added to the configuration hierarchy after a software release is made, it is not changed. Because of this, creating an interface and modifying its parameters may seem overly complex, but it is done for a good reason: to ensure that 10 years from now the general structure of creating an interface is backward-compatible.

Interfaces come in two types: logical and physical. A physical interface is an actual device that someone can touch and a cable of some sort goes into it. A logical interface is an entity that has a protocol and a network address assigned to it. A physical interface can also be called an *IFD* and a logical interface is called an *IFL*, terms sometimes sprinkled around in the documentation or in various Junos material.

An interface is named in a common format and the format is shared regardless of the interface type. The first part of an interface name is the media type. Table 3-3 lists a few of the common media types and their abbreviations.

Table 3-3. Interface media types

Name	Media type
fe	Fast Ethernet 10/100
ge	Gigabit Ethernet 1000
xe	10 gigabit Ethernet
t1	T1 interface
vlan	Virtual interface that resides in a virtual LAN (VLAN)

There are many different types of interfaces, and only a handful are represented in Table 3-3. For more information on the various interface types refer to the Junos documentation set at *http://www.juniper.net/techpubs*.

Interface names also include the location in which they are found in the chassis. This portion of the interface name consists of three numbers: the FPC number, the physical interface card (PIC) number, and the port number.

FPC stands for *flexible PIC concentrator*, and it is simply a slot in a chassis. The differentiation of FPCs typically determines how the FPC plugs into the backplane of the device. A PIC represents a physical or pluggable (both terms are seen and sometimes used interchangeably) interface card on which interfaces or ports reside. The numbering for an interface is represented in an *X*/*Y*/*Z* pattern, with *X* being the FPC, *Y* being the PIC, and *Z* being the port. An example of a complete interface name is "ge-0/0/0".

> A few interface types do not fit into this format. One of these is fxp0, which is used as a management port. You can configure it with most of the options that an interface can use, such as IP addresses, but this interface cannot route traffic because it is not a transient interface. We will discuss the fxp0 interface in Chapter 10.

Each physical interface has some physical properties that you can configure, such as speed, duplex, and auto-negotiation; these properties vary based on interface type. Because of all the variations that are possible, it's best to check the latest Junos documentation to get the most up-to-date configuration options. But in most cases, the command-line help, using ?, will give you what you need.

When an interface is configured for use on the network it must always be configured with what is known as a *unit*. A unit is a logical entity that is applied to an interface. A physical interface must have at least one unit, but it can have as many as 16,000, depending on the need. This is a departure from other operating systems.

To communicate with other hosts and pass traffic through the device, protocols must be configured. Junos supports numerous protocols for network communication and several can be configured per unit. The most common protocol that is used is IPv4. This is the current standard on the Internet and in most networks. IPv6 is growing in popularity, and because of this, Junos has support for it as well. When configuring an interface, a protocol is called a *family*. This is because a protocol is often a family of protocols; an example is IP, as IP uses ICMP, TCP, and UDP for messaging purposes.

Configuring an interface is simple, even though it has several parts to it. Let's create an interface configured with an IP address on it. Although there are many different protocols and permutations, we will use IPv4, as it is fairly common.

```
[edit interfaces]
root@SRX210-A# set ge-0/0/0 unit 0 family inet address 1.2.3.4/30
```

```
[edit interfaces]
root@SRX210-A# show
ge-0/0/0 {
    unit 0 {
        family inet {
            address 1.2.3.4/30;
        }
    }
}
```

In this command set the IP address of 1.2.3.4 with a bit mask of 30 bits is used. It is applied to interface ge-0/0/0 and unit 0. Although any unit number can be used, it's common to use 0 when only one unit is used. When VLANs are implemented, it's common to have the unit name match the VLAN tag; although this is not required, it helps when other administrators need to look through a configuration.

Instead of having to type out "unit" when running a command, you can use a period (.) instead of the word *unit* when configuring an interface. It's a nice shortcut:

```
[edit interfaces]
root@SRX210-A# set ge-0/0/0.0 family inet address 1.2.3.4/30

[edit interfaces]
root@SRX210-A# show ge-0/0/0
unit 0 {
    family inet {
        address 1.2.3.4/30;
    }
}

[edit interfaces]
root@SRX210-A#
```

Adding a VLAN tag is a simple configuration. To start the configuration the interface needs to have tagging enabled on it, before it can be enabled on the logical interface:

```
[edit interfaces]
root@SRX210-A# set ge-0/0/0 vlan-tagging

[edit interfaces]
root@SRX210-A# set ge-0/0/0.100 vlan-id 100

[edit interfaces]
root@SRX210-A# set ge-0/0/0.100 family inet address 1.2.3.4/30

[edit interfaces]
root@SRX210-A# show ge-0/0/0
vlan-tagging;
unit 100 {
    vlan-id 100;
    family inet {
        address 1.2.3.4/30;
    }
}
```

```
[edit interfaces]
root@SRX210-A#
```

Switching (Branch)

On the branch SRX Series (see Chapter 1), most Ethernet interfaces support the ability to do switching. The switching capabilities in the branch SRX Series are inherited from Juniper Networks' EX Series Ethernet Switches, so the functionality and configuration are nearly identical.

The most common configuration type is an *access port*. An access port is a port that does not accept VLAN tagged packets, but rather tags the packets internally to the switch. It will also allow the packet to exit as a tagged packet on a trunk port. (A VLAN must be assigned to an interface even if the traffic will never exit the device as a packet tagged with the VLAN. In cases such as these, the actual VLAN tag used is irrelevant.)

```
[edit interfaces ge-0/0/2.0]
root@JunosBook# set family ethernet-switching

[edit interfaces ge-0/0/2.0]
root@JunosBook# set family ethernet-switching port-mode access

[edit interfaces ge-0/0/2.0]
root@JunosBook# show
unit 0 {
    family ethernet-switching {
        port-mode access;
        vlan {
            members 100;
        }
    }
}

[edit interfaces ge-0/0/2.0]
root@JunosBook#
```

Here, `ethernet-switching` was added as a family (remember that a family represents a protocol suite, and in this case it represents switching). The port was set to `access` mode, which internally tags the packet after it enters the port. It is tagged with VLAN 100, as that is what is configured under the `vlan` stanza. An access port can only have a single VLAN configured. When configuring a VLAN it can be specified with the tag number or a configured VLAN name. We will discuss VLAN configuration later in this section.

Most of the branch SRX Series devices have several ports that you can configure for switching. In some cases, up to 24 sequential ports can be used for switching. Instead of having to configure all of the ports by hand, it's possible to use the `interface range` command. This configuration allows you to select several ports and then apply the same commands across all of the interfaces:

```
[edit interfaces]
root@JunosBook# show
interface-range interfaces-trust {
    member ge-0/0/1;
    member fe-0/0/2;
    member fe-0/0/3;
    member fe-0/0/4;
    member fe-0/0/5;
    member fe-0/0/7;
    unit 0 {
        family ethernet-switching {
            vlan {
                port-mode access;
                members 100;
            }
        }
    }
}
```

An interface range must be given a unique name, and then one or more interfaces can be added as members of the range. At this point, any configuration option that can normally be added to an interface can be added here. Because of this, the use of interface ranges is not just limited to switching. For example, unit 0 was created with Ethernet switching and VLAN 100. Upon commit, all interfaces have the same configuration applied to them.

Up to this point, all VLANs have been used with just a number tag. It is also possible to create VLANs and give them a name which allows for easier management and identification in the configuration. You can use the VLAN name instead of the tag name anywhere in the configuration:

```
[edit vlans]
root@JunosBook# show
vlan-trust {
    vlan-id 100;
    interface {
        fe-0/0/6.0;
    }
    l3-interface vlan.0;
}

[edit vlans]
root@JunosBook#
```

Each VLAN is given a custom name. This name must be unique and must not overlap with any other existing VLAN name. You also must assign a VLAN ID to the VLAN. You can configure several other options under a VLAN, the most common of which concern the direct configuration of interfaces. Previously, when Ethernet switching was configured on each interface, a VLAN had to be configured. In this configuration example, the VLAN can be configured from one central location directly under the VLAN. Either option is valid; the usage is based on personal preference.

The other common option is the use of a VLAN interface. A VLAN interface allows for the termination of traffic that can then be routed out another interface on the device. The VLAN interface is accessible from any port that is a member of that VLAN. The interface is configured just like any other interface type:

```
[edit]
root@JunosBook# edit interfaces

[edit interfaces]
root@JunosBook# set vlan.0 family inet address 1.2.3.4/24

[edit interfaces]
root@JunosBook# edit interfaces

[edit interfaces]
root@JunosBook# show vlan
unit 0 {
    family inet {
        address 1.2.3.4/24;
    }
}

[edit interfaces]
root@JunosBook#
```

A *trunk port* is a port that has two or more VLANs configured on it and traffic entering a trunk port must be tagged with a VLAN tag. A trunk port is typically used when connecting the SRX to another switch:

```
[edit]
root@JunosBook# edit interfaces

[edit interfaces]
root@JunosBook# set ge-0/0/2.0 family ethernet-switching port-mode trunk

[edit interfaces]
root@JunosBook# set ge-0/0/2.0 family ethernet-switching vlan members 200

[edit interfaces]
root@JunosBook# show ge-0/0/2.0
family ethernet-switching {
    port-mode trunk;
    vlan {
        members [ 100 200 ];
    }
}

[edit interfaces]
root@JunosBook#
```

As you can see, the configuration here is very similar to an access port. The differences are minor, as the port mode is configured as a trunk and multiple VLAN members are added to the port. Traffic entering the port must be tagged and must match the VLANs configured on the port.

Zones

A zone is a logical construct that is applied to an interface and is used as a building block for security policies on the SRX Series Services Gateways and the Juniper Networks J Series Services Routers. The concept of the zone originated on the ScreenOS platform from NetScreen Technologies. When creating a security policy, the idea is to allow traffic from a source to go to a destination. The zone adds another dimension to that by allowing for the concept of a source zone and a destination zone. This was very different from all of the existing firewall products of the time. The division of a security policy base into multiple smaller policy sets, or contexts, enhanced performance and simplified management.

Creating a security zone is simple, as the minimum requirement is just a name. In the past on NetScreen products, there was a concept of having prenamed zones called *Trust*, *Untrust*, and *DMZ*. These zone names were always left in place because the original ScreenOS devices actually used these as the interface names. Juniper has moved away from having the default names, and now allows users to name the zones whatever they want. Security zones are located under the `security zones` stanza:

```
[edit security zones]
root@SRX210-A# show
security-zone SuperZone {
    interfaces {
        ge-0/0/0.0;
    }
}

[edit security zones]
root@SRX210-A#
```

Security zones offer little to no value without the addition of interfaces. In the example shown here, the ge-0/0/0.0 interface is added to the new zone named `SuperZone`. The zone is now ready to be used in security policies. We will cover security policies in detail in Chapter 4.

At least one interface must be bound in a zone to be able to use it to create security policies. Multiple interfaces can be added to a zone as well, and this may be helpful depending on the goal of the network design. An interface can only be a member of one zone at a time. Logical interfaces are added to a zone, and so it's possible to have multiple logical interfaces that are a member of the same physical interface to be members of multiple zones.

Functional zones are a logical entity that is applied to the interface to enable it to have a special function. Interfaces that are a member of a functional zone cannot be used in a security zone. On the SRX, the only functional zone that is used is *management*. Adding an interface into the management zone allows the interface to be used for out-of-band management, a helpful tool for devices such as the branch SRX Series devices, which do not have a dedicated interface for management.

```
[edit security zones]
root@JunosBook# set functional-zone management interfaces fe-0/0/6.0

[edit security zones]
root@JunosBook# edit functional-zone management

[edit security zones functional-zone management]
root@JunosBook# show
interfaces {
    fe-0/0/6.0;
}
host-inbound-traffic {
    system-services {
        all;
    }
}

[edit security zones functional-zone management]
root@JunosBook#
```

Adding an interface to a functional zone is the same as using a security zone. A new element shown in this configuration is `host inbound traffic`. The `host inbound traffic` stanza can be configured under any zone, and it allows for the acceptance of two different types of traffic to the SRX itself. If the host inbound traffic is not configured, traffic will not be accepted. This is different from creating a security policy, as a security policy is only for transit traffic and not for traffic terminating on the device.

```
root@JunosBook# set host-inbound-traffic system-services ?
Possible completions:
  all                  All system services
  any-service          Enable services on entire port range
  dns                  DNS and DNS-proxy service
  finger               Finger service
  ftp                  FTP
  http                 Web management service using HTTP
  https                Web management service using HTTP secured by SSL
  ident-reset          Send back TCP RST to IDENT request for port 113
  ike                  Internet Key Exchange
  lsping               Label Switched Path ping service
  netconf              NETCONF service
  ntp                  Network Time Protocol service
  ping                 Internet Control Message Protocol echo requests
  reverse-ssh          Reverse SSH service
  reverse-telnet       Reverse telnet service
  rlogin               Rlogin service
  rpm                  Real-time performance monitoring
  rsh                  Rsh service
  sip                  Enable Session Initiation Protocol service
  snmp                 Simple Network Management Protocol service
  snmp-trap            Simple Network Management Protocol traps
  ssh                  SSH service
  telnet               Telnet service
  tftp                 TFTP
  traceroute           Traceroute service
  xnm-clear-text       JUNOScript API for unencrypted traffic over TCP
```

```
  xnm-ssl               JUNOScript API service over SSL
[edit security zones functional-zone management]
root@JunosBook# set host-inbound-traffic protocols ?
Possible completions:
  all                   All protocols
  bfd                   Bidirectional Forwarding Detection
  bgp                   Border Gateway Protocol
  dvmrp                 Distance Vector Multicast Routing Protocol
  igmp                  Internet Group Management Protocol
  ldp                   Label Distribution Protocol
  msdp                  Multicast Source Discovery Protocol
  ndp                   Enable Network Discovery Protocol
  nhrp                  Next Hop Resolution Protocol
  ospf                  Open Shortest Path First
  ospf3                 Open Shortest Path First version 3
  pgm                   Pragmatic General Multicast
  pim                   Protocol Independent Multicast
  rip                   Routing Information Protocol
  ripng                 Routing Information Protocol next generation
  router-discovery      Router Discovery
  rsvp                  Resource Reservation Protocol
  sap                   Session Announcement Protocol
  vrrp                  Virtual Router Redundancy Protocol
[edit security zones functional-zone management]
root@JunosBook# set host-inbound-traffic protocols
```

The first type of host inbound traffic is called *system services*. System services traffic is related to any service that is used for management on the SRX. This includes SSH, Telnet, and DNS. The other type of host inbound traffic is *protocols*. These are routing protocols or other protocols that are used for communicating with other network devices. Each individual service can be turned on, or all of them can be turned on, using the `all` flag.

Given that an SRX is most often deployed as a security device, it's a best practice to reduce the total number of host inbound protocols.

Host inbound traffic can also be enabled on a per-interface basis. This is a good idea when multiple interfaces are in a zone. Also, some protocols such as DHCP can only be enabled on a single interface and not on a per-zone basis. DHCP will not be allowed unless specifically enabled under the interface.

```
root@host# set interfaces fe-0/0/6.0 host-inbound-traffic system-services dhcp

[edit security zones functional-zone management]
root@JunosBook# show
interfaces {
    fe-0/0/6.0 {
        host-inbound-traffic {
            system-services {
                dhcp;
```

```
                }
            }
        }
    }
    host-inbound-traffic {
        system-services {
            all;
        }
    }

    [edit security zones functional-zone management]
    root@JunosBook#
```

Summary

Junos is a large-scale and extensible operating system. It is designed to give administrators flexible configuration options that allow for extreme customization of the device. It also allows full control over what happens to the traffic that passes through the device. For administrators who are looking for more information on how to use the Junos operating system there are four great resources.

The first resource is the Juniper Networks Technical Library (of which this book is a part), covering the Junos operating system. These books are published by O'Reilly and have "Junos" in the main title. You can discover more about them at *http://www.oreilly.com* or at *http://www.juniper.net/books*. The series includes books such as *Junos Cookbook* (*http://oreilly.com/catalog/9780596100148/*) by Aviva Garrett, which provides valuable tips that apply to all Junos-based devices. For those of you who are migrating from other vendors and platforms, look for *Junos Fundamentals* (scheduled for publication in November 2010). This book covers all the basics and will prepare you for the JNCIA, Juniper's foundation certification track.

In addition, Juniper publishes a series of how-to booklets called the Day One series (*http://www.juniper.net/dayone*). These mini-books are full of information focused on specific topics. They are free and cover a wide variety of topics.

Lastly, the Junos documentation covers every nook and cranny of the operating system and is the best place to find information on how to use a command or review a concept.

These resources can fill in where this short chapter had to leave off. The rest of the book assumes you can find your way around the CLI. If need be, review this chapter, and the aforementioned resources, if you need more basic instruction. The authors assume you have an intermediate familiarity with using a CLI, and we will try to introduce you gradually to the finer points of configuring, administering, and monitoring your SRX Series Services Gateway device.

Chapter Review Questions

1. What are the two different modes of operation in the Junos command line?
2. What topics are covered on the built-in help on the command line?
3. In configuration mode, what command is used to place a statement into the configuration?
4. What is the benefit of having a configuration that is based on a hierarchy?
5. What is a unit on an interface?
6. What is the commit model for the configuration?
7. Where is the concept of the commit model inherited from?
8. What is a zone?
9. What does the root user do?
10. What platform can support Ethernet switching?

Chapter Review Answers

1. Operational mode and configuration mode are the two different modes of operation in the Junos command line.
2. A full copy of the Junos documentation is configured on every Junos device. All of the available commands and topics are accessible.
3. The `set` command places a new configuration statement into the configuration. The `delete` command can be used to remove a command from the configuration.
4. A hierarchy-based configuration allows an administrator to enter a specific part of the configuration that he wishes to edit. It also provides the ability to restrict access to specific stanzas by using access classes.
5. A unit is a logical interface that is applied to a physical interface. A unit is an abstraction that allows for the use of multiple VLANs or protocols to be enabled on the same physical interface.
6. The commit model allows for the application of the configuration when the user specifies. This is different from traditional network operating systems which applied the configuration immediately to the device.
7. The commit model was inherited from revision control software for source code. It enables the ability to commit, roll back, and save several revisions of configurations.
8. A zone is a logical entity that interfaces can become a member of. Zones are used in creating security policies and they provide a clear source and destination for traffic regardless of IP address. It's also possible to create a functional zone to place an interface in management mode so that it cannot pass traffic.

9. The root user is the ultimate administrator for a Junos device. It is the only user that is configured by default. A new user should be configured and used to manage the device. The root user should only be used for initial configuration of the device.
10. Currently, the branch platform can configure Ethernet switching. In the future, the capability will be made available to data center SRX Series devices.

CHAPTER 4

Security Policy

Security policies, sometimes called firewall rules, are a method of selectively allowing traffic through a network. In a sense, security policies control who can talk to whom (or rather, what systems can talk to which other systems), and more importantly, how the conversation takes place. Security policies also provide the means for logging, authentication, and accounting of network traffic. The SRX evaluates every packet that passes through its zones and determines whether the traffic is permitted, dropped, logged, or more deeply inspected, or if it requires further authentication. This chapter explores how the SRX evaluates traffic and performs security policy lookups, how to configure those security policies, and some common issues to avoid.

Security Policy Overview

As illustrated in Figure 4-1, when a packet enters the SRX, the flow daemon (flowd) performs a session lookup. It does this to see whether the packet is already part of an existing session. If the packet is part of an existing session, it takes what is referred to as the *fast path*. If it is not found to be part of an existing session, it goes down the *slow path*. The fast path has fewer steps involved in checking the packet, and as a result, it is much faster at processing the packet.

Why does the security policy lookup take place after so many other checks?

The SRX is a zone-based firewall, meaning that all security policies are associated with zones and those zones are tied to interfaces. The SRX must perform a route lookup to determine the destination zone context before it can examine the correct security policies. In fact, before the firewall can do a security policy evaluation for a flow, it must perform three actions: a screen check (detailed in Chapter 6), a route lookup, and finally, a route lookup to determine the destination security zone. Any of these steps might result in the packet being dropped, even before security policy evaluation.

By default, three security zones come preconfigured on the SRX: the Trust zone, the Untrust zone, and the junos-global zone. It's best to use custom zones with clear names describing their role and placement in the network. An example of this would be calling

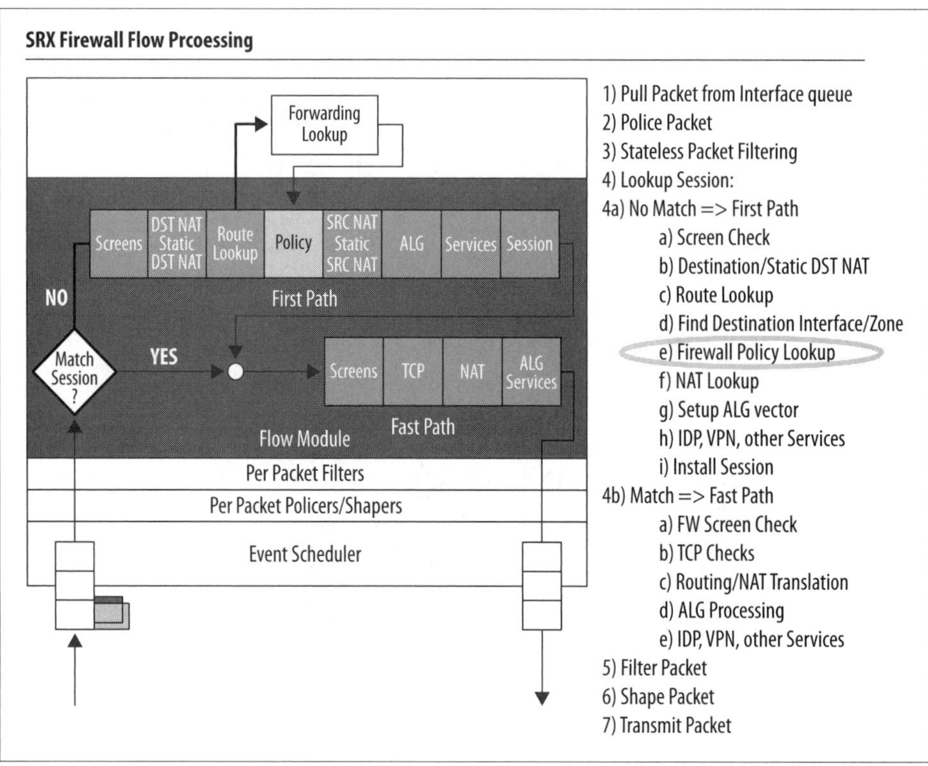
SRX Firewall Flow Prcoessing
Forwarding Lookup
Screens
DST NAT Static DST NAT
Route Lookup
Policy
SRC NAT Static SRC NAT
ALG
Services
Session
First Path
NO
Match Session ?
YES
Screens
TCP
NAT
ALG Services
Fast Path
Flow Module
Per Packet Filters
Per Packet Policers/Shapers
Event Scheduler
1) Pull Packet from Interface queue
2) Police Packet
3) Stateless Packet Filtering
4) Lookup Session:
4a) No Match => First Path
a) Screen Check
b) Destination/Static DST NAT
c) Route Lookup
d) Find Destination Interface/Zone
e) Firewall Policy Lookup
f) NAT Lookup
g) Setup ALG vector
h) IDP, VPN, other Services
i) Install Session
4b) Match => Fast Path
a) FW Screen Check
b) TCP Checks
c) Routing/NAT Translation
d) ALG Processing
e) IDP, VPN, other Services
5) Filter Packet
6) Shape Packet
7) Transmit Packet

Figure 4-1. Where policy evaluation in the SRX packet flow takes place

the accounting department network segment "accounting-dept" or even "Dept-A." This will be far more user-friendly than a generic name such as "Trust" when an administrator returns to this zone configuration in the future.

Let's create a new security zone:

```
[edit]
juniper@SRX5800> edit security
[edit security]
juniper@SRX5800> set zones security-zone accounting-dept
```

The new zone is called `accounting-dept`. Once a new zone has been created there are a few features that can be turned on. The most important feature is called TCP-RST. TCP-RST will send a RESET packet for any non-TCP SYN packet that doesn't already match an existing session. What does that mean? Well, it basically means that if a session has timed out or is started improperly, the SRX will tell the source node that it needs to restart the TCP connection. It is recommended by the authors that TCP-RST remain disabled unless it is required on your network. This makes the SRX visible when it drops packets and can be abused by a malicious user to probe the SRX's security policies.

Additional zone configuration items include:

`Host-inbound-traffic`
: This tells the SRX what to allow to this security zone. For example, if you want to ping the SRX's interface, you need to configure ping under the zone's **`host-inbound-traffic`** profile. Any protocols or system services that need to be allowed to go to the SRX should be configured under **`host-inbound-traffic`**. Here's a quick example:

```
juniper@SRX5800> set zones security-zone accounting-dept host-inbound-traffic
system-services ping
```

Screen
: Screens are high-performance denial-of-service (DoS) and distributed denial-of-service (DDoS) protections that are extremely efficient and can block a number of floods and attacks in hardware. We will cover screens thoroughly in Chapter 7.

The last step in configuring a security zone is to apply the interface to the zone:

```
[edit security]
juniper@SRX5800> set zones security-zone accounting-dept interfaces ge-0/0/0
```

The new zone configuration is:

```
[edit security]
juniper@SRX5800>  show zones security-zone accounting-dept
host-inbound-traffic {
    system-services {
        ping;
    }
}
interfaces {
    ge-0/0/0.0;
}
```

These are the fundamentals of zones, so let's take a look at a quick security policy. The format and configuration of a simple security policy that the firewall administrator has previously configured might look something like the following:

```
juniper@SRX5800> show configuration security policies
from-zone trust to-zone Internet {
    policy allow-users {
        match {
            source-address inside-users;
            destination-address any;
            application any;
        }
        then {
            permit;
        }
    }
}
```

Security policy configurations are composed of six major elements all used within this sample security policy:

Source zone
: The source zone is referred to as `from-zone` and is labeled as `trust`.

Destination zone
: The destination, or `to-zone`, is labeled as `Internet`.

Policy
: This is a descriptive name assigned to the policy. In the preceding example, it's called `allow-users`.

Source address
: The source address group is `inside-users`. A source address is a collection or a single IP address used in policy to dictate whom is initiating this connection.

Destination address
: In the example `allow-users` policy, the destination address is `any`. The destination address again is a collection or a single IP address that the source is talking to. In this case, `any` means any destination.

Service
: In the example `allow-users` policy, the service is `any`. The service is a single port or port range such as HTTP (TCP port 80), SSH (TCP port 22), or, for example, DNS (UDP port 53).

These items are all a part of the `match` statement which details to what and to whom this policy applies.

The last line of the example policy is an action configured to take place if the traffic matches the criteria of the first lines, referred to as the `then` statement. If traffic is initiated from the Trust zone, has a destination address in the Internet zone, and is from the `inside-users` segment, the SRX permits the traffic. The `then` statement describes what action should be taken. An action can include logging, denying, permitting, or sending for deeper inspection in cases such as Intrusion Detection and Protection (IDP) and Unified Threat Management (UTM). We will cover both IDP and UTM later in the book, but for now it's important to understand that they are enabled and triggered by the `then` statement in security policies. The security policy is what matches traffic and tells the SRX to send the packet or flow for deeper inspection.

Keep in mind that multiple actions can be configured inside the `then` statement.

SRX Policy Processing

In step 4 of Figure 4-1's illustrated SRX packet flow, the SRX builds a list of configured policies and the order in which they are processed. When the network security process determines a source and destination zone, the SRX evaluates only those policies configured between those two zones and continues to evaluate them (in a top-down order) until a matching condition is found, as shown in Figure 4-2. As the network security process evaluates an incoming packet, if a matching policy is found no further policies will be evaluated.

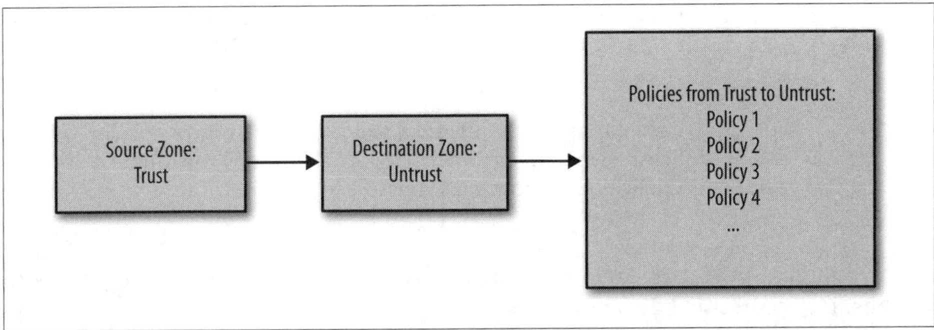

Figure 4-2. SRX policy processing

There are two important things to note in the SRX policy process shown in Figure 4-2. First, not all configured policies are evaluated when the SRX does its policy processing. Only the policies that have been configured between the matching `from-zone to-zone` are evaluated. Second, the policy tables are evaluated in a top-down fashion, which means the order of your policies is very important. When the SRX finds a matching policy it takes whatever action that policy has.

Let's look at an example of a configuration error that has not taken into account the fact that the policies are evaluated in a top-down fashion:

```
juniper@SRX5800> show configuration security policies
from-zone trust to-zone Internet {
    policy allow-users {
        match {
            source-address inside-users;
            destination-address any;
            application any;
        }
        then {
            permit;
        }
    }
    policy protect_inside_users {
        match {
            source-address inside-users;
            destination-address bad_hosts;
            application any;
        }
        then {
            deny;
        }
    }
}
```

When read, the first policy to be evaluated is permitting `inside-users` to connect to any address using any application, and the second policy that is evaluated is to keep the `inside-users` from connecting to a list of known, bad hosts, but it is *after* the permit policy. So, in this instance, when the SRX does its policy lookup, the second policy never gets hit and the `inside-users` network is never protected from accessing those bad hosts.

For legacy ScreenOS users, it's important to note that there is no global security policy in the SRX policy system today. This means you cannot write global policies that apply to all zones.

We will discuss proper policy processing throughout this chapter. It really is key to establishing secure and efficient premises, and it depends on how you create the policies. The SRX will do exactly what you tell it to do. Now that we've briefly discussed what a security policy is and how the SRX handles its processing let's take a look at some real policy tables.

A helpful tip that catches many users is where Network Address Translation (NAT) is applied and how that relates to policy. Destination NAT is applied *before* the policy lookup takes place, and source NAT is applied after. That means when you are configuring policies you must ensure that if a destination NAT is configured, the security policies are using the new NATed address instead of the nontranslated original address.

Viewing SRX Policy Tables

Within the SRX there are multiple ways to view the details of the configured security policies and their order. While viewing the security policies you can issue the optional `detail` command at the end of any policy lookup. The `detail` switch gives you additional information regarding the security policies, such as their address books and applications.

Before using the `detail` command, let's look at example output that shows how to view all configured security policies using the `show security policies` command:

```
juniper@SRX5800> show security policies
Default policy: deny-all
From zone: trust, To zone: trust
  Policy: default-permit, State: enabled, Index: 4, Sequence number: 1
    Source addresses: any
    Destination addresses: any
    Applications: any
    Action: permit
From zone: trust, To zone: Internet
  Policy: default-permit, State: enabled, Index: 5, Sequence number: 1
```

```
      Source addresses: any
      Destination addresses: any
      Applications: any
      Action: permit
    Policy: protect_inside_users, State: enabled, Index: 7, Sequence number: 2
      Source addresses: inside-users
      Destination addresses: bad_hosts
      Applications: any
      Action: deny
  From zone: Internet, To zone: trust
    Policy: default-deny, State: enabled, Index: 6, Sequence number: 1
      Source addresses: any
      Destination addresses: any
      Applications: any
      Action: deny
```

Did you notice in the preceding output that this SRX is configured with a default policy of `deny-all`, meaning that it will deny all traffic by default? Policies must be written to allow traffic to pass between the security zones.

By default, there are two configured policies: the `default-permit` from Trust to Internet and the `default-deny` from Internet to Trust. Any additional behaviors must be configured to block or permit the desired traffic. Remember, if additional access is needed from the Internet zone to the Trust zone when a new security policy is configured, it must be placed *before* the `default-deny`. The order of policies is very important.

Now, let's get more information by adding `detail` at the end of the command:

```
juniper@SRX5800> show security policies detail
Default policy: deny-all
Policy: default-permit, action-type: permit, State: enabled, Index: 4
  Sequence number: 1
  From zone: trust, To zone: trust
  Source addresses:
    any: 0.0.0.0/0
  Destination addresses:
    any: 0.0.0.0/0
  Application: any
    IP protocol: 0, ALG: 0, Inactivity timeout: 0
      Source port range: [0-0]
      Destination port range: [0-0]
Policy: default-permit, action-type: permit, State: enabled, Index: 5
  Sequence number: 1
  From zone: trust, To zone: Internet
  Source addresses:
    any: 0.0.0.0/0
  Destination addresses:
    any: 0.0.0.0/0
  Application: any
    IP protocol: 0, ALG: 0, Inactivity timeout: 0
```

```
        Source port range: [0-0]
        Destination port range: [0-0]
```

Here the `show security policies detail` command displays a lot more information than what we saw in the previous output. Now, the true source/destination address IPs are displayed as `any`, or `0.0.0.0/0`, and the application port ranges and protocols are listed.

Instead of viewing all policies configured on the SRX, it is often easier to view policies between two specific zones by using the additional command options `from-zone <zone> to-zone <zone>`:

```
juniper@SRX5800> show security policies from-zone trust to-zone Internet
From zone: trust, To zone: Internet
  Policy: default-permit, State: enabled, Index: 5, Sequence number: 1
    Source addresses: any
    Destination addresses: any
    Applications: any
    Action: permit
  Policy: protect_inside_users, State: enabled, Index: 7, Sequence number: 2
    Source addresses: inside-users
    Destination addresses: bad_hosts
    Applications: any
    Action: deny
```

In this example output of only the security policies between the Trust and Internet zones, you should notice that the policies are still out of order, and that the `protect_inside_users` policy is still *after* the `default-permit` policy. We'll fix this later in the chapter.

Another way to view a specific policy instead of looking at a large list is to view it by `policy-name`. The `policy-name` option shows only *that* specific policy and provides you with the same level of information as the previous examples, if the name of the policy is already known (in our case it's `protect_inside_users`). In this example, the `detail` command has been used to provide further information about the `protect_inside_users` policy:

```
juniper@SRX5800> show security policies policy-name protect_inside_users detail
Policy: protect_inside_users, action-type: deny, State: enabled, Index: 7
  Sequence number: 2
  From zone: trust, To zone: Internet
  Source addresses:
    inside-users: 10.1.1.0/24
  Destination addresses:
    bad_hosts: 198.133.219.25/32
  Application: any
    IP protocol: 0, ALG: 0, Inactivity timeout: 0
      Source port range: [0-0]
      Destination port range: [0-0]
```

Viewing Policy Statistics

To enable policy statistics the then action must include the count flag. The count statement then enables counters for the specific policy.

Here, count is added to default-deny from Internet to Trust:

```
juniper@SRX5800# edit security policies from-zone Internet to-zone trust
[edit security policies from-zone Internet to-zone trust]
juniper@SRX5800# set policy default-deny then count
```

The configuration ends up looking like this:

```
juniper@SRX5800> show conf security policies from-zone Internet to-
zone trust
policy default-deny {
    match {
        source-address any;
        destination-address any;
        application any;
    }
    then {
        deny;
        count;
    }
}
```

Notice that both the then action and the count action are deny. This tells the SRX to keep track of statistics on this policy.

You must configure counting directly on each policy on which counting is needed.

Now, when the policy is viewed, new statistics are shown:

```
juniper@SRX5800> show security policies policy-name default-deny detail
Policy: default-deny, action-type: deny, State: enabled, Index: 6
  Sequence number: 1
  From zone: Internet, To zone: trust
  Source addresses:
    any: 0.0.0.0/0
  Destination addresses:
    any: 0.0.0.0/0
  Application: any
    IP protocol: 0, ALG: 0, Inactivity timeout: 0
      Source port range: [0-0]
      Destination port range: [0-0]
  Policy statistics:
    Input  bytes     :              200               5 bps
    Output bytes     :              500               10 bps
    Input  packets   :              23               2 pps
    Output packets   :              45               4 pps
```

```
Session rate     :              3              1 sps
Active sessions  :              2
Session deletions:              1
Policy lookups   :              3
```

Notice that the input/output rates are shown, as well as the session ramp rate. The session ramp rate is the number of sessions per second (`sps` in the preceding output) that the SRX has handled as a result of this policy.

Policy counters allow for much more visibility into the details of a policy, but do proceed with caution. Policy counters can add a bit of overhead to the policy processing, and if the device is a lower-end SRX it might be wise to limit the number of policies that have counters enabled to only those that are truly needed. On the higher-end models, policy counters will add a minor amount of overhead, but it is much less noticeable.

To reset policy counters back to zero use the `clear security policies statistics` command.

It's also possible to set alarms based upon predefined traffic count thresholds so that if the number of policy hits exceeds your preconfigured kilobytes-per-minute or bytes-per-second threshold, the SRX can send an alarm or, if an event script is written, take an advanced next-step action such as adding a firewall filter or access control list (ACL) to block the host.

An event script is an automated script that runs directly on the SRX when triggered by a certain event or log. Event scripts are outside the scope of this book. For more information about event scripts, visit *http://www.juniper.net/techpubs/*.

The code to configure thresholds and alarm for a policy looks something like this:

```
juniper@SRX5800# edit security policies from-zone Internet to-zone trust
[edit security policies from-zone Internet to-zone trust]
juniper@SRX5800# set policy default-deny then count alarm per-minute-threshold 100
```

The configuration will look something like this:

```
juniper@SRX5800# show security policies from-zone Internet to-zone trust
policy default-deny {
    match {
        source-address any;
        destination-address any;
        application any;
    }
    then {
        deny;
        count {
            alarm per-minute-threshold 100;
        }
    }
}
```

It's also possible to alarm the local log or an external logging device such as the Network and Security Manager (NSM), a syslog server, or a Simple Network Management Protocol (SNMP) collector on both permit and deny policies on a kilobytes-per-minute or bytes-per-second basis.

Viewing Session Flows

Once traffic has gone through the SRX packet flow, and assuming that the traffic has been permitted, the details of that session go into the SRX's session table. The session table is a real-time list of current sessions going through the SRX. Only connections that are active or haven't been timed out show up in the session table.

One very important thing to note is that if a flow is in the session table, it has already been permitted by policy and the session has been created—the SRX has allowed this connection and all return traffic for this flow to pass through. At this point, the SRX is only doing some minor checks via the *fast path*, as we saw in Figure 4-1 earlier in this chapter.

Here's an example of what a session looks like:

```
juniper@SRX5800> show security flow session
Session ID: 4785, Policy name: default-permit/1, Timeout: 1800
  In: 10.10.1.1/49229 --> 10.1.1.254/23;tcp, If: ge-0/0/0.0
  Out: 10.1.1.254/23 --> 10.10.1.1/49229;tcp, If: ge-0/0/1.0
```

You can learn a lot of useful information about this short session:

- The policy name that allowed this traffic is `default-permit`.
- The timeout is 1,800 seconds or 30 minutes; 30 minutes is the default timeout for TCP traffic.
- Both the source IP, 10.10.1.1, and the destination IP, 10.1.1.254, are shown with their respective source/destination ports, and the session is TCP port 23 or Telnet.
- The source interface is ge-0/0/0.0 and the destination interface for this session is ge-0/0/1.0.

To view the session table at a higher level you would use the `summary` command, which gives a breakdown of the different types of sessions and how many sessions there are:

```
juniper@SRX5800> show security flow session summary
Session summary:
  Unicast-sessions: 20
  Multicast-sessions: 0
  Failed-sessions: 0
  Sessions-in-use: 20
  Maximum-sessions: 65536
```

Be aware that session tables are often quite large, with thousands or even millions of sessions at any given time. Even so, the ability to search through the session table is extremely important, and Juniper has added some great filters to assist with this. As always, use the question mark (?) in the command-line interface (CLI) to show the list of possible options, as shown in the following output:

```
juniper@SRX5800> show security flow session ?
Possible completions:
  <[Enter]>            Execute this command
  application          Show session for specified application or application set
  destination-port     Show each session that uses specified destination port
  destination-prefix   Show each session that matches destination prefix
  idp                  Show IDP sessions
  interface            Show each session that uses specified interface
  protocol             Show each session that uses specified IP protocol
  resource-manager     Show resource-manager sessions
  session-identifier   Show session with specified session identifier
  source-port          Show each session that uses specified source port
  source-prefix        Show each session that matches source prefix
  summary              Show summary of sessions
  tunnel               Show tunnel sessions
  |                    Pipe through a command
```

Keep in mind that you can apply multiple filters to the search.

Another feature that has been added in Junos but was not available in ScreenOS is the ability to not only search by a source IP or destination IP, but also by an *entire* subnet.

This is important because it enables you to search for all traffic coming from or going to an entire subnet:

```
juniper@SRX5800> show security flow session destination-prefix 10.1.1/24
Session ID: 4785, Policy name: default-permit/1, Timeout: 1800
  In: 10.10.1.1/49229 --> 10.1.1.254/23;tcp, If: ge-0/0/0.0
  Out: 10.1.1.254/23 --> 10.10.1.1/49229;tcp, If: ge-0/0/1.0
Session ID: 4787, Policy name: default-permit/1, Timeout: 1800
  In: 10.10.1.5/49131 --> 10.1.1.254/23;tcp, If: ge-0/0/0.0
  Out: 10.1.1.254/23 --> 10.10.1.5/49131;tcp, If: ge-0/0/1.0
2 sessions displayed
```

In the following example, we are filtering the session table by `destination-port 23` or Telnet:

```
juniper@SRX5800> show security flow session destination-port 23
Session ID: 4785, Policy name: default-permit/1, Timeout: 1800
  In: 10.10.1.1/49229 --> 10.1.1.254/23;tcp, If: ge-0/0/0.0
  Out: 10.1.1.254/23 --> 10.10.1.1/49229;tcp, If: ge-0/0/1.0
Session ID: 4787, Policy name: default-permit/1, Timeout: 1800
  In: 10.10.1.5/49131 --> 10.1.1.254/23;tcp, If: ge-0/0/0.0
  Out: 10.1.1.254/23 --> 10.10.1.5/49131;tcp, If: ge-0/0/1.0
2 sessions displayed
```

And finally, here's how you can apply multiple filters to filter the session output even further. In the following output, two filters have been applied: the source-prefix filter and the destination port filter. This snippet shows only the sessions that match both of these requirements:

```
juniper@SRX5800> show security flow sess source-prefix 10.10.1.5
destination-port 23
Session ID: 4787, Policy name: default-permit/1, Timeout: 1800
  In: 10.10.1.5/49131 --> 10.1.1.254/23;tcp, If: ge-0/0/0.0
  Out: 10.1.1.254/23 --> 10.10.1.5/49131;tcp, If: ge-0/0/1.0
1 sessions displayed
```

Policy Structure

Earlier in the chapter we broke down an example security policy into its core elements. Now, let's discuss how to create the various objects that go into those security policies and toy with some of the advanced configuration options.

Security Zones

The first thing we need to do is to create a new security zone and assign it to the corresponding interface:

```
juniper@SRX5800> edit
Entering configuration mode
[edit]
juniper@SRX5800# set security zones security-zone web-dmz
juniper@SRX5800# set security zones security-zone web-dmz interfaces fe-0/0/2.0
```

Now we need to configure the IP address of the web servers. IP addresses or DNS names are configured in what's called address-books. These address-books store the IP or DNS information used in security policies. Additionally, address-books are tied to a single security zone; it's not possible to assign the same address-book to two different security zones.

The important thing to note is that it's not possible to configure IP addresses *directly* into the security policy—it must be done within an address-book.

```
juniper@SRX5800> edit
Entering configuration mode
[edit]
juniper@SRX5800# edit security zones security-zone web-dmz
[edit security zones security-zone web-dmz]
juniper@SRX5800# set address-book address web1 172.31.100.60
```

Here, a new address-book has been created on web-dmz that was previously configured. The new address-book has been assigned the label of web1, and the IP address of web1 is 172.31.100.60.

You create a second address-book for the second web server on web-dmz in the same way:

```
juniper@SRX5800>
[edit security zones security-zone web-dmz]
juniper@SRX5800# set address-book address web2 172.31.100.61
```

The third address-book that is configured is slightly different. This time, instead of using IP addresses, the address-book is configured with a DNS name:

```
juniper@SRX5800> edit security zones security-zone Internet
[edit security zones security-zone Internet]
juniper@SRX5800# set address-book address hackers_web hackers.com
```

Here, the address-book hackers_web was configured to the Internet security zone. The hackers_web address-book includes the DNS name hackers.com.

Some address-book names are reserved internally for the SRX and cannot be used. The prefixes are static_nat_, incoming_nat_, and junos_.

In situations where the policy calls for multiple IP addresses, ranges, or DNS names, instead of writing multiple security policies that all take the same action it's possible to use an address-set. An address-set is simply a grouping of address books.

Think of the address-book as a business card with information such as a phone number and name. Those business cards can all be stored into a single Rolodex or an address-set. Creating an address-set is similar to creating an address-book. Address-sets are also assigned to security zones and configured in the same manner:

```
juniper@SRX5800> edit security zones security-zone web-dmz
Entering configuration mode
[edit security zones security-zone web-dmz]
juniper@SRX5800# set address-book address-set web-servers address web1
[edit security zones security-zone web-dmz]
juniper@SRX5800# set address-book address-set web-servers address web2
```

A new address-set has been configured and is called web-servers, and the two web server address-books have been assigned to it. Now, when policy is written later, instead of writing policy for both web1 and web2 we can just use web-servers and it is applied to both.

We can verify the configuration by looking at the web-dmz zone to confirm that the proper addresses are assigned to the zone, and that the address-set is configured properly:

```
juniper@SRX5800> show configuration security zones security-zone web-dmz
address-book {
    address web1 172.31.100.60/32;
    address web2 172.31.100.61/32;
    address-set web-servers {
        address web1;
```

```
        address web2;
    }
}
```

Service Configuration

The next object to configure in our policy structure is the *application* (or service, as it was previously known in ScreenOS). Applications are used in policy to state how the source and destination can talk to each other, with some examples including HTTP, SSH, DNS, and SIP.

The SRX comes with a large list of preconfigured applications with much of the hard work already done. The protocol, source port, destination port, and other values have already been configured. All we need to do is to assign it to a policy.

These predefined applications start with `junos-`. To view a list of the predefined services use the `show configuration groups junos-defaults applications` command:

```
juniper@SRX5800> show configuration groups junos-defaults applications
#
# File Transfer Protocol
#
application junos-ftp {
    application-protocol ftp;
    protocol tcp;
    destination-port 21;
}
#
# Trivial File Transfer Protocol
#
application junos-tftp {
    application-protocol tftp;
    protocol udp;
    destination-port 69;
}
#
# Real Time Streaming Protocol
#
application junos-rtsp {
    application-protocol rtsp;
    protocol tcp;
    destination-port 554;
```

To view the details of a specific application use the syntax `show configuration groups junos-defaults applications application junos-<application name>`:

```
juniper@SRX5800> show conf groups junos-defaults app app junos-telnet
protocol tcp;
destination-port 23;
```

Much like `address-books` and `address-sets`, it is also possible to configure `application-sets`. This is a useful feature that replaces the need to write the same policy again and again just to permit a single additional service. Here's a web-management `application-set` that allows the network administrator to manage the servers on `web-dmz`:

```
juniper@SRX5800> edit applications application-set
Entering configuration mode
[edit applications application-set]
juniper@SRX5800# set web_mgt application junos-ssh
[edit applications application-set]
juniper@SRX5800# set web_mgt application junos-ping

[edit applications application-set]
juniper@SRX5800# set web_mgt application junos-pc-anywhere
```

The `application-set web_mgt` has been created and then configured for SSH, ping, and pcAnywhere as a part of that web management group.

If there is a custom program on the network, or perhaps an application isn't already configured on the SRX, it's easy to create a custom application. Say the local system administrators don't use pcAnywhere, but instead use a different remote access solution that goes over TCP port 4999. Now we'll have to create a custom application for them to use.

You must configure the following items when configuring a custom application:

Application name
: This is a label assigned to the custom application.

Protocol
: This specifies what protocol is used: TCP, UDP, ICMP, and so on.

`Source-port`
: This is the source port for the application. Keep in mind that most of the time the source port is a randomly assigned port between 1024 and 65535. `Any` is not an accepted configuration option; however, a range can be used.

`Destination-port`
: This is the destination port or range.

`Inactivity-timeout`
: This is how long the SRX will let the connection go idle before removing it from the session table. This value is configured in seconds and is optional. If you don't configure a value, the default timeout for the protocol will apply. For TCP the default is 30 minutes, and for UDP it is 2 minutes.

Here is an example of a custom `remote_mgt` application created for the system administrators to access into their web servers. This application allows them to connect to TCP port 4999, and because no `inactivity-timeout` is configured, it's automatically set for 30 minutes, the TCP default:

```
juniper@SRX5800> edit applications application
Entering configuration mode
[edit applications application]
```

```
juniper@SRX5800# set remote_mgt protocol tcp source-port 1024-65535
destination-port 4999
```

Now that the application has been configured, it's time to create the policies for the web-dmz zone. The first policy to create is to allow system administrators on the Trust zone to manage the web servers on the web-dmz zone and log the traffic.

```
juniper@SRX5800# edit security policies from-zone trust to-zone web-dmz
[edit security policies from-zone trust to-zone web-dmz]
juniper@SRX5800# set policy webdmz_mgt match source-address any
destination-address web-servers application web_mgt
[edit security policies from-zone trust to-zone web-dmz]
juniper@SRX5800# set policy webdmz_mgt then permit
[edit security policies from-zone trust to-zone web-dmz]
juniper@SRX5800# set policy webdmz_mgt then log session-close session-init
```

Now let's confirm the `webdmz_mgt` policy configuration:

```
juniper@SRX5800# show security policies from-zone trust to-zone web-dmz
policy webdmz_mgt {
    match {
        source-address any;
        destination-address web-servers;
        application web_mgt;
    }
    then {
        permit;
        log {
            session-init;
            session-close;
        }
    }
}
```

The next step is to set up access from the Internet zone to the web-dmz zone to allow users on the Internet to access the web servers via HTTP and keep statistics on the traffic:

```
juniper@SRX5800# edit security policies from-zone Internet to-zone web-dmz
[edit security policies from-zone Internet to-zone web-dmz]
juniper@SRX5800# set policy http-access match source-address any
destination-address web-servers application junos-http
[edit security policies from-zone Internet to-zone web-dmz]
juniper@SRX5800# set policy http-access then permit
[edit security policies from-zone Internet to-zone web-dmz]
juniper@SRX5800# set policy http-access then count
```

Keep in mind that, as stated earlier, unless something is explicitly permitted, it will be denied. So, there is no reason to write a `deny` when evaluating traffic from the Internet zone to the web-dmz zone, as only HTTP is permitted (as currently configured), unless you want to modify the deny policy for logging purposes:

```
juniper@SRX5800> show conf security policies from-zone Internet to-zone web-dmz
policy http-access {
    match {
        source-address any;
```

```
            destination-address web-servers;
            application junos-http;
        }
        then {
            permit;
            count;
        }
    }
```

To recap what we have done so far, we created a new zone named web-dmz; assigned two web server addresses to the `web-servers address-set`; created an `application-set` called `web_mgt` for system administrator access; and wrote a policy between both the Internet zone and the web-dmz zone for HTTP access in addition to a policy between the Trust zone and the web-dmz zone for management. Figure 4-3 shows that user `Dept-A` can now connect to the web application servers.

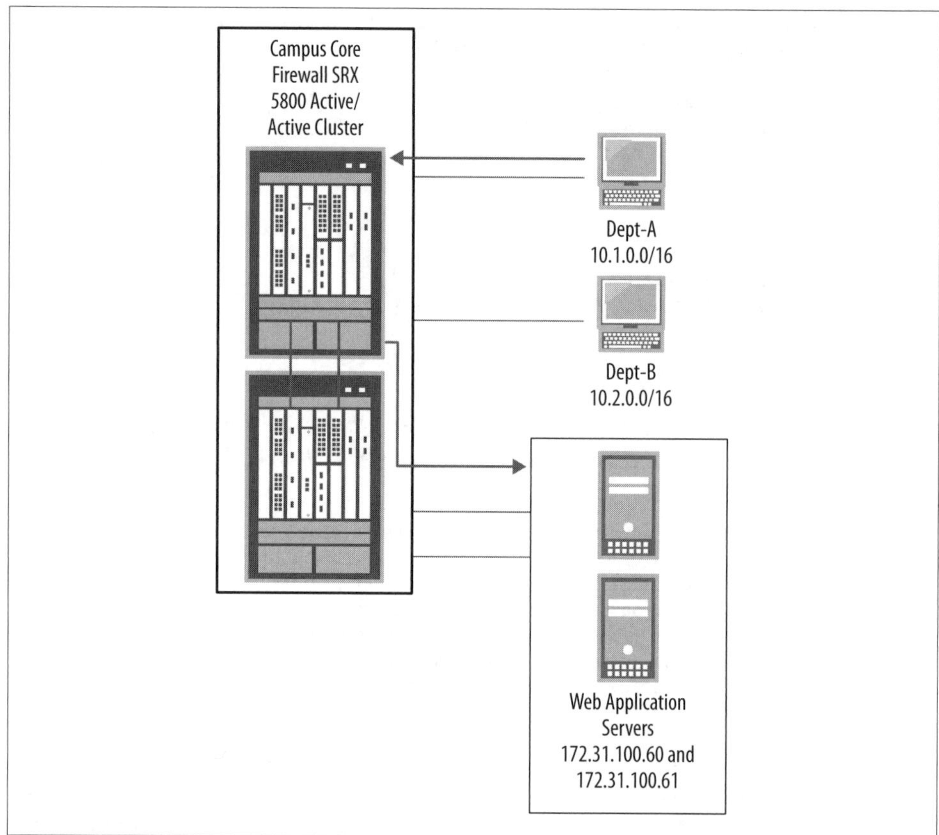

Figure 4-3. Dept-A data path to web servers

Blocking Unwanted Traffic

The next thing we need to do as we explore our sample policy structure is to deny unwanted outbound traffic from the users zone. In cases of Trust to Untrust, there is a default permit. Network operators may wish to block undesired programs and protocols from being used on the network using this default permit, such as instant messaging clients, outbound email (with the exception of email going through the corporate email servers), and many popular P2P applications. In this type of situation, we would need to explicitly block them.

Let's configure the SRX to block some of these services per the Campus Core's Internet access policy. The goal is to have the SRX silently deny all of these applications, as shown in Figure 4-4.

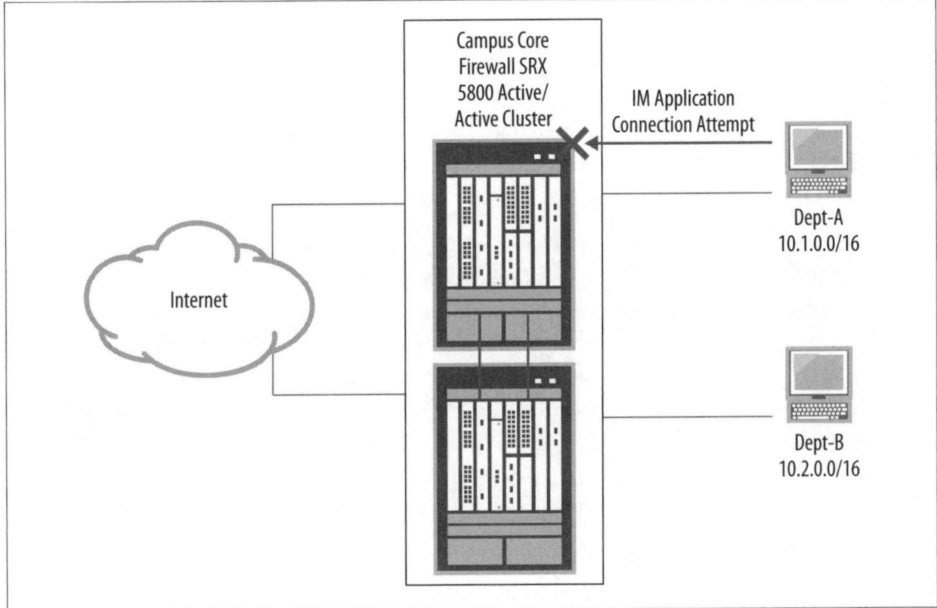

Figure 4-4. Blocking unwanted traffic with the SRX

Let's start our configuration:

```
juniper@SRX5800# edit applications application-set
[edit applications application-set]
juniper@SRX5800# set deny_services application junos-ymsg
[edit applications application-set
juniper@SRX5800# set deny_services application junos-smtp
[edit applications application-set
juniper@SRX5800# set deny_services application junos-msn
[edit applications application-set
juniper@SRX5800# set deny_services application junos-irc
[edit applications application-set
```

```
juniper@SRX5800# set deny_services application junos-gnutella
[edit applications application-set
juniper@SRX5800# set deny_services application junos-aol
```

Now, we'll create an open policy that applies to everyone going to any destination (any source to any destination):

```
juniper@SRX5800# edit security policies from-zone trust to-zone Internet
[edit security policies from-zone trust to-zone Internet]
juniper@SRX5800# set policy denied_apps match source-address any
destination-address any application deny_services
```

When blocking traffic on the SRX you have a couple of options that are very different in terms of how they go about dropping traffic:

`deny`
: The `deny` flag will *silently* drop the connection. The packet is dropped and logged (if configured to do so).

`reject`
: The `reject` flag has a key difference from the `deny` flag. Although `reject` drops the packet and logs (if configured to do so), it will also send an ICMP Port Unreachable packet to the initiating source for every packet that is rejected. This is used to inform the end host that the traffic was dropped.

Obviously, you must be careful with the `reject` flag because a large number of rejected packets could cause the SRX's performance to degrade due to flooding ICMP messages. In nearly all cases, the authors of this book highly recommend using `deny` instead of `reject`. For the same reason as the zone TCP-RST configuration, policies configured with `reject` could allow for malicious users to notice the SRX on your network and assist in mapping out your security policies. With that in mind, let's proceed with our blocking traffic policy:

```
[edit security policies from-zone trust to-zone Internet]
juniper@SRX5800# set policy denied_apps then deny log session-close session-init
```

Now let's confirm the deny policy's configuration:

```
juniper@SRX5800# show security policies from-zone trust to-zone Internet
policy denied_apps
match {
    source-address any;
    destination-address any;
    application deny_services;
}
then {
    deny;
    log {
        session-init;
        session-close;
    }
}
```

Always remember to evaluate policy ordering—since the policy that was just created is after the permit-any policy it must be moved before the permit-any policy to take effect. To do this use the `insert` command and insert `denied_apps` before `default-permit`:

```
[edit]
juniper@SRX5800# insert security policies from-zone trust to-zone Internet
policy denied_apps before policy default-permit
```

A quick confirmation shows that the policies are in the correct order:

```
juniper@SRX5800> show security policies from-zone trust to-zone Internet
From zone: trust, To zone: Internet
  Policy: denied_apps, State: enabled, Index: 13, Sequence number: 1
    Source addresses: any
    Destination addresses: any
    Applications: deny_services
    Action: deny, log
  Policy: default-permit, State: enabled, Index: 5, Sequence number: 2
    Source addresses: any
    Destination addresses: any
    Applications: any
    Action: permit
  Policy: protect_inside_users, State: enabled, Index: 6, Sequence number: 3
    Source addresses: inside-users
    Destination addresses: bad_hosts
    Applications: any
    Action: deny
```

Policy Logging

We briefly covered policy logging from a configuration standpoint earlier in this chapter. Here we'll discuss the details of policy logging and how to configure and view the logs.

For legacy NetScreen readers, policy logging is very different on the SRX. The logging system is more of a local syslog server than the traditional traffic log found on NetScreen devices, and nearly everything that could be done with the ScreenOS traffic logs can be done on the SRX's logfiles.

To log on the SRX you must configure the following two items:

- Policy logging must be enabled on the policy via the `session-init` and `session-close` configuration items.
- A filter and traffic logfile must be created on the SRX.

First, to enable policy logging, configure `log session-close session-init` on the specific policy on which logging is desired. The `session-close` flag tells the SRX to log whenever it tears down a session's connection (a session could close for many reasons, including a timeout, a FIN packet, or an RST packet). The `session-init` flag tells the SRX to log traffic for that policy when a session is built.

Here's an example of a policy with logging enabled (that was actually configured earlier in the chapter). This example policy logs both the creation and the teardown of these connections and works on policies that permit traffic as well as policies that deny traffic:

```
[edit]
juniper@SRX5800# set security policies from-zone trust to-zone web-dmz
policy webdmz_mgt then log session-close session-init
```

The next item we need to configure is a location for the traffic logs to go to. You can name the traffic logfile whatever you want, although it's always best to give the log a descriptive name, such as `traffic-log` or `policy-log`, just so other users know where to look for the logs.

Here the traffic logfile is called `traffic-log`. The second line of the config tells the SRX to send all traffic matching `RT_FLOW_SESSION`, which is a string that shows up in the policy messages:

```
[edit]
juniper@SRX5800# set system syslog file traffic-log any any
juniper@SRX5800# set system syslog file traffic-log match "RT_FLOW_SESSION"
```

Now, to view the traffic logs, use the `show log <filename>` command to display the entire traffic log:

```
juniper@SRX5800> show log traffic-log
Jan  7 12:07:24  SRX5800 RT_FLOW: RT_FLOW_SESSION_CREATE: session created
10.1.1.100/53910->172.31.100.60/22 junos-ssh
10.1.1.100/53910->172.31.100.60/22 None None 6 webdmz_mgt trust web-dmz 59
Jan  7 12:07:25  SRX5800 RT_FLOW: RT_FLOW_SESSION_CLOSE: session closed TCP RST:
10.1.1.100/53908->172.31.100.60/22 junos-ssh 10.1.1.100/53908->172.31.100.60/22
None None 6 webdmz_mgt trust web-dmz 57 1(64) 1(40) 3
```

Here is a detailed breakdown of the different types of messages, followed by an example (borrowed from the SRX documentation):

Session creation

`<source-address>/<source-port>-><destination-address>/`
`<destination-port>,<protocol-id>: <policy-name>`

```
RT_FLOW_SESSION_CREATE: session created 10.1.1.100/53908->172.31.100.60/22 junos-
ssh 10.1.1.100/53908->172.31.100.60/22 None None 6 webdmz_mgt trust web-dmz 57
```

Session close

`session closed <reason>: <source-address>/<source-port>->`
`<destination-address>/<destination-port>,<protocol-id>:<policy-name>,`
`<inbound-packets>, <inbound-bytes>,<outbound-bytes> <elapsed-time>`

```
RT_FLOW_SESSION_CLOSE: session closed TCP RST: 10.1.1.100/53907->172.31.100.60/22
junos-ssh 10.1.1.100/53907->172.31.100.60/22 None None 6 webdmz_mgt trust web-dmz
56 1(64) 1(40) 2
```

Session deny

`session denied <source-address>/<source-port>-><destination-address>/<destination-port>,<protocol-id>(<icmp-type>):<policy-name>`

```
RT_FLOW_SESSION_DENY: session denied 10.1.1.100/2->10.2.0.254/25931 icmp 1(8)
web_deny trust web-dmz
```

There are no built-in filters, as there were on the NetScreen platform. Instead, the SRX has some very powerful methods for filtering the displayed data that are built into the Junos operating system. Although a deep dive into all of the different filter options is outside the scope of this chapter, let's cover a few ways to filter through the traffic log. Just remember, this is only a small sample of what's possible.

The simplest way to filter the traffic log (or any syslog file, for that matter) is to use the `| match <data>` command, which filters the output to only that which matches the data that was input:

```
juniper@SRX5800> show log traffic-log | match 3389
Jan  7 12:06:38  SRX5800 RT_FLOW: RT_FLOW_SESSION_CREATE: session created
10.1.1.100/53904->172.31.100.60/3389 None 10.1.1.100/53904->172.31.100.60/
3389 None None 6 webdmz_mgt trust web-dmz 49
```

In this example, the match condition was `3389` (in this case, a port for Windows Remote Desktop). The `match` command is very powerful, and even allows for regular-expression-type searches, such as this match filter matching on the string `3389 OR 22`:

```
juniper@SRX5800> show log traffic-log | match "3389|22"
Jan  7 12:06:38  SRX5800 RT_FLOW: RT_FLOW_SESSION_CREATE: session created
10.1.1.100/53904->172.31.100.60/3389 None 10.1.1.100/53904->172.31.100.60/
3389 None None 6 webdmz_mgt trust web-dmz 49
Jan  7 12:07:22  SRX5800 RT_FLOW: RT_FLOW_SESSION_CREATE: session created
10.1.1.100/53907->172.31.100.60/22 junos-ssh 10.1.1.100/53907->172.31.100.60/22
None None 6 webdmz_mgt trust web-dmz 56
Jan  7 12:07:23  SRX5800 RT_FLOW: RT_FLOW_SESSION_CREATE: session created
10.1.1.100/53908->172.31.100.60/22 junos-ssh 10.1.1.100/53908->172.31.100.60/22
None None 6 webdmz_mgt trust web-dmz 57
```

Additional methods for viewing the traffic log include the ability to do a Unix-tail-type command. For example, the `last` command displays the last *X* number of lines. Here, the `last` filter is used to display only the last two lines of the traffic log:

```
juniper@SRX5800> show log traffic-log | last 2
Jan  7 12:07:25  SRX5800 RT_FLOW: RT_FLOW_SESSION_CLOSE: session closed TCP RST:
10.1.1.100/53909->172.31.100.60/22 junos-ssh 10.1.1.100/53909->172.31.100.60/22
None None 6 webdmz_mgt trust web-dmz 58 1(64) 1(40) 2
Jan  7 12:07:25  SRX5800 RT_FLOW: RT_FLOW_SESSION_CLOSE: session closed TCP RST:
10.1.1.100/53910->172.31.100.60/22 junos-ssh 10.1.1.100/53910->172.31.100.60/22
None None 6 webdmz_mgt trust web-dmz 59 1(64) 1(40) 1
```

Keep in mind that you can use multiple pipe filters together to form powerful commands. For example, if your goal is to determine how many times a certain IP, or segment, showed up in the traffic log, you could use a combination of `match` and `count`:

```
juniper@SRX5800> show log traffic-log | match 172.31.100.60 | count
Count: 13 lines
```

In the preceding output, 172.31.100.60 shows up 13 times in the traffic log.

You also can see what the firewall has dropped. Assuming that logging has been enabled on the deny policy, a simple filter on `deny` shows dropped traffic:

```
juniper@SRX5800> show log traffic-log | match DENY
Jan  7 12:07:05  SRX5800 RT_FLOW: RT_FLOW_SESSION_DENY: session denied
10.1.1.100/53906->172.31.100.60/21 junos-ftp 6(0) web_deny trust web-dmz
Jan  7 12:07:06  SRX5800 RT_FLOW: RT_FLOW_SESSION_DENY: session denied
10.1.1.100/53906->172.31.100.60/21 junos-ftp 6(0) web_deny trust web-dmz
Jan  7 12:07:11  SRX5800 RT_FLOW: RT_FLOW_SESSION_DENY: session denied
10.1.1.100/0->10.2.0.254/25931 icmp 1(8) web_deny trust web-dmz
Jan  7 12:07:12  SRX5800 RT_FLOW: RT_FLOW_SESSION_DENY: session denied
10.1.1.100/1->10.2.0.254/25931 icmp 1(8) web_deny trust web-dmz
Jan  7 12:07:13  SRX5800 RT_FLOW: RT_FLOW_SESSION_DENY: session denied
10.1.1.100/2->10.2.0.254/25931 icmp 1(8) web_deny trust web-dmz
```

It is also possible to log the policy denies to their own logfile—for example, if you wish to keep a separate copy of dropped traffic. You can do this by creating a new logfile and adjusting the `match` condition:

```
[edit]
juniper@SRX5800# set system syslog file traffic-deny any any
[edit]
juniper@SRX5800# set system syslog file traffic-deny match "RT_FLOW_SESSION_DENY"
```

A helpful trick to make it easier to troubleshoot traffic when a lot of data is going to the traffic logfile is to filter with more specific matching conditions. For example, if we were troubleshooting connectivity to 172.31.100.60, or wanted to log that specific traffic to a different logfile for later evaluation, we could filter only that traffic to a different file. Here, 172.31.100.60 is filtered to a new logfile called `troubleshooting_traffic`:

```
[edit]
juniper@SRX5800# set system syslog file troubleshooting_traffic any any
[edit]
juniper@SRX5800# set system syslog file troubleshooting_traffic match
"172.31.100.60"
```

Now, it's possible to view the traffic log for just 172.31.100.60:

```
juniper@SRX5800> show log troubleshooting_traffic
Jan 7 12:24:42 SRX5800 clear-log[1377]: logfile cleared
Jan  7 12:24:46  SRX5800 RT_FLOW: RT_FLOW_SESSION_CREATE: session created
10.1.1.100/53989->172.31.100.60/22 junos-ssh 10.1.1.100/53989->172.31.100.60/22
None None 6 webdmz_mgt trust web-dmz 91
Jan  7 12:24:47  SRX5800 RT_FLOW: RT_FLOW_SESSION_CLOSE: session closed TCP RST:
```

```
10.1.1.100/53989->172.31.100.60/22 junos-ssh 10.1.1.100/53989->172.31.100.60/22
None None 6 webdmz_mgt trust web-dmz 91 1(64) 1(40) 2
```

Once you get the hang of it, you'll see that there are many ways to filter out and count the data in logfiles using various commands. We've just scratched the surface here. Use the CLI question mark (?) to display all the different command possibilities:

```
juniper@SRX5800> show log troubleshooting_traffic | ?
Possible completions:
  count                Count occurrences
  display              Show additional kinds of information
  except               Show only text that does not match a pattern
  find                 Search for first occurrence of pattern
  hold                 Hold text without exiting the --More-- prompt
  last                 Display end of output only
  match                Show only text that matches a pattern
  no-more              Don't paginate output
  request              Make system-level requests
  resolve              Resolve IP addresses
  save                 Save output text to file
  trim                 Trim specified number of columns from start of line
```

Oops, I almost forgot to mention another very useful feature, the `monitor` command. Use the `monitor` command so that the SRX displays the output of the traffic log in real time to the console. It's very useful when troubleshooting or evaluating traffic.

```
juniper@SRX5800> monitor start traffic-log
```

Then, as data is written to the traffic logfile, it's displayed to the console. Use the `monitor stop` command to turn off the monitoring:

```
juniper@SRX5800>
*** traffic-log ***
Jan  7 12:07:13  SRX5800 RT_FLOW: RT_FLOW_SESSION_DENY: session denied
10.1.1.100/2->10.2.0.254/25931 icmp 1(8) web_deny trust web-dmz
```

On the high-end lines such as the SRX5800 a limited amount of logging is available to the local logs. There simply isn't enough disk space or processing to log the high rate of sessions that the high-end SRX devices are capable of handling. Logging to the local disk should be limited on these platforms to only critical policies.

Troubleshooting Security Policy and Traffic Flows

In most cases, simple policy logging of the traffic that is being denied and permitted is sufficient to verify what the SRX is doing with the data. However, in some instances more information is needed. On the NetScreen platform this information was gained via debugs, typically via `debug flow basic`. Juniper has taken into account how often debugs are used when troubleshooting traffic flows, in addition to policies, and has improved on this feature with traceoptions.

Within traceoptions you can accomplish the equivalent of a "debug flow basic" via `basic-datapath traceoption`. Traceoptions monitor and log traffic flows going into and out of the SRX and, much like the NetScreen debugs, filters tend to be very resource-intensive. The authors of this book highly suggest that when you use traceoptions you always have a packet filter set, and that the packet filter is as specific as possible to avoid any adverse system impacts.

Unlike on the NetScreen platform, on the SRX you can configure only one expression per packet filter. To examine bidirectional communication you need multiple packet filters, one for each direction.

Troubleshooting Sample

Our sample problem is as follows: while configuring a new web server, users are complaining that they cannot access the website. It has already been confirmed that policy is written correctly and traffic logs session initiation. It's all shown somewhat briefly in Figure 4-5.

The source is 10.1.1.100, a local workstation on the Trust zone in `Dept-A` via port ge-0/0/0.0.

The destination is 10.2.0.3, a new web server on the web-dmz zone via port fe-0/0/2.0.

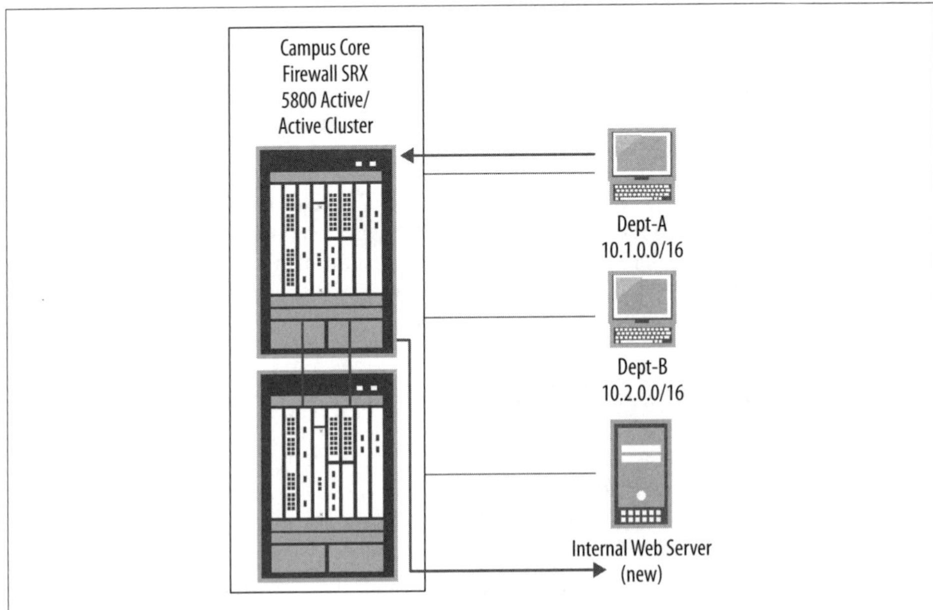

Figure 4-5. Sample problem showing users unable to access the website

The first thing we should do is to configure a logfile for the `traceoption` output. We can do this using the `file <file_name>` command. Here, the output file is named *tshoot_web*:

```
juniper@SRX5800# edit security flow traceoptions
[edit security flow traceoptions]
juniper@SRX5800# set file tshoot_web
```

Next we need to set the filters. It's worth noting that nothing takes effect until the configuration is committed, so it's perfectly safe to change the order in which these items are configured:

```
[edit security flow traceoptions]
juniper@SRX5800# set packet-filter trust_to_web source-prefix 10.1.1.100/32
destination-prefix 10.2.0.3/32
[edit security flow traceoptions]
juniper@SRX5800# set packet-filter web_to_trust source-prefix 10.2.0.3/32
destination-prefix 10.1.1.100/32
```

In the preceding output, two packet filters have been configured. The first filter is for 10.1.1.100 to 10.2.0.3 and the second filter is for the reverse traffic flow 10.2.0.3 talking to 10.1.1.100.

The last item we need to configure is the actual traceoption flag. Here, it is `basic-datapath`, as this should give us all the information we need:

```
[edit security flow traceoptions]
juniper@SRX5800# set flag basic-datapath
```

If you haven't heard it before, it's always wise to review the configuration before applying:

```
juniper@SRX5800# show security flow traceoptions
file tshoot_web;
flag basic-datapath;
packet-filter trust_to_web {
    source-prefix 10.1.1.100/32;
    destination-prefix 10.2.0.3/32;
}
packet-filter web_to_trust {
    source-prefix 10.2.0.3/32;
    destination-prefix 10.1.1.100/32;
}
[edit]
```

The output of the config looks correct. All of the required configuration options are there: a traceoptions file, a traceoptions flag, and two packet filters for bidirectional traffic. Since everything looks OK, we can commit the configuration and the workstation can initiate some traffic so that we can monitor it. Once the test traffic has been completed, all the data to troubleshoot our problem should be in the *tshoot_web* traceoptions file.

The output contains a lot of detailed information regarding what the SRX is doing with the packet as it passes through its hardware and does its series of checks, and the reality is that you can overlook much of this information in the output because it's for developers who are troubleshooting and does not apply to what you need to know. Also, the traceoptions output will likely change over the printed lifetime of this book, as the developers add and remove information.

Troubleshooting Output

The output of the packet's details is shown in its entirety in Example 4-1. Look through it and then we'll break down what each portion means or does and what we can overlook.

This output is from a single first packet as it enters the SRX in our troubleshooting scenario (see Figure 4-5).

Example 4-1. Output of the packet's details, in its entirety

```
juniper@SRX5800> show log tshoot_web
Jan 17 12:35:51 12:35:50.1249501:CID-0:RT:<10.1.1.100/51510-
>10.2.0.3/80;6> matched filter trust_to_web:
Jan 17 12:35:51 12:35:50.1249501:CID-0:RT:packet [48] ipid = 57203,
@423f6b9e
Jan 17 12:35:51 12:35:50.1249501:CID-0:RT:---- flow_process_pkt: (thd
1): flow_ctxt type 13, common flag 0x0, mbuf 0x423f6a00
Jan 17 12:35:51 12:35:50.1249501:CID-0:RT: flow process pak fast ifl
68 in_ifp ge-0/0/0.0
Jan 17 12:35:51 12:35:50.1249501:CID-0:RT:  ge-
0/0/0.0:10.1.1.100/51510->10.2.0.3/80, tcp, flag 2 syn
Jan 17 12:35:51 12:35:50.1249501:CID-0:RT: find flow: table
0x4d5c8238, hash 1430(0xffff), sa 10.1.1.100, da 10.2.0.3, sp 51510,
dp 80, proto 6, tok 384
Jan 17 12:35:51 12:35:50.1249501:CID-0:RT:  no session found, start
first path. in_tunnel - 0, from_cp_flag - 0
Jan 17 12:35:51 12:35:50.1249501:CID-0:RT:  flow_first_create_session
Jan 17 12:35:51 12:35:50.1249501:CID-0:RT:  flow_first_in_dst_nat: in
<ge-0/0/0.0>, out <N/A> dst_adr 10.2.0.3, sp 51510, dp 80
Jan 17 12:35:51 12:35:50.1249501:CID-0:RT:  chose interface ge-
0/0/0.0 as incoming nat if.
Jan 17 12:35:51 12:35:50.1249501:CID-0:RT:flow_first_rule_dst_xlate:
DST no-xlate: 0.0.0.0(0) to 10.2.0.3(80)
Jan 17 12:35:51 12:35:50.1249501:CID-0:RT:flow_first_routing: call
flow_route_lookup(): src_ip 10.1.1.100, x_dst_ip 10.2.0.3, in ifp ge-
0/0/0.0, out ifp N/A sp 51510, dp 80, ip_proto 6, tos 0
Jan 17 12:35:51 12:35:50.1249501:CID-0:RT:Doing DESTINATION addr
route-lookup
Jan 17 12:35:51 12:35:50.1249501:CID-0:RT:  routed (x_dst_ip
10.2.0.3) from trust (ge-0/0/0.0 in 0) to ge-0/0/0.0, Next-hop:
10.1.1.1
Jan 17 12:35:51 12:35:50.1249501:CID-0:RT:  policy search from zone
trust-> zone trust
```

```
Jan 17 12:35:51 12:35:50.1249501:CID-0:RT:  app 6, timeout 1800s,
curr ageout 20s
Jan 17 12:35:51 12:35:50.1249501:CID-0:RT:flow_first_src_xlate:
10.1.1.100/51510 -> 10.2.0.3/80 | 10.2.0.3/80 -> 0.0.0.0/51510:
nat_src_xlated: False, nat_src_xlate_failed: False
Jan 17 12:35:51 12:35:50.1249501:CID-0:RT:flow_first_src_xlate: src
nat 0.0.0.0(51510) to 10.2.0.3(80) returns status: 0, rule/pool id:
0/0, pst_nat: False.
Jan 17 12:35:51 12:35:50.1249501:CID-0:RT:  dip id = 0/0,
10.1.1.100/51510->10.1.1.100/51510
Jan 17 12:35:51 12:35:50.1249501:CID-0:RT:flow_first_get_out_ifp:
1000 -> cone nat test
Jan 17 12:35:51 12:35:50.1249501:CID-0:RT:  choose interface ge-
0/0/0.0 as outgoing phy if
Jan 17 12:35:51 12:35:50.1249501:CID-0:RT:is_loop_pak: No loop: on
ifp: ge-0/0/0.0, addr: 10.2.0.3, rtt_idx:0
Jan 17 12:35:51 12:35:50.1249501:CID-0:RT:policy is NULL (wx/pim
scenario)
Jan 17 12:35:51 12:35:50.1249501:CID-0:RT:sm_flow_interest_check:
app_id 0, policy 4, app_svc_en 0, flags 0x2. not interested
Jan 17 12:35:51 12:35:50.1249501:CID-0:RT:sm_flow_interest_check:
app_id 1, policy 4, app_svc_en 0, flags 0x2. not interested
Jan 17 12:35:51 12:35:50.1249501:CID-
0:RT:flow_first_service_lookup(): natp(0x4b9f2198):
local_pak(0x3fdedc70.0x423f6a00):  TCP proxy NOT interested: 0.
Jan 17 12:35:51 12:35:50.1249501:CID-0:RT:  service lookup identified
service 6.
Jan 17 12:35:51 12:35:50.1249501:CID-0:RT:  flow_first_final_check:
in <ge-0/0/0.0>, out <ge-0/0/0.0>
Jan 17 12:35:51 12:35:50.1249501:CID-0:RT:  existing vector list 2-
446fe828.
Jan 17 12:35:51 12:35:50.1249501:CID-0:RT:  Session (id:9270) created
for first pak 2
Jan 17 12:35:51 12:35:50.1249501:CID-0:RT:
flow_first_install_session======> 0x4b9f2198
Jan 17 12:35:51 12:35:50.1249501:CID-0:RT: nsp 0x4b9f2198, nsp2
0x4b9f2204
Jan 17 12:35:51 12:35:50.1249501:CID-0:RT:
make_nsp_ready_no_resolve()
Jan 17 12:35:51 12:35:50.1249501:CID-0:RT:  route lookup: dest-ip
10.1.1.100 orig ifp ge-0/0/0.0 output_ifp ge-0/0/0.0 orig-zone 6 out-
zone 6 vsd 0
Jan 17 12:35:51 12:35:50.1249501:CID-0:RT:  route to 10.1.1.100
Jan 17 12:35:51 12:35:50.1249501:CID-0:RT:Installing c2s NP session
wing
Jan 17 12:35:51 12:35:50.1249501:CID-0:RT:Installing s2c NP session
wing
Jan 17 12:35:51 12:35:50.1249501:CID-0:RT:  flow got session.
Jan 17 12:35:51 12:35:50.1249501:CID-0:RT:  flow session id 9270
Jan 17 12:35:51 12:35:50.1249501:CID-0:RT:  tcp flags 0x2, flag 0x2
Jan 17 12:35:51 12:35:50.1249501:CID-0:RT:  Got syn,
10.1.1.100(51510)->10.2.0.3(80), nspflag 0x1021, 0x20
Jan 17 12:35:51 12:35:50.1249501:CID-0:RT:mbuf 0x423f6a00, exit nh
0x30010
```

```
Jan 17 12:35:51 12:35:50.1249501:CID-0:RT: ----- flow_process_pkt rc
0x0 (fp rc 0)
```

That's a lot to digest. To make this easier (quicker) to read, a helpful tip is to use the `trim` command option. The `trim` command removes a specified number of characters. For instance, you can use it to remove the date and time to make the code a lot easier to read or fit on a screen. Example 4-2 shows the trace file trimmed. `Trim 42` removes the date and time as well as the `CID-0:RT:`, leaving just the important data.

Example 4-2. Trimmed trace file

```
juniper@SRX5800> show log tshoot_web | trim 42
<10.1.1.100/51510->10.2.0.3/80;6> matched filter trust_to_web:
packet [48] ipid = 57203, @423f6b9e
---- flow_process_pkt: (thd 1): flow_ctxt type 13, common flag 0x0,
mbuf 0x423f6a00
 flow process pak fast ifl 68 in_ifp ge-0/0/0.0
  ge-0/0/0.0:10.1.1.100/51510->10.2.0.3/80, tcp, flag 2 syn
 find flow: table 0x4d5c8238, hash 1430(0xffff), sa 10.1.1.100, da
10.2.0.3, sp 51510, dp 80, proto 6, tok 384
  no session found, start first path. in_tunnel - 0, from_cp_flag - 0
  flow_first_create_session
  flow_first_in_dst_nat: in <ge-0/0/0.0>, out <N/A> dst_adr 10.2.0.3,
sp 51510, dp 80
  chose interface ge-0/0/0.0 as incoming nat if.
flow_first_rule_dst_xlate:  DST no-xlate: 0.0.0.0(0) to 10.2.0.3(80)
flow_first_routing: call flow_route_lookup(): src_ip 10.1.1.100,
x_dst_ip 10.2.0.3, in ifp ge-0/0/0.0, out ifp N/A sp 51510, dp 80,
ip_proto 6, tos 0
Doing DESTINATION addr route-lookup
  routed (x_dst_ip 10.2.0.3) from trust (ge-0/0/0.0 in 0) to ge-
0/0/0.0, Next-hop: 10.1.1.1
  policy search from zone trust-> zone trust
  app 6, timeout 1800s, curr ageout 20s
flow_first_src_xlate: 10.1.1.100/51510 -> 10.2.0.3/80 | 10.2.0.3/80 -
> 0.0.0.0/51510: nat_src_xlated: False, nat_src_xlate_failed: False
flow_first_src_xlate: src nat 0.0.0.0(51510) to 10.2.0.3(80) returns
status: 0, rule/pool id: 0/0, pst_nat: False.
  dip id = 0/0, 10.1.1.100/51510->10.1.1.100/51510
flow_first_get_out_ifp: 1000 -> cone nat test
  choose interface ge-0/0/0.0 as outgoing phy if
is_loop_pak: No loop: on ifp: ge-0/0/0.0, addr: 10.2.0.3, rtt_idx:0
policy is NULL (wx/pim scenario)
sm_flow_interest_check: app_id 0, policy 4, app_svc_en 0, flags 0x2.
not interested
sm_flow_interest_check: app_id 1, policy 4, app_svc_en 0, flags 0x2.
not interested
flow_first_service_lookup(): natp(0x4b9f2198):
local_pak(0x3fdedc70.0x423f6a00):  TCP proxy NOT interested: 0.
  service lookup identified service 6.
  flow_first_final_check: in <ge-0/0/0.0>, out <ge-0/0/0.0>
  existing vector list 2-446fe828.
  Session (id:9270) created for first pak 2
  flow_first_install_session======> 0x4b9f2198
```

```
 nsp 0x4b9f2198, nsp2 0x4b9f2204
  make_nsp_ready_no_resolve()
  route lookup: dest-ip 10.1.1.100 orig ifp ge-0/0/0.0 output_ifp ge-
0/0/0.0 orig-zone 6 out-zone 6 vsd 0
  route to 10.1.1.100
Installing c2s NP session wing
Installing s2c NP session wing
  flow got session.
  flow session id 9270
  tcp flags 0x2, flag 0x2
  Got syn, 10.1.1.100(51510)->10.2.0.3(80), nspflag 0x1021, 0x20
mbuf 0x423f6a00, exit nh 0x30010
 ----- flow_process_pkt rc 0x0 (fp rc 0)
```

Bidirectional Traffic

For a quick way to verify bidirectional traffic—for example, if you need to confirm whether an end host is responding—you can perform a quick `match` command. Keep in mind that this will not tell you what has happened, only that the traffic is bidirectional. Notice how 10.1.1.100 is shown as the source on the `trust_to_dmz` filter and 172.31.100.60 is shown as the source on the `dmz_to_trust` filter:

```
juniper@SRX5800> show log tracetest | match matched
Jan 21 23:32:21 23:32:21.807167:CID-0:RT:<10.1.1.100/58543-
>172.31.100.60/80;6> matched filter Trust_to_dmz:
Jan 21 23:32:21 23:32:21.823519:CID-0:RT:<172.31.100.60/80-
>10.1.1.100/58543;6> matched filter dmz_to_trust:
Jan 21 23:32:21 23:32:21.825358:CID-0:RT:<10.1.1.100/58543-
>172.31.100.60/80;6> matched filter Trust_to_dmz:
Jan 21 23:32:21 23:32:21.825358:CID-0:RT:<10.1.1.100/58543-
>172.31.100.60/80;6> matched filter Trust_to_dmz:
Jan 21 23:32:22 23:32:21.935552:CID-0:RT:<172.31.100.60/80-
>10.1.1.100/58543;6> matched filter dmz_to_trust:
Jan 21 23:32:22 23:32:21.937322:CID-0:RT:<10.1.1.100/58543-
>172.31.100.60/80;6> matched filter Trust_to_dmz:
```

Now, let's analyze the data from the traceoption's output shown in Example 4-2.

The first line, shown here, displays the source IP 10.1.1.100 and destination IP 10.2.0.3, as well as the ports used to communicate. It then documents that this traffic matched the `trust_to_web` traceoptions filter.

```
<10.1.1.100/60218->10.2.0.3/80;6> matched filter trust_to_web:
```

The next line gives us the IPID, which is 57203 in this example:

```
packet [48] ipid = 57203, @423f6b9e
```

These two lines are basically useful to internal developers for troubleshooting hardware/software issues, and not for our problem at hand:

```
---- flow_process_pkt: (thd 1): flow_ctxt type 13, common flag 0x0,
mbuf 0x423f6a00
 flow process pak fast ifl 68 in_ifp ge-0/0/0.0
```

Notice that the inbound interface is ge-0/0/0.0 and the protocol is TCP, and that this is a SYN packet:

```
ge-0/0/0.0:10.1.1.100/60218->10.2.0.3/80, tcp, flag 2 syn
```

Here is the output as the SRX performs its 5-tuple lookup. The 5-tuple includes the source, destination, source port, destination port, and protocol. Protocol number 6 is TCP.

```
find flow: table 0x4d5c8238, hash 1430(0xffff), sa 10.1.1.100, da 10.2.0.3, sp
51510, dp 80, proto 6, tok 384
```

The Internet Assigned Numbers Authority (IANA) has assigned numbers to all protocols. Here is a link to a list that IANA updates periodically: *http://www.iana.org/assignments/protocol-numbers/*.

Now that the 5-tuple lookup has been completed, a flow lookup is done. At this point, as shown by the output, the SRX determines if there is an existing session for this packet and whether it can take the fast path, or if this is a new session and it needs to go down the slow path. The example packet that is being broken down is, in fact, a first packet of a new session, and as such, the SRX determines that no existing session has been found and one must be created:

```
no session found, start first path. in_tunnel - 0, from_cp_flag - 0
  flow_first_create_session
```

The SRX then checks to see if there are any destination NAT configurations that apply. In this case, there are none, so no NAT is applied:

```
flow_first_in_dst_nat: in <ge-0/0/0.0>, out <N/A> dst_adr 10.2.0.3, sp 51510,
dp 80
  chose interface ge-0/0/0.0 as incoming nat if.
flow_first_rule_dst_xlate:  DST no-xlate: 0.0.0.0(0) to 10.2.0.3(80)
```

After the destination NAT has been looked up and applied, a route lookup can be done if one exists. The route lookup must take place after a destination NAT for routing purposes:

```
10.2.0.3, in ifp ge-0/0/0.0, out ifp N/A sp 51510, dp 80, ip_proto 6, tos 0
Doing DESTINATION addr route-lookup
  routed (x_dst_ip 10.2.0.3) from trust (ge-0/0/0.0 in 0) to ge-0/0/0.0,
Next-hop: 10.1.1.1
```

Once a route lookup is done on the destination, the SRX can determine the source and destination zones via a zone lookup. It then does a policy search to see if this traffic is denied/rejected/permitted or some other action, but in our case, it's permitted:

```
policy search from zone trust-> zone web-dmz
  app 6, timeout 1800s, curr ageout 20s
```

If it had been denied by policy, a message such as this would have shown up, saying that the packet was denied and dropped:

```
packet dropped, denied by policy
packet dropped, policy deny.
flow find session returns error.
----- flow_process_pkt rc 0x7 (fp rc -1)
```

But that's not the case, and now that the policy has been evaluated, the SRX checks to see if any source NAT configuration applies. In this case, there is no source NAT and everything returns `false`:

```
flow_first_src_xlate: 10.1.1.100/51510 -> 10.2.0.3/80 | 10.2.0.3/80 ->
0.0.0.0/51510: nat_src_xlated: False, nat_src_xlate_failed: False
flow_first_src_xlate: src nat 0.0.0.0(51510) to 10.2.0.3(80) returns status: 0,
rule/pool id: 0/0, pst_nat: False.
  dip id = 0/0, 10.1.1.100/51510->10.1.1.100/51510
flow_first_get_out_ifp: 1000 -> cone nat test
```

The SRX then determines the outgoing interface for this packet:

```
choose interface ge-0/0/0.0 as outgoing phy if
is_loop_pak: No loop: on ifp: ge-0/0/0.0, addr: 10.2.0.3, rtt_idx:0
```

Next, the SRX does some additional policy checks to see if items such as TCP proxy and WX apply:

```
policy is NULL (wx/pim scenario)
sm_flow_interest_check: app_id 0, policy 4, app_svc_en 0,
flags 0x2. not interested
sm_flow_interest_check: app_id 1, policy 4, app_svc_en 0,
flags 0x2. not interested
flow_first_service_lookup(): natp(0x4b9f2198): local_pak(0x3fdedc70.0x423f6a00):
TCP proxy NOT interested: 0.
  service lookup identified service 6.
```

In the preceding output, notice the policy number, `policy 4`. All security policies are assigned an index number. This index number is mainly for internal reference, but it can be viewed within the `show security policies` command, as shown in the following output, where you can see that policy 4 is a `default-permit`:

```
juniper@SRX5800> show security policies | match index
  Policy: default-permit, State: enabled, Index: 4, Sequence number: 1
  Policy: default-permit, State: enabled, Index: 5, Sequence number: 1
  Policy: protect_inside_users, State: enabled, Index: 6, Sequence number: 2
  Policy: webdmz_mgt, State: enabled, Index: 8, Sequence number: 1
  Policy: web_deny, State: enabled, Index: 9, Sequence number: 2
  Policy: default-deny, State: enabled, Index: 7, Sequence number: 1
  Policy: http-access, State: enabled, Index: 10, Sequence number: 1
  Policy: deny-all, State: enabled, Index: 11, Sequence number: 2
```

Back to our SRX output ... the packet is sent out as the last checks are completed, as indicated here:

```
flow_first_final_check: in <ge-0/0/0.0>, out <ge-0/0/0.0>
  existing vector list 2-446fe828.
```

```
    Session (id:9270) created for first pak 2
    flow_first_install_session======> 0x4b9f2198
  nsp 0x4b9f2198, nsp2 0x4b9f2204
    make_nsp_ready_no_resolve()
    route lookup: dest-ip 10.1.1.100 orig ifp ge-0/0/0.0 output_ifp ge-0/0/0.0
orig-zone 6 out-zone 6 vsd 0
    route to 10.1.1.100
Installing c2s NP session wing
Installing s2c NP session wing
    flow got session.
    flow session id 9270
    tcp flags 0x2, flag 0x2
    Got syn, 10.1.1.100(51510)->10.2.0.3(80), nspflag 0x1021, 0x20
mbuf 0x423f6a00, exit nh 0x30010
 ----- flow_process_pkt rc 0x0 (fp rc 0)
```

Although the output from traceoptions is a bit cryptic and hard to read, sometimes it's much easier to understand if you look at it line by line, like we just did.

So, from the output in the *tshoot_web* file, it appears that traffic is going out the *incorrect* interface. From the preceding output, the route lookup is done and it appears that traffic is exiting the same interface on which it is entering. The `ifp` is the inbound interface and the `output_ifp` is the outbound interface.

```
route lookup: dest-ip 10.1.1.100 orig ifp ge-0/0/0.0 output_ifp ge-0/0/0.0
orig-zone 6 out-zone 6 vsd 0
```

Look at the routing table to confirm that traffic is not exiting the proper interface:

```
juniper@SRX5800> show route 10.2.0.3
inet.0: 4 destinations, 4 routes (4 active, 0 holddown, 0 hidden)
+ = Active Route, - = Last Active, * = Both
0.0.0.0/0          *[Static/5] 6d 11:52:38
                    > to 10.1.1.1 via ge-0/0/0.0
```

The routing is incorrect. A quick static route should fix this problem and route traffic out the proper interface:

```
juniper@SRX5800> edit
[edit]
juniper@SRX5800> set routing-options static route 10.2.0.0/24 next-hop 10.2.1.1
```

Fix the problem and return to the `show route` command. Once a correct route is added, the traffic works for all users on the internal LAN:

```
juniper@SRX5800> show route 10.2.0.3
inet.0: 5 destinations, 5 routes (5 active, 0 holddown, 0 hidden)
+ = Active Route, - = Last Active, * = Both
10.2.0.0/24     *[Static/5] 00:02:32
                    > 10.2.1.1 via fe-0/0/2.0
```

Turning Off Traceoptions

After you have completed any troubleshooting in your network, is it highly recommended that you turn off traceoptions. Unless there is a very good reason to leave them running, you should always disable them as soon as you have finished troubleshooting, as traceoptions can consume SRX resources, and depending on the amount of traffic being debugged, SRX performance could be impacted.

There are two ways to turn off traceoptions. The first method is to just deactivate the configuration. This leaves the traceoptions configuration in the SRX, but it is turned off until it is reactivated at a later date when troubleshooting has resumed.

To deactivate everything use the `deactivate security flow traceoptions` command. However, be careful when using the `deactivate` command, because much like the `delete` command, if you use it incorrectly, it can have a severe impact on the SRX.

```
[edit]
juniper@SRX5800# deactivate security flow traceoptions
```

To confirm that the traceoptions have been disabled, just look at the configuration with the `show` command. Junos will tell you that this portion of the configuration is inactive:

```
juniper@SRX5800# show security flow traceoptions
##
## inactive: security flow traceoptions
##
file tshoot_web;
flag basic-datapath;
packet-filter trust_to_web {
    source-prefix 10.1.1.100/32;
    destination-prefix 10.2.0.3/32;
}
packet-filter web_to_trust {
    source-prefix 10.2.0.3/32;
    destination-prefix 10.1.1.100/32;
}
```

The second method to turn off traceoptions is to delete the traceoptions configuration. If the traceoptions configuration is no longer needed and troubleshooting has been completed, it's wise to delete the configuration from the SRX.

To do this, use the `delete` command coupled with the `security flow traceoptions` configuration:

```
[edit]
juniper@SRX5800# delete security flow traceoptions
```

Now confirm that the traceoptions configuration is gone:

```
[edit]
juniper@SRX5800# show security flow traceoptions
[edit]
juniper@SRX5800#
```

The authors recommend that whenever you use the `delete` command you issue a `show | compare` before committing the configuration. This will display all changes to the configuration that are applied when a commit is done. It also ensures that no unintended configurations are made, or in this case, deleted:

```
juniper@SRX5800# show | compare
[edit security]
-   flow {
-       traceoptions {
-           file tshoot_web;
-           flag basic-datapath;
-           packet-filter trust_to_web {
-               source-prefix 10.1.1.100/32;
-               destination-prefix 10.2.0.3/32;
-           }
-           packet-filter web_to_trust {
-               source-prefix 10.2.0.3/32;
-               destination-prefix 10.1.1.100/32;
-           }
-       }
-   }
[edit]
```

As shown, only the traceoptions configuration has been deleted, so it's safe to do a `commit` and exit configuration mode.

To remove old troubleshooting logfiles, use the `file delete <file name>` command. It's always a best practice to remove old, unused files when you no longer need them.

Application Layer Gateway Services

Application layer gateways (ALGs) are advanced application-inspecting features available on the SRX that serve two primary purposes. The first is to dynamically pinhole traffic for applications allowing return inbound packets (e.g., for FTP there may be multiple sessions for control and data for the same data connection between the source and destination). The second role of an ALG is to provide a deeper layer of inspection and a more granular layer of application security. ALGs can be better described as extra intelligence built to assist with certain applications that have problems with stateful firewalls.

This type of extra security and inspection is possible because an ALG understands the application protocol and how it is supposed to function. The SRX can prevent many types of SCCP DoS attacks, such as call flooding, from taking place on the network. We will cover these configurable application screens in detail in Chapter 7, but in a nutshell, ALGs are application (Layer 7)-aware packet processing (Layer 4).

It's worth noting that not all ALGs are available in the higher-end SRX models. For example, at the time of this writing, SCCP and H323 are not available on the high-end SRX devices, while the branch SRX Series has full support for all listed ALGs.

Here is a list of ALGs currently built into the SRX, along with a brief explanation of what each one does:

REAL
: RealAudio/RealVideo are proprietary formats developed by RealNetworks and they use what is called Progressive Network Audio (PNA) or Progressive Network Media (PNM) to send streaming audio data. PNA packets are sent over a TCP connection and act like a control channel. The audio data itself is sent over a UDP connection. The ALG dynamically allows these UDP data connections and performs any NAT that needs to take place.

RTSP
: Real-Time Streaming Protocol is used to establish and control media connections between end hosts. RTSP handles all client-to-media server requests such as play and pause, and is used to control real-time playback of the media files from the server. RTSP does not, however, stream any media data. Commonly, that is left to Real-time Transport Protocol (RTP), and the two are used in combination to deliver media to the clients.

DNS
: The Domain Name System ALG monitors DNS queries and response packets. Since DNS is UDP and is a simple request-response type of flow, the DNS ALG monitors for the `response` flag and then closes down the UDP session. This is very useful; otherwise, the SRX would wait two minutes before timing out the session, which is the default for UDP.

FTP
: The File Transfer Protocol ALG monitors the FTP connection for PORT, PASV, and 227 commands. The ALG will handle all NAT functions and pinholing of any additional ports necessary. Additional security options can be leveraged by configuring the FTP ALG to block specific FTP functions, such as FTP put or FTP get.

TFTP
: The Trivial File Transfer Protocol ALG monitors the initiation of a TFTP connection and pinholes a connection through the SRX permitting the reverse direction.

TALK
: TALK is a legacy chat-type application for Unix platforms developed in the early 1980s. TALK communicates on UDP port 517/518 for control-channel-type functions. The TALK ALG will handle all NAT functions in addition to any pinholing that needs to take place.

RSH

RSH stands for Remote Shell. RSH is a Unix-type program that can execute commands across a network. RSH typically uses TCP port 514. RSH has largely been replaced by SSH as RSH communicates unencrypted. The RSH ALG handles all NAT functions as well as any pinholing that needs to take place.

PPTP

Point-to-Point Tunneling Protocol is a Layer 2 protocol used for tunneling PPP over an IP network. PPTP is often used as a way to implement virtual private networks (VPNs) and is tunneled over TCP and a Generic Route Encapsulation (GRE) tunnel encapsulating the PPP packets. The PPTP ALG handles all NAT functions and pinholing for functions of PPTP, such as Call IDs of PAC and PNS.

SQL

The Structured Query Language ALG handles SQL TNS response frames and then evaluates the packet for IP address and port information. The SQL ALG handles all NAT functions and pinholing for the TCP data channel.

H323

This is a suite of protocols that provides audio-visual communication sessions over an IP network. The H.323 standard includes call signaling, call control, multimedia transport, multimedia control, and bandwidth control. The H323 ALG handles all NAT functions in addition to gatekeeper discovery, endpoint registration/admission/status, and call control/call setup. The H323 ALG also has many application screens that provide additional protections at an application level.

SIP

Session Initiation Protocol is a signaling protocol used for initiating, modifying, and terminating multimedia sessions such as voice and video calls over IP. The SIP ALG on the SRX only supports Session Description Protocol (SDP), even though SIP can use a variety of different description protocols to describe the session. The SIP ALG monitors SIP connections and dynamically pinholes for the SIP traffic.

SCCP

Skinny Client Control Protocol is a Cisco protocol for VoIP call signaling to the Cisco CallManager. The SCCP ALG will look within the control packets and allow the RTP port number and IP address of the media termination, dynamically pinholing for the RTP flows. In addition to pinholing, the SCCP ALG also handles all NAT functions and application layer protections.

MGCP

Media Gateway Control Protocol is a signaling and call control protocol used in VoIP between the media gateway and media controller. The MGCP ALG handles the dynamic pinholing for any additional connections needed, as well as handling all NAT functions. The MGCP ALG also inspects the VoIP signaling data and ensures that it complains to RFC standards blocking any malformed packets or attacks. Additional application layer protections are also configurable within the ALG.

RPC
: Remote Procedure Call is a secure interprocess communication that handles data exchange and invocation to a different process, typically to a machine on the local network or across the Internet. The RPC ALG handles dynamic port negotiation and pinholing as well as all NAT functions.

IKE/ESP
: IKE (Internet Key Exchange) and ESP (Encapsulating Security Payload) are a part of the IP Security (IPsec) protocol. In situations where the SRX is inline and an IPsec VPN passes through the SRX and NAT is enabled, IPsec VPNs can have issues. This is a common problem with IPsec and address translation. The IKE/ESP ALG should help with that problem, enabling the SRX to go inline and not interfere with VPN flows.

ALGs all perform the same type of function: they inspect the applications control channel and handle either NAT, dynamic pinholing of ports, or both. The ALG process does not inspect or monitor the actual data channel, something to keep in mind when working with ALGs.

To view which ALGs are currently enabled on the SRX, use the `show security alg status` command to display the ALGs:

```
juniper@SRX5800> show security alg status
ALG Status :
  DNS       : Enabled
  FTP       : Enabled
  H323      : Enabled
  MGCP      : Enabled
  MSRPC     : Enabled
  PPTP      : Enabled
  RSH       : Enabled
  RTSP      : Enabled
  SCCP      : Enabled
  SIP       : Enabled
  SQL       : Enabled
  SUNRPC    : Enabled
  TALK      : Enabled
  TFTP      : Enabled
```

How to Configure an ALG

Let's use the FTP ALG as our first configuration example, because if you remember from earlier in this chapter, it was configured for web-dmz administration.

From the trust network the web administrators are now requesting FTP access to the web1 server so that files can be uploaded to the server. In a secured network, their request should be denied because FTP transmits everything in clear text as it is an insecure protocol. The web administrators should be told to use SFTP. However, for this example, let's assume that SFTP is not available and FTP must be used. Sadly, cases such as this widely exist due to many legacy platforms and applications.

Enabling the FTP ALG is simple, since there is already a policy that allows the web administrators to connect to the web-dmz:

```
juniper@SRX5800> show security policies from-zone trust to-zone web-dmz
From zone: trust, To zone: web-dmz
  Policy: webdmz_mgt, State: enabled, Index: 8, Sequence number: 1
    Source addresses: any
    Destination addresses: web-servers
    Applications: web_mgt
    Action: permit, log
  Policy: web_deny, State: enabled, Index: 9, Sequence number: 2
    Source addresses: any
    Destination addresses: any
    Applications: any
    Action: deny, log
```

All we need to do is add the Junos-FTP service to the `web_mgt application-set`:

```
[edit]
juniper@SRX5800# set applications application-set web_mgt application junos-ftp
[edit]
juniper@SRX5800# commit and-quit
commit complete
Exiting configuration mode
```

Look at the applications the Junos-FTP service shows under `web_mgt`:

```
juniper@SRX5800> show configuration applications application-set web_mgt
application junos-ssh;
application junos-ping;
application junos-pc-anywhere;
application windows_rdp;
application junos-http;
application junos-ftp;
```

A more detailed look at the `webdmz_mgt` policy shows the new ALG information:

```
juniper@SRX5800> show security policies from-zone trust to-zone web-dmz
policy-name webdmz_mgt detail
Policy: webdmz_mgt, action-type: permit, State: enabled, Index: 8
  Sequence number: 1
  From zone: trust, To zone: web-dmz
  Source addresses:
    any: 0.0.0.0/0
  Destination addresses:
    web2: 10.2.0.2/32
    web1: 172.31.100.60/32
  Application: web_mgt
    IP protocol: tcp, ALG: 0, Inactivity timeout: 1800
      Source port range: [0-0]
      Destination port range: [22-22]
    IP protocol: 1, ALG: 0, Inactivity timeout: 60
      ICMP Information: type=255, code=0
    IP protocol: udp, ALG: 0, Inactivity timeout: 60
      Source port range: [0-0]
      Destination port range: [5632-5632]
    IP protocol: tcp, ALG: 0, Inactivity timeout: 1800
```

```
      Source port range: [1024-65535]
      Destination port range: [3389-3389]
    IP protocol: tcp, ALG: 0, Inactivity timeout: 1800
      Source port range: [0-0]
      Destination port range: [80-80]
    IP protocol: tcp, ALG: ftp, Inactivity timeout: 1800
      Source port range: [0-0]
      Destination port range: [21-21]
  Session log: at-create, at-close
```

Let's confirm that FTP does work to the server and that the web administrators can now upload their files as needed:

```
ftp> open 172.31.100.60
Connected to 172.31.100.60.
220-FileZilla Server version 0.9.34 beta
220-written by Tim Kosse (Tim.Kosse@gmx.de)
220 Please visit http://sourceforge.net/projects/filezilla/
Name (172.31.100.60:tle4729):
331 Password required for tle4729
Password:
```

Now view this connection on the SRX:

```
juniper@SRX5800> show security flow session application ftp
Session ID: 11663, Policy name: webdmz_mgt/8, Timeout: 788
  In: 10.1.1.100/59832 --> 172.31.100.60/21;tcp, If: ge-0/0/0.0
  Out: 172.31.100.60/21 --> 10.1.1.100/59832;tcp, If: fe-0/0/2.0
Session ID: 11664, Policy name: webdmz_mgt/8, Timeout: 790
  In: 10.1.1.100/59834 --> 172.31.100.60/21;tcp, If: ge-0/0/0.0
  Out: 172.31.100.60/21 --> 10.1.1.100/59834;tcp, If: fe-0/0/2.0
2 sessions displayed
```

Voilà! Some ALGs are simple to set up, as easy as using the prebuilt Junos application. ALGs such as FTP, TFTP, and DNS are perfect examples of this type of ALG. Other, more complex ALGs have more optional configuration knobs.

Our second ALG configuration example concerns the SIP ALG. The SIP ALG has a lot more configuration options than the FTP ALG, but the SIP ALG is applied in the same way the FTP ALG is applied: via security policy and Junos-SIP as the application.

Although SIP has various configuration knobs under the `security alg sip` stanza, I'll cover just a few here. First, set the SIP ALG `maximum-call-duration` setting to 1,000 minutes (that's more than 15 hours!):

```
[edit]
juniper@SRX5800# set security alg sip maximum-call-duration 1000
```

The next optional configuration is the timeout value (this value is in seconds):

```
[edit]
juniper@SRX5800# set security alg sip inactive-media-timeout 60
```

Overall, the SIP ALG is pretty easy to set up and configure. Problems arise when vendors do not follow RFC guidelines or they write their own one-off SIP implementations. If issues start after the SIP ALG is configured, the primary things to check are the SIP counters for errors. For inoperability issues, one possible workaround is to enable the `unknown-message` option; by default, the SRX's SIP ALG drops all unsupported messages for security purposes. Note that this disables that security feature:

```
[edit]
juniper@SRX5800# set security alg sip application-screen unknown-message
permit-routed
```

Another common issue is when vendors implement proprietary headers into their SIP packets. Per standards, the call-id header should contain a hostname or source IP address, and in some cases, vendors adjust or change this. To disable the call-id enforcement use the following:

```
[edit]
juniper@SRX5800# set security alg sip disable-call-id-hiding
juniper@SRX5800# edit security policies from-zone trust to-zone voip-dmz
```

Once that has been applied, the base SIP configuration is finished. SIP calls can be made and should have no problems going through. Let's verify the SIP stats by using the `show security alg sip counters` command to view the counters, including errors on decoding packets:

```
juniper@SRX5800> show security alg sip counters
   Method          T       1xx       2xx       3xx      4xx       5xx     6xx
                  RT        RT        RT        RT       RT        RT      RT
   INVITE          2         1         0         0        2         0       0
                   0         0         0         0        0         0       0
   CANCEL          0         0         0         0        0         0       0
                   0         0         0         0        0         0       0
      ACK          2         0         0         0        0         0       0
                   0         0         0         0        0         0       0
      BYE          0         0         0         0        0         0       0
                   0         0         0         0        0         0       0
 REGISTER         28         0         8         0       20         0       0
                   0         0         0         0        0         0       0
  OPTIONS          0         0         0         0        0         0       0
                   0         0         0         0        0         0       0
     INFO          0         0         0         0        0         0       0
                   0         0         0         0        0         0       0
  MESSAGE          0         0         0         0        0         0       0
                   0         0         0         0        0         0       0
   NOTIFY          0         0         0         0        0         0       0
                   0         0         0         0        0         0       0
    PRACK          0         0         0         0        0         0       0
                   0         0         0         0        0         0       0
  PUBLISH          0         0         0         0        0         0       0
                   0         0         0         0        0         0       0
    REFER          0         0         0         0        0         0       0
                   0         0         0         0        0         0       0
SUBSCRIBE          0         0         0         0        0         0       0
                   0         0         0         0        0         0       0
   UPDATE          0         0         0         0        0         0       0
                   0         0         0         0        0         0       0
 BENOTIFY          0         0         0         0        0         0       0
                   0         0         0         0        0         0       0
```

```
    SERVICE       0       0       0       0       0       0       0
                  0       0       0       0       0       0       0
      OTHER       0       0       0       0       0       0       0
                  0       0       0       0       0       0       0
  SIP Error Counters:
    Total Pkt-in                   : 76
    Total Pkt dropped on error     : 13
    Transaction error              : 0
    Call error                     : 0
    IP resolve error               : 0
    NAT error                      : 0
    Resource manager error         : 0
    RR header exceeded max         : 0
    Contact header exceeded max    : 0
    Call Dropped due to limit      : 0
    SIP stack error                : 0
    SIP decode error               : 13
    SIP unknown method error       : 0
    RTO message sent               : 0
    RTO message received           : 0
    RTO buffer allocation failure  : 0
    RTO buffer transmit failure    : 0
    RTO send processing error      : 0
    RTO receive processing error   : 0
    RTO receive invalid length     : 0
```

To view a higher-level overview of calls, use the `show security alg sip calls` command as the optional detail flag at the end to display even more information about the call:

```
juniper@SRX5800> show security alg sip calls
Total number of calls: 2 (# of call legs 4)
   Call leg1: zone 3
      UAS callid:120ed748-11121207-04c1279d-0bbb7e18@172.31.100.50 (pending tsx 1)
      Local tag
      Remote tag: 120ed748111212e264b0a951-5cbb0a95
      State: STATE_DISCONNECTED
   Call leg2: zone 2
      UAC callid:120ed748-11121207-04c1279d-0bbb7e18@172.31.100.50 (pending tsx 1)
      Local tag: 120ed748111212e264b0a951-5cbb0a95
      Remote tag
      State: STATE_DISCONNECTED
   Call leg1: zone 3
      UAS callid:120ed748-11121207-04c1279d-0bbb7e18@172.31.100.50 (pending tsx 1)
      Local tag:  120f90542e7e64cd724880f5-65db2f99
      Remote tag: 120ed748111212e264b0a951-5cbb0a95
      State: STATE_ESTABLISHED
   Call leg2: zone 2
      UAC callid:120ed748-11121207-04c1279d-0bbb7e18@172.31.100.50 (pending tsx 1)
      Local tag:  120ed748111212e264b0a951-5cbb0a95
      Remote tag: 120f90542e7e64cd724880f5-65db2f99
```

To view transactions, use the `show security alg sip transaction` command:

```
 juniper@SRX5800> show security alg sip transaction
Total number of transactions: 1
       Transaction Name   Method  CSeq  State        Timeout  VIA RSC ID
```

```
UAS:gsn0x5a06ddf1    BYE     101    Proceeding        -1          -
UAC:gsn0x5a06f615    BYE     101    Calling           25          8184
```

And to view the overall health of the SIP ALG, use `show security alg sip rate`:

```
juniper@SRX5800> show security alg sip rate
CPU ticks per microseconds is 3735928559
Time taken for the last message is 0 microseconds
Total time taken for 0 messages is 0 microseconds(in less than 10 minutes)
Rate: 3735928559 messages/second
```

ALGs provide an additional layer of security and handle NAT as well as dynamic pinholing when needed. With that deeper layer of inspection come more processing and additional potential problems. Oftentimes when Juniper writes ALGs, they are written to follow and enforce RFC specifications. The problem most commonly comes when vendors write one-off applications or their own additions to the protocol, or to the service, and the ALG doesn't know how to properly handle it.

Juniper has incorporated as many workarounds as possible, such as `called-hiding` and `unknown-message`, in the SIP ALG. However, sometimes issues still occur. In these events, the only option may be to open more port ranges than the vendor has provided.

Policy Schedulers

Policy schedulers are rules that you can enable or disable based on time and date. Schedulers are configured on a per-policy basis and only one scheduler can be configured per policy. However, multiple policies can reference a single scheduler.

You can use schedulers in a number of different situations and for several different purposes:

Internet browsing access
: You can write a scheduler to allow Internet access from the employees' network only during nonbusiness hours. For example, from 5:00 p.m. to 8:00 a.m. and from noon to 1:00 p.m. (lunch hour) employees are allowed to access the Internet via HTTP as this is during nonbusiness hours.

Access to payroll systems
: You can write a scheduler to allow the HR department to access the payroll system only during business hours—for example, from 8:00 a.m. to 6:00 p.m. This can prevent rogue access when nobody is on-site or in the office.

In both of the preceding examples, you can use schedules to restrict or permit access based on the time or date. Schedulers can assist in enforcing company policies and in increasing security, and you can be quite creative based on the habits of typical network users.

You can enable schedules by first creating the scheduler and then applying it to the policy.

Let's create a few sample schedulers and then discuss what was done.

```
juniper@SRX5800# set schedulers scheduler deny-web daily start-time 08:00
stop-time 17:00
[edit]
```

In the preceding output, a scheduler was created called deny-web that is enforced daily from 8:00 a.m. to 5:00 p.m., thus applying this scheduler to anything that you do not want done during office hours.

Now, let's apply that scheduler to a policy that denies access to HTTP:

```
juniper@SRX5800# edit security policies from-zone trust to-zone Internet
[edit security policies from-zone trust to-zone Internet]
juniper@SRX5800# set policy deny_daytime_websurfing match source-address any
destination-address any application junos-http
[edit security policies from-zone trust to-zone Internet]
juniper@SRX5800# set Internet policy deny_daytime_websurfing then deny
[edit security policies from-zone trust to-zone Internet]
juniper@SRX5800# set policy deny_daytime_websurfing scheduler-name deny-web
```

In the preceding output, a security policy was written from the Trust zone going to the Internet zone for any HTTP traffic. Then an action of deny was applied, and finally the scheduler deny-web was configured to be active during those time frames in deny-web.

It is also possible to add days to exclude, as in the following:

```
juniper@SRX5800# edit schedulers scheduler
[edit schedulers scheduler]
juniper@SRX5800# set network-access daily start-time 09:00 stop-time 20:00
[edit schedulers scheduler]
juniper@SRX5800# set network-access saturday exclude
[edit schedulers scheduler]
juniper@SRX5800# set network-access sunday exclude
```

The scheduler called network-access runs daily from 9:00 a.m. to 8:00 p.m. (This scheduler might be used to control remote access into the network.) Notice that two additional lines were configured for both Saturday and Sunday to be excluded. In other words, remote users will not be able to access the network on weekends once this scheduler is applied to the proper policy.

Just like the first policy, let's configure this setup to allow the contractor subnet access to everything on the web-dmz zone during the defined times in network-access:

```
juniper@SRX5800#set security zones security-zone trust address-book address
contractor_subnet 10.3.0.0/24
[edit]
juniper@SRX5800# edit security policies from-zone trust to-zone web-dmz
[edit security policies from-zone trust to-zone web-dmz]
juniper@SRX5800# set policy contractor_access match source-address
contractor_subnet destination-address any application any

[edit security policies from-zone trust to-zone web-dmz]
juniper@SRX5800# set policy contractor_access then permit
```

```
[edit security policies from-zone trust to-zone web-dmz]
juniper@SRX5800# set policy contractor_access scheduler-name network-access
```

Now look at the configuration to check that everything is in order:

```
juniper@SRX5800# show security policies from-zone trust to-zone web-dmz policy
contractor_access
match {
    source-address contractor_subnet;
    destination-address any;
    application any;
}
then {
    permit;
}
scheduler-name network-access;
[edit]
```

One-Time Schedulers

One-time schedulers can also be configured to run for a predefined period of time. After that period of time, the scheduler becomes inactive and does not activate the policy. You can use this in situations where access should be granted on a temporary basis or something needs to be blocked for a period of time.

An example of a one-time scheduler is a scheduler that grants access to a vendor for a window of time to troubleshoot or fix a problem. If the web servers we configured earlier were having problems, we could configure a policy that allowed Microsoft to access them remotely. The security department should have a problem with granting this type of access permanently, so we would use a scheduler to ensure that access is removed after a previously agreed upon time frame. Here's a one-time scheduler granting temporary access into the network:

```
[edit]
juniper@SRX5800# set schedulers scheduler microsoft_remote_access
start-date 2010-02-14.09:00 stop-date 2010-02-15.09:00
[edit]
juniper@SRX5800#
```

This one-time scheduler is called `microsoft_remote_access` and is set to enable on February 14, 2010 at 9:00 a.m. It will end 24 hours later. Here is the permit that will no longer apply after 24 hours:

```
juniper@SRX5800# edit
[edit]
juniper@SRX5800# set security zones security-zone Internet address-book address
ms_support 207.46.197.32

[edit]
juniper@SRX5800# set security policies from-zone Internet to-zone web-dmz

[edit security policies from-zone Internet to-zone web-dmz]
juniper@SRX5800# set policy temp_ms_access match source-address ms_support
```

```
destination-address web1 application any
[edit security policies from-zone Internet to-zone web-dmz]
juniper@SRX5800# set policy temp_ms_access scheduler-name microsoft_remote_access

[edit security policies from-zone Internet to-zone web-dmz]
juniper@SRX5800# set policy temp_ms_access then permit
[edit security policies from-zone Internet to-zone web-dmz]
juniper@SRX5800#
```

In the preceding output, a new address book was created for Microsoft's source IP address. Then a policy was written to allow that IP access to the web1 server via any application. The third item configured was the scheduler `microsoft_remote_access` that was applied. Now, this scheduler will be active from February 14 until February 15 to allow Microsoft to remotely access the server.

Let's look at the configuration as a whole:

```
juniper@SRX5800# show security policies from-zone Internet to-zone web-dmz
policy temp_ms_access
match {
    source-address ms_support;
    destination-address web1;
    application any;
}
then {
    permit;
}
scheduler-name microsoft_remote_access;
[edit]
```

You can view configured schedulers with the `show schedulers` command. Here is the output from the three already configured schedulers. Right now it appears that there are two active schedulers and one inactive scheduler. The output will also list the next time a scheduler is set to turn on or off.

```
juniper@SRX5800> show schedulers
Scheduler name: deny-web, State: active
  Next deactivation: Fri Jan 22 17:00:00 2010
Scheduler name: microsoft_remote_access, State: inactive
  Next activation: Sun Feb 14 09:00:00 2010
Scheduler name: network-access, State: active
  Next deactivation: Fri Jan 22 20:00:00 2010
```

Let's look at a detailed policy output to confirm that the schedule is applied and it is active (the state should show `enabled`):

```
juniper@SRX5800> show security policies from-zone trust to-zone web-dmz
policy-name contractor_access detail
Policy: contractor_access, action-type: permit, State: enabled, Index: 14
  Sequence number: 3
  From zone: trust, To zone: web-dmz
  Source addresses:
    contractor_subnet: 10.3.0.0/24
  Destination addresses:
    any: 0.0.0.0/0
```

```
Application: any
  IP protocol: 0, ALG: 0, Inactivity timeout: 0
    Source port range: [0-0]
    Destination port range: [0-0]
Scheduler name: network-access
```

Web and Proxy Authentication

The SRX can also be used as an inline web proxy, forcing users to authenticate for access, or as a pass-through authentication forcing Telnet, FTP, and HTTP to authenticate, adding an additional layer of security while keeping a historical log for later review and auditing.

Web Authentication

Figure 4-6 illustrates the stages of the web authentication process.

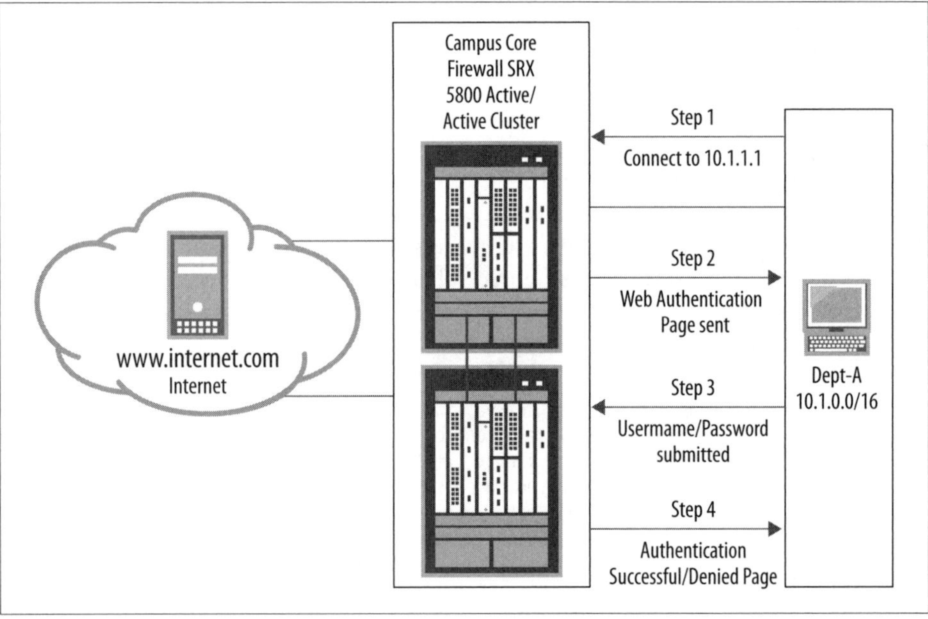

Figure 4-6. How web authentication works

Configuring web authentication is relatively painless. The largest task is creating the user profiles that would be needed for authentication.

The first step is to enable authentication on the interface itself. Here we apply web authentication to an already existing interface, ge-0/0/0, of which the Trust zone is a part:

```
[edit]
juniper@SRX5800# set interfaces ge-0/0/0 unit 0 family inet
address 10.1.0.254/24 web-authentication http
[edit]
juniper@SRX5800#
```

Next, we need to create a user or list of users that have permission to access the Web. Here we use the volunteer sample user `Tim_Eberhard` which has been set up under `access profile web-allow-group`. The access profile will be referenced later in the configuration.

```
[edit]
juniper@SRX5800# set access profile web-allow-group client Tim_Eberhard
firewall-user password letmeinpls
```

An alternative to using local user lists on the SRX is to authenticate users to an external database on a RADIUS, RSA, or LDAP server.

Let's begin a web authentication configuration example to an external RADIUS server. A RADIUS server could be configured with thousands of individual accounts:

```
[edit]
juniper@SRX5800# set access profile web-allow-group_radius
radius-server 10.3.4.100 secret radius_secret_key retry 2
```

Next we will configure the SRX to try the RADIUS server first; if that server fails, the SRX will resort back to the local database (this way, if the RADIUS server ever fails, it's possible to have a default account that allows access during emergencies):

```
[edit]
juniper@SRX5800# set access profile web-allow-group authentication-order radius
authentication-order password
```

Now we'll apply the web authentication to the policy, adding the `permit-http` policy from the Trust zone to the Internet zone:

```
[edit]
juniper@SRX5800# set security policies from-zone trust to-zone Internet
policy permit-http then permit firewall-authentication web-authentication
```

Let's look at the configuration as a whole:

```
[edit]
juniper@SRX5800# show access profile web-allow-group
authentication-order [ radius password ];
client Tim_Eberhard {
    firewall-user {
        password "$9$hISclM7NbgaUX7wgoZkqCtuORS7Nb2oG"; ## SECRET-DATA
    }
}
radius-server {
    10.3.4.100 {
        secret "$9$iq5Fn6AOBEP5hrvM-d6/CuIcKvLN-wKM7VbsZGREclvLdVYgJD";
## SECRET-DATA
        retry 2;
    }
```

```
}
[edit]
juniper@SRX5800# show interfaces ge-0/0/0
description "Inside network";
speed 100m;
link-mode full-duplex;
unit 0 {
    family inet {
        address 10.1.0.254/24 {
            web-authentication http;
        }
    }
}
juniper@SRX5800# show security policies from-zone trust to-zone Internet
policy permit-http {
    match {
        source-address any;
        destination-address any;
        application junos-http;
    }
    then {
        permit {
            firewall-authentication {
                web-authentication;
            }
        }
    }
}
```

This basic web authentication will prompt users when they try to use HTTP. Web authentication is basically a portal that will authenticate a user's traffic through.

Pass-Through Authentication

Another method of authentication that you can use on the SRX is called *pass-through authentication*. Pass-through authentication is different from web authentication as it just prompts the user to enter his account information for authentication somewhat transparently. Pass-through can be triggered by HTTP, Telnet, and FTP traffic.

From a user standpoint, the authentication process looks as though the website or Telnet, or the FTP session, is prompting the user for his account information, whereas with web authentication users need to go to a certain IP address and authenticate before attempting to send any other traffic.

Figure 4-7 illustrates the pass-through authentication process.

Configuring pass-through authentication is much like configuring web authentication. The first thing you need to do is to turn on pass-through authentication and assign it to a profile. For the following example, we'll reuse `web-allow-group` since it already had a user account and RADIUS server configured. The second thing you need to do is to set a banner to inform the user what to submit for authentication.

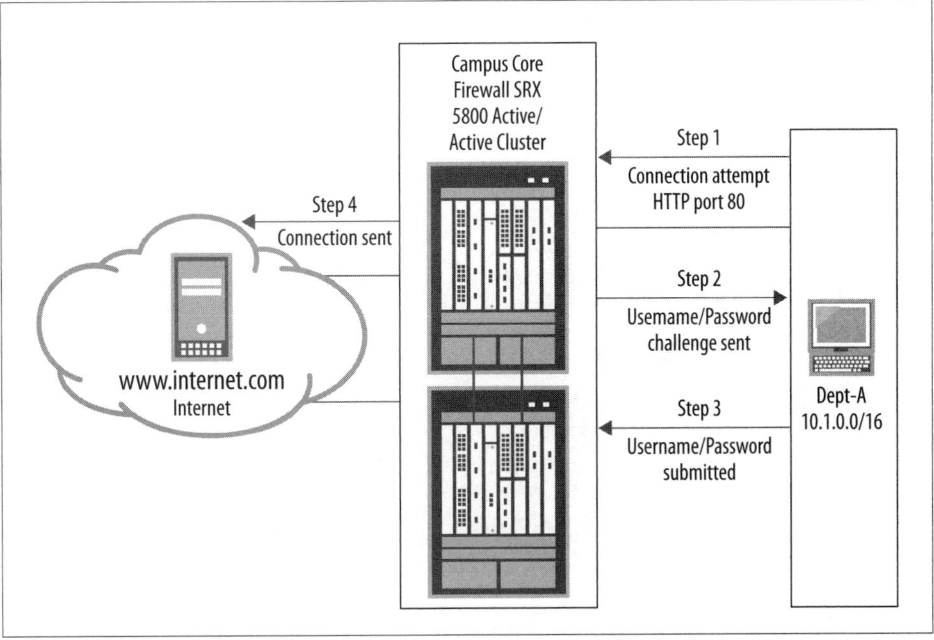

Figure 4-7. How pass-through authentication works

A banner should provide a phone number or an email address that users can use for support if they cannot get past the inline challenge.

We'll use the Telnet service for our example. Since Telnet is an insecure protocol that must sometimes be supported due to legacy applications and systems, using inline authentication here is an additional layer of security that we can apply to our connection.

```
juniper@SRX5800# edit access firewall-authentication pass-through
[edit access firewall-authentication pass-through]
juniper@SRX5800# set default-profile web-allow-group
[edit access firewall-authentication pass-through]
juniper@SRX5800# set telnet banner success "PLEASE ENTER IN YOUR ACCOUNT INFO.
FOR SUPPORT PLEASE CALL THE NOC AT 1-800-555-1212"
[edit access firewall-authentication pass-through]
juniper@SRX5800# top
[edit]
juniper@SRX5800# edit security policies from-zone trust to-zone web-dmz
[edit security policies from-zone trust to-zone web-dmz]
juniper@SRX5800# set policy permit-telnet match source-address any
destination-address any
[edit security policies from-zone trust to-zone web-dmz]
juniper@SRX5800# set policy permit-telnet match application junos-telnet
[edit security policies from-zone trust to-zone web-dmz]
```

```
juniper@SRX5800# set policy permit-telnet then permit firewall-authentication
pass-through access-profile web-allow-group
```

And here is what that configuration looks like all together:

```
juniper@SRX5800# show | compare
[edit security policies from-zone trust to-zone web-dmz]
      policy web_deny { ... }
+     policy permit-telnet {
+         match {
+             source-address any;
+             destination-address any;
+             application junos-telnet;
+         }
+         then {
+             permit {
+                 firewall-authentication {
+                     pass-through {
+                         access-profile web-allow-group;
+                     }
+                 }
+             }
+         }
+     }
```

We can view active authenticated information about the SRX's authentications using the following output:

```
juniper@SRX5800# show security firewall-authentication users
Firewall authentication data:
  Total users in table: 1
          Id Source Ip       Src zone Dst zone Profile    Age Status   User
           4 10.3.0.12     Trust    Internet      webauth-     4 Success  Tim
```

The `show security firewall-authentication history` command shows all active and authenticated users currently passing through the SRX:

```
juniper@SRX5800> show security firewall-authentication history
History of firewall authentication data: Authentications: 2 Id Source Ip
Date Time Duration Status User
1 10.1.0.120 2010-01-12 18:20:02 0: 00:22 Failed bob
2 10.1.0.125 2010-01-13 12:22:48 0: 00:21 Success bill
```

Firewall authentication provides an additional layer of security as well as logs. It can be used to enforce company access policies or better protect network boundaries and access. It is a very simple way to improve the overall security strategy of anything from the smallest home office to a large corporate network.

Case Study 4-1

Objective: Set up basic firewall policy for the company's network, including web and email access for the users, and inbound as well as outbound access for the servers.

Our strategies to achieve that objective are as follows:

- Create a security policy that allows access to the web server DMZ from anywhere on the Internet.
- Allow access to the mail servers on the mail server DMZ from the internal user networks 10.1.0.0/24 and 10.1.2.0/24, and inbound/outbound mail access to the mail server from the Internet.
- Create a custom application with a 60-minute timeout for TCP port 6667 and apply that custom application on the web server DMZ to the Internet.
- Create a policy that requires users on the trust network 10.1.0.0/24 to authenticate for web browsing during business hours to comply with the company's Internet access policy.

Figure 4-8 shows our topology for Case Study 4-1.

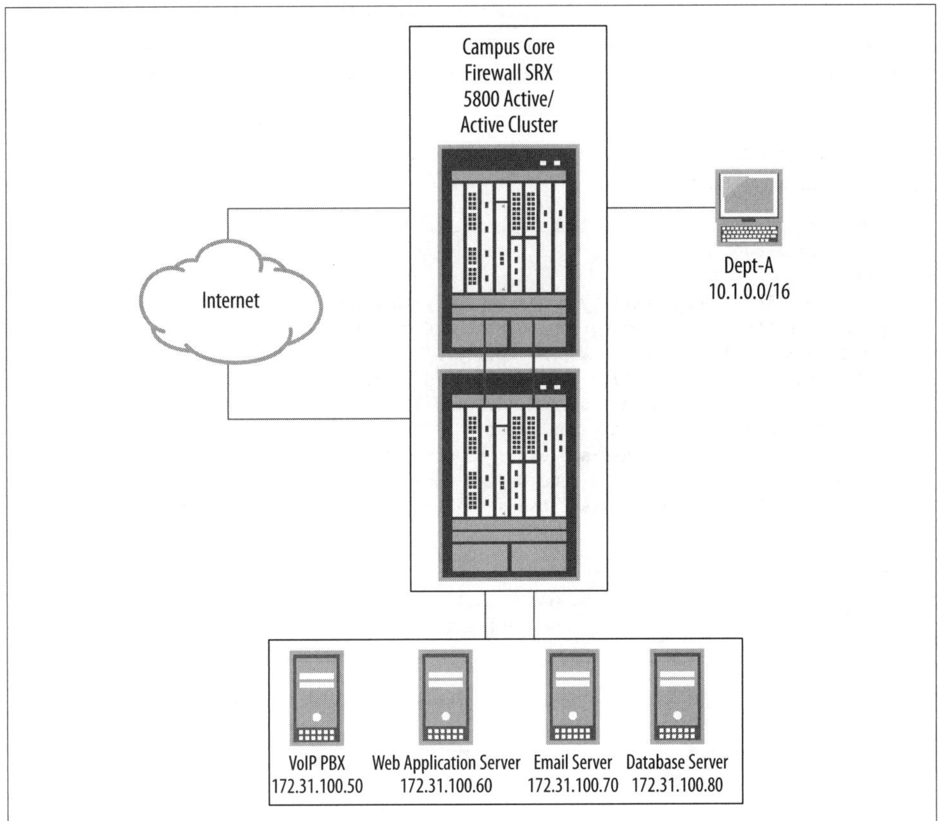

Figure 4-8. Case Study 4-1's objective

First, we need to write a policy for access to the web server DMZ from the Internet. This is a basic permit policy with any source. Since it's a web server facing the public Internet logging will be enabled. Let's start with the following:

```
[edit]
juniper@SRX5800# set security zones security-zone web-dmz address-book address
web_server 172.31.100.60/32
[edit]
juniper@SRX5800# edit security policies from-zone internet to-zone web-dmz
[edit security policies from-zone internet to-zone web-dmz]
juniper@SRX5800# set policy "allow_http_from_web" match source-address any
destination-address web1 application junos-http
[edit security policies from-zone internet to-zone web-dmz]
juniper@SRX5800# set policy "allow_http_from_web" then permit
[edit security policies from-zone internet to-zone web-dmz]
juniper@SRX5800# set policy "allow_http_from_web" then log session-close
session-init
```

Next, we need to write a couple of policies that make the mail server work. To do this, we'll create one policy that allows the user segments to access the mail server and another policy to allow both inbound and outbound mail access from the mail server itself.

First we need to create the `address-books`. An `address-set` will combine both user segments into a single `address-set`:

```
[edit security policies from-zone internet to-zone web-dmz]
juniper@SRX5800# top
[edit]
juniper@SRX5800# edit security zones security-zone dept-a address-book
[edit security zones security-zone dept-a address-book]
juniper@SRX5800# set address users1 10.1.0.0/24
[edit security zones security-zone dept-a address-book]
juniper@SRX5800# set address users2 10.1.2.0/24
[edit security zones security-zone dept-a address-book]
juniper@SRX5800# set address-set users_segments address users1
[edit security zones security-zone dept-a address-book]
juniper@SRX5800# set address-set users_segments address users2
```

Now, we need to create the mail server DMZ and configure an `address-book` for that server:

```
[edit security zones security-zone dept-a address-book]
juniper@SRX5800# top
[edit]
juniper@SRX5800# set security zones security-zone mail-dmz
[edit]
juniper@SRX5800# set security zones security-zone mail-dmz address-book
address mail_server 172.31.100.70/32
```

We need to configure an `application-set` to allow the various mail services:

```
juniper@SRX5800# edit applications application-set
[edit applications application-set]
juniper@SRX5800# set mail_services application junos-imap
[edit applications application-set]
juniper@SRX5800# set mail_services application junos-smtp
[edit applications application-set]
juniper@SRX5800# set mail_services application junos-pop3
```

Once that is complete, we can configure the first policy that allows users to access the mail server:

```
[edit applications application-set]
juniper@SRX5800# top
[edit]
juniper@SRX5800# edit security policies from-zone dept-a to-zone mail-dmz
[edit security policies from-zone dept-a to-zone mail-dmz]
juniper@SRX5800# set policy "allow_users_to_mail" match source-address
users_segments destination-address mail_server application mail_services
[edit security policies from-zone dept-a to-zone mail-dmz]
juniper@SRX5800# set policy "allow_users_to_mail" then permit
```

Now that users are allowed to access the mail servers, the mail servers need to send email out as well as receive mail from the Internet.

Here is the code to send email from mail-dmz to the Internet:

```
[edit security policies from-zone dept-a to-zone mail-dmz]
juniper@SRX5800# top
[edit]
juniper@SRX5800# edit security policies from-zone mail-dmz to-zone internet
[edit security policies from-zone mail-dmz to-zone internet]
juniper@SRX5800# set policy "permit_outbound_mail"
match source-address mail_server destination-address any
application mail_services
[edit]
juniper@SRX5800# set policy "permit_outbound_mail" then permit
```

Now, here's the code to reverse connectivity:

```
juniper@SRX5800# top
[edit]
juniper@SRX5800# edit security policies from-zone internet to-zone mail-dmz
[edit security policies from-zone internet to-zone mail-dmz]
juniper@SRX5800# set policy "permit_inbound_mail" match source-address any
destination-address mail_server application mail_services
[edit security policies from-zone internet to-zone mail-dmz]
juniper@SRX5800# set policy "permit_inbound_mail" then permit
[edit security policies from-zone internet to-zone mail-dmz]
juniper@SRX5800# set policy "permit_inbound_mail" then log session-init
session-close
```

You might have noticed that logging was enabled. It is a best practice to log anything coming in from the Internet, at the very least. Here, both the web server and the mail server inbound connections from the Internet are logged.

Another service that needs to be permitted is TCP port 6667 with an inactivity timeout of 60 minutes; we also need to allow the web server to connect to any destination on the Internet with that port. Since timeouts are configured in seconds, our timeout will need to be 3,600 seconds:

```
juniper@SRX5800# top
[edit]
juniper@SRX5800# set applications application tcp_6667 protocol tcp
source-port 6667 destination-port 1-65000 inactivity-timeout 3600
[edit]
juniper@SRX5800# edit security policies from-zone web-dmz to-zone internet
[edit security policies from-zone web-dmz to-zone internet]
juniper@SRX5800# set policy "permit_irc" match source-address web1
destination-address any application tcp_6667
[edit]
juniper@SRX5800# set policy "permit_irc" then permit
```

The last few configurations we need to make are to create a policy that forces users on the `Dept-A` segment to authenticate for HTTP access during business hours. We can do this by creating a scheduler and then configuring pass-through authentication for HTTP.

But before we can configure anything, we must set a scheduler for the normal business hours of 8:00 a.m. to 5:00 p.m., excluding weekends, to enforce company policy:

```
juniper@SRX5800# top
[edit]
juniper@SRX5800# edit schedulers scheduler
[edit schedulers scheduler]
juniper@SRX5800# set "http-business-hours" daily start-time 08:00:00
stop-time 17:00:00
[edit schedulers scheduler]
juniper@SRX5800# set "http-business-hours" sunday exclude
[edit schedulers scheduler]
juniper@SRX5800# set  "http-business-hours" saturday exclude
```

Now we can set up a pass-through authentication profile:

```
juniper@SRX5800# top
[edit]
juniper@SRX5800# set access profile web-allow-group radius-server 10.3.4.100
secret radius_secret_key retry 2
[edit]
juniper@SRX5800# set access firewall-authentication pass-through
default-profile web-allow-group http banner login
"PLEASE ENTER IN YOUR ACCOUNT INFO. FOR SUPPORT PLEASE CALL THE NOC AT
1-800-555-1212"
```

OK, now we need to write our policy to reference both the scheduler and the pass-through access profile:

```
[edit]
juniper@SRX5800# edit security policies from-zone dept-a to-zone internet
[edit security policies from-zone dept-a to-zone internet]
juniper@SRX5800# set policy "http_auth" match source-address users_segments
```

```
destination-address any application junos-https
[edit security policies from-zone dept-a to-zone internet]
juniper@SRX5800# set policy "http_auth" scheduler-name http-business-hours
[edit security policies from-zone dept-a to-zone internet]
juniper@SRX5800# set policy "http_auth" then permit firewall-authentication
pass-through access-profile web-allow-group
```

Finally, let's take a look at the entire configuration and ensure that everything commits correctly:

```
juniper@SRX5800# show | compare
[edit security zones security-zone web-dmz address-book]
       address web2 { ... }
+      address web_server 172.31.100.60/32;
[edit security zones]
     security-zone CDN { ... }
+    security-zone internet;
+    security-zone dept-a {
+        address-book {
+            address users1 10.1.0.0/24;
+            address users2 10.1.2.0/24;
+            address-set users_segments {
+                address users1;
+                address users2;
+            }
+        }
+    }
+    security-zone mail-dmz {
+        address-book {
+            address mail_server 172.31.100.70/32;
+        }
+    }
[edit security]
+   policies {
+       from-zone internet to-zone web-dmz {
+           policy allow_http_from_web {
+               match {
+                   source-address any;
+                   destination-address web1;
+                   application junos-http;
+               }
+               then {
+                   permit;
+                   log {
+                       session-init;
+                       session-close;
+                   }
+               }
+           }
+       }
+       from-zone dept-a to-zone mail-dmz {
+           policy allow_users_to_mail {
+               match {
+                   source-address users_segments;
+                   destination-address mail_server;
+                   application mail_services;
```

```
+                }
+                then {
+                    permit;
+                }
+            }
+        }
+        from-zone mail-dmz to-zone internet {
+            policy permit_outbound_mail {
+                match {
+                    source-address mail_server;
+                    destination-address any;
+                    application mail_services;
+                }
+                then {
+                    permit;
+                }
+            }
+        }
+        from-zone internet to-zone mail-dmz {
+            policy permit_inbound_mail {
+                match {
+                    source-address any;
+                    destination-address mail_server;
+                    application mail_services;
+                }
+                then {
+                    permit;
+                    log {
+                        session-init;
+                        session-close;
+                    }
+                }
+            }
+        }
+        from-zone web-dmz to-zone internet {
+            policy permit_irc {
+                match {
+                    source-address web1;
+                    destination-address any;
+                    application tcp_6667;
+                }
+                then {
+                    permit;
+                }
+            }
+        }
+        from-zone dept-a to-zone internet {
+            policy http_auth {
+                match {
+                    source-address users_segments;
+                    destination-address any;
+                    application junos-https;
+                }
+                then {
+                    permit {
```

```
+                        firewall-authentication {
+                            pass-through {
+                                access-profile web-allow-group;
+                            }
+                        }
+                    }
+                }
+                scheduler-name http-business-hours;
+            }
+        }
+    }
[edit]
+  access {
+      profile web-allow-group {
+          radius-server {
+              10.3.4.100 {
+                  secret
"$9$VZsoGDjq5T3gonCuOcSjikPz6pu1hclpOEyrex7F36Au1SyKMX-";
## SECRET-DATA
+                  retry 2;
+              }
+          }
+      }
+      firewall-authentication {
+          pass-through {
+              default-profile web-allow-group;
+              http {
+                  banner {
+                      login "PLEASE ENTER IN YOUR ACCOUNT INFO.
FOR SUPPORT PLEASE CALL THE NOC AT 1-800-555-1212";
+                  }
+              }
+          }
+      }
+  }
[edit applications]
    application windows_rdp { ... }
+   application tcp_6667 {
+       protocol tcp;
+       source-port 6667;
+       destination-port 1-65000;
+       inactivity-timeout 3600;
+   }
[edit applications]
    application-set web_mgt { ... }
+   application-set mail_services {
+       application junos-imap;
+       application junos-smtp;
+       application junos-pop3;
+   }
[edit]
+  schedulers {
+      scheduler http-business-hours {
+          daily {
+              start-time 08:00:00 stop-time 17:00:00;
```

```
+             }
+             sunday exclude;
+             saturday exclude;
+         }
+ }
[edit]
juniper@SRX5800# commit check
configuration check succeeds
```

After reviewing the changes and performing a `commit` check, everything looks good. Our SRX is now set up for the company when users come into the office.

Case Study 4-2

Objective: A new department is being added and their network configured on the company's network, and while in a meeting to talk about their access requirements they stated they need the following networking requirements:

- Full unfiltered Internet access
- Full unfiltered access to the web and mail servers
- Access from the Internet into their network segment so that they can host customer-facing web servers

Our strategy to achieve that objective is to evaluate how best to give them the requested access while maintaining network security. Figure 4-9 illustrates their needs.

This case study is more real-world than you might think. All too often, users (including management) do not understand the needs of their business or how to incorporate security into the workflow. External servers should never be on the same segment as users, and unfiltered access may sound like a good idea from a "getting things done" point of view, but in reality, policies can be written to allow the user department to do everything that they need to do while maintaining an acceptable level of security.

Corporate security policies should apply to everyone. They exist for a reason, and if it's a corporation's security policy to block P2P apps on its network, this should be done globally.

First, let's set up their Internet access. We need to create a new zone for `Dept-B`, and we need to create `address-books` which should be put into an `address-set`.

```
[edit]
juniper@SRX5800# edit security zones security-zone
[edit security zones security-zone]
juniper@SRX5800# set dept-b
[edit security zones security-zone]
juniper@SRX5800# set dept-b address-book address users3 10.2.1.0/24
[edit security zones security-zone]
juniper@SRX5800# set dept-b address-book address users4 10.2.2.0/24
[edit security zones security-zone]
juniper@SRX5800# set dept-b address-book address users5 10.2.3.0/24
```

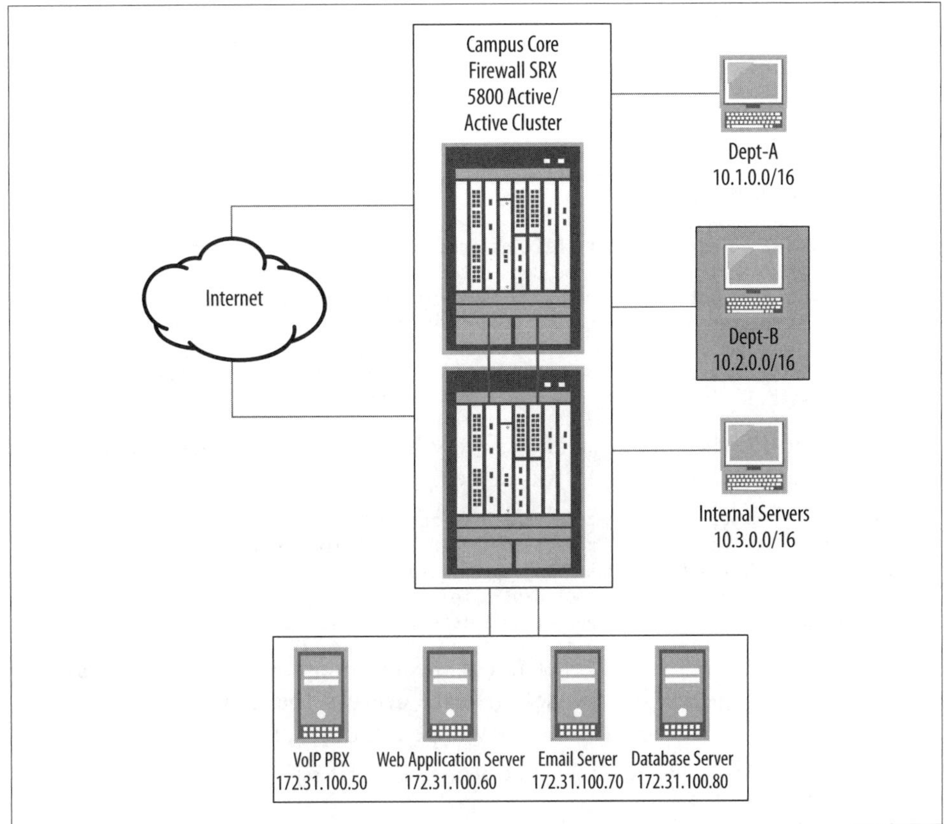

Figure 4-9. Case Study 4-2's objectives

```
[edit security zones security-zone]
juniper@SRX5800# set dept-b address-book address-set dept_b_users address users3
[edit security zones security-zone]
juniper@SRX5800# set dept-b address-book address-set dept_b_users address users4
[edit security zones security-zone]
juniper@SRX5800# set dept-b address-book address-set dept_b_users address users5
```

Next, we should block a group of predetermined applications from accessing the Internet. We should put these applications into an `address-set` for ease of policy engineering, and we need to deny those applications via policy.

```
[edit security zones security-zone]
juniper@SRX5800# top
[edit]
juniper@SRX5800# edit applications application-set
[edit applications application-set]
juniper@SRX5800# set deny_services application junos-ymsg
[edit applications application-set]
juniper@SRX5800# set deny_services application junos-smtp
[edit applications application-set]
juniper@SRX5800# set deny_services application junos-msn
```

```
[edit applications application-set]
juniper@SRX5800# set deny_services application junos-irc
[edit applications application-set]
juniper@SRX5800# set deny_services application junos-gnutella
[edit applications application-set]
juniper@SRX5800# set deny_services application junos-aol
[edit applications application-set]
juniper@SRX5800# top
[edit]
juniper@SRX5800# edit security policies from-zone dept-b to-zone internet
[edit security policies from-zone dept-b to-zone internet]
juniper@SRX5800# set policy "deny_bad_apps" match source-address dept_b_users
destination-address any application deny_services
[edit security policies from-zone dept-b to-zone internet]
juniper@SRX5800# set policy "deny_bad_apps" then deny log session-close
session-init
```

Don't forget to add the policy that allows everything else! The new department's users might be upset if all of their traffic was denied.

```
[edit security policies from-zone dept-b to-zone internet]
juniper@SRX5800# set policy "permit-to-internet-any" match source-address
dept_b_users destination-address any application any
[edit security policies from-zone dept-b to-zone internet]
juniper@SRX5800# set policy "permit-to-internet-any" then permit
```

Now that we've taken care of Internet access, the next order of business is access to the mail server. Using the `application-set` and `mail address-book` that we created earlier, all we really need to do is to create a policy to permit the traffic.

```
[edit security policies from-zone dept-b to-zone internet]
juniper@SRX5800# top
[edit]
juniper@SRX5800# edit security policies from-zone dept-b to-zone mail-dmz
[edit security policies from-zone dept-b to-zone mail-dmz]
juniper@SRX5800# set policy "permit_b_to_mail" match source-address dept_b_users
destination-address mail_server application mail_services
[edit security policies from-zone dept-b to-zone mail-dmz]
juniper@SRX5800# set policy "permit_b_to_mail" then permit
```

The last item is to address this new web server that `Dept-B` wants on the network. The web server should be moved to its own DMZ and policy specifically for that web server needs to be written:

```
[edit security policies from-zone dept-b to-zone mail-dmz]
juniper@SRX5800# top
[edit]
juniper@SRX5800# set security zones security-zone Bweb-dmz
[edit]
juniper@SRX5800# set security zones security-zone Bweb-dmz address-book
address web5 10.3.0.1/32
[edit]
juniper@SRX5800# edit security policies from-zone internet to-zone Bweb-dmz
[edit security policies from-zone internet to-zone Bweb-dmz]
juniper@SRX5800# set policy "permit_to_bweb" match source-address any
destination-address web5 application junos-http
```

```
[edit security policies from-zone internet to-zone Bweb-dmz]
juniper@SRX5800# set policy "permit_to_bweb" then permit
[edit security policies from-zone internet to-zone Bweb-dmz]
juniper@SRX5800# set policy "permit_to_bweb" then log session-close session-init
```

And if you noticed, as always, it's suggested that you log the traffic from the Internet.

Now, let's take a look at the entire configuration for `Dept-B`:

```
juniper@SRX5800# show | compare
[edit security zones]
     security-zone mail-dmz { ... }
+    security-zone dept-b {
+        address-book {
+            address users3 10.2.1.0/24;
+            address users4 10.2.2.0/24;
+            address users5 10.2.3.0/24;
+            address-set dept_b_users {
+                address users3;
+                address users4;
+                address users5;
+            }
+        }
+    }
+    security-zone Bweb-dmz {
+        address-book {
+            address web5 10.3.0.1/32;
+        }
+    }
[edit security policies]
     from-zone dept-a to-zone internet { ... }
+    from-zone dept-b to-zone internet {
+        policy deny_bad_apps {
+            match {
+                source-address dept_b_users;
+                destination-address any;
+                application deny_services;
+            }
+            then {
+                deny;
+                log {
+                    session-init;
+                    session-close;
+                }
+            }
+        }
+        policy permit-to-internet-any {
+            match {
+                source-address dept_b_users;
+                destination-address any;
+                application any;
+            }
+            then {
+                permit;
+            }
+        }
```

```
+     }
+     from-zone dept-b to-zone mail-dmz {
+         policy permit_b_to_mail {
+             match {
+                 source-address dept_b_users;
+                 destination-address mail_server;
+                 application mail_services;
+             }
+             then {
+                 permit;
+             }
+         }
+     }
+     from-zone internet to-zone Bweb-dmz {
+         policy permit_to_bweb {
+             match {
+                 source-address any;
+                 destination-address web5;
+                 application junos-http;
+             }
+             then {
+                 permit;
+                 log {
+                     session-init;
+                     session-close;
+                 }
+             }
+         }
+     }
[edit applications]
    application-set mail_services { ... }
+   application-set deny_services {
+       application junos-ymsg;
+       application junos-smtp;
+       application junos-msn;
+       application junos-irc;
+       application junos-gnutella;
+       application junos-aol;
+   }
[edit]
juniper@SRX5800# commit check
configuration check succeeds
```

The `commit` check appears to be successful and the configuration looks good. The new department can now come online without any issues and the security of the company has not been compromised.

Converters and Scripts

To help bridge the gap between the NetScreen system and the SRX system several tools have been developed. One such tool is the S2JES (ScreenOS to Junos-ES) converter. This is a free tool (it requires a valid login to *http://www.juniper.net*) that will convert a ScreenOS configuration file or syntax to Junos-ES. It can help with migration from a

ScreenOS policy base to Junos policy. You can find the tool at *https://i2j.juniper.net/s2jes/index.jsp*.

Op scripts will also assist in migration efforts. Op scripts are SLAX or XSLT-based scripts that run directly on the SRX. These scripts are often developed by Juniper and by external users. You can use op scripts to view information in a summarized format or, for example, to run a series of health checks.

One of my favorite op scripts for the SRX is the policy test script. The policy test script will take input such as a source IP, destination IP, source port, or destination port and find any matching policies. All of these fields are optional, so the match can be as broad or as narrow as you want it to be.

Here is example output of the policy test script:

```
user@cli# op policy-test source-address 10.1.1.1 destination-address 10.2.2.2
From-Zone     To-Zone      Name              Src-Addr         Dst-Addr
Application  Action trust        untrust      ftp-permit       any              any
junos-ftp    permit trust        untrust      http-https-rej  any              any
junos-https  reject                                              junos-http
```

The policy test script found two policies that match the source/destination address. From the preceding output it appears that only FTP is allowed and HTTP/HTTPS is explicitly denied.

Other scripts mimic the output of ScreenOS-type commands, such as "get interface," "get service," and "get policy." You can find these scripts in a number of places, but two of the major sites are:

http://www.juniper.net/us/en/community/junos/script-automation/library/
http://code.google.com/p/junoscriptorium/

You can find the policy test script shown earlier at the following URL:

http://www.juniper.net/us/en/community/junos/script-automation/library/configuration/policy-test/

Summary

The SRX security policy system is extremely flexible and straightforward. We will use security policies in later chapters to perform functions such as VPN, IDP, UTM, and more. The SRX exemplifies why a zone-based firewall is a better choice than a traditional interface-based firewall, and with more granular security and less work involved in assigning levels of trusts to their various zones, will make your life as a security engineer much better.

Although the SRX policy system doesn't have complete feature parity with NetScreen's, Juniper continues to make progress with its large resource base that is working on the SRX. New features such as additional ALGs are being deployed regularly with no signs of slowing down.

Chapter Review Questions

1. How do you write a global security policy on an SRX?
2. When writing security policies for traffic that the destination is NATed to, which IP address would you put in the security policy—the true destination address or the NATed IP address?
3. What is the difference between `deny` and `reject` actions in a security policy?
4. How do you view all active sessions from the 192.168.0.0 subnet?
5. How do you filter denied traffic to a file called *Deny_log*?
6. What are traceoptions and why would you use them to troubleshoot security policies?
7. What are ALGs and what do they do?
8. How can you, as the SRX administrator, limit access to specific network segments during nonbusiness hours?
9. At what step does firewall policy lookup take place in the SRX flow process?
10. What is the difference between a fast path and a slow path?

Chapter Review Answers

1. Global security policies are not supported on the SRX. They are a legacy NetScreen feature and are not available today on the SRX platform.
2. Destination NAT is applied *before* security policy is evaluated. As a result, all security policies must be written for the NATed address. Source NAT is applied after the security policy is evaluated and should be written for the nontranslated IP address.
3. The `deny` action will silently drop the packet, where `reject` will send back an ICMP Port Unreachable to the source IP address. The `deny` action is usually the preferred method, unless it's critical that the source IP address be notified that its traffic has been dropped by a firewall.
4. To view all active sessions from the 192.168.0.0 subnet, use either:

   ```
   juniper@SRX5800> show security flow session source-prefix 192.168/16
   ```

   or:

   ```
   juniper@SRX5800> show security flow session source-prefix 192.168.0.0/16
   ```

   Either method is acceptable.
5. To filter denied traffic to a file called *Deny_log*, first you will need to ensure that the security policy has logging enabled. Without that, nothing will be sent to the local syslogs. Once that is complete, you'll need to specify a syslog file and filter for the `RT_FLOW_SESSION_DENY` string:

```
[edit]
juniper@SRX5800# set system syslog file Deny_log any any
[edit]
juniper@SRX5800# set system syslog file Deny_log match "RT_FLOW_SESSION_DENY"
```

6. Traceoptions are much like debugs on the NetScreen platform. Traceoptions will monitor and record the packet as it's evaluated through the various stages of packet processing. You can use traceoptions to verify that a packet is arriving on the correct interface and is being evaluated by the correct policy. You can also use traceoptions to ensure that the correct action is being taken (deny, permit, IDP, etc.) and to verify return traffic.
7. Application layer gateways are Layer 6 and Layer 7 inspections of certain protocols by the SRX. They are used to assist with certain applications that have problems with stateful firewalls, and can be used to provide an additional layer of application security. ALGs monitor the control channel of a data connection for specific information so that the SRX can dynamically handle firewall pinholing and NAT translation.
8. This is a perfect example of when to use policy schedulers. Policy schedulers can control when traffic is allowed (or denied) to network segments or services. Using policy schedulers, an SRX admin could lock down the payroll servers during nonbusiness hours by writing a policy scheduler that only permits traffic from 8:00 a.m. to 5:00 p.m. Monday through Friday.
9. As shown in Figure 4-1 at the beginning of this chapter, security policy lookup takes place just after route lookup/destination zone lookup. It is critical to understand the flow processing, as it will often be used while troubleshooting traffic down the road.
10. As a packet arrives on the interface of an SRX, an existing session lookup takes place. The SRX looks at the packet and tries to match it to an already established connection in the session table. If one is found, the SRX sends it down the fast path. If no session match is found, it is sent down the slow path.

    When a packet is sent down the slow path, the SRX must initially perform several checks when the new session is created, such as NAT, route lookup, and policy lookup, among others. Once those have been completed and the traffic is permitted, the SRX will build a session in the session table and all additional packets for that connection will take the fast path.

    The fast path just does some basic TCP checks and screens to ensure that everyone is playing nicely on this already allowed connection. Additionally, the SRX will do some ALG processing, and if an action such as IDP of VPNs exists, the action will also be processed.

CHAPTER 5

Network Address Translation

This chapter details the Junos Network Address Translation (NAT) features for the SRX. NAT provides a versatile set of tools for overcoming IPv4 address exhaustion, merging networks, migrating networks, redirecting traffic, or simply hiding network topologies. Put simply, NAT is the means for modifying the IP addresses and TCP/UDP ports in IP packets.

This chapter has three main sections that correspond to the three main types of NAT on the SRX:

- Source NAT
- Destination NAT
- Static NAT

Source NAT translates the source IP addresses and TCP/UDP ports of matching flows. Destination NAT translates the destination IP addresses and TCP/UDP ports of matching flows. And static NAT translates configured prefixes symmetrically whether they are the sources initiating flows or the destinations receiving them.

This chapter shows you how to configure NAT with step-by-step tutorials using the Junos command-line interface (CLI). It also includes a case study at the end of each main section.

How the SRX Processes NAT

The Junos operating system provides a complete and integrated set of NAT tools for the SRX. It departs both from the earlier ScreenOS security policy model and the Junos services interface model of NAT configuration. It depends neither on the disparate MIPs, DIPs, and VIPs of ScreenOS security policy, nor on the logical interface traffic steering of the packet mode Junos `services` stanza.

NAT is configured in the SRX under the Junos `security` stanza. It is fully integrated with stateful flow processing, while it is logically separate from security policy configuration. A given traffic flow can match, at most, a single NAT rule, and must match just a single security policy. There is no direct correspondence between NAT rules and security policies—the flows matched by one NAT rule may then be matched by one or several security policies. Flows matched by one security policy may have matched zero, one, or several NAT rules. But once a flow is matched by a NAT rule, the effect of the NAT rule will be fully integrated with the creation of a session table flow such that translation takes place symmetrically for both directions of IP conversation.

Figure 5-1 illustrates the processing of NAT in relation to the SRX flow model.

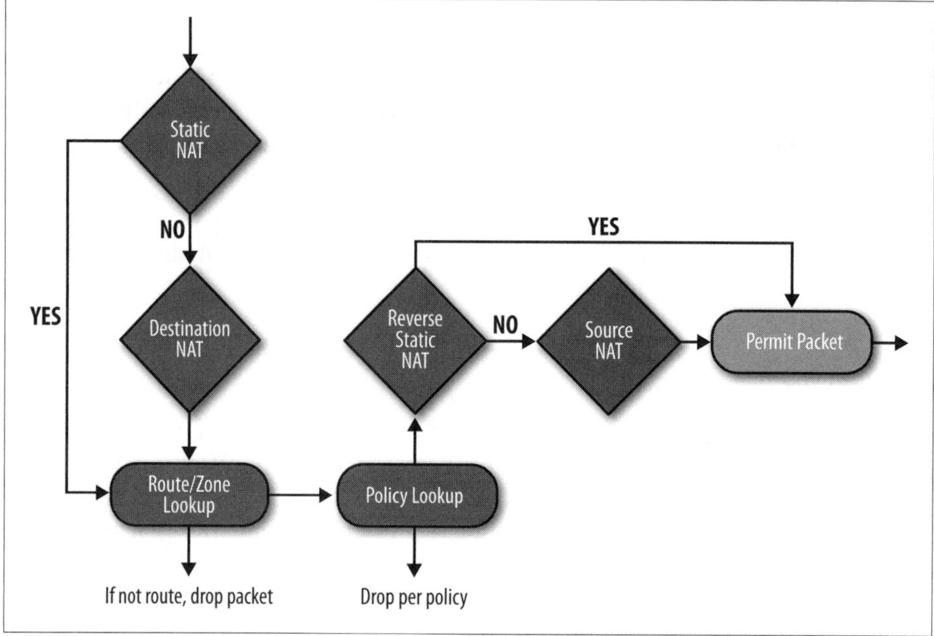

Figure 5-1. NAT processing within SRX flow

Notice that static NAT and destination NAT rules are matched before the route and zone lookups that must precede security policy evaluation. Source NAT and the reverse of static NAT rules are matched after security policy evaluation. In other words:

- Translations that change the *destination* IP addresses of packets always take place *before* the route lookups that depend on those destination addresses for determining the best matching route. As a result, security policy (which depends on route lookup for zone determination) is written to the translated destination IP address.
- Translations that change the *source* IP addresses of packets always take place *after* route lookups, as the source address does not affect traditional

destination-based routing decisions. As a result, security policy is written to the original (pre-translation) source IP address.

When a static NAT rule-set matches a given flow, it will take precedence over either a source or a destination NAT rule-set that would otherwise match the same flow.

The SRX NAT model enables more flexible and precise NAT configuration, as the absence of security policy dependencies makes network topology and address translation redesign possible, even as security policies remain in place.

Each NAT rule-set must be implemented from the context of an interface, zone, or routing instance. Because source translations follow route and zone lookups, their rule-sets must be configured with the context of both the ingress and egress interface, zone, or routing instance. As static and destination translations precede route and zone lookups, their rule-sets must be configured with the context of just the ingress interface, zone, or routing instance (given that the egress interface, zone, or routing instance is not determined until the route lookup following the translation).

When multiple NAT rule-sets contain contexts matching a given flow, the rule-set with the most specific context is used to determine the translation action. As shown in Figure 5-2, a rule-set with a matching interface context is preferred over one with a matching zone context, which is preferred over one with a matching routing instance context. Then within the chosen rule-set, rules are evaluated in order, with the first matching the flow utilized to determine the translation action.

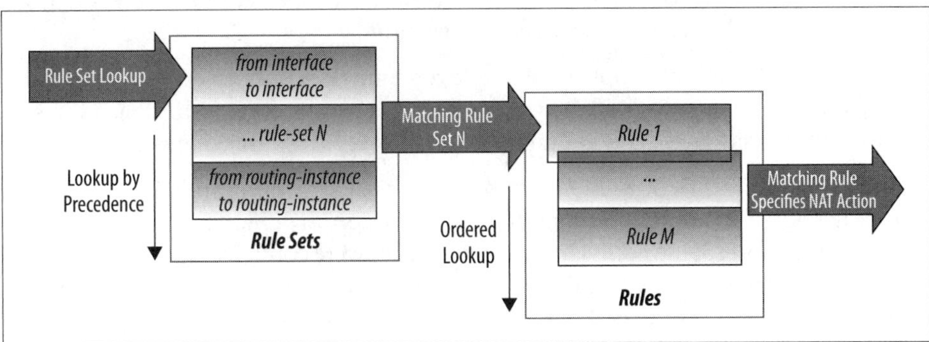

Figure 5-2. NAT rule-set precedence

Source NAT

Source NAT is the translation of source IP addresses and TCP/UDP ports in the headers of IP flows. It is most commonly used for the translation of private IP address space to public globally routable address space.

Source NAT on the SRX enables the translation of one or more private source IP addresses to a group of public IP addresses of equal or smaller size. TCP and UDP port translation may be used to scale translations when a larger group of private source IP addresses is overloading onto a smaller group of public IP addresses. The post-translation IP addresses may be configured in a pool, or the translations may be overloaded to the IP address configured on the egress interface of the matching flows.

In Figure 5-3, a source NAT is shown in action. Here the internal source IP address and port of an IP packet are translated to a different public source IP address and port, as the packet egresses the device.

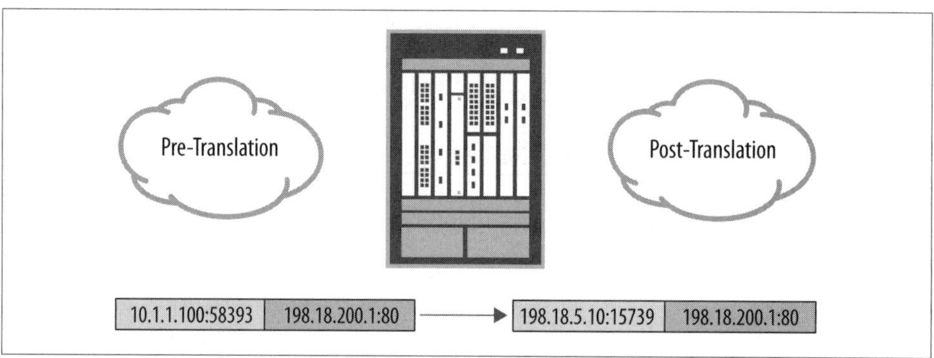

Figure 5-3. Source NAT

Source NAT implementation in Junos for the SRX is a superset of the ScreenOS DIP security policy and NAT mode interface translation.

Source NAT is commonly implemented to overcome IPv4 public address exhaustion. Systems within an organization are configured with private RFC 1918 IPv4 addresses and then translated to globally routable IPv4 addresses at a public network boundary.

Figure 5-4 shows the Dept-A and Dept-B networks of Organization-XYZ (this book's sample network topology) and the path through the core SRX5800 cluster to the public Internet. In Chapter 3, the necessary security policies were configured to allow Internet-bound traffic from Dept-A and Dept-B systems to successfully reach systems on the public Internet. However, the IPv4 address space used in Dept-A and Dept-B is not globally routable. It is private IPv4 address space as defined in RFC 1918.

Public Internet routers do not have reachability information with which to direct traffic toward private RFC 1918 address space. When systems with private IPv4 addresses in Dept-A and Dept-B attempt to communicate with systems on the public Internet, the return traffic from those public Internet systems toward the private IPv4 addresses must fail. The first public Internet router hop returns an ICMP Unreachable message, as the private addresses are unknown. Meanwhile the systems in Dept-A and Dept-B remain idle with flows which never receive responses.

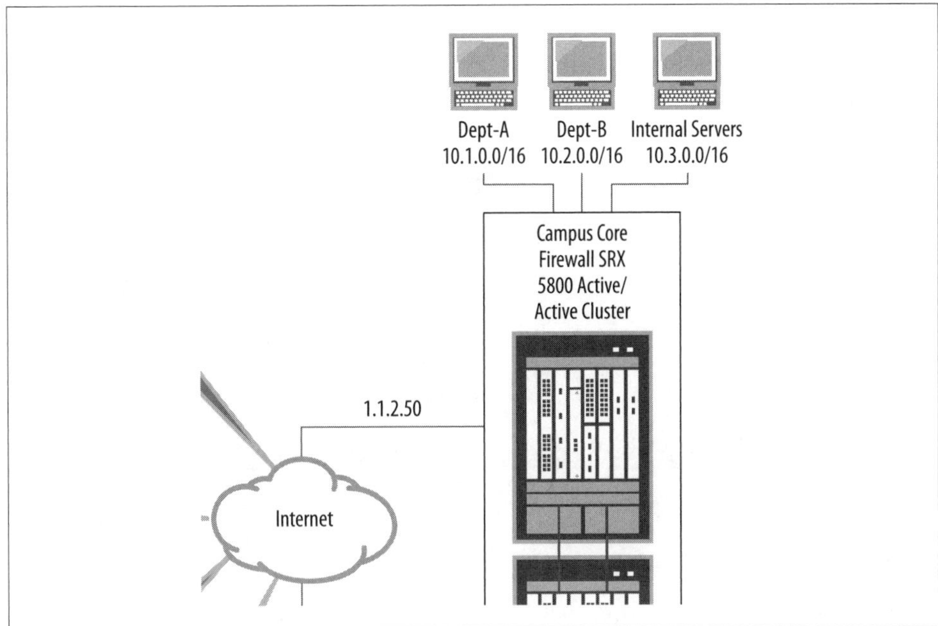

Figure 5-4. Dept-A and Dept-B path to public Internet

For bidirectional communication to the public Internet to succeed, the private IPv4 address space of the Dept-A and Dept-B systems must be translated to globally routable public IPv4 address space.

Interface NAT

SRX platforms support NAT configurations where the source IP addresses in flows are translated to the address assigned to the security platform's own outgoing interface. This behavior is commonly called *interface NAT* and is similar to the *NAT mode* interface configuration in ScreenOS. Interface NAT overloads one or more internal source IP addresses to the single public interface IP address via Port Address Translation (PAT), as shown in Figure 5-5. Here, the source IP address and port are translated to a new port of the SRX interface IP address 198.18.5.50.

The Junos implementation of interface NAT for the SRX departs from the limited ScreenOS behavior where translation took effect exclusively for traffic originated from an ingress "Trust" zone interface in "NAT mode" toward an egress "Untrust" zone interface. In contrast, Junos allows wide flexibility in the implementation of interface NAT between any zones, interfaces, or routing instances. The source IP addresses of flows can be explicitly translated to an interface address or to pool addresses, or simply excluded from translation altogether through configuration of the SRX's powerful NAT rule-sets.

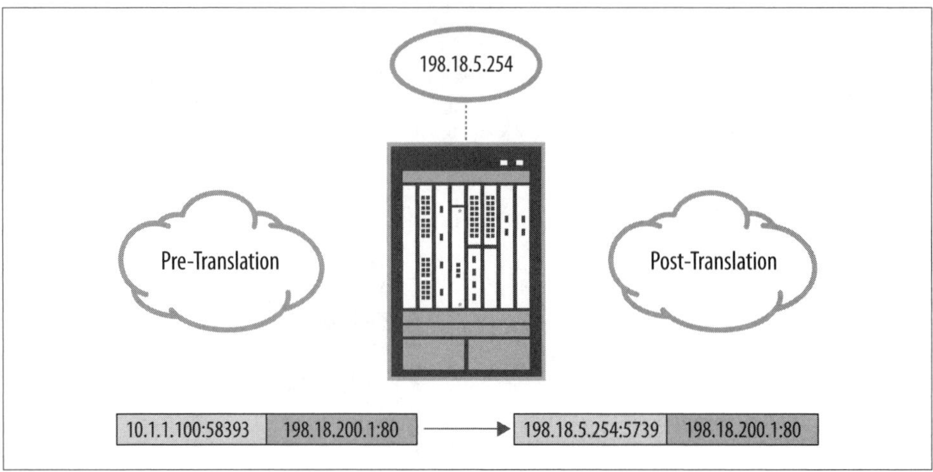

Figure 5-5. Interface NAT

Implementing a source NAT rule-set

In the Junos CLI configuration that follows, a simple source NAT rule-set is implemented between the Dept-A zone and the Inet zone. Use the **edit** command to enter configuration mode:

```
james@SRX5800-1> edit
Entering configuration mode
```

Here you access command-line help (?) for the NAT configuration hierarchy:

```
[edit]
james@SRX5800-1# edit security nat ?
Possible completions:
  <[Enter]>           Execute this command
> destination         Configure Destination NAT
> proxy-arp           Configure Proxy ARP
> source              Configure Source NAT
> static              Configure Static NAT
> traceoptions        NAT trace options
  |                   Pipe through a command
```

The SRX has three major categories of NAT: destination, source, and static. Here you access the command-line help for the *source* NAT configuration hierarchy:

```
[edit]
james@SRX5800-1# edit security nat source ?
Possible completions:
  <[Enter]>           Execute this command
> interface           Configure interface port overloading for persistent NAT
> pool                Define a source address pool
> pool-utilization-alarm  Configure pool utilization alarm
> port-randomization  Configure Source NAT port randomization
> rule-set            Configurate a set of rules
  |                   Pipe through a command
```

The two major elements of a source NAT configuration are the `pool` and `rule-set`. Use the `edit` command to move to the source NAT `rule-set` hierarchy:

```
[edit]
james@SRX5800-1# edit security nat source rule-set Dept-A-to-Inet

[edit security nat source rule-set Dept-A-to-Inet]
james@SRX5800-1# set ?
Possible completions:
> rule                 Source NAT rule
> from                 Where is the traffic from
> to                   Where is the traffic to
+ apply-groups         Groups from which to inherit configuration data
+ apply-groups-except  Don't inherit configuration data from these groups
```

The command-line help output shows the options for a source NAT `rule-set`. A source NAT `rule-set` must define both where traffic will be coming `from` as well as where it will be going `to`. View the command-line help for the `from` context:

```
[edit security nat source rule-set Dept-A-to-Inet]
james@SRX5800-1# set from ?
Possible completions:
+ interface            Source interface list
+ routing-instance     Source routing instance list
+ zone                 Source zone list
```

You discover that traffic may come `from` a zone, interface, or routing instance. Use the `set` command to limit the scope of this `rule-set` to traffic initiated from the Dept-A zone:

```
[edit security nat source rule-set Dept-A-to-Inet]
james@SRX5800-1# set from zone Dept-A
```

Now access the command-line help for the rule-set's `to` context:

```
[edit security nat source rule-set Dept-A-to-Inet]
james@SRX5800-1# set to ?
Possible completions:
+ interface            Destination interface list
+ routing-instance     Destination routing instance list
+ zone                 Destination zone list
```

You discover that traffic may go `to` a zone, interface, or routing instance. Use the `set` command to limit the scope of this `rule-set` to traffic destined toward the Inet zone:

```
[edit security nat source rule-set Dept-A-to-Inet]
james@SRX5800-1# set to zone Inet
```

Access command-line help for the configuration of rules within the source NAT `rule-set`:

```
[edit security nat source rule-set Dept-A-to-Inet]
james@SRX5800-1# set rule intNAT ?
Possible completions:
  <[Enter]>            Execute this command
+ apply-groups         Groups from which to inherit configuration data
+ apply-groups-except  Don't inherit configuration data from these groups
```

```
  > match                Specify Source NAT rule match criteria
  > then                 Then action
    |                    Pipe through a command
```

A rule-set must contain one or more rules. Every rule must have a name. This rule is named intNAT. Each rule must contain both a match criterion and a then action. Here you access command-line help for the source NAT rule match conditions:

```
[edit security nat source rule-set Dept-A-to-Inet]
james@SRX5800-1# set rule intNAT match ?
Possible completions:
+ apply-groups           Groups from which to inherit configuration data
+ apply-groups-except    Don't inherit configuration data from these groups
+ destination-address    Destination address
> destination-port       Destination port
+ source-address         Source address
```

A source NAT rule may match source IP addresses, destination IP addresses, and destination TCP/UDP ports. Use the set command to match this rule to traffic from the 10.1.0.0/16 address prefix:

```
[edit security nat source rule-set Dept-A-to-Inet]
james@SRX5800-1# set rule intNAT match source-address 10.1/16
```

Here you examine command-line help for source NAT rule actions:

```
[edit security nat source rule-set Dept-A-to-Inet]
james@SRX5800-1# set rule intNAT then source-nat ?
Possible completions:
+ apply-groups           Groups from which to inherit configuration data
+ apply-groups-except    Don't inherit configuration data from these groups
> interface              Use egress interface address
  off                    No action
> pool                   Use Source NAT pool
```

A source NAT rule may translate via an interface, a pool, or not at all (off). Use the set command to configure the source NAT rule action of PAT overloading on the IP address of the SRX device's egress interface:

```
[edit security nat source rule-set Dept-A-to-Inet]
james@SRX5800-1# set rule intNAT then source-nat interface
```

Note that PAT overloading is implied by the use of interface NAT. Examine your new source NAT rule-set with the show command:

```
[edit security nat source rule-set Dept-A-to-Inet]
james@SRX5800-1# show
from zone Dept-A;
to zone Inet;
rule intNAT {
    match {
        source-address 10.1.0.0/16;
    }
    then {
        source-nat {
            interface;
```

```
            }
        }
    }
```

This `rule-set` matches flows originated from the Dept-A zone's 10.1.0.0/16 IP address range and destined toward the Inet zone. Flows matching these conditions are translated by the SRX device via PAT to the interface IP address configured on the SRX device's Inet zone egress interface.

Once you're satisfied that your configuration work is complete, execute the `commit` command to move your candidate configuration to the active running configuration on the SRX device:

```
[edit security nat source rule-set Dept-A-to-Inet]
james@SRX5800-1# commit and-quit
configuration check succeeds
commit complete
Exiting configuration mode

james@SRX5800-1>
```

Viewing interface NAT in the session table

Now you examine a live flow in the SRX device's session table from the operational CLI. You find that this flow has been translated by your new source NAT rule-set:

```
james@SRX5800-1> show security flow session
Session ID: 2299, Policy name: webdmz_mgt/8, Timeout: 1792
  In: 10.1.1.100/49783 --> 198.18.200.1/80;tcp, If: ge-0/0/0.0
  Out: 198.18.200.1/80 --> 198.18.5.50/15653;tcp, If: ge-0/0/2.0

1 sessions displayed

james@SRX5800-1>
```

You note that the pre-translation source IP address of the flow is 10.1.1.100 in the initiating direction (`In:`). You also see that return traffic for the flow (`Out:`) comes back to a post-translation IP address of 198.18.5.50 (the SRX interface IP address) as the destination.

The port that this flow's traffic returns to (15653) on the translated public IP address (198.18.5.50) is different from the port (49783) that the original pre-translation IP address (10.1.1.100) utilized to initiate the traffic. This change of ports is PAT in action. This PAT makes it possible to overload such a large range of internal address space (the 10.1.0.0/16 Dept-A network) to the single Inet zone interface IP address (198.18.5.50).

Viewing traffic flow logs for interface NAT

Traffic flow logging is a useful tool for troubleshooting and forensics. Here you examine the logs for your translated flow with the `show log` command:

```
james@SRX5800-1> show log traffic-log
Jan 19 09:32:28  SRX210 RT_FLOW: RT_FLOW_SESSION_CREATE: session created
```

```
10.1.1.100/49783->198.18.200.1/80 junos-http 198.18.5.50/15653->198.18.200.1/80
intNAT None 6 webdmz_mgt trust Inet 2293

Jan 19 09:32:30  SRX210 RT_FLOW: RT_FLOW_SESSION_CLOSE: session closed TCP FIN:
10.1.1.100/49783->198.18.200.1/80 junos-http 198.18.5.50/15653->198.18.200.1/80
intNAT None 6 webdmz_mgt trust Inet 2293 6(330) 4(436) 3
james@SRX5800-1>
```

Fortunately, flow logging has already been enabled for both the session initiation and the session closure in the configuration of the security policy matching this flow (see Chapter 2 for more information about the actual configuration of security policy logging).

Both the session initiation and the session closure logs show the following:

- The matching NAT rule (`intNAT`)
- The pre-translation source IP address and port of the packets entering the Dept-A zone (`10.1.1.100` and `49783`)
- The post-translation source IP address and port of the packets that egress the Inet zone interface (`198.18.5.50` and `15653`)

Operational commands for interface NAT

Now you examine the NAT rule itself in the Junos operational CLI:

```
james@SRX5800-1> show security nat source rule all
Total rules: 1

source NAT rule: intNAT              Rule-set: Dept-A-to-Inet
  Rule-Id                    : 1
  Rule position              : 1
  From zone                  : Dept-A
  To zone                    : Inet
  Match
    Source addresses         : 10.1.0.0       - 10.1.255.255
  Action                     : interface
    Persistent NAT type      : N/A
    Inactivity timeout       : 0
    Max session number       : 0
  Translation hits           : 9

james@SRX5800-1>
```

The output shows all aspects of the NAT rule configuration:

- The context of the traffic (in this case, traffic initiated from zone Dept-A toward zone Inet)
- The rule-set name (`Dept-A-to-Inet`)
- The rule name (`intNAT`)
- The position of the rule within that rule-set (`1`, or first)

- The rule conditions for matching traffic (source addresses of 10.1.0.0 through 10.1.255.255)
- The action to be taken (translate to the `interface` address)
- The number of flows that have been translated by this NAT rule (`Translation hits : 9`)

Next, as this is an *interface* NAT configuration (which thereby intrinsically utilizes PAT), you can examine the availability and allocation of TCP/UDP ports on the egress interface's IP address:

```
james@SRX5800-1> show security nat interface-nat-ports
Pool   Total  Single ports  Single ports  Twin ports  Twin ports
index  ports     allocated     available   allocated   available
    0  64510             0         63486           0        1024
    1  64510             0         63486           0        1024
    2  64510             0         63486           0        1024
    3  64510             1         63485           0        1024
    4  64510             0         63486           0        1024
    5  64510             0         63486           0        1024
    6  64510             0         63486           0        1024
    7  64510             0         63486           0        1024

james@SRX5800-1>
```

Here the output shows that a total of 64,510 ports are available while just a single port is allocated.

Tracing interface NAT flows

Lastly, you access the most comprehensive NAT troubleshooting tool through the configuration of `security flow traceoptions`. When `security flow traceoptions` are enabled for a given flow, the SRX records a comprehensive breakdown of the handling of the translated IP packets (a "debug flow" in the language of legacy ScreenOS software).

Here you begin enabling security flow tracing by entering configuration mode on the SRX device:

```
james@SRX5800-1> edit
Entering configuration mode
```

You move the configuration mode prompt to the `security flow traceoptions` hierarchy and then use command-line help to view the configuration options within it:

```
[edit]
james@SRX5800-1# edit security flow traceoptions

[edit security flow traceoptions]
james@SRX5800-1# set ?
Possible completions:
+ apply-groups         Groups from which to inherit configuration data
+ apply-groups-except  Don't inherit configuration data from these groups
```

```
> file                  Trace file information
> flag                  Events and other information to include in trace output
  no-remote-trace       Disable remote tracing
> packet-filter         Flow packet debug filters
  rate-limit            Limit the incoming rate of trace messages (0..4294967295)
```

A minimum flow traceoptions configuration must include both a target `file` and a `flag`. The target `file` determines where the flow trace output will be recorded. The `flag` defines what type of flow trace data will be collected. The `packet-filter` option should also be used to narrow the trace to specific flows.

Here you define a target flow trace logfile named `tracetest` (which will automatically be placed in the */var/log* directory upon `commit` completion):

```
[edit security flow traceoptions]
james@SRX5800-1# set file tracetest
```

You now view command-line help for the `flag` option:

```
[edit security flow traceoptions]
james@SRX5800-1# set flag ?
Possible completions:
  all                  All events
  basic-datapath       Basic packet flow
  packet-drops         Packet drops
```

The `basic-datapath` flag is the most common flag for flow tracing and provides functionality roughly equivalent to the "debug flow basic" command in legacy ScreenOS systems. Add this `flag` to the configuration with the `set` command:

```
[edit security flow traceoptions]
james@SRX5800-1# set flag basic-datapath
```

You now view command-line help for the optional `packet-filter` configuration:

```
[edit security flow traceoptions]
james@SRX5800-1# set packet-filter NATfilter ?
Possible completions:
+ apply-groups         Groups from which to inherit configuration data
+ apply-groups-except  Don't inherit configuration data from these groups
  destination-port     Match TCP/UDP destination port
  destination-prefix   Destination IPv4 address prefix
  interface            Logical interface
  protocol             Match IP protocol type
  source-port          Match TCP/UDP source port
  source-prefix        Source IPv4 address prefix
```

The `packet-filter` option restricts traces to flows matching your specified IP protocol numbers, IP addresses, and TCP/UDP ports. This narrows the trace results collected in the target logfile, making it easier for you to find relevant information when troubleshooting.

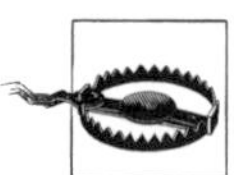

It is *very* important to trace only the traffic you need, as significant *additional* processing overhead is required on the SRX for packet tracing.

Without the packet-filter, this traceoptions configuration would impact all traffic passing the SRX device and potentially lead to significant performance degradation.

Use the set command to restrict flow traces to packets with a source IP address in the range of 10.1.0.0/16:

```
[edit security flow traceoptions]
james@SRX5800-1# set packet-filter NATfilter source-prefix 10.1/16
```

Note that this only matches one direction of the flows. An additional packet-filter must be defined with a condition matching the same address range as a destination in order to capture traces for the opposite direction of the flows. For now, you will just trace the one direction of the translated flows. Use the set command to also restrict flow traces to packets with a destination port of 80 (the typical port for HTTP):

```
[edit security flow traceoptions]
james@SRX5800-1# set packet-filter NATfilter destination-port 80
```

An additional packet-filter must likewise be defined here as well for this same port as a source in order to capture traces for the opposite direction of the flows. Again, you will just trace the one direction of the translated flows in this example. Now check your completed traceoptions configuration with the show command. Pipe the output to a compare so that you can quickly see only the changes you have made:

```
[edit security flow traceoptions]
james@SRX5800-1# show | compare

[edit security]
+   flow {
+       traceoptions {
+           file NATtrace;
+           flag basic-datapath;
+           packet-filter NATfilter {
+               source-prefix 10.1.0.0/16;
+               destination-port 80;
+           }
+       }
+   }
```

And finally, enable the new security flow traceoptions with the commit command:

```
[edit security flow traceoptions]
james@SRX5800-1# commit and-quit
commit complete
Exiting configuration mode

james@SRX5800-1>
```

The security flow traceoptions configuration begins collecting the basic-datapath information for packets initiated from 10.1.0.0/16 toward a destination port of 80. Now you can check the logs for your new trace data.

Here's a tip. You can pipe the `security flow traceoptions` logfile output to a `trim` command in order to eliminate the leading characters from each line (which include timestamp and module identification) for ease of readability. Use the `show log` command to view the flow trace results:

```
james@SRX5800-1> show log NATtrace | trim 41
<10.1.1.100/49783->198.18.200.1/80;6> matched filter NATfilter:
packet [64] ipid = 26698, @423f279e

---- flow_process_pkt: (thd 1): flow_ctxt type 13, common flag 0x0,
mbuf 0x423f2600
 flow process pak fast ifl 68 in_ifp ge-0/0/0.0

  ge-0/0/0.0:10.1.1.100/49783->198.18.200.1/80, tcp, flag 2 syn
 find flow: table 0x4d5c8220, hash 38079(0xffff), sa 10.1.1.100, da 198.18.200.1,
sp 49783, dp 80, proto 6, tok 384
  no session found, start first path. in_tunnel - 0, from_cp_flag - 0
  flow_first_create_session
```

Here you see your `packet-filter` named `NATfilter` matching the TCP flow (IP protocol number "6") sourced from IP address 10.1.1.100 on TCP port 49783 toward a destination IP address of 198.18.200.1 on TCP port 80 (the traditional identification of HTTP traffic) entering interface ge-0/0/0.0.

Your `security flow traceoptions packet-filter` has succeeded in narrowing the trace to the packets you have chosen.

Most importantly, the trace output shows that there is no existing session for this packet (`no session found, start first path`). The system must evaluate this packet as a potential new flow.

Continuing to examine the output:

```
  flow_first_in_dst_nat: in <ge-0/0/0.0>, out <N/A> dst_adr 198.18.200.1,
sp 49783, dp 80
  chose interface ge-0/0/0.0 as incoming nat if.
flow_first_rule_dst_xlate:  DST no-xlate: 0.0.0.0(0) to 198.18.200.1(80)
flow_first_routing: call flow_route_lookup(): src_ip 10.1.1.100, x_dst_ip
198.18.200.1, in ifp ge-0/0/0.0, out ifp N/A sp 49783, dp 80, ip_proto 6, tos 10
Doing DESTINATION addr route-lookup
  routed (x_dst_ip 198.18.200.1) from trust (ge-0/0/0.0 in 0) to ge-0/0/2.0,
Next-hop: 198.18.5.51
```

And here the trace output shows that the route lookup for the destination IP address 198.18.200.1 results in a next hop of 198.18.5.51 via the ge-0/0/2.0 interface.

Next, the trace output shows the policy search between security zones Dept-A and Inet. This shows that the ingress interface ge-0/0/0.0 is configured in security zone Dept-A and that the egress interface ge-0/0/2.0 is configured in security zone Inet:

```
policy search from zone Dept-A-> zone Inet
policy has timeout 900
app 6, timeout 1800s, curr ageout 20s
```

The trace output here shows that the source IP address and port of the flow have been translated from 10.1.1.100 and 49783 to 198.18.5.50 and 15653:

```
flow_first_src_xlate: 10.1.1.100/49783 -> 198.18.200.1/80 | 198.18.200.1/80 ->
0.0.0.0/49783: nat_src_xlated: False, nat_src_xlate_failed: False
flow_first_src_xlate: src nat 0.0.0.0(49783) to 198.18.200.1(80)
returns status: 1, rule/pool id: 1/2, pst_nat: False.
  dip id = 2/0, 10.1.1.100/49783->198.18.5.50/15653
  dip id = 2/0, 10.1.1.100/49783->198.18.5.50/15653
flow_first_get_out_ifp: 1000 -> cone nat test
  choose interface ge-0/0/2.0 as outgoing phy if
is_loop_pak: No loop: on ifp: ge-0/0/2.0, addr: 198.18.200.1, rtt_idx:0
policy is NULL (wx/pim scenario)
sm_flow_interest_check: app_id 0, policy 8, app_svc_en 0, flags 0x2.
not interested
sm_flow_interest_check: app_id 1, policy 8, app_svc_en 0, flags 0x2.
not interested
flow_first_service_lookup(): natp(0x4b6cea18): local_pak(0x3fdedc70.0x423f2600):
TCP proxy NOT interested: 0.
  service lookup identified service 6.
  flow_first_final_check: in <ge-0/0/0.0>, out <ge-0/0/2.0>
flow_first_final_check: flow_set_xlate_vector.
  existing vector list 1002-446f8628.
  Session (id:2299) created for first pak 1002
  flow_first_install_session======> 0x4b6cea18
 nsp 0x4b6cea18, nsp2 0x4b6cea84
  make_nsp_ready_no_resolve()
  route lookup: dest-ip 10.1.1.100 orig ifp ge-0/0/0.0 output_ifp ge-0/0/0.0
orig-zone 6 out-zone 6 vsd 0
  route to 10.1.1.100
```

And finally, notice that the trace output shows that both `wings` (directions) of the flow have been installed successfully into the session table with the identifier 2299:

```
Installing c2s NP session wing
Installing s2c NP session wing
  flow got session.
  flow session id 2299
  tcp flags 0x2, flag 0x2
  Got syn, 10.1.1.100(49783)->198.18.200.1(80), nspflag 0x1021, 0x20
  post addr xlation: 198.18.5.50->198.18.200.1.
mbuf 0x423f2600, exit nh 0x50010
 ----- flow_process_pkt rc 0x0 (fp rc 0)

james@SRX5800-1>
```

Before leaving the device, make sure the `security flow traceoptions` configuration is removed.

Removing the `security flow traceoptions` configuration upon completion of your troubleshooting eliminates any potential performance impact to your SRX device and traffic passing through it.

Enter configuration mode and use the `delete` command to remove the `security flow traceoptions` configuration:

```
james@SRX5800-1> edit
Entering configuration mode

[edit]
james@SRX5800-1# delete security flow traceoptions
```

Review your configuration changes with the `show` command:

```
[edit]
james@SRX5800-1# show | compare
[edit security]
-   flow {
-       traceoptions {
-           file tracetest;
-           flag basic-datapath;
-           flag all;
-           packet-filter NATfilter {
-               source-prefix 10.1.0.0/16;
-               destination-port 80;
-           }
-       }
-   }
```

You see that the `security flow traceoptions` configuration has been deleted in this candidate configuration. Implement your configuration changes with the `commit` command:

```
[edit]
james@SRX5800-1# commit and-quit
commit complete
Exiting configuration mode

james@SRX5800-1>
```

Address Pools

Although interface NAT is a simple and often used tool, the SRX offers an even more powerful NAT tool: *address pools*. Address pools are often used instead of the simple interface NAT when:

- PAT is not an option for a given application flow.
- More than a single post-translation IP address is needed to achieve the required NAT scaling.
- More complex or powerful translations are necessary to the given NAT design.

Figure 5-6 shows the translation of a source address and port to a new IP address and port from an address pool defined within the SRX device.

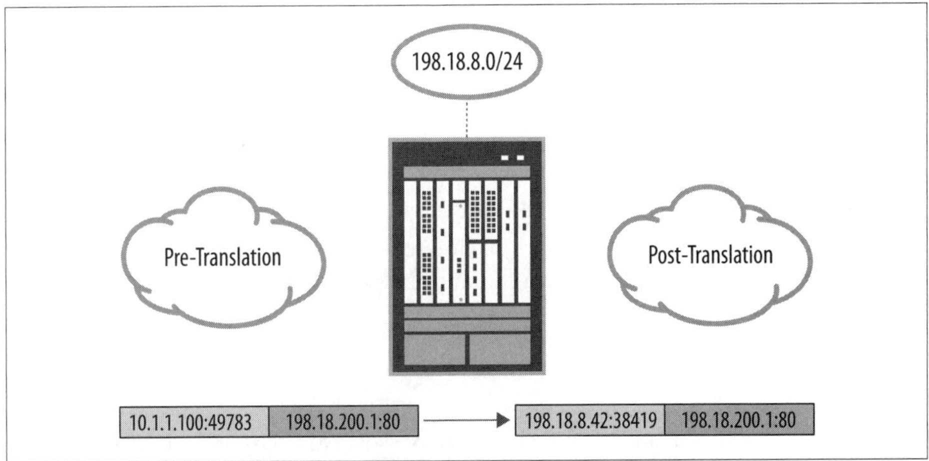

Figure 5-6. Source NAT with address pools

NAT address pools are configured with one or more address ranges or prefixes. They may be configured with PAT (by default) or without PAT (utilizing a `port no-translation` option). When configured with PAT, the range of ports used for translation can be specified with the `port` option. When a given pool is exhausted, it may then reference a completely different `overflow-pool` for additional translations.

Implementing a source NAT address pool

In the example source NAT address pool configuration which you're about to begin, the interface NAT configuration is replaced with a pool NAT (while renaming the NAT rule from `intNAT` to `poolNAT` for good measure).

The process isn't that difficult, so you'll start by entering configuration mode again and moving the configuration prompt back to the source NAT hierarchy. Use command-line help to get a list of all the options at the source NAT configuration hierarchy:

```
james@SRX5800-1> edit
Entering configuration mode

[edit]
james@SRX5800-1# edit security nat source

[edit security nat source]
james@SRX5800-1# set ?
Possible completions:
  address-persistent    Allow source address to maintain same translation
+ apply-groups          Groups from which to inherit configuration data
+ apply-groups-except   Don't inherit configuration data from these groups
> interface             Configure interface port overloading for persistent NAT
> pool                  Define a source address pool
> pool-utilization-alarm  Configure pool utilization alarm
> port-randomization    Configure Source NAT port randomization
> rule-set              Configurate a set of rules
```

Here you can see the special `address-persistent` option.

The `address-persistent` option is configured when all PAT translations for a given host must be translated through the same public IP address.

Without the `address-persistent` option, different flows from a given source address may be translated through entirely different public IP addresses.

Farther down the same command line help output, you also see the `port-randomization` option.

The SRX randomizes the translated port chosen for each translated flow by default. The `port-randomization disable` option disables this behavior.

Although port randomization is more secure and can mitigate some attacks, it requires additional system resources to achieve the randomization behavior.

Use command-line help for the source NAT address pool configuration:

```
[edit security nat source]
james@SRX5800-1# set pool ipPool ?
Possible completions:
> address               Add address to pool
+ apply-groups          Groups from which to inherit configuration data
+ apply-groups-except   Don't inherit configuration data from these groups
> host-address-base     The base of host address
> overflow-pool         Specify an overflow pool
> port                  Config port attribute to pool
> routing-instance      Routing instance
```

Junos reveals that the following:

- One or more addresses, prefixes, or ranges may be configured in a pool.
- Port ranges may be defined for pool translations.
- As discussed earlier, an `overflow-pool` may be referenced for use when this pool itself is exhausted.

Use the `set` command to define the prefix 10.10.10.192/29 for use in the `ipPool` source NAT address pool:

```
[edit security nat source]
james@SRX5800-1# set pool ipPool address 10.10.10.192/29
```

Now move the configuration prompt to the rule-set hierarchy to complete your work:

```
[edit security nat source]
james@SRX5800-1# edit rule-set Dept-A-to-Inet
```

Rename the previous `intNAT` rule to `poolNAT`:

```
[edit security nat source rule-set Dept-A-to-Inet]
james@SRX5800-1# rename rule intNAT to rule poolNAT
```

Use the command-line help to see the source NAT rule actions for address pools:

```
[edit security nat source rule-set Dept-A-to-Inet]
james@SRX5800-1# set rule poolNAT then source-nat pool ?
Possible completions:
  <pool-name>          Name of Source NAT pool
+ apply-groups         Groups from which to inherit configuration data
+ apply-groups-except  Don't inherit configuration data from these groups
  ipPool
> persistent-nat       Persistent NAT info
```

The `ipPool` address pool you just created is already listed in the command-line help output as a configuration option.

Also shown is the `persistent-nat` configuration option which allows the mapping of source translations to be maintained over time across multiple flows (and is discussed later in this chapter).

Now use the `set` command to change the NAT rule's action to reference your new address pool named `ipPool`:

```
[edit security nat source rule-set Dept-A-to-Inet]
james@SRX5800-1# set rule poolNAT then source-nat pool ipPool
```

Use the `show` command to see your completed configuration changes including the replacement of the previous interface NAT with the new pool NAT:

```
[edit security nat source]
james@SRX5800-1# show | compare
[edit security nat source]
+  pool ipPool {
+      address {
+          10.10.10.192/29;
+      }
+  }
[edit security nat source rule-set Dept-A-to-Inet]
+   rule poolNAT {
+       match {
+           source-address 10.10.0/16;
+       }
+       then {
+           source-nat {
+               pool {
+                   ipPool;
+               }
+           }
+       }
```

```
+   }
-   rule intNAT {
-       match {
-           source-address 10.1.0.0/16;
-       }
-       then {
-           source-nat {
-               interface;
-           }
-       }
-   }
```

And finally, use the `commit` command to implement the configuration changes on the running SRX system:

```
[edit]
james@SRX5800-1# commit and-quit
configuration check succeeds
commit complete
Exiting configuration mode

james@SRX5800-1>
```

The configuration is now active on the SRX device. The source addresses of flows originated from the Dept-A zone's 10.1.0.0/16 IP address range toward the Inet zone will now be translated by the SRX to the `ipPool` prefix of 10.10.10.192/29.

Viewing pool NAT in the session table

Now you show a new flow as it is translated by the modified NAT rule-set:

```
james@SRX5800-1> show security flow session
Session ID: 2321, Policy name: webdmz_mgt/8, Timeout: 1782
  In: 10.1.1.100/49794 --> 198.18.200.1/80;tcp, If: ge-0/0/0.0
  Out: 198.18.200.1/80 --> 10.10.10.197/16137;tcp, If: ge-0/0/2.0

1 sessions displayed

james@SRX5800-1> show security flow session session-identifier 2321
Session ID: 2321, Status: Normal
Flag: 0x0
Policy name: webdmz_mgt/8
Source NAT pool: ipPool, Application: junos-http/6
Maximum timeout: 1800, Current timeout: 1778
Start time: 4371, Duration: 22
   In: 10.1.1.100/49794 --> 198.18.200.1/80;tcp,
    Interface: ge-0/0/0.0,
    Session token: 0x180, Flag: 0x4129
    Route: 0x40010, Gateway: 10.1.1.100, Tunnel: 0
    Port sequence: 0, FIN sequence: 0,
    FIN state: 0,
   Out: 198.18.200.1/80 --> 10.10.10.197/16137;tcp,
    Interface: ge-0/0/2.0,
    Session token: 0x200, Flag: 0x4128
    Route: 0x50010, Gateway: 198.18.200.1, Tunnel: 0
```

```
        Port sequence: 0, FIN sequence: 0,
        FIN state: 0,

1 sessions displayed

james@SRX5800-1>
```

Two key distinctions relative to the earlier interface NAT section can be seen in this session table output:

- The `ipPool` address pool is shown in the detailed session table entry accessed via the specific session identifier (`Source NAT pool: ipPool`).
- The return direction of the flow (`Out`) shows a post-translation IP address of 10.10.10.197, which is indeed from the configured `ipPool` address pool.

Note that PAT is still in action as the TCP port is changed from 49794 to 16137. This is expected as the `port no-translation` option was absent from your `ipPool` address pool's configuration earlier.

Viewing traffic flow logs for pool NAT

Show and examine the logs for the initiation and closure of this session:

```
james@SRX5800-1> show log traffic-log
Jan 19 09:35:43  SRX210 RT_FLOW: RT_FLOW_SESSION_CREATE: session created
10.1.1.100/49794->198.18.200.1/80 junos-http 10.10.10.197/16137->198.18.200.1/80
poolNAT None 6 webdmz_mgt trust Inet 2313

Jan 19 09:35:46  SRX210 RT_FLOW: RT_FLOW_SESSION_CLOSE: session closed TCP FIN:
10.1.1.100/49794->198.18.200.1/80 junos-http 10.10.10.197/16137->198.18.200.1/80
poolNAT None 6 webdmz_mgt trust Inet 2313 7(384) 5(488) 3
james@SRX5800-1>
```

Both the session initiation and the session closure logs show the following:

- The matching NAT rule `poolNAT`.
- The pre-translation source IP address and port (`10.1.1.100` and `49794`) of the packets entering the Dept-A zone.
- The post-translation source IP address and port (`10.10.10.197` and `16137`) of the packets that ultimately egress via the Inet zone interface.

Operational commands for pool NAT

Now examine your `poolNAT` rule from the operational CLI:

```
[edit]

james@SRX5800-1> show security nat source rule all
Total rules: 1

source NAT rule: poolNAT                Rule-set: Dept-A-to-Inet
  Rule-Id                    : 2
```

```
  Rule position             : 1
  From zone                 : Dept-A
  To zone                   : Inet
  Match
    Source addresses        : 10.1.0.0        - 10.1.255.255
  Action                    : ipPool
    Persistent NAT type     : N/A
    Inactivity timeout      : 0
    Max session number      : 0
  Translation hits          : 4

james@SRX5800-1>
```

This output shows all aspects of the NAT rule configuration, including the following:

- The context of traffic (traffic initiated from zone Dept-A toward zone Inet)
- The rule-set name (`Dept-A-to-Inet`)
- The rule name (`poolNAT`)
- The position of the rule within that rule-set (`1`, or first)
- The rule conditions for matching traffic (source addresses of 10.1.0.0 through 10.1.255.255)
- The action to be taken (translate to the `ipPool` address pool)
- The number of flows that have been translated by this NAT rule (`Translation hits : 4`)

Next you examine the `ipPool` address pool:

```
james@SRX5800-1> show security nat source pool all
Total pools: 1

Pool name          : ipPool
Pool id            : 4
Routing instance   : default
Host address base  : 0.0.0.0
Port               : [1024, 63487]
Total addresses    : 8
Translation hits   : 4
Address range                        Single Ports   Twin Ports
       10.10.10.192 - 10.10.10.197      1              0

james@SRX5800-1>
```

And the output shows the following:

- The number of addresses in the pool (`Total Addresses : 8`)
- The range of ports available for PAT (`Port : [1024, 63487]`)
- The address range (`10.10.10.192 - 10.10.10.197`)
- The number of flows that have been translated using this pool (`Translation hits : 4`)
- The number of ports currently allocated from this PAT pool (`1`)

Tracing pool NAT flows

Finally, you examine the trace logfile after restoring the **security flow traceoptions** configuration from the earlier interface NAT section (configuration not repeated here for brevity):

```
james@SRX5800-1> show log NATtrace | trim 41
<10.1.1.100/49794->198.18.200.1/80;6> matched filter NATfilter:
packet [64] ipid = 8085, @423efd1e
---- flow_process_pkt: (thd 1): flow_ctxt type 13, common flag 0x0,
mbuf 0x423efb80
 flow process pak fast ifl 68 in_ifp ge-0/0/0.0
  ge-0/0/0.0:10.1.1.100/49794->198.18.200.1/80, tcp, flag 2 syn
 find flow: table 0x4d5c8220, hash 26127(0xffff), sa 10.1.1.100,
da 198.18.200.1, sp 49794, dp 80, proto 6, tok 384
  no session found, start first path. in_tunnel - 0, from_cp_flag - 0
  flow_first_create_session
  flow_first_in_dst_nat: in <ge-0/0/0.0>, out <N/A> dst_adr 198.18.200.1,
sp 49794, dp 80
  chose interface ge-0/0/0.0 as incoming nat if.
flow_first_rule_dst_xlate:  DST no-xlate: 0.0.0.0(0) to 198.18.200.1(80)
flow_first_routing: call flow_route_lookup(): src_ip 10.1.1.100, x_dst_ip
198.18.200.1, in ifp ge-0/0/0.0, out ifp N/A sp 49794, dp 80, ip_proto 6, tos 10
Doing DESTINATION addr route-lookup
  routed (x_dst_ip 198.18.200.1) from Dept-A (ge-0/0/0.0 in 0) to ge-0/0/2.0,
Next-hop: 198.18.200.1
  policy search from zone Dept-A-> zone Inet
  policy has timeout 900
  app 6, timeout 1800s, curr ageout 20s
flow_first_src_xlate: 10.1.1.100/49794 -> 198.18.200.1/80 | 198.18.200.1/80 ->
 0.0.0.0/49794: nat_src_xlated: False, nat_src_xlate_failed: False
flow_first_src_xlate: src nat 0.0.0.0(49794) to 198.18.200.1(80)
returns status: 1, rule/pool id: 2/4, pst_nat: False
  dip id = 4/0, 10.1.1.100/49794->10.10.10.197/16137
  dip id = 4/0, 10.1.1.100/49794->10.10.10.197/16137
```

Here the pool NAT is shown taking effect, as the pre-translation address and port (10.1.1.100 and 49794) are changed to the post-translation address and port (10.10.10.197 and 16137). And the remainder of the output:

```
flow_first_get_out_ifp: 1000 -> cone nat test
  choose interface ge-0/0/2.0 as outgoing phy if
is_loop_pak: No loop: on ifp: ge-0/0/2.0, addr: 198.18.200.1, rtt_idx:0
policy is NULL (wx/pim scenario)
sm_flow_interest_check: app_id 0, policy 8, app_svc_en 0, flags 0x2.
not interested
sm_flow_interest_check: app_id 1, policy 8, app_svc_en 0, flags 0x2.
not interested
flow_first_service_lookup(): natp(0x4b6d03e8): local_pak(0x3fdedc70.0x423efb80):
TCP proxy NOT interested: 0.
  service lookup identified service 6.
  flow_first_final_check: in <ge-0/0/0.0>, out <ge-0/0/2.0>
flow_first_final_check: flow_set_xlate_vector.
  existing vector list 1002-446f8628.
  Session (id:2313) created for first pak 1002
```

```
  flow_first_install_session======> 0x4b6d03e8
 nsp 0x4b6d03e8, nsp2 0x4b6d0454
  make_nsp_ready_no_resolve()
  route lookup: dest-ip 10.1.1.100 orig ifp ge-0/0/0.0 output_ifp ge-0/0/0.0
orig-zone 6 out-zone 6 vsd 0
  route to 10.1.1.100
Installing c2s NP session wing
Installing s2c NP session wing
  flow got session.
  flow session id 2313
  tcp flags 0x2, flag 0x2
  Got syn, 10.1.1.100(49794)->198.18.200.1(80), nspflag 0x1021, 0x20
  post addr xlation: 10.10.10.197->198.18.200.1.
mbuf 0x423efb80, exit nh 0x50010
 ----- flow_process_pkt rc 0x0 (fp rc 0)

james@SRX5800-1>
```

This shows both directions (`wings`) of the flow successfully installed in the session table. The address and port translation from the configured `ipPool` address pool will now take effect statefully for both directions of conversation.

Removing PAT

The SRX supports the creation of NAT address pools without PAT via the `port no-translation` option. In this model each internal IP address will be translated directly to a different corresponding public IP address from the pool. The TCP and UDP ports pass through the device unchanged. Although these translations can be simpler for applications and users to work with, they will more rapidly deplete your address pools as each private IP address requires its own unique public IP address from the pool.

A translation without PAT is shown in Figure 5-7, where the source address is changed from 10.1.1.100 to 1.1.1.1, while the source port remains fixed at 58393.

Now you will continue on to modify your configuration from the previous section to likewise disable PAT. The existing `ipPool` pool contains just eight unique IP addresses (from the 10.10.10.192/29 address pool) while it is translating a potentially much larger body of hosts (the 10.1.0.0/16 Dept-A zone). This worked fine with PAT where tens of thousands of ports were available for unique source IP address translations. But now without PAT, you'll need to use the `overflow-pool` configuration option to allow the translation of flows for additional hosts in the likely event that this small pool is exhausted.

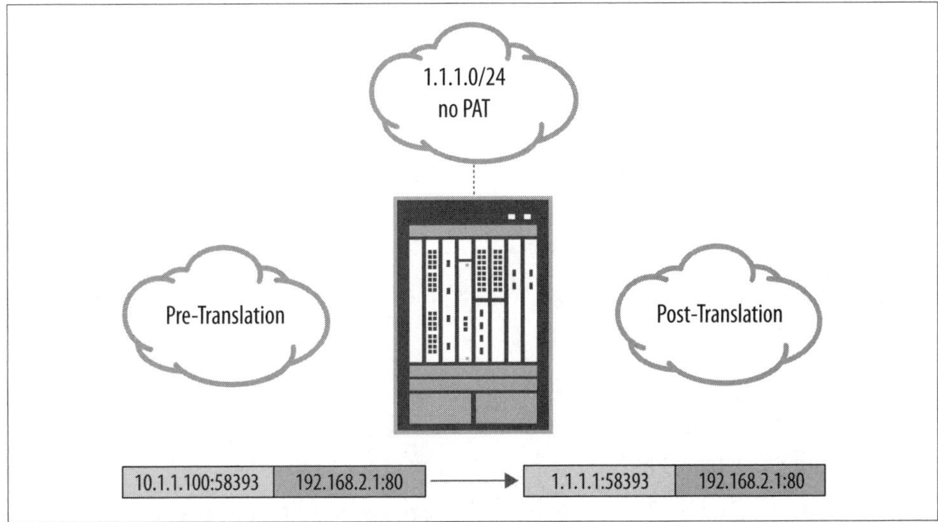

Figure 5-7. Source NAT without PAT

Implementing source NAT without PAT

To begin, enter configuration mode and move the configuration prompt to the source NAT pool hierarchy:

```
james@SRX5800-1> edit
Entering configuration mode

[edit]
james@SRX5800-1# edit security nat source pool ipPool
[edit security nat source pool ipPool]
```

Use the `set` command to disable PAT for this pool:

```
james@SRX5800-1# set port no-translation
```

Use the `set` command to create an `overflow-pool` directing excess translations to an interface NAT:

```
[edit security nat source pool ipPool]

james@SRX5800-1# set overflow-pool interface
```

Although up to eight Dept-A zone IP addresses may be concurrently translated to unique pool IP addresses (from the existing 10.10.10.192/29 `ipPool` pool's prefix) with PAT now disabled, any situation with more than eight addresses concurrently creating flows through this pool will now result in the translation of these additional flows via PAT overloading on the IP address of the egress *interface* (198.18.5.50 in this case). Without this `overflow-pool`, the additional addresses' flows would simply fail to be translated.

Show the completed configuration changes and then **commit** to the running configuration on the SRX device:

```
[edit security nat source pool ipPool]
james@SRX5800-1# show | compare
[edit security nat source pool ipPool]
+      port no-translation;
+      overflow-pool interface;

[edit security nat source pool ipPool]
james@SRX5800-1# commit and-quit
configuration check succeeds
commit complete
Exiting configuration mode

james@SRX5800-1>
```

Viewing source NAT without PAT

And now you view a new flow translated through the modified rule-set:

```
james@SRX5800-1> show security flow session
Session ID: 2330, Policy name: webdmz_mgt/8, Timeout: 1782
  In: 10.1.1.100/49832 --> 198.18.200.1/80;tcp, If: ge-0/0/0.0
  Out: 198.18.200.1/80 --> 10.10.10.195/49832;tcp, If: ge-0/0/2.0

1 sessions displayed

james@SRX5800-1>
```

Here in the session table output, the internal source IP address 10.1.1.100 is translated to the 10.10.10.195 pool address (visible in the `Out` return direction) while the source port remains unchanged at 49832.

Here you show the corresponding traffic log for this same flow's initiation:

```
james@SRX5800-1> show log traffic-log
Jan 19 09:39:47  SRX210 RT_FLOW: RT_FLOW_SESSION_CREATE: session created
10.1.1.100/49832->198.18.200.1/80 junos-http 10.10.10.195/49832->198.18.200.1/80
poolNAT None 6 webdmz_mgt Dept-A Inet 2330

james@SRX5800-1>
```

This session initiation log entry likewise shows the translation of the source IP address from 10.1.1.100 to 10.10.10.195, while the source port remains fixed at 49832. It also shows the matching NAT rule (`poolNAT`).

And here is the modified `ipPool` address pool in the operational CLI:

```
james@SRX5800-1> show security nat source pool all
Total pools: 1

Pool name          : ipPool
Pool id            : 4
Routing instance   : default
Host address base  : 0.0.0.0
```

```
Port                 : no translation
Total addresses      : 8
Translation hits     : 2
Address range                        Single Ports   Twin Ports
       10.10.10.192 - 10.10.10.197       1              0

james@SRX5800-1>
```

And sure enough, PAT has been disabled for the `ipPool` address pool (`Port : no translation`).

Proxy ARP

The address pool we used in the preceding sections used a prefix that existed only virtually within the SRX device. It did not exist anywhere physically on a real network. Reachability for this pool necessarily depends upon simple IP routing lookups (whether through a static or a dynamic routing entry).

The SRX also supports the configuration of address pools that reside within the bounds of subnets on the SRX device's *own* physical interfaces, as shown in Figure 5-8.

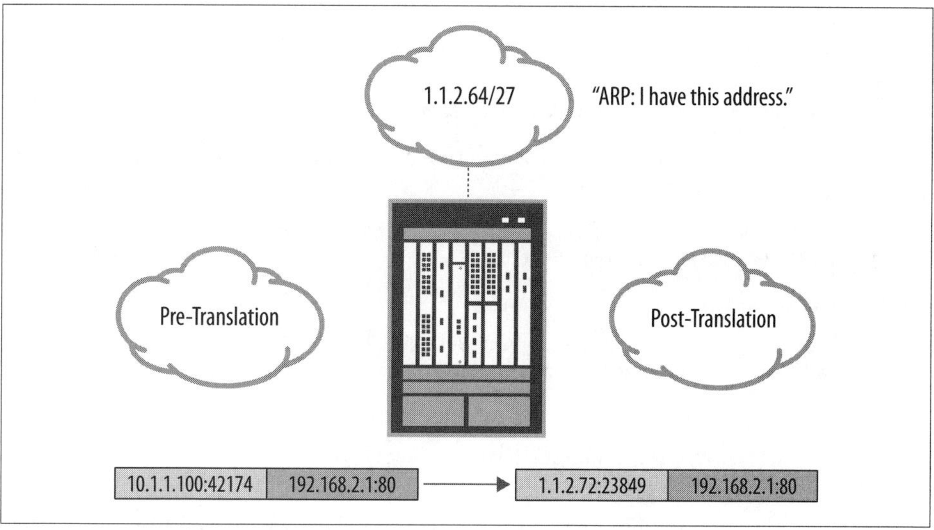

Figure 5-8. Source NAT with Proxy ARP

The Proxy ARP feature must be engaged in these cases to allow reachability for these pools. As the pool exists within a presumably already routable IP network (or else the SRX device itself would be unreachable), the key is to provide reachability at the Ethernet layer (rather than the IP layer as in previous examples).

The last hop IP routing device must send an ARP request on the local Ethernet network, seeking the Media Access Control (MAC) address for each given pool address, in order to pass data to that NAT device.

The Proxy ARP feature allows the SRX device to respond to these ARP requests on behalf of the pool addresses, and in so doing, the SRX device provides its own MAC address as the Ethernet layer destination for packets sent to a pool address at the IP layer. Once packets are received, the SRX device continues flow processing as normal.

Implementing proxy ARP

Now you will put the Proxy ARP feature to use by creating a new source NAT rule-set for the Dept-B zone network. First, enter configuration mode and move to the source NAT configuration hierarchy:

```
james@SRX5800-1> edit
Entering configuration mode

[edit]
james@SRX5800-1# edit security nat source
```

Configure a new source NAT pool from a portion of the Inet zone interface's IP network range:

```
[edit security nat source]
james@SRX5800-1# set pool phyPool address 198.18.5.64/27
```

Now create a new rule-set that will utilize the new pool:

```
[edit]
james@SRX5800-1# edit rule-set Dept-B-to-Inet
```

Use the `set` command to configure the new rule-set for traffic originated from the Dept-B zone:

```
[edit security nat source rule-set Dept-B-to-Inet]
james@SRX5800-1# set from zone Dept-B
```

And for traffic destined to the Inet zone:

```
[edit security nat source rule-set Dept-B-to-Inet]
james@SRX5800-1# set to zone Inet
```

Move the configuration prompt to the `rule` hierarchy:

```
[edit security nat source rule-set Dept-B-to-Inet]
james@SRX5800-1# edit rule phypoolNAT
```

Use the `set` command to configure the `rule` to match flows originated from a source IP address in the 10.2.0.0/16 range:

```
[edit security nat source rule-set Dept-B-to-Inet rule phypoolNAT]
james@SRX5800-1# set match source-address 10.2/16
```

And then to take the new `phyPool` pool as a source NAT action:

```
[edit security nat source rule-set Dept-B-to-Inet rule phypoolNAT]
james@SRX5800-1# set then source-nat phyPool
```

Next you move the configuration prompt up three levels in the hierarchy:

```
[edit security nat source rule-set Dept-B-to-Inet rule phypoolNAT]
james@SRX5800-1# up 3
```

And here you configure Proxy ARP for the 198.18.5.64/27 range (the same as the phyPool address pool) on the ge-0/0/2.0 interface (which is within the Inet zone):

```
[edit security nat]
james@SRX5800-1# set proxy-arp interface ge-0/0/2.0 address 198.18.5.64/27
 [edit security nat]
```

Use the show command to see the completed Proxy ARP, NAT pool, and rule-set configuration changes for Dept-B:

```
james@SRX5800-1# show | compare
[edit security nat source]
    pool ipPool { ... }
+   pool phyPool {
+       address {
+           198.18.5.64/27;
+       }
+   }
[edit security nat source]
    rule-set Dept-A-to-Inet { ... }
+   rule-set Dept-B-to-Inet {
+       from zone Dept-B;
+       to zone web-dmz;
+       rule phypoolNAT {
+           match {
+               source-address 198.18.11.0/24;
+           }
+           then {
+               source-nat {
+                   pool {
+                       phyPool;
+                   }
+               }
+           }
+       }
+   }
[edit security nat]
+  proxy-arp {
+      interface ge-0/0/2.0 {
+          address {
+              198.18.5.64/27;
+          }
+      }
+  }
```

And after confirming, commit the new configuration:

```
[edit security nat]
james@SRX5800-1# commit and-quit
configuration check succeeds
commit complete
Exiting configuration mode

james@SRX5800-1>
```

The source addresses of flows originated from the Dept-B zone's 10.2.0.0/16 IP address range toward the Inet zone will now be translated by the SRX device to the 198.18.5.64/27 address pool that exists within the SRX device's egress Inet zone network. The SRX device will now also answer ARP requests for addresses in the same 198.18.5.64/27 range when they're received on the ge-0/0/2.0 interface.

Viewing proxy ARP in action

Now you see a flow translated via the new rule-set:

```
james@SRX5800-1> show security flow session
Session ID: 2336, Policy name: webdmz_mgt/8, Timeout: 1796
  In: 10.2.1.15/49842 --> 198.18.200.1/80;tcp, If: ge-0/0/0.0
  Out: 198.18.200.1/80 --> 198.18.5.78/2615;tcp, If: ge-0/0/2.0

1 sessions displayed

james@SRX5800-1>
```

Here, the internal source IP address 10.2.1.15 is translated to the 198.18.5.78 pool address (visible in the `Out` return direction) while the source port is translated from 49842 to 2615. PAT overloading is engaged (as it was *not specifically disabled*).

The corresponding traffic log for this flow is:

```
james@SRX5800-1> show log traffic-log
Jan 19 09:41:59  SRX210 RT_FLOW: RT_FLOW_SESSION_CREATE: session created
10.2.1.15/49842->198.18.200.1/80 junos-http 198.18.5.78/2615->198.18.200.1/80
phypoolNAT None 6 webdmz_mgt Dept-B web-dmz 2336

james@SRX5800-1>
```

This session initiation log entry shows the translation of the internal source IP address and port from 10.2.1.15 and 49842 to the public address and port of 198.18.5.78 and 2615. It also shows the matching NAT rule (`phypoolNAT`).

Show the new rule in the operational CLI:

```
james@SRX5800-1> show security nat source rule phypoolNAT

source NAT rule: phypoolNAT              Rule-set: Dept-B-to-Inet
  Rule-Id                     : 2
  Rule position               : 1
  From zone                   : Dept-B
  To zone                     : Inet
  Match
    Source addresses          : 198.18.5.64      - 198.18.5.95
  Action                      : phyPool
    Persistent NAT type       : N/A
    Inactivity timeout        : 0
    Max session number        : 0
  Translation hits            : 1

james@SRX5800-1>
```

And the new pool:

```
james@SRX5800-1> show security nat source pool all
Total pools: 1

Pool name          : phyPool
Pool id            : 5
Routing instance   : default
Host address base  : 0.0.0.0
Port               : [1024, 63487]
Total addresses    : 32
Translation hits   : 1
Address range                        Single Ports   Twin Ports
      198.18.5.64 - 198.18.5.95          1              0

james@SRX5800-1>
```

Persistent NAT

The persistent NAT feature in the SRX makes it possible to maintain address and port translation mappings over time and across multiple flows. True to its name, it literally makes NAT a *persistent* behavior.

Persistent NAT behavior was often called *Cone NAT* in the past.

Here you will run through an example persistent NAT implementation. Persistent NAT is configured in the SRX under the hierarchy for pool actions within a source NAT rule.

Implementing persistent NAT

You'll get started by moving the configuration prompt to the right hierarchy within the source NAT rule:

```
james@SRX5800-1> edit
Entering configuration mode

[edit]
james@SRX5800-1# edit security nat source rule-set Dept-B-to-Inet
rule phypoolNAT then source-nat pool persistent-nat
```

Check out the command-line help for the persistent NAT hierarchy:

```
[edit security nat source rule-set Dept-B-to-Inet rule poolNAT
then source-nat pool persistent-nat]
james@SRX5800-1# set ?
Possible completions:
+ apply-groups         Groups from which to inherit configuration data
+ apply-groups-except  Don't inherit configuration data from these groups
  inactivity-timeout   Inactivity timeout value (60..7200)
```

```
  max-session-number   The maximum session number value (8..100)
> permit               Persistent NAT permit configure
```

The `inactivity-timeout` option defines how long a persistent NAT mapping will remain in the persistent NAT table. The value is defined in increments of seconds from a minimum of one minute to a maximum of two hours. The default is five minutes.

The `max-session-number` option defines how many concurrent entries may be created in the session table for a given persistent NAT mapping. The default is 30 sessions, but this can be tuned to between eight and 100 concurrent sessions.

Use command-line help again to find the permissible types of persistent NAT mappings:

```
[edit security nat source rule-set Dept-B-to-Inet rule poolNAT
then source-nat pool persistent-nat]
james@SRX5800-1# set permit ?
Possible completions:
  any-remote-host      Permit any remote host
  target-host          Permit target host
  target-host-port     Permit target host port
```

Once enabled, all of these options ensure that any flows initiated from a given internal IP address and port pair are translated to the same public IP address and port pair consistently for the duration of the persistent NAT mapping. The distinction between them is in the externally initiated traffic which is translated by the NAT rule.

The `any-remote-host` option allows translations for all external hosts initiating traffic into the public IP address on which the internal host is being translated by the persistent NAT mapping. Of course, security policy continues to be evaluated and may block the externally initiated flows depending on the configuration. (See Chapter 3 for more information on security policy configuration.)

The `target-host` option differs in that it only permits the translation of externally initiated flows from hosts that have already received flows initiated from the internal host with the persistent NAT mapping. Any external host which has not received traffic initiated from the internal host will not be translated by the NAT rule.

The `target-host-port` option goes one step further by only allowing the translation of externally initiated flows on the specific ports on which the external hosts have received traffic initiated from the internal host within the persistent NAT mapping. Any externally initiated flow that does not match both the IP addresses and ports of a previous internally initiated flow in the persistent NAT mapping will fail to be translated. In this example, you configure the `target-host-port` option:

```
[edit security nat source rule-set Dept-B-to-Inet rule poolNAT
then source-nat pool persistent-nat]
james@SRX5800-1# set permit target-host-port
```

Check the completed persistent NAT configuration changes:

```
[edit security nat source rule-set Dept-B-to-Inet rule poolNAT
then source-nat pool persistent-nat]
```

```
james@SRX5800-1# show | compare
[edit security nat source rule-set Dept-B-to-Inet rule poolNAT
then source-nat pool]
+  persistent-nat {
+      permit target-host-port;
+  }
```

And `commit` the persistent NAT configuration on the SRX device:

```
[edit security nat source rule-set Dept-B-to-Inet rule poolNAT
then source-nat pool]
james@SRX5800-1# commit and-quit
commit complete
Exiting configuration mode

james@SRX5800-1>
```

Viewing persistent NAT in action

Now you view a flow translated via the new persistent NAT configuration:

```
james@SRX5800-1> show security flow session
Session ID: 60178, Policy name: webdmz_mgt/14, Timeout: 1768
  In: 10.2.1.17/52538 --> 198.18.200.1/80;tcp, If: ge-0/0/0.0
  Out: 198.18.200.1/80 --> 198.18.5.68/16754;tcp, If: ge-0/0/2.0

1 sessions displayed
james@SRX5800-1>
```

As you can see in the session table output, the internal source IP address 10.2.1.17 and source port 52538 are translated to the 198.18.5.68 pool address and 16754 source port (visible in the `Out` return direction).

Next you see the corresponding traffic logs for this flow:

```
james@SRX5800-1> show log traffic-log
Feb  1 03:44:19  SRX210 RT_FLOW: RT_FLOW_SESSION_CREATE: session created
10.2.1.17/52538->198.18.200.1/80 None 198.18.200.159/16754->198.18.200.1/80
phypoolNAT None 6 webdmz_mgt Dept-B Inet 60023

Feb  1 03:44:40  SRX210 RT_FLOW: RT_FLOW_SESSION_CLOSE: session closed TCP FIN:
10.2.1.17/52538->198.18.200.1/80 None 198.18.200.159/16754->198.18.200.1/80
phypoolNAT None 6 webdmz_mgt Dept-B Inet 60023 8(1145) 5(1036) 22

james@SRX5800-1>
```

Here the log entries each show the translation of the internal source IP address and port from 10.2.1.17 and 52538 to the public address and port of 198.18.5.68 and 16754. They also show the matching NAT rule (`phypoolNAT`).

Now look at the modified rule in the operational CLI:

```
james@SRX5800-1> show security nat source rule phypoolNAT

source NAT rule: phypoolNAT              Rule-set: Dept-B-to-Inet
  Rule-Id                    : 2
```

```
  Rule position              : 1
  From zone                  : Dept-B
  To zone                    : Inet
  Match
    Source addresses         : 198.18.5.64     - 198.18.5.95
  Action                     : phyPool
    Persistent NAT type      : target-host-port
    Inactivity timeout       : 300
    Max session number       : 8
  Translation hits           : 110

james@SRX5800-1>
```

Here the key change is that the `Action` now shows a specific persistent NAT type (`target-host-port`), persistent NAT inactivity timeout (`300`), and maximum number of sessions per persistent NAT mapping (`8`).

Here you see that the pool itself has not been changed:

```
james@SRX5800-1> show security nat source pool all
Total pools: 1

Pool name          : phyPool
Pool id            : 5
Routing instance   : default
Host address base  : 0.0.0.0
Port               : [1024, 63487]
Total addresses    : 32
Translation hits   : 2
Address range                          Single Ports   Twin Ports
      198.18.5.64 - 198.18.5.95            1              0

james@SRX5800-1>
```

And last is the most significant operational CLI distinction between working with a persistent NAT and an ordinary source NAT:

```
james@SRX5800-1> show security nat source persistent-nat-table all
Internal                Reflective          Source      Type
Left_time/  Curr_Sess_Num/  Source
 In_IP          In_Port Ref_IP          Ref_Port NAT Pool
Conf_time   Max_Sess_Num    NAT Rule
10.2.1.17   52538   198.18.5.68   16754     phyPool    target-host-port  186/300
 0/8            phypoolNAT

james@SRX5800-1>
```

You can see that persistent NAT maintains a separate mapping in a persistent NAT table that includes:

- The pre-translation source IP address (`10.2.1.17`)
- The pre-translation source port (`52538`)
- The post-translation source IP address (`198.18.5.68`)
- The post-translation source port (`16754`)

- The source NAT pool (`phyPool`)
- The persistent NAT mode (`target-host-port`)
- The time left for this persistent NAT mapping in seconds (`186`)
- The timeout configured for this mapping in seconds (`300`)
- The current number of sessions using this persistent NAT mapping (`0`)
- The maximum number of sessions that may use this mapping (`8`)
- The matching source NAT rule (`phypoolNAT`)

The maintenance of this persistent NAT mapping table, and the resultant association of future translations with this persistent mode of NAT, is the key distinction between persistent NAT and traditional source NAT.

Case Study 5-1: ISP Redundancy via PAT

When an organization is unable to obtain adequate public IPv4 address space (and is thus in need of PAT overloading), it is usually also the case that the organization's address space is too small to meet the minimum requirements for global routing advertisement. For instance, large Internet service providers (ISPs) will decline to accept route advertisements smaller than /24 address blocks from peers.

If an organization has been designated with an address block smaller than a /24 by its upstream ISP, it isn't possible to implement a redundant advertisement of this address block. The address block will be summarized into a larger address block, owned by the ISP, when it is advertised on to the ISP's global Internet peers, as shown in Figure 5-9.

The challenge with this approach is that any flap of the organization's connectivity with its upstream ISPs will remain invisible to the global Internet community. The advertisement of the upstream ISP's larger summarized block will be entirely unaffected by a loss of connectivity to any one downstream customer. Traffic to the small organization's address block will simply be black-holed down an unusable path in the event of a connectivity failure.

An imperfect, but necessary, solution to this challenge is the implementation of distinct PAT rules per upstream ISP, as shown in Figure 5-9. Each ISP will provide its own globally routable address space. These two ranges of addresses are then separately advertised within these ISPs' own larger summarized blocks of address space. In this way, the customer organization has two distinct paths to the public Internet via these two ISPs, but the return path for each ISP is to a different block of address space.

The redundancy exists in the received routes (likely just a default route, as shown in Figure 5-9). Traffic leaves the customer via whichever ISP's route is preferred. It is translated according to the specific PAT rule implemented for that egress zone. This NAT rule then uses the egress ISP's address block for the PAT. The return traffic comes back via the correct ISP through the summarized route, containing this PAT pool, which is advertised to the global Internet.

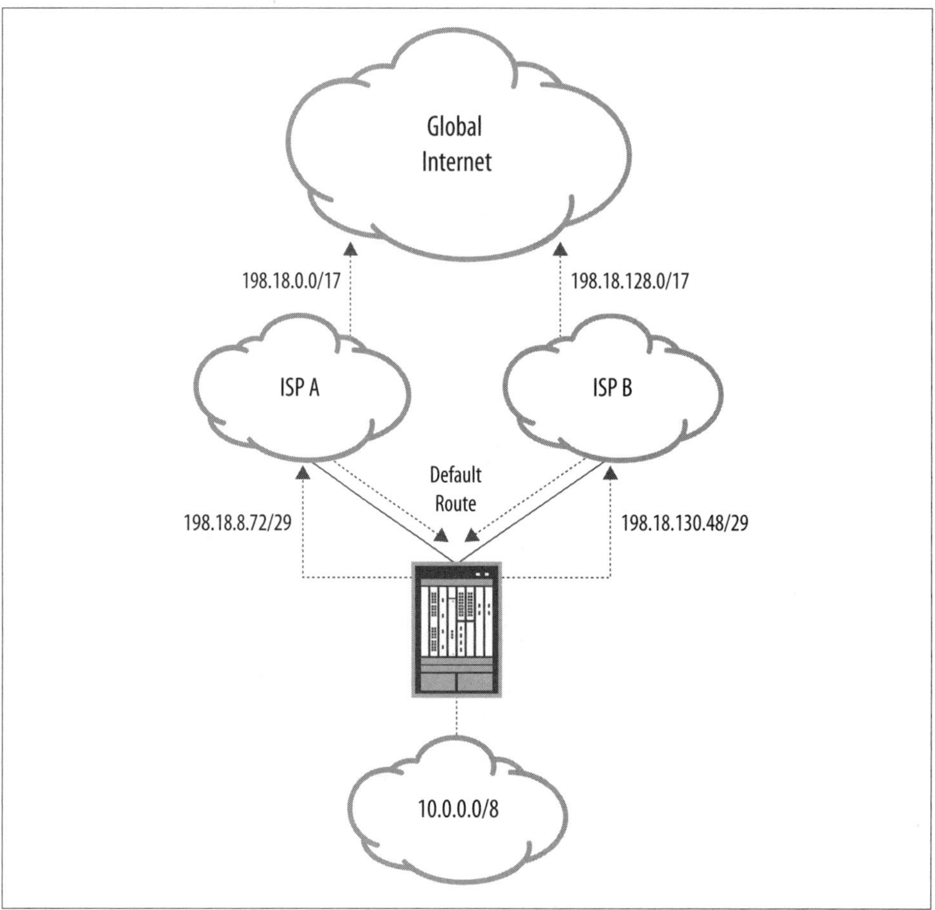

Figure 5-9. ISP redundancy via PAT

In the event of a failover, the traffic exits via the other ISP and the different PAT rule for that ISP's egress zone. The traffic would thereby return through that second ISP's own summarized address advertisement containing this second different PAT pool.

Although many applications will break as connectivity is failed over to the redundant path (as the translated source IP addresses will change for the hosts), it would nonetheless be possible to restart many applications and user flows following the failover. This would provide a level of redundancy, though a very imperfect one.

Implementing redundant ISP PAT

You will implement a redundant ISP PAT configuration step by step over the next few pages. The first step is to enter configuration mode and create a source PAT address pool for traffic to ISP-A:

```
james@SRX5800-1> edit
Entering configuration mode

[edit]
james@SRX5800-1# edit security nat source

[edit security nat source]
james@SRX5800-1# set pool ISP-A-Pool address 198.18.8.72/29
```

Then a source PAT address pool is created for traffic to ISP-B:

```
[edit security nat source]
james@SRX5800-1# set pool ISP-B-Pool address 198.18.130.48/29
```

Now a source NAT rule-set is created for traffic from Dept-A to ISP-A:

```
[edit]
james@SRX5800-1# edit rule-set Dept-A-to-ISP-A

[edit security nat source rule-set Dept-A-to-ISP-A]
james@SRX5800-1# set from zone Dept-A

[edit security nat source rule-set Dept-A-to-ISP-A]
james@SRX5800-1# set to zone ISP-A
```

Now you configure the NAT rule-set for traffic from Dept-A to ISP-A to match all traffic (`source-address 0/0`) and translate to the `ISP-A-Pool` address pool that you created earlier:

```
[edit security nat source rule-set Dept-A-to-ISP-A]
james@SRX5800-1# set rule ISP-A-PAT match source-address 0/0

[edit security nat source rule-set Dept-A-to-ISP-A]
james@SRX5800-1# set rule ISP-A-PAT then source-nat pool ISP-A-Pool
```

And now you create a separate source NAT rule-set for traffic from Dept-A to ISP-B:

```
[edit security nat source rule-set Dept-A-to-ISP-A]
james@SRX5800-1# up

[edit security nat source]
james@SRX5800-1# edit rule-set Dept-A-to-ISP-B

[edit security nat source rule-set Dept-A-to-ISP-B]
james@SRX5800-1# set from zone Dept-A

[edit security nat source rule-set Dept-A-to-ISP-B]
james@SRX5800-1# set to zone ISP-B
```

The NAT rule-set for traffic from Dept-A to ISP-B is configured to match all traffic (`source-address 0/0`) and translate to the `ISP-B-Pool` address pool created earlier:

```
[edit security nat source rule-set Dept-A-to-ISP-B]
james@SRX5800-1# set rule ISP-B-PAT match source-address 0/0

[edit security nat source rule-set Dept-A-to-ISP-B]
james@SRX5800-1# set rule ISP-B-PAT then source-nat pool ISP-B-Pool
```

Check your completed redundant ISP PAT configuration:

```
[edit security nat source rule-set Dept-A-to-ISP-B]
james@SRX5800-1# show | compare
[edit security nat source]
+ pool ISP-A-Pool {
+     address {
+         198.18.8.72/29;
+     }
+ }
+ pool ISP-B-Pool {
+     address {
+         198.18.130.48/29;
+     }
+ }
+ rule-set Dept-A-to-ISP-A {
+     from zone Dept-A;
+     to zone ISP-A;
+     rule ISP-A-PAT {
+         match {
+             source-address 0.0.0.0/0;
+         }
+         then {
+             source-nat {
+                 pool {
+                     ISP-A-Pool;
+                 }
+             }
+         }
+     }
+ }
+ rule-set Dept-A-to-ISP-B {
+     from zone Dept-A;
+     to zone ISP-B;
+     rule ISP-B-PAT {
+         match {
+             source-address 0.0.0.0/0;
+         }
+         then {
+             source-nat {
+                 pool {
+                     ISP-B-Pool;
+                 }
+             }
+         }
+     }
+ }
```

Everything looks good. Commit the configuration to complete your work:

```
[edit security nat source rule-set Dept-A-to-ISP-B]
james@SRX5800-1# commit and-quit
commit complete
Exiting configuration mode

james@SRX5800-1>
```

Conclusion

Our review of Source NAT on the SRX covered a very powerful set of tools for modifying the source IP addresses and TCP/UDP ports of IP packets. You learned about interface NAT, pool NAT (both with and without PAT), Proxy ARP, and persistent NAT. With these simple tools, you can now fulfill the great majority of real-world NAT needs. But not quite all. In the next sections, you will go on to learn about the two remaining pillars of NAT on SRX devices: destination NAT and static NAT.

Destination NAT

Destination NAT enables the translation of one destination address to another, a destination address and port to another destination address and port, or a group of destination addresses to another group of equal size. Figure 5-10 shows a simple example where a public IP address is mapped directly to a private internal IP address while maintaining the original port number.

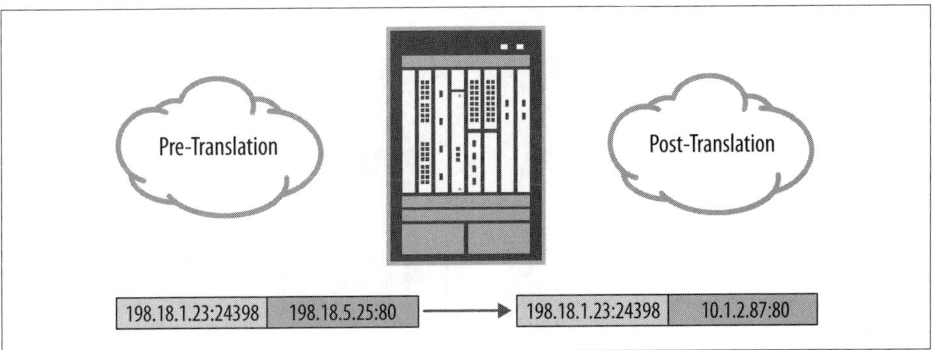

Figure 5-10. Destination NAT

Destination NAT in SRX Junos is a superset of ScreenOS VIP and security policy destination translations. Figure 5-11 shows the equivalent of a ScreenOS VIP translation where both the destination port and destination IP address are translated.

Destination NAT is most commonly used for hiding internal servers, migrating servers, or mapping different services on a single public address to multiple internal systems.

Figure 5-12 shows a snippet of our book's topology (see Figure P-1 in the Preface), the Internal-Servers network of Organization-XYZ and its path through the core SRX5800 cluster to the public Internet. In Chapter 3, the necessary security policies were configured to allow inbound Internet traffic to the Internal-Servers network's devices. But like Dept-A and Dept-B earlier, the IPv4 address space used for Internal-Servers is not globally routable. It is also private IPv4 address space as defined in RFC 1918.

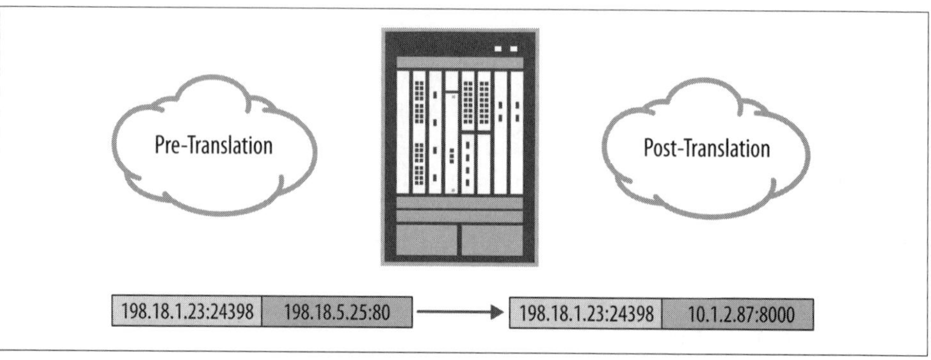

Figure 5-11. Destination NAT with PAT

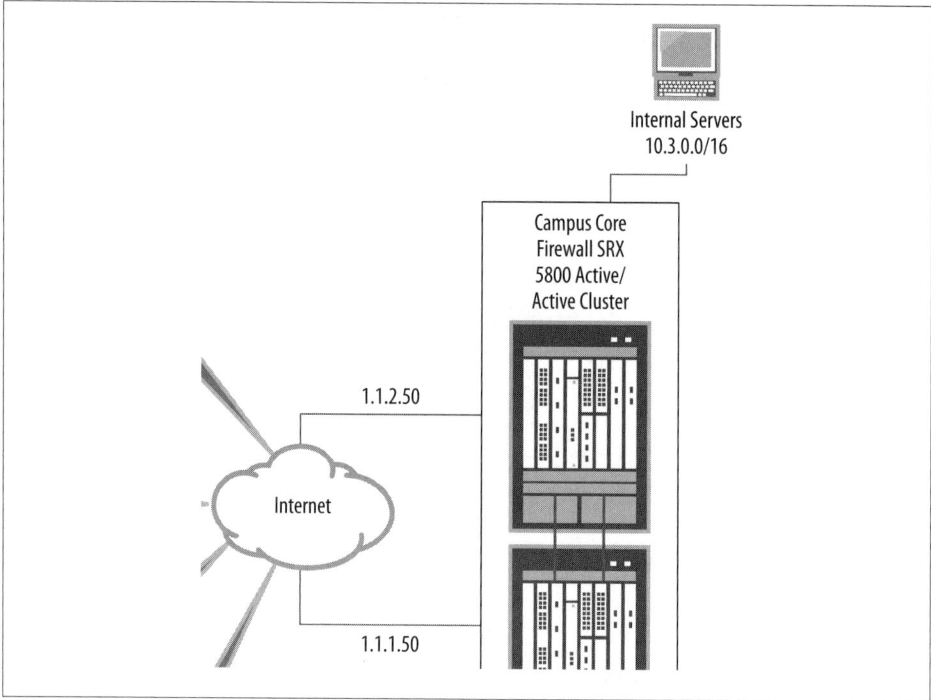

Figure 5-12. Destination NAT with PAT

So, here your sample configuration objective is to implement a basic destination NAT rule-set enabling global connectivity to the devices in the Internal-Servers network.

Implementing Destination NAT

Begin by entering configuration mode and moving the configuration prompt to the destination NAT hierarchy:

```
james@SRX5800-1> edit
Entering configuration mode

[edit]
james@SRX5800-1# edit security nat destination
```

Use the `set` command to create a destination NAT pool `serverPool` targeting a private 10.3.1.45 IP address on port 80:

```
[edit security nat destination]
james@SRX5800-1# set pool serverPool address 10.3.1.45/32 port 80
```

Move the configuration prompt to the `Internet` rule-set hierarchy:

```
[edit security nat destination]
james@SRX5800-1# edit rule-set Internet
```

And again use the `set` command to configure the new rule-set for traffic originated from the Inet zone:

```
[edit security nat destination rule-set Internet]
james@SRX5800-1# set from zone Inet
```

Destination NAT rule-sets do not use a `to` context as the destination route will not be determined until after the destination IP address translation has been completed.

Move the configuration prompt to the `serverNAT` rule hierarchy:

```
[edit security nat destination rule-set Internet]
james@SRX5800-1# edit rule serverNAT
```

Use the `set` command to configure the rule to match all possible source addresses:

```
[edit security nat destination rule-set Internet rule serverNAT]
james@SRX5800-1# set match source-address 0/0
```

And once again to configure the rule to match a destination address of 198.18.12.1 specifically:

```
[edit security nat destination rule-set Internet rule serverNAT]
james@SRX5800-1# set match destination-address 198.18.12.1/32
```

Now configure the rule to match a destination port of 80:

```
[edit security nat destination rule-set Internet rule serverNAT]
james@SRX5800-1# set match destination-port 80
```

And finally, use the `set` command to configure the rule for translation via the `serverPool` address pool defined earlier (10.3.1.45/32 port 80):

```
[edit security nat destination rule-set Internet rule serverNAT]
james@SRX5800-1# set then destination-nat pool serverPool
```

Now check your completed configuration changes:

```
[edit security nat destination rule-set Internet rule serverNAT]
james@SRX5800-1# show | compare
[edit security nat]
+    destination {
```

```
+         pool serverPool {
+             address 10.3.1.45/32 port 80;
+         }
+         rule-set Internet {
+             from zone Inet;
+             rule serverNAT {
+                 match {
+                     source-address 0.0.0.0/0;
+                     destination-address 198.18.12.1/32;
+                     destination-port 80;
+                 }
+                 then {
+                     destination-nat pool serverPool;
+                 }
+             }
+         }
+     }
```

Nice. Now `commit` the configuration so that the destination NAT rule-set takes effect:

```
[edit security nat destination rule-set Internet rule serverNAT]
james@SRX5800-1# commit and-quit
configuration check succeeds
commit complete
Exiting configuration mode

james@SRX5800-1>
```

Viewing Destination NAT

Now you view a flow translated by the new destination NAT rule-set:

```
james@SRX5800-1> show security flow session destination-port 80
Session ID: 2416, Policy name: webdmz_mgt/8, Timeout: 1794
  In: 198.18.11.100/50073 --> 198.18.12.1/80;tcp, If: ge-0/0/0.0
  Out: 10.3.1.45/80 --> 198.18.11.100/50073;tcp, If: ge-0/0/2.0

1 sessions displayed

james@SRX5800-1>
```

The output shows the flow initiated toward the 198.18.12.1 address on port 80 (matching the `serverNAT` rule configured earlier). The return direction of the flow (`Out`) is sourced from 10.3.1.45 on port 80 (the address and port pairing defined in the `serverPool` address pool). Now you drill down into the log for the session creation:

```
james@SRX5800-1> show log traffic-log
Jan 19 09:59:08  SRX210 RT_FLOW: RT_FLOW_SESSION_CREATE: session created
198.18.11.100/50073->198.18.12.1/80 junos-http 198.18.11.100/50073->10.3.1.45/80
None serverNAT 6 webdmz_mgt trust web-dmz 2416

james@SRX5800-1>
```

And as you can see, the log shows much of the same information as in the session table entry. The destination address and port are translated from 198.18.12.1 and 80 when entering the Inet zone interface, to 10.3.1.45 and 80 when leaving the Internal-Servers zone interface. The NAT rule performing the translation is also clearly shown (`server NAT`). Now you view the summary of the destination NAT configuration:

```
james@SRX5800-1> show security nat destination summary
Total pools: 1
Pool name       Address                         Routing       Port  Total
                Range                           Instance            Addres
serverPool      10.3.1.45      - 10.3.1.45      default       80    1

Total rules: 1
Rule name       Rule set       From             Action
serverNAT       Internet Internal-Servers       serverPool

james@SRX5800-1>
```

There is one rule named `serverNAT` within the Internet rule-set matching traffic from the Internal-Servers zone, which is then translated via the `serverPool` address pool containing the address 10.3.1.45 and port 80.

You examine the operational CLI output showing the destination NAT rule:

```
james@SRX5800-1> show security nat destination rule all
Total destination-nat rules: 1

Destination NAT rule: serverNAT            Rule-set: Internet
  Rule-Id                    : 1
  Rule position              : 1
  From zone                  : Internal-Servers
  Match
    Source addresses         : Any              - 255.255.255.255
    Destination addresses    : 198.18.12.1    - 198.18.12.1
  Action                     : serverPool
  Destination port           : 80
  Translation hits           : 2

james@SRX5800-1>
```

And here you see the `serverNAT` rule in the `Internet` rule-set matching traffic from the Internal-Servers zone with any source address and a 198.18.12.1 destination address and 80 destination port. This output shows that matching traffic is then translated via the `serverPool` address pool. Two flows have been translated via this rule thus far (`Translation hits : 2`). Now you take a look at the destination pool:

```
james@SRX5800-1> show security nat destination pool all
Total destination-nat pools: 1

Pool name       : serverPool
Pool id         : 1
Routing instance: default
Total address   : 1
Translation hits: 2
```

```
Address range                          Port
    10.3.1.45 - 10.3.1.45           80

james@SRX5800-1>
```

Here the output shows the destination NAT pool **serverPool** with an address of 10.3.1.45 and port of 80. Two flows have been translated via this pool thus far (`Translation hits: 2`).

Tracing Destination NAT Flows

And finally, here is the `security flow traceoptions` logfile output showing the first translated packet of this flow.

```
james@SRX5800-1> show log NATtrace | trim 41
<198.18.11.100/50073->198.18.12.1/80;6> matched filter NATfilter:
packet [64] ipid = 64159, @423f279e
---- flow_process_pkt: (thd 1): flow_ctxt type 13, common flag 0x0,
mbuf 0x423f2600
 flow process pak fast ifl 68 in_ifp ge-0/0/0.0
  ge-0/0/0.0:198.18.11.100/50073->198.18.12.1/80, tcp, flag 2 syn
 find flow: table 0x4d5c8220, hash 16311(0xffff), sa 198.18.11.100,
da 198.18.12.1, sp 50073, dp 80, proto 6, tok 384
  no session found, start first path. in_tunnel - 0, from_cp_flag - 0
check self-traffic on ge-0/0/0.0, in_tunnel 0x0
  flow_first_create_session
  flow_first_in_dst_nat: in <ge-0/0/0.0>, out <N/A> dst_adr 198.18.12.1,
sp 50073, dp 80
  chose interface ge-0/0/0.0 as incoming nat if.
flow_first_rule_dst_xlate:  DST xlate: 198.18.12.1(80) to 10.3.1.45(80),
rule/pool id 1/1.
```

The output shows the destination translation as the address 198.18.12.1 and port 80 are translated to 10.3.1.45 and 80. Note that the rule and pool identification numbers (`1` and `1`) match the same identification numbers shown for the **serverNAT** rule and `serverPool` address pool in the earlier operational CLI outputs. You examine a little more output:

```
flow_first_routing: call flow_route_lookup(): src_ip 198.18.11.100, x_dst_ip
10.3.1.45, in ifp ge-0/0/0.0, out ifp N/A sp 50073, dp 80, ip_proto 6, tos 10
Doing DESTINATION addr route-lookup
  routed (x_dst_ip 10.3.1.45) from Inet (ge-0/0/0.0 in 0) to ge-0/0/2.0,
Next-hop: 10.3.1.45
```

And you find that having translated the destination IP address of the packet, the SRX device now performs the destination route lookup on the translated 10.3.1.45 IP address. The next hop identified is the directly connected 10.3.1.45 server, reachable via the ge-0/0/2.0 interface.

Following the route lookup, the zones corresponding to the ingress and egress interfaces are identified (Inet zone to Internal-Servers zone):

```
policy search from zone Inet-> zone Internal-Servers
  policy has timeout 900
```

So, the policy chain can now be searched successfully as well.

```
app 6, timeout 1800s, curr ageout 20s
flow_first_src_xlate: 198.18.11.100/50073 -> 198.18.12.1/80 | 10.3.1.45/80 ->
0.0.0.0/50073: nat_src_xlated: False, nat_src_xlate_failed: False
flow_first_src_xlate: src nat 0.0.0.0(50073) to 10.3.1.45(80) returns status: 0,
rule/pool id: 0/0, pst_nat: False.
  dip id = 0/0, 198.18.11.100/50073->198.18.11.100/50073
flow_first_get_out_ifp: 1000 -> cone nat test
  choose interface ge-0/0/2.0 as outgoing phy if
is_loop_pak: No loop: on ifp: ge-0/0/2.0, addr: 10.3.1.45, rtt_idx:0
policy is NULL (wx/pim scenario)
sm_flow_interest_check: app_id 0, policy 8, app_svc_en 0, flags 0x2.
not interested
sm_flow_interest_check: app_id 1, policy 8, app_svc_en 0, flags 0x2.
not interested
flow_first_service_lookup(): natp(0x4b6dc1d0): local_pak(0x3fdedc70.0x423f2600):
TCP proxy NOT interested: 0.
  service lookup identified service 6.
  flow_first_final_check: in <ge-0/0/0.0>, out <ge-0/0/2.0>
flow_first_final_check: flow_set_xlate_vector.
  existing vector list 1002-446f8628.
  Session (id:2416) created for first pak 1002
  flow_first_install_session======> 0x4b6dc1d0
 nsp 0x4b6dc1d0, nsp2 0x4b6dc23c
  make_nsp_ready_no_resolve()
  route lookup: dest-ip 198.18.11.100 orig ifp ge-0/0/0.0 output_ifp ge-0/0/0.0
orig-zone 6 out-zone 6 vsd 0
  route to 198.18.11.100
```

And now your last look through the remaining output shows that both directions (`wings`) of the flow are installed successfully in the session table:

```
Installing c2s NP session wing
Installing s2c NP session wing
  flow got session.
  flow session id 2416
  tcp flags 0x2, flag 0x2
  Got syn, 198.18.11.100(50073)->198.18.12.1(80), nspflag 0x1021, 0x30
  post addr xlation: 198.18.11.100->10.3.1.45.
mbuf 0x423f2600, exit nh 0x50010
 ----- flow_process_pkt rc 0x0 (fp rc 0)
```

Here, the destination address and port translation from the configured `serverNAT` rule and `serverPool` pool have taken effect statefully for both directions of the conversation.

Case Study 5-2: Virtual IP NAT

For your case study on destination NAT, a common NAT scenario is inherited from the old ScreenOS VIP NAT feature. This is a destination NAT scenario where one public IP address (the virtual IP address) appears to offer multiple public services, but in reality is mapped to multiple function-specific internal servers, as shown in Figure 5-13.

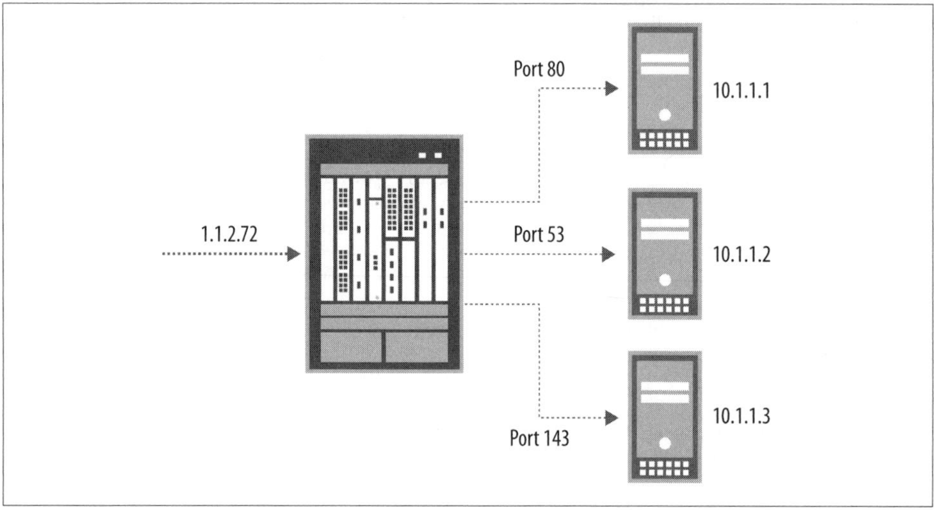

Figure 5-13. Virtual IP with NAT

This form of NAT allows best-of-breed servers to be leveraged for each server application, while one common face (the virtual IP) is maintained to the public Internet community.

For your case study, you'll configure the virtual IP scenario shown in Figure 5-13 from the Junos CLI.

Implementing VIP NAT

You begin by entering configuration mode and creating the destination NAT address pool for the internal HTTP server (`HTTP-VIP`):

```
james@SRX5800-1> edit
Entering configuration mode

[edit]
james@SRX5800-1# edit security nat destination

[edit security nat destination]
james@SRX5800-1# set pool HTTP-VIP address 10.1.1.1 port 80
```

Create the destination NAT address pool for the internal DNS server (`DNS-VIP`):

```
[edit security nat destination]
james@SRX5800-1# set pool DNS-VIP address 10.1.1.2 port 53
```

Create the destination NAT address pool for the internal IMAP server (`IMAP-VIP`):

```
[edit security nat destination]
james@SRX5800-1# set pool IMAP-VIP address 10.1.1.3 port 143
```

Create the new destination NAT rule-set (`Virtual-IP`) for traffic initiated from the Inet zone:

```
[edit security nat destination]
james@SRX5800-1# edit rule-set Virtual-IP

[edit security nat destination rule-set Virtual-IP]
james@SRX5800-1# set from zone Inet
```

Create a new destination NAT rule for mapping HTTP traffic destined to the public IP address through to the private HTTP server:

```
[edit security nat destination rule-set Virtual-IP]
james@SRX5800-1# set rule HTTP match destination-address 198.18.5.72

[edit security nat destination rule-set Virtual-IP]
james@SRX5800-1# set rule HTTP match destination-port 80

[edit security nat destination rule-set Virtual-IP]
james@SRX5800-1# set rule HTTP then destination-nat pool HTTP-VIP
```

Create a new destination NAT rule for mapping DNS traffic destined to the public IP address through to the private DNS server:

```
[edit security nat destination rule-set Virtual-IP]
james@SRX5800-1# set rule DNS match destination-address 198.18.5.72

[edit security nat destination rule-set Virtual-IP]
james@SRX5800-1# set rule DNS match destination-port 53

[edit security nat destination rule-set Virtual-IP]
james@SRX5800-1# set rule DNS then destination-nat pool DNS-VIP
```

Finally, create a new destination NAT rule for mapping IMAP traffic destined to the public IP address through to the private IMAP server:

```
[edit security nat destination rule-set Virtual-IP]
james@SRX5800-1# set rule IMAP match destination-address 198.18.5.72

[edit security nat destination rule-set Virtual-IP]
james@SRX5800-1# set rule IMAP match destination-port 143

[edit security nat destination rule-set Virtual-IP]
james@SRX5800-1# set rule IMAP then destination-nat pool IMAP-VIP
```

Examine your destination NAT configuration changes:

```
[edit security nat destination rule-set Virtual-IP]
james@SRX5800-1# show | compare
[edit security nat destination]
```

```
+ pool HTTP-VIP {
+     address 10.1.1.1/32 port 80;
+ }
+ pool DNS-VIP {
+     address 10.1.1.2/32 port 53;
+ }
+ pool IMAP-VIP {
+     address 10.1.1.3/32 port 143;
+ }
+ rule-set Virtual-IP {
+     from zone Inet;
+     rule HTTP {
+         match {
+             destination-address 198.18.5.72/32;
+             destination-port 80;
+         }
+         then {
+             destination-nat pool HTTP-VIP;
+         }
+     }
+     rule DNS {
+         match {
+             destination-address 198.18.5.72/32;
+             destination-port 53;
+         }
+         then {
+             destination-nat pool DNS-VIP;
+         }
+     }
+     rule IMAP {
+         match {
+             destination-address 198.18.5.72/32;
+             destination-port 143;
+         }
+         then {
+             destination-nat pool IMAP-VIP;
+         }
+     }
+ }
```

That should do the trick. Now you can `commit` and go get a drink!

```
[edit security nat destination rule-set Virtual-IP]
james@SRX5800-1# commit and-quit
commit complete
Exiting configuration mode

james@SRX5800-1>
```

Static NAT

Static NAT enables the translation of flows initiated both to and from a configured address or range of addresses. It accomplishes in one rule-set what would otherwise require a combination of separate source and destination NAT rule-sets. Static

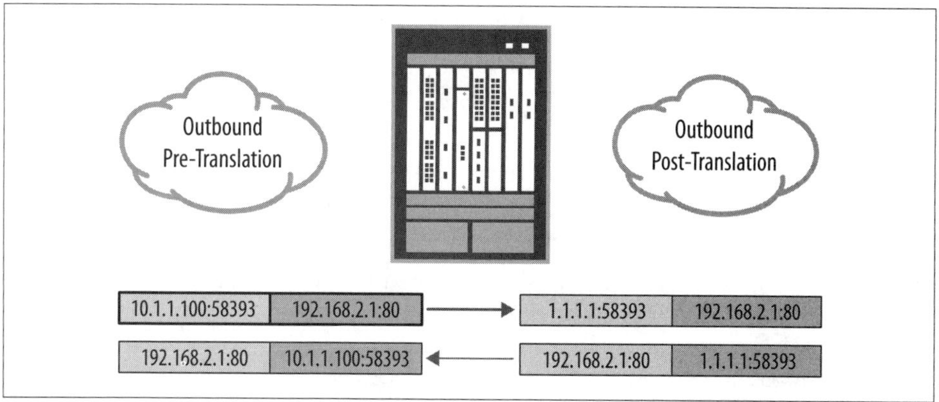

Figure 5-14. Static NAT

translations are always between one address and another address, or one range of addresses and another of equal size. In other words, static NAT requires a one-to-one correspondence between the pre-translation and post-translation addresses. Thus, static NAT provides a simple and effective method of migrating systems to new address space.

Figure 5-14 shows this bidirectional nature of static NAT, where a given host's IP address is translated whether it is initiating communication outbound or whether it is receiving communication initiated from elsewhere inbound.

Static NAT in the SRX is a superset of ScreenOS MIP configuration.

Now you will walk through an example creating a static NAT rule-set that statically translates flows originating from the Inet zone and destined to a specific /24 network.

First enter configuration mode and move the configuration prompt to the static NAT rule-set hierarchy in Junos:

```
james@SRX5800-1> edit
Entering configuration mode

[edit]
james@SRX5800-1# edit security nat static rule-set Internet
```

Now use the `set` command to configure the new static NAT rule-set for traffic originated from the Internal-Servers zone:

```
[edit security nat static rule-set Internet]
james@SRX5800-1# set from zone Inet
```

Move the configuration prompt to the static NAT rule hierarchy:

```
[edit security nat static rule-set Internet]
james@SRX5800-1# edit rule 1to1NAT
```

Use the `set` command to match your new rule to flows destined toward the 198.18.31.0/24 address range (the public addresses of this particular static NAT):

```
[edit security nat static rule-set Internet rule 1to1NAT]
james@SRX5800-1# set match destination-address 198.18.31.0/24
```

And now configure the rule to translate matched traffic to the private 10.3.10.0/24 prefix:

```
[edit security nat static rule-set Internet rule 1to1NAT]
james@SRX5800-1# set then static-nat prefix 10.3.10/24
```

These last two commands have created a direct static NAT correspondence between 1.1.1.0/24 and 10.3.10.0/24. Flows initiated toward a destination of 1.1.1.1 will translate to a destination of 10.3.10.1 (and vice versa: flows initiated from 10.3.10.1 will be translated to a source of 1.1.1.1). And the same correspondence continues through the range. Flows initiated toward 1.1.1.200 will be translated to 10.3.10.200 (and vice versa: flows initiated from 10.3.10.200 will be translated to a source of 1.1.1.200).

Now check your completed static NAT configuration:

```
 [edit security nat static rule-set Internet rule 1to1NAT]
james@SRX5800-1# show | compare
[edit security nat]
+    static {
+        rule-set Internet {
+            from zone Inet;
+            rule 1to1NAT {
+                match {
+                    destination-address 198.18.31.0/24;
+                }
+                then {
+                    static-nat prefix 10.3.10.0/24;
+                }
+            }
+        }
+    }
```

And `commit` to the active configuration on the SRX device:

```
[edit security nat static rule-set Internet rule 1to1NAT]
james@SRX5800-1# commit and-quit
commit complete
Exiting configuration mode
```

You view your new static NAT rule here in the Junos operational CLI:

```
james@SRX5800-1> show security nat static rule all
Total static-nat rules: 1

Static NAT rule: 1to1NAT              Rule-set: Internet
  Rule-Id                    : 1
```

```
Rule position              : 3
From zone                  : Inet
Destination addresses      : 198.18.31.0
Host addresses             : 10.3.10.0
Netmask                    : 255.255.255.0
Host routing-instance      : N/A
Translation hits           : 41859
```

Case Study 5-3: Double NAT

Double NAT occurs when both the source IP address and destination IP address leave the translating system changed. Double NAT is commonly used for merging two networks with overlapping address space. This has become an increasingly common scenario as more organizations have moved to using RFC 1918 private address space for their internal addressing in an effort to overcome public IPv4 address exhaustion. When these organizations merge, they are left with overlapping RFC 1918 addressing. In these cases, double NAT must be leveraged until systems can be readdressed.

Figure 5-15 shows a double NAT scenario where the source client and destination server share the identical IP address configuration. This seemingly impossible communication scenario is made quite possible by double NAT.

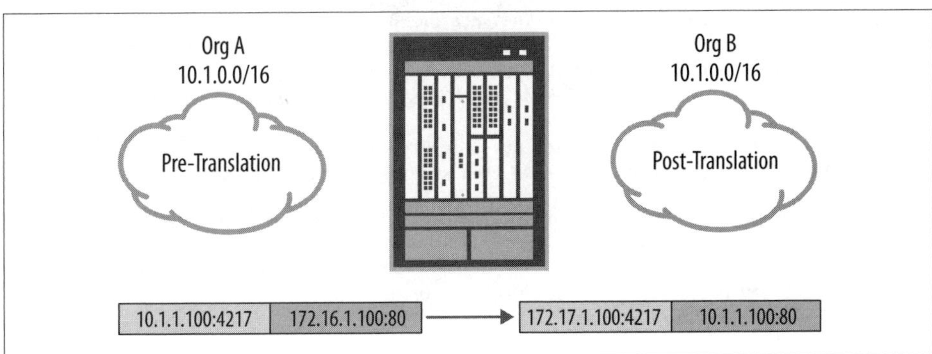

Figure 5-15. Double NAT

For this double NAT case study, you will create a double NAT configuration facilitating communication between `Org-A` and `Org-B` routing instances with overlapping 10.1.0.0/16 IP address space.

Enter configuration mode and create a new rule-set for traffic originated in the `Org-A` routing instance:

```
james@SRX5800-1> edit
Entering configuration mode

[edit]
james@SRX5800-1# edit security nat static rule-set Org-A-to-Org-B
```

```
[edit security nat static rule-set Org-A-to-Org-B]
james@SRX5800-1# set from routing-instance Org-A
```

Configure a rule-set matching traffic destined to the public IP address range designated for `Org-B` (172.31.0.0/16) and translate it to the overlapping private address range (10.1.0.0/16) for communication with the real `Org-B` hosts:

```
[edit security nat static rule-set Org-A-to-Org-B]
james@SRX5800-1# set rule Orb-B-hide match destination-address 172.31/16

[edit security nat static rule-set Org-A-to-Org-B]
james@SRX5800-1# set rule Orb-B-hide then static-nat prefix 10.1/16
```

Now use the `up` command to move your configuration prompt and create a new rule-set matching traffic destined to the public IP address range designated for `Org-A` (172.30.0.0/16) and translate it to the overlapping private address range (10.1.0.0/16), for communication with the real `Org-A` hosts:

```
[edit security nat static rule-set Org-A-to-Org-B]
james@SRX5800-1# up

[edit security nat static]
james@SRX5800-1# edit rule-set Org-B-to-Org-A

[edit security nat static rule-set Org-B-to-Org-A]
james@SRX5800-1# set from routing-instance Org-B

[edit security nat static rule-set Org-B-to-Org-A]
james@SRX5800-1# set rule Org-A-hide match destination-address 172.30/16

[edit security nat static rule-set Org-B-to-Org-A]
james@SRX5800-1# set rule Org-A-hide then static-nat prefix 10.1/16
```

As always, it is best to review your configuration before making it active on your SRX device:

```
[edit security nat static rule-set Org-B-to-Org-A]
james@SRX5800-1# show | compare
[edit security]
+   nat {
+       static {
+           rule-set Org-A-to-Org-B {
+               from routing-instance Org-A;
+               rule Orb-B-hide {
+                   match {
+                       destination-address 172.31.0.0/16;
+                   }
+                   then {
+                       static-nat prefix 10.1.0.0/16;
+                   }
+               }
+           }
+           rule-set Org-B-to-Org-A {
+               from routing-instance Org-B;
+               rule Org-A-hide {
```

```
+                   match {
+                       destination-address 172.30.0.0/16;
+                   }
+                   then {
+                       static-nat prefix 10.1.0.0/16;
+                   }
+               }
+           }
+       }
+   }
[edit]
+  routing-instances {
+      Org-A {
+          instance-type virtual-router;
+      }
+      Org-B {
+          instance-type virtual-router;
+      }
+  }
```

Your careful review has approved the double NAT configuration and you `commit` to the active configuration on your SRX device. You can now move on to concluding this chapter with a review and some study questions.

```
[edit security nat static rule-set Org-B-to-Org-A]
james@SRX5800-1# commit and-quit
commit complete
Exiting configuration mode

james@SRX5800-1>
```

Summary

You covered a lot of ground in this chapter implementing an array of source, destination, and static address translations on SRX devices. You are now empowered to solve a wide array of address translation projects in the real world.

Whether grappling with the global challenge of IPv4 address exhaustion, the more local challenge of corporate mergers, or simply implementing unique server DMZs in a data center, you now have the tools to solve these challenges with grace and ease.

Chapter Review Questions

1. What is NAT?
2. What is source NAT?
3. What is destination NAT?
4. What is static NAT?
5. What is PAT?

6. What is a pool?
7. What type of NAT hides hosts behind an interface address in Junos for the SRX?
8. What type of NAT is best used for overcoming IPv4 address exhaustion?
9. What type of NAT is best used for hiding servers in a data center?
10. What type of NAT is best used for integrating overlapping privately addressed networks during corporate mergers?

Chapter Review Answers

1. NAT stands for Network Address Translation. It is the translation of IP addresses and TCP/UDP ports in the headers of IP packets.
2. Source NAT is the translation of source IP addresses and TCP/UDP ports in the headers of IP packets.
3. Destination NAT is the translation of destination IP addresses and TCP/UDP ports in the headers of IP packets.
4. Static NAT is the symmetrical translation of flows for a given IP prefix whether it is initiating the flows as the source, or receiving them as the destination.
5. PAT stands for Port Address Translation. It is a subset of NAT where TCP/UDP ports are translated. The most typical variant of PAT is *source PAT* where a larger private source address range is overloaded to a smaller public address range. This is typically accomplished through PAT overloading. PAT overloading occurs when more than one private IP address shares the same public IP address. This is achieved by using different TCP/UDP ports of the same public IP address.
6. A pool is an IP prefix, IP range, or collection of IP prefixes and/or IP ranges that can be used for translating either the source or destination IP addresses in the headers of IP packets. Pools may also define TCP/UDP port ranges for PAT.
7. Interface NAT is accomplished through the source NAT feature set in Junos for the SRX.
8. Source NAT is best used for overcoming IPv4 address exhaustion by hiding the source IP addresses of privately addressed hosts behind one or more public IP addresses.
9. Destination NAT is the most effective tool for hiding the real IP addresses of systems providing services for other devices on the network.
10. Static NAT is the most effective tool for integrating overlapping private IP address ranges. Static NAT can most easily be applied to large IP prefixes where hosts will need to both initiate and receive translated traffic.

CHAPTER 6

IPsec VPN

The SRX product suite combines the robust IP Security virtual private network (IPsec VPN) features from ScreenOS into the legendary networking platform of Junos. IPsec VPNs have become a central component of modern computer networks for securing the data between different sites and remote users. As more critical applications and sensitive information has been transferred into electronic format, the demand to secure this information has grown. IPsec VPNs are sometimes confused with Layer 2 or Layer 3 VPNs which do not actually encrypt the data, but rather tunnel the traffic that flows through the VPNs; however, IPsec VPNs are VPNs that provide encryption and authentication to secure traffic. In the past, IPsec VPNs were widely used out of convenience to securely deliver data between sites, and also to provide remote access for mobile users. After numerous high-profile security breaches resulting in the compromise of sensitive data, many regulations (PCI, SOX, HIPAA) have been enacted to help prevent such incidents. Although the high-profile data breaches were not the result of compromise from a lack of IPsec VPNs, many of these regulations require that data is encrypted in transit and at rest. Since VPNs satisfy the encryption of data in transit, they have been widely deployed for this purpose.

There are two high-level uses for IPsec VPNs: to secure data between two or more computer networks, and to secure data between a remote user and a computer network. This chapter details the technologies behind both site-to-site and remote access VPNs and how these technologies are implemented on the SRX. After a thorough discussion of the technology and the implementation of the IPsec VPNs on the SRX, we will examine verification and troubleshooting features and conclude with some case studies to provide you with a few real-world implementation examples.

VPN Architecture Overview

VPNs not only secure communication between two devices, but they also create a virtual channel that data can traverse. In this section, we will examine two primary VPN architectures: site-to-site and remote access. Although the underlying technologies are essentially the same, the manner in which the VPNs interconnect varies between the different models.

Site-to-Site IPsec VPNs

Site-to-site IPsec VPNs connect two sites together to allow for secure communication between the two sites, as shown in Figure 6-1. Site-to-site VPNs are most often deployed to secure data between sites in an organization, or between an organization and a partner organization. Site-to-site VPNs are more common over the Internet than across private networks; however, many organizations are encrypting data between sites on private networks, to secure the communication. Internet site-to-site VPNs also offer a cost and availability benefit over private site-to-site links, making them a good choice for securing data, especially when performance is not a major concern. The Internet site-to-site VPNs may also serve as a backup link to private links, in the event the private link should fail. There are a couple of variations of site-to-site VPNs besides the direct site-to-site architecture; these include hub and spoke, full mesh, and multipoint VPNs.

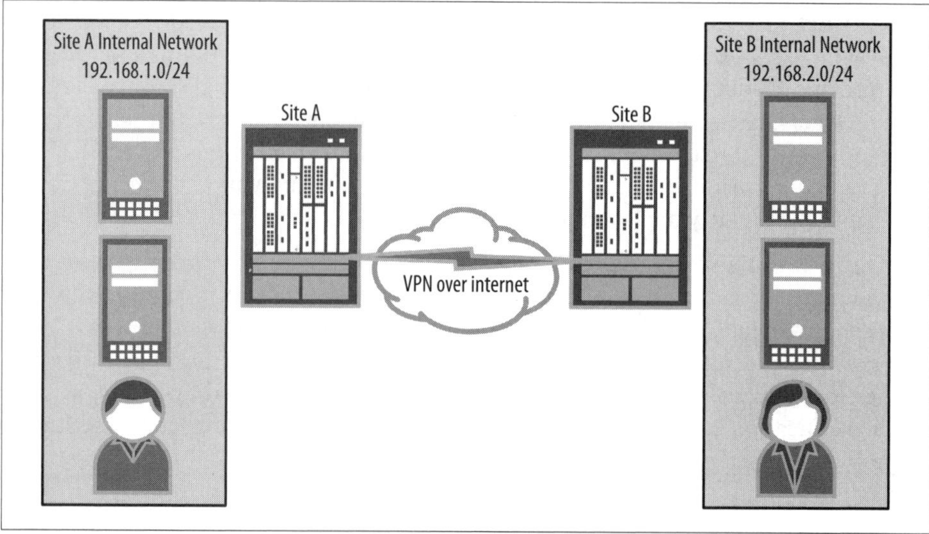

Figure 6-1. Sample site-to-site VPN

Hub and Spoke IPsec VPNs

Many enterprise networks have one or more large offices, with multiple branch offices. In some cases, branch offices need to access resources in all other branches; in other cases, they may only need to access resources in the central sites. In the latter case, hub and spoke VPN networks provide a simple method of accomplishing this goal, as illustrated in Figure 6-2. Each remote site connects into the central site, but they do not connect into each other directly; rather, they connect through the central site, hence the hub and spoke moniker.

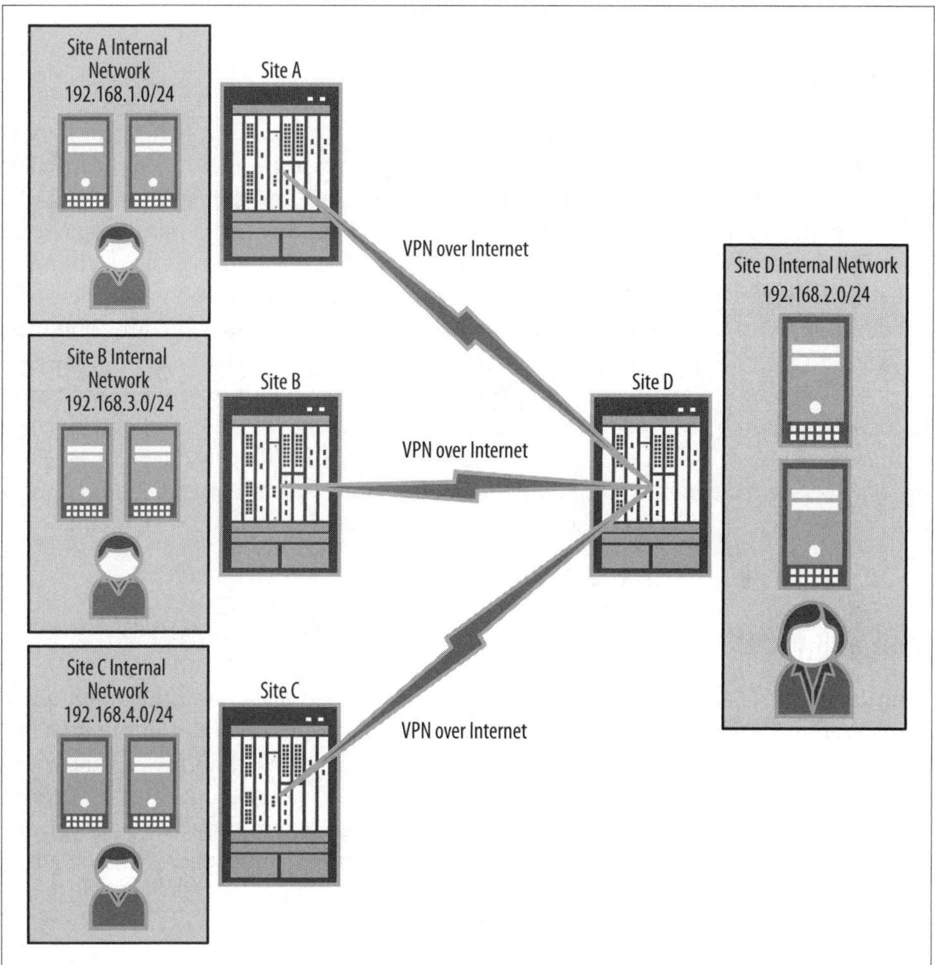

Figure 6-2. Sample hub and spoke VPN

From a management perspective, hub and spoke networks are straightforward to administer since all spokes connect to the hub. They are easy to scale because there is a minimum amount of state that must be maintained. (Only *N* VPNs must be maintained, where *N* is the number of VPNs, or remote sites; full mesh VPNs, which we will discuss next, require $N(N - 1)/2$ VPNs. This means that with 10 remote sites, only 10 VPNs would need to be maintained in a hub and spoke network, whereas 25 would need to be maintained in a full mesh network.) And finally, it is much easier to secure hub and spoke networks, as well as provide services for each connected network, because the security and services can be administered centrally at the hub rather than occurring at all of the spokes (this, as you can imagine, equates to cost savings).

Full Mesh VPNs

Although hub and spoke VPNs might be commonplace because of their simplicity, there are a few factors that might make this model undesirable for your particular network. First, all traffic must go from the spoke to the hub and then to the other spoke when trying to send traffic between spokes. This can result in a lag in performance and can cause latency issues, as the hub site must process all of the traffic. This is a common issue in modern networks that run real-time applications such as VoIP and video conferencing, which are sensitive to bandwidth and latency issues and generally work better when the sites can communicate directly with each other. Therefore, full mesh is most typically implemented for connecting remote offices *within* an organization (and is not so common between *separate* organizations) because it allows each site to communicate directly with all other sites, as shown in Figure 6-3. The disadvantages of full mesh VPNs are the complexity of implementation (since all sites must be interconnected), the inability to scale, and the management overhead associated with maintaining all of the VPNs.

Multipoint VPNs

Multipoint VPNs are a hybrid of hub and spoke and full mesh, and they attempt to combine the advantages of each model, as depicted in Figure 6-4. In multipoint VPNs, some spokes also have direct connections between each other to improve bandwidth and latency without constricting the hub site. Suffice it to say that multipoint VPNs do have some different mechanisms to establish themselves dynamically; they are typically implemented to connect remote offices with the hub, and in some cases with each other, within an organization.

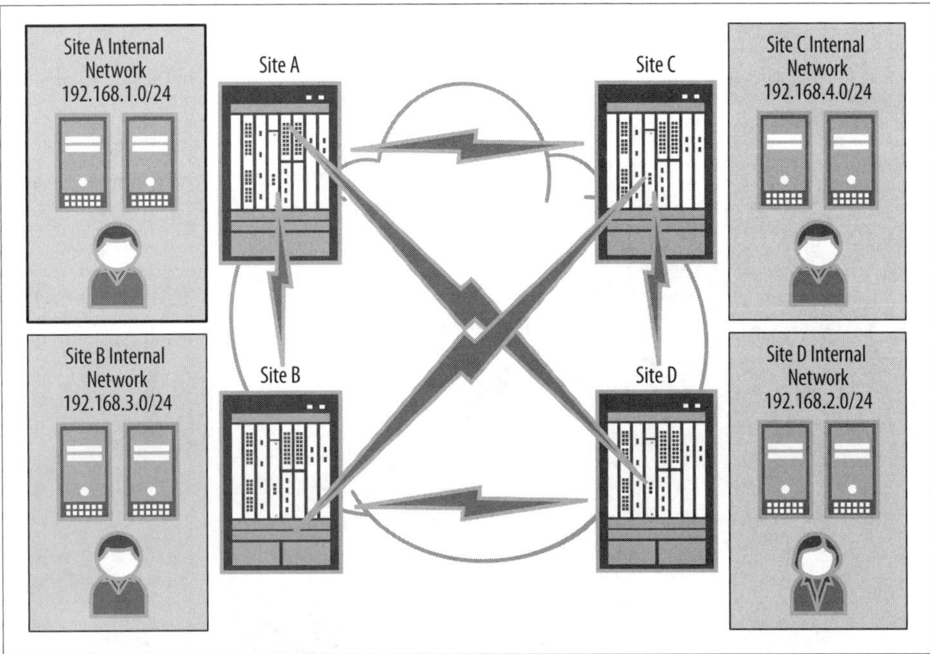

Figure 6-3. Sample full mesh VPN

The obvious advantage of multipoint VPNs is that the remote offices still connect to the hub, but also can connect to each other. This is common in environments with some real-time applications that may need to connect to each other for performance reasons. When a VPN must be established between spokes, the spokes negotiate the connections dynamically, and shut the VPNs down after the communication has ceased.

ScreenOS supported an example of multipoint VPNs, called auto-connect VPNs (AC-VPNs). At the time of this writing, the SRX does not support AC-VPNs.

Remote Access VPNs

Whereas site-to-site VPNs commonly connect sites together, another form of IPsec VPN allows a remote user to connect to a true site for remote access. The underlying technologies of site-to-site and remote access IPsec VPNs are essentially the same; the main difference is that a site-to-site VPN is typically terminated between two VPN gateways, such as two SRX platforms. There is no requirement for software on any of the end systems. In fact, the end systems do not have to be aware that there is a VPN at all; the VPN is completely transparent to the end systems, the applications, and the

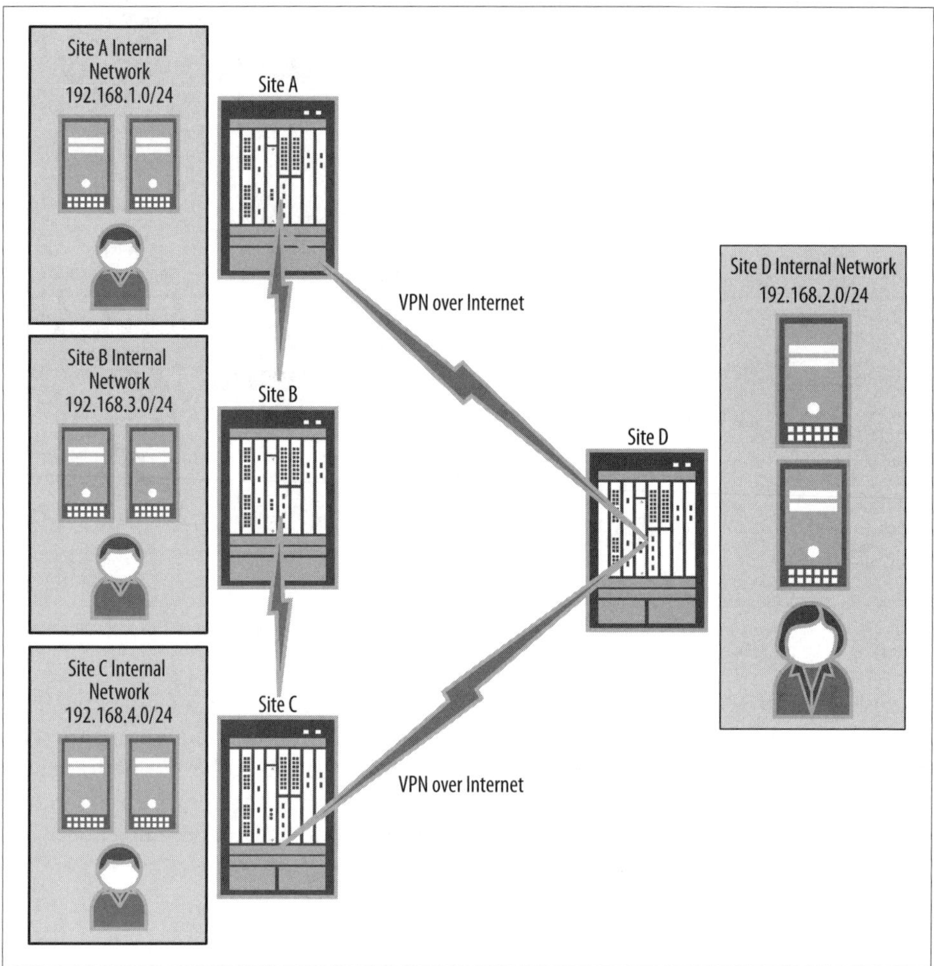

Figure 6-4. Sample multipoint VPN

users. The problem is that site-to-site VPNs are not always possible to implement because of the requirement for the additional hardware. To help alleviate this requirement, and empower remote users to be able to access corporate resources, remote access VPNs are used to provide this functionality.

Remote access VPNs are created by running software on the end systems which will establish a VPN to the central site VPN gateway such as an SRX, as shown in Figure 6-5.

Remote access VPNs are commonly available in two forms: IPsec VPNs and SSL VPNs. Although the functionality is essentially transparent to the user, there are differences between IPsec VPNs and SSL VPNs:

IPsec VPNs
: IPsec VPNs utilize underlying Layer 3 encryption to establish secure VPNs between a host and VPN gateway. The user traffic may or may not be tunneled, and IPsec processing is optimized for processing network traffic. IPsec VPNs also are considered to have the strongest security of any kind of remote access.

SSL VPNs
: SSL VPNs are widely deployed for their simplicity, in part because they often utilize the Secure Sockets Layer (SSL) of a web browser (although SSL VPNs may also use separate applications to process this traffic as well). SSL VPNs (including the Juniper Networks Secure Access SSL VPN Gateway) gained popularity because of their interoperability with end systems and their ability to function within most networks.

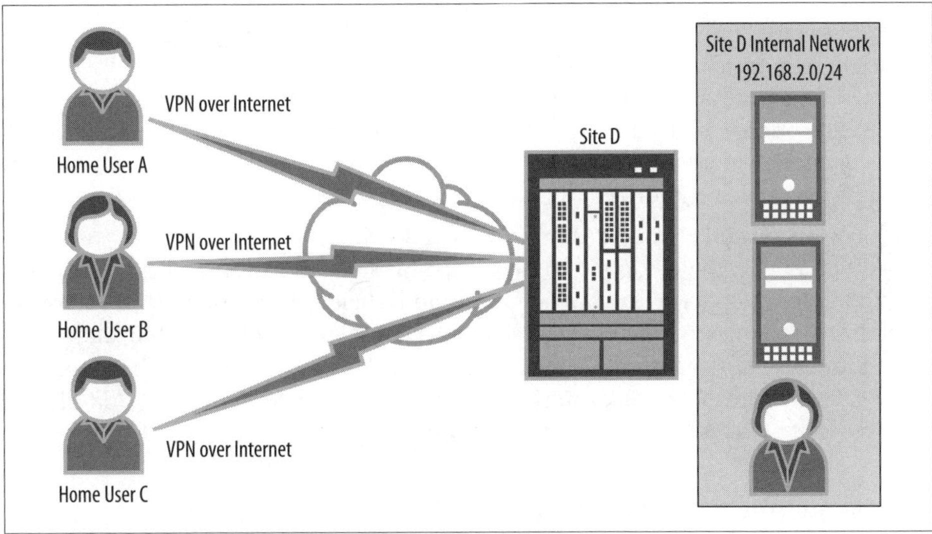

Figure 6-5. Sample remote access VPN

IPsec VPN Concepts Overview

IPsec VPNs come in many different flavors and support a multitude of configuration options in order to adapt to the needs of various networks while securing the data which travels in the VPN. This adaptive variation, and the fact that IPsec VPNs are popularly deployed, demand that we take a little time to demystify these options and provide you with some insight into how the different features can be used.

IPsec Encryption Algorithms

Encryption serves VPNs by obfuscating unencrypted traffic into a form that only the two sides of the VPN can understand. The SRX supports the use of the following standards-based encryption algorithms for this purpose. (For the sake of brevity, we have condensed our explanation of how the different encryption algorithms actually function, and instead we examine the strength and performance impact.)

Data Encryption Standard (DES)
: DES was one of the first widely deployed encryption algorithms for IPsec. It is lightweight in terms of processing power; thus, this algorithm is more susceptible to brute force attacks since there is not as large of a key space to encrypt the traffic. It's largely been replaced with the newer encryption algorithms of 3DES and AES. Best security practices tend for DES not to be used unless security is not a concern, and only basic encryption is desired.

Triple Data Encryption Standard (3DES)
: 3DES is a more powerful version of DES and subjects the data to additional rounds of encryption, making it more difficult to identify clear-text traffic. Although 3DES does require more processing power than DES, it is considered to be a safe algorithm to implement for data that is of medium sensitivity.

Advanced Encryption Standard (AES)
: AES is an encryption algorithm developed by the National Institute of Standards and Technology (NIST) to provide secure and efficient encryption for very sensitive data. AES comes in different key bit lengths, most commonly 128, 256, and 384—the longer the key length the more secure the data. Note also that the longer the key length, the more processing power is required to encrypt the data. AES should be used to encrypt the most sensitive traffic.

IPsec Authentication Algorithms

IPsec authentication, also known as *hashing*, protects the authenticity of the source of the encryption traffic. Without authentication, the two VPN endpoints would be unable to ensure that the traffic arrived unmodified, or even that it came from its original source. IPsec authentication performs this task by using a hashing algorithm. A hashing algorithm essentially calculates a special value based on the data which it hashes. Even a change of a single bit of data results in a completely different hash result. Also, a hash algorithm is meant to be nonreversible, so if an attacker had the result of the hash algorithm, it would still be difficult for him to determine the original contents. Although there is a possibility that two or more data sets could produce the same hash result, this is very unlikely, and even if there is a collision whereby two values create the same hash, it is unlikely that the two data sets would be interchangeable in clear-text form.

The SRX supports three different hash algorithms to provide IPsec authentication:

Message-Digest algorithm 5
: MD5 is a widely deployed hash algorithm that consists of a 128-bit hash space. Although acceptable as a hashing algorithm, it is not recommended for the most sensitive applications.

Secure Hash Algorithm 1
: SHA-1 is an improvement over MD5, using a more robust algorithm with a larger key space (168-bit) to provide more security over MD5. SHA-1 is recommended for sensitive data that needs more powerful security than MD5. SHA-1 is slowly being replaced with the new SHA-2 algorithm, although deployment of SHA-2, at the time of this writing, is not common.

Secure Hash Algorithm 2
: SHA-2 is a very powerful secure hash algorithm which is supported on the SRX. It uses a larger key space than both MD5 and SHA-1 to provide maximum security, and also has some modifications to help maximize performance and security.

IKE Version 1 Overview

IPsec can establish a VPN in one of two ways: via the Internet Key Exchange (IKE) protocol or via manual key exchange. Manual key exchange is exactly that: both sides exchange the keys in some manual fashion (e.g., phone or email), and once everything is configured the VPN can be established. IKE is a more involved process that negotiates the VPN between both VPN endpoints. It should be strongly noted that using IKE to negotiate VPNs between two endpoints is much more common and much more secure than manual key exchange. IKE allows both sides to renegotiate VPNs on the fly so that the encryption keys are constantly changing, making it more difficult for an eavesdropper to compromise the security of the network. Manual keys do not change (or at least not automatically), so if the keys are somehow determined, administrative intervention must take place to change the keys.

Two versions of the IKE standard are available: IKE version 1 and IKE version 2.

This book will focus on IKE version 1, as IKE version 2 is not supported by the SRX at the time of this writing (although it is supported in ScreenOS as of version 6.1).

Further, IKE negotiation takes place in two phases, known as Phase 1 and Phase 2. The purpose of Phase 1 is to authenticate the identities of both sides of the VPN, and to establish a secure communication channel between both sides for further negotiation. In Phase 2, the remainder of the VPN negotiation process completes, and the encryption keys are exchanged to be used to secure the data that traverses the VPN.

Let's drill down just a little into Phase 1 and Phase 2 of IKE version 1 negotiations just to ensure that you understand the process. Numerous options may be implemented, and those options will be examined further in "Phase 1 IKE Negotiations" on page 259.

IKE Phase 1

IKE Phase 1 is responsible for establishing a secure communication channel through which to negotiate the VPN encryption keys. During this process, different messages are exchanged between the two VPN gateways, depending on whether Phase 1 is negotiated in Main mode or in Aggressive mode (to be detailed shortly). In Phase 1, three events take place, along with optional exchanges depending on the configuration. The actual negotiation itself will vary depending on whether Main mode or Aggressive mode is used.

1. The encryption and authentication algorithms to be used are negotiated to secure the communication.
2. A secure communication channel is established using Diffie-Hellman key exchange.
3. The peer's identity is authenticated using either the preshared key or certificates, along with the IKE identity.
4. Phase 1 will also negotiate various options such as Network Address Translation traversal (NAT-T) and Dead Peer Detection (DPD).

During these initial Phase 1 IKE negotiations, a secure channel must be established between the two VPN peers; however, a question may arise: how do you form a secure communication channel that can be negotiated over an insecure network? The answer is to use the Diffie-Hellman key exchange method. The intimate details of this exchange are beyond the scope of this book and are not necessary to understand VPN configuration. Suffice it to say that essentially, Diffie-Hellman key exchange uses public key encryption whereby each party shares each other's public keys, while retaining the private keys. They then encrypt the authentication parameter (e.g., password) and send it to the other peer, which decrypts it with their private key. This happens in both directions. If both peers cannot successfully authenticate the other peer, Phase 1 cannot be established.

Diffie-Hellman *groups* refer to the size of the key length used for negotiating the VPN. There are several different groups, not all of which are supported by all vendors. When setting up a VPN with another party, the Diffie-Hellman groups must match on both peers; otherwise, the VPN connection will not establish, and error messages should detail the failure. The larger the key length, the stronger it is considered to be, because there are more possibilities for bit combinations. For instance, a 1-bit key would have two values, 0 and 1. A 2-bit key would have four values, 0, 1, 2, and 3, which in binary is 00, 01, 10, and 11. Therefore, the larger the key, the more possibilities for different keys and the more difficult it is to guess the correct key used for encryption. Consider these three groups and their escalating strength:

Group 1: 768-bit strength
Group 2: 1,024-bit strength
Group 5: 1,536-bit strength

IKE Phase 2

IKE Phase 2 is responsible for generating the encryption keys used to encrypt the data traffic within the VPN. Just like in Phase 1, messages are exchanged between the two VPN gateways, and there are some similarities. Unlike Phase 1, however, there is only one negotiation mode, called Quick mode. In Quick mode, the following events always occur during Phase 2:

1. The encryption and authentication algorithms to be used to encrypt the data traffic are negotiated.
2. The method to be used to encrypt the data traffic is negotiated: either Encapsulating Security Payload (ESP) or Authentication Header (AH).
3. Proxy IDs which identify the traffic to be encrypted are negotiated.
4. Phase 2 optional processing, including Perfect Forward Secrecy (PFS), is negotiated.

Do not confuse IKE Phase 1 and Phase 2 with IKE version 1 and version 2. As mentioned, IKE version 1 is the only version that is supported on the SRX at the time of this writing. Version 2 is supported by ScreenOS, and the SRX will support this in the future.

IPSec VPN Protocol

Two different VPN protocols can be used for IPsec VPNs, regardless of what IKE parameters are used to establish the VPN. The two protocols are Encapsulating Security Payload (ESP) and Authentication Header (AH):

ESP
: This performs encryption and authentication on the traffic within the VPN, thus protecting the confidentiality of the traffic within the VPN. It also authenticates the data within the VPN, ensuring that it has not been modified and that it originated from the correct source.

AH
: This protocol does not encrypt the traffic within the VPN, but simply authenticates the traffic to ensure that it came from the correct source, and has not been modified.

ESP is much more widely deployed than AH, because typically, organizations want to ensure that data originated from the correct location and that it wasn't modified (they may also want to ensure that the data is confidential). Since additional effort is not required to configure the encryption on the VPN gateway, most network administrators or organizations simply encrypt and authenticate. Note that additional processing must take place to perform both the encryption and the authentication, so ESP may not perform as well as AH, but the security benefits of ESP far outweigh any performance impact it might have.

IPsec VPN Mode

In addition to the choice of VPN protocol, there are two different *modes* which will determine how the traffic is exchanged in the VPN:

Tunnel mode
: Tunnel mode encapsulates the original IP packet within another packet in the VPN tunnel. This is most commonly used when hosts within separate private networks want to communicate over a public network. Both VPN gateways establish the VPN tunnel to each other, and all traffic between the two gateways appears to be from the two gateways, with the original packet embedded within the exterior IPsec packet. Note that whether the original packet is encrypted depends on whether ESP or AH mode has been selected. ESP encapsulates, encrypts, and authenticates the original Layer 3 through Layer 7 IP traffic, whereas AH only encapsulates and authenticates the original Layer 3 through Layer 7 IP traffic.

Transport mode
: Transport mode does not encapsulate the original packet in a new packet, like Tunnel mode does; rather, it sends the packet directly between the two hosts that have established the IPsec tunnel. Depending on whether ESP or AH mode is used, the data is either encrypted and authenticated, or just authenticated. This includes encryption and authentication for Layer 4 through Layer 7 in ESP mode, or just authentication for AH for Layer 4 through Layer 7 of the original IP packet.

Tunnel mode is the most common VPN mode on the Internet because it easily allows entire networks (particularly those with private address space) to communicate over public IP networks. Transport mode is primarily used when encrypting traffic between two hosts to secure communication where IP address overlap is not an issue (such as between a host and a server on a private network).

IPsec Manual Keys

In certain situations, IKE negotiations are not preferable. Although an individual IKE negotiation may not require too many resources to establish, setting up hundreds or thousands of VPNs per second can be very difficult due to the key generation that must take place for each VPN. Another non-IKE-preferred scenario is when an organization does not want the keys to expire.

In both scenarios, manual key IPsec VPNs, as we discussed in "IKE Version 1 Overview" on page 255, may be the optimal choice. The disadvantage is that manual keys do not automatically get renegotiated (which happens by default every 24 hours for

Phase 1, and every hour for Phase 2). Therefore, the keys remain the same, and if they are somehow compromised, manual intervention must take place in order to change the keys. With manual keys, there is no VPN negotiation process; the IPsec keys are hardcoded, along with the encryption, authentication, protocol, and mode for the VPN. Essentially, manual keys skip the Phase 1 and Phase 2 negotiation and just produce the keys that would normally be generated in Phase 2. All of the same concepts in terms of encryption and authentication algorithms—ESP versus AH, Tunnel versus Transport mode—apply with manual keys.

Phase 1 IKE Negotiations

Now that you know a little more about how the VPN negotiation takes place, let's drill down into a detailed discussion and break down the individual components of Phase 1 IKE negotiation.

IKE Authentication

A few pages back you learned about Diffie-Hellman at the initial stages of a Phase 1 IKE negotiation, but Diffie-Hellman only provides the ability to establish a secure channel over which two parties can communicate—it does not actually authenticate the other VPN peer. This is where IKE authentication is used to ensure that the other party is authorized to establish the VPN. The details of Diffie-Hellman authentication are beyond the scope of this book; there is an abundance of information available on the Internet, including on Wikipedia (*http://en.wikipedia.org/wiki/Diffie-Hellman_key_exchange*).

IKE authentication comes in two forms: preshared key (password) and certificate authentication.

Preshared key authentication

The most common way to establish a VPN connection is to use preshared keys, which is essentially a password that is the same for both parties. This password must be exchanged in advance in some out-of-band mechanism, such as over the phone, via a verbal exchange, or via less secure mechanisms, even email. The parties then authenticate each other by encrypting the preshared key with the peer's public key, which was obtained in the Diffie-Hellman exchange.

Preshared keys are commonly deployed for site-to-site IPsec VPNs, either within a single organization or between different organizations. Preshared key authentication is popular because the keys do not require the overhead of certificates, and many administrators are much more familiar with passwords than they are with certificates. To ensure that preshared keys are used in the most secure fashion, a preshared key must consist of at least 8 characters (12 or more is recommended) using a combination of letters, numbers, and nonalphanumeric characters, along with different cases for the letters (i.e., the preshared key should not use a dictionary word). An example of a complex password is *H7bK1Mc2$#cNa*.

When using nonalphanumeric characters, make sure they are not special characters which could be mistaken by some operating systems. A common example is the question mark (?), which can typically trigger a command-line interface (CLI) to think the user is requesting context-sensitive help. And although most operating systems support the use of a control sequence, some do not, so you may want to avoid using a control sequence if you are unsure whether the peer supports it.

Certificate authentication

Certificate-based authentication is considered more secure than preshared key authentication because the certificate key cannot be compromised easily (as can a weak preshared key). In addition, optional mechanisms can be used within certificate authentication to ensure that a certificate is still valid. Finally, certificates are not easily vulnerable to visual eavesdropping, like a preshared key might be, although certificates can still be compromised if access to the filesystem that they are stored on is obtained.

Certificates are composed of a public and private key, and can be "signed" by a master certificate known as a *certificate authority* (CA). In this way, certificates can be checked to see if they are signed with a CA which is trusted. Certificates can also be revoked should they be compromised, or if they expire (since certificates are generated with an expiration date, although there is no standard time frame for generated certificates).

The many aspects of certificate-based authentication could fill an entire book, so all the intricate details of this form of authentication are not covered here. For the purposes of this chapter, we expect you to have a working understanding of Public Key Infrastructure (PKI), including certificates, CAs, and the technologies that deliver these capabilities. Later in this chapter we will discuss the configuration specifics on the SRX to get you working with this technology.

IKE Identities

You can think of the IKE identity as the username that is associated with the authentication method (preshared key or certificate). Although that isn't exactly the purpose of this feature, IKE identity performs a similar functionality.

The SRX platform supports a few different types of IKE identities, and you can use them to identify the identity (along with other attributes such as the preshared key or certificate) of the remote party.

IP address
: The most common form of IKE identity for site-to-site VPNs is the IP address. Typically, this is automatically derived from the configuration of a peer gateway, by using the IP address. IP addresses are not commonly used for remote access

VPNs because the client IP address is typically not static, but there is nothing technically wrong with using an IP address for the client IKE identity.

Hostname
: The hostname, or fully qualified domain name (FQDN), is essentially a string that identifies the end system. This does not strictly have to match the actual FQDN of the end system; however, this is recommended for ease of management.

User FQDN
: A user FQDN (UFQDN) is also known as a *user-at-hostname*. It is a simple string that follows the same format as an email address: *user@company.com*. Note that this doesn't have to match the user's actual hostname; however, it is recommended that you use the same email address as the user's actual email address for ease of management.

Distinguished name
: The distinguished name (DN) is the full name that is used in certificates to identify a unique user in a certificate. An example of a DN is "CN=user, DC=company, DC=com," the ASN.1 encoding standard.

When using site-to-site VPNs the most common type of IKE identity is the IP address, assuming that the host has a static IP address. If the host does not have a static IP address, a hostname can be used. When a dial-up remote access client (rather than a gateway) is used, a UFQDN is the most common IKE identity. And if certificates are used, the DN or a subset of the name can be used to identify the users of an organization or a unit of the organization.

Phase 1 IKE Negotiation Modes

IPsec VPNs can use two different modes when negotiating the IKE in Phase 1. The two modes of negotiation of Phase 1 are called Main mode and Aggressive mode. Only one mode is used for negotiation of Phase 1 of the VPN tunnel, and the mode must be configured the same on both sides of the tunnel; otherwise, Phase 1 is not able to complete.

Main mode

When building site-to-site VPNs, Main mode is the most common and secure way to establish the VPN because it provides additional security during the setup phase of the VPN tunnel and requires that six messages be exchanged during the negotiation. The advantage in security of Main mode over Aggressive mode is that the IKE identities are encrypted and cannot be determined by eavesdroppers. Main mode does require additional processing, and is typically used when the IP address of the client is not fixed, or known in advance.

The following sequence of message exchange occurs during Main mode:

1. Initiator proposes the encryption and authentication algorithms to be used to establish the VPN.
2. Responder must accept the proposal and provide the other VPN gateway with a proposal of the encryption and authentication algorithm.
3. Initiator starts the Diffie-Hellman key exchange process by presenting a generated public key, along with a pseudorandom number.
4. Responder responds to the initiator with its public key as part of the Diffie-Hellman key exchange. After message 4, both parties communicate via an encrypted channel.
5. Initiator sends the responder its IKE identity to authenticate itself.
6. Responder sends the initiator its IKE identity. Message 6 completes Phase 1 of the IKE negotiation.

Aggressive mode

Aggressive mode is an alternative to Main mode IPsec negotiation and it is most common when building VPNs from client workstations to VPN gateways, where the client's IP address is neither known in advanced nor fixed. Aggressive mode requires half of the messages that Main mode does when establishing Phase 1, but it does so at the cost of disclosing the IKE identities in clear text; thus, it is a little aggressive in its security negotiations.

Aggressive mode uses the following sequence of messages:

1. Initiator proposes the encryption and authentication algorithms to be used, begins the Diffie-Hellman key exchange, and sends its IKE identity and pseudorandom number.
2. Responder must accept the proposal, and will provide the initiator with a pseudorandom number and the IKE identity of the responder. The responder will have also authenticated the initiator in this stage.
3. Initiator authenticates the responder and confirms the exchange. At this point, both parties have established a secure channel for negotiating the IPsec VPN in Phase 2 and Phase 1 is now complete.

Phase 2 IKE Negotiations

Phase 2 of IKE negotiations establishes the security associations (encryption/decryption key) that are used to secure the IPsec data within the VPN. IKE Phase 2 only has a single mode, known as *Quick mode*, which negotiates the Phase 2 IPsec keys.

Additional processing may optionally take place either in Phase 2, or between Phase 1 and Phase 2. XAuth is an authentication mechanism that commonly is used for remote client IPsec VPNs, and it takes place between Phase 1 and Phase 2. We will cover XAuth later in this chapter.

Perfect Forward Secrecy

PFS renegotiates Phase 1 before proceeding to negotiate Phase 2. The purpose of PFS is because in Phase 1, the exchange of keys and other encryption components can present a risk, particularly in Aggressive mode where IKE identities are sent in the clear.

PFS mitigates those concerns by renegotiating Phase 1 in the same secure channel that Phase 1 previously built. The new Phase 1 channel is used to renegotiate Phase 2. In terms of properties, PFS essentially allows the user to suggest a different Diffie-Hellman group; however, the encryption and authentication algorithms are the same as the ones used for the original Phase 1 negotiation.

Quick Mode

The only mode of negotiating Phase 2 in IPsec, known as Quick mode, exchanges three messages:

Encryption/authentication algorithms
: The encryption and authentication algorithms which are used as part of the IPsec VPN

Proxy IDs
: The proxy IDs which identify what traffic is part of the VPN

Mode and encapsulation
: The VPN protocol and mode the VPN uses (ESP/AH and Tunnel/Transport)

There are some additional parameters which can be configured as part of Phase 2, and they may or may not be negotiated as part of the Quick mode process.

Proxy ID Negotiation

A proxy ID is a mechanism for identifying the traffic carried within the VPN, and it contains two components: the local and remote IP prefix, and the service. Within IKE version 1, only a single prefix can be defined per local and remote IP value, along with a single service.

Strictly speaking, the proxy IDs do not really need to match the traffic at all, but both parties must match what they are negotiating in the VPN. Proxy IDs have long been considered a nuisance when configuring VPNs because they are not really needed, and in large part because different vendors have determined the proxy IDs differently. There is an exception to this that was supported in ScreenOS (multiple proxy IDs), but this isn't supported today in the SRX.

The issue is that the proxy IDs are defined within the IKE RFC, which strictly defines how they are formatted and what they contain. However, the RFC doesn't exactly state how the proxy IDs should be derived, and therefore vendors have interpreted this differently. Ultimately, this has caused interoperability issues when trying to establish VPN tunnels, so be advised that some tuning may be required.

Flow Processing and IPsec VPNs

It is important to understand where IPsec processing of traffic happens in the traffic processing chain. When a session is created on the SRX (as discussed in Chapter 5) we perform all of the flow processing steps, which includes services at the end of the processing chain. If a flow is destined for a VPN (whether it is route- or policy-based) the traffic will be sent into the VPN as one of the last steps in the processing chain (just before actually sending the traffic out of the physical media itself). Placing the VPN at the end of the processing chain allows other services to take place on the plain-text traffic (such as UTM, IPS, NAT, ALG, etc.) and the reverse operation can happen after the traffic is decrypted, returning from another IPsec peer. If the VPN is not already established when the traffic is destined for a VPN peer, the SRX will queue the traffic while it establishes the VPN, and then will send it out as soon as the VPN is established—or drop it if the VPN cannot be established. Just like clear-text traffic, VPN-bound traffic is fully flow-aware (and is enforced by flow processing). The IPsec tunnel is just an abstraction layer on top of the standard flow processing itself.

SRX VPN Types

Two types of VPNs can be configured on the SRX—policy-based VPNs and route-based VPNs—and their underlying IPsec functionality is essentially the same in terms of traffic being encrypted. It's the implementation that's different and that can be used to leverage administrative functionality.

Not all vendors provide both policy- and route-based VPNs; however, there are no compatibility issues with running a policy-based VPN to a route-based VPN, with one exception: when running dynamic routing protocols such as Routing Information Protocol (RIP), Open Shortest Path First (OSPF), Intermediate System-to-Intermediate System (IS-IS), or Protocol-Independent Multicast (PIM) on the VPN, only route-based VPNs can be used.

Policy-Based VPNs

Policy-based VPNs utilize the power of a firewall security policy to define what traffic should be passed through a VPN. Policy-based VPNs allow traffic to be directed to a VPN on a policy-by-policy basis, including the ability to match traffic based on the source IP, destination IP, application, and respective to and from zones. When using policy-based VPNs the action of "Tunnel" is used, which implies that the traffic is permitted, along with defining the VPN to be used in that policy. Additional policy processing such as application services (IPS, URL filtering, antivirus, logging, etc.) can be used in policy-based VPNs.

When using policy-based VPNs, the proxy IDs are derived from the firewall policy that is used. The policy's source address maps to the proxy ID's local ID, the destination address maps to the remote ID, and the service maps to the application for traffic that is destined for the tunnel (to be encrypted; e.g., Trust to Untrust). In the case where traffic is arriving encrypted from the VPN (to be decrypted; e.g., Untrust to Trust) the proxy ID source address will be the remote ID, the destination address is the local ID, and the service is the application.

Determining the Proxy IDs on Policy-Based VPNs

When address object sets, or multicelled source or destination addresses, are used, the respective IDs will be negotiated as 0.0.0.0/0. In the case of service, when either an application set or multicelled applications are used, the service will be negotiated as Any. Although the same proxy ID can be used multiple times on the platform, it can only be defined once per VPN endpoint. For instance, if three different VPNs negotiate the proxy IDs as Local: 0.0.0.0/0, Remote 0.0.0.0/0, and Service Any, that is fine; however, the same VPN can only have this once. If it is defined multiple times for a single VPN, the SRX will issue a commit error due to the overlapping proxy IDs. Proxy IDs can be manually hardcoded by the administrator for the VPN rather than being derived automatically from the policies. The main thing to take away is how the proxy IDs can be derived, as the proxy IDs must match on both sides for VPN negotiation to be successful.

With policy-based VPNs, you can override the proxy IDs which are derived from the policy by defining them (like you would with route-based VPNs) in the Phase 2 configuration. We will discuss the configuration for defining the proxy IDs later in this chapter.

Policy-based VPNs are primarily used for simple site-to-site VPNs and for remote access VPNs. For more advanced needs, route-based VPNs should be considered.

Route-Based VPNs

The alternative to policy-based VPNs is route-based VPNs. Route-based VPNs use a virtual interface known as a *secure tunnel interface* (st0 interface) in which all traffic routed into the interface will be sent into a VPN. The traffic is directed into the interface just like any other traffic decision through the use of routing, hence the term *route-based VPN*. Route-based VPNs still have a secure policy applied to them; however, the security policy does not use the action of Tunnel, but rather the action of Permit. The routing decision causes the traffic to be sent into the VPN. The interesting part of route-based VPNs is that they can be used to leverage advanced features such as use of dynamic routing protocols. Dynamic routing protocols allow easier administration and the ability to fail traffic over to different links. Note that dynamic routing is not required for route-based VPNs; static routes will work just fine as well.

The negotiation of proxy IDs for route-based VPNs is relatively simple. Because they must be manually defined for each VPN, they are not derived from a policy or other source. Just like policy-based VPNs, only a single proxy ID combination can be used per VPN; however, proxy IDs from different VPNs can overlap.

The st0 interface must be configured within a security zone just like any other logical interface. Prior to versions 10.0r3, 10.1r2, and 10.2r2, placing the st0 interface in a non-Inet.0 virtual router (VR) was not supported, but in these and later releases this was fixed.

Generally, when using site-to-site VPNs route-based VPNs are preferred over policy-based VPNs because they are more flexible and they allow the use of dynamic routing over the VPNs; however, there is some added complexity over using policy-based VPNs.

Numbered versus unnumbered st0 interfaces

In a point-to-point VPN configuration, the st0 interface can function similarly to a Point-to-Point Protocol (PPP) interface in that it doesn't have to be numbered (configured with an IP address) since there are only two hosts on the communication channel (the IPsec VPN). In the case that you use an unnumbered interface, you will essentially borrow the IP address of another interface rather than using an explicit IP address for the interface itself. Typically, it is a good idea to just configure IP addresses on the interface rather than using unnumbered interfaces because you can always use private IP addressing within the IPsec VPN since, as the name implies, it is private (not only is it encrypted, but also the actual network within the IPsec tunnel is not impacted by the IP addressing of the network it is running over).

Point-to-point versus point-to-multipoint VPNs

Route-based VPNs offer two different types of architectures: point-to-point and point-to-multipoint. Point-to-point VPNs map a single VPN to a single logical interface unit, so the SRX connects directly to a single peer VPN gateway on the interface. Point-to-multipoint VPNs allow the device to connect to multiple peer gateways on a single logical interface. Refer to Figure 6-1 for a point-to-point architecture, and to Figure 6-2 for a point-to-multipoint architecture.

An important design consideration to make when building a VPN infrastructure is when to use point-to-point and when to use point-to-multipoint. Point-to-point VPNs are an obvious design decision when only a single peer needs to be connected; when multiple peers need to be connected point-to-multipoint should be considered.

But point-to-multipoint also has the advantage of conserving IP subnets along with the number of logical interfaces that are used. For example, in the case of point-to-point VPNs, an IP subnet and logical interface must be used for each VPN. When only a few VPNs are used the consumption of IP subnets and logical interfaces may not be much of a concern. However, when thousands of VPNs are used, platform limits may occur with point-to-point VPNs.

On the other hand, point-to-point VPNs have the advantage of being able to define each logical interface to a separate zone, whereas point-to-multipoint VPNs are all part of the same zone. Note that even when point-to-multipoint is used, each VPN can still be segmented by security policies, since intra-zone blocking is hardcoded into each zone.

Typically, when connecting to other trading partners that are not part of your organization, point-to-point VPNs should be used rather than point-to-multipoint.

Special point-to-multipoint attributes

It is important to understand that point-to-multipoint VPNs require additional configuration to be supported. First, on the hub's st0 interface, you must also specify that it is a multipoint interface, as shown in the following output:

```
[edit]
root@SRX5800-1# show interfaces st0
unit 0 {
    multipoint;
    family inet {
        address 192.168.100.5/24;
    }
}
```

Also, if you are using auto Next-Hop Tunnel Binding (NHTB), no additional configuration is required, but if your peer device doesn't support auto NHTB you must manually specify these entries, as shown in the following output. If you do not specify this information, your point-to-multipoint VPN will not be able to properly establish and route traffic accordingly.

```
[edit]
root@SRX5800-1# show interfaces st0
unit 0 {
   multipoint;
   family inet {
      next-hop-tunnel 192.168.100.1 ipsec-vpn East-Branch;
```

```
            next-hop-tunnel 192.168.100.2 ipsec-vpn West-Branch;
            next-hop-tunnel 192.168.100.3 ipsec-vpn South-Branch;
            address 192.168.100.5/24;
        }
    }
```

Point-to-multipoint NHTB

Point-to-multipoint VPNs allow you to bind multiple VPNs to a single interface on the hub. For this to work properly, the SRX must know not only which VPN to send the traffic into on the st0 interface to which it is bound, but also which next-hop will be used for routing that traffic on the interface. To accomplish this, the SRX uses a mechanism called a Next-Hop Tunnel Binding (NHTB) table on the interface to map all of this information.

On the SRX, if you are going to another SRX or ScreenOS device and you are using static routing, the SRX can automatically exchange the next-hop tunnel information with the peer as part of the optional vendor attribute exchanges in Phase 2 (also known as auto NHTB). If you are not using an SRX or ScreenOS device, and the peer doesn't support these attributes (it should just ignore them), you will need to manually enter the table mappings to show what the next-hop should be (also known as manual NHTB). Alternatively, if you are using a dynamic routing protocol (such as RIP, OSPF, or Border Gateway Protocol [BGP]), you will not need to make a manual mapping entry because the SRX can build the table automatically from the routing updates matching the next-hop to the tunnel it came out of.

Other SRX VPN Components

There are several other VPN components of the SRX platform, many of which are optional enhancements, although some happen automatically and can be altered manually if desired. It is important to have a thorough understanding of the individual features before enabling them, because enabling the features in the incorrect fashion may lead to undesirable effects. Knowledge is power, especially with a powerful device such as the SRX.

Dead Peer Detection

One particular issue that IKE does not account for is if the VPN peer suddenly fails during communication. Since the VPN gateway is not typically initiating traffic (except in the case of dynamic routing protocols), it typically doesn't notice if or when the VPN has failed, at least, not until the IPsec keys expire and the VPN needs to be renegotiated.

To help improve the detection of such failures, a standards-based feature called *Dead Peer Detection* (DPD) can be implemented. DPD essentially sends a User Datagram Protocol (UDP) message at defined intervals, and if messages are not responded to, the peer is considered to be down. By using DPD, a gateway can perform some alternative action such as defaulting to another VPN whenever a failure is detected.

DPD is primarily used with VPNs where dynamic routing is *not* used (such as OSPF), because dynamic routing protocols can both detect a failure and default over to another path without the need for DPD.

VPN Monitoring

One issue with DPD is that it doesn't necessarily mean the underlying VPN is up and running, just that the peer is up and responding. VPN monitoring is not an IPsec standard feature, but it utilizes Internet Control Message Protocol (ICMP) to determine if the VPN is up. VPN monitoring allows the SRX to send ICMP traffic either to the peer gateway, or to another destination on the other end of the tunnel (such as a server), along with specifying the source IP address of the ICMP traffic. If the ICMP traffic fails, the VPN is considered down.

An SRX VPN monitoring option, called Optimized, sends only the ICMP traffic through the tunnel when there is an absence of user traffic. If user traffic is traversing the tunnel, the SRX assumed it to be up, and does not send the ICMP messages. If the traffic ceases, the SRX starts sending the ICMP messages until user traffic begins again.

Even though VPN monitoring is not an IPsec standard feature like DPD, it can be used with other vendors' devices and does not require the VPN peer gateway. You can think of VPN monitoring as Track IP specifically designed for VPNs.

XAuth

XAuth is an SRX feature that allows extensible authentication to IPsec VPN negotiation. XAuth actually takes place between Phase 1 and Phase 2 processing, and is a standards-based feature. Typically, XAuth is used with client remote access VPNs to provide further authentication, such as authentication to a corporate directory service such as Active Directory, which IKE does not allow. XAuth is used in addition to the authentication which takes place in IKE Phase 1.

At the time of this writing, the SRX only supports authenticating XAuth clients, but cannot act as an XAuth client itself. This is typically not an issue, because XAuth authentication is usually used to authenticate remote clients, not VPN peer gateways. Also, SRX XAuth authentication is only supported for authenticating clients to remote authentication sources, and does not support authenticating XAuth users locally.

NAT Traversal

One issue with terminating IPsec remote access clients on VPN gateways in contemporary networks is that often the users are located behind a device that performs source Network Address Translation (source NAT). When performing source NAT on IPsec traffic a device can modify the source address and UDP port in the packet, and therefore make the hash (which was calculated on the original packet) invalid. To help resolve this common scenario, *NAT Traversal* (NAT-T) was created.

NAT-T encapsulates the original ESP or AH traffic in an additional UDP packet. When the VPN gateway receives the UDP traffic it will simply decapsulate the ESP or AH packet from the UDP layer.

NAT-T also uses UDP port 4500 (by default) rather than the standard UDP port 500 (which is only used for IKE negotiations, not ESP or AH), because the VPN gateway may try to process the traffic as IKE rather than as actual data traffic which is to be processed. NAT-T works with either ESP or AH, and with either Tunnel or Transport mode.

On the SRX, NAT-T support is enabled by default, and must be explicitly disabled on a VPN-by-VPN basis. It's recommended that you *enable* NAT-T whenever remote access VPNs are deployed.

Anti-Replay Protection

One liability of IPsec VPNs is that an attacker can capture valid packets and replay them into the network to try to confuse the VPN gateway or remote host. Although the attacker cannot determine the contents of the IPsec message, he may be able to cause a denial of service (DoS) by injecting the traffic.

IPsec protects against this attack by using a sequence of numbers which are built into the IPsec packet—the system does not accept a packet for which it has already seen the same sequence number. Each sequence number is unique and is not based on the original data packet itself, but is maintained by the gateway; even in the case of TCP retransmissions, the sequence number is different. If the remote gateway sees a packet with a duplicate sequence number, it is considered to be *replayed*.

If Anti-Replay protection is enabled, and a duplicate is seen, the packet is dropped and a log message is generated. If Anti-Replay protection is not enabled, the traffic is processed (decrypted), although other security features such as stateful firewall, application layer gateways (ALGs), and Intrusion Detection and Prevention (IDP) may drop the decrypted packet later in the processing chain.

Anti-Replay protection can be enabled independently on each side of the VPN. Since the IPsec messages always contain the sequence number, the option for Anti-Replay is essentially whether or not the VPN gateway monitors the connection to determine the existence of a replayed packet.

Fragmentation

Data networks enforce maximum sizes for frames and packets. Originally, on multi-access networks that shared a collision domain (such as systems connected by an Ethernet hub), use of data sizes that were too large greatly increased the likelihood of collisions, so limits were placed on packet size to optimize packet processing.

Collisions weren't the only issue with regulating frame size, because when packets were too large, small packets could be delayed for processing behind larger packets, and systems couldn't be optimized for efficient packet processing.

Maximum Transmission Unit (MTU) and Maximum Segment Size (MSS)

MTU can refer to the size of a Layer 2 frame or the size of a Layer 3 packet (depending on the vendor). Juniper refers to the MTU as the complete Layer 2 frame, including the header. Standard Ethernet uses an MTU of 1,500 bytes of Layer 3 (including the IP header, Layer 4 header, and data), along with the 14-byte Ethernet header, for a total of 1,514 bytes. The IP header takes up 20 bytes, and the Layer 4 header (either TCP or UDP) will take up 20 bytes. This means that with a 1,514-byte Layer 2 MTU, and 54 bytes of Layer 2 through Layer 4 headers, there can be 1,460 bytes of user data. Note that different media can employ different MTU sizes; for example, the SRX can support Ethernet jumbo frames of up to 9,192 bytes.

Fragmentation comes into play when a packet is sent that is too large to meet the constraints of the underlying transmission medium's MTU. When a network device receives a packet that is too large to be transmitted on the egress transmission medium, it has a choice of either fragmenting the packet (chopping the packet into smaller messages) or dropping the packet.

It is common to employ fragmentation in VPN processing because there is additional overhead in the messages sent over the VPN, including the ESP or AH header, and in Tunnel mode the original packet is encapsulated in another IP packet. Furthermore, in remote access VPNs with NAT-T, the packet is encapsulated yet again in a UDP packet. So, when a gateway receives the original packet, if it is 1,500 bytes all of the additional overhead of the IPsec headers will make it too big to be sent over a standard 1,514-byte Ethernet network. In this case, the gateway must fragment the packet or drop it.

When configuring an SRX VPN it is important to be cognizant of the underlying MTU and the MSS that is derived from the MTU (MTU – Layer 4 header overhead = MSS).

There is also an option for processing the *Don't Fragment* (DF) bit in IP messages—the bit can be ignored, set, or cleared when processing the original packet.

Differentiated Services Code Point

Differentiated Services Code Point (DSCP) is an 8-bit field in an IP header which helps to classify the packet from a Quality of Service (QoS) perspective so that network devices can properly provide the appropriate precedence when processing the packet. DSCP bits don't force the network devices to provide a certain level of service, but they can be leveraged to do so.

The SRX automatically copies the DSCP bits from the original packet to the IPsec packet so that the network devices between the two VPN gateways can provide the appropriate processing on the encrypted traffic.

IKE Key Lifetimes

Keys are generated in both Phase 1 and Phase 2 IPsec. The keys in Phase 1 are generated to create a secure channel for the Phase 2 keys to be negotiated. The Phase 2 keys are the keys that are used to negotiate the user traffic. In both Phase 1 and Phase 2, the keys are considered active for a certain period of time, known as the *key lifetime*. Phase 1 is always negotiated as a period of time, but Phase 2 can be either a period of time or a certain amount of data that is transmitted in kilobytes. Key lifetimes are important because the longer that keys are active, the more potential there is for compromised security. That isn't to say that IPsec is insecure—quite the opposite; however, the longer the same keys are used the more potential there is to determine what those keys are and decrypt the content that is transmitted. Again, when properly configured, this is not a major concern, but something to keep in mind when selecting key lifetime.

Each phase allows the ability to configure the key lifetime for that individual phase. The shorter the lifetime, the more often the keys are renegotiated. Although renegotiating often provides some security advantage, it can be costly from a performance perspective on the VPN gateways when operating on a large scale.

IPSec does not have any official default timers for IPsec key negotiation, but uses default key lifetimes (if not explicitly defined) of 86,400 seconds for Phase 1 and 3,600 seconds for Phase 2. This means Phase 2 times out before the Phase 1 key lifetime, which is an ideal event because only the keys in Phase 2 are used to encrypt the actual data, whereas the Phase 1 keys are only used to create a secure channel to negotiate the Phase 2 keys.

It's important to understand that different vendors' devices may choose different key lifetimes, and that sometimes a mismatch in key lifetimes may cause VPN establishment issues and even stability issues, so it's important to match the values wherever possible.

Network Time Protocol

Network Time Protocol (NTP) is not a strict requirement for IPsec VPNs, but there is good cause for enabling it. First, the obvious need is to have the time properly synchronized for many reasons related to management (timestamps, schedulers, etc.), so this is just a best practice in general. But also, for IPsec with certificates, it is very important because certificates are dependent on accurate time to ensure that they have not expired. If the time is not synchronized, this could make the SRX think the certificate has expired (or has been generated for a future time) when in reality it hasn't. Finally, the less obvious reason pertains to the high-end SRX. The high-end SRX is a distributed processing system with Services Processing Units (SPUs) which operate independently. This also means they may not maintain the same time, and this can create some issues, particularly with VPNs and retrieving information from the SPUs. To ensure no issues, you should always enable NTP on the platform to ensure that the SPUs are synchronized (since the route engine [RE] will sync the time down to the SPUs when NTP is enabled).

Certificate Validation

One of the strengths of certificate-based IPsec authentication is that the certificate can be revoked should it be compromised in any way, in addition to the SRX being able to validate the certificate itself to ensure that it has been signed by the correct CA certificate. By default, if you only upload the CA certificate to the SRX, the SRX can only determine whether the proposed certificate is signed by the CA certificate; it cannot determine whether the certificate had been revoked or is on hold. A certificate on hold is not permanently revoked, but in this state it cannot be used for authentication. To determine if the certificate has been revoked, the SRX must poll the CA itself to determine which certificates have been revoked. Typically, there are two ways to do this: via certificate revocation lists (CRLs) or via Online Certificate Status Protocol (OCSP).

CRL

With this method, the SRX will poll the CA for a list of all of the serial numbers of the revoked or on-hold certificates. Typically, this is done either manually or on a periodic basis. When the SRX needs to validate a certificate it will then check to make sure the certificate is signed by the CA, and if that succeeds, it will check the CRL to see if it includes the proposed certificate's serial number. If the serial number is not on the CRL, the certificate will be considered valid; if it is on the CRL, the certificate will be considered revoked and the authentication will fail. Also note that a certificate that is expiring will not be on the CRL, although it will be considered invalid if it has expired. Furthermore, the CRL itself has a lifetime which can be used to ensure that the CRL is not valid after a long period of time.

At the time of this writing, the SRX supports CRL collection via HTTP or LDAP. If configured to use CRL checking, the SRX will try to download the CRL that is specified in the CA certificate itself, and if that fails, the SRX will follow the configuration, which specifies the CRL path.

OCSP

OSCP is not supported at the time of this writing. It is primarily used to authenticate X.509 certificates similar to CRL checking, but is slightly different in a few ways. First, it doesn't need to download the entire CRL (which is good when the CRL grows very large), but instead queries the OCSP server to determine if an individual certificate is valid, revoked, or on hold. Next, OCSP can query for certificate status in real time, on an as-needed basis. This also helps to ensure that certificates have not expired between CRL polling periods. Finally, OCSP can cache individual certificate authentication responses rather than having to poll for each certificate every time (within a timeout, e.g., 10 minutes).

Simple Certificate Enrollment Protocol

When using large-scale certificate deployments, the simple task of deploying and managing certificates can become a nightmare very quickly. To help alleviate the management needs of large-scale certificate environments, the SRX supports the use of Simple Certificate Enrollment Protocol (SCEP). SCEP is used on SRX devices to be able to reach out to the CA for certificate-related management tasks. These include initial certificate enrollment (get the initial client certificate on the SRX), client certificate renewal, CA certificate renewal, and the ability to get new certificates before the old ones expire. The CA is typically software which runs on a server such as Microsoft Certificate Authority or INSTA-CA, and other CAs that are maintained by certificate signing organizations. When using SCEP the SRX simply acts as a client to update its own certificates and CA certificates; it is not used to authenticate other certificates like CRL or OCSP checking is.

Group VPN

Starting in version 10.2 the branch SRX Series devices support a VPN technology called Group VPN (also known by the Cisco implementation GETVPN), based on RFC 3547. Group VPN is intended to solve the issue of large-scale IPsec implementations that connect branch locations to central hub sites in a scalable and automated fashion over a private network such as MPLS/virtual private LAN service (VPLS). The Juniper Group VPN solution is largely compatible with the Cisco GETVPN solution, since they are based on the same RFC. Covering Group VPN is outside the scope of this book (in part because thorough coverage of the feature is enough to fill a book in itself). If you are interested in gaining more information on this topic, it is covered in the Junos 10.2

documentation, and an AppNote will likely be posted on the Juniper website. Of course, reading the RFC also provides a wealth of information as well.

Dynamic VPN

Dynamic VPN is a feature that is specific to branch SRX Series devices which allows client systems to create remote access VPNs that are terminated on the branch SRX Series gateways. Essentially, this provides a streamlined way to provision and connect users to an SRX over the Internet or other private network. The client that is installed on the user machine is downloaded from the SRX gateway's web interface and is automatically installed. Then, when the user wishes to connect to the SRX, he simply does so by logging in to the SRX's Dynamic VPN Web Interface, which will trigger the VPN session on the user's PC. The administrator does not need to provision any software or configuration as this is automatically installed on the user's system. Additionally, if upgrades to the client are required, this is automatically performed without the need for administrative intervention.

It is important to understand a few things when it comes to Dynamic VPNs. The following limitations exist at the time of this writing:

- To use the Dynamic VPN feature you must purchase and install licenses for the clients. This isn't a limitation on the number of clients, but rather the number of clients which can connect at the same time. See the data sheets for more information on platform-specific limits.
- The Dynamic VPN client can only use IPsec to create a secure connection to the SRX. SSL support will come at a later point in time.
- Only Windows XP and Vista (both 32- and 64-bit) are supported by the Dynamic VPN client. Windows 7 support will come in the future, so stay tuned for the release notes.
- Dynamic VPN requires XAuth, and XAuth does not support local authentication in 10.2. This means you must use a RADIUS server to authenticate the remote clients. Local XAuth authentication will be supported.

Selecting the Appropriate VPN Configuration

The previous sections of this chapter gave you a lot of information—some generalized, some SRX-specific. It's time to make use of that information and provide you with some real-world guidance on how to select the appropriate properties for your SRX VPN configuration.

As you've come to realize by now, there are many different VPN configuration options. However, deciding which options to select is quite easy once you understand them. Here we'll detail 12 key configuration options with recommendations and tips on when and where you might use them:

AutoKey IKE versus manual keys

The first decision you should make when determining how to deploy your VPNs is whether IKE will be used to negotiate the VPN keys, or whether to use manual keys. For just about every scenario, AutoKey IKE should be used over manual key encryption because AutoKey IKE is dynamic and renegotiates the keys used rather than using the same key indefinitely. The only exception to this rule is if security isn't much of a concern, due to the impact that AutoKey negotiation would put on your system. Although individual IKE negotiation may not put much load on the system, negotiating lots of VPN tunnels simultaneously can be very computationally intensive, thus making manual keys preferable.

ESP versus AH

ESP is the most widely deployed VPN protocol because it not only performs authentication, but also provides security by encrypting the data. Although encrypting the data is a computationally intensive process, it typically can be offloaded by using some hardware acceleration. Therefore, unless there is a specific reason to only provide authentication, ESP should be used to provide both encryption and authentication.

Tunnel mode versus Transport mode

Tunnel mode is the most common mode for VPN site-to-site encryption, particularly when going over the Internet. Since Tunnel mode encapsulates the original packet within the encrypted tunnel packet, it allows communication between two privately addressed hosts over a public network (the Internet). Both Tunnel mode and Transport mode allow for encryption, but Tunnel mode does have more overhead in terms of packet size because it must add an additional IP header to the packet on top of the ESP or AH header. Transport mode may be desirable when there is host-to-host IPsec traffic rather than gateway-to-gateway traffic, or when IPsec traffic is communicating over a private network. Transport mode has become popular as a solution for IPsec encryption of multicast traffic, as the contents of the data remain confidential, but the packets can be routed and replicated in the network. If there is any doubt as to which mode should be used, Tunnel mode should be selected.

Main mode versus Aggressive mode

The rule of thumb when it comes to Main mode versus Aggressive mode is that if both nodes have a static IP address (or an address which can be resolved via Domain Name System [DNS]), Main mode should be used. However, if a gateway or host has a dynamic IP address, typically Aggressive mode should be used for the best interoperability (although depending on the implementation of the VPN gateways Main mode may be able to be used).

Diffie-Hellman group number

Diffie-Hellman key exchange is used to negotiate Phase 1 and PFS aspects of IPsec. The larger the key, the more difficult it will be to compromise the security of the negotiation, but the more computationally intensive the negotiation will be.

Typically, Diffie-Hellman Group 2 is considered secure at the time of this writing, although larger key lengths (e.g., Group 5, 14, etc.) are more secure, but may be unnecessary. Remember that Diffie-Hellman is used to negotiate the secure channel to negotiate the Phase 2 keys, but does not actually encrypt the data itself.

Preshared keys versus certificate authentication
: As previously discussed, you can authenticate IPsec peers in two ways: via preshared keys and via certificates. Preshared keys are easier to deploy, and are the most common form of authentication. Certificates are a very powerful form of authentication, as you can scale them to large implementations and you can revoke certificates and authenticate certificates dynamically. Certificates do have a certain amount of overhead when it comes to generation, signing, checking status, and renewing, however, and therefore they are most commonly used for large implementations. When just using simple site-to-site VPNs, or VPNs between other organizations, preshared keys are easier to use. If you are deploying site-to-site or client VPNs within an organization on the scale of several hundred or several thousand, certificates should be examined, as they provide some scaling advantages.

IKE identity
: IKE identity is commonly overlooked as a major component of a VPN; however, it is important to select the appropriate IKE identity. The IKE identity essentially acts as the username for the IKE authentication in a roundabout way. Typically, when both sides of a site-to-site VPN have static IP addresses, the IKE identity is the IP address for both nodes. When a single node is using a dynamic IP address, that node typically uses the `Hostname` attribute, which can be a simple name to identify the peer. But when a user is connecting to a gateway, that user should use the UFQDN. It is important to make sure both sides can properly authenticate the other peer with the method that the other side is expecting, as a mismatch or improper IKE identity causes failure.

Configure remote identity when you do not know the remote peer's IP address. Configure local identity if you do not have a static IP address (e.g., your gateway uses Dynamic Host Configuration Protocol [DHCP]).

VPN encryption algorithm
: When selecting the VPN encryption algorithm, the important things to remember are the sensitivity of the data within the VPN, the amount of data that is sent over the VPN in terms of throughput, and whether the algorithm that is used will be accelerated by hardware. DES is largely considered to be an obsolete encryption algorithm by today's standards because the key space is only 56 bits and it can be broken with modern computers in a few months' time. 3DES and AES are widely considered to be much better algorithms and are secure against attacks with modern computer hardware. If the data is extremely sensitive and needs to be protected

against attacks under extremely powerful computing power, both now and in the future, you should use an algorithm such as AES-256; otherwise, 3DES or AES-128 should be sufficient for most scenarios.

VPN authentication algorithm
: The VPN authentication algorithm is used to create a hash of the traffic to ensure that it has not been modified or forged. Two hash algorithms are implemented in the SRX at the time of this writing: MD5 and SHA-1. SHA-1 is considered to be a stronger hash algorithm than MD5, and since both are implemented in hardware, it is recommended that you use SHA-1 rather than MD5, although MD5 isn't necessarily an obsolete algorithm.

Perfect Forward Secrecy
: PFS is a mechanism used to renegotiate the Phase 1 keys over an established Phase 1 channel. It is primarily meant to help provide additional security to Aggressive mode authentication where the IKE identities are negotiated in clear text, but it can also be used to renegotiate Phase 1 for additional security. It is recommended that you use PFS when using Aggressive mode, or in the most sensitive of security environments, and it is very important to choose the correct preshared key (if you're using preshared keys), along with the proper encryption and authentication algorithms.

Policy-based VPNs versus route-based VPNs
: Policy-based VPNs are common when configuring simple site-to-site VPNs or remote access VPNs, especially when interoperating with VPN products from other vendors. When only a few VPNs are needed, or if the VPNs are simple, it might make sense to use policy-based VPNs because they are easier to set up and have fewer components (from a configuration perspective) than route-based VPNs. When you're setting up a VPN infrastructure with a large number of remote access tunnels, or when multicast or dynamic routing protocols are used, you should use route-based VPNs. In general, route-based VPNs are more powerful than policy-based VPNs, so they are generally preferred over policy-based VPNs, but simple implementations can still utilize policy-based VPNs.

Predefined proposal sets versus custom proposal sets
: To help ease configuration, the SRX has predefined proposal sets for both Phase 1 and Phase 2 IKE negotiations. You can choose to use these predefined sets or create your own. It is really just a matter of preference. There are three predefined proposals: basic, standard, and compatible. Typically, it is best to just define your own, since it takes the guesswork out of configuring the VPNs, especially if you are establishing a VPN to another vendor (which may not use the same terminology). Additionally, if you use predefined sets, you might have to go through several proposals with the peer before finding a match (which would leave a log trail as well), so it is best to just configure identical proposals as the peer.

IPsec VPN Configuration

Now that we have broken down the individual components of IPsec VPNs, let's examine how to put these features into practice on the SRX with the configuration of a hub and spoke VPN.

Since certain aspects of VPNs can only have single attributes (e.g., preshared key or certificates, but not both), we will cover some configuration elements that do not apply to our actual VPN infrastructure. Figure 6-6 shows a network diagram of the IPsec VPN infrastructure that is being implemented. We'll cover the various configuration elements in the order they should be configured, since certain elements reference other aspects of the configuration.

Configuring NTP

Although we covered NTP configuration earlier in the book, it is a very important function of VPN, so we will reiterate how to configure it here. The following configuration assumes that you already have network connectivity and routing set up (you can also use domain names as your NTP servers, so long as you have DNS configured; also, note that the SRX will resolve the name and place it into the final configuration):

```
[edit]
root@SRX3600-1# set system name-server 4.2.2.2

[edit]
root@SRX3600-1# set system ntp server pool.ntp.org

[edit]
root@SRX3600-1# show system
host-name SRX3600-1;
domain-name jnpr.net;
name-server {
    4.2.2.2;
}
ntp {
    server 74.207.249.60;
}
```

Certificate Preconfiguration Tasks

When configuring your SRX for certificate authentication for Phase 1 you need to do several things before you can use certificate authentication to its fullest advantage (if you are using preshared keys only, this section does not apply).

In this example, we will do the following things to prepare our SRX for certificate authentication. Not all of these are strictly required, but to cover all of the common scenarios we will cover them in a single example.

- Generate a locally generated certificate called IPSEC.

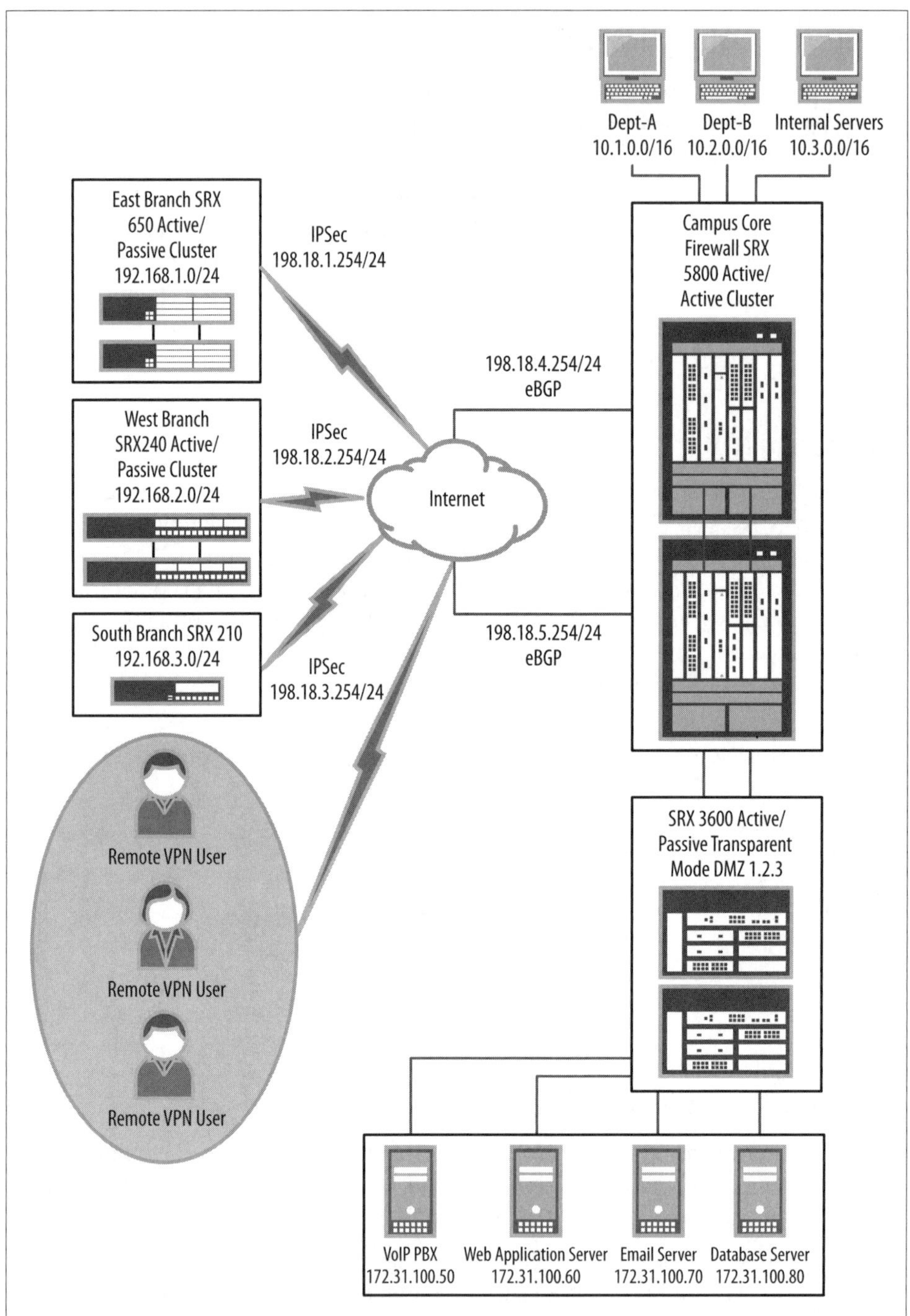

Figure 6-6. IPsec VPN infrastructure

- Create a CA profile called CAPROFILE. The CA profile should be configured to use CRL checking and to download the CRL from *http://172.31.100.50* every two hours. The name of the CA server identifier is CASERVER.
- Configure SCEP to enroll a certificate to an SCEP server. SCEP should also be configured to automatically grab the CA certificate, reenroll the certificate before it expires, and download the new CA certificate before it expires. The SRX should retry every 3,600 seconds to download a new certificate.
- Use HTTP-based CRL checking to ensure that certificates proposed by the client are valid certificates that have not been revoked. This should be polled every two hours for an updated CRL.

```
root@SRX3600-1> request security pki generate-key-pair certificate-id IPSEC
Generated key pair IPSEC, key size 1024 bits

root@SRX3600-1> edit

[edit]
root@SRX3600-1# edit security pki ca-profile CAPROFILE

[edit security pki ca-profile CAPROFILE]
root@SRX3600-1# set ca-identity CASERVER revocation-check crl refresh-interval 2
url http://172.31.100.50

[edit security pki ca-profile CAPROFILE]
root@SRX3600-1# set enrollment retry-interval 3600

[edit security pki ca-profile CAPROFILE]
root@SRX3600-1# up

[edit security pki]
root@SRX3600-1# set auto-re-enrollment certificate-id CAPROFILE ca-profile-name
qqq challenge-password aaa re-enroll-trigger-time-percentage 10
re-generate-keypair

[edit security pki ca-profile CAPROFILE]
root@SRX3600-1# run request pki ca-certificate enroll ca-profile CAPROFILE

Fingerprint:
75:1b:2f:a7:95:bc:2e:3b:54:d0:71:ae:86:42:09:e2:cc:75:34:d1 (sha1)
C1:4d:cc:fc:8f:10:d2:04:e9:80:09:68:4c:01:bd:42 (md5)
Do you want to load the above CA certificate ? [yes,no]

## Enroll the Local Certificate to Microsoft SCEP Server##

[edit security pki ca-profile CAPROFILE]
root@SRX3600-1# set enrollment url http://172.31.100.50/certsrv/mscep/mscep.dll

[edit security pki ca-profile CAPROFILE]
root@SRX3600-1# run request security pki local-certificate enroll ca-profile
CAPROFILE
certificate-id qqq challenge-password aaa domain-name my.company.com
```

```
email qqq@company.com ip-address 10.10.10.10 subject DC=company,
CN=SRX, OU=IT, O=my, L=sunnyvale, ST=california, C=us
```

Phase 1 IKE Configuration

Let's begin with the Phase 1 configuration, which has several different configuration elements (some optional, some required) for proper IPsec establishment. The important thing to remember as part of the Phase 1 configuration is that Phase 1 is not actually used to encrypt the data within the VPN, but rather to establish the secure channel to negotiate the Phase 2 keys that will be used to establish the IPsec VPN.

One great thing about configuring VPNs in the SRX compared to ScreenOS is that the configuration is not immediately applied and can be altered without removing all instances of the configuration to edit elements. This means that as long as you don't commit the configuration, these settings can be made in any particular order—an enormous advantage over ScreenOS and many other vendors' products. Another major advantage is that Junos separates the Phase 1 elements into three areas: proposal, policy, and gateway. This is advantageous when multiple gateways use the same policy and/or proposals, and allows for template-like functionality for VPNs.

Our Phase 1 IKE configuration follows this process:

1. Configure the elements of the Phase 1 proposal, which defines the encryption and authentication policies.
2. Define the Phase 1 mode, preshared key or certificate, and proposal.
3. Configure the actual Phase 1 gateway properties.

Configuring Phase 1 proposals

The Phase 1 proposal provides the framework for the encryption and authentication parameters that are used in policy and gateway functionality. All Phase 1 proposals are configured under the `[security ike proposal <proposal-name>]` level in the configuration hierarchy. In our example, we will configure the following elements (they can be configured in any order within the Phase 1 proposal):

Authentication method
: The authentication method defines whether preshared keys or certificates are used for Phase 1 authentication. Note that the `rsa-signatures` attribute signifies certificates using RSA key generation. This step does not refer to the authentication algorithm of Phase 1, but rather to how Phase 1 peers can authenticate each other.

Diffie-Hellman group
: The Diffie-Hellman group defines which group or key length will be used for the Phase 1 keys. The larger the key, the more secure it is, but also the more computationally complex it is to establish.

Encryption algorithm
: The encryption algorithm determines which algorithm will be used to encrypt the data within the Phase 1 secure channel. The SRX supports DES, 3DES, AES-128, AES-192, and AES-256, which are the most powerful (in that order) and the most demanding, although hardware acceleration makes this less of a concern. (Note that CBC stands for Cipher Block Chaining and it has to do with the fact that these algorithms are using block encryption rather than stream encryption, but it is not a detail that you need to be concerned with.)

Authentication parameter
: The authentication parameter defines what authentication algorithm is used to ensure that data has been received from the correct VPN peer, and that it hasn't been modified.

Key lifetimes
: Key lifetimes determine how long the VPN keys are active until they expire, and then must be renegotiated when Phase 1 needs to be renegotiated.

Configuration for Remote-Office1 proposal with preshared keys. Configure the following properties for the Remote-Office-PSK proposal:

- Preshared key authentication
- Diffie-Hellman Group 2
- 3DES-CBC encryption algorithm
- SHA-1 authentication algorithm
- Key lifetime of 86,400 seconds

```
[edit]
root@SRX5800#edit security ike proposal Remote-Office-PSK

[edit security ike proposal Remote-Office-PSK]
root@SRX5800#set authentication-method pre-shared-keys

[edit security ike proposal Remote-Office-PSK]
root@SRX5800#set dh-group group2

[edit security ike proposal Remote-Office-PSK]
root@SRX5800#encryption-algorithm 3des-cbc

[edit security ike proposal Remote-Office-PSK]
root@SRX5800#set authentication algorithm sha1

[edit security ike proposal Remote-Office-PSK]
root@SRX5800#set lifetime-seconds 86400

[edit security ike proposal Remote-Office-PSK]
root@SRX5800# show
authentication-method pre-shared-keys;
dh-group group2;
authentication-algorithm sha1;
encryption-algorithm 3des-cbc;
```

```
lifetime-seconds 86400;

[edit security ike proposal Remote-Office-PSK]
root@SRX5800#top commit
```

Configuration for Remote-Office1 proposal with certificates. Alternatively, configure the following properties for the Remote-Office-Cert proposal:

- Certificate authentication
- Diffie-Hellman Group 2
- 3DES-CBC encryption algorithm
- SHA-1 authentication algorithm
- Key lifetime of 86,400 seconds

```
[edit]
root@SRX5800#edit security ike proposal Remote-Office-Cert

[edit security ike proposal Remote-Office-Cert]
root@SRX5800#set authentication-method certificates

[edit security ike proposal Remote-Office-Cert]
root@SRX5800#set dh-group group2

[edit security ike proposal Remote-Office-Cert]
root@SRX5800#encryption-algorithm 3des-cbc

[edit security ike proposal Remote-Office-Cert]
root@SRX5800#set authentication algorithm sha1

[edit security ike proposal Remote-Office-Cert]
root@SRX5800#set lifetime-seconds 86400

[edit security ike proposal Remote-Office-Cert]
root@SRX5800# show
authentication-method certificates;
dh-group group2;
authentication-algorithm sha1;
encryption-algorithm 3des-cbc;
lifetime-seconds 86400;

[edit security ike proposal Remote-Office-Cert]
root@SRX5800#top commit
```

Configuring Phase 1 policies

Phase 1 policies define the actual criteria of the VPN tunnel as well as which proposals can be used as part of the Phase 1 negotiation. Note that Junos supports up to four Phase 1 proposals in a single policy. Basically, if the peer initiates the VPN, the SRX will allow any of the listed proposals. If the SRX is initiating the VPN, it will try the different proposals in the order they are listed until either a proposal is accepted by the peer, or negotiations fail. Keep in mind that for Phase 1, preshared keys *or* certificates can be used with any combination of the parameters and proposals, but they are exclusive in that only one method can be used, not both.

Configuring Phase 1 mode
: Main mode or Aggressive mode should be selected depending on the configuration of the tunnel.

Configuring preshared keys
: Preshared keys are used for each peer to authenticate each other during Phase 1. Preshared keys can be entered as either a clear-text string (ASCII text) or hexadecimal text. This must be specified when entering the preshared key. Typically, ASCII text will be used to specify the password, since it can support human-readable strings, whereas hexadecimal is 0–9, a–f text.

Configuring certificates
: Certificates can be used as an alternative to preshared keys because they offer more dynamic support for strong authentication than preshared keys. You need to specify a few parameters, including the local certificate to use, the Trusted CA with which to authenticate the peer certificate (it must be loaded on the SRX), and the peer certificate type which defines the peer's certificate format.

Configuring the local certificate
: This is the certificate to be presented to the IPsec peer.

Configuring the trusted CA
: This is used to authenticate the peer's certificate.

Configuring the peer certificate type
: The SRX supports negotiation with either PKCS7 or X.509 signature encoding. A peer certificate type must be defined for the certificates that are being negotiated. The type of certificate depends on which encoding process the certificate is generated with and must be negotiated with the peer gateway.

Configuring proposals
: A proposal or set of proposals must be chosen for the IKE policy to define which encryption and/or authentication algorithms are used when negotiating the peer IPsec VPN. Up to four proposals can be selected, although only a single proposal is required. There are also some predefined proposals that can be used.

Configuring Phase 1 IKE policy with preshared key, Main mode. Configure the Remote-Office-Static Phase 1 IKE policy using the following values:

- IKE Phase 1 Main mode
- A preshared key of $up3r$ecReT
- The Remote-Office-PSK proposal

```
[edit]
root@SRX5800#edit security ike policy Remote-Office-Static

[edit security ike policy Remote-Office-Static]
```

```
root@SRX5800#set mode main

[edit security ike policy Remote-Office-Static]
root@SRX5800#set pre-shared-key ascii-text $up3r$ecReT

[edit security ike policy Remote-Office-Static]
root@SRX5800#set proposals Remote-Office-PSK

[edit security ike policy Remote-Office-Static]
root@SRX5800#show
mode main;
proposals Remote-Office-PSK;
pre-shared-key ascii-text "$9$JTUHq5Tz9tO5QhSlex7bsYgoGiHm5zns2Q3";
## SECRET-DATA

[edit security ike policy Remote-Office-Static]
root@SRX5800#top commit
```

Configuring Phase 1 IKE policy with preshared key, Aggressive mode. Configure the Remote-Office-Dynamic Phase 1 IKE policy for gateways with dynamic IP addresses using the following values:

- IKE Phase 1 Aggressive mode
- A preshared key of $up3r$ecReT
- The Remote-Office1 proposal

```
[edit]
root@SRX5800#edit security ike policy Remote-Office-Dynamic

[edit security ike policy Remote-Office-Dynamic]
root@SRX5800#set mode aggressive

[edit security ike policy Remote-Office-Dynamic]
root@SRX5800#set pre-shared-key ascii-text $up3r$ecReT

[edit security ike policy Remote-Office-Dynamic]
root@SRX5800#set proposals Remote-Office-PSK

[edit security ike policy Remote-Office-Dynamic]
root@SRX5800#show
mode aggressive;
proposals Remote-Office-PSK;
pre-shared-key ascii-text "$9$JTUHq5Tz9tO5QhSlex7bsYgoGiHm5zns2Q3";
## SECRET-DATA
```

Configuring Phase 1 IKE policy with certificates. For this example, we will create a Phase 1 IKE policy using certificates that builds on our previous work creating a local certificate and setting up the CA profile:

- Create an IKE policy called Remote-Office-Static-Cert which uses certificate authentication rather than preshared key authentication.
- This policy should use Main mode for the Phase 1 IKE mode.

- You should trust any valid certificate signed by a CA which you have configured to trust.
- Use the local-certificate IPSEC which we generated earlier for authentication to your peer. This certificate should be in the PKCS7 format.
- Use Remote-Office1 for the proposal.

```
[edit]
root@SRX5800#edit security ike policy Remote-Office-Static-Cert

[edit security ike policy Remote-Office-Static-Cert]
root@SRX5800#set mode main

[edit security ike policy Remote-Office-Static-Cert]
root@SRX5800#set certificate local-certificate IPSEC

[edit security ike policy Remote-Office-Static-Cert]
root@SRX5800#set certificate trusted-ca use-all

[edit security ike policy Remote-Office-Static-Cert]
root@SRX5800#set certificate peer-certificate-type pkcs7

[edit security ike policy Remote-Office-Static-Cert]
root@SRX5800#set Office1 proposals Remote-Office1

[edit security ike policy Remote-Office-Static-Cert]
root@SRX5800# show
mode main;
proposals Remote-Office1;
certificate {
    local-certificate IPSEC;
    trusted-ca use-all;
    peer-certificate-type pkcs7;
}

root@SRX5800#top commit
```

Configuring Phase 1 gateways

The last aspect of Phase 1 which must be configured is the actual gateway itself. The gateway identifies the remote peer the IPsec VPN peers with, and defines the appropriate parameters for that IPsec VPN. As we discussed earlier in this chapter, there are two types of gateways: those with static IP addresses and those with dynamic IP addresses (including remote clients).

The SRX allows you to define multiple gateways with the same policies, which is a feature that can greatly simplify configuration, particularly if multiple gateways have the same proposal and policy. Here we'll cover the aspects of configuring both static and dynamic IP gateways and the various properties for IPsec VPN gateways.

Configuring remote gateways with a static IP address
: The optimal setup for two VPN gateways is to have both of them use static IP addresses. This simplifies the Phase 1 setup between the two gateways, as well as potential troubleshooting since the IP address of the gateway is always known.

In addition to the primary IP address defined in the gateway definition, up to four backup gateways can also be defined should the primary gateway fail.

Configuring remote gateways with a dynamic IP address
: When the remote IPsec gateway does not have a static IP address, but rather is assigned via DHCP, or is perhaps a gateway which moves between different locations, dynamic IKE identities are used rather than configuring a fixed IP address. A few properties may have to be defined as part of this configuration:

  Configuring local identities
  : Local identities are required when a device is using a dynamic IP address to identify itself to the other gateway. This can be either a DN, an FQDN, an IP address, or a UFQDN. Typically, for site-to-site VPNs, the FQDN or hostname is used to define the local identity and the DN is used for certificate-based authentication. UFQDN is typically used for remote client VPNs.

  Configuring remote identities
  : Remote identities are required when the remote party does not have a static IP address, and therefore must use a dynamic IKE identity. The identity types are the same for the remote identities as they are for the local identities.

Configuring the external interface
: The external interface is the interface on which the SRX terminates the IPsec VPN. The interface that the traffic terminates on must match the interface defined for that gateway or Phase 1 negotiations will fail. This is often overlooked in the configuration and is a source of confusion when experiencing issues establishing the VPN. Note that the interface must also include the IPsec unit number; if it is not defined, it is set as unit 0, but if the unit is not correct, establishment issues will occur. Note that prior to v10.4, termination of IPsec VPNs on non-Inet.0 VRs is not supported.

Configuring interfaces and zones to allow IKE traffic
: On top of configuring the external interface on which the IPsec VPN is terminated, you must also make sure that IKE traffic is allowed on the interface and/or zone on the SRX; otherwise, the SRX will drop the traffic before the IKE daemon can process it. This is a security precaution to prevent DoS attacks against IKE gateways on interfaces that shouldn't be allowed to accept the IKE traffic. Additionally, further restrictions can be made through the use of interface access lists that can

prevent IKE traffic based on stateless firewall filters, so it is important to make sure such filters are not interfering with the traffic.

Configuring IKE policy
: The IPsec VPN gateway must define the IKE policy previously configured. The IKE policy defines the preshared key or certificates used, along with the other properties of the IPsec tunnel such as the encryption and authentication algorithms. The name of the IKE policy does not have to match the name of the gateway, but this is often done for simplicity. Also, IKE policies can be reused by other gateways assuming that the properties are the same.

Configuring NAT-T
: NAT-T is required when the remote IPsec gateway or client is behind a device performing NAT. By default, NAT-T is enabled on the SRX, so it must be explicitly disabled to turn it off on a gateway-by-gateway basis.

Configuring NAT keepalives
: NAT keepalives (also known as *session keepalives*) may be required when the remote client or gateway is behind a device performing NAT. The NAT device maintains a table that maps the translations of each session (including that of the IPsec VPN session). The sessions and their corresponding translations typically time out after a certain period of time if no traffic is received (known as an *idle timeout*). If the VPN is expected to have large periods of inactivity where the session and translation may time out, NAT keepalives should be enabled to generate "artificial" traffic to keep the session active on the NAT device.

Configuring DPD
: DPD allows the two gateways to determine if the peer gateway is up and responding to the DPD messages which are negotiated during IPsec establishment.

Configuring an IKE gateway with static IP address and DPD. Configure the Remote-Office1 IKE gateway with the following parameters:

- IP address of 198.18.1.254
- External interface of ge-0/0/0.0
- Accept inbound IKE traffic on host ge-0/0/0.0 in the Untrust zone
- Remote-Office1 IKE policy
- Enable DPD with an interval of every 10 seconds and a threshold of 3
- Don't have DPD always send keepalives; only send in the absence of traffic

```
[edit]
root@SRX5800#edit security ike gateway Remote-Office1

[edit security ike gateway Remote-Office1]
root@SRX5800#set address 198.18.1.254

[edit security ike gateway Remote-Office1]
root@SRX5800#set external-interface ge-0/0/0.0
```

```
[edit security ike gateway Remote-Office1]
root@SRX5800#set ike-policy Remote-Office1

[edit security ike gateway Remote-Office1]
root@SRX5800#set dead-peer-detection interval 10

[edit security ike gateway Remote-Office1]
root@SRX5800#set dead-peer-detection threshold 3

[edit security ike gateway Remote-Office1]
root@SRX5800# show
ike-policy Remote-Office1;
address 198.18.1.254;
dead-peer-detection {
    interval 10;
    threshold 3;
}
external-interface ge-0/0/0.0;

[edit security ike gateway Remote-Office1]
root@SRX5800#top edit security zones security-zone untrust
interfaces ge-0/0/0.0 host-inbound-traffic system-services

[edit security zones security-zone untrust interfaces ge-0/0/0.0
host-inbound-traffic system-services]
root@SRX5800#set ike

[edit security zones security-zone untrust interfaces ge-0/0/0.0
host-inbound-traffic system-services]
root@SRX5800#show
ike;

[edit security zones security-zone untrust interfaces ge-0/0/0.0
host-inbound-traffic system-services]
root@SRX5800#top commit
```

Configuring dynamic gateways and remote access clients

Some properties of IKE Phase 1 apply only to remote clients connecting to the SRX. These are primarily centered on XAuth and IKE IDs:

Configuring XAuth
: XAuth negotiation technically takes place between Phase 1 and Phase 2 of the VPN establishment, but is herewith discussed as part of the Phase 1 negotiation. The SRX only supports authenticating clients with XAuth and not authenticating itself to another XAuth-capable peer. Also, the SRX must use RADIUS to authenticate remote users, and cannot use local XAuth users like ScreenOS can (at the time of this writing). A few things must be configured as part of the XAuth configuration, including the XAuth access profile, the XAuth RADIUS server configuration, and the XAuth configuration within IKE. Also, when configuring remote users, an IKE gateway must be configured to define the IKE identity of the user.

Configuring IKE connection sharing
: IKE connection sharing allows an administrator to define a single IKE gateway object that allows multiple users to connect to it with the same properties. This is most commonly performed when using multiple remote clients that are also using XAuth to authenticate; however, this is not a requirement. It is primarily used as a matter of convenience for the administrator so that she doesn't have to configure multiple gateways as well as remote clients with separate configuration files, but rather can use a single remote configuration and single gateway configuration. This is known as a shared-IKE ID.

Configuring an IKE gateway with a dynamic IP address. Configure the Remote-Office3 gateway which uses a dynamic IP address with the following properties:

- Remote-Office-Dynamic IKE policy
- Remote-Office3.company.com used as identity of Remote-Office3
- External interface of ge-0/0/0.0
- IKE processing enabled on interface ge-0/0/0.0

```
[edit]
root@SRX5800#edit security ike gateway Remote-Office3

[edit security ike gateway Remote-Office3]
root@SRX5800#set dynamic hostname Remote-Office3.company.com

[edit security ike gateway Remote-Office3]
root@SRX5800#set external-interface ge-0/0/0.0

set security zones security-zone untrust interfaces ge-0/0/0.0
host-inbound-traffic system-services ike

[edit security ike gateway Remote-Office3]
root@SRX5800#set ike-policy Remote-Office-Dynamic

[edit security ike gateway Remote-Office3
root@5800# show
ike-policy Remote-Office-Dynamic;
dynamic hostname Remote-Office3.company.com;
external-interface ge-0/0/0.0;

[edit security ike gateway Remote-Office3]
root@SRX5800#top edit security zones security-zone untrust interfaces
ge-0/0/0.0 host-inbound-traffic system-services

[edit security zones security-zone untrust interfaces ge-0/0/0.0
host-inbound-traffic system-services]
root@SRX5800#set ike

[edit security zones security-zone untrust interfaces ge-0/0/0.0
host-inbound-traffic system-services]
root@SRX5800#show
ike;
```

```
[edit security zones security-zone untrust interfaces ge-0/0/0.0
host-inbound-traffic system-services]
root@SRX5800#top commit
```

Configuring an IKE remote access client. Configure the following properties for a remote client connection:

- The remote client's identity should be a shared IKE ID type, with up to 25 simultaneous connections.
- The user should use the UFQDN *Remote-Client@company.com*.
- The VPNs should be terminated on the ge-0/0/0.0 interface, and ensure that IKE traffic can be processed on this interface.
- The Remote-Office-Dynamic IKE policy should be selected.
- XAuth will be used for this connection with an access profile of Remote-Client, via RADIUS server 10.3.1.50, with a secret of RadiU$Secr3+.

```
[edit]
root@SRX5800# edit security ike gateway Remote-Client

[edit security ike gateway Remote-Client]
root@SRX5800# set dynamic user-at-hostname Remote-Client@company.com

[edit security ike gateway Remote-Client]
root@SRX5800# set external-interface ge-0/0/0.0

[edit security ike gateway Remote-Client]
root@SRX5800# set ike-policy Remote-Office-Dynamic

[edit security ike gateway Remote-Client]
root@SRX5800# set xauth access-profile Remote-Client

[edit security ike gateway Remote-Client]
root@SRX5800# set dynamic connection-limit 25

[edit security ike gateway Remote-Client]
root@SRX5800# set Dynamic dynamic ike-user-type shared-ike-id

[edit security ike gateway Remote-Client
root@SRX5800# show
ike-policy Remote-Office-Dynamic;
dynamic {
    user-at-hostname Remote-Client@company.com;
    connections-limit 25;
    ike-user-type shared-ike-id;
}
local-identity hostname HQ.company.com;
external-interface ge-0/0/0.0;
xauth access-profile Remote-Client;

[edit security ike gateway Remote-Client]
root@SRX5800#top edit security zones security-zone untrust interfaces
```

```
ge-0/0/0.0 host-inbound-traffic system-services

[edit security zones security-zone untrust interfaces ge-0/0/0.0
host-inbound-traffic system-services
root@SRX5800#set ike

[edit security zones security-zone untrust interfaces ge-0/0/0.0
host-inbound-traffic system-services
root@SRX5800#show
ike;

[edit security zones security-zone untrust interfaces ge-0/0/0.0
host-inbound-traffic system-services
root@SRX5800# top edit access profile Remote-Client

[edit access profile Remote-Client]
root@SRX5800# set authentication-order radius

[edit access profile Remote-Client]
root@SRX5800# set radius-server 10.3.1.50 secret RaDiU$Secr3+

[edit access profile Remote-Client]
root@SRX5800# show
authentication-order radius;
radius-server {
        10.3.1.50 secret "$9$PTn9AtOEhyQFrKvWXxjik.PQn6AuBE/9Ec";
## SECRET-DATA
    }

[edit access profile Remote-Client]
root@SRX5800#top commit
```

Phase 2 IKE Configuration

Phase 2 IKE configuration requires several parameters to be defined for the IPsec VPN to establish. Phase 2 primarily deals with securing the data traffic located within the IPsec VPN tunnel. This communication takes place on top of the secure communication channel formed in Phase 1.

In this section, we will cover the following regarding Phase 2 configuration: Phase 2 proposal, Phase 2 policy, and common VPN components.

Configuring Phase 2 proposals

Phase 2 IKE proposals are similar to Phase 1 IKE proposals in that encryption and authentication algorithms are selected, along with key lifetimes. As mentioned before, the purpose of the Phase 2 encryption and authentication algorithms differs with that of Phase 1 encryption and authentication algorithms, but the actual components of the proposals are essentially the same. It is important to note that the names of the proposals, policies, and VPNs do not have to match those of the Phase 1 policies used, since they will be referenced accordingly, but name matching is often done for simplicity of management.

Configuring the encryption algorithm
: The encryption algorithm defines which encryption algorithm is used to encrypt the data within the IPsec VPN. This is only applicable when using ESP, as AH does not encrypt the actual content of the VPN.

Configuring the authentication algorithm
: The authentication algorithm is used to ensure that the data has arrived from the correct source and has not been modified.

Configuring the IPsec protocol
: ESP or AH must be selected for determining the type of VPN. ESP provides both encryption and authentication, while AH only provides authentication.

Configuring the key lifetimes
: Key lifetimes for Phase 2 can be configured in seconds or as kilobytes. If the goal is to ensure that Phase 2 keys are active for only a certain period of time, seconds is the appropriate choice; if the goal is to keep keys active until a certain amount of data has been sent (based on VPN usage), kilobytes is preferred. If you do not specify the value, by default 3,600 seconds (or one hour) will be used for the Phase 2 key lifetime.

Configuring a Phase 2 proposal for remote offices and client connections. Configure the following properties for the Remote-Office Phase 2 proposal that will be used for all remote offices and client connections:

- Use AES-256 for the encryption algorithm.
- Use SHA-1 for the authentication algorithm.
- Use ESP as the IPsec protocol.
- Set a lifetime of one hour for the Phase 2 keys.

```
[edit]
root@SRX5800# edit security ipsec proposal Remote-Office-Client

[edit security ipsec proposal Remote-Office-Client]
root@SRX5800# set encryption-algorithm aes-256-cbc

[edit security ipsec proposal Remote-Office-Client]
root@SRX5800# set authentication-algorithm hmac-sha1-96

[edit security ipsec proposal Remote-Office-Client]
root@SRX5800# set protocol esp

[edit security ipsec proposal Remote-Office-Client]
root@SRX5800# set lifetime-seconds 3600

[edit security ipsec proposal Remote-Office-Client]
root@SRX5800# show
protocol esp;
```

```
authentication-algorithm hmac-sha1-96;
encryption-algorithm aes-256-cbc;
lifetime-seconds 3600;

[edit security ipsec proposal Remote-Office-Client]
root@SRX5800#top commit
```

Configuring Phase 2 IPsec policy

The Phase 2 IPsec policy defines how the VPN is established. A few properties are defined in the IPsec policy, including which proposals are to be used, as well as whether PFS is to be used on the VPN.

Configuring the IPsec proposals
: Up to four proposals can be negotiated for the IPsec tunnel, although only one is used for the actual IPsec traffic encryption and authentication. Essentially, the initiator tries to negotiate each IPsec tunnel until a proposal is accepted by the peer or there are no other IPsec proposals left to negotiate.

Configuring PFS
: If PFS is to be used, it is configured in the IPsec policy, and actually takes effect *after* Phase 1 but before Phase 2 is negotiated. As part of the configuration, the Diffie-Hellman group must be defined to be negotiated for the PFS. It does not have to match the Diffie-Hellman group negotiated in Phase 1.

Configuring an IPsec policy defining the Phase 2 proposal. You must configure an IPsec policy which defines which Phase 2 proposal will be selected, and if PSK will be used for the VPN, if applicable. Configure the Remote-Office-Client Phase 2 IPsec policy, which will be used for all remote office and client connections with the following properties:

- Use the Remote-Office-Client proposal.
- Use PFS with Diffie-Hellman Group 5 for additional security.

```
[edit]
root@SRX5800# edit security ipsec policy Remote-Office-Client

[edit security ipsec policy Remote-Office-Client]
root@SRX5800# set proposals Remote-Office-Client

[edit security ipsec policy Remote-Office-Client]
root@SRX5800# set perfect-forward-secrecy keys group5

[edit security ipsec policy Remote-Office-Client]
root@SRX5800# show
perfect-forward-secrecy {
    keys group5;
}
proposals Remote-Office-Client;

[edit security ipsec policy Remote-Office-Client]
root@SRX5800#top commit
```

Configuring common IPsec VPN components

Now that the IPsec proposal and the policy have been configured, the VPN object can be completed with the final configuration of Phase 2. This information includes the proxy IDs, the IPsec policy, the tunnel binding (if route-based VPNs are used), and other properties of the VPN tunnel including replay detection, fragmentation, and VPN monitoring. We'll begin with the VPN configuration components that are common to both policy-based and route-based VPNs, and then cover the components specific to policy- and route-based VPNs, respectively. Some of the components covered in this section are optional and will be noted as such.

Configuring the IPsec VPN gateway
: The IPsec VPN gateway must be configured in Phase 2. This references the IKE VPN gateway object configured in Phase 1.

Configuring the IPsec policy
: The IPsec policy defines the proposal and PFS configuration for the VPN.

Configuring VPN establishment
: The VPN can be established immediately when the configuration is applied (and subsequently whenever the VPN expires), or it can be established on-traffic when there is user data traffic. By default, VPNs are established on-traffic.

Configuring fragmentation
: Fragmentation may be required on VPN traffic because of the overhead associated with IPsec VPNs (either ESP/AH overhead or overhead associated with Tunnel mode) and the underlying MTU of the physical data links. A few options can be selected for the fragmentation. You can alternatively clear the `DF` bit, set the `DF` bit, and copy the `DF` bit. If fragmentation is required but the `DF` bit is set (and honored by the SRX), that traffic will be dropped.

Configuring Anti-Replay detection
: By default, Anti-Replay detection is enabled. It essentially consists of checking the sequence numbers and enforcing the check, rather than just ignoring the sequence numbers. Anti-Replay detection can be disabled manually if desired on a VPN-by-VPN basis.

Configuring VPN monitoring
: VPN monitoring is a proprietary method of ensuring that the VPN is actually established (which goes beyond the VPN gateway availability of DPD to actually ensure that the VPN itself is up). A few parameters must be configured as part of VPN monitoring, including what device to ping, what source interface is used, and whether the traffic is optimized. The optimized setting omits sending the pings when user data is present.

Configuring a common site-to-site VPN component. Configure a VPN called East-Branch, which will serve as the site-to-site VPN for the East Branch to Campus site:

- Use an IKE gateway called East-Branch.

- Use an IPsec policy called `Remote-Office-Client`.
- Establish the VPNs immediately and automatically rekey.
- Disable Anti-Replay detection.
- Always clear the Don't Fragment (`DF`) bit.
- Monitor the VPN by pinging the IP address 192.168.1.50 using a method in which the pings are only sent in the absence of traffic every three seconds with a failure threshold of 3.

```
[edit]
root@SRX5800# edit security ipsec vpn East-Branch

[edit security ipsec vpn East-Branch]
root@SRX5800# set ike gateway East-Branch

[edit security ipsec vpn East-Branch]
root@SRX5800# set ike ipsec-policy Remote-Office-Client

[edit security ipsec vpn East-Branch]
root@SRX5800# set establish-tunnels immediately

[edit security ipsec vpn East-Branch]
root@SRX5800# set df-bit clear

[edit security ipsec vpn East-Branch]
root@SRX5800# set ike no-anti-replay

[edit security ipsec vpn East-Branch]
root@SRX5800# set vpn-monitor optimized source-interface st0.0
destination-ip 192.168.1.50

[edit security ipsec vpn East-Branch]
root@SRX5800# show
df-bit clear;
vpn-monitor {
    optimized;
    destination-ip 192.168.1.50;
}
ike {
    gateway East-Branch;
    no-anti-replay;
}
ipsec-policy Remote-Office-Client;

[edit security ipsec vpn East-Branch]
root@SRX5800# up

[edit security ipsec]
root@SRX5800# set vpn-monitor-options inverval 3 threshold 3


[edit security ipsec]
root@SRX5800# show
vpn-monitor-options {
```

```
        interval 3;
        threshold 3;
    }

    [edit security ipsec]
    root@SRX5800#top commit
```

Configuring policy-based VPNs

The main thing that needs to be configured as part of policy-based VPNs is the tunnel action of the appropriate security policy rule. One thing that is often forgotten when it comes to configuring policy-based VPNs is that a route may still be needed to force the traffic to go to the correct destination zone. This is not special to the VPN configuration, as it also applies to standard traffic to determine the egress interface and egress zone.

Configuring a policy-based VPN for the East Branch to the Central site VPN. In this example, we will be configuring a policy-based VPN for the East Branch to the Central site VPN. Use the following properties for creating this policy-based VPN:

- Allow any HTTP traffic to or from the 10.0.0.0/8 network to 192.168.1.0/24 for the East-Branch VPN created in the previous steps.
- Log the connections on session close.

```
[edit]
root@SRX5800# set security zones security-zones trust address-book
address 10.0.0.0/8 10.0.0.0/8

[edit]
root@SRX5800# show security zones security-zone trust address-book
address 10.0.0.0/8 10.0.0.0/8


[edit]
root@SRX5800# set security zones security-zones untrust address-book
address 192.168.1.0/24 192.168.1.0/24

[edit]
root@SRX5800# show security zones security-zone untrust address-book
address 192.168.1.0/24 192.168.1.0/24

[edit]
root@SRX5800# edit security policies from-zone trust to-zone untrust policy
East-Branch-Outbound

[edit security policies from-zone trust to-zone untrust policy
East-Branch-Outbound]
root@SRX5800# set match source-address 10.0.0.0/8 destination-address
192.168.1.0/24 application junos-http

[edit security policies from-zone trust to-zone untrust policy
East-Branch-Outbound]
root@SRX5800# set then permit tunnel ipsec-vpn East-Branch pair-policy
East-Branch-Inbound
```

```
[edit security policies from-zone trust to-zone untrust policy
East-Branch-Outbound]
root@SRX5800# set then log session-close

[edit security policies from-zone trust to-zone untrust policy
East-Branch-Outbound]
root@SRX5800# show
match {
        source-address 10.0.0.0/8;
        destination-address 192.168.1.0/24;
        application junos-http;
        }
 then {
        permit {
               tunnel {
                 ipsec-vpn East-Branch;
                 pair-policy East-Branch-Inbound;
                }
         }
            log {
                session-close;
            }
  }

[edit security policies from-zone trust to-zone untrust policy
East-Branch-Outbound]
root@SRX5800#top edit security policies from-zone untrust to-zone
trust policy East-Branch-Inbound

[edit security policies from-zone trust to-zone untrust policy
East-Branch-Inbound]
root@SRX5800# show
match {
        source-address 192.168.1.0/24;
        destination-address 10.0.0.0/8;
        application junos-http;
        }
 then {
        permit {
               tunnel {
                 ipsec-vpn East-Branch;
                 pair-policy East-Branch-Outbound;
                }
         }
            log {
                session-close;
            }
  }

[edit security policies from-zone trust to-zone untrust policy
East-Branch-Inbound]
root@SRX5800#top commit
```

Configuring route-based VPNs

Route-based VPNs require a few extra components over policy-based VPNs, as outlined here:

Configuring secure tunnel interfaces
: Secure tunnel interfaces are virtual interfaces that place all of the traffic that arrives in them into VPNs that are bound to the tunnel interface. They are required for route-based VPNs, where the traffic destined to the VPN is routed into the secure tunnel interface. It is important to understand that just like standard logical interfaces, the units can be in different zones from each other, so they can be separate.

Configuring interface binding
: Once the st0.*x* interface has been created, the VPN must be bound to the appropriate secure tunnel interface. This is done within the Phase 2 configuration.

Configuring proxy IDs
: Proxy IDs must be configured for route-based VPNs since they cannot be derived from anything like policy-based VPNs can. Policy-based VPNs can also be overwritten by defining the proxy IDs manually. At the time of this writing, only a single proxy ID can be defined per VPN on the SRX.

Configuring routing
: The SRX must know how to reach the destination networks. This can be done through the use of static routing or dynamic routing. In this example configuration, static routing is used.

Although route-based VPNs do not require a policy with the Tunnel action, security policies to allow the traffic are still required. The policy is a regular policy, with the standard Permit action. The following syntax shows the Then action of the policy, followed by a complete example of a match policy:

```
[edit]
root@SRX5800# set interfaces st0 unit 0 family inet address 192.168.100.1/24

root@SRX5800# show interfaces st0
unit 0 {
    family inet {
        address 192.168.100.1/24;
    }
}

[edit]
root@SRX5800# edit security ipsec vpn East-Branch

[edit security ipsec vpn East-Branch]
root@SRX5800# set bind-interface st0.0

[edit security ipsec vpn East-Branch]
root@SRX5800# set ike proxy-identity local 10.0.0.0/8 remote 192.168.1.0/24
service junos-http
```

```
[edit security ipsec vpn East-Branch]
root@SRX5800# set ike gateway East-Branch

[edit security ipsec vpn East-Branch]
root@SRX5800# set ipsec-policy Remote-Office-Client


[edit security ipsec vpn East-Branch]
root@SRX5800# show
bind-interface st0.0;
ike {
    gateway East-Branch;
    proxy-identity {
        local 10.0.0.0/8;
        remote 192.168.1.0/24;
        service junos-http;
    }
    ipsec-policy Remote-Office-Client;
}

[edit security ipsec vpn East-Branch]
root@SRX5800# top


[edit]
root@SRX5800# set routing-options static route 192.168.1.0/24
next-hop 192.168.100.254

[edit]
root@SRX5800# show routing-options static route 192.168.1.0/24
next-hop 192.168.100.254

[edit]
root@SRX5800# set security zones security-zones trust address-book
address 10.0.0.0/8 10.0.0.0/8

[edit]
root@SRX5800# show security zones security-zone trust address-book
address 10.0.0.0/8 10.0.0.0/8

[edit]
root@SRX5800# set security zones security-zones untrust address-book
address 192.168.1.0/24 192.168.1.0/24

[edit]
root@SRX5800# show security zones security-zone untrust address-book
address 192.168.1.0/24 192.168.1.0/24

[edit]
root@SRX5800# edit security policies from-zone trust to-zone untrust policy
East-Branch-Outbound

[edit security policies from-zone trust to-zone untrust policy
East-Branch-Outbound]
root@SRX5800# set match source-address 10.0.0.0/8 destination-address
```

```
192.168.1.0/24 application junos-http

[edit security policies from-zone trust to-zone untrust policy
East-Branch-Outbound]
root@SRX5800# set then permit

[edit security policies from-zone trust to-zone untrust policy
East-Branch-Outbound]
root@SRX5800# set then log session-close

[edit security policies from-zone trust to-zone untrust policy
East-Branch-Outbound]
root@SRX5800# show
match {
        source-address 10.0.0.0/8;
        destination-address 192.168.1.0/24;
        application junos-http;
        }
 then {
        permit
        log {
                session-close;
            }
  }

[edit security policies from-zone trust to-zone untrust policy
East-Branch-Outbound]
root@SRX5800#top edit security policies from-zone untrust to-zone trust policy
East-Branch-Inbound

[edit security policies from-zone untrust to-zone trust policy
East-Branch-Inbound]
root@SRX5800# set match source-address 192.168.1.0/24 destination-address
192.168.1.0/24 application junos-http

[edit security policies from-zone untrust to-zone trust policy
East-Branch-Inbound]
root@SRX5800# set then permit

[edit security policies from-zone untrust to-zone trust policy
East-Branch-Inbound]
root@SRX5800# set then log session-close


[edit security policies from-zone untrust to-zone trust policy
East-Branch-Inbound]
root@SRX5800# show
match {
        source-address 192.168.1.0/24;
        destination-address 10.0.0.0/8;
        application junos-http;
        }
 then {
        permit
        log {
```

```
                session-close;
            }
    }

[edit security policies from-zone untrust to-zone trust policy
East-Branch-Inbound]
root@SRX5800#top commit
```

Configuring Manual Key IPsec VPNs

In certain circumstances, an administrator may find that the benefits of IKE are not worth the overhead in processing, and may elect to use manual key VPNs instead. The configuration is much lighter with manual key VPNs because there are no Phase 1 or Phase 2 negotiations; each side can just start sending the data at will with the administratively defined IPsec keys. Of course, both sides must be configured appropriately, or else the data will be dropped by either side.

The following parameters must be defined for manual key encryption:

Gateway
: This is the gateway object for the manual key encryption. This must be either an IP address or a resolvable hostname.

Encryption
: Encryption defines the encryption algorithm and the encryption key itself (in either ASCII text or hexadecimal). The encryption algorithm can be DES-CBC, 3DES-CBC, AES-128-CBC, AES-192-CBC, or AES-256-CBC. Note that the encryption key length must be 8 bytes for DES, 24 bytes for 3DES, 16 bytes for AES-128, 24 bytes for AES-192, and 32 bytes for AES-256.

Authentication
: Authentication defines the authentication algorithm and the authentication key to be used (in either ASCII text or hexadecimal). The authentication algorithm can be either HMAC-MD5-96 or HMAC-SHA1-96. Note that this key length must be 16 bytes for MD5 and 20 bytes for SHA-1.

External interface
: This is the interface on which the IPsec VPN will terminate. This must be the correct interface (including the correct unit) or the VPN negotiation will fail.

Protocol
: The protocol must be defined as either ESP or AH.

Security Parameter Index (SPI)
: The SPI is a number the VPN gateways use to identify which VPN keys are used for the VPN. The SPIs must match or else there will be a decryption failure on the peer device because it will not be able to identify which keys are applicable to decrypt the traffic for the VPN. Remember that two peers can have more than one active VPN at the same time, to each other, and therefore they must use SPIs to identify which VPN the packet belongs to so that it can be decrypted accordingly.

Configuring a manual key IPsec VPN

Build the following scenario using manual key encryption between two IPsec VPN peers:

- Connect an SRX5800 to Remote-Office-Manual via manual key encryption.
- Configure the encryption algorithm to be AES-256-CBC and the authentication algorithm to be HMAC-SHA1-96.
- Encryption keys should be EncryptionKey1234567890123456789.
- Authentication keys should be AuthenticationKey123.
- The protocol should be ESP.
- Use 1003 for the SPI.
- The external interface should be ge-0/0/0.0.

```
[edit]
root@SRX5800# edit security ipsec vpn Remote-Office-Manual manual

[edit security ipsec vpn Remote-Office-Manual manual]
root@SRX5800# set gateway 198.18.10.254

[edit security ipsec vpn Remote-Office-Manual manual]
root@SRX5800# set external-interface ge-0/0/0.0

[edit security ipsec vpn Remote-Office-Manual manual]
root@SRX5800# set protocol esp

[edit security ipsec vpn Remote-Office-Manual manual]
root@SRX5800# set spi 1003

[edit security ipsec vpn Remote-Office-Manual manual]
root@SRX5800# set authentication algorithm hmac-sha1-96

[edit security ipsec vpn Remote-Office-Manual manual]
root@SRX5800# set authentication key ascii-text AuthenticationKey123

[edit security ipsec vpn Remote-Office-Manual manual]
root@SRX5800# set encryption algorithm aes-256-cbc

[edit security ipsec vpn Remote-Office-Manual manual]
root@SRX5800# set encryption key ascii-text EncryptionKey1234567890123456789

[edit security ipsec vpn Remote-Office-Manual manual]
root@SRX5800#show
gateway 198.18.10.254;
external-interface ge-0/0/0.0;
protocol esp;
spi 1003;
authentication {
    algorithm hmac-sha1-96;
    key ascii-text "$9$7j-dwoJDqPQwYJDHmF3revWX-ws4aJDwYDkPQ9CylK8x-
Y2aZjqY25Qn6At"; ## SECRET-DATA
}
```

```
encryption {
    algorithm aes-256-cbc;
    key ascii-text "$9$fTznEhrvMXEcoGUDPfRhSrK8oaU.PQuOhreM-dHq.fFnCtuIhSpu7-
wYoaCtpOhSylKMLxhcwY24ZGCtpOhSWLx7Vwx7"; ## SECRET-DATA
}

[edit security ipsec vpn Remote-Office-Manual manual]
root@SRX5800#top commit
```

Dynamic VPN

In this example, we will demonstrate how to leverage the built-in Dynamic VPN client on the branch SRX Series devices to connect remote clients to the corporate network.

Phase 1 proposal
: Create a proposal called Dynamic-VPN that uses 3DES-SHA1, preshared keys, Diffie-Hellman Group 2, and a lifetime of four hours, and set a description.

Phase 1 policy
: Create a policy called Dynamic-VPN-Policy that uses aggressive mode, the preshared key DialUp4123, and the Dynamic-VPN proposal, and set a description.

Phase 1 gateway
: Create an IKE gateway called Dynamic-VPN-Gateway. You will use the XAuth parameters that we defined earlier in the chapter for our XAuth profile called XAuth. Limit the number of connections to five using a shared IKE ID of *dynvpn@company.com*. This VPN should be terminated on interface ge-0/0/0.0 using the IKE policy Dynamic-VPN-Policy. Ensure that the ge-0/0/0.0 interface allows inbound IKE and HTTP/HTTPS connections so that the user can access the web interface and to make sure VPNs can establish properly.

Phase 2 proposal
: Create a proposal called Dynamic-VPN using AES256-SHA1 with ESP as the IPsec protocol, set the lifetime to 3,600 seconds, and provide a description for the proposal.

Phase 2 policy
: Create a policy called Dynamic-VPN-Policy which uses the Dynamic-VPN Phase 2 proposal with PDF Diffie-Hellman Group 2.

Phase 2 VPN
: Create a Phase 2 VPN called Dynamic-VPN which uses Dynamic-VPN-Gateway as the gateway and Dynamic-VPN-Policy as the Phase 2 policy.

Dynamic VPN client configuration
: Create a Dynamic VPN client configuration called Dynamic-VPN-Clients which uses the Dynamic-VPN configuration we defined for user `dynvpn`. This profile should allow users to access the resource 10.0.0.0/8 behind the firewall when they are connected. Use the XAuth profile XAuth, and also force the client to upgrade if an upgrade to the client is necessary upon login.

Local certificate

Finally, generate a local certificate which can be used to host HTTPS on the web server on the ge-0/0/0.0 interface. This is needed so that we can allow users to log in securely. You must also ensure that the ge-0/0/0.0 interface allows the HTTPS connection inbound.

```
[edit]
root@SRX210# edit security ike proposal Dynamic-VPN

[edit security ike proposal Dynamic-VPN]
root@SRX210# set authentication-method pre-shared-keys dh-group group2
authentication-algorithm sha1 encryption algorithm 3des-cbc lifetime-seconds
12000 description "Dynamic VPN Proposal"

[edit security ike proposal Dynamic-VPN]
root@SRX210# show
description "Dynamic VPN Proposal";
authentication-method pre-shared-keys;
dh-group group2;
authentication-algorithm sha1;
encryption-algorithm 3des-cbc;
lifetime-seconds 12000;

[edit security ike proposal Dynamic-VPN]
root@SRX210#up

[edit security ike]
root@SRX210# edit policy Dynamic-VPN-Policy

[edit security ike policy Dynamic-VPN-Policy]
root@SRX210# set mode aggressive description "Dynamic-VPN IKE Policy" proposals
Dynamic-VPN pre-shared-key ascii-text DialUp4123

[edit security ike policy Dynamic-VPN-Policy]
root@SRX210# show
mode aggressive;
description "Dynamic-VPN IKE Policy";
proposals Dynamic-VPN;
pre-shared-key ascii-text "$9$K8zvWXY2aZGi7-.f5T9CM8LxVw24aUik"; ## SECRET-DATA

[edit security ike policy Dynamic-VPN-Policy]
root@SRX210# up

[edit security ike]
root@SRX210# edit gateway Dynamic-VPN-Gateway

[edit security ike gateway Dynamic-VPN-Gateway]
root@SRX210# set external-interface ge-0/0/0.0 ike-policy Dynamic-VPN-Policy
xauth access-profile XAuth

[edit security ike gateway Dynamic-VPN-Gateway]
root@SRX210# set dynamic connection-limit 5 user-at-hostname dynvpn@company.com
ike-user-type shared-ike-id
```

```
[edit security ike gateway Dynamic-VPN-Gateway]
root@SRX210# show
ike-policy Dynamic-VPN-Policy;
dynamic {
    user-at-hostname "dynvpn@company.com";
    connections-limit 5;
    ike-user-type shared-ike-id;
}
external-interface ge-0/0/0;
xauth access-profile XAuth;

[edit security ike gateway Dynamic-VPN-Gateway]
root@SRX210# top

[edit]
root@SRX210# show access-profile
XAuth;

[edit]
root@SRX210# show access profile XAuth
authentication-order radius;
radius-server {
    192.168.224.60 {
        port 1812;
        secret "$9$pf5hB1hrev7dbgoJDk.zFIEclMX"; ## SECRET-DATA
        source-address 192.168.224.3;
    }
}

[edit]
root@SRX210# show security zones security-zone trust
interfaces {
    ge-0/0/0.0 {
        host-inbound-traffic {
            system-services {
                http;
                https;
                ping;
                ike;
            }
            protocols {
                ospf;
            }
        }
    }
}

[edit]
root@SRX210# edit security ipsec proposal Dynamic-VPN

[edit security ipsec proposal Dynamic-VPN]
root@SRX210# set description "Dynamic VPN Proposal" authentication-algorithm
hmac-sha1-96 encryption-algorithm aes-256-cbc lifetime-seconds 3600 protocol esp

[edit security ipsec proposal Dynamic-VPN]
```

```
root@SRX210# show
description "Dynamic VPN Proposal";
protocol esp;
authentication-algorithm hmac-sha1-96;
encryption-algorithm aes-256-cbc;
lifetime-seconds 3600;

[edit security ipsec proposal Dynamic-VPN]
root@SRX210# up

[edit security ipsec]
root@SRX210# edit policy Dynamic-VPN-Policy

[edit security ipsec policy Dynamic-VPN-Policy]
root@SRX210# set description "Dynamic VPN Phase 2 Policy" proposals Dynamic-VPN
perfect-forward-secrecy keys group2

[edit security ipsec policy Dynamic-VPN-Policy]
root@SRX210# show
description "Dynamic VPN Phase 2 Policy";
perfect-forward-secrecy {
    keys group2;
}
proposals Dynamic-VPN;

[edit security ipsec policy Dynamic-VPN-Policy]
root@SRX210 up

[edit security ipsec]
root@SRX210# edit vpn Dynamic-VPN

[edit security ipsec vpn Dynamic-VPN]
root@SRX210# set ike gateway Dynamic-VPN-Gateway ipsec-policy Dynamic-VPN-Policy

[edit security ipsec vpn Dynamic-VPN]
root@SRX210# show
ike {
    gateway Dynamic-VPN-Gateway;
    ipsec-policy Dynamic-VPN-Policy;
}

[edit security ipsec vpn Dynamic-VPN]
root@SRX210# up 2

[edit security]
root@SRX210# edit dynamic-vpn

[edit security dynamic-vpn
root@SRX210# set clients Dynamic-VPN-Clients remote-protected-resources
10.0.0.0/8

[edit security dynamic-vpn]
root@SRX210# set clients Dynamic-VPN-Clients user dynvpn

[edit security dynamic-vpn]
```

```
root@SRX210# set clients Dynamic-VPN-Clients ipsec-vpn Dynamic-VPN

[edit security dynamic-vpn]
root@SRX210# set force-upgrade

[edit security dynamic-vpn]
root@SRX210# set access-profile XAuth

[edit security dynamic-vpn]
root@SRX210# show
force-upgrade;
access-profile XAuth;
clients {
    Dynamic-VPN-Clients {
        remote-protected-resources {
            10.0.0.0/8;
        }
        ipsec-vpn Dynamic-VPN;
        user {
            dynvpn;
        }
    }
}

[edit security dynamic-vpn]
root@SRX210# top

[edit]
root@SRX210# run request security pki generate-key-pair certificate-id HTTPS
Generated key pair HTTPS, key size 1024 bits

[edit]
root@SRX210# set system services web-management https
system-generated-certificate interface ge-0/0/0.0

[edit]
root@SRX210# show system services web-management
https {
    system-generated-certificate;
    interface ge-0/0/0.0;
}
```

VPN Verification and Troubleshooting

Once the configuration of the VPN is complete and committed, you should take some additional steps to ensure that the VPN is operational. You can also use these steps whenever there appears to be an issue with VPN establishment or connectivity. This section details the useful commands that can help provide information on the status of VPNs, as well as troubleshooting steps and available facilities that can provide advanced diagnostics for resolving VPN issues.

Useful VPN Commands

The SRX has several useful commands when it comes to determining the state of VPNs, including commands that identify specific aspects of VPNs.

show security ike security-associations

The `show security ike security-associations` command shows any VPNs that have passed Phase 1 and have an active IKE security association for Phase 1.

This command is important because if IKE fails to complete Phase 1, it can't proceed to Phase 2. (An exception is that if the IKE Phase 1 lifetime expires before the Phase 2 lifetime expires, there may not be a listing for the IKE security association while there will be one for Phase 2. However, when the Phase 2 security association expires, the Phase 1 IKE security association will need to be renegotiated first.)

The following output shows an actively established Phase 1 security association, first without the `detail` argument and then with the `detail` argument. There are lots of useful reasons for using the `detail` command to show the properties of the tunnel itself. It's often most useful to define the peer gateway before the detail to only show a specific gateway's status. When troubleshooting VPN establishment, you must first verify that Phase 1 is completing successfully before moving on to Phase 2, and this command helps provide that information.

```
root@SRX210> show security ike security-associations
Index   Remote Address  State  Initiator cookie  Responder cookie  Mode
1484    198.18.1.1    UP     27c96e043fb9f80c  73ec1d49b689f198  Main

root@SRX210> show security ike security-associations detail
IKE peer 198.18.1.1, Index 1484,
  Role: Initiator, State: UP
  Initiator cookie: 27c96e043fb9f80c, Responder cookie: 73ec1d49b689f198
  Exchange type: Main, Authentication method: Pre-shared-keys
  Local: 198.18.1.254:500, Remote: 198.18.1.1:500
  Lifetime: Expires in 28239 seconds
  Algorithms:
   Authentication        : sha1
   Encryption            : aes-cbc (256 bits)
   Pseudo random function: hmac-sha1
  Traffic statistics:
   Input  bytes  :                 780
   Output bytes  :                 992
   Input  packets:                   4
   Output packets:                   5
  Flags: Caller notification sent
  IPSec security associations: 1 created, 0 deleted
  Phase 2 negotiations in progress: 0
```

show security ipsec security-associations

Once Phase 1 has been established, you might need to determine whether Phase 2 has been successfully completed. A very useful command is the `show security ipsec security-associations` command. It will show the established Phase 2 security associations and applicable properties. There is also the `detail` command that provides much more information regarding the state of the VPN.

```
root@SRX210> show security ipsec security-associations
  Total active tunnels: 1
  ID     Gateway          Port  Algorithm       SPI      Life:sec/kb  Mon vsys
  <131073 198.18.1.1  500   ESP:aes-256/sha1 20b3bf2e 1673/ unlim  -   0
  >131073 198.18.1.1  500   ESP:aes-256/sha1 3958d177 1673/ unlim  -   0

root@SRX210> show security ipsec security-associations detail
  Virtual-system: Root
  Local Gateway: 198.18.1.254, Remote Gateway: 198.18.1.1
  Local Identity: ipv4_subnet(any:0,[0..7]=172.31.0.0/16)
  Remote Identity: ipv4_subnet(any:0,[0..7]=192.168.0.0/16)
    DF-bit: clear
    Direction: inbound, SPI: 20b3bf2e, AUX-SPI: 0
    Hard lifetime: Expires in 1073 seconds
    Lifesize Remaining:  Unlimited
    Soft lifetime: Expires in 436 seconds
    Mode: tunnel, Type: dynamic, State: installed, VPN Monitoring: -
    Protocol: ESP, Authentication: hmac-sha1-96, Encryption: aes-cbc (256 bits)
    Anti-replay service: enabled, Replay window size: 64

    Direction: outbound, SPI: 3958d177, AUX-SPI: 0
    Hard lifetime: Expires in 1073 seconds
    Lifesize Remaining:  Unlimited
    Soft lifetime: Expires in 436 seconds
    Mode: tunnel, Type: dynamic, State: installed, VPN Monitoring: -
    Protocol: ESP, Authentication: hmac-sha1-96, Encryption: aes-cbc (256 bits)
    Anti-replay service: enabled, Replay window size: 64
```

show security ipsec statistics

It's always useful to gather high-level information regarding how the platform is processing security information, including issues with encryption and decryption. The command `show security ipsec statistics` provides such useful information, including the number of encrypted and decrypted ESP and AH packets, as well as the different types of failures. You can check this command multiple times when trying to determine if the number of failures and errors is increasing.

```
root@SRX210> show security ipsec statistics
ESP Statistics:
  Encrypted bytes:         192721984
  Decrypted bytes:          90699752
  Encrypted packets:         1535730
  Decrypted packets:         1646906
AH Statistics:
  Input bytes:                     0
```

```
    Output bytes:                0
    Input packets:               0
    Output packets:              0
  Errors:
    AH authentication failures: 0, Replay errors: 0
    ESP authentication failures: 0, ESP decryption failures: 0
    Bad headers: 0, Bad trailers: 0
```

You can clear the information with the `clear security ipsec statistics` command.

VPN Tracing and Debugging

When the information contained within the output of the `show` commands is not enough to determine the root cause of VPN negotiation failures, more detailed information is required to determine where the message breakdown occurs. The SRX offers detailed breakdowns of the debugging of VPN establishment, even down to the individual IPsec messages that are sent and received by the SRX. So, let's cover the individual troubleshooting steps that you can use to help troubleshoot a VPN issue. Then we'll discuss how to perform tracing, and finally what to look for in the output.

VPN troubleshooting process

Follow these steps when troubleshooting a VPN issue:

1. Verify that the peer gateway is reachable.

   If there is an issue with routing to the remote gateway, or if a device is limiting access (e.g., IKE traffic, ESP/AH traffic, NAT-T tunneled traffic), VPN establishment will fail. Basic tests could include ping and traceroute (assuming that these services are available on the remote device) to ensure that routing is functioning properly and there are no Internet service provider (ISP) issues. The following services should not be blocked by *any* device between the SRX and the remote peer:

   a. UDP port 500 (default port for IKE negotiation). If this is blocked, IKE negotiation will fail, with messages on the initiating gateway indicating that the connection limit has been reached. On the responder device, there will be no messages at all because the IKE traffic will not have reached the gateway.

   b. IP Protocol 50 (ESP) if using ESP. If this is blocked, IKE negotiation may complete successfully, but VPN traffic will not be able to communicate when using ESP.

   c. IP Protocol 51 (AH) if using AH. If this is blocked, IKE negotiation may complete successfully, but VPN traffic will not be able to communicate when using AH.

   d. UDP port 4500 (default port for NAT-T). If this is blocked, IKE negotiation may complete successfully, but VPN traffic will not be able to communicate when using NAT-T.

2. Check the access lists and zone settings.

   On the SRX, if an access list is enabled on the external interface terminating the VPN or the lo0 interface that blocks any of the services mentioned in step 1, the VPN will not be able to establish. Additionally, the SRX requires IKE to be enabled on the interface, or in the zone of the external interface as a host-inbound-traffic system service (it can be at the zone or interface level, with the interface level overriding the zone level). Make sure this is enabled; otherwise, the VPN will fail to establish.

3. Check whether hostnames are used for the gateway.

   You can optionally define the gateway address as a DNS address rather than an IP address. In this case, DNS must be enabled and functioning properly to be able to identify the remote gateway. Configuring multiple DNS servers often helps in case of a DNS server failure.

4. Check whether the VPN is terminating on the correct interface.

   In Phase 1 of the VPN, you must define on which interface the VPN will terminate. If the VPN is trying to terminate on a different interface (even if the logical unit is wrong), the VPN will fail to establish.

5. Check whether the Phase 1 modes match on both gateways.

   Both gateways must use the same Phase 1 mode, either Main mode or Aggressive mode. If the modes don't match, the VPN establishment will fail.

6. Check whether the Phase 1 proposals match.

   The Phase 1 proposals must match on both VPN gateways. If they do not match, negotiations will fail. The SRX supports up to four proposals, so if the first proposal negotiation fails, it will try the other proposals if available, but if there are no matches the negotiations will fail in Phase 1. Check the proper combination of certificate versus PSK, encryption and authentication algorithms, along with the proper Diffie-Hellman groups.

7. Check whether the IKE identities are configured correctly.

   As mentioned, there are a few different types of IKE identities, namely, IP address, FQDN, and UFQDN. You can define the local identity (to be presented to the peer) and the peer identity (to be presented by the peer). The local/peer must match on the respective systems or else Phase 1 will fail.

8. Check whether the Phase 1 authentication is properly configured.

   There are two types of Phase 1 authentication: preshared keys and certificates. In the case of preshared keys, the preshared keys must match on both VPN gateways for the VPN to complete Phase 1. In the case of certificates, the certificate presented must be signed by a trusted CA (configured to work for the VPN). Next, if certificate revocation checking is enabled, the certificate must not be revoked for the authentication to pass.

9. If XAuth is used, check whether authentication is succeeding.

   XAuth occurs between Phase 1 and Phase 2 of the VPN establishment process. At the time of this writing, XAuth is only supported for authentication of RADIUS users, and not local users on the firewall. If XAuth authentication does not succeed, authentication will fail before Phase 2.

10. Check whether PFS is configured.

    If PFS is configured, it must be configured on both gateways. Additionally, the same Diffie-Hellman groups must be used between the peers for PFS. Note that the Diffie-Hellman groups do not need to be the same as what is used in Phase 1; however, both peers must use the same in the PFS configuration.

11. Check whether Phase 2 proposals match.

    Just like Phase 1, the Phase 2 proposals must match on both ends (including encryption and authentication algorithms). If they don't match, Phase 2 negotiations will fail. Up to four proposals may be defined and will be negotiated in order of definition if the previous proposal fails, but if no proposal matches, the Phase 2 proposals will fail.

12. Check whether the proxy IDs match.

    This is probably the most common reason for VPN negotiations to fail, especially when trying to establish VPNs between different vendors. Proxy IDs can be manually defined in the Phase 2 IPsec VPN configuration, or they can be derived from the respective policies which are used for the VPN in the case of policy-based VPNs. Doing a trace will show whether the VPN is failing due to proxy ID mismatch, but this is something to be aware of.

13. Check whether the key lifetimes match.

    This isn't an explicitly required parameter, but sometimes this may matter with other vendors' implementations of IPsec VPNs, so it is best to set the VPNs to support the same key lifetimes to ensure proper interoperability.

14. If policy-based VPNs are enabled, check whether the correct policy is being matched.

    With policy-based VPNs, the traffic should match the correct policy. If it is not matching the correct policy, this might be a result of the incorrect policy configuration, or a routing issue or misconfiguration. Remember that even in the case of policy-based VPNs, the SRX must know what the egress interface and, thus, the egress zone is to match the correct From/To zone pair. It doesn't matter whether static or dynamic routing is used; the routing must be properly configured. Doing a simple flow trace will identify whether the traffic is being matched to the correct policy along with the correct routing information. Also, make sure the policy is configured to tunnel the traffic to the correct VPN.

15. If route-based VPNs are configured, check whether proper routing and security policies are configured.

    With a route-based VPN, you still need to define the correct security policy to permit the traffic. If the traffic is not being permitted by policy, it cannot enter the VPN. You can determine this by doing a flow debug to enable logging on the policies to ensure that the traffic is being permitted. Additionally, with route-based VPNs, the appropriate routing must be configured to route the traffic into the correct tunnel interface. Both static and dynamic routing can be used, but in the case of dynamic routing, you must make sure the applicable protocols are enabled on the tunnel interface (from the protocol configuration, along with the host-inbound-traffic protocol configuration).

16. If route-based VPNs are configured, check whether the VPN is bound to the correct interface.

    Route-based VPNs must be bound to the correct interface. If they are bound to the wrong interface, VPN negotiation may establish, but the traffic will not go through the right VPN.

17. Check whether NAT is occurring between the two VPN gateways.

    If so, NAT-T must be enabled (primarily for remote access VPNs and not site-to-site VPNs) because the ESP/AH packets will be modified, which will invalidate the hash for integrity checking.

18. If all else fails, check the release notes to see if there are any known issues for the release of Junos you are running, and check the Knowledge Base. If you still cannot find an answer, contact the Juniper Networks Technical Assistance Center (JTAC) for additional assistance in troubleshooting.

Configuring and analyzing VPN tracing

You can do a trace on a VPN in two different ways. The first option is to simply trigger a trace between two VPN peers with a hidden command called `request security ike debug-enable`. The second option is to turn on wholesale IKE debugging on the entire platform. The first method is best if you know the IP address of your remote VPN which you would like to trace for; the second method is good for other scenarios where you might want to troubleshoot more than just a single IPsec negotiation. Another difference is that the first method is done by operational mode commands, whereas the second is done by the standard tracefile configuration. The following output shows how to briefly troubleshoot between two hosts, the local SRX 192.168.100.5 and the remote peer 192.168.100.3, and logs the output to */var/log/kmd*:

```
root@SRX5800> request security ike debug-enable local 192.168.100.5 remote
192.168.100.3 level 15

root@SRX5800> show log kmd

root@SRX5800> request security ike debug-disable
```

By default, Junos logs some information related to VPN establishment to the file */var/log/kmd*. The tracing configuration is the same regardless of the type of VPN.

Here are a few additional configuration options you can enable to provide more information:

Enable IKE tracing
: By default, IKE tracing is not enabled. IKE tracing allows you to view the information in Phase 1. Although this can be logged to a file other than */var/log/kmd*, direct all logs to that file for simplicity.

Enable IPsec tracing
: IPsec tracing will allow more detailed information to be logged to the *.kmd* file, but note that the destination is not configurable. If IPsec tracing is not enabled, the */var/log/kmd* file will only show high-level VPN status.

Trigger VPN establishment (on traffic)
: If the VPN is not configured to automatically establish (using the "establish immediately" Phase 2 option), some traffic must be generated before the VPN will attempt to establish.

View VPN trace output
: After the VPN has attempted to establish, view the output of the trace log.

Disable tracing after solving the issue
: It is important to disable tracing when you are not using it. In the case of VPN tracing, it isn't so much a matter of performance; rather, it generates a lot of logs, so when it's not needed, it is best to disable it.

Troubleshoot traffic flows
: If you have determined that the VPN is properly established, but the traffic is not passing through the VPN as expected (whether using policy- or route-based VPNs), refer to the discussion of flow tracing in Chapter 3.

Here are the configurations to enable the additional VPN tracing options:

```
[edit]
root@SRX5800# edit security ike traceoptions

[edit security ike traceoptions]
root@SRX5800# set flag ike

[edit security ike traceoptions]
root@SRX5800# set file kmd

[edit security ike traceoptions]
root@SRX5800# top edit security ipsec traceoptions

[edit security ike traceoptions]
root@SRX5800# show
file kmd;
flag ike;
```

```
[edit security ipsec traceoptions]
root@SRX5800# set flag all

[edit security ipsec traceoptions]
root@SRX5800#show
flag all;

[edit security ipsec traceoptions]
root@SRX5800#top commit and-quit
```

Troubleshooting a site-to-site VPN

After the VPN establishment has been triggered, you can look at the */var/log/kmd* file to determine exactly what is happening.

The file contains a lot of information regarding the particular IKE entries. Use the following sample output to help you sift through the file and find the relevant information to extract the root cause of the failure:

```
Phase 1 Proposal Failure

root@SRX5800> show log kmd

##
Use the sample output below to help you sift through it and find the relevant
information to extract the root cause of the failure.

Received first packet from peer 198.18.1.1
##

Aug 14 21:06:11 jnp_ike_connect: Start, remote_name = 198.18.1.1:500, xchg = 2,
flags = 00000000
Aug 14 21:06:11 ike_sa_allocate: Start, SA = { a677627c 13dce62b - 00000000
00000000 }
Aug 14 21:06:11 ike_init_isakmp_sa: Start, remote = 198.18.1.1:500, initiator = 1
Aug 14 21:06:11 jnp_ike_connect: SA = { a677627c 13dce62b - 00000000 00000000},
nego = -1
Aug 14 21:06:11 ike_st_o_sa_proposal: Start
Aug 14 21:06:11 ike_policy_reply_isakmp_vendor_ids: Start
Aug 14 21:06:11 ike_st_o_private: Start
Aug 14 21:06:11 ike_policy_reply_private_payload_out: Start
Aug 14 21:06:11 ike_encode_packet: Start, SA = { 0xa677627c 13dce62b - 00000000
00000000 } / 00000000, nego = -1

##
Send response to source packet with src-ip 198.18.1.3
##

Aug 14 21:06:11 ike_send_packet: Start, send SA = { a677627c 13dce62b - 00000000
00000000}, nego = -1, src = 198.18.1.3:500, dst = 198.18.1.1:500,
routing table id = 0

##
Got second exchange from the peer, start decoding it
##
```

```
Aug 14 21:06:11 ike_get_sa: Start, SA =
{ a677627c 13dce62b - 2b282cfa fb5b7e9e } / 00000000, remote = 198.18.1.1:500
Aug 14 21:06:11 ike_sa_find: Not found SA =
{ a677627c 13dce62b - 2b282cfa fb5b7e9e }
Aug 14 21:06:11 ike_sa_find_half: Found half SA =
{ a677627c 13dce62b - 00000000 00000000 }
Aug 14 21:06:11 ike_sa_upgrade: Start, SA =
{ a677627c 13dce62b - 00000000 00000000 } -> { ... - 2b282cfa fb5b7e9e }
Aug 14 21:06:11 ike_alloc_negotiation: Start, SA =
{ a677627c 13dce62b - 2b282cfa fb5b7e9e}
Aug 14 21:06:11 ike_decode_packet: Start
Aug 14 21:06:11 ike_decode_packet: Start, SA =
{ a677627c 13dce62b - 2b282cfa fb5b7e9e} / 00000000, nego = 0

##
No valid proposal was choosen.  At this point you should contact the peer to
make sure that the Phase 1 proposal matches exactly, including the following
properties:  Main/Aggressive Mode, Encryption and Authentication Algorithims,
Preshared Key/Certificate, Diffie-Hellman Group
##

Aug 14 21:06:11 ike_st_i_n: Start, doi = 1, protocol = 1,
code = No proposal chosen (14), spi[0..16] = a677627c 13dce62b ...,
data[0..8] = 00080004 00000000 ...
Aug 14 21:06:11 198.18.1.3:500 (Responder) <-> 198.18.1.1:500
{ a677627c 13dce62b - 2b282cfa fb5b7e9e [0] / 0x00000000 }
Info; Received notify err = No proposal chosen (14) to isakmp sa, delete it

##
Message has been sent to inform the peer that no proposal has been chosen,
now SRX will delete its current negotiation and await another attempt
##

Aug 14 21:06:11 ike_st_i_private: Start
Aug 14 21:06:11 ike_send_notify: Connected, SA =
{ a677627c 13dce62b - 2b282cfa fb5b7e9e}, nego = 0
Aug 14 21:06:11 ike_delete_negotiation: Start, SA =
{ a677627c 13dce62b - 2b282cfa fb5b7e9e}, nego = 0
Aug 14 21:06:11 ike_free_negotiation_info: Start, nego = 0
Aug 14 21:06:11 ike_free_negotiation: Start, nego = 0
Aug 14 21:06:11 ike_remove_callback: Start, delete SA =
{ a677627c 13dce62b - 2b282cfa fb5b7e9e}, nego = -1
Aug 14 21:06:11 198.18.1.3:500 (Initiator) <-> 198.18.1.1:500
{ a677627c 13dce62b - 2b282cfa fb5b7e9e [-1] / 0x00000000 } IP;
Connection got error = 14, calling callback
Aug 14 21:06:11 ike_delete_negotiation: Start, SA =
{ a677627c 13dce62b - 2b282cfa fb5b7e9e}, nego = -1
Aug 14 21:06:11 jnp_ike_tunnel_table_entry_delete: Deleting tunnel_id:
1748 from IKE tunnel table
Aug 14 21:06:11 ike_sa_delete: Start, SA =
{ a677627c 13dce62b - 2b282cfa fb5b7e9e }


Phase 2 Proxy-ID Failure
```

```
root@SRX5800> show log kmd

##
Receive first packet in IKE negotiation, decode and evaluate
##

Aug  14 20:48:43 ike_sa_find_ip_port: Remote = 198.18.1.1:500,
Found SA = { 07a7f08c 798b8bd8 - d94d344c 834c287f}
Aug  14 20:48:43 ike_alloc_negotiation: Start, SA =
{ 07a7f08c 798b8bd8 - d94d344c 834c287f}
Aug  14 20:48:43 jnp_ike_create_delete_internal: SA =
{ 07a7f08c 798b8bd8 - d94d344c 834c287f}, nego = 0
Aug  14 20:48:43 ike_encode_packet: Start, SA =
{ 0x07a7f08c 798b8bd8 - d94d344c 834c287f } / 78353525, nego = 0
Aug  14 20:48:43 ike_send_packet: Start, send SA =
{ 07a7f08c 798b8bd8 - d94d344c 834c287f}, nego = 0, src = 198.18.1.3:500,
dst = 198.18.1.1:500, routing table id = 0
Aug  14 20:48:43 ike_delete_negotiation: Start, SA =
{ 07a7f08c 798b8bd8 - d94d344c 834c287f}, nego = 0
Aug  14 20:48:43 ike_free_negotiation_info: Start, nego = 0
Aug  14 20:48:43 ike_free_negotiation: Start, nego = 0
Aug  14 20:48:43 Group/Shared IKE ID VPN configured: 2
Aug  14 20:48:43 jnp_ike_connect_ipsec: Start, remote_name = 198.18.1.1:500,
flags = 00010000
Aug  14 20:48:43 ike_sa_find_ip_port: Remote = 198.18.1.1:500,
Found SA = { 07a7f08c 798b8bd8 - d94d344c 834c287f}
Aug  14 20:48:43 ike_alloc_negotiation: Start, SA =
{ 07a7f08c 798b8bd8 - d94d344c 834c287f}
Aug  14 20:48:43 jnp_ike_connect_ipsec: SA =
{ 07a7f08c 798b8bd8 - d94d344c 834c287f}, nego = 0

##
Phase 1 has completed IKE negotiations, start Phase 2 Quick Mode
##

Aug  14 20:48:43 ike_init_qm_negotiation: Start, initiator = 1,
message_id = 65c239c7
Aug  14 20:48:43 ike_st_o_qm_hash_1: Start
Aug  14 20:48:43 ike_st_o_qm_sa_proposals: Start
Aug  14 20:48:43 ike_st_o_qm_nonce: Start
Aug  14 20:48:43 ike_policy_reply_qm_nonce_data_len: Start
Aug  14 20:48:43 ike_st_o_qm_optional_ke: Start
Aug  14 20:48:43 ike_st_o_qm_optional_ids: Start
Aug  14 20:48:43 ike_st_qm_optional_id: Start
Aug  14 20:48:43 ike_st_qm_optional_id: Start
Aug  14 20:48:43 ike_st_o_private: Start
Aug  14 20:48:43 ike_policy_reply_private_payload_out: Start
Aug  14 20:48:43 ike_policy_reply_private_payload_out: Start
Aug  14 20:48:43 ike_st_o_encrypt: Marking encryption for packet
Aug  14 20:48:43 ike_encode_packet: Start, SA =
{ 0x07a7f08c 798b8bd8 - d94d344c 834c287f } / 65c239c7, nego = 0
Aug  14 20:48:43 ike_finalize_qm_hash_1: Hash[0..20] = 23467739 e92dd45f ...
Aug  14 20:48:43 ike_send_packet: Start, send SA =
{ 07a7f08c 798b8bd8 - d94d344c 834c287f}, nego = 0, src = 198.18.1.3:500,
```

```
dst = 198.18.1.1:500, routing table id = 0

##
Initial quick mode packet has been sent, waiting for reply
##

Aug  14 20:48:43 kmd_diff_config_now, configuration diff complete
Aug  14 20:48:43 ike_get_sa: Start, SA =
{ 07a7f08c 798b8bd8 - d94d344c 834c287f } / 170e3079, remote = 198.18.1.1:500
Aug  14 20:48:43 ike_sa_find: Found SA =
{ 07a7f08c 798b8bd8 - d94d344c 834c287f }
Aug  14 20:48:43 ike_alloc_negotiation: Start, SA =
{ 07a7f08c 798b8bd8 - d94d344c 834c287f}
Aug  14 20:48:43 ike_init_qm_negotiation: Start, initiator = 0,
message_id = 170e3079

##
Reply from peer has arrived, decode it
##

Aug  14 20:48:43 ike_decode_packet: Start
Aug  14 20:48:43 ike_decode_packet: Start, SA =
{ 07a7f08c 798b8bd8 - d94d344c 834c287f} / 170e3079, nego = 1
Aug  14 20:48:43 ike_decode_payload_sa: Start
Aug  14 20:48:43 ike_decode_payload_t: Start, # trans = 1
Aug  14 20:48:43 ike_st_i_encrypt: Check that packet was encrypted succeeded
Aug  14 20:48:43 ike_st_i_qm_hash_1: Start, hash[0..20] = 0fe63361 f217367a ...
Aug  14 20:48:43 ike_st_i_qm_nonce: Nonce[0..32] = 7762f152 69ac6961 ...
Aug  14 20:48:43 ike_st_i_qm_ke: Ke[0..128] = 8150e601 70a4fab9 ...
Aug  14 20:48:43 ike_st_i_qm_sa_proposals: Start
Aug  14 20:48:43 KMD_INTERNAL_ERROR: Phase2 finish: No sa_cfg found!
Aug  14 20:48:43 KMD_PM_P2_POLICY_LOOKUP_FAILURE: Policy lookup for Phase-2
[responder] failed for p1_local=ipv4(udp:500,[0..3]=198.18.1.3)
p1_remote=ipv4(udp:500,[0..3]=198.18.1.1)
p2_local=ipv4_subnet(any:0,[0..7]=172.31.0.0/16)
p2_remote=ipv4_subnet(any:0,[0..7]=192.168.0.0/16)

##
Previous messages indicate that there has been a Phase 2 lookup error and
it shows what Proxy-ID's the peer is trying to propose Local-ID=172.31.0.0/16,
Remote-ID=192.168.0.0/16.  At this point you should contact the peer
and make sure that their proxy-ID configuration matches what you are expecting,
or modify your configuration to match this proxy-ID.  The above message
also seems to implicitly indicate that the Phase 2 Proposal (Encryption/
Authentication/PFS &c) is ok, but that the negotiations failed
on the Proxy-ID negotiation.  The SRX will now send a message to the peer
indicating that the Phase 2 negotiations were not successful, although it
will not explicitly state why, this information is only located on
the responder.  The SRX will then clear the state of the negotiation and await
another attempt.
##

Aug  14 20:48:43 ike_qm_sa_reply: Start
Aug  14 20:48:43 198.18.1.3:500 (Responder) <-> 198.18.1.1:500
{ 07a7f08c 798b8bd8 - d94d344c 834c287f [1] / 0x170e3079 } QM;
```

```
= No proposal chosen (14)
Aug  14 20:48:43 ike_alloc_negotiation: Start, SA =
{ 07a7f08c 798b8bd8 - d94d344c 834c287f}
Aug  14 20:48:43 ike_encode_packet: Start, SA =
{ 0x07a7f08c 798b8bd8 - d94d344c 834c287f } / a0a22239, nego = 2
Aug  14 20:48:43 ike_send_packet: Start, send SA =
{ 07a7f08c 798b8bd8 - d94d344c 834c287f}, nego = 2, src = 198.18.1.3:500,
dst = 198.18.1.1:500, routing table id = 0
Aug  14 20:48:43 ike_delete_negotiation: Start, SA =
{ 07a7f08c 798b8bd8 - d94d344c 834c287f}, nego = 2

***Disable Tracing***

root@SRX5800> edit

[edit]
root@SRX5800#rollback 1

[edit]
root@SRX5800#commit comment "Disabling VPN Tracing by reverting to config
without it" and-quit
```

Troubleshooting a remote access VPN

After the VPN establishment has been triggered, you can look at the */var/log/kmd* file to determine exactly what is happening.

The file contains a lot of information for the particular IKE entries. Just as we did for the site-to-site VPN, use the following sample output to help you sift through the remote access VPN and find the relevant information to extract the root cause of the failure:

```
root@SRX5800> show log kmd

Aug 14 21:07:38 ike_get_sa: Start, SA =
{ d3622295 fb67acf0 - 00000000 00000000 } / 00000000, remote = 198.18.1.100:500
Aug 14 21:07:38 ike_sa_allocate: Start, SA = { d3622295 fb67acf0 - 8980eab2 eb47
3562 }
Aug 14 21:07:38 ike_init_isakmp_sa: Start, remote = 198.18.1.100:500,
initiator = 0
Aug 14 21:07:38 ike_decode_packet: Start
Aug 14 21:07:38 ike_decode_packet: Start, SA = { d3622295 fb67acf0 - 8980eab2 eb
473562} / 00000000, nego = -1
Aug 14 21:07:38 ike_decode_payload_sa: Start
Aug 14 21:07:38 ike_decode_payload_t: Start, # trans = 1
Aug 14 21:07:38 ike_st_i_vid: VID[0..44] = 47bbe7c9 93f1fc13 ...
Aug 14 21:07:38 ike_st_i_vid: VID[0..8] = da8e9378 80010000 ...
Aug 14 21:07:38 ike_st_i_vid: VID[0..16] = afcad713 68a1f1c9 ...
Aug 14 21:07:38 ike_st_i_vid: VID[0..8] = 09002689 dfd6b712 ...
Aug 14 21:07:38 ike_st_i_vid: VID[0..16] = 4485152d 18b6bbcd ...
Aug 14 21:07:38 ike_st_i_vid: VID[0..16] = 90cb8091 3ebb696e ...

##
Use the sample output below to help you sift through it and find the relevant
information to extract the root cause of the failure.
```

```
Here the first IKE packet is received and the SRX begin the IKE decode
##

Aug 14 21:07:38 ike_st_i_id: Start
Aug 14 21:07:38 ike_st_i_sa_proposal: Start
Aug 14 21:07:38 ike_isakmp_sa_reply: Start
Aug 14 21:07:38 ike_st_i_nonce: Start, nonce[0..32] = 35c16d86 b96558c9 ...
Aug 14 21:07:38 ike_st_i_cert: Start
Aug 14 21:07:38 ike_st_i_hash_key: Start, no key_hash
Aug 14 21:07:38 ike_st_i_ke: Ke[0..128] = 817323c0 1a4eefbe ...
Aug 14 21:07:38 ike_st_i_cr: Start
Aug 14 21:07:38 ike_st_i_private: Start
Aug 14 21:07:38 ike_st_o_sa_values: Start
Aug 14 21:07:38 ike_st_o_ke: Start
Aug 14 21:07:38 ike_st_o_nonce: Start
Aug 14 21:07:38 ike_policy_reply_isakmp_nonce_data_len: Start
Aug 14 21:07:38 ike_st_o_id: Start
Aug 14 21:07:38 ike_policy_reply_isakmp_id: Start
Aug 14 21:07:38 ike_st_o_certs_base: Start
Aug 14 21:07:38 ike_st_o_sig_or_hash: Start, auth_method = 4
Aug 14 21:07:38 ike_st_o_hash: Start
Aug 14 21:07:38 ike_find_pre_shared_key: Find pre shared key key for
198.18.1.1:500, id = ipv4(udp:500,[0..3]=198.18.1.1) -> 198.18.1.100:500, id =
usr@fqdn(udp:500,[0..18]=johndoe@company.com)
Aug 14 21:07:38 ike_policy_reply_find_pre_shared_key: Start
Aug 14 21:07:38 ike_calc_mac: Start, initiator = false, local = true
Aug 14 21:07:38 ike_policy_reply_isakmp_vendor_ids: Start
Aug 14 21:07:38 ike_st_o_status_n: Start
Aug 14 21:07:38 ike_st_o_private: Start
Aug 14 21:07:38 ike_policy_reply_private_payload_out: Start
Aug 14 21:07:38 ike_policy_reply_private_payload_out: Start
Aug 14 21:07:38 ike_policy_reply_private_payload_out: Start
Aug 14 21:07:38 ike_st_o_calc_skeyid: Calculating skeyid
Aug 14 21:07:38 ike_encode_packet: Start, SA =
{ 0xd3622295 fb67acf0 - 8980eab2 eb473562 } / 00000000, nego = -1
Aug 14 21:07:38 ike_send_packet: Start, send SA =
{ d3622295 fb67acf0 - 8980eab2 eb473562}, nego = -1, src = 198.18.1.1:500,
dst = 198.18.1.100:500, routing table id = 0

##
In the previous statements the SRX determines that the IKE packet is from
198.18.1.100 destined to 198.18.1.1 (our interface) with an IKE ID of
type user at hostname (or UFQDN) johndoe@company.com.  The SRX also checks
the value in the preshared key to make sure that it matches properly.
##

Aug 14 21:07:38 ike_get_sa: Start, SA =
{ d3622295 fb67acf0 - 8980eab2 eb473562 } / 00000000, remote = 198.18.1.100:500
Aug 14 21:07:38 ike_sa_find: Found SA = { d3622295 fb67acf0 - 8980eab2 eb473562 }
Aug 14 21:07:38 ike_decode_packet: Start
Aug 14 21:07:38 ike_decode_packet: Start, SA =
{ d3622295 fb67acf0 - 8980eab2 eb473562} / 00000000, nego = -1
Aug 14 21:07:38 ike_st_i_hash: Start, hash[0..20] = 52e59171 a54dad00 ...
Aug 14 21:07:38 ike_calc_mac: Start, initiator = false, local = false
Aug 14 21:07:38 ike_st_i_cert: Start
```

```
Aug 14 21:07:38 ike_st_i_status_n: Start, doi = 1, protocol = 1,
code = Replay status notification (24577),
spi[0..16] = d3622295 fb67acf0 ..., data[0..4] = 00000000 00000000 ...
Aug 14 21:07:38 ike_st_i_status_n: Start, doi = 1, protocol = 1, code = Initial
contact notification (24578), spi[0..16] = d3622295 fb67acf0 ..., data[0..0] =
00000000 00000000 ...
Aug 14 21:07:38 ike_st_i_private: Start
Aug 14 21:07:38 ike_st_o_wait_done: Marking for waiting for done
Aug 14 21:07:38 ike_st_o_all_done: MESSAGE: Phase 1 { 0xd3622295 fb67acf0 -
0x8980eab2 eb473562 } / 00000000, version = 1.0, xchg = Aggressive,
auth_method = Pre shared keys with XAuth (initiator), Responder,
cipher = aes-cbc, hash = sha1, prf = hmac-sha1, life = 0 kB /
Aug 14 21:07:38 198.18.1.1:500 (Responder) <-> 198.18.1.100:500
{ d3622295 fb67acf0 - 8980eab2 eb473562 [-1] / 0x00000000 } Aggr; MESSAGE:
Phase 1 version = 1.0, auth_method = Pre shared keys with XAuth (initiator),
= aes-cbc, hash = sha1, prf = hmac-sha1, life = 0 kB /

##
The previous statements show that the SRX is using Aggressive Mode, with
Pre-Shared Keys and XAuth for client negotiation.  The proposed Cipher is AES128-
SHA1 (128 is implied) and that the key lifetime is not defined.  This
negotiation is clearly for a remote client VPN, typical IPSec Site-to-site would
show Main Mode, and would not typically have XAuth.
##

Aug 14 21:07:38 ike_send_notify: Connected, SA = { d3622295 fb67acf0 - 8980eab2
eb473562}, nego = -1
Aug 14 21:07:38 jnp_ike_connect_cfg: Start, remote_name = 198.18.1.100:500,
flags = 00008000
Aug 14 21:07:38 ike_sa_find_ip_port: Remote = 198.18.1.100:500,
Found SA = { d3622295 fb67acf0 - 8980eab2 eb473562}
Aug 14 21:07:38 ike_alloc_negotiation: Start, SA =
{ d3622295 fb67acf0 - 8980eab2 eb473562}
Aug 14 21:07:38 jnp_ike_connect_cfg: SA =
{ d3622295 fb67acf0 - 8980eab2 eb473562}, nego = 0
Aug 14 21:07:38 ike_init_cfg_negotiation: Start, initiator = 1,
message_id = 3fdb5840
Aug 14 21:07:38 ike_st_o_gen_hash: Start
Aug 14 21:07:38 ike_st_o_cfg_attr: Start
Aug 14 21:07:38 ike_st_o_private: Start
Aug 14 21:07:38 ike_st_o_encrypt: Marking encryption for packet
Aug 14 21:07:38 ike_encode_packet: Start, SA =
{ 0xd3622295 fb67acf0 - 8980eab2 eb473562 } / 3fdb5840, nego = 0
Aug 14 21:07:38 ike_send_packet: Start, send SA =
{ d3622295 fb67acf0 - 8980eab2 eb473562}, nego = 0, src = 198.18.1.1:500,
dst = 198.18.1.100:500, routing table id = 0

##
The SRX responds to the IKE message from the client
##

Aug 14 21:07:43 ike_retransmit_callback: Start,
retransmit SA = { d3622295 fb67acf0 - 8980eab2 eb473562}, nego = 0
Aug 14 21:07:43 ike_send_packet: Start, retransmit previous packet SA =
{ d3622295 fb67acf0 - 8980eab2 eb473562}, nego = 0, src = 198.18.1.1:500,
```

```
dst = 198.18.1.100:500, routing table id = 0
Aug 14 21:07:44 ike_get_sa: Start, SA =
{ d3622295 fb67acf0 - 8980eab2 eb473562 } / 3fdb5840, remote = 198.18.1.100:500
Aug 14 21:07:44 ike_sa_find: Found SA = { d3622295 fb67acf0 - 8980eab2 eb473562 }
Aug 14 21:07:44 ike_st_o_done: ISAKMP SA negotiation done
Aug 14 21:07:44 ike_send_notify: Connected, SA =
{ d3622295 fb67acf0 - 8980eab2 eb473562}, nego = -1
Aug 14 21:07:44 ike_free_negotiation_isakmp: Start, nego = -1
Aug 14 21:07:44 ike_free_negotiation: Start, nego = -1
Aug 14 21:07:44 ike_decode_packet: Start
Aug 14 21:07:44 ike_decode_packet: Start, SA =
{ d3622295 fb67acf0 - 8980eab2 eb473562} / 3fdb5840, nego = 0
Aug 14 21:07:44 ike_decode_payload_attr: Start
Aug 14 21:07:44 ike_st_i_encrypt: Check that packet was encrypted succeeded
Aug 14 21:07:44 ike_st_i_gen_hash: Start, hash[0..20] = f431a256 ac900477 ...
Aug 14 21:07:44 ike_st_i_cfg_attr: Start
Aug 14 21:07:44 ike_st_i_private: Start
Aug 14 21:07:44 ike_st_o_cfg_wait_done: Marking for waiting for done
Aug 14 21:07:44 ike_st_o_cfg_wait_done: MESSAGE: CFG Mode wait done
Aug 14 21:07:44 198.18.1.1:500 (Initiator) <-> 198.18.1.100:500
{ d3622295 fb67acf0 - 8980eab2 eb473562 [0] / 0x3fdb5840 } CFG; MESSAGE: CFG Mode wait done

##
At this point Phase 1 establishment is completed, the SRX begins Phase 2
negotiation
##

Aug 14 21:07:44 ike_send_notify: Connected, SA =
{ d3622295 fb67acf0 - 8980eab2 eb473562}, nego = 0
Aug 14 21:07:44 jnp_ike_connect_cfg: Start, remote_name = 198.18.1.100:500,
flags = 00008000
Aug 14 21:07:44 ike_sa_find_ip_port: Remote = 198.18.1.100:500,
Found SA = { d3622295 fb67acf0 - 8980eab2 eb473562}
Aug 14 21:07:44 ike_alloc_negotiation: Start, SA =
{ d3622295 fb67acf0 - 8980eab2 eb473562}
Aug 14 21:07:44 jnp_ike_connect_cfg: SA =
{ d3622295 fb67acf0 - 8980eab2 eb473562}, nego = 1
Aug 14 21:07:44 ike_init_cfg_negotiation: Start, initiator = 1,
message_id = 7e56b115
Aug 14 21:07:44 ike_st_o_gen_hash: Start
Aug 14 21:07:44 ike_st_o_cfg_attr: Start
Aug 14 21:07:44 ike_st_o_private: Start
Aug 14 21:07:44 ike_st_o_encrypt: Marking encryption for packet
Aug 14 21:07:44 ike_encode_packet: Start, SA =
{ 0xd3622295 fb67acf0 - 8980eab2 eb473562 } / 7e56b115, nego = 1
Aug 14 21:07:44 ike_send_packet: Start, send SA =
{ d3622295 fb67acf0 - 8980eab2 eb473562}, nego = 1, src = 198.18.1.1:500,
dst = 198.18.1.100:500, routing table id = 0
Aug 14 21:07:44 ike_get_sa: Start, SA =
{ d3622295 fb67acf0 - 8980eab2 eb473562 } / 7e56b115, remote = 198.18.1.100:500
Aug 14 21:07:44 ike_sa_find: Found SA = { d3622295 fb67acf0 - 8980eab2 eb473562 }
Aug 14 21:07:44 ike_decode_packet: Start
Aug 14 21:07:44 ike_decode_packet: Start, SA =
{ d3622295 fb67acf0 - 8980eab2 eb473562} / 7e56b115, nego = 1
Aug 14 21:07:44 ike_decode_payload_attr: Start
```

```
Aug 14 21:07:44 ike_st_i_encrypt: Check that packet was encrypted succeeded
Aug 14 21:07:44 ike_st_i_gen_hash: Start, hash[0..20] = dfcaa88c 40f3697e ...
Aug 14 21:07:44 ike_st_i_cfg_attr: Start
Aug 14 21:07:44 ike_st_i_private: Start
Aug 14 21:07:44 ike_st_o_cfg_wait_done: Marking for waiting for done
Aug 14 21:07:44 ike_st_o_cfg_wait_done: MESSAGE: CFG Mode wait done
Aug 14 21:07:44 198.18.1.1:500 (Initiator) <-> 198.18.1.100:500
{ d3622295 fb67acf0 - 8980eab2 eb473562 [1] / 0x7e56b115 } CFG; MESSAGE: CFG Mode wait done
Aug 14 21:07:44 ike_send_notify: Connected, SA =
{ d3622295 fb67acf0 - 8980eab2 eb473562}, nego = 1
Aug 14 21:07:44 ike_get_sa: Start, SA =
{ d3622295 fb67acf0 - 8980eab2 eb473562 } / c8ef4ee3, remote = 198.18.1.100:500
Aug 14 21:07:44 ike_sa_find: Found SA = { d3622295 fb67acf0 - 8980eab2 eb473562 }
Aug 14 21:07:44 ike_alloc_negotiation: Start, SA =
{ d3622295 fb67acf0 - 8980eab2 eb473562}
Aug 14 21:07:44 ike_init_qm_negotiation: Start, initiator = 0,
message_id = c8ef4ee3

##
In the above lines the SRX has received the first packet for Phase 2 Quick Mode
negotiation, the SRX decrypts the packet (which matches a SA negotiated in
Phase 1) and parse out the fields to begin checking whether the Phase 2 Proposal
matches a configured proposal
##

Aug 14 21:07:44 ike_decode_packet: Start
Aug 14 21:07:44 ike_decode_packet: Start, SA = { d3622295 fb67acf0 - 8980eab2
eb473562} / c8ef4ee3, nego = 2
Aug 14 21:07:44 ike_decode_payload_sa: Start
Aug 14 21:07:44 ike_decode_payload_t: Start, # trans = 1
Aug 14 21:07:44 ike_st_i_encrypt: Check that packet was encrypted succeeded
Aug 14 21:07:44 ike_st_i_qm_hash_1: Start, hash[0..20] = f5431c9c 5a41ae04 ...
Aug 14 21:07:44 ike_st_i_qm_nonce: Nonce[0..32] = 847152b6 e30c41d0 ...
Aug 14 21:07:44 ike_st_i_qm_ke: Ke[0..128] = 5591055a 49022ca1 ...
Aug 14 21:07:44 ike_st_i_qm_sa_proposals: Start
Aug 14 21:07:44 KMD_INTERNAL_ERROR: Phase2 finish: No sa_cfg found!
Aug 14 21:07:44 KMD_PM_P2_POLICY_LOOKUP_FAILURE: Policy lookup for Phase-2
[responder] failed for p1_local=ipv4(udp:500,[0..3]=198.18.1.1)
p1_remote=usr@fqdn(udp:500,[0..18]=johndoe@company.com)
p2_local=ipv4_subnet(any:0,[0..7]=192.168.100.0/24)
p2_remote=ipv4(any:0,[0..3]=198.18.1.100)

##
The output below shows the Phase 2 proposal is failing policy lookup.
Please see the end of this debug for steps to take to determine what the
root cause can be.  In this output, the SRX shows the proposal.  In this case,
the lookup failure has to do with the fact that the VPN is attempting to
terminate on the wrong interface.  Below is the output that you should see
if the connection succeeds Phase 2:
##

Aug 14 17:09:22 198.18.1.1:500 (Responder) <-> 198.18.1.100:500
{ cdf1c372 0f946928 - ad6b9fbb 4594cb35 [2] / 0xf4f71bbc } QM; MESSAGE: Phase 2
connection succeeded, No PFS, group = 0
Aug 14 17:09:22 ike_qm_call_callback: MESSAGE: Phase 2 connection succeeded, No
```

```
PFS, group = 0
Aug 14 17:09:22 198.18.1.1:500 (Responder) <-> 198.18.1.100:500
{ cdf1c372 0f946928 - ad6b9fbb 4594cb35 [2] / 0xf4f71bbc } QM; MESSAGE:
SA[0][0] = ESP 3des, life = 0 kB/0 sec, group = 0, tunnel, hmac-sha1-96,
key len = 0, key rounds = 0
Aug 14 17:09:22 ike_qm_call_callback: MESSAGE: SA[0][0] = ESP 3des,
life = 0 kB/0 sec, group = 0, tunnel, hmac-sha1-96, key len = 0, key rounds = 0
Aug 14 17:09:22 ike_st_o_qm_wait_done: Marking for waiting for done

***Disable Tracing***

root@SRX5800> edit

[edit]
root@SRX5800#rollback 1

[edit]
root@SRX5800#commit comment "Disabling VPN Tracing by reverting to config
without it" and-quit
```

Case Studies

Although there are truly limitless combinations of VPN configurations that we could discuss, most often VPN configurations will be quite similar. This section discusses the two main types of VPNs: a site-to-site VPN (with multiple remote sites) and a VPN that connects a remote IPsec client.

Case Study 6-1: Site-to-Site VPN

The goal of this case study is to establish site-to-site VPNs between the Campus Core and the three remote offices (East, West, and South Branches). The following properties should be present for this configuration, as shown in Figure 6-7:

- VPNs should use Main mode in a point-to-multipoint configuration.
- OSPF should be used as a dynamic routing protocol for this example on the tunnel interfaces, with all st0 interfaces in Area 0. Since this isn't true broadcast, define neighbors in the configuration.

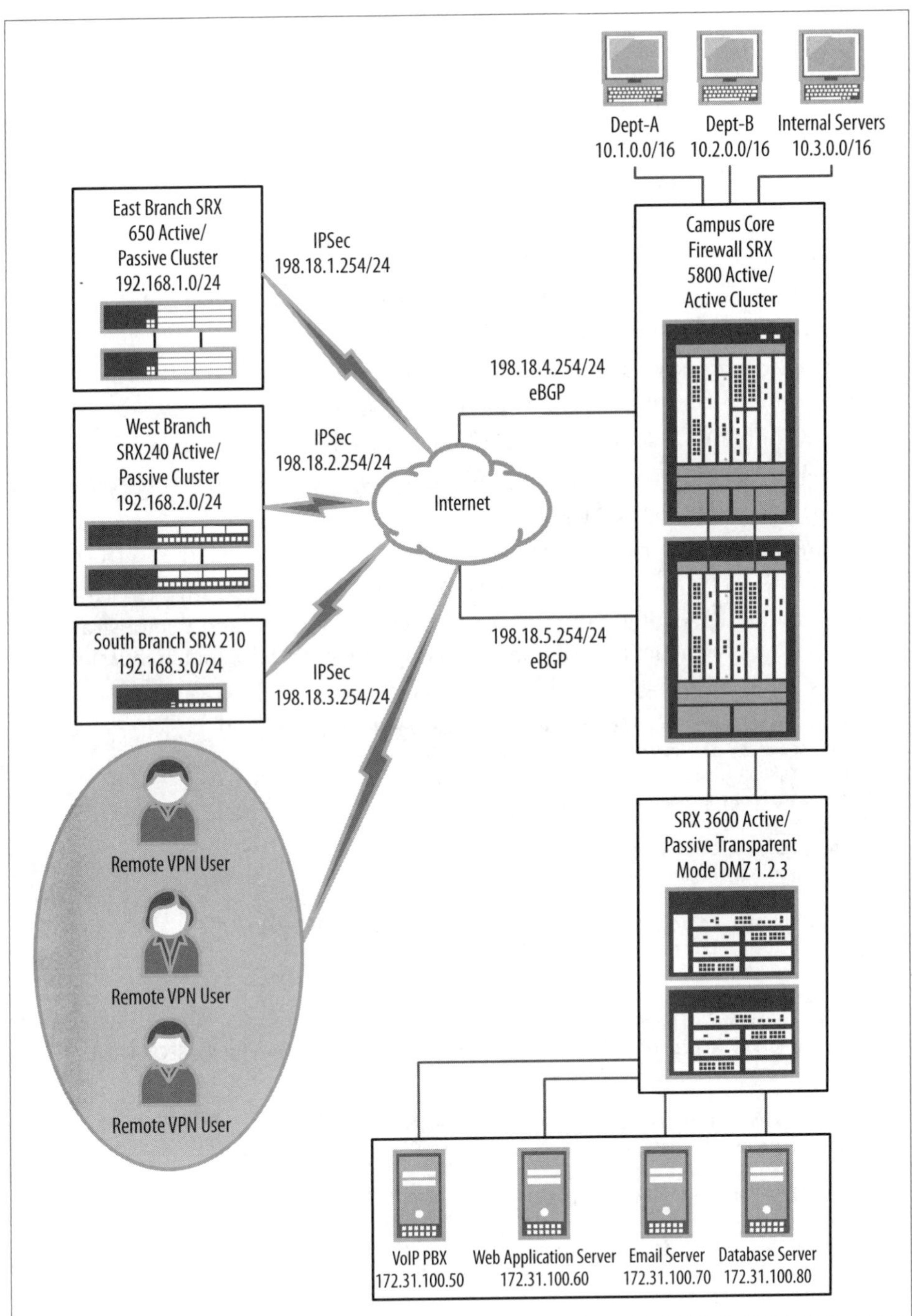

Figure 6-7. Case study network diagram

- The architecture will be hub and spoke (utilizing point-to-multipoint VPNs).
- The st0 interface should be in the VPN zone. Use the following IP addressing for the st0 interfaces on the Campus Core and the remote offices:
  - —Campus Core: 192.168.100.5/24
  - —East Branch: 192.168.100.1/24
  - —West Branch: 192.168.100.2/24
  - —South Branch: 192.168.100.3/24
- Only the respective networks for each side should be allowed through the VPN, with any service allowed between the networks.
- The Phase 1 proposal should use 3DES SHA-1 with preshared keys. The key will be 8aifMhau%% using Diffie-Hellman Group 2.
- Phase 2 of the VPN should use AES128-SHA1 as the proposal, and no PFS.
- Branch VPN gateways should use 198.18.5.254 as the primary VPN connection and 198.18.4.254 as the backup.
- Ensure that IKE can be terminated on the external interfaces in the Untrust zone.
- For the proxy ID just use local-id 0.0.0.0/0, remote-id 0.0.0.0, and service Any to simplify the IKE configuration to the respective gateways, and demonstrate that proxy IDs only impact negotiation by making sure both sides match, but not what traffic can pass through the VPN.

```
/*This Phase 1 Proposal is Applied to Campus and Remote Offices*/
[edit security ike proposal Remote-Office-PSK]
root@SRX5800# show
authentication-method pre-shared-keys;
dh-group group2;
authentication-algorithm sha1;
encryption-algorithm 3des-cbc;

/*This Phase 1 Policy is Applied to Campus and Remote Offices*/
[edit security ike policy Remote-Office-Static]
root@SRX5800#show
mode main;
proposals Remote-Office-PSK;
pre-shared-key ascii-text "$9$hA7cvWLX-VwgEc7dVsJZUjHqT3AtuREc"; ## SECRET-DATA


/*Getway Configuration on the Campus Core SRX*/
[edit security ike gateway Eastbranch-Remote-Office]
root@SRX5800# show
ike-policy Remote-Office-Static;
address 198.18.1.254;
dead-peer-detection {
    interval 10;
    threshold 3;
}
no-nat-traversal;
external-interface ge-0/0/0.0;
```

```
[edit security ike gateway Westbranch-Remote-Office]
root@SRX5800# show
ike-policy Remote-Office-Static;
address 198.18.2.254;
dead-peer-detection {
    interval 10;
    threshold 3;
}
no-nat-traversal;
external-interface ge-0/0/0.0;

[edit security ike gateway Southbranch-Remote-Office]
root@SRX5800# show
ike-policy Remote-Office-Static;
address 198.18.3.254;
dead-peer-detection {
    interval 10;
    threshold 3;
}
no-nat-traversal;
external-interface ge-0/0/0.0;

/*Gateway Configuration on the Remote Offices*/
[edit security ike gateway Eastbranch-Remote-Office]
root@SRX650# show
ike-policy Remote-Office-Static;
address [ 198.18.5.254 198.18.4.254 ];
dead-peer-detection {
    interval 10;
    threshold 3;
}
no-nat-traversal;
external-interface ge-0/0/0.0;

/*This Zone Configuration is Applied to Campus and Remote Offices*/
[edit security zones security-zone untrust host-inbound-traffic system-services]
root@SRX5800#show
ike;

/*Phase 2 Proposal is applied to Campus and Remote Offices*/
[edit security ipsec proposal Remote-Offices]
root@SRX5800# show
protocol esp;
authentication-algorithm hmac-sha1-96;
encryption-algorithm aes-128-cbc;

/*Phase 2 Proposal is applied to Campus and Remote Offices*/
[edit security ipsec policy Remote-Offices]
root@SRX5800# show
proposals Remote-Offices

/*Phase 2 VPN Configuration for Campus Core*/
[edit security ipsec vpn East-Branch]
root@SRX5800# show
```

```
bind-interface st0.0;
ike {
    gateway East-Branch;
    proxy-identity {
        local 0.0.0.0/0;
        remote 0.0.0.0/0;
        service any;
    }
    ipsec-policy Remote-Offices;
}

[edit security ipsec vpn West-Branch]
root@SRX5800# show
bind-interface st0.0;
ike {
    gateway West-Branch;
    proxy-identity {
        local 0.0.0.0/0;
        remote 0.0.0.0/0;
        service any;
    }
    ipsec-policy Remote-Offices;
}

[edit security ipsec vpn South-Branch]
root@SRX5800# show
bind-interface st0.0;
ike {
    gateway South-Branch;
    proxy-identity {
        local 0.0.0.0/0;
        remote 0.0.0.0/0;
        service any;
    }
    ipsec-policy Remote-Offices;
}

/*Phase 2 VPN Configuration for Remote Gateways*/
[edit security ipsec vpn Campus-Core]
root@SRX650# show
bind-interface st0.0;
ike {
    gateway Campus-Core;
    proxy-identity {
        local 0.0.0.0/0;
        remote 0.0.0.0/0;
        service any;
    }
    ipsec-policy Remote-Offices;
}


/*ST0 Configuration for Campus Core*/
[edit interfaces st0]
```

```
root@SRX5800#
unit 0 {
    multpoint;
    family inet {
        address 192.168.100.5/24;
    }
}

/*ST0 Configuration for East-Branch*/
[edit interfaces st0]
root@SRX650#
unit 0 {
    family inet {
        address 192.168.100.1/24;
    }
}

/*ST0 Configuration for West-Branch*/
[edit interfaces st0]
root@SRX240#
unit 0 {
    family inet {
        address 192.168.100.2/24;
    }
}

/*ST0 Configuration for South-Branch*/
[edit interfaces st0]
root@SRX210#
unit 0 {
    family inet {
        address 192.168.100.3/24;
    }
}

/*ST0 Zone Configuration Configuration for Campus Core and Remote Offices*/
[edit security zones security-zones vpn]
root@SRX5800#show
interfaces {
        st0.0 {
            host-inbound-traffic {
                system-services {
                    ike;
                }
                protocols {
                    ospf;
                }
}

/*OSPF Protocol Configuration Configuration for Campus Core*/
[edit protocols]
root@SRX5800#show
ospf {
    area 0.0.0.0 {
        interface st0.0 {
```

```
            neighbor 192.168.100.1;
           neighbor 192.168.100.2;
           neighbor 192.168.100.3;
        interface-type p2mp;
        dynamic-neighbor
        }
    }
}
```

/*OSPF Protocol Configuration Configuration for Remote Offices*/

```
[edit protocols]
root@SRX5800#show
ospf {
    area 0.0.0.0 {
        interface st0.0 {
            neighbor 192.168.100.5;
          dynamic-neighbor;
        }
    }
}
```

/*Security Policies for Route Based VPN Campus Core*/

```
[edit]
root@SRX5800# show security zones security-zone trust address-book
address 10.0.0.0/8 10.0.0.0/8;


[edit]
root@SRX5800# show security zones security-zone vpn address-book
address 192.168.1.0/24 192.168.1.0/24;
address 192.168.2.0/24 192.168.2.0/24;
address 192.168.3.0/24 192.168.3.0/24;



[edit security policies from-zone trust to-zone vpn policy Remote-Offices]
root@SRX5800# show
match {
        source-address 10.0.0.0/8;
        destination-address [ 192.168.1.0/24 192.168.2.0/24 192.168.3.0/24 ];
        application any;
        }
 then {
        permit
        log {
                session-close;
            }
  }

[edit security policies from-zone vpn to-zone trust policy Remote-Offices]
root@SRX5800# show
match {
        source-address [ 192.168.1.0/24 192.168.2.0/24 192.168.3.0/24 ];
```

```
        destination-address 10.0.0.0/8;
        application any;
        }
 then {
        permit
        log {
               session-close;
            }
  }
```

/*Security Policies for Route Based VPN East-Branch Core*/

```
[edit]
root@SRX650# show security zones security-zone vpn address-book
address 10.0.0.0/8 10.0.0.0/8;
address 192.168.2.0/24 192.168.2.0/24;
address 192.168.3.0/24 192.168.3.0/24;



[edit]
root@SRX650# show security zones security-zone trust address-book
address 192.168.1.0/24 192.168.1.0/24;



[edit security policies from-zone trust to-zone vpn policy Remote-Offices]
root@SRX650# show
match {
        source-address 192.168.1.0/24;
        destination-address [10.0.0.0/8 192.168.2.0/24 192.168.3.0/24 ];
        application any;
        }
 then {
        permit
        log {
               session-close;
            }
  }

[edit security policies from-zone vpn to-zone trust policy Remote-Offices]
root@SRX650# show
match {
        source-address [ 10.0.0.0/8 192.168.2.0/24 192.168.3.0/24 ];
        destination-address 192.168.1.0/24;
        application any;
        }
 then {
        permit
        log {
               session-close;
            }
  }
```

/*Security Policies for Route Based VPN West-Branch Core*/

```
[edit]
root@SRX240# show security zones security-zone vpn address-book
address 10.0.0.0/8 10.0.0.0/8;
address 192.168.1.0/24 192.168.1.0/24;
address 192.168.3.0/24 192.168.3.0/24;



[edit]
root@SRX240# show security zones security-zone trust address-book
address 192.168.2.0/24 192.168.2.0/24;



[edit security policies from-zone trust to-zone vpn policy Remote-Offices]
root@SRX240# show
match {
        source-address 192.168.2.0/24;
        destination-address [10.0.0.0/8 192.168.1.0/24 192.168.3.0/24 ];
        application any;
        }
 then {
        permit
        log {
                session-close;
            }
  }

[edit security policies from-zone vpn to-zone trust policy Remote-Offices]
root@SRX240# show
match {
        source-address [ 10.0.0.0/8 192.168.1.0/24 192.168.3.0/24 ];
        destination-address 192.168.2.0/24;
        application any;
        }
 then {
        permit
        log {
                session-close;
            }
  }
```

/*Security Policies for Route Based VPN South-Branch Core*/

```
[edit]
root@SRX210# show security zones security-zone vpn address-book
address 10.0.0.0/8 10.0.0.0/8;
address 192.168.1.0/24 192.168.1.0/24;
address 192.168.2.0/24 192.168.2.0/24;
```

```
[edit]
root@SRX210# show security zones security-zone trust address-book
address 192.168.3.0/24 192.168.3.0/24;



[edit security policies from-zone trust to-zone vpn policy Remote-Offices]
root@SRX210# show
match {
        source-address 192.168.3.0/24;
        destination-address [10.0.0.0/8 192.168.1.0/24 192.168.2.0/24 ];
        application any;
        }
 then {
        permit
        log {
                session-close;
            }
  }

[edit security policies from-zone vpn to-zone trust policy Remote-Offices]
root@SRX210# show
match {
        source-address [ 10.0.0.0/8 192.168.1.0/24 192.168.2.0/24 ];
        destination-address 192.168.3.0/24;
        application any;
        }
 then {
        permit
        log {
                session-close;
            }
  }
```

Case Study 6-2: Remote Access VPN

The goal of this case study is to configure an IPSec client VPN on the SRX. The configurations will largely be the same as in the preceding case study, except where noted. The configuration should be set up as follows:

- Phase 1 should use Aggressive mode, and PFS (Diffie-Hellman Group2) should be used to secure the VPN, terminated on the ge-0/0/0 Untrust interface.
- For the standard-based IPSec client, use an IKE identity of *ipsecike@company.com*. No specific client software will be examined here; however, any standards-based client implementation should interoperate with this example.
- Phase 1 should use 3DES-MD5 for the proposal with Diffie-Hellman Group 2.
- Use the preshared key 71hajfy44.
- Phase 2 should use AES128-SHA1 with ESP Tunnel mode for the proposal.

- Use a policy-based VPN for this configuration to allow the clients access to the Campus Core networks (10.0.0.0/8).

```
/* IPSec Remote Client*/
[edit security ike proposal Remote-Client]
root@SRX5800# show
authentication-method pre-shared-keys;
dh-group group2;
authentication-algorithm md5;
encryption-algorithm 3des-cbc;

[edit security ike policy Remote-Client]
root@SRX5800#show
mode aggressive;
proposals Remote-Office-PSK;
pre-shared-key ascii-text "$9$VWYJGDikqmTX74ZDif5revM7-s24"; ## SECRET-DATA

[edit security ike gateway Remote-Client]
root@SRX5800# show
ike-policy Remote-Client;
dynamic {
    user-at-hostname ipsecike@company.com;
}
external-interface ge-0/0/0.0;

[edit security ipsec proposal Remote-Client]
root@SRX5800# show
protocol esp;
authentication-algorithm hmac-sha1-96;
encryption-algorithm aes-128-cbc;

[edit security ipsec policy Remote-Client]
root@SRX5800# show
perfect-forward-secrecy {
    keys group2;
}
proposals Remote-Client;

[edit security ipsec vpn Remote-Client]
root@SRX5800# show
ike {
    gateway Remote-Client;
}
ipsec-policy Remote-Client;

[edit security zones security-zones trust address-book]
root@SRX5800# show
address 10.0.0.0/8 10.0.0.0/8;

[edit security policies from-zone untrust to-zone trust policy Remote-Client]
root@SRX5800# show
match {
        source-address any;
        destination-address 10.0.0.0/8;
        application any;
```

```
        }
then {
        permit {
                tunnel {
                  ipsec-vpn Remote-Client;
                 }
         }
            log {
                session-close;
            }
 }

[edit security zones security-zone untrust host-inbound-traffic system-services]
root@SRX5800#show
ike;
```

Summary

IPsec VPNs provide a secure mechanism to connect remote networks together. Although many concepts and components apply to IPsec VPNs, many VPNs follow very similar configuration techniques which can be easily scaled and replicated. In the past, IPsec VPNs were primarily used to secure remote sites and clients over the Internet, but in contemporary networks, there is also a growing trend to secure intra-organizational traffic with IPsec VPNs. This applies not only to traffic crossing leased lines and private networks, but also traffic within LANs. It is clear that IPsec VPNs will continue to play a very important role for securing networks and the valuable information carried over them for the foreseeable future.

Chapter Review Questions

1. What is the purpose of Phase 1 in IPsec negotiations?
2. What is the difference between Main and Aggressive modes, and in which phase of negotiations do they occur?
3. Why would Aggressive mode be necessary instead of Main mode?
4. How many Phase 1 and Phase 2 proposals can be configured on the SRX, and how are they evaluated?
5. What is PFS and what purpose does it serve?
6. What are the advantages and disadvantages of policy-based VPNs versus route-based VPNs?
7. What is the difference between point-to-point and point-to-multipoint VPNs?
8. What is the difference between DPD and VPN monitoring?
9. What is NAT-T and when must NAT-T be used?
10. What are the advantages and disadvantages of certificate Phase 1 authentication versus preshared key Phase 1 authentication?

11. What is a proxy ID, how is it used in IPsec negotiations, and why is it a common cause of VPN establishment issues?

Chapter Review Answers

1. Phase 1 is used to create a secure channel to negotiate the Phase 2 encryption keys which will be used to secure the traffic.
2. Both Main and Aggressive modes occur in Phase 1 of IPsec negotiations. The difference is that Main mode negotiates the Phase 1 security with a six-message exchange with the IKE identities encrypted, whereas Aggressive mode negotiates them in a three-message exchange with the IKE identities in clear text.
3. Aggressive mode is necessary when the IP address of the remote peer is dynamic and another mechanism such as dynamic DNS is not used to help identify the host.
4. The SRX supports up to four Phase 1 and four Phase 2 IPsec proposals per gateway. They are evaluated in order from first to last, until a proposal can be matched with the peer, or negotiations fail because a proposal cannot be chosen.
5. PFS stands for Perfect Forward Secrecy and is an optional configuration option which can be used to trigger a renegotiation of Phase 1 keys after Phase 1 has been completed. This is most often performed when using Aggressive mode for Phase 1 authentication.
6. Policy-based VPNs are good for simple VPNs where dynamic routing and a complex policy configuration are not required. Route-based VPNs are more powerful, with the ability to not only control traffic, but also interact with dynamic routing protocols, provide automatic failover, and integrate more generally into the network architecture.
7. Point-to-point VPNs map a single VPN to a single st0 interface, while point-to-multipoint VPNs map multiple VPNs to a single st0 interface, where all VPNs will be in the same zone and the st0 interfaces will be in the same subnet.
8. DPD stands for Dead Peer Detection and is a standard IKE capability to detect if the peer gateway is up by sending IKE pings. It is negotiated in Phase 1. VPN monitoring is not a standard IKE component, but rather relies on sending peers from the gateway through the IPsec tunnel to determine if it is up. It is a more reliable mechanism because it allows one to take into account not only whether the peer is up, but also whether the VPN is up. VPN monitoring and DPD results can then be used by the SRX to consider the VPN up or down, and make alternative arrangements if available to send the traffic over another VPN.
9. NAT-T is a technique for encapsulating IPsec traffic in UDP traffic so that it can pass through a NAT device (most commonly used for remote clients that are behind a NAT gateway). This is required because NAT can alter fields that will then make the authentication invalid. By encapsulating the IPsec traffic in a UDP packet, the

UDP packet is NATed, and then, when it arrives at the gateway, the UDP headers are stripped off and the IPsec traffic is processed as normal.

10. Preshared keys are simple to implement, with little overhead. They are best used for site-to-site VPNs where only a few VPNs are used, or for remote access VPNs when there are only a few clients. The disadvantage of preshared key VPNs is that they don't scale easily without compromising security (by using the same key). Certificates have the ability to dynamically update a certificate's status, along with the ability to provide a unique certificate to each client. More overhead is associated with certificate authentication because it requires a CA to be generated, also called certificate generation (revocation and expiry). Other mechanisms such as CRL/OCSP can be used to ensure the validity of a certificate.

11. Proxy IDs are negotiated in Phase 2 and are meant to provide information about the type of traffic that will be carried over the VPN. In reality, proxy IDs do not enforce any real control over the actual traffic that passes over the VPN; however, they must match in order to establish the VPNs. Proxy IDs are a common source of issues when establishing IPsec VPNs, particularly when establishing them between different vendors, because the IKEv1 standard did not specify exactly how the proxy IDs should be derived, and therefore different vendors derive them differently. This means the proxy IDs might not match, and therefore will require tuning for proper configuration.

CHAPTER 7

High-Performance Attack Mitigation

Attack prevention and mitigation is what separates a high-end, state-of-the-art firewall from your basic run-of-the-mill firewall. Firewalls have been around for a long time, and these days even routers and load balancers can do basic stateful IP filtering and vendors claim their device is a "firewall." But the SRX has some of the most advanced attack prevention capabilities on the market today. With such built-in features as screens, AppDoS, and AppDDoS, the SRX is capable of blocking most well-known attacks extremely efficiently and can even mitigate huge amounts of denial-of-service (DoS) traffic and distributed denial-of-service (DDoS) attacks without any interruption to normal traffic processing.

Over the course of this chapter, you'll learn about the various SRX screens and some of the major types of attacks seen in the real world, and how to mitigate those attacks with screens. You'll learn how to protect the SRX's control plane from direct attacks and how to protect critical services behind the SRX via screens, firewall filters, and Intrusion Detection and Prevention (IDP).

To simplify the discussion, we have categorized the types of attacks into five major areas. Realize that some attacks may be included in multiple categories, depending on how the attacks are implemented.

The following is a high-level summary of the five different types of malicious traffic:

Network reconnaissance
: Network recon is the first thing an attacker does when attempting to break into the network. Attackers use network reconnaissance to gain knowledge of or access to the network and the elements within by essentially probing the network to map it, gain as much information as possible, and find different vectors to attack or breach. Network reconnaissance includes port scanning, version scanning, Internet Control Message Protocol (ICMP) sweeps, and firewalking.

Basic IP attacks
: These attacks take advantage of the lack of security within TCP/IP and are often meant to bypass perimeter security measures or cause harm to end hosts via

malicious packets. Some basic IP attacks include SYN/FIN packets, IP spoofing packets, and SYN fragments. These types of packets should never be seen on a production network and can almost always be safely blocked.

Canned DoS attacks
: These basic attacks are 10 to 15 years old at this point. However, they can still be seen in IDS logs on many large networks. Old attacks such as Teardrop and Land attacks can still cause a poorly written application or platform to behave in unexpected ways. So, although these are very old and are not a major risk, they can still be used, and you need to ensure that these attacks never reach your internal trusted networks or servers.

Application layer attacks
: Application attacks are typically higher-end attacks that take advantage of application vulnerabilities or design issues with the intent to take end hosts or services offline. Typically, they are legitimate requests, but with malicious intentions of flooding or consuming resources. A simple example of this is a Skinny Client Control Protocol (SCCP) call flood.

Flooding and resource exhaustion
: One of the oldest forms of DoS attacks, flooding is used to take a host or service offline or to impair it, degrading the service it provides. A good example of this is a large contingent of infected hosts sending requests or bogus packets to a server or network in an attempt to fill up the network bandwidth or consume sockets/connections so that legitimate users or requests cannot access the resources.

In this chapter, we will discuss how the SRX can block, stop, and guard against these types of attacks. First we'll look at the tools at our disposal and then we'll discuss how to configure them and create production profiles. We'll round out our discussion with details on how to harden the SRX and protect against attacks made directly to the SRX and its resources.

Network Protection Tools Overview

There are methods to protect and block bad stuff from your network. Although there is no single solution for all types of attacks, many different tools are available for different layers of protection. You can use these methods in combination to form a complete layered network security solution. Learning how to properly use the features available to you on the SRX will better protect your network and the performance of your SRX.

Firewall Filters

Firewall filters are stateless filters that can block or drop traffic based on Layer 2 or Layer 3 header information. For those of you who are familiar with the Cisco IOS firewalls, firewall filters are the equivalent of access control lists (ACLs). Firewall filters are applied to the ingress or the egress interface, and you can use them to drop traffic as quickly and efficiently as possible.

It's highly recommended that you apply firewall filters to the inbound port to control traffic before the SRX processes it. Why spend cycles processing traffic just to drop it as it exits the interface?

You can use firewall filters to block unwanted traffic altogether. For example, on the perimeter of many networks, firewall filters block large network segments from which attacks tend to originate, such as APNIC; during the days of the SQL Slammer attack, many networks blocked port 1434 to prevent a flood of propagation attempts from infected hosts.

Although it's possible to block this type of traffic with security policies, it's simply more efficient to block it with stateless firewall filters. Firewall filters are applied as traffic enters the interface before any kind of session, screen, route, or policy lookup is done, as shown in Figure 7-1. This means the SRX spends as little effort as possible to drop this traffic.

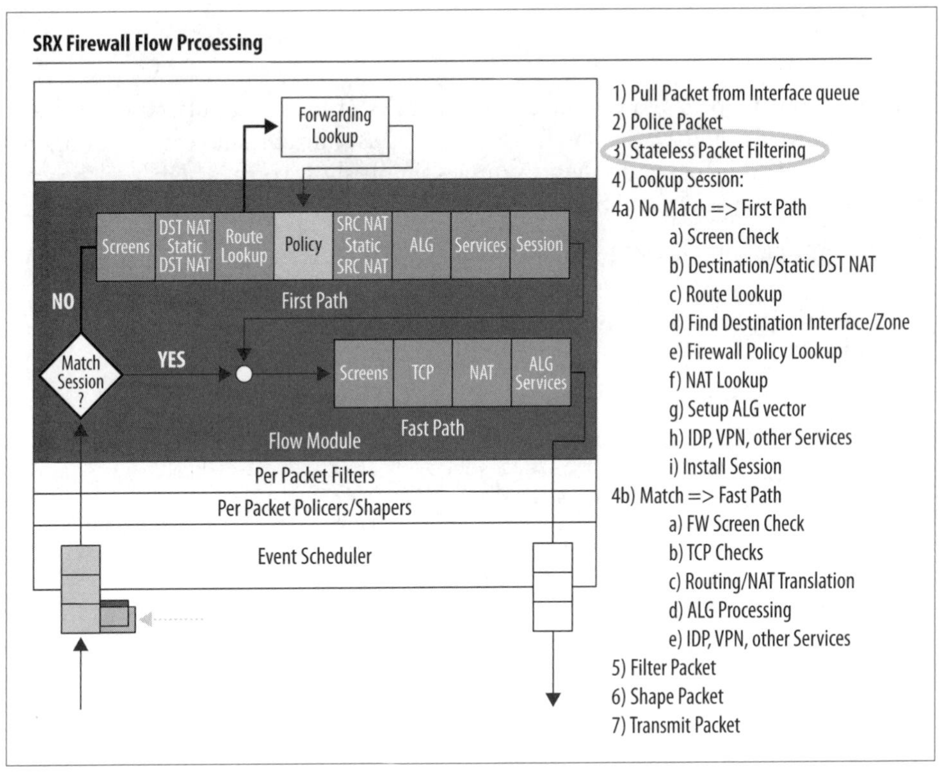
SRX Firewall Flow Prcoessing
Forwarding Lookup
Screens
DST NAT Static DST NAT
Route Lookup
Policy
SRC NAT Static SRC NAT
ALG
Services
Session
NO
First Path
Match Session ?
YES
Screens
TCP
NAT
ALG Services
Flow Module
Fast Path
Per Packet Filters
Per Packet Policers/Shapers
Event Scheduler
1) Pull Packet from Interface queue
2) Police Packet
3) Stateless Packet Filtering
4) Lookup Session:
4a) No Match => First Path
a) Screen Check
b) Destination/Static DST NAT
c) Route Lookup
d) Find Destination Interface/Zone
e) Firewall Policy Lookup
f) NAT Lookup
g) Setup ALG vector
h) IDP, VPN, other Services
i) Install Session
4b) Match => Fast Path
a) FW Screen Check
b) TCP Checks
c) Routing/NAT Translation
d) ALG Processing
e) IDP, VPN, other Services
5) Filter Packet
6) Shape Packet
7) Transmit Packet

Figure 7-1. Where firewall filters take place in the SRX packet flow

If you experience a large-scale attack that impacts your SRX's performance, often you can put a firewall filter in place to mitigate and block the traffic more efficiently.

A firewall filter is composed of the following:

Match condition
: Much like a security policy, you must tell the SRX the kind of traffic to which you want this firewall filter applied. A firewall filter can match on Layer 3, Layer 2, TCP, and ICMP header fields.

Action
: This portion of the firewall filter tells the SRX what action it should take if the match conditions are met. You can count, pass, drop, analyze, or even police the packets.

Interface
: Much like an ACL, a firewall filter is applied on the physical interface. You can apply the firewall filter inbound or outbound to the interface.

Firewall filters cannot be used on aggregate Ethernet interfaces.

The following snippets show some quick examples of matching different traffic and taking actions. Obviously, firewall filters are very customizable and can be configured in hundreds of different ways. These examples simply show you at a high level the ways in which you can use firewall filters.

In the following output, a firewall filter is used to count ICMP packets and pass them along:

```
juniper@SRX5800# show firewall filter count_icmp
term 1 {
    from {
        protocol icmp;
    }
    then {
        count icmp_packets;
        accept;
    }
}
term 2 {
    then accept;
}
```

Here is an example of a firewall filter to block a source network. If a large number of attacks are coming from a netblock, it might make sense to block them at a firewall filter level.

```
juniper@SRX5800# show firewall filter badnetwork
term 1 {
    from {
        source-address {
            198.133.219.0/24;
        }
    }
    then {
        count badnet;
        discard;
    }
}
term 2 {
    then accept;
}
```

Here is a quick firewall filter to block the SQL Slammer worm. In this example, anything matching the destination port of 1434 will be dropped to a bit bucket.

```
juniper@SRX5800# show firewall filter block_slammer
term 1 {
    from {
        destination-port 1434;
    }
    then {
        discard;
    }
}
term 2 {
    then accept;
}
```

Screens

A screen is a built-in tunable protection mechanism that performs a variety of security functions to keep the network safe. Screens are extremely efficient and can be tuned to operate in a small enterprise or in the largest carrier networks. Screens are widely used to add additional protections both at the edge of the network and to internal segments to protect the network from attacks and internal misconfigurations that could impact network availability. Screens are good at detecting and preventing many types of malicious traffic.

Screen checks take place very early in packet processing to make mitigation as efficient and fast as possible. Although they take more processing power than a firewall filter, they are able to look deeper into the packet and at the entire session flow, essentially enabling the SRX to block very large and complex attacks. On the higher-end SRX models, many of these screens are handled in hardware, so the traffic is dropped extremely close to the ingress interface.

When you compare the packet processing in Figure 7-1 to that in Figure 7-2 you may notice that the screen checks take place on both the slow path and the fast path. Once

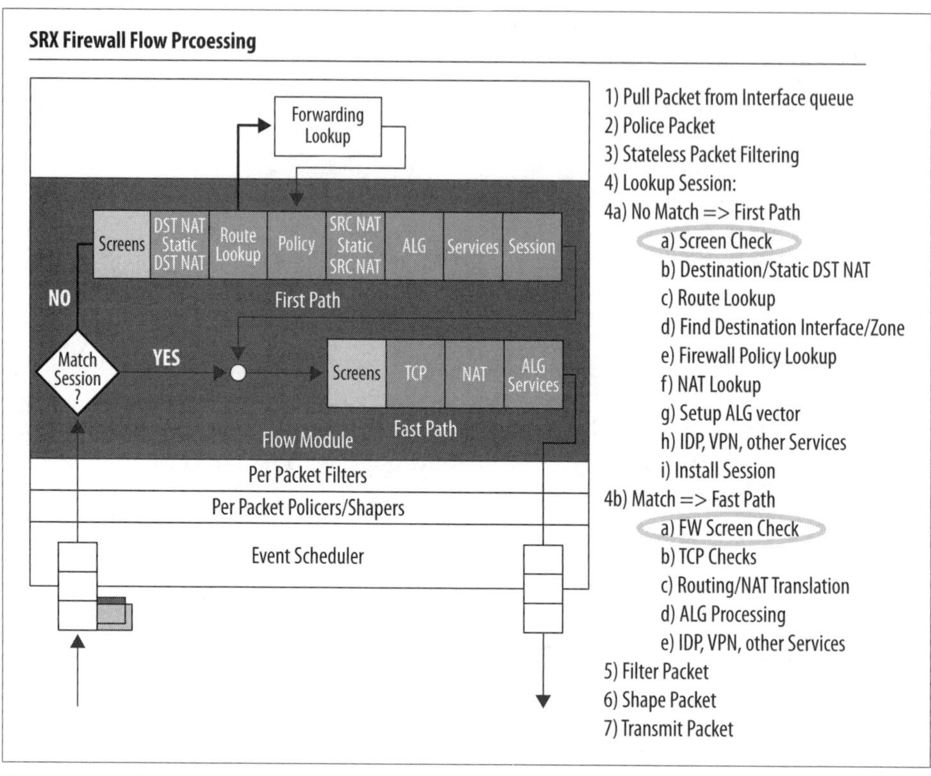
SRX Firewall Flow Prcoessing
Forwarding Lookup
Screens
DST NAT Static DST NAT
Route Lookup
Policy
SRC NAT Static SRC NAT
ALG
Services
Session
NO
First Path
Match Session ?
YES
Screens
TCP
NAT
ALG Services
Flow Module
Fast Path
Per Packet Filters
Per Packet Policers/Shapers
Event Scheduler
1) Pull Packet from Interface queue
2) Police Packet
3) Stateless Packet Filtering
4) Lookup Session:
4a) No Match => First Path
a) Screen Check
b) Destination/Static DST NAT
c) Route Lookup
d) Find Destination Interface/Zone
e) Firewall Policy Lookup
f) NAT Lookup
g) Setup ALG vector
h) IDP, VPN, other Services
i) Install Session
4b) Match => Fast Path
a) FW Screen Check
b) TCP Checks
c) Routing/NAT Translation
d) ALG Processing
e) IDP, VPN, other Services
5) Filter Packet
6) Shape Packet
7) Transmit Packet

Figure 7-2. Where screen checks take place in the SRX packet flow

a session is permitted by policy and is established, the SRX continues to monitor that connection for signs of any malicious traffic or flooding beyond its preconfigured thresholds. If it sees any malicious traffic, it blocks and drops the packets.

Screens are evaluated on the *inbound* zone. So, as a session is created, only the source zone's screens are applied to the traffic. When traffic comes into the Untrust zone destined for the Trust zone, only the Untrust screens are evaluated.

Screens are grouped into screen profiles, and those profiles are then applied to a zone. This is different from the NetScreen way of applying screens and allows for a single profile to be applied to multiple interfaces.

Be careful when designing screens, as even return traffic will not be evaluated by the Trust's screens since the traffic is a part of the initial session that was created with a source zone of Untrust. Additionally, you can use `alarm-without-drop` when deploying any new screens to research what traffic would potentially be dropped by the screen profile.

Security Policy

We covered security policies in detail in Chapter 4. However, since they are part of the multiple layers of security that the SRX can apply to the network, we will briefly cover them again here. Security policies are stateful and can drop traffic based on Layer 3 header information. They are less efficient than firewall filters and screens, but they can be more powerful in terms of evaluating entire flows of traffic at a Layer 3 level, and thus enforce states based on that information, as shown in Figure 7-3. You can use security policies to allow certain types of connections from specific sources or networks.

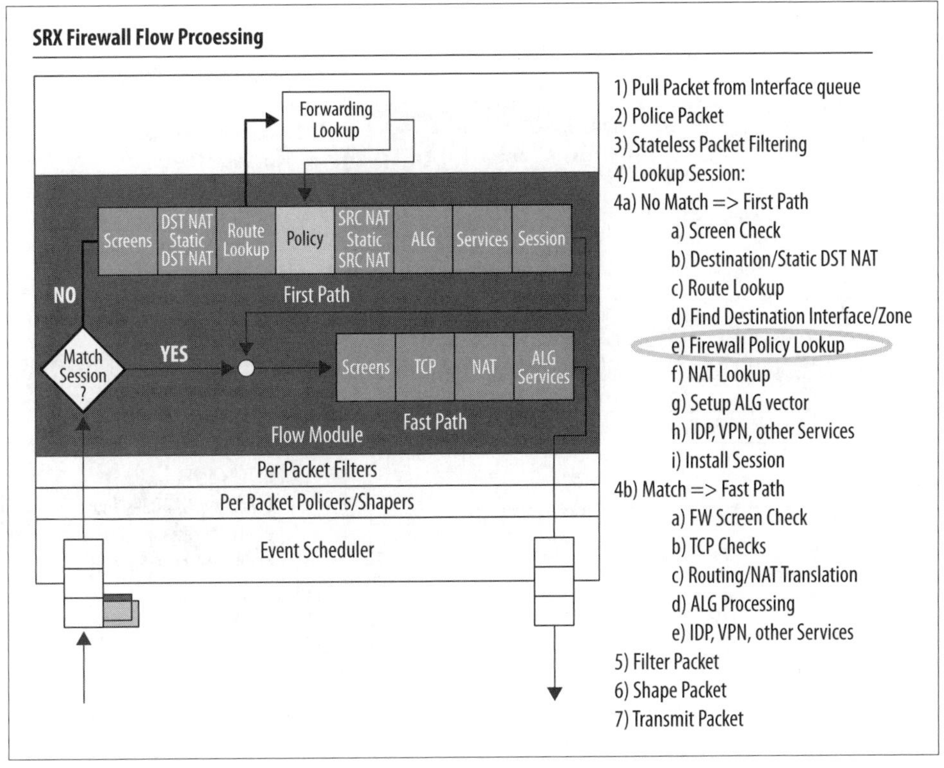
SRX Firewall Flow Prcoessing
Forwarding Lookup
Screens
DST NAT Static DST NAT
Route Lookup
Policy
SRC NAT Static SRC NAT
ALG
Services
Session
NO
First Path
Match Session ?
YES
Screens
TCP
NAT
ALG Services
Fast Path
Flow Module
Per Packet Filters
Per Packet Policers/Shapers
Event Scheduler
1) Pull Packet from Interface queue
2) Police Packet
3) Stateless Packet Filtering
4) Lookup Session:
4a) No Match => First Path
a) Screen Check
b) Destination/Static DST NAT
c) Route Lookup
d) Find Destination Interface/Zone
e) Firewall Policy Lookup
f) NAT Lookup
g) Setup ALG vector
h) IDP, VPN, other Services
i) Install Session
4b) Match => Fast Path
a) FW Screen Check
b) TCP Checks
c) Routing/NAT Translation
d) ALG Processing
e) IDP, VPN, other Services
5) Filter Packet
6) Shape Packet
7) Transmit Packet

Figure 7-3. Where security policy lookups take place in the SRX packet flow

Say you wanted to block port 1434 inbound, but you needed to allow the network's SQL servers to initiate communication or allow a specific host inbound. In this situation, a firewall filter might not be the best option; the easiest solution would be to write a security policy allowing the traffic from the internal trusted SQL server outbound. This would permit return traffic for any SQL connection initiated from the internal SQL server, but would still deny any inbound requests from the outside.

That's just a quick example of a security policy. For all the depth you might wish on security policies, refer to Chapter 4.

IPS and AppDoS

IPS and AppDoS are the most powerful, and thus, the least efficient method of dropping traffic on the SRX, because IPS and AppDoS tend to take up the most processing cycles. That's because they take place *after* the policy lookup (see Figure 7-4) and they look deep into the packet or the entire packet flow to try to determine if the traffic is malicious.

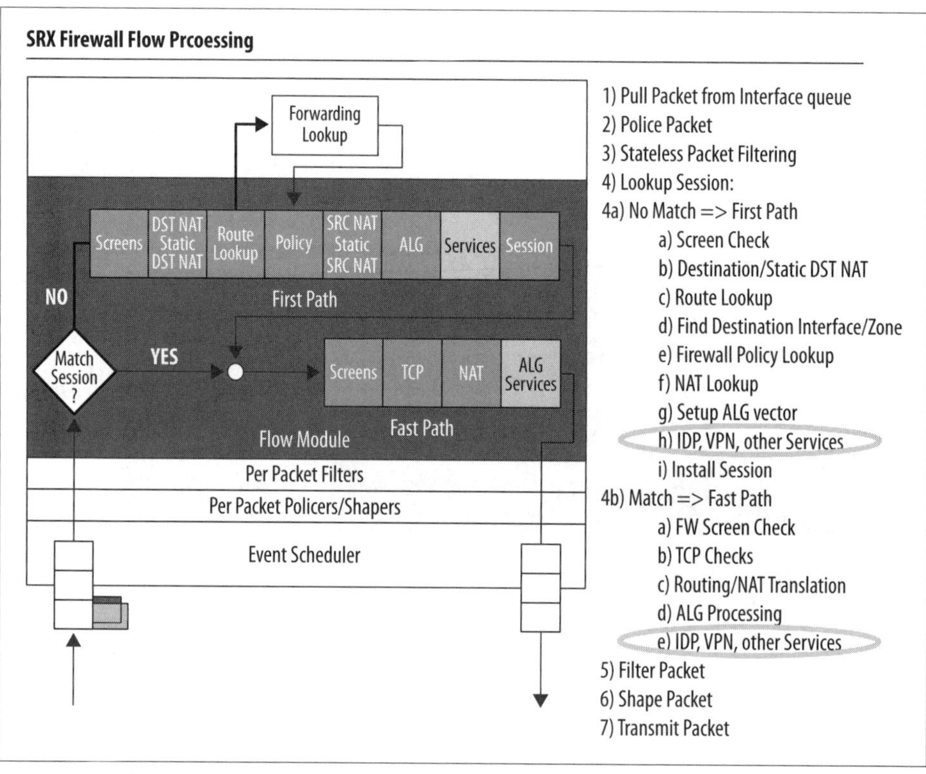
SRX Firewall Flow Prcoessing
Forwarding Lookup
Screens
DST NAT Static DST NAT
Route Lookup
Policy
SRC NAT Static SRC NAT
ALG
Services
Session
NO
First Path
Match Session ?
YES
Screens
TCP
NAT
ALG Services
Flow Module
Fast Path
Per Packet Filters
Per Packet Policers/Shapers
Event Scheduler
1) Pull Packet from Interface queue
2) Police Packet
3) Stateless Packet Filtering
4) Lookup Session:
4a) No Match => First Path
a) Screen Check
b) Destination/Static DST NAT
c) Route Lookup
d) Find Destination Interface/Zone
e) Firewall Policy Lookup
f) NAT Lookup
g) Setup ALG vector
h) IDP, VPN, other Services
i) Install Session
4b) Match => Fast Path
a) FW Screen Check
b) TCP Checks
c) Routing/NAT Translation
d) ALG Processing
e) IDP, VPN, other Services
5) Filter Packet
6) Shape Packet
7) Transmit Packet

Figure 7-4. Where IPS and AppDoS take place in the SRX packet flow

IPS and AppDoS have the ability to dig deep into the packet flow and compare it with known attacks or known patterns of attacks. This enables the SRX to block attacks all the way up to Layer 7 flow information.

For example, you can use IPS instead of dropping all inbound port 80 or HTTP traffic into your network so that you can drop malicious attempts at performing a SQL injection attack that could potentially compromise your backend databases.

AppDoS, on the other hand, has the ability to look at patterns of traffic-and-block based on known behaviors. For example, in a DDoS attack with legitimate infected hosts or a botnet, a protection mechanism such as a SYN cookie or SYN proxy just isn't enough because the infected hosts will respond to the SYN-ACK. Instead, AppDoS can evaluate the traffic patterns and determine that these 10,000 hosts are all doing a simple HTTP request every two minutes. Since it's not normal human behavior to wait precisely 120 seconds before repeatedly requesting data, the AppDoS process starts blocking those attempts from getting to the internal server, mitigating the DDoS attempt.

For more information on IPS and AppDoS see Chapter 8.

Protecting Against Network Reconnaissance

Before breaking into your network, bad guys will scan and probe various parts of the network, looking for attack vectors or weak points of security. With easy-to-use tools such as Nmap and Firewalk, mapping a network from the outside is simple. Nmap can scan an entire network in minutes or probe a single host for open sockets.

Although the first of our five types of network attacks, network reconnaissance, is nearly impossible to stop altogether, it can be limited, throttled, or obscured.

The first location to harden is the perimeter of the network. In this book's example network (see Figure P-1 in the Preface), it's the Campus Core SRX5800 cluster. However, this is only the starting point, as network reconnaissance could come from not only outside your network, but also inside it. Internal threats also need to be taken into account and protected against—the threat could be the result of a breach of the actual physical network, or it could have come from a malicious employee or contractor.

The SRX has multiple built-in protection mechanisms to prevent and mitigate many common types of reconnaissance. Keep in mind that there is no single cookie-cutter solution for preventing reconnaissance—security is always a compromise, and to make something completely secure you have to unplug it and store it in a safe. The moment you bring a server or network online, it will be vulnerable to attack. So, many of the methods that prevent network reconnaissance also prevent network and system administrators from being able to map out their own network, and potentially limit their troubleshooting tools.

For example, in some situations you might not be able to block all ICMP packets, so the compromise is to rate-limit the number of ICMP packets to a reasonable amount and size. This enables users to run standard pings, but a rapid ping or a large ping packet will fail.

If blocking inbound ICMP is an option, it is highly recommended that you deploy, as it can prevent many types of network reconnaissance and remove a large number of attack vectors on the network infrastructure, as well as on the end nodes themselves.

Firewall Filtering

Although you can block all ICMP packets with security policies, to do it more efficiently you can block them on the inbound interface via a firewall filter such as the following:

```
juniper@SRX5800> edit
[edit]
juniper@SRX5800> edit firewall filter
[edit firewall filter]
juniper@SRX5800> set block-icmp term 1 from protocol icmp
juniper@SRX5800> set block-icmp term 1 then count
juniper@SRX5800> set block-icmp term 1 then discard
juniper@SRX5800> set block-icmp term 2 then accept
```

Since this is the first firewall filter you've seen in this book, let's go over the basics.

Firewall filters consist of a basic *match condition*. In our example, `from protocol icmp` is our match condition. Then, much like a security policy, there is a *then action*. In `term 1` there are two actions: the first is a `count` to count the number of packets that match protocol ICMP, and the second is a `discard` to discard these packets. Counting the number of packets is useful when understanding how much traffic is being dropped and/or at what rate. You can view these firewall counters via the `show log filter` command.

The second of two actions is in the `term 2` that has an action of `accept`. This is critical, as firewall filters will `discard` by default, unless there is an `accept` at the end of the filter.

Although firewall filters can be very powerful and you can use them to block all kinds of specific traffic such as ICMP codes of certain ICMP types, a more detailed discussion of them is out of the scope of this chapter. For more information on specific filtering and matching conditions, please review Juniper's technical documentation on firewall filter match conditions at *http://www.juniper.net/techpubs*. The documentation will provide you with an extensive list of what types of packets you can match and filter on.

Once you have built the firewall filter, you need to apply it to the interface. In our case, you want to apply the firewall filter on the Internet-facing interface blocking ingress traffic, or in plain English, traffic coming from the Internet into the interface. For example:

```
juniper@SRX5800> edit
[edit]
juniper@SRX5800>  set interface ge-0/0/0 unit 0 family inet filter
input block-icmp
```

Screening

In the event that ICMP must be allowed on the network, or certain hosts need to be permitted, a screen can add an additional layer of protection to keep any rogue or misconfigured hosts from scanning or flooding the network.

The first thing to limit is what's called an IP sweep. IP sweeps are used to compile a list of hosts that are online on the network and actively respond to traffic. Typically, an ICMP echo request is used in an IP sweep in an attempt to get an ICMP response. Once the attacker gathers a list of hosts, his next step may be additional port scanning and OS fingerprinting.

The ICMP sweep screen is configured with a threshold per source IP. In other words, a single source IP can generate 10 ICMP packets to different destinations per configured threshold (in microseconds). This can be configured from 1,000 microseconds to 1 million microseconds. For reference, 1,000 microseconds is 1 millisecond. So, you can allow as few as 10 ICMP packets per millisecond or as many as 10 ICMP packets per second. The larger the threshold, the longer the duration and the less ICMP packets that are permitted:

```
juniper@SRX5800> edit
[edit]
juniper@SRX5800> set security screen ids-option untrusted-internet
icmp ip-sweep threshold 1000000
```

Sending 10 ICMP packets per second to different hosts seems like a lot for a single host. So, that is what we'll block. With this screen configured, a single host out on the Internet would only be able to ping 10 hosts per second. This would hardly prevent the attacker from mapping out your network nodes, but it may skew the results, or slow them down, as the SRX will silently drop above the configured threshold, limiting any potential impact to the network from these sweeps.

A new set of screens in Junos 10.2 expands on IP sweep protection. Juniper has added two additional screens to protect against TCP and UDP sweeps. Most advanced reconnaissance will avoid ICMP altogether, as bad guys tend to know that ICMP is limited/blocked at the perimeter of the network. However, by sending a SYN sweep or UDP sweep, it's possible to find more interesting results and map out services in the process. Tools such as Nmap are extremely good at doing precisely this.

The TCP and UDP sweeps are configured the same way as ICMP sweep screens. The threshold value, like the ICMP sweep screen, is in microseconds.

The following configuration enables protection against these types of sweeps:

```
juniper@SRX5800> edit
[edit]
juniper@SRX5800> set security screen ids-option untrusted-internet
tcp tcp-sweep threshold 1000000
[edit]
juniper@SRX5800> set security screen ids-option untrusted-internet
udp ucp-sweep threshold 1000000
```

Port Scan Screening

Once a network has been scanned for responding hosts, the attacker typically gathers more information about these up hosts. Attackers often want to know what version of OS they're running, and what open ports or services they have. This is called *port scanning*, or scanning for open sockets to potentially attack.

The SRX has the ability to limit the number of SYN packets a single source can send per microsecond. Now, this doesn't come close to blocking all types of port scans, as Nmap has the ability to do many different types of scans, but it does limit the majority of port scanning.

Let's add `port-scan` to our `untrusted-internet` screen profile. `port-scan` has the same upper and lower durations as the IP sweep screen:

```
juniper@SRX5800> edit
[edit]
juniper@SRX5800> set security screen ids-option untrusted-internet
tcp port-scan threshold 1000000
```

Here, the port scan screen is configured with a threshold of 1 second. This means a single source host can send one SYN packet to 10 different ports per second. Again, this does not block all port scan attempts, but it will limit the attack and hopefully prevent the system from taking any kind of performance hit.

FIN scans are another method of port scanning. An attacker typically sends a FIN packet to a port and then listens. The end host, assuming the socket is listening, sees a FIN packet arrive for a connection that it does not have established, so it responds with a "reset packet."

Blocking this type of scan is easy. Here, it is added to our `untrusted-internet` screen profile:

```
juniper@SRX5800> edit
[edit]
juniper@SRX5800> set security screen ids-option untrusted-internet tcp fin-no-ack
```

Ideally, this type of scan, and other types such as the null scan, is already prevented by the SRX's `tcp-syn-checking` system. However, if that is disabled, the SRX does not require a SYN packet to create a new TCP connection, and it would allow for these types of attacks.

Additional reconnaissance methods include the use of record route, timestamp, stream ID, source route, and security. These are all IP options that have no place or right to be in most networks, so we'll block them from entering our perimeter:

```
juniper@SRX5800> edit

[edit]
juniper@SRX5800> edit security screen ids-option

[edit security screen ids-option]
```

```
juniper@SRX5800# set untrusted-internet ip record-route-option

[edit security screen ids-option]
juniper@SRX5800# set untrusted-internet ip timestamp-option

[edit security screen ids-option]
juniper@SRX5800# set untrusted-internet ip security-option

[edit security screen ids-option]
juniper@SRX5800# set untrusted-internet ip stream-option

[edit security screen ids-option]
juniper@SRX5800# set untrusted-internet ip loose-source-route-option

[edit security screen ids-option]
juniper@SRX5800# set untrusted-internet ip strict-source-route-option

[edit security screen ids-option]
juniper@SRX5800# set untrusted-internet ip source-route-option
```

Sometimes these IP options are ways to map out the network by requesting return traffic to take different network paths. As stated previously, they are typically not used inside a network and should especially get dropped when coming inbound from the Internet.

So far, here is what our `untrusted-internet` screen profile looks like:

```
juniper@SRX5800# show | compare
[edit security screen]
+    ids-option untrusted-internet {
+        icmp {
+            ip-sweep threshold 1000000;
+        }
+        ip {
+            record-route-option;
+            timestamp-option;
+            security-option;
+            stream-option;
+            source-route-option;
+            loose-source-route-option;
+            strict-source-route-option;
+        }
+        tcp {
+            fin-no-ack;
+            port-scan threshold 1000000;
+        }
+    }
```

Summary

Blocking network reconnaissance is not always 100% possible. You can gain an additional layer of security by using IPS to block advanced sweeps, scans, and other information-gathering attempts. It's also possible to *shun* or *blackhole* a host that has been caught attempting to gather information about the network.

Ideally, firewall filters, screens, security policy, and IPS would be used in an efficient security design to prevent as much network reconnaissance as possible. When designing each layer, try to block as much as possible at the lower levels. If all ICMP is blocked at a firewall filter, the security policy blocking ICMP from the Internet zone does not have to process any traffic; the same goes for the IPS signatures for ICMP information gathering. And they can work harder at other security processes.

Each design needs to be tailored to the needs and flows of your network. Remember, traffic flows can be immensely different from an ISP's network-to-enterprise network. Additionally, certain troubleshooting methods of services may rely on ICMP or routing options.

It's not possible to configure a cookie-cutter security design to protect all the different network types and sizes out there, but the SRX is as close as you can get to applying security solutions as fast as you need them.

Protecting Against Basic IP Attacks

In the preceding section, we addressed many of the basic IP attacks. This section discusses how to block additional common attacks, and the tricks you can use to circumvent other prevention mechanisms.

Blocking these basic IP attacks at a screen level lessens the load on the IPS layer (as many of these attacks can also be blocked there, albeit at the expense of more processing and evaluation).

Basic IP Protections

One common IP attack is the malformed packet. Attackers and security researchers have found that incorrectly formatting packets or sending incomplete packets can produce unintended consequences on both network infrastructure and end hosts. It is not unheard of to witness these types of packets crashing services or even the server itself. Today's operating systems tend to prevent this from happening, but it is a best practice to block such packets before they enter your network and reach your end hosts. Let's enter the security screen:

```
juniper@SRX5800> edit

[edit]
juniper@SRX5800# edit security screen

[edit security screen]
juniper@SRX5800# set ids-option untrusted-internet ip bad-option
```

Along the same lines as the malformed packet that should never be seen as legitimate traffic entering the network, it is also best to block IP packets with an unknown protocol ID:

```
[edit security screen]
juniper@SRX5800# set ids-option untrusted-internet ip unknown-protocol
```

Fragments are often used to circumvent attack preventions and detections by splitting an attack payload across multiple fragmented packets—and sending a large number of fragmented packets can harm any session-aware device or end node, as the device or end node has to reassemble those packets to evaluate them. The SRX has the ability to block fragmented IP packets altogether to prevent these types of attacks.

Although it is potentially dangerous, you have the ability to block all fragmented IP packets using the `set security screen ids-option untrusted-internet ip block-frag` command. But since our network has IP fragments, let's leave this screen disabled. It's a good example of the things you need to consider when configuring screens, because not all of them should be used on every network. Each screen should be evaluated and the flows and traffic of the network should be taken into account when applying the screen.

The last and most important of the basic IP protections that you'll apply is the *spoofing* screen. The spoofing screen attempts to prevent an attacker from falsifying his source IP address. The SRX checks the source IP address in the packet header and then compares that to its routing table. If it knows that network segment or host exists elsewhere, it determines that the IP packet it is evaluating is spoofed. This is based on Reverse Path Forwarding (RPF) loose checking.

In other words, and as shown in Figure 7-5, if a packet arrives on the outside Internet-facing interface with a source IP address of an internal network—say, 10.1.0.201 destined for 172.31.100.60—the SRX determines that 10.1.0.201 exists within the internal network, and therefore it must be a spoof attack.

Let's configure our SRX to block these spoofing attempts:

```
[edit security screen]
juniper@SRX5800# set ids-option untrusted-internet ip spoofing
```

You must be careful with asymmetric routing, as it can cause the spoofing screen to drop legitimate traffic. You can configure additional granular protections from specific IP packets via firewall filters. A quick and simple example of this is to block the record route IP options:

```
juniper@SRX5800> edit
[edit]
juniper@SRX5800> edit firewall filter
[edit firewall filter]
juniper@SRX5800> set block-recordroute term 1 from ip-options record-route
juniper@SRX5800> set block-recordroute term 1 then count
juniper@SRX5800> set block-recordroute term 1 then discard
juniper@SRX5800> set block-recordroute term 2 then accept
```

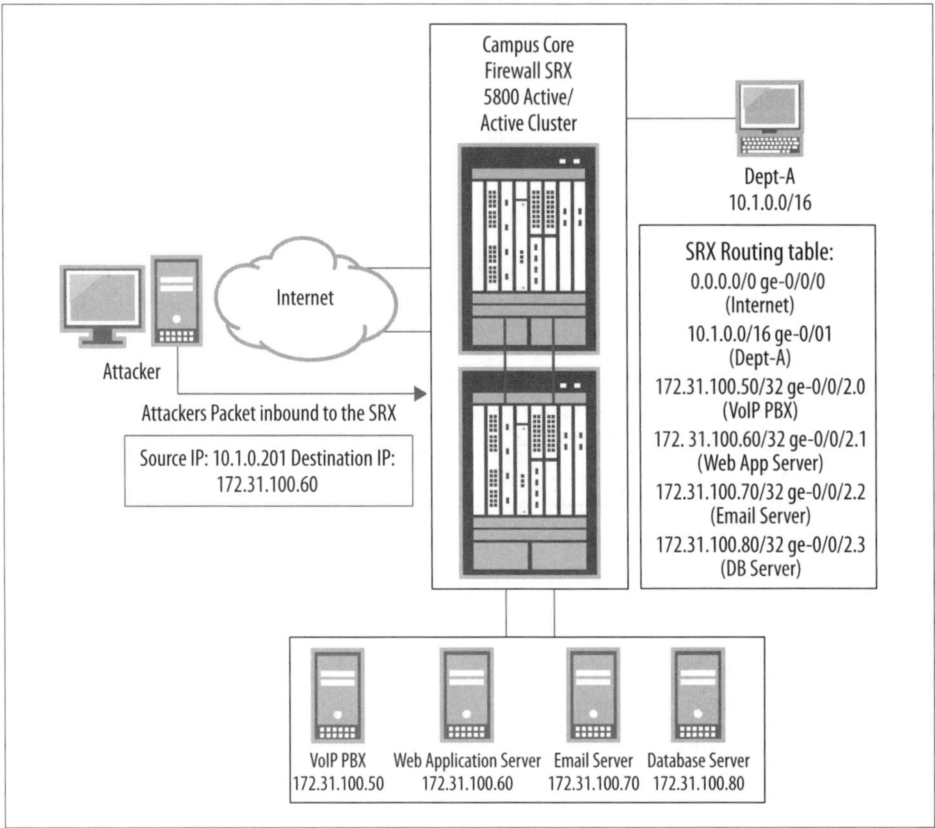

Figure 7-5. The spoof attack

Remember that `then accept` is critical before applying the firewall filter to the interface:

```
juniper@SRX5800> edit
[edit]
juniper@SRX5800>  set interface ge-0/0/0 unit 0 family inet filter input block-
recordroute
```

Basic ICMP Protections

You can defend yourself against ICMP abuse by limiting the size and fragmentation of ICMP packets. ICMP is a tool used to test network performance and stability, so limiting ICMP's size and ability to fragment will potentially limit ICMP tunneling problems and protect against large ICMP packet floods or fragmentation attacks:

```
[edit security screen]
juniper@SRX5800# set ids-option untrusted-internet icmp fragment
[edit security screen]
juniper@SRX5800# set ids-option untrusted-internet icmp large
```

Basic TCP Protections

The misuse of TCP is a common occurrence and it is often used to attack network hosts. The SRX can protect against many of the basic TCP attacks via screens, with additional protection coming from the IPS. Screens can do some basic sanity checks of the TCP flags to ensure that they are legitimate packets.

The `fin-no-ack` screen was already enabled in "Protecting Against Network Reconnaissance" on page 349 to prevent FIN packets from illegitimately entering the network. In addition to blocking TCP packets with the FIN flag but not the ACK flag set, the SRX has screens to prevent TCP packets with no flags and SYN-FIN flags set. Both of these types of packets should never be seen in a working network such as ours, and can therefore be blocked via the screens:

```
[edit security screen]
juniper@SRX5800# set ids-option untrusted-internet tcp tcp-no-flag

[edit security screen]
juniper@SRX5800# set ids-option untrusted-internet tcp syn-fin
```

The SRX also has the ability to block packets with a SYN flag that is configured as a fragment. Again, this type of packet should never be seen on a production network, so it's safe to block at our border:

```
[edit security screen]
juniper@SRX5800# set ids-option untrusted-internet tcp syn-frag
```

Now, let's look at our current `untrusted-internet` profile thus far:

```
juniper@SRX5800# show security screen ids-option untrusted-internet
icmp {
    ip-sweep threshold 1000000;
    fragment;
    large;
}
ip {
    bad-option;
    record-route-option;
    timestamp-option;
    security-option;
    stream-option;
    spoofing;
    source-route-option;
    loose-source-route-option;
    strict-source-route-option;
    unknown-protocol;
}
tcp {
    syn-fin;
    fin-no-ack;
    tcp-no-flag;
    syn-frag;
    port-scan threshold 1000000;
}
```

You can use most of these IP screens and filters on all networks; however, you must closely evaluate items such as the fragmentation screen and spoofing to ensure that they do not impact legitimate traffic flows.

It's always recommended when applying new screens, or a new screen profile, that you closely monitor the logs for any unexpected drops or false positives.

Basic Denial-of-Service Screens

Let's start our coverage of defense from the second general category of attacks with a blast from the past. Juniper has also implemented screens for you to use to block many of the popular attacks from the 1990s. Yes, the 1990s. Although these attacks were patched many, many years ago, Juniper wrote screens to protect against them because they do show up as hackers attempt to cash in on a newer generation of network security engineers. For more up-to-date protections against exploits and attacks from this grand decade of the Internet, use of the IPS system is recommended.

Winnuke is an attack screen that blocks an attack on the Windows 95/NT/3.1 platforms. Winnuke attacked port 139 (NetBIOS) with some out-of-band data in an attempt to crash the system. You can block winnuke using the `set security screen ids-option untrusted-internet tcp winnuke` command.

A second attack from the mid-1990s is the Ping of Death attack. This attack involves sending a ping packet at the maximum possible size, which is 65,535 bytes. Sending a ping packet of this size would cause the end host to crash. To block this attack use the `set security screen ids-option untrusted-internet icmp ping-death` command.

A more sophisticated DoS attack from the 1990s that seems to come back to life every now and again is the Teardrop attack. The Teardrop attack was most recently found to crash Windows 7 boxes by attacking the SMB2 protocol. The Teardrop attack is two fragmented packets that overlap each other, as shown in Figure 7-6. The idea is that when the end application that is listening reassembles the two fragmented packets, it causes the application or host to crash.

This is the only DoS screen that we'll apply to our screen profile:

```
[edit security screen]
juniper@SRX240# set ids-option untrusted-internet ip tear-drop
```

Our last attack from the past is the Land attack. This attack, much like Teardrop, seems to come back every now and then as Microsoft seems to forget it exists. Most recently, Windows XP SP2 and Windows 2003 were found to be vulnerable to a Land attack. A Land attack is typically a SYN packet with a source IP/port that is the same as the destination IP/port. The theory is that when the destination IP attempts to process the packet it will cause unexpected behavior when it sees that the packet is from itself, as

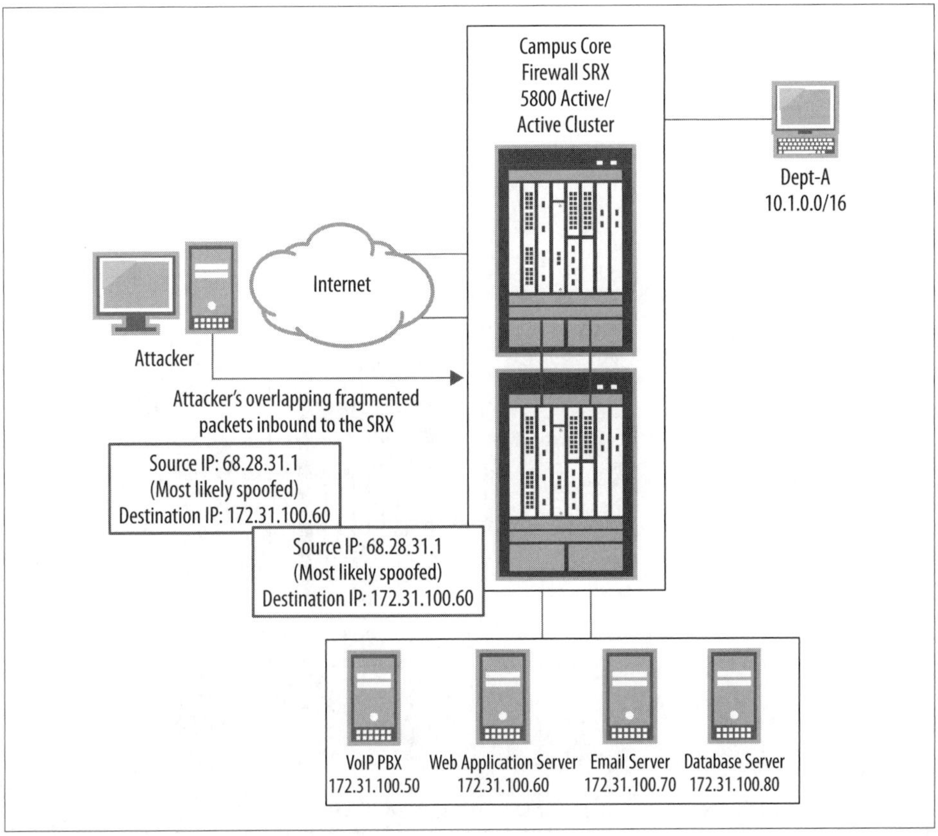

Figure 7-6. The old Teardrop attack

shown in Figure 7-7. In most cases, the spoof screen prevents this attack from occurring; however, let's add it to our `untrusted-internet` profile for the next time Microsoft is vulnerable:

```
[edit security screen]
juniper@SRX240# set ids-option untrusted-internet tcp land
```

Although not all of the basic DoS screens are applicable to today's threats, you can put some of them in place as safeguards against future potential vulnerabilities. Attacks such as Teardrop and Land appear to be timeless and continue to pop up every now and again, while others seem to provide a history lesson for younger administrators working network security.

If you want to prevent current-day DoS attacks and other such exploits, use the built-in IPS functionality on the SRX.

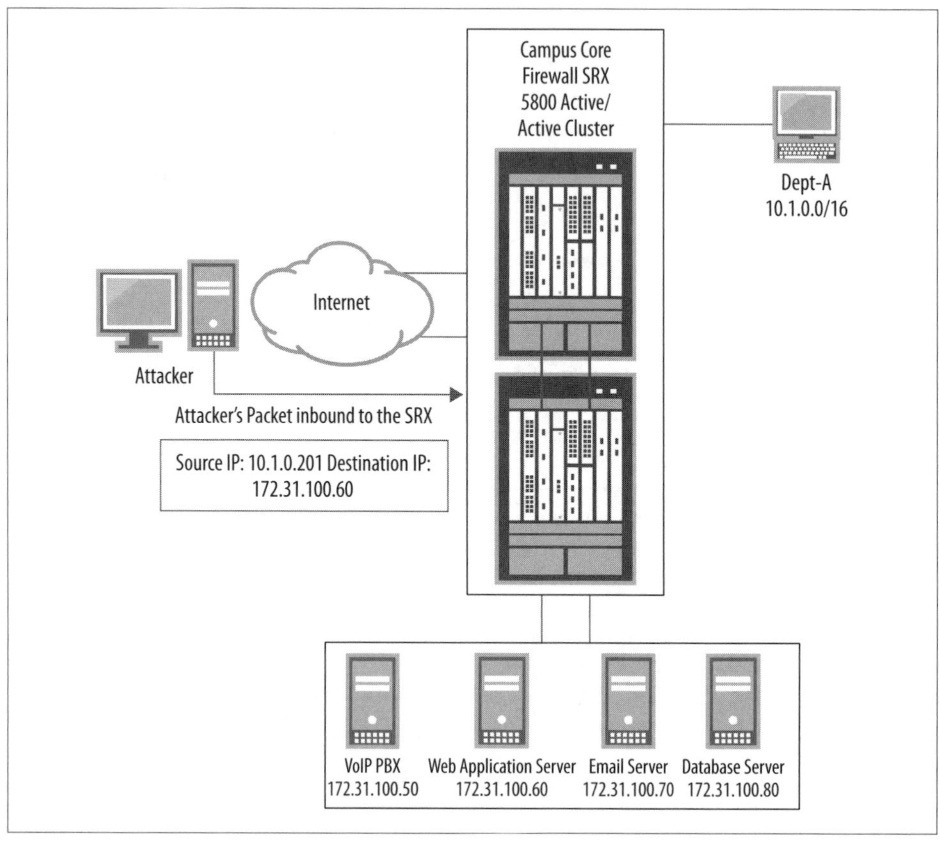

Figure 7-7. The Land attack

So far, our updated untrusted-internet screen profile looks like this:

```
juniper@SRX240# show security screen ids-option untrusted-internet
icmp {
    ip-sweep threshold 1000000;
    fragment;
    large;
}
ip {
    bad-option;
    record-route-option;
    timestamp-option;
    security-option;
    stream-option;
    spoofing;
    source-route-option;
    loose-source-route-option;
    strict-source-route-option;
    unknown-protocol;
    tear-drop;
```

```
    }
    tcp {
        syn-fin;
        fin-no-ack;
        tcp-no-flag;
        syn-frag;
        port-scan threshold 1000000;
        land;
    }
```

Let's move on to the more advanced DoS attacks and the years coming right at us.

Advanced Denial-of-Service and Distributed Denial-of-Service Protection

Here we'll look at various methods in which the SRX can prevent or mitigate advanced DoS and DDoS flooding attacks. A DoS flood is a flood of packets to a host or network that is meant to depredate or reduce the availability of the service/network. There are many types of DoS flooding attacks, but they can be categorized into two main flavors:

Service flood
: A DoS flood is an attempt to overrun a system or service with requests (valid or invalid) which overrun the system's ability to process legitimate requests. An example is an HTTP request flood, as shown in Figure 7-8. The idea of the HTTP flood is to overrun the web server with thousands (or millions) of bogus requests, knocking the website offline and preventing it from serving its customers.

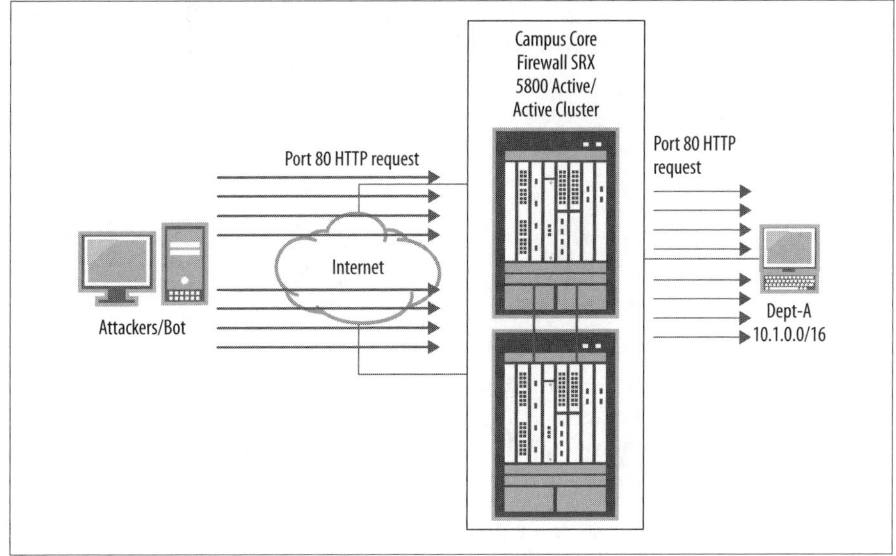

Figure 7-8. A service flood attack

Bandwidth flood

A bandwidth flood is similar to a service flood, with the exception that the bandwidth flood may not be attacking a single destination; instead, it's attempting to fill up the network links or network infrastructure's processing capacity. Typically, you see these types of floods as large UDP packets with spoofed sources, as shown in Figure 7-9. Assuming the destination node or network's smallest link in the network path is an OC3, which is approximately 155 Mb, to attack the availability of this network and its ability to serve legitimate customers an attack simply has to send, at most, 155 Mb of UDP packets.

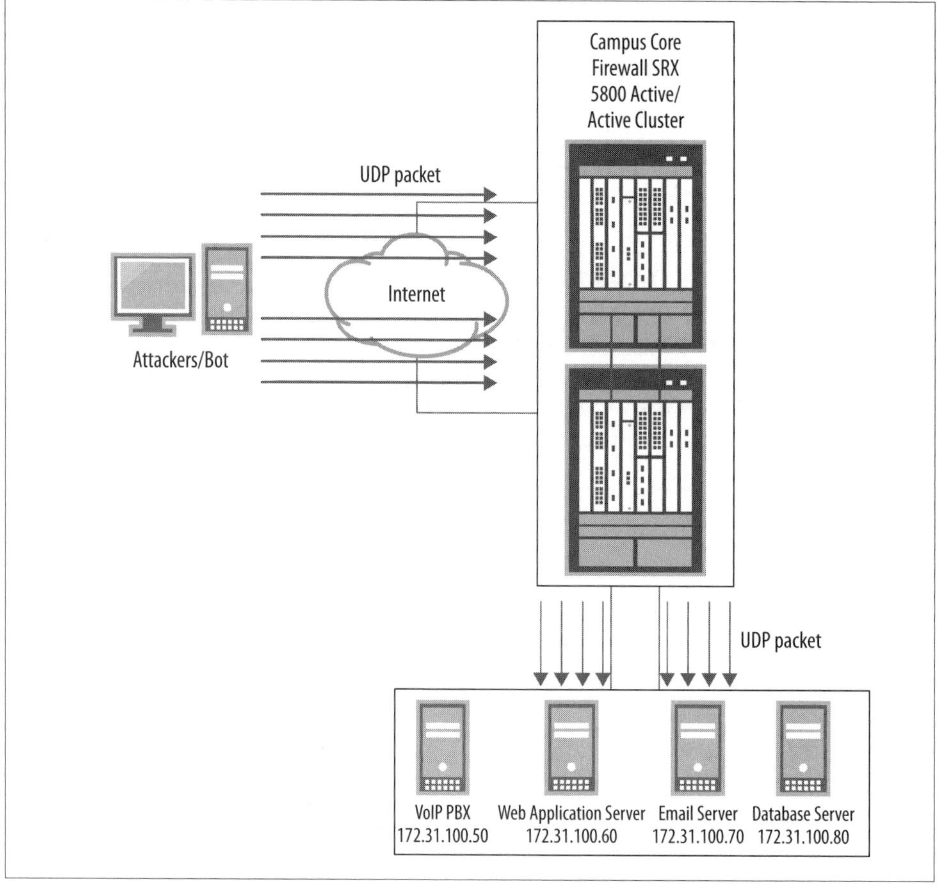

Figure 7-9. A bandwidth flood attack

Both bandwidth floods and service floods are very common attacks. They are trivial to execute yet can be dangerous when distributed. Presently, there are two major methods for flooding a target. The first involves cloud computing and the second is the DDoS attack.

Today it is becoming increasingly common to leverage the cloud computing phenomenon in attack scenarios. A malicious user can rent a very large server farm with extremely large Internet links within these cloud computing services, and all for a small fee. With a precanned program or a custom script, this malicious user could then do a lot of damage.

In the DDoS attack, a small army of compromised hosts are used on high-speed bandwidth connections that combine their data connections to overrun the destination network's connection. DDoS attacks were made popular in early 2000, and made the mainstream news when a young Canadian attacker took down many popular sites, including Yahoo!, Amazon, Dell, eBay, and CNN. The compromised hosts that perform the attack are typically called *bots*, and a collection of these bots is referred to as a *botnet*.

Botnets are extremely dangerous. They have the unique ability to connect to a central location for instructions. Originally, these bots would just flood a site; however, they can delay their connections or attempt to download items from the target.

Botnet owners historically were bored teenagers, experimenting hackers, or possibly a malicious person seeking revenge. Today's botnet owners are much more devious and are driven by money—they use their botnets and bots for extortion: click fraud, identity/service theft, and spam.

How do you mitigate these major types of DoS floods on the SRX? Keep in mind that a DoS attack only has to be effective as the weakest link in the chain. Having an SRX5800 on the network perimeter is great for mitigating huge numbers of floods, but if your uplink to the Internet is only a 25 MB circuit the attacker simply has to fill that 25 MB uplink to get the desired results. So, analyze your network from the outside in, looking at the external facing links, inline devices (routers, load balancers, switches), and external facing services.

You should place weaker servers and load balancers behind an SRX for protection, whereas most routers can typically defend themselves via ACLs, reverse ACLs, and other built-in mechanisms.

ICMP Floods

An ICMP flood is one of the easiest and most preventable types of floods. ICMP is often processed differently than normal packets, and in many cases, such as ICMP echo-reply or traceroute, it requires a response packet. These floods are often referred to as *ping floods*.

The most obvious way to mitigate a ping flood is to block ICMP altogether at the perimeter of your network via firewall filters, if this is possible. Assuming it's not, you can leverage some of the built-in ICMP flood protection features within the SRX, such as configuring IP sweep protection and blocking large ICMP packets, which we already discussed in this chapter. You can improve on this, however, by limiting the rate at which a single source can send ICMP packets.

Unlike previous screens that apply on a per-source basis, the flood screens are zone-wide. So, it's important to understand what is considered normal as far as number of ICMP packets seen, and not to set the threshold too low. If any ICMP packets are used for keepalives or device state monitoring, that makes ICMP flood protection even riskier.

In your perimeter zone screen profile, you should limit the number of ICMP packets to what you determined to be a normal number. This threshold is per *second*, unlike previous thresholds, which were per *microsecond*. After careful analysis, the following configuration is applied:

```
[edit]
juniper@SRX5800# set security screen ids-option untrusted-internet
icmp flood threshold 8000
```

Your configured threshold is set for 8,000 ICMP packets per second. This is across the entire zone for the `untrusted-internet` screen. This should allow for enough valid ICMP traffic to pass through the zone from the Internet without impacting any legitimate traffic, while limiting the impact of any potential inbound ICMP floods.

UDP Floods

UDP packet floods tend to be one of the more popular generic floods out there. It seems that all basic bots or attackers who are not very familiar with networking or programming tend to use UDP floods, probably due to UDP's simplistic stateless nature. But UDP floods can be very effective at getting through firewall rules and ACLs, and large packet UDP floods can clog circuits at a rapid pace. Hence, they carry a large risk when leveraged properly. Even greater is the risk of blocking legitimate UDP traffic over your network due to thresholds being set too low on your screen profile.

Again, this UDP threshold value is zone-wide and per-second. You must be extremely cautious when enabling this screen, as it has the very real ability to drop legitimate UDP traffic. Think for a moment about what type of UDP traffic can traverse your network: streaming video and audio, webcasts, VoIP services, Domain Name System (DNS) traffic, authentication traffic, IP Security (IPsec) traffic, and more. The list of critical services using UDP is long and must be taken into consideration; when that threshold is met for the UDP flood screen, anything above that is dropped, legitimate or not. So, let's go through a mini case study.

Let's say you have evaluated your company's traffic loads over the course of a few weeks and determined that 500 UDP packets per second during peak are the most that are ever seen over this zone. Just to be safe, you double that value to 1,000 UDP packets per second. This configuration runs fine for months without a problem, and then a small UDP flood is pointed at one of your servers. The UDP flood isn't enough to soak up the bandwidth on your Internet links, nor is it large enough to impact the firewall, but it gets capped by that new UDP flood screen. Crisis adverted? Not really.

Shortly after noticing the screen alarms and the increase in UDP traffic, you receive calls from various users and system administrators across the network. DNS is working intermittently, VoIP calls are failing, and the company's webcast demo for sales is failing. Everyone is mad and business is being adversely affected.

Understanding the risks involved with capping an entire protocol such as UDP must be taken into account. In most cases, the upper threshold should be set for the worst-case scenario. What is the absolute maximum amount of UDP traffic that the servers and network can handle before other things start to be impacted? When this UDP threshold is hit it should be triggered at the point at which the network or service must be saved, and all UDP traffic going over this zone has now been deemed optional.

After careful evaluation and monitoring, the following configuration is applied for UDP flood protection:

```
[edit]
juniper@SRX5800# set security screen ids-option untrusted-internet
udp flood threshold 50000
```

Wow, 50,000 UDP packets per second? Why so high? When would this ever get hit?

Well, the answer is "hopefully never." Hopefully, you'll never see a UDP flood great enough to cause your infrastructure to have to start blocking all UDP traffic, but it will do so in order to protect the network. By using various test equipment to generate a large number of UDP packets, it is determined that the supporting equipment behind the SRX can handle up to 70,000 UDP packets per second without failing. So, setting the threshold just below that allows for normal, or even elevated, traffic loads.

If this screen was ever hit hard, you would want to evaluate the sources and/or the destination IP addresses or ports, and perhaps manually block them via a firewall filter. You could even automate this to some level via event scripts.

SYN/TCP Floods

SYN floods are, by far, the most common type of DDoS attacks, and they are typically directed at a service such as HTTP. A SYN packet is the first packet sent from the host to a server requesting a connection via TCP. All TCP connections must be set up via the three-way handshake per TCP RFC 793. Figure 7-10 shows an example of a normal TCP setup.

The SYN flood attack is attempting to exploit the way TCP sets up its connections. Once a SYN packet is sent, the server sends a SYN/ACK packet in return and listens

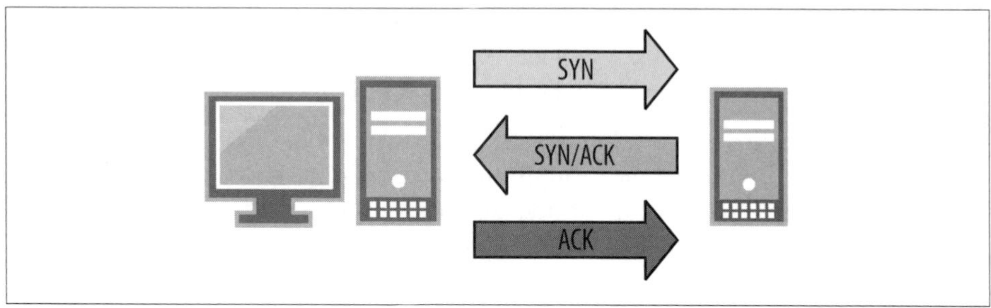

Figure 7-10. TCP Three-way handshake

for the acknowledgment. This causes the server to hang as it listens and waits for that ACK packet.

Multiple vectors are being attacked with a SYN flood. The first major vector concerns the fact that the server is processing the initial SYN request and creating a SYN/ACK packet to reply with, which obviously exhausts resources. The second major vector is the number of idle and hanging sockets that are opened while waiting for the ACK packet to come back from the originating source. This could be an issue on any item that keeps state, such as load balancers, firewalls, proxies, servers, and so on.

So, how do you prevent these types of SYN floods from impacting your elements and infrastructure? The first preventive measure, as with every other flood configuration, is to understand how your network flows. Traffic should be monitored via JFlow/NetFlow sniffers to understand the normal level of TCP traffic. How many SYNs per second is the baseline? You should understand the average number of new TCP connection requests per second, as well as the peak number of connections per second.

The SYN flood protection screen has the following configuration options:

Attack threshold
: This is the number of SYN packets per predestination address and port number per second. Once this number is reached, the SRX begins proxying TCP connection attempts to that destination or port. This threshold is on a per-destination and per-service basis. (We will discuss the proxying process in more detail shortly.)

Alarm threshold
: This is the number of SYN packets per second that will send an alarm to the event log. This is useful for notifications and alarms in addition to testing your attack threshold values.

Source threshold
: This is the number of SYN packets per IP address, and it can be to any destination IP address or port number. The source threshold blocks any SYN packets above the threshold, instead of proxying, like the attack threshold does.

Destination threshold
: This is the number of SYN packets per destination IP address, and it can be from any source IP address or port number. The destination threshold operates like the source threshold; it blocks any SYN packets above the threshold, instead of proxying, like the attack threshold.

Timeout
: The timeout value is the amount of time the embryonic or initial sessions (sessions that haven't created a three-way handshake) are in the session table. By default, this value is 20 seconds. You can set this value more aggressively if there is a risk of your session table filling up.

A SYN flood looks something akin to Figure 7-11.

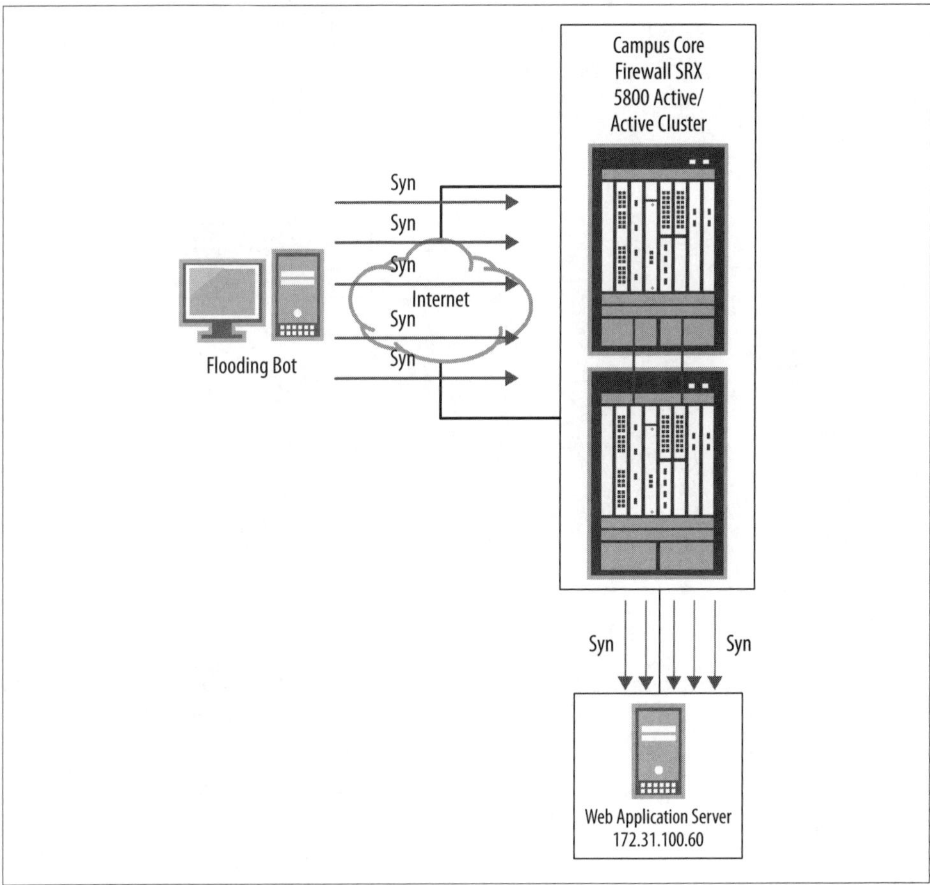

Figure 7-11. An example SYN flood to the HTTP web server

Figure 7-12 shows what it looks like when the SYN attack threshold is met. Note that the attack threshold was hit after the second SYN—this is extremely low and only for diagram purposes.

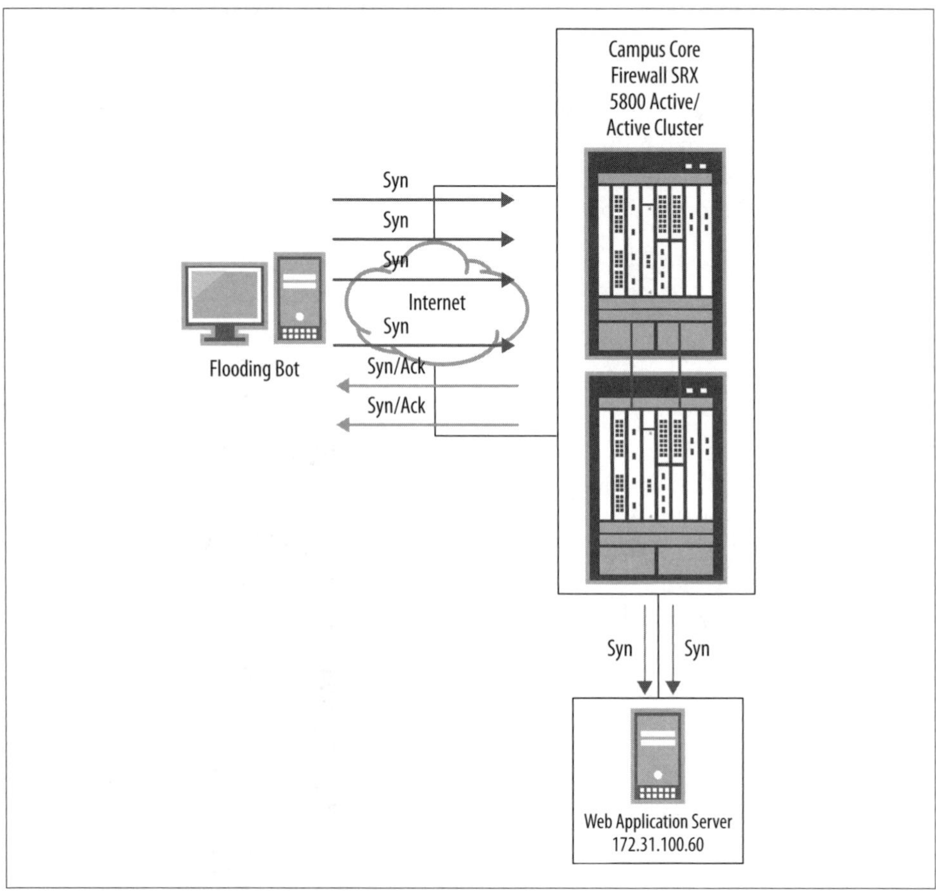

Figure 7-12. The same SYN flood with SYN protection enabled

The first two SYN packets are allowed through. Once the threshold of 2 is met, the SRX proxies the connection, sending a SYN/ACK back to the source. This is used to determine if it is a legitimate request or just a drone flooding SYN requests.

In the source- and destination-based SYN flooding protections, the SYN packets are not proxied but dropped to the floor. Anything above that configured threshold is dropped. This is a dangerous setting, and you must be cautious when designing these thresholds. Figure 7-13 shows an example of the SRX's source and destination behavior.

Here is the configuration that was applied to our perimeter SRXs. These values were set very high due to the web-based frontend servers and the large traffic load seen on

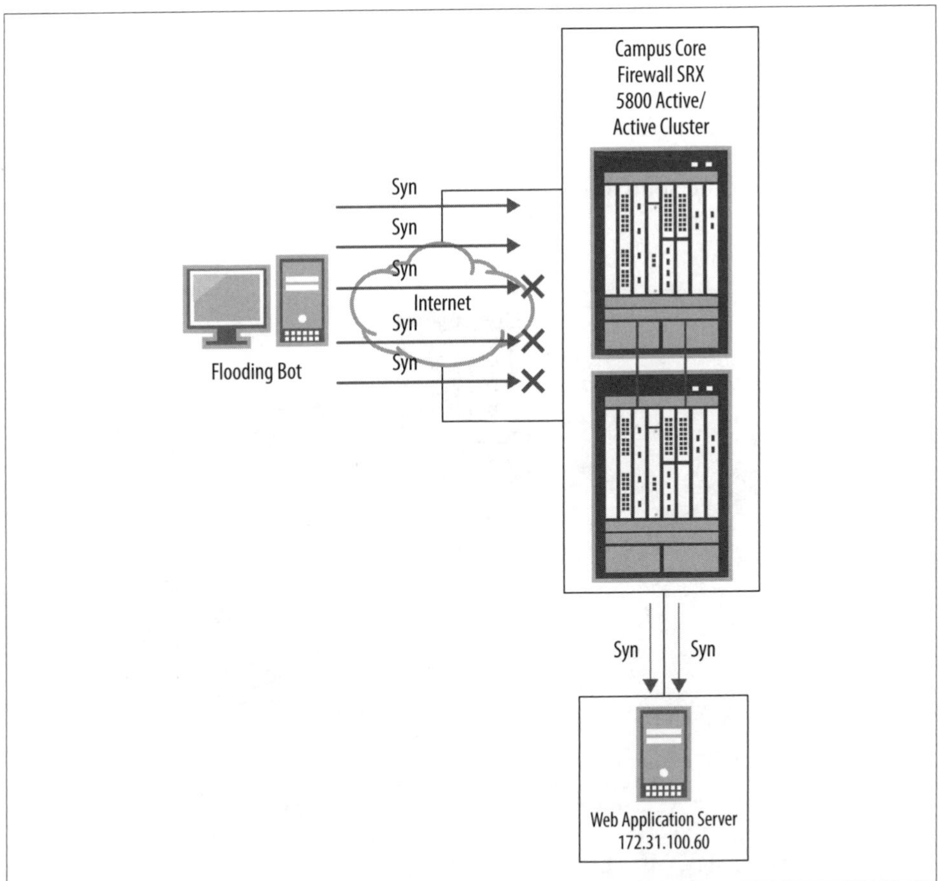

Figure 7-13. The same SYN flood hitting the threshold

the network. As stated before, you need to design these settings carefully for your own particular network and requirements.

```
[edit]
juniper@SRX5800# set security screen ids-option untrusted-internet tcp
syn-flood timeout 10

[edit]
juniper@SRX5800# set security screen ids-option untrusted-internet tcp
syn-flood attack-threshold 1500

[edit]
juniper@SRX5800# set security screen ids-option untrusted-internet tcp
syn-flood source-threshold 200

[edit]
juniper@SRX5800# set security screen ids-option untrusted-internet tcp
syn-flood destination-threshold 10000
```

SYN Cookies

The next layer of security that the SRX can provide is called *SYN cookie* protection, shown in Figure 7-14. SYN cookie protection is a stateless SYN proxy that you can use to defend against SYN floods from spoofed source IP addresses. A SYN cookie doesn't add much value if the source IP addresses are legitimate and reply to the SYN/ACK packet.

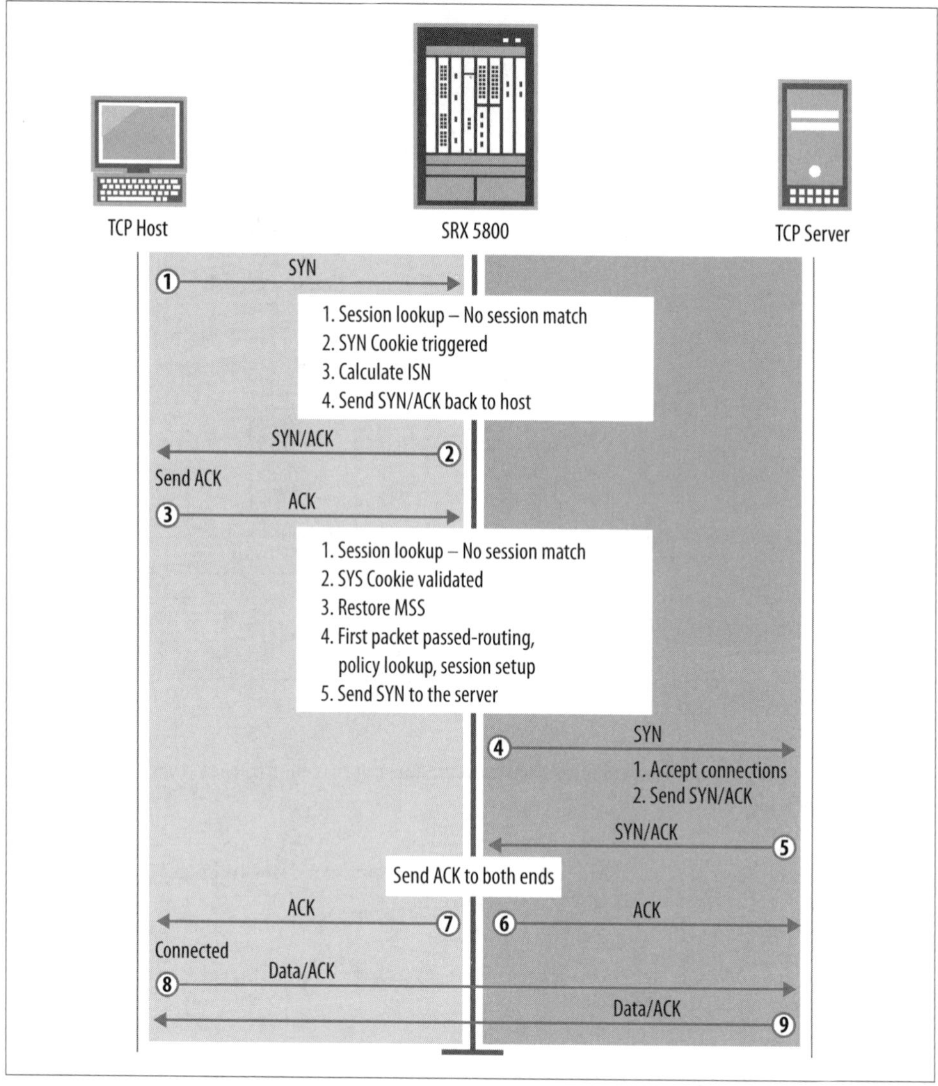

Figure 7-14. How a SYN cookie works

A SYN cookie is very efficient due to the fact that it's stateless. No route lookups or policy lookups are performed upon receipt of the SYN packet.

When a SYN cookie is enabled the SRX proxies all TCP negotiations for the destinations. The SRX replies to all incoming SYN packets with a specially marked SYN/ACK packet containing the original source and destination addresses and port numbers via a Message-Digest algorithm 5 (MD5) hash.

To configure SYN cookie protection, add the following configurations to your SRX:

```
[edit]
juniper@SRX5800# set security flow syn-flood-protection-mode syn-cookie
```

SYN-ACK-ACK Proxies

Another type of TCP attack is the SYN-ACK-ACK proxy. Remembering our three-way handshake, once the SYN/ACK is sent in Figure 7-10 an attack will continue to send acknowledgment packets over and over again in an attempt to flood the host or connection table. You can prevent this type of attack with the SYN-ACK-ACK screen, which again applies a threshold for the number of connections from a single source.

Figure 7-15 shows an example of this type of attack.

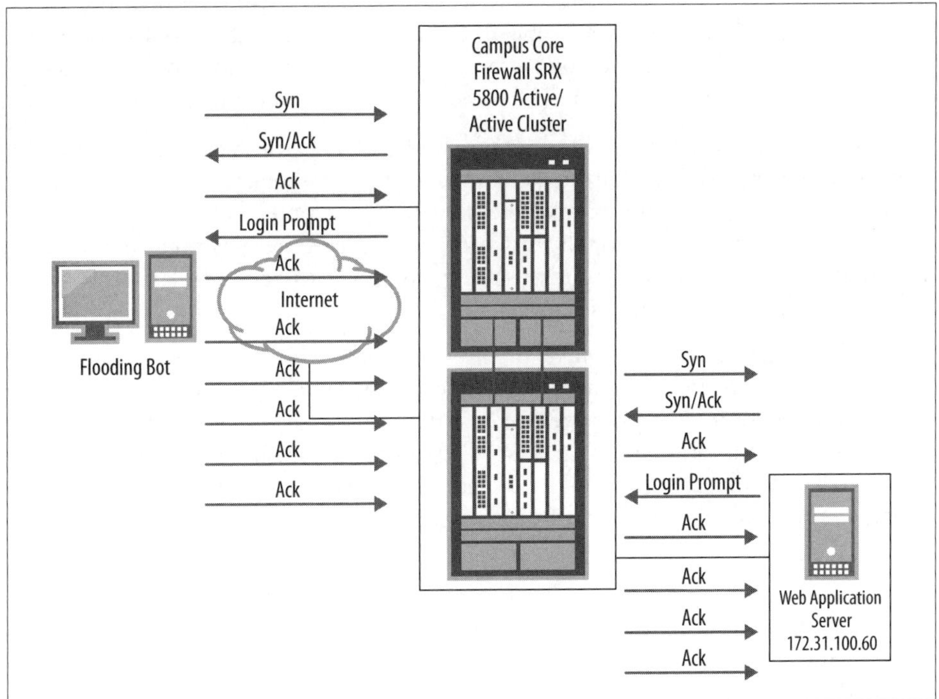

Figure 7-15. An example of a SYN-ACK-ACK proxy

The solution is easy enough, by configuring a screen under our `untrusted-internet` profile:

```
[edit]
juniper@SRX5800# set security screen ids-option untrusted-internet tcp
syn-ack-ack-proxy threshold 500
```

Session Limitation

Now that we have our base screens set to protect against the various types of flooding, let's configure some session limitations. A session screen is configured in two ways:

Source-based
: The source-based session limitation is the number of connections a source IP is allowed to have. For example, if the limit was 100, traffic entering this zone would only be permitted 100 connections per source IP. This is useful for limiting inbound Internet traffic and restricting the number of connections external IPs can open to your hosts or servers.

Destination-based
: This is the total number of sessions to a single destination. This is typically used to limit the number of connections to a server or service. You must be careful when applying this screen. Remember, these are zone-wide specific settings. So, for example, 5,000 sessions to a single IP address may seem abnormal until all the employees concurrently log on to the domain at the same time, or all users click the company intranet page for the latest company announcement at the same time.

Both source- and destination-based screen limitations can protect your session table while keeping any single host from generating a large number of connections and possibly flooding other hosts or parts of the network with connection attempts. It could be a misconfigured device, a malicious user, or just an extremely abnormal flood of legitimate traffic. The session-limiting settings should be there to regulate your session table and keep things running smoothly.

Like all limiting features of the SRX, you must be careful when using session limitation. You need to understand the number of connections an average source uses, as well as the number of connections per average destination. You also must take into account and plan for any abnormalities or peaks. When a session threshold is hit any additional sessions that fall into that threshold are silently dropped—and that, from a user standpoint, would mean intermittent connectivity or sporadic failures.

The source and destination session limitation screens are applied on the inbound zone, like all screen settings. So, as you apply this to your Internet-facing zone, the source session screens apply to traffic on the Internet coming *inbound*. The destination screens are your internal network or servers. Traffic initiated from the inside and heading outbound does not hit this set of screens.

As always, after careful evaluation and monitoring of traffic, you have determined that any single destination inbound to your network should receive, at most, 10,000 concurrent sessions. To be safe, set this at 20,000 to accommodate any influx in traffic to your web server. Also, let's say you found that the average source IP only had two connections inbound to your network. To be safe, and to prevent an impact to your customers who are possibly behind a proxy, let's set the source screen limit at 200:

```
[edit]
juniper@SRX5800#  set security screen ids-option untrusted-internet
limit-session limit-session destination-ip-based 20000

[edit]
juniper@SRX5800# set security screen ids-option untrusted-internet
limit-session limit-session source-ip-based 200
```

So, in this design, a single-source IP address on the Internet would be able to initiate up to 200 inbound connections at any given time. All the Internet IP addresses would be able to generate up to 20,000 connections to any single destination concurrently.

This helps us prevent the flood of connections from flooding the network or servers and potentially filling up the session tables. It also helps throttle traffic inbound into our network. With 200 connections, that would not stop attackers from scanning, sweeping the network, or mirroring our website, but it would limit them and keep them from impacting our availability.

It's worth mentioning again that it's possible to just alarm on a screen hit versus dropping the traffic. This is handy when deploying a new untested screen profile:

```
juniper@SRX5800# set security screen ids-option untrusted-internet
alarm-without-drop
```

Let's take a moment to review what our screen profile looks like at this point:

```
juniper@SRX5800# show security screen
ids-option untrusted-internet {
    icmp {
        ip-sweep threshold 1000000;
        fragment;
        large;
        flood threshold 8000;
    }
    ip {
        bad-option;
        record-route-option;
        timestamp-option;
        security-option;
        stream-option;
        spoofing;
        source-route-option;
        loose-source-route-option;
        strict-source-route-option;
        unknown-protocol;
        tear-drop;
    }
```

```
        tcp {
            syn-fin;
            fin-no-ack;
            tcp-no-flag;
            syn-frag;
            port-scan threshold 1000000;
            syn-ack-ack-proxy threshold 500;
            syn-flood {
                attack-threshold 1500;
                source-threshold 200;
                destination-threshold 20000;
                timeout 10;
            }
            land;
        }
        udp {
            flood threshold 50000;
        }
        limit-session {
            source-ip-based 200;
            destination-ip-based 10000;
        }
    }

    [edit]
```

To view the configured screens and their thresholds issue a `show security screen ids-option untrusted-internet` command:

```
juniper@SRX5800> show security screen ids-option untrusted-internet
Screen object status:

Name                                              Value
  ICMP flood threshold                            8000
  UDP flood threshold                             50000
  TCP port scan threshold                         1000000
  ICMP address sweep threshold                    1000000
  IP tear drop                                    enabled
  TCP SYN flood attack threshold                  1500
  TCP SYN flood alarm threshold                   512
  TCP SYN flood source threshold                  200
  TCP SYN flood destination threshold             20000
  TCP SYN flood timeout                           10
  IP spoofing                                     enabled
  IP source route option                          enabled
  TCP land attack                                 enabled
  TCP SYN fragment                                enabled
  TCP no flag                                     enabled
  IP unknown protocol                             enabled
  IP bad options                                  enabled
  IP record route option                          enabled
  IP timestamp option                             enabled
  IP security option                              enabled
  IP loose source route option                    enabled
  IP strict source route option                   enabled
  IP stream option                                enabled
```

```
  ICMP fragmentation                     enabled
  ICMP large packet                      enabled
  TCP SYN FIN                            enabled
  TCP FIN no ACK                         enabled
  TCP SYN-ACK-ACK proxy threshold        500
  Session source limit threshold         200
  Session destination limit threshold    10000
```

Once you have reviewed the configured screens and confirmed that they are set at the correct thresholds, apply the screen profile to the outside zone:

```
[edit]
juniper@SRX5800# set security zones security-zone internet screen
untrusted-internet
```

You can see which screen profiles are bound to the different zones by issuing a `show security zones` command. Notice the screen profile `untrusted-internet` is bound to the Internet security zone:

```
juniper@SRX5800> show security zones | find Internet

Security zone: Internet
  Send reset for non-SYN session TCP packets: Off
  Policy configurable: Yes
  Screen: untrusted-internet
  Interfaces bound: 0
  Interfaces:

Security zone: web-dmz
  Send reset for non-SYN session TCP packets: Off
  Policy configurable: Yes
  Interfaces bound: 1
  Interfaces:
    fe-0/0/2.0
```

You can view the screen counters at a zone level or an interface level. To view the screens for the profile just applied, issue a `show security screen statistics zone internet` command:

```
juniper@SRX5800> show security screen statistics zone internet
Screen statistics:

 IDS attack type                         Statistics
  ICMP flood                             147
  UDP flood                              0
  TCP winnuke                            0
  TCP port scan                          0
  ICMP address sweep                     0
  IP tear drop                           0
  TCP SYN flood                          10
  IP spoofing                            0
  ICMP ping of death                     0
  IP source route option                 0
  TCP land attack                        0
  TCP SYN fragment                       0
  TCP no flag                            0
```

```
IP unknown protocol                    0
IP bad options                         0
IP record route option                 0
IP timestamp option                    0
IP security option                     0
IP loose source route option           0
IP strict source route option          0
IP stream option                       0
ICMP fragment                          0
ICMP large packet                      0
TCP SYN FIN                            0
TCP FIN no ACK                         24
Source session limit                   0
TCP SYN-ACK-ACK proxy                  0
IP block fragment                      0
Destination session limit              3
```

You can view the same statistics at the interface level. It's the same information, so you can use whichever method you prefer for viewing data:

```
juniper@SRX5800> show security screen statistics interface ge-0/0/0
Screen statistics:

 IDS attack type                          Statistics
  ICMP flood                              147
  UDP flood                               0
  TCP winnuke                             0
  TCP port scan                           0
  ICMP address sweep                      0
  IP tear drop                            0
  TCP SYN flood                           10
  IP spoofing                             0
  ICMP ping of death                      0
  IP source route option                  0
  TCP land attack                         0
  TCP SYN fragment                        0
  TCP no flag                             0
  IP unknown protocol                     0
  IP bad options                          0
  IP record route option                  0
  IP timestamp option                     0
  IP security option                      0
  IP loose source route option            0
  IP strict source route option           0
  IP stream option                        0
  ICMP fragment                           0
  ICMP large packet                       0
  TCP SYN FIN                             24
  TCP FIN no ACK                          0
  Source session limit                    0
  TCP SYN-ACK-ACK proxy                   0
  IP block fragment                       0
  Destination session limit               3
```

You can find the statistics on SYN protection and address spoofing under the `statistics detail` command. Here the `flow error` pipe is used to only show the packet-dropped counters:

```
juniper@SRX5800> show interfaces ge-0/0/0 statistics detail | find "flow error"
    Flow error statistics (Packets dropped due to):
      Address spoofing:                   12
      Authentication failed:              0
      Incoming NAT errors:                0
      Invalid zone received packet:       0
      Multiple user authentications:      0
      Multiple incoming NAT:              0
      No parent for a gate:               0
      No one interested in self packets: 0
      No minor session:                   0
      No more sessions:                   0
      No NAT gate:                        0
      No route present:                   0
      No SA for incoming SPI:             0
      No tunnel found:                    0
      No session for a gate:              0
      No zone or NULL zone binding        0
      Policy denied:                      956
      Security association not active:   0
      TCP sequence number out of window: 0
      Syn-attack protection:              602
      User authentication errors:         0
    Protocol inet, MTU: 1500, Generation: 152, Route table: 0
      Flags: Is-Primary
      Addresses, Flags: Is-Default Is-Preferred Is-Primary
        Destination: 192.168.1/24, Local: 192.168.1.254, Broadcast:
192.168.1.255, Generation: 142
```

AppDoS

Another method to protect against floods and DoS/DDoS attacks is called AppDoS (and in the case of DDoS attacks, AppDDoS). AppDoS is a groundbreaking new feature from Juniper that is intended to analyze large traffic patterns and look for suspicious trends or activities. This goes beyond basic proxying and flood prevention. AppDoS takes a detailed look at the traffic behaviors over a period of time and uses an intelligence engine to determine if the traffic is legitimate or is part of an attack. AppDoS is covered in depth in Chapter 8.

Application Protection

We covered application layer gateways (ALGs) in Chapter 4, but we didn't cover the built-in SRX protection mechanisms for the different ALGs. The SRX has many built-in application protections that can, for example, protect against the flooding of calls on your VoIP system. Protecting your internal infrastructure from misconfiguration or rogue users is critical to providing the percentage of uptime that current network users demand from their applications and services.

SIP

A proxy server is one of the most important pieces of equipment in a Session Initiation Protocol (SIP) setup. As such, the SRX can provide some level of protection to ensure availability of the proxy server to its users. The SIP DoS protection monitors invite requests and the proxy server replies. Any invite requests that are redirected, errored, or failed are placed into a table that is denied for a predefined duration. This prevents any invite floods to your proxy servers.

This SIP DoS protection is a global configuration and is not tied to a single zone.

The following configuration applies specifically to our VoIP server (you can leave this not configured to apply to *all* SIP proxy servers) and places users into the blocked table for 20 seconds:

```
[edit]
juniper@SRX5800# set security alg sip application-screen protect deny
destination-ip 172.31.100.50

[edit]
juniper@SRX5800# set security alg sip application-screen protect deny timeout 20
```

Figure 7-16 illustrates an example of the blocking table process. As 10.1.1.140 makes an INVITE request to the VoIP PBX 172.31.100.50, the server sends back a 400 Error or client error. The SRX monitors this response and then adds the source 10.1.1.140 to its blocked list for 20 seconds. During this time, the proxy server will not forward the source address's invite requests.

MGCP

Media Gateway Control Protocol is used between the media gateway and the media controller. The SRX can add a layer of protection in front of the media gateway by limiting the number of remote access service (RAS) messages and connections per second. The MGCP flood threshold drops any messages above the configured threshold.

You can configure two flood thresholds on the MGCP application screen. The first is for RAS messages with a value between 2 and 50,000 messages per second per gateway; the second is the number of create connection commands with a value of 2 to 10,000 connection requests per second.

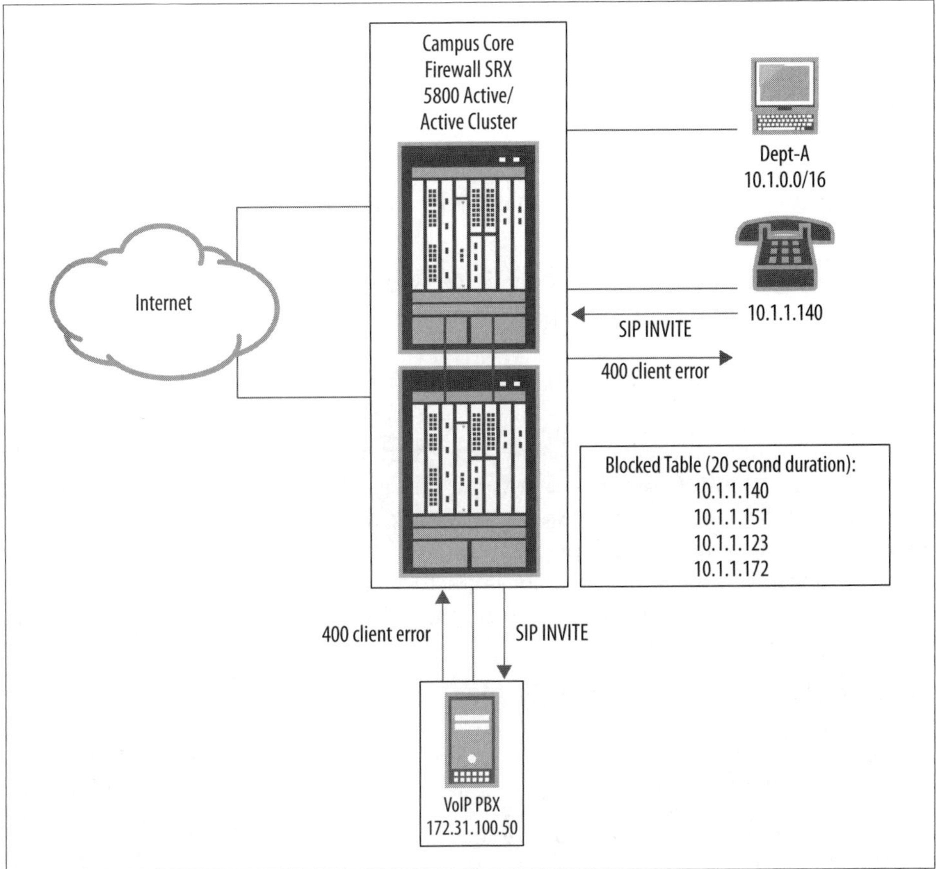

Figure 7-16. Blocking table process

Our example here limits the number of RAS messages to 15,000 and the number of connections per second to 2,000:

```
[edit]
juniper@SRX5800# set security alg mgcp application-screen message-
flood threshold 15000

[edit]
juniper@SRX5800# set security alg mgcp application-screen connection-
flood threshold 2000
```

To view the flood counters for MGCP for evidence of being hit or dropping any traffic, issue a `show security alg mgcp counters` command to display the data. Filtering on the keyword `flood` displays only the flood counters:

```
juniper@SRX5800> show security alg mgcp counters | match flood

  Connection flood drop          : 15
  Message flood drop             : 28
```

SCCP

SCCP is a VoIP protocol used by Cisco for its CallManager call signaling. The SCCP ALG application screens can limit the number of calls per client per second. This is extremely useful for protecting your CallManager infrastructure from attacks and network floods. Since this configuration is on a per-client basis when this threshold is hit only the client is blocked. The threshold can be configured from two calls to 1,000 call attempts per second.

The following configuration limits our SCCP setup to just 10 calls per second. This seems more than reasonable for our environment.

```
[edit]
juniper@SRX5800# set security alg sccp application-screen call-flood
threshold 10
```

As the SRX becomes more Layer 7 state aware with the ALGs, we will see more application screens from Juniper. This is a very exciting area of development, as it adds a good additional level of security to some very critical aspects of the network. The availability of a VoIP system is absolutely crucial and is one of those services that tend to get a lot of visibility and cause a major impact to a business when they're down. Providing 100% availability ensures that everyone is happy and that the network administrators get a good night's rest.

Here is our application screen configuration:

```
juniper@SRX5800# show security alg
mgcp {
    application-screen {
        message-flood threshold 15000;
        connection-flood threshold 2000;
    }
}
sccp {
    application-screen {
        call-flood threshold 10;
    }
}
sip {
    application-screen {
        protect {
            deny {
                destination-ip {
                    172.31.100.50;
                }
                timeout 20;
            }
        }
    }
}
```

Protecting the SRX

Thus far in this chapter, we have covered how to protect the network and services *behind* the SRX. This section covers how to protect the SRX itself from attack. It's critical to harden the SRX's control plane from any potential attacks and to ensure availability.

The first item to put in place is a firewall filter applied to the loopback interface. All traffic destined for the route engine (RE) goes through the loopback interface. To throttle and limit traffic that can enter the RE, we can apply a firewall filter to the loopback interface.

This acts much like a receive ACL on Cisco Systems routers.

The first thing you need to do when designing a loopback firewall filter is to document the traffic types that enter the RE. Traffic such as Simple Network Management Protocol (SNMP), Network Time Protocol (NTP), management protocols, and syslog should be examined. For the ScreenOS crowd, firewall filters are the only way to reproduce the `manager-ip` settings and restrict what IP addresses or segments can access the management plane of the SRX.

Here are the different devices and networks that need to talk to the SRX:

Management network: 10.1.10.1/24
SNMP server: 10.1.30.101
NTP server: 10.1.20.100
Backup NTP server: 10.1.30.100

So, let's configure the traffic types that need to enter the RE. Yours may be different, of course, depending on your network and configuration, so pay attention to the process:

```
[edit]
juniper@SRX5800# edit firewall filter SRX_Protection

[edit firewall filter SRX_Protection]
juniper@SRX5800# set term in-ssh from source-address 10.1.20.1/24

[edit firewall filter SRX_Protection]
juniper@SRX5800# set term in-ssh from protocol tcp

[edit firewall filter SRX_Protection]
juniper@SRX5800# set term in-ssh from destination-port ssh

[edit firewall filter SRX_Protection]
juniper@SRX5800# set term in-ssh then accept
```

```
[edit firewall filter SRX_Protection]
juniper@SRX5800# set term snmp from source-address 10.1.30.101/32

[edit firewall filter SRX_Protection]
juniper@SRX5800# set term snmp from protocol udp

[edit firewall filter SRX_Protection]
juniper@SRX5800# set term snmp from port snmp

[edit firewall filter SRX_Protection]
juniper@SRX5800# set term snmp then accept

[edit firewall filter SRX_Protection]
juniper@SRX5800# set term ntp from source-address 10.1.20.100/32

[edit firewall filter SRX_Protection]
juniper@SRX5800# set term ntp from source-address 10.1.30.100/32

[edit firewall filter SRX_Protection]
juniper@SRX5800# set term ntp from protocol udp

[edit firewall filter SRX_Protection]
juniper@SRX5800# set term ntp from port ntp

[edit firewall filter SRX_Protection]
juniper@SRX5800# set term ntp then accept

[edit firewall filter SRX_Protection]
juniper@SRX5800# set term deny-any-other-ssh from protocol tcp

[edit firewall filter SRX_Protection]
juniper@SRX5800# set term deny-any-other-ssh from port ssh

[edit firewall filter SRX_Protection]
juniper@SRX5800# set term deny-any-other-ssh from port telnet

[edit firewall filter SRX_Protection]
juniper@SRX5800# set term deny-any-other-ssh from port ftp

[edit firewall filter SRX_Protection]
juniper@SRX5800# set term deny-any-other-ssh from port ftp-data

[edit firewall filter SRX_Protection]
juniper@SRX5800# set term deny-any-other-ssh then discard

[edit firewall filter SRX_Protection]
juniper@SRX5800# set term deny-any-other-udp from protocol udp

[edit firewall filter SRX_Protection]
juniper@SRX5800# set term deny-any-other-udp from port snmp

[edit firewall filter SRX_Protection]
juniper@SRX5800# set term deny-any-other-udp from port snmptrap
```

```
[edit firewall filter SRX_Protection]
juniper@SRX5800# set term deny-any-other-udp from port ntp

[edit firewall filter SRX_Protection]
juniper@SRX5800# set term deny-any-other-udp then discard

[edit firewall filter SRX_Protection]
juniper@SRX5800# set term allow-everything-else then accept
```

Now, the firewall filter needs to be applied to the loopback interface:

```
[edit]
juniper@SRX5800# set interface lo0 unit 0 family inet filter input SRX_Protection
```

Although this is an example loopback filter that limits the different services that are allowed to talk with the RE, you can gain additional security from rate-limiting traffic inbound to the RE. Here is an example rate-limited policy:

```
 [edit]
firewall {
    policer lo-police1 {
        loopback-interface-policer;
        if-exceeding {
            bandwidth-limit 100m;
            burst-size-limit 500k;
        }
        then {
            discard;
        }
    }
}
```

Now that the management plane has been protected, we need to address the services and allow inbound traffic. To configure the interface to, for example, respond to pings and traceroutes, we need to configure what's called a *host-inbound-traffic system service*. This is done at the interface level, although it's highly recommended if you do allow services such as ping and traceroute that you apply a policer to reduce the chance of any potential attacks leveraging ICMP.

```
[edit]
juniper@SRX5800# set security zones security-zone trust interfaces
ge-0/0/0.0 host-inbound-traffic system-services ping
```

Ping and traceroute are just a sample of the full services available for configuration that you can find on your SRX model of system services allowed. Use the help prompt in this manner:

```
juniper@SRX5800# set security zones security-zone trust interfaces
ge-0/0/0.0 host-inbound-traffic system-services ?
Possible completions:
  all                    All system services
  any-service            Enable services on entire port range
  bootp                  Bootp and dhcp relay-agent service
  dhcp                   Dynamic Host Configuration Protocol
  dns                    DNS and DNS-proxy service
```

```
  finger                Finger service
  ftp                   FTP
  http                  Web management service using HTTP
  https                 Web management service using HTTP secured by SSL
  ident-reset           Send back TCP RST to IDENT request for port 113
  ike                   Internet Key Exchange
  lsping                Label Switched Path ping service
  netconf               NETCONF service
  ntp                   Network Time Protocol service
  ping                  Internet Control Message Protocol echo requests
  reverse-ssh           Reverse SSH service
  reverse-telnet        Reverse telnet service
  rlogin                Rlogin service
  rpm                   Real-time performance monitoring
  rsh                   Rsh service
  sip                   Enable Session Initiation Protocol service
  snmp                  Simple Network Management Protocol service
  snmp-trap             Simple Network Management Protocol traps
  ssh                   SSH service
  telnet                Telnet service
  tftp                  TFTP
  traceroute            Traceroute service
  xnm-clear-text        JUNOScript API for unencrypted traffic over TCP
  xnm-ssl               JUNOScript API service over SSL
```

Additionally, all routing protocols that you're going to run need to be configured under that interface. Let's run an example. Assume you're going to run Border Gateway Protocol (BGP) on the outside interface that needs to be configured, so it can be allowed in the interface *and* zone:

```
[edit]
juniper@SRX5800# set security zones security-zone trust interfaces
ge-0/0/0.0 host-inbound-traffic protocols bgp
```

Here's a full list of allowed protocols. Of course, there is an `all` option, but that is not recommended—it's always best to only allow the specific protocols and services that are needed for your network.

```
juniper@SRX5800# set security zones security-zone trust interfaces
ge-0/0/0.0 host-inbound-traffic protocols ?
Possible completions:
  all                   All protocols
  bfd                   Bidirectional Forwarding Detection
  bgp                   Border Gateway Protocol
  dvmrp                 Distance Vector Multicast Routing Protocol
  igmp                  Internet Group Management Protocol
  ldp                   Label Distribution Protocol
  msdp                  Multicast Source Discovery Protocol
  nhrp                  Next Hop Resolution Protocol
  ospf                  Open Shortest Path First
  pgm                   Pragmatic General Multicast
  pim                   Protocol Independent Multicast
  rip                   Routing Information Protocol
  router-discovery      Router Discovery
  rsvp                  Resource Reservation Protocol
```

```
sap                     Session Announcement Protocol
vrrp                    Virtual Router Redundancy Protocol
```

To protect the session table from filling up, Juniper has provided a feature called *aggressive ageout*. Under normal situations, the SRX would use its service timeouts to remove idle connections from the connection table. However, in situations where the session table is reaching capacity, the SRX can start aggressively aging out idle sessions dynamically.

Let's configure the early ageout time to be 20 seconds. During this time in which the session table is at risk of being filled up, what would normally be a five-minute idle timeout for HTTP would now be 20 seconds:

```
[edit]
juniper@SRX5800# set security flow aging early-ageout 20
```

This has the potential to age out valid sessions very quickly with the intent to protect the session table, because if the session table fills up, the SRX no longer is able to build any new sessions and new traffic would start to fail. The idea is to prevent, at all costs, the session table from filling up to provide availability to new connections.

Finally, you need to configure *when* you want the aggressive aging out to take effect and at what point it can return to normal ageout times. These are called *high watermark* and *low watermark*.

The high watermark is the percentage of the session table that must be filled before aggressive aging out is activated. Once it's activated, the low watermark is the percentage that the session table must reduce to before aggressive ageout is disabled.

```
[edit]
juniper@SRX5800# set security flow aging high-watermark 90 low-watermark 70
```

Protecting your SRX from attacks and limiting the vectors of attacks on the SRX itself is critical to providing availability to the network the SRX serves. Although many network administrators tend to overlook security screens and may even view them as optional, hardening the SRX and protecting it from attacks should never be overlooked or skipped.

Summary

In this chapter, we covered how to protect the perimeter of your network from reconnaissance, basic attacks, floods, and applications. Keep in mind that as important as it is to apply these protections to the perimeter, it is also very important to configure these protections on the other, more trusted zones. Internal segments, DMZs, server farms, and backend systems also should be evaluated. Although the same screens and limitations may not apply, putting thresholds on floods and sessions prevents any foul play or misconfigurations from adversely impacting the network and protects other segments.

Careful design and configuration of firewall filters, screens, security policies, and IPS signatures is an excellent start to layered network security design. Blocking unwanted traffic at the most efficient point will keep your SRX healthy and enable you to add the more performance-intensive security layers such as AppDoS and IPS without running out of capacity on your SRX.

Chapter Review Questions

1. What are the various ways to prevent a TCP DoS/DDoS attack?
2. What is the most efficient way to prevent infected SQL Slammer hosts from trying to propagate on your network?
3. What two methods can be used to protect the SRX session table from running out of capacity?
4. When a screen profile is applied to a zone what traffic does the screen evaluate?
5. What screens should I use to protect my network?
6. How do you enable a screen profile to log screen hits but not drop traffic?
7. How do you protect the routing engine/management plane from attacks?
8. What kind of IP sweeps can the SRX protect against?
9. What are some common network reconnaissance tools used by bad guys?
10. How does a SYN cookie work?

Chapter Review Answers

1. You can set some basic screens out of the gate to prevent some TCP misbehaviors:

   ```
   -tcp-no-flag
   -syn-fin
   -syn-frag
   ```

   You can also set more advanced configurations. You do need to tweak and tune these settings, but they provide an excellent layer of protection against many TCP DoS/DDoS attacks:

   ```
   -syn-flood protection
   -syn cookie
   -syn-ack-ack proxy
   ```

   Although not specific to TCP session limiting, screens could be used to limit the number of connections a DoS/DDoS attack can take, creating a bottleneck.

2. A firewall filter configured to block TCP port 1434 is the most efficient way to prevent infected SQL Slammer hosts from trying to propagate on your network. Slammer could be blocked by a security policy, or an IPS signature; however, a firewall filter would be the most efficient method. A good-layered security design tries to block these at the lowest level. With that in mind, maintaining a large firewall filter set is more difficult and less straightforward when compared to security policies, and you should limit their use to only the "heavy hitters" that you see on your network.
3. If you use a combination of source and destination session screen limits to prevent a single IP or destination from filling up your session table, along with early or aggressive ageout, filling up the SRX session table will be very difficult, even for a wily hacker.
4. When a screen profile is applied to a zone the screen evaluates all ingress traffic. At this time, you cannot set exceptions for screens. Any traffic coming inbound to that zone will be evaluated by the screen profile. If traffic is initiated in the Trust zone with a screen profile of `protect_trust` and then exits the Untrust zone with a screen profile of `protect_untrust`, *only* the `protect_trust` screen profile will be evaluated, not both. This also applies to return traffic of that same session.
5. There is no simple canned configuration to prevent attacks. Each network has different flows and patterns and careful planning is necessary to understand the traffic profiles and potential threats. Analyze your network for attack vectors. What needs to be protected? This could include DNS servers, DHCP servers, NTP servers, web servers, Active Directory servers, core switches, VoIP PBX systems, and so on.

   What are the normal loads like? What are they during abnormal but legitimate loads? If you're a major online retailer, your traffic load for 50 weeks per year will be much lower than the 2 weeks before Christmas. The last thing you want is the protections you put in place to cause an impact to your legitimate traffic flow.
6. Screen profiles can be configured with the `alarm-without-drop` flag. This will allow a new screen profile to be evaluated with real-world traffic before it is configured to drop anything. This would enable a network administrator to test items such as traffic failover, heavy abnormal (but legitimate) load, and other such situations before any blocking is done.
7. You can protect the management plane by placing a firewall filter on the loopback interface. All traffic going to the management plane must traverse the loopback interface, also known as lo0. Applying a firewall filter that limits who can talk to the SRX and how will limit the scope of any potential attack vectors.
8. Since the 10.2 code version, the SRX can protect against ICMP, TCP, and UDP sweeps with screens.

9. The good news is that most of the tools used by bad guys can be found with very little effort. You can use them to take a look at your network and try to evaluate security from an outsider's view, as well as test any reconnaissance protections that you've put in place. Here are the websites for a few of these tools:

   Nmap: *http://nmap.org/* or *http://insecure.org/*
   Hping/Hping2: *http://www.hping.org/*
   Xprobe: *http://ofirarkin.wordpress.com/xprobe/*
   Firewalk: *http://www.packetstormsecurity.org/UNIX/audit/firewalk/*

10. SYN cookie protection is a stateless SYN proxy. A SYN cookie proxies all initial TCP negotiations for the destination to add a layer of security and protect the destination. For details, refer back to Figure 7-14.

CHAPTER 8

Intrusion Prevention

Although stateful firewall technology is a powerful mechanism for controlling cyber threats and preventing denials of service, controlling targeted exploitation requires deeper inspection and control of the application layer traffic itself. The SRX platform integrates the power of stateful firewalling, routing, Network Address Translation (NAT), and virtual private networks (VPNs), along with the power of Juniper Intrusion Detection and Prevention (IDP) technology, into a single unit. Make no mistake: this is true IPS, not a subset of inspection capabilities, and it's all done within integrated network purposed hardware so that additional types of components are not needed.

This chapter details the Juniper IPS functionality built into the SRX. It starts with an overview of IPS—what it does, why it's necessary, and how it compares to other technologies, including Juniper's standalone IDP and ISG with IDP platforms. Then we have some fun configuring IPS on the SRX, as well as IPS tuning and troubleshooting. After that, we'll look at a real-world case study to help solidify the concepts we've discussed. And as with all the chapters in this book, questions at the end of the chapter should help those taking Juniper's security certification to prepare for their exam.

The Need for IPS

Despite what some flashy vendor advertisements and blogs may say, stateful firewalling is not dead, nor will it be anytime soon. Stateful firewalling provides a core layer of security, to ensure that network traffic is restricted to only that which a policy dictates from the networking layer and the transport layer (Layers 3 and 4, respectively). It also goes a step further to ensure that the exchanges follow the exchanges that are expected in Layers 3 and 4.

This is a critical layer of network security; however, it should not be the only layer of network security you apply to protect a network infrastructure. The problem with stateful firewalling by itself is that it can go only so far to limit which source IP addresses can communicate to which destination IP addresses, and on which Layer 3 and Layer 4 protocols the communication can be exchanged. See Figure 8-1.

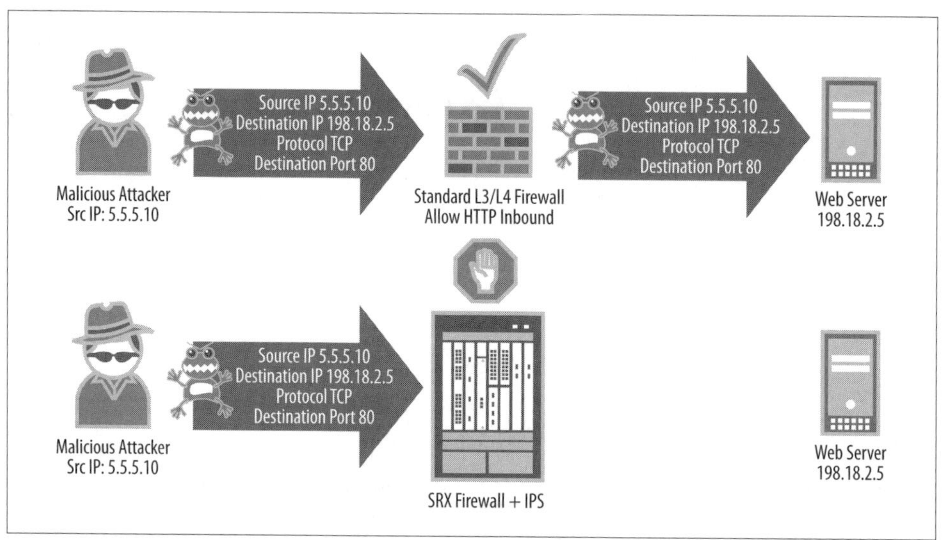

Figure 8-1. Firewall versus IPS

Stateful firewalling cannot actually limit what can be exchanged within the channels of permitted Layer 3 and Layer 4 communication. For instance, if your organization hosts a public web server to serve as the portal for the Internet (say, to get information about your company), assuming you're using standard ports and protocols you would need to open a firewall rule that would allow any source IP address to be able to connect to the destination IP address of your web server on TCP port 80. From that perspective, the firewall would ensure that (barring no additional configuration to permit otherwise) only Internet connections to your web server on TCP port 80 would be allowed (no File Transfer Protocol [FTP], Domain Name System [DNS], Simple Mail Transfer Protocol [SMTP], Server Message Block [SMB], etc.).

Limiting access to only the essentials is very important; however, the capabilities of stateful firewalling alone do little to control what is actually exchanged within these connections. You can make the analogy that IPS is to networking what airport screening checkpoints are to physical security. (Although we like to think that network-based IPS can do an even better job than airport security, and won't take your 3.5 ounce bottle of shampoo away either!) In airport screening, not only are you inspected to determine where you are coming from and where you are going, but also your contents are searched via a combination of X-rays, metal detectors, chemical analysis, and sometimes airport security personnel. Although determining where you are coming from and where you are going may be important to security at some level, the items you carry with you are also extremely important to security. Computer networking is no different from physical airport security in the need to inspect and secure communications.

Luckily, although the task of security computer network communications is daunting, powerful tools within the SRX exist to make this task practical for security administrators.

How Does IPS Work?

At a high level, IPS works by scrutinizing all of the bits contained within packets to look for both known and unknown attacks, as shown in Figure 8-2. Traditional firewalls primarily look only at Layers 3 and 4 when it comes to security, and ignore the actual contents of the payloads themselves. This makes for efficient processing, which can be accelerated in hardware, but it alone does not provide protection for traffic that is permitted by firewall policies.

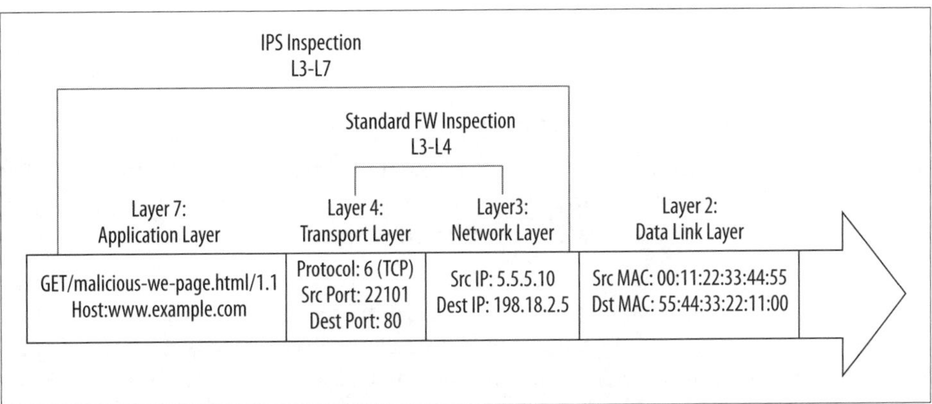

Figure 8-2. Firewall inspection of attack versus IPS

So, why do we still need stateful firewalling at all if we can just use IPS to ensure that traffic is "scrubbed" to only permit desired traffic, regardless of where it comes from or what port it is on?

That's an excellent question, and one that some vendors claim the use of their IPS products will answer. The fact of the matter is that no security is perfect, and although in a perfect world using only IPS might be a valid solution, this is not a perfect world. By utilizing firewalling as a layer of security, you can weed out undesired traffic early in the process so that you don't have to utilize any more resources than are necessary for processing traffic that you know early on you don't want. It's important, because IPS is a very computationally expensive process that cannot be easily assisted through the use of application-specific integrated circuit (ASIC)-based inspection. By blocking traffic early on, you ensure that neither the IPS nor the destination servers have to process traffic unnecessarily. Resources are always going to be finite, and often expensive.

Eliminate processing of undesired traffic as early in the process as possible to ensure that no more resources than necessary are required.

Licensing

Licenses are required to download the Juniper attack objects and policy templates. If you are just using the IPS functionality and you want to only use your own attack objects, you can do so without the need for a license (although you will see a license warning).

Note that the IPS licenses have a lifetime plan. Typically, licenses are distributed in one-year increments (including multiyear licenses), and if the license expires the ability to download attack object updates is prevented. Contact your Juniper reseller for information on getting licenses.

IPS and antivirus

If you have IPS, do you still need antivirus?

The short answer to this question is "yes"; as mentioned before, best practice rules that IPS is not a substitute for antivirus. Cyber threats come in many different forms, but let's classify them as network-based or file-based protection.

Traditionally, IPS is primarily concerned with network-based threats and securing communication between different hosts as shown in Figure 8-4. File-based protection is another story. Although files can certainly be exchanged over networks, they can also be exchanged through other mechanisms such as USB drives, CD/DVDs, and sometimes secure communication channels such as IP Security (IPsec) VPNs that are not terminated on the IPS itself. This is true both for network-based antivirus servers and for IPS.

True security is best executed by providing layered security (see Figure 8-3); that is, using IPS for what it is best at, by securing communications between hosts, but on those hosts providing additional security through the use of host-based IPS and antivirus protection. Network-based antivirus is an excellent perimeter tool as well, but just like IPS, it doesn't completely remove the need for host-based protection because it is often difficult to inspect encrypted files and not all files may be exchanged over the network.

It is important to understand that, at the time of this writing, the Juniper SRX does not focus on inspecting the content of files, so it cannot serve as a network-based antivirus appliance. The IPS can search for patterns within communication, so technically it can detect patterns within the payloads of files; however, specific signatures are not written to perform this type of functionality. For the most precise antivirus matching, the files must be fully reassembled before they can be scanned. To provide inline antivirus protection, TCP proxying must be used, and this is not a goal of the IPS system.

Although the SRX does not focus on inspecting the contents of files, most contemporary threats try to spread themselves over the network, or "phone home" to command and control servers. Here the SRX can be used to not only identify these types of infection and control attempts, but also to actually block them and alert administrators to this activity. (See Figure 8-4.)

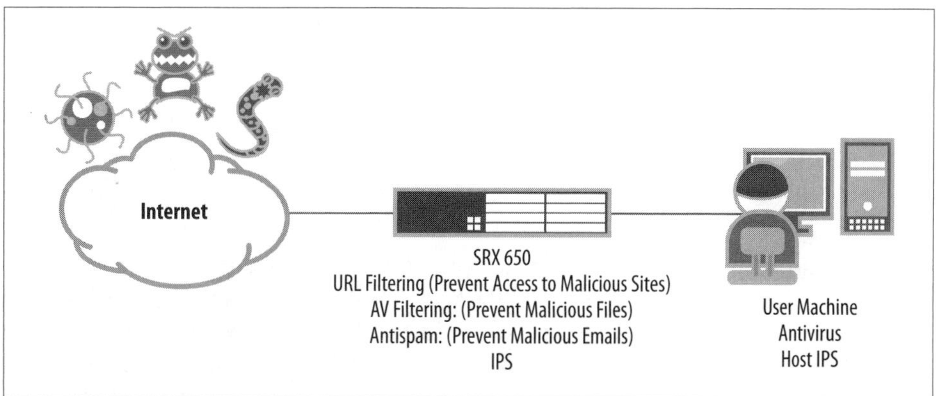

Figure 8-3. Layered security

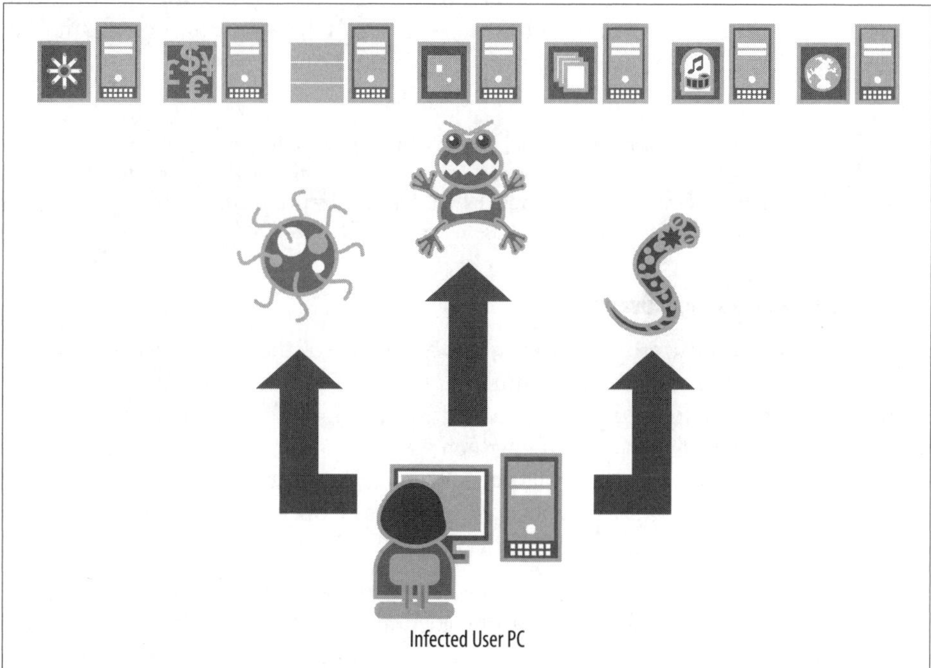

Figure 8-4. Infected host attempting to propagate

What is the difference between full IPS and deep inspection/IPS lite?

Previous generations of Juniper firewalls such as the NetScreen and SSG series (along with many other competitors) offer deep inspection or IPS lite functionality. This provides a limited subset of inspection capability by inspecting the traffic at Layer 7, but it is for only a handful of signatures. Deep inspection/IPS lite does not provide full inspection; therefore, it isn't really geared toward true security, and it has become more of a checkbox security feature that auditors tend to look for. If you are truly concerned about providing real security for your environment, full IPS should be a requirement. When evaluating solutions, it is important to determine exactly what level of IPS is performed. On the SRX platforms (from the SRX100 to the SRX5800), IPS is a full-featured inspection technology that cuts no corners.

Is it IDP or IPS?

Many SRX administrators may be familiar with the previous generations of IPS products offered by Juniper Networks, including the standalone IDP appliance and the ISG with IDP security modules. In the past, these products referred to IPS functionality as IDP or intrusion detection and prevention, which originated from SecureOne (developer of the first IPS [rather than IDS] platform). SecureOne was later acquired by NetScreen, which was acquired by Juniper.

To move more in line with industry-standard terms, Juniper Networks has begun to call its IDP *IPS*. You can still find a lot of references to "IDP" in the SRX configuration, but over the lifetime of this book, this will be migrated to IPS.

Juniper does not typically change command-line interface (CLI) configuration statements without a formal process, so for the short and medium terms, you might notice that IDP is referenced rather than IPS. You can effectively refer to these terms equally.

False positives and false negatives in IPS

Some network administrators are weary of IPS because of the risk of *false positives*. A false positive is when something legitimate is detected as something malicious. If the administrator has configured protection against malicious attacks, it is likely that IPS might actually block legitimate traffic, which we all know can cause a few headaches. A *false negative* is when a real attack is deemed as legitimate traffic, and therefore is not detected. False negatives are as much a concern as false positives, although without an IPS in place, they would get through anyway.

False positives occur for several reasons, one of which may be that it isn't a false positive at all; that is, the IPS may detect the traffic accurately as it is instructed to do. Often, particularly in the case of protocol anomaly protection, if a vendor does not follow a standard implementation (e.g., an RFC or manufacturer spec) of a protocol, the IPS detects this as an attack, just like it is programmed to do. In other cases, a signature may be too broad in detection and may identify both malicious and legitimate traffic. And finally, false negatives might occur because the IPS isn't actually inspecting for such activity, the detection may be disabled, or the signatures may not detect particular iterations of an attack.

The good news is that the SRX goes to great lengths to minimize both false positives and false negatives, and this chapter details how the SRX does this through the use of intelligent application matching, protocol decoding, and context-based inspection. This chapter also discusses fine-tuning of the SRX so that you can minimize occurrences of false positives.

Management IPS functionality on the SRX

Administrators familiar with prior generations of Juniper IPS products such as the standalone IDP appliance and the ISG with IDP security modules know that the Network and Security Manager (NSM) management platform was required to manage the IPS functionality on the IDP and ISG, respectively. The SRX is different in that it does not require the NSM for any IPS functionality at all, although the NSM can certainly manage the SRX IPS functionality. The SRX allows you to fully manage the SRX IPS via the CLI, and most functions are available via J-Web as well. Although some tasks, such as viewing the contents of attack objects, are easier on the NSM than on the platform itself, the functionality is completely in the platform and doesn't require any additional software systems to manage it.

Stages of a system compromise

Understanding the stages of an attack is critical to being able to provide comprehensive security. Many security books go into great detail regarding the different stages of an attack, but for our purposes let's simplify them into four common stages or aspects of an attack. Note that not all stages are necessary for an attack, but are common to most attacks.

Reconnaissance
: The first phase of an attack typically identifies vulnerable hosts. Often, this includes port scanning, banner grabbing, and other techniques to get information to leak from the system regarding what platform it is and its respective software.

  The SRX can help to protect against different types of sweeps and scans through the use of screens, but also there are a large number of attack objects in the IPS that are associated with information leakage attempts. You can also use IP actions (discussed later in this chapter) to shun traffic from sources that are attempting such reconnaissance techniques.

Vulnerability exploitation
: Once a vulnerable system is identified, the attacker tries to exploit the vulnerability in the system. There is a lot of confusion about this stage, because technically, the vulnerability exploitation does one of two things: it crashes the system or service (a denial of service or DoS), or it changes the control of execution on the system. As part of the latter case, the attacker often injects code known as *shellcode* which allows for further exploitation.

  The SRX provides comprehensive protection of vulnerability exploitation with thousands of attack objects that protect against exploitation using both protocol anomaly and signature-based attack objects. These attack objects can protect against both attacks that cause a system or service to crash, and attacks that try to compromise the system.

Shellcode execution
: Assuming that the attack is meant to compromise the system rather than simply crash it, the attacker typically injects shellcode as part of the vulnerability exploitation stage. Shellcode is code that is executed in place of the regular application, to further compromise the system. Examples of what shellcode can do include opening a backdoor on the system, creating outbound control connections, modifying the system by creating users or elevating access, and injecting malicious applications. Without the use of shellcode, the exploited system would not likely be compromised (controlled) even if the vulnerability was exploited.

  Not only does the SRX detect and prevent the exploitation of vulnerabilities, but it can also detect shellcode, so even if it somehow missed the actual exploit, it would likely be able to detect the shellcode. Numerous shellcode attack signatures can be blocked in addition to the actual exploit itself.

Infection attempts/phone-home traffic
: Once a system is compromised, it typically tries to infect other machines, or phone home to the control servers, or do both.

  The SRX can detect these infection and phone-home techniques, depending on the nature of the infection method and the communication to the command and control system. The SRX can often detect attempts to infect other machines, with the ability to block those attempts and identify compromised machines. Additionally, the SRX may be able to identify command and control and phone-home traffic. Sometimes this traffic is encrypted, so the SRX may not be able to identify what the machine is controlled by, but the SRX can identify encrypted traffic streams (and block them if so desired).

As you can see, the SRX can do quite a lot to prevent attacks, minimize their impact, and identify and control the spread of machines that may be infected (such as a laptop that is infected in a foreign network). By implementing a *layered security approach*, the SRX can offer real security to the networks that it protects.

IPS Packet Processing on the SRX

To understand how IPS processing on the SRX works, you must first understand where IPS sits in the path of packet processing, what components are utilized for IPS processing, and the actual composition of the IPS functionality itself. Let's examine how SRX IPS fits into the big picture of your network security exactly in that order.

Packet processing path

We already discussed the packet flow on the SRX when it comes to session setup, steady state processing, and session close. Now let's focus in more depth on what happens to packet processing in terms of the IPS. It is important to remember that for the high-end SRX, a session is always anchored to a single Services Processing Unit (SPU) for the duration of its lifetime. The same holds true in the case of IPS. IPS is always going to be inspected on the same SPU as that of the firewall flow. Unlike previous generations of Juniper IDP platforms and many other vendors' products, the SRX does not require special hardware to perform its IPS processing. Instead, all IPS services are processed in the SPU itself. If additional IPS processing power is required, the administrator need only add additional SPUs.

In the case of the branch SRX Series, there is only one network processor where *all* processing is performed.

The SRX IPS functionality is tightly tied to its firewall functionality.

In the case of the branch SRX Series, if packet mode is used, that traffic cannot be inspected by the IPS engine. At the time of this writing, the high-end SRX does not support selective processing; it only supports flow mode.

Figure 8-5 illustrates a high-level flowchart of how packet processing operates in the SRX with regard to the different services. Note that IPS is one of the last things to be processed in the services chain. That means if the traffic is not permitted by a firewall policy (which must also reference it to be inspected by IPS) the traffic never hits the IPS engine. This is intentional, because you don't want to burden the IPS with inspecting traffic that is ultimately going to be dropped by some other mechanism anyway.

One of the great things about the SRX IPS implementation is that it offers a great deal of granularity. Unlike many other vendors' implementations, the SRX allows you to enable IPS processing on a firewall rule-by-rule basis, rather than just turning on inspection across the board. This means traffic that is not marked by a firewall rule to be processed by IPS completely bypasses the IPS altogether. Traffic that is marked for IPS processing is then handed off to the IPS engine.

In addition to referencing IPS processing on a firewall rule-by-rule basis, within the IPS rulebase you still have extremely granular rulebase control over how the IPS is enforced. We will cover this in depth later in the chapter.

As I mentioned, all IPS-bound traffic must be processed by the stateful firewall flow engine first (known as *flowd*). For now, suffice it to say that if the IPS engine needs to process traffic, the traffic will be handed off after the firewall has completed its

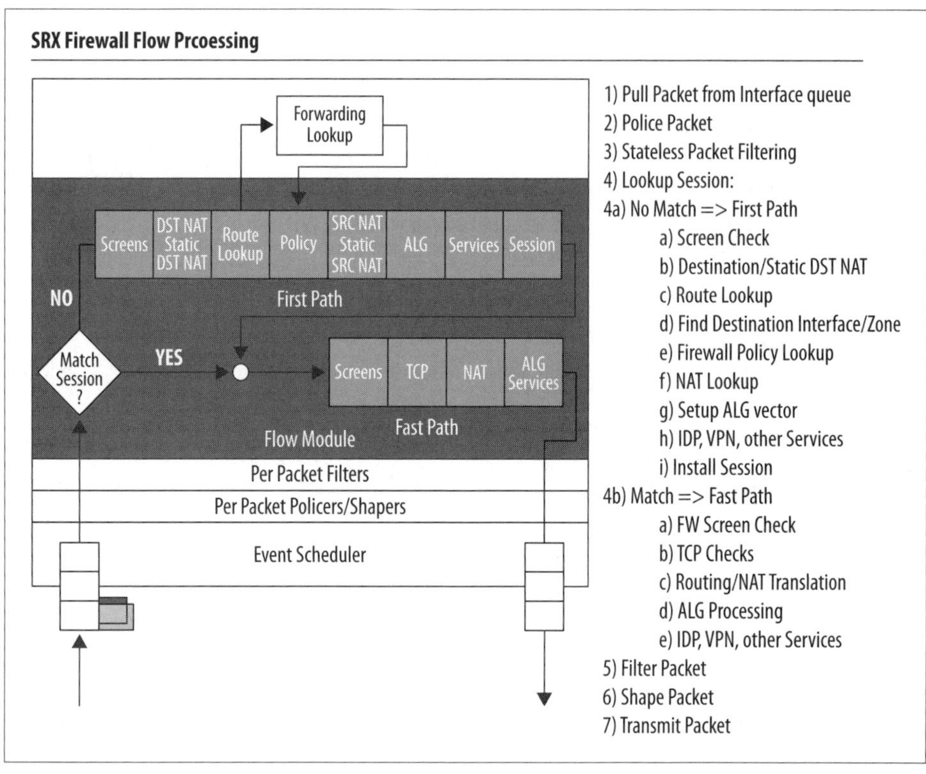

SRX Firewall Flow Prcoessing
Forwarding Lookup
Screens
DST NAT Static DST NAT
Route Lookup
Policy
SRC NAT Static SRC NAT
ALG
Services
Session
First Path
NO
Match Session ?
YES
Screens
TCP
NAT
ALG Services
Flow Module
Fast Path
Per Packet Filters
Per Packet Policers/Shapers
Event Scheduler
1) Pull Packet from Interface queue
2) Police Packet
3) Stateless Packet Filtering
4) Lookup Session:
4a) No Match => First Path
a) Screen Check
b) Destination/Static DST NAT
c) Route Lookup
d) Find Destination Interface/Zone
e) Firewall Policy Lookup
f) NAT Lookup
g) Setup ALG vector
h) IDP, VPN, other Services
i) Install Session
4b) Match => Fast Path
a) FW Screen Check
b) TCP Checks
c) Routing/NAT Translation
d) ALG Processing
e) IDP, VPN, other Services
5) Filter Packet
6) Shape Packet
7) Transmit Packet

Figure 8-5. First path packet processing

processing (and only for permitted traffic). Within the IPS engine there are several stages of processing, as illustrated in Figure 8-6.

IPS processing on the SRX can be broken down into eight general stages of processing:

Stage 1: Fragmentation processing
: The first thing that must happen before you can really get to the inspection is that the SRX must process fragmented traffic (if present). To ensure that common IDS evasion techniques using fragmentation are not effective, it rebuilds any fragmented traffic from a Layer 3 perspective. This stage also provides countermeasures against fragment-based attacks such as missing fragments, underlapping or overlapping fragments, duplicate fragments, and other fragment-based anomalies. Many of these values are also configurable in the IPS sensor configuration section, although defaults should suffice in most cases.

Stage 2: IPS flow setup
: After any Layer 3 fragments are processed, the SRX examines the traffic to see whether it has an existing session for it or if there is an existing session which might need some special processing. The IPS session table is different from the firewall session table, because additional IPS state related to the traffic is required.

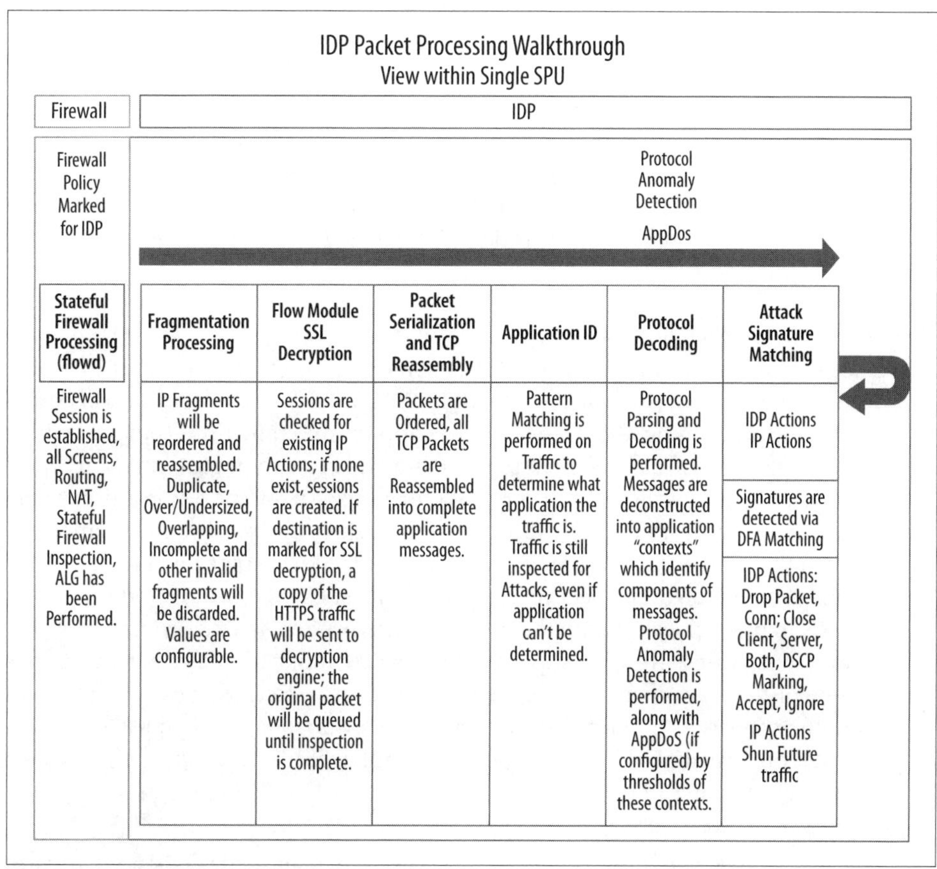

IDP Packet Processing Walkthrough
View within Single SPU
Firewall
IDP
Firewall Policy Marked for IDP
Protocol Anomaly Detection
AppDos
Stateful Firewall Processing (flowd)
Fragmentation Processing
Flow Module SSL Decryption
Packet Serialization and TCP Reassembly
Application ID
Protocol Decoding
Attack Signature Matching
Firewall Session is established, all Screens, Routing, NAT, Stateful Firewall Inspection, ALG has been Performed.
IP Fragments will be reordered and reassembled. Duplicate, Over/Undersized, Overlapping, Incomplete and other invalid fragments will be discarded. Values are configurable.
Sessions are checked for existing IP Actions; if none exist, sessions are created. If destination is marked for SSL decryption, a copy of the HTTPS traffic will be sent to decryption engine; the original packet will be queued until inspection is complete.
Packets are Ordered, all TCP Packets are Reassembled into complete application messages.
Pattern Matching is performed on Traffic to determine what application the traffic is. Traffic is still inspected for Attacks, even if application can't be determined.
Protocol Parsing and Decoding is performed. Messages are deconstructed into application "contexts" which identify components of messages. Protocol Anomaly Detection is performed, along with AppDoS (if configured) by thresholds of these contexts.
IDP Actions
IP Actions
Signatures are detected via DFA Matching
IDP Actions: Drop Packet, Conn; Close Client, Server, Both, DSCP Marking, Accept, Ignore
IP Actions Shun Future traffic

Figure 8-6. IPS processing flowchart

Stage 3: SSL decryption (if applicable)
: If SSL decryption is configured, and traffic is destined to a web server that is configured to be decrypted, decryption happens in this phase. See "SSL Inspection" on page 421 for more information.

Stage 4: Serialization and reassembly
: For accurate IPS processing, all messages must be processed in order, in a flow, and the messages must be reassembled if they span multiple packets. Without reassembly, an IPS engine can be easily evaded, which would result in lots of false positives. The SRX IPS engine ensures that before traffic is processed, it is ordered and reassembled in this stage of the processing.

Stage 5: Application identification
: The SRX has the ability to detect what application is running on any Layer 4 port. This is important because it allows the device to determine what traffic is running in a given flow regardless of whether it is running on a standard port. Even if the

application cannot be identified, the SRX can still inspect it as a bytestream. This stage typically happens within the first couple of kilobytes of traffic, and the SRX utilizes both directions of the traffic to identify the application.

Starting with 10.2 of the High End SRX, the Application Identification portion of the appID detection has been moved from the IPS module into the firewall module for future support of AppSecure functionality, which can perform application-based enforcement and services.

Stage 6: Protocol decoding
: Once the application is identified (or is simply classified as a stream), the SRX decodes the application from a protocol level, a process known as *protocol decoding*. Protocol decoding allows the SRX to chop up the traffic into *contexts*, which are specific parts of different messages. Contexts are very important to IPS processing because they allow the SRX to look for attacks in the specific location where they actually occur, not just blindly by byte matching across all traffic that passes through the SRX. After all, you wouldn't want the SRX to block an email conversation between you and a peer discussing the latest exploit; you would only want the SRX to block the exploit in the precise location where it actually occurs. At the time of this writing, the SRX supports almost 600 application contexts. Contexts are one of the ways that the SRX seeks to eliminate false positives. The protocol decoding stage is also where the SRX performs protocol anomaly protection and Application Distributed Denial of Service (AppDDoS) protection, both of which we will discuss later in this chapter.

Stage 7: Stateful signature detection
: The attack objects that rely on signatures (rather than anomaly detection) are processed in the stateful signature stage of the device's processing. These signatures are not blind pattern matches, but are highly accurate stateful signatures that not only match attacks within the contexts in which they occur, but also can be composed of multiple match criteria (using Boolean expressions between individual criteria). Typically, the attack signatures do not seek to detect a specific exploit, but rather protect against the vulnerability itself. This is important because attack exploits can vary, so writing signatures around a particular exploit is not a great tactic, but protecting against the actual vulnerability is much more powerful.

Stage 8: IDP/IP actions
: Once an attack object in the IPS policy is matched, the SRX can execute an action on that specific session, along with actions on future sessions. The ability to execute an action on that particular session is known as an *IDP action*. IDP actions can be one of the following: No-Action, Drop-Packet, Drop-Connection, Close-Client, Close-Server, Close-Client-and-Server, DSCP-Marking, Recommended, or Ignore. IP actions are actions that can be enforced on future sessions. These actions include

IP-Close, IP-Block, IP-Notify, and IP-Ratelimit, which we will cover in more depth later in the chapter.

Direction-specific detection

One theme in IPS processing that reoccurs throughout this chapter (and in other references) is the notion of client-to-server versus server-to-client traffic. There are typically two directions of traffic flow in modern client/server applications (with the exception of, say, multicast, which is primarily the multicast server sending to the clients). The client is always considered the device that initiates the connection (the source) while the server is the device that is accepting the connection (the destination). This is true even if the client is uploading data to the server.

This is important to know as an IPS administrator, and it's very important for creating custom attack objects. With said explanation, let's explore the significance of client-to-server versus server-to-client attacks:

Client-to-server attacks
: These are what most administrators think IPS does, which is to protect their server infrastructure from attacks generated by malicious clients to compromise or DoS a system. These attacks primarily work only when the client has access to the server, and firewalls can help mitigate access to unnecessary services on that server. IPS can help to detect and prevent attacks that are generated on permitted services (such as a web server listening on HTTP, TCP port 80).

  In this case, the attack is in the traffic generated from the client-to-server direction.

Server-to-client attacks
: Although attacking servers with client-to-server attacks allows attackers to pick their targets, most organizations use firewalls to limit inbound connections to only necessary systems wherever possible. As a result, attackers have changed their tactics, since they can't directly connect to the assets they are trying to compromise. Now, attackers make their victims come to them. There are many different ways to get a victim to come to the attacker (e.g., spam emails with malicious links, social networking, and other social engineering-based attempts). An example of this type of attack is when an attacker is running a web server that serves malicious HTML pages that exploit a JavaScript vulnerability in Internet Explorer, such as the Aurora exploit. Although the attacker may not always have control over which victims visit his malicious site, he typically doesn't have to worry about firewalls blocking this access because users are usually allowed to make connections outbound.

  In this case, the attack is in the traffic generated from the server-to-client direction.

SRX IPS modes

Three different modes can be configured in SRX IPS: integrated, dedicated, and inline tap modes.

At the time of this writing, the branch SRX Series platform only supports integrated mode. However, the high-end SRX supports all three (but only one mode at a time).

Integrated mode
: Traffic processed by the firewall process within the Network Processing Unit or NPU (branch) and SPU (high end), and any traffic that is destined to be sent to have IPS processing, is handled by the firewall process itself. This means the firewall process, rather than a separate process, handles the IPS processing. Because SRX processors are multicore, multithreaded processors, multiple flows can be processed concurrently. This is the default option for the high-end SRX.

  Advantages
  : Integrated mode is the only choice for the branch SRX Series, but on the high-end SRX it is good for situations where the IPS engine needs to process only a little bit of traffic. This mode also has the advantage of inline tap mode, in that all IPS-bound traffic is inspected before being passed out the unit, so it will not allow attacks that it is configured to block if they are single packet attacks.

  Disadvantages
  : Integrated mode IPS processing can impact the performance of both firewall and IPS processing if the IPS engine becomes exceptionally busy, since all processing (firewall and IPS) is done directly in the firewall process. Also, if the firewall process crashes (due to either a firewall-related issue or an IPS-related issue), the entire data plane will be restarted. If high availability (HA) clustering is configured, this will trigger a failure of the data plane to the other node, while the data plane is restarted. Finally, for the high-end SRX, each flow SPU can support 1 million firewall sessions, but in integrated mode, although 1 million firewall sessions are supported, only 128,000 of those sessions can be processed by IPS. Finally, in integrated mode there is additional latency when processing traffic with IPS compared to the firewall.

Dedicated mode (high end only)
: In dedicated mode, the firewall and IPS are handled by separate processes. (Keep in mind that a single session will be processed by both the firewall and IPS in the same SPU for the high-end SRX.) Dedicated mode also allows the administrator to define how much of the SPU is dedicated to the firewall versus the IPS. There are three different weights: equal (half firewall, half IPS), firewall (two-thirds firewall, one-third IPS), and IPS (one-third firewall, two-thirds IPS). Traffic is first processed by the firewall process, and traffic marked for IPS processing is then passed to the IPS process; assuming everything checks out, it is then handed back to the firewall process for forwarding. While the IPS is processing the packets, the firewall process is kept busy processing other packets, so resources do not sit idle. Note that at the time of this writing, no SPU can be dedicated exclusively to firewall or to IPS processing, and the allocation is the same across all SPUs in the SRX.

Advantages

Dedicated mode insulates the performance impact of IPS processing from firewall-only traffic, if the IPS engine becomes busy. In dedicated mode, all 1 million sessions can be processed both as firewall and as IPS in each flow SPU. The SRX can be configured to define how much of the processor is allocated to firewall versus IPS to allow the administrator to customize the processor implementation to best suit the needs of the environment. This mode also has the advantage of inline tap mode in that all IPS-bound traffic will be inspected before being passed out the unit, so it will not allow attacks that it is configured to block if they are single packet attacks.

Disadvantages

If only a little bit of IPS is needed, integrated mode might be the best choice—or dedicated mode balanced to firewall. Otherwise, if only a little bit of IPS is required and dedicated mode is used, IPS resources are wasted, while firewall resources may be overutilized. Although firewall processing is insulated from the IPS, should the IPS become busy, IPS traffic will still be impacted (unlike inline mode). Finally, in dedicated mode, there is additional latency when processing traffic with IPS compared to firewall.

Inline tap mode (high end only)

In inline tap mode, the same separation of processing exists as in dedicated mode, but instead of passing IPS-bound traffic to the IPS engine and waiting for the IPS engine to complete processing before forwarding it on, the firewall process makes a copy of the packet and sends it to the IPS engine, and then directly processes the traffic without waiting for the IPS engine to send the traffic back for forwarding.

Advantages

Both firewall and IPS traffic are insulated from performance issues if the IPS engine becomes busy because the firewall traffic is directly processed, and IPS-bound traffic is copied to the IPS engine while the original packets are forwarded. There is no additional latency using inline tap mode. Failures in the IPS engine do not result in interruptions of traffic because the IPS traffic is copied to the IPS engine and then forwarded. If there is a failure of the IPS engine, traffic in that SPU will be processed by the firewall only while the IPS engine is restarted. All new IPS-bound flows will then be processed by the IPS engine.

Disadvantages

Since traffic is forwarded before being inspected there is a possibility that some attacks might pass through the SRX; however, additional actions can still be taken on the flows themselves (e.g., drop/close the flow, along with IP actions). If only a little bit of traffic needs to be processed by the SRX, the firewall resources might be overutilized.

When using a high-end SRX, the question of which mode to use arises. Integrated mode is the default and is appropriate for implementations that require only a small amount of IPS processing. If you want to maximize IPS performance and don't want to allow for the possibility that an attack that is configured to be blocked might pass through the SRX, dedicated mode is recommended because all traffic is processed by the IPS engine before being forwarded. If performance (and lack of impact to traffic if the IPS engine gets busy) is the primary concern, inline tap mode is the right choice.

SRX deployment options

Traditionally, there are a few different modes for deploying an IPS in the network. In the past, often an IPS was a device that sat transparently in the network, simply inspecting traffic as it passed through. Another option was that you could use *sniffer mode*, which passively listened for attacks out-of-band from the network traffic. This is typically accomplished via SPAN port or network tap. Rarely was an IPS deployed in routed mode, although some standalone IPS systems support that.

The SRX is a different story, because it is a full-featured router, firewall, and IPS device that can fill all of these needs. On the branch SRX Series, only Layer 3 mode is supported, so you can deploy the branch SRX in Layer 3. On the high-end SRX, both Layer 2 and Layer 3 modes are supported for IPS. You can deploy multiple segments concurrently on the SRX, even separating the security policy of the different segments (via zones).

One thing that is missing on the SRX is support for true sniffer mode. You can accomplish this functionality by mirroring traffic to an SRX and putting the interface on the SRX in promiscuous mode. You will still need to configure routing on the SRX to "route" the traffic to an egress interface, which can be the same as the ingress interface, and then you just need to configure the appropriate policy (e.g., Trust to Trust, with a rule permitting anything for IDP processing). In this mode, you should also disable "SYN" and "Sequence checking" under "Set security flow" because these settings can interfere with session establishment.

Attack Object Types

Attack objects can be categorized into two different types: protocol anomaly and stateful signature-based attack objects. Both types of attack objects come bundled with the SRX signature updates and provide security against both known and unknown (zero-day) attacks.

Protocol anomaly attack objects
: These are predefined objects developed by the Juniper Security Team to detect activity that is outside the bounds of a protocol. Typically, the enforcement for what is considered acceptable behavior for protocols is based on an RFC specification; or a manufacturer spec if there is no RFC. Protocol anomaly detection is built into the detector engine and is not based on any specific pattern.

Administrators cannot create protocol anomaly objects, as this is code that is built into the detector engines; however, you can configure custom attack objects that utilize protocol anomaly objects as part of a compound attack object.

Signature-based attack objects
: These are provided by the Juniper Security Team along with protocol anomaly attack objects, firmware, and detector engine updates. Signature-based attack objects are attack objects that actually match specific patterns through the use of a regular expression engine. The use of a regular expression engine provides the ability to match a range of patterns rather than a specific pattern. Additionally, a single attack object can be composed of multiple patterns that can be evaluated as a Boolean expression to make complex matches. As mentioned earlier in the chapter, signature-based attack objects are stateful signatures that match the attack object within the specific location in which it actually occurs in the attack itself (known as a context). You can create custom signature-based attack objects to use alongside predefined attack objects, as we will discuss in "Custom attack objects and groups" on page 406.

Application contexts

To aid in the accuracy and performance of IPS inspection, the SRX uses a concept called *contexts* to match an attack in the specific place where it occurs in the application protocol. This helps to ensure that performance is optimized by not searching for attacks where they would not occur, and it limits false positives. There may be many contexts within a single message. The SRX supports about 600 contexts at the time of this writing. Here is an example of an HTTP Header message and the associated values and contexts (in bold, not found in the actual message) in that message:

```
GET /index.html Http1.1 http-get-url
Host: www.company.com http-header-host
Accept: image/gif, image/x-xbitmap, image/jpeg, image/pjpeg http-header-accept
Accept-Language: en http-header-accept-language
Accept-Encoding: gzip, deflate http-header-content-encoding
User-Agent: Mozilla/4.0 (compatible; MSIE 5.5; Windows NT 4.0)
http-header-user-agent
```

Juniper maintains documentation that describes all of the different contexts and their associated function. You can find the documentation by searching the Juniper Support Knowledge Base.

Predefined attack objects and groups

Juniper provides predefined attack objects (both protocol anomaly and signatures) individually and in predefined groups to customers who have active licenses. The predefined attack objects cannot be edited for the most part; however, you can use these as a basis for creating custom attack objects. At the time of this writing, there are about 6,000 predefined attack objects, and the number is growing every day as new threats emerge. Another feature of Juniper predefined attack objects is that customers can view the actual patterns that are used for signature-based attack objects. Many other vendors keep their signatures closed, which impacts customers because they cannot view how the IPS is matching patterns (particularly with pattern matching). Juniper keeps only some signatures closed if they are providing protection prior to when the vendor has a chance to patch the vulnerability to ensure that the protection is not going to impact the community.

Custom attack objects and groups

In addition to the vast number of predefined attack objects that are provided as part of the IPS license, you also have a great deal of control over creating your own signature-based attack objects in the SRX. Additionally, you can create custom objects for application identification on the SRX so that you can identify not only custom attacks, but also custom applications. We covered this in greater detail in "Attack Object Types" on page 404.

Two types of custom attack groups can be configured in the SRX: static attack groups and dynamic attack groups. The primary difference is that static attack groups are exactly that: you must manually add or remove any attacks into this group. The only thing that will change is if an attack object itself is changed as part of an update, and then its contents will be updated; otherwise, the group does not change. Dynamic attack groups give you the ability to define filters that select which attacks are added into the attack group. The filters can be complex and can consist of multiple factors to identify attack objects to be selected for the dynamic attack group.

Severities

Multiple severity levels are used to define the impact an attack can have on a system:

Critical
: Critical attacks are attacks that try to gain "root" level access to a system to crash the entire system. Critical attacks are also certain malicious evasion techniques that are clearly used for nefarious purposes.

Major
: Major attacks are attacks that try to gain "user" level access to a system to crash a particular service or application.

Minor
: Minor attacks are attacks that try to perform information leakage techniques, including those that exploit vulnerabilities to reveal information about the target.

Warning
: Warning attacks are attacks that are suspicious in nature, such as scans and other reconnaissance attempts. Juniper also may drop the severity of legacy attacks to Warning after they are no longer deemed a threat (e.g., Windows 3.1 and 95 vulnerabilities).

Information

Information attacks are not typically malicious activity, but rather can provide valuable information about activity on the network, such as applications that are running, potential vulnerable software, and best-practice violations.

Signature performance impacts

A common question that many IPS administrators have concerns what impact different signatures have on the performance of their IPS (or in this case, the SRX). There is no simple answer to this question, in part because the impact that individual signatures have is not linear and based on the number of signatures, as some signatures have more of a performance impact than others. Generally speaking, the signatures that perform "context"-based matching are going to be the most efficient, since they only perform inspection based on specific locations of protocols; these would be followed by stream signatures, which inspect the entire stream up to a certain limit (e.g., 1 Kb). Signatures that inspect the entire stream for the duration of the session will generally have the worst performance. Juniper attempts to take the guesswork out of signature performance by classifying the signatures with the greatest impact on performance as being low-performing. These signatures are placed under the MISC category, and also have a field called Performance. You can filter on the Performance values in dynamic attack groups, or just avoid the MISC signatures wherever possible.

It is important to understand that when you add signatures into the policy, regardless of whether you are permitting, blocking, or exempting them, you are performing inspection first and then determining what to do once an attack is found. For instance, the traffic is examined by the detector engine, and then it is examined again after a signature is matched based on what has been compiled into the policy. After a signature has been matched, the SRX will do a policy lookup to determine what the action should be for the respective traffic (based on the rulebase). This is the case regardless of the action or of whether it is exempted in the policy. The key takeaway is that by having a signature anywhere in the policy, you are going to take a performance hit for traffic matching that protocol. If you do not add an attack object into the policy, it will not be compiled into the policy, and therefore it won't impact performance. As mentioned earlier, attack objects don't all have the same performance impacts. The reason is that some signatures require more pattern matching than others, resulting in more computational cycles being spent on packet processing.

Understanding the performance impacts of the signatures is not meant to discourage you from deploying a sensible policy, but rather to empower you to understand how policies are impacted by their contents. When performance is the primary concern, you should craft your policy to only the essential attack objects that are necessary to inspect the traffic and provide adequate coverage. Rather than deploying a broad policy, you should create a policy which is very specific in the attack objects that are included. You can do this by using both static and dynamic attack object groups to select the signatures that should be added based on the components of the traffic itself. If your concerns are more around coverage rather than security, you can deploy a policy which has broader protection, but also signatures that are meant to provide protection or visibility for the traffic. As we progress through this chapter, we will explore the mechanisms to configure and tune an effective policy for the SRX.

IPS Policy Components

A key feature that sets the SRX apart from other platforms that perform firewall and other services together is that the SRX provides extremely granular configuration and application of IPS inspection against processed traffic. The SRX offers exact control over what traffic is processed by the IPS engine, as well as *within* the IPS policy itself.

You should understand several components in order to create and apply effective security policies on the SRX, including rulebases, match criteria, actions, and packet logging. Let's cover the various components and how to apply them.

Rulebases

The IPS functionality in the SRX is composed of rulebases. Each rulebase consists of rules that define what traffic to match, and then what action to take on that traffic. At the time of this writing, three rulebases are part of the SRX IPS policy:

IPS rulebase
: The IPS rulebase defines what traffic should be inspected and what measures should be taken for traffic that matches the IPS attack objects defined in the policy. This is the traditional IPS rulebase used to define attacks and other applications that are enforced by the policy.

Application-DDoS rulebase
: The Application-DDoS rulebase is part of the AppDDoS suite that is only offered on the high-end SRX at the time of this writing. The Application-DDoS rulebase essentially defines the policy to be enforced to protect servers from application-level DoS attacks. We will cover Application-DDoS protection in detail in "AppDDoS Protection" on page 423.

Exempt rulebase
: The Exempt rulebase complements the IPS rulebase and provides a simple mechanism to override detected attacks. The Exempt rulebase provides a rulebase for a single location to bypass actions taken by the IPS engine in the IPS rulebase. Rather than having to make a complex IPS rulebase with these overrides, the Exempt rulebase provides a separate location to do this so that the IPS rulebase remains clean and focused on the attacks. Most often, the Exempt rulebase is used to ignore false positives or certain attack scenarios—traffic is first matched in the IPS rulebase, but then also examined in the Exempt rulebase, and if it matches a rule in the Exempt rulebase, it is permitted and nothing will be logged. We will cover examples of this at length in this chapter.

Match criteria

Each rule has match criteria to identify which traffic will have a particular action applied to it. There are several components of the match criteria, many of which are also present in the firewall policy. These criteria are not redundant, since the firewall policy identifies what traffic is to be sent to the IPS engine, and then the IPS engine applies IPS inspection based on the contents of that traffic. The following criteria are evaluated as part of the different rulebases:

From zone
: Matches traffic based on the zone from which the traffic originates. This can be used to match traffic arriving on a particular logical interface, including per-virtual LAN (VLAN) matching.

To zone
: Matches traffic based on which zone the traffic is going to as it leaves the SRX. The To zone is determined by a route lookup, or in the case of transparent mode, by a bridge lookup to determine what the egress interface is, and therefore the egress zone.

Source address
: The source address defines the IP address of the client, and is defined in the address book for the respective From zone. It is important to remember that IPS processing happens after NAT transformations, so you must configure your source address to match the translated addresses. You can use individual source address objects, address sets, or any combination of object and group in this field.

Destination address
: The destination address defines the IP address of the server and is defined in the address book for the respective To zone. It is important to remember that IPS processing happens after NAT transformations, so you must configure your destination address to match the translated address. You can use individual destination address objects, address sets, or any combination of object and group in this field.

Application
: The SRX IPS engine has the ability to match attacks on any port for the given Layer 4 protocol (TCP/UDP). By default, an attack is tied to a particular application (Layer 4 protocol) which may or may not have a specific list of ports on which the application will be detected. When the IPS is set to match the Application Default, it inspects the traffic for specific protocols on the ports they are listed for in the `application-id` object for that attack. You can override checking for applications on the default ports on a rule-by-rule basis.

Attacks
: This applies to the IPS and Exempt rulebases only. The Attacks field defines what attacks to match as part of this rule. You can combine predefined and custom

attacks within a single rule, along with using any combination of static or dynamic groups.

Application-DDoS
: This applies to the Application-DDoS only. The Application-DDoS field defines the Application-DDoS profiles that are used to enforce the connection and application thresholds used for the Application-DDoS enforcement. Since Application-DDoS protection does not provide IPS, but rather is protecting against Application-DDoS attacks, the Attacks field is not required in the Application-DDoS rulebase, just like Application-DDoS is not required in the IPS or Exempt rulebase.

Then actions

On an IPS rule-by-rule basis, you can define what actions should be taken when the appropriate criteria are matched in the IPS engine. You can enforce two types of actions on the traffic: IPS actions and IP actions.

IPS actions perform an action on the offending traffic, while IP actions can take actions on future sessions (such as preventing them). They are exclusive of each other, so you can configure one, or the other, but it usually makes sense to configure IPS actions if you are using IP actions for a session. Additionally, you can configure logging and packet capture on a rule-by-rule basis.

The following lists define the IPS and IP actions available for the SRX. Note that these are available for the IPS and the Application-DDoS rulebases, since the Exempt rulebase simply defines scenarios for which no action should be taken when an attack is matched. Although you can essentially do the same in the IPS and Application-DDoS rulebase, it is much simpler to have the exemptions in one place.

IPS actions. The following IPS actions are available for the SRX:

No-Action
: No-Action means exactly what it says: no action will be taken on the session for this match. That isn't to say that another rule might not perform a drop or close on the traffic, since even when a rule matches, the IPS processing is not complete. So, you need to be aware of the fact that even with a No-Action defined, that doesn't mean other rules might not block this traffic.

Ignore-Connection
: Ignore-Connection means the traffic will be permitted, but also that the IPS engine will ignore the rest of the connection and will not process it at all. This is useful for identifying connections (such as custom applications) that you do not want to inspect. After a session has been marked Ignore-Connection, the IPS engine will not process it. It's important to keep that in mind, because an attack could be present later in the connection, but the IPS would not see it. If you only want to ignore a specific attack, but not ignore the rest of the connection, either put that attack in the Exempt rulebase (recommended) or configure the rule with No-Action.

Drop-Packet
: Drop-Packet will drop an individual offending packet, but not the rest of the session. Typically, you want to use the Drop-Connection action when malicious activity is detected on a flow, but in some cases, you might just want to prevent a particular activity which might be contained within a session (such as a file transfer) without dropping the entire session. Of course, this is highly dependent on the application's architecture, so when in doubt, either research the application or just use Drop-Connection. Drop-Packet may be useful for attacks that consist of only a single packet (such as SQL Slammer), but this isn't very common. Note that Drop-Packet will not have any impact in inline tap mode, since the original packet (not the copied one to the IPS engine) has already made it through the SRX and will be recorded as action DISMISS in the logs.

Drop-Connection
: Drop-Connection drops all packets (including the offending ones) of a connection, so essentially, if an attack is triggered, all packets of the session will be silently dropped. This is effective for all supported protocols. If inline tap mode is used, the original offending packet might make it through, but all future packets are dropped by the SRX. Drop-Connection is useful for silently dropping the connection without alerting the client or server that the session is being dropped.

Close-Client
: If TCP is used as the protocol, the SRX can send a TCP Reset to the client (which will appear to be from the server, but is actually spoofed by the SRX) along with blocking all future packets in the flow. With the Close-Client option, the server will not be alerted that the session has been closed. This is useful when you want to protect a client from an attack from the server (such as an Internet Explorer exploit generated by the server). Since you are sending a TCP Reset, the web client won't just sit there and time out, but will immediately inform the user that the connection was reset. If the Layer 4 protocol of the flow is not TCP, and the action is Close-Client, the action will effectively be Drop-Connection, as there will be no TCP Reset, but the traffic for the offending flow will still be silently dropped.

Close-Server
: If TCP is used as the protocol, the SRX can send a TCP Reset to the server (which will appear to be from the client, but is actually spoofed by the SRX) along with blocking all future packets in the flow. With the Close-Server option, the client will not be alerted that the session has been closed. This is useful for protecting the server from client-based attacks such as resource utilization attacks against the server. By sending a reset, the server does not spend any more time holding the connection open and immediately closes the session out. If the Layer 4 protocol of the flow is not TCP, and the action is Close-Server, the action will effectively be Drop-Connection, as there will be no TCP Reset, but the traffic for the offending flow will still be silently dropped.

Close-Client-and-Server
: If TCP is used as the protocol, the SRX can send a TCP Reset to both the client and the server. The resets are spoofed by the SRX and appear to be from the client (from the server's perspective) and from the server (from the client's perspective). Additionally, the SRX blocks all future packets in the connection. This is useful when you want to close the connections, and inform both the client and the server so that they don't continue to retransmit packets or believe that the connection is still open when it really isn't (which can cause application issues). If the Layer 4 protocol of the flow is not TCP, and the action is Close-Client-Server, the action will effectively be Drop-Connection, as there will be no TCP Reset, but the traffic for the offending flow will still be silently dropped.

Mark-Diffserv
: The SRX is capable of rewriting the Differentiated Services Code Point (DSCP) bits of an IP header to a defined value within the IPS rulebase. This is useful if you want to use the IPS to identify applications such that upstream or downstream devices can perform Quality of Service (QoS) processing on the flows (such as on a router). At the time of this writing, the SRX does not honor the DSCP marking performed in the IPS engine because the classification phase of QoS on the SRX happens when traffic arrives, not after it has been processed by the IPS. DSCP marking is most useful for identifying actual applications from a Layer 7 perspective, which a standard router or switch would not be able to do. In the near future, and depending on when you are reading this, the SRX will be able to enforce its own DSCP policy along with shaping traffic based on the IPS policy.

Recommended
: Recommended uses the Whatever action and is defined within a predefined attack object (or within a custom attack object, whatever is configured by the administrator). Predefined attack objects come with a Recommended action set by the Juniper Security Team based on the nature of the attack and the suggested action to perform.

Notification actions. The following notification actions are available for the SRX:

Log attacks
: On a rule-by-rule basis, you can configure logging similar to how it is done on a rule-by-rule basis in a firewall policy. Additionally, the alert flag can be set to help security engineers identify significant events.

Severity
: The severity level can be configured on a rule-by-rule basis to signify events in the logs and to override the default severity levels defined within the attack objects.

Packet logging
: Packet logging is configured under the notification section of a rule and it is covered in detail in the next section.

Packet logging. Starting in Junos 10.2, you can collect packet captures when IPS events are triggered. When an IPS rule is triggered, it collects the appropriate packets and puts them in PCAP format which is then sent to an external device via DMI. Support for packet logging to the STRM will be coming soon; please check the release notes or contact your Juniper sales staff. Juniper is working with other vendors to provide support for this as well.

The packet capture feature is flexible. You can configure it on an IPS rule-by-rule basis, and also define how many packets both before and after the attack should be included. You do need to exercise some caution when enabling packet captures. When packet captures are enabled, you can log packets both prior to and following the attack. To accommodate this functionality, the SRX must buffer packets in all flows prior to and following an attack. This requires memory and other system resources to maintain this information. On top of that, if you are logging lots of attacks, you must also send the packet captures externally. For all of these reasons, packet logging should be strictly applied, and not applied across the board with all attacks. Besides the ability to apply packet captures on an IPS rule-by-rule basis, there are also a few parameters that you can configure:

Host
: This is the host that receives the PCAP information. You also define the UDP port that will be used to send the data. This configuration is required.

Source-Address
: This is part of the configuration for sending the PCAP information to the logging host. This IP address is arbitrary, and you do not have to have it be the IP address of the SRX, but typically it's a best practice to do so.

Max Sessions
: You can configure a percentage value (1% to 100%) of sessions that are tracked with packet logs. This is an important way to limit how many sessions are processed for resource purposes.

Total-Memory
: You can define the percentage of memory that can be allocated to the packet capture feature.

Policy Configuration

Within an IPS security policy, you can define how the packets should be logged on the SRX. And within the rule, you can define the following values (which should be used with care to ensure that memory is not overused for buffering and processing the packets):

Pre-Attack

You can capture from one to 255 packets before an attack is triggered. This is accomplished by buffering all packets for the session up to the number of packets logged for the pre-attack limit for that particular rule.

Post-Attack

You can log from zero to 255 packets after an attack occurs. Note that if the attack triggers a drop or close connection, there may not be any more packets in the attack.

Post-Attack-Timeout

When an attack is triggered, the SRX may not know how many packets will follow the attack (e.g., if you configure 20 packets to be logged after the attack, the SRX will not send the PCAP until it has all 20 packets). To ensure that the SRX does not hold on to the packets indefinitely, you configure a Post-Attack-Timeout to define how long the SRX should wait while holding on to the packets before sending them out.

IP actions. The following IP actions are available for the SRX:

IP-Notify

IP-Notify will simply generate a log when a connection is detected from a host that was previously identified for IP actions. This is useful if you don't want to block future connections that are identified by IP action, but you do want to identify any future connections made by that host based on the target/timeout.

IP-Block

IP-Block allows you to silently block (drop) future connections made by hosts which were marked by IP-Block in a previous attack. This is tracked based on the target and timeout that are defined in the rule on which the attack was triggered.

IP-Close

IP-Close is similar to IP-Block, except TCP Resets will be sent in addition to dropping all of the packets as part of that flow. This is tracked based on the target and timeout that are defined in the rule on which the attack was triggered. If the Layer 4 protocol is not TCP, a silent Drop-Connection will be applied.

IP Connection-Rate-Limit

This is used to rate-limit how many connections per second a host can initiate in the future after it has been added to the IP Action Table. Particularly with DDoS scenarios, you may want to limit the number of connections a host can make rather than block them outright. You can use the same strategy when certain attacks are detected so that you don't block all future connections, but rather limit how many can be initiated.

Targets and timeouts. Targets define which hosts have IP actions applied to them based on the information matched in the attack that triggered the IP action.

Destination-Address
: This performs the appropriate IP action on the destination address of the connection, so if IP-Block is the action, connections to the Destination-Address are blocked. This is good for blacklisting traffic to a botnet server, or other restricted destinations.

Service
: This performs the appropriate IP action on the source IP, destination IP, destination port, and protocol, so it's very selective in which connections are blocked. This is good if you want to prevent future connections from a source to a destination on a particular service (destination port and protocol such as TCP port 80).

Source-Address
: This matches future connections from a particular source address (regardless of which zone is used). This is useful if you want to protect a server from clients that attempt malicious activity. By using IP-Block or IP-Close with the Source-Address target, you can prevent future connections until the timeout expires.

Source-Zone
: This is somewhat of a legacy feature, which will actually block the entire source zone at the time of this writing (that's right, we confirmed this with the developers!). It originally came out of the ISG with IDP feature set. Note that there is talk of improving this to take the source address itself into account, but at the time of this writing, if you enable this target it will enforce it on the entire source zone on which the attack was triggered.

Zone-Service
: This is similar to Service, but is also takes into account the Source-Zone in the event of IP overlaps.

The timeout defines how long the IP action is in effect for a given target—for instance, how long a connection will be blocked with IP-Block. You can configure this on a rule-by-rule basis in the IPS engine, so it's not a global configuration, but rather can be applied very granularly. If a timeout of 0 is configured, the timeout will not automatically expire, but rather will only be cleared via a manual clear of the IP action entry or a reboot.

Terminate Match

Terminate Match is somewhat of a legacy feature that arose from the earlier days of the standalone IDP to make it function similar to a firewall. By default, for IPS processing (both standalone IDP and SRX), even after a match is made for an attack, the rulebase continues to process that traffic to see if any other rules match. The IPS will always take the most stringent action (e.g., drop connection if a rule with Drop-Connection and No-Action is matched), but some customers may want to restrict this even further. By enabling Terminate Match, the IPS rulebase acts more like a firewall, in that once it finds a rule which matches the To/From zones, source IP, destination IP, and application, it will do whatever that rule says if the attack is detected; if not, it will not process that traffic any further. Generally, you should not use Terminate Match, especially with No-Action rules, because it can cause you to overlook potentially malicious traffic. Use this feature with caution unless you really know what you're doing!

Security Packages

Cyber threats are dynamic in nature and require vigilance to provide up-to-date protection. To provide up-to-date security capabilities, attack updates are provided on a daily basis (if new signatures are required) and as emergencies if a zero-day threat is released.

The important thing to note is that a new attack object may not be required for new attacks, as the Juniper Security Team tries to create attack objects to protect against vulnerabilities and anomalous behavior rather than writing signatures against specific exploits (which may change very frequently). For instance, the Aurora Internet Explorer exploit which was discovered in December 2009 was already covered by the HTTP:STC:SCRIPT:FUNC-REASSIGN attack object (released August 2009, well ahead of the exploit), so customers were fully protected from this zero-day attack.

The security packages themselves are composed of several different components which are updated when a new version of the signature database and detector engines is available. You can either manually trigger the SRX to download the attack objects, or configure the SRX to automatically go and retrieve the updates. The following subsections describe the different components of Juniper security packages.

Attack database

The attack database contains all of the attack objects (both signature- and protocol anomaly-based) and is provided by the Juniper Security Team. New updates are typically posted daily, although sometimes there may not be a new exploit (which isn't already covered by existing signatures). When the attack database is downloaded, it contains the full attack database in a compressed form. If the attack database is downloaded directly to the SRX, it is stored in */var/db/idpd/sec-download* for staging. If it is downloaded from the NSM, it is stored in */var/db/idpd/nsm-download*. The */var/db/idpd/sec-repository* folder contains the attack, groups, applications, and detector engine files.

You can sign up for Technical Bulletins on the Juniper Support page so that you receive email updates on the release of new attack databases, detector engines, and Junos firmware. See *http://kb.juniper.net/KB9890*.

Attack object updates versus full updates

You can perform two types of updates for attack objects.

A standard update downloads the complete attack database to the SRX. You can automate this process so that it occurs at predefined intervals, or you can manually trigger it at your leisure.

Full updates include both the attack database and the latest detector engine. Typically, detector engine updates are released once per quarter, while attack databases are released daily (if there are updates to attack objects). Detector engine updates will provide bug fixes for the detector engine, new inspection capabilities, and new support for different application decoding.

Policy template updates are something that you must manually perform and are not included as part of the attack object updates.

Application objects

Starting with Junos 10.1, the SRX provides objects that detail applications which are used for application ID matching, called *application objects*. These are stored separately from the attack objects, even though there isn't much difference between application ID objects and attack objects.

Application objects primarily detect applications by using signature-based pattern matching for well-known transactions initiated by the respective applications, rather than looking for an actual exploit attempt. The mechanisms are virtually identical, but they are defined separately for administrative organization. The application objects are released with the attack updates; however, typically there are not as many applications being created as there are discovered exploits and vulnerabilities for those applications, so new application objects are released only when there are new Layer 7 applications.

Detector engines

The detector engine is a module run by the IPS process on the SRX to execute protocol anomaly protection as well as signature-based pattern matching. Detector engine updates are released quarterly, and provide new protocol decoding capabilities, enhancements to protocol anomaly protection, and bug fixes. The detector engine is not installed by default with a signature update; rather, you must trigger a manual "full update" to download the detector engine and install it. The SRX allows for two detector engines to be installed concurrently when an update is applied so that all new sessions utilize the new detector engine, while the old sessions will still be processed by the previous detector engine. When all sessions from the old detector engine are closed, the original detector engine is removed. The installation of the new detector engine does not have any performance impact because of this graceful installation process. Just like the signature updates, you can sign up for notifications when new detector engines are available. The notifications also include release notes that detail all of the new features, addressed issues, and known limitations for that detector engine.

Policy templates

To assist administrators with new IPS installations, Juniper provides several different predefined policies that administrators can download and install. Although these are helpful to understand the basic mechanics of the IPS policies, every environment is going to be different, with different applications and different administrative goals. So, best practice recommends creating a customized policy for true enforcement.

The good news is that this chapter details how to deploy and tune an IPS policy effectively, minimizing false positives and providing real security. But in the meantime, you might want to take a look at the policy templates for examples. The policy templates are updated informally by the Juniper Security Team, so you need to stay tuned to the version numbers for new policy templates.

Scheduling updates

Updates can be scheduled to automatically download and optionally install attack object updates which include application object updates. When attack updates are scheduled, you can define the interval and schedule for when they should be downloaded, along with whether the SRX should install the new version. Of course, if you are using a central management system such as NSM or Junos Space, you can also trigger installations automatically from there.

Sensor Attributes

Although the SRX's predefined sensor attributes should be just fine for most environments, in some situations you may want to override the default behavior for the IPS sensor to better fit your environment. A large number of attributes can be modified, and covering them all is simply outside the scope of this book. Instead, we will provide their location and discuss what you can configure under the sensor configuration hierarchy. Then, if necessary, you can investigate what you need to change and make those changes accordingly.

As the following output shows, all of the options for sensor attributes are configured under the [edit security idp sensor-configuration] hierarchy level:

```
{primary:node0}[edit security idp sensor-configuration]
root@SRX5800-2# set ?
Possible completions:
> log          IDP Log Configuration
> application-identification Application identification
> flow          Flow configuration
> re-assembler      Re-assembler configuration
> ips          Ips configuration
> global          Global configuration
> detector        Detector Configuration
> ssl-inspection     SSL inspection
```

Let's briefly examine each one.

Logging sensor attributes

The SRX provides the ability to customize the behavior of the SRX IPS logging facility. By default, logs are suppressed should the same event occur rapidly. This is to prevent both the SRX and the syslog server from having to process the same information. You can override the default settings by configuring the threshold of events to start logging, how large to set the buffer for log messages, or even to disable log suppression altogether.

Application identification attributes

By default, the SRX attempts to use application identification to identify what the actual traffic is within a flow so that the protocol decoding engine can accurately detect attacks You can optionally disable application identification processing if you would like to perform the protocol decoding strictly on a Layer 4 port basis. Additionally, a number of parameters can be tuned for optimal memory use for application identification, session table size, application caching, and whether to look for nested applications (e.g., the ability to look for Facebook as an application, since normally it would be detected as the parent application HTTP).

Typically, you should not alter memory attributes unless the Juniper Networks Technical Assistance Center (JTAC) has recommended that you do, as doing so might result in IPS inspection issues.

Flow attributes

The SRX IPS functionality is flow-based, and classifies traffic into flows very similar to how the IPS session table it set up in the firewall session table. You can configure additional attributes in the IPS around flow processing such as queue sizes, behavior of UDP timeouts, flow table size, and other timers and behaviors related to policy installation.

Typically, you should not configure queue and flow table sizes without consulting JTAC, as this can cause IPS inspection issues.

Reassembler attributes

Before true IPS inspection can occur, application traffic must be reassembled into the complete state that it normally would be processed (on the client and server). This is particularly true when the application transactions span several packets. As a part of this processing, internal values are set for the amount of memory used and different queue sizes to be implemented.

Typically, you should modify these values only with recommendation from JTAC, as the default values should be appropriate for most environments.

IPS attributes

There are a few settings under the IPS hierarchy, but it is more of a miscellaneous field than anything else. Typically, you shouldn't need to modify these values, such as ignoring server-to-client traffic, shellcode, and regular expression processing.

Global attributes

Similar to the IPS attributes, these attributes typically do not need to be modified. There are a few attributes around policy caching and memory limits, but usually you can just leave them alone.

Detector attributes

You may need to occasionally change certain default values around inspection thresholds. These thresholds are available on a protocol-by-protocol basis, and will not be the same across different protocols. For instance, HTTP has several predefined thresholds, such as how many failed login attempts should trigger an attack, or how long a cookie can be (in bytes). For most users, the predefined values should be just fine, but there is no such thing as a default network, so you may need to adjust your detector engine attributes accordingly if you are noticing that certain threshold-based attacks are being generated incorrectly.

SSL inspection attributes

If you are using the SSL decryption functionality to inspect Secure Sockets Layer (SSL) encrypted traffic, you may need to tweak values under the SSL Inspection Attributes section of the configuration, especially if you are very demanding about performance.

At the time of this writing, SSL decryption is supported only for the high-end SRX, and is not supported in the branch SRX Series devices. You should modify these values only with recommendations from JTAC.

SSL Inspection

Web services are a critical piece of infrastructure for most organizations today. Web presence for many started as a way to provide information for customers, but even for modest organizations that aren't web-focused, many have deployed web applications that are critical to their infrastructure. To help ensure that customer data is not compromised, many of these web applications are delivered via HTTPS which provides encryption for standard HTTP sessions. The problem is that the encrypted traffic between the client and the web server cannot be simply inspected for attacks, other than attacks against SSL itself. Further, SSL does nothing to prevent attacks against web services; if anything, it makes it harder to detect because the IPS cannot simply view the information.

To help counteract a potential hole in network security, you can configure the SRX to inspect SSL encrypted traffic between the client and the server to protect against client-to-server attacks.

Note the following limitations:

Platform support
: At the time of this writing, SSL decryption is supported only on the high-end SRX devices, and not on the branch.

Inspection of traffic
: This is supported for both client-to-server and server-to-client directions, if the SSL key is installed; otherwise, only attacks on SSL itself can be detected.

SSL server keys
: For the SRX to inspect encrypted traffic, it must have the private keys for the web servers whose traffic it is inspecting prior to the session being establish. These keys are installed on the SRX for this configuration. Note that forward proxy support (where clients terminate their SSL connections on the SRX) is not available on the SRX at the time of this writing, but is available on the Juniper standalone IDP product. This functionality should arrive on the SRX during the print life of this book.

Only HTTPS support
: Today, HTTPS is the only SSL encapsulated application that is supported, so there is no support for other protocols, such as FTP Secure (FTPS); however, such support is possible in the future.

SSL decryption/inspection overview

Before we see how to configure SSL inspection, a few things should be mentioned regarding implementation of the SSL decryption functionality to give you a better idea of how it works, and the benefits of using it:

Hardware-assisted
: The actual SSL decryption is performed in the SPU processor via encryption/decryption hardware, so the heavy lifting is offloaded to separate hardware rather than being processed by software. This greatly improves the performance of SSL decryption (I clocked in at 1 Gbps of decryption + inspection for an SPU with the Recommended IPS policy!)

Automatic port detection
: The SRX uses application ID to identify traffic when the SSL private key is known by the SRX, to decrypt the traffic, so no configuration is necessary to define the ports which the SRX should listen to for the SSL traffic.

Decryption and inspection
: For sessions that are flagged for SSL processing, the SSL decrypts the traffic, while queuing the original SSL traffic. The decrypted traffic is inspected, and if there is an attack, the appropriate action is taken. If there is no attack, the original SSL packets are forwarded (this helps with throughput). Of course, packets do need to be exchanged throughout the communication, so packets are passed as needed for proper bidirectional communication.

Configuration
: The configuration is quite simple for SSL decryption and inspection. The only additional configuration that is required beyond standard IPS configuration is the private key that is loaded and associated with a server. Any traffic that is decrypted by SSL is inspected according to the standard IPS policy.

Supported modes
: Integrated, dedicated, and inline tap modes are all supported for SSL decryption.

Alternatives to SSL decryption and inspection

Not all SRX platforms support SSL decryption, but the good news is that you can still inspect SSL traffic with the assistance of other devices. For instance, in the case of a branch SRX Series device, client-to-server SSL connections can be terminated on a reverse proxy, such as an Apache Web Server, or on another device. The SRX sits between the reverse proxy and the actual web server that transmits HTTP which the SRX can inspect, as shown in Figure 8-7. This also has the advantage of off-loading the encryption/decryption from the web server, and alleviating the SRX from having to decrypt it.

Inspecting client SSL traffic is a bit more complex, because the SRX does not know the server private keys, like it would for specific server inspection. To inspect client SSL traffic you need to use proxy server chaining so that clients terminate their SSL connections on an HTTPS proxy (such as Squid), which then passes the traffic to an egress

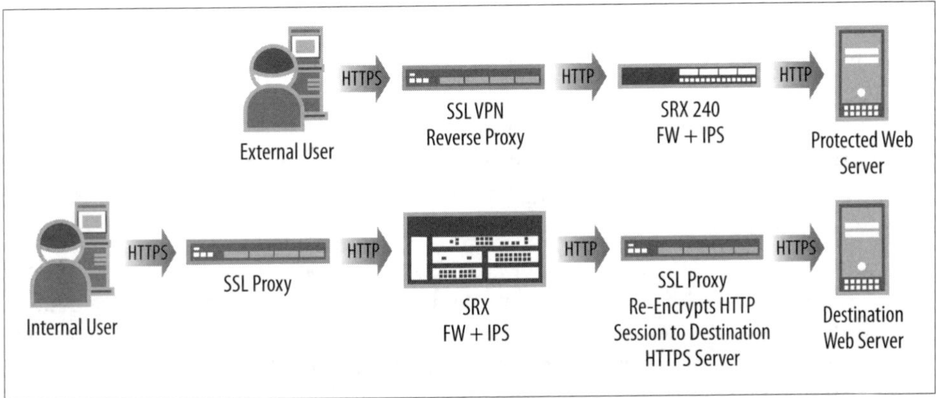

Figure 8-7. Reverse proxy

proxy over HTTP (so that the SRX can inspect it), where the egress proxy would initiate the HTTPS connection to the destination server. Also note that on the Juniper standalone IDP platforms (IDP 75, IDP 250, IDP 800, and IDP 8200) running 5.0r2+ SSL, forward proxy is supported, where the client proxies its connection on the IDP itself. SSL forward proxy is not supported on the SRX at the time of this writing, but it likely will be in the near future, or perhaps by the time you are reading this.

AppDDoS Protection

AppDDoS is a relatively new breed of attacks that do not exploit a specific vulnerability, but rather try to inundate an application service with lots of activity to make it unavailable. AppDDoS attacks are not simple packet floods, or malicious traffic; they are seemingly valid traffic that is replicated on a large scale to bring down a victim server. Because the traffic won't match any malicious attack objects, nor is it a flood that triggers most thresholds, it is a very difficult attack to block. Or was; AppDDoS protection is a solution that is integrated into the IPS engine to profile the servers that AppDDoS is protecting, and can identify hosts that cross the application thresholds to enforce an action on them.

AppDDoS essentially takes place in the protocol decoding phase of IPS processing, by matching on contexts within the application and then enforcing rate limiting on the application contexts. To understand how this works, let's examine how AppDDoS protection is triggered, and then how it is enforced.

1. *Firewall policy:* First, traffic must match a permitted rule in the firewall policy which has the Application-Service IDP. This triggers the traffic to be sent to the IPS engine.
2. *IPS engine:* Once the traffic is passed to the IPS engine, it is inspected as usual. During the protocol decoding phase, the SRX will attempt to determine if the

thresholds have been met or surpassed in the Application-DDoS rulebase. The following stages occur for AppDDoS processing:

a. *Connection threshold monitoring (stage 1):* The first phase of AppDDoS processing is to monitor for a connection rate threshold (at the Layer 4 level) against a particular server. This is measured in connections per second. Until this threshold is reached, no additional monitoring is performed for AppDDoS.

b. *Context profiling (stage 2):* Once the connection rate threshold has been passed in stage 1, the SRX begins to monitor the connections for a rate limit for context matching. If a certain number of contexts are met (within 60 seconds) along with a certain threshold for an individual value for that threshold, one of two things can happen:

   Application screening: Strict application limits can be placed on the traffic to limit the absolute number of connections that match the associated context and values. These connections can be dropped, closed, or permitted.

   Botnet protection: The SRX advances to the beginning of the next stage, stage 3.

3. *Botnet protection (Stage 3):* Once the threshold of context and value has been met for the monitored server (for all connections matching the AppDDoS profiles), final action can be taken against offenders. The botnet protection stage monitors clients on a source IP basis, to see if individual source IPs go over the threshold. Because normal users typically would not request the same web page 50 times in two seconds (thresholds are configurable and granular), the AppDDoS protection can identify automated hosts performing attacks, versus legitimate users. Source IPs that have been identified as botnet clients will have whatever action is defined for that rule.

   a. *Actions:* Actions are taken on the flow that crosses the threshold defined for AppDDoS. Four actions can be taken as part of AppDDoS at the time of this writing.

      The Close-Server action sends a TCP RST to the destination web server monitored by AppDDoS and blocks all further traffic from being transmitted in this flow. There is only a Close-Server action, and not a Close-Client or Close-Client-and-Server action, because the device is primarily trying to protect the servers from malicious clients, and to do so, it must minimize the resources consumed by the malicious activity on the server.

      The Drop-Connection action silently drops the connection in both directions.

      The Drop-Packet action silently drops the packet that crossed the threshold in the flow (typically used only for UDP/non-TCP flows).

      The No-Action action performs no action on the offending flow.

   b. *IP Actions:* IP Actions are the actions that can be taken on future flows. In the case of AppDDoS, these are always taken on the source IP, which is unlike the

IPS rulebase that performs these actions according to a number of other factors. The reason for this is that the device is primarily concerned with protecting servers from malicious clients with AppDDoS, so the configuration and functionality reflect that. IP Actions also have the timeout value configurable to determine how long the offending hosts should have the IP Action enforced. This is configurable in seconds on an AppDDoS rule-by-rule basis. Finally, IP Actions can be logged (IP-Notify will implicitly log) if logging is enabled for that IP Action rule.

The IP-Block action silently prevents any connections from the offending source from being established until the timeout period has expired in the IP Action Table.

With the IP-Close action, any future connections made by the offending source are closed (and all traffic is blocked, so no session will be passed to the server) until the timeout associated with that host has expired. This is useful for explicitly notifying the host that the connection is being closed, rather than silently dropping it.

With the IP-Rate-Limit action, as of Junos 10.1 administrators can rate-limit connections from offending sources from being established (in connections per second) once the threshold has been met. This action can be enforced on the source until the timeout has expired.

The IP-Notify action simply generates a log when a source that has been placed in the IP Action Table has surpassed its connection limit, and tries to create new sessions. The new sessions will be permitted but a log is generated. It's a useful tool for allowing administrators to investigate suspicious hosts without interfering with the traffic.

Note that IPS inspection can be combined with AppDDoS. IPS inspection happens after AppDDoS for any given flow, and can provide additional protection against exploit-specific attacks. AppDDoS performs much better than IPS because it does not require as much in-depth packet processing (where IPS must do extensive attack matching), but adding AppDDoS *in addition to* IPS processing does not have as significant an impact compared to just IPS itself, since AppDDoS inspection is built on the infrastructure that IPS would normally perform anyway.

AppDDoS profiles

AppDDoS profiles are to the Application-DDoS rulebase what attack objects are to the IPS rulebase. Just as attack objects define what to match as part of the IPS rulebase, AppDDoS profiles define the thresholds that should be met as part of the Application-DDoS rulebase. As mentioned in the preceding section, there are three stages of AppDDoS processing within the IPS engine.

Here are the properties of the AppDDoS profile:

Connection-Rate-Threshold
: This defines the number of connections per second to move from stage 1 to stage 2 of AppDDoS processing.

Service
: This defines the Layer 7 application that this profile is inspecting. As of Junos 10.2, only HTTP and DNS are officially supported, and therefore the rest of the applications are hidden, but may still be configured. More support for applications should be coming in future Junos releases, so check the release notes and documentation.

Context
: One or more application contexts can be defined for a single AppDDoS profile. This is the application context described earlier in the chapter (such as `http-url-get`) and is used to define threshold setting for different contexts. Within a context there are several values that can, or must, be configured, to define the stage 2 and stage 3 behaviors:

  `Hit-Rate-Threshold`
  : This defines how many times the context must be "hit" within a 60-second period, also known as a *tick*. For instance, if the `Hit-Rate-Threshold` was 100 for `http-url-get`, 100 matches would have to be executed on `http-url-get` that matched that application profile defined in the AppDDoS rulebase. This is mandatory to configure.

  `Value-Hit-Rate-Threshold`
  : Whereas `Hit-Rate-Threshold` refers to a context match, `Value-Hit-Rate-Threshold` defines the threshold that a "value" within a context is hit in 60 seconds before passing the threshold. It is used in conjunction with `Hit-Rate-Threshold` to move from stage 2 to stage 3 of processing, and it is a mandatory component. For example, in the case of the `http-url-get` context, the value within that context would be the URL of the resource that is being requested, such as "index.html" or "story.html". Note that you do not configure what contexts to match, because the system automatically tracks those contexts individually as part of `Value-Hit-Rate-Threshold`. Once `Hit-Rate-Threshold` (on a context) and `Value-Hit-Rate-Threshold` (on the value within a context) have surpassed the thresholds defined, the AppDDoS protection can either perform an action to rate-limit access across the board, or move from stage 2 to stage 3. This is mandatory to configure.

  `Max-Context-Values`
  : As mentioned in the description for `Value-Hit-Rate-Threshold`, the system automatically tracks the values within a context for you, and no additional configuration is needed. The problem here is that it can take a lot of resources for the SRX to monitor if AppDDoS is inspecting a lot of contexts and servers. To help focus on the most important values to track, you can define how many

contexts to track with the `Max-Context-Values` parameter. Think of this as the top *X* values that are tracked. For instance, if you defined this as 100, the top 100 values within that context are tracked. Up to 10,000 values are supported. This configuration is optional.

`Exclude-Context-Values`
: Since the system automatically classifies the values, you may have some specific values that you don't want to track. The `Exclude-Context-Values` command allows you to explicitly define which values to ignore, so these won't impact the tracking of the different thresholds. For instance, on a web server, you might be most interested in matching the most computationally expensive requests, but ignoring the others. You can define regular expression values for which contexts to ignore. This configuration is optional.

`Time-Binding-Count`
: Once `Hit-Rate-Threshold` and `Value-Hit-Rate-Threshold` of stage 2 have been hit, if stage 3 botnet protection is enabled the `time-binding-count` will define how many times an individual source host triggers the context/value pair before it is in violation of the thresholds. This goes hand in hand with `Time-Binding-Period` to define the threshold. Essentially, the system tracks each individual source IP for how many times it hits the context/value pairs, and if it goes above `Time-Binding-Count` within `Time-Binding-Period`, it is flagged for being in violation of the AppDDoS profile and the actions defined in the AppDDoS rule are taken. This is mandatory when doing stage 3 botnet protection.

`Time-Binding-Period`
: This is the period in seconds that is used to define the threshold that must be surpassed for stage 3. The threshold is expressed as `Time-Binding-Count/Time-Binding-Period`.

Custom Attack Groups and Objects

SRX IPS offers an extremely powerful feature that enables you to define your own groups (of both predefined and custom attack objects) along with your own custom attack objects. Although the casual IPS administrator may not need to define custom attack objects, the ability to customize attacks into groups is key to being able to make the administration of an IPS policy much easier to enforce.

Static attack groups

A static attack group is essentially a group that you manually add attack objects and groups to (both predefined and custom) which will not add members during attack updates. If attack objects are modified as part of an attack update, they are updated in the group; if they are deleted, they are removed from the group. But no new attack objects are added to this group. Static groups are very useful if you want strict control over adding new attacks into attack groups during signature updates to ensure that you don't cause unexpected results with new attack objects. The only things you need to define for static groups are the members that are added to this group.

Dynamic attack groups

Dynamic attack groups provide administrators with a powerful ability to adjust to new threats when new attack objects are downloaded from Juniper. Whereas static attack groups allow you to create groups that don't automatically change with signature attack updates, dynamic attack groups do change. And they have very intelligent controls for defining what should be added or removed with attack updates. Dynamic attack groups utilize filters to define the attributes of attack objects that would select them to be implemented in the group. Additionally, you can override members in the groups to exclude them if need be.

You can use filter categories to select the attacks for the group. When you define multiple filters, they essentially form a logical AND between filters. For instance, if you define Category=HTTP and Severity=Critical, only attacks that are of that category and severity are present in this group. When new attacks are downloaded, if they fit this criterion they are added to the group. Here's more detail on filter fields you can dial:

Category
: Category defines the Juniper-defined categories for attacks. These are one of the most useful filters to define because they are the applications themselves, such as HTTP, FTP, DNS, and other types of attacks, such as spyware, viruses, Trojan horses, and worms.

Direction
: Direction defines the direction in which the attack takes place, either client-to-server or server-to-client.

False-Positives
: False-Positives is a field that is defined for each object, which defines how frequently false positives are likely to occur with the individual object. Juniper defines these for predefined attack objects; you can configure this field in your custom attack objects.

Performance
: Juniper tries to specify the attack object performance for the attack objects. This is not an exact science, and performance is typically holistic for the policy as a whole, rather than for an individual attack object. You can also specify this for custom attack objects and you can use this filter to only select the appropriate attacks based on performance impacts. The performance impact of signatures is as follows: 0 = Unknown, 1 = Fast, 5 = Normal, and 9 = Slow. You can use performance filtering in the dynamic attack groups to filter out slow-performing attack objects. Note that generally, Juniper will put slow-performing attack objects under the MISC attack group.

Products
: Juniper defines products to which the predefined attack objects apply—for instance, protecting against attacks on specific operating systems, services, applications, and other software.

Recommended
: This filter is simply a field. If Recommended is selected, only attacks that are marked with the `Recommended` attribute are selected. Juniper defines the `Recommended` flag for attacks that are part of the recommended policy, and you can specify this flag for custom attacks as well.

Service
: Service defines the actual application protocol (e.g., HTTP, FTP, DNS, SMB, SMTP, etc.) that the attack belongs to. This is similar to some of the attacks defined under the category configuration.

Severity
: You can use the Severity field (as we did earlier in this chapter) to define what traffic should be selected based on the severity defined for the attack object.

Custom attack objects

Thousands of predefined attack objects are available from Juniper as part of the company's security subscription services, but sometimes you may need to define your own custom attack signatures. For instance, if you have in-house developed applications or applications that use specialized protocols that are not standard, Juniper may not have any protection for these types of applications. Additionally, you may want to use the IPS to prevent against certain communication, such as users accessing certain websites or downloading certain types of files. You can control all of these easily through the SRX IPS functionality, but it may take just a bit of work upfront to configure. Once you understand the process, it is simple to create new attack objects, and you can do so quite quickly.

Juniper also has a comprehensive signature creation guide that is available by searching the Juniper Support Knowledge Base for *custom attack objects*.

Finally, if you are having an issue creating a custom signature, and you have a valid Juniper IPS support agreement, you can open a case with JTAC. Be sure to include your configuration and a PCAP of the traffic you are trying to classify so that they can better assist you.

The following parameters are part of the IPS configuration for custom attack objects:

Recommended Action
: Recommended Action allows you to define the recommended action that is used should this attack object be selected in an IPS rule which says that the action should be recommended. This is not a required field.

Severity

Severity defines the severity at which this attack should be listed. This can have significance on more than just the logs themselves; it can also impact the object's placement if referencing severities elsewhere such as in dynamic attack groups.

Time-Binding

Time-Binding is an optional attribute you can use to define events that may not be malicious, but if triggered multiple times (such as through an authentication failure) should be considered malicious. As part of Time-Binding, you can define the count (or events per minute) that the attack must be triggered before considering the attack valid, and the Scope, which defines whether the binding is based on a source (one source, multiple destinations), a destination (multiple sources, one destination), or peer (one source, one destination). For authentication failures, it is typically based on the "peer" scope. IP actions are useful when Time-Bindings are met to prevent the same attacker from initiating new connections.

Attack-Type

The Attack-Type defines whether the attack is a protocol anomaly, a signature, or a compound (chain) attack object:

Protocol anomaly

Protocol anomaly attack detection must be programmed into the detector engine, but you can still create your own custom attack objects based on the predefined protocol anomaly objects.

Direction specifies in which stream of the communication the detection should be applied. This can be Client to Server, Server to Client, or Both. It is recommended that you only apply the custom signature in the direction that it occurs to improve performance.

Service defines the Layer 7 application within which the protocol anomaly attack object should be checking for a condition.

Shellcode defines the platform that the victim is running to determine the applicable shellcode for that platform.

Test defines the actual protocol anomaly test condition that is used within the attack object to define a violation condition to trigger the attack object.

Signature

Signature-based attack objects will be the most common form of attack object to configure. This is where you use regular expression matching to define what attack objects should be matched by the detector engine.

Direction specifies in which stream of the communication the detection should be applied. This can be Client to Server, Server to Client, or Both. It is recommended that you only apply the custom signature in the direction that it will occur to improve performance.

Contexts are for signature-based attack objects to define where to look in the message for the attack. About 600 contexts are available at the time of this writing. Specifying the correct context is important to ensure accuracy and performance. You also have generic contexts such as "streams" which identify where in the bytestream to search for the attack objects.

Pattern is the actual regular expression used to detect the signature within the context within which it occurs. This is mandatory for signature-based attack objects.

There is a lot of confusion over RegExp and Pattern. Pattern is required to provide matching within the context. Technically, Pattern is not based on Perl Compatible Regular Expressions (PCREs), although it is very similar. RegExp allows you to add an additional layer of matching using PCRE on top of Pattern to match attacks. This comes at a decrease in performance compared to pattern matching. If you don't need RegExp, you should omit it.

Protocol defines additional parameters that might be found in the IP, ICMP, TCP, or UDP headers. This allows you to provide additional factors for attack detection. For instance, you can match specific TCP flags such as SYN, ACK, FIN, Window Size, Sequence Number, and so forth.

Protocol-Binding defines the Layer 7 application in which the attack should be detected. This information is used with the application ID engine to select the relevant contexts and attacks that can be detected in that flow. Additionally, starting in Junos 10.1, nested applications are supported, such as Layer 7 applications that run over another Layer 7 application. The most common example of this is web applications running over HTTP, such as Facebook, YouTube, and other web apps.

Shellcode defines what platform the victim will be running so that the associated shellcode can be checked for. This is not mandatory.

Negate allows you to specify that the attack object should be triggered if none of the specified criteria are matched. This should be used with caution, and is typically done in chain objects.

Chain

Chain attack objects are objects that reference multiple attack objects (custom or predefined) and can be composed of protocol anomaly and/or signature-based attack objects. Chains allow you to define Boolean expressions and ordering to make complex matching on a single criterion as well as on multiple factors.

Expression defines a Boolean expression to use to evaluate the defined members and find a match. For instance, this could be an expression with AND, OR, NOT logic among the attack members.

Member defines other predefined or custom attack objects that are evaluated as part of this chain attack object. Up to 32 members can be defined for a single chain object. If no expression is used, all members must be matched for the chain object to be triggered.

Order is just a flag in the chain object to define whether the "order" in which the members are defined should be the order in which they are detected. This can go hand in hand with Expression, but remember that if you are using both Order and Expression, the order in which the attacks are detected must be the order the attack objects are listed (top to bottom) in addition to satisfying the Expression. If you are only using Order, all attack members must be matched in the order they are listed.

Protocol-Binding defines the Layer 7 application in which the attack should be detected. This information is used with the application ID engine to select the relevant contexts and attacks that can be detected in that flow. Additionally, starting in Junos 10.1, nested applications are supported, such as Layer 7 applications that run over another Layer 7 application. The most common example of this is web applications running over HTTP, such as Facebook, YouTube, and other web apps.

The `reset` flag indicates that multiple matches in the same flow should trigger a new alert.

Two scopes can be defined: known as Session and Transaction. Session matches items within the same flow, but across actual transactions (e.g., different Layer 7 messages), while Transaction is the attacks within the same transaction (Layer 7 message). When in doubt, use Session.

Although creating custom signatures may seem like an advanced task, especially with the use of regular expressions, lots of content on building effective regular expressions is available and it can be very helpful. Of course, you can always search the Internet, but the widely acclaimed regular expression book, *Mastering Regular Expressions (http://oreilly.com/catalog/9780596528126/)* by Jeffrey E.F. Friedl (O'Reilly), may be your best source.

Configuring IPS Features on the SRX

Wow. If you have read this far, you've gone through a detailed explanation of just about every component of SRX IPS functionality. Now you can learn how to actually configure these different features within the SRX.

From here on out, you will learn the configuration of the individual elements, as well as focus on common "real-world" implementations of these features. Let's get started.

Getting Started with IPS on the SRX

We should perform a few steps before we configure SRX IPS. Here is a list of things to do before configuring the SRX for IPS functionality:

1. Install the license.

   You must install an IDP license before you can download any attack objects. If you are using only custom attack objects, you don't need to install a license (earlier versions had a bug where they required it), but if you want to download Juniper predefined attack objects, you must have this license. Juniper provides you with the ability to download a 30-day trial license to permit this functionality for a brief period of time to evaluate the functionality. We covered license installation earlier in the book; all you need is the `request system license add` command either specifying a file, or copying and pasting it into the terminal.

2. Configure network access.

   Before you can download the attack objects, you must have network connectivity to either the Juniper download server or a local server from which the signatures can be downloaded. This typically requires network configuration (IP/Netmask, routing, and DNS) and permitted access to reach the server. At the time of this writing, HTTP proxies are not supported, but you can configure a local web server from which to serve the files.

3. Download attack objects.

   Before deploying the IPS, you must first download the attack objects from which the policy will be compiled. Triggering a manual download does not configure the SRX to download them in the future, so you must configure automatic updates to download them.

4. Install attack objects.

   Once the download has been completed, you must install the attack updates before they are actually used in a policy. If you already have a policy configured, you do not need to recommit the policy—installing the updates adds them to the policy. The installation process compiles the attack objects which have been downloaded to a stage directory into the configured policy.

5. Download policy templates (optional).

   You can optionally download and install predefined IPS policies known as policy templates provided by Juniper to get started. After finishing this chapter, you should be able to configure your own policy, so you probably won't need policy templates.

If you are attempting to download the attack objects in an HA chassis cluster, you should use the fxp0 interface configuration as described in Chapter 4 If you do not use the fxp0 interface, the secondary control plane will not be able to download its update.

Getting started example

Our first example shows the basic configuration and download of attack objects and how to install them prior to actually configuring a security policy. The steps in this example are as follows:

1. Check IPS status.
2. Download attack objects including sensor updates.
3. Install attack objects and sensor updates.
4. Download policy templates.
5. Install policy templates.

```
root@SRX5800-1> show security idp security-package-version
node0:
--------------------------------------------------------------------------

 Attack database version:1551(Thu Feb 25 13:37:46 2009)
 Detector version :10.2.140100209


root@SRX5800-1> request security idp security-package download full-update
node0:
--------------------------------------------------------------------------
Will be processed in async mode. Check the status using the status checking CLI


root@SRX5800-1> request security idp security-package download status
node0:
--------------------------------------------------------------------------
Done;Successfully downloaded from
(https://services.netscreen.com/cgi-bin/index.cgi).
Version info:1621(Fri Mar 5 12:56:13 2010, Detector=10.3.140100209)


root@SRX5800-1> request security idp security-package install
node0:
--------------------------------------------------------------------------
Will be processed in async mode. Check the status using the status checking CLI


root@SRX5800-1> request security idp security-package install status
node0:
--------------------------------------------------------------------------
Done;Attack DB update : successful - [UpdateNumber=1621,ExportDate=Fri
Mar 5 12:56:13 2010,Detector=10.3.140100209]
   Updating control-plane with new detector : successful
   Updating data-plane with new attack or detector : successful

root@SRX5800-1> show security idp status
node0:
--------------------------------------------------------------------------
State of IDP: 2-default,    Up since: 2010-03-04 13:25:32 PST (4d 03:45 ago)
```

```
Packets/second: 5601        Peak: 7289 @ 2010-03-04 13:25:32 PST
KBits/second :        Peak: 2219660 @ 2010-03-04 13:25:32 PST
Latency (microseconds): [min: 67] [max: 105] [avg: 96]

Packet Statistics:
 [ICMP: 0] [TCP: 0] [UDP: 0] [Other: 0]

Flow Statistics:
 ICMP: [Current: 17] [Max: 26 @ 2010-03-04 13:25:32 PST]
 TCP: [Current: 460] [Max: 851 @ 2010-03-04 13:25:32 PST]
 UDP: [Current: 623] [Max: 694 @ 2010-03-04 13:25:32 PST]
 Other: [Current: 15] [Max: 22 @ 2010-03-04 13:25:32 PST]

Session Statistics:
 [ICMP: 17] [TCP: 460] [UDP: 623] [Other: 15]

Number of SSL Sessions : 0


 Policy Name : SRX5800-IDP
 Running Detector Version : 10.3.1400100209

Forwarding process mode : regular
```

It's important to understand that compiling and applying an IPS policy can take time (up to 20 minutes depending on the number of attack objects and the size of the policy). On the SRX, when you update attack objects or commit a new IPS configuration the SRX essentially triggers a job to start to compile the IPS attack objects into a policy that the detector engine understands. This is done by a low-priority process in the control plane, and no change is made to the data plane until the policy has been fully compiled, at which point the new policy is applied to the data plane. Running the `show security idp status` command gives some insight regarding whether the new policy has been successfully compiled, but if you want more detail, you need to run a trace on the IDP process to determine if it finished compiling (we will cover this in "Troubleshooting IPS" on page 457).

Configuring automatic updates

Although updating the SRX manually is a powerful way to inspect the new signatures before actually deploying them, it does require much more administrative dedication to keep signatures updated. You can configure the SRX to automatically update itself on an interval of your choosing to ensure that the SRX has up-to-date signatures without administrative intervention. This example demonstrates how to configure this functionality with the following objectives:

Enable automatic downloads to start May 7 at midnight, and attempt to download every 24 hours if there is an update. If the update stalls for more than five minutes, after a new version has been downloaded the SRX should install it.

```
{primary:node0}[edit]
root@SRX5800-1# edit security idp security-package
```

```
{primary:node0}[edit security idp security-package]
root@SRX5800-1# set install automatic start-time 05-07.00:00 interval 24
download-timeout 5 enable
```

Useful IPS files

At the time of this writing, Juniper was still enhancing the CLI and J-Web to make them more usable for viewing predefined IPS objects (attacks, groups, applications, etc.). The exception is NSM, which has these laid out nicely in a table. Until then, all of the information is available on the SRX. You just need to know where to look.

You should download the attack signatures before viewing these files for the updated version.

/var/db/idpd/sec-download/SignatureUpdate.xml
: This file is the entire attack database. It details every attack, and for signature-based attack objects, it also provides the patterns used to match signatures. This file is the motherload of the attack objects and provides you with the most information, but it's in XML format, so you will need to either load it into an XML browser or look at the file with a text editor.

/var/db/idpd/sec-download/groups.xml
: This file is the list of different predefined groups and the attack objects that fit into them. It's essentially a list of dynamic attack object groups that define the properties that attack objects should match to be part of the group.

/var/db/idpd/sec-repository/attack.list
: This file lists all attacks known by the SRX in their appropriate name format.

/var/db/idpd/sec-repository/attack-group.list
: This file lists all attack groups on the SRX based on their categories.

/var/db/idpd/sec-repository/application.list
: This file lists all the AppID applications that are known to the system and their respective standard ports.

Here's how to access each file, and include a snippet of the content within it:

```
root@SRX5800-1> file show /var/db/idpd/sec-download/SignatureUpdate.xml |
find Metasploit
  <Name>SCAN:METASPLOIT:LSASS</Name>
  <DisplayName>SCAN: Metasploit LSASS Exploit</DisplayName>
  <Severity>Major</Severity>
  <Category>SCAN</Category>
  <Keywords>metasploit</Keywords>
  <Recommended>true</Recommended>
  <RecommendedAction>Drop</RecommendedAction>
  <Description>This signature detects the security-audit tool Metasploit
```

```
as it uses the LSASS Exploit to attack a host. This can be a probe from a
security test, or it could be an attacker using Metasploit to compromise your
network.</Description>
  <References>
  <CVE>CVE-2003-0533</CVE>
  <BugTraq>10108</BugTraq>
  <URL>http://www.microsoft.com/technet/security/bulletin/MS04-011.mspx</URL>
  </References>
  <Supersedes />
  <Attacks>
  <Attack>
   <Type>chain</Type>
   <InternalID>917</InternalID>
   <ExportID>3</ExportID>
   <LastModified>2009-11-18</LastModified>
   <ActivationDate>2005-08-08</ActivationDate>
   <FalsePositives>unknown</FalsePositives>
   <Performance>0</Performance>
   <Service>SMB</Service>
   <TimeBinding>
   <Scope>none</Scope>
   <Count>1</Count>
   </TimeBinding>
   <Hidden>false</Hidden>
   <Port />
   <Application />
   <Expression />
   <Order>no</Order>
   <Reset>no</Reset>
   <ScopeOption />
   <Members>
   <Attack>
    <Member>m01</Member>
    <Type>Signature</Type>
    <Direction>CTS</Direction>
    <Flow>control</Flow>
    <Shellcode>no</Shellcode>
    <Context>smb-open-filename</Context>
    <Negate>false</Negate>
    <Offset>0</Offset>
    <Pattern><![CDATA[\\?\[lsarpc\].*]]></Pattern>
    <Regex />
   </Attack>
   <Attack>
    <Member>m02</Member>
    <Type>Signature</Type>
    <Direction>CTS</Direction>
    <Flow>control</Flow>
    <Shellcode>no</Shellcode>
    <Context>smb-native-lanman</Context>
    <Negate>false</Negate>
    <Offset>0</Offset>
    <Pattern><![CDATA[(Metasploit\sFramework|LameCiscoIDSDevelopers)]]></Pattern>
    <Regex />
   </Attack>
```

```
      </Members>
      <Versions>
      <Version>idp-srx9.2</Version>
      </Versions>
    </Attack>
    </Attacks>
    <Direction>
    <Value>CTS</Value>
    </Direction>
    <FalsePositives>
    <Value>unknown</Value>
    </FalsePositives>
    <Performance>
    <Value>0</Value>
    </Performance>
    <Service>
    <Value>smb</Value>
    </Service>
    <Type>
    <Value>Signature</Value>
    </Type>
  </Entry>
  <Entry>

root@SRX5800-1> file show /var/db/idpd/sec-download/groups.xml | find
"HTTP - Critical"
    <Name>HTTP - Critical</Name>
    <Type>dynamic</Type>
    <Filters>
    <Filter>
      <Field>Category</Field>
      <Values>
      <Value>HTTP</Value>
      </Values>
    </Filter>
    <Filter>
      <Expression>And</Expression>
      <Field>Direction</Field>
      <Values>
      <Value>cts</Value>
      <Value>!stc</Value>
      <Value>!any</Value>
      </Values>
    </Filter>
    <Filter>
      <Field>Performance</Field>
      <Values>
      <Value>0</Value>
      <Value>1</Value>
      <Value>5</Value>
      </Values>
    </Filter>
    <Filter>
      <Field>Severity</Field>
      <Values>
```

```
   <Value>Critical</Value>
   </Values>
  </Filter>
  </Filters>
 </Group>

root@SRX5800-1> file show /var/db/idpd/sec-repository/attack.list
"APP:AFP-LEN-OF"
"APP:AI:NO-MATCH"
"APP:AI:PARTIAL-MATCH"
"APP:AJP12-SHUTDOWN"
"APP:AMANDA:AMANDA-ROOT-OF1"
"APP:AMANDA:AMANDA-ROOT-OF2"
"APP:APT-WWW-PROXY:AWPLOG-DOS"
"APP:ARKEIA:AGENT-ACCESS"
"APP:ARKEIA:AGENT-CONFIG"
"APP:ARKEIA:DEFAULT-ADMIN-PW"
"APP:ARKEIA:DEFAULT-PASSWORD"
"APP:ARKEIA:TYPE-77-OF"
"APP:BAKBON-NETVAULT-INT-OF"
"APP:BORLAND:VISIBROKER"
"APP:BRG-MAIL-US-PASS"
"APP:CA:ALERT-SRV-OF"
"APP:CA:ARCSRV:BCK-MSG"
"APP:CA:ARCSRV:CAMEDIASRV"
"APP:CA:ARCSRV:DIRTRAV"
"APP:CA:ARCSRV:FILE-UPLOAD"
"APP:CA:ARCSRV:HSM-OF"
"APP:CA:ARCSRV:LND-FILE-MANIP"
"APP:CA:ARCSRV:LND-OF"
---(more)---

root@SRX5800-1> file show /var/db/idpd/sec-repository/attack-group.list
"APP"
"APP - All"
"APP - Critical"
"APP - Info"
"APP - Major"
"APP - Minor"
"APP - Warning"
"Additional Web Services - Critical"
"Additional Web Services - Info"
"Additional Web Services - Major"
"Additional Web Services - Minor"
"Additional Web Services - Warning"
"All Attacks"
"Anomaly"
"Anomaly - All"
"Anomaly - Critical"
"Anomaly - Info"
"Anomaly - Major"
"Anomaly - Minor"
"Anomaly - Warning"
"Attack Type"
"BSD"
```

```
"BSD - Services - All"
---(more)---

root@SRX5800-1> file show /var/db/idpd/sec-repository/application.list
"ApplicationID:AIM" 61
"ApplicationID:APPLEJUICE" 125
"ApplicationID:ARES" 95
"ApplicationID:BGP" 201
"ApplicationID:BITTORRENT" 60
"ApplicationID:BITTORRENT-DHT" 131
"ApplicationID:BITTORRENT-TRACKER-URL" 68
"ApplicationID:CHARGEN" 39
"ApplicationID:CUPS" 146
"ApplicationID:CVS" 147
"ApplicationID:DHCP" 34
"ApplicationID:DIRECTCONNECT" 98
"ApplicationID:DISCARD" 13
"ApplicationID:DNP3" 175
"ApplicationID:DNS" 191
"ApplicationID:DOT-NET" 182
"ApplicationID:DRDA" 183
"ApplicationID:ECHO" 12
"ApplicationID:EDONKEY" 100
"ApplicationID:EDONKEY-TCP" 189
"ApplicationID:FINGER" 8
"ApplicationID:FREECAST" 163
"ApplicationID:FTP" 63
---(more)---
```

The output of these commands shares lot of details regarding the individual components and the different predefined lists available on the SRX. At the time of this writing, the only graphical way to view this information is through the NSM. In the future, the attacks and the attack groupings will likely be added into J-Web and Junos Space to improve the user experience so that you can graphically view, modify, and create the objects, as well as the groups themselves.

Configuring static and dynamic attack groups

Unless you are going to use predefined attack groups, or the attack objects themselves, you should find yourself configuring static and dynamic attack groups prior to defining the policies. Defining these groups is quite simple, especially when you are familiar with the predefined attack object groups and attacks. This example shows how to configure the following groups:

- A static attack group named Aurora which includes the attacks HTTP:STC:SCRIPT:UNI-SHELLCODE and HTTP:STC:SCRIPT:FUNC-REASSIGN, which are two known attack objects that are triggered by the Aurora Internet Explorer exploit
- A static attack group named Protect-FTP which contains the predefined attack groups FTP – Critical, FTP – Major, and FTP – Minor

- A dynamic attack group called Malicious-Activity that contains all shellcode, worms, spyware, viruses, and Trojan horse signatures of severity Critical, Major, and Minor
- A dynamic attack group called Protect-Internal-Clients that contains all server-to-client attacks that are of severity Critical, Major, and Minor

```
{primary:node0}[edit]
root@SRX5800-1# edit security idp custom-attack-group Aurora

{primary:node0}[edit security idp custom-attack Aurora]
root@SRX5800-1#set group-members [ HTTP:STC:SCRIPT:UNI-SHELLCODE
HTTP:STC:SCRIPT:FUNC-REASSIGN ]

{primary:node0}[edit security idp custom-attack Aurora]
root@SRX5800-1# show
group-members [ HTTP:STC:SCRIPT:UNI-SHELLCODE HTTP:STC:SCRIPT:FUNC-REASSIGN ];

{primary:node0}[edit security idp custom-attack-group Aurora]
root@SRX5800-1# up

{primary:node0}[edit security idp]
root@SRX5800-1# edit custom-attack-group Protect-FTP

{primary:node0}[edit security idp custom-attack-group Protect-FTP]
root@SRX5800-1# set group-members [ "FTP - Critical" "FTP - Major"
"FTP - Minor" ]

{primary:node0}[edit security idp custom-attack-group Protect-FTP]
root@SRX5800-1# show
group-members [ "FTP - Critical" "FTP - Major" "FTP - Minor" ];

{primary:node0}[edit security idp custom-attack-group Protect-FTP]
root@SRX5800-1# up

{primary:node0}[edit security idp]
root@SRX5800-1# edit dynamic-attack-group Malicious-Activity

{primary:node0}[edit security idp dynamic-attack-group Malicious-Activity]
root@SRX5800-1# set filters severity values [ critical major minor ]

{primary:node0}[edit security idp dynamic-attack-group Malicious-Activity]
root@SRX5800-1# set category values [ SHELLCODE VIRUS WORMS SPYWARE TROJAN]

{primary:node0}[edit security idp dynamic-attack-group Malicious-Activity]
root@SRX5800-1# show
filters {
  severity {
    values [ critical major minor ];
  }
  category {
    values [ SHELLCODE VIRUS WORMS SPYWARE TROJAN ];
  }
}
```

```
{primary:node0}[edit security idp dynamic-attack-group Malicious-Activity]
root@SRX5800-1# up

{primary:node0}[edit security idp]
root@SRX5800-1# edit dynamic-attack-group Protect-Internal-Clients

{primary:node0}[edit security idp dynamic-attack-group Protect-Internal-Clients]
root@SRX5800-1# set filters direction values server-to-client

{primary:node0}[edit security idp dynamic-attack-group Protect-Internal-Clients]
root@SRX5800-1# set filters severity values [ critical major minor ]

{primary:node0}[edit security idp dynamic-attack-group Protect-Internal-Clients]
root@SRX5800-1# show
filters {
  direction {
    values server-to-client;
  }
  severity {
    values [ critical major minor ];
  }
}

{primary:node0}[edit security idp dynamic-attack-group Protect-Internal-Clients]
root@SRX5800-1# top

{primary:node0}[edit]
root@SRX5800-1# commit
node0:
configuration check succeeds
node1:
commit complete
node0:
commit complete
```

Creating a custom attack object

There are many cases in which a customer might want to block against a behavior that may not exploit an actual vulnerability, or perhaps protect an in-house application from an exploit which was discovered internally, while the development team works on correcting the application. For these types of scenarios, you typically have to develop your own signatures to prevent the undesirable conditions. In this example, two different custom attack objects are configured, one a signature-based attack object and the other a compound attack object. Note that we are going to assume a fundamental understanding of regular expressions, as the actual theory behind regular expressions is outside the scope of this book.

- Create a signature-based attack object called Block-Facebook. This attack object is used to block any HTTP traffic going to **.facebook.com* from internal users. Set the severity to Warning.

- Create a compound signature called Compound-Attack which is composed of three members: FTP-User, FTP-DMG, and FTP-EXE. FTP-User is a custom attack object which matches any FTP account with the name User. FTP-DMG matches any request to get a file with the *.dmg* extension, and FTP-EXE does the same but for *.exe* files. This attack should match any session where the login is "user" and they are trying to download a file with an extension of either **.exe* or **.dmg*. Set the severity to Major.

```
[edit]
root@SRX5800-1# edit security idp custom-attack Block-Facebook

[edit security idp custom-attack Block-Facebook]
root@SRX5800-1# set attack-type signature context http-header-host pattern
".*\.\[facebook\.com\]" direction client-to-server

[edit security idp custom-attack Block-Facebook]
root@SRX5800-1# set severity warning

[edit security idp custom-attack Block-Facebook]
root@SRX5800-1#up

[edit security idp]
root@SRX5800-1# edit custom-attack Compound-Attack

[edit security idp custom-attack Compound-Attack]
root@SRX5800-1# set attack-type chain member FTP-DMG attack-type signature
context ftp-get-filename pattern ".*\.\[dmg\]" direction client-to-server

[edit security idp custom-attack Compound-Attack]
root@SRX5800-1# set attack-type chain member FTP-EXE attack-type signature
context ftp-get-filename pattern ".*\.\[exe\]" direction client-to-server

[edit security idp custom-attack Compound-Attack]
root@SRX5800-1# set attack-type chain member FTP-USER attack-type signature
context ftp-username pattern "^user$" direction client-to-server

[edit security idp custom-attack Compound-Attack]
root@SRX5800-1# set attack-type chain expression "(FTP-EXE OR FTP-DMG) AND
FTP-USER"

[edit security idp custom-attack Compound-Attack]
root@SRX5800-1# set severity major

[edit security idp custom-attack Block-Facebook]
root@SRX5800-1#up

[edit security idp]
root@SRX5800-1# show | find custom-attack

[edit security idp]
root@SRX5800# show | find custom-attack
custom-attack Block-Facebook {
    severity warning;
    attack-type {
```

```
            signature {
                context http-header-host;
                pattern ".*\.\[facebook\.com\]";
                direction client-to-server;
            }
        }
    }
    custom-attack Compound-Attack {
        severity major;
        attack-type {
            chain {
                expression "(FTP-EXE OR FTP-DMG) AND FTP-USER";
                member FTP-DMG {
                    attack-type {
                        signature {
                            context ftp-get-filename;
                            pattern ".*\.\[dmg\]";
                            direction client-to-server;
                        }
                    }
                }
                member FTP-EXE {
                    attack-type {
                        signature {
                            context ftp-get-filename;
                            pattern ".*\.\[exe\]";
                            direction client-to-server;
                        }
                    }
                }
                member FTP-USER {
                    attack-type {
                        signature {
                            context ftp-username;
                            pattern "^user$";
                            direction client-to-server;
                        }
                    }
                }
            }
        }
    }

    [edit security idp custom-attack Compound-Attack]
    root@SRX5800-1# top

    [edit]
    root@SRX5800-1# commit
```

Let's examine some of the patterns used in this example. In the Block-Facebook example, we have the pattern `".*\.\[facebook\.com\]"`. All patterns are surrounded by quotations to indicate where the expression starts and stops for the Junos CLI. The `.*` in the beginning indicates that anything can precede or follow the example. The `\.` means we use the \ escape character to take the regular expression literally rather than as a control character. Next we have the \[, which means this will be the beginning of a case-insensitive match (since we don't want to be evaded by any changes in case). Then we have the string `facebook`, followed by `\.com\]`, which indicates that we want to match `.com`, and we close out the case-insensitive match.

In the compound attack example, we use a chain attack composed of three members. The FTP-DMG and FTP-EXE members are essentially the same, just different extensions, so we'll just cover the FTP-EXE example. The pattern `".*\.\[exe\]"` begins with `.*` to indicate that anything can precede or follow the pattern, which is then followed by `\.\[exe\]`, which is used to indicate that we should take the `.` literally as a character rather than as a control character. This is followed by `\[exe\]`, where the `\[` and `\]` indicate that the characters within the boundary will be matched case-insensitively so that we can't be fooled by changes in case. Next, we match the username `user` exactly. We want to ensure that we are not matching a username that merely has the string `user` in it, but rather that the string is exactly `user`, so we use the ^ character to indicate the beginning of the match and the `$` to indicate that there is nothing else in the match. In this example, we don't care about the case, since the username `user` is going to be authenticated by our system. Finally, we use the Boolean expression `(FTP-EXE OR FTP-DMG) AND FTP-USER` to indicate that we will only match when the filename has an *.exe* or *.dmg* extension (since a file will only have one of these) and that the name is `user` for that flow.

Creating, activating, and referencing IPS

Before you can actually perform any inspection, you must define an IPS rulebase, apply it as the active IPS policy (at this time only one IPS policy can be active at a time), and reference this policy in the SRX security policy (firewall) rulebase. Although you could use a predefined policy template for your rulebase, you are going to create your own, since it's much more fun that way.

In this example, you will do the following:

- Create an IPS rulebase called Protect-Everything. You are going to be using the IPS rulebase. For all rules, you should match from Untrust to Trust, log events, and match any source, destination, or default application.
- The first rule should match any attack for the two static groups that you created, and silently drop their connections. Call this rule `Static-Groups`.
- For the two dynamic groups you created, you'll create a rule to match their connections and close both the client and the server, as well as silently drop traffic from future flows for 120 seconds. Call this rule `Dynamic-Groups`.
- You'll perform all of this from the Untrust to Trust direction for any traffic, and then log all of these events.

```
{primary:node0}[edit]
root@SRX5800-1# edit security idp idp-policy Protect-Everything rulebase-ips
```

```
{primary:node0}[edit security idp idp-policy Protect-Everything rulebase-ips]
root@SRX5800-1# set rule Static-Groups match from-zone untrust to-zone trust
source-address any destination-address any application default attacks custom-
attack-groups [ Aurora Protect-FTP ]

{primary:node0}[edit security idp idp-policy Protect-Everything rulebase-ips]
root@SRX5800-1# set rule Static-Groups then action drop-connection

{primary:node0}[edit security idp idp-policy Protect-Everything rulebase-ips]
root@SRX5800-1# set rule Static-Groups then notification log-attacks

{primary:node0}[edit security idp idp-policy Protect-Everything rulebase-ips]
root@SRX5800-1# show
rule Static-Groups {
  match {
    from-zone untrust;
    source-address any;
    to-zone trust;
    destination-address any;
    application default;
    attacks {
      custom-attack-groups [ Aurora Protect-FTP ];
    }
  }
  then {
    action {
      drop-connection;
    }
    notification {
      log-attacks;
    }
  }
}

{primary:node0}[edit security idp idp-policy Protect-Everything rulebase-ips]
root@SRX5800-1# set rule Dynamic-Groups match from-zone untrust to-zone trust
source-address any destination-address any application default attacks dynamic-
attack-groups [ Malicious-Activity Protect-Internal-Clients ]

{primary:node0}[edit security idp idp-policy Protect-Everything rulebase-ips]
root@SRX5800-1# set rule Dynamic-Groups then action close-client-and-server

{primary:node0}[edit security idp idp-policy Protect-Everything rulebase-ips]
root@SRX5800-1# set rule Dynamic-Groups then ip-action ip-block log target
source-address timeout 120

{primary:node0}[edit security idp idp-policy Protect-Everything rulebase-ips]
root@SRX5800-1# set rule Dynamic-Groups then notification log-attacks

{primary:node0}[edit security idp idp-policy Protect-Everything rulebase-ips]
root@SRX5800-1# show rule Dynamic-Groups
match {
  from-zone untrust;
  source-address any;
  to-zone trust;
```

```
    destination-address any;
    application default;
    attacks {
      dynamic-attack-groups [ Malicious-Activity Protect-Internal-Clients ];
    }
  }
  then {
    action {
      close-client-and-server;
    }
    ip-action {
      ip-block;
      target source-address;
      log;
      timeout 120;
    }
    notification {
      log-attacks;
    }
  }

{primary:node0}[edit security idp idp-policy Protect-Everything rulebase-ips]
root@SRX5800-1# up 2

{primary:node0}[edit security idp]
root@SRX5800-1# set active-policy Protect-Everything


{primary:node0}[edit security idp]
root@SRX5800-1# show active-policy
active-policy Protect-Everything;

{primary:node0}[edit security idp]
root@SRX5800-1# top

{primary:node0}[edit]
root@SRX5800-1# edit security policies from-zone untrust to-zone trust

{primary:node0}[edit security policies from-zone untrust to-zone trust]
root@SRX5800-1# set policy Inspect-IPS match source-address any
destination-address any application any

{primary:node0}[edit security policies from-zone untrust to-zone trust]
root@SRX5800-1# set policy Inspect-IPS then permit application-services idp

{primary:node0}[edit security policies from-zone untrust to-zone trust]
root@SRX5800-1# set policy Inspect-IPS then log session-close

{primary:node0}[edit security policies from-zone untrust to-zone trust]
root@SRX5800-1# show
policy Inspect-IPS {
  match {
    source-address any;
    destination-address any;
    application any;
```

```
      }
      then {
        permit {
          application-services {
            idp;
          }
        }
        log {
          session-close;
        }
      }
    }

{primary:node0}[edit security policies from-zone untrust to-zone trust]
root@SRX5800-1# top

{primary:node0}[edit]
root@SRX5800-1# commit
node0:
configuration check succeeds
node1:
commit complete
node0:
commit complete
```

A lot is going on in this example. You have configured your IPS policy and rules, and configured the IPS to assign the active policy and associated firewall rules to send traffic to the IPS engine. Without these steps, the traffic would never be sent to the IPS. One important thing to note is that when you apply this in your environment, it may take some time to compile and apply the IPS policy. It all happens automatically, and no traffic will be disrupted. The best thing to do is to check the output of the `show security idp status` command to see if your active policy (in our case, `Protect-Everything`) has been applied and is active.

Exempt rulebase

Even with the best of intentions, you may find yourself in an IPS scenario where you have unexpectedly blocked legitimate traffic. For instance, if you are running protocol anomaly protection and you have mistaken some nonstandard application behavior that is not really malicious as an attack, it will be dropped according to your policy. To help make a clean IPS rulebase, with simple yet granular overrides, Juniper employs the Exempt rulebase to ensure that we can easily ignore certain scenarios, and at the same time not ignore inspection for the entire connection. In this example, you'll perform the following:

After applying the IPS policy in the last example, some users are complaining that they are not able to access the web server. It turns out that their machines are infected with the FunWebProducts spyware, which adds a toolbar in Internet Explorer applications. It is more of a nuisance than actual malicious software, so you don't want to block your customers from accessing your web server at 172.31.100.60. Create an Exempt policy to not block this attack from the Internet to the 172.31.100.60 web server with the FunWebProducts attack object.

```
{primary:node0}[edit]
root@SRX5800-1# set security zones security-zone trust address-book address
Web-Server-172.31.100.60/32 172.31.100.60/32

{primary:node0}[edit security zones security-zone trust address-book]
root@SRX5800-1# show
address Web-Server-172.31.100.60/32 172.31.100.60/32;

{primary:node0}[edit]
root@SRX5800-1# edit security idp idp-policy Protect-Everything rulebase-exempt

{primary:node0}[edit security idp idp-policy Protect-Everything rulebase-exempt]
root@SRX5800-1# set rule FunWebProducts match from-zone untrust to-zone trust
source-address any destination-address Web-Server-172.31.100.60/32 attacks
predefined-attacks SPYWARE:BH:FUNWEBPRODUCTS

{primary:node0}[edit security idp idp-policy Protect-Everything rulebase-exempt]
root@SRX5800-1# show
rule FunWebProducts {
  match {
    from-zone untrust;
    source-address any;
    to-zone trust;
    destination-address Web-Server-172.31.100.60/32;
    attacks {
      predefined-attacks SPYWARE:BH:FUNWEBPRODUCTS;
    }
  }
}

{primary:node0}[edit security policies from-zone untrust to-zone trust]
root@SRX5800-1# top

{primary:node0}[edit]
root@SRX5800-1# commit
node0:
configuration check succeeds
node1:
commit complete
node0:
commit complete
```

AppDDoS protection

DoS attacks against applications are very difficult attacks to prevent; however, the SRX has the ability to implement a powerful mechanism to protect against these attacks.

AppDDoS is supported only on the high-end SRX at this time.

In this example you are going to use the following parameters:

- Protect the web server defined in the Exempt example from attacks against its HTTP web server.
- Typically, there should be no more than 100 connections per second from clients to the web server.
- The web server is providing static content. Typically, no more than 200 accesses against the HTTP-URL-PARSED context will be triggered, with fewer than 20 hits against a specific value.
- Only track the top 20 values for this profile.
- No client should be accessing the content more than three times within 60 seconds. If a client accesses the content more than three times per minute, you should drop their connection, and reset future connections for 10 minutes.

```
{primary:node0}[edit]
root@SRX5800-1# edit security idp application-ddos Protect-Web-Server

{primary:node0}[edit security idp application-ddos Protect-Web-Server]
root@SRX5800-1# set service http

{primary:node0}[edit security idp application-ddos Protect-Web-Server]
root@SRX5800-1# set connection-rate-threshold 100

{primary:node0}[edit security idp application-ddos Protect-Web-Server]
root@SRX5800-1# set context http-url-parsed hit-rate-threshold 200
value-hit-rate-threshold 20 max-context-values 20 time-binding-count 3 time-
binding-period 60

{primary:node0}[edit security idp application-ddos Protect-Web-Server]
root@SRX5800-1# show
service http;
connection-rate-threshold 100;
context http-url-parsed {
  hit-rate-threshold 200;
  value-hit-rate-threshold 20;
  max-context-values 20;
  time-binding-count 3;
  time-binding-period 60;
}

{primary:node0}[edit security idp application-ddos Protect-Web-Server]
root@SRX5800-1# up

{primary:node0}[edit]
root@SRX5800-1# edit idp-policy Protect-Everything rulebase-ddos


{primary:node0}[edit security idp idp-policy Protect-Everything rulebase-ddos]
root@SRX5800-1# show
rule Protect-Web-Server {
  match {
    from-zone untrust;
```

```
      source-address any;
      to-zone trust;
      destination-address Web-Server-172.31.100.60/32;
      application default;
      application-ddos {
        Protect-Web-Server;
      }
    }
    then {
      action {
        drop-connection;
      }
      ip-action {
        ip-close;
        log;
        timeout 600;
      }
    }
  }

{primary:node0}[edit security idp idp-policy Protect-Everything rulebase-ddos]
root@SRX5800-1# set rule Protect-Web-Server match from-zone untrust to-zone
trust source-address any destination-address Web-Server-172.31.100.60/32
application default application-ddos Protect-Web-Server

{primary:node0}[edit security idp idp-policy Protect-Everything rulebase-ddos]
root@SRX5800-1# set rule Protect-Web-Server then action drop-connection

{primary:node0}[edit security idp idp-policy Protect-Everything rulebase-ddos]
root@SRX5800-1# set rule Protect-Web-Server then ip-action
ip-close log timeout 600

{primary:node0}[edit security idp idp-policy Protect-Everything rulebase-ddos]
root@SRX5800-1# top

{primary:node0}[edit]
root@SRX5800-1# commit
node0:
configuration check succeeds
node1:
commit complete
node0:
commit complete
```

SSL decryption

Many modern web applications deal with sensitive information such as credit card and Social Security numbers, medical and financial records, and other forms of authentication that require privacy. The problem from a security perspective is that when SSL is used, if it is terminated on the web server itself the IPS device (in this case, the SRX) can't simply view the traffic within that communication. To help provide inspection for the secured traffic, the SRX supports the ability to inspect the SSL secured traffic for servers in which you install the SSL private keys. In this example, you'll perform the following configuration:

- Configure SSL inspection for the web server at 172.31.100.60. Use the private key /var/tmp/Web-Server-Private-Key.cert which has a password to secure the private key: Unahy371.
- Enable SSL inspection in the configuration for up to 100,000 sessions (per SPU).

```
{primary:node0}[edit]
root@SRX5800-1# run request security idp ssl-inspection key
add Private-Server-Key file /var/tmp/Web-Server-Private-Key.cert server
172.31.100.60 password Unahy371

{primary:node0}[edit]
root@SRX5800-1# set security idp sensor-configuration ssl-inspection
sessions 100000

root@SRX5800-1# show security idp sensor-configuration
ssl-inspection {
  sessions 10000;
}

{primary:node0}[edit security idp idp-policy Protect-Everything rulebase-ddos]
root@SRX5800-1# top

{primary:node0}[edit]
root@SRX5800-1# commit
node0:
configuration check succeeds
node1:
commit complete
node0:
commit complete
```

One nifty thing to note for SSL decryption is that it automatically detects on which port to decrypt the SSL for any server for which it is providing SSL inspection. It does this by utilizing AppID on those ports to determine if the traffic is SSL, and therefore if it should inspect it.

Configuring IPS modes

The high-end SRX platform has the ability to define three different modes for operating: integrated, dedicated (9.6+), and inline tap (10.2+). Integrated mode is the default, but you can optionally configure the other modes. With dedicated and inline tap modes, you can also adjust the SRX to allocate more resources for firewall versus IPS processing.

Changing modes requires a reboot (both members, if in a cluster, but this can be staggered).

In this example you'll demonstrate the following:

- The configuration for integrated mode (or the lack of configuration)
- Dedicated mode weighted Equally
- Dedicated mode weighted Firewall
- Dedicated mode weighted IPS
- Inline tap mode weighted Equally
- Inline tap mode weighted Firewall
- Inline tap mode weighted IPS

```
## Integrated Mode, Delete IDP Maximize Sessions ##
{primary:node0}[edit]
root@SRX5800-1# delete security forwarding-process application-services maximize-
idp-sessions

## Dedicated Mode, Equal Weighting ##
{primary:node0}[edit]
root@SRX5800-1# set security forwarding-process application-services
maximize-idp-sessions weight equal

## Dedicated Mode, Firewall Weighting ##
{primary:node0}[edit]
root@SRX5800-1# set security forwarding-process application-services
maximize-idp-sessions weight firewall

## Dedicated Mode, IPS Weighting ##
{primary:node0}[edit]
root@SRX5800-1# set security forwarding-process application-services
maximize-idp-sessions weight idp

## Inline Tap Mode, Equal Weighting ##
{primary:node0}[edit]
root@SRX5800-1# set security forwarding-process application-services
maximize-idp-sessions inline-tap weight equal

## Inline Tap Mode, Firewall Weighting ##
{primary:node0}[edit]
root@SRX5800-1# set security forwarding-process application-services
maximize-idp-sessions inline-tap weight firewall

## Inline Tap Mode, IPS Weighting ##
{primary:node0}[edit]
root@SRX5800-1# set security forwarding-process application-services
maximize-idp-sessions inline-tap weight idp

{primary:node0}[edit]
root@SRX5800-1# commit
node0:
configuration check succeeds
node1:
commit complete
node0:
```

```
commit complete

{primary:node0}[edit]
root@SRX5800-1# run request system reboot
Reboot the system ? [yes,no] (no) yes
```

Of course, you would only select one of those modes at a time, but this example was to demonstrate how to configure the different modes. You can also view the current configured mode with the `show security idp status` operational mode command.

Deploying and Tuning IPS

Deploying IPS requires a slight learning curve. You could memorize every command and feature by heart, and still have a rocky deployment. The challenge is that every environment is different, just like a fingerprint or DNA. There are different applications, different volumes of the applications, different policies on what is accepted activity, and different resources to protect; all which can make for different goals for the IPS. Although this book can't tell you exactly what your policy should be, it can certainly help you to build and deploy that policy.

First Steps to Deploying IPS

Before you get too caught up in the actual deployment do a bit of legwork and map out the policy which you want to deploy. Think of it as brainstorming for your IPS. You should identify the assets you want to protect, and identify the systems and applications and how they interact with others in your network. You may need to contact the application owners beforehand to identify this information. You should also determine your IPD protection goals. This would include the types of threats you want to prevent, and any other factors that might limit the scope of the deployment. (Often this involves management approval so that there aren't any surprises.)

Building the Policy

Once you have identified the assets and the goals of the IPS, and you have gotten all of the necessary approvals, you should be ready to build your IPS policy on the SRX. Remember that if you are using predefined attack objects, you must purchase and install the IPS license. You should then download and install the latest and greatest attack objects and detector engine using the full update. This ensures that you have all of the latest attack objects when writing your policy. With those prerequisite tasks taken care of you should create your policy based on the skills you gained earlier in the chapter. If you want a decent place to start, you can download and install the policy templates, and then modify them to suit your needs. Don't apply the policy just yet, though...

Testing Your Policy

The authors would like to tell you to just deploy your IPS policy and let it go from there, but this is not the case for IPS (in our combined broad experience, with many competitor IPS systems, it is no different for them, either).

As mentioned, different environments with different applications make it difficult to make a one-size-fits-all policy with no adverse effects. The best thing that you can do is to test your policy before actually deploying it into production.

This can mean different things for different organizations. If you are a large organization which has lots of resources, you probably have a production lab in which you can replicate your production environment. You could place your SRX in that environment with the appropriate policy deployed and then see what happens. Since it is a lab, you can work out any of the kinks (such as false positives) there, without impacting production. Alternatively, you might be able to make a mirrored segment of the production segments on which you want to deploy the SRX using switchport mirroring (SPAN) or network taps so that even if the SRX has a false positive, it is on the mirrored segment rather than on the production segment.

On the other hand, many organizations don't have the luxury of full test labs. Fear not, because even in these environments you can still deploy with caution and confidence. The other option (which is a good idea to use even if you have the production lab) is to deploy the SRX, but not block anything in the IPS engine. You can do this by using the No-Action actions in the SRX IPS policy so that the SRX is not interfering with any traffic, but is still performing all of the inspection. In this configuration, you should have the SRX log the output to a syslog server such as the STRM so that you can evaluate the output and determine if any false positives are occurring, and if there is anything that should be tuned.

As part of the tuning process, you will likely be adding exceptions into the Exempt rulebase, tuning thresholds (especially if using AppDDoS protection), and getting accustomed to the facilities that provide visibility into the SRX IPS and the actual traffic itself. Just like IPS policies, there is no standard length of time to perform this phase; however, typically you want to ensure that you have a good cycle of traffic. This means if you have certain applications which only run at certain times you want to wait until they have been given a chance to run with IPS enabled to see if there are any adverse effects. If you are pressed for a single time frame, best practice says to let it run a month before enabling blocking (vary this shorter or longer depending on the environment), but any time frames can be worked with as something is better than nothing.

By carefully performing this measured approach, you are going a long way toward ensuring the success of the SRX IPS deployment, and mitigating the risk of issues that might occur in production.

Actual Deployment

After you have completed your testing phase you are ready to deploy in an active blocking mode; unless your goal is just to keep it in an IDS state, in which case your work is finished.

If you did all of the legwork upfront to build and tune the policy, typically the only thing to do here is to change the actions on the appropriate rules to the appropriate actions, rather than just taking no action. If all goes well, there really shouldn't be any surprises in this process. IPS is always going to be in somewhat of a state of evolution, since the threats themselves are always evolving, so it is not a set-and-forget technology as an unmanaged switch would be.

Day-to-Day IPS Management

Once you have completed the initial deployment, you (or your coworkers or external monitoring party) must still maintain the IPS and examine incidents. In terms of maintenance, it comes down to keeping the attack database on the SRX properly updated (not necessarily with the latest and greatest updates, but you should make sure you investigate updates and don't let them lapse too long) with detector engines and new features to help protect against new attacks.

Keeping the device updated can be automated. If you are concerned about new attacks being false positives, you should use static groups for the rules in which you block attacks, and only monitor new attacks with the `no-action` parameter so that you don't block new exploits without ensuring that it is safe to do so first. This means you have to manually add the new attack objects that you want to block into the static groups, but it provides the best balance of updated protection and stability.

The next thing you will likely do on a day-to-day basis is to monitor the IPS logs. Since you will probably see thousands of events per day (maybe more in large environments), you need a rational way to manage the alerts and to somehow investigate only the important ones. The authors recommend that you use reporting, such as that in the STRM, which can not only generate a report, but also allow you to drill down into that report (all the way to the offending logs themselves). This way, you will not go blind watching logs whiz by on the screen, but rather start from a high-level human-readable report that summarizes the pertinent events. Typically, you will have lots of different reports (e.g., worms, shellcode, server-to-client exploits, and more), but they will at least provide a good starting point. Then you can drill down where necessary to identify events that should be investigated in more detail.

Of course, simply logging and reporting all by itself probably does not provide everything you need. Generally, you are going to want to layer your implementation to provide different functionality for different events. For instance, some attacks you want to block when they occur, to protect the system's infrastructure, and other attacks you may not want to block, but you want to be notified when they occur. This can typically be accomplished with logging plus action on the syslog server to generate an email, or trap of some sort, to alert you that an event has occurred. (Be careful that you don't trigger a DoS yourself with too many alerts!) Next, you will have events that you don't want to block, and you don't need to be alerted right when they happen, but they are of interest (such as users running unauthorized games). This is where logging and reporting come in handy. You can review your logs at a later point to determine if further action is required.

Troubleshooting IPS

The SRX has a wealth of facilities that you can use to gain lots of information about IPS functionality and the security state of the inspection events for traffic that is passing through the SRX. So, in addition to the security events of the SRX there are also troubleshooting facilities to look at in the IPS policy commit process. In this section, we have broken down troubleshooting into several sections with examples of the commands, their output, and things to look for.

Checking IPS Status

First off, it is important to make sure the SRX is up and running with an active IPS policy and that it is seeing traffic. If you don't see the information, the SRX is not inspecting traffic.

This first example shows the SRX without the IPS configured; the second example uses an active configuration. Note that on top of these steps, you can also add flow debugging to the list of things to examine. Although flow debugging won't get into the gory details of IPS debugging, it will give you a good idea of what is happening prior to IPS processing.

```
## Inactive IPS example, note Policy Name, No Detector Engine ##
root@SRX5800-1> show security idp status
node0:
--------------------------------------------------------------------------
State of IDP: 2-default,    Up since: 1987-07-02 12:00:52 UTC (1179w6d 06:24 ago)

Packets/second: 0         Peak: 0 @ 1987-07-02 12:00:52 UTC
KBits/second : 0         Peak: 0 @ 1987-07-02 12:00:52 UTC
Latency (microseconds): [min: 0] [max: 0] [avg: 0]

Packet Statistics:
 [ICMP: 0] [TCP: 0] [UDP: 0] [Other: 0]

Flow Statistics:
 ICMP: [Current: 0] [Max: 0 @ 1987-07-02 12:00:52 UTC]
 TCP: [Current: 0] [Max: 0 @ 1987-07-02 12:00:52 UTC]
 UDP: [Current: 0] [Max: 0 @ 1987-07-02 12:00:52 UTC]
 Other: [Current: 0] [Max: 0 @ 1987-07-02 12:00:52 UTC]
```

```
Session Statistics:
 [ICMP: 0] [TCP: 0] [UDP: 0] [Other: 0]

Number of SSL Sessions : 0


 Policy Name : none

Forwarding process mode : maximizing sessions

## Active IPS policy, note detector engine and active stats ##
```

Checking Security Package Version

It is important to keep track of the active IPS security update version and the detector engine version. It's easy to check, by simply issuing the following command:

```
{primary:node0}
root@SRX5800-1> show security idp security-package-version
node0:
--------------------------------------------------------------------------

 Attack database version:1621(Fri Mar 5 12:56:13 2010)
 Detector version :10.3.140100209
 Policy template version :1
```

IPS Attack Table

Viewing the list of attacks detected will not give you the specifics of the attacks, so it's very useful to view the numbers to give you a better idea of your environment. You can also use modifiers to count or only match specific attacks, as shown here:

```
root@SRX5800-1> show security idp attack table
node0:
--------------------------------------------------------------------------
IDP attack statistics:

 Attack name                    #Hits
 TCP:OPTERR:NONSYN-MSS              9496
 TCP:AUDIT:S2C-OLD-ESTB              1923
 TCP:AUDIT:C2S-FUTURE-ACK             516
 HTTP:AUDIT:URL                 120
 POP3:AUDIT:REQ-NESTED-REQUEST           83
 TCP:AUDIT:OPTIONS-UNNEGOT-TS            74
 POP3:AUDIT:REQ-INVALID-STATE            62
 IMAP:AUDIT:REQ-INVALID-STATE            56
 TCP:AUDIT:OLD-3WH-ACK              56
 TCP:AUDIT:S2C-FUTURE-ACK             40
 SMTP:AUDIT:REQ-NESTED-REQUEST           27
 APP:AI:PARTIAL-MATCH               19
 FTP:AUDIT:REQ-UNKNOWN-CMD             17
 PROTOCOLS:TRAFFIC:NOT-FTP             16
 HTTP:SQL:INJ:SQL-INJ-URL              15
```

```
 HTTP:SQL:INJ:CMD-CHAIN-1            14
 HTTP:SQL:INJ:CMD-IN-URL            14
 HTTP:SQL:INJ:CMD-CHAIN-2            10
 HTTP:REQERR:REQ-MALFORMED-URL          9
 HTTP:SQL:INJ:GENERIC             6
 HTTP:STC:SCRIPT:UNI-SHELLCODE          6
 CHAT:IRC:NICK               5
 HTTP:STC:ACTIVEX:UNCOMMON-AX          5
 CHAT:IRC:SRV-RESPONSE            4
 HTTP:STC:SCRIPT:UNICODE-SLED          4
 HTTP:EXT:METAFILE              3
 NNTP:AUDIT:NESTED-REQ             3
 HTTP:AUDIT:LENGTH-OVER-256           2
 HTTP:AUDIT:LENGTH-OVER-512           2
 HTTP:INFO:HTTPPOST-GETSTYLE           2
 HTTP:STC:STREAM:CONTENT-TYPE          2
 LPR:AUDIT:PORT               2
 POP3:EXT:DOT-WMF               2
 PROTOCOLS:PORT:FTP              2
 RTSP:EXPLOIT:INVALID-PORT           2
 VNC:SESSION                2
 CHAT:AUDIT:IRC-CMD              1
 CHAT:IRC:OVERFLOW:LINE             1
 FTP:CISCO-VPN-ACCESS             1
 FTP:OVERFLOW:LINE-TOO-LONG           1
 HTTP:AUDIT:LENGTH-OVER-1024          1
 HTTP:AUDIT:LENGTH-OVER-2048          1
 HTTP:AUDIT:LENGTH-OVER-4096          1

{primary:node0}
root@SRX5800-1> show security idp attack table | count
Count: 124 lines

{primary:node0}
root@SRX5800-1> show security idp attack table | match HTTP | match SQL
 HTTP:SQL:INJ:SQL-INJ-URL            15
 HTTP:SQL:INJ:CMD-CHAIN-1            14
 HTTP:SQL:INJ:CMD-IN-URL            14
 HTTP:SQL:INJ:CMD-CHAIN-2            10
 HTTP:SQL:INJ:GENERIC             6
```

Application Statistics

Just like the attack tables, it's often helpful to the administrator to get a bird's eye view of the application distributions that the SRX is processing. Of course, other mechanisms such as AppTrack can provide this detailed information as well. The following output is but a snippet of the application lists (since they would be quite long to print here):

```
{primary:node0}
root@SRX5800-1> show security idp application-statistics
node0:
--------------------------------------------------------------------------
IDP applications:
```

```
application type                    packet count
ECHO                             0
DISCARD                            0
CHARGEN                            0
FTP                              724
SSH                              0
TELNET                            108
SMTP                             4305
DNS                              23
GOPHER                            0
FINGER                            0
HTTP                             8016
POP3                             3634
PORTMAPPER                             1658
IDENT                             0
SMB                              518
IMAP                             5012
REXEC                             0
RLOGIN                            40
```

IPS Counters

Several IPS counters are valuable to examine when determining the status of the IPS, the traffic that the IPS is processing, and the events that the IPS is taking. Several counters are worthwhile to examine, but we'll focus on the flow output in this example:

```
{primary:node0}
root@SRX5800-1> show security idp counters ?
Possible completions:
 application-ddos   Show the Application DDOS counters
 application-identification Show Application Identification counters
 dfa          Show IDP DFA counters
 flow          Show IDP Flow counters
 ips          Show IPS counters
 log          Show IDP Log counters
 node          Show IDP counters on specific node
 packet         Show IDP Packet counters
 policy-manager    Show IDP Policy counters
 ssl-inspection    Show SSL Inspection counters
 tcp-reassembler   Show IDP Reassembler counters

{primary:node0}
root@SRX5800-1> show security idp counters flow node 0 | no-more
node0:
--------------------------------------------------------------------------
IDP counters:

 IDP counter type                       Value
 Fast-path packets                        53655
 Slow-path packets                        2289
 Session construction failed                       0
 Session limit reached                       0
 Memory limit reached                      0
```

```
Not a new session                                0
Invalide index at ageout                         0
Packet logging                                   0
Busy packets                                     0
Busy packet Errors                               0
Dropped queued packets (async mode)              0
Reinjected packets (async mode)                  0
Policy cache hits                                802
Policy cache misses                              1771
Maximum flow hash collisions                     0
Flow hash collisions                             0
Gates added                                      0
Gate matches                                     0
Sessions deleted                                 2052
Sessions aged-out                                0
Sessoins in-use while aged-out                   0
TCP flows marked dead on RST/FIN                 1670
Policy init failed                               0
Number of Sessions exceeds high mark             0
Number of Sessions drops below low mark          0
Memory of Sessions exceeds high mark             0
Memory of Sessions drops below low mark          0
Sessions constructed                             2289
SM Sessions ignored                              1890
SM Sessions interested                           0
SM Sessions not interested                       0
SM Sessions interest error                       0
Sessions destructed                              2138
SM Session Create                                2289
SM Packet Process                                0
SM Session close                                 0
SM Client-to-server packets                      0
SM Server-to-client packets                      0
SM Client-to-server L7 bytes                     13395204
SM Server-to-client L7 bytes                     25598889
```

IP Action Table

When a violation occurs (IPS or AppDDoS) the administrator has the option to perform an action not only on that connection, but also on future connections depending on configuration. This is known as IP Action, and you can view the contents of this table, including using modifiers to select specific entries:

```
{primary:node0}
root@SRX5800-1>show security flow ip-action

Src-Addr  Src-Port  Dst-Addr  Proto/Dst-Port  Timeout(sec)
 16.0.80.0 0        0.0.0.0    0/0          598/600      0   close

 16.0.66.15 0        0.0.0.0    0/0          596/600      0   close

 16.0.74.17 0        0.0.0.0    0/0          595/600      0   close

 16.0.0.47 0        0.0.0.0    0/0          596/600      0   close
```

```
16.0.80.56 0        0.0.0.0    0/0          596/600        0    close

16.0.22.59 0        0.0.0.0    0/0          596/600        0    close

16.0.78.76 0        0.0.0.0    0/0          598/600        0    close
```

From the output of the `show security flow ip-table` command you can determine if a host has been shunned (source, destination, protocol, destination port) and the timeout remaining in the maximum time. In this example, the shunned host shows a timeout of 600 seconds which counts down. The entries remain in the table until they time out.

AppDDoS Useful Commands

AppDDoS is the next generation of protection against DDoS attacks. It has very powerful functionality, but it is not a one-size-fits-all component, and you must tune it to the appropriate thresholds of your environment. You can easily determine what the appropriate thresholds should be for your environment by enabling AppDDoS protection without blocking traffic to determine a baseline threshold. The following commands highlight different areas of importance:

```
{primary:node0}
root@SRX5800-1# show security idp application-ddos application http-url-parsed
node0:
--------------------------------------------------------------------------

Zone     Server        Application         Conn/sec  Context         Contexts/tick
trust    172.31.100.60       http-url-parsed      2197/sec  http-url-parsed   26179/60sec
```

The preceding output shows that our 172.31.100.60 web server is receiving 2,197 connections per second, with 26,179 hits against the **http-url-parsed** context in a 60-second period. You can use these values to further tune your AppDDoS profile to define the appropriate thresholds.

```
{primary:node0}
root@SRX5800-1# show security idp application-ddos application http-url-parsed
detail
node0:
--------------------------------------------------------------------------

 Zone: trust Server: 172.31.100.60 Application: http-url-parsed Connections/sec:
44/sec

Context: http-url-parsed Contexts/tick: 10423/60sec
 Value: 2f 69 6e 64 65 78 2e 68 74 6d 6c          /index.html
 Context values/tick : 12/60sec
```

You can also get the output for individual values and thresholds, as shown in the following output, where the value is `/index.html` and it is hitting that 12 times every 60 seconds:

```
root@SRX5800-1# run show security idp counters application-ddos
node0:
--------------------------------------------------------------------------
IDP counters:

 IDP counter type                                            Value
 App-DDOS inspected flows                                      1011519
 App-DDOS failed flows                                       0
 App-DDOS ignored flows                                       6121
 App-DDOS first path failed                                     0
 App-DDOS first path succeeded                                   1017640
 App-DDOS dropped packets                                      15452
 App-DDOS processed packets                                     2692028
 App-DDOS connection table process succeeded                            1017611
 App-DDOS connection table process failed                             0
 App-DDOS context process succeeded                                221232
 App-DDOS context process failed                                 0
 App-DDOS ignore context                                      1
 App-DDOS context values excluded                                 0
 App-DDOS context value process succeeded                             221232
 App-DDOS context value process failed                              0
 App-DDOS context value prune failed                               0
 App-DDOS no action                                          0
 App-DDOS drop connection action                                 0
 App-DDOS drop packet action                                   0
 App-DDOS close server action                                   15452
 App-DDOS IP Action notify                                     0
 App-DDOS IP Action rate-limit                                   0
 App-DDOS IP Action block                                      0
 App-DDOS IP Action close                                      15452
 App-DDOS logs sent                                          0
```

Here the output displays a high-level overview of the different activity and associated actions that have taken place. This is useful output, particularly when troubleshooting, to see if values are increasing.

Troubleshooting the Commit/Compilation Process

It is pretty rare to have the IPS compilation process fail. In most cases, it is just taking a while to fully compile. The compilation process occurs in the control plane, and then once it is complete, it pushes down to each flow SPU on the data plane. There are several ways to troubleshoot the IPS compilation process.

The first thing to do is to check the IPS status to ensure that the IPS is running with an active policy. If this does not show an active policy and detector engine, the compilation process has not been completed. This can happen after a reboot, or when you are applying an initial policy. It will just take some time to apply.

```
{primary:node0}
root@SRX5800-1> show security idp status
node0:
--------------------------------------------------------------------------
State of IDP: 2-default,    Up since: 1987-07-02 12:00:51 UTC (1180w0d 02:06 ago)
```

```
Packets/second: 4          Peak: 196837 @ 1987-07-03 03:12:24 UTC
KBits/second : 1          Peak: 502775 @ 1987-07-03 03:12:29 UTC
Latency (microseconds): [min: 0] [max: 0] [avg: 0]

Packet Statistics:
 [ICMP: 13] [TCP: 64555645] [UDP: 16157404] [Other: 263]

Flow Statistics:
 ICMP: [Current: 0] [Max: 18 @ 1987-07-02 12:43:32 UTC]
 TCP: [Current: 238] [Max: 410084 @ 1987-07-03 03:11:57 UTC]
 UDP: [Current: 0] [Max: 174756 @ 1987-07-03 03:10:45 UTC]
 Other: [Current: 0] [Max: 4 @ 1987-07-02 12:40:55 UTC]

Session Statistics:
 [ICMP: 0] [TCP: 119] [UDP: 0] [Other: 2]

Number of SSL Sessions : 0


 Policy Name : Brad-IDP
 Running Detector Version : 10.3.140100209

Forwarding process mode : maximizing sessions
```

This output shows that there is an active policy and detector engine. If you are committing a new policy, this new policy may not have completed yet. If you wish, you can apply a trace on the IPS process; this primarily traces the compilation process, but not the actual IPS inspection. Here the trace file is given the name *IDP-Debug*, but it doesn't really matter what you call it:

```
{primary:node0}[edit]
root@SRX5800-1# set security idp traceoptions flag all

{primary:node0}[edit]
root@SRX5800-1# set security idp traceoptions level all

{primary:node0}[edit]
root@SRX5800-1# set security idp traceoptions file IDP-Debug

{primary:node0}[edit]
root@SRX5800-1# show security idp traceoptions
file IDP-Debug;
flag all;
level all;

{primary:node0}[edit]
root@SRX5800-1# commit
node0:
commit complete
```

Now that you have applied the trace, you can either manually view the file or "tail" the logs to the terminal window using the `monitor start` command:

```
{primary:node0}
root@SRX5800-1> show log IDP-Debug
Feb 11 13:51:49 idpd_need_policy_compile:467 Active policy path
/var/db/idpd/sets/Brad-IDP.set
Feb 11 13:51:50 Active Policy (Brad-IDP) rule base configuration is changed
so need to recompile active policy
Feb 11 13:51:51 Compiling policy Brad-IDP....
Feb 11 13:51:51 Apply policy configuration, policy ops bitmask = 41
Feb 11 13:51:52 Starting policy(Brad-IDP) compile with compress dfa...

{primary:node0}
root@SRX5800-1> monitor start IDP-Debug
```

While this process is executing, you can check the process table to get a good idea if the process is still running while you're waiting for the compilation to complete. High utilization on the IDPD process will indicate that the IDPD process is still compiling.

```
{primary:node0}
root@SRX5800-1> show system processes extensive
node0:
--------------------------------------------------------------------------
last pid: 4121;  load averages: 0.99, 0.65, 0.30 up 0+19:23:25  13:55:36
132 processes: 5 running, 110 sleeping, 17 waiting

Mem: 361M Active, 128M Inact, 112M Wired, 297M Cache, 69M Buf, 1101M Free
Swap: 2048M Total, 2048M Free


  PID USERNAME THR PRI NICE  SIZE  RES STATE  TIME  WCPU COMMAND
 4111 root      1 130   0  219M  147M RUN    3:32 92.14% idpd
 1145 root      1   8   0 42528K 18288K nanslp 38:27 1.90% chassisd
   20 root     1 -68 -187    0K   12K RUN    4:35 0.15% irq10: em0 em1+++*
   13 root     1 -20 -139    0K   12K WAIT   2:46 0.05% swi7: clock sio
   11 root     1 171  52    0K   12K RUN   17.9H 0.00% idle
 1164 root      1  96   0  206M  148M select 19:35 0.00% idpd
   12 root     1 -40 -159    0K   12K WAIT   3:15 0.00% swi2: net
 1030 root      1  76   0    0K   12K       1:52 0.00% bcmLINK.0
   15 root     1 -16   0    0K   12K -      0:55 0.00% yarrow
 1313 root      1   4   0    0K   12K peer_s  0:52 0.00% peer proxy
 1163 root      1  96   0 72812K 17792K select  0:43 0.00% appidd
 1288 root      1  96   0 25192K 22028K select  0:28 0.00% snmpd
```

When you see the following information (either by manually showing the IDP log or by using the `monitor start` command), the successful compilation has occurred. If you used the `monitor start` command, you can issue the `monitor stop` command to stop the tailing:

```
Feb 11 13:59:07 IDP policy[/var/db/idpd/bins/Brad-IDP.bin.gz.v] and
detector[/var/db/idpd/sec-repository/installed-detector/
libidp-detector.so.tgz.v] loaded successfully.

{primary:node0}
root@SRX5800-1> monitor stop
```

Case Study 8-1

There is a lot to be said for putting the theory of IPS into action in a production network. The good news is that we will look at a few example policies that can be used to secure an enterprise network against internal and external threats. In this case study, we will examine the ability to provide protection under three different scenarios:

DMZ network
: In the DMZ, several servers must be protected against attacks by clients, including HTTP, HTTPS, FTP, SMTP, and DNS servers. We also want to make sure these machines are not compromised and start to infect other machines in the network or the Internet at large with spyware, worms, Trojan horses, and viruses. The DMZ server can only talk outbound on HTTP and HTTPS for updates. All logs should be taken in this example. Assume that the DMZ zone uses the interface Reth4.

Internal clients
: We want to protect internal clients against attacks from malicious servers in the wild. These hosts will only be allowed to communicate over HTTP, HTTPS, FTP, IM, and out to the Internet; all other services are restricted by the firewall policy itself. We also want to identify and block any hosts that are infected by spyware, worms, Trojan horses, or viruses for two hours, along with setting the `alert` flag in the logs. Assume that the Internal-Clients zone is composed of Dept-A and Dept-B with interfaces Reth2 and Reth3, respectively.

Internal servers
: Clients are permitted to access a wide variety of services on the internal servers. Currently, your organization does not restrict services between internal clients and servers, but it does wish to provide additional security. At this time, management is hesitant to interfere with internal traffic, but they would like to provide visibility, so you should just log the attacks at this point. The internal servers are allowed to talk out to the Internet via HTTP and HTTPS for updates. Additionally, we want to identify any servers which may be infected by spyware, worms, Trojan horses, or viruses. Assume that the Internal-Servers zone uses interface Reth5.

For these examples, we will leverage the power of dynamic groups. The most significant attacks will be located in the Critical, Major, and Minor severities. We will also use category, direction, and performance filters as well to ensure that our policy is as specific and lean as possible, while still providing serious coverage. Figure 8-8 shows an overview of the case study.

First, we will define our network elements, their zones, and the firewall policy which will be used to pass the traffic to the IPS for inspection. We will assume that the NAT has already been taken care of, since it will not change the objects in our policies.

```
[edit]
root@SRX5800# edit security zones security-zone DMZ

[edit security zones security-zone DMZ]
```

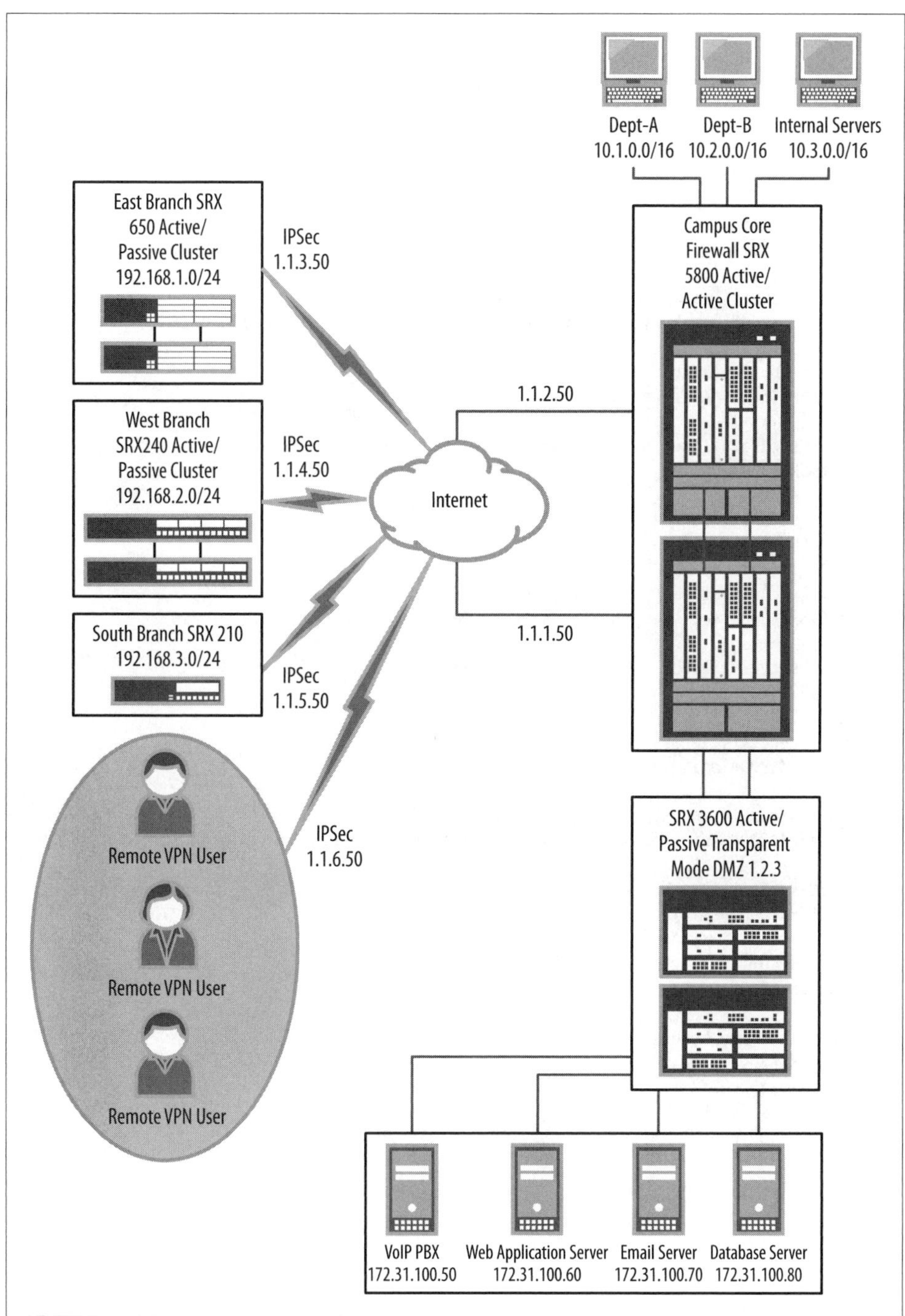

Figure 8-8. Case Study 8-1

```
root@SRX5800# set address-book address DMZ-Server-172.31.100.0/24 172.31.100.0/24

[edit security zones security-zone DMZ]
root@SRX5800# set interfaces reth4

[edit security zones security-zone DMZ]
root@SRX5800# up

[edit security zones]
root@SRX5800# edit security-zone Dept-A

[edit security zones security-zone Dept-A]
root@SRX5800# set address-book address Dept-A-10.1.0.0/16 10.1.0.0/16

[edit security zones security-zone Dept-A]
root@SRX5800# set interfaces reth2

[edit security zones security-zone Dept-A]
root@SRX5800# up

[edit security zones]
root@SRX5800# edit security-zone Dept-B

[edit security zones security-zone Dept-B]
root@SRX5800# set address-book address Dept-B-10.2.0.0/16 10.2.0.0/16

[edit security zones security-zone Dept-B]
root@SRX5800# up

[edit security zones]
root@SRX5800# edit security-zone Internal-Servers

[edit security zones security-zone Internal-Servers]
root@SRX5800# set address-book address Internal-Servers-10.3.0.0/16 10.3.0.0/16

[edit security zones security-zone Internal-Servers]
root@SRX5800# set interfaces reth5

[edit security zones security-zone Internal-Servers]
root@SRX5800# up

[edit security zones]
root@SRX5800# show
security-zone DMZ {
    address-book {
        address DMZ-Server-172.31.100.0/24 172.31.100.0/24;
    }
    interfaces {
        reth4.0;
    }
}
security-zone Dept-A {
    address-book {
        address Dept-A-10.1.0.0/16 10.1.0.0/16;
    }
```

```
    interfaces {
        reth2.0;
    }
}
security-zone Dept-B {
    address-book {
        address Dept-B-10.2.0.0/16 10.2.0.0/16;
    }
}
security-zone Internal-Servers {
    address-book {
        address Internal-Servers-10.3.0.0/16 10.3.0.0/16;
    }
    interfaces {
        reth5.0;
    }
}

[edit security zones]
root@SRX5800# top

[edit]
root@SRX5800# set applications application-set DMZ-Services application
junos-http

[edit]
root@SRX5800# set applications application-set DMZ-Services application
junos-https

[edit]
root@SRX5800# set applications application-set DMZ-Services application
junos-ftp

[edit]
root@SRX5800# set applications application-set DMZ-Services application
junos-smtp

[edit]
root@SRX5800# set applications application-set DMZ-Services application
junos-dns-udp

[edit]
root@SRX5800# set applications application-set Allowed-Outbound application
junos-http

[edit]
root@SRX5800# set applications application-set Allowed-Outbound application
junos-https

[edit]
root@SRX5800# set applications application-set Allowed-Outbound application
junos-ftp

[edit]
root@SRX5800# set applications application-set Allowed-Outbound application
```

```
junos-aol

[edit]
root@SRX5800# set applications application-set Allowed-Outbound application
junos-ymsg

[edit]
root@SRX5800# show applications
application-set DMZ-Services {
    application junos-http;
    application junos-https;
    application junos-ftp;
    application junos-smtp;
    application junos-dns-udp;
}
application-set Allowed-Outbound {
    application junos-http;
    application junos-https;
    application junos-ftp;
    application junos-aol;
    application junos-ymsg;
}

[edit]
root@SRX5800# edit security policies from-zone Dept-A to-zone DMZ

[edit security policies from-zone Dept-A to-zone DMZ]
root@SRX5800# set policy Dept-A-to-DMZ match source-address Dept-A-10.1.0.0/16
destination-address DMZ-Server-172.31.100.0/24 application DMZ-Services

[edit security policies from-zone Dept-A to-zone DMZ]
root@SRX5800# set policy Dept-A-to-DMZ then permit application-services idp

[edit security policies from-zone Dept-A to-zone DMZ]
root@SRX5800# set policy Dept-A-to-DMZ then log session-close

[edit security policies from-zone Dept-A to-zone DMZ]
root@SRX5800# up

[edit security policies]
root@SRX5800# edit from-zone Dept-B to-zone DMZ

[edit security policies from-zone Dept-B to-zone DMZ]
root@SRX5800# set policy Dept-B-to-DMZ match source-address Dept-B-10.2.0.0/16
destination-address DMZ-Server-172.31.100.0/24 application DMZ-Services

[edit security policies from-zone Dept-B to-zone DMZ]
root@SRX5800# set policy Dept-B-to-DMZ then permit application-services idp

[edit security policies from-zone Dept-B to-zone DMZ]
root@SRX5800# set policy Dept-B-to-DMZ then log session-close

[edit security policies from-zone Dept-B to-zone DMZ]
root@SRX5800# up
```

```
[edit security policies]
root@SRX5800# edit from-zone Dept-A to-zone Internal-Servers

[edit security policies from-zone Dept-A to-zone Internal-Servers]
root@SRX5800# set policy Dept-A-to-Internal-Servers match source-address Dept-A-
10.1.0.0/16 destination-address Internal-Servers-10.3.0.0/16 application any

[edit security policies from-zone Dept-A to-zone Internal-Servers]
root@SRX5800# set policy Dept-A-to-Internal-Servers then permit application-
services idp

[edit security policies from-zone Dept-A to-zone Internal-Servers]
root@SRX5800# set policy Dept-A-to-Internal-Servers then log session-close

[edit security policies from-zone Dept-A to-zone Internal-Servers]
root@SRX5800# up

[edit security policies]
root@SRX5800# edit from-zone Dept-B to-zone Internal-Servers

[edit security policies from-zone Dept-B to-zone Internal-Servers]
root@SRX5800# set policy Dept-B-to-Internal-Servers match source-address Dept-B-
10.2.0.0/16 destination-address Internal-Servers-10.3.0.0/16 application any

[edit security policies from-zone Dept-B to-zone Internal-Servers]
root@SRX5800# set policy Dept-B-to-Internal-Servers then permit application-
services idp

[edit security policies from-zone Dept-B to-zone Internal-Servers]
root@SRX5800# set policy Dept-B-to-Internal-Servers then log session-close

[edit security policies from-zone Dept-B to-zone Internal-Servers]
root@SRX5800# up

[edit security policies]
root@SRX5800# edit from-zone untrust to-zone DMZ

[edit security policies from-zone untrust to-zone DMZ]
root@SRX5800# set policy untrust-to-DMZ match source-address any destination-
address DMZ-Server-172.31.100.0/24 application DMZ-Services

[edit security policies from-zone untrust to-zone DMZ]
root@SRX5800# set policy untrust-to-DMZ then permit application-services idp

[edit security policies from-zone untrust to-zone DMZ]
root@SRX5800# set policy untrust-to-DMZ then log session-close

[edit security policies from-zone untrust to-zone DMZ]
root@SRX5800# up

[edit security policies]
root@SRX5800# edit from-zone Dept-A to-zone untrust

[edit security policies from-zone Dept-A to-zone untrust]
root@SRX5800# set policy Dept-A-to-untrust match source-address
```

```
Dept-A-10.1.0.0/16 destination-address any application Allowed-Outbound

[edit security policies from-zone Dept-A to-zone untrust]
root@SRX5800# set policy Dept-A-to-untrust then permit application-services idp

[edit security policies from-zone Dept-A to-zone untrust]
root@SRX5800# set policy Dept-A-to-untrust then log session-close

[edit security policies from-zone Dept-A to-zone untrust]
root@SRX5800# up

[edit security policies]
root@SRX5800# edit from-zone Dept-B to-zone untrust

[edit security policies from-zone Dept-B to-zone untrust]
root@SRX5800# set policy Dept-B-to-untrust match source-address
Dept-B-10.2.0.0/16 destination-address any application Allowed-Outbound

[edit security policies from-zone Dept-B to-zone untrust]
root@SRX5800# set policy Dept-B-to-untrust then permit application-services idp

[edit security policies from-zone Dept-B to-zone untrust]
root@SRX5800# set policy Dept-B-to-untrust then log session-close

[edit security policies from-zone Dept-B to-zone untrust]
root@SRX5800# up

[edit security policies]
root@SRX5800# edit from-zone DMZ to-zone untrust

[edit security policies from-zone DMZ to-zone untrust]
root@SRX5800# set policy DMZ-to-untrust match source-address DMZ-Server-
172.31.100.0/24 destination-address any application [ junos-http junos-https ]

[edit security policies from-zone DMZ to-zone untrust]
root@SRX5800# set policy DMZ-to-untrust then permit application-services idp

[edit security policies from-zone DMZ to-zone untrust]
root@SRX5800# set policy DMZ-to-untrust then log session-close

[edit security policies from-zone DMZ to-zone untrust]
root@SRX5800# up

[edit security policies]
root@SRX5800# edit from-zone Internal-Servers to-zone untrust

[edit security policies from-zone Internal-Servers to-zone untrust]
root@SRX5800# set policy Internal-Servers-to-untrust match source-address
Internal-Servers-10.3.0.0/16 destination-address any application [ junos-http
junos-https ]

[edit security policies from-zone Internal-Servers to-zone untrust]
root@SRX5800# set policy Internal-Servers-to-untrust then permit application-
services idp
```

```
[edit security policies from-zone Internal-Servers to-zone untrust]
root@SRX5800# set policy Internal-Servers-to-untrust then log session-close

[edit security policies]
root@SRX5800# top

from-zone Dept-A to-zone DMZ {
    policy Dept-A-to-DMZ {
        match {
            source-address Dept-A-10.1.0.0/16;
            destination-address DMZ-Server-172.31.100.0/24;
            application DMZ-Services;
        }
        then {
            permit {
                application-services {
                    idp;
                }
            }
            log {
                session-close;
            }
        }
    }
}
from-zone Dept-B to-zone DMZ {
    policy Dept-B-to-DMZ {
        match {
            source-address Dept-B-10.2.0.0/16;
            destination-address DMZ-Server-172.31.100.0/24;
            application DMZ-Services;
        }
        then {
            permit {
                application-services {
                    idp;
                }
            }
            log {
                session-close;
            }
        }
    }
}
from-zone Dept-B to-zone Internal-Servers {
    policy Dept-B-to-Internal-Servers {
        match {
            source-address Dept-B-10.2.0.0/16;
            destination-address Internal-Servers-10.3.0.0/16;
            application any;
        }
        then {
            permit {
                application-services {
                    idp;
```

```
                }
            }
            log {
                session-close;
            }
        }
    }
}
from-zone Dept-A to-zone Internal-Servers {
    policy Dept-A-to-Internal-Servers {
        match {
            source-address Dept-A-10.1.0.0/16;
            destination-address Internal-Servers-10.3.0.0/16;
            application any;
        }
        then {
            permit {
                application-services {
                    idp;
                }
            }
            log {
                session-close;
            }
        }
    }
}
from-zone untrust to-zone DMZ {
    policy untrust-to-DMZ {
        match {
            source-address any;
            destination-address DMZ-Server-172.31.100.0/24;
            application DMZ-Services;
        }
        then {
            permit {
                application-services {
                    idp;
                }
            }
            log {
                session-close;
            }
        }
    }
}
from-zone Dept-A to-zone untrust {
    policy Dept-A-to-untrust {
        match {
            source-address Dept-A-10.1.0.0/16;
            destination-address any;
            application Allowed-Outbound;
        }
        then {
            permit {
```

```
                application-services {
                    idp;
                }
            }
            log {
                session-close;
            }
        }
    }
}
from-zone Dept-B to-zone untrust {
    policy Dept-B-to-untrust {
        match {
            source-address Dept-B-10.2.0.0/16;
            destination-address any;
            application Allowed-Outbound;
        }
        then {
            permit {
                application-services {
                    idp;
                }
            }
            log {
                session-close;
            }
        }
    }
}
from-zone DMZ to-zone untrust {
    policy DMZ-to-untrust {
        match {
            source-address DMZ-Server-172.31.100.0/24;
            destination-address any;
            application [ junos-http junos-https ];
        }
        then {
            permit {
                application-services {
                    idp;
                }
            }
            log {
                session-close;
            }
        }
    }
}
from-zone Internal-Servers to-zone untrust {
    policy Internal-Servers-to-untrust {
        match {
            source-address Internal-Servers-10.3.0.0/16;
            destination-address any;
            application [ junos-http junos-https ];
        }
```

```
            then {
                permit {
                    application-services {
                        idp;
                    }
                }
                log {
                    session-close;
                }
            }
        }
    }
```

Next, we will create the dynamic group objects that will be used for the IPS policy to protect our infrastructure.

```
[edit]
root@SRX5800# edit security idp dynamic-attack-group Protect-DMZ
[edit security idp dynamic-attack-group Protect-DMZ]

[edit security idp dynamic-attack-group Protect-DMZ]
root@SRX5800# set filters category values [ HTTP SSL SMTP DNS SHELLCODE
WORM TROJAN ]

[edit security idp dynamic-attack-group Protect-DMZ]
root@SRX5800# set filters direction values client-to-server

[edit security idp dynamic-attack-group Protect-DMZ]
root@SRX5800# set filters severity values [ critical major minor ]

[edit security idp dynamic-attack-group Protect-DMZ]
root@SRX5800# set filters performance values [ fast normal unknown ]


[edit security idp dynamic-attack-group Protect-DMZ]
root@SRX5800# up

[edit security idp]
root@SRX5800# edit dynamic-attack-group Protect-Clients

[edit security idp dynamic-attack-group Protect-Clients]
root@SRX5800# set filters severity values [ critical major minor ]

[edit security idp dynamic-attack-group Protect-Clients]
root@SRX5800# set filters performance values [ fast normal unknown ]

[edit security idp dynamic-attack-group Protect-Clients]
root@SRX5800# set filters direction values server-to-client

[edit security idp dynamic-attack-group Protect-Clients]
root@SRX5800# set filters category values [ HTTP SSL FTP CHAT SHELLCODE WORM
SPYWARE TROJAN VIRUS ]

[edit security idp dynamic-attack-group Protect-Clients]
root@SRX5800# up
```

```
[edit security idp]
root@SRX5800# edit dynamic-attack-group Detect-Infection

[edit security idp dynamic-attack-group Detect-Infection]
root@SRX5800# set filters performance values [ fast normal unknown ]

[edit security idp dynamic-attack-group Detect-Infection]
root@SRX5800# set filters direction values client-to-server

[edit security idp dynamic-attack-group Detect-Infection]
root@SRX5800# set filters severity values [ critical major minor ]

[edit security idp dynamic-attack-group Detect-Infection]
root@SRX5800# set filters category values [ WORM SPYWARE TROJAN VIRUS SHELLCODE ]

[edit security idp dynamic-attack-group Detect-Infection]
root@SRX5800# up

[edit security idp dynamic-attack-group Detect-Infection]
root@SRX5800# up

[edit security idp]
root@SRX5800# edit dynamic-attack-group Protect-Servers

[edit security idp dynamic-attack-group Protect-Servers]
root@SRX5800# set filters severity values [ critical major minor ]

[edit security idp dynamic-attack-group Protect-Servers]
root@SRX5800# set filters performance values [ fast normal unknown ]

[edit security idp dynamic-attack-group Protect-Servers]
root@SRX5800# set filters direction values client-to-server

[edit security idp dynamic-attack-group Protect-Servers]
root@SRX5800# up

[edit security idp dynamic-attack-group Protect-Servers]
root@SRX5800# show | find dynamic-attack-group
dynamic-attack-group Protect-DMZ {
    filters {
        direction {
            values client-to-server;
        }
        severity {
            values [ critical major minor ];
        }
        performance {
            values [ fast normal unknown ];
        }
        category {
            values [ HTTP SSL FTP SMTP DNS SHELLCODE WORM TROJAN ];
        }
    }
}
dynamic-attack-group Protect-Clients {
```

```
        filters {
            direction {
                values server-to-client;
            }
            severity {
                values [ critical major minor ];
            }
            performance {
                values [ fast normal unknown ];
            }
            category {
                values [ HTTP SSL FTP CHAT SHELLCODE WORM SPYWARE TROJAN VIRUS ];
            }
        }
    }
    dynamic-attack-group Detect-Infection {
        filters {
            direction {
                values client-to-server;
            }
            severity {
                values [ critical major minor ];
            }
            performance {
                values [ fast normal unknown ];
            }
            category {
                values [ WORM SPYWARE TROJAN VIRUS SHELLCODE ];
            }
        }
    }
    dynamic-attack-group Protect-Servers {
        filters {
            direction {
                values client-to-server;
            }
            severity {
                values [ critical major minor ];
            }
            performance {
                values [ fast normal unknown ];
            }
        }
    }
```

Now that we have defined all of the objects, firewall policy, and IPS attack groups, we will finally define the actual IPS policy to take everything into account in the objectives and put it into place.

```
[edit security idp]
root@SRX5800# edit idp-policy IDP rulebase-ips rule Protect-DMZ

[edit security idp idp-policy IDP rulebase-ips rule Protect-DMZ]
root@SRX5800# set match from-zone untrust to-zone DMZ source-address any
destination-address DMZ-Server-172.31.100.0/24 application default attacks
```

```
dynamic-attack-groups Protect-DMZ

[edit security idp idp-policy IDP rulebase-ips rule Protect-DMZ]
root@SRX5800# set then action drop-connection

[edit security idp idp-policy IDP rulebase-ips rule Protect-DMZ]
root@SRX5800# set then notification log-attacks

[edit security idp idp-policy IDP rulebase-ips rule Protect-DMZ]
root@SRX5800# up

[edit security idp idp-policy IDP rulebase-ips]
root@SRX5800# edit rule Protect-Clients-Dept-A

[edit security idp idp-policy IDP rulebase-ips rule Protect-Clients-Dept-A]
root@SRX5800# set match from-zone Dept-A to-zone untrust source-address Dept-A-
10.1.0.0/16 destination-address any application default attacks dynamic-attack-
groups [ Protect-Clients Detect-Infection ]

[edit security idp idp-policy IDP rulebase-ips rule Protect-Clients-Dept-A]
root@SRX5800# set then action drop-connection

[edit security idp idp-policy IDP rulebase-ips rule Protect-Clients-Dept-A]
root@SRX5800# set then notification log-attacks alert

[edit security idp idp-policy IDP rulebase-ips rule Protect-Clients-Dept-A]
root@SRX5800# set then ip-action ip-block target source-address timeout 7200 log

[edit security idp idp-policy IDP rulebase-ips rule Protect-Clients-Dept-A]
root@SRX5800# up

[edit security idp idp-policy IDP rulebase-ips]
root@SRX5800# edit rule Protect-Clients-Dept-B

[edit security idp idp-policy IDP rulebase-ips rule Protect-Clients-Dept-B]
root@SRX5800# set match from-zone Dept-B to-zone untrust source-address Dept-B-
10.2.0.0/16 destination-address any application default attacks dynamic-attack-
groups [ Protect-Clients Detect-Infection ]

[edit security idp idp-policy IDP rulebase-ips rule Protect-Clients-Dept-B]
root@SRX5800# set then action drop-connection

[edit security idp idp-policy IDP rulebase-ips rule Protect-Clients-Dept-B]
root@SRX5800# set then ip-action ip-block target source-address log timeout 7200

[edit security idp idp-policy IDP rulebase-ips rule Protect-Clients-Dept-B]
root@SRX5800# set then notification log-attacks alert

[edit security idp idp-policy IDP rulebase-ips rule Protect-Clients-Dept-B]
root@SRX5800# up

[edit security idp idp-policy IDP rulebase-ips rule Protect-Clients-Dept-B]
root@SRX5800# up

[edit security idp idp-policy IDP rulebase-ips]
```

```
root@SRX5800# edit rule Protect-DMZ-Outbound

[edit security idp idp-policy IDP rulebase-ips rule Protect-DMZ-Outbound]
root@SRX5800# set match from-zone DMZ to-zone untrust source-address DMZ-Server-
172.31.100.0/24 destination-address any application default attacks
dynamic-attack-groups [ Protect-Clients Detect-Infection ]

[edit security idp idp-policy IDP rulebase-ips rule Protect-DMZ-Outbound]
root@SRX5800# set then action drop-connection

[edit security idp idp-policy IDP rulebase-ips rule Protect-DMZ-Outbound]
root@SRX5800# set then ip-action ip-block target source-address log timeout 7200

[edit security idp idp-policy IDP rulebase-ips rule Protect-DMZ-Outbound]
root@SRX5800# set then notification log-attacks alert

[edit security idp idp-policy IDP rulebase-ips rule Protect-DMZ-Outbound]
root@SRX5800# up

[edit security idp idp-policy IDP rulebase-ips]
root@SRX5800# edit rule Protect-Servers-Outbound

[edit security idp idp-policy IDP rulebase-ips rule Protect-Servers-Outbound]
root@SRX5800# set match from-zone Internal-Servers to-zone untrust
source-address Internal-Servers-10.3.0.0/16 destination-address any application
default attacks dynamic-attack-groups [ Protect-Clients Detect-Infection ]

[edit security idp idp-policy IDP rulebase-ips rule Protect-Servers-Outbound]
root@SRX5800# set then action drop-connection

[edit security idp idp-policy IDP rulebase-ips rule Protect-Servers-Outbound]
root@SRX5800# set then ip-action ip-block target source-address log timeout 7200

[edit security idp idp-policy IDP rulebase-ips rule Protect-Servers-Outbound]
root@SRX5800# set then notification log-attacks alert

[edit security idp idp-policy IDP rulebase-ips rule Protect-Servers-Outbound]
root@SRX5800# up

[edit security idp idp-policy IDP rulebase-ips rule Protect-Servers-Outbound]
root@SRX5800# up

[edit security idp idp-policy IDP rulebase-ips]
root@SRX5800# edit rule Protect-Servers

[edit security idp idp-policy IDP rulebase-ips rule Protect-Servers]
root@SRX5800# set match from-zone any to-zone Internal-Servers source-address
any destination-address Internal-Servers-10.3.0.0/16 application default attacks
dynamic-attack-groups Protect-Servers

[edit security idp idp-policy IDP rulebase-ips rule Protect-Servers]
root@SRX5800# set then action no-action

[edit security idp idp-policy IDP rulebase-ips rule Protect-Servers]
root@SRX5800# set then notification log-attacks
```

```
[edit security idp idp-policy IDP rulebase-ips rule Protect-Servers]
root@SRX5800# up 3

[edit security idp]
root@SRX5800# set active-policy IDP

[edit security idp]
root@SRX5800# show idp-policy IDP
rulebase-ips {
    rule Custom {
        match {
            source-address any;
            destination-address any;
            attacks {
                custom-attacks [ Block-Facebook Compound-Attack ];
            }
        }
        then {
            action {
                drop-connection;
            }
        }
    }
    rule Protect-DMZ {
        match {
            from-zone untrust;
            source-address any;
            to-zone DMZ;
            destination-address [ edit security idp dynamic-attack-group Detect-
Infection DMZ-Server-172.31.100.0/24 ];
            application default;
            attacks {
                dynamic-attack-groups Protect-DMZ;
            }
        }
        then {
            action {
                drop-connection;
            }
            notification {
                log-attacks;
            }
        }
    }
    rule Protect-Clients-Dept-A {
        match {
            from-zone Dept-A;
            source-address Dept-A-10.1.0.0/16;
            to-zone untrust;
            destination-address any;
            application default;
            attacks {
                dynamic-attack-groups [ Protect-Clients Detect-Infection ];
            }
```

```
        }
        then {
            action {
                drop-connection;
            }
            ip-action {
                ip-block;
                target source-address;
                log;
                timeout 7200;
            }
            notification {
                log-attacks {
                    alert;
                }
            }
        }
    }
    rule Protect-Clients-Dept-B {
        match {
            from-zone Dept-B;
            source-address Dept-B-10.2.0.0/16;
            to-zone untrust;
            destination-address any;
            application default;
            attacks {
                dynamic-attack-groups [ Protect-Clients Detect-Infection ];
            }
        }
        then {
            action {
                drop-connection;
            }
            ip-action {
                ip-block;
                target source-address;
                log;
                timeout 7200;
            }
            notification {
                log-attacks {
                    alert;
                }
            }
        }
    }
    rule Protect-DMZ-Outbound {
        match {
            from-zone DMZ;
            source-address DMZ-Server-172.31.100.0/24;
            to-zone untrust;
            destination-address any;
            application default;
            attacks {
                dynamic-attack-groups [ Protect-Clients Detect-Infection ];
```

```
        }
    }
    then {
        action {
            drop-connection;
        }
        ip-action {
            ip-block;
            target source-address;
            log;
            timeout 7200;
        }
        notification {
            log-attacks {
                alert;
            }
        }
    }
}
rule Protect-Servers-Outbound {
    match {
        from-zone Internal-Servers;
        source-address Internal-Servers-10.3.0.0/16;
        to-zone untrust;
        destination-address any;
        application default;
        attacks {
            dynamic-attack-groups [ Protect-Clients Detect-Infection ];
        }
    }
    then {
        action {
            drop-connection;
        }
        ip-action {
            ip-block;
            target source-address;
            log;
            timeout 7200;
        }
        notification {
            log-attacks {
                alert;
            }
        }
    }
}
rule Protect-Servers {
    match {
        from-zone any;
        source-address any;
        to-zone Internal-Servers;
        destination-address Internal-Servers-10.3.0.0/16;
        application default;
        attacks {
```

```
                dynamic-attack-groups Protect-Servers;
            }
        }
        then {
            action {
                no-action;
            }
            notification {
                log-attacks;
            }
        }
    }
}

[edit security idp]
root@SRX5800# show active-policy
active-policy IDP;

[edit security idp]
root@SRX5800# top

[edit]
root@SRX5800# commit
```

Summary

Although access lists and stateful firewalls were adequate protection for the early threats of the Internet, today's threats require much more vigilance. The IPS that the SRX offers is but a piece of the protection that the threats in the wild today call for. The SRX provides comprehensive IPS protection—not just a subset, but a full implementation of IPS features to provide security for the servers and for the clients of the enterprise. Traditionally, full IPS functionality required completely separate server class devices in addition to dedicated firewalls to provide adequate protection. As threats have advanced over time, so have the protection capabilities offered by the industry; most notably Juniper. Juniper has provided a long lineage of IPS products, from the standalone IDP, to the ISG with security module blades, to the latest SRX Series, all of which have integrated IPS. As an administrator today, you have many more cost-effective options for securing your network, and one of the most powerful tools at your disposal is the SRX Gateway.

Chapter Review Questions

1. What is the difference between full IPS and deep inspection/IPS lite?
2. How can the attack object updates be downloaded, and what is the difference between standard and "full" updates?
3. What is the difference between signature-based attack objects and protocol anomaly detection?

4. What is the difference between an actual exploit and shellcode?
5. What is the difference between client-to-server and server-to-client attacks?
6. What is SSL decryption and how does it work?
7. How is AppDDoS different from IPS and screens?
8. What is the difference between static and dynamic attack groups?
9. Can you create custom protocol anomaly objects?
10. Describe a chain (compound) attack object.

Chapter Review Answers

1. Full IPS provides a much more complete inspection capability than deep inspection/IPS lite. This includes much more in the way of protocol inspection, decoding, application identification, and anomaly-based detection. Deep inspection is typically a small subset of IPS capabilities.
2. The standard update only provides the attack database itself, while the full update will provide the attack database and the detector engine. You can schedule standard updates as part of the configuration, along with being able to manually trigger an update.
3. Signature-based attack objects use detection based on stateful signatures and regular expressions, while protocol anomaly-based attack objects are coded into the detector engine to detect anomalous behavior, but this is not strictly a predefined regular expression pattern; rather, it is more intelligent detection.
4. An exploit is a piece of code which gains control over a victim machine, typically by assuming control over the execution of that program. Shellcode takes the attack a step further to perform some actions after the system execution has been commandeered.
5. Client-to-server attacks are attacks that are generated from the client which is attacking the server of the connection. Server-to-client attacks are those in which the server attacks the client that made the connection to the server.
6. SSL decryption is a feature of the high-end SRX (at the time of this writing) and provides organizations the ability to inspect SSL encrypted sessions with IPS. The SRX must have the private key for the web server installed, and will use that to decrypt the SSL flows to inspect them before passing the traffic on.
7. AppDDoS is a technology (supported on the high-end SRX at the time of this writing) which looks at the big picture of sessions across the different flows on the platform to determine if an attack is taking place, and then what to do about it. Unlike IPS, which is looking for specific patterns or anomalous behavior, AppDDoS attacks are typically meant to tie up resources making lots of valid requests. Screens, on the other hand, deal with lower-level (Layers 3 and 4) anomalies which might occur in the packet processing. These are typically dealt with in the NPU or

in the SPU. AppDDoS functions in the SPU and inspects the higher Layer 7 aspects of the flows. AppDDoS, screens, and IPS can all go hand in hand to provide maximum security.

8. Static groups are groups which you add members into manually, and the groups' membership will not be changed during updates. Dynamic attack groups are specifically set up to define filters that define the criteria regarding which attack objects to add into the group.
9. You cannot define the protocol anomaly code itself, since that must be handled by the Juniper Security Team. However, you can create your own attack objects which are composed of protocol anomaly conditions.
10. Chain attack objects, sometimes referred to as compound attack objects, are used to define multiple criteria for detecting attacks. This is done by first defining the member attack objects (which can be signature and attack objects), and then defining how they fit together to match the overall attack object. You can do this using a Boolean expression and ordered pattern matching.

CHAPTER 9

Unified Threat Management

Unified Threat Management (UTM) is a set of features designed to provide application-layer inspection of traffic as it traverses a network. Similar to Intrusion Detection and Prevention (IDP), security devices that support UTM features decode and inspect upper-layer protocols to detect malicious, or simply disallowed, traffic.

In fact, the IDP feature is often considered part of the UTM feature set. It is only a matter of convention, but as far as Juniper Networks goes, the UTM and IDP features are considered to be independent. At the time of this writing, the UTM feature set is only supported on branch SRX Series gateways.

This chapter explores the UTM features in the SRX, how to identify those features, and how to configure and use them in your own network.

What Is UTM?

So, what features are found on the SRX under the UTM umbrella? Well, the simple answer is anything, apart from IDP, that requires Layer 7 inspection. This includes antivirus, web filtering, content filtering, and antispam.

There is a common trade-off between how detailed the traffic analysis is and how much traffic can be processed. A firewall that protects thousands of hosts inherently has less capacity than the cumulative processing power of all the hosts behind it. When the number of hosts to protect is large, this trade-off would seem to suggest that the ideal place to do the inspection is at the hosts.

However, host-based security suffers from severe limitations in management—it's hard to keep all systems updated with the latest patterns and engines. Also, some features, such as web filtering, require large databases that are best maintained centrally.

So, obviously, the idea is to divide the labor to allow large networks to work in a co-operative way. CPU-intensive tasks such as antivirus scanning are distributed across the network, but to mitigate management problems such as patch updates, centralized security gateways can be used to look for the latest in-the-wild attacks.

And last but not least, whenever there is an imminent threat, security administrators can focus solely on a few devices capable of stopping the latest attacks, so perimeter security devices are commonly kept up-to-date with daily or hourly security patches. These frequent updates, and the fact that the devices are always on, make them especially attractive for performing UTM functions.

All of these factors leverage a common infrastructure built on top of the traditional firewall session table, and a component called the *session manager* allows applications (here referring to the UTM applications themselves, such as the antivirus module) to register interest in a session. As part of the slow path, sessions are marked by one (or more) UTM applications to be processed and the packets from such sessions are sent to the interested applications, which determine if the traffic is allowed.

Whenever an SRX UTM application detects some harmful traffic, it has several options:

- Drop the packet.
- Notify the session manager to silently drop the session.
- Close the session.
- Send a reset.
- In some cases, applications can also embed messages to be sent to users to notify them of problems.

Although this is a very simplistic UTM overview, it already hints at some of the infrastructure required for applications to perform their jobs. Since notification messages must be sent to the users (think about web filtering: if a particular URL is deemed harmful or against policy, users must be notified that access to that site is not allowed), all traffic must be sent through a transparent proxy, which, as we shall see, further defines how a UTM policy works.

Application Proxy

Security policies are used to associate traffic to a UTM policy. UTM policies are profiles used to store all the configuration options for the different features in the UTM feature set. Once a security policy specifies a UTM policy, a transparent proxy processes all matching traffic and, in the case of this book's SRX devices, modifies the contents of the traffic or generate error messages back to the user.

To proxy a session, an SRX device acts both as a TCP client and as a server terminating and originating a TCP session. This uses significant resources, in terms of both memory and CPU, which puts some constraints on the total number of sessions an SRX can proxy (and, in turn, the total number of concurrent sessions using UTM features).

The TCP proxy code feeds a data stream to the protocol parser which, in turn, can decode the protocols supported by UTM, namely FTP, HTTP, SMTP, POP3, and IMAP. The protocol parser extracts the relevant content from each protocol and sends it to the appropriate engine for processing, all of which is depicted in Figure 9-1.

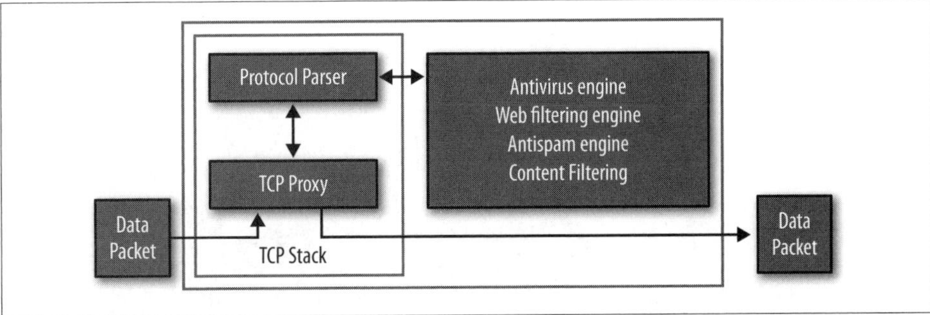

Figure 9-1. How SRX proxies a session

Web Filtering

The SRX web filtering feature, available as part of the UTM feature set, provides a way to control access to websites based on user-defined policies.

For web filtering to be possible, all sites available on the Internet are categorized and a database is created containing the list of all known sites (identified by the site's URLs) and their categories. Juniper has partnered with Websense to provide the category database. Depending on the requirements, two different methods are supported:

- The SurfControl integrated method (note that SurfControl is now part of Websense, but for historic reasons, it is still referred to as the SurfControl solution)
- The Websense redirect method

Both methods provide a way for users to specify a list of site categories that are allowed or denied. The main difference between them concerns where the site's database is located, and where the policies are stored and evaluated.

The SurfControl integrated solution (see Figure 9-2) uses a server hosted and updated by SurfControl that stores the category database. When enabled, the SRX extracts the URL from HTTP messages and queries over the Internet the SurfControl server to determine the site's category. Once a category is obtained, the SRX uses this information to determine if the site is allowed (in this case, the site database is hosted over the Internet and the SRX evaluates the policy).

The Websense redirect solution takes a different approach, which uses a Websense server hosted locally, storing the site's database and web filtering policies. When an HTTP request is received, the SRX forwards the request to the local Websense server, as shown in Figure 9-3, which determines if the request is allowed.

Because the SRX only forwards the request to a Websense server owned and maintained by the user, no license is required to use this mode (as opposed to the SurfControl integrated mode that does require a license).

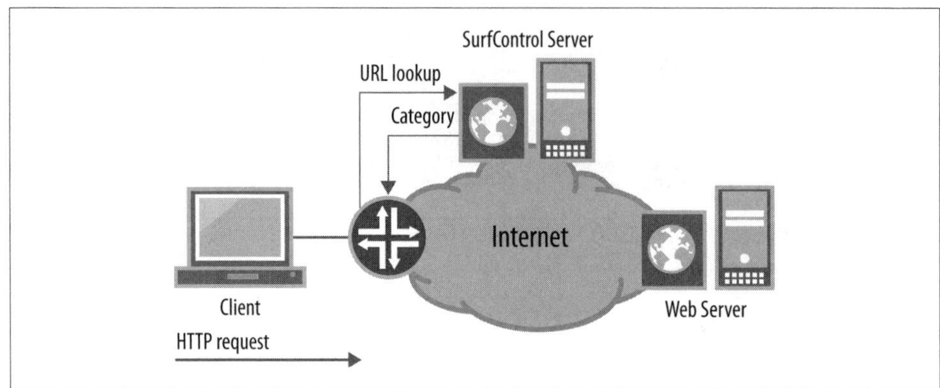

Figure 9-2. SurfControl integrated web filtering

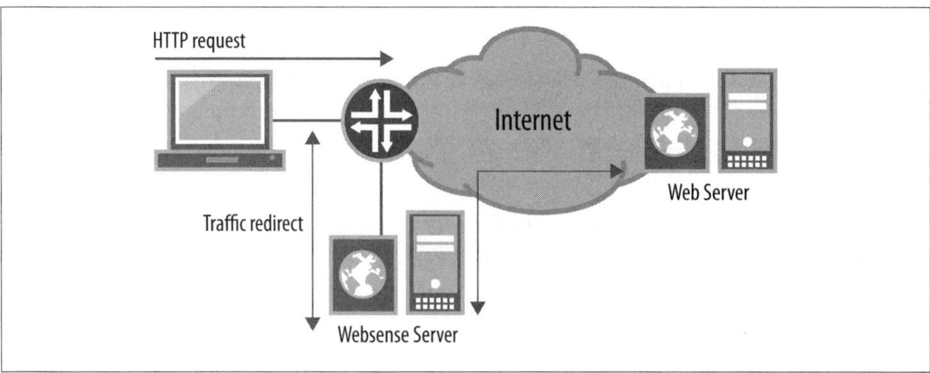

Figure 9-3. Websense redirect web filtering

Configuring web filtering using SurfControl

Let's get our hands dirty and configure web filtering in one of our branch offices, in order to see how things truly work.

First, clients must be allowed in the Trust zone to have Internet access (which requires Network Address Translation [NAT] and a security policy allowing the Trust→Untrust traffic), so a basic configuration would look something like this:

```
nat {
    source {
        rule-set internet {
            from zone trust;
            to zone untrust;
            rule nat-all {
                match {
                    source-address 0.0.0.0/0;
                    destination-address 0.0.0.0/0;
                }
```

```
                then {
                    source-nat {
                        interface;
                    }
                }
            }
        }
    }
}
zones {
    security-zone trust {
        interfaces {
            ge-0/0/1.0;
        }
    }
    security-zone untrust {
        interfaces {
            ge-0/0/0.0;
        }
    }
}
```

Now our web filtering task force has decided that network users in the Trust zone of our small branch office should not have access to gambling sites. So, let's create a UTM policy with web filtering enabled that is used to block access to gambling sites:

```
[edit security utm feature-profile web-filtering]
set surf-control-integrated profile no-gamblig category Gambling action block
set surf-control-integrated profile no-gamblig default permit

[edit security utm]
set utm-policy wf-only web-filtering http-profile no-gambling
```

From the configuration, we can see that our UTM policy, named `wf-only`, points to a web filtering profile (named `no-gambling`). This profile contains the list of both allowed and blocked categories. The default category action is used to determine what to do when either the action for a category has not been explicitly configured, or the category of a URL is unknown (this happens whenever the SurfControl database has no category information for such URL).

To enable the newly created UTM policy, use security policies to select the traffic that uses the `wf-only` policy:

```
[security policies]
set from-zone trust to-zone untrust policy utm-wf-policy match source-address any
set from-zone trust to-zone untrust policy utm-wf-policy match
destination-address any
set from-zone trust to-zone untrust policy utm-wf-policy match application
junos-http
set from-zone trust to-zone untrust policy utm-wf-policy then permit
application-services utm-policy wf-only
```

This might seem a bit convoluted at first, but the underlying assumption is that it is better to create profiles that can be referenced multiple times (i.e., by multiple policies) so that configuration changes can be done in a single place.

That's why in the SRX a security policy points to a UTM policy, which in turn specifies a feature profile to use for each protocol supported by UTM (and for each supported feature), as shown in Figure 9-4.

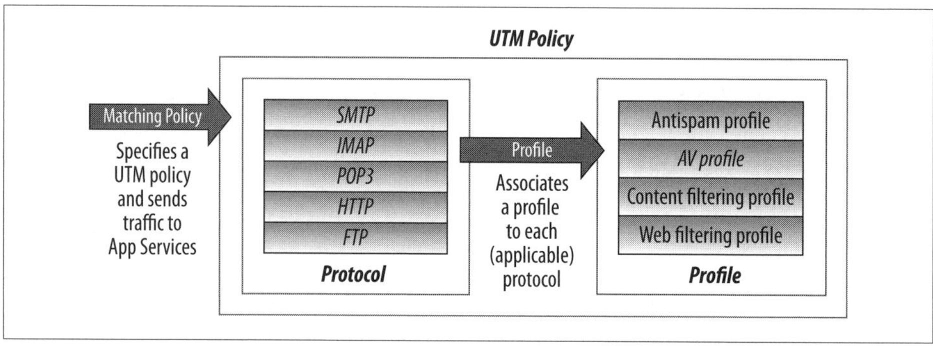

Figure 9-4. UTM policy evaluation

With our sample configuration, a user trying to access a gambling site is denied access and is shown a page with some default message, such as "Corporation XYZ Web Filtering has been set to block this site."

But suppose that our small branch office issues a large amount of traffic early in the mornings, most of it to only a few sites. Wouldn't it be better to maintain a local database holding the results from the latest queries, to reduce the latencies associated with querying the SurfControl server?

We can do this by enabling caching. The cache size determines the number of URIs to keep in memory, while the timeout specifies the maximum time (in seconds) after which a record is removed, as shown in this sample configuration:

```
[edit security utm feature-profile web-filtering]
set surf-control-integrated cache timeout 600
set surf-control-integrated cache size 1000000
```

Now that we looked at some of the configuration options, here is the inside scoop. Some users do not need such granular control over the categories and sites that are allowed or blocked. After all, we can all guess which categories should be allowed or blocked. Instead of doing a lengthy configuration, we can simply use the `junos-wf-cpa-default` profile:

```
[edit security utm]
set utm-policy wf-only web-filtering http-profile junos-wf-cpa-default
```

For those of you who are interested, Table 9-1 lists the allowed/denied categories in the default profile.

Table 9-1. Allowed/denied categories in the default profile

Category	Action
Adult_Sexually_Explicit	Block
Advertisements	Block
Arts_Entertainment	Permit
Chat	Permit
Computing_Internet	Permit
Criminal_Skills	Block
Drugs_Alcohol_Tobacco	Block
Education	Permit
Finance_Investment	Permit
Food_Drink	Permit
Gambling	Block
Games	Block
Glamour_Intimate_Apparel	Permit
Government_Politics	Permit
Hacking	Block
Hate_Speech	Block
Health_Medicine	Permit
Hobbies_Recreation	Permit
Hosting_Sites	Permit
Job_Search_Career_Development	Permit
Kids_Site	Permit
Lifestyle_Culture	Permit
Motor_Vehicles	Permit
News	Permit
Personals_Dating	Block
Photo_Searches	Permit
Real_Estate	Permit
Reference	Permit
Religion	Permit
Remote_Proxies	Block
Sex_Education	Block
Search_Engines	Permit
Shopping	Permit
Sports	Permit

Category	Action
Streaming_Media	Permit
Travel	Permit
Usenet_News	Permit
Violence	Block
Weapons	Block
Web_based_Email	Permit

It's odd that the Sex_Education category is blocked but the Glamour_Intimate_Apparel category is permitted.

Configuring web filtering using Websense redirect

Let's try the previous configuration using the Websense redirect feature. Remember that the Websense server manages the list of allowed categories, so the web filtering profile must only specify the address of the server and port.

Please refer to the Websense documentation for configuration examples on how to set up the server.

Note that the SRX configuration uses a web filtering feature profile that requires setting the web filtering type to `websense-redirect`. The configuration of the web filtering type was not required when using the SurfControl integrated engine, as it is the default option.

```
[edit security utm]
set feature-profile web-filtering type websense-redirect
set feature-profile web-filtering websense-redirect profile ws-server1
server host 10.155.206.13
set feature-profile web-filtering websense-redirect profile ws-server1
server port 15868
set utm-policy utm-wf-websense web-filtering http-profile ws-server1
```

Of course, the UTM policy is applied to a security policy, just like in our previous example:

```
[edit security policies]
set security from-zone trust to-zone untrust policy utm-wf-policy match
source-address any
set security from-zone trust to-zone untrust policy utm-wf-policy match
destination-address any
set security from-zone trust to-zone untrust policy utm-wf-policy match
application any
set security from-zone trust to-zone untrust policy utm-wf-policy
then permit application-services utm-policy utm-wf-websense
```

With each profile, it is also possible to specify an account that the Websense server will use to determine which web filtering policy to use. When configured, the account is passed on to the server with every HTTP request. This can be useful when creating multiple security policies that require different web filtering policies.

Let's go just a little further and consider the case where traffic from the Trust to Untrust zones requires blocking access to hacking sites, but traffic from the Engineering zone to the Untrust zone should not (so that the IT team can learn about the latest exploits). This requires two web filtering profiles, each passing a different account that the server uses to choose the appropriate filtering policy. Here is the first web filtering profile:

```
[edit security utm]
set feature-profile web-filtering type websense-redirect
set feature-profile web-filtering websense-redirect profile ws-engineering
server host 10.155.206.13
set feature-profile web-filtering websense-redirect profile ws-engineering
server port 15868
set feature-profile web-filtering websense-redirect profile ws-engineering
account engineering
set feature-profile web-filtering websense-redirect profile ws-trust
server host 10.155.206.13
set feature-profile web-filtering websense-redirect profile ws-trust
server port 15868
set feature-profile web-filtering websense-redirect profile ws-trust
account trust
set utm-policy utm-wf-websense-engineering web-filtering http-profile
ws-engineering
set utm-policy utm-wf-websense-trust web-filtering http-profile ws-trust
```

And here is the second one:

```
[edit security policies]
set from-zone trust to-zone untrust policy utm-wf-policy match source-address any
set from-zone trust to-zone untrust policy utm-wf-policy match
destination-address any
set from-zone trust to-zone untrust policy utm-wf-policy match
application junos-http
set from-zone trust to-zone untrust policy utm-wf-policy then
permit application-services utm-policy utm-wf-websense-trust
set from-zone engineering to-zone untrust policy utm-wf-policy-eng match
source-address any
set from-zone engineering to-zone untrust policy utm-wf-policy-eng match
destination-address any
set from-zone engineering to-zone untrust policy utm-wf-policy-eng match
application junos-http
set from-zone engineering to-zone untrust policy utm-wf-policy-eng then
permit application-services utm-policy utm-wf-websense-engineering
```

Since multiple HTTP requests can arrive simultaneously, the requests are automatically load-balanced between the different sockets, so, naturally, there is a trade-off between the load that each SRX can create to a Websense server and the maximum number of requests that can be resolved in parallel. In most cases, the default configuration is adequate, but it's possible to limit the maximum number of simultaneous connections an SRX can create for a given profile by changing the sockets option (between one and eight connections are supported):

```
[edit security utm feature-profile web-filtering]
set profile ws-trust server host 10.155.206.13
set profile ws-trust server port 15868
set profile ws-trust sockets 4
set profile ws-trust account trust
```

Creating custom category lists

It is often useful to control access to some internal servers that are not accessible to the categorization engines, or to explicitly allow or deny access to a particular URL. *Custom category lists* provide this functionality on the SRX, and since these lists take precedence over classification servers, it is possible to overwrite the categorization that they perform. When an HTTP request is received, the custom category lists are checked, and if a match is found, the traffic is allowed or denied based on the configuration, without the need to query the web filtering servers.

The first thing to configure is a URL pattern, consisting of one or more URLs. The wildcard character (*) is supported (meaning one or more characters of any type) at the beginning of the site name, and it must be followed by a period (.). The question mark character (?), which matches any single character, is only supported after the last "." in the URL.

Since we are dealing with URLs, the *http://* prefix is required. As an example, the following patterns are correctly expanded:

http://www.juniper.net/
http://.juniper.net*
http://www.juniper.???
http://www.juniper.ne?
http://.juniper.???*

These patterns are not:

http://ww.juniper.net*
http://???.juniper.net
http://www..net*
*http://www.juniper.**
http://???.???.???

Creating a URL list is quite simple. Just add the list of URL patterns as shown here:

```
[edit security utm custom-objects]
set url-pattern allowed-urls value http://www.thenewnetworkishere.com
set url-pattern allowed-urls value http://www.netscreen.com
set url-pattern blocked-urls value
http://www.thenewnetworkishere.com/us/en/new_network/
set url-pattern blocked-urls value "http://???.netscreen.com"
```

Once the URL lists are created, you can create custom categories consisting of one (or more) URL list(s). The custom categories are used to create whitelists and blacklists to allow or deny access to matching URLs, regardless of the web filtering engine used (e.g., SurfControl integrated or Websense redirect). Blacklists are evaluated first, and therefore they take precedence over whitelists (and server processing). The evaluation order of whitelists and blacklists is shown more explicitly in Figure 9-5.

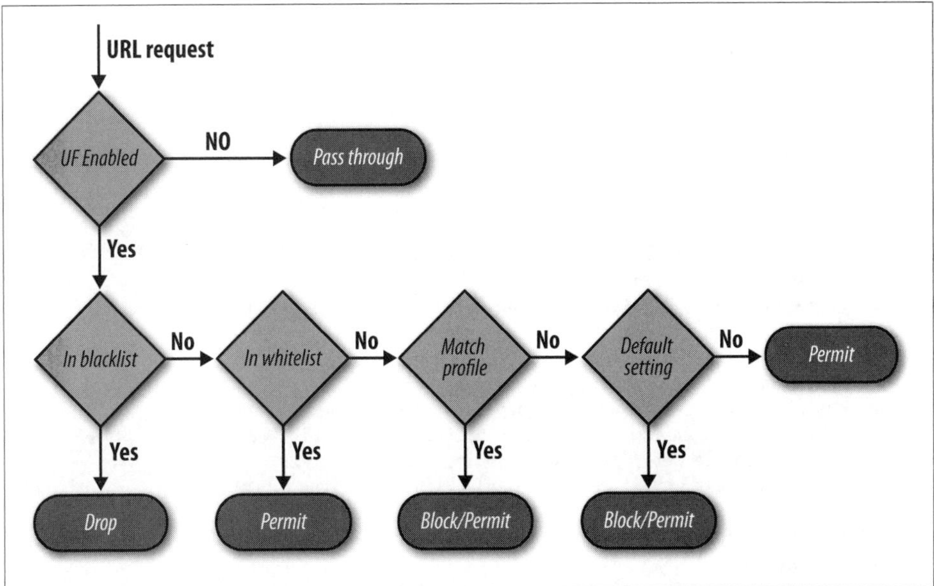

Figure 9-5. Web filtering evaluation order

Let's use the newly create URL lists to create new categories to be used for blacklists and whitelists:

```
[edit security utm custom-objects]
set custom-url-category good-sites value allowed-urls
set custom-url-category bad-sites value blocked-urls

[edit security utm feature-profile]
set web-filtering url-whitelist good-sites
set web-filtering url-blacklist bad-sites
```

Here, access to *http://www.thenewnetworkishere.com/us/en/new_network/* is allowed because the URL belongs to the whitelist, whereas access to any other URL in the *http://www.thenewnetworkishere.com* domain is denied. But if you try to access *http://www.netscreen.com*, you'll find that access is allowed even though the blacklist contains the *http://???.netscreen.com* pattern. Why is that? Aren't blacklists supposed to have priority over whitelists?

A closer look at the configuration reveals the problem. The *http://???.netscreen.com* URL, although valid, will not be treated as a wildcard pattern because the "?" wildcard is only allowed after the last "." (thus, it will only match a request to *http://???.netscreen.com*, and not to, say, *http://www.netscreen.com*).

Using local classification only

I mentioned that the SurfControl integrated and Websense redirect solutions have some added costs associated with them: the SurfControl integrated solution requires a license, and Websense redirect can only be used with an external Websense server (which requires purchase of the Websense software).

For networks that only need local classification using blacklists and whitelists, a local engine on the SRX that does not require any license is provided. The configuration is the same as for the other two engine types, but only custom categories on URL lists are supported. We can redo our previous configuration, this time using the local engine:

```
[edit security utm]
set custom-objects url-pattern allowed-urls value
http://www.thenewnetworkishere.com
set custom-objects url-pattern allowed-urls value http://www.netscreen.com
set custom-objects url-pattern blocked-urls value
http://www.thenewnetworkishere.com/us/en/new_network/
set custom-objects url-pattern blocked-urls value "http://???.netscreen.com"
set custom-objects custom-url-category good-sites value allowed-urls
set custom-objects custom-url-category bad-sites value blocked-urls
set feature-profile web-filtering url-whitelist good-sites
set feature-profile web-filtering url-blacklist bad-sites
set feature-profile web-filtering type juniper-local
set feature-profile web-filtering juniper-local profile local-engine
default permit
set utm-policy utm-wf-local web-filtering http-profile local-engine

[edit security policy]
set from-zone trust to-zone untrust policy utm-wf-policy match source-address any
set from-zone trust to-zone untrust policy utm-wf-policy match
destination-address any
set from-zone trust to-zone untrust policy utm-wf-policy match
application junos-http
set from-zone trust to-zone untrust policy utm-wf-policy then
permit application-services utm-policy utm-wf-websense-trust
```

Antivirus

Building on the same SRX infrastructure as web filtering, the antivirus engine can proxy all connections, decode and extract files from the upper-layer protocols, and scan the extracted files for viruses. Once a file is detected, it is stored in memory and passed on to the scanning engine.

Three different scanning engines are supported:

- The Kaspersky full antivirus engine
- The Juniper Express engine

- The Sophos in-the-cloud engine

Each has its own set of advantages and trade-offs which you should try to match to the demands and needs of your network. Let's get started with the Kaspersky antivirus engine.

Kaspersky full antivirus

The Kaspersky full antivirus database and engine provide the most comprehensive solution to scanning for viruses, for at the time of this writing, half a million records were included in the database. The engine is also capable of using some heuristics methods to detect polymorphic and metamorphic viruses (viruses that constantly change their code while keeping their functionality, making them difficult to detect using traditional pattern-matching engines).

All this flexibility comes at the expense of computational complexity and the full antivirus solution significantly reduces the maximum performance of a device when a large portion of the traffic is scanned.

Before we start the configuration, you need to download and install the latest antivirus engine and database. The SRX can download the updates automatically, provided that it has Internet connectivity (and at least a name server is configured and reachable).

Since multiple engines are available, we must specify which engine to use (at the time of this writing, only a single engine can be used at any given time):

```
set security utm feature-profile anti-virus type kaspersky-lab-engine
```

The operational command `request security utm anti-virus` triggers a pattern update:

```
root@SRX650-1# run request security utm anti-virus kaspersky-lab-engine pattern-
update
Anti-virus update request results: av_mgr: pattern updater 2644 is started,
downloading from http://update.juniper-updates.net/AV/SRX650/.
```

Once a pattern is downloaded and installed, the antivirus engine status command shows the engine and database version as well as the number of records in the database:

```
root@SRX650-1# run show security utm anti-virus status
 UTM anti-virus status:

    Anti-virus key expire date: 2011-09-02 00:00:00
    Update server: http://update.juniper-updates.net/AV/SRX650/
           Interval: 60 minutes
           Pattern update status: next update in 57 minutes
           Last result: already have latest database
    Anti-virus signature version: 01/13/2010 06:30 GMT, virus records: 536362
    Anti-virus signature compiler version: N/A
    Scan engine type: kaspersky-lab-engine
    Scan engine information: last action result: No error(0x00000000)
```

This command also provides a hint of the default update frequency of the engine as you can see from the output, where the SRX queries the update server every hour and automatically updates the engine and signatures if new ones are available.

You can control this behavior from the [security utm feature-profile anti-virus kaspersky-lab-engine pattern-update] hierarchy (it is available for every antivirus engine supported). For instance, we can disable the automatic update so that administrators can choose to manually update the signatures on maintenance windows:

```
[edit security utm feature-profile anti-virus kaspersky-lab-engine]
set pattern-update no-autoupdate
```

Let's move on and practice configuring some antivirus policies using the Kaspersky engine. As a reminder, Figure 9-6 shows what our simple branch network looks like.

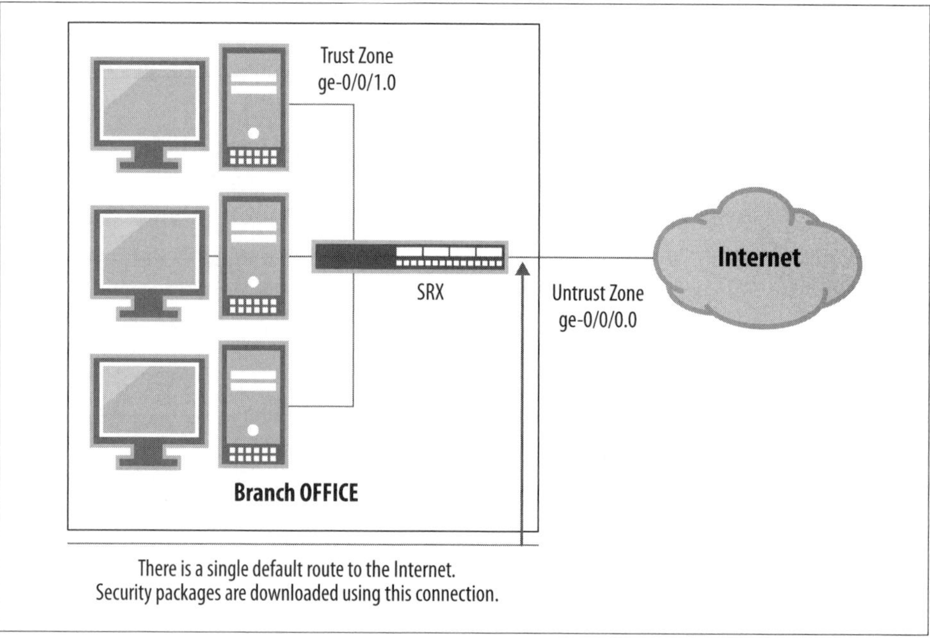

Figure 9-6. How SRX proxies a session

Just like in our web filtering examples, a single policy from Trust to Untrust is used. The following specifies the UTM policy to use which, in turn, lists the antivirus profiles used for each protocol:

```
[edit security nat]
set source rule-set internet from zone trust
set source rule-set internet to zone untrust
set source rule-set internet rule nat-all match source-address 0.0.0.0/0
set source rule-set internet rule nat-all match destination-address 0.0.0.0/0
set source rule-set internet rule nat-all then source-nat interface
```

```
[edit security policies]
set from-zone trust to-zone untrust policy utm-av-policy match source-address any
set from-zone trust to-zone untrust policy utm-av-policy match
destination-address any
set from-zone trust to-zone untrust policy utm-av-policy match application any
set from-zone trust to-zone untrust policy utm-av-policy then
permit application-services utm-policy kaspesky-av-only

[edit security utm]
set feature-profile anti-virus type kaspersky-lab-engine
set feature-profile anti-virus kaspersky-lab-engine profile karspersky-basic
scan-options intelligent-prescreening
set utm-policy kaspesky-av-only anti-virus http-profile karspersky-basic
set utm-policy kaspesky-av-only anti-virus ftp upload-profile karspersky-basic
set utm-policy kaspesky-av-only anti-virus ftp download-profile karspersky-basic
set utm-policy kaspesky-av-only anti-virus smtp-profile karspersky-basic
set utm-policy kaspesky-av-only anti-virus pop3-profile karspersky-basic
set utm-policy kaspesky-av-only anti-virus imap-profile karspersky-basic
```

Note that the only thing configured in the antivirus profile is an option to enable intelligent prescreening. Since antivirus scanning is quite computationally expensive, several techniques are used to bypass scanning for harmless content, and intelligent prescreening is one of them. When enabled, intelligent prescreening uses the first few packets of a file to determine if malicious code could be present. Based on this first pass, the engine can determine if the file contents are likely to be infected, and can bypass scanning (without the need to store and scan the whole file) if the file is determined to not be infected.

Following the same kind of adjustments, the scan-mode knob controls whether all files are scanned. When scan-by-extension is set, only files with extensions matching one of the extensions in the extension list are scanned.

Before enhancing our configuration, there are two more important scan options that should be mentioned. In an attempt to bypass the antivirus engines, it is common for viruses to be sent in compressed files. The SRX can decompress the files before scanning them, but sometimes files can be compressed multiple times—for instance, when ZIP files contain one or more ZIP files. To put a bound to the CPU resources used by the engine, it is possible to limit the number of decompressions that a single file can undergo.

The last scan option worth mentioning is the content size limit. Since the full content of files has to be stored in memory for a file to be scanned (unless intelligent prescreening has determined that the file is not infected), it is possible to limit the max file size, after which the engine can decide to either drop or allow the file (we will cover how to control this behavior later in this chapter when we discuss how to control fallback).

Let's put some of these options into our antivirus policy:

```
[edit security utm]
set feature-profile anti-virus type kaspersky-lab-engine
```

```
set feature-profile anti-virus kaspersky-lab-engine profile
karspersky-by-extension scan-options intelligent-prescreening
set feature-profile anti-virus kaspersky-lab-engine profile
karspersky-by-extension scan-options scan-mode by-extension
set feature-profile anti-virus kaspersky-lab-engine profile
karspersky-by-extension scan-options content-size-limit 20000
set feature-profile anti-virus kaspersky-lab-engine profile
karspersky-by-extension scan-options decompress-layer-limit 4
set utm-policy kaspesky-av-only anti-virus http-profile
karspersky-by-extension
set utm-policy kaspesky-av-only anti-virus ftp upload-profile
karspersky-by-extension
set utm-policy kaspesky-av-only anti-virus ftp download-profile
karspersky-by-extension
set utm-policy kaspesky-av-only anti-virus smtp-profile
karspersky-by-extension
set utm-policy kaspesky-av-only anti-virus pop3-profile
karspersky-by-extension
```

You might notice that the policy specified scanning by extension, but where is the extension list? Well, it turns out that a default extension list containing these extensions is used:

```
386;ACE;ARJ;ASP;BAT;BIN;BZ2;CAB;CHM;CLA;CMD;COM;CPL;DLL;DOC;DOT;DPL;DRV;DWG;
ELF;EMF;EML;EXE;FON;FPM;GEA;GZ;HA;HLP;HTA;HTM;HTML;HTT;HXS;ICE;INI;ITSF;JAR;
JPEG;JPG;JS;JSE;LHA;LNK;LZH;MBX;MD?;MIME;MSG;MSI;MSO;NWS;OCX;OTM;OV?;PDF;PHP;
PHT;PIF;PK;PL;PLG;PP?;PRG;PRJ;RAR;REG;RTF;SCR;SH;SHS;SWF;SYS;TAR;TGZ;THE;TSP;
VBE;VBS;VXD;WSF;WSH;XL?;XML;ZIP;
```

This list cannot be modified. Instead, it's possible to create a new list with additional extensions to scan. For instance, let's add `xslt` to the list of extensions to scan:

```
[edit security utm]
set custom-objects filename-extension my-extensions value XSLT
set feature-profile anti-virus kaspersky-lab-engine profile
karspersky-by-extension scan-options scan-extension my-extensions
```

The Kaspersky full antivirus engine leverages all the strength of its knowledge of antivirus technology. With more than half a million signatures, it provides a comprehensive solution to the virus detection problem. Often, when client computers protected by the SRX already have an antivirus engine installed, a full scanning solution is not needed. Instead, a lightweight centralized solution that can be updated quickly and easily is the perfect complement to a host-based solution. This is the main idea behind the Juniper Express antivirus engine, which we'll discuss in the next section.

Juniper Express antivirus

The Kaspersky antivirus engine provides the most complete solution to the virus detection problem, but it might not always be the best idea to use it. At the beginning of this chapter, I pointed out that in many circumstances (particularly with a large number of computers behind an SRX and a large amount of traffic), it's best to offload the task of looking for viruses to the endpoints (the computers behind the SRX). In such circumstances, the SRX can still play an important role by scanning for only a subset of the full antivirus database, but doing so in a more efficient way. This is the idea behind the Juniper Express antivirus engine.

With this solution, the SRX uses pattern-matching techniques, which can be offloaded to specific hardware. The virus database is still provided by Kaspersky, but only a subset of the full database, with the most recent and critical signatures are distributed.

On SRX platforms with hardware acceleration (all branch SRX devices including the SRX210, SRX240, and SRX650), the matching is offloaded into hardware, whereas in legacy platforms (J Series), the main CPU performs all the matching operations.

The configuration is quite similar to the full antivirus solution, but some of the options, such as scan-by-extension and scanning compressed files, are not supported (keep in mind that the main advantage of using this solution is to improve performance; having to decompress files would defeat the purpose of using the Express engine). Let's take a look at a Juniper Express antivirus configuration for our branch office:

```
[edit security policies]
set from-zone trust to-zone untrust policy utm-av-policy match source-address any
set from-zone trust to-zone untrust policy utm-av-policy match
destination-address any
set from-zone trust to-zone untrust policy utm-av-policy match application any
set from-zone trust to-zone untrust policy utm-av-policy then
permit application-services utm-policy express-av-only

[edit security utm]
set feature-profile anti-virus type juniper-express-engine
set feature-profile anti-virus juniper-express-engine profile
juniper-express scan-options no-intelligent-prescreening
set utm-policy express-av-only anti-virus http-profile juniper-express
set utm-policy express-av-only anti-virus ftp upload-profile juniper-express
set utm-policy express-av-only anti-virus ftp download-profile juniper-express
set utm-policy express-av-only anti-virus smtp-profile juniper-express
set utm-policy express-av-only anti-virus pop3-profile juniper-express
set utm-policy express-av-only anti-virus imap-profile juniper-express
```

If you have been following the examples, at this point your antivirus database should be loaded with the Kaspersky Full antivirus database. Do not forget to load the Juniper Express antivirus database before testing this configuration. The `request security utm anti-virus juniper-express-engine pattern-update` operational mode command can be used to load the new database.

Using the Juniper Express engine, it is possible to leverage the strengths of a packet-based engine, such as high performance and low scanning latencies, to provide a lightweight, hardware-assisted virus detection solution. Devices are still constrained by the size of the virus signature database and administrators still have to make sure the database is up-to-date. The last approach to antivirus uses an in-the-cloud solution, removing the need to keep a local database and eliminating the burden of the local database administrator.

Sophos in-the-cloud antivirus

The latest addition to the antivirus feature set is the Sophos in-the-cloud solution and it tackles the scalability problem in a different way.

Most malicious traffic (and in fact, most traffic) these days is carried over HTTP, so a repudiation-based system provides an effective way to block content from well-known malicious sites. This is done in a similar way to how web filtering is performed, but instead of returning the category of a site, the Sophos server indicates if the site is known to host malicious code.

Obviously, this only works for HTTP-based traffic. For non-HTTP traffic, files can still be scanned by computing a checksum of the file and comparing the result against a malware database. Not all viruses can be detected this way, particularly polymorphic, metamorphic, or, in general, nonstatic malware. But at least for the time being, static malware constitutes the majority of attacks.

On the Sophos engine, the two URL methods and file checksum checking can be used simultaneously. First (and for HTTP only), the URL is checked against the repudiation database. If allowed (or if the protocol is not HTTP, in which case the URL check does not apply), the contents are downloaded and a checksum is computed for all the embedded files. URL checks can be disabled in the antivirus profile using a `no-url-check` option.

At the time of this writing, a checksum can be computed for the following file types (files of other types are not scanned):

> *.exe*; *.zip*; *.rar*; *.swf*; *.pdf*; *.ole2* (*.doc*, *.xls*)

Here's an example configuration that uses the Sophos engine to scan HTTP traffic:

```
[edit security]
set policies from-zone trust to-zone untrust policy Internet-Access match
source-address any
set policies from-zone trust to-zone untrust policy Internet-Access match
destination-address any
set policies from-zone trust to-zone untrust policy Internet-Access match
application junos-http
set policies from-zone trust to-zone untrust policy Internet-Access then
permit application-services utm-policy Sophos-AV-Only

set utm feature-profile anti-virus type sophos-engine
set utm feature-profile anti-virus sophos-engine profile Sophos-AV
scan-options uri-check
set utm utm-policy Sophos-AV-Only anti-virus http-profile Sophos-AV
```

Just as with the other engines, it's necessary to download the antivirus pattern engine before you can use the feature. But if the virus and URL database are stored in the Sophos servers, why do we have to download any pattern files? In this case, the pattern files contain some of the logic the engine uses to compute the file checksums and identify the file types. So, you still have to make sure the latest engine is used.

The main advantage of the Sophos in-the-cloud solution is that, since the database is stored and maintained outside the SRX, the number of signatures that can be detected is not bound by the SRX's memory.

Antivirus trickling

When using any of the antivirus solutions, the SRX must locally store the contents of the files that need to be scanned (these files can be embedded or downloaded through HTTP or FTP, or be part of email attachments).

Remember that the SRX proxies all the connections that require UTM services. Large files present the biggest problem in that, while they are being downloaded and later scanned by the SRX, the client connection can time out if the SRX does not send any information back to the client.

To prevent this from happening, the SRX can leak some of the file contents back to the client. This is referred to as *trickling*, and it can be configured under the antivirus profile. When enabled, the SRX sends small fragments of the file to the client in regular intervals (controlled by the timeout interval):

```
[edit security utm feature-profile anti-virus]
set sophos-engine profile Sophos-AV trickling timeout 10
```

Whitelists

Since the antivirus scanning operation is very CPU-intensive, best practice advocates avoiding scanning traffic when such traffic is known to be harmless.

For instance, in situations where the content in a particular resource is under the administrator's control and is guaranteed to be clean, scanning the traffic from that resource could be avoided. Figure 9-7 shows the whitelist processing.

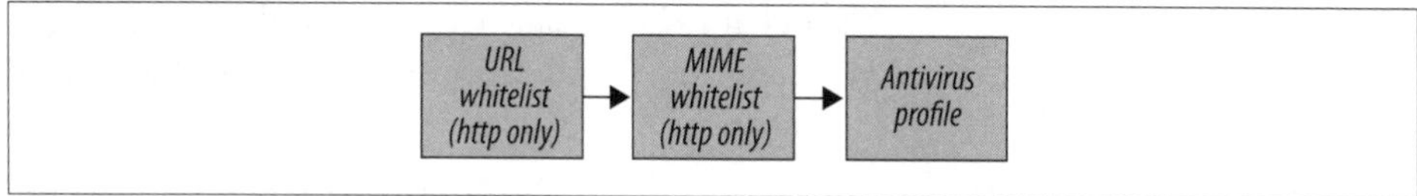

Figure 9-7. Whitelist evaluation order

In the same spirit, administrators have the option of identifying certain file types that are not considered harmful and subsequently are not scanned. When available, the MIME headers of a file can be used to obtain information about the file's type. The `mime-whitelist` is used to indicate the MIME types that do not need to be scanned. It is also possible to configure an exception list, indicating more specific MIME types that must be scanned even if their type is included in the `mime-whitelist`. For example, we can define a `mime-whitelist` that does not scan video files except for Windows media files by creating a `mime-whitelist` with MIME type `video/` and an associated exception list for MIME type `video/x-ms-wmv`.

To be consistent with the web filtering feature, the URL whitelist command references a custom URL category (not a URL pattern). This is useful for reusing custom URL categories used in a web filtering profile to allow traffic to some internal sites (as shown in "Creating custom category lists" on page 496).

URL patterns and MIME patterns are defined under the `[security utm custom-objects]` Junos hierarchy:

```
[edit security utm]
set custom-objects mime-pattern video value video/
set custom-objects mime-pattern windows-media value video/x-ms-wmv
set custom-objects url-pattern internal-server value http://intranet.company.com
set custom-objects url-pattern another-internal-server value
http://extranet.company.com
set custom-objects custom-url-category internal-sites value internal-server
set custom-objects custom-url-category internal-sites
value another-internal-server

set feature-profile anti-virus mime-whitelist list video
set feature-profile anti-virus mime-whitelist exception windows-media
set feature-profile anti-virus url-whitelist internal-sites
```

Notifications

So far, we have discussed how to enable some of the features included in the UTM feature set, and we worked our way through some simple configurations. What we haven't discussed, however, is how users are notified whenever traffic is blocked.

Notification options are similar across all UTM features. When offending traffic is detected, the protocol content is modified with an embedded user message (e.g., for HTTP, a new page is generated with a customizable notification message to the user).

In the case of FTP, it's also possible to generate a protocol-specific error so that the FTP application is notified of the problem. UTM features that can block FTP traffic (antivirus and content filtering) generate these notifications when dealing with FTP traffic.

Since we have been experimenting most recently with antivirus, it seems appropriate to customize the notification messages sent to the user when a virus is found. The following configuration shows how to customize the notification options for our antivirus profile:

```
[edit security policies]
set from-zone trust to-zone untrust policy Internet-Access match
source-address any
set from-zone trust to-zone untrust policy Internet-Access match
destination-address any
set from-zone trust to-zone untrust policy Internet-Access match
application junos-http
```

```
set from-zone trust to-zone untrust policy Internet-Access match
application junos-ftp
set from-zone trust to-zone untrust policy Internet-Access then p
ermit application-services utm-policy AV-notifications

[edit security utm]
set feature-profile anti-virus type kaspersky-lab-engine
set feature-profile anti-virus kaspersky-lab-engine pattern-update
set feature-profile anti-virus kaspersky-lab-engine profile full-av
scan-options intelligent-prescreening

#Message sent to the user when a virus is found
set feature-profile anti-virus kaspersky-lab-engine profile full-av
notification-options virus-detection custom-message
"Virus Found! File blocked by SRX"

set utm-policy AV-notifications anti-virus http-profile full-av
set utm-policy AV-notifications anti-virus ftp upload-profile full-av
set utm-policy AV-notifications anti-virus ftp download-profile full-av
```

Users accessing infected files through HTTP are presented with the configured error message. Trying to download an infected file using FTP results in both an error message sent to the client and the context of the file being replaced with the error message.

It's also possible to configure the profile to only generate protocol error messages for FTP, while leaving the file contents blank:

```
[edit security utm]
set notification-options virus-detection type message
```

When an email message is discovered carrying an infected file, the SRX can generate a notification email message for both the original email sender and the local network administrator.

For these notification messages to be sent, the SRX must be configured with an SMTP server (and account information) used to forward the emails. The SMTP server configuration can be found under the [smtp] hierarchy:

```
[edit smtp]
set primary-server address <smtp server address>
set primary-server login "administrator@network.net" password <password>
```

The notification options control the contents of the notification emails, and where these emails will be sent:

```
[edit security utm]
set feature-profile anti-virus kaspersky-lab-engine profile full-av notification-
options virus-detection custom-message-subject "SRX AV engine: Virus Found"
set feature-profile anti-virus kaspersky-lab-engine profile full-av notification-
options virus-detection notify-mail-sender
```

Each feature profile allows the customization of notification options so that you can alert users when some traffic is blocked by one of the UTM features, but how can you view when some content has been blocked? Better yet, how can you view and filter the information that each UTM feature can supply?

Those are good questions to answer, but before we work on them with the rest of the UTM configuration, let's provide some insight into how the UTM logs are generated.

Viewing the UTM Logs

By default, all messages generated by the system are stored under the */var/log/messages* file.

The default log configuration filters all messages except for the critical ones, which means that, in most cases, UTM logs are discarded unless they are specifically allowed.

In Junos, the eventd daemon controls how the system logs are stored and forwarded. The configuration for this daemon can be found under the `[system syslog]` hierarchy, and it allows administrators to filter the messages and send them to a remote syslog server, a local file, or an actual user terminal.

System logs can be generated using standard syslog or structured syslog format; the latter is shown in Figure 9-8.

```
<priority>version timestamp hostname process processid tag [AVP list] text
```

Figure 9-8. Structured syslog message format

Figure 9-8 shows that a structured syslog message includes the following elements:

- An 8-bit integer value used to encode the facility and severity of the message (see Table 9-2)
- The log version
- A timestamp
- The hostname of the device generating the message
- The process name and process ID of the process generating the message
- A message tag (the tag is a string used to identify the message and it is very useful when filtering logs)
- A list of attribute value pairs (used to encode information relevant to that message, such as IP addresses, virus names, etc.)
- (Optional) A text string that describes the event that caused the log

Table 9-2. Log facility and severity encoding

Facility number	Severity emergency	Alert	Critical	Error	Warning	Notice	Info	Debug
kernel (0)	1	1	2	3	4	5	6	7
user (1)	8	9	10	11	12	13	14	15

Facility number	Severity emergency	Alert	Critical	Error	Warning	Notice	Info	Debug
mail (2)	16	17	18	19	20	21	22	23
daemon (3)	24	25	26	27	28	29	30	31
authorization (4)	32	33	34	35	36	37	38	39
syslog (5)	40	41	42	43	44	45	46	47
printer (6)	48	49	50	51	52	53	54	55
news (7)	56	57	58	59	60	61	62	63
uucp (8)	64	65	66	67	68	69	70	71
clock (9)	72	73	74	75	76	77	78	79
authorization-private (10)	80	81	82	83	84	85	86	87
ftp (11)	88	89	90	91	92	93	94	95
ntp (12)	96	97	98	99	100	101	102	103
security (13)	104	105	106	107	108	109	110	111
console (14)	112	113	114	115	116	117	118	119
local0 (16)	128	129	130	131	132	133	134	135
dfc (17)	136	137	138	139	140	141	142	143
local2 (18)	144	145	146	147	148	149	150	151
firewall (19)	152	153	154	155	156	157	158	159
pfe (20)	160	161	162	163	164	165	166	167
conflict-log (21)	168	169	170	171	172	173	174	175
change-log (22)	176	177	178	179	180	181	182	183
interactive-commands (23)	184	185	186	187	188	189	190	191

It is very useful to classify the logs, and send logs from different modules to different files, so administrators can easily find the logs from a given module. Toward this end, a very common practice is to configure the devices to log web filtering, antivirus, and firewall session logs to different files. Here's how you can do this:

```
[edit system syslog]
set file sessions user info
set file sessions match RT_FLOW
set file sessions structured-data brief
set file interfaces any any
set file interfaces match SNMP_TRAP_LINK
set file interfaces structured-data brief
set file viruses user info
set file viruses match AV_
set file viruses structured-data brief
set file webfilter daemon any
set file webfilter match WEBFILTER_
set file webfilter structured-data brief
```

Though it's short, there are a few things to note in this configuration. First, the facility of the logs generated by the data plane (i.e., traffic-driven logs) is `user`. This might be counterintuitive and it is due to the fact that the data-plane threads forward all the logs to a daemon running on user space in the control plane (running on the routing engines in the SRX3000 and SRX5000 lines, and running in a separate hardware thread on single-processor SRX devices). This daemon collects all the logs from the different forwarding threads and forwards them to the event management subsystem.

Careful readers might notice that logs from the web filtering subsystem do not use facility `user` but use facility `daemon` instead. It turns out that the code in charge of querying the SurfControl servers to obtain the category for a particular URL runs in the control plane, which explains why the logs use a different facility.

The `match` statements in the configuration are used to filter the logs. Any regular expression can be used (given that the logs are simple text strings, any part of the log can be used to match on), but, since logs generated by a given subsystem always use the same prefix in the log `TAG`, a very simple regular expression matching on the `TAG` prefix allows one to filter the logs by the originating subsystem.

Some of the most common prefixes present in the logs are:

`ANTISPAM_`
: Used by the antispam module.

`AV_`
: Used by the antivirus module.

`CONTENT_FILTERING_`
: Used by the content filtering module.

`IDP_`
: Used by the IDP module.

`RT_FLOW_`
: Used by the flow module (which handles session establishment and teardown, among other things). The flow logs include the packet's 5-tuple (source and destination IP addresses, source and destination ports, and protocol), translated addresses (showing the effects of NAT) and zones, among other information.

`FWAUTH_`
: Used by the firewall authentication module.

`RT_SCREEN_`
: Used by the screens associated to zones (and generates logs for invalid packets, session limits, etc.).

For instance, when session logging and web filtering are enabled an HTTP request will result in a session open log, followed by a web filtering log indicating the requested URL and category, followed by a session close log. Of course, the granularity of the logs is configurable in such a way that logs are generated only for session open or session close events (or both).

Let's take a look at the output from an HTTP request:

```
root@SRX650-1# run show log sessions

<14>1 2010-01-25T01:47:59.294Z SRX650-1 RT_FLOW - RT_FLOW_SESSION_CREATE
[junos@2636.1.1.1.2.40 source-address="10.1.1.101" source-port="38090"
destination-address="96.17.215.148" destination-port="80"
service-name="junos-http" nat-source-address="172.19.101.26"
nat-source-port="3732" nat-destination-address="96.17.215.148"
nat-destination-port="80" src-nat-rule-name="nat-all"
dst-nat-rule-name="None" protocol-id="6" policy-name="Internet-Access"
source-zone-name="trust" destination-zone-name="untrust" session-id-32="58"]

<14>1 2010-01-25T01:48:24.209Z SRX650-1 RT_FLOW - RT_FLOW_SESSION_CLOSE
[junos@2636.1.1.1.2.40 reason="TCP FIN" source-address="10.1.1.101" source-
port="38090" destination-address="96.17.215.148" destination-port="80" service-
name="junos-http" nat-source-address="172.19.101.26" nat-source-port="3732" nat-
destination-address="96.17.215.148" nat-destination-port="80" src-nat-rule-
name="nat-all" dst-nat-rule-name="None" protocol-id="6" policy-name="Internet-
Access" source-zone-name="trust" destination-zone-name="untrust"
session-id-32="58" packets-from-client="6" bytes-from-client="544" packets-from-
server="5" bytes-from-server="1531" elapsed-time="25"]

root@SRX650-1# run show log webfilter

<29>1 2010-01-25T01:47:59.240Z SRX650-1 utmd 1077 WEBFILTER_SERVER_CONNECTED
[junos@2636.1.1.1.2.40 name="cpa.surfcpa.com"]
<28>1 2010-01-25T01:47:59.299Z SRX650-1 utmd 1077 WEBFILTER_URL_PERMITTED
[junos@2636.1.1.1.2.40 source-address="10.1.1.101" source-port="38090"
destination-address="96.17.215.148" destination-port="80"
name="Computing_Internet" error-message="by predefined category"
profile-name="wf-surfcontrol" object-name="www.juniper.net" pathname="/"]
```

In the session logs you can observe two messages, one for the session open and another one for the session close. These messages include a lot of useful information, such as the names of the matching security and NAT policies. The session close log also includes traffic statistics (at the time of the session open event, no traffic statistics are available!) and the close reason.

The web filtering logs show that there was a connection to the category server (`cpa.surfcpa.com`). When the web filtering cache is enabled, this message is generated only if the requested URL is not in the cache. In our example, the visited URL was *http://www.juniper.net/*, categorized as belonging to a `"Computing_Internet"` site and allowed by the UTM policy (clearly shown by the message `TAG WEBFILTER_URL_PERMITTED`).

External log collectors, including the Juniper Networks STRM product, can be used to store and correlate the logs and can create useful reports that include (but are not limited to) the following:

- Top URL categories
- Most visited sites
- Top talkers (in total bytes or number of sessions)

- Top attacks
- Top viruses
- Top rejected URLs
- Top spammers

The following configuration has session logging enabled. Session logs are stored in the */var/logs/session* file, while web filtering logs are stored in the */var/log/webfilter* file.

```
[edit security]
set nat source rule-set internet from zone trust
set nat source rule-set internet to zone untrust
set nat source rule-set internet rule nat-all match source-address 0.0.0.0/0
set nat source rule-set internet rule nat-all match destination-address 0.0.0.0/0
set nat source rule-set internet rule nat-all then source-nat interface

set policies from-zone trust to-zone untrust policy Internet-Access match source-
address any
set policies from-zone trust to-zone untrust policy Internet-Access match
destination-address any
set policies from-zone trust to-zone untrust policy Internet-Access match
application junos-http
set policies from-zone trust to-zone untrust policy Internet-Access then permit
application-services utm-policy WF-only
set policies from-zone trust to-zone untrust policy Internet-Access then log
session-init
set policies from-zone trust to-zone untrust policy Internet-Access then log
session-close

set utm feature-profile web-filtering surf-control-integrated profile wf-
surfcontrol category Weapons action block
set utm feature-profile web-filtering surf-control-integrated profile wf-
surfcontrol category News action permit
set utm feature-profile web-filtering surf-control-integrated profile wf-
surfcontrol category Computing_Internet action permit
set utm utm-policy WF-only web-filtering http-profile wf-surfcontrol
```

Although this detailed log information is useful for debugging and troubleshooting purposes, it is difficult to get a general idea of traffic trends. This is why, as of Junos 10.4, the web UI provides some reports of the overall network and threat activity, as shown in Figure 9-9.

Of course, the log storage capacity of each platform determines how many logs can be analyzed, but from small branch deployments the on-box reporting capabilities provide an easy way to inspect the traffic forwarded by the SRX and assess the network's vulnerabilities.

Please exercise caution when locally storing log information into devices that use flash storage. These memories wear out after a limited number of write cycles.

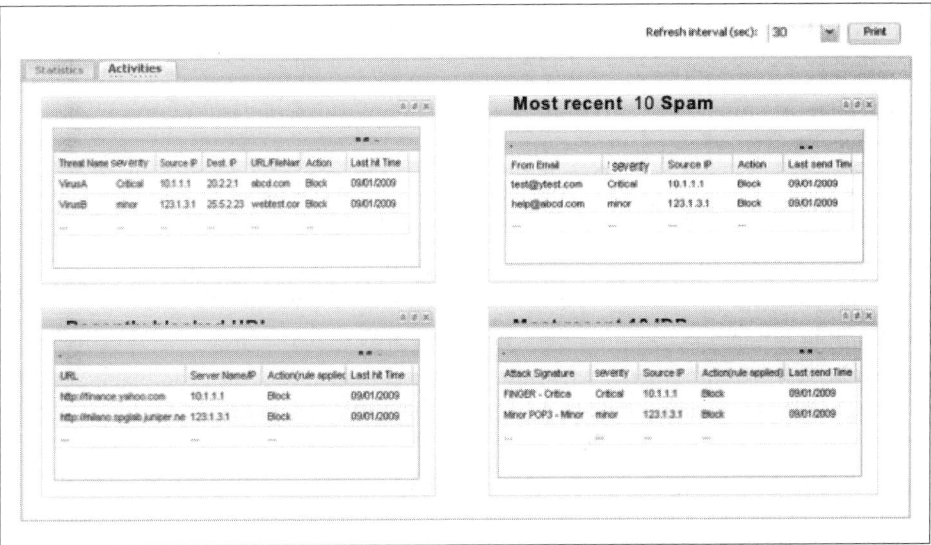

Figure 9-9. The web UI of an SRX showing the security events

Figure 9-10 shows some of the reports available, including general per-feature hit counts, most recent threats, and threat count over the past 24 hours, in a variety of information graphics types.

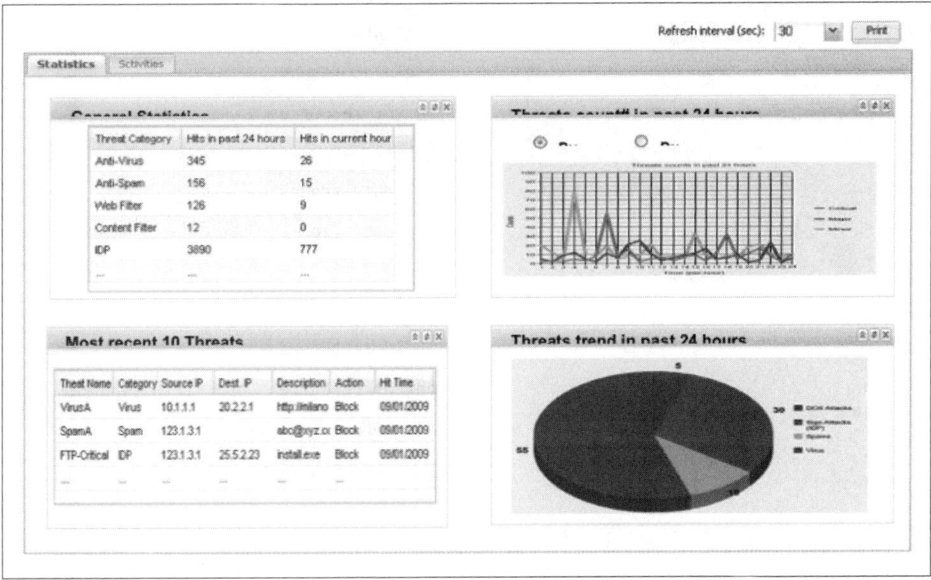

Figure 9-10. The web UI showing traffic statistics

Also available are per-activity reports showing the most recent attacks, viruses, spams, and blocked URLs.

Controlling What to Do When Things Go Wrong

As much as you would like the network to be available all the time, it is a bad idea to design systems pretending that connectivity problems, bugs, or a lack of resources never happens.

What devices and network administrators can do is to establish a set of rules regarding what to do when problems occur.

Chapter 10 deals with how to cluster devices to provide redundant hardware, data, and control planes. Here, in the context of UTM, let's configure the SRX gateway to react when things fail despite the measures taken to improve the network's availability.

The web filtering and antivirus feature profiles can specify a set of fallback actions. They control what to do (either allow or block the traffic) when the UTM engine cannot process any more traffic.

Table 9-3 shows a list of the different events that can trigger a fallback.

Table 9-3. Fallback events

Feature	Engine	Events
Web filtering	SurfControl integrated and Websense redirect	`server-connectivity`
		Timeout
		`too-many-requests`
Antivirus	Sophos and Juniper Express	`content-size`
		`engine-not-ready`
		`out-of-resources`
		Timeout
		`too-many-requests`
	Kaspersky	`content-size`
		`corrupt-file`
		`decompress-layer`
		`engine-not-ready`
		`out-of-resources`
		`password-file`
		`too-many-requests`

So, you can choose to allow messages while the antivirus engine is being uploaded, while blocking files that are larger than the max file size. Search back into this chapter's antivirus policy configs and this should all make perfect sense:

```
[edit security]
set policies from-zone trust to-zone untrust policy Internet-Access match source-
address any
```

```
set policies from-zone trust to-zone untrust policy Internet-Access match
destination-address any
set policies from-zone trust to-zone untrust policy Internet-Access match
application junos-http
set policies from-zone trust to-zone untrust policy Internet-Access match
application junos-ftp
set policies from-zone trust to-zone untrust policy Internet-Access then permit
application-services utm-policy KS-AV-Only
set policies from-zone trust to-zone untrust policy Internet-Access then log
session-init
set policies from-zone trust to-zone untrust policy Internet-Access then log
session-close

set utm feature-profile anti-virus type kaspersky-lab-engine
set utm feature-profile anti-virus kaspersky-lab-engine profile KS-FullAV
fallback-options decompress-layer block
set utm feature-profile anti-virus kaspersky-lab-engine profile KS-FullAV
fallback-options content-size block
set utm feature-profile anti-virus kaspersky-lab-engine profile KS-FullAV
fallback-options engine-not-ready log-and-permit
set utm feature-profile anti-virus kaspersky-lab-engine profile KS-FullAV scan-
options intelligent-prescreening
set utm feature-profile anti-virus kaspersky-lab-engine profile KS-FullAV scan-
options content-size-limit 10000

set utm utm-policy KS-AV-Only anti-virus http-profile KS-FullAV
```

As you can see with this configuration, an attempt to download a large file generates a user notification (for HTTP it displays an error page) and the following log message indicating the fallback action, cause, endpoint addresses, and name of the offending file:

```
<12>1 2010-01-29T10:59:59.660Z SRX650-1 RT_UTM - AV_HUGE_FILE_DROPPED_MT
[junos@2636.1.1.1.2.40 source-address="10.2.1.101" source-port="80" destination-
address="10.1.1.103" destination-port="51727" filename="10.2.1.101/images/junos-
srxsme-10.2-20100106.0-domestic.tgz"]
```

When one is downloading a file while the engine is loading a new database (this can be tested by forcing a reload with the `request security utm anti-virus kaspersky-lab-engine pattern-reload` command) the SRX still logs a message, but allows the file through:

```
<12>1 2010-01-29T11:27:11.670Z SRX650-1 RT_UTM - AV_SCANNER_ERROR_SKIPPED_MT
[junos@2636.1.1.1.2.40 source-address="10.2.1.101" source-port="80" destination-
address="10.1.1.103" destination-port="40732"
filename="10.2.1.101/images/eicar.com" error-code="14" error-message="scan
engine is not ready"]
```

Before leaving for the next UTM feature, let's end with this simple tip that you can specify a default fallback action, which indicates the action to take for an event that is not configured:

```
set utm feature-profile anti-virus kaspersky-lab-engine profile KS-FullAV
fallback-options default block
```

Content Filtering

In this chapter, you have looked at, and hopefully learned, how to drop traffic based on some analysis of the files transported, and in the particular case of HTTP traffic, how to use the URLs to classify the sites and then use that information to allow or block access to a particular site.

It's a good time to examine the SRX content filtering feature which allows you to look at the protocol commands used by the various protocols supported by the UTM feature set, and blocking or allowing these commands. *What?* Why would you want to restrict some *commands* from any given protocol?

Well, you should already know that some content types are more susceptible to carrying malicious traffic—for instance, although signed, ActiveX code embedded in web pages can carry malicious code which, when executed, can run with the same privilege level as the logged user. ActiveX code is normally signed, and when it is signed by a valid certificate authority (CA) it is known that it hasn't been tampered with. The problem is that the CA signing the code does not normally evaluate the security of the code. Worse yet, many times the code is unsigned or is signed by an unknown CA. The browser generates a warning in these cases, but users are still allowed to download and execute the code.

For situations such as this, many administrators want to restrict access to some of the protocol commands for sites they do not trust. The content filtering feature was designed to provide a simple way for admins to block such traffic. When complex matches are required (i.e., using regular expressions) or when the UTM parsing engine does not support the protocol in question (i.e., it's not HTTP, FTP, SMTP, IMAP, or POP3), the IDP engine can be used to provide more feature-rich functionality, but at the expense of configuration complexity and lack of good user notification mechanisms.

A large part of the work required to extract files from the different protocols consists of decoding the protocols, identifying the various protocol contexts, and storing the transported files so that they can be passed to the different scanning engines.

The content filtering feature leverages all the processing done by the UTM parsing engine. As part of the protocol decoding process, the engine identifies the different commands exchanged between client and server. Administrators can then create lists of content types or commands that are allowed or denied by the SRX gateway.

What content or commands can be allowed or blocked highly depends on the protocol in question. Perhaps the best way to explain what you can do with this feature is to show you.

Filtering FTP traffic

Although it has been around for some time, FTP provides a simple yet flexible way to exchange files among computers. The protocol has been extended over the years to allow clients to restart interrupted transfers, provide strong authentication, and support IPv6, among other things.

It is not the objective of this section to describe FTP in detail, but rather to show you how to prevent users from logging in to an FTP server using the root user. When an FTP connection is established, the `USER` command is passed from the client to the server to indicate the username used to log in to the server. The content filtering feature is used to block this command so that even when allowed by the server, the root account will not be accessible.

It is sometimes useful to see the list of commands supported by FTP. The following is not a comprehensive list; it has been extracted from the Unix manpages of the VSFTPD server, and it shows some of the commands supported by this server:

> `ABOR`: Abort previous command
> `ACCT`: Specify account (ignored)
> `ADAT`: Send an authentication protocol message
> `ALLO`: Allocate storage (vacuously)
> `APPE`: Append to a file
> `AUTH`: Specify an authentication protocol to be performed
> `CCC`: Set the command channel protection mode to Clear (no protection)
> `CDUP`: Change to parent of current working directory
> `CWD`: Change working directory
> `DELE`: Delete a file
> `ENC`: Send a privacy and integrity protected command
> `HELP`: Give help information
> `LIST`: Give list files in a directory (`ls -lgA`)
> `MIC`: Send an integrity protected command
> `MKD`: Make a directory
> `MDTM`: Show last modification time of file
> `MODE`: Specify data transfer mode
> `NLST`: Give name list of files in directory
> `NOOP`: Do nothing
> `PASS`: Specify password
> `PASV`: Prepare for server-to-server transfer
> `PBSZ`: Specify a protection buffer size
> `PORT`: Specify a data connection port
> `PROT`: Specify a protection level under which to protect data transfers
> `PWD`: Print the current working directory
> `QUIT`: Terminate session
> `REST`: Restart incomplete transfer
> `RETR`: Retrieve a file
> `RMD`: Remove a directory
> `RNFR`: Specify rename-from filename
> `RNTO`: Specify rename-to filename

`SIZE`: Return size of file
`STAT`: Return status of server
`STOR`: Store a file
`STOU`: Store a file with a unique name
`STRU`: Specify data transfer structure
`SYST`: Show operating system type of server system
`TYPE`: Specify data transfer type
`USER`: Specify username

Blocking some of these commands allows administrators to enforce certain security postures at the gateway, without having to configure every single protected server (and, frankly, sometimes the servers are not under the control of the SRX administrator).

For instance, default FTP server configurations allow for simple, clear-text authentication. This is particularly dangerous because the account information can be easily obtained from a packet capture. Consider the network shown in Figure 9-11. If traditional user authentication were allowed to the FTP servers, any user could snoop the FTP login and be able to extract the username and password information from users accessing the server.

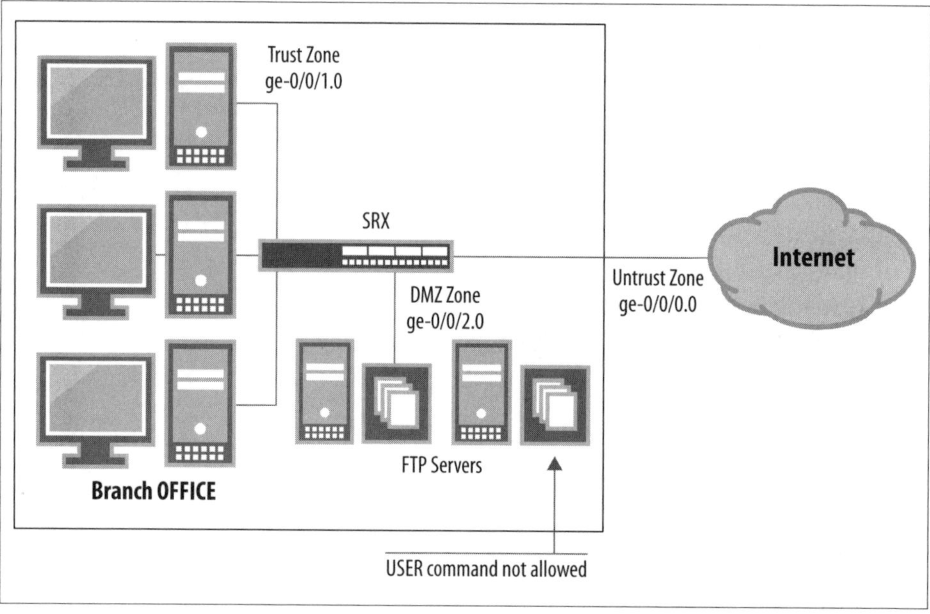

Figure 9-11. Using content filtering with FTP servers

To illustrate this point, this is what an extract of packet capture, displayed in ASCII format between an FTP client and server, looks like:

```
tcpdump -r ftp.pcap -A -g -n
...
```

```
07:50:53.816847 IP 10.1.1.102.42808 > 10.2.1.103.21: Flags [P.], seq 1:12,
ack 21, win 32748, length 11
E..3.[......
..f
..g.8..$wKU:N..P...m...USER test

07:50:53.816899 IP 10.2.1.103.21 > 10.1.1.102.42808: Flags [.],
ack 12, win 5840, length 0
E..(.>@.@.s.
..g
..f...8:N..$wK`P...u...
07:50:53.817400 IP 10.2.1.103.21 > 10.1.1.102.42808: Flags [P.], seq 21:55,
ack 12, win 5840, length 34
E..J.?@.@.s.
..g
..f...8:N..$wK`P.......331 Please specify the password.

07:50:53.817815 IP 10.1.1.102.42808 > 10.2.1.103.21: Flags [.],
ack 55, win 32734, length 0
E..(.\......
..f
..g.8..$wK`:N.%P............
07:50:56.387967 IP 10.1.1.102.42808 > 10.2.1.103.21: Flags [P.], seq 12:26,
ack 55, win 32734, length 14
E..6._......
..f
..g.8..$wK`:N.%P.../...PASS test123
```

Modern FTP servers support stronger authentication mechanisms. Using the content filtering feature, we can make sure no clients are allowed to use the `USER` command (used for legacy user authentication).

Let's assume that connections to the FTP server are only allowed from the Trust to the DMZ zones. The configuration would be the same if connections from the Untrust zone were considered, but this way, we don't need to deal with how to NAT the traffic from the Internet (not until later, at least, in the next case study):

```
[edit security policies]
set from-zone trust to-zone DMZ policy FTP-inbound-access match
source-address any
set from-zone trust to-zone DMZ policy FTP-inbound-access match
destination-address any
set from-zone trust to-zone DMZ policy FTP-inbound-access match
application junos-ftp
set from-zone trust to-zone DMZ policy FTP-inbound-access then permit
application-services utm-policy CF-ftp

[edit security zones]
set security-zone untrust interfaces ge-0/0/0.0
set security-zone trust interfaces ge-0/0/1.0
set security-zone DMZ interfaces ge-0/0/2.0

[edit security utm]
set custom-objects protocol-command ftp-root-login value USER
set feature-profile content-filtering profile ftp-no-root block-command ftp-root-
```

```
login
set utm-policy CF-ftp content-filtering ftp upload-profile ftp-no-root
set utm-policy CF-ftp content-filtering ftp download-profile ftp-no-root
```

When our tester tries to log in using the USER command, this is what he sees:

```
root@pato-vm2:~# ftp -n 10.2.1.103
Connected to 10.2.1.103.
220 (vsFTPd 2.0.5)
ftp> user
(username) test
550 10.1.1.102:39384->10.2.1.103:21 Requested action not taken
and the request is dropped for Content Filtering command block list.
Login failed.
```

You can also create file extension lists so that whenever a request command exchanges a filename, if the extension is found in the block extension list, the command will be blocked:

```
set custom-objects filename-extension some-images value gif
set custom-objects filename-extension some-images value tif
set custom-objects filename-extension some-images value twf
set custom-objects filename-extension some-images value tiff
set custom-objects filename-extension some-images value svg
set custom-objects filename-extension some-images value ai
set custom-objects filename-extension some-images value bmp
set custom-objects filename-extension some-images value drw
set custom-objects filename-extension some-images value dwg
set custom-objects filename-extension some-images value eps
set custom-objects filename-extension some-images value jpg
set custom-objects filename-extension some-images value png
set feature-profile content-filtering profile no-images block-extension
some-images
set utm-policy CF-ftp content-filtering ftp upload-profile no-images
set utm-policy CF-ftp content-filtering ftp download-profile no-images
```

Filtering HTTP traffic

Just as you can block FTP commands and file extensions, you can do the same with HTTP. In this case, the HTTP commands refer to the different HTTP methods that clients can request (e.g., GET, POST, PUT, DELETE, HEAD, OPTIONS, CONNECT). As in our FTP case, this is useful when, for security reasons, it's desirable to disable a particular method. For example, the TRACE method is meant to be used for debugging purposes, but it also can open some attack vectors.

You could also use this to filter some content—in particular, cookies, ActiveX components, Java applets, and *.zip* and *.exe* files.

As in our previous scenario, shown in Figure 9-10, HTTP connections are allowed from the Trust to the Untrust networks, but sites wishing to push ActiveX components will be blocked. Users are displayed an error page (and a log is generated) when attempting to access such sites.

```
[edit security]
set policies from-zone trust to-zone untrust policy Restricted-HTTP match source-
address any
set policies from-zone trust to-zone untrust policy Restricted-HTTP match
destination-address any
set policies from-zone trust to-zone untrust policy Restricted-HTTP match
application junos-http
set policies from-zone trust to-zone untrust policy Restricted-HTTP then permit
application-services utm-policy HTTP-no-activex

set utm feature-profile content-filtering profile no-activex block-content-type
activex
set utm feature-profile content-filtering profile no-activex block-content-type
java-applet
set utm feature-profile content-filtering profile no-activex block-content-type
http-cookie

set utm utm-policy HTTP-no-activex content-filtering http-profile no-activex
```

Since no database has to be updated for this feature, no license is required to use it.

Antispam

The last feature in our UTM feature list is antispam. Following in the spirit of antivirus, antispam is meant to be used in conjunction with host-based antispam solutions.

Antispam provides a repudiation-based filtering solution—the SRX extracts the address of the message sender (or relaying agent) and uses it to query a repudiation database hosted and maintained by Sophos.

The Spam Block List (SBL) server maintains a database with the IP addresses of known spammers or hosts that are considered to be compromised. Whitelists and blacklists of servers can also be created which allow users to override the classification done by the SBL server, as shown in Figure 9-12. In addition, these lists support not only IP addresses, but also domain names (in which case they are compared against the domain name obtained from an email's From: field).

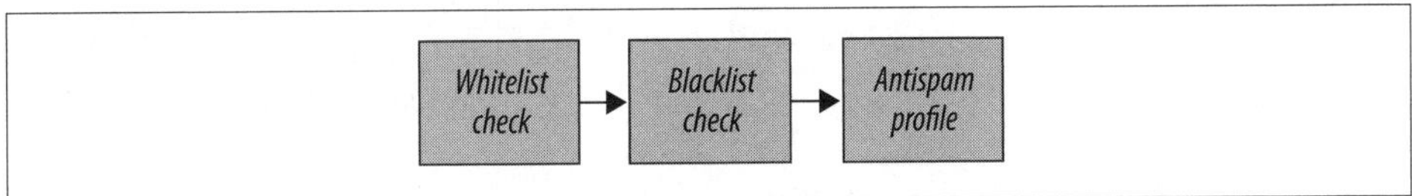

Figure 9-12. Antispam order of evaluation

The SMTP decoder extracts three fields from each email message:

1. The source IP address of the connection—either the sender or, if a relay server was used, the address of the last relay
2. The sender's domain name, obtained from the From: field of the message

3. The sender's address, obtained from the trace information present in the message, if the message was sent through a forwarder

These three fields are used to determine if a message is considered spam, by performing the following three corresponding checks:

1. The sender IP address is first checked against the whitelist and then the blacklist, and finally the SLB server. If the address matches any of the addresses in the whitelist the message will be allowed. A match on the blacklist or the SLB database will flag the message as spam.
2. The sender domain is checked against the whitelist and blacklist (the SLB server does not maintain domain names).
3. Finally, the sender address is checked against the whitelist and blacklist.

Once a message is classified as spam, the antispam profile is used to determine if the message is either discarded or tagged. The profile also indicates if the tag message is included in the subject line or the email header.

At the time of this writing, only SMTP is supported (i.e., there is no IMAP or POP3 support).

By now, we should be able to almost guess how this feature is configured. The configuration follows the same structure as the previous ones. You can add an SMTP server to the branch office, and use the antispam feature to prescreen the messages received, as shown in Figure 9-13.

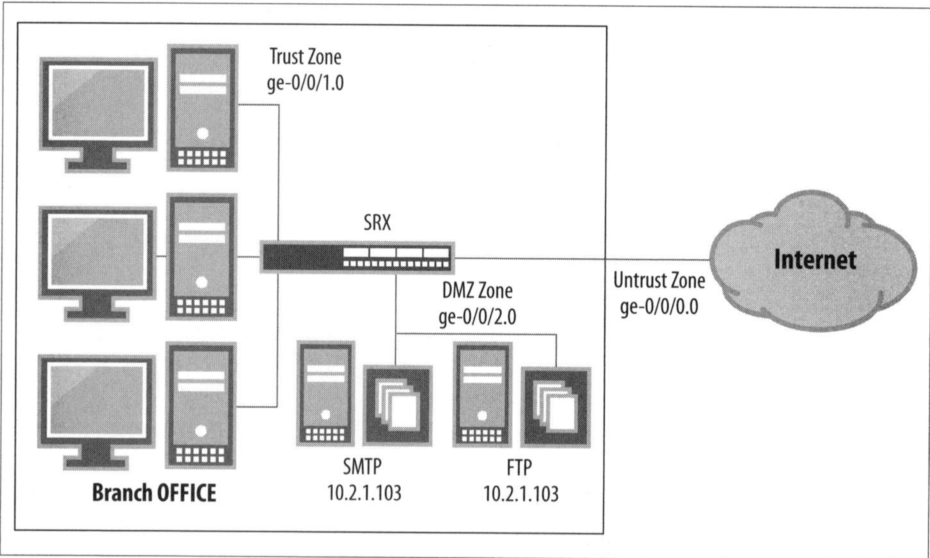

Figure 9-13. Branch office with SMTP server

UTM Monitoring

So far we have covered the main features of the UTM in the SRX. We looked at each feature, discussed its application, and analyzed configuration examples for you to follow and adapt to your needs and networks.

Now it's time explore how to troubleshoot the operation of the different UTM features.

The first thing to check is that each feature used is enabled with an updated database. The command to do this is `show security utm <feature name> status`.

Let's go back to the scenario depicted in Figure 9-5 where a host in the Trust network is going through an SRX with antivirus enabled. The `show security utm anti-virus status` command displays information about the status of the antivirus engine:

```
root@SRX650-1# show security utm anti-virus status
 UTM anti-virus status:

    Anti-virus key expire date: 2011-03-04 00:00:00
    Update server: http://update.juniper-updates.net/AV/SRX650/
           Interval: 60 minutes
           Pattern update status: next update in 3 minutes
           Last result: already have latest database
    Anti-virus signature version: 02/08/2010 02:28 GMT, virus records: 531278
    Anti-virus signature compiler version: N/A
    Scan engine type: kaspersky-lab-engine
    Scan engine information: last action result: No error(0x00000000)
```

You can see from the output if a valid antivirus license is installed (and its expiration date), the database version, and the number of records in it. The last line, showing `last action result`, is useful for checking the status of the engine or an ongoing pattern update (as we discussed in "Antivirus" on page 498).

You can also check what happens if you manually restart the antivirus feature:

```
root@SRX650-1#run restart utmd

AUTM Daemon started, pid 11188

[edit]
root@SRX650-1#

[edit]
root@SRX650-1# run show security utm anti-virus status
 UTM anti-virus status:

    Anti-virus key expire date: 2011-03-04 00:00:00
    Update server: http://update.juniper-updates.net/AV/SRX650/
           Interval: 60 minutes
           Pattern update status: in process
           Last result: downloading list file
    Anti-virus signature version: not loaded
    Anti-virus signature compiler version: N/A
```

```
        Scan engine type: kaspersky-lab-engine
        Scan engine information: last action result: Engine not ready(0x80000009)
```

After the utmd daemon is back up, the engine status will revert to `No error`:

```
root@SRX650-1# run show security utm anti-virus status
 UTM anti-virus status:

    Anti-virus key expire date: 2011-03-04 00:00:00
    Update server: http://update.juniper-updates.net/AV/SRX650/
           Interval: 60 minutes
           Pattern update status: next update in 58 minutes
           Last result: new database loaded
    Anti-virus signature version: 02/08/2010 02:28 GMT, virus records: 531278
    Anti-virus signature compiler version: N/A
    Scan engine type: kaspersky-lab-engine
    Scan engine information: last action result: No error(0x00000000)
```

Given that the packets must be processed by multiple different components, it's a useful exercise to trace the processing of the traffic from a given session, when one or more UTM features are enabled.

Start by looking at the session logs and session table. Remember that security policies are used to determine which traffic is processed by the different UTM features, so it is only natural to start the trace by looking at the information maintained in the session table.

Let's see what happens when an HTTP request is generated from the Trust zone. The `show security flow session` command displays the information found in the session table:

```
root@SRX650-1# run show security flow session application http extensive
Session ID: 115197, Status: Normal
Flag: 0x2
Policy name: utm-av-policy/6
Source NAT pool: interface, Application: junos-http/6
Maximum timeout: 120, Current timeout: 108
Session State: Valid
Start time: 186996, Duration: 12
   In: 10.1.1.103/49170 --> 66.129.230.17/80;tcp,
    Interface: ge-0/0/1.0,
    Session token: 0x1c0, Flag: 0x0x2621
    Route: 0x70010, Gateway: 10.1.1.103, Tunnel: 0
    Port sequence: 0, FIN sequence: 0,
    FIN state: 0,
    Pkts: 12, Bytes: 1142
   Out: 66.129.230.17/80 --> 172.19.101.26/1083;tcp,
    Interface: ge-0/0/0.0,
    Session token: 0x180, Flag: 0x0x2620
    Route: 0x60010, Gateway: 172.19.101.1, Tunnel: 0
    Port sequence: 0, FIN sequence: 3415875481,
    FIN state: 1,
    Pkts: 9, Bytes: 1642
```

Among other things, this table shows the matching policy and application. Based on the application and the UTM policy, you can work your way backward to determine the feature profile used to process the packets from this session:

```
root@SRX650-1# show security policies | display set | match utm-av-policy
set security policies from-zone trust to-zone untrust policy utm-av-policy match
source-address any
set security policies from-zone trust to-zone untrust policy utm-av-policy match
destination-address any
set security policies from-zone trust to-zone untrust policy utm-av-policy match
application any
set security policies from-zone trust to-zone untrust policy utm-av-policy then
permit application-services utm-policy kaspersky-av-only
```

Since we know that the `kaspersky-av-only` UTM policy is used to process this traffic, you can determine which feature profiles were used from the UTM policy configuration:

```
root@SRX650-1# show security utm | display set | match kaspersky-av-only
set security utm utm-policy kaspersky-av-only anti-virus
http-profile kaspersky-by-extension
set security utm utm-policy kaspersky-av-only anti-virus ftp upload-profile
kaspersky-by-extension
set security utm utm-policy kaspersky-av-only anti-virus ftp download-profile
kaspersky-by-extension
set security utm utm-policy kaspersky-av-only anti-virus smtp-profile
kaspersky-by-extension
set security utm utm-policy kaspersky-av-only anti-virus pop3-profile
kaspersky-by-extension
set security utm utm-policy kaspersky-av-only anti-virus imap-profile
kaspersky-by-extension

[edit]
root@SRX650-1# show security utm | display set | match karspersky-by-extension
set security utm feature-profile anti-virus kaspersky-lab-engine profile
kaspersky-by-extension scan-options intelligent-prescreening
set security utm feature-profile anti-virus kaspersky-lab-engine profile
kaspersky-by-extension scan-options scan-mode by-extension
set security utm feature-profile anti-virus kaspersky-lab-engine profile
kaspersky-by-extension scan-options scan-extension my-extensions
set security utm feature-profile anti-virus kaspersky-lab-engine profile
kaspersky-by-extension scan-options content-size-limit 20000
set security utm feature-profile anti-virus kaspersky-lab-engine profile
kaspersky-by-extension scan-options decompress-layer-limit 4
```

In addition, each UTM feature maintains counters for all traffic they process. You can look at these counters in our antivirus example by using the `show security utm <feature> statistics` command:

```
root@SRX650-1# run show security utm anti-virus statistics
 UTM Anti Virus statistics:

 Intelligent-prescreening passed:       0
 MIME-whitelist passed:                 0
 URL-whitelist passed:                  0
```

```
Scan Mode:
    scan-all:                          0
    Scan-extension:                    4
Scan Request:

 Total          Clean          Threat-found    Fallback
      4             4                0              0
Fallback:

                          Log-and-permit        Block
 Engine not ready:              0                    0
 Password file:                 0                    0
 Decompress layer:              0                    0
 Corrupt files:                 0                    0
 Out of resources:              0                    0
 Timeout:                       0                    0
 Maximum content size:          0                    0
 Too many requests:             0                    0
 Others:                        0                    0
```

The counters are pretty self-explanatory, but it is instructional to check the total number of threats found, and the number of fallback actions taken (which indicate the reasons some content was not processed by the engine and was allowed without scanning or being blocked).

Another useful source of information is to examine the logs generated by the different engines. The configuration shown in "Viewing the UTM Logs" on page 508 shows how to configure branch SRX boxes to send the UTM to different files. Looking at the logfiles you can obtain information about the different viruses found, fallback actions, URLs visited, spam found, and, in general, any content blocked by one of the UTM engines.

For example, when trying to download the EICAR AV test file (a well-known test file that contains a harmless pattern, recognized as a virus by most antivirus engines and used for testing purposes) information about the virus name is found (EICAR-Test-File), the zone where the virus was received (Untrust), the address/port of the requesting host (10.1.1.103:54612), the requested URL (*http://www.eicar.org/download/eicar.com*), and the filename (*eicar.com*):

```
root@SRX650-1# run show log viruses
<12>1 2010-02-08T08:29:28.565Z SRX650-1 RT_UTM - AV_VIRUS_DETECTED_MT
[junos@2636.1.1.1.2.40 source-address="188.40.238.250" source-port="80"
destination-address="10.1.1.103" destination-port="47095" source-zone-
name="untrust" filename="www.eicar.org/download/eicar.com" temporary-
filename="www.eicar.org/download/eicar.com" name="EICAR-Test-File"
url="EICAR-Test-File"]
```

Notification messages also generate logs, as evident from the message obtained while doing an HTTP request after having restarted utmd:

```
<12>1 2010-02-08T08:35:44.215Z SRX650-1 RT_UTM - AV_SCANNER_DROP_FILE_MT
[junos@2636.1.1.1.2.40 source-address="74.125.155.147" source-port="80"
destination-address="10.1.1.103" destination-port="33578"
```

```
filename="www.google.com/" error-code="14" error-message="scan engine is not
ready"]
```

You can find a list of all the messages the UTM subsystem logged in the *Junos System Log Messages Reference* manual available at *http://www.juniper.net/techpubs*.

Licensing

As you might know by now, some of the UTM features require a license to operate. The `show system license` operational command displays the licenses that are installed, used, and required:

```
>show system license
License usage:
                                 Licenses   Licenses   Licenses  Expiry
  Feature name                       used  installed     needed
  bgp-reflection                        0         14          0  permanent
  av_key_kaspersky_engine               0          1          0  2011-03-03
16:00:00 PST
  av_key_sophos_engine                  0          1          0  2012-01-05
16:00:00 PST
  anti_spam_key_sbl                     0          1          0  2011-09-01
17:00:00 PDT
  wf_key_surfcontrol_cpa                0          1          0  2011-09-01
17:00:00 PDT
  idp-sig                               0          1          0  2011-09-01
17:00:00 PDT
  ax411-wlan-ap                         0         14          0  permanent
...
```

Licenses are tied to the chassis serial number (so it has to be supplied when ordering a license) and, when working in high availability (HA), both member nodes require a license to operate. Once purchased, licenses are easy to install by either loading the license file into the device and using the `request system license add <filename>` command or, more commonly, directly copying the license information from the command-line interface (CLI):

```
>request system license add terminal
[Type ^D at a new line to end input,
 enter blank line between each license key]
<Feature X LICENSE INFO>

<Feature Y LICENSE INFO>

...
^D
```

To summarize, Table 9-4 shows the different UTM features and license requirements.

Table 9-4. UTM features and license requirements

Feature	License required?
SurfControl integrated WF	Yes
Websense redirect WF	No
Juniper local WF	No
Kaspersky full AV	Yes
Juniper Express AV	Yes
Sophos in-the-cloud AV	Yes
Sophos AS	Yes
Content filtering	No

Tracing UTM Sessions

You can leverage the Junos tracing infrastructure to obtain debugging information by using traceoptions, configured under each feature profile, to control the debug messages generated as each module processes sessions.

This tracing is quite verbose and has a high impact on the devices' performance, so be careful not to enable it on a heavily used production device:

```
[edit security utm]
feature-profile {
    anti-virus {
        traceoptions {
            flag all;
        }
    }
}
```

Tracing files are stored under the */var/log* directory and are named after each UTM feature using the `utmd-` prefix. For example, the antivirus engine stores its logs in a file named *utmd-av*.

By looking at how a trace request to a clean site is processed, you can get an idea of how traffic is treated under normal circumstances. So, let's try a Google page. As you can see, none of the content embedded in the page was deemed to be dangerous (no file with an extension matching the default extension list was found when using scan-extension mode):

```
Feb  8 08:51:11 [2]av_mgr: scan params 6000000: layer: 4, max-size: 20000;
mode: 1; hint: 1; [XSLT;:]
Feb  8 08:51:11 [2]av_mgr: find idle worker 2.
Feb  8 08:51:11 {11994} av_worker: recv event 3 len 1048.
Feb  8 08:51:11 {11994} scanner 2: recv event 3.
Feb  8 08:51:11 {11994} scanner 2: scan file www.google.com/ for 1 times ...
Feb  8 08:51:11 AV scan file [www.google.com/]: MD5
```

```
f27724d1d57d36cab6b77f8fc53b6bc7, size 1161
Feb  8 08:51:11 scan file: [/var/run/utm/utmfile181989376]
Feb  8 08:51:11 scan mode: 1, type 2
Feb  8 08:51:11 set mem limit 645795840.
Feb  8 08:51:11 scan begin: /var/run/utm/utmfile181989376
Feb  8 08:51:11 scan ext mode skip check: www.google.com/
Feb  8 08:51:11 file do not have entension, scan.
Feb  8 08:51:11 Object inform: /var/run/utm/utmfile181989376,  level 0
Feb  8 08:51:11 scan done: /var/run/utm/utmfile181989376, 0x00000000
Feb  8 08:51:11 Result:
Feb  8 08:51:11 last error: 0x00000000, No error
```

Instead, a request to download the EICAR file is scanned by the antivirus engine and a virus is detected:

```
Feb  8 08:53:30 [2]av_mgr: scan params 6000000: layer: 4, max-size: 20000;
mode: 1; hint: 0; [XSLT;:]
Feb  8 08:53:30 [2]av_mgr: find idle worker 2.
Feb  8 08:53:30 [2]av_mgr -> 2: event scan_file len 1044.
Feb  8 08:53:30 {11994} av_worker: recv event 3 len 1048.
Feb  8 08:53:30 {11994} scanner 2: recv event 3.
Feb  8 08:53:30 {11994} scanner 2: scan file www.eicar.org/download/eicar.com
for 1 times ...
Feb  8 08:53:30 AV scan file [www.eicar.org/download/eicar.com]: MD5
44d88612fea8a8f36de82e1278abb02f, size 68
Feb  8 08:53:30 scan file: [/var/run/utm/utmfile181989376]
Feb  8 08:53:30 scan mode: 1, type 0
Feb  8 08:53:30 set mem limit 645742592.
Feb  8 08:53:30 scan begin: /var/run/utm/utmfile181989376
Feb  8 08:53:30 scan ext mode skip check: www.eicar.org/download/eicar.com
Feb  8 08:53:30 ext is ;COM;, list XSLT;, ,
386;ACE;ARJ;ASP;BAT;BIN;BZ2;CAB;CHM;CLA;CMD;COM;CPL;DLL;DOC;DOT;DPL;DRV;DWG;ELF;
EMF;EML;EXE;FON;FPM;GEA;GZ;HA;HLP;HTA;HTM;HTML;HTT;HXS;ICE;INI;ITSF;JAR;JPEG;JPG;
JS;JSE;LHA;LNK;LZH;MBX;MD?;MIME;MSG;MSI;MSO;NWS;OCX;OTM;OV?;PDF;PHP;PHT;PIF;PK;
PL;PLG;PP?;PRG;PRJ;RAR;REG;RTF;SCR;SH;SHS;SWF;SYS;TAR;TGZ;THE;TSP;VBE;VBS;VXD;
WSF;WSH;XL?;XML;ZIP;
Feb  8 08:53:30 hit 1. !!!
Feb  8 08:53:30 hit default list, scan
Feb  8 08:53:30 Object inform: /var/run/utm/utmfile181989376,  level 0
Feb  8 08:53:30 Detect inform: EICAR-Test-File
Feb  8 08:53:30 scan done: /var/run/utm/utmfile181989376, 0x00000004
Feb  8 08:53:30 Result:
Feb  8 08:53:30 last error: 0x00000000, No error
Feb  8 08:53:30
Feb  8 08:53:30 {11994} scanner 2 sends result: 1.
Feb  8 08:53:30 [2]av_mgr: recv event, len 648.
Feb  8 08:53:30 [2]av_mgr <- 2: event scan_result, it takes 5600 usecs.
```

Administrators are encouraged to try out several traffic patterns and features to become familiar with how the different UTM modules process traffic.

Now let's put what you have learned so far to good use.

Case Study 9-1: Small Branch Office

Let's put everything together to get a complete picture of how a typical branch office SRX is deployed.

In this case study, you will focus on a branch office with the characteristics listed here and shown in Figure 9-14:

- The DMZ zone should provide inbound access to an HTTP and FTP server.
- The Trust zone should require antivirus and web filtering services.
- The FTP server should allow only downloads; uploading of files is not permitted.
- Since only FTP downloads are allowed and the FTP server will not have HTTP or mail access, no virus scanning is needed.
- Traffic from the Trust to the Untrust zones will be NATed using the address of the egress interface.
- Traffic from the Untrust to the DMZ zones will be NATed using the address of the Untrust interface. Traffic to port 80 will be sent to the HTTP server, while traffic to port 21 will be sent to the FTP server (using destination NAT with port forwarding).
- Access to the SRX from the Untrust network is only allowed for SSH and HTTPS. HTTP access from the Untrust zone cannot be allowed as this traffic will be forwarded to the HTTP server in the DMZ zone.

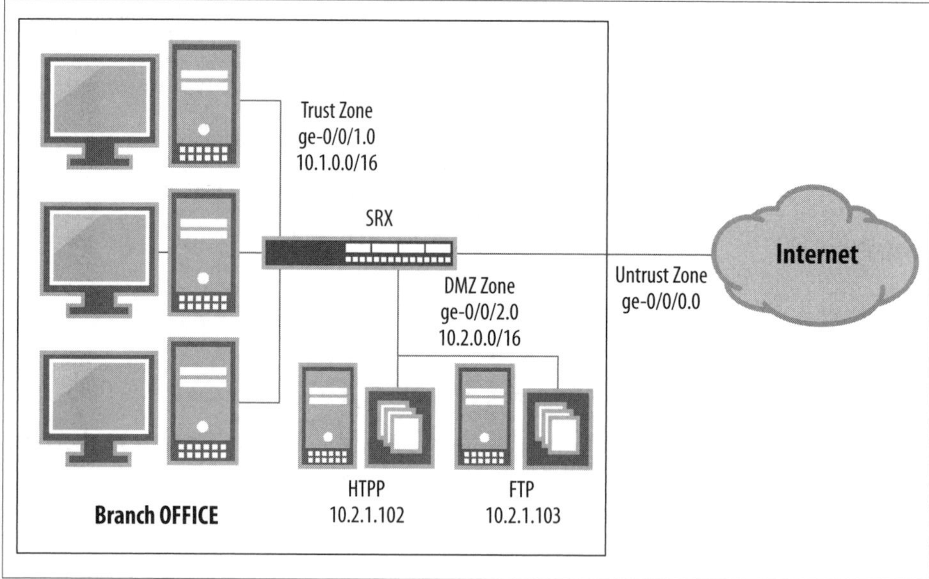

Figure 9-14. Reference branch office

Follow along with the configurations. First let's set the NTP and DNS configuration:

```
set system host-name SRX650-1
#NTP and DNS configuration
set system name-server 4.2.2.2
set system ntp server pool.ntp.org
```

Now set the management protocols:

```
set system services ssh protocol-version v2
set system services web-management http interface ge-0/0/1.0
set system services web-management https system-generated-certificate
set system services web-management https interface ge-0/0/0.0
```

Configure the logging:

```
set system syslog user * any emergency
set system syslog file messages any critical
set system syslog file sessions user info
set system syslog file sessions match RT_FLOW
set system syslog file sessions structured-data brief
set system syslog file antivirus user info
set system syslog file antivirus match AV_
set system syslog file antivirus structured-data brief
set system syslog file webfilter daemon any
set system syslog file webfilter match WEBFILTER_
set system syslog file webfilter structured-data brief
set system syslog file contentfilter user info
set system syslog file contentfilter match CONTENT_FILTERING_
set system syslog file contentfilter structured-data brief

#Interfaces
set interfaces ge-0/0/0 unit 0 family inet dhcp
set interfaces ge-0/0/0 description "Internet Connection"
set interfaces ge-0/0/1 unit 0 family inet address 10.1.1.26/16
set interfaces ge-0/0/1 description "Trust Net"
set interfaces ge-0/0/2 unit 0 family inet address 10.2.1.26/16
set interfaces ge-0/0/1 description "DMZ Net"
```

Configure the NAT configuration and the interface NAT for egress traffic:

```
set security nat source rule-set trust-untrust from zone trust
set security nat source rule-set trust-untrust to zone untrust
set security nat source rule-set trust-untrust rule nat-all-egress match source-
address 0.0.0.0/0
set security nat source rule-set trust-untrust rule nat-all-egress match
destination-address 0.0.0.0/0
set security nat source rule-set trust-untrust rule nat-all-egress then
source-nat interface
```

Now configure the port forwarding to access the HTTP and FTP servers:

```
set security nat destination pool http-server address 10.2.1.103/32
set security nat destination pool http-server address port 80
set security nat destination pool ftp-server address 10.2.1.102/32
set security nat destination pool ftp-server address port 21
set security nat destination rule-set to-dms from zone dmz
set security nat destination rule-set to-dms rule to-http-server match
```

```
source-address 0.0.0.0/0
set security nat destination rule-set to-dms rule to-http-server match
destination-address 0.0.0.0/0
set security nat destination rule-set to-dms rule to-http-server match
destination-port 80
set security nat destination rule-set to-dms rule to-http-server then
destination-nat pool http-server
set security nat destination rule-set to-dms rule to-ftp-server match
source-address 0.0.0.0/0
set security nat destination rule-set to-dms rule to-ftp-server match
destination-address 0.0.0.0/0
set security nat destination rule-set to-dms rule to-ftp-server match
destination-port 21
set security nat destination rule-set to-dms rule to-ftp-server then
destination-nat pool ftp-server
```

Set the screens to filter some malformed packets and limit the max number of inbound connections from the Internet:

```
set security screen ids-option untrust-screen icmp ip-sweep threshold 5000
set security screen ids-option untrust-screen icmp fragment
set security screen ids-option untrust-screen icmp large
set security screen ids-option untrust-screen icmp ping-death
set security screen ids-option untrust-screen ip bad-option
set security screen ids-option untrust-screen ip record-route-option
set security screen ids-option untrust-screen ip source-route-option
set security screen ids-option untrust-screen ip loose-source-route-option
set security screen ids-option untrust-screen ip strict-source-route-option
set security screen ids-option untrust-screen tcp port-scan threshold 5000
set security screen ids-option untrust-screen tcp winnuke
set security screen ids-option untrust-screen limit-session source-ip-based 200
```

Set the security zones configuration:

```
set security zones security-zone untrust screen untrust-screen
set security zones security-zone untrust host-inbound-traffic system-services ssh
set security zones security-zone untrust host-inbound-traffic
system-services https
set security zones security-zone untrust interfaces ge-0/0/0.0
set security zones security-zone trust address-book address
net-10.1/16 10.1.0.0/16
set security zones security-zone trust host-inbound-traffic system-services ping
set security zones security-zone trust host-inbound-traffic system-services ssh
set security zones security-zone trust host-inbound-traffic system-services http
set security zones security-zone trust host-inbound-traffic system-services https
set security zones security-zone trust interfaces ge-0/0/1.0
set security zones security-zone dmz address-book address
ftp-server 10.2.1.102/32
set security zones security-zone dmz address-book address
http-server 10.2.1.103/32
set security zones security-zone dmz interfaces ge-0/0/2.0
```

Security Policies

First let's set the outbound traffic from the Trust to the Untrust that is sent to the antivirus and web filtering engines (MAIL and HTTP):

```
set security policies from-zone trust to-zone untrust policy outbound-AV_WF
match source-address net-10.1/16
set security policies from-zone trust to-zone untrust policy outbound-AV_WF
match destination-address any
set security policies from-zone trust to-zone untrust policy outbound-AV_WF
match application junos-http
set security policies from-zone trust to-zone untrust policy outbound-AV_WF
match application junos-smtp
set security policies from-zone trust to-zone untrust policy outbound-AV_WF
match application junos-pop3
set security policies from-zone trust to-zone untrust policy outbound-AV_WF
match application junos-imap
set security policies from-zone trust to-zone untrust policy outbound-AV_WF
then permit application-services utm-policy AV_WF_HTTP_MAIL
```

Set the various protocols allowed from Trust to Untrust which do not require any UTM scanning (DNS, NTP, and encrypted protocols):

```
set security policies from-zone trust to-zone untrust policy outboud-no-services
match source-address net-10.1/16
set security policies from-zone trust to-zone untrust policy outboud-no-services
match destination-address any
set security policies from-zone trust to-zone untrust policy outboud-no-services
match application junos-dns-udp
set security policies from-zone trust to-zone untrust policy outboud-no-services
match application junos-https
set security policies from-zone trust to-zone untrust policy outboud-no-services
match application junos-imaps
set security policies from-zone trust to-zone untrust policy outboud-no-services
match application junos-ntp
set security policies from-zone trust to-zone untrust policy outboud-no-services
then permit
```

Allow inbound FTP traffic to the FTP server using a UTM policy to block some FTP commands:

```
set security policies from-zone untrust to-zone dmz policy inbound_to_ftp_server
match source-address any
set security policies from-zone untrust to-zone dmz policy inbound_to_ftp_server
match destination-address ftp-server
set security policies from-zone untrust to-zone dmz policy inbound_to_ftp_server
match application junos-ftp
set security policies from-zone untrust to-zone dmz policy inbound_to_ftp_server
then permit application-services utm-policy FTP_NO_MODIFY
```

Allow inbound traffic to the HTTP server in the DMZ zone, but scan all the traffic to the HTTP server:

```
set security policies from-zone untrust to-zone dmz policy inbound_to_http_server
match source-address any
set security policies from-zone untrust to-zone dmz policy inbound_to_http_server
```

```
match destination-address http-server
set security policies from-zone untrust to-zone dmz policy inbound_to_http_server
match application junos-http
set security policies from-zone untrust to-zone dmz policy inbound_to_http_server
then permit application-services utm-policy AV_ONLY
```

Finally, allow NTP and DNS traffic from the Untrust zone to the Internet:

```
set security policies from-zone dmz to-zone untrust policy dmz-out match source-
address ftp-server
set security policies from-zone dmz to-zone untrust policy dmz-out match source-
address http-server
set security policies from-zone dmz to-zone untrust policy dmz-out match
destination-address any
set security policies from-zone dmz to-zone untrust policy dmz-out match
application junos-dns-udp
set security policies from-zone dmz to-zone untrust policy dmz-out match
application junos-ntp
set security policies from-zone dmz to-zone untrust policy dmz-out then permit
```

Drop all traffic not explicitly allowed:

```
set security policies default-policy deny-all
```

UTM Policies and Profiles

Let's set the antivirus feature profile to use intelligent prescreening:

```
set security utm feature-profile anti-virus kaspersky-lab-engine profile KS_AV
fallback-options corrupt-file block
set security utm feature-profile anti-virus kaspersky-lab-engine profile KS_AV
fallback-options password-file log-and-permit
set security utm feature-profile anti-virus kaspersky-lab-engine profile KS_AV
fallback-options decompress-layer log-and-permit
set security utm feature-profile anti-virus kaspersky-lab-engine profile KS_AV
fallback-options content-size log-and-permit
set security utm feature-profile anti-virus kaspersky-lab-engine profile KS_AV
fallback-options engine-not-ready log-and-permit
set security utm feature-profile anti-virus kaspersky-lab-engine profile KS_AV
fallback-options timeout log-and-permit
set security utm feature-profile anti-virus kaspersky-lab-engine profile KS_AV
fallback-options out-of-resources log-and-permit
set security utm feature-profile anti-virus kaspersky-lab-engine profile KS_AV
fallback-options too-many-requests log-and-permit
set security utm feature-profile anti-virus kaspersky-lab-engine profile KS_AV
scan-options intelligent-prescreening
set security utm feature-profile anti-virus kaspersky-lab-engine profile KS_AV
scan-options scan-mode all
set security utm feature-profile anti-virus kaspersky-lab-engine profile KS_AV
scan-options content-size-limit 10000
set security utm feature-profile anti-virus kaspersky-lab-engine profile KS_AV
scan-options decompress-layer-limit 2
set security utm feature-profile anti-virus kaspersky-lab-engine profile KS_AV
notification-options virus-detection type message
set security utm feature-profile anti-virus kaspersky-lab-engine profile KS_AV
notification-options virus-detection notify-mail-sender
```

```
set security utm feature-profile anti-virus kaspersky-lab-engine profile KS_AV
notification-options virus-detection custom-message-subject "VIRUS WARNING"
set security utm feature-profile anti-virus kaspersky-lab-engine profile KS_AV
notification-options fallback-block type message
set security utm feature-profile anti-virus kaspersky-lab-engine profile KS_AV
notification-options fallback-block notify-mail-sender
set security utm feature-profile anti-virus kaspersky-lab-engine profile KS_AV
notification-options fallback-block custom-message-subject "VIRUS WARNING"
set security utm feature-profile anti-virus kaspersky-lab-engine profile KS_AV
notification-options fallback-non-block notify-mail-recipient
set security utm feature-profile anti-virus kaspersky-lab-engine profile KS_AV
notification-options fallback-non-block custom-message-subject "VIRUS WARNING"
```

For the web filtering profile, let's block access to some commonly blocked categories:

```
set security utm feature-profile web-filtering type surf-control-integrated
set security utm feature-profile web-filtering surf-control-integrated
cache timeout 600
set security utm feature-profile web-filtering surf-control-integrated
cache size 10000
set security utm feature-profile web-filtering surf-control-integrated
profile safe-sites category Adult_Sexually_Explicit action block
set security utm feature-profile web-filtering surf-control-integrated
profile safe-sites category Criminal_Skills action block
set security utm feature-profile web-filtering surf-control-integrated
profile safe-sites category Drugs_Alcohol_Tobacco action block
set security utm feature-profile web-filtering surf-control-integrated
profile safe-sites category Gambling action block
set security utm feature-profile web-filtering surf-control-integrated
profile safe-sites category Glamour_Intimate_Apparel action block
set security utm feature-profile web-filtering surf-control-integrated
profile safe-sites category Personals_Dating action block
set security utm feature-profile web-filtering surf-control-integrated
profile safe-sites category Hacking action block
set security utm feature-profile web-filtering surf-control-integrated
profile safe-sites category Remote_Proxies action block
set security utm feature-profile web-filtering surf-control-integrated
profile safe-sites category Weapons action block
set security utm feature-profile web-filtering surf-control-integrated
profile safe-sites category Violence action block
set security utm feature-profile web-filtering surf-control-integrated
profile safe-sites default permit
set security utm feature-profile web-filtering surf-control-integrated
profile safe-sites custom-block-message "Site not allowed by corporate policy"
set security utm feature-profile web-filtering surf-control-integrated
profile safe-sites fallback-settings default log-and-permit
set security utm feature-profile web-filtering surf-control-integrated
profile safe-sites fallback-settings server-connectivity log-and-permit
set security utm feature-profile web-filtering surf-control-integrated
profile safe-sites fallback-settings timeout log-and-permit
set security utm feature-profile web-filtering surf-control-integrated
profile safe-sites fallback-settings too-many-requests log-and-permit
```

Set the command list to block all FTP commands that could modify the contents of the FTP server:

```
set security utm custom-objects protocol-command no-modify-content value PUT
set security utm custom-objects protocol-command no-modify-content value DELE
set security utm custom-objects protocol-command no-modify-content value MKD
set security utm custom-objects protocol-command no-modify-content value RMD
set security utm custom-objects protocol-command no-modify-content value STOR
set security utm custom-objects protocol-command no-modify-content value STOU
```

Create the content filtering profile, denying commands in the `no-modify-content` command list:

```
set security utm feature-profile content-filtering profile ftp-no-modify-content
block-command no-modify-content
set security utm feature-profile content-filtering profile ftp-no-modify-content
notification-options type protocol-only
```

This UTM policy is used to send traffic both to the web filtering engine and, if allowed by web filtering, to the antivirus engine for scanning:

```
set security utm utm-policy AV_WF_HTTP_MAIL anti-virus http-profile KS_AV
set security utm utm-policy AV_WF_HTTP_MAIL anti-virus smtp-profile KS_AV
set security utm utm-policy AV_WF_HTTP_MAIL anti-virus pop3-profile KS_AV
set security utm utm-policy AV_WF_HTTP_MAIL anti-virus imap-profile KS_AV
set security utm utm-policy AV_WF_HTTP_MAIL web-filtering http-profile safe-sites
```

Let's limit the number of sessions that a single client can simultaneously use:

```
set security utm utm-policy AV_WF_HTTP_MAIL traffic-options sessions-per-client
limit 300
set security utm utm-policy AV_WF_HTTP_MAIL traffic-options sessions-per-client
over-limit block
```

This is the UTM policy used to block some FTP commands. Note that the session limit is set to 10, as it should be quite unlikely for a single client to simultaneously download so many files. Clients reaching the session quota will trigger a log message but will be allowed to continue (it's useful to tune the limit to make sure no false positives result in legitimate traffic being dropped).

```
set security utm utm-policy FTP_NO_MODIFY content-filtering ftp upload-profile
ftp-no-modify-content
set security utm utm-policy FTP_NO_MODIFY content-filtering ftp download-profile
ftp-no-modify-content
set security utm utm-policy FTP_NO_MODIFY traffic-options sessions-per-client
limit 10
set security utm utm-policy FTP_NO_MODIFY traffic-options sessions-per-client
over-limit log-and-permit
```

And last but not least, this policy is used to scan traffic from the Internet to the HTTP server for viruses. As in the FTP case, it is a good practice to limit the maximum number of sessions per client, after finding the appropriate threshold for a given network:

```
set security utm utm-policy AV_ONLY anti-virus http-profile KS_AV
set security utm utm-policy AV_ONLY traffic-options sessions-per-client limit 300
set security utm utm-policy AV_ONLY traffic-options sessions-per-client
```

```
over-limit
log-and-permit
```

Now we'll use the `show` command to check our work and the `commit` command to get our Branch Office SRX deployed and working. As always, monitor the flows and use traceoptions to check the logs.

Summary

The UTM feature set provides powerful tools for blocking viruses, undesired web content, files, and emails, giving administrators fine-grained control over the traffic allowed through the network. However, these features come at the expense of computational complexity, which is why Juniper Networks decided to provide a range of solutions, from full on-box scanning capabilities to in-the-cloud-based approaches aimed at providing different detection capabilities with different performance characteristics.

Chapter Review Questions

1. Which features comprise the UTM solution?
2. If the combined CPU power of devices protected by an SRX is likely to be much larger than the power of the SRX, why does a CPU-intensive feature such as antivirus still make sense?
3. Where are web filtering policies evaluated when using the Websense redirect solution?
4. Which UTM features require a license?
5. What is intelligent prescreening?
6. Does the SRX transmit the file contents to a central server when using the Sophos in-the-cloud antivirus solution?
7. When using the SurfControl integrated engine, URLs are evaluated against the engine as well as against whitelists and blacklists. What is the order of evaluation?
8. Which protocols are decoded (and therefore supported) by the UTM protocol parser?
9. The antispam SMTP protocol decoder extracts three fields. Which ones?
10. What facility do the data-plane-generated logs use?

Chapter Review Answers

1. The UTM feature set is composed of the following features:
    - Web filtering
    - Antivirus

- Antispam
- Content filtering

2. A CPU-intensive feature such as antivirus still makes sense in this case because a network-based solution is simpler to administrate and keep updated. A two-tier approach is recommended in which the first tier (the network) is used to detect recent in-the-wild attacks, while host-based solutions can be used to stop less commonly found attacks.
3. With the Websense redirect solution, the web filtering policies are evaluated by the Websense server and not by the SRX. After a URL is evaluated, the Websense server sends an allow/block command to the SRX.
4. All the antivirus solutions—the SurfControl integrated solution and the Sophos antispam solution—require a license.
5. Intelligent prescreening is a technique used to optimize the scanning of files by trying to determine if a file is potentially harmful by looking at the first few bites. If the file is determined to be harmless, scanning can be avoided.
6. The SRX does not transmit the file contents to a central server when using the Sophos in-the-cloud antivirus solution. The in-the-cloud solution only transmits checksums of the files.
7. Blacklists are evaluated first, followed by whitelists and the SurfControl engine.
8. The protocol decoder supports the following protocols:
   - FTP
   - HTTP
   - SMTP
   - IMAP
   - POP3
9. The antispam SMTP protocol decoder extracts the source IP address of the connection, the sender name, and the sender address.
10. Data-plane logs are tagged with the `user` facility.

CHAPTER 10
High Availability

Failure is not an option.

—Eugene F. Kranz, *Apollo 13* moon mission

Information availability is a daily part of modern society. People make phone calls, read the news, stream songs, check sports scores, and watch television all over the Internet or on their local provider's network. At any given time, at any given location, almost any bit of information can be made available over the Internet. Today, and in the near future, it's expected that there should be no interruptions to the access of this flow of information. Failure to provide all of the world's information at any user's fingertips at any time, day or night, will create great wrath on whomever's network is in the way. Welcome to the 21st century.

The average user of the Internet's services is unable to comprehend why the information he desires is not available. All he knows is that it isn't, and that is no longer acceptable. Consumers clamor for compensation and complain to all available outlets. Business users call the help desk and demand explanations, while escalating their lost connection to all levels. Revenue is lost and the world looks bleak. Information must always be *highly* available, not just available.

The most likely location of a failure somewhere in the network is typically between the client device and the server. This chapter is dedicated to training network administrators on how to ensure that their SRX is not the device that brings down the network. Firewalls are placed in the most critical locations in the network, and when problems occur, trust us, users notice.

A router handles each packet as its own entity. It does not process traffic as though the packets had a relationship to each other. The packet could be attempting to start a new connection, end a connection, or have all sorts of strange data inside. A router simply looks at the Layer 3 header and passes the packet on. Because of this, packets can come in any order and leave the router in any way. If the router only sees one packet out of an entire connection and never sees another, it doesn't matter. If one router failed, another router can easily pick up all of the traffic utilizing dynamic routing. Designing for high availability (HA) with stateful firewalls is different because of their stateful nature.

Stateful firewalls need to see the creation and teardown of the communication between two devices. All of the packets in the middle of this communication need to be seen as well. If some of the packets are missed, the firewall will start dropping them as it misses changes in the state of communications. Once stateful firewalls came into the picture, the nature of HA changed. The state of traffic must be preserved between redundant firewalls. If one firewall fails, the one attempting to take over for it must have knowledge of all of the traffic that is passing through it. All established connections will be dropped if the new firewall does not have knowledge of these sessions. This creates the challenge of ensuring that state synchronization can occur between the two devices. If not, the whole reason for having redundancy in the firewalls is lost.

Understanding High Availability in the SRX

The design of the SRX is extremely robust regardless of the model or platform. It has a complete operating system and many underlying processors and subsystems. Depending on the platform, it could have dozens of processors. Because of this, the SRX implements HA in a radically different way than most firewalls. Common features such as configuration and session synchronization are still in the product, but *how* the two chassis interact is different.

Chassis Cluster

An SRX HA cluster implements a concept called *chassis cluster*. A chassis cluster takes the two SRX devices and represents them as a single device. The interfaces are numbered in such a way that they are counted starting at the first chassis and then end on the second chassis. Figure 10-1 shows a chassis cluster. On the left chassis, the flexible PIC concentrator (FPC) starts counting as normal; on the second chassis, the FPCs are counted as though they were part of the first chassis.

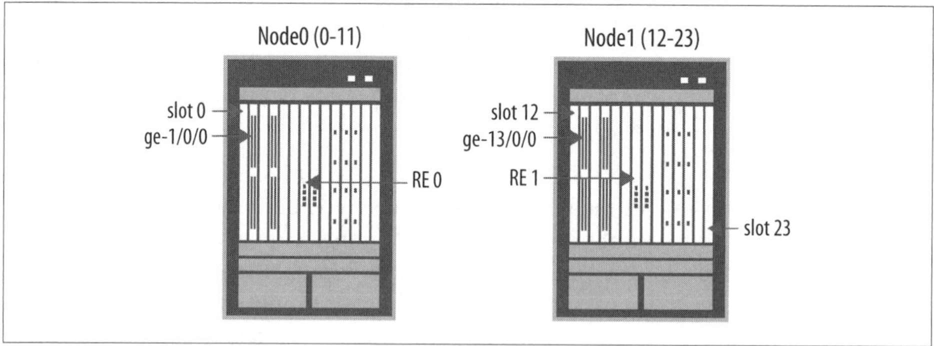

Figure 10-1. Chassis cluster FPC numbering

FPCs, PICs, and Ports, Oh My!

Junos-based devices use a specific naming convention for their interfaces and interface devices. An FPC is a flexible PIC concentrator. The FPC is the device that holds the interface cards or PIC. The FPC connects into the fabric of the chassis. A PIC is a physical interface card. The PIC contains network processors and typically one or more ports. A port may be a WAN interface or one or more Ethernet interfaces.

Interfaces are numbered in the following format: media-FPC/PIC/PORT. The media represents the type of media. This may be fast Ethernet (fe), 10 gigabit Ethernet (xe), or a T1 (t1). The FPC/PIC/PORT represents the physical location in the chassis. The FPC number is the FPC's number. FPC counting starts at zero. An FPC may contain one or more PICs. Similar to FPCs, the PICs are numbered from zero and then counted up from there. Lastly, ports are counted from zero and upward from there.

In Chapter 1, we discussed the concept of the route engine (RE). In an SRX cluster, each SRX has one active RE. When the cluster is created the two REs work together to provide redundancy. This is similar to the Juniper M Series, T Series, and MX Series routing platforms that support dual REs. The Junos operating system is currently limited to supporting two REs per device. Because of this, the SRX cluster can only have one RE per chassis. When the chassis are combined and act as a single chassis, the devices reach the two-RE limit.

Multiple REs in a single SRX are currently not supported.

The chassis cluster concept, although new to the SRX, is not new to Juniper Networks. The SRX utilizes the code infrastructure from the TX Matrix products. The TX Matrix is a multichassis router that is considered one of the largest routers in the world. Only the largest service providers and cloud networks utilize the product. Because of its robust design and reliable infrastructure, it's great to think that the code from such a product sits inside every SRX. When the SRX was designed the engineers at Juniper looked at the current available options and saw that the TX Matrix provided the infrastructure they needed. This is a great example of how using the Junos operating system across multiple platforms benefits all products.

To run a device in clustering mode there are a set of specific requirements. For the SRX3000 and SRX5000 lines the devices must have an identical number of SPCs and the SPCs must be in identical locations. The SRXs, however, may have any number of interface cards and they do not have to be in the same slots. Best practice suggests, though, that you deploy interfaces in the same FPCs and or PIC slots, as this will make it easier to troubleshoot in the long run.

For most network administrators, this concept of a single logical chassis is very different from traditional HA firewall deployment. To provide some comparison, in ScreenOS, for example, the two devices were treated independently of each other. The configuration, as well as network traffic state, was synchronized between the devices, but each device had its own set of interfaces.

On the branch SRX Series products, Ethernet switching as of Junos 10.2 is not supported when the devices are in chassis cluster mode. Before enabling clustering, Ethernet switching must be disabled.

The Control Plane

As discussed throughput this book, the SRX has a separated control plane and data plane. Depending on the SRX platform architecture, the separation varies from being separate processes running on separate cores to completely physically differentiated subsystems. For the purposes of this discussion, however, it's enough to know that the control and data planes are separated.

The control plane is used in HA to synchronize the kernel state between the two REs. It also provides a path between the two devices to send hello messages between them. On the RE, a process or daemon runs, called *jsrpd*. This stands for *Junos stateful redundancy protocol daemon*. This daemon is responsible for sending the messages and doing failovers between the two devices. Another kernel, *ksyncd*, is used for synchronizing the kernel state between the two devices. All of this occurs over the control plane link.

The control plane is always in an *active/backup* state. This means only one RE can be the master over the cluster's configuration and state. This ensures that there is only one ultimate truth over the state of the cluster. If the primary RE fails, the secondary takes over for it. Creating an *active/active* control plane makes synchronization more difficult because many checks would need to be put in place to validate which RE is right.

The two devices' control planes talk to each other over a control link. This link is reserved for control plane communication. It is critical that the link maintain its integrity to allow for communication between the two devices. For more, see "Upgrading the Cluster" on page 584.

The Data Plane

The data plane's responsibility in the SRX is to pass data and processes based on the administrator's configuration. All session and service states are maintained on the data plane. The REs and/or control plane are not responsible for maintaining state (the RE simply requests data and statistics from the data plane and returns it to the administrator).

The data plane has a few responsibilities when it comes to HA implementation. First and foremost is state synchronization. The state of sessions and services is shared between the two devices. Sessions are the state of the current set of traffic that is going through the SRX, and services are other items such as the virtual private network (VPN), intrusion protection service (IPS), and application layer gateways (ALGs).

On the branch SRX Series, synchronization happens between the flowd daemon running on the data plane. The SRX Series for the branch, as discussed in Chapter 1, runs a single multicore processor with a single multithreaded flowd process. The data center SRX distributed architecture state synchronization is handled in a similar fashion. Figure 10-2 shows a detailed example.

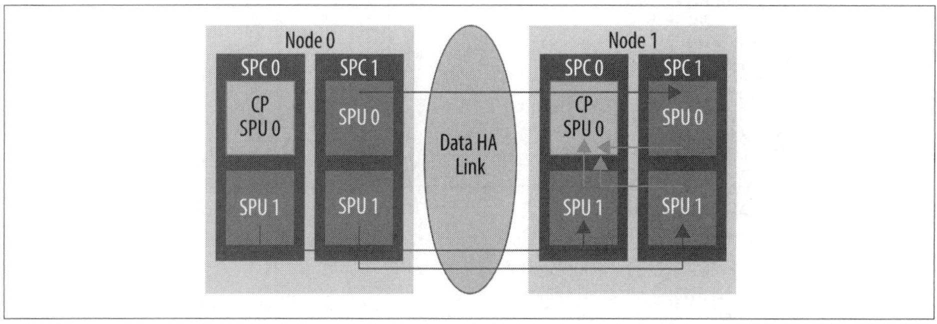

Figure 10-2. Data center SRX state synchronization

In Figure 10-2, two SRX data center platforms are shown. Node 0 is shown on the left and node 1 is on the right. Each device is depicted with two SPCs. SPC 0 is the SPC that contains the central point (CP) Services Processing Unit (SPU) and a second flow SPU. In SPC 1, both SPUs are flow SPUs. Both SRX data center platforms are required to have the same number and location of SPCs and Network Processing Cards (NPCs). This is required because the SPUs talk to their peer SPU in the same FPC and PIC location. As seen in the back of Figure 10-2, the flow SPU in FPC 0 on node 0 sends a message to node 1 on FPC 0 in PIC 1. This is the session synchronization message. Once the SPU on node 1 validates and creates the session, it sends a message to its local CP. As stated in Chapter 1, the central point processors are responsible for maintaining the state for all of the exiting sessions on the SRX. The secondary device now has all of the necessary information to handle the traffic in the event of a failover.

Information is synchronized in what is known as a real-time object (RTO). This RTO contains the necessary information to synchronize the data to the other node. The remote side does not send an acknowledgment of the RTO because doing so would slow down the session creation process, and frankly, an acknowledgment is rarely needed. There are many different RTO message types. New ones may be added based on the creation of new features on the SRX. The most commonly used message types are the ones for session creation and session closure.

The second task the SRX needs to handle is forwarding traffic between the two devices. This is also known as *data path* or *Z path forwarding*. Figure 10-3 illustrates this. Under most configuration deployments, Z path forwarding is not necessary. However, in specific designs, this operation may be very common. (The details are further explored in "Deployment Concepts" on page 548.) In the event that traffic is received by a node, the node will always forward the traffic to a node on which the traffic will egress.

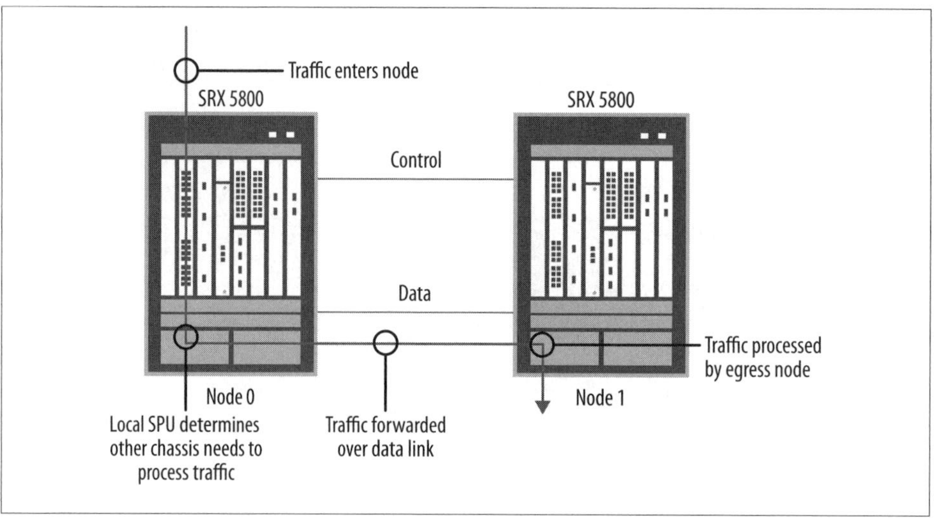

Figure 10-3. Data path or Z path forwarding

The last task for the data link is to send jsrpd messages between the two devices. The jsrpd daemon passes messages over the data plane to validate that it is operating correctly. These are similar to the messages that are sent over the control link, except that they go through the data plane. By sending these additional messages over the data plane, the RE ensures that the data plane is up and capable of passing traffic. On the branch SRX Series devices, the message exits the control plane, passes through flowd and over the data link, and then to the second device. The second device receives the packet, flowd, and passes the packet to the control plane and on to jsrpd. Depending on the platform, the rate for the messages will vary.

All of these data plane messages pass over the data link. The data link is also known as the *fabric link* depending on the context of the discussion. The size of the link varies based on the requirements. These requirements consist of the amount of data forwarding between devices and the number of new connections per second:

- On the SRX100 and SRX210, a 100 MB Ethernet link is acceptable for the link.
- For the SRX650 and SRX240, it's suggested that you use a 1 GB link.
- On the data center SRXs, a 1 GB link is acceptable unless data forwarding is going to occur.
- Even on an SRX5000 Series with a maximum of 350,000 new connections per second, a 1 GB link can sustain the RTOs.
- If data forwarding is in the design, a 10 GB link is suggested.

Junos High Availability Concepts

This chapter started with the concept of the chassis cluster because it's the fundamental concept for the entire chapter. There are several important aspects to the chassis cluster; some concern how the cluster is configured, and others are simply key to the fault tolerance the chassis cluster provides. In this section, we will explore the deeper concepts of the chassis cluster.

Cluster ID

Each cluster must share a unique identifier among all of its members. This identifier is used in a few different ways, but most importantly it is used when two devices are communicating with each other. Fifteen cluster IDs are available for use when creating a cluster. The cluster ID is also used when determining Media Access Control (MAC) addresses for the redundant Ethernet interfaces.

Node ID

The node ID is the unique identifier for a device within a cluster. There are two node IDs: 0 and 1. The node with an ID of 0 is considered the base node. The node ID does not give the device any sort of priority over its mastership, only in interface ordering. Node 0 is the first node for the interface numbering in the chassis cluster. The second node, node 1, is the second and last node in the cluster.

Redundancy groups

In an HA cluster, the goal is the ability to fail over resources in case something goes wrong. A *redundancy group* is a collection of resources that need to fail over between the two devices. Only one node at a time can be responsible for a redundancy group; however, a single node can be the primary node for any number of redundancy groups.

Two different items are placed in a redundancy group: the control plane and the interfaces. The default redundancy group is group 0. Redundancy group 0 represents the control plane. The node that is the master over redundancy group 0 has the active RE.

The active RE is responsible for controlling the data plane and pushing new configurations. It is considered the *ultimate truth* in matters regarding what is happening on the device.

The data plane components for redundancy groups exist in numbers 1 and greater. The different SRX platforms support different numbers of redundancy groups. A data plane redundancy group contains one or more Redundant Ethernet Interfaces (Reths). Each member in the cluster has a physical interface bound into a Reth. The active node's physical interface will be active and the backup node's interface will be passive and will not pass traffic. It is easier to think of this as a binary switch. Only one of the members of the Reth is active at any given time. "Deployment Concepts" on page 548 details the use of data plane redundancy groups.

Interfaces

A network device doesn't help a network without participating in traffic processing. An SRX has two different interface types that it can use to process traffic. The first is the Reth. A Reth is a Junos aggregate Ethernet interface and it has special properties compared to a traditional aggregate Ethernet interface. The Reth allows the administrator to add one or more child links per chassis. Figure 10-4 shows an example of this where node 0 is represented on the left and node 1 is represented on the right.

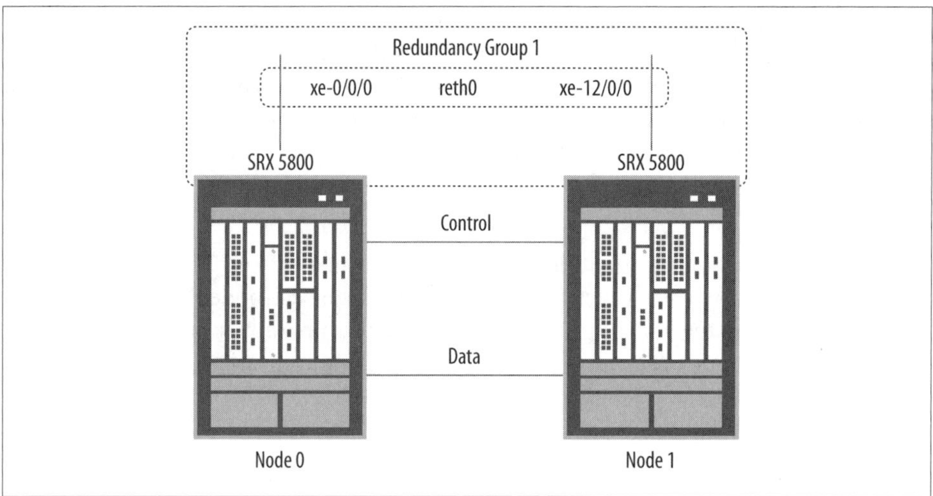

Figure 10-4. Reth example

In the figure, node 0 has interface xe-0/0/0 as a child link of reth0 and node 1 has interface xe-12/0/0. The interface reth0 is a member of redundancy group 1. The node, in this case node 0, has its link active. Node 1's link is in an up state but it does not accept or pass traffic. Upon a failover between nodes, the newly active node sends out Gratuitous ARPs (GARPs). Both nodes share the same MAC address on the Reth. The surrounding switches will learn the new port that has the Reth MAC address. The hosts are still sending their data to the same MAC, so they do not have to relearn anything.

The MAC address for the Reth is based on a combination of the cluster ID and the Reth number. Figure 10-5 shows the algorithm that determines the MAC address. In the figure, there are two types of fields: the hex field represents one bit by using a hexadecimal representation of a byte using two base 16 digits; the bit field represents a number in binary with eight bits.

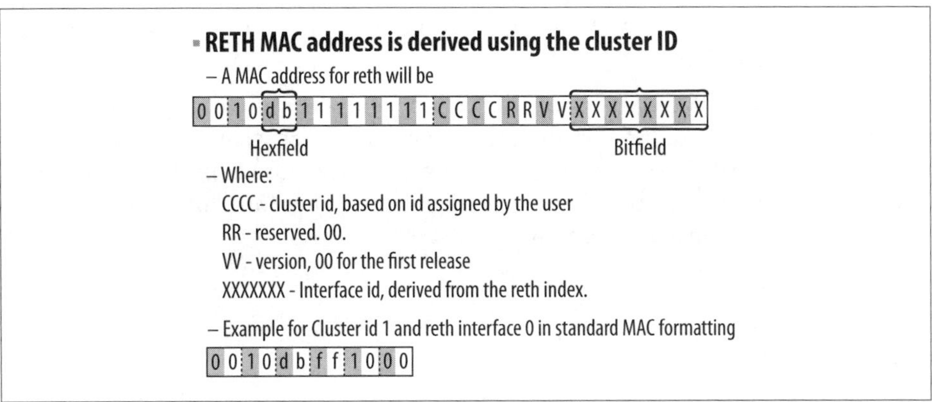

Figure 10-5. Reth MAC address

The first four of the six bytes are fixed. They do not change between cluster deployments. The last two bytes vary based on the cluster ID and the Reth index. In the figure, *CCCC* represents the cluster ID in binary. With four bits, the maximum number is 15, which is the same number of cluster IDs supported. Next, the *RR* represents a reserved field for future expansion. It is currently set to 0 for both bits. The *VV* represents the version of the chassis cluster, which today is set at 0 for both of the bits. Last is the field filled with *XXXXXXXXX*, and this represents the redundant Ethernet index ID. Based on Figure 10-5, it's easy to see that collision of MAC addresses between clusters can be avoided.

When configured in a chassis cluster the SRX is also able to support local interfaces. A local interface is an interface that is configured local to a specific node. This method of configuration on an interface is the same method of configuration on a standalone device. The significance of a local interface in an SRX cluster is that it does not have a backup interface on the other chassis, meaning that it is part of neither a Reth nor a redundancy group. If this interface were to fail, its IP address would not fail over to the other node. Although this feature may seem perplexing at first, it actually provides a lot of value in complex network topologies, and it will be further explored later in this chapter.

Deployment Concepts

It's time to apply all these concepts to actual deployment scenarios. For HA clusters, there is a lot of terminology for the mode of actually deploying devices, and this section attempts to give administrators a clear idea of what methods of deployment are available to them.

Earlier in this chapter we discussed control plane redundancy, whereby the control plane is deployed in an active/passive fashion. One RE is active for controlling the cluster, and the second RE is passive. The secondary RE performs some basic maintenance for the local chassis, and synchronizes the configuration as well as checks that the other chassis is alive.

In this section, we will discuss what can be done with the redundancy groups on the data plane. The configuration on the data plane determines what mode the SRXs are operating in. The SRX doesn't have an idea of being forced into a specific mode of HA, but operates in that mode based on the configuration. There are three basic modes of operation, and one creative alternative:

- Active/passive
- Active/active
- Mixed mode
- The six pack

Active/passive

In the active/passive mode, the first SRX data plane is actively passing traffic while the second SRX data plane is sitting in a passive setting *not* passing traffic. Upon a fault condition, of course, the passive data plane will take over and begin passing traffic. To accomplish this, the SRX utilizes one data plane redundancy group and one or more redundant Ethernet interfaces. Figure 10-6 illustrates an example of this active/passive process.

As shown in Figure 10-6, node 0, on the left, is currently active and node 1 is passive. In this example, there are two Reth interfaces: reth0 and reth1. Reth0 goes toward the Internet and reth1 goes toward the internal network. Because node 0 is currently active, it is passing all of the traffic between the Internet and the internal network. Node 1's data plane is (patiently) waiting for any issue to arise so that it can take over and continue to pass traffic. The interfaces on node 1 that are in the reth0 and reth1 groups are physically up but are unable to pass traffic. Since node 0 is currently active, it synchronizes any new sessions that are created to node 1. When node 1 needs to take over for node 0, it will have the same session information locally.

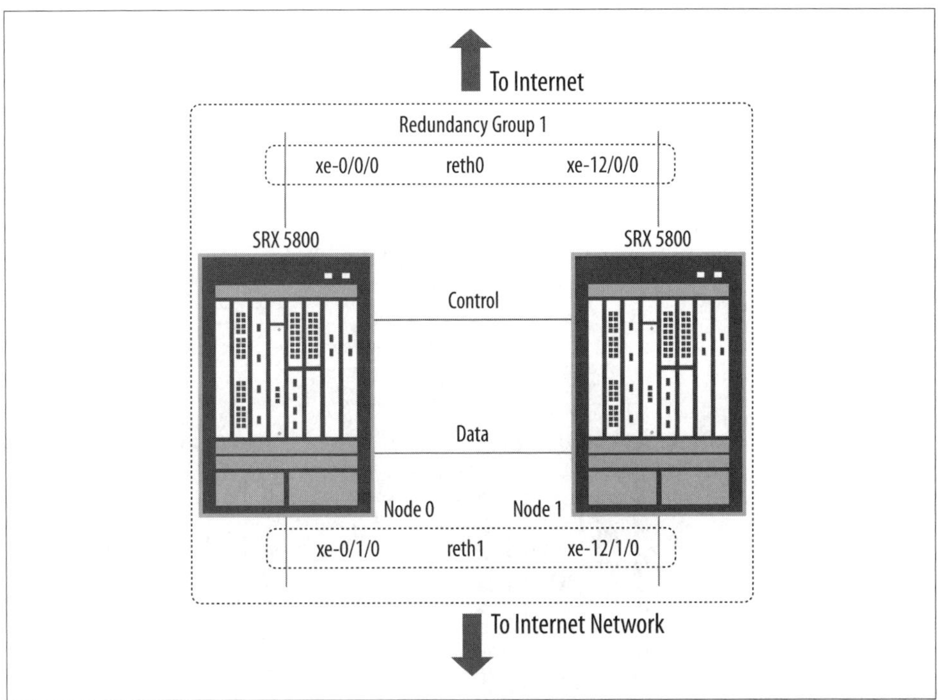

Figure 10-6. Active/passive cluster

Active/active

In an active/active deployment, both SRXs are simultaneously passing traffic. Although it sounds difficult, the concept is simple—active/active is merely active/passive but done twice. In this case, each member of the cluster is active for its own redundancy group and the other device is passive for the redundancy group. In the event of a failure, the remaining node will take over for the traffic for the failed device. Synchronization happens between both nodes. Sessions for both redundancy groups are available on both nodes.

So, the question remains: what does this type of deployment mean for the administrator? The biggest advantage is that passing traffic over the backup node ensures that the backup data plane is ready and correctly functioning. Nothing is worse than having an HA cluster running for months and then, during the moment of truth, a failure occurs, and the second node is in a degraded state and no one discovered this ahead of time. A good example of avoiding this is to have one of the redundancy groups passing a majority of the traffic while the other redundancy group is used to pass only a single health check. This is a great design because the second device is verified and the administrator doesn't have to troubleshoot load-sharing scenarios.

Active/active deployments can also be used to share load between the two hosts. The only downside to this design is that it may be difficult to troubleshoot flows going through the two devices, but ultimately that varies on the administrator and the environment, and it's probably better to have the option available in the administrator's tool chest than not. Figure 10-7 shows an example of an active/active cluster.

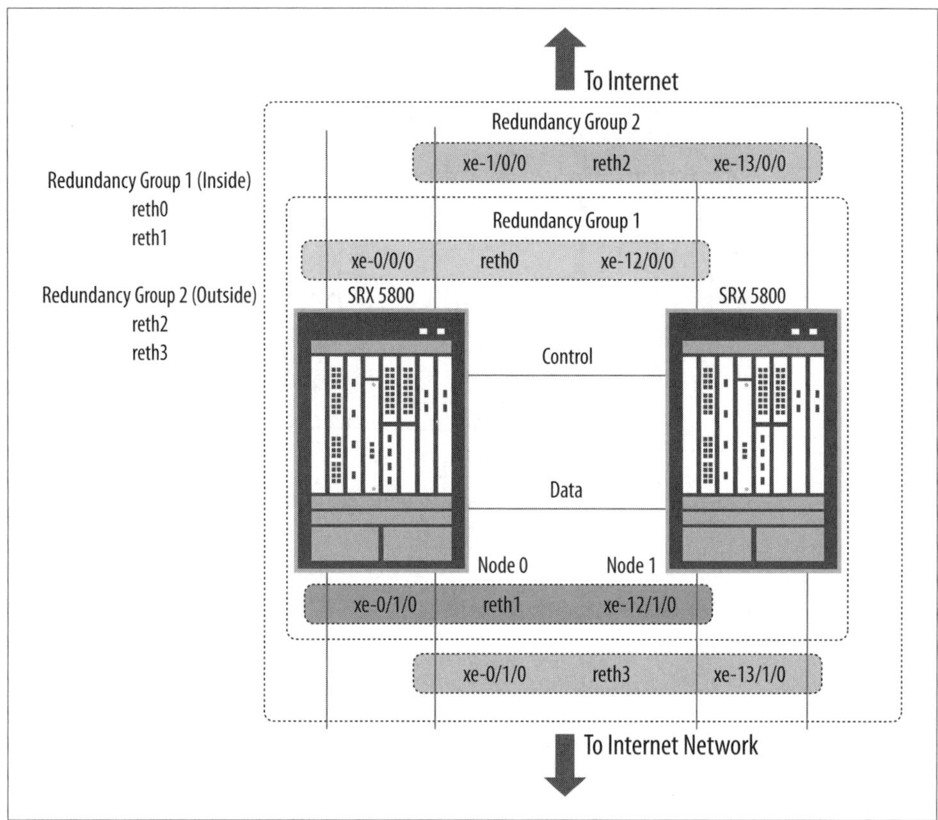

Figure 10-7. Active/active cluster

Figure 10-7 shows an active/active cluster as simply two active/passive configurations. Building from Figure 10-6, the example starts with the same configuration as before. The clusters had a single redundancy group 1 and two Reths, reth0 and reth1, with node 0 being the designated primary. In this example, a second redundancy group is added, redundancy group 2, and two additional Reths are added to accommodate it. reth2 is on the Internet-facing side of the firewalls and reth3 is toward the internal network. This redundancy group, however, has node 1 as the primary, so traffic that is localized to redundancy group 2 is only sent through node 1 unless a failure occurs.

Mixed mode

Mixed mode, perhaps the most interesting HA configuration, builds on the concepts already demonstrated but expands to include local interfaces. As we discussed earlier, a local interface is an interface that has configurations local to the node for which it is attached. The other node is not required to have a backup to this interface as in the case of a Reth.

This option has significance in two specific use cases.

The first use case is WAN interfaces. For this use case there are two SRX210s, each with a T1 interface and a single Reth to present back to the LAN, as depicted in Figure 10-8. Node 0 on the left has a T1 to provider A and node 1 on the right has a T1 to provider B. Each node has a single interface connected to the LAN switch . These two interfaces are bound together as reth0. The reth0 interface provides a redundant, reliable gateway to present to clients. Because of the way a T1 works, it is not possible to have a common Layer 2 domain between the two T1 interfaces, so each T1 is its own local interface to the local node.

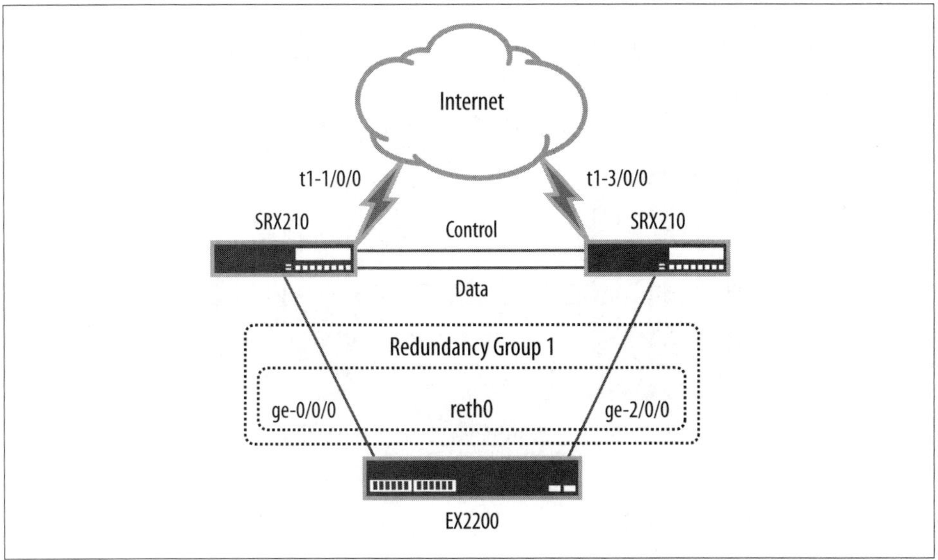

Figure 10-8. Mixed mode with WAN interfaces

Traffic can enter or exit either T1 interface, and it is always directed out to the correct interface. In Figure 10-8's case, that would be reth0, as it is the only other interface configured. The benefit of this design is that the two T1s provide redundancy and increased capacity, and sessions between the two interfaces are synchronized. It's great when you are using T1 interfaces as connections to a remote VPN site.

A second great use case for mixed mode is with data centers using a dynamic routing integration design. The design is similar to our previous example, but in this case all of the interfaces are Ethernet. The two SRXs each have two interfaces connected into two different M120 routers, all of which can be seen in Figure 10-9. Having two links each going to two different routers provides a better level of redundancy in case links or routers fail. The Open Shortest Path First (OSPF) routing protocol is enabled between the SRXs and the upstream routers, allowing for simplified failover between the links and ensuring that the four devices can determine the best path to the upstream networks. If a link fails, OSPF recalculates and determines the next best path.

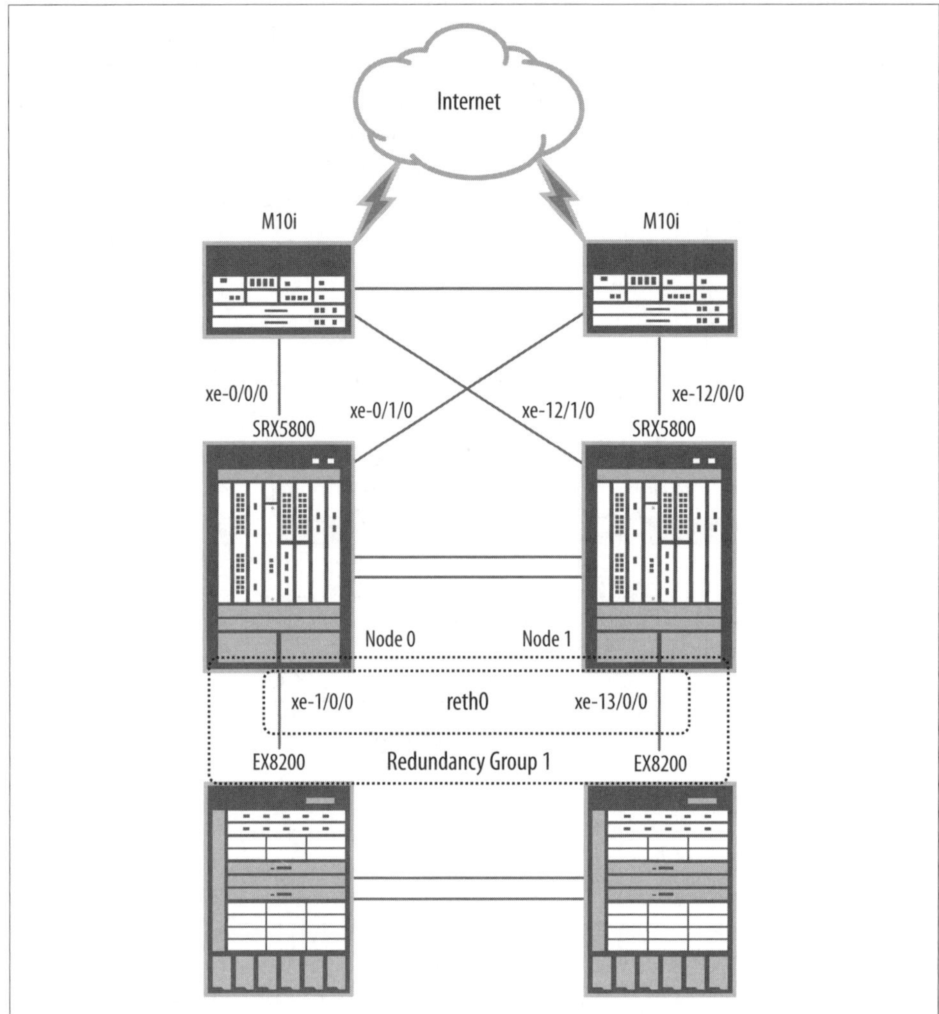

Figure 10-9. Data center mixed mode design

You can see in Figure 10-9 that the southbound interfaces connect into two EX8200 core switches. These switches provide a common Layer 2 domain between the southbound interfaces, which allows for the creation of reth0 (similar to the rest of the designs seen in this chapter).

Six pack

It's possible to forgo redundant Ethernet interfaces altogether and use only local interfaces. This is similar to the data center mixed mode design, except it takes the idea one step further and uses local interfaces for both the north- and southbound connections. A common name for this design is *six pack*. It uses four routers and two firewalls and is shown in Figure 10-10.

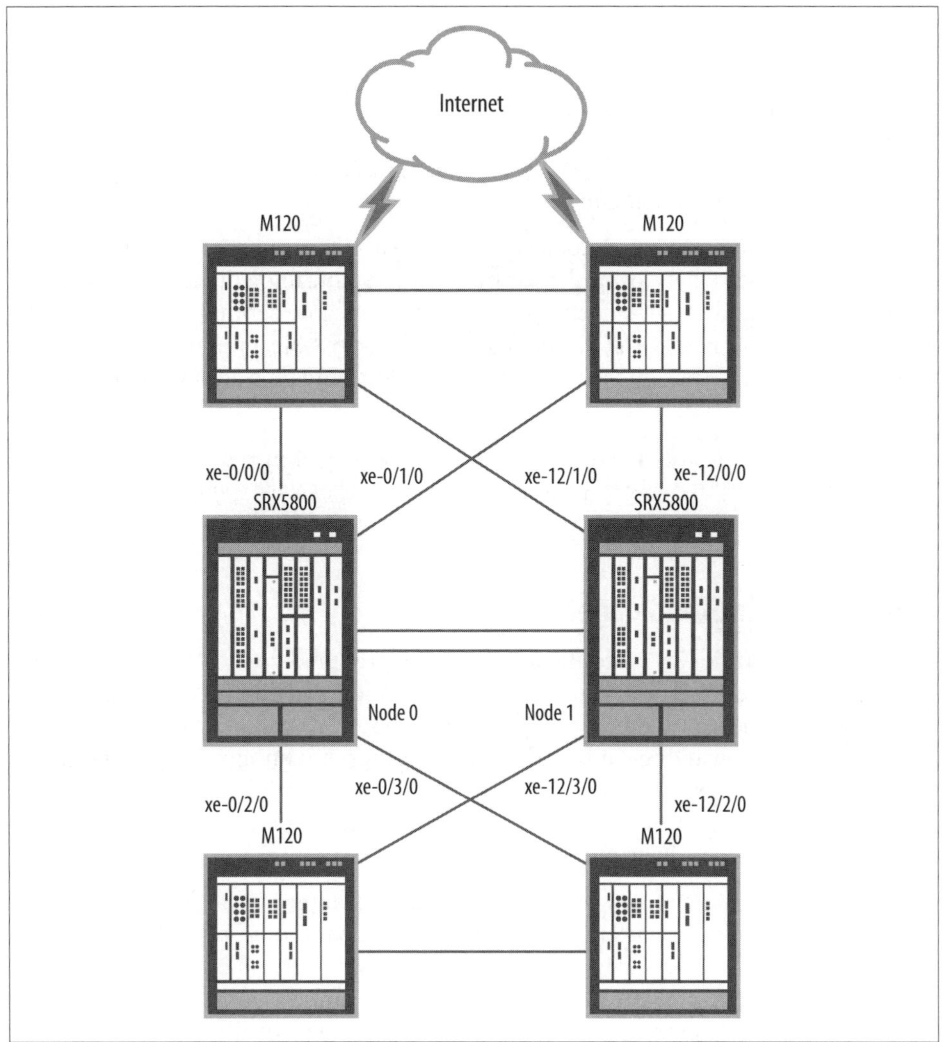

Figure 10-10. Six pack HA design

Much like the mixed mode design, the two northbound routers in Figure 10-10 are connected to the SRXs with two links. Each router has a connection to each SRX. On the southbound routers, the same design is replicated. This allows for a fully meshed, active/active, and truly HA network to exist. In this case, the SRXs are acting more like how a traditional router would be deployed. OSPF is used for the design to direct traffic through the SRXs, and it's even possible to use equal cost multipath routing to do balancing for upstream hosts.

The six pack design shows just how flexible the SRXs can be to meet the needs of nearly any environment. These deployments can even be done in either the traditional Layer 3 routing mode or Layer 2 transparent mode.

Configuration

Understanding how a chassis cluster works is half the battle in attaining acceptable HA levels. The rest concerns configuring a cluster.

To be fair, the configuration is actually quite easy—it's just a few steps to get the cluster up and running. Setting it up correctly is the key to a stable implementation, and needless to say, rushing through some important steps can cause serious pain later on. So, we suggest that you start with fresh configurations, if possible, even if this means clustering the devices starting with a minimal configuration and then adding on from there.

If there is an existing configuration, set it aside and then create the cluster. After the cluster is running happily, then migrate the configuration back on.

Differences from Standalone

When an administrator enters configuration mode on a standalone SRX, all of the active users who log in to the device can see the configuration and edit it. When each user's changes can be seen by the other users on the device, it's called a *shared configuration*. Once chassis clustering is enabled, the devices must be configured in what is called *configure private*, or *private*, mode, which enforces each administrator to see only her own configuration changes. This imposes several restrictions on the end administrator while using configure private mode.

The first notable restriction is that all configuration commits must be done from the root, or top, of the configuration hierarchy. Second, the option to do `commit confirmed` is no longer allowed, which, as you know, allows for a rollback to the previous configuration if things go wrong. Both are very nice features that are not available when in clustering mode. The reason these are disabled is simple: stability.

A lot of communication is going on between the two SRXs when they are in a clustered mode, so when committing a change it is best to minimize the chances of differences between the two devices' local configurations at the time of the commit. If each node had a user modifying the configuration at the same time, this would add an unneeded level of complexity to ensure that the configurations are synchronized. Because of this, private mode is required while making configuration changes.

Activating JSRPD (Juniper Services Redundancy Protocol)

The first step in creating a cluster is to place the device into cluster mode. By default, the SRX does not run the jsrpd daemon, so this must be triggered. To enable the jsrpd daemon and turn the device into an eligible chassis cluster member, a few special bits must be set in the NVRAM on the device, triggering the SRX, upon boot, to enable jsrpd and enter chassis cluster mode.

These settings are permanent until they are otherwise removed. An initial reboot is required after setting the cluster ID to get the jsrpd daemon to start. The daemon will start every time the bits are seen in the NVRAM.

It takes a single command, and it takes effect only upon reboot. Although it is unfortunate that a reboot is required, it is required only once. You must run the command from operational mode and as a user with super-user privileges.

```
root@SRX210-H> set chassis cluster cluster-id 1 node 0 reboot
Successfully enabled chassis cluster. Going to reboot now

root@SRX210-H>
*** FINAL System shutdown message from root@SRX210-H ***
System going down IMMEDIATELY
```

For this command to work we needed to choose the cluster ID and the node ID. For most implementations, cluster ID 1 is perfectly acceptable, as we discussed earlier in the chapter. The node ID is easy too: for the first node that is being set up use node 0, and for the second node use node 1. There isn't a specific preference between the two. Being node 0 or node 1 doesn't provide any special benefit; it's only a unique identifier for the device.

Once the device comes back up, it's easy to notice the changes. Right above the shell prompt is a new line:

```
{primary:node0} #<----new to the the prompt
root>
```

This line tells the administrator two important pieces of information. The part on the left of the colon is the current status of the cluster control plane in relevance to the cluster, and it will define which state the RE is in.

This only shows the control plane status. This *does not* show which device has the active data plane. This is a common mistake for those using the SRX. That message should be on its own page all by itself as it's that important to remember.

There are several different options for control plane status, as listed in Table 10-1. Upon boot, the device enters the hold state. During this state the control plane is preparing itself to enter the cluster. Next the device enters the secondary state when the RE checks to see if there is already a primary RE in the cluster. If not, it then transitions to the primary state.

Table 10-1. Control plane states

State	Meaning
Hold	This is the initial state upon boot. The RE is preparing to join the cluster.
Secondary	The RE is in backup state and is ready to take over for the primary.
Primary	The RE is the controller for the cluster.
Ineligible	Something has occurred that makes the RE no longer eligible to be part of the cluster.
Disabled	The RE is no longer eligible to enter the cluster. It must be rebooted to rejoin the cluster.
Unknown	A critical failure has occurred. The device is unable to determine its current state. It must be rebooted to attempt to reenter the cluster.
Lost	Communication with the other node is lost. A node cannot be in a lost state; this is only listed under the `show chassis cluster status` command when the other device was never detected.
Secondary-hold	A device enters secondary-hold when it is identified as a secondary but the configured hold-down timer has not yet expired. In the event of a critical failure, the redundancy group can still fail over.

After the primary states are three states that occur only when something goes wrong. *Ineligible* occurs when something happens that invalidates the member from the cluster. From there the device enters the *disabled* state after a period of time while being ineligible. The last state, *unknown*, can occur only if some disastrous, unexpected event occurs.

Once the system is up, and in either the final primary or secondary state, there are a few steps you can take to validate that the chassis cluster is indeed up and running. First check that the jsrpd daemon is up and running. If the new cluster status message is above the prompt, it's pretty certain that the daemon is running:

```
{primary:node0}
root> show system processes | match jsrpd
  863  ??  S      0:00.24 /usr/sbin/jsrpd -N

{primary:node0}
root> show chassis cluster status
Cluster ID: 1
Node                  Priority          Status  Preempt  Manual failover
```

```
Redundancy group: 0 , Failover count: 1
    node0                   1          primary      no       no
    node1                   0          lost         n/a      n/a

{primary:node0}
root>
```

The greatest friend of anyone using the chassis cluster is the `show chassis cluster status` command. It is the most common command for looking at the current status of the cluster and it is full of information. The first bit of information is the cluster ID, the one that was initially configured and will likely stay that way until cleared. Next is information regarding all of the redundancy groups that are configured; the first one in our case is redundancy group 0. This represents the control plane only and has no relevance on who is actively passing traffic.

Under each redundancy group, each node is listed along with its priorities, status, preempt status, and whether the device is in manual failover. By default, redundancy group 0 is created without user intervention. Each device is given a default priority of 1. Because of this, the first node that becomes primary will be primary until a failure occurs. Next the status is listed. The last two columns are preempt and manual failover. Preempt is the ability to configure the device with the higher priority to preempt the device with the lower priority. The manual failover column will state if the node was manually failed-over to by the administrator.

Managing Cluster Members

Most Junos devices have a special interface named fxp0. This interface is used to manage the SRXs. It is typically connected to the RE, although some devices, such as the SRX100 and SRX200 Series, do not have a dedicated port for fxp0 because the devices are designed to provide the maximum number of ports for branch devices. However, when SRX devices are configured in a cluster, the secondary node cannot be directly managed unless it has either a local interface or the fxp0 port. To ease management of the SRX100 and SRX200 Series, the fe-0/0/6 port automatically becomes the fxp0 port. In "Node-Specific Information" on page 567 we will discuss how to configure this port.

The fxp0 interface exists on the majority of Junos devices. This is due to the devices' service-provider-like design. Fxp0 allows for secure out-of-band management, enabling administrators to access the device no matter what is happening on the network. Because of this, many of the capabilities and management services often operate best through the fxp0 port. Tools such as Network and Security Manager (NSM) and Junos Space operate best when talking to an fxp0 port. Also, updates for Intrusion Detection and Prevention (IDP) and Unified Threat Management (UTM) will work best through this interface.

Configuring the Control Ports

Now that the devices are up and running, it's time to get the two devices talking. There are two communication paths for the devices to talk over; the first leads to the second. The control port is the first, and by configuring the control port it's possible to get the devices communicating early on. Then, once the devices are in a cluster, the configuration is automatically synchronized for a consistent second method. This can cut the administrator's work in half as he has to configure both devices only once.

Different platforms have different requirements for configuring the control port. Table 10-2 lists each platform and the control port location. Since each platform has different subsystems under the hood, so to speak, there are different ways to configure the control port. The only device that requires manual intervention is the SRX5000. Some devices also support dual or redundant control ports.

Table 10-2. Control ports by platform

Device	Control port	Description	Dual support?
SRX100 and SRX210	fe-0/0/7	Dedicated as a control port upon enabling clustering	No
SRX240 and SRX600	ge-0/0/1	Dedicated as a control port upon enabling clustering	No
SRX3000	Both located on the switch fabric board (SFB)	No user configuration required	Yes
SRX5000	Located on the Services Processing Card (SPC)	Manual configuration required	Yes

When connecting control ports you connect the control port from each device to the other device. It is not recommended that you join two primary devices together—it's best to reboot the secondary and then connect the control port. Upon reboot, the two devices will begin to communicate.

For all of the SRX devices, except the SRX5000, you can do this right after the initial cluster configuration. For the SRX5000 Series two reboots are required.

The SRX5000 Series control ports are located on the SPC, because when Juniper was creating the SRX5000 the SPC was the only part that was created from scratch and the remaining parts were taken from the MX Series. Ultimately, locating the control ports on the SPC removes the control ports from other components while adding some additional resiliency. The SPC and its underlying traffic processing are physically separate from the control ports even though they are located on the same card. The SRX5000 must use fiber SFPs to connect the two chassis.

Enabling Dual Control Links

The data center SRX is designed with many hardware components. Because of this, it requires additional hardware to enable dual control links. Inside each chassis there are two physically separate Ethernet control networks. By default, only one of the two networks is up and operational. This network is enabled by the RE in each chassis.

To enable the secondary network that will allow for the use of dual control links an additional piece of hardware is needed. On the SRX5000 Series a second RE is needed. This RE is only used to enable the secondary control network and then turns off. On the SRX3000 Series an SRX clustering module or SCM is used. It serves a similar function, but it is a different part than a standard RE. An RE on the SRX3000 also contains the component that controls all of the line cards. This part is removed on the SCM.

Two physically separate control networks are used to provide complete redundancy. Although it would be possible to use two links between the chassis and use a protocol such as Spanning Tree Protocol to prevent Layer 2 loops, no one would want such a critical feature relying on Spanning Tree.

To configure the control ports on the SRX5000, the administrator first needs to determine which ports he wants to configure, which he can do based on which FPC the control port is located within. Next, he must identify the port number (either port 0 or port 1):

```
{primary:node0}[edit chassis cluster]
root@SRX5800A# set control-ports fpc 1 port 0
root@SRX5800A# set control-ports fpc 2 port 1
root@SRX5800A# show
control-link-recovery;
control-ports {
    fpc 1 port 0;
    fpc 2 port 1;
}
root@SRX5800A# commit
```

There is logic in how the control ports should be configured on the SRX5000s. The control ports can be on the same FPC, but ideally, the SRX should not be configured that way. If possible, do not place the control port on the same card as the CP or central point processor. The reason is that the CP is used as a hop for the data link. If the FPC with the CP fails, and the control link is on it and it's a single control link, the SRX cluster can go into *split brain* or *dual mastership*. Because of this, separating the two is recommended. So, if an administrator is going to utilize dual control links, it's recommended that he place each control link on separate SPCs and the CP on a third SPC. This would require at least three SPCs, but this is the recommendation for the ultimate in HA.

Once the control links are up and running, and the secondary node is rebooted and up and running, it's time to check that the cluster is communicating. Again, we go back to the `show chassis cluster status` command:

```
{primary:node0}
root> show chassis cluster status
Cluster ID: 1
Node                Priority      Status    Preempt  Manual failover

Redundancy group: 0 , Failover count: 1
    node0                  1             primary        no       no
    node1                  1             secondary      no       no

{primary:node0}
root>
```

Both devices should be able to see each other, as shown here, with one device being primary and the other secondary.

Next, since there are two devices, it's possible to check communications between the two, this time using the `show chassis cluster statistics` command:

```
{primary:node0}
root> show chassis cluster control-plane statistics
Control link statistics:
    Control link 0:
        Heartbeat packets sent: 217
        Heartbeat packets received: 21
        Heartbeat packet errors: 0
Fabric link statistics:
    Probes sent: 4286
    Probes received: 0
    Probe errors: 0
```

At this point in the cluster creation, you should see only heartbeat messages on the control link, such as under the statistic `Heartbeat packets received:`. In the preceding output, 21 packets have been received. Typically, the number of heartbeat packets sent and received will not match, as one device started before the other and did not receive messages for a period of time. But once the sent and received numbers consistently match, everything on the control plane should be in order.

The SRX3000 and the SRX5000 are able to utilize two control links that are provided for redundancy only. In the event that one of the control links on the device fails, the second is utilized. But to utilize the second control link an additional component is needed. The SRX3000 uses a component called the SRX Clustering Module (SCM), which is used to activate and control the secondary control link. On the SRX5000, a standard RE can be used. The RE needs to have Junos 10.0 or later loaded to operate the control link. Both the SCM and the secondary RE are loaded into the second RE port on the platform. These modules do not act as an RE or backup to the RE, but rather are used only for the backup control link.

These components must be placed into the chassis while it is powered off. Upon boot, the secondary link will be up and functional.

A quick look at the output of the `show chassis cluster control-plane statistics` command shows the second control link working:

```
root > show chassis cluster control-plane statistics
Control link statistics:
    Control link 0:
        Heartbeat packets sent: 1114
        Heartbeat packets received: 217
        Heartbeat packet errors: 0
    Control link 1:
        Heartbeat packets sent: 1114
        Heartbeat packets received: 217
        Heartbeat packet errors: 0
Fabric link statistics:
    Probes sent: 1575937
    Probes received: 1575224
    Probe errors: 0
```

A final configuration option needs to be configured for the control link. That option is control link recovery. Control link recovery allows for automated recovery of the secondary chassis in the event that the control link fails. If the single or both control links fail, then the secondary device will go into the disabled state.

On the data center SRXs, a feature called *unified in-service software upgrade* (ISSU) can be utilized. This method is a graceful upgrade method and allows for the SRXs to upgrade without losing sessions or traffic.

As of Junos 10.2, VPN is not supported during the upgrade process. However, everything else will work.

The process may take some time to complete. This is because the kernel on the two devices must synchronize and the software must be updated. It is suggested that you have all of the redundancy groups on a single member in the cluster. The process is similar to the other, except the upgrade only needs to be run on one SRX:

```
{primary:node0}
root@SRX5800-1> request system software in-service-upgrade
junos-srx5000-10.2R2.6-domestic.tgz reboot
```

The command will upgrade each node and reboot them as needed. No further commands are required.

There is one last option that the unified ISSU process can use: the `no-old-master-upgrade` command, which leaves the master in a nonupgraded state. This ensures that there is a working box should the software upgrade fail. Upon successful completion of the upgrade, the old master is manually upgraded, as shown here:

```
{primary:node0}
root@SRX5800-1> request system software in-service-upgrade
junos-srx5000-10.2R3.10-domestic.tgz no-old-master-upgrade

##next on the old master

{primary:node0}
root@SRX5800-1> request system software add junos-srx5000-10.2R3.10-domestic.tgz

{primary:node0}
root@SRX5800-1> request chassis cluster in-service-upgrade abort

{primary:node0}
root@SRX5800-1> request system reboot
```

If things do go wrong and both nodes are unable to complete the upgrade in the unified ISSU process, the upgraded node needs to be rolled back. This is simple to do. First you must abort the unified ISSU process, then roll back the software on that node, and then reboot the system:

```
{primary:node0}
root@SRX5800-1> request chassis cluster in-service-upgrade abort
Exiting in-service-upgrade window

{primary:node0}
root@SRX5800-1> request system software rollback

{primary:node0}
root@SRX5800-1> request system reboot
```

To recover, the device must be rebooted. The risk is that the device may not be able to see the primary upon reboot, so if that occurs, dual mastership or split brain will result. The better option is to enable control link recovery. It only takes a single command to enable, as shown in the next example:

```
{primary:node0}[edit chassis cluster]
root# set control-link-recovery

{primary:node0}[edit chassis cluster]
root# show
control-link-recovery;
```

Once control link recovery is enabled, a user can manually reconnect the control link. After the control link has been up for about 30 seconds and the SRXs have determined that the link is healthy, the secondary node will reboot. Upon recovering from the reboot, the cluster will be up and synchronized and ready to operate. Although a reboot seems harsh for such a recovery, it is the best way to ensure that the backup node is up and completely operational.

Configuring the Fabric Links

The second half of the chassis cluster communication equation is the fabric connection. Unlike the control link, the fabric link provides several functions and a great deal of value to the cluster, the most important being *session synchronization*. Without session synchronization, there would be little value to an SRX cluster. A second feature of the fabric link is the ability to forward traffic between the two chassis. The egress chassis is responsible for processing the traffic, so traffic is forwarded to the other cluster member only if the egress interface is on that chassis.

Each node in the chassis needs its own fabric interface configured. The interfaces should be directly connected to each other. Creating the fabric link between the two chassis requires the creation of a special interface called the *fab* interface. The fab interface is a special version of the aggregate Ethernet interface that allows for the binding of one or more interfaces into a special bundle. Interfaces are added to the fab interface with node 0's fabric interface, called fab0, and node 1's fabric interface, called fab1. Set the interface thusly:

```
{primary:node0}[edit interfaces]
root# set fab0 fabric-options member-interfaces fe-0/0/4

{primary:node0}[edit interfaces]
root# set fab1 fabric-options member-interfaces fe-2/0/4

{primary:node0}[edit]
root# show interfaces
fab0 {
    fabric-options {
        member-interfaces {
            fe-0/0/4;
        }
    }
}
fab1 {
    fabric-options {
        member-interfaces {
            fe-2/0/4;
        }
    }
}

{primary:node0}[edit]
root# run show interfaces terse
Interface               Admin Link Proto    Local                 Remote
ge-0/0/0                up    down
ge-0/0/1                up    down
fe-0/0/2                up    down
fe-0/0/3                up    down
fe-0/0/4                up    up
fe-0/0/4.0              up    up   aenet    --> fab0.0
fe-0/0/5                up    up
fe-0/0/6                up    up
```

```
fe-0/0/7                up    up
ge-2/0/0                up    down
ge-2/0/1                up    down
fe-2/0/2                up    down
fe-2/0/3                up    down
fe-2/0/4                up    up
fe-2/0/4.0              up    up   aenet    --> fab1.0
fe-2/0/5                up    up
fe-2/0/6                up    up
fe-2/0/7                up    up
fab0                    up    up
fab0.0                  up    up   inet     30.17.0.200/24
fab1                    up    up
fab1.0                  up    up   inet     30.18.0.200/24
fxp0                    up    up
fxp0.0                  up    up   inet     10.0.1.210/24
fxp1                    up    up
fxp1.0                  up    up   inet     129.16.0.1/2
                                   tnp      0x1100001
fxp2                    up    up
gre                     up    up
ipip                    up    up
lo0                     up    up
lo0.16384               up    up   inet   127.0.0.1          --> 0/0
lo0.16385               up    up   inet   10.0.0.1           --> 0/0
                                          10.0.0.16          --> 0/0
                                          128.0.0.1          --> 0/0
                                          128.0.1.16         --> 0/0
                                   inet6  fe80::224:dcff:fed4:e000
lo0.32768               up    up
lsi                     up    up
mtun                    up    up
pimd                    up    up
pime                    up    up
pp0                     up    up
st0                     up    up
tap                     up    up
vlan                    up    down
{primary:node0}[edit]
root#
```

As shown in the preceding output, interfaces fe-0/0/4 and fe-2/0/4 are members of an `aenet` bundle. Interface fe-0/0/4 is a member of fab0.0, and fe-2/0/4 is a member of fab1.0. If you look closely at fab0.0 and at fab1.0, each is given an internal IP address. The address is used for internal communication and does not need to be configured by the administrator.

You should verify that the two SRXs are talking over the fabric link. The send and receive statistics should be increasing.

```
{primary:node0}[edit interfaces]
root# set fab0 fabric-options member-interfaces fe-0/0/4

{primary:node0}[edit interfaces]
root# set fab1 fabric-options member-interfaces fe-2/0/4
```

```
{primary:node0}[edit]
root# show interfaces
fab0 {
    fabric-options {
        member-interfaces {
            fe-0/0/4;
        }
    }
}
```

When the SRX needs to forward traffic across the data plane it encapsulates the entire packet and then forwards it over the link. The fabric link is automatically configured using *jumbo frames*, or frames that are larger than the standard 1,514-byte frame. Juniper supports up to a 9,192-byte frame. The difficulty here is that the SRX cannot take a maximum size frame and then encapsulate it because it would be far too large to push over the fabric link, and the SRX is not able to fragment the packet. So, it's best to set the maximum transmission unit (MTU) on the SRX interfaces to less than 8,900 to ensure that the packets are able to pass over the fabric link.

If you're using an active/passive cluster this should not be an issue.

As of Junos 10.2, *all* SRX platforms are able to use redundant fabric link ports, unlike control link redundancy, which is restricted to the data center SRXs only. Adding a second link is identical to creating the first link and it also requires a second link to be physically cabled between the two chassis. For some platforms, such as the SRX100 or SRX210, that may seem excessive because adding a second fabric link would mean half of the ports on the chassis would be taken up by links for HA: one control link, two fabric links, and a management link. Only three are required, but the fourth is optional.

There are good reasons to add a redundant fabric link on the smaller SRX devices. The first is that there is an important level of redundancy on the critical links between the SRXs, and it helps to prevent split brain, a critical requirement especially in a remote branch location. (We will discuss dealing with split brain further in "Fault Monitoring" on page 586 and "Troubleshooting the Cluster" on page 606.) For larger networks, an interesting use is to utilize the smaller branch boxes to test and learn on less expensive units or provide training.

To configure the second fabric link utilize the following commands:

```
{primary:node0}[edit interfaces]
root# set fab0 fabric-options member-interfaces fe-0/0/5

{primary:node0}[edit interfaces]
root# set fab1 fabric-options member-interfaces fe-2/0/5
```

```
{primary:node0}[edit]
root# show interfaces
fab0 {
    fabric-options {
        member-interfaces {
            fe-0/0/4;
           fe-0/0/5;
        }
    }
}
fab1 {
    fabric-options {
        member-interfaces {
            fe-2/0/4;
            fe-2/0/5;
        }
    }
}
{primary:node0}
root> show interfaces terse
Interface               Admin Link Proto    Local           Remote
ge-0/0/0                up    down
ge-0/0/1                up    down
fe-0/0/2                up    down
fe-0/0/3                up    down
fe-0/0/4                up    up
fe-0/0/4.0              up    up   aenet    --> fab0.0
fe-0/0/5                up    up
fe-0/0/5.0              up    up   aenet    --> fab0.0
fe-0/0/6                up    up
fe-0/0/7                up    up
ge-2/0/0                up    down
ge-2/0/1                up    down
fe-2/0/2                up    down
fe-2/0/3                up    down
fe-2/0/4                up    up
fe-2/0/4.0              up    up   aenet    --> fab1.0
fe-2/0/5                up    up
fe-2/0/5.0              up    up   aenet    --> fab1.0
fe-2/0/6                up    up
fe-2/0/7                up    up
fab0                    up    up
fab0.0                  up    up   inet     30.17.0.200/24
fab1                    up    up
fab1.0                  up    up   inet     30.18.0.200/24
fxp0                    up    up
fxp0.0                  up    up   inet     10.0.1.210/24
fxp1                    up    up
fxp1.0                  up    up   inet     129.16.0.1/2
                                   tnp      0x1100001
fxp2                    up    up
gre                     up    up
ipip                    up    up
lo0                     up    up
lo0.16384               up    up   inet     127.0.0.1       --> 0/0
```

```
lo0.16385               up    up   inet     10.0.0.1          --> 0/0
                                            10.0.0.16         --> 0/0
                                            128.0.0.1         --> 0/0
                                            128.0.1.16        --> 0/0
                                   inet6    fe80::224:dc0f:fcd4:e000
lo0.32768               up    up
lsi                     up    up
mtun                    up    up
pimd                    up    up
pime                    up    up
pp0                     up    up
ppd0                    up    up
ppe0                    up    up
st0                     up    up
tap                     up    up
vlan                    up    down

{primary:node0}
root>
```

In this output's configuration, each fabric link has a second member interface added to it. So, fe-0/0/5 is added to fab0, and fe-2/0/5 is added to fab1. Since a fab link is like an aggregate Ethernet interface, the configuration also looks similar. Note that packets will only pass over one fab link at a time, as the second fab link is only used as a backup.

Node-Specific Information

A chassis cluster HA configuration takes two devices and makes them look as though they are one. However, the administrator may still want some elements to be unique between the cluster members, such as the hostname and the IP address on fxp0, which are typically unique per device. No matter what unique configuration is required or desired, it's possible to achieve it by using Junos *groups*. Groups provide the ability to create a configuration and apply it anywhere inside the configuration hierarchy. It's an extremely powerful feature, and here we'll use it to create a group for each node.

Each group is named after the node it is applied to, and it's a special naming that the SRX looks for. Upon commit, only the group that matches the local node name is applied, as shown in the following configuration:

```
{primary:node0}[edit groups]
root# show
node0 {
    system {
        host-name SRX210-A;
    }
    interfaces {
        fxp0 {
            unit 0 {
                family inet {
                    address 10.0.1.210/24;
                }
            }
```

```
        }
    }
}
node1 {
    system {
        host-name SRX210-B;
    }
    interfaces {
        fxp0 {
            unit 0 {
                family inet {
                    address 10.0.1.211/24;
                }
            }
        }
    }
}

{primary:node0}[edit groups]
root#
```

In this configuration example, there are two groups, created under the **groups** hierarchy which is at the top of the configuration tree. The **node0** group has its hostname set as **SRX210-A** and **node1** has its hostname set as **SRX210-B**. To apply the groups, the administrator needs to use the **apply-groups** command at the root of the configuration. When the configuration is committed to the device, Junos will see the command and merge the correct group to match the node name:

```
{primary:node0}[edit]
root# set apply-groups "${node}"

{primary:node0}[edit]
root# show apply-groups
## Last changed: 2010-03-31 14:25:09 UTC
apply-groups "${node}";

{primary:node0}[edit]
root#

root# show interfaces | display inheritance
fab0 {
    fabric-options {
        member-interfaces {
            fe-0/0/4;
            fe-0/0/5;
        }
    }
}
fab1 {
    fabric-options {
        member-interfaces {
            fe-2/0/4;
            fe-2/0/5;
        }
    }
```

```
}
##
## 'fxp0' was inherited from group 'node0'
##
fxp0 {
    ##
    ## '0' was inherited from group 'node0'
    ##
    unit 0 {
        ##
        ## 'inet' was inherited from group 'node0'
        ##
        family inet {
            ##
            ## '10.0.1.210/24' was inherited from group 'node0'
            ##
            address 10.0.1.210/24;
        }
    }
}

{primary:node0}[edit]
root#
```

To apply the configurations to the correct node, a special command was used: the `set apply-groups "${node}"` command. The variable `"${node}"` is interpreted as the local node name. Next in the output example is the `show | display inheritance` command which shows the components of the configuration that are inherited from the group—the component that is inherited has three lines above it that all begin with `##`, with the second line specifying from which group the value is inherited.

As discussed, the fxp0 management port can be configured like a standard interface providing a management IP address for each device, but it's also possible to provide a shared IP address between each device so that when connecting to the IP it is redirected back to the primary RE. This way, the administrator does not have to figure out which is the master RE before connecting to it. The administrator can connect to what is called the *master-only* IP.

To do so, a tag is added to the end of the command when configuring the IP address, which is configured in the main configuration and not in the groups (since the tag is applied to both devices, there is no need to place it in the groups):

```
{primary:node0}[edit]
root# set interfaces fxp0.0 family inet address 10.0.1.212/24 master-only

{primary:node0}[edit]
root# show interfaces fxp0
unit 0 {
    family inet {
        address 10.0.1.212/24 {
            master-only;
        }
    }
```

```
}

{primary:node0}
root@SRX210-A> show interfaces fxp0 terse
Interface               Admin Link Proto    Local                 Remote
fxp0                    up    up
fxp0.0                  up    up   inet     10.0.1.210/24
                                            10.0.1.212/24

{primary:node0}
root@SRX210-A>
```

Configuring Heartbeat Timers

The SRX sends heartbeat messages on both the control and data links to ensure that the links are up and running. Although the device itself could look to see if the link is up or down, that is not enough to validate it. Heartbeat messages provide three layers of validation: link, daemon, and internal paths.

The message requires the two jsrpd daemons to successfully communicate, ensuring that the other daemon isn't in a state of disarray and validating the internal paths between the two daemons, including the physical link and the underlying subsystems. For the data link, the packets are even sent through the data plane, validating that the flow daemons are communicating properly.

Each platform has default heartbeat timers that are appropriate for that device. The reason for the differences is due to the ability of the kernel to guarantee the time to the jsrpd daemon. Generally, the larger the device, the larger the processor on the RE; the larger the processor, the faster it can process tasks; and the faster the device can process tasks, the quicker it can move on to the next task.

This begs the question of how fast an administrator needs a device to fail over. Of course, the world would like zero downtime and guaranteed reliability for every service, but the answer is as fast as a device can fail over in a reasonable amount of time while maintaining stability.

Table 10-3 lists the various configuration options for heartbeat timers based on the SRX platform. The branch platforms utilize a higher timer because they use slower processors to ensure stability at the branch. Although a faster failover may be desired, stability is the most important goal. If the device fails over but is lost in the process, it is of no use.

Table 10-3. Control plane heartbeats

Platform	Control plane timer min (ms)	Control plane timer max (ms)	Missed heartbeat threshold min (sec)	Missed heartbeat threshold max (sec)	Min missing peer detection time (sec)
SRX100	2,000	2,000	8	8	16
SRX210	2,000	2,000	8	8	16
SRX240	2,000	2,000	8	8	16
SRX650	2,000	2,000	8	8	16
SRX3400	1,000	2,000	3	8	3
SRX3600	1,000	2,000	3	8	3
SRX5600	1,000	2,000	3	8	3
SRX5800	1,000	2,000	3	8	3

As of Junos 10.2, it is not possible to modify the heartbeat settings on the branch SRX Series devices. They are set at a default of 16 seconds. This means that if the primary node were to go offline, it would take 16 seconds for the backup to take over. In most branch locations, where HA is needed but a graceful failover is accepted, this is fine. The data center SRXs have a default failover detection time of three seconds, and these platforms can be modified. To do so is simple. There are two options to set: threshold and interval.

```
{primary:node0}[edit chassis cluster]
root@SRX210-A# set heartbeat-interval 2000

{primary:node0}[edit chassis cluster]
root@SRX210-A# set heartbeat-threshold 8

{primary:node0}[edit chassis cluster]
root@SRX210-A# show control-link-recovery;
heartbeat-interval 2000;
heartbeat-threshold 8;

{primary:node0}[edit chassis cluster]
root@SRX210-A#
```

Redundancy Groups

Redundancy groups are the core of the failover mechanism for the SRX and they are used for both the control and data planes. On any SRX cluster there can be at least one redundancy group at a minimum, and up to 129 at a maximum. How many you deploy of course varies by platform and deployment scenario.

A redundancy group is a collection of objects and it represents which node is the owner of the objects. The objects are either interfaces or the control plane. Whichever node is the primary owner for the redundancy group is the owner of the items in the redundancy group. On ScreenOS firewalls this was called a *VSD* (virtual security device). When a cluster is created, redundancy group 0 is also created by default. No additional configuration is required to make it work.

Each node is given a priority within a redundancy group. The higher-priority device is given mastership over the redundancy group. This depends on a few options, and one of them, by default, is that a node with a higher priority will not preempt the device with the lower priority. The result is that if a lower-priority node were to have ownership of a redundancy group and then a node with the higher priority were to come online, it would not give ownership to the higher-priority device. To enable this, the preempt option would need to be enabled, and the device with the higher priority would take ownership of the redundancy group when it was healthy to do so. Most organizations do not use this option—they want to manually move the redundancy group back to the node after the failover is investigated.

Creating a redundancy group is the same for the control or data plane, with the only difference seen when configuring the interfaces. Let's create an example with redundancy group 0. Remember that this is not required, but doing so helps to create the redundancy group and set the node priorities, because if the node priorities are not set they default to 1.

Most organizations use node 0 as the higher-priority device. It's best when configuring the cluster to keep the configuration logical. When troubleshooting in the middle of the night it's great to know that node 0 should be the higher-priority node and that it is the same across the whole organization.

Let's create the redundancy group:

```
Default:
root@SRX210-A> show chassis cluster status
Cluster ID: 1
Node                 Priority        Status    Preempt  Manual failover

Redundancy group: 0 , Failover count: 1
    node0                 1               primary        no        no
    node1                 1           secondary      no        no

{primary:node0}
root@SRX210-A>

{primary:node0}[edit chassis cluster]
root@SRX210-A# set redundancy-group 0 node 0 priority 254

{primary:node0}[edit chassis cluster]
root@SRX210-A# set redundancy-group 0 node 1 priority 1

{primary:node0}[edit chassis cluster]
root@SRX210-A# show redundancy-group 0
```

```
    node 0 priority 254;
    node 1 priority 1;

root@SRX210-A> show chassis cluster status
Cluster ID: 1
Node                    Priority       Status     Preempt  Manual failover

Redundancy group: 0 , Failover count: 1
    node0                     254          primary        no       no
    node1                     1            secondary      no       no

{primary:node0}
root@SRX210-A>
```

Now let's create redundancy group 1. The most common firewall deployment for the SRX is a Layer 3-routed active/passive deployment. This means the firewalls are configured as a router and that one device is active and the other is passive. To accomplish this, a single data plane redundancy group is created. It uses the same commands as used to create redundancy group 0 except for the name **redundancy-group 1**:

```
{primary:node0}[edit chassis cluster]
root@SRX210-A# set redundancy-group 1 node 0 priority 254

{primary:node0}[edit chassis cluster]
root@SRX210-A# set redundancy-group 1 node 1 priority 1

{primary:node0}[edit chassis cluster]
root@SRX210-A# set chassis cluster reth-count 2

{primary:node0}[edit chassis cluster]
root@SRX210-A# show
control-link-recovery;
reth-count 2;
heartbeat-interval 2000;
heartbeat-threshold 8;
redundancy-group 0 {
    node 0 priority 254;
    node 1 priority 1;
}
redundancy-group 1 {
    node 0 priority 254;
    node 1 priority 1;
}

{primary:node0}[edit chassis cluster]
root@SRX210-A#
{primary:node0}
root@SRX210-A> show chassis cluster status
Cluster ID: 1
Node                    Priority      Status     Preempt  Manual failover

Redundancy group: 0 , Failover count: 1
    node0                     254          primary        no       no
    node1                     1            secondary      no       no
```

```
Redundancy group: 1 , Failover count: 1
    node0                   254         primary        no        no
    node1                   1           secondary      no        no

{primary:node0}
root@SRX210-A>
```

To keep things consistent, redundancy group 1 also gives node 0 a priority of 254 and node 1 a priority of 1. To be able to commit the configuration at least one Reth has to be enabled (it's shown here but is further discussed in the next section). After commit, the new redundancy group can be seen in the cluster status. It looks exactly like redundancy group 0 and contains the same properties.

When creating an active/active configuration and utilizing redundant Ethernet interfaces the SRX needs to have at least two redundancy groups. Each node in the cluster will have an active redundancy group on it. You configure this redundancy group in the same way as you did the other redundancy group, except that the other node will be configured with a higher priority. In this case, node 1 will have priority 254 and node 0 will have priority 1:

```
{primary:node0}[edit chassis cluster]
root@SRX210-A# set redundancy-group 2 node 0 priority 1

{primary:node0}[edit chassis cluster]
root@SRX210-A# set redundancy-group 2 node 1 priority 254

{primary:node0}[edit chassis cluster]
root@SRX210-A# show
control-link-recovery;
reth-count 2;
heartbeat-interval 2000;
heartbeat-threshold 8;
redundancy-group 0 {
    node 0 priority 254;
    node 1 priority 1;
}
redundancy-group 1 {
    node 0 priority 254;
    node 1 priority 1;
}
redundancy-group 2 {
    node 0 priority 1;
    node 1 priority 254;
}

{primary:node0}[edit chassis cluster]
root@SRX210-A#

{primary:node0}
root@SRX210-A> show chassis cluster status
Cluster ID: 1
Node                 Priority      Status     Preempt  Manual failover

Redundancy group: 0 , Failover count: 1
```

```
    node0                   254         primary        no         no
    node1                   1           secondary      no         no

Redundancy group: 1 , Failover count: 1
    node0                   254         primary        no         no
    node1                   1           secondary      no         no

Redundancy group: 2 , Failover count: 0
    node0                   1           secondary      no         no
    node1                   254         primary        no         no

{primary:node0}
root@SRX210-A>
```

Now three redundancy groups are listed. The newest redundancy group, redundancy group 2, has node 1 as its primary and node 0 as its secondary. In this case, all of the traffic for redundancy group 2 will be flowing through node 1 and redundancy group 1's traffic will be flowing through node 0. In the event of a failover, each node backs up the other. So, it's possible for either node to take over all of the redundancy groups.

It's important to plan for the possibility that a single device might have to handle all of the traffic for all of the redundancy groups. If you don't plan for this, the single device can be overwhelmed.

Each redundancy group needs a minimum of one Reth in it to operate. Because of this, the total number of redundancy groups is tied to the total number of Reths per platform, plus one for redundancy group 0. Table 10-4 lists the number of supported redundancy groups per SRX platform.

Table 10-4. Redundancy groups per platform

Platform	Redundancy groups
SRX100	9
SRX210	9
SRX240	25
SRX650	69
SRX3400	129
SRX3600	129
SRX5600	129
SRX5800	129

As previously discussed, it's possible to have the node with the higher priority preemptively take over the redundancy group. By default, the administrator would need to manually fail over the redundancy group to the other node. Configuring a preempt only requires a single command under the redundancy group as shown here, but redundancy groups also have a default hold-down timer, or the time that the redundancy group must wait until it can preempt. On redundancy group 1 and greater it is set to one second. On redundancy group 0 it is set to 300 seconds or 5 minutes to prevent instability on the control plane.

```
{primary:node0}[edit chassis cluster]
root@SRX210-A# set redundancy-group 1 preempt

{primary:node0}[edit chassis cluster]
root@SRX210-A# show
control-link-recovery;
reth-count 2;
heartbeat-interval 2000;
heartbeat-threshold 8;
redundancy-group 0 {
    node 0 priority 254;
    node 1 priority 1;
}
redundancy-group 1 {
    node 0 priority 254;
    node 1 priority 1;
    preempt;
}

{primary:node0}[edit chassis cluster]
root@SRX210-A#

{primary:node0}
root@SRX210-A> show chassis cluster status
Cluster ID: 1
Node                  Priority          Status     Preempt  Manual failover

Redundancy group: 0 , Failover count: 1
    node0                   254         primary      no        no
    node1                   1           secondary    no        no

Redundancy group: 1 , Failover count: 1
    node0                   254         primary      yes       no
    node1                   1           secondary    yes       no

{primary:node0}
root@SRX210-A>
```

A hold-down timer can be set to prevent unnecessary failovers in a chassis cluster, used in conjunction with preempt as the number of seconds to wait until the redundancy group can fail over. As previously mentioned, default hold-down timers are configured: for redundancy group 1 it's one second, and for redundancy group 0 it's 300 seconds. You can customize the timer and set it between zero and 1,800 seconds, but best practice suggests to never set redundancy group 0 to less than 300 seconds to prevent instability on the control plane.

It's best to set a safe number for the redundancy groups to ensure that the network is ready for the failover, and in the event of a hard failure on the other node, the redundancy group will fail over as fast as possible:

```
{primary:node0}[edit chassis cluster]
root@SRX210-A# set redundancy-group 1 hold-down-interval 5

{primary:node0}[edit chassis cluster]
root@SRX210-A# show
control-link-recovery;
reth-count 2;
heartbeat-interval 2000;
heartbeat-threshold 8;
redundancy-group 0 {
    node 0 priority 254;
    node 1 priority 1;
}
redundancy-group 1 {
    node 0 priority 254;
    node 1 priority 1;
    preempt;
    hold-down-interval 5;
}

{primary:node0}[edit chassis cluster]
root@SRX210-A#
```

Configuring Interfaces

A firewall without interfaces is like a car without tires—it's just not going to get you very far. In the case of chassis clusters, there are two different options: the redundant Ethernet interface (Reth) and the local interface. A Reth is a special type of interface that integrates the features of an aggregate Ethernet interface together with redundancy groups.

Before redundant Ethernet interfaces are created, the total number of interfaces in the chassis must be specified. This is required because the Reth is effectively an aggregate Ethernet interface and an interface needs to be provisioned before it can work.

It is suggested that you only provision the total number of interfaces that are required to conserve resources.

Let's set the number of interfaces in the chassis and then move on to create redundancy groups 1+ and configure the interfaces:

```
{primary:node0}[edit chassis cluster]
root@SRX210-A# set reth-count 2

{primary:node0}[edit chassis cluster]
```

```
root@SRX210-A# show
control-link-recovery;
reth-count 2;
redundancy-group 0 {
    node 0 priority 254;
    node 1 priority 1;
}
redundancy-group 1 {
    node 0 priority 254;
    node 1 priority 1;
}

{primary:node0}[edit chassis cluster]
root@SRX210-A#

{primary:node0}
root@SRX210-A> show interfaces terse | match reth
reth0                   up    up
reth1                   up    up
```

Each SRX platform has a maximum number of Reths that it can support, as listed in Table 10-5.

Table 10-5. Reth count per platform

Platform	Redundant Ethernet interfaces
SRX100	8
SRX210	8
SRX240	24
SRX650	68
SRX3400	128
SRX3600	128
SRX5600	128
SRX5800	128

Now let's create a Reth. When using a Reth, each member of the cluster has one or more local interfaces that participate in the Reth:

```
{primary:node0}[edit interfaces]
root@SRX210-A# set fe-0/0/2 fastether-options redundant-parent reth0

{primary:node0}[edit interfaces]
root@SRX210-A# set fe-2/0/2 fastether-options redundant-parent reth0

{primary:node0}[edit interfaces]
root@SRX210-A# set reth0.0 family inet address 172.16.0.1/24

{primary:node0}[edit]
root@SRX210-A# set interfaces reth0 redundant-ether-options redundancy-group 1
```

```
{primary:node0}[edit interfaces]
root@SRX210-A# show
fe-0/0/2 {
    fastether-options {
        redundant-parent reth0;
    }
}
fe-2/0/2 {
    fastether-options {
        redundant-parent reth0;
    }
}
fab0 {
    fabric-options {
        member-interfaces {
            fe-0/0/4;
            fe-0/0/5;
        }
    }
}
fab1 {
    fabric-options {
        member-interfaces {
            fe-2/0/4;
            fe-2/0/5;
        }
    }
}
fxp0 {
    unit 0 {
        family inet {
            address 10.0.1.212/24 {
                master-only;
            }
        }
    }
}
reth0 {
    redundant-ether-options {
        redundancy-group 1;
    }
    unit 0 {
        family inet {
            address 172.16.0.1/24;
        }
    }
}

{primary:node0}[edit]
root@SRX210-A#
```

In this configuration example, interfaces fe-0/0/2 and fe-2/0/2 have reth0 specified as their parent. Then the reth0 interface is specified as a member of redundancy group 1, and finally the interface is given an IP address. From here the interface can be configured with a zone so that it can be used in security policies for passing network traffic.

Upon commit, there are two places to validate that the interface is functioning properly, as shown in the following output. First, the user can look at the interface listing to show the child links and also the Reth itself. Second, under the chassis cluster status, Junos shows if the interface is up or not. The reason to use the second method of validation is that although the child links may be physically up, the redundancy groups may have a problem, and the interface may be down as far as jsrpd is concerned (we will discuss this further in "Troubleshooting the Cluster" on page 606).

```
{primary:node0}
root@SRX210-A> show interfaces terse | match reth0
fe-0/0/2.0              up    up    aenet    --> reth0.0
fe-2/0/2.0              up    up    aenet    --> reth0.0
reth0                   up    up
reth0.0                 up    up    inet     172.16.0.1/24

{primary:node0}
root@SRX210-A> show chassis cluster interfaces
Control link 0 name: fxp1

Redundant-ethernet Information:
    Name         Status      Redundancy-group
    reth0        Up          1
    reth1        Down        Not configured

{primary:node0}
root@SRX210-A>
```

With the data center SRX firewalls, it's possible to utilize multiple child links per node in the cluster, meaning that each node may have up to eight links configured together for its Reth interface. The requirement for this to work is that both nodes must have the same number of links on each chassis. It works exactly like a traditional Reth where only one chassis will have its links active, and the secondary node's links are still waiting until a failover occurs. Configuring this is similar to what was done before; the noted difference is that additional interfaces are made child members of the Reth:

```
{primary:node0}[edit interfaces
root@SRX5800-1# set xe-6/2/0 gigether-options redundant-parent reth0

{primary:node0}[edit interfaces]
root@SRX5800-1# set xe-6/3/0 gigether-options redundant-parent reth1

{primary:node0}[edit interfaces]
root@SRX5800-1# set xe-18/2/0 gigether-options redundant-parent reth0

{primary:node0}[edit interfaces]
root@SRX5800-1# set xe-18/3/0 gigether-options redundant-parent reth1

{primary:node0}[edit interfaces]
root@SRX5800-1# show interfaces
xe-6/0/0 {
    gigether-options {
        redundant-parent reth0;
    }
```

```
}
xe-6/1/0 {
    gigether-options {
        redundant-parent reth1;
    }
}
xe-6/2/0 {
    gigether-options {
        redundant-parent reth0;
    }
}
xe-6/3/0 {
    gigether-options {
        redundant-parent reth1;
    }
}
xe-18/0/0 {
    gigether-options {
        redundant-parent reth0;
    }
}
xe-18/1/0 {
    gigether-options {
        redundant-parent reth1;
    }
}
xe-18/2/0 {
    gigether-options {
        redundant-parent reth0;
    }
}
xe-18/3/0 {
    gigether-options {
        redundant-parent reth1;
    }
}
reth0 {
    redundant-ether-options {
        redundancy-group 1;
    }
    unit 0 {
        family inet {
            address 1.0.0.1/16;
        }
    }
}
reth1 {
    redundant-ether-options {
        redundancy-group 1;
    }
    unit 0 {
        family inet {
            address 2.0.0.1/16;
        }
    }
```

```
}

{primary:node0}[edit]
root@SRX5800-1#

{primary:node0}
root@SRX5800-1> show interfaces terse | match reth
xe-6/0/0.0              up    up    aenet    --> reth0.0
xe-6/1/0.0              up    up    aenet    --> reth1.0
xe-6/2/0.0              up    down  aenet    --> reth0.0
xe-6/3/0.0              up    down  aenet    --> reth1.0
xe-18/0/0.0             up    up    aenet    --> reth0.0
xe-18/1/0.0             up    up    aenet    --> reth1.0
xe-18/2/0.0             up    up    aenet    --> reth0.0
xe-18/3/0.0             up    up    aenet    --> reth1.0
reth0                   up    up
reth0.0                 up    up    inet     1.0.0.1/16
reth1                   up    up
reth1.0                 up    up    inet     2.0.0.1/16

{primary:node0}
root@SRX5800-1> show chassis cluster interfaces
Control link 0 name: em0
Control link 1 name: em1

Redundant-ethernet Information:
    Name         Status      Redundancy-group
    reth0        Up          1
    reth1        Up          1

{primary:node0}
root@SRX5800-1>
```

As seen here, the configuration is identical except that additional interfaces are added as members of the Reth. As far as the switch it is connected to, the interface is considered an *aggregate Ethernet*, *link agg group*, or *EtherChannel* depending on the vendor. It's also possible to use LACP as well.

When a failover occurs to the secondary node, the node must announce to the world that it is now owner of the MAC address associated with the Reth interface (since the Reth's MAC is shared between nodes). It does this using gratuitous ARPs or *GARPs*. A GARP is an ARP that is broadcast but not specifically requested. Once a GARP is sent, the local switch will be able to update its MAC table to map which port the MAC address is associated with. By default, the SRX sends four gratuitous ARPs per Reth on a failover. These are sent from the control plane and out through the data plane. To modify the number of GARPs sent, this must be configured on a per-redundancy-group basis. Use the `set gratuitous-arp-count` command and a parameter between 1 and 16:

```
{primary:node0}[edit chassis cluster redundancy-group 1]
root@SRX210-A# set gratuitous-arp-count 5

{primary:node0}[edit chassis cluster redundancy-group 1]
root@SRX210-A# show
```

```
node 0 priority 254;
node 1 priority 1;
gratuitous-arp-count 5;

{primary:node0}[edit]
root@SRX210-A#
```

One last item to mention is the use of local interfaces. A local interface is not bound or configured to a redundancy group; it's exactly what the name means: a local interface. It is configured like any traditional type of interface on a Junos device and is used in an active/active scenario. It does not have a backup interface on the second device. To refresh yourself on how to configure a local interface, please refer to Chapter 3.

Integrating Dynamic Routing

The SRX devices provide a very rich set of dynamic routing features. To get the most out of the cluster there are a few important points to note. These points should be considered the best-practice guidelines for using dynamic routing with an SRX cluster.

As of Junos 10.2, the SRX does not support nonstop routing or NSR, meaning that the state of dynamic routing protocols is not synchronized between the two REs.

If the data plane fails over between the two SRX devices, there is no direct impact, but if the control plane fails over, the dynamic routing state is lost, along with all of the routes. This can be a huge problem. If there isn't a matching route, the packet and, ultimately, the session is lost.

There are a few ways to mitigate this. The first is to prevent the control plane from failing over, and you can do that by allowing the control plane to only fail over in the event of a critical failure. The second option is to enable the dynamic routing integration feature called *graceful restart*. When graceful restart is enabled and the control plane fails over, the routes on the secondary node are not immediately removed, buying the SRX some time to replace the routes with the routes learned from a newly formed adjacency.

The standard function of graceful restart is to allow a router to restart without disrupting the network. Before the device restarts, it will send a message to its peers stating not to send additional route updates during this time. When a failure occurs on the primary node the secondary node sends out the graceful restart opaque link-state advertisement (LSA). Ideally, the surrounding routers should support graceful restart as well.

Enabling graceful restart is fairly easy, as it only requires one command to turn it on (it can also be tweaked on a per-protocol basis):

```
{primary:node0}[edit]
root@SRX210-A# set routing-options graceful-restart

{primary:node0}[edit]
root@SRX210-A# show routing-options
graceful-restart;

{primary:node0}[edit]
root@SRX210-A#
```

At a minimum, graceful restart should be enabled when using dynamic routing on the SRX to preserve routes on the data plane. Ideally, your surrounding routers should support graceful restart as well. Note that although Junos does support graceful restart, other vendors may not. *Junos High Availability (http://oreilly.com/catalog/9780596523053/)* by James Sonderegger, Orin Blomberg, Kieran Milne, and Senad Palislamovic (O'Reilly) provides an in-depth exposition on using graceful restart in the network.

Upgrading the Cluster

There are two ways to upgrade an SRX cluster: graceful and immediate. As of Junos 10.2, the graceful method is only available on the larger, data center SRX devices. The feature is planned for the branch devices in a future release and may be available as you are reading this book.

To upgrade the clusters ungracefully, each member is updated individually to the same releases, then both devices are rebooted at the same time. This will cause a network outage during that time, but it should be minimal. The reason both devices must be rebooted at the same time is to ensure that there is no conflict between the old and new versions.

Here's a config example that shows the software update and the command to reboot:

```
{primary:node0}
root@SRX210-A> request system software add junos-srxsme-10.2R2.6-domestic.tgz
reboot

{primary:node0}
root@SRX210-A> request system reboot

{secondary:node1}
root@SRX210-B> request system software add junos-srxsme-10.2R2.6-domestic.tgz

{secondary:node1}
root@SRX210-B> request system reboot
```

On the larger, data center SRXs, unified ISSU can be utilized. This method is a graceful upgrade method and allows for the SRXs to upgrade without losing sessions or traffic.

As of Junos 10.2, VPN is not supported during the upgrade process. However, everything else will upgrade.

Note that the process may take some time to complete. This is because the kernel on the two devices must synchronize and the software must be updated. It is suggested that you have all of the redundancy groups on a single member in the cluster. The process for graceful upgrade is similar to an immediate upgrade, except the upgrade only needs to be run on one SRX:

```
{primary:node0}
root@SRX5800-1> request system software in-service-upgrade
junos-srx5000-10.2R2.6-domestic.tgz reboot
```

This command will upgrade each node and reboot them as needed. No further commands are required.

Another option that the unified ISSU process can use is the `no-old-master-upgrade` process, which leaves the master in a nonupgraded state. This ensures that there is a working box if the software upgrade were to fail. Upon successful competition of the upgrade, the old master needs to be manually upgraded, as shown here:

```
{primary:node0}
root@SRX5800-1> request system software in-service-upgrade
junos-srx5000-10.2R3.10-domestic.tgz no-old-master-upgrade

##next on the old master

{primary:node0}
root@SRX5800-1> request system software add junos-srx5000-10.2R3.10-domestic.tgz

{primary:node0}
root@SRX5800-1> request chassis cluster in-service-upgrade abort

{primary:node0}
root@SRX5800-1> request system reboot
```

If things go wrong, and both nodes are unable to complete the upgrade in the unified ISSU process, the upgraded node needs to be rolled back. This is simple to do. First the unified ISSU process needs to be aborted. Then the software on that node must be rolled back, and lastly the system must be rebooted:

```
{primary:node0}
root@SRX5800-1> request chassis cluster in-service-upgrade abort
Exiting in-service-upgrade window

{primary:node0}
root@SRX5800-1> request system software rollback

{primary:node0}
root@SRX5800-1> request system rebootw
```

Fault Monitoring

"In the event of a failure, your seat cushion may be used as a flotation device." If your plane were to crash and you were given notice, you would take the appropriate action to prevent disaster. When working with a chassis cluster, an administrator wants to see the smoke before the fire. That is what happens when an administrator configures monitoring options in the chassis cluster. The admin is looking to see if the plane is going down and to take evasive action before it's too late. By default, the SRX monitors for various internal failures such as hardware and software issues. But what if other events occur, such as interfaces failing, or upstream gateways going away? If the administrator wants to take action based on these events, he must configure the SRX to take action.

The SRX monitoring options are configured on a per-redundancy-group basis, meaning that if specific items were to fail, that redundancy group can fail over to the other chassis. In complex topologies, this gives the administrator extremely flexible options on what to fail over and when. Two integrated features can be used to monitor the redundancy groups: interface monitoring and IP monitoring.

And there are two situations the SRXs can be in when a failure occurs. The first is that the SRXs are communicating and the two nodes in the cluster are both functional. If this is the case, and a failure occurs, the failover between the two nodes will be extremely fast because the two nodes can quickly transfer responsibility for passing traffic between them. The second scenario is when the two nodes lose communication. This could be caused by a loss of power or other factors. In this case, all heartbeats between the chassis must be missed before the secondary node can take over for the primary, taking anywhere from 3 to 16 seconds, depending on the platform.

In this section, each failure scenario is outlined so that the administrator can gain a complete understanding of what to expect if or when a failure occurs.

Interface Monitoring

Interface monitoring monitors the physical status of an interface. It checks to see if the interface is in an up or down state. When one or more monitored interfaces fail, the redundancy group fails over to the other node in the cluster.

The determining factor is when a specific weight is met, and in this case it is 255. The weight of 255 is the redundancy group threshold that is shared between interface monitoring and IP monitoring. Once enough interfaces have failed to meet this weight, the failover for the redundancy group occurs. In most situations, interface monitoring is configured in such a way that if one interface were to fail, the entire redundancy group would fail over. However, it could be configured that two interfaces need to fail. In this first configuration, only one interface needs to fail to initiate a failover:

```
{primary:node0}[edit chassis cluster redundancy-group 1]
root@SRX210-A# set interface-monitor fe-0/0/2 weight 255
```

```
{primary:node0}[edit chassis cluster redundancy-group 1]
root@SRX210-A# set interface-monitor fe-2/0/2 weight 255

{primary:node0}[edit chassis cluster redundancy-group 1]
root@SRX210-A# show
node 0 priority 254;
node 1 priority 1;
interface-monitor {
    fe-0/0/2 weight 255;
    fe-2/0/2 weight 255;
}

{primary:node0}[edit chassis cluster redundancy-group 1]
root@SRX210-A#
root@SRX210-A> show chassis cluster interfaces
Control link 0 name: fxp1

Redundant-ethernet Information:
    Name         Status      Redundancy-group
    reth0        Up          1
    reth1        Down        Not configured

Interface Monitoring:
    Interface         Weight    Status    Redundancy-group
    fe-2/0/2          255       Up        1
    fe-0/0/2          255       Up        1

{primary:node0}
root@SRX210-A>
```

In this example, interfaces fe-0/0/2 and fe-2/0/2 are configured with a weight of 255. In the event that either interface fails, the redundancy group will fail over.

In the next example, the interface has failed. Node 0 immediately becomes secondary and its priority becomes zero for redundancy group 1. This means it will only be used as a last resort for the primary of redundancy group 1. Upon restoring the cables, everything becomes normal again:

```
{primary:node0}
root@SRX210-A> show chassis cluster interfaces
Control link 0 name: fxp1

Redundant-ethernet Information:
    Name         Status      Redundancy-group
    reth0        Up          1
    reth1        Down        Not configured

Interface Monitoring:
    Interface         Weight    Status    Redundancy-group
    fe-2/0/2          255       Up        1
    fe-0/0/2          255       Down      1

{primary:node0}
root@SRX210-A> show chassis cluster status
```

```
Cluster ID: 1
Node                  Priority          Status     Preempt  Manual failover

Redundancy group: 0 , Failover count: 1
    node0                  254          primary        no       no
    node1                  1            secondary      no       no

Redundancy group: 1 , Failover count: 2
    node0                  0            secondary      no       no
    node1                  1            primary        no       no

{primary:node0}
root@SRX210-A>
```

In this example:

```
{primary:node0}[edit]
root@SRX210-A# set interfaces fe-0/0/3 fastether-options redundant-parent reth1

{primary:node0}[edit]
root@SRX210-A# set interfaces fe-2/0/3 fastether-options redundant-parent reth1

{primary:node0}[edit]
root@SRX210-A# set interfaces reth0 redundant-ether-options redundancy-group 1

{primary:node0}[edit]
root@SRX210-A# set interfaces reth1 redundant-ether-options redundancy-group 1

{primary:node0}[edit]
root@SRX210-A# set interfaces reth1.0 family inet address 172.17.0.1/24

{primary:node0}[edit]
root@SRX210-A# show interfaces ## Truncated to only show these interfaces
fe-0/0/3 {
    fastether-options {
        redundant-parent reth1;
    }
}
fe-2/0/3 {
    fastether-options {
        redundant-parent reth1;
    }
}
reth1 {
    redundant-ether-options {
        redundancy-group 1;
    }
    unit 0 {
        family inet {
            address 172.17.0.1/24;
        }
    }
}

{primary:node0}[edit chassis cluster redundancy-group 1]
root@SRX210-A# set interface-monitor fe-0/0/2 weight 128
```

```
{primary:node0}[edit chassis cluster redundancy-group 1]
root@SRX210-A# set interface-monitor fe-2/0/2 weight 128

{primary:node0}[edit chassis cluster redundancy-group 1]
root@SRX210-A# show
node 0 priority 254;
node 1 priority 1;
interface-monitor {
    fe-0/0/2 weight 128;
    fe-2/0/2 weight 128;
}

{primary:node0}[edit chassis cluster redundancy-group 1]
root@SRX210-A#

{primary:node0}
root@SRX210-A> show chassis cluster interfaces
Control link 0 name: fxp1

Redundant-ethernet Information:
    Name         Status      Redundancy-group
    reth0        Up          1
    reth1        Up          1

Interface Monitoring:
    Interface          Weight    Status    Redundancy-group
    fe-2/0/2           128       Up        1
    fe-0/0/2           128       Up        1

{primary:node0}
root@SRX210-A>
```

both interfaces are needed to trigger a failover. The next sequence shows where node 0 will lose one interface from each of its Reths. This causes a failover to occur on node 1.

```
{primary:node0}[edit]
root@SRX210-A# show chassis cluster redundancy-group 1
node 0 priority 254;
node 1 priority 1;
interface-monitor {
    fe-0/0/2 weight 128;
    fe-0/0/3 weight 128;
}

{primary:node0}[edit]
root@SRX210-A#

{primary:node0}
root@SRX210-A> show chassis cluster status
Cluster ID: 1
Node                  Priority      Status    Preempt  Manual failover

Redundancy group: 0 , Failover count: 1
```

```
    node0                  254        primary        no       no
    node1                  1          secondary      no       no

Redundancy group: 1 , Failover count: 3
    node0                  254        primary        no       no
    node1                  1          secondary      no       no

{primary:node0}
root@SRX210-A> show chassis cluster interfaces
Control link 0 name: fxp1

Redundant-ethernet Information:
    Name         Status      Redundancy-group
    reth0        Up          1
    reth1        Up          1

Interface Monitoring:
    Interface          Weight    Status     Redundancy-group
    fe-0/0/3           128       Up         1
    fe-0/0/2           128       Up         1

{primary:node0}
root@SRX210-A>

{primary:node0}
root@SRX210-A> show chassis cluster interfaces
Control link 0 name: fxp1

Redundant-ethernet Information:
    Name         Status      Redundancy-group
    reth0        Up          1
    reth1        Up          1

Interface Monitoring:
    Interface          Weight    Status     Redundancy-group
    fe-0/0/3           128       Down       1
    fe-0/0/2           128       Down       1

{primary:node0}
root@SRX210-A> show chassis cluster status
Cluster ID: 1
Node                  Priority       Status    Preempt  Manual failover

Redundancy group: 0 , Failover count: 1
    node0                  254        primary        no       no
    node1                  1          secondary      no       no

Redundancy group: 1 , Failover count: 4
    node0                  0          secondary      no       no
    node1                  1          primary        no       no

{primary:node0}
root@SRX210-A>
```

And here it required both interfaces to go down to fail over to the other node.

Only physical interfaces can be monitored. The Reths themselves can't be monitored.

Interface monitoring should be done on nonzero redundancy groups and not on the control plane, because best practice urges you to only allow the control plane to fail over in the event of a hard failure.

IP Monitoring

As of Junos 10.2, IP monitoring is only available on the data center SRX platforms. It allows for the monitoring of upstream gateways. When using IP monitoring the ping probe validates the entire end-to-end path from the SRX to the remote node and back. The feature is typically used to monitor its next hop gateway, ensuring the gateway is ready to accept packets from the SRX. This is key, as the SRX's link to its local switch may be working but the upstream devices may not.

IP monitoring is configured per redundancy group and has some similarities to interface monitoring. It also uses weights, and when the weights add up to exceed the redundancy group weight, a failover is triggered. But with IP monitoring, the SRX is monitoring remote gateways, not interfaces.

In each redundancy group there are four global options that affect all of the hosts that are to be monitored:

- The first option is the global weight. This is the weight that is subtracted from the redundancy group weight for all of the hosts being monitored.
- The second option is the global threshold. This is the number that needs to be met or exceeded by all of the cumulative weights of the monitored IPs to trigger a failover.
- The last two options are the retry attempts for the ping. The first is the retry count which is the number of times to retry between failures. The minimum setting is five retries.
- And the last is the retry interval, and this value specifies the number of seconds between replies. The default retry time is one second.

Here the configuration options can be seen using the help prompt:

```
root@SRX5800-1# set redundancy-group 1 ip-monitoring ?
Possible completions:
+ apply-groups         Groups from which to inherit configuration data
+ apply-groups-except  Don't inherit configuration data from these groups
> family               Define protocol family
  global-threshold     Define global threshold for IP monitoring (0..255)
  global-weight        Define global weight for IP monitoring (0..255)
  retry-count          Number of retries needed to declare reachablity failure
(5..15)
  retry-interval       Define the time interval in seconds between retries.
(1..30)
```

```
{primary:node0}[edit chassis cluster]
root@SRX5800-1#
```

These IP monitoring options can be overwhelming, but they are designed to give the user more flexibility. The redundancy group can be configured to fail over if one or more of the monitored IPs fail, or if a combination of the monitored IPs and interfaces fail.

In the next example, two monitored IPs are going to be configured. Both of them need to fail to trigger a redundancy group failure. The SRX will use routing to resolve which interface should be used to ping the remote host (you could also go across virtual routers as of Junos 10.1 and later):

```
{primary:node0}[edit chassis cluster redundancy-group 1]
root@SRX5800-1# set ip-monitoring family inet 1.2.3.4 weight 128

{primary:node0}[edit chassis cluster redundancy-group 1]
root@SRX5800-1# set ip-monitoring family inet 1.3.4.5 weight 128

{primary:node0}[edit chassis cluster redundancy-group 1]
root@SRX5800-1# show
node 0 priority 200;
node 1 priority 100;
ip-monitoring {
    global-weight 255;
    global-threshold 255;
    family {
        inet {
            1.2.3.4 weight 128;
            1.3.4.5 weight 128;
        }
    }
}

{primary:node0}[edit chassis cluster redundancy-group 1]
root@SRX5800-1#


{primary:node0}[edit chassis cluster redundancy-group 1]
root@SRX5800-1# run show chassis cluster ip-monitoring status
node0:
--------------------------------------------------------------------------

Redundancy group: 1

IP address   Status       Failure count  Reason
1.3.4.5      unreachable    1            redundancy-group state unknown
1.2.3.4      unreachable    1            redundancy-group state unknown

node1:
----------------------------------------------------------------------

Redundancy group: 1
```

```
IP address     Status        Failure count  Reason
1.3.4.5        unreachable     1            redundancy-group state unknown
1.2.3.4        unreachable     1            redundancy-group state unknown

{primary:node0}[edit chassis cluster redundancy-group 1]
root@SRX5800-1# run show chassis cluster status
Cluster ID: 1
Node                  Priority          Status    Preempt  Manual failover

Redundancy group: 0 , Failover count: 1
    node0                  200          primary        no       no
    node1                  100          secondary      no       no

Redundancy group: 1 , Failover count: 1
    node0                  0            primary        no       no
    node1                  0            secondary      no       no

{primary:node0}[edit chassis cluster redundancy-group 1]
root@SRX5800-1#
```

After you have studied that, the next example uses a combination of both IP monitoring *and* interface monitoring, and shows how the combined weight of the two will trigger a failover:

```
{primary:node0}[edit chassis cluster redundancy-group 1]
root@SRX5800-1# show
node 0 priority 200;
node 1 priority 100;
interface-monitor {
    xe-6/1/0 weight 255;
}
ip-monitoring {
    global-weight 255;
    global-threshold 255;
    family {
        inet {
            1.2.3.4 weight 128;
        }
    }
}

{primary:node0}[edit]
root@SRX5800-1# run show chassis cluster status
Cluster ID: 1
Node                  Priority          Status    Preempt  Manual failover

Redundancy group: 0 , Failover count: 1
    node0                  200          primary        no       no
    node1                  100          secondary      no       no

Redundancy group: 1 , Failover count: 2
    node0                  200          secondary      no       no
    node1                  100          primary        no       no

{primary:node0}[edit]
```

```
root@SRX5800-1# run show chassis cluster ip-monitoring status
node0:
--------------------------------------------------------------------------

Redundancy group: 1

IP address   Status       Failure count  Reason
1.2.3.4      unreachable  1              redundancy-group state unknown

node1:
--------------------------------------------------------------------------

Redundancy group: 1

IP address   Status       Failure count  Reason
1.2.3.4      unreachable  1              redundancy-group state unknown

{primary:node0}[edit]
root@SRX5800-1# run show chassis cluster interfaces ?
Possible completions:
  <[Enter]>            Execute this command
  |                    Pipe through a command
{primary:node0}[edit]
root@SRX5800-1# run show chassis cluster interfaces
Control link 0 name: em0
Control link 1 name: em1

Redundant-ethernet Information:
    Name         Status      Redundancy-group
    reth0        Up          1
    reth1        Up          1
    reth2        Down        1
    reth3        Up          1

Interface Monitoring:
    Interface         Weight    Status     Redundancy-group
    xe-6/1/0          128       Up         1

{primary:node0}[edit]
root@SRX5800-1#
```

Here the ping for IP monitoring is sourced from the Reth's active device, with the IP address configured on the specified interface. Optionally, it's possible to configure a secondary IP to trigger the ping to come from the configured secondary IP address and from the backup interface, allowing the administrator to check the backup path coming from the secondary node. This would ensure that before a failover occurs, the backup path is working. Let's configure this option. It only takes one additional step *per* monitored IP:

```
{primary:node0}[edit chassis cluster redundancy-group 1]
root@SRX5800-1# set ip-monitoring family inet 1.2.3.4 weight 255
interface reth0.0 secondary-ip-address 1.0.0.10

{primary:node0}[edit chassis cluster redundancy-group 1]
```

```
root@SRX5800-1# show
node 0 priority 200;
node 1 priority 100;
ip-monitoring {
    global-weight 255;
    global-threshold 255;
    family {
        inet {
            1.2.3.4 {
                weight 255;
                interface reth0.0 secondary-ip-address 1.0.0.10;
            }
        }
    }
}

{primary:node0}[edit]
root@SRX5800-1# run show chassis cluster ip-monitoring status
node0:
--------------------------------------------------------------------------

Redundancy group: 1

IP address                Status        Failure count  Reason
1.2.3.4                   unreachable     0            no route to host

node1:
--------------------------------------------------------------------------

Redundancy group: 1

IP address                Status        Failure count  Reason
1.2.3.4                   unreachable     0            no route to host

{primary:node0}[edit]
root@SRX5800-1#
```

As mentioned, the monitor IP feature exists only on the data center SRX (as of Junos 10.2). This is because it works only in the data plane, and has not been included on the branch devices yet. The SRX5000 Series products can create up to 64 monitored IPs and the SRX3000 Series can create 32. The ping is generated from the second SPU on the system, which is the first non-CP SPU, and because of that, it is not limited to scheduling or processing restrictions found on the RE.

Manual Failover

Although the SRX has control over which node is in charge of each redundancy group, sometimes the administrator needs to fail over a redundancy group—say, for maintenance or troubleshooting purposes. No matter the reason, it's possible to manually fail over any of the redundancy groups. By executing a manual failover, the SRX will place the new master node with a priority of 255 (you can't configure this priority as it is only used for a manual failover).

The only event that can take over a manual failover is a hard failure, such as the device failing. When using a manual failover it's best to unset the manual failover flag so that the SRX can manage it from there.

In this example, redundancy group 1 will be failed over between the two chassis and then reset to the default state:

```
{primary:node0}
root@SRX210-A> show chassis cluster status
Cluster ID: 1
Node                Priority           Status     Preempt  Manual failover

Redundancy group: 0 , Failover count: 1
    node0               254          primary        no       no
    node1               1            secondary      no       no

Redundancy group: 1 , Failover count: 5
    node0               254          primary        no       no
    node1               1            secondary      no       no

{primary:node0}
root@SRX210-A> request chassis cluster failover redundancy-group 1 node 1
node1:
-----------------------------------------------------------------------

Initiated manual failover for redundancy group 1

{primary:node0}
root@SRX210-A> show chassis cluster status
Cluster ID: 1
Node               Priority           Status     Preempt  Manual failover

Redundancy group: 0 , Failover count: 1
    node0               254          primary        no       no
    node1               1            secondary      no       no

Redundancy group: 1 , Failover count: 6
    node0               254          secondary      no       yes
    node1               255          primary        no       yes

{primary:node0}
root@SRX210-A> request chassis cluster failover reset redundancy-group 1
node0:
----------------------------------------------------------------------
No reset required for redundancy group 1.

node1:
----------------------------------------------------------------------
Successfully reset manual failover for redundancy group 1

{primary:node0}
root@SRX210-A> request chassis cluster failover redundancy-group 1 node 0
node0:
```

```
----------------------------------------------------------------------
Initiated manual failover for redundancy group 1

root@SRX210-A> show chassis cluster status
Cluster ID: 1
Node                Priority          Status    Preempt  Manual failover

Redundancy group: 0 , Failover count: 1
    node0               254           primary        no       no
    node1               1             secondary      no       no

Redundancy group: 1 , Failover count: 7
    node0               255           primary        no       yes
    node1               1             secondary      no       yes

{primary:node0}
root@SRX210-A> request chassis cluster failover reset redundancy-group 1
node0:
----------------------------------------------------------------------
Successfully reset manual failover for redundancy group 1

node1:
----------------------------------------------------------------------
No reset required for redundancy group 1.

{primary:node0}
root@SRX210-A>
```

Here redundancy group 1 is failed over to node 1. Then, as you can see, the priority is set to 255 and the manual failover flag is set. Once this flag is set, another manual failover cannot occur until it is cleared. Next, the failover is reset for redundancy group 1, using the `request chassis cluster failover reset redundancy group 1` command, allowing the redundancy group to be failed over again. Next, the redundancy group is failed over back to the original node and the manual failover is reset. If a hold-down timer was configured, the manual failover cannot go over the hold-down timer, meaning that a manual failover cannot occur until the hold-down timer has passed.

It is also possible to do this for the control plane. However, it's best to not rapidly fail over the control plane, and best practice recommends that you use a 300-second hold-down timer to prevent excessive flapping of the control plane (which is discussed further in "Preserving the Control Plane" on page 605).

Now, in this manual failover example, redundancy group 0 will be failed over and then the hold-down timer will prevent a manual failover:

```
{primary:node0}
root@SRX210-A> show configuration chassis cluster
control-link-recovery;
reth-count 2;
heartbeat-interval 2000;
heartbeat-threshold 8;
redundancy-group 0 {
    node 0 priority 254;
```

```
        node 1 priority 1;
        hold-down-interval 300;
    }
    redundancy-group 1 {
        node 0 priority 254;
        node 1 priority 1;
        interface-monitor {
            fe-2/0/2 weight 255;
            fe-0/0/2 weight 255;
        }
    }

{primary:node0}
root@SRX210-A> show chassis cluster status
Cluster ID: 1
Node                Priority          Status    Preempt  Manual failover

Redundancy group: 0 , Failover count: 1
    node0               254         primary        no       no
    node1               1           secondary      no       no

Redundancy group: 1 , Failover count: 7
    node0               254         primary        no       no
    node1               1           secondary      no       no

{primary:node0}
root@SRX210-A> request chassis cluster failover redundancy-group 0 node 1
node1:
--------------------------------------------------------------------------
Initiated manual failover for redundancy group 0

{primary:node0}
root@SRX210-A> show chassis cluster status
Cluster ID: 1
Node                Priority          Status    Preempt  Manual failover

Redundancy group: 0 , Failover count: 2
    node0               254         secondary-hold no       yes
    node1               255         primary        no       yes

Redundancy group: 1 , Failover count: 7
    node0               254         primary        no       no
    node1               1           secondary      no       no

{secondary-hold:node0}
root@SRX210-A> request chassis cluster failover reset redundancy-group 0
node0:
--------------------------------------------------------------------------
No reset required for redundancy group 0.

node1:
--------------------------------------------------------------------------
Successfully reset manual failover for redundancy group 0

{secondary-hold:node0}
```

```
root@SRX210-A> request chassis cluster failover redundancy-group 0 node 0
node0:
--------------------------------------------------------------------------
Manual failover is not permitted as redundancy-group 0 on node0 is in secondary-
hold state.

{secondary-hold:node0}
root@SRX210-A> show chassis cluster status
Cluster ID: 1
Node                Priority          Status    Preempt  Manual failover

Redundancy group: 0 , Failover count: 2
    node0               254           secondary-hold no        no
    node1               1             primary        no        no

Redundancy group: 1 , Failover count: 7
    node0               254           primary        no        no
    node1               1             secondary      no        no

{secondary-hold:node0}
root@SRX210-A>
```

Here redundancy group 0 is failed over from node 0 to node 1. This is just as before. It creates the priority on the new primary to 255 and sets the manual failover to `yes`. However, now node 0 shows `secondary-hold` as its status, indicating that it is in secondary mode but is also on a hold-down timer. When the timer expires, it will show `secondary`. In the event of a critical failure to the primary device, the `secondary-hold` unit can still take over. Lastly, an attempt to manually fail over the node is made, and it's not possible to fail over since the node is on a hold-down timer.

Hardware Monitoring

On the SRX, there is a daemon running called *chassisd*. This process is designed to run and control the system hardware, and it is also used to monitor for faults. If the chassisd determines that the system has experienced specific faults, it will trigger a failover to the other node. Depending on the SRX platform, various components can fail before a complete failover is triggered.

The majority of the branch platforms are not component-based. This means the entire system consists of a single board, and if anything were to go wrong on the main board, generally the complete system would fail. The branch SRX devices also have interface cards, and if the cards fail, the local interfaces are lost. Interface monitoring can be used to detect if the interface has failed.

The data center devices are a different story. These devices have many different boards and system components, and because of this, the failover scenarios can get fairly complex. Both Juniper Networks and customers thoroughly test the reliability of the devices and each component is failed in a matrix of testing scenarios to ensure that failovers are correctly covered.

Route engine

The route engine (RE) is the local brain of a chassis. Its job is to maintain control over the local cards in the chassis. It ensures that all of them are up and running and it allows the administrator to manage the device. If the RE fails, it can no longer control the local chassis, and if that RE was the primary for the cluster, the secondary engineer will pause until enough heartbeats are missed that it assumes mastership.

During this period, the local chassis will continue to forward (the data plane without an RE will continue to run for up to three minutes), but as soon as the other RE contacts the SPUs, they will no longer process traffic. By this time, the secondary data plane will have taken over for the traffic.

In the event that the secondary RE fails, that chassis immediately becomes lost. After the heartbeat threshold is passed, the primary RE will assume the other chassis has failed and any active traffic running on the chassis in redundancy groups will fail over to the remaining node. Traffic that used local interfaces must utilize another protocol, such as OSPF, to fail over to the other node.

Switch control board

The switch control board (SCB) is a component that is unique to the SRX5000 Series. This component contains three important systems: the switch fabric, the control plane network, and the carrier slot for the RE. It's a fairly complex component as it effectively connects everything in the device. The SRX5600 requires one SCB and can have a second for redundancy. The SRX5800 requires two SCBs and can have a third for redundancy.

If an SCB fails in the SRX5600, it will fail over to the second SCB. Its redundancy, however, causes a brief blip in traffic and then things start moving along. The second SCB also requires the use of a local RE, the same simple RE that is used to bring up dual control links. The second RE is needed to activate the local control plane switching chip on the second SCB—if this was not in place, the RE would be unable to talk to the rest of the chassis.

The SRX5800's behavior is different because, by default, it has two SCBs. These are required to provide full throughput to the entire chassis, and if one were to fail, the throughput would be halved until a new SCB is brought online. The same conditions as the SRX5600 also apply here. If the SCB containing the RE were to fail, a secondary RE would need to be in the second SCB to provide the backup control network for the RE to communicate. If the SCB that does not contain the primary RE fails, the maximum throughput of the chassis is cut in half. This means all of the paths in the box are halved. If a third SCB is installed, it will take over for either of the failed SCBs. It cannot provide a redundant control link as it is not able to contain an RE, and when the switchover happens to the third SCB it will briefly interrupt traffic as the switchover occurs.

Now, all of this should pose the question to the careful reader: if the RE is contained in an SCB and the SCB fails, will this affect the RE? The answer depends on the type of failure. If the fabric chips fail, the RE will be fine, as the SCB simply extends the connections from the back plane into the RE. The engineers put the RE in the SCB to conserve slots in the chassis and reserve them for traffic processing cards. It is possible for an SCB to fail in such a way that it will disable the engineer; it's unlikely, but possible.

Switch fabric board

The switch fabric board (SFB) is a unique component to the SRX3000 Series platform. It contains the switch fabric, the primary control plane switch, the secondary control plane switch, an interface card, and the control ports. If this component were to fail, the chassis would effectively be lost. The SFB's individual components can fail as well, causing various levels of device degradation. In the end, once the integrity of the card is lost, the services residing in that chassis will fail over to the remaining node.

Services Processing Card

The Services Processing Card (SPC) contains one or two SPUs, depending on the model of the SRX. Each SPU is monitored directly by the SRX's local RE chassisd process. If any SPU fails, several events will immediately occur. The RE will reset all of the cards on the data plane, including interfaces and NPCs. Such an SPU failure causes the chassis monitoring threshold to hit 255. This causes all of the data plane services to fail over to the secondary chassis. Messages relating to SPUs failing can be seen in the jsrpd logs. The entire data plane is reset because it is easier to ensure that everything is up and running after a clean restart, rather than having to validate many individual subsystems. Each subsystem is validated upon a clean restart of the chassis.

Network Processing Card

A separate Network Processing Card (NPC) is unique to the SRX3000 Series (these items are located on the interface cards on the SRX5000). They were separated out to lower the component costs and to lower the overall cost of the chassis. The SRX3000 has static bindings to each interface, so if an NPC were to fail the interface bound to it would effectively be lost as it would not have access to the switching fabric. The chassis will be able to detect this by using simple health checks; alternatively, IP monitoring can be used to validate the next hop. This message would be sent from the SPC and then through the NPC. Because the NPC has failed, the messages will not make it out of the chassis. At this point, IP monitoring triggers a failover to the other node. The NPC failure ultimately triggers a failover to the remaining node in the chassis and the chassis with the failure restarts all of the cards. If the NPC with the failure is unable to restart, the interfaces are mapped to new NPCs, assuming there are some remaining. Although the device can run in a degraded state, it's best to leave all of the traffic on the good node and replace the failed component.

Interface card

The SRX data center devices have both types of interface cards, often referred to as input/output cards (IOCs). However, there are stark differences between the two. The IOCs on the SRX3000 contain a switching chip (used to connect multiple interfaces to a single bus) and an FPGA to connect into the fabric. The IOCs on the SRX5000s contain two or more sets of NPUs, fabric connect chips, and physical interfaces. If an SRX5000 Series interface card fails and it does not contain a monitored interface, or the only fabric link, the SRX will rely on the administrator to use interface monitoring or IP monitoring to detect a failure. The same goes with the SRX3000 Series platforms. On the SRX5000 Series, it is also possible to hot-swap interfaces to replace the card, while the SRX3000 requires that the chassis be powered off to replace a card.

Control link

The control link is a critical component in the system. It allows the two brains, the REs, to talk to each other. If the control link physically goes down and the fabric link is up, the secondary RE immediately goes into ineligible state. Eventually, it will go into disabled state. Once it becomes ineligible, the only way to recover the secondary node is to reboot the device. If control link recovery is enabled, the device will reboot itself after one minute of successful communications. (Using control link recovery is the best option in this scenario, since it allows the device to reboot when it knows communications are working correctly.) The important item here is that for this scenario to work, at least one fabric link must still be up. With the fabric link still remaining, the primary RE knows that the secondary is still alive but a problem has occurred.

The secondary node goes into disabled state to prevent split brain (the state when two devices both think they are master). If this occurs, effectively two nodes are fighting to be the primary node for the cluster. They will use GARPs to try to take over and process the traffic on the network, typically causing an outage. This is a good reason you should use dual control links and data links when possible.

Data link

The data link uses jsrpd heartbeat messages to validate that the path is up and is actively working. This is similar to the control link. However, the data link is more forgiving. It can take up to 120 seconds for the data link to detect that it is down. This is because it's possible for the data link to get completely full of RTOs, or data forwarding messages, hence the data link is more forgiving in missing messages from the other node. However, after the required amount of time has passed, the secondary node will become disabled just like the control link. There isn't an automatic reboot like the control link—the secondary node must be manually rebooted to recover it.

Control link and data link failure

Rarely do both the fabric and data links go down at the same time, meaning within the same second. But we all know this can occur for all sorts of reasons, from hardware failures to a machete-wielding utility helper chopping up cables in the data center. It's a common request and test that Juniper Networks receives, so it's best that we cover it than to leave administrators wondering.

If the control link and the data link were to fail at the same time, the worst possible scenario would occur, split brain, leaving the cluster members thinking the other node has failed, which will effectively cause an outage. There are several ways to prevent this.

As of Junos 10.2, it is possible to use dual fabric links on the branch SRX Series devices. Even if a control link and a fabric link were to fail, the last remaining control link would prevent split brain from occurring. So, generally speaking, split brain will not occur on the branch platforms.

For the data center platforms, utilizing dual control links and dual fabric links will provide the same level of split brain prevention, with one point to note. On the SRX5000 Series, the control port is on the SPC, and the SPC containing the CP is a part of the data path. So, if the administrator were to configure the control link, and the CP is on the same SPC and it failed, split brain would occur. The CP is always located on the SPU in the lowest numbered FPC and PIC slot.

You can use the `show chassis fpc pic-status` command to identify the location of the FPC.

The best practice is to place the control port on any SPC other than the one containing the CP. If redundant control links are required, it's best to place them on two separate SPCs. This would mean that on an SRX5000 Series, three SPCs with one containing the CP and the other two each containing a control link would be used for the best level of redundancy. The same goes for the fabric link. Placing each redundant fabric link on a separate SPC would be the best practice for availability. Although this may seem like overkill, if ultimate availability is required, this is the suggested deployment.

Though it does look like the CP is a single point of failure, that isn't true. If the CP fails, the data plane will be reset. As soon as the SPCs receive power, the control links will come up rapidly, allowing the cluster to continue control plane communications and preventing split brain.

Power supplies

It's obvious that if the device's sole source of power fails, the device shuts off. This will cause the remaining node to perform Dead Peer Detection (DPD) to determine if the other node is alive. DPD is done with jsrpd heartbeats. If the remaining node is the primary device for the control and data planes, it continues to forward traffic as is. It notes that the other node is down since it cannot communicate with it. If the remaining node was secondary, it will wait until all of the heartbeats are missed before it determines that the node has failed. Once the heartbeats have been passed, it assumes mastership of the node.

For devices with redundant power supplies, the remaining power supply will power the chassis and it will continue to operate. This is applicable to the SRX650 and the SRX3400. The SRX3600 has up to four power supplies, and it requires at least two to operate. The other two are used for redundancy. So, in the best availability deployment, four should be deployed.

The SRX5000 Series devices each have up to four power supplies. At a suggested minimum, three should be used. Depending on the total number of cards running in the chassis, a single power supply can be used. If the total draw from the installed components exceeds the available power, all of the cards will be turned off. The RE will continue attempting to start the cards until the power is available. It's always best to deploy the SRXs with the highest amount of available power supply to ensure availability.

Software Monitoring

The SRX is set up to monitor the software that is running, and this is true for both the control and data planes. The SRX attempts to detect a failure within the system as soon as it happens, and if and when it can detect a failure within the system it must react accordingly. The SRX platform has some fairly complex internals, but it is built to protect against failures, so if the RE has a process that fails, it can restart it, and the failure is logged for additional troubleshooting.

The branch's data plane consists of a core flowd process. The RE is in constant communication to watch if it is acting correctly. In the event that the flowd process crashes, or hangs up, the control plane quickly fails over to the other node. This will happen in less than the time it would take to detect a dead node. In any failure case where the two nodes are still in communication, the failover time is quite fast. These cases include IP monitoring, manual failover, and interface monitoring.

On the data center SRX's data plane, each SPU has both control and data software running on it. The RE talks directly to each SPU's control software for status updates and for configuration changes. Because of this, the RE will know if the data plane fails. If the flowd processes crash on the data plane (there is one per SPU), the entire data plane will be hard-reset, which means all of the line cards will be reset. This is done to ensure that the control plane is completely up to an acceptable running standard. To do this, the data plane is failed over to the secondary node.

Preserving the Control Plane

If a device is set up to rapidly fail over, it's possible that it could be jumping the gun and attempting a failover for no reason. When it's time to move between two firewalls, it's best to ensure that the time is correct for the failover. There are methods in dynamic routing to do extremely fast failover using a protocol called *bidirectional forwarding detection* (BFD). This protocol is used in conjunction with a routing protocol such as OSPF. It can provide 50 ms failovers. That is extremely fast but provides little threat to the network. In this case, BFD is rerouting around a link or device failure typically in a stateless manner. Because it's done stateless, there is little threat to the traffic.

When a stateful firewall does a failover, there is much more in play than simply rerouting traffic. The new device needs to accept all of the traffic and match up the packets with the existing sessions that are synchronized to the second node. Also, the primary device needs to relinquish control of the traffic. On the data plane, it's a fairly stable process to fail over and fail back between nodes. In fact, this can be done rapidly and nearly continuously without much worry. It's best to let the control plane fail over only in the event of a failure, as there simply isn't a need to fail over the control plane unless a critical event occurs.

The biggest reason for any concern is that the control plane talks to the various daemons on the other chassis and on the data plane. If rapid failover were to occur, it's possible to destabilize the control plane. This is not a rule, it's an exception, just as the owner of a car isn't going to jam the car into reverse on the highway. Often, administrators want to test the limits of the SRX and drop them off shelves and whatnot, so it's fair to call this out as a warning before it's tested in production.

Using Junos Automation

Junos automation is the ability to use several underlying technologies in Junos to automate certain tasks, including the ability for an administrator to make his own commands, validate the configuration upon commit, and react to various events that may occur. It's an extremely powerful feature to offer to an administrator, allowing him to create his own features on the SRX shaped to his own demands.

Automation is a common feature that can be used across most Junos devices; examples for this book's audience might be the creation of custom IP monitoring features, or having the SRX fail over interfaces based on specific events, or even creating a command to completely validate the node.

Junos automation is an expansive feature that is further covered in Chapter 13, but it truly deserves its own book to cover the amazing features it can accomplish.

Juniper Networks publishes a series of booklets on Junos automation in its Day One series, freely available at *http://www.juniper.net/dayone*.

Some networks completely manage their SRXs using automation and others rely on it for complete HA on the SRX, even past the built-in features. Whether or not you use it for HA, Junos automation is a feature that everyone should check out and utilize in his Junos-powered network.

Troubleshooting the Cluster

From time to time things can go wrong. You can be driving along in your car and a tire can blow out; sometimes a firewall can crash. Nothing that is made by humans is precluded from undergoing an unseen failure. Because of this, the administrator must be prepared to deal with the worst possible scenarios. In this section, we will discuss various methods that show the administrator how to troubleshoot a chassis cluster gone awry.

First Steps

There are a few commands to use when trying to look into an issue. The administrator needs to first identify the cluster status and determine if it is communicating.

The `show chassis cluster status` command, although simple in nature, shows the administrator the status of the cluster. It shows who is the primary member for each redundancy group and the status of those nodes, and it will give insight into who should be passing traffic in the network. Here's a sample:

```
{primary:node1}
root@SRX210-B> show chassis cluster status
Cluster ID: 1
Node                  Priority          Status    Preempt  Manual failover

Redundancy group: 0 , Failover count: 1
    node0                   254          secondary      no       no
    node1                   1            primary        no       no

Redundancy group: 1 , Failover count: 2
    node0                   254          primary        no       no
    node1                   1            secondary      no       no

{primary:node1}
root@SRX210-B>
```

You should have seen this many times in this chapter, as it is used frequently. Things to look for here are that both nodes show as up, both have a priority greater than zero, both have a status of either primary, secondary, or secondary-hold, and one and only one node is primary for each redundancy group. Generally, if those conditions are met, things in the cluster should be looking OK. If not, and for some reason one of the nodes does not show up in this output, communication to the other node has been lost. The administrator should then connect to the other node and verify that it can communicate.

To validate that the two nodes can communicate the `show chassis cluster control-plane statistics` command is used, showing the messages that are being sent between the two members. The send and receive numbers should be incrementing between the two nodes. If they are not, something may be wrong with both the control and fabric links. Here is an example with the statistics highlighted:

```
{primary:node0}
root@SRX210-A> show chassis cluster control-plane statistics
Control link statistics:
    Control link 0:
        Heartbeat packets sent: 124
        Heartbeat packets received: 95
        Heartbeat packet errors: 0
Fabric link statistics:
    Probes sent: 122
    Probes received: 56
    Probe errors: 0

{primary:node0}
root@SRX210-A>
```

Again, this command should be familiar as it has been used in this chapter. If these (highlighted) numbers are not increasing, check the fabric and control plane interfaces. The fabric interfaces method is the same across all SRX products.

Next let's check the fabric links. It's important to verify that the fabric link and the child links show they are in an up state:

```
{primary:node0}
root@SRX210-A> show interfaces terse
Interface               Admin Link Proto    Local              Remote
--snip--
fe-0/0/4.0              up    up   aenet    --> fab0.0
fe-0/0/5                up    up
fe-0/0/5.0              up    up   aenet    --> fab0.0
--snip--
fe-2/0/4.0              up    up   aenet    --> fab1.0
fe-2/0/5                up    up
fe-2/0/5.0              up    up   aenet    --> fab1.0
--snip--
fab0                    up    up
fab0.0                  up    up   inet     30.17.0.200/24
fab1                    up    up
fab1.0                  up    up   inet     30.18.0.200/24
--snip--
{primary:node0}
root@SRX210-A>
```

If any of the child links of the fabric link, `fabX`, show in a down state, this would show the interface that is physically down on the node. This must be restored to enable communications.

The control link is the most critical to verify, and it varies per SRX platform type. On the branch devices, the interface that is configured as the control link must be checked. This is specified in Table 10-2's control ports by platform. The procedure would be the same as any physical interface. Here an example from an SRX210 was used, and it shows that the specified interfaces are up:

```
{primary:node0}
root@SRX210-A> show interfaces terse
Interface               Admin Link Proto    Local                 Remote
--snip--
fe-0/0/7                up    up
--snip--
fe-2/0/7                up    up
--snip--

{primary:node0}
root@SRX210-A>
```

On the data center SRXs, there is no direct way to check the state of the control ports; since the ports are dedicated off of switches inside the SRX and they are not typical interfaces, it's not possible to check them. It is possible, however, to check the switch that is on the SCB to ensure that packets are being received from that card. Generally, though, if the port is up and configured correctly, there should be no reason why it won't communicate. But checking the internal switch should show that packets are passing from the SPC to the RE. There will also be other communications coming from the card as well, but this at least provides insight into the communication. To check, the node and FPC that has the control link must be known. In the following command, the specified port coincides with the FPC number of the SPC with the control port:

```
{primary:node0}
root@SRX5800-1> show chassis ethernet-switch statistics 1 node 0
node0:
------------------------------------------------------------------
Displaying port statistics for switch 0
Statistics for port 1 connected to device FPC1:
  TX Packets 64 Octets          7636786
  TX Packets 65-127 Octets      989668
  TX Packets 128-255 Octets     37108
  TX Packets 256-511 Octets     35685
  TX Packets 512-1023 Octets    233238
  TX Packets 1024-1518 Octets   374077
  TX Packets 1519-2047 Octets   0
  TX Packets 2048-4095 Octets   0
  TX Packets 4096-9216 Octets   0
  TX 1519-1522 Good Vlan frms   0
  TX Octets                     9306562
  TX Multicast Packets          24723
```

```
    TX Broadcast Packets        219029
    TX Single Collision frames  0
    TX Mult. Collision frames   0
    TX Late Collisions          0
    TX Excessive Collisions     0
    TX Collision frames         0
    TX PAUSEMAC Ctrl Frames     0
    TX MAC ctrl frames          0
    TX Frame deferred Xmns      0
    TX Frame excessive deferl   0
    TX Oversize Packets         0
    TX Jabbers                  0
    TX FCS Error Counter        0
    TX Fragment Counter         0
    TX Byte Counter             1335951885
    RX Packets 64 Octets        6672950
    RX Packets 65-127 Octets    2226967
    RX Packets 128-255 Octets   39459
    RX Packets 256-511 Octets   34332
    RX Packets 512-1023 Octets  523505
    RX Packets 1024-1518 Octets  51945
    RX Packets 1519-2047 Octets  0
    RX Packets 2048-4095 Octets  0
    RX Packets 4096-9216 Octets  0
    RX Octets                   9549158
    RX Multicast Packets        24674
    RX Broadcast Packets        364537
    RX FCS Errors               0
    RX Align Errors             0
    RX Fragments                0
    RX Symbol errors            0
    RX Unsupported opcodes      0
    RX Out of Range Length      0
    RX False Carrier Errors     0
    RX Undersize Packets        0
    RX Oversize Packets         0
    RX Jabbers                  0
    RX 1519-1522 Good Vlan frms 0
    RX MTU Exceed Counter       0
    RX Control Frame Counter    0
    RX Pause Frame Counter      0
    RX Byte Counter             999614473

{primary:node0}
root@SRX5800-1>
```

The output looks like standard port statistics from a switch. Looking in here will validate that packets are coming from the SPC. Since the SRX3000 has its control ports on the SFB, and there is nothing to configure for the control ports, there is little to look at on the interface. It is best to focus on the result from the `show chassis cluster control-plane statistics` command.

If checking the interfaces yields mixed results where they seem to be up but they are not passing traffic, it's possible to reboot the node in the degraded state. The risk here is that the node may come up in split brain. Since that is a possibility, it's best to disable its interfaces, or physically disable all of them except the control or data link. The ports can even be disabled on the switch they are connected to. This way, upon boot, if the node determines it is master it will not interrupt traffic. A correctly operating node using the minimal control port and fabric port configuration should be able to communicate to its peer. If, after a reboot, it still cannot communicate to the other node, it's best to verify the configuration and cabling. Lastly, the box or cluster interfaces may be bad.

Checking Interfaces

Interfaces are required to pass traffic through the SRX, and for the SRX to be effective in its job it needs to have interfaces up and able to pass traffic. The SRX can use both local and redundant Ethernet interfaces, and for our purposes here, both have similar methods of troubleshooting.

To troubleshoot an interface, first check to see if the interface is physically up. Use the `show interfaces terse` command to quickly see all of the interfaces in both chassis:

```
{primary:node0}
root@SRX210-A> show interfaces terse
Interface               Admin Link Proto    Local               Remote
ge-0/0/0                up    down
ge-0/0/1                up    down
fe-0/0/2                up    up
```

This should be familiar if you've been reading through this chapter, and certainly throughout the book. The other item to check is the status of the Reth within a redundancy group to see if the interface is up or down inside the Reth. It's possible that the Reth could be physically up but logically down (in the event that there was an issue on the data plane). To check the status of a Reth interface use the `show chassis cluster interfaces` command:

```
root@SRX210-A> show chassis cluster interfaces
Control link 0 name: fxp1

Redundant-ethernet Information:
    Name         Status      Redundancy-group
    reth0        Up          1
    reth1        Up          1

Interface Monitoring:
    Interface          Weight     Status     Redundancy-group
    fe-0/0/2           255        Up         1
    fe-2/0/2           255        Up         1

{primary:node0}
root@SRX210-A>
```

If the interfaces are physically up but the redundant interfaces show that they are in a down state, it's time to look at the data plane.

Verifying the Data Plane

The data plane on the SRX passes and processes the traffic. Since it is an independent component from the RE, it could be down while the administrator is still in the RE. There are a few things to check on the SRX to validate the data plane.

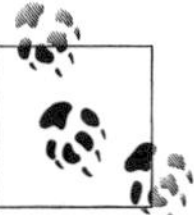

Because the data plane is very different between the branch SRX platform and the data center platform, there will be some variance between the commands.

Verifying the FPCs and PICs is the first step, and this shows the status of the underlying hardware that needs to be up to process the data traffic. On the branch SRX, the data plane is a single multithreaded process, however, so running the `show chassis fpc pic-status` command shows the status of the data plane:

```
root@SRX210-A> show chassis fpc pic-status
node0:
--------------------------------------------------------------------------
Slot 0   Online       FPC
  PIC 0  Online       2x GE, 6x FE, 1x 3G

node1:
--------------------------------------------------------------------------
Slot 0   Online       FPC
  PIC 0  Online       2x GE, 6x FE, 1x 3G

{primary:node0}
root@SRX210-A>
```

As you can see, this output is from an SRX210, but the command will list the status of the data plane on each SRX. Here it shows a single FPC and a single PIC. Although the output does not mention anything about flowd or the data plane, the output shows that the SRX is up and ready to pass traffic.

Now let's show node 1 with a failed data plane:

```
{primary:node0}
root@SRX210-A> show chassis fpc pic-status
node0:
--------------------------------------------------------------------------
Slot 0   Online       FPC
  PIC 0  Online       2x GE, 6x FE, 1x 3G

node1:
--------------------------------------------------------------------------
Slot 0   Offline      FPC

{primary:node0}
root@SRX210-A>
```

Here, node 1's data plane went offline, caused by the loss of the flowd process. Another event that can be seen is that redundancy groups one and greater will have their priority as zero (to be discussed in the next section).

The output of the `pic status` command should correlate with the hardware that is in the chassis, which can be seen in the output of `show chassis hardware`:

```
{primary:node0}
root@SRX210-A> show chassis hardware
node0:
--------------------------------------------------------------------------
Hardware inventory:
Item             Version  Part number  Serial number  Description
Chassis                                AD2609AA0497   SRX210h
Routing Engine   REV 28   750-021779   AAAH2307       RE-SRX210-HIGHMEM
FPC 0                                                 FPC
  PIC 0                                               2x GE, 6x FE, 1x 3G
Power Supply 0

node1:
--------------------------------------------------------------------------
Hardware inventory:
Item             Version  Part number  Serial number  Description
Chassis                                AD2909AA0346   SRX210h
Routing Engine   REV 28   750-021779   AAAH4743       RE-SRX210-HIGHMEM
FPC 0                                                 FPC
  PIC 0                                               2x GE, 6x FE, 1x 3G
Power Supply 0

{primary:node0}
root@SRX210-A>
```

Here the command shows the hardware in PIC 0, which is the same as shown in the `pic status` command. This command is more useful on the data center platform because on the data center SRX, it's a little more complex, as there are typically many different processors.

For example, here's the PIC status of an SRX5800:

```
{primary:node0}
root@SRX5800-1> show chassis fpc pic-status
node0:
--------------------------------------------------------------------------
Slot 0   Online       SRX5k SPC
  PIC 0  Online       SPU Cp
  PIC 1  Online       SPU Flow
Slot 1   Online       SRX5k SPC
  PIC 0  Online       SPU Flow
  PIC 1  Online       SPU Flow
Slot 3   Online       SRX5k SPC
  PIC 0  Online       SPU Flow
  PIC 1  Online       SPU Flow
Slot 6   Online       SRX5k DPC 4X 10GE
  PIC 0  Online       1x 10GE(LAN/WAN) RichQ
  PIC 1  Online       1x 10GE(LAN/WAN) RichQ
```

```
  PIC 2  Online       1x 10GE(LAN/WAN) RichQ
  PIC 3  Online       1x 10GE(LAN/WAN) RichQ
Slot 11  Online       SRX5k DPC 40x 1GE
  PIC 0  Online       10x 1GE RichQ
  PIC 1  Online       10x 1GE RichQ
  PIC 2  Online       10x 1GE RichQ
  PIC 3  Online       10x 1GE RichQ

node1:
--------------------------------------------------------------------------
Slot 0   Online      SRX5k SPC
  PIC 0  Online      SPU Cp
  PIC 1  Online      SPU Flow
Slot 1   Online      SRX5k  SPC
  PIC 0  Online      SPU Flow
  PIC 1  Online      SPU Flow
Slot 3   Online      SRX5k SPC
  PIC 0  Online      SPU Flow
  PIC 1  Online      SPU Flow
Slot 6   Online      SRX5k DPC 4X 10GE
  PIC 0  Online      1x 10GE(LAN/WAN) RichQ
  PIC 1  Online      1x 10GE(LAN/WAN) RichQ
  PIC 2  Online      1x 10GE(LAN/WAN) RichQ
  PIC 3  Online      1x 10GE(LAN/WAN) RichQ
Slot 11  Online      SRX5k DPC 40x 1GE
  PIC 0  Online      10x 1GE RichQ
  PIC 1  Online      10x 1GE RichQ
  PIC 2  Online      10x 1GE RichQ
  PIC 3  Online      10x 1GE RichQ

{primary:node0}
root@SRX5800-1>
```

Here the command shows the SPCs that are online, which SPU is the CP, and the interface cards. A correctly operating device should have all of its SPCs online, and unless they are disabled, the interfaces should be online. Cards that have not booted yet will be offline or present. In a data center SRX, it can take up to five minutes for the data plane to completely start up. As the cards come online, the following messages will be sent to the command prompts. These messages should only come up once during the process and then they will be logged to the messages file:

```
{primary:node0}
root@SRX5800-1>
Message from syslogd@SRX5800-1 at Mar 13 22:01:48  ...
SRX5800-1 node0.fpc1.pic0 SCHED: Thread 4 (Module Init) ran for 1806 ms without
yielding

Message from syslogd@SRX5800-1 at Mar 13 22:01:49  ...
SRX5800-1 node0.fpc1.pic1 SCHED: Thread 4 (Module Init) ran for 1825 ms without
yielding


{primary:node0}
root@SRX5800-1>
```

If these messages are coming up on the command-line interface (CLI), the SPUs are constantly restarting and should identify a problem, perhaps because not enough power is being sent to the data plane and the SPUs are restarting.

Let's show the hardware that should match up to the output of the `show chassis cluster fpc pic-status` command in the previous example. This will show all of the FPCs that are SPCs, and the administrator should be able to match up which PICs should be online and active:

```
{primary:node0}
root@SRX5800-1> show chassis hardware
node0:
--------------------------------------------------------------------------
Hardware inventory:
Item             Version  Part number  Serial number  Description
Chassis                                JN112A0AEAGA   SRX 5800
Midplane         REV 01   710-024803   TR8821         SRX 5800 Backplane
FPM Board        REV 01   710-024632   WX3786         Front Panel Display
PDM              Rev 03   740-013110   QCS12365066    Power Distribution Module
PEM 0            Rev 01   740-023514   QCS1233E066    PS 1.7kW; 200-240VAC in
PEM 1            Rev 01   740-023514   QCS1233E02V    PS 1.7kW; 200-240VAC in
PEM 2            Rev 01   740-023514   QCS1233E02E    PS 1.7kW; 200-240VAC in
Routing Engine 0 REV 03   740-023530   9009007746     RE-S-1300
CB 0             REV 03   710-024802   WX5793         SRX5k SCB
CB 1             REV 03   710-024802   WV8373         SRX5k SCB
FPC 0            REV 12   750-023996   XS7597         SRX5k SPC
  CPU            REV 03   710-024633   XS6648         SRX5k DPC PMB
  PIC 0                   BUILTIN      BUILTIN        SPU Cp
  PIC 1                   BUILTIN      BUILTIN        SPU Flow
FPC 1            REV 08   750-023996   XA7212         SRX5k SPC
  CPU            REV 02   710-024633   WZ0740         SRX5k DPC PMB
  PIC 0                   BUILTIN      BUILTIN        SPU Flow
  PIC 1                   BUILTIN      BUILTIN        SPU Flow
FPC 3            REV 12   750-023996   XS7625         SRX5k SPC
  CPU            REV 03   710-024633   XS6820         SRX5k DPC PMB
  PIC 0                   BUILTIN      BUILTIN        SPU Flow
  PIC 1                   BUILTIN      BUILTIN        SPU Flow
FPC 6            REV 17   750-020751   WY2754         SRX5k DPC 4X 10GE
  CPU            REV 02   710-024633   WY3706         SRX5k DPC PMB
  PIC 0                   BUILTIN      BUILTIN        1x 10GE(LAN/WAN) RichQ
    Xcvr 0       REV 02   740-011571   C831XJ039      XFP-10G-SR
  PIC 1                   BUILTIN      BUILTIN        1x 10GE(LAN/WAN) RichQ
    Xcvr 0       REV 01   740-011571   C744XJ021      XFP-10G-SR
  PIC 2                   BUILTIN      BUILTIN        1x 10GE(LAN/WAN) RichQ
  PIC 3                   BUILTIN      BUILTIN        1x 10GE(LAN/WAN) RichQ
FPC 11           REV 14   750-020235   WY8697         SRX5k DPC 40x 1GE
  CPU            REV 02   710-024633   WY3743         SRX5k DPC PMB
  PIC 0                   BUILTIN      BUILTIN        10x 1GE RichQ
--snip--
  PIC 1                   BUILTIN      BUILTIN        10x 1GE RichQ
--snip--
  PIC 2                   BUILTIN      BUILTIN        10x 1GE RichQ
--snip--
  PIC 3                   BUILTIN      BUILTIN        10x 1GE RichQ
```

```
    Xcvr 0         REV 01   740-013111   8280380        SFP-T
--snip--
Fan Tray 0         REV 05   740-014971   TP8104         Fan Tray
Fan Tray 1         REV 05   740-014971   TP8089         Fan Tray

{primary:node0}
root@SRX5800-1>
```

Core Dumps

A core dump occurs when things have gone wrong and a process crashes. The memory for the process is then dumped to local storage. If something goes wrong and a process crashes on the SRX, the core dump is stored to several different directories on the local RE. Here's an example of how to find core dumps:

```
{primary:node0}
root@SRX5800-1> show system core-dumps
node0:
--------------------------------------------------------------------------
/var/crash/*core*: No such file or directory
/var/tmp/*core*: No such file or directory
/var/crash/kernel.*: No such file or directory
/tftpboot/corefiles/*core*: No such file or directory

node1:
--------------------------------------------------------------------------
/var/crash/*core*: No such file or directory
-rw-rw----  1 root  wheel   104611 Feb 26 22:22 /var/tmp/csh.core.0.gz
-rw-rw----  1 root  wheel   108254 Feb 26 23:11 /var/tmp/csh.core.1.gz
-rw-rw----  1 root  wheel   107730 Feb 26 23:11 /var/tmp/csh.core.2.gz
/var/crash/kernel.*: No such file or directory
/tftpboot/corefiles/*core*: No such file or directory
total 3

{primary:node0}
root@SRX5800-1>
```

If core dumps are found, there isn't much for the users to troubleshoot. Although sometimes core dumps from CSH or a C shell can occur when a user uses Ctrl-c to terminate a program, these generally can be ignored. However, if a core dump for flowd or other processes exists, it should be reported to the Juniper Networks Technical Assistance Center (JTAC), as it may be an indicator of a more complex problem.

The Dreaded Priority Zero

For most administrators the following output is a disaster:

```
{primary:node0}
root@SRX210-A> show chassis cluster status
Cluster ID: 1
Node                  Priority      Status     Preempt  Manual failover
```

```
Redundancy group: 0 , Failover count: 1
    node0                   254     primary        no       no
    node1                   1       secondary      no       no

Redundancy group: 1 , Failover count: 1
    node0                   254     primary        no       no
    node1                   0       secondary      no       no

{primary:node0}
root@SRX210-A>
```

Seeing a priority of zero tends to leave administrators in a state of confusion, but the simple reason this occurs may be due to a problem on the data plane. Determining the problem can be difficult. Although some of the troubleshooting steps we already discussed can be helpful, you might try another. Everything that happens with jsrpd is logged to the file *jsrpd*, in the directory */var/log*. You can view the file by using the `show log jsrpd` command. The contents of the file vary, based on the events that occur with jsrpd, but the file is typically quite readable.

There are some specific items to check for. The first is coldsync, which is the initial synchronization between the kernels on the two REs. A failed coldsync will cause the priority to be set to zero. If there is a problem and coldsync cannot complete, the coldsync monitoring weight will be set to 255. If it completes, it is set to zero. Here's an example of a coldsync log:

```
{primary:node0}
root@SRX210-A> show log jsrpd | match coldsync

Apr 11 08:44:14 coldsync is completed for all the PFEs. cs monitoring weight
is set to ZERO
Apr 11 13:09:38 coldsync status message received from PFE: 0, status: 0x1
Apr 11 13:09:38 duplicate coldsync completed message from PFE: 0 ignored
Apr 11 13:09:38 coldsync is completed for all the PFEs. cs monitoring weight
is set to ZERO
Apr 11 13:11:20 coldsync status message received from PFE: 0, status: 0x1
Apr 11 13:11:20 duplicate coldsync completed message from PFE: 0 ignored
Apr 11 13:11:20 coldsync is completed for all the PFEs. cs monitoring weight
is set to ZERO
Apr 11 13:19:05 coldsync status message received from PFE: 0, status: 0x1
Apr 11 13:19:05 duplicate coldsync completed message from PFE: 0 ignored
Apr 11 13:19:05 coldsync is completed for all the PFEs. cs monitoring weight
is set to ZERO
```

If coldsync fails, it's possible to do two things. First, on either device issue a `commit full` command, which will resend the complete configuration to the data and control planes (this may impact traffic as it reapplies all of the policies). The other option is to reboot the secondary node and attempt the coldsync process again. (As a last resort, read the next section.)

In the logfile, the history of interfaces going up and down, node mastership, and other events are kept. Most of the events are quite obvious to the administrator and should provide a road map to what happened on the device.

Additional information can be gathered by turning on the traceoptions; just be aware that a lot of additional processing can be required based on the type of traceoptions you enable. If *all events are enabled* it will spike the chassis process to 100% utilization.

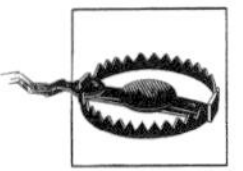

Do not enable traceoptions for more than a few minutes!

There have been countless times where administrators have left traceoptions enabled for all events, and all sorts of trouble has occurred, from service outages to crashing devices, if traceoptions stays active for a long enough period of time.

When All Else Fails

The SRX is a complex and feature-rich product, and Junos provides all sorts of configuration knobs that are not available on other products, all of it engineered with an appreciation of uptime and that to any organization it is critical. We began this chapter with a quote: "Failure is not an option."

If the SRX is going to be deployed in a complex environment, the administrator should become familiar with the product before deployment. The administrator's knowledge and understanding of the product is the first line of defense for ensuring that the product is going to work in the environment. The more critical the environment, the more detailed an administrator should be in his testing and knowledge about the product. Before deployment, some administrators spend months learning and staging the SRX. Although that may seem like an excessive amount for you and your network needs, it's a fact that the most prepared administrators have the fewest issues. It's one of the reasons we wrote this book, and hopefully, you've read this far into it.

There are other sources for studying and analyzing the SRX. For instance, the J-Net community allows users and product experts to communicate, sharing solutions and issues about Juniper products (*http://forums.juniper.net/*). It's also a really great set of resources to learn from what other users are doing. Another great resource is the juniper-nsp mailing list. This mailing list has been around for many years and the SRX has become a popular topic (*http://puck.nether.net/mailman/listinfo/juniper-nsp*).

You might also look at a new and budding series of Day One booklets from Juniper Networks that are free and that cover the SRX product line (*http://www.juniper.net/dayone*).

But truly, when all else fails, it's a good idea to contact JTAC for support (*http://www.juniper.net/support/requesting-support.html*). When contacting JTAC it's important to provide the correct information. If you share the correct data with JTAC they can quickly get to the root of the problem.

First collect the output from the command `request support information`. The output can be quite large. If possible, save it locally to the RE, then transfer it off the box by using `request support information | save SupportInfo.txt`, and then use the following sequence of commands to copy off the file:

```
{primary:node0}
root@SRX5800-1> copy file SupportInfo.txt ftp://tester:password@myftpserver.com:/

OR

{primary:node0}
root@SRX5800-1> copy file SupportInfo.txt scp://172.19.100.50:
root@172.19.100.50's password:
SupportInfo.txt
100% 7882     7.7KB/s   00:00

{primary:node0}
root@SRX5800-1>
```

JTAC may also request the contents of the */var/log* directory. If possible, when opening a case, have the support information file, the */var/log* contents, any core dumps, and a simple topology diagram readily available. By providing this, you will solve half the battle for JTAC in getting to the root of the issue. If some event occurs and it's not reflected in the logs, there isn't much JTAC can do. Be sure to document the event and share what was observed in the network. JTAC can take it from there and work with you to resolve the issue.

Summary

Because the SRX will be placed in a mission-critical location in the network, it is extremely important to ensure that it is up and functional. Firewalls are placed in between the untrusted and trusted locations within a network. If the firewall fails, there is nothing left to bring the two networks together, causing a major outage. As you saw in this chapter, the SRX has a robust HA architecture that can survive the worst of tragedies.

The biggest benefit to the SRX HA design is the flexibility it gives to the end user. The ability to use redundancy groups and mix and match them with local interfaces is very powerful. It allows you to overcome the traditional limitations of a redundant firewall configuration and explore new design scenarios. At first, the new paradigm of mixing redundant interfaces, redundancy groups, and local interfaces is overwhelming. Hopefully, this chapter will allow you to think more freely and move away from past firewall limitations.

Chapter Review Questions

1. What is the purpose of the control link?
2. What are the three types of communication that pass over the fabric link?

3. Can configuration groups be used for any other tasks on a Junos device? Be specific.
4. What feature needs to be enabled when using dynamic routing?
5. What are the two most important commands when troubleshooting an SRX cluster?
6. From what Juniper product did the SRX get part of its HA code infrastructure?
7. Which platform supports the automatic upgrade of the secondary node?
8. Are acknowledgments sent for session synchronization messages?
9. What is a redundancy group?
10. Why is the control port so important?

Chapter Review Answers

1. The control link is used for the two route engines to talk to each other. The kernels synchronize state between each other, the REs talk to the data plane on the other node, and jsrpd communicates. The jsrpd daemon sends heartbeat messages to validate that the other side is up and running.
2. Heartbeats are sent by the jsrpd daemon to ensure that the remote node is up and healthy. The heartbeats pass through the data planes of both devices and back to the other side. This validates the entire path end to end, making sure it is able to pass traffic. In the event that traffic needs to be forwarded between the two nodes, it is done over the data link. Last but not least, the data link is used to synchronize RTO messages between the two chassis. RTOs are real-time objects that are used in the maintenance of the state between the two devices. This includes session creation and session closing messages.
3. Node-specific information is configured using Junos groups. This was one of the fundamental features that was created in Junos. Junos groups can also be thought of as configuration templates or snippets. They can be used to do such things as enabling logging on all firewall policies and configuring specific snippets of information. Using Junos groups where it makes sense simplifies the administration of the SRX and makes reading the configuration easier.
4. When using dynamic routing the graceful restart feature should be enabled. It allows the data plane to keep dynamic routes active if the control plane fails over. It also allows for other routers that surround the SRX to assist it during a control plane failover.
5. The two most important commands are `show chassis cluster status` and `show chassis cluster statistics`. This will allow for the current state of the cluster and the current status of communication between the two nodes. Anyone who is administering a cluster will use these two commands the most.
6. The SRX utilized code from the TX Series products. The TX Series are some of the largest and most scalable routing products in the world.

7. The data center SRXs support unified in-service software upgrades. This feature allows for an automatic upgrade of the backup node without impacting network availability.
8. Session synchronization messages are not acknowledged. This would take additional time and resources away from the processors by forcing the processing of an additional message.
9. A redundancy group is a logical collection of objects. It can contain either the control plane (redundancy group 0 only) or interfaces (redundancy group 1+).
10. The control port provides critical communication between the two route engines. If this link is lost, the two REs cannot synchronize the state of the kernels. Because of this, if the control link goes down, the secondary node will go into a disabled state.

CHAPTER 11

Routing

This chapter will show you the Internet Protocol (IP) routing features of Junos for the SRX. IP routing is, very simply, the means by which IP packets are moved across IP networks. This is true whether the network is the global Internet or the smaller IP networks in businesses, schools, and homes.

The SRX is the first platform for which Juniper Networks brought its decade-long experience in IP security from the earlier ScreenOS platforms into the Junos operating system with its equally rich decade of IP routing experience.

Junos was the operating system built for mission-critical IP routing. Junos platforms are deployed at the core of the global Internet and many of the world's largest enterprises. This chapter is not meant to replace the already excellent coverage of Junos's extensive IP routing capabilities in O'Reilly's earlier *Junos Enterprise Routing (http://oreilly.com/catalog/9780596514426/)* by Doug Marschke and Harry Reynolds and *Junos Cookbook (http://oreilly.com/catalog/9780596100148/)* by Aviva Garrett. The goal of this chapter is to offer a solid grounding for network professionals who are new to IP routing in the Junos operating system.

In this chapter you will find all that you'll need to get IP routing up and running on your SRX device. This chapter has seven main sections touching all aspects of IP routing on the SRX:

- How the SRX "routes" IP packets
- Static routing
- Dynamic routing
- Internet peering
- Routing policy
- Routing instances
- Filter-based forwarding

This chapter shows you how to configure IP routing with direct tutorials in the Junos command-line interface (CLI). It also includes case studies at the end of some of the major sections.

How the SRX "Routes" IP Packets

How do you route packets in Junos?

It can seem counterintuitive at first blush, but in Junos terminology, the IP packets passing through a Junos device are not routed. They are *forwarded*. Packet *forwarding* is performed in the SRX's *data plane*. The SRX's data plane makes its forwarding decisions via a *forwarding table*.

Forwarding Tables

A forwarding table contains relatively simple information, just the essentials to decide where a packet needs to be sent. An entry in the table identifies a destination and how it will be reached. That's it.

Here you examine a small IP forwarding table in the Junos CLI with the `show route forwarding-table` command:

```
jamesq@srx5800-1> show route forwarding-table
Destination    Type RtRef Next hop          Type Index NhRef Netifn
default        user     1 0:21:59:80:d0:2  ucst   357     4 ge-11/0/5.0
```

The `default` forwarding table entry directs traffic to a next hop Ethernet Media Access Control (MAC) address of `0:21:59:80:d0:2` reachable via the `ge-11/0/5.0` interface. Every packet with a destination IP address which is otherwise unknown in the forwarding table will have its Ethernet layer destination address rewritten to `0:21:59:80:d0:2` before being transmitted out the `ge-2/0/1.0` interface (should it successfully pass the SRX's security inspection, of course).

Not all entries in the forwarding table will lead to literal packet forwarding actions. The next entry in this same forwarding table shows an action for discarding packets (`dcsd`) destined to an address of `0.0.0.0/32`:

```
0.0.0.0/32         perm     0                         dscd     34      1
```

In other words, all packets with a literal `0.0.0.0` in the destination IP address field will be silently dropped.

This next series of forwarding table entries is different in that they refer to an IP network configured on an actual logical interface of the SRX itself:

```
10.2.1.0/24    intf  0                   rslv   593     1 ge-11/0/5.0
10.2.1.0/32    dest  0 10.2.1.0         recv   591     1 ge-11/0/5.0
10.2.1.10/32   dest  0 0:21:59:80:d0:2   ucst    613     3 ge-11/0/5.0
10.2.1.11/32   intf  0 10.2.1.11        locl   592     2
```

```
10.2.1.11/32   dest  0 10.2.1.11       locl  592    2
10.2.1.255/32  dest  0 10.2.1.255      bcst  590    1 ge-11/0/5.0
```

The IP address configured on the SRX's `ge-11/0/5.0` logical interface (`intf`) is `10.2.1.11/32` which is thereby considered local (`locl`) to the SRX itself. The larger IP network on this interface (`intf`) is the `10.2.1.0/24` prefix. The other addresses residing within this subnet must be resolved (`rslv`) through Address Resolution Protocol (ARP). One neighboring IP address (`10.2.1.10/32`) has completed successful ARP resolution pointing it to a unicast (`ucst`) Ethernet MAC address of `0:21:59:80:d0:2` (reachable out of the same `ge-11/0/5.0` logical interface, of course). The broadcast (`bcst`) address for this network is `10.2.1.255/32`.

And last in this forwarding table, you find a unicast (`ucst`) entry for `10.32.1.1/32` that is reachable via the neighboring `10.2.1.10` device reachable on logical interface `ge-11/0/5.0`:

```
10.32.1.1/32      user     0 10.2.1.10     ucst    613    3 ge-11/0/5.0
```

Like the default route earlier, this is known as a `user` entry in the forwarding table. Unlike the interface entries that are known via the Junos kernel itself, these `user` entries are created by the Junos routing protocol daemon (RPD) process which exists in Junos's "userland" from an operating system perspective.

As depicted in Figure 11-1, `rpd` is a *control plane* process. It is responsible for all IP routing in Junos. It populates the *routing table* that is synthesized to create the *forwarding table* that will ultimately be pushed down to the *data plane*. The tools for `rpd` to create these routing tables and forwarding tables are the subject of this chapter.

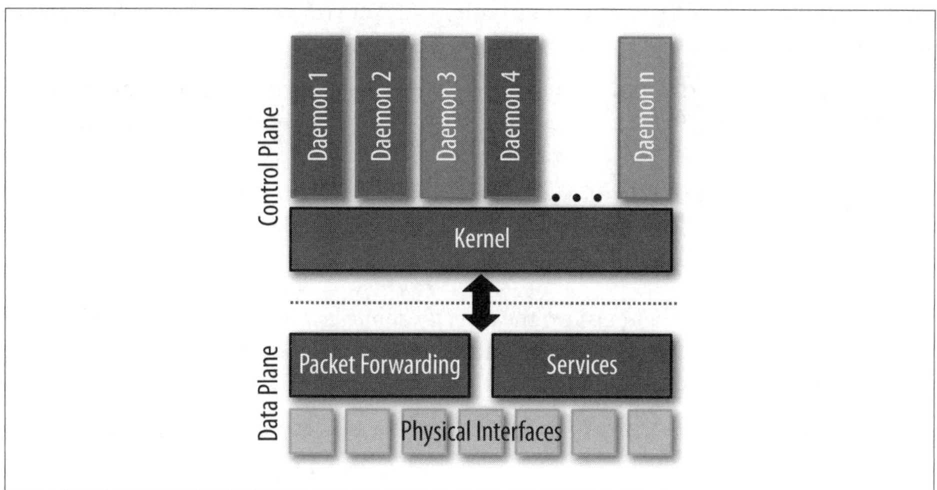

Figure 11-1. Junos control plane and data plane

IP Routing

Now that you've explored the IP forwarding table, you investigate the IP routing table with a `show route` command:

```
jamesq@SRX5800-1> show route

inet.0: 18 destinations, 4 routes (4 active, 0 holddown, 0 hidden)
Restart Complete
+ = Active Route, - = Last Active, * = Both

0.0.0.0/0          *[Static/5] 2w2d 21:29:27
                    > to 10.2.1.10 via ge-11/0/5.0
```

The primary IPv4 routing table on all Junos devices is called `inet.0`. Above you see that the default route (`0.0.0.0/0`) in the `inet.0` routing table is a `Static` route reachable via the next hop IP address `10.2.1.10` on the `ge-11/0/5.0` logical interface. A *static* route is one that is *statically* created by the network administrator within the local Junos configuration itself. A static route is dependent on the reachability of its next hop IP address. It lacks the resilience of a *dynamic* route that can adapt to changing network conditions.

Unlike forwarding tables, routing tables do not contain any Ethernet layer reachability information. IP routing tables contain only IP reachability information.

As you'll see later, these IP layer routing table entries are translated to the Ethernet layer reachability information of the forwarding table via ARP.

Next you see that the `10.2.1.0/24` prefix configured on the logical interface `ge-11/0/5.0` is called a `Direct` route, though the IP address belonging to the SRX itself on that segment (`10.2.1.11/32`) is called a `Local` route:

```
10.2.1.0/24      *[Direct/0] 2w0d 22:19:31
                      > via ge-11/0/5.0
10.2.1.11/32     *[Local/0] 2w2d 21:27:28
                        Local via ge-11/0/5.0
```

`Direct` routes are those that exist on the *directly connected* interfaces of the SRX. They do not belong to the SRX itself. `Local` routes are the entries pointing to the IP addresses owned by the SRX.

Finally, you see that the remaining `10.32.1.1/32` entry is from the *dynamic routing protocol* `IS-IS`:

```
10.32.1.1/32         *[IS-IS/15] 00:49:17, metric 10
                    > to 10.2.1.10 via ge-11/0/5.0
```

Dynamic routing protocols provide a far more resilient means of IP routing. Dynamic routing works through the continuous exchange of IP reachability information between neighboring IP network devices, also known as *IP routers*.

As the SRX is built on the Junos operating system, every SRX device has the capability to function as a very powerful IP router. Junos for the SRX supports the three most common dynamic interior gateway protocols (IGPs): Open Shortest Path First (OSPF), Intermediate System-to-Intermediate System (IS-IS), and Routing Information Protocol (RIP). IGPs are most often used to exchange IP reachability information within a single organization's network. IGPs assume a common level of trust for the IP routing information exchanged between routers within the IGP's domain.

Junos for the SRX also supports Border Gateway Protocol (BGP). BGP is the protocol used around the world for *Internet peering* between organizations. BGP assumes no trust between organizations and so it comes with a powerful complement of tools for controlling the propagation of IP routes.

Asymmetric Routing

One last key concept to note about integrating the SRX into complex routing environments is how easily it copes with *asymmetric routing*. As depicted in Figure 11-2, asymmetric routing occurs when one direction of an IP conversation traverses a different path than the return direction.

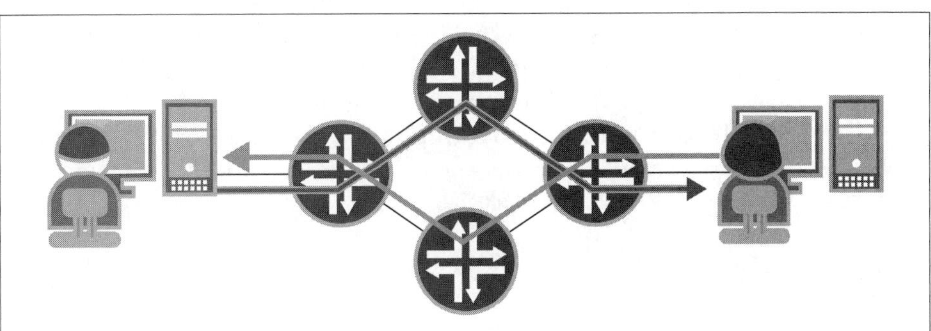

Figure 11-2. Asymmetric routing

Traditional security devices were not built to cope with such complex routed environments. Their packet handling would rigidly enforce symmetric packet flow. They would simply drop the return traffic for any flows similar to the one depicted in Figure 11-2.

The SRX is a fundamentally different type of device. It is built to solve *both* your security needs *and* your routing needs.

The SRX works flawlessly in asymmetrically routed environments. Return traffic for a flow can come back through literally *any* interface and work perfectly and with fully stateful security enforcement intact. In fact, the SRX's flexibility is even greater than this. For the SRX, traffic need not even return on the same *chassis*. In the high availability (HA) clusters that we will explore in the next chapter, a flow's traffic may return on any interface in *either* chassis and continue to work flawlessly with fully stateful security inspection. The SRX is that powerful.

The SRX still enforces *security policy* in asymmetrically routed environments. Although return traffic may return through any interfaces, those interfaces must be configured in the correct *security zone* to statefully match the existing security policy enforcement.

Address Resolution Protocol (ARP)

ARP is the glue that ties IP addresses to Ethernet MAC addresses, thereby making it possible for IP packets to traverse Ethernet links. At its most basic level, ARP consists of, first, an Ethernet layer broadcast *request* for a mapping between an IP address and an Ethernet MAC address and, second, the Ethernet layer *unicast* reply containing the requested mapping information.

Before leaving this section, you examine an ARP table with the `show arp` command in the Junos CLI:

```
jamesq@SRX5800-1> show arp
MAC Address       Address         Name                Interface     Flags
00:21:59:80:d0:02 10.2.1.10       hello.jnpr.net      ge-11/0/5.0   none
```

The preceding ARP table output shows that the IP address `10.2.1.10` has been successfully resolved to an Ethernet layer MAC address of `00:21:59:80:d0:02` on the `ge-11/0/5.0` logical interface. This ARP table mapping makes it possible for this SRX device to transmit IP packets destined to `10.2.1.10` or with a next hop of `10.2.1.10` out of the `ge-11/0/5.0` logical interface with the correct Ethernet header containing the destination MAC address `00:21:59:80:d0:02`.

Static Routing

Static routing is the simplest and most basic form of IP routing. A static route consists of a destination IP prefix and a next hop IP address through which it can be reached. As shown in Figure 11-3, static routes are literally configured by the administrator on the local SRX device itself.

When you need a quick solution for getting routes up on an SRX device, static routing is the easiest one available.

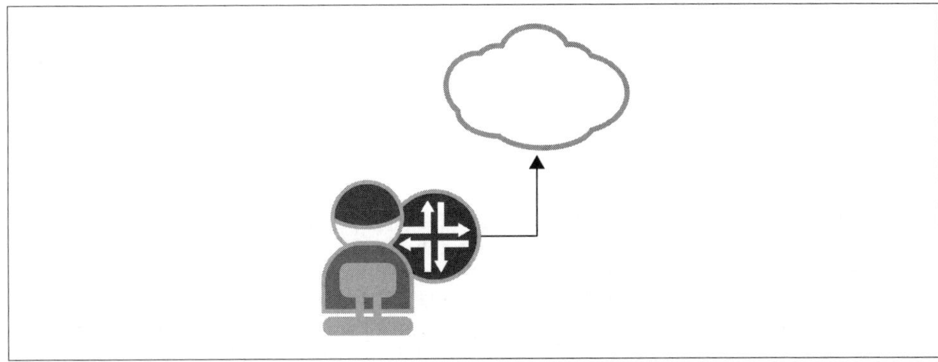

Figure 11-3. Network administrator configures static route

Creating a Static Route

In the Junos CLI configuration that follows, you will create a new static route. You enter configuration mode and move to the static route configuration hierarchy using the `edit` command:

```
jamesq@SRX5800-1> edit
Entering configuration mode

[edit]
jamesq@SRX5800-1# edit routing-options static
```

You access the CLI help for the static route hierarchy:

```
[edit routing-options static]
jamesq@SRX5800-1# set ?
Possible completions:
+ apply-groups          Groups from which to inherit configuration data
+ apply-groups-except   Don't inherit configuration data from these groups
> defaults              Global route options
  rib-group             Routing table group
> route                 Static route
```

And you find the `route` option for creating a static route.

You begin building a `route` toward the 10.0.0.0/0 network (which you smartly abbreviate `10/0`, a well-understood abbreviation for the Junos CLI) and examine the CLI help:

```
[edit routing-options static]
jamesq@SRX5800-1# set route 10/0 ?
Possible completions:
  active                Remove inactive route from forwarding table
+ apply-groups          Groups from which to inherit configuration data
+ apply-groups-except   Don't inherit configuration data from these groups
> as-path               Autonomous system path
  backup-pe-group       Multicast source redundancy group
> bfd-liveness-detection  Bidirectional Forwarding Detection (BFD) options
> color                 Color (preference) value
```

```
> color2                Color (preference) value 2
+ community             BGP community identifier
  discard               Drop packets to destination; send no ICMP unreachables
  install               Install route into forwarding table
> metric                Metric value
> metric2               Metric value 2
> metric3               Metric value 3
> metric4               Metric value 4
+ next-hop              Next hop to destination
  next-table            Next hop to another table
  no-install            Don't install route into forwarding table
  no-readvertise        Don't mark route as eligible to be readvertised
  no-resolve            Don't allow resolution of indirectly connected next hops
  no-retain             Don't always keep route in forwarding table
  passive               Retain inactive route in forwarding table
> preference            Preference value
> preference2           Preference value 2
> qualified-next-hop    Next hop with qualifiers
  readvertise           Mark route as eligible to be readvertised
  receive               Install a receive route for the destination
  reject                Drop packets to destination; send ICMP unreachables
  resolve               Allow resolution of indirectly connected next hops
  retain                Always keep route in forwarding table
> tag                   Tag string
> tag2                  Tag string 2
```

And here in this exhaustive list of static routing options you see a hint of the power of the IP routing tool set in Junos. Junos offers no fewer than 32 options for the configuration of a "simple" static route.

Fortunately, it is not necessary to understand all of these fine gradations of options because, for your purposes, you need just one, the `next-hop`:

```
[edit routing-options static]
jamesq@SRX5800-1# set route 10/8 next-hop 10.2.1.100
```

And before you even realized it, you have succeeded in creating your very own static route in the Junos configuration!

You view your results with the `show` command:

```
[edit routing-options static]
jamesq@SRX5800-1# show | compare
[edit routing-options static]
   route 0.0.0.0/ { ... }
+  route 10.0.0.0/8 next-hop 10.2.1.100;
```

You `commit` the configuration to the SRX:

```
[edit routing-options static]
james@SRX5800-1# commit and-quit
configuration check succeeds
commit complete
Exiting configuration mode

james@SRX5800-1>
```

Verifying a Static Route

Now that you have a new static route pointing the `10.0.0.0/8` prefix to the next hop neighboring router, you test connectivity to a known `10.1.1.1` device with the `ping` command:

```
jamesq@SRX5800-1> ping 10.1.1.1
PING 10.1.1.1 (10.1.1.1): 56 data bytes
^C
--- 10.1.1.1 ping statistics ---
4 packets transmitted, 0 packets received, 100% packet loss
```

But the `ping` test fails! What could have happened?

You stay calm and check your new configuration in the `inet.0` routing table with the `show route 10.1.1.1` command:

```
jamesq@srx5800-1> show route 10.1.1.1

inet.0: 19 destinations, 22 routes (19 active, 0 holddown, 0 hidden)
Restart Complete
+ = Active Route, - = Last Active, * = Both

10.0.0.0/8         *[Static/5] 00:07:01
                    > to 10.2.1.100 via ge-11/0/5.0
```

Excellent! There's the `10.0.0.0/8` static route entry in the `inet.0` table as expected. Good stuff.

But how does this routing table entry translate to the actual forwarding table?

You check with the `show route forwarding-table` command:

```
jamesq@srx5800-1> show route forwarding-table
Destination  Type RtRef Next hop          Type Index NhRef Netifn
default      user     1 0:21:59:80:d0:2 ucst    357     4 ge-11/0/5.0
10.0.0.0/8   user     0 10.2.1.100        hold   601     3 ge-11/0/5.0
```

That's not what you want to see. The `10.0.0.0/8` forwarding table entry points to the `10.2.1.100` as the next hop, but it mysteriously says `hold`. You continue down the forwarding table and find that the next hop for the `10.2.1.100/32` also says `hold`.

```
10.2.1.0/24    intf  0                    rslv   593      1 ge-11/0/5.0
10.2.1.0/32    dest  0 10.2.1.0           recv   591      1 ge-11/0/5.0
10.2.1.10/32   dest  0 0:21:59:80:d0:2    ucst   613      3 ge-11/0/5.0
10.2.1.11/32   intf  0 10.2.1.11          locl   592      2
10.2.1.100/32  dest  0 10.2.1.100         hold   601      3 ge-11/0/5.0
```

That's not right. There should be an Ethernet MAC address as the next hop for `10.2.1.100`.

Wait! Of course!

You quickly check the ARP table:

```
jamesq@SRX5800-1> show arp
MAC Address       Address         Name            Interface      Flags
```

```
00:21:59:80:d0:02 10.2.1.10    hello.jnpr.net    ge-11/0/5.0    none
Total entries: 1

jamesq@SRX5800-1>
```

Just as expected, there's no ARP entry for `10.2.1.100`.

Oops! It was all just a typo. The next hop IP address for the static route should have been `10.2.1.10` instead!

Time to fix the mistake:

```
jamesq@SRX5800-1> edit

[edit]
jamesq@SRX5800-1# edit routing-options static route 10/8

[edit routing-options static route 10.0.0.0/8]
jamesq@SRX5800-1# show
next-hop 10.2.1.100;
```

There it is—the fat-fingered next hop IP address!

You remove the error with the `delete` command:

```
[edit routing-options static route 10.0.0.0/8]
jamesq@SRX5800-1# delete
Delete everything under this level? [yes,no] (no) yes
```

And then `set` the correct next hop to `10.2.1.10`:

```
[edit routing-options static route 10.0.0.0/8]
james@SRX5800-1# set next-hop 10.2.1.10
```

You check the configuration with the `show` command:

```
james@SRX5800-1# show | compare
[edit routing-options static]
     route 172.19.100.176/32 { ... }
-    route 10.0.0.0/8 next-hop 10.2.1.100;
+    route 10.0.0.0/8 next-hop 10.2.1.10;
```

And `commit` your changes:

```
[edit routing-options static]
james@SRX5800-1# commit and-quit
configuration check succeeds
commit complete
Exiting configuration mode

james@SRX5800-1>
```

You test again with the `ping` command:

```
james@SRX5800-1> ping 10.1.1.1
PING 10.1.1.1 (10.1.1.1): 56 data bytes
64 bytes from 10.1.1.1: icmp_seq=0 ttl=64 time=2.706 ms
64 bytes from 10.1.1.1: icmp_seq=1 ttl=64 time=2.512 ms
64 bytes from 10.1.1.1: icmp_seq=2 ttl=64 time=3.035 ms
```

```
^C
--- 10.1.1.1 ping statistics ---
3 packets transmitted, 3 packets received, 0% packet loss
round-trip min/avg/max/stddev = 2.512/2.751/3.035/0.216 ms

james@SRX5800-1>
```

Success!

As you can see, static routing is very susceptible to human fallibility. It's equally susceptible to *network* fallibility. That's why it is time to move on to dynamic routing where the routers can use their own smarts.

Dynamic Routing

In the simplest terms, dynamic routing serves exactly the same purpose as static routing. It associates destination IP prefixes with the next hop IP addresses through which they can be reached, thereby allowing the construction of forwarding table entries for reaching them.

But dynamic routing is different from static routing in that it is based not on static configuration, but on the dynamic interplay of *routing protocols* across a live IP network, as shown in Figure 11-4.

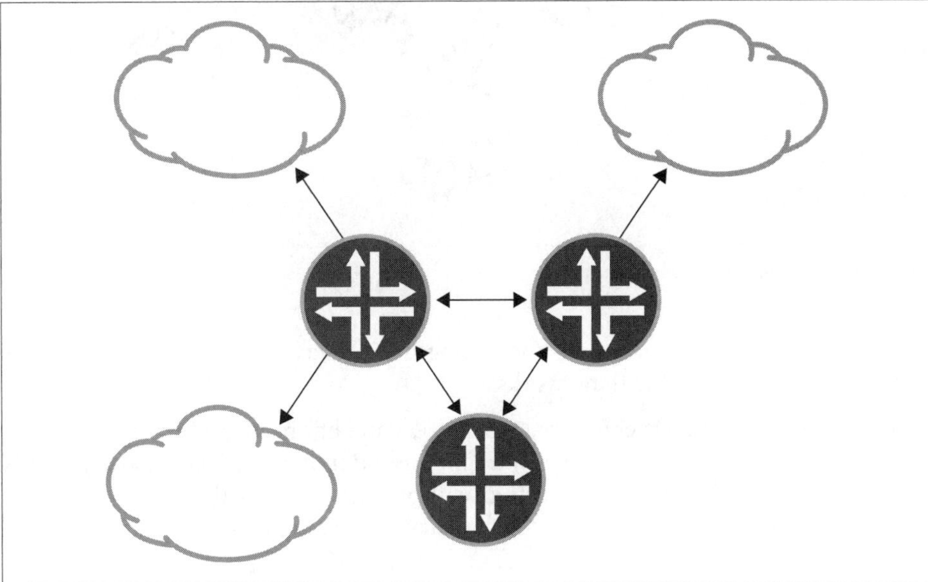

Figure 11-4. Dynamic routing communication

This dynamic interplay is what makes dynamic routing so much more powerful and resilient in the real world. Routing protocols continually exchange and update routing information between IP routing devices as network conditions change.

Real networks are not predictable or static. Devices fail. Connections fail. Whole networks fail. When these unpredictable events occur, network administrators are held accountable by their organizations. This is why dynamic routing is so important.

Where a simple static route may easily (and unknowingly) point toward an unusable network path, a dynamic route has the power to change through newly learned information, as shown in Figure 11-5.

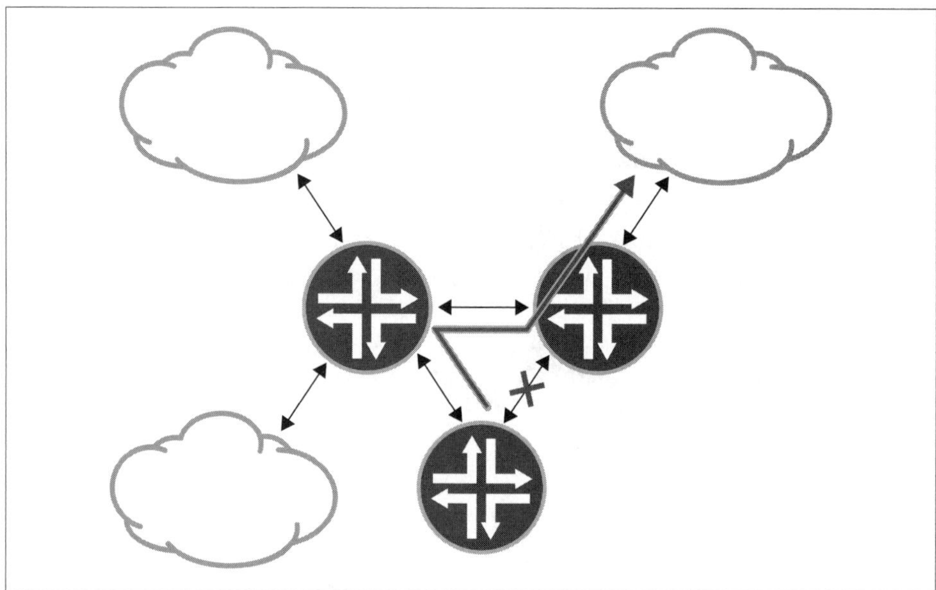

Figure 11-5. Dynamic routing convergence

This simple concept of dynamically converging around network failures is fundamental to building highly available IP networks.

Dynamic routing is, however, a very large subject and has been the basis for innumerable books, including the excellent *Junos Enterprise Routing* and *Junos Cookbook* publications mentioned earlier. This section will provide you just the taste of dynamic routing that you'll need to get your SRX device up and running in a dynamically routed IP network.

Configuring OSPF Routing

Open Shortest Path First (OSPF) is the most commonly used dynamic routing protocol in modern IP networks. It is an IGP in that an OSPF routing domain is typically built within just one organization's network (in contrast to *exterior* protocols such as BGP which are built for peering between organizations).

Figure 11-6 shows an OSPF topology overlaying Organization-XYZ's internal IP networks.

OSPF is a *link-state* routing protocol in that it is designed to flood *link-state advertisements* (LSAs) between all routers within an OSPF *area* (such as the OSPF area drawn in Figure 11-6). These LSAs contain all of the local routing information from each OSPF router in the area, including the IP addressing for each of a router's local interfaces.

All routers within an OSPF area form a common view of their network topology through this exchange of LSAs and through the creation of a common and synchronized LSA database. The *Shortest Path First* (SPF) in the name OSPF refers to the algorithm used by OSPF routers for computing actual IP routes from the information in the LSA database.

Although OSPF is a complex and powerful routing protocol that is largely beyond the scope of this book, a simple OSPF configuration can be constructed very easily.

In the Junos CLI configuration that follows, you will establish a basic OSPF adjacency joining your SRX to an OSPF routing domain. You enter configuration mode with the `edit` command:

```
jamesq@SRX5800-1> edit
Entering configuration mode
```

And move to the OSPF configuration hierarchy:

```
[edit]
jamesq@SRX5800-1# edit protocols ospf
```

You access the CLI help for the OSPF hierarchy:

```
[edit protocols ospf]
jamesq@SRX5800-1# set ?
Possible completions:
+ apply-groups         Groups from which to inherit configuration data
+ apply-groups-except  Don't inherit configuration data from these groups
> area                 Configure an OSPF area
> backup-spf-options   Configure options for backup SPF
> database-protection  Configure database protection attributes
  disable              Disable OSPF
+ export               Export policy
  external-preference  Preference of external routes
> graceful-restart     Configure graceful restart attributes
+ import               Import policy (for external routes or setting priority)
  no-nssa-abr          Disable full NSSA functionality at ABR
  no-rfc-1583          Disable RFC1583 compatibility
> overload             Set the overload mode (repel transit traffic)
  preference           Preference of internal routes
  prefix-export-limit  Maximum number of prefixes that can be exported (0..4294967295)
  reference-bandwidth  Bandwidth for calculating metric defaults (9600..1000000000000)
  rib-group            Routing table group for importing OSPF routes
```

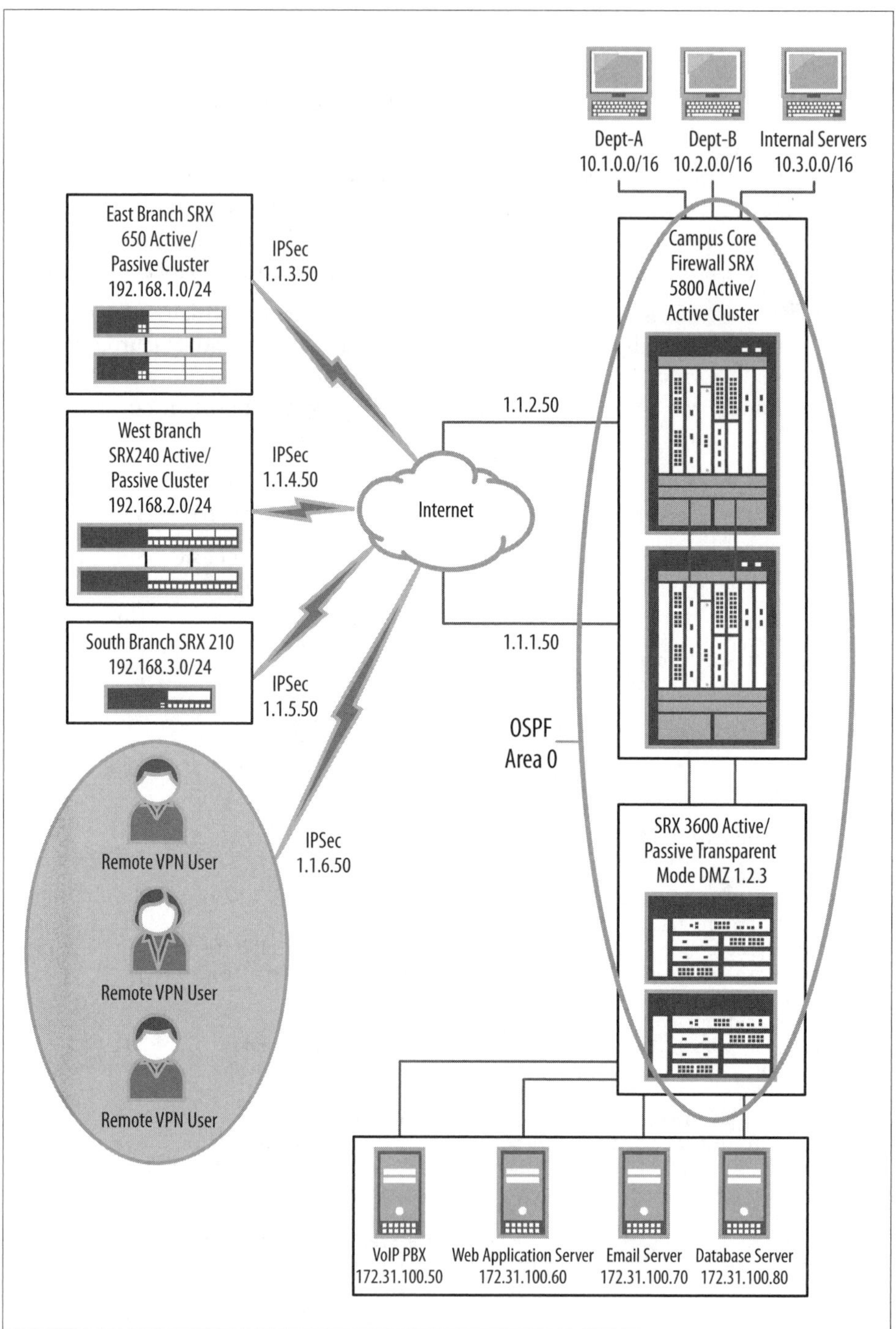

Figure 11-6. Organization-XYZ's OSPF routing topology

```
> spf-options          Configure options for SPF
> topology             Topology parameters
> traceoptions         Trace options for OSPF
> traffic-engineering  Configure traffic engineering attributes
```

Again, Junos shows itself replete with tools for the manipulation of IP routing. But fortunately just a few of these knobs are necessary for your basic OSPF network. It will be enough to simply configure the relevant logical interfaces within an OSPF **area** stanza.

Here, in one command, you both create an OSPF link-state **area 0** (as shown in Figure 11-6) and you place the **ge-11/0/5.0** logical interface into this new area:

```
[edit protocols ospf]
jamesq@SRX5800-1# set area 0 interface ge-11/0/5.0
```

Area 0 is the most common OSPF area. In a single area OSPF network topology (such as the one you are building here), any area number is allowed. Just make sure you match your OSPF area configuration for each SRX interface to the OSPF area that is used by the neighboring OSPF devices (with which the SRX will need to match areas to form successful OSPF neighbor adjacencies).

Note that in a multi-area OSPF topology (which is beyond the scope of this book), there must be at least one **area 0** acting as a *backbone* area interconnecting all of the other OSPF areas. A multi-area OSPF topology is impossible without at least one area numbered zero.

Adding the logical interface **ge-11/0/5.0** to OSPF **area 0** causes OSPF to do two things:

- It adds the IP prefixes configured on interface **ge-11/0/5.0** to the OSPF Router LSA it creates and floods across the OSPF area.
- It begins transmitting OSPF Hello packets out of interface **ge-11/0/5.0** while likewise listening for Hello packets on the same interface. In this way, the SRX device seeks an OSPF *adjacency* with any neighboring OSPF devices sharing the same Layer 2 network.

As a matter of best practice, you also place your loopback as a passive interface in the OSPF area:

```
[edit protocols ospf]
jamesq@SRX5800-1# set area 0 interface lo0.0 passive
```

By including the loopback interface in the OSPF area, you ensure that the SRX's router identification for OSPF is derived from the loopback IP address that exists virtually within the SRX. This is preferable to deriving OSPF router identification from an IP address configured on a real interface. If the router identification were derived from a real interface, that interface could go down, forcing the identification to change and creating unnecessary OSPF churn as the area reconverged around the seemingly "new" OSPF device with its new router identification.

Also note the passive knob configured on the loopback interface. As OSPF would ordinarily attempt to form adjacencies on all interfaces configured in an area, this knob tells OSPF not to bother transmitting Hello packets or listening for them on this loopback interface which exists only virtually within the SRX.

Your basic OSPF network configuration is now complete. You examine it with the show command:

```
[edit protocols ospf]
root@SRX5800-1# show
area 0.0.0.0 {
    interface ge-11/0/5.0;
    interface lo0.0 passive;
}
```

And finally commit your new configuration:

```
[edit protocols ospf]
james@SRX5800-1# commit and-quit
configuration check succeeds
commit complete
Exiting configuration mode

james@SRX5800-1>
```

Now that the SRX has a live OSPF configuration, it is time for you to confirm that it has successfully formed an OSPF adjacency with the neighboring OSPF router on the ge-11/0/5.0 interface. You investigate with the show ospf neighbor command:

```
james@SRX5800-1> show ospf neighbor

james@SRX5800-1>
```

That's not what you expect to see! There are no OSPF neighbors visible to the SRX. It's time to troubleshoot the new OSPF configuration.

Troubleshooting OSPF adjacencies

You confirm that OSPF is running on the ge-11/0/5.0 interface with the show ospf interface command:

```
jamesq@SRX5800-1> show ospf interface
Interface     State   Area          DR ID          BDR ID       Nbrs
ge-11/0/5.0   DR      0.0.0.0       198.18.16.2    0.0.0.0         0
lo0.0         DRother 0.0.0.0       0.0.0.0        0.0.0.0         0
```

That's good! OSPF is running on the configured interfaces. But there are no neighbors on ge-11/0/5.0. What could the problem be?

It's time to dig deeper. You go back into configuration mode to set up OSPF traceoptions for some live troubleshooting on the SRX:

```
jamesq@srx5800-1> edit
Entering configuration mode
```

```
[edit]
jamesq@SRX5800-1# edit protocols ospf
```

After entering the OSPF hierarchy, you examine CLI help for `traceoptions`:

```
[edit protocols ospf]
jamesq@SRX5800-1# set traceoptions ?
Possible completions:
+ apply-groups         Groups from which to inherit configuration data
+ apply-groups-except  Don't inherit configuration data from these groups
> file                 Trace file options
> flag                 Tracing parameters
```

A complete OSPF `traceoptions` configuration requires both a `file` and a `flag` configuration. The `flag` defines what troubleshooting information will be collected. The `file` specifies where the information will be written in the */var/log* directory.

You examine the CLI help for the `flag` configuration:

```
[edit protocols ospf]
jamesq@SRX5800-1# set traceoptions flag ?
Possible completions:
  all                  Trace everything
  database-description  Trace database description packets
  error                Trace errored packets
  event                Trace OSPF state machine events
  flooding             Trace LSA flooding
  general              Trace general events
  graceful-restart     Trace graceful restart
  hello                Trace hello packets
  lsa-ack              Trace LSA acknowledgment packets
  lsa-analysis         Trace LSA analysis
  lsa-request          Trace LSA request packets
  lsa-update           Trace LSA update packets
  normal               Trace normal events
  nsr-synchronization  Trace NSR synchronization events
  packet-dump          Dump the contents of selected packet types
  packets              Trace all OSPF packets
  policy               Trace policy processing
  route                Trace routing information
  spf                  Trace SPF calculations
  state                Trace state transitions
  task                 Trace routing protocol task processing
  timer                Trace routing protocol timer processing
```

Again Junos is overflowing with options! But where are you to begin troubleshooting?

There it is! You need to figure out why the OSPF `hello` packet exchange is not leading to an adjacency:

```
[edit protocols ospf]
jamesq@SRX5800-1# set traceoptions flag hello
```

Now you examine CLI help for the `file` option:

```
[edit protocols ospf]
jamesq@SRX5800-1# set traceoptions file ?
```

```
Possible completions:
  <filename>            Name of file in which to write trace information
  files                 Maximum number of trace files (2..1000)
  no-world-readable     Don't allow any user to read the log file
  size                  Maximum trace file size (10240..4294967295)
  world-readable        Allow any user to read the log file
```

And you point the OSPF trace data to the *ospftrace* file in the */var/log* directory:

```
[edit protocols ospf]
jamesq@SRX5800-1# set traceoptions file ospftrace
```

And `commit` your changes:

```
[edit protocols ospf]
jamesq@SRX5800-1# commit and-quit
configuration check succeeds
commit complete
Exiting configuration mode
```

After waiting a minute for your new `ospftrace` logfile to collect some data, you check out the results with the `show log` command:

```
jamesq@srx5800-1> show log ospftrace
Apr 11 15:40:21 trace_on: Tracing to "/var/log/ospftrace" started
Apr 11 15:40:21.821379 OSPF sent Hello 10.2.1.11 -> 224.0.0.5
(ge-11/0/5.0 IFL 80 area 0.0.0.0)
Apr 11 15:40:21.821444   Version 2, length 44, ID 198.18.16.2, area 0.0.0.0
Apr 11 15:40:21.821454   mask 255.255.255.0, hello_ivl 10, opts 0x2, prio 128
Apr 11 15:40:21.821461   dead_ivl 40, DR 10.2.1.11, BDR 0.0.0.0
Apr 11 15:40:21.822530 OSPF sent Hello 10.2.1.11 -> 224.0.0.5
(ge-11/0/5.0 IFL 80 area 0.0.0.0)
Apr 11 15:40:21.822558   Version 2, length 44, ID 198.18.16.2, area 0.0.0.0
Apr 11 15:40:21.822567   mask 255.255.255.0, hello_ivl 10, opts 0x2, prio 128
Apr 11 15:40:21.822574   dead_ivl 40, DR 10.2.1.11, BDR 0.0.0.0
Apr 11 15:40:30.057636 OSPF periodic xmit from 10.2.1.11 to 224.0.0.5
(IFL 80 area 0.0.0.0)
Apr 11 15:40:38.222314 OSPF periodic xmit from 10.2.1.11 to 224.0.0.5
(IFL 80 area 0.0.0.0)
Apr 11 15:40:45.819123 OSPF periodic xmit from 10.2.1.11 to 224.0.0.5
(IFL 80 area 0.0.0.0)
Apr 11 15:40:55.678602 OSPF periodic xmit from 10.2.1.11 to 224.0.0.5
(IFL 80 area 0.0.0.0)
Apr 11 15:41:03.862275 OSPF periodic xmit from 10.2.1.11 to 224.0.0.5
(IFL 80 area 0.0.0.0)
Apr 11 15:41:13.611732 OSPF periodic xmit from 10.2.1.11 to 224.0.0.5
(IFL 80 area 0.0.0.0)
Apr 11 15:41:22.080391 OSPF periodic xmit from 10.2.1.11 to 224.0.0.5
(IFL 80 area 0.0.0.0)
```

The SRX is sending OSPF Hello packets every few seconds out the `ge-11/0/5.0` interface to the `224.0.0.5` multicast address (the address used for speaking to OSPF routers). But it never sees any neighbor Hello packets come back.

Why would the SRX *control plane* not receive OSPF packets being sent by a neighboring OSPF router on an interface correctly configured for OSPF?

That's it! The SRX isn't just a router. It's also a *security* device!

OSPF security zone configuration

You confirm that interface `ge-11/0/5.0` is in the `trust` zone with the `show security zones` command:

```
jamesq@SRX5800-1> show security zones trust
Security zone: trust
  Send reset for non-SYN session TCP packets: Off
  Policy configurable: Yes
  Interfaces bound: 3
  Interfaces:
    ge-11/0/5.0
```

All data plane interfaces on an SRX device must be configured in `security zones`. The OSPF-speaking `ge-11/0/5.0` interface you are using here is no different.

You jump back into configuration mode to complete your SRX `zones` configuration for support of OSPF:

```
jamesq@SRX5800-1> edit
Entering configuration mode

[edit]
jamesq@SRX5800-1# edit security zones
```

You check the CLI help for the `security zones` hierarchy:

```
[edit security zones]
jamesq@SRX5800-1# set security-zone trust ?
Possible completions:
  <[Enter]>            Execute this command
> address-book         Address book entries
  application-tracking  Enable Application tracking support for this zone
+ apply-groups         Groups from which to inherit configuration data
+ apply-groups-except  Don't inherit configuration data from these groups
> host-inbound-traffic  Allowed system services & protocols
> interfaces           Interfaces that are part of this zone
  screen               Name of ids option object applied to the zone
  tcp-rst              Send RST for TCP SYN packet not matching session
  |                    Pipe through a command
```

There it is. The `host-inbound-traffic` configuration option in the `zones` configuration controls the communication of routing protocols with the SRX control plane. That was blocking OSPF!

You look at the CLI help for the `host-inbound-traffic protocols` configuration:

```
[edit security zones]
jamesq@SRX5800-1# set security-zone trust host-inbound-traffic protocols ?
Possible completions:
  all                  All protocols
  bfd                  Bidirectional Forwarding Detection
  bgp                  Border Gateway Protocol
  dvmrp                Distance Vector Multicast Routing Protocol
```

```
igmp                 Internet Group Management Protocol
msdp                 Multicast Source Discovery Protocol
ndp                  Enable Network Discovery Protocol
nhrp                 Next Hop Resolution Protocol
ospf                 Open Shortest Path First
ospf3                Open Shortest Path First version 3
pgm                  Pragmatic General Multicast
pim                  Protocol Independent Multicast
rip                  Routing Information Protocol
ripng                Routing Information Protocol next generation
sap                  Session Announcement Protocol
vrrp                 Virtual Router Redundancy Protocol
```

There are options to permit traffic for every major control plane protocol, and even the option to permit `all` of them at once. You use the `set` command to add configuration for permitting OSPF:

```
[edit security zones]
jamesq@SRX5800-1# set security-zone trust host-inbound-traffic protocols ospf
```

And `commit` the new configuration:

```
[edit protocols ospf]
james@SRX5800-1# commit and-quit
configuration check succeeds
commit complete
Exiting configuration mode
```

Time to check out the *ospftrace* file again with the `show log` command:

```
jamesq@srx5800-1> show log ospftrace | last
Apr 11 16:05:37.932833 OSPF rcvd Hello 10.2.1.10 -> 224.0.0.5
(ge-11/0/5.0 IFL 80 area 0.0.0.0)
Apr 11 16:05:37.932892  Version 2, length 48, ID 10.32.1.1, area 0.0.0.0
Apr 11 16:05:37.932899  checksum 0x0, authtype 0
Apr 11 16:05:37.932908  mask 255.255.255.0, hello_ivl 10, opts 0x2, prio 128
Apr 11 16:05:37.932943  dead_ivl 40, DR 10.2.1.10, BDR 0.0.0.0
```

Excellent! You're receiving OSPF Hello packets from your neighbor `10.2.1.10`. This is the first step to negotiating a successful OSPF adjacency.

```
Apr 11 16:05:37.934746 OSPF sent Hello 10.2.1.11 -> 224.0.0.5
(ge-11/0/5.0 IFL 80 area 0.0.0.0)
Apr 11 16:05:37.934773  Version 2, length 48, ID 198.18.16.2, area 0.0.0.0
Apr 11 16:05:37.934781  mask 255.255.255.0, hello_ivl 10, opts 0x2, prio 128
Apr 11 16:05:37.934789  dead_ivl 40, DR 10.2.1.11, BDR 0.0.0.0
Apr 11 16:05:37.942947 RPD_OSPF_NBRUP: OSPF neighbor 10.2.1.10
realm ospf-v2 ge-11/0/5.0 area 0.0.0.0) state changed from Init to ExStart due
to 2WayRcvd (event reason: initial DBD packet was received)
Apr 11 16:05:37.943622 OSPF sent Hello 10.2.1.11 -> 224.0.0.5
ge-11/0/5.0 IFL 80 area 0.0.0.0)
Apr 11 16:05:37.943652  Version 2, length 48, ID 198.18.16.2, area 0.0.0.0
Apr 11 16:05:37.943662  mask 255.255.255.0, hello_ivl 10, opts 0x2, prio 128
Apr 11 16:05:37.943669  dead_ivl 40, DR 10.2.1.11, BDR 0.0.0.0
Apr 11 16:05:37.944153 OSPF rcvd Hello 10.2.1.10 -> 224.0.0.5
ge-11/0/5.0 IFL 80 area 0.0.0.0)
Apr 11 16:05:37.944178  Version 2, length 48, ID 10.32.1.1, area 0.0.0.0
```

```
Apr 11 16:05:37.944185   checksum 0x0, authtype 0
Apr 11 16:05:37.944193   mask 255.255.255.0, hello_ivl 10, opts 0x2, prio 128
Apr 11 16:05:37.944200   dead_ivl 40, DR 10.2.1.11, BDR 10.2.1.10
Apr 11 16:05:37.944291 OSPF sent Hello 10.2.1.11 -> 224.0.0.5
ge-11/0/5.0 IFL 80 area 0.0.0.0)
Apr 11 16:05:37.944301   Version 2, length 48, ID 198.18.16.2, area 0.0.0.0
Apr 11 16:05:37.944309   mask 255.255.255.0, hello_ivl 10, opts 0x2, prio 128
Apr 11 16:05:37.944316   dead_ivl 40, DR 10.2.1.11, BDR 10.2.1.10
Apr 11 16:05:37.944364 OSPF sent Hello 10.2.1.11 -> 224.0.0.5 (
ge-11/0/5.0 IFL 80 area 0.0.0.0)
Apr 11 16:05:37.944373   Version 2, length 48, ID 198.18.16.2, area 0.0.0.0
Apr 11 16:05:37.944380   mask 255.255.255.0, hello_ivl 10, opts 0x2, prio 128
Apr 11 16:05:37.944387   dead_ivl 40, DR 10.2.1.11, BDR 10.2.1.10
Apr 11 16:05:38.020642 RPD_OSPF_NBRUP: OSPF neighbor 10.2.1.10 (
realm ospf-v2 ge-11/0/5.0 area 0.0.0.0) state changed from Loading
to Full due to LoadDone (event reason: OSPF loading completed)
```

And there it is! The *ospftrace* file shows a `Full` adjacency with `10.2.1.10` on interface `ge-11/0/5.0`.

For consistency, you go back and check the `show ospf neighbor` command:

```
jamesq@SRX5800-1> show ospf neighbor
Address          Interface              State     ID               Pri  Dead
10.2.1.10      ge-11/0/5.0            Full      10.32.1.1          128    36
```

Great! You quickly see if the SRX is receiving any OSPF routes with the `show route` command:

```
jamesq@SRX5800-1> show route protocol ospf

inet.0: 20 destinations, 23 routes (20 active, 0 holddown, 0 hidden)
Restart Complete
+ = Active Route, - = Last Active, * = Both

10.32.1.1/32         *[OSPF/10] 00:13:15, metric 1
                    > to 10.2.1.10 via ge-11/0/5.0
224.0.0.5/32        *[OSPF/10] 20:42:16, metric 1
                      MultiRecv
```

And there is a new OSPF route for `10.32.1.1/32` pointing to the `10.2.1.10` OSPF neighbor!

You were able to quickly drill down to just the OSPF routes by using the `protocol` option to the `show route` command. Junos comes built with an array of options for filtering routing table output:

```
jamesq@SRX5800-1> show route ?
Possible completions:
  <[Enter]>            Execute this command
  <destination>        IP address and optional prefix length of destination
  active-path          Show active paths
  advertising-protocol  Show information in format intended for
particular routing protocol
  all                  Show all entries, including hidden entries
  aspath-regex         BGP AS path regular expression for entries to match
```

```
  best                  Show longest matching route
  brief                 Display brief output
+ community             Identifier for community (can include wildcards)
  community-name        Name of configured community policy to match
  damping               Show entries subjected to particular kind of route damping
  detail                Display detailed output
  exact                 Show routes that match exactly
  export                Show instance export information
  extensive             Display extensive output
  flow                  Show flow routing information
  forwarding-table      Show entries in all forwarding tables
  hidden                Show hidden entries
  inactive-path         Show inactive paths
  inactive-prefix       Show inactive route destinations
  instance              Show routing instances information
  logical-system        Name of logical system, or 'all'
  martians              Show martian networks
  next-hop              IP address of next hop that is destination for entries
  no-community          Show entries with no associated community
  output                Show entries sent out a particular interface
  private               Show private table routes
  protocol              Name of protocol that is source for entries
  range                 Show all entries in prefix range
  rd-prefix             Route distinguisher with ip prefix (rd:prefix)
  receive-protocol      Show information in format received from
particular routing protocol
  resolution            Show next-hop resolution database
  rib-groups            Show group of routing tables
  snooping              Show routes for multicast snooping
  source-gateway        IP address of source router for entries
  summary               Show routing table statistics
  table                 Name of routing table
  terse                 Display terse output
  |                     Pipe through a command
```

But again, all of the preceding options are for filtering output from the Junos *routing tables*. By examining `show route protocol ospf`, you see the routes that the routing table `inet.0` has accepted from OSPF. But you can also view routing information from the perspective of the OSPF protocol itself with the `show ospf route` command:

```
jamesq@SRX5800-1> show ospf route
Topology default Route Table:

Prefix          Path  Route      NH     Metric NextHop       Nexthop
                Type  Type       Type          Interface     Address/LSP
10.32.1.1       Intra Router     IP          1 ge-11/0/5.0 10.2.1.10
10.32.1.1/32    Intra Network    IP          1 ge-11/0/5.0 10.2.1.10
198.18.16.2/32  Intra Network    IP          0 lo0.0
10.2.1.0/24     Intra Network    IP          1 ge-11/0/5.0
```

And here you see two additional routes for `198.18.16.2/32` (the local SRX's loopback interface IP address) and `10.2.1.0/24` (the network where the SRX has formed the new OSPF adjacency). These are routes that OSPF knows about, but they are not routes that Junos has taken from OSPF.

Rather, Junos views 198.18.16.2/32 as a directly connected interface route:

```
jamesq@SRX5800-1> show route 198.18.16.2/32

inet.0: 20 destinations, 23 routes (20 active, 0 holddown, 0 hidden)
Restart Complete
+ = Active Route, - = Last Active, * = Both

198.18.16.2/32          *[Direct/0] 16:05:21
                        > via lo0.0
```

And 10.2.1.0/24 is likewise viewed as a directly connected interface route but also containing a smaller 10.2.1.11/32 local address within it:

```
jamesq@SRX5800-1> show route 10.2.1.0/24

inet.0: 20 destinations, 23 routes (20 active, 0 holddown, 0 hidden)
Restart Complete
+ = Active Route, - = Last Active, * = Both

10.2.1.0/24       *[Direct/0] 20:59:39
                    > via ge-11/0/5.0
10.2.1.11/32      *[Local/0] 20:59:43
                      Local via ge-11/0/5.0
```

Notice the [Direct/0] designation for both of the routes that superseded OSPF in the routing table. The zero corresponds to the preference that Junos has for that type of route.

As shown in Table 11-1, OSPF internal routes have a preference of 10 where directly connected networks have the better preference of 0 (lower is better). OSPF may know about directly connected networks, but it will never be responsible for contributing them to a Junos routing table.

Table 11-1. Junos routing preferences

Type of route	Default preference
Directly connected network	0
System routes	4
Static	5
OSPF internal route	10
IS-IS Level 1 internal route	15
IS-IS Level 2 internal route	18
Default	20
Redirects	30
Kernel	40
SNMP	50
Router discovery	55

Type of route	Default preference
RIP	100
RIPng	100
PIM	105
DVMRP	110
Routes to interfaces that are down	120
Aggregate	130
OSPF AS external routes	150
IS-IS Level 1 external route	160
IS-IS Level 2 external route	165
BGP	170
MSDP	175

Before leaving the OSPF section, let's examine one advanced command, `show ospf database`:

```
jamesq@SRX5800-1> show ospf database

    OSPF database, Area 0.0.0.0
Type       ID               Adv Rtr          Seq          Age  Opt  Cksum  Len
Router     10.32.1.1        10.32.1.1        0x80000034   799  0x22 0xc633  48
Router    *198.18.16.2      198.18.16.2      0x80000016   798  0x22 0x17f3  48
Network   *10.2.1.11        198.18.16.2      0x80000001   798  0x22 0xae02  32
```

The `show ospf database` command displays the complete LSA database for OSPF. This SRX has three LSAs in its database, one for each of the two routers in the OSPF area and the last representing the multiaccess (Ethernet) network between them. The starred (*) LSAs were created by the local SRX itself.

The full complexity of the LSA database is beyond the scope of this book, but for a little taste, here you examine CLI help underneath the `show ospf database` command:

```
jamesq@SRX5800-1> show ospf database ?
Possible completions:
  <[Enter]>            Execute this command
  advertising-router   Router ID of advertising router
  area                 OSPF area ID
  asbrsummary          Summary AS boundary router link-state advertisements
  brief                Display brief output (default)
  detail               Display detailed output
  extensive            Display extensive output
  external             External link-state advertisements
  instance             Name of OSPF instance
  link-local           Link local link-state advertisements
  logical-system       Name of logical system, or 'all'
  lsa-id               Link-state advertisement ID
  netsummary           Summary network link-state advertisements
  network              Network link-state advertisements
```

```
nssa                    Not-so-stubby area link-state advertisements
opaque-area             Opaque area-scope link-state advertisements
router                  Router link-state advertisements
summary                 Display summary output
|                       Pipe through a command
```

And you see the array of LSA types and options for filtering the LSA database. Only the `router` and `network` LSA types are relevant to the simple single-area OSPF network built in this section.

You dig a little deeper with the `extensive` option to the `show ospf database` command:

```
jamesq@SRX5800-1> show ospf database extensive

    OSPF database, Area 0.0.0.0
 Type       ID              Adv Rtr          Seq      Age  Opt  Cksum  Len
Router   10.32.1.1        10.32.1.1      0x80000034   802  0x22 0xc633  48
  bits 0x0, link count 2
  id 10.2.1.11, data 10.2.1.10, Type Transit (2)
    Topology count: 0, Default metric: 1
  id 10.32.1.1, data 255.255.255.255, Type Stub (3)
    Topology count: 0, Default metric: 0
  Topology default (ID 0)
    Type: Transit, Node ID: 10.2.1.11
      Metric: 1, Bidirectional
  Aging timer 00:46:37
  Installed 00:13:21 ago, expires in 00:46:38
```

The Router LSA `10.32.1.1` shows that the neighboring OSPF router has two interfaces (`10.32.1.1` and `10.2.1.10`) attached to it.

Next you see the SRX's own `198.18.16.2` Router LSA also showing two interfaces (`198.18.16.2` and `10.2.1.11`) attached:

```
Router  *198.18.16.2  198.18.16.2    0x80000016   801  0x22 0x17f3  48
  bits 0x0, link count 2
  id 10.2.1.11, data 10.2.1.11, Type Transit (2)
    Topology count: 0, Default metric: 1
  id 198.18.16.2, data 255.255.255.255, Type Stub (3)
    Topology count: 0, Default metric: 0
  Topology default (ID 0)
    Type: Transit, Node ID: 10.2.1.11
      Metric: 1, Bidirectional
  Gen timer 00:36:38
  Aging timer 00:46:38
  Installed 00:13:21 ago, expires in 00:46:39, sent 00:13:21 ago
  Last changed 00:13:21 ago, Change count: 2, Ours
```

And last the `10.2.1.0/24` Network LSA created by this SRX itself (known as the OSPF *designated router* for the multiaccess Ethernet segment) showing both the SRX itself (`198.18.16.2`) and the neighboring router (`10.32.1.1`) attached to the network:

```
Network *10.2.1.11  198 .18.16.2    0x80000001   801  0x22 0xae02  32
  mask 255.255.255.0
  attached router 198.18.16.2
  attached router 10.32.1.1
```

```
Topology default (ID 0)
  Type: Transit, Node ID: 10.32.1.1
    Metric: 0, Bidirectional
  Type: Transit, Node ID: 198.18.16.2
    Metric: 0, Bidirectional
Gen timer 00:36:38
Aging timer 00:46:38
Installed 00:13:21 ago, expires in 00:46:39, sent 00:13:21 ago
Last changed 00:13:21 ago, Change count: 1, Ours
```

Case Study 11-1: Securing OSPF Adjacencies

OSPF, like all IGPs, is a very trusting protocol *by default*. It will assume that any neighboring device speaking OSPF to it on a configured interface is a legitimate member of its OSPF domain with legitimate routes to share. A clueful attacker *could* engage in a variety of very damaging denial-of-service (DoS) and man-in-the-middle attacks on an OSPF routed network by exploiting such undeserved trust.

Worse still, OSPF is built to communicate over IP, the protocol used across the global Internet. Now, in practice, no OSPF speaking router should permit an OSPF packet to be forwarded beyond the local network segment on which it saw the packet transmitted. However, this still leaves a significant security hole open for any attacker who gains access to one of those local segments facing your OSPF devices.

In the Junos CLI configuration that follows, you will enable a Message-Digest algorithm 5 (MD5) hashed authentication key value to secure the OSPF communication on the `ge-11/0/5.0` link.

You return to configuration mode with the `edit` command:

```
jamesq@SRX5800-1> edit
Entering configuration mode
```

And drill down to the `ge-11/0/5.0` link's OSPF configuration:

```
[edit]
jamesq@SRX5800-1# edit protocols ospf area 0 interface ge-11/0/5.0
```

You examine OSPF's `interface` configuration options in CLI help:

```
[edit protocols ospf area 0.0.0.0 interface ge-11/0/5.0]
jamesq@SRX5800-1# set ?
Possible completions:
+ apply-groups         Groups from which to inherit configuration data
+ apply-groups-except  Don't inherit configuration data from these groups
> authentication
> bandwidth-based-metrics  Configure bandwidth based metrics
> bfd-liveness-detection  Bidirectional Forwarding Detection options
  dead-interval        Dead interval (seconds) (1..65535)
  disable              Disable OSPF on this interface
  dynamic-neighbors    Learn neighbors dynamically on a p2mp interface
  hello-interval       Hello interval (seconds) (1..255)
  interface-type       Type of interface
  ipsec-sa             IPSec security association name
```

```
  link-protection      Protect interface from link faults only
  metric               Interface metric (1..65535)
  no-eligible-backup   Not eligible to backup traffic from protected interfaces
  no-neighbor-down-notification  Don't inform other protocols about
neighbor down events
  node-link-protection  Protect interface from both link and node faults
> passive              Do not run OSPF, but advertise it
  priority             Designated router priority (0..255)
  retransmit-interval  Retransmission interval (seconds) (1..65535)
  secondary            Treat interface as secondary
  te-metric            Traffic engineering metric (1..4294967295)
> topology             Topology specific attributes
  transit-delay        Transit delay (seconds) (1..65535)
```

And drill down into the OSPF `authentication` configuration, choosing the most secure option (MD5):

```
[edit protocols ospf area 0.0.0.0 interface ge-11/0/5.0]
jamesq@SRX5800-1# set authentication ?
Possible completions:
+ apply-groups         Groups from which to inherit configuration data
+ apply-groups-except  Don't inherit configuration data from these groups
> md5                  MD5 authentication key
  simple-password      Authentication key
[edit protocols ospf area 0.0.0.0 interface ge-11/0/5.0]
jamesq@SRX5800-1# set authentication md5 ?
Possible completions:
  <key-id>             Key ID for MD5 authentication (0..255)
[edit protocols ospf area 0.0.0.0 interface ge-11/0/5.0]
jamesq@SRX5800-1# set authentication md5 1 ?
Possible completions:
  key            MD5 authentication key value
  start-time     Start time for key transmission (YYYY-MM-DD.HH:MM)
```

It's important to note that *both* sides of an OSPF adjacency must be configured with the identical `authentication` configuration lest the adjacency be broken and interrupt traffic. In your case, you're lucky that your colleague is furiously typing away on the facing OSPF router to make sure your new configuration will match up. If that were not the case, you could use the `start-time` configuration knob here to synchronize the timing of the implementation of the new `authentication` scheme.

You continue drilling down and set the new MD5 key to the very memorable `junos rocks!` value:

```
[edit protocols ospf area 0.0.0.0 interface ge-11/0/5.0]
jamesq@SRX5800-1# set authentication md5 1 key ?
Possible completions:
  <key>                MD5 authentication key value
[edit protocols ospf area 0.0.0.0 interface ge-11/0/5.0]
jamesq@SRX5800-1# set authentication md5 junosrocks!
```

And with your new MD5 key set you jump back to the `top` of the Junos configuration:

```
[edit protocols ospf area 0.0.0.0 interface ge-11/0/5.0]
jamesq@SRX5800-1# top
```

You inspect the changes with the show command:

```
[edit]
jamesq@SRX5800-1# show | compare
[edit protocols ospf area 0.0.0.0 interface ge-11/0/5.0]
+      authentication {
+          md5 1 key "$9$rFCKWxbs4Di.s2T3/9B1LxNbwgkqfznCsY"; ## SECRET-DATA
+      }
```

You note that Junos does not display the MD5 key value as you typed it, but rather displays a secure hashed representation of it.

You complete your changes with the commit command:

```
[edit]
jamesq@SRX5800-1# commit and-quit
configuration check succeeds
commit complete
Exiting configuration mode
```

And now check your colleague's typing with the show ospf neighbor command:

```
jamesq@SRX5800-1> show ospf neighbor
Address          Interface      State     ID             Pri  Dead
10.2.1.10      ge-11/0/5.0      Full      10.32.1.1      128    35
```

Success! You and your colleague did not break anything. You both can keep your jobs. Phew.

Just to see the authentication in action, you also check out the earlier OSPF trace file with the show log command:

```
jamesq@SRX5800-1> show log ospftrace | last
Apr 14 11:04:53.651889 OSPF sent Hello 10.2.1.11 -> 224.0.0.5 (
ge-11/0/5.0 IFL 80 area 0.0.0.0)
Apr 14 11:04:53.651918   Version 2, length 48, ID 198.18.16.2, area 0.0.0.0
Apr 14 11:04:53.651927   mask 255.255.255.0, hello_ivl 10, opts 0x2, prio 128
Apr 14 11:04:53.651934   dead_ivl 40, DR 10.2.1.11, BDR 10.2.1.10
Apr 14 11:04:54.488421 OSPF rcvd Hello 10.2.1.10 -> 224.0.0.5 (
ge-11/0/5.0 IFL 80 area 0.0.0.0)
Apr 14 11:04:54.488479   Version 2, length 48, ID 10.32.1.1, area 0.0.0.0
Apr 14 11:04:54.488486   checksum 0x0, authtype 2
Apr 14 11:04:54.488495   mask 255.255.255.0, hello_ivl 10, opts 0x2, prio 128
Apr 14 11:04:54.488501   dead_ivl 40, DR 10.2.1.11, BDR 10.2.1.10
```

And there you have it, the SRX is successfully receiving OSPF Hello packets with authtype 2 (the value for MD5) and your adjacency remains Full.

Great job! Your network (or at least this OSPF link) is now secure from hackers.

Case Study 11-2: Redundant Paths and Routing Metrics

Although the previous sections saw your SRX connected successfully into an OSPF routing domain, they didn't give a taste for the type of dynamic resilience to failures as shown in Figure 11-5 earlier.

In the Junos CLI configuration that follows, you will enable the second *redundant* link between your OSPF routers. First, you check the current OSPF interface with the `show ospf interface extensive` command:

```
jamesq@SRX5800-1> show ospf interface extensive
Interface       State   Area        DR ID           BDR ID        Nbrs
ge-11/0/5.0     DR      0.0.0.0     198.18.16.2     10.32.1.1     1
  Type: LAN, Address: 10.2.1.11, Mask: 255.255.255.0, MTU: 1500, Cost: 1
  DR addr: 10.2.1.112, BDR addr: 10.2.1.10, Priority: 128
  Adj count: 1
  Hello: 10, Dead: 40, ReXmit: 5, Not Stub
  Auth type: None
  Protection type: None
  Topology default (ID 0) -> Cost: 1
lo0.0       DRother 0.0.0.0    0.0.0.0          0.0.0.0          0
  Type: LAN, Address: 198.18.16.2, Mask: 255.255.255.255, MTU: 65535, Cost: 0
  Adj count: 0, Passive
  Hello: 10, Dead: 40, ReXmit: 5, Not Stub
  Auth type: None
  Protection type: None
  Topology default (ID 0) -> Passive, Cost: 0
```

And you find the single gigabit Ethernet (`ge-11/0/5.0`) link between the routers with a metric cost of 1 (`Cost: 1`). This is the lowest and best possible OSPF metric, and the default for any gigabit speed link.

You also check the OSPF route for the `10.32.1.1/32` network, finding it still reachable via the `10.2.1.10` router on interface `ge-11/0/5.0`:

```
jamesq@SRX5800-1> show route protocol ospf

inet.0: 24 destinations, 28 routes (25 active, 0 holddown, 0 hidden)
Restart Complete
+ = Active Route, - = Last Active, * = Both

10.32.1.1/32         *[OSPF/10] 00:55:46, metric 1
                    > to 10.2.1.10 via ge-11/0/5.0
224.0.0.5/32        *[OSPF/10] 00:57:15, metric 1
                      MultiRecv
```

You jump back into configuration mode with the `edit` command:

```
jamesq@SRX5800-1> edit
Entering configuration mode
```

Then down to the OSPF hierarchy:

```
[edit]
jamesq@SRX5800-1# edit protocols ospf
```

And check the OSPF configuration with a `show` command:

```
[edit protocols ospf]
jamesq@SRX5800-1# show
area 0.0.0.0 {
    interface ge-11/0/5.0;
    interface lo0.0 {
```

```
            passive;
        }
    }
```

It's time to build the new `ge-11/0/6.0` interface configuration, but with a twist. You add the `metric 10` configuration option to ensure that this new interface's path will be less preferred than the existing `ge-11/0/5.0` link:

```
[edit protocols ospf]
jamesq@SRX5800-1# set area 0 interface ge-11/0/6.0 metric 10
```

You `show` your configuration changes:

```
[edit protocols ospf]
jamesq@SRX5800-1# show | compare
[edit protocols ospf area 0.0.0.0]
      interface lo0.0 { ... }
+     interface ge-11/0/6.0 {
+         metric 10;
+     }
```

Before executing a `commit` command to make them active:

```
[edit protocols ospf]
jamesq@SRX5800-1# commit and-quit
configuration check succeeds
commit complete
Exiting configuration mode
```

You check your work with the `show ospf neighbor` command:

```
jamesq@SRX5800-1> show ospf neighbor
Address          Interface         State     ID          Pri  Dead
10.2.1.10     ge-11/0/5.0          Full      10.32.1.1   128    34
10.3.3.10     ge-11/0/6.0          Full      10.32.1.1   128    33
```

Good job! You now have two OSPF adjacencies to the `10.32.1.1` router. You check the `10.32.1.1/32` route with the `show route` command:

```
jamesq@SRX5800-1> show route protocol ospf

inet.0: 25 destinations, 28 routes (25 active, 0 holddown, 0 hidden)
Restart Complete
+ = Active Route, - = Last Active, * = Both

10.32.1.1/32         *[OSPF/10] 00:56:18, metric 1
                    > to 10.2.1.10 via ge-11/0/5.0
224.0.0.5/32        *[OSPF/10]  00:57:47, metric 1
                       MultiRecv
```

Perfect, the `10.32.1.1/32` route is still taking the preferred path through `ge-11/0/5.0`.

Now it's time to test the OSPF network's resiliency. You break the `ge-11/0/5.0` link and thereby bring down its OSPF adjacency, as shown in the `show log` output:

```
jamesq@SRX5800-1> show log messages | last
Apr 14 11:54:19  SRX5800-1 mib2d[1301]: SNMP_TRAP_LINK_DOWN:
ifIndex 521, ifAdminStatus up(1), ifOperStatus down(2), ifName
```

```
ge-11/0/5
Apr 14 11:54:19  SRX5800-1 rpd[1276]: RPD_OSPF_NBRDOWN: OSPF neighbor
10.2.1.10 (realm ospf-v2 ge-11/0/5.0 area 0.0.0.0) state changed from
Full to Down due to KillNbr (event reason: interface went down)
```

And success! Your OSPF topology has reconverged, as depicted in Figure 11-7, to reach the `10.32.1.1/32` network via the new `ge-11/0/6.0` link's adjacency, as shown in the `show route` output:

```
jamesq@SRX5800-1> show route protocol ospf

inet.0: 24 destinations, 25 routes (24 active, 0 holddown, 0 hidden)
Restart Complete
+ = Active Route, - = Last Active, * = Both

10.32.1.1/32        *[OSPF/10] 00:53:09, metric 10
                    > to 10.3.3.10 via ge-11/0/6.0
224.0.0.5/32       *[OSPF/10] 01:53:19, metric 1
                      MultiRecv
```

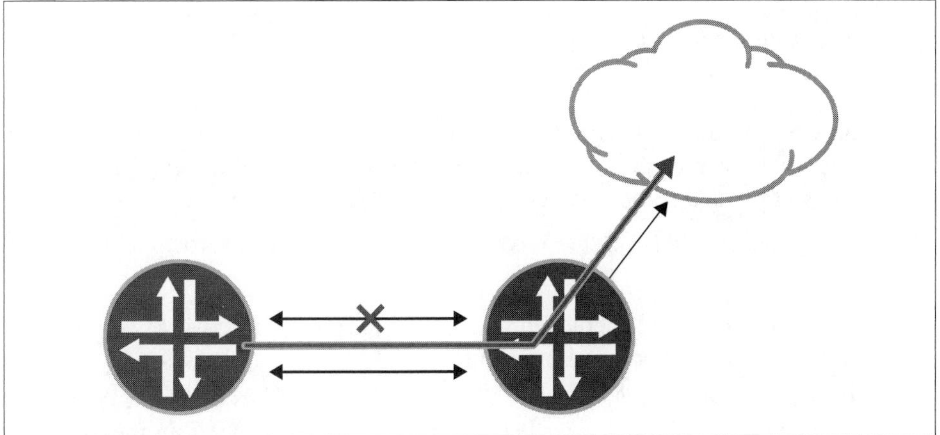

Figure 11-7. Routing around link failure

Growing OSPF Networks

OSPF is a powerful protocol that can grow with the needs of your organization. As organizations grow larger, it often makes sense to leverage the hierarchy in OSPF's design. OSPF routers can be segmented into multi-area topologies, as shown in Figure 11-8, or even integrated with other routing protocols (as we'll explore in "Routing Policy" on page 664).

Please consult O'Reilly's excellent *JUNOS Enterprise Routing* and *Junos Cookbook* publications, mentioned earlier, for coverage of the more complex OSPF topologies, such as those involving multiple areas.

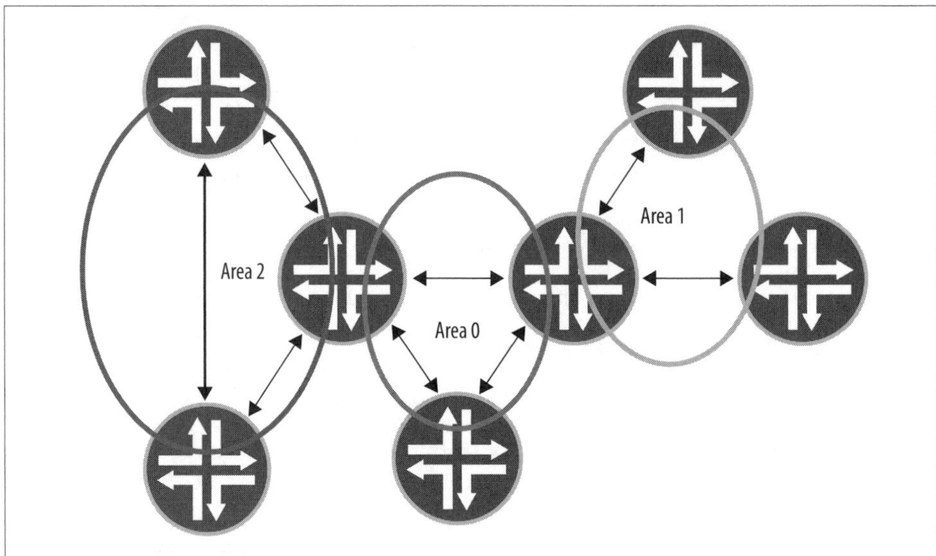

Figure 11-8. OSPF multi-area topology

IS-IS

Although OSPF is the most common IGP routing protocol, there is one other very successful IGP known as IS-IS (for *Intermediate System to Intermediate System* in the terminology of the ISO standards body that defined it).

IS-IS is very similar to OSPF in that it is also a *link-state* routing protocol, but there are key differences:

- IS-IS is more commonly deployed in large service provider networks where OSPF is most often used in enterprise networks.
- IS-IS achieves hierarchy through *levels* rather than the *areas* of OSPF. IS-IS levels are segmented on physical links between routers rather than within the routers as is the case for OSPF areas.
- IS-IS link-state information is flooded in larger *link-state packets* (LSPs) rather than the fine-grained LSAs used in OSPF.
- Though IS-IS is used to communicate IP routing information, IS-IS itself encapsulates packets in ISO rather than IP packets. OSPF instead uses IP packets for communicating between routers.

Fortunately, when it comes to joining an SRX to a simple IS-IS topology, as you will do in the next section, only the last bullet will be important for the new configuration you are building.

Configuring IS-IS

In this section, you will replace your OSPF configuration with an equivalently functioning IS-IS configuration. Here you enter configuration mode with the `edit` command:

```
jamesq@SRX5800-1> edit
Entering configuration mode
```

And examine the old OSPF configuration with the `show` command:

```
[edit]
jamesq@SRX5800-1# show protocols
ospf {
    area 0.0.0.0 {
        interface ge-11/0/5.0;
        interface lo0.0 passive;
    }
}
```

Then you blow it away with the `delete` command:

```
[edit]
jamesq@SRX5800-1# delete protocols
```

Time to begin exploring IS-IS in the Junos CLI help:

```
[edit]
jamesq@SRX5800-1# set protocols isis ?
Possible completions:
+ apply-groups         Groups from which to inherit configuration data
+ apply-groups-except  Don't inherit configuration data from these groups
  disable              Disable IS-IS
+ export               Export policy
> graceful-restart     IS-IS graceful restart options
  ignore-attached-bit  Ignore the attached bit in Level 1 LSPs
> interface            Interface configuration
> level                Configure global level attributes
  loose-authentication-check  Verify authentication only if PDU has
authentication TLV
  lsp-lifetime         Lifetime of LSPs (350..65535 seconds)
  max-areas            Maximum number of advertised Areas (3..36)
  no-adjacency-holddown  Disable adjacency hold down
  no-authentication-check  Disable authentication checking
  no-ipv4-routing      Disable IPv4 routing
> overload             Set the overload bit (no transit traffic)
  reference-bandwidth  Bandwidth for calculating metric defaults
(9600..1000000000000)
> rib-group            Routing table group for importing IS-IS routes
> spf-options          Configure SPF attributes
> topologies           Enable topologies
> traceoptions         Trace options for IS-IS
```

Junos again offers a fountain of knobs for tuning IS-IS, but fortunately for your small project you need to add just the two interfaces.

You use the set command to add the ge-11/0/5.0 and lo0.0 logical interfaces to IS-IS:

```
[edit]
jamesq@SRX5800-1# set protocols isis interface ge-11/0/5.0

[edit]
jamesq@SRX5800-1# set protocols isis interface lo0.0 passive
```

And your IS-IS configuration is done. That's it.

But that won't be enough to get IS-IS up and running. Remember, IS-IS does not use IP for communication. It uses the ISO protocol. You need to configure ISO on both ge-11/0/5.0 and lo0.0 before IS-IS will work:

```
[edit]
jamesq@SRX5800-1# set interfaces ge-11/0/5.0 family iso

[edit]
jamesq@SRX5800-1# set interfaces lo0.0 family iso address 49.0002.0002.0002.00
```

That last statement for lo0.0 is not just a best practice, as it was for OSPF, but a basic requirement for a working IS-IS configuration. There must be a loopback interface configured with a correctly formatted ISO address for an IS-IS router to identify itself to the other routers in the IS-IS domain.

You look at your configuration changes with the show command:

```
[edit]
james@SRX5800-1# show | compare
[edit interfaces ge-11/0/5 unit 0]
+      family iso;
[edit interfaces]
+   lo0 {
+       unit 0 {
+           family iso {
+               address 49.0002.0002.0002.00;
+           }
+       }
+   }
[edit protocols]
+   isis {
+       interface ge-11/0/5.0;
+       interface lo0.0 passive;
+   }
-   ospf {
-       area 0.0.0.0 {
-           interface ge-11/0/5.0;
-           interface lo0.0 passive;
-       }
-   }
```

And now that you're *really* done, you go ahead and commit the work:

```
[edit]
jamesq@SRX5800-1# commit and-quit
configuration check succeeds
```

```
commit complete
Exiting configuration mode
```

Verifying IS-IS

Fingers crossed, you check out the new IS-IS setup with the `show isis adjacency` command:

```
james@SRX5800-1> show isis adjacency
Interface       System          L State    Hold (secs) SNPA
ge-11/0/5.0     SRX3400-1       1  Up                8  0:21:59:80:d0:2
ge-11/0/5.0     SRX3400-1       2  Up                8  0:21:59:80:d0:2
```

Success! The IS-IS adjacency is `Up`. Or rather, *both adjacencies* (plural) are `Up`. Remember again that IS-IS divides levels on the links between routers. This means IS-IS separately negotiates its backbone (level 2) and non-backbone (level 1) adjacencies over the local network links. In default configuration, it negotiates both a level 1 and a level 2 adjacency. Even though IS-IS is configured on just one external interface (`ge-11/0/5.0`) toward just one external peer, *two* adjacencies are formed between the routers over this single link.

This can, of course, be changed with configuration, and this is where the hierarchy of IS-IS comes in. It is by simply pruning level 1 or level 2 from IS-IS adjacencies that the link-state hierarchy of multi-level IS-IS networks is created. Fortunately, for the purposes of the present project, a single link-state topology works just fine, so you leave the default behavior intact.

One surprise you might note here is that the IS-IS adjacency is up without any changes to the `security zone` configuration. Nothing has explicitly permitted IS-IS as was necessary for a working OSPF configuration.

As IS-IS runs directly over the ISO protocol (*not* IP), IS-IS packets do not pass through the SRX security engine. The SRX is built for securing *IP* communication, not ISO. No security configuration is necessary for a successful configuration of IS-IS.

Next you check out the IS-IS routes in the `inet.0` routing table with the `show route` command:

```
root@SRX5800-1> show route protocol isis

inet.0: 20 destinations, 23 routes (20 active, 0 holddown, 0 hidden)
Restart Complete
+ = Active Route, - = Last Active, * = Both

10.32.1.1/32          [IS-IS/15] 1d 06:47:55, metric 10
                    > to 10.2.1.10 via ge-11/0/5.0

iso.0: 1 destinations, 1 routes (1 active, 0 holddown, 0 hidden)
Restart Complete

jamesq@SRX5800-1>
```

Good stuff! The same `10.32.1.1/32` route is learned from the neighbor via IS-IS as was learned earlier via OSPF.

Also note the new `iso.0` routing table. This was created as a consequence of configuring an ISO address on the loopback interface, as shown in this routing table output:

```
jamesq@SRX5800-1> show route table iso.0

iso.0: 1 destinations, 1 routes (1 active, 0 holddown, 0 hidden)
Restart Complete
+ = Active Route, - = Last Active, * = Both

49.0002.0002.0002/56
                   *[Direct/0] 1d 06:54:42
                    > via lo0.0
```

You decide to dig a little deeper into IS-IS by looking at the IS-IS LSP database with the `show isis database` command:

```
jamesq@SRX5800-1> show isis database
IS-IS level 1 link-state database:
LSP ID                      Sequence Checksum Lifetime Attributes
SRX3400-1.00-00                  0x2   0x2440     1182 L1 L2
SRX3400-1.02-00                  0x1   0x9408     1182 L1 L2
SRX5800-1.00-00                  0x2   0x2ce5     1184 L1 L2
  3 LSPs

IS-IS level 2 link-state database:
LSP ID                      Sequence Checksum Lifetime Attributes
SRX3400-1.00-00                  0x2   0x2440     1182 L1 L2
SRX3400-1.02-00                  0x1   0x9408     1182 L1 L2
SRX5800-1.00-00                  0x3   0x60dd     1185 L1 L2
  3 LSPs
```

And just like OSPF, there are three LSPs for IS-IS as there were three LSAs for OSPF. Note that there are *two* sets of these same three LSPs: one set is for the level 1 area and the other is for the level 2 area. Both sets will be essentially identical as the IS-IS configuration made no effort to prune level 1 or level 2 adjacencies from any links.

Also note that IS-IS actually resolves the routers' ISO addresses to clear hostnames (`SRX-3400-1` and `SRX5800-1`). This is much easier for administrators than interpreting the long ISO addresses.

Next you look deeper with the `show isis database extensive` command:

```
jamesq@SRX5800-1> show isis database extensive
IS-IS level 1 link-state database:

SRX3400-1.00-00 Sequence: 0xdc, Checksum: 0x5e26, Lifetime: 830 secs
   IS neighbor: SRX3400-1.02                  Metric:       10
     Two-way fragment: SRX3400-1.02-00, Two-way first fragment: SRX3400-1.02-00
   IP prefix: 10.32.1.1/32                 Metric:        0 Internal Up
   IP prefix: 10.2.1.0/24                  Metric:       10 Internal Up

  Header: LSP ID: SRX3400-1.00-00, Length: 145 bytes
```

```
    Allocated length: 284 bytes, Router ID: 10.32.1.1
    Remaining lifetime: 830 secs, Level: 1, Interface: 80
    Estimated free bytes: 139, Actual free bytes: 139
    Aging timer expires in: 830 secs
    Protocols: IP

  Packet: LSP ID: SRX3400-1.00-00, Length: 145 bytes, Lifetime : 1198 secs
    Checksum: 0x5e26, Sequence: 0xdc, Attributes: 0x3 <L1 L2>
    NLPID: 0x83, Fixed length: 27 bytes, Version: 1, Sysid length: 0 bytes
    Packet type: 18, Packet version: 1, Max area: 0

  TLVs:
    Area address: 49 (1)
    Speaks: IP
    IP router id: 10.32.1.1
    IP address: 10.32.1.1
    Hostname: SRX3400-1
    IS neighbor: SRX3400-1.02, Internal, Metric: default 10
    IS extended neighbor: SRX3400-1.02, Metric: default 10
      IP address: 10.2.1.10
      Local interface index: 83, Remote interface index: 0
    IP prefix: 10.2.1.0/24, Internal, Metric: default 10, Up
    IP prefix: 10.32.1.1/32, Internal, Metric: default 0, Up
    IP extended prefix: 10.2.1.0/24 metric 10 up
    IP extended prefix: 10.32.1.1/32 metric 0 up
  No queued transmissions
```

In the preceding output, you have the LSP for the neighboring IS-IS router in the level 1 (non-backbone) database. It identifies both networks that this router touches (`10.32.1.1/32` and `10.2.1.0/24`) much as an OSPF router LSA does for an OSPF speaking router.

IS-IS passes routing information within the LSP in the highly extensible `TLV` (*type-length-value*) fields. These fields make IS-IS very adaptable as network technology progresses.

Next in the level 1 database is a slightly different entry known as a *Pseudonode* LSP:

```
SRX3400-1.02-00 Sequence: 0xdb, Checksum: 0xdee2, Lifetime: 998 secs
   IS neighbor: SRX3400-1.00                    Metric:        0
     Two-way fragment: SRX3400-1.00-00, Two-way first fragment: SRX3400-1.00-00
   IS neighbor: SRX5800-1.00                    Metric:        0
     Two-way fragment: SRX5800-1.00-00, Two-way first fragment: SRX5800-1.00-00

  Header: LSP ID: SRX3400-1.02-00, Length: 76 bytes
    Allocated length: 284 bytes, Router ID: 0.0.0.0
    Remaining lifetime: 998 secs, Level: 1, Interface: 80
    Estimated free bytes: 208, Actual free bytes: 208
    Aging timer expires in: 998 secs

  Packet: LSP ID: SRX3400-1.02-00, Length: 76 bytes, Lifetime : 1198 secs
    Checksum: 0xdee2, Sequence: 0xdb, Attributes: 0x3 <L1 L2>
    NLPID: 0x83, Fixed length: 27 bytes, Version: 1, Sysid length: 0 bytes
    Packet type: 18, Packet version: 1, Max area: 0
```

```
    TLVs:
      IS neighbor: SRX3400-1.00, Internal, Metric: default 0
      IS neighbor: SRX5800-1.00, Internal, Metric: default 0
      IS extended neighbor: SRX3400-1.00, Metric: default 0
      IS extended neighbor: SRX5800-1.00, Metric: default 0
    No queued transmissions
```

The Pseudonode LSP represents a multiaccess segment (such as the Ethernet broadcast segment, in this case) as well as the IS-IS routers that are connected to that segment. This LSP effectively functions very much like the Network LSA in OSPF. In the preceding output, you see that both the **SRX3400-1** and **SRX5800-1** IS-IS routers are connected to the multiaccess link represented in this Pseudonode LSP.

And last in the level 1 database you have your own SRX's LSP representing the two networks (**198.18.16.2/32** and **10.2.1.0/24**) that it touches:

```
SRX5800-1.00-00 Sequence: 0xe6, Checksum: 0xa59, Lifetime: 956 secs
   IS neighbor: SRX3400-1.02            Metric:       10
     Two-way fragment: SRX3400-1.02-00, Two-way first fragment: SRX3400-1.02-00
   IP prefix: 198.18.16.2/32             Metric:        0 Internal Up
   IP prefix: 10.2.1.0/24                Metric:       10 Internal Up

  Header: LSP ID: SRX5800-1.00-00, Length: 145 bytes
    Allocated length: 1492 bytes, Router ID: 198.18.16.2 `
    Remaining lifetime: 956 secs, Level: 1, Interface: 0
    Estimated free bytes: 1295, Actual free bytes: 1347
    Aging timer expires in: 956 secs
    Protocols: IP

  Packet: LSP ID: SRX5800-1.00-00, Length: 145 bytes, Lifetime : 1198 secs
    Checksum: 0xa59, Sequence: 0xe6, Attributes: 0x3 <L1 L2>
    NLPID: 0x83, Fixed length: 27 bytes, Version: 1, Sysid length: 0 bytes
    Packet type: 18, Packet version: 1, Max area: 0

  TLVs:
    Area address: 49 (1)
    Speaks: IP
    IP router id: 198.18.16.2
    IP address: 198.18.16.2
    Hostname: SRX5800-1
    IS neighbor: SRX3400-1.02, Internal, Metric: default 10
    IS extended neighbor: SRX3400-1.02, Metric: default 10
      IP address: 10.2.1.11
      Local interface index: 80, Remote interface index: 0
    IP prefix: 10.2.1.0/24, Internal, Metric: default 10, Up
    IP prefix: 198.18.16.2/32, Internal, Metric: default 0, Up
    IP extended prefix: 10.2.1.0/24 metric 10 up
    IP extended prefix: 198.18.16.2/32 metric 0 up
  No queued transmissions
```

And given the very simple topology (one common link, one IS-IS neighbor, and both levels of adjacency), the level 2 database is essentially identical to the level 1 database:

```
IS-IS level 2 link-state database:
```

```
SRX3400-1.00-00 Sequence: 0xdd, Checksum: 0x5c27, Lifetime: 1043 secs
   IS neighbor: SRX3400-1.02             Metric:       10
     Two-way fragment: SRX3400-1.02-00, Two-way first fragment: SRX3400-1.02-00
   IP prefix: 10.32.1.1/32               Metric:        0 Internal Up
   IP prefix: 10.2.1.0/24                Metric:       10 Internal Up

  Header: LSP ID: SRX3400-1.00-00, Length: 145 bytes
    Allocated length: 284 bytes, Router ID: 10.32.1.1
    Remaining lifetime: 1043 secs, Level: 2, Interface: 80
    Estimated free bytes: 139, Actual free bytes: 139
    Aging timer expires in: 1043 secs
    Protocols: IP

  Packet: LSP ID: SRX3400-1.00-00, Length: 145 bytes, Lifetime : 1198 secs
    Checksum: 0x5c27, Sequence: 0xdd, Attributes: 0x3 <L1 L2>
    NLPID: 0x83, Fixed length: 27 bytes, Version: 1, Sysid length: 0 bytes
    Packet type: 20, Packet version: 1, Max area: 0

  TLVs:
    Area address: 49 (1)
    Speaks: IP
    IP router id: 10.32.1.1
    IP address: 10.32.1.1
    Hostname: SRX3400-1
    IS neighbor: SRX3400-1.02, Internal, Metric: default 10
    IS extended neighbor: SRX3400-1.02, Metric: default 10
      IP address: 10.2.1.10
      Local interface index: 83, Remote interface index: 0
    IP prefix: 10.2.1.0/24, Internal, Metric: default 10, Up
    IP prefix: 10.32.1.1/32, Internal, Metric: default 0, Up
    IP extended prefix: 10.2.1.0/24 metric 10 up
    IP extended prefix: 10.32.1.1/32 metric 0 up
  No queued transmissions

SRX3400-1.02-00 Sequence: 0xda, Checksum: 0xe0e1, Lifetime: 1043 secs
   IS neighbor: SRX3400-1.00             Metric:        0
     Two-way fragment: SRX3400-1.00-00, Two-way first fragment: SRX3400-1.00-00
   IS neighbor: SRX5800-1.00             Metric:        0
     Two-way fragment: SRX5800-1.00-00, Two-way first fragment: SRX5800-1.00-00

  Header: LSP ID: SRX3400-1.02-00, Length: 76 bytes
    Allocated length: 284 bytes, Router ID: 0.0.0.0
    Remaining lifetime: 1043 secs, Level: 2, Interface: 80
    Estimated free bytes: 208, Actual free bytes: 208
    Aging timer expires in: 1043 secs

  Packet: LSP ID: SRX3400-1.02-00, Length: 76 bytes, Lifetime : 1198 secs
    Checksum: 0xe0e1, Sequence: 0xda, Attributes: 0x3 <L1 L2>
    NLPID: 0x83, Fixed length: 27 bytes, Version: 1, Sysid length: 0 bytes
    Packet type: 20, Packet version: 1, Max area: 0

  TLVs:
    IS neighbor: SRX3400-1.00, Internal, Metric: default 0
    IS neighbor: SRX5800-1.00, Internal, Metric: default 0
    IS extended neighbor: SRX3400-1.00, Metric: default 0
```

```
      IS extended neighbor: SRX5800-1.00, Metric: default 0
    No queued transmissions

  SRX5800-1.00-00 Sequence: 0xea, Checksum: 0x25d, Lifetime: 956 secs
     IS neighbor: SRX3400-1.02             Metric:      10
       Two-way fragment: SRX3400-1.02-00, Two-way first fragment: SRX3400-1.02-00
     IP prefix: 198.18.16.2/32             Metric:       0 Internal Up
     IP prefix: 10.2.1.0/24                Metric:      10 Internal Up

    Header: LSP ID: SRX5800-1.00-00, Length: 145 bytes
      Allocated length: 1492 bytes, Router ID: 198.18.16.2
      Remaining lifetime: 956 secs, Level: 2, Interface: 0
      Estimated free bytes: 1295, Actual free bytes: 1347
      Aging timer expires in: 956 secs
      Protocols: IP

    Packet: LSP ID: SRX5800-1.00-00, Length: 145 bytes, Lifetime : 1198 secs
      Checksum: 0x25d, Sequence: 0xea, Attributes: 0x3 <L1 L2>
      NLPID: 0x83, Fixed length: 27 bytes, Version: 1, Sysid length: 0 bytes
      Packet type: 20, Packet version: 1, Max area: 0

    TLVs:
      Area address: 49 (1)
      Speaks: IP
      IP router id: 198.18.16.2
      IP address: 198.18.16.2
      Hostname: SRX5800-1
      IS neighbor: SRX3400-1.02, Internal, Metric: default 10
      IS extended neighbor: SRX3400-1.02, Metric: default 10
        IP address: 10.2.1.11
        Local interface index: 80, Remote interface index: 0
      IP prefix: 10.2.1.0/24, Internal, Metric: default 10, Up
      IP prefix: 198.18.16.2/32, Internal, Metric: default 0, Up
      IP extended prefix: 10.2.1.0/24 metric 10 up
      IP extended prefix: 198.18.16.2/32 metric 0 up
    No queued transmissions
```

And there you have it, a solid IS-IS configuration. Great job!

Configuring BFD

Both OSPF and IS-IS serve as excellent routing protocols, but neither was designed for the *subsecond* convergence demanded in modern networks for supporting real-time traffic. Not even a hiccup is tolerated when real-time communication, such as voice, video, or financial market data, is at stake. Both OSPF and IS-IS are hamstrung by keepalive timers measured in *seconds*, rather than the *milliseconds* that would be necessary for rapid reconvergence.

Bidirectional forwarding detection (BFD) was developed for rapid failure detection in these demanding real-time networks. Rather than replacing IP routing protocols like OSPF and IS-IS, BFD simply augments them and extends their capabilities with subsecond keepalives.

In the Junos CLI configuration that follows, you will extend your existing IS-IS configuration with subsecond BFD failure detection.

You enter configuration mode and jump to the IS-IS hierarchy using the `edit` command:

```
jamesq@SRX5800-1> edit
Entering configuration mode

[edit]
jamesq@SRX5800-1# edit protocols isis
```

And examine CLI help for the `bfd-liveness-detection` statement:

```
[edit protocols isis]
jamesq@SRX5800-1# show interface ge-11/0/5.0 bfd-liveness-detection ?
Possible completions:
+ apply-groups         Groups from which to inherit configuration data
+ apply-groups-except  Don't inherit configuration data from these groups
> authentication       Authentication options
> detection-time       Detection-time options
  minimum-interval     Minimum transmit and receive interval (1..255000 milliseconds)
  minimum-receive-interval  Minimum receive interval (1..255000 milliseconds)
  multiplier           Detection time multiplier (1..255)
  no-adaptation        Disable adaptation
> transmit-interval    Transmit-interval options
  version              BFD protocol version number
```

Two simple `set` commands defining the `minimum-interval` (in milliseconds) at which BFD keepalive packets will be sent and the `multiplier` for the number of missed packets to trigger failure detection, and the BFD configuration is built:

```
[edit protocols isis]
jamesq@SRX5800-1# set interface ge-11/0/5.0 bfd-liveness-detection
minimum-interval 300

[edit protocols isis]
jamesq@SRX5800-1# set interface ge-11/0/5.0 bfd-liveness-detection multiplier 3
```

But just like OSPF Hello packets, BFD packets ride over IP and require `security zone` permissions. You make a quick configuration change in the `security zone` hierarchy using the `top set` command:

```
[edit protocols isis]
jamesq@SRX5800-1# top set security zones security-zone trust
host-inbound-traffic protocols bfd
```

You check out your new BFD configuration with the `show` command:

```
[edit protocols isis]
jamesq@SRX5800-1# show | compare
[edit protocols isis interface ge-11/0/5.0]
+      bfd-liveness-detection {
+          minimum-interval 300;
+          multiplier 3;
+      }
[edit security zones security-zone trust host-inbound-traffic protocols]
```

```
        ospf { ... }
+       bfd;
```

And `commit` the new configuration:

```
[edit protocols isis]
jamesq@SRX5800-1# commit and-quit
configuration check succeeds
commit complete
Exiting configuration mode
```

You confirm with the `show bfd session` command that BFD is happily exchanging keepalive packets every 300 milliseconds:

```
jamesq@SRX5800-1> show bfd session
                                                 Detect   Transmit
Address      State     Interface       Time     Interval  Multiplier
10.2.1.10    Up        ge-11/0/5.0     0.900     0.300        3

1 sessions, 2 clients
Cumulative transmit rate 3.3 pps, cumulative receive rate 3.3 pps
```

Success! BFD is ready and waiting to detect any failures on the `ge-11/0/5.0` link *in less than one second*. Congratulations!

Configuring RIP

Last (and very possibly least) is Routing Information Protocol (RIP). RIP is the oldest IGP protocol supported in Junos. It is generally considered obsolete. It is most often used only when a neighboring device, typically an older server, must use it.

Unlike OSPF or IS-IS, RIP is a distance-vector routing protocol. It relies on the number of router hops as its primary metric of determining the best network paths. Where BFD supports subsecond convergence and OSPF and IS-IS by themselves each support multisecond convergence, RIP convergence can be more on the order of *minutes*.

In a nutshell, you'll only use RIP when you must.

But it looks like there is one of those pesky old servers on your network, so you jump back into Junos configuration mode:

```
jamesq@SRX5800-1> edit
Entering configuration mode
```

And check out CLI help for RIP configuration:

```
[edit]
jamesq@SRX5800-1# set protocols rip ?
Possible completions:
+ apply-groups         Groups from which to inherit configuration data
+ apply-groups-except  Don't inherit configuration data from these groups
  authentication-key   Authentication key (password)
  authentication-type  Authentication type
  check-zero           Check reserved fields on incoming RIPv2 packets
> graceful-restart     RIP graceful restart options
> group                Instance configuration
```

```
  holddown             Hold-down time (10..180 seconds)
+ import               Import policy
  message-size         Number of route entries per update message (25..255)
  metric-in            Metric value to add to incoming routes (1..15)
  no-check-zero        Don't check reserved fields on incoming RIPv2 packets
> receive              Configure RIP receive options
> rib-group            Routing table group for importing RIP routes
  route-timeout        Delay before routes time out (30..360 seconds)
> send                 Configure RIP send options
> traceoptions         Trace options for RIP
  update-interval      Interval between regular route updates (10..60 seconds)
```

Junos places interfaces into RIP through group configuration:

```
[edit]
jamesq@SRX5800-1# set protocols rip group ?
Possible completions:
  <group_name>         Group name
[edit]
jamesq@SRX5800-1# set protocols rip group Servers ?
Possible completions:
  <[Enter]>            Execute this command
+ apply-groups         Groups from which to inherit configuration data
+ apply-groups-except  Don't inherit configuration data from these groups
> bfd-liveness-detection  Bidirectional Forwarding Detection options
+ export               Export policy
+ import               Import policy
  metric-out           Default metric of exported routes (1..15)
> neighbor             Neighbor configuration
  preference           Preference of routes learned by this group
  route-timeout        Delay before routes time out (30..360 seconds)
  update-interval      Interval between regular route updates (10..60 seconds)
  |                    Pipe through a command
```

Somewhat counterintuitively, RIP interfaces are configured under a neighbor statement in Junos. Here you add the ge-11/0/4.0 interface to the RIP configuration:

```
[edit]
jamesq@SRX5800-1# set protocols rip group Servers neighbor ge-11/0/4.0
```

Of course, you must allow RIP to pass in the security zone configuration:

```
[edit]
jamesq@SRX5800-1# set security zones security-zone trust
host-inbound-traffic protocols rip
```

You check out your new RIP configuration with a show command:

```
[edit]
jamesq@SRX5800-1# show | compare
[edit protocols]
+   rip {
+       group Servers {
+           neighbor ge-11/0/4.0;
+       }
+   }
[edit security zones security-zone trust host-inbound-traffic protocols]
```

```
        bfd { ... }
+       rip;
```

And execute a commit to complete the changes:

```
[edit]
jamesq@SRX5800-1# commit and-quit
configuration check succeeds
commit complete
Exiting configuration mode
```

Verifying RIP

With your RIP configuration complete, you confirm that RIP is up and running with the show rip neighbor command:

```
jamesq@SRX5800-1> show rip neighbor
                     Source          Destination     Send   Receive   In
Neighbor       State Address         Address         Mode   Mode      Met
--------       ----- -------         -----------     ----   -------   ---
ge-11/0/4.0       Up 172.16.1.11  224.0.0.9         mcast  both        1
```

Everything looks good, so next you check your learned routes in the inet.0 routing table with the show route command:

```
jamesq@SRX5800-1> show route protocol rip

inet.0: 20 destinations, 22 routes (20 active, 0 holddown, 0 hidden)
Restart Complete
+ = Active Route, - = Last Active, * = Both

198.18.16.0/20          *[RIP/100] 00:55:15, metric 2, tag 0
                       > to 172.16.1.10 via ge-11/0/4.0
224.0.0.9/32          *[RIP/100] 00:59:26, metric 1
                        MultiRecv

jamesq@SRX5800-1>
```

And there you have it, a 198.18.16.0/20 RIP route successfully learned from the 172.16.1.10 neighbor.

One special caveat about RIP is that Junos only *receives* RIP learned routes by default. Junos will not *advertise* routes through RIP unless an explicit export routing policy is defined. The routing policy technology that makes this possible is covered in the next section.

Routing Policy

Routing policy is at the center of what makes IP routing on Junos so special. It is the glue that interconnects the disparate routing protocols and it is your instrument for manipulating routes and controlling their propagation.

In the Junos CLI configuration that follows, you use routing policy to advertise your *RIP* learned `198.18.16.0/20` route through your *IS-IS* routing domain. You enter configuration mode with the `edit` command:

```
jamesq@SRX5800-1> edit
Entering configuration mode
```

And `edit` a new `policy-statement` that you will later apply to your IS-IS configuration:

```
[edit]
jamesq@SRX5800-1# edit policy-options policy-statement into-isis
```

You check your options with CLI help:

```
[edit policy-options policy-statement into-isis]
jamesq@SRX5800-1# set ?
Possible completions:
+ apply-groups         Groups from which to inherit configuration data
+ apply-groups-except  Don't inherit configuration data from these groups
  dynamic-db           Object may exist in dynamic database
> from                 Conditions to match the source of a route
> term                 Policy term
> then                 Actions to take if 'from' and 'to' conditions match
> to                   Conditions to match the destination of a route
```

The basic unit of routing policy configuration is the `term`. Each `term` has its own administrator configurable name. Here you `edit` a new `term` that you have named `rip-to-isis`:

```
[edit policy-options policy-statement into-isis]
jamesq@SRX5800-1# edit term rip-to-isis
```

And investigate the CLI help for `term` configuration:

```
[edit policy-options policy-statement into-isis term rip-to-isis]
jamesq@SRX5800-1# set ?
Possible completions:
+ apply-groups         Groups from which to inherit configuration data
+ apply-groups-except  Don't inherit configuration data from these groups
> from                 Conditions to match the source of a route
> then                 Actions to take if 'from' and 'to' conditions match
> to                   Conditions to match the destination of a route
```

Perfect, a routing policy `term` has just three basic elements:

- The `from` statement identifying the origin of routes
- The `to` statement identifying the destination for routes
- The `then` statement identifying the actions to be taken on the routes

Junos routing policy is both that simple and that powerful.

You look at the CLI help for the `from` statement:

```
[edit policy-options policy-statement into-isis term rip-to-isis]
jamesq@SRX5800-1# set from ?
```

```
Possible completions:
  aggregate-contributor  Match more specifics of an aggregate
+ apply-groups           Groups from which to inherit configuration data
+ apply-groups-except    Don't inherit configuration data from these groups
  area                   OSPF area identifier
+ as-path                Name of AS path regular expression (BGP only)
+ as-path-group          Name of AS path group (BGP only)
  color                  Color (preference) value
  color2                 Color (preference) value 2
+ community              BGP community
+ condition              Condition to match on
> external               External route
  family
  instance               Routing protocol instance
+ interface              Interface name or address
  level                  IS-IS level
  local-preference       Local preference associated with a route
  metric                 Metric value
  metric2                Metric value 2
  metric3                Metric value 3
  metric4                Metric value 4
> multicast-scope        Multicast scope to match
+ neighbor               Neighboring router
+ next-hop               Next-hop router
  next-hop-type          Next-hop type
  origin                 BGP origin attribute
+ policy                 Name of policy to evaluate
  preference             Preference value
  preference2            Preference value 2
> prefix-list            List of prefix-lists of routes to match
> prefix-list-filter     List of prefix-list-filters to match
+ protocol               Protocol from which route was learned
  rib                    Routing table
> route-filter           List of routes to match
  route-type             Route type
> source-address-filter  List of source addresses to match
  state                  Route state
+ tag                    Tag string
  tag2                   Tag string 2
```

There are so many options for identifying routes, but for your project you'll need just two: the routing `protocol` name and the `route-filter` for matching the specific `198.18.16.0/20` route prefix.

Here you use the `protocol` statement to match RIP routes only:

```
[edit policy-options policy-statement into-isis term rip-to-isis]
jamesq@SRX5800-1# set from protocol rip
```

And then you work on setting up a `route-filter` for the `198.18.16.0/20` network (again smartly abbreviating to `198.18.16/20` for brevity) by examining the options in CLI help:

```
[edit policy-options policy-statement into-isis term rip-to-isis]
jamesq@SRX5800-1# set from route-filter 198.18.16/20 ?
Possible completions:
  exact                  Exactly match the prefix length
```

```
  longer               Mask is greater than the prefix length
  orlonger             Mask is greater than or equal to the prefix length
  prefix-length-range  Mask falls between two prefix lengths
  through              Route falls between two prefixes
  upto                 Mask falls between two prefix lengths
```

Perfect, you want to match just the `exact` route `198.18.16.0/20` and not any of the smaller (more specific) routes within the `198.18.16.0/20` range. You complete your configuration statement using the `exact` option:

```
[edit policy-options policy-statement into-isis term rip-to-isis]
jamesq@SRX5800-1# set from route-filter 198.18.16/20 exact
```

Now it's time to do something with these routes. You check out the CLI help for the `then` statement:

```
[edit policy-options policy-statement into-isis term rip-to-isis]
jamesq@SRX5800-1# set then ?
Possible completions:
  accept               Accept a route
+ apply-groups         Groups from which to inherit configuration data
+ apply-groups-except  Don't inherit configuration data from these groups
> as-path-expand       Prepend AS numbers prior to adding local-as (BGP only)
  as-path-prepend      Prepend AS numbers to an AS path (BGP only)
> color                Color (preference) value
> color2               Color (preference) value 2
> community            BGP community properties associated with a route
  damping              Define BGP route flap damping parameters
  default-action       Set default policy action
  destination-class    Set destination class in forwarding table
> external             External route
  forwarding-class     Set source or destination class in forwarding table
> install-nexthop      Choose the next hop to be used for forwarding
  label-allocation     Set label allocation mode
> load-balance         Type of load balancing in forwarding table
> local-preference     Local preference associated with a route
> map-to-interface     Set output logical interface
> metric               Metric value
> metric2              Metric value 2
> metric3              Metric value 3
> metric4              Metric value 4
  next                 Skip to next policy or term
> next-hop             Set the address of the next-hop router
  origin               BGP path origin
> preference           Preference value
> preference2          Preference value 2
  priority             Set priority for route installation
  reject               Reject a route
  source-class         Set source class in forwarding table
> tag                  Tag string
> tag2                 Tag string 2
  trace                Log matches to a trace file
```

Again, there are so many options. But again, you don't want to do anything fancy. You are not trying to change the routing protocol `metric` value, the `next-hop` to the destination, or the QoS `forwarding-class`, or to `load-balance` the traffic (see Case Study 11-3 later for an example of that). You just want to `accept` the route:

```
[edit policy-options policy-statement into-isis term rip-to-isis]
jamesq@SRX5800-1# set then accept
```

You pop `up` one level:

```
[edit policy-options policy-statement into-isis term rip-to-isis]
jamesq@SRX5800-1# up
```

And check out your completed `policy-statement into-isis` with the `show` command:

```
[edit policy-options policy-statement into-isis]
jamesq@SRX5800-1# show
term rip-to-isis {
    from {
        protocol rip;
        route-filter 198.18.16.0/20 exact;
    }
    then accept;
}
```

And it looks beautiful! Time to jump to the `top` of the configuration hierarchy:

```
[edit policy-options policy-statement into-isis]
jamesq@SRX5800-1# top
```

And apply your new `policy-statement into-isis` as an `export` policy for the IS-IS configuration:

```
[edit]
jamesq@SRX5800-1# set protocols isis export into-isis
```

Remember, routing policy is written from the perspective of the Junos routing tables, *not* the routing protocols. In the preceding output, you defined an `export` statement to take a RIP route from the routing table and communicate it *out* through the IS-IS protocol.

Conversely, an `import` policy is used for controlling the routing information taken *into* a routing table from a routing protocol.

Last, you check out your completed configuration with the `show` command:

```
[edit]
jamesq@SRX5800-1# show | compare
[edit protocols]
+   isis {
+       export into-isis;
+   }
[edit policy-options]
+   policy-statement into-isis {
+       term rip-to-isis {
+           from {
+               protocol rip;
+               route-filter 198.18.16.0/20 exact;
```

```
+           }
+           then accept;
+       }
+   }
```

And commit the configuration changes:

```
[edit]
jamesq@SRX5800-1# commit and-quit
configuration check succeeds
commit complete
Exiting configuration mode
```

You check out your results in the operational CLI with the show isis database command:

```
jamesq@SRX5800-1> show isis database
IS-IS level 1 link-state database:
LSP ID                        Sequence Checksum Lifetime Attributes
SRX3400-1.00-00                    0x2   0x65f9     1123 L1 L2
SRX3400-1.02-00                    0x1   0x9408     1123 L1 L2
SRX5800-1.00-00                   0x12   0xd2b7     1125 L1 L2
  3 LSPs

IS-IS level 2 link-state database:
LSP ID                        Sequence Checksum Lifetime Attributes
SRX3400-1.00-00                    0x3   0x93ef     1123 L1 L2
SRX3400-1.02-00                    0x1   0x9408     1123 L1 L2
SRX5800-1.00-00                   0x13   0xc7ee     1125 L1 L2
  3 LSPs
```

There are no new LSPs in the databases, but you do see a higher sequence number (0x13) on the local SRX5800 LSP. Something must have changed!

You investigate the SRX5800 LSP with the extensive option to the show isis database command:

```
jamesq@SRX5800-1> show isis database SRX5800 extensive
IS-IS level 1 link-state database:

SRX5800-1.00-00 Sequence: 0x12, Checksum: 0xd2b7, Lifetime: 1086 secs
   IS neighbor: SRX3400-1.02              Metric:       10
     Two-way fragment: SRX3400-1.02-00, Two-way first fragment: SRX3400-1.02-00
   IP prefix: 198.18.16.0/20              Metric:        2 External Up
   IP prefix: 198.18.16.2/32              Metric:        0 Internal Up
   IP prefix: 10.2.1.0/24                 Metric:       10 Internal Up
```

And there it is!

You still see the original two Internal IS-IS routes from the ge-11/0/5.0 and lo0.0 interfaces configured *within* the IS-IS domain, but now there is also a new External route for the 198.18.16.0/20 prefix that is inherited from RIP *outside* the IS-IS routing domain via the brand-new export routing policy into-isis.

```
Header: LSP ID: SRX5800-1.00-00, Length: 167 bytes
    Allocated length: 1492 bytes, Router ID: 198.18.16.2
```

```
    Remaining lifetime: 1086 secs, Level: 1, Interface: 0
    Estimated free bytes: 1277, Actual free bytes: 1325
    Aging timer expires in: 1086 secs
    Protocols: IP

  Packet: LSP ID: SRX5800-1.00-00, Length: 167 bytes, Lifetime : 1198 secs
    Checksum: 0xd2b7, Sequence: 0x12, Attributes: 0x3 <L1 L2>
    NLPID: 0x83, Fixed length: 27 bytes, Version: 1, Sysid length: 0 bytes
    Packet type: 18, Packet version: 1, Max area: 0

  TLVs:
    Area address: 49 (1)
    Speaks: IP
    IP router id: 198.18.16.2
    IP address: 198.18.16.2
    Hostname: SRX5800-1
    IP prefix: 10.2.1.0/24, Internal, Metric: default 10, Up
    IP prefix: 198.18.16.2/32, Internal, Metric: default 0, Up
    IP extended prefix: 10.2.1.0/24 metric 10 up
    IP extended prefix: 198.18.16.2/32 metric 0 up
    IP external prefix: 198.18.16.0/20, Internal, Metric: default 2, Up
    IP extended prefix: 198.18.16.0/20 metric 2 up
    IS neighbor: SRX3400-1.02, Internal, Metric: default 10
    IS extended neighbor: SRX3400-1.02, Metric: default 10
      IP address: 10.2.1.11
      Local interface index: 80, Remote interface index: 0
  No queued transmissions
```

And, of course, you see the 198.18.16.0/20 prefix successfully included in the IS-IS TLVs.

Case Study 11-3: Equal Cost Multipath (ECMP)

Now that you have the power of routing policy in your tool set, you can go a step beyond your work in Case Study 9-2 earlier where you built redundant OSPF paths between routers. You now have the tools to *load balance* across those redundant paths.

You begin with both links (ge-11/0/5.0 and ge-11/0/6.0) restored to OSPF and set to equal metric costs as shown in the routing table entry for 10.32.1.1/32:

```
jamesq@SRX5800-1> show route 10.32.1.1/32

inet.0: 25 destinations, 28 routes (25 active, 0 holddown, 0 hidden)
Restart Complete
+ = Active Route, - = Last Active, * = Both

10.32.1.1/32        *[OSPF/10] 00:00:55, metric 1
                     to 10.2.1.10 via ge-11/0/5.0
                   > to 10.3.3.10 via ge-11/0/6.0
```

You confirm that only one link (ge-11/0/6.0) is used in the actual forwarding table entry for 10.32.1.1/32:

```
jamesq@SRX5800-1> show route forwarding-table
Routing table: default.inet
Internet:
Destination    Type RtRef Next hop          Type Index NhRef Netif
default        user     2 0:10:db:40:1a:85 ucst   333     4 fxp0.0
default        perm     0                   rjct    36     4
0.0.0.0/32     perm     0                   dscd    34     1
10.32.1.1/32   user     0 10.3.3.10         ucst   600     4 ge-11/0/6.0
```

You go back to configuration mode:

```
jamesq@SRX5800-1> edit
Entering configuration mode
```

And you create a simple new routing policy consisting of a single statement containing the `load-balance per-packet` action:

```
[edit]
jamesq@SRX5800-1# set policy-options policy-statement ecmp then
load-balance per-packet
```

The Junos load balancing action is called `per-packet`, though it actually represents a *per-flow* load balancing behavior. The very first Junos router, the M40, was built on an early data plane application-specific integrated circuit (ASIC) that could not load-balance flows, and so it truly did load-balance *per packet* as the name suggests. However, every subsequent Junos platform in existence (including all further M Series, T Series, MX Series, and, indeed, SRX Series) has load balanced traffic *per flow* when this knob is applied to the forwarding table configuration.

Though this is a *routing* policy, it must be applied to the *forwarding* table, which you do here by configuring it under the `forwarding-table export` statement:

```
[edit]
jamesq@SRX5800-1# set routing-options forwarding-table export ecmp
```

You double-check your configuration work with the `show` command:

```
[edit]
jamesq@SRX5800-1# show | compare
[edit routing-options]
+   forwarding-table {
+       export ecmp;
+   }
[edit policy-options]
+   policy-statement ecmp {
+       then {
+           load-balance per-packet;
+       }
+   }
```

And then `commit`:

```
[edit]
jamesq@SRX5800-1# commit and-quit
```

```
configuration check succeeds
commit complete
Exiting configuration mode
```

You return to the show route 10.32.1.1/32 output and it remains unchanged:

```
jamesq@SRX5800-1# show route 10.32.1.1/32

inet.0: 25 destinations, 28 routes (25 active, 0 holddown, 0 hidden)
Restart Complete
+ = Active Route, - = Last Active, * = Both

10.32.1.1/32       *[OSPF/10] 00:07:59, metric 1
                    to 10.2.1.10 via ge-11/0/5.0
                  > to 10.3.3.10 via ge-11/0/6.0
```

But now you look at the real results in the show route forwarding-table output:

```
jamesq@SRX5800-1# show route forwarding-table
Routing table: default.inet
Internet:
Destination  Type RtRef Next hop           Type Index NhRef Netif
default      user     2 0:10:db:40:1a:85   ucst   333     4 fxp0.0
default      perm     0                    rjct    36     4
0.0.0.0/32   perm     0                    dscd    34     1
10.32.1.1/32 user     0                    ulst 1048574     2
                        10.2.1.10          ucst   599     5 ge-11/0/5.0
                        10.3.3.10          ucst   600     3 ge-11/0/6.0
```

Success! The forwarding table now contains *two* next hop entries for reaching 10.32.1.1/32. The SRX will load-balance *flows* toward the 10.32.1.1/32 destination. Great job!

Internet Peering

You've learned the ins and outs of integrating SRX into your organization's own routed networks, but what if you need to connect an SRX to the global Internet? This section gives you the tools to do just that.

Although there's a plethora of choices for gluing together your *internal* routed networks (OSPF, IS-IS, RIP), there is just one protocol for the global Internet: Border Gateway Protocol (BGP).

BGP has been central to the functioning of the global Internet for two decades. It was created in the time when "the Internet" was just a handful of educational and research institutions connected together via the government-funded National Science Foundation Network (NSFNET). BGP has survived, to its creators' great surprise, through to the enormous and privately funded global spider web of service providers and corporations that is called "the Internet" today.

BGP is very different from the *interior* gateway protocols such as OSPF, IS-IS, and RIP that you reviewed earlier. It is the sole surviving *exterior* gateway protocol (EGP) in use today. It is designed specifically for router peering *between* organizations. Where IGP protocols assume some level of trust and freely pass their routing information between routers once adjacencies are formed, an EGP protocol can never take trust for granted. This is why the *routing policy* covered in the preceding section is so fundamental to building any *real-world* BGP configuration.

BGP must cope with a much larger routing world. Whereas the largest IGP networks contain, at most, a couple thousand routers and possibly several thousand unique IP routes, the one major BGP network in use today (the Internet) represents, very possibly, millions of routers and billions of IP routes. Two things make this level of scale possible: path-vector routing and summarization.

BGP is a path-vector routing protocol. Where the atomic unit of an IGP routing topology is an individual router, the atomic unit of a BGP routing topology is an entire organization. BGP abstracts away all of the routers within an organization's network to just one identifier: the organization's autonomous system (AS) number.

As shown in Figure 11-9, path-vector routing works by finding the shortest AS path or the smallest number of distinct organizations through which traffic must pass to reach a destination.

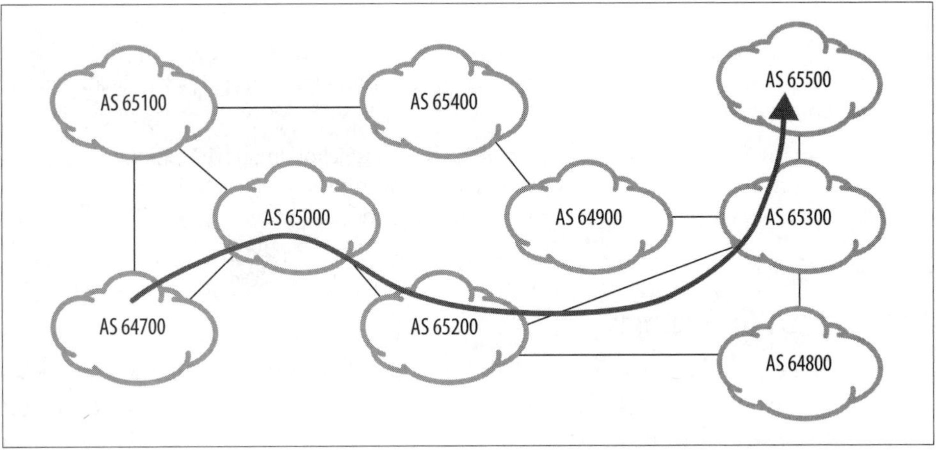

Figure 11-9. BGP path-vector routing

Summarization is the second key to global BGP scaling. Although there might well be billions of IP routes across the globe, BGP only needs to worry about a few of them. As a matter of routing policy, the largest Internet service providers (ISPs) in the world require that all organizations connecting to them summarize their routes to a much smaller number. Where an organization might have hundreds of small /26 IP subnets visible within its IGP (each /26 encompassing as many as 62 IP hosts), a global ISP might only accept a much larger /16 prefix advertisement (encompassing up to 1,024 of the smaller /26 networks) in its routing policy for the organization.

Through this combination of BGP's path-vector design and the prudent enforcement of summarization in ISP routing policy, BGP has survived at the center of the Internet far beyond its designers' expectations. Nonetheless, global Internet routing tables have grown massively in that time—from mere hundreds of routes to, as of this writing, tier-1 ISPs (the very largest) reporting BGP tables in excess of 300,000 globally unique IP routes.

SRX Forwarding Table Convergence

Although the SRX *control plane* is fully capable of running BGP with all the power that Junos routing offers (even supporting full BGP routing tables in the higher-end platforms), the SRX *data plane* is optimized for IP services processing rather than for rapid convergence of very large IP forwarding tables.

Though other Junos platforms such as the M Series, T Series, and MX Series have data planes specifically designed for extraordinarily nimble forwarding table reconvergence even with massive tables of hundreds of thousands of entries, the SRX data plane is designed today only for rapid forwarding table reconvergence at IGP scale (a few thousand routes).

The SRX is most effectively used for Internet peerings where a BGP default route suffices. For Internet borders where full BGP tables of hundreds of thousands of routes are a requirement, using an SRX as the BGP border router is discouraged. It can be done, but forwarding table convergence will be too time-consuming for nearly all real-world deployments.

Of course, the SRX is a platform undergoing constantly evolving development and this limitation may be removed in the future. Please consult the Juniper Networks website at *http://www.juniper.net* for the latest recommendations.

Configuring BGP Peerings

In the Junos CLI configuration that follows, you will establish a BGP peering to an external organization (AS `65400`). You will use routing policy to accept only the default route (`0.0.0.0/0`) and advertise only a summary of your network (`198.18.16.0/20`). You enter configuration mode and move to the BGP configuration hierarchy with the `edit` command:

```
jamesq@SRX5800-1> edit
Entering configuration mode

[edit]
jamesq@SRX5800-1# edit protocols bgp
```

You examine CLI help for the BGP hierarchy:

```
[edit protocols bgp]
jamesq@SRX5800-1# set ?
Possible completions:
```

```
  accept-remote-nexthop  Allow import policy to specify a non-directly
connected next-hop
> advertise-external    Advertise best external routes
  advertise-inactive    Advertise inactive routes
  advertise-peer-as     Advertise routes received from the same autonomous system
+ apply-groups          Groups from which to inherit configuration data
+ apply-groups-except   Don't inherit configuration data from these groups
  authentication-algorithm  Authentication algorithm name
  authentication-key    MD5 authentication key
  authentication-key-chain  Key chain name
> bfd-liveness-detection  Bidirectional Forwarding Detection (BFD) options
  cluster               Cluster identifier
  damping               Enable route flap damping
  description           Text description
  disable               Disable BGP
+ export                Export policy
> family                Protocol family for NLRIs in updates
> graceful-restart      BGP graceful restart options
> group                 Define a peer group
  hold-time             Hold time used when negotiating with a peer
> idle-after-switch-over  Stop peer session from coming up after
> nonstop-routing switch-over
+ import                Import policy
  include-mp-next-hop   Include NEXT-HOP attribute in multiprotocol updates
  ipsec-sa              IPSec SA name
  keep                  How to retain routes in the routing table
  local-address         Address of local end of BGP session
> local-as              Local autonomous system number
  local-interface       Local interface for IPv6 link local EBGP peering
  local-preference      Value of LOCAL_PREF path attribute
  log-updown            Log a message for peer state transitions
> metric-out            Route metric sent in MED
  mtu-discovery         Enable  TCP path MTU discovery
> multihop              Configure an EBGP multihop session
  no-advertise-peer-as  Don't advertise routes received from the
same autonomous system
  no-aggregator-id      Set router ID in aggregator path attribute to 0
  no-client-reflect     Disable intracluster route redistribution
  out-delay             How long before exporting routes from routing
table (0..65535)
> outbound-route-filter  Dynamically negotiated cooperative route filtering
  passive               Do not send open messages to a peer
> path-selection        Configure path selection strategy
  peer-as                Autonomous system number in plain number or
'higher 16bits'.'Lower 16 bits' (asdot notation) format
  preference            Preference value
  remove-private        Remove well-known private AS numbers
  tcp-mss               Maximum TCP segment size (1..4096)
> traceoptions          Trace options for BGP
  vpn-apply-export      Apply BGP export policy when exporting VPN routes
```

Many BGP attributes can be defined globally for the entire protocol at this level, but actual BGP peers are built under `group` configuration. Here you begin to configure a `group` named `ISP` and access CLI help for this level of the hierarchy:

```
[edit protocols bgp]
jamesq@SRX5800-1# set group ISP ?
Possible completions:
  accept-remote-nexthop  Allow import policy to specify a non-directly
connected next-hop
> advertise-external    Advertise best external routes
  advertise-inactive    Advertise inactive routes
  advertise-peer-as     Advertise routes received from the same autonomous system
+ allow                 Configure peer connections for specific networks
+ apply-groups          Groups from which to inherit configuration data
+ apply-groups-except   Don't inherit configuration data from these groups
  as-override           Replace neighbor AS number with our AS number
  authentication-algorithm  Authentication algorithm name
  authentication-key    MD5 authentication key
  authentication-key-chain  Key chain name
> bfd-liveness-detection  Bidirectional Forwarding Detection (BFD) options
  cluster               Cluster identifier
  damping               Enable route flap damping
  description           Text description
+ export                Export policy
> family                Protocol family for NLRIs in updates
> graceful-restart      BGP graceful restart options
  hold-time             Hold time used when negotiating with a peer
> idle-after-switch-over  Stop peer session from coming up after
> nonstop-routing switch-over
+ import                Import policy
  include-mp-next-hop   Include NEXT-HOP attribute in multiprotocol updates
  ipsec-sa              IPSec SA name
  keep                  How to retain routes in the routing table
  local-address         Address of local end of BGP session
> local-as              Local autonomous system number
  local-interface       Local interface for IPv6 link local EBGP peering
  local-preference      Value of LOCAL_PREF path attribute
  log-updown            Log a message for peer state transitions
> metric-out            Route metric sent in MED
  mtu-discovery         Enable TCP path MTU discovery
> multihop              Configure an EBGP multihop session
> multipath             Allow load sharing among multiple BGP paths
> neighbor              Configure a neighbor
  no-advertise-peer-as  Don't advertise routes received from the
same autonomous system
  no-aggregator-id      Set router ID in aggregator path attribute to 0
  no-client-reflect     Disable intracluster route redistribution
  out-delay             How long before exporting routes from routing
table (0..65535)
> outbound-route-filter  Dynamically negotiated cooperative route filtering
  passive               Do not send open messages to a peer
  peer-as                Autonomous system number in plain number or
'higher 16bits'.'Lower 16 bits' (asdot notation) format
  preference            Preference value
  remove-private        Remove well-known private AS numbers
```

```
    tcp-mss                Maximum TCP segment size (1..4096)
  > traceoptions           Trace options for BGP
    type                   Type of peer group
    vpn-apply-export       Apply BGP export policy when exporting VPN routes
```

Again, there are many options for BGP configuration in Junos, but the basic building blocks for your simple BGP peering will be a **neighbor** statement identifying the BGP peer IP address and a **peer-as** statement identifying the AS number of that peer's organization. As this is your first BGP configuration, you must also configure your organization's own AS number under `routing-options autonomous-system` from the top of the configuration hierarchy.

It is also a best practice to configure a `local-address` statement defining the IP address that the SRX will use in exchanging BGP packets with the peer. BGP packets are sent using TCP to the well-known port 179. As such, there is no fundamental restriction on the interface or IP address a BGP speaker will use in initiating a peering. However, the IP addresses must match between peers for Junos routers to accept and establish BGP peerings. Thus, leaving out the `local-address` statement can lead to unexpected results (broken peerings).

You begin configuring the `neighbor` statement for the `198.18.4.10` peer and view CLI help under this hierarchy:

```
[edit protocols bgp]
jamesq@SRX5800-1# set group ISP neighbor 198.18.4.10 ?
Possible completions:
  <[Enter]>            Execute this command
  accept-remote-nexthop  Allow import policy to specify a non-directly
connected next-hop
> advertise-external   Advertise best external routes
  advertise-inactive   Advertise inactive routes
  advertise-peer-as    Advertise routes received from the same autonomous system
+ apply-groups         Groups from which to inherit configuration data
+ apply-groups-except  Don't inherit configuration data from these groups
  as-override          Replace neighbor AS number with our AS number
  authentication-algorithm  Authentication algorithm name
  authentication-key   MD5 authentication key
  authentication-key-chain  Key chain name
> bfd-liveness-detection  Bidirectional Forwarding Detection (BFD) options
  cluster              Cluster identifier
  damping              Enable route flap damping
  description          Text description
+ export               Export policy
> family               Protocol family for NLRIs in updates
> graceful-restart      BGP graceful restart options
  hold-time            Hold time used when negotiating with a peer
> idle-after-switch-over  Stop peer session from coming up after
nonstop-routing switch-over
+ import               Import policy
  include-mp-next-hop  Include NEXT-HOP attribute in multiprotocol updates
  ipsec-sa             IPSec SA name
  keep                 How to retain routes in the routing table
  local-address        Address of local end of BGP session
```

```
> local-as                 Local autonomous system number
  local-interface          Local interface for IPv6 link local EBGP peering
  local-preference         Value of LOCAL_PREF path attribute
  log-updown               Log a message for peer state transitions
> metric-out               Route metric sent in MED
  mtu-discovery            Enable TCP path MTU discovery
> multihop                 Configure an EBGP multihop session
> multipath                Allow load sharing among multiple BGP paths
  no-advertise-peer-as  Don't advertise routes received from the same
autonomous system
  no-aggregator-id         Set router ID in aggregator path attribute to 0
  no-client-reflect        Disable intracluster route redistribution
  out-delay                How long before exporting routes from routing table
(0..65535)
> outbound-route-filter  Dynamically negotiated cooperative route filtering
  passive                  Do not send open messages to a peer
  peer-as                   Autonomous system number in plain number or 'higher
16bits'.'Lower 16 bits' (asdot notation) format
  preference               Preference value
  remove-private           Remove well-known private AS numbers
  tcp-mss                  Maximum TCP segment size (1..4096)
> traceoptions             Trace options for BGP
  vpn-apply-export         Apply BGP export policy when exporting VPN routes
  |                        Pipe through a command
```

Again, many of the same configuration knobs that existed at the global BGP configuration level and at the `group` configuration level also exist here under the individual `neighbor` configuration level. You may configure these knobs wherever it makes sense for your deployment. For larger deployments, it may make sense to configure common values at global or `group` levels. When the same knob is configured at multiple levels, the most specific level for that `neighbor` takes effect. A configuration at the `neighbor` level will supersede a configuration at the `group` level which will in turn supersede a configuration at the global level.

You finish off the `neighbor` statement for `198.18.4.10` by configuring its AS number with the `peer-as` statement:

```
[edit protocols bgp]
jamesq@SRX5800-1# set group ISP neighbor 198.18.4.10 peer-as 65400
```

You configure the SRX to initiate the BGP peering from the `local-address` `198.18.4.254` on the `ge-9/0/5.0` interface directly connected to the `198.18.4.10` peer:

```
[edit protocols bgp]
jamesq@SRX5800-1# set group ISP local-address 198.18.4.254
```

It is key that the BGP peering is initiated between IP addresses on a directly connected Layer 2 network. Though BGP utilizes TCP for communication and can ride over your IGP routed infrastructure to communicate over a larger IP network, the default BGP behavior will transmit packets with an IP time-to-live (TTL) value of just 1. This means the first router hop a BGP packet traverses will decrement the TTL value to 0, drop the packet, and return an ICMP TTL Exceeded message.

This behavior can be altered with the `multihop` configuration knob. This is commonly done to enable eBGP peerings between loopback IP addresses, similar to the common practice for internal BGP (IBGP) peerings within an organization's AS (outside the coverage of this book; please consult O'Reilly's excellent Junos routing publications).

Last in the BGP configuration stanza, you define both the `export` routing policy for the routes that the SRX will send to the BGP peer and the `import` routing policy for the routes that the SRX will accept in from the BGP peer:

```
[edit protocols bgp]
jamesq@SRX5800-1# set group ISP export ISP-out

[edit protocols bgp]
jamesq@SRX5800-1# set group ISP import ISP-in
```

And you `show` your completed BGP configuration (Junos correctly noting that you have not yet created the new routing policies that you have referenced):

```
[edit protocols bgp]
jamesq@SRX5800-1# show
group ISP {
    local-address 198.18.4.254;
    import ISP-in; ## 'ISP-in' is not defined
    export ISP-out; ## 'ISP-out' is not defined
    neighbor 198.18.4.10 {
        peer-as 65400;
    }
}
```

It is time to jump back to the `top` of the configuration hierarchy to complete your project:

```
[edit protocols bgp]
jamesq@SRX5800-1# top
```

The SRX's own `autonomous-system` number is defined globally at the `routing-options` hierarchy of the configuration:

```
[edit protocols bgp]
jamesq@SRX5800-1# set routing-options autonomous-system 65100
```

And now you set out to create your new routing policies for BGP. First, you `edit` the `ISP-in` policy controlling the routes accepted in from the BGP neighbor:

```
[edit protocols bgp]
jamesq@SRX5800-1# edit policy-options policy-statement ISP-in
```

You configure a `term` to `accept` only the default route (`0.0.0.0/0` abbreviated as `0/0`) from the peer:

```
[edit policy-options policy-statement ISP-in]
jamesq@SRX5800-1# set term default-in from route-filter 0/0 exact

[edit policy-options policy-statement ISP-in]
jamesq@SRX5800-1# set term default-in then accept
```

And then configure a final term to reject all other routes from the peer:

```
[edit policy-options policy-statement ISP-in]
jamesq@SRX5800-1# set term block then reject
```

You check your new policy configuration with the show command:

```
[edit policy-options policy-statement ISP-in]
jamesq@SRX5800-1# show
term default-in {
    from {
        route-filter 0.0.0.0/0 exact;
    }
    then accept;
}
term block {
    then reject;
}
```

Then jump up one level:

```
[edit policy-options policy-statement ISP-in]
jamesq@SRX5800-1# up
```

You edit the new outbound ISP-out routing policy controlling routes advertised to the BGP peer:

```
[edit policy-options policy-statement]
jamesq@SRX5800-1# edit policy-statement ISP-out
```

You create a new term advertising the aggregate route of 198.18.16.0/20 (abbreviated as 198.18.16/20) summarizing your networks:

```
[edit policy-options policy-statement ISP-out]
jamesq@SRX5800-1# set term OrgXYZ from protocol aggregate

[edit policy-options policy-statement ISP-out]
jamesq@SRX5800-1# set term OrgXYZ from route-filter 198.18.16/20 exact

[edit policy-options policy-statement ISP-out]
jamesq@SRX5800-1# set term OrgXYZ then accept
```

You show your new one term policy:

```
[edit policy-options policy-statement ISP-out]
jamesq@SRX5800-1# show
term OrgXYZ {
    from {
        protocol rip;
        route-filter 198.18.16.0/20 exact;
    }
    then accept;
}
```

And you pop back to the top of the configuration hierarchy:

```
[edit policy-options policy-statement ISP-out]
jamesq@SRX5800-1# top
```

And create this new `aggregate` route of `198.18.16.0/20` under the `routing-options` stanza:

```
[edit]
jamesq@SRX5800-1# set routing-options aggregate route 198.18.16/20
```

An `aggregate` route is, just like it sounds, a route that encompasses smaller (more specific) routes within its prefix range. An `aggregate` route is similar to a `static` route, but without the literal actions such as `next-hop` and `discard`. More specific routes within the defined prefix range must be present in the same routing table for an `aggregate` route to likewise be active and present in the routing table.

In the case of the `198.18.16.0/20` route, we know from earlier in the chapter that there is a more specific `198.18.16.2/32` address configured on the SRX's own `lo0.0` interface creating the necessary, more specific route for this `aggregate` route to become active.

You inspect your completed configuration with a `show` command:

```
[edit]
jamesq@SRX5800-1# show | compare
[edit routing-options]
+   aggregate {
+       route 198.18.16.0/20;
+   }
+   autonomous-system 65100;
[edit]
+  protocols {
+      bgp {
+          group ISP {
+              local-address 198.18.4.254;
+              import ISP-in;
+              export ISP-out;
+              neighbor 198.18.4.10 {
+                  peer-as 65400;
+              }
+          }
+      }
+  }
+  policy-options {
+      policy-statement ISP-in {
+          term default-in {
+              from {
+                  route-filter 0.0.0.0/0 exact;
+              }
+              then accept;
+          }
+          term block {
+              then reject;
+          }
+      }
+      policy-statement ISP-out {
+          term OrgXYZ {
+              from {
+                  protocol aggregate;
+                  route-filter 198.18.16.0/20 exact;
```

```
+                   }
+                   then accept;
+               }
+           }
+   }
```

And `commit` the changes:

```
[edit]
jamesq@SRX5800-1# commit and-quit
configuration check succeeds
commit complete
Exiting configuration mode
```

BGP is much like RIP in having timers measured on the order of *minutes*, so your new BGP peering will not come up instantaneously. But BGP can fortunately be extended with BFD configuration (much like OSPF and IS-IS) for subsecond failure detection after the BGP peering is established.

After waiting a requisite couple of minutes, you view your BGP configuration results in the Junos operational CLI with the `show bgp summary` command:

```
jamesq@SRX5800-1> show bgp summary
Groups: 1 Peers: 1 Down peers: 0
Table    Tot Paths  Act Paths Suppressed    History Damp State    Pending
inet.0          1          0          0          0          0          0
Peer                AS      InPkt     OutPkt    OutQ   Flaps Last Up/Dwn State
|#Active/Received/Accepted/Damped...
198.18.4.10     65400          3          3       0       0     1 0/1/1/0
0/0/0/0
```

Success! You can see that the peering is fully `Established` as the SRX is receiving a route from the peer (the `0/1/1/0` under `Active/Received/Accepted/Damped` shown in the output).

You'll note that this BGP peering came up without resorting to any new `security zone` configuration. This is because BGP utilizes TCP for communication. Typically both BGP peers will attempt to initiate the TCP flow (each by sending its own SYN flagged packets), but only one TCP flow is necessary for a successful BGP peering.

As the SRX data plane will happily pass control plane traffic *outbound* without respect to security policy, the TCP connection initiated by the local SRX itself was able to successfully negotiate for the BGP peering. The SRX, being a *stateful* firewall device, allowed the traffic from the other BGP peer to return within the context of this same TCP flow. Nonetheless, for absolute best practices, it would be a good idea to explicitly permit BGP in the `security zone` configuration of the BGP configured interface.

BGP Routing Tables

For even the simplest BGP peering, there are always at least three routing tables. First, there is the received routes table (the *Adj-RIB-In* in BGP terminology) which represents the routes as they are received from the BGP peer before the application of routing policy. Inspecting this table can be very useful in troubleshooting `import` routing policies. Here you examine this table with the `show route receive-protocol bgp` command:

```
jamesq@SRX5800-1> show route receive-protocol bgp 198.18.4.10

inet.0: 17 destinations, 20 routes (17 active, 0 holddown, 0 hidden)
Restart Complete
  Prefix          Nexthop              MED     Lclpref    AS path
  0.0.0.0/0       198.18.4.10                             65400 I
```

The second table is the more ordinary primary routing table (`inet.0` in Junos) that contains received BGP routes *after* the application of routing policy (which may alter or filter routes out entirely) and is also the source of routes for the `export` routing policies that will determine the routing information shared outbound with BGP peers. This table can be examined more simply with the `show route protocol bgp` command:

```
jamesq@SRX5800-1> show route protocol bgp

inet.0: 23 destinations, 26 routes (23 active, 0 holddown, 0 hidden)
Restart Complete
+ = Active Route, - = Last Active, * = Both

0.0.0.0/0          *[BGP/170] 01:46:07, localpref 100
                      AS path: 65400 I
                    > to 198.18.4.10 via ge-9/0/5.0
```

Good job! The SRX is successfully accepting the BGP learned `0.0.0.0/0` default route into the `inet.0` table.

Last, the third table is the advertised routes table (the *Adj-RIB-Out* in BGP terminology) which represents the routes advertised to the BGP peer after the application of `export` routing policies. Here you examine this table with the `show route advertising-protocol bgp` command:

```
jamesq@SRX5800-1> show route advertising-protocol bgp 198.18.4.10

inet.0: 18 destinations, 21 routes (18 active, 0 holddown, 0 hidden)
Restart Complete
  Prefix          Nexthop              MED     Lclpref    AS path
* 198.18.16.0/20       Self                                   I

{primary:node0}
root@SRX5800-1>
```

Perfect! The SRX is successfully advertising the `198.18.16.0/20` aggregate route to the BGP peer.

Case Study 11-4: Internet Redundancy

Much like the OSPF section before Case Study 9-2 earlier in the chapter, you have a single point of failure in your new BGP configuration. There is only one upstream BGP path to the public Internet. As shown in Figure 11-10, there is a well-known concept

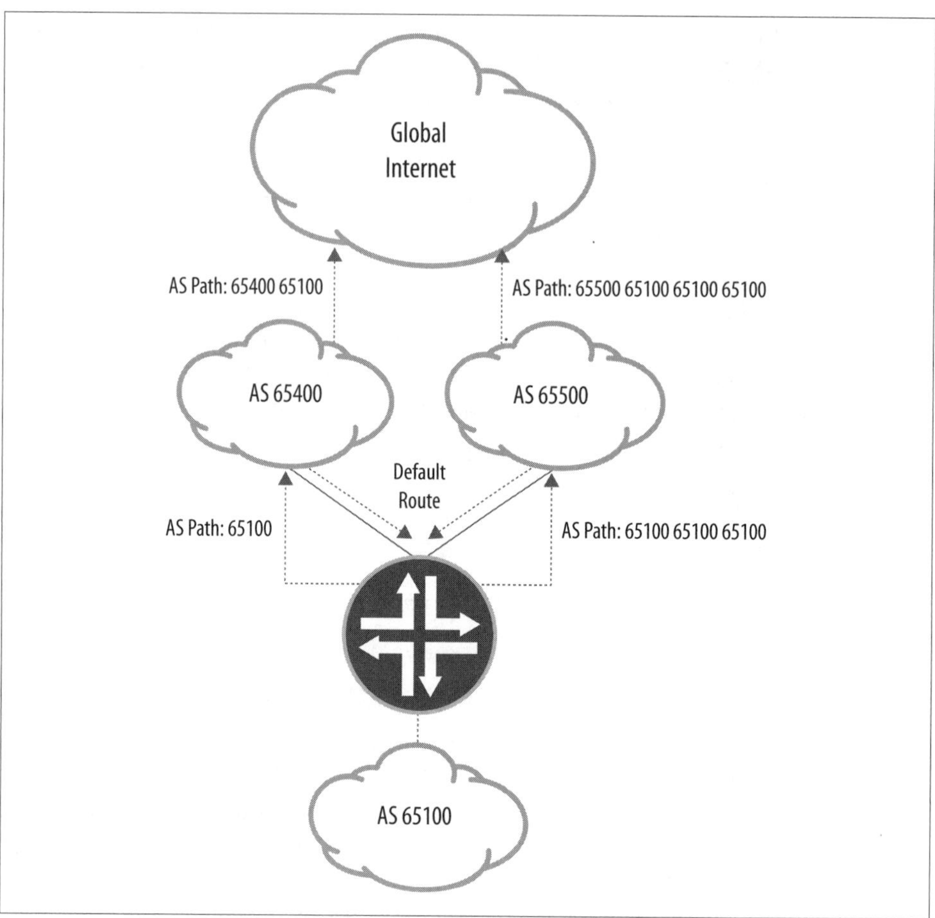

Figure 11-10. BGP multihoming

of *BGP multihoming* in the Internet community where an organization is BGP-peered redundantly to two different upstream ISPs.

In the Junos CLI configuration that follows, you will create a second BGP peering to a redundant ISP. Although this new path will be fully available for failover, you will make it the less preferred path using the concepts of BGP Local Preference and AS path prepending (as pictured in Figure 11-10).

You begin by entering configuration mode with the `edit` command:

```
jamesq@SRX5800-1> edit
Entering configuration mode
```

And create a new BGP configuration `group` named `ISP-redundant`:

```
[edit]
jamesq@SRX5800-1# edit protocols bgp group ISP-redundant
```

From within this new group hierarchy, you configure the neighbor 198.18.5.10 and its peer-as 65500:

```
[edit protocols bgp group ISP-redundant]
jamesq@SRX5800-1# set neighbor 198.18.5.10 peer-as 65500
```

You define the local-address 198.18.5.254 to match the ge-9/0/6.0 link directly connecting to the peer:

```
[edit protocols bgp group ISP-redundant]
jamesq@SRX5800-1# set local-address 198.18.5.254
```

And reference the soon-to-be-created import and export policies for route exchange with the peer:

```
[edit protocols bgp group ISP-redundant]
jamesq@SRX5800-1# set import redundant-ISP-in

[edit protocols bgp group ISP-redundant]
jamesq@SRX5800-1# set export redundant-ISP-out
```

You show your completed BGP configuration group (Junos, as before, correctly noting that you have not yet created the new routing policies that you have referenced):

```
[edit protocols bgp group ISP-redundant]
jamesq@SRX5800-1# show
local-address 198.18.5.254;
import redundant-ISP-in; ## 'redundant-ISP-in' is not defined
export redundant-ISP-out; ## 'redundant-ISP-out' is not defined
neighbor 198.18.5.10 {
    peer-as 65500;
}
```

You jump back to the top of the configuration hierarchy:

```
[edit protocols bgp group ISP-redundant]
jamesq@SRX5800-1# top
```

And edit the new redundant-ISP-in policy controlling the routes that the SRX will accept from the redundant ISP's BGP peering:

```
[edit]
jamesq@SRX5800-1# edit policy-options policy-statement redundant-ISP-in
```

Much as with the earlier BGP peer's configuration, the new policy likewise allows only a default route (0.0.0.0/0 abbreviated as 0/0):

```
[edit policy-options policy-statement redundant-ISP-in]
jamesq@SRX5800-1# set term redundant-default-in from route-filter 0/0 exact
```

But you configure this new policy with a lower (less preferred) local-preference value of 50 (the default value being 100), ensuring that the SRX will prefer the other BGP peer's routes:

```
[edit policy-options policy-statement redundant-ISP-in]
jamesq@SRX5800-1# set term redundant-default-in then local-preference 50
```

```
[edit policy-options policy-statement redundant-ISP-in]
jamesq@SRX5800-1# set term redundant-default-in then accept
```

And, as before, you create a final term to reject all other routes from this new BGP peer:

```
[edit policy-options policy-statement redundant-ISP-in]
jamesq@SRX5800-1# set term block then reject
```

You jump up one level:

```
[edit policy-options policy-statement redundant-ISP-in]
jamesq@SRX5800-1# up
```

And now edit the new redundant-ISP-out policy controlling the routes that the SRX will advertise out to the redundant ISP peering:

```
[edit policy-options]
jamesq@SRX5800-1# edit policy-statement redundant-ISP-out
```

As before, you advertise only the 198.18.16.0/20 (abbreviated as 198.18.16/20) aggregate route:

```
[edit policy-options policy-statement redundant-ISP-out]
jamesq@SRX5800-1# set term OrgXYZ-prepend from protocol aggregate

[edit policy-options policy-statement redundant-ISP-out]
jamesq@SRX5800-1# set term OrgXYZ-prepend from route-filter 198.18.16/20 exact
```

But now you also as-path-prepend with your AS number three times, encouraging Internet routers to prefer the much shorter AS path through your original BGP peering with the first ISP:

```
[edit policy-options policy-statement redundant-ISP-out]
jamesq@SRX5800-1# set term OrgXYZ-prepend then as-path-prepend
"65100 65100 65100"

[edit policy-options policy-statement redundant-ISP-out]
jamesq@SRX5800-1# set term OrgXYZ-prepend then accept
```

You jump back to the top of the configuration:

```
[edit policy-options policy-statement redundant-ISP-out]
jamesq@SRX5800-1# top
```

And show the completed additions:

```
[edit]
jamesq@SRX5800-1# show | compare
[edit protocols bgp]
     group ISP { ... }
+    group ISP-redundant {
+        local-address 198.18.5.254;
+        import redundant-ISP-in;
+        export redundant-ISP-out;
+        neighbor 198.18.5.10 {
+            peer-as 65500;
+        }
+    }
```

```
[edit policy-options]
+   policy-statement redundant-ISP-in {
+       term redundant-default-in {
+           from {
+               route-filter 0.0.0.0/0 exact;
+           }
+           then {
+               local-preference 50;
+               accept;
+           }
+       }
+       term block {
+           then reject;
+       }
+   }
+   policy-statement redundant-ISP-out {
+       term OrgXYZ-prepend {
+           from {
+               protocol aggregate;
+               route-filter 198.18.16.0/20 exact;
+           }
+           then {
+               as-path-prepend "65100 65100 65100";
+               accept;
+           }
+       }
+   }
```

Before the commit:

```
[edit]
jamesq@SRX5800-1# commit and-quit
configuration check succeeds
commit complete
Exiting configuration mode
```

After waiting a couple of minutes, you view your BGP configuration results in the Junos operational CLI with the `show bgp summary` command:

```
jamesq@SRX5800-1> show bgp summary
Groups: 2 Peers: 2 Down peers: 0
Table      Tot Paths  Act Paths Suppressed    History Damp State    Pending
inet.0             2          0          0          0          0          0
Peer                 AS      InPkt     OutPkt    OutQ   Flaps Last Up/Dwn
State|#Active/Received/Accepted/Damped...
198.18.4.10       65400        628        636       0       1     1:06:40
0/1/1/0           0/0/0/0
198.18.5.10       65500          3          5       0       0          28
0/1/1/0           0/0/0/0
```

Great job! You now have BGP peerings to redundant ISPs (AS numbers `65400` and `65500`), each showing one accepted route. You dig a little deeper with the `show route` command:

```
jamesq@SRX5800-1> show route protocol bgp

inet.0: 20 destinations, 24 routes (20 active, 0 holddown, 0 hidden)
Restart Complete
+ = Active Route, - = Last Active, * = Both

0.0.0.0/0          *[BGP/170] 01:06:50, localpref 100
                      AS path: 65400 I
                    > to 198.18.4.10 via ge-9/0/5.0
                    [BGP/170] 00:00:38, localpref 50
                      AS path: 65500 I
                    > to 198.18.5.10 via ge-9/0/6.0
```

And there you have it, a redundant default route (showing the less preferred `localpref 50`) toward the new `198.18.5.10` peer.

And finally, you confirm that the SRX is advertising the `198.18.16.0/20` route with the correct AS path prepending to the `198.18.5.10` peer using the `show route` command:

```
jamesq@SRX5800-1> show route advertising-protocol bgp 198.18.5.10

inet.0: 20 destinations, 24 routes (20 active, 0 holddown, 0 hidden)
Restart Complete
  Prefix             Nexthop      MED     Lclpref    AS path
* 198.18.16.0/20        Self    65100        65100 65100 [65100] I
```

Congratulations! You now have fully redundant Internet peerings!

Routing Instances

This and the next section ("Filter-Based Forwarding" on page 693) will move beyond the more customary IP routing topics to some of what makes IP routing in the Junos operating system so unique.

The Junos control plane is far more versatile than that of a typical IP router. Junos is not limited to one monolithic routing table, but rather can support hundreds and even *thousands* of distinct routing tables on the highest-end platforms.

Likewise, the Junos data plane is not restricted by traditional destination-based routing when making forwarding decisions (as you'll explore in both this and the next section). It can make forwarding decisions based on nearly any relevant fields in the Layer 3 and Layer 4 headers.

The power and flexibility that is put in your hands by this combination of highly unique control plane and equally unique data plane is extraordinary. In an age when *virtualization* has become a buzzword, IP routing in Junos is the real deal. You will scratch the surface of Junos's power in the following sections.

Configuring Routing Instances

The `routing-instance` is the basic building block for constructing the multiplicity of custom routing tables, forwarding entries, and routing protocol instantiations that are possible with the Junos operating system.

In the Junos CLI configuration that follows, you will create a custom `routing-instance` with its own routing table, interface, and OSPF, as depicted in Figure 11-11.

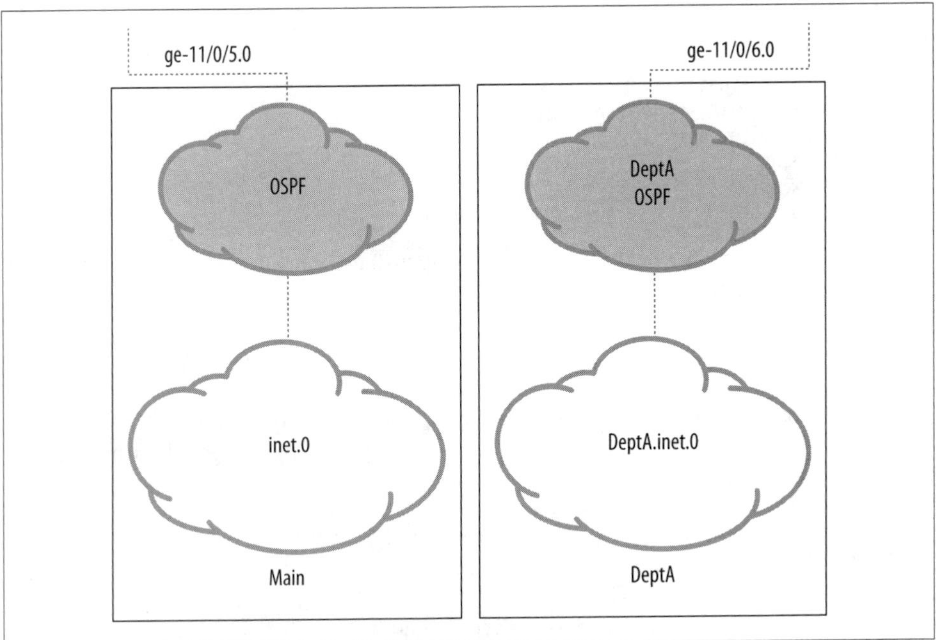

Figure 11-11. Routing instances

Here you enter configuration mode with the **`edit`** command:

```
jamesq@SRX5800-1> edit
Entering configuration mode
```

And **`edit`** your new `routing-instances DeptA`:

```
[edit]
jamesq@SRX5800-1# edit routing-instances DeptA
```

You view the CLI help for `routing-instance` configuration:

```
[edit routing-instances DeptA]
jamesq@SRX5800-1# set ?
Possible completions:
> access               Network access configuration
> access-profile       Access profile for this instance
+ apply-groups         Groups from which to inherit configuration data
+ apply-groups-except  Don't inherit configuration data from these groups
```

```
  description          Text description of routing instance
  instance-type        Type of routing instance
> interface            Interface name for this routing instance
  no-irb-layer-2-copy  Disable transmission of layer-2 copy of packets of irb
routing-interface
> pbb-options          Provider backbone bridging options for routing-instance
> protocols            Routing protocol configuration
> routing-options      Protocol-independent routing option configuration
> service-groups       Service group configuration for routing-instance
```

You have the option to introduce interfaces, routing protocols, and custom static routes to the `routing-instance` configuration, but an `instance-type` *must* be defined:

```
[edit routing-instances DeptA]
jamesq@SRX5800-1# set instance-type ?
Possible completions:
  forwarding           Forwarding instance
  no-forwarding        Nonforwarding instance
  virtual-router       Virtual routing instance
```

A `forwarding` instance contains distinct routing and forwarding tables but no instance level routing protocols or interfaces.

A `no-forwarding` instance is a vehicle for creating routing tables that will populate forwarding tables outside the instance.

A `virtual-router` instance is the full package, encompassing the ability to configure interfaces, routing protocols, routing tables, and forwarding tables all within the one `routing-instance`.

For maximum flexibility in this project, you configure your new `routing-instance` as a `virtual-router`:

```
[edit routing-instances DeptA]
jamesq@SRX5800-1# set instance-type virtual-router
```

The configuration of routing protocols within a `routing-instance` requires the inclusion of at least one logical interface. You move the `ge-9/0/6.0` interface to the new `routing-instance`:

```
[edit routing-instances DeptA]
jamesq@SRX5800-1# set interface ge-9/0/6.0
```

And then configure it within `area 0` of OSPF:

```
[edit routing-instances DeptA]
jamesq@SRX5800-1# set protocols ospf area 0 interface ge-9/0/6.0
```

You hop up to the `top` of the configuration:

```
[edit routing-instances DeptA]
jamesq@SRX5800-1# top
```

And view your changes with the `show` command:

```
[edit]
jamesq@SRX5800-1# show | compare
```

```
[edit routing-instances]
+   DeptA {
+       instance-type virtual-router;
+       interface ge-9/0/6.0;
+       protocols {
+           ospf {
+               area 0.0.0.0 {
+                   interface ge-9/0/6.0;
+               }
+           }
+       }
+   }
```

And decide to `commit`:

```
[edit]
jamesq@SRX5800-1# commit and-quit
[edit security zones security-zone trust]
  'interfaces ge-9/0/6.0'
    Interface ge-9/0/6.0 must be in the same routing instance as other
interfaces in the zone
error: configuration check-out failed
```

Oops!

And this is where SRX is different from an ordinary Junos router. On the SRX, interfaces don't just live in routing instances; they also live in security zones.

All interfaces configured within the same security zone must also be configured within the same routing instance.

As the security zone cannot span more than one routing instance, you will either need to remove the `ge-9/0/6.0` interface from the new routing instance or place it in a different security zone. Given the goal of the present project, you remove the `ge-9/0/6.0` interface from the `trust` zone:

```
[edit]
jamesq@SRX5800-1# delete security zones security-zone trust interfaces ge-9/0/6.0
```

And place it in a new `DeptA` zone:

```
[edit]
jamesq@SRX5800-1# set security zones security-zone DeptA interfaces ge-9/0/6.0
```

Which you also quickly configure to allow `all` traffic for the control plane:

```
[edit]
jamesq@SRX5800-1# set security zones security-zone DeptA host-inbound-
traffic protocols all

[edit]
jamesq@SRX5800-1# set security zones security-zone DeptA host-inbound-
traffic system-services all
```

And now again you view your changes with the show command:

```
[edit]
jamesq@SRX5800-1# show | compare
[edit security zones security-zone trust interfaces]
-     ge-9/0/6.0;
[edit security zones]
     security-zone Mu { ... }
+    security-zone DeptA {
+        host-inbound-traffic {
+            system-services {
+                all;
+            }
+            protocols {
+                all;
+            }
+        }
+        interfaces {
+            ge-9/0/6.0;
+        }
+    }
[edit routing-instances]
+   DeptA {
+       instance-type virtual-router;
+       interface ge-9/0/6.0;
+       protocols {
+           ospf {
+               area 0.0.0.0 {
+                   interface ge-9/0/6.0;
+               }
+           }
+       }
+   }
```

And commit the changes:

```
[edit]
jamesq@SRX5800-1# commit and-quit
configuration check succeeds
commit complete
Exiting configuration mode
```

You add the instance option to the show ospf neighbor command to check the adjacency within your new instance of OSPF:

```
jamesq@SRX5800-1> show ospf neighbor instance DeptA
Address          Interface     State     ID              Pri  Dead
198.18.5.10     ge-9/0/6.0     Full      198.18.5.10     128    34
```

Great! The adjacency is in a Full state.

Next you add the table option to the show route command to see the new instance's custom routing table:

```
jamesq@SRX5800-1> show route table DeptA

DeptA.inet.0: 4 destinations, 4 routes (4 active, 0 holddown, 0 hidden)
```

```
+ = Active Route, - = Last Active, * = Both

0.0.0.0/0          *[OSPF/150] 00:00:25, metric 0, tag 0
                    > to 198.18.5.10 via ge-9/0/6.0
198.18.5.0/24      *[Direct/0] 00:00:42
                    > via ge-9/0/6.0
198.18.5.254/32    *[Local/0]  00:00:42
                      Local via ge-9/0/6.0
224.0.0.5/32       *[OSPF/10] 00:00:43, metric 1
                      MultiRecv
```

Beautiful!

And through the magic of routing instances your SRX now has two entirely separate default routes, the one in the main `inet.0` routing table and the second in the new instance's `DeptA.inet.0` table, as shown in this `show route` output:

```
jamesq@SRX5800-1> show route 0/0 exact

inet.0: 18 destinations, 21 routes (18 active, 0 holddown, 0 hidden)
Restart Complete
+ = Active Route, - = Last Active, * = Both

0.0.0.0/0          *[BGP/170] 00:12:28, localpref 100
                      AS path: 65400 I
                    > to 198.18.4.10 via ge-9/0/5.0

DeptA.inet.0: 4 destinations, 4 routes (4 active, 0 holddown, 0 hidden)
+ = Active Route, - = Last Active, * = Both

0.0.0.0/0          *[OSPF/150] 00:01:18, metric 0, tag 0
                    > to 198.18.5.10 via ge-9/0/6.0

jamesq@SRX5800-1>
```

Filter-Based Forwarding

Filter-based forwarding (FBF) combines the firewall filter tools explored in Chapter 6 with the `routing-instance` tools of the preceding section to create an entirely new instrument for manipulating traffic flow.

FBF brings the virtualization of the control plane's `routing-instance` down into the data plane's forwarding table. Rather than segmenting routing and forwarding simply at the interface level as you did in the preceding section, FBF empowers you to slice and dice traffic as you see fit.

As depicted in Figure 11-12, if you want web traffic going down one path to the Internet and all other traffic going down another path, you can do that. If you want your workstation using one link to the data center for VoIP calls and another for backups, you can do that too. In fact, there isn't much that can be dreamt up in the realm of routing and forwarding that cannot be accomplished with the careful application of FBF.

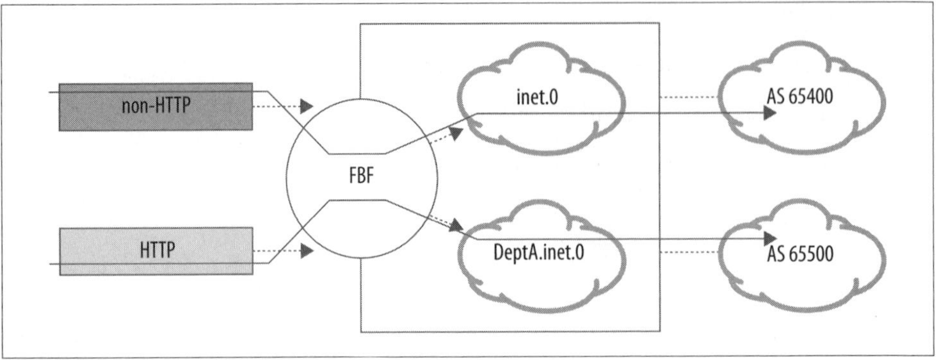

Figure 11-12. Filter-based forwarding

FBF is sometimes confused with the policy-based routing (PBR) features of legacy and competing platforms. FBF goes far beyond PBR. PBR is, at best, a more extensible version of a static route. FBF is PBR on steroids. FBF has all the same traffic matching capabilities, but it ties them directly into the power of Junos's full complement of dynamic routing protocols.

Ultimately, all this power in FBF is made possible through the existence of just one simple knob, the `then routing-instance` action in firewall filter terms. Traffic can first be divided with all the versatility of firewall filter `from` criteria, and then it can be acted upon with the equal versatility of an array of unique `routing-instance` dynamic routing configuration.

Configuring Filter-Based Forwarding

In the Junos CLI configuration that follows, you will build a simple example of FBF splitting of HTTP traffic off to the `DeptA` instance built in the preceding section.

You begin by entering configuration mode with the `edit` command:

```
jamesq@SRX5800-1> edit
Entering configuration mode
```

And move to the `firewall filter` configuration hierarchy, creating a new filter named `fbf-redirect`:

```
[edit]
jamesq@SRX5800-1# edit firewall filter fbf-redirect
```

You inspect CLI help for the *very* wide array of `from` options for matching traffic in `firewall filter` terms:

```
[edit firewall filter fbf-redirect]
jamesq@SRX5800-1# set term HTTP from ?
Possible completions:
> address              Match IP source or destination address
+ apply-groups         Groups from which to inherit configuration data
+ apply-groups-except  Don't inherit configuration data from these groups
```

```
> destination-address  Match IP destination address
+ destination-port     Match TCP/UDP destination port
+ destination-port-except  Do not match TCP/UDP destination port
> destination-prefix-list  Match IP destination prefixes in named list
+ dscp                 Match Differentiated Services (DiffServ) code point
+ dscp-except          Do not match Differentiated Services (DiffServ) code point
+ esp-spi              Match IPSec ESP SPI value
+ esp-spi-except       Do not match IPSec ESP SPI value
  first-fragment       Match if packet is the first fragment
+ forwarding-class     Match forwarding class
+ forwarding-class-except  Do not match forwarding class
  fragment-flags       Match fragment flags (in symbolic or hex formats)
- (Ingress only)
+ fragment-offset      Match fragment offset
+ fragment-offset-except  Do not match fragment offset
+ icmp-code            Match ICMP message code
+ icmp-code-except     Do not match ICMP message code
+ icmp-type            Match ICMP message type
+ icmp-type-except     Do not match ICMP message type
> interface            Match interface name
+ interface-group      Match interface group
+ interface-group-except  Do not match interface group
> interface-set        Match interface in set
+ ip-options           Match IP options
+ ip-options-except    Do not match IP options
  is-fragment          Match if packet is a fragment
+ packet-length        Match packet length
+ packet-length-except  Do not match packet length
+ port                 Match TCP/UDP source or destination port
+ port-except          Do not match TCP/UDP source or destination port
+ precedence           Match IP precedence value
+ precedence-except    Do not match IP precedence value
> prefix-list          Match IP source or destination prefixes in named list
+ protocol             Match IP protocol type
+ protocol-except      Do not match IP protocol type
  service-filter-hit   Match if service-filter-hit is set
> source-address       Match IP source address
+ source-port          Match TCP/UDP source port
+ source-port-except   Do not match TCP/UDP source port
> source-prefix-list   Match IP source prefixes in named list
  tcp-established      Match packet of an established TCP connection
  tcp-flags            Match TCP flags (in symbolic or hex formats)
  tcp-initial          Match initial packet of a TCP connection
```

And settle on just two `from` options to tease out the HTTP traffic you want to match. You match on `port 80` (the well-known TCP port—here matching regardless of direction, source, or destination port will do) and `protocol 6` (the IP protocol number for TCP):

```
[edit firewall filter fbf-redirect]
jamesq@SRX5800-1# set term http from port 80

[edit firewall filter fbf-redirect]
jamesq@SRX5800-1# set term http from protocol 6
```

And now the key, you configure a `then routing-instance DeptA` action to send this HTTP traffic to the new `DeptA` instance created in the preceding section:

```
[edit firewall filter fbf-redirect]
jamesq@SRX5800-1# set term http then routing-instance DeptA
```

Of course, packets cannot actually be "sent" to something that only exists virtually (such as a routing instance). In reality, "sending" traffic to the `DeptA` routing instance simply means the forwarding table lookup for this traffic will be derived from the unique `DeptA.inet.0` routing table of that instance.

The default action of a `firewall filter` is to drop unmatched traffic (even when it is built for FBF purposes), so you must configure a final `term` matching and permitting all other traffic to steer clear of creating an outage:

```
[edit firewall filter fbf-redirect]
jamesq@SRX5800-1# set term accept then accept
```

You view your completed `firewall filter` with a `show` command:

```
[edit firewall filter fbf-redirect]
jamesq@SRX5800-1# show
term http {
    from {
        protocol 6;
        port 80;
    }
    then {
        routing-instance DeptA;
    }
}
term accept {
    then accept;
}
```

And then jump to the `top` of the configuration hierarchy:

```
[edit firewall filter fbf-redirect]
jamesq@SRX5800-1# top
```

To apply the new `firewall filter fbf-redirect` against traffic entering the `ge-9/0/1.0` interface:

```
[edit]
jamesq@SRX5800-1# set interfaces ge-9/0/1.0 family inet filter input fbf-redirect
```

You check out the final configuration changes with a `show` command:

```
[edit]
jamesq@SRX5800-1# show | compare
[edit interfaces ge-9/0/1 unit 0 family inet]
+       filter {
+           input fbf-redirect;
+       }
[edit firewall]
    filter test { ... }
+   filter fbf-redirect {
```

```
+       term http {
+           from {
+               protocol 6;
+               port 80;
+           }
+           then {
+               routing-instance DeptA;
+           }
+       }
+       term accept {
+           then accept;
+       }
+   }
```

And `commit` the changes:

```
[edit]
jamesq@SRX5800-1# commit and-quit
configuration check succeeds
commit complete
Exiting configuration mode

jamesq@SRX5800-1>
```

Case Study 11-5: Dynamic Traffic Engineering

In this case study, you will build upon the redundant Internet topology from Case Study 9-4, but this time you'll use the fresh twists of FBF and routing instances. You will create precisely the sort of unique traffic engineered solution that is so special to Junos.

To make all of this magic work, you will use one new concept. The `rib-group` (RIB for *Routing Information Base*, which is just a fancy name for a routing table) is the configuration vehicle that enables Junos to combine multiple routing tables into *groups* and to thereby populate routes across multiple routing tables simultaneously.

In the Junos CLI configuration that follows, you will pick out two lucky /24 ranges of your Organization-XYZ hosts and *dynamically* route each through *opposite* preferred Internet paths, all while they are otherwise traveling over the identical topology and using the very same routes, as depicted in Figure 11-13.

You will start by building two `forwarding` type routing instances and a new `firewall filter` steering the respective /24 host ranges each to its own routing instance.

You will modify your existing `import` BGP routing policies to manipulate the `local-preference` values of the received default Internet routes as they are passed to the instance routing tables. These routing policy modifications will make each instance's routing table act as the mirror image of the other. Both instances' tables will see the *identical* two BGP default routes from the identical two Internet peers, but each table will view these same two routes with *opposite* `local-preference` values.

This will in turn lead Junos to create opposite forwarding actions for traffic passed by the `firewall filter` to the two routing instances. The two chosen /24 ranges of hosts

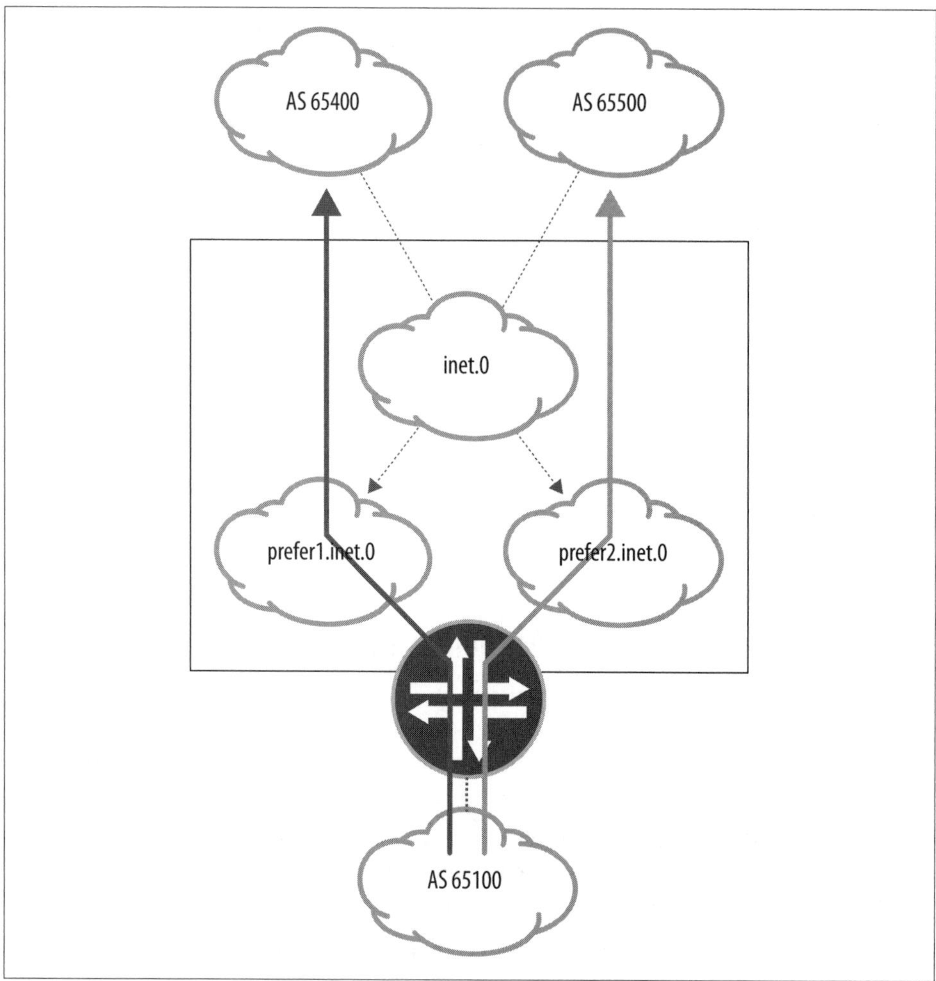

Figure 11-13. Dynamic traffic engineering

will route to the public Internet through opposite Internet connections. This will happen despite the fact that their traffic is otherwise identical and entering the SRX through the very same `ge-9/0/4.0` interface.

Meanwhile, thanks to the power of Junos, all of this traffic engineering flexibility is achieved without the loss of one bit of dynamic routing redundancy. Despite opposite preferred routes, each routing table will nonetheless see the redundant route through the counterpart's preferred Internet connection. This redundant route will simply be placed in each table with a Local Preference opposite to that of the other table.

You begin your work by entering configuration mode with the `edit` command:

```
jamesq@SRX5800-1> edit
Entering configuration mode
```

And create your two new routing instances named prefer1 and prefer2:

```
[edit]
jamesq@SRX5800-1# set routing-instances prefer1 instance-type forwarding

[edit]
jamesq@SRX5800-1# set routing-instances prefer2 instance-type forwarding
```

Both routing instances are as simple as could be. Each contains the required instance-type statement and nothing more. As forwarding instances, they will both act as headless containers for new routing and forwarding tables. Neither will contain any interfaces or routing protocols.

You apply a new firewall filter named prefer to your inbound DeptA zone interface ge-9/0/4.0:

```
[edit]
jamesq@SRX5800-1# set interfaces ge-9/0/4.0 family inet filter input prefer
```

Then you jump to the firewall filter configuration hierarchy to actually create this new filter:

```
[edit]
jamesq@SRX5800-1# edit firewall filter prefer
```

You build the first term prefer1 to match traffic sourced from the 10.1.1.0/24 range (abbreviated as 10.1.1/24) and pass it to the prefer1 routing instance:

```
[edit firewall filter prefer]
jamesq@SRX5800-1# set term prefer1 from source-address 10.1.1/24

[edit firewall filter prefer]
jamesq@SRX5800-1# set term prefer1 then routing-instance prefer1
```

You build the second term prefer2 to match traffic sourced from the 10.1.2.0/24 range (abbreviated as 10.1.2/24) and pass it to the prefer2 routing instance:

```
[edit firewall filter prefer]
jamesq@SRX5800-1# set firewall filter prefer term prefer2 from
source-address 10.1.2/24

[edit firewall filter prefer]
jamesq@SRX5800-1# set firewall filter prefer term prefer2 then
routing-instance prefer2
```

As all firewall filters drop unmatched traffic by default, you create a closing term to accept all other traffic into the ge-9/0/4.0 interface:

```
[edit firewall filter prefer]
jamesq@SRX5800-1# set firewall filter prefer term accept then accept
```

You hop to the top of the configuration hierarchy:

```
[edit firewall filter prefer]
jamesq@SRX5800-1# top
```

And edit the import routing policy for the primary Internet peering:

```
[edit]
jamesq@SRX5800-1# edit policy-options policy-statement ISP-in
```

You show the routing policy before you begin making changes:

```
[edit policy-options policy-statement ISP-in]
jamesq@SRX5800-1# show
term default-in {
    from {
        route-filter 0.0.0.0/0 exact;
    }
    then accept;
}
term block {
    then reject;
}
```

You create a new term named higher that will modify all matching received routes with a higher (more preferred) BGP Local Preference value of 200 when they are passed to the prefer1.inet.0 routing table:

```
[edit policy-options policy-statement ISP-in]
jamesq@SRX5800-1# set term higher to rib prefer1.inet.0

[edit policy-options policy-statement ISP-in]
jamesq@SRX5800-1# set term higher then local-preference 200
```

The prefer1.inet.0 RIB is the new IPv4 routing table from the new prefer1 routing instance (in the same way that inet.0 is the IPv4 routing table outside the routing instances).

You insert this new higher term at the front of the policy chain before the existing default-in term:

```
[edit policy-options policy-statement ISP-in]
jamesq@SRX5800-1# insert term higher before term default-in
```

You show the modified routing policy:

```
[edit policy-options policy-statement ISP-in]
jamesq@SRX5800-1# show
term higher {
    to rib prefer1.inet.0;
    then {
        local-preference 200;
    }
}
term default-in {
    from {
        route-filter 0.0.0.0/0 exact;
    }
    then accept;
}
term block {
```

```
        then reject;
    }
```

Note that the new `higher` term, as configured, would not be enough to accomplish your goal. It does not itself `accept` any routes. The final `block` term would `reject` the matched routes were it not for the second term `default-in` matching and accepting the `0.0.0.0/0` prefix as before. This existing `default-in` term is already generic enough to `accept` the default route into any relevant routing table.

> Routing policy itself has no effect on populating routes to additional routing tables. That is accomplished through the `rib-group` configuration later in this section. Routing policy only acts to modify or filter the routes that otherwise would be passed wholesale by the default `rib-group` configuration.

You pop `up` one level in the configuration hierarchy:

```
[edit policy-options policy-statement ISP-in]
jamesq@SRX5800-1# up
```

And `edit` the import routing policy for the second Internet peering:

```
[edit policy-options policy-statement]
jamesq@SRX5800-1# edit policy-statement redundant-ISP-in
```

You again `show` the routing policy before making changes:

```
[edit policy-options policy-statement redundant-ISP-in]
jamesq@SRX5800-1# show
term redundant-default-in {
    from {
        route-filter 0.0.0.0/0 exact;
    }
    then {
        local-preference 50;
        accept;
    }
}
term block {
    then reject;
}
```

Here you first `delete` the existing `local-preference` policy action:

```
[edit policy-options policy-statement redundant-ISP-in]
jamesq@SRX5800-1# delete term redundant-default-in then local-preference 50
```

Before creating another new term named `higher` that will likewise modify all matching received routes with a higher (more preferred) BGP Local Preference value of `200` when they are passed to the `prefer2.inet.0` routing table through this policy:

```
[edit policy-options policy-statement redundant-ISP-in]
jamesq@SRX5800-1# set term higher to rib prefer2.inet.0
```

```
[edit policy-options policy-statement redundant-ISP-in]
jamesq@SRX5800-1# set term higher then local-preference 200
```

You insert this new higher term at the front of the policy chain before the existing redundant-default-in term:

```
[edit policy-options policy-statement redundant-ISP-in]
jamesq@SRX5800-1# insert term higher before term redundant-default-in
```

And now show this modified routing policy as well:

```
[edit policy-options policy-statement redundant-ISP-in]
jamesq@SRX5800-1# show
term higher {
    to rib prefer2.inet.0;
    then {
        local-preference 200;
    }
}
term redundant-default-in {
    from {
        route-filter 0.0.0.0/0 exact;
    }
    then accept;
}
term block {
    then reject;
}
```

You hop to the top of the configuration to complete your work:

```
[edit policy-options policy-statement redundant-ISP-in]
jamesq@SRX5800-1# top
```

You configure BGP to associate all of its IPv4 routes with a new rib-group named bgprib:

```
[edit]
jamesq@SRX5800-1# set protocols bgp family inet unicast rib-group bgprib
```

You configure this new rib-group bgprib to push the routes (*import* them, in Junos terminology) to not only the default inet.0 routing table, but also the new prefer1.inet.0 and prefer2.inet.0 routing tables:

```
[edit]
jamesq@SRX5800-1# set routing-options rib-groups bgprib import-rib
[ inet.0 prefer1.inet.0 prefer2.inet.0 ]
```

And finally, you show your now completed FBF, routing instance, and RIB group configuration:

```
[edit]
jamesq@SRX5800-1# show | compare
[edit interfaces]
+   ge-9/0/4 {
+       unit 0 {
+           family inet {
```

```
+               filter {
+                   input prefer;
+               }
+           }
+       }
+   }
[edit routing-options]
+  rib-groups {
+      bgprib {
+          import-rib [ inet.0 prefer1.inet.0 prefer2.inet.0 ];
+      }
+  }
[edit protocols bgp]
+    family inet {
+        unicast {
+            rib-group bgprib;
+        }
+    }
[edit policy-options policy-statement ISP-in]
+    term higher {
+        to rib prefer1.inet.0;
+        then {
+            local-preference 200;
+        }
+    }
     term default-in { ... }
[edit policy-options policy-statement redundant-ISP-in]
+    term higher {
+        to rib prefer2.inet.0;
+        then {
+            local-preference 200;
+        }
+    }
     term redundant-default-in { ... }
[edit policy-options policy-statement redundant-ISP-in term
redundant-default-in then]
-      local-preference 50;
[edit firewall]
    filter test { ... }
+   filter prefer {
+       term prefer1 {
+           from {
+               source-address {
+                   10.1.1.0/24;
+               }
+           }
+           then {
+               routing-instance prefer1;
+           }
+       }
+       term prefer2 {
+           from {
+               source-address {
+                   10.1.2.0/24;
+               }
```

```
+           }
+           then {
+               routing-instance prefer2;
+           }
+       }
+       term accept {
+           then accept;
+       }
+   }
[edit routing-instances]
+   prefer1 {
+       instance-type forwarding;
+   }
+   prefer2 {
+       instance-type forwarding;
+   }
```

You `commit` the changes:

```
[edit]
jamesq@SRX5800-1# commit and-quit
configuration check succeeds
commit complete
Exiting configuration mode
```

And then check out the results with the `show route protocol bgp` command:

```
jamesq@SRX5800-1> show route protocol bgp

inet.0: 23 destinations, 27 routes (23 active, 0 holddown, 0 hidden)
Restart Complete
+ = Active Route, - = Last Active, * = Both

0.0.0.0/0          *[BGP/170] 01:57:50, localpref 100
                      AS path: 65400 I
                    > to 198.18.4.10 via ge-9/0/5.0
                    [BGP/170] 01:57:46, localpref 100
                      AS path: 65500 I
                    > to 198.18.5.10 via ge-9/0/6.0

prefer1.inet.0: 1 destinations, 2 routes (1 active, 0 holddown, 0 hidden)
+ = Active Route, - = Last Active, * = Both

0.0.0.0/0          *[BGP/170] 00:00:15, localpref 200
                      AS path: 65400 I
                    > to 198.18.4.10 via ge-9/0/5.0
                    [BGP/170] 00:00:15, localpref 100
                      AS path: 65500 I
                    > to 198.18.5.10 via ge-9/0/6.0

prefer2.inet.0: 1 destinations, 2 routes (1 active, 0 holddown, 0 hidden)
+ = Active Route, - = Last Active, * = Both

0.0.0.0/0          *[BGP/170] 00:00:15, localpref 200
                      AS path: 65500 I
                    > to 198.18.5.10 via ge-9/0/6.0
                    [BGP/170] 00:00:15, localpref 100
```

```
                AS path: 65400 I
              > to 198.18.4.10 via ge-9/0/5.0
```

Excellent job!

The default `inet.0` table shows the redundant paths through both AS 65400 and AS 65500 with equal Local Preference values of `100`, and so it chooses the first path through AS 65400 for its lower router identification (the next relevant tiebreaker).

But the `prefer1.inet.0` and `prefer2.inet.0` tables each have more deliberate tiebreakers.

The `prefer1.inet.0` table prefers the AS 65400 path for its carefully engineered Local Preference value of `200`, while it retains the AS 65500 path as a backup at a default Local Preference value of `100`.

The `prefer2.inet.0` table prefers the opposite AS 65500 path for its own carefully engineered Local Preference value of `200`, while it retains the AS 65400 path as a backup at the default Local Preference value of `100`.

Just as you designed, each table is a mirror image of the other. Your firewall filter `prefer` will now dynamically engineer traffic from the `10.1.1.0/24` and `10.1.2.0/24` prefixes through opposite Internet paths.

Summary

With Junos for the SRX, you now have in your hands the most powerful routing platform in the business. And not just in the security business, it is the most powerful routing platform in the *routing* business. Junos was built for and is used by the largest and most complex IP networks in the world.

In this chapter, you've had a little taste of the possibilities. You started with the basics and then explored nearly all of the major IP routing features of Junos for the SRX. You built static and dynamic routing. You connected your SRX to the global Internet. And then you explored the most powerful tools of the best router jocks in the business, routing instances and filter-based forwarding.

But again, this chapter is not meant to replace the extensive coverage of IP routing in Junos. For more information, see the Juniper Networks Technical Library books published by O'Reilly at either *http://www.oreilly.com* or *http://www.juniper.net/books*. Titles include *Junos Fundamentals*, *Junos Enterprise Routing*, and the *Junos Cookbook*. Please check out these excellent books and expand your horizons even more!

Chapter Review Questions

1. What are the differences between a routing table and a forwarding table?
2. What does Address Resolution Protocol accomplish?
3. Why is dynamic routing typically a better solution than static routing?
4. What interior gateway protocols are supported in Junos?
5. How are routes passed between protocols in Junos?
6. How is equal cost multipath enabled in Junos?
7. What are the most preferred types of routes in a Junos routing table?
8. What protocol is used for Internet peering?
9. What is a routing instance in Junos?
10. What does filter-based forwarding accomplish?

Chapter Review Answers

1. Routing tables contain Layer 3 IP reachability information at a control plane level where forwarding tables contain data plane level actions for building Layer 2 headers and moving packets through toward their destinations. The control plane uses the information in the routing table to create the forwarding table.
2. Address Resolution Protocol (ARP) is used for resolving Layer 3 IP addresses to their Layer 2 Ethernet MAC addresses. This makes it possible for IP packets to be forwarded over Layer 2 Ethernet links.
3. Dynamic routing improves the availability of a network by allowing systems to respond to the inevitable failures by forwarding traffic around them. Static routing makes a fixed forwarding decision which does not change, even in the event of downstream failures.
4. OSPF, IS-IS, and RIP are the interior gateway protocols (IGPs) supported in Junos. Where OSPF and IS-IS are modern link-state protocols, RIP is a deprecated distance-vector protocol typically used for supporting legacy infrastructure.
5. Junos supports *routing policy* for the exchange of routes between routing protocols (often termed "route redistribution" within the industry).
6. Equal cost multipath (ECMP) is configured in Junos through a routing policy applied to the forwarding table.
7. The most preferred routes in a Junos routing table are those for networks directly connected to the Junos device. The most preferred user-configurable routes are static routes. And, of course, the preference of a routing protocol is also user-configurable in Junos.
8. Border Gateway Protocol (BGP) is used for peerings between organizations across the global Internet.

9. A routing instance is a virtual container for, variously, interfaces, routing protocols, and routing tables within Junos.
10. Filter-based forwarding (FBF) combines Junos firewall filters with routing instances to create powerful new forwarding table actions that can be based on a variety of other Layer 3 and Layer 4 header criteria besides the traditional destination IP address based forwarding decisions typical of IP routers. Uniquely in Junos, this can all be accomplished with full dynamic routing redundancy.

CHAPTER 12

Transparent Mode

There are two common challenges to deploying traditional Layer 3 network firewalls into a network. The first challenge is that you typically must change the IP routing to support the new firewall into the network, which can be a particularly difficult task, especially when dealing with readdressing segments. The other challenge with traditional firewalls is that they are very weak routers, at least in terms of dynamic routing protocol support, not to mention the fact that the security teams which managed the firewalls are typically separate from the teams which managed the routing infrastructure.

Since the SRX runs Junos, you're already equipped with the best routing platform there is, so routing support isn't an issue for the SRX, even though it is for many competitive firewalls and the previous generation of ScreenOS devices.

Transparent mode essentially allows the SRX to act as a Layer 2 bridge with the added security functionality of being a stateful firewall, as well as providing additional services such as intrusion protection services (IPS). At the time of this writing, transparent mode is only supported on the high-end SRX platforms and not on the branch SRX Series. However, support is likely to come on the branch SRX platforms in the near future, and quite possibly while you're reading these pages.

Transparent Mode Overview

Fundamentally, transparent mode is very similar to Layer 3 routed mode on the SRX platform. There are some limitations that are discussed later in this chapter that you should be aware of when balancing the decision to deploy transparent mode, but this is a feature that certainly has its place in contemporary networking. First this chapter reviews the reasons for deployment, how the technology functions, and the different components and concepts to be aware of when deploying transparent mode. After this review, actual configuration examples are shown. Even if you believe you are already savvy on the concepts of transparent mode, try to avoid the urge to skip the review, because these configurations assume your knowledge is current and up-to-date.

Why Use Transparent Mode?

You should consider using transparent mode because certain networking scenarios are not ideal for a Layer 3 implementation of a firewall. The good news is that transparent mode can be a viable alternative for administrators who want to avoid deployment dilemmas that Layer 3 implementations can cause.

Here are a few common scenarios in which to implement transparent mode:

Segmenting a Layer 2 domain

Sometimes day-to-day operations require that a firewall be placed where it did not exist before, a common example being for compliance with security standards such as PCI, HIPAA, SOX, and other international security standards. For instance, these standards may require that firewalling is present between a web server farm and a database server farm existing in a DMZ. Although integrating a Layer 3 firewall might be an option, it would require you to make IP address changes on at least one set of the devices. This can be easier than it sounds, especially if you have lots of hooks accessing the applications by IP address, and if the applications cannot easily change their IP address. In this situation, you can simply implement a transparent mode firewall between the web and server farms, without having to change any IP addresses or make any changes on the application side. At the same time, you can now enforce security between these different segments.

Figure 12-1 shows a before and after view of how a transparent mode SRX can be inserted into a network to provide security.

As you can see, if the firewall is in Layer 3 mode, it can't separate hosts on the same Layer 2 domain because of where it is logically placed. If you wanted to insert a Layer 3 firewall, you could, but you would need to re-IP-address your network to accommodate the changes. Transparent mode firewalls, on the other hand, do not segment your network from a Layer 3 perspective, and therefore they can sit between hosts on the same Layer 2 network to protect them from other hosts on the same Layer 2 network, along with enforcing security against remote attacks.

Complex routing environments

Traditional firewalls typically did not make good routers, both from a routing capacity perspective and from a feature perspective. Now that Juniper offers a firewall that is on Junos, there is a very complete routing infrastructure on the firewall itself, so this may not be as big a concern as it is with other products. Nevertheless, some environments may feel more comfortable with firewalls only performing security functions, and leaving routing up to separate routers. In these environments, firewalls can sit between routers transparently and simply inspect the traffic and forward it like a Layer 2 switch.

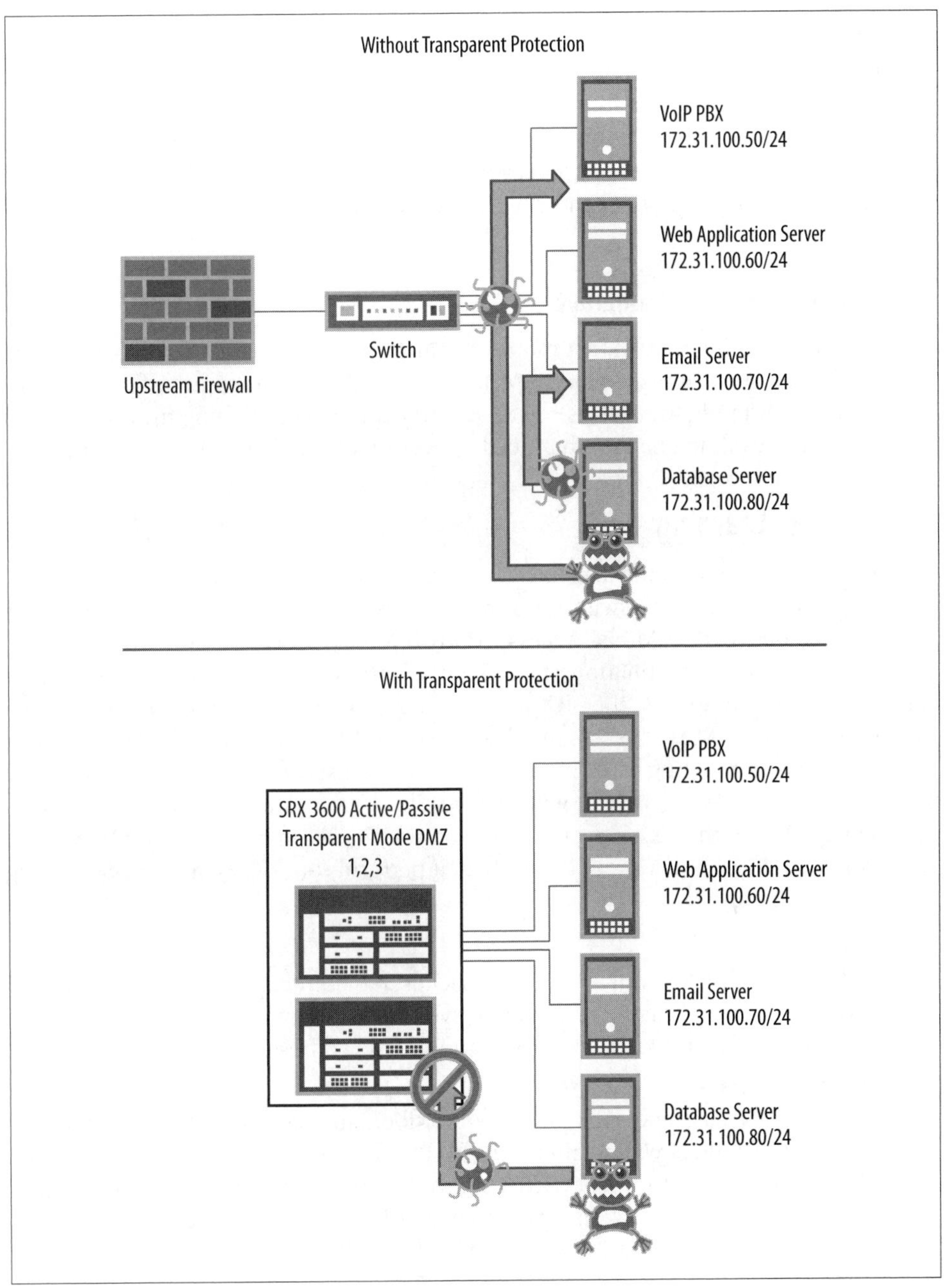

Figure 12-1. Segmenting a Layer 2 domain

Separation of duties

In some environments, separate teams manage the routing, switching, firewalling, and IPS services, or some combination of these roles. In these environments, having routing on the firewalls might mean separate teams have to be involved, which may not be ideal. Although there is no technical reason for using transparent mode in this scenario, other factors such as logistical and political issues can make transparent mode more ideal.

Existing transparent mode infrastructure

Sometimes an existing transparent mode firewall infrastructure is in place that must be upgraded. In these scenarios, swapping out the existing transparent mode firewalls with new transparent mode firewalls is the easiest transition, as switching from Layer 2 to Layer 3 would result in changes that need to occur with the Layer 3 infrastructure.

MAC Address Learning

An SRX in transparent mode acts like a switch with regard to how it forwards traffic. As you know, a true Layer 2 switch does not forward based on IP addresses, but rather based on the destination Media Access Control (MAC) addresses of the frames it receives. To forward to a destination, the SRX must learn where the MAC addresses "live" on the network. To do this, the SRX learns which ports are a path to a MAC address based on the source MAC address that is learned on that particular port. These entries are cached into a bridging table on the SRX and are used for packet forwarding, including policy lookup, as we will discuss in "Transparent Mode Flow Process" on page 721. If the SRX does not know on which port in the virtual LAN (VLAN) the destination MAC address can be reached, it performs one of two actions depending on the configuration:

Flood the frame
: By default, the SRX simply floods the packet out all interfaces in the same VLAN except the port on which the packet arrived. This is how a switch normally functions when it doesn't know the destination MAC address.

ARP with traceroute
: In some cases, customers may not wish to flood any packets out for security reasons, so Junos offers you an alternative to flooding the traffic, which is to send an Address Resolution Protocol (ARP) and optionally an Internet Control Message Protocol (ICMP) packet with a time to live (TTL) of 1, while queuing the packet. If no destination responds, the original packet is dropped.

Transparent Mode and Bridge Loops, Spanning Tree Protocol

One thing you must be aware of when working with transparent mode firewalls is that if you do not properly configure a transparent mode firewall you may trigger a *bridge loop*. If you are connecting the SRX directly to routed interfaces on peer devices, this should not be an issue, but if you are connecting the SRX to switch interfaces, you need to give some thought to your design. Because at the time of this writing the SRX does not actively participate in Spanning Tree Protocol (STP) itself, it does forward the Bridge Protocol Data Units (BPDUs) and the STP messages. Additionally, you may need to tweak your spanning tree configuration to properly forward traffic to the active SRX node. If you do not do this, traffic may not pass through the SRX, or failovers between nodes may not function properly. These different configurations are examined throughout this chapter.

Transparent Mode Limitations

At the time of this writing, there are some limitations when it comes to transparent mode on the SRX, particularly in contrast to ScreenOS. You should be aware of the following limitations before configuring transparent mode:

Transparent mode is only supported on the high-end SRX platform
: The biggest limitation of transparent mode today is that it is only available on the high-end SRX platforms and not on the branch SRX Series platforms (see Chapter 1 for exact definitions of these platforms). There are plans to bring transparent mode support into the product in the near future; however, the configuration may vary on the branch SRX Series.

The branch SRX Series does support Ethernet switching, but when forwarding traffic in a flow-based manner, traffic must be routed through the branch SRX Series device.

Virtual private network (VPN) support
: At the time of this writing, VPN termination on Integrated Routing and Bridging (IRB) interfaces is not supported in transparent mode. This termination is supported on virtual LAN (VLAN) interfaces in ScreenOS, but it is not yet supported on the SRX in transparent mode. This feature will likely be supported in the future.

Mixed mode Layer 2/Layer 3 support
: At the time of this writing, you can only configure Layer 2 or Layer 3, but not both, simultaneously. This was never supported on ScreenOS, however, and is likely to be supported in the near future on SRX.

IPv6 pass-through
: At the time of this writing, IPv6 pass-through is not supported on the SRX in transparent mode, even with the `bypass-all-non-ip` flag set. IPv6 in transparent mode will be supported in the future on the SRX.

Network Address Translation (NAT)
: At the time of this writing, NAT is not supported in transparent mode. Policy NAT is supported in ScreenOS starting with version 6.1, but this is not yet supported in the SRX for transparent mode.

Some application layer gateways (ALGs)
: Most, but not all, ALGs are supported in transparent mode. You should consult the documentation for the release you are planning to use, to ensure that the ALG you need is supported in the release.

Virtual router support
: At the time of this writing, you cannot place IRB interfaces into different virtual routers; they must remain in the `Inet.0` routing table.

QinQ tunneling
: QinQ tunneling is not supported on the high-end SRX (either in Layer 3 or in Layer 2) at the time of this writing.

Changing modes
: To change from Layer 3 to Layer 2 mode (or vice versa) you must reboot the chassis.

Transparent Mode Components

There are several components of transparent mode, some common to Layer 3 and some specific to transparent mode itself. This section examines the different components of transparent mode; configuration examples follow later in the chapter. These components are also the building blocks of the case study at the end of the chapter.

Interfaces, family bridge, and bridge domains in transparent mode

Transparent mode ushers in a few new concepts concerning interfaces and forwarding. Transparent mode follows the same interface model as standard Layer 3 interfaces, with the use of physical interface properties, followed by logical interface configuration. The main differences that exist are as follows:

Family bridge
: Rather than using family Inet, Inet6, ISO, and so on, since there is no explicit IP address configuration, we will use the family bridge, which is the same as what the MX Series uses for its platform.

Interface addressing
: In transparent mode, there is no IP address assigned to a logical interface. The SRX functions as a switch and not as a router. Traffic is switched toward the SRX by listening for MAC addresses and determining that they live on the other side of the SRX. The interfaces do have MAC addresses, but the source/destination MAC addresses of transit traffic will never be of the SRX's interfaces themselves. A concept of IRB interfaces allows you to send management traffic to the SRX, but other than that, the traffic will not be addressed to the SRX itself.

Bridge domains
: These are the Layer 2 equivalent of virtual routers in Layer 3 mode. Essentially, bridge domains allow you to separate the Layer 2 traffic, including spanning tree domains, and other forwarding options. We will cover bridge domains and how they influence transparent mode in "Configuring Integrated Routing and Bridging" on page 729.

Interface Modes in Transparent Mode

In transparent mode, there are two different modes in which you can place an interface: access mode and trunk mode. If you have any experience with the EX Series or MX Series platforms, the SRX follows the same convention here, although unlike the EX Series platform (and like the MX Series platform) the SRX uses the family bridge convention.

Access mode
: Access mode is the default mode family bridge interfaces. In access mode, the interface only has a single unit that uses a single VLAN member, which can be configured for the interface. Traffic arriving on the interface is classified with the VLAN which is configured. The term *access mode* comes from the fact that most end systems that access the network on these types of interfaces are configured on a switch. For the SRX, however, access mode simply means there is only a single VLAN configured on the interface.

Trunk mode
: The SRX supports the ability to terminate multiple VLANs on a single interface, through the use of 802.1q trunking. To accommodate this, you will need to configure an interface in trunk mode, which uses VLAN tagging to differentiate VLANs for the purposes of separation and classification of traffic. You can use a native VLAN, which is untagged, or you can use an interface with all tagged VLANs. When using trunk mode, you can configure multiple units (logical interfaces), each having one or more VLAN members present on it.

You cannot mix both access mode units and trunk mode units on a single interface, and, if you are using access mode, you can only have a single unit present. Just like Layer 3 mode, you can put different logical interface units into different zones, and you can put different VLANs into different bridge domains (similar to how you can put different logical interface units into different virtual routers in Layer 3 mode).

Bridge Domains

As mentioned earlier in this chapter, bridge domains are used to logically separate traffic on the SRX. In reality, they are very similar to VLANs in terms of how the traffic is processed in the system; however, the bridge domain allows Junos to abstract the

VLANs and their associated tags from the actual traffic processing. Typically, most implementations require that you configure a separate bridge domain for each VLAN, although this isn't a strict requirement; you can bridge multiple VLANs together if you wish.

Within a bridge domain, you can configure either a single or multiple VLANs to be part of the same bridge domain; however, you can only configure an IRB interface in a bridge domain if you are using a single VLAN for the bridge domain.

IRB Interfaces

As mentioned, the standard logical interfaces on the SRX do not support IP addresses when the SRX is configured in transparent mode; however, the SRX does support a special type of interface called an *IRB interface*. You can think of an IRB interface as a VLAN interface from Junos' switching capabilities. IRB interfaces are virtual interfaces that allow you to configure IP addressing on the interface so that even in transparent mode you can communicate with the SRX on data plane interfaces. Of course, even in transparent mode you can manage the device through the fxp0 interface, which does have full management capabilities. The purpose of IRB interfaces is so that you can manage a transparent mode device on the data plane by making an addressable interface. At the time of this writing, the IRB interface cannot route traffic itself; rather, you can use it to accept inbound management connections, including pings, SSH, Telnet, and HTTP, and you can make outbound connections on the IRB interface to other devices.

In transparent mode, you cannot put IRB interfaces into different virtual routing instances, because different virtual routers are not supported.

Transparent Mode Zones

For those of you who have a rich experience working with ScreenOS, there is a slight difference with the way security zones are defined in Junos. Unlike ScreenOS, where you were required to prepend a Layer 2 security zone name with `L2-<name>`, in Junos there is no requirement for any special naming convention. Security zones are associated with Layer 2 by the interfaces that are in them, and therefore the system is smart enough to know it is a Layer 2 zone without any special naming requirements. So, in reality, there are no differences between Layer 2 and Layer 3 security zones from a configuration perspective. Just like Layer 3 security zones, you place the logical interfaces (e.g., ge-0/0/4.20) into the security zones, so the SRX can support not only access mode interfaces but also 802.1q VLANs that are bound to a specific unit on a trunk link. One exception is that IRB interfaces themselves are not placed within security zones, but the surrounding Layer 2 interfaces are, so you can still filter out traffic for them. We will cover this in more detail in the configuration examples later in this chapter.

Transparent Mode Security Policy

Security policies in transparent mode are almost identical to those in Layer 3, with the only exception being that VPN is not supported in transparent mode, so therefore policy-based VPNs would not be supported in the security policies.

For those of you who do not have experience with ScreenOS, the Layer 2 security policies in Junos are pretty straightforward. In transparent mode, the security policy is no different from a Layer 3 policy. The transparent mode policy is still composed of filtering based on From/To zones, source addresses, destination addresses, and applications (source port, destination port, and protocol). However, one thing to keep in mind is that unlike ScreenOS, intrazone blocking is always enforced (for both Layer 2 and Layer 3 modes), so you always need a security policy, even for traffic coming from and going to the *same* zone (e.g., from Trust to Trust). Also note that in transparent mode, you cannot filter on Layer 2 components (again, we will cover this later in this chapter).

Transparent Mode Specific Options

Transparent mode supports the following flow configurations that are not supported in Layer 3:

Block all non-IP packets
: If the SRX sees non-IP packets (or packets that are not involved with IP, such as ARP, Internet Group Management Protocol [IGMP], or Dynamic Host Configuration Protocol [DHCP], for example), the SRX will silently drop them. This includes broadcast and multicast traffic.

Bypass all non-IP unicast traffic
: This option permits non-IP unicast traffic to be sent through the box. Note that this does not include IPv6, which is dropped if you attempt to forward it through the SRX. If you do need to forward IPv6 through the SRX, the recommendation is to use Generic Route Encapsulation (GRE) tunneling on the routers.

No packet flooding
: By default, the SRX floods all packets with an unknown destination MAC address out all interfaces in the same VLAN on which the packet arrived, except the source interface. This is the standard behavior for bridging/switching devices when they do not know on which port the destination MAC address can be reached. Some administrators would like to avoid this behavior if the destination MAC address is not known, and have the SRX ARP for the destination MAC address. There are two options for this: ARP and send an ICMP traceroute, or just simply ARP.

QoS in Transparent Mode

Starting in Junos 10.1, the SRX supports the ability to perform Quality of Service (QoS) in transparent mode. Transparent mode QoS allows you to perform classification and rewriting based on 802.1p values, along with being able to do standard shaping and priority processing based on these QoS values. Note that transparent mode does not support classification or rewriting based on IP precedence or Differentiated Services Code Point (DSCP) values, only on the Layer 2 802.1p values, so if you need to classify based on IP precedence or DSCP, you should do it upstream or downstream and copy the equivalent values into the 802.1p field so that the SRX can apply the appropriate QoS in transparent mode. "Configuring Transparent Mode QoS" on page 736 takes a deep look at this functionality.

VLAN Rewriting

Many network engineers consider VLAN rewriting (also known as VLAN retagging) as the NAT of Layer 2 VLAN tags when in Layer 2 mode. In some networks, VLAN rewriting is used to ensure that "clean" traffic that may be on the same VLAN has passed through a firewall; to do this, we can use different VLAN tags on different sides of the firewall. In other cases, there may be a handoff between different network boundaries (e.g., between a customer and an Internet service provider [ISP]), so to keep things simple on the customer end, VLAN rewriting can be used to ensure that there is no VLAN overlap. In Layer 3 mode, networks can be segmented simply by routing the traffic between VLANs (including performing other services such as firewalling and IPS); however, in Layer 2 mode, a device does not perform any of the routing transforms to route traffic between Layer 3 networks. When you want to transform the VLAN on one side of the firewall in transparent mode, you would want to use VLAN rewriting. Essentially, VLAN rewriting simply defines how the VLANs are translated by mapping VLANs on a one-to-one ratio. For instance, in Figure 12-2, we are mapping VLAN 20 to VLAN 80. We will cover this concept later in the configuration example section.

Only tagged traffic on VLANs can be translated. This means the traffic on the native VLAN cannot be translated since there is no tag. You would need to make sure the surrounding networking devices tagged this native VLAN on their end, for you to translate the VLAN on the SRX.

High Availability with Transparent Mode

The SRX supports the ability to operate an SRX chassis cluster in transparent mode. Chassis clustering in transparent mode operates very similarly to Layer 3 mode, but with the same differences as standalone Layer 3 compared to standalone Layer 2.

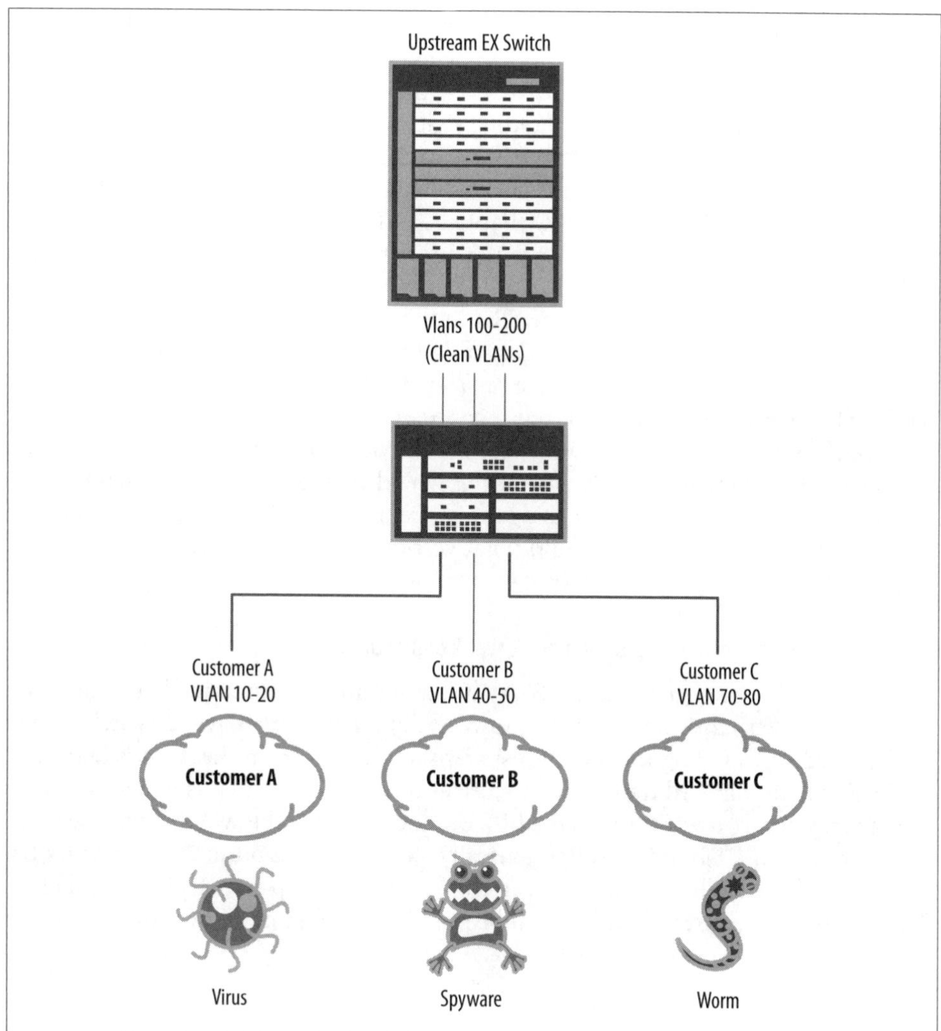

Figure 12-2. VLAN rewriting

Transparent mode features have been developed over time, so you should be aware of the following high availability (HA) transparent mode features:

Active/passive clusters
: Active/passive transparent mode HA is supported in Junos 9.6 and later.

Active/active clusters
: Active/active transparent mode HA is supported in Junos 10.2 and later.

IDP support in clusters
: IDP is supported in Layer 2 chassis clusters as of Junos 10.0 for active/passive and active/active.

When operating in transparent mode HA clusters, you need to be especially aware of bridge loops, and how transparent mode triggers traffic failovers. In Layer 3 mode, the SRX will send Gratuitous ARPs (GARPs) out the new active Reth interface member after a failover to signal to the surrounding switches that the SRX's MAC address has moved to a new interface (that of the new active Reth member). In transparent mode, there is no active MAC address or IP address on which to terminate the traffic, so no GARPs can be sent. Instead, the SRX flaps the old active interfaces up and down to trigger an STP recalculation. If STP is not properly configured on the surrounding switches (if applicable), it can lead to traffic not failing over, or other disruptions. Note that in active/passive mode, only one SRX in the cluster has its data plane active at a time (just like in active/passive Layer 3 mode). In Layer 2 active/active mode, an individual redundancy group is only active on a single SRX data plane at a time, but both SRX data planes can have different redundancy groups active on them, just like Layer 3 active/active. Of course, you can't have an individual redundancy group active on both cluster members at the same time, as this would cause a bridge loop. This chapter's case study includes an example of using transparent mode in HA. In addition, the next section details where to use STP and what version of STP you should be using, and Chapter 9 discusses chassis clustering in great detail.

Spanning Tree Protocol in transparent mode Layer 2 deployments

When Layer 3 devices surround the SRX cluster in transparent mode, there really isn't much of a concern for spanning tree. However, in many cases, Layer 2 switching will be deployed surrounding the SRX transparent mode cluster. In these cases, although the SRX will not forward traffic that it receives on an interface that is not active for its redundancy group, it will forward the BPDUs, and therefore the switches will view this as a network loop. Disabling STP is generally a bad idea in a production network because if someone makes a mistake, it can trigger a bridge loop since STP is disabled. At the same time, using standard STP can be nonideal because of failover timings (up to 50 seconds after a topology change).

It doesn't really matter if you are using active/passive or active/active. The concerns are going to be the same.

Here are some guidelines for what you should use for the transparent mode switching architecture:

Transparent mode without VLAN trunking
: If you are not using VLAN trunking on your transparent mode Reth interfaces, you can simply use Rapid Spanning Tree Protocol (RSTP), which will provide much better failover times and reliability than standard STP.

Multiple Spanning Trees Protocol (MSTP)
: MSTP is actually preferable to RSTP, although in the case of no VLAN trunking, it shouldn't make much of a difference.

Transparent mode with VLAN trunking
: If VLAN trunking is used, it is possible that a bridge loop may occur within an individual VLAN, but not on the entire trunk itself. RSTP does not provide any way to prevent bridge loops within VLANs on a trunk unless the entire link has a loop on the native VLAN. Instead, you can use MSTP, which enables you to provide separate instances of STP. This gives you the same benefits of RSTP in terms of redundancy, but with the ability to separate STP domains similar to PVST+.

> You can use Cisco proprietary protocols such as PVST+ and RPVST, but there really isn't much of a point with the standardized implementations of STP that exist.

Transparent Mode Flow Process

The transparent mode flow process is very similar to that of the routed Layer 3 mode flow process. Essentially, the differences between Layer 2 and Layer 3 are in the forwarding process, and at the same time, there are some features that are not supported in transparent mode. There is no difference in the packet flow in terms of the flow between the Network Processing Unit (NPU), control point (CP), and Services Processing Unit (SPU) on the high-end SRXs; all of this occurs in the same fashion. However, the actual process within the SPU varies slightly.

Figure 12-3 shows the transparent mode packet flow.

Slow-path packet SPU packet processing

Slow-path packet processing consists of the following steps:

1. The initial packet is forwarded from the NPU to the CP, and then from the CP to the SPU which the CP selects to process the flow.
2. The policing, stateless filtering, and screens can be performed on the SPU (although this can also occur elsewhere). Most of the screens are performed on the NPU, but a few screens are performed on the SPU. These screens are typically related to processing session limits (in conjunction with the CP, which knows about the session numbers of all source/destination IP addresses being processed on the box).
3. The SPU will determine if it knows about the session or not. If the session is known, it will fast-path the session, but in the case of a new session, additional processing must be performed.
4. Transparent mode differs from Layer 3 routed mode because not only is there no IP address on its interfaces, but also it does not perform forwarding based on a

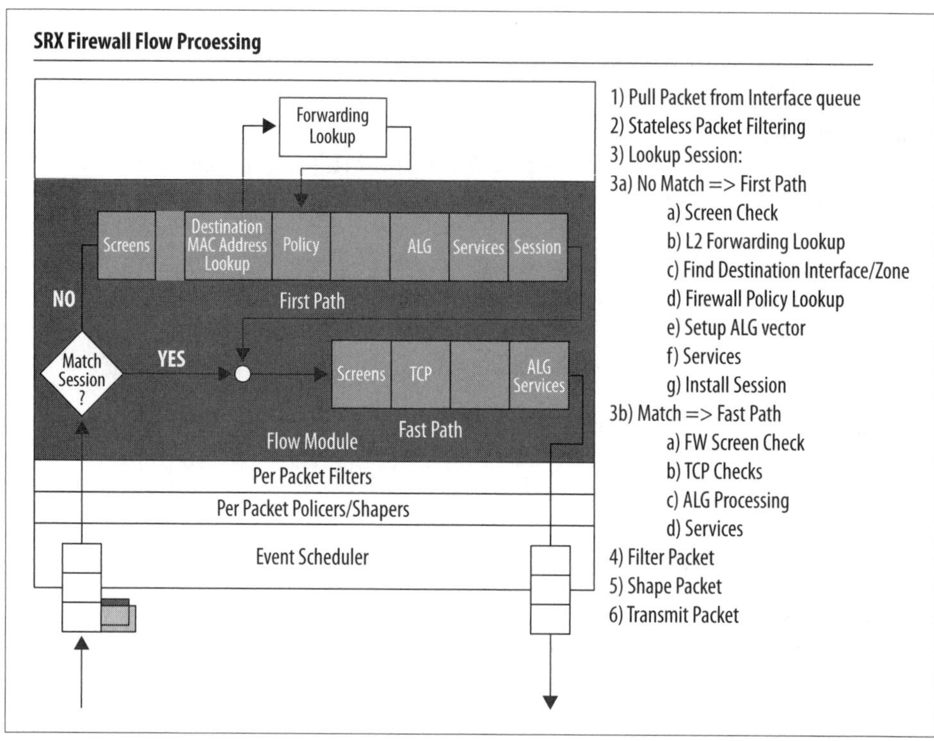
SRX Firewall Flow Prcoessing
Forwarding Lookup
Screens
Destination MAC Address Lookup
Policy
ALG
Services
Session
NO
First Path
Match Session ?
YES
Screens
TCP
ALG Services
Flow Module
Fast Path
Per Packet Filters
Per Packet Policers/Shapers
Event Scheduler
1) Pull Packet from Interface queue
2) Stateless Packet Filtering
3) Lookup Session:
3a) No Match => First Path
a) Screen Check
b) L2 Forwarding Lookup
c) Find Destination Interface/Zone
d) Firewall Policy Lookup
e) Setup ALG vector
f) Services
g) Install Session
3b) Match => Fast Path
a) FW Screen Check
b) TCP Checks
c) ALG Processing
d) Services
4) Filter Packet
5) Shape Packet
6) Transmit Packet

Figure 12-3. Packet flow diagram

routing lookup, but rather based on a bridging lookup, since both network segments are within the same Layer 3 domain. Two scenarios occur during packet processing:

a. If the destination MAC address is known, it is "learned" similar to how a bridge or switch would normally function by simply listening for packets and examining the source MAC address. When a new source MAC address is learned, it is added to the bridging table. If the destination MAC address for the packet that the SRX is forwarding is known, it determines the egress interface (and therefore the egress zone) based on the bridging lookup.

b. If the destination MAC address is unknown, the SRX must try to determine what port the destination MAC address lives on (even if only two interfaces are present). By default, the SRX simply floods the packet out all interfaces in the same VLAN, except for the port on which the packet arrived. This is how a switch normally functions when it doesn't know the destination MAC address. In some cases, customers may not wish to flood any packets out for security reasons. For this reason, Junos offers you an alternative to flooding the traffic, which is to send an ARP and optionally a traceroute, while queuing the packet. If no destination responds, the original packet is dropped. You can configure how the platform responds to unknown destination MAC addresses in the flow configuration, configured later in this chapter.

5. Step 4 determined what destination interface to forward the traffic out of, and therefore the destination zone is known. The source zone is known as soon as the packet arrives, because the system knows what interface it arrived on, and therefore what the source zone is. With the knowledge of the source and destination zones in hand, the SRX can then do a policy lookup in the from/to zone context. The SRX performs a policy lookup in the specific from/to zone context to match traffic on the source IP, destination IP, and application (source/destination ports and protocol).
6. If ALGs are configured, such as File Transfer Protocol (FTP), the SRX must examine any control traffic which is matched to an ALG. An example of this would be port 21 for FTP, although custom ports can also be used by the ALG which is configured in a custom application object. For ALG control traffic, the SRX must do several things. First it must perform packet reassembly if fragmentation is used, along with TCP reassembly if the application message spans multiple TCP packets, and then the ALG determines if any additional data sessions need to be opened on the SRX.
7. After the ALG stage is processed (if present), the SRX performs additional services, such as IPS, if configuration is present.
8. The last stage of packet processing before forwarding the initial packet is to install the session. In the case of the high-end SRX, the session will be installed on the ingress/egress NPUs along with the CP, and of course, the session table of the SPU processing the traffic itself.
9. The packet is sent to the egress NPU where it will be forwarded out the egress interface.

Fast-path SPU processing

In Figure 12-3, you can see fast-path processing by following the flowchart and taking the Match Session "Yes" track. The fast-path packet process consists of the following steps:

1. An inbound packet is received by an interface and sent to the NPU, which provides processing for that interface. The NPU performs a session lookup and determines that it knows the session and the SPU processing it. The NPU then forwards the packet directly to the SPU which owns the session.
2. Policing, stateless filtering, and screens are performed. Technically, the screens that are applied after the initial packet setup are all on the NPU on the high-end SRX platforms.
3. The SPU determines if it knows about the session already, which in this case it does. The session entry will provide cached instructions on how to process the packet so that the SRX does not have to do any forwarding or policy checks, as these have already been determined in the first packet processing. Note that if the

egress interface which the session is tied to fails, the SRX will attempt to find a new forwarding path for the destination MAC address, if possible. It either floods the packet or sends an ARP, and optionally a traceroute, depending on your configuration.

4. If ALGs are configured, such as FTP, the SRX must examine any control traffic which is matched to an ALG. An example of this would be port 21 for FTP, although custom ports can also be used by the ALG, which are configured as custom application objects. For ALG control traffic, the SRX must do several things. First it must perform packet reassembly if fragmentation is used, along with TCP reassembly if the application message spans multiple TCP packets. The ALG then determines if any additional data sessions need to be opened on the SRX.
5. After the ALG stage is processed (if present), the SRX performs additional services such as IPS, if configuration is present.
6. The packet is sent to the egress NPU where it is forwarded out the egress interface.

Session teardown

All sessions must come to an end at some point. A session may be terminated for several different reasons:

TCP
: A FIN or RESET is sent.

Session timeout
: Sessions that do not have any traffic after the defined idle timeout for that service will be cleared as a *session ageout*.

ALG
: An ALG can terminate a session based on the control traffic. This may terminate the control and/or data portion of the session.

Other
: There are other reasons why a session may be cleared out, such as an IPS closing a session due to an attack being detected. Changes to policies or policy schedules can also trigger a session to close.

After a session has been closed, the SPU signals to the ingress/egress NPUs, the CP, and if in an HA chassis cluster, its peer SPU that the session has closed.

Configuring Transparent Mode

Now that you have learned the various components of transparent mode, you can evaluate the configuration of the SRX in transparent mode. This section covers examples of the different concepts of transparent mode in the same order in which they were introduced in the preceding section. Additionally, a transparent mode HA example is provided in the chapter's case study.

Configuring Transparent Mode Basics

This example creates four interfaces. Two of the interfaces are going to be in access mode and two are going to be in trunk mode. Additionally, there are six different VLANs and six different bridge domains.

The interfaces and VLANS are as follows:

- ge-0/0/1 will be in access mode, with VLAN 10 as its VLAN for unit 0.
- ge-0/0/2 will be in access mode, with VLAN 20 as its VLAN for unit 0.
- ge-0/0/3 will be in trunk mode, with VLAN 10 on unit 10, VLAN 30 on unit 30, and VLAN 40 on unit 40.
- ge-0/0/4 will be in trunk mode, with VLAN 20 on unit 10, VLAN 50 on unit 50, and VLAN 60 on unit 60.

The six bridge domains are each called `L2-VLAN-XX` where *XX* is the VLAN number. The bridge domains logically separate the traffic for the different VLANs.

Let's go:

```
{secondary:node0}[edit]
root@SRX3400-1# edit interfaces ge-0/0/1 unit 0 family bridge

{secondary:node0}[edit interfaces ge-0/0/1 unit 0 family bridge]
root@SRX3400-1# set interface-mode access vlan-id 10

{secondary:node0}[edit interfaces ge-0/0/1 unit 0 family bridge]
root@SRX3400-1# up 3

{secondary:node0}[edit interfaces]
root@SRX3400-1# edit ge-0/0/2 unit 0 family bridge

{secondary:node0}[edit interfaces ge-0/0/2 unit 0 family bridge]
root@SRX3400-1# set interface-mode access vlan-id 20

{secondary:node0}[edit interfaces ge-0/0/2 unit 0 family bridge]
root@SRX3400-1# up 3

{secondary:node0}[edit interfaces]
root@SRX3400-1# edit ge-0/0/3

{secondary:node0}[edit interfaces ge-0/0/3]
root@SRX3400-1# set unit 10 family bridge interface-mode trunk vlan-id-list 10

{secondary:node0}[edit interfaces ge-0/0/3]
root@SRX3400-1# set unit 30 family bridge interface-mode trunk vlan-id-list 30

{secondary:node0}[edit interfaces ge-0/0/3]
root@SRX3400-1# set unit 40 family bridge interface-mode trunk vlan-id-list 40

{secondary:node0}[edit interfaces ge-0/0/3]
root@SRX3400-1# set vlan-tagging
```

```
{secondary:node0}[edit interfaces ge-0/0/3]
root@SRX3400-1# up

{secondary:node0}[edit interfaces]
root@SRX3400-1# edit ge-0/0/4

{secondary:node0}[edit interfaces ge-0/0/4]
root@SRX3400-1# set unit 20 family bridge interface-mode trunk vlan-id-list 20

{secondary:node0}[edit interfaces ge-0/0/4]
root@SRX3400-1# set unit 50 family bridge interface-mode trunk vlan-id-list 50

{secondary:node0}[edit interfaces ge-0/0/4]
root@SRX3400-1# set unit 60 family bridge interface-mode trunk vlan-id-list 60

{secondary:node0}[edit interfaces ge-0/0/3]
root@SRX3400-1# set vlan-tagging

{secondary:node0}[edit interfaces ge-0/0/4]
root@SRX3400-1# up

{secondary:node0}[edit interfaces]
root@SRX3400-1# show
ge-0/0/1 {
    unit 0 {
        family bridge {
            interface-mode access;
            vlan-id 10;
        }
    }
}
ge-0/0/2 {
    unit 0 {
        family bridge {
            interface-mode access;
            vlan-id 20;
        }
    }
}
ge-0/0/3 {
    vlan-tagging;
    unit 10 {
        family bridge {
            interface-mode trunk;
            vlan-id-list 10;
        }
    }
    unit 30 {
        family bridge {
            interface-mode trunk;
            vlan-id-list 30;
        }
    }
    unit 40 {
        family bridge {
```

```
            interface-mode trunk;
            vlan-id-list 40;
        }
    }
}
ge-0/0/4 {
    vlan-tagging;
    unit 20 {
        family bridge {
            interface-mode trunk;
            vlan-id-list 20;
        }
    }
    unit 50 {
        family bridge {
            interface-mode trunk;
            vlan-id-list 50;
        }
    }
    unit 60 {
        family bridge {
            interface-mode trunk;
            vlan-id-list 60;
        }
    }
}

{secondary:node0}[edit interfaces]
root@SRX3400-1# up

{secondary:node0}[edit]
root@SRX3400-1# set bridge-domains L2-VLAN-10 domain-type bridge vlan-id 10

{secondary:node0}[edit]
root@SRX3400-1# set bridge-domains L2-VLAN-20 domain-type bridge vlan-id 20

{secondary:node0}[edit]
root@SRX3400-1# set bridge-domains L2-VLAN-30 domain-type bridge vlan-id 30

{secondary:node0}[edit]
root@SRX3400-1# set bridge-domains L2-VLAN-40 domain-type bridge vlan-id 40

{secondary:node0}[edit]
root@SRX3400-1# set bridge-domains L2-VLAN-50 domain-type bridge vlan-id 50

{secondary:node0}[edit]
root@SRX3400-1# set bridge-domains L2-VLAN-60 domain-type bridge vlan-id 60

{secondary:node0}[edit]
root@SRX3400-1# show bridge-domains
L2-VLAN-10 {
    domain-type bridge;
    vlan-id 10;
}
L2-VLAN-20 {
```

```
        domain-type bridge;
        vlan-id 20;
    }
    L2-VLAN-30 {
        domain-type bridge;
        vlan-id 30;
    }
    L2-VLAN-40 {
        domain-type bridge;
        vlan-id 40;
    }
    L2-VLAN-50 {
        domain-type bridge;
        vlan-id 50;
    }
    L2-VLAN-60 {
        domain-type bridge;
        vlan-id 60;
    }
```

Before you can switch from Layer 3 to Layer 2, you must reboot the firewalls in the cluster. This is required whenever switching from Layer 3 to Layer 2, or vice versa, at the time of this writing:

```
{secondary:node0}[edit]
root@SRX3400-1# commit and-quit
warning: Interfaces are changed from route mode to transparent mode. Please
reboot the device or all nodes in the HA cluster!
node0:
configuration check succeeds
node1:
warning: Interfaces are changed from route mode to transparent mode. Please
reboot the device or all nodes in the HA cluster!
commit complete
node0:
commit complete

{primary:node0}
root@SRX3400-1> request system reboot

{secondary:node2}
root@SRX3400-2> request system reboot
```

You might be asking yourself, why is `vlan-id` used for the access mode interfaces, and `vlan-id-list` for the trunk mode interfaces? This is because access mode interfaces can only have a single VLAN ID (which is untagged). With trunk mode interfaces, you can have multiple units each with different VLANs, or you can tie a group of VLANs to a single trunk mode logical interface. These will be bridged separately (if they are part of different bridge domains), but it essentially allows you to take a shortcut with defining the interfaces themselves.

One important thing to note from this example is that for the trunk interfaces with this configuration, any untagged packets are dropped (or packets tagged for VLANs that you are not looking for). If you would like to accept untagged packets, you would want to use the following code:

```
{secondary:node0}[edit interfaces ge-0/0/3]
root@SRX3400-1# set native-vlan-id 5
```

Configuring Integrated Routing and Bridging

Transparent mode does not use Layer 3 IP addresses on its interfaces; therefore, there is no way to communicate with it directly, or to send traffic from the transparent mode interfaces themselves. To solve this issue, the SRX supports IRB interfaces, so you can send traffic from the SRX as well as manage the SRX on these interfaces. IRB interfaces are not required in transparent mode, but they are required if you want to send traffic out the data plane, or receive traffic directed at the SRX on the data plane in transparent mode. In this example, the SRX is configured to send syslog messages out the IRB.0 interface in transparent mode, along with allowing inbound management via SSH and ping. To do this, configure the following:

- Configure the IRB.0 interface in VLAN 60, with an IP address of 192.168.60.1/24.
- Route traffic to syslog server 192.16.15.20 via next-hop 192.168.60.254.
- Allow inbound SSH and pings for the IRB.0 interface.

```
{primary:node0}[edit]
root@SRX3400-1# set interfaces irb unit 0 family inet address 192.168.60.1/24


{primary:node0}[edit]
root@SRX3400-1# show interfaces irb
unit 0 {
    family inet {
        address 192.168.60.1/24;
    }
}

{primary:node0}[edit]
root@SRX3400-1# set routing-options static route 192.168.15.20 next-hop
192.168.60.254

{primary:node0}[edit]
root@SRX3400-1# show routing-options
static {
    route 192.168.15.20/32 next-hop 192.168.60.254;
}

{primary:node0}[edit]
root@SRX3400-1# set bridge-domains L2-VLAN-60 routing-interface irb.0

{primary:node0}[edit]
root@SRX3400-1# show bridge-domains L2-VLAN-60
domain-type bridge;
vlan-id 60;
```

```
routing-interface irb.0;

{primary:node0}[edit]
root@SRX3400-1# set system services ssh


{primary:node0}[edit]
root@SRX3400-1# show system services
ssh;

{primary:node0}[edit]
root@SRX3400-1# edit firewall family inet filter Services term Inbound

{primary:node0}[edit firewall family inet filter Services term Inbound]
root@SRX3400-1# set Inbound from protocol tcp


{primary:node0}[edit firewall family inet filter Services term Inbound]
root@SRX3400-1# set from destination-port 22

{primary:node0}[edit firewall family inet filter Services term Inbound]
root@SRX3400-1# set then accept

{primary:node0}[edit firewall family inet filter Services term Inbound]
root@SRX3400-1# up

{primary:node0}[edit firewall family inet filter Services]
root@SRX3400-1# edit term ICMP

{primary:node0}[edit firewall family inet filter Services term ICMP]
root@SRX3400-1# set from protocol icmp icmp-type echo-request

{primary:node0}[edit firewall family inet filter Services term ICMP]
root@SRX3400-1# set then accept

{primary:node0}[edit firewall family inet filter Services term ICMP]
root@SRX3400-1# up


{primary:node0}[edit firewall family inet filter Services]
root@SRX3400-1# show
term Inbound {
    from {
        protocol tcp;
        destination-port 22;
    }
    then accept;
}
term ICMP {
    from {
        protocol icmp;
        icmp-type echo-request;
    }
    then accept;
}
```

```
{primary:node0}[edit]
root@SRX3400-1# set interfaces irb unit 0 family inet filter input Services


{primary:node0}[edit]
root@SRX3400-1# show interfaces irb
unit 0 {
    family inet {
        filter {
            input Services;
        }
        address 192.168.60.1/24;
    }
}
```

If you want to restrict what services to listen on for the IRB interface, you should limit the system services allowed on the surrounding interfaces in the zones the VLANs are in, and use standard Junos firewall filters to limit what services are listened for on the IRB interfaces.

Configuring Transparent Mode Security Zones

Now that you have seen the interfaces and placed them into their respective bridge domains, let's add them into security zones on the SRX. As mentioned earlier in the chapter, the Layer 2 security zones don't have any special properties to them, and the configuration is just like Layer 3. In this example, the interfaces that were created two examples ago are configured as follows:

- Place interface ge-0/0/1.0 into the Trust zone.
- Place interface ge-0/0/2.0 into the Untrust zone.
- Place interfaces ge-0/0/3.40, ge-0/0/4.20, and ge-0/0/4.60 into the Trust zone.
- Place interfaces ge-0/0/3.10, ge-0/0/3.30, and ge-0/04.50 into the Untrust zone.
- Enable ping and SSH for all interfaces in the Trust zone; only allow ping for interfaces in the Untrust zone.

```
{primary:node0}[edit]
root@SRX3400-1# edit security zones security-zone trust

{primary:node0}[edit security zones security-zone trust]
root@SRX3400-1# show
host-inbound-traffic {
    system-services {
        ping;
        ssh;
    }
}
interfaces {
    ge-0/0/1.0;
```

```
        ge-0/0/3.40;
        ge-0/0/4.20;
        ge-0/0/4.60;
    }

{primary:node0}[edit security zones security-zone trust]
root@SRX3400-1# up

{primary:node0}[edit security zones]
root@SRX3400-1# edit security-zone untrust

{primary:node0}[edit security zones security-zone untrust]
root@SRX3400-1# set interfaces ge-0/0/2.0

{primary:node0}[edit security zones security-zone untrust]
root@SRX3400-1# set interfaces ge-0/0/3.10

{primary:node0}[edit security zones security-zone untrust]
root@SRX3400-1# set interfaces ge-0/0/3.30

{primary:node0}[edit security zones security-zone untrust]
root@SRX3400-1# set interfaces ge-0/0/4.50

{primary:node0}[edit security zones security-zone untrust]
root@SRX3400-1# set host-inbound-traffic system-services ping

{primary:node0}[edit security zones security-zone untrust]
root@SRX3400-1# show
host-inbound-traffic {
    system-services {
        ping;
    }
}
interfaces {
    ge-0/0/2.0;
    ge-0/0/3.10;
    ge-0/0/3.30;
    ge-0/0/4.50;
}
```

Configuring Transparent Mode Security Policies

Now that the separate logical Layer 2 interfaces have been created and assigned to security zones, let's create security policies to dictate what traffic is or isn't allowed to pass through the device between the various zones.

In this example, the following properties are configured:

- Create a rule from Trust to Untrust which allows any HTTP, HTTPS, Simple Mail Transfer Protocol (SMTP), and FTP traffic to go from the three trust networks 172.31.20.0/24, 172.31.40.0/24, and 172.31.60.0/24 to the three untrust networks 172.31.10.0/24, 172.31.30.0/24, and 172.31.50.0/24.

- Create a rule which allows only UDP-DNS and PING to return from the three untrust networks to the three trust networks.
- Log all policies on session close.
- Set the default policy to Deny-All (it should be set as this by default).

```
{primary:node0}[edit]
root@SRX3400-1# set security zones security-zones trust addreess-book address
172.31.20.0/24 172.31.20.0/24

{primary:node0}[edit]
root@SRX3400-1# set security zones security-zones trust address-book address
172.31.40.0/24 172.31.40.0/24

{primary:node0}[edit]
root@SRX3400-1# set security zones security-zones trust address-book address
172.31.60.0/24 172.31.60.0/24

{primary:node0}[edit]
root@SRX3400-1# set security zones security-zones untrust address-book address
172.31.10.0/24 172.31.10.0/24

{primary:node0}[edit]
root@SRX3400-1# set security zones security-zones untrust address-book address
172.31.30.0/24 172.31.30.0/24

{primary:node0}[edit]
root@SRX3400-1# set security zones security-zones untrust address-book address
172.31.50.0/24 172.31.50.0/24

{primary:node0}[edit]
root@SRX3400-1# show security zones
security-zone untrust {
    address-book {
        address 172.31.10.0/24 172.31.10.0/24;
        address 172.31.30.0/24 172.31.30.0/24;
        address 172.31.50.0/24 172.31.50.0/24;
    }
    host-inbound-traffic {
        system-services {
            ping;
        }
    }
    interfaces {
        ge-0/0/2.0;
        ge-0/0/3.10;
        ge-0/0/3.30;
        ge-0/0/4.50;
    }
}
security-zone trust {
    address-book {
        address 172.31.20.0/24 172.31.20.0/24;
        address 172.31.40.0/24 172.31.40.0/24;
        address 172.31.60.0/24 172.31.60.0/24;
```

```
        }
        host-inbound-traffic {
            system-services {
                ping;
                ssh;
            }
            protocols {
                all;
            }
        }
        interfaces {
            ge-0/0/1.0;
            ge-0/0/3.40;
            ge-0/0/4.20;
            ge-0/0/4.60;
        }
    }

{primary:node0}[edit]
root@SRX3400-1# edit security policies from-zone trust to-zone untrust policy
Allow-Traffic

{primary:node0}[edit security policies from-zone trust to-zone untrust policy
Allow-Traffic]
root@SRX3400-1# set match source-address [ 172.31.20.0/24 172.31.40.0/24
172.31.60.0/24 ]

{primary:node0}[edit security policies from-zone trust to-zone untrust policy
Allow-Traffic]
root@SRX3400-1# set match destination-address [ 172.31.10.0/24 172.31.30.0/24
172.31.50.0/24 ]

{primary:node0}[edit security policies from-zone trust to-zone untrust policy
Allow-Traffic]
root@SRX3400-1# set match application [ junos-http junos-https junos-smtp
junos-ftp ]

{primary:node0}[edit security policies from-zone trust to-zone untrust policy
Allow-Traffic]
root@SRX3400-1# set then permit

{primary:node0}[edit security policies from-zone trust to-zone untrust policy
Allow-Traffic]
root@SRX3400-1# set then log session-close

{primary:node0}[edit security policies from-zone trust to-zone untrust policy
Allow-Traffic]
root@SRX3400-1# up 2

{primary:node0}[edit security policies]
root@SRX3400-1# edit from-zone untrust to-zone trust policy Allow-Inbound

{primary:node0}[edit security policies from-zone untrust to-zone trust policy
Allow-Inbound]
```

```
root@SRX3400-1# set match source-address [ 172.31.10.0/24 172.31.30.0/24
172.31.50.0/24 ]

{primary:node0}[edit security policies from-zone untrust to-zone trust policy
Allow-Inbound]
root@SRX3400-1# set match destination-address [ 172.31.20.0/24 172.31.40.0/24
172.31.60.0/24 ]

{primary:node0}[edit security policies from-zone untrust to-zone trust policy
Allow-Inbound]
root@SRX3400-1# set match application [ junos-dns-udp junos-ping ]

{primary:node0}[edit security policies from-zone untrust to-zone trust policy
Allow-Inbound]
root@SRX3400-1# set then permit

{primary:node0}[edit security policies from-zone untrust to-zone trust policy
Allow-Inbound]
root@SRX3400-1# set then log session-close

{primary:node0}[edit security policies from-zone untrust to-zone trust policy
Allow-Inbound]
root@SRX3400-1# up 2

{primary:node0}[edit security policies]
root@SRX3400-1# set default-policy deny-all


{primary:node0}[edit security policies]
root@SRX3400-1# show
from-zone trust to-zone untrust {
    policy Allow-Traffic {
        match {
            source-address [ 172.31.20.0/24 172.31.40.0/24 172.31.60.0/24 ];
            destination-address [ 172.31.10.0/24 172.31.30.0/24 172.31.50.0/24 ];
            application [ junos-http junos-https junos-smtp junos-ftp ];
        }
        then {
            permit;
            log {
                session-close;
            }
        }
    }
}
from-zone untrust to-zone trust {
    policy Allow-Inbound {
        match {
            source-address [ 172.31.10.0/24 172.31.30.0/24 172.31.50.0/24 ];
            destination-address [ 172.31.20.0/24 172.31.40.0/24 172.31.60.0/24 ];
            application [ junos-dns-udp junos-ping ];
        }
        then {
            permit;
            log {
```

```
                    session-close;
                }
            }
        }
    }
    default-policy {
        deny-all;
    }
```

Configuring Bridging Options

Several bridging options can be configured on the SRX to manipulate how it processes packets and performs learning operations in transparent mode. Typically, you won't need to alter the configuration of these options, but just in case, this section demonstrates how to do exactly that.

In this example, the following configurations are performed:

- Your network has some legacy applications which require IPX, DECNET, AppleTalk, and Banyan VINES. Since the SRX does not support these protocols, configure the firewall to just bypass them from the firewall for processing.
- Your security posture is strict in terms of information leakage, so configure the SRX not to flood any packets with an unknown MAC address.

```
{primary:node0}[edit]
root@SRX3400-1# edit security flow bridge

{primary:node0}[edit security flow bridge]
root@SRX3400-1# set bypass-non-ip-unicast

{primary:node0}[edit security flow bridge]
root@SRX3400-1# set no-packet-flooding

{primary:node0}[edit security flow bridge]
root@SRX3400-1# show
bypass-non-ip-unicast;
no-packet-flooding;
```

Configuring Transparent Mode QoS

QoS in transparent mode is essentially the same as Layer 3 mode, with the primary exceptions of how the classification is performed and how the rewriting can be performed (802.1p bits only).

- Classify traffic matching the 802.1p bits 011 to the Expedited Forwarding Class (low loss priority), and 802.1p bits 111 to the Assured Forwarding Class (high loss priority) on interfaces reth0 and reth1.
- On reth0 and reth1, rewrite the outgoing 802.1p bits from 011 to 000 and 111 to 101, respectively.

```
[edit]
root@SRX3600-1# edit class-of-service classifiers ieee-802.1 011

[edit class-of-service classifiers ieee-802.1 011]
root@SRX3600-1# set forwarding-class expedited-forwarding loss-priority low code-
points 011

[edit class-of-service classifiers ieee-802.1 011]
root@SRX3600-1# up 1

[edit class-of-service classifiers]
root@SRX3600-1# edit ieee-802.1 111

[edit class-of-service classifiers ieee-802.1 111]
root@SRX3600-1# set forwarding-class assured-forwarding loss-priority high code-
points 111

[edit class-of-service classifiers ieee-802.1 111]
root@SRX3600-1# up 2

[edit class-of-service]
root@SRX3600-1# edit rewrite-rules

[edit class-of-service rewrite-rules]
root@SRX3600-1# edit ieee-802.1 011

[edit class-of-service rewrite-rules ieee-802.1 011]
root@SRX3600-1# set forwarding-class expedited-forwarding loss-priority low code-
point 000

[edit class-of-service rewrite-rules ieee-802.1 011]
root@SRX3600-1# up

[edit class-of-service rewrite-rules]
root@SRX3600-1# edit ieee-802.1 111

[edit class-of-service rewrite-rules ieee-802.1 111]
root@SRX3600-1# set forwarding-class assured-forwarding loss-priority high code-
point 101

[edit class-of-service rewrite-rules ieee-802.1 111]
root@SRX3600-1# up 2

[edit class-of-service]
root@SRX3600-1# set interfaces reth0 unit 0 classifiers ieee-802.1 011

[edit class-of-service]
root@SRX3600-1# set interfaces reth0 unit 0 rewrite-rules ieee-802.1 011

[edit class-of-service]
root@SRX3600-1# set interfaces reth1 unit 0 classifiers ieee-802.1 111

[edit class-of-service]
root@SRX3600-1# set interfaces reth1 unit 0 rewrite-rules ieee-802.1 111
```

```
[edit class-of-service]
root@SRX3600-1# show
classifiers {
    ieee-802.1 011 {
        forwarding-class expedited-forwarding {
            loss-priority low code-points 011;
        }
    }
    ieee-802.1 111 {
        forwarding-class assured-forwarding {
            loss-priority high code-points 111;
        }
    }
}
interfaces {
    reth0 {
        unit 0 {
            classifiers {
                ieee-802.1 011;
            }
            rewrite-rules {
                ieee-802.1 011;
            }
        }
    }
    reth1 {
        unit 0 {
            classifiers {
                ieee-802.1 111;
            }
            rewrite-rules {
                ieee-802.1 111;
            }
        }
    }
}
rewrite-rules {
    ieee-802.1 011 {
        forwarding-class expedited-forwarding {
            loss-priority low code-point 000;
        }
    }
    ieee-802.1 111 {
        forwarding-class assured-forwarding {
            loss-priority high code-point 101;
        }
    }
}
```

Configuring VLAN Rewriting

Earlier in this chapter, I mentioned that you can use VLAN rewriting to rewrite one VLAN to another on an interface. This example does exactly that, with the following configuration:

- On interface ge-0/0/3, configure VLAN retagging to translate VLAN 100 to VLAN 10. Use unit 10 for this translation.
- On interface ge-0/0/4, configure VLAN retagging to translate VLAN 200 to VLAN 20. Use unit 20 for this translation.

```
{primary:node0}[edit]
root@SRX3400-1# edit interfaces ge-0/0/3

{primary:node0}[edit interfaces ge-0/0/3]
root@SRX3400-1# set unit 10 family bridge vlan-rewrite translate 100 10

{primary:node0}[edit interfaces ge-0/0/3]
root@SRX3400-1# show
vlan-tagging;
unit 10 {
    family bridge {
        interface-mode trunk;
        vlan-id-list 10;
        vlan-rewrite {
            translate 100 10;
        }
    }
}
unit 30 {
    family bridge {
        interface-mode trunk;
        vlan-id-list 30;
    }
}
unit 40 {
    family bridge {
        interface-mode trunk;
        vlan-id-list 40;
    }
}

{primary:node0}[edit interfaces ge-0/0/3]
root@SRX3400-1# up

{primary:node0}[edit interfaces]
root@SRX3400-1# edit ge-0/0/4

{primary:node0}[edit interfaces ge-0/0/4]
root@SRX3400-1# set unit 20 family bridge vlan-rewrite translate 200 20

{primary:node0}[edit interfaces ge-0/0/4]
root@SRX3400-1# show
vlan-tagging;
unit 20 {
    family bridge {
        interface-mode trunk;
        vlan-id-list 20;
        vlan-rewrite {
            translate 200 20;
```

```
            }
        }
    }
    unit 50 {
        family bridge {
            interface-mode trunk;
            vlan-id-list 50;
        }
    }
    unit 60 {
        family bridge {
            interface-mode trunk;
            vlan-id-list 60;
        }
    }
```

As you can see here, you need to configure `vlan-rewrite` under a logical unit that is configured as a trunk link. In the case of ge-0/0/3, traffic that arrives inbound, tagged with VLAN 100, is translated on ingress to VLAN 10 and processed accordingly. When traffic on VLAN 10 is leaving the SRX on that interface, it is reverse-translated on egress to VLAN 100. The same is true for ge-0/0/4 translating from VLAN 200 to 20 and vice versa. The main command that empowers this is the `set interfaces <interface> unit <unit> family bridge interface-mode trunk translate <incoming-vlan> <translated-vlan>` command. In addition, you must define the VLANs which are present on the unit using the `vlan-id-list` command.

Transparent Mode Commands and Troubleshooting

Troubleshooting issues in transparent mode are almost identical to troubleshooting Layer 3, with a few exceptions which are the focus here. First, this section lists some of the useful commands in Layer 2 that you should be aware of, and then we will work our way through a step-by-step troubleshooting plan.

The next few commands are unique to transparent mode. We will cover the rest of the steps in "Transparent Mode Troubleshooting Steps" on page 743.

The show bridge domain Command

The `show bridge domain` command lists all of the active bridge domains on the device, along with the associated VLANs and interfaces for those domains. If you are experiencing an issue where traffic isn't flowing, you should check this out first to make sure you have the correct interface, VLAN, and bridge domain configuration.

```
root@SRX3400-1> show bridge domain

Routing instance     Bridge domain        VLAN ID     Interfaces
default-switch       L2-VLAN-10           10
                                                      ge-0/0/1.0
                                                      ge-0/0/3.10
```

```
default-switch        L2-VLAN-20           20
                                                      ge-0/0/2.0
                                                      ge-0/0/4.20
default-switch        L2-VLAN-30           30
                                                      ge-0/0/3.30
default-switch        L2-VLAN-40           40
                                                      ge-0/0/3.40
default-switch        L2-VLAN-50           50
                                                      ge-0/0/4.50
default-switch        L2-VLAN-60           60
                                                      ge-0/0/4.60
```

The show bridge mac-table Command

The `show bridge mac-table` command is important for looking at the bridge MAC learning table. If you do not see the MAC addresses for the hosts in the correct bridge domain on the correct interface of this output, either the SRX is not seeing the MAC addresses at all (check the surrounding networking devices) or you're seeing them on the wrong interface/bridge domain (which might require some configuration changes).

```
{primary:node0}
root@SRX3400-1> show bridge mac-table

MAC flags (S -static MAC, D -dynamic MAC,
           SE -Statistics enabled, NM -Non configured MAC)

Routing instance : default-switch
 Bridging domain : L2-VLAN-20, VLAN : 20
   MAC                 MAC      Logical
   address             flags    interface
   00:1f:12:31:d3:21   D        ge-0/0/2.0
   00:1f:12:f4:ef:1c   D        ge-0/0/2.0
```

The show l2-learning global-information Command

This command lists the global configuration for the SRX bridge domains:

```
{primary:node0}
root@SRX3400-1> show l2-learning global-information
Global Configuration:

MAC aging interval     : 300
MAC learning           : Enabled
MAC statistics         : Disabled
MAC limit Count        : 131071
MAC limit hit          : Disabled
MAC packet action drop: Disabled
LE  aging time         : 1200
LE  BD aging time      : 1200
```

The show l2-learning global-mac-count Command

You may also want to check how many MAC addresses your system currently knows about, to ensure that the table is not full. At the time of this writing, the SRX supports 64,000 MAC address entries in the table.

```
{primary:node0}
root@SRX3400-1> show l2-learning global-mac-count
2 dynamic and static MAC addresses learned globally
```

The show l2-learning interface Command

Although the SRX doesn't support STP natively at the time of this writing, it will forward the BPDUs to ensure that there are no bridge loops. Additionally, there may be reasons why an interface is forwarding, or VLANs within an interface are not forwarding, such as the physical interface being down, as shown in this example:

```
{primary:node0}
root@SRX3400-1> show l2-learning interface
Routing Instance Name : default-switch
Logical Interface flags (DL -disable learning, AD -packet action drop,
                         LH - MAC limit hit, DN - Interface Down )
Logical             BD         MAC        STP          Logical
Interface           Name       Limit      State        Interface flags
ge-0/0/1.0                     131071
                    L2-VLA..   131071     Forwarding
Routing Instance Name : default-switch
Logical Interface flags (DL -disable learning, AD -packet action drop,
                         LH - MAC limit hit, DN - Interface Down )
Logical             BD         MAC        STP          Logical
Interface           Name       Limit      State        Interface flags
ge-0/0/3.30                    131071
                    L2-VLA..   131071     Discarding
Routing Instance Name : default-switch
Logical Interface flags (DL -disable learning, AD -packet action drop,
                         LH - MAC limit hit, DN - Interface Down )
Logical             BD         MAC        STP          Logical
Interface           Name       Limit      State        Interface flags
ge-0/0/3.40                    131071
                    L2-VLA..   131071     Discarding
Routing Instance Name : default-switch
Logical Interface flags (DL -disable learning, AD -packet action drop,
                         LH - MAC limit hit, DN - Interface Down )
Logical             BD         MAC        STP          Logical
Interface           Name       Limit      State        Interface flags
ge-0/0/4.20                    131071
                    L2-VLA..   131071     Discarding
Routing Instance Name : default-switch
Logical Interface flags (DL -disable learning, AD -packet action drop,
                         LH - MAC limit hit, DN - Interface Down )
Logical             BD         MAC        STP          Logical
Interface           Name       Limit      State        Interface flags
ge-0/0/2.0                     131071
```

```
                    L2-VLA..   131071     Forwarding
Routing Instance Name : default-switch
Logical Interface flags (DL -disable learning, AD -packet action drop,
                         LH - MAC limit hit, DN - Interface Down )
Logical              BD         MAC        STP           Logical
Interface            Name       Limit      State         Interface flags
ge-0/0/4.50                     131071
                    L2-VLA..   131071     Discarding
Routing Instance Name : default-switch
Logical Interface flags (DL -disable learning, AD -packet action drop,
                         LH - MAC limit hit, DN - Interface Down )
Logical              BD         MAC        STP           Logical
Interface            Name       Limit      State         Interface flags
ge-0/0/4.60                     131071
                    L2-VLA..   131071     Discarding
Routing Instance Name : default-switch
Logical Interface flags (DL -disable learning, AD -packet action drop,
                         LH - MAC limit hit, DN - Interface Down )
Logical              BD         MAC        STP           Logical
Interface            Name       Limit      State         Interface flags
ge-0/0/3.10                     131071
                    L2-VLA..   131071     Discarding
```

Transparent Mode Troubleshooting Steps

Here are some recommended sequential troubleshooting steps for working in transparent mode:

1. Check the spanning tree.

   An issue with the spanning tree is the most common issue when traffic is not flowing through the SRX properly, since surrounding networking gear with spanning tree enabled may put the data interfaces into a blocking state. This is not an issue with the SRX itself, but you will need to run the respective commands on the surrounding networking gear to determine if any of the interfaces that are connected to the SRX are in the blocking state. In the Juniper Networks EX Series Ethernet Switches, you would do this in Junos with the `show spanning-tree interface` command to look for interfaces in the `BLK` state. On the MX Series, you would look in Junos with the `show l2-learning interface` command.

   This is particularly important when dealing with HA clusters, since the interfaces may be in the blocking state for one member and not the other. You should test failover to ensure it works properly.

2. Check to see if MAC addresses are being learned.

   The absence of MAC addresses in the SRX bridging table certainly indicates that there is an issue, along with MAC addresses not appearing on the correct VLANs or interfaces. On the SRX, you can use the `show bridge mac-table` command.

3. Check the configuration.

   The first common issue that occurs with transparent mode is often a configuration mistake, including the wrong VLAN IDs or incorrect bridge domains. You must check the configuration on the surrounding networking devices along with the SRX. On the SRX, you would want to start by looking at the `show bridge domain` command to make sure the VLAN configuration is properly mapped to the correct domains. You might also want to review the configuration of the surrounding devices.

4. Check that the native VLANs are properly configured.

   On both the SRX and the surrounding networking devices, you must make sure the correct native VLANs are used (if any), or else there may be an issue with interpreting the traffic. The same is true for properly matching the correct traffic to the correct VLAN. If you do not have the correct mappings, there will be issues. Note that the units do not technically need to match between the two devices, but making sure the correct tags and the correct classification are used is essential.

5. Check that sessions are being established.

   If the traffic appears to be arriving on the SRX on the correct interfaces and VLANs, you should check to make sure the sessions are being established and matched to the correct rule. You can do this initially by just looking at the session table using the `show security flow session <modifiers>` command along with running the standard flow tracing operations covered in Chapter 3. For instance, you can enable the `basic-datapath` debug and send the output to the file *L2Debug*. Additionally, you should configure a packet filter based around the traffic you are looking for to ensure that you don't match unnecessary traffic. Make sure to turn the debugging off after the issue has been resolved to ensure that performance isn't impacted.

```
{primary:node0}[edit]
root@SRX3400-1# edit security flow traceoptions

{primary:node0}[edit security flow traceoptions]
root@SRX3400-1# set flag basic-datapath

{primary:node0}[edit security flow traceoptions]
root@SRX3400-1# set file L2Debug

{primary:node0}[edit security flow traceoptions]
root@SRX3400-1# set packet-filter MatchTraffic interface ge-0/0/1.0 source-prefix
 172.31.0.0/16 destination-prefix 192.168.1.1

{primary:node0}[edit security flow traceoptions]
root@SRX3400-1# show
file L2Debug;
flag basic-datapath;
packet-filter MatchTraffic {
    source-prefix 172.31.0.0/16;
    destination-prefix 192.168.1.1/32;
```

```
        interface ge-0/0/1.0;
    }
```

6. Examine the debug output.

   From your debugs, you should be able to determine that the traffic is entering and exiting the correct interfaces, along with being matched by the correct security policy. If this isn't happening, the output in the debug should provide you with hints about what you need to change to resolve the issue.

7. Check if you are using any unsupported features or running into a known issue.

   Remember that some SRX features are not yet supported in transparent mode. We covered them in the beginning of this chapter, and you might check with the Juniper documentation for actual timing of these features. For known issues, you should check the release notes of the version you are running, along with any subsequent releases for issues that have been resolved in case it sounds like a bug. If you are using these features, that could be causing the issue. Check with the Juniper Networks Technical Assistance Center (JTAC) if you suspect this.

8. Troubleshoot the surrounding networking equipment.

   If the SRX appears to be processing the traffic properly and the traffic appears to be entering and exiting the SRX, you should access the neighboring devices to make sure the traffic is actually reaching them, and that they are processing the traffic correctly. The methodology you would follow on the other devices depends on the device, but if you can, do an end-to-end packet trace to try to determine where things are breaking down. That is definitely useful when all other steps seem to yield no information.

9. Check the Juniper Knowledge Base.

   The Juniper Knowledge Base (*http://kb.juniper.net/*) may have additional information for troubleshooting these issues, along with potential major known issues.

10. Call JTAC.

    If all else fails, and you have gathered all of the data from your troubleshooting steps, you should call JTAC for additional assistance in troubleshooting the issue. Having information such as network diagrams, packet captures, and access to the devices is very helpful for finding a speedy resolution (see Chapter 9 for a series of commands to run whose output JTAC may want or need to see).

Case Study 12-1

Now that you have covered all of the concepts related to transparent mode, let's bring it all together and provide a full configuration example, along with the use of chassis clustering to achieve an HA solution.

There really isn't much difference between clustering a transparent mode pair and clustering a Layer 3 mode pair, from a configuration or concept perspective—you just need to be aware of the surrounding networking configuration to accommodate transparent mode.

This case study performs the following configuration according to this book's network diagram (see Figure 12-4):

- Create a chassis cluster with the two SRX3600s that protect the DMZ. Configure all of the properties of the HA cluster as you see fit (except the interfaces as described shortly). Use ge-0/0/9 and ge-13/0/9 for the data links.
- Support trunk link reth0, which will serve as the backbone link. Reth0 will have two tagged VLANs, one for VLAN 100 and another which allows VLAN 30 inbound, but translates it to VLAN 1. Reth0 will be composed of the physical interfaces ge-0/0/0 and ge-13/0/0.
- There will be four other Reth interfaces which connect into a switch before connecting to the end servers. These will all use the access mode interfaces. Reth1 will belong to the VoIP PBX zone and will be composed of ge-0/0/1 and ge-13/0/1. Reth2 will be in the WebApp zone and will be composed of ge-0/0/2 and ge-13/0/2. Reth3 will be in the Email-Server zone and will be composed of ge-0/0/3 and ge-13/0/3. Finally, reth4 will be in the Database zone and will be composed of ge-0/0/4 and ge-13/0/4. All of these interfaces will be in VLAN 30.
  - —Create the respective bridge domains.
  - —Create an IRB.30 interface with an IP address of 172.31.30.254/24.
- For your policies create the following:
  - —Allow Dept-A and Dept-B to talk to the PBX via RTSP and vice versa.
  - —Allow inbound HTTP and HTTPS to the web server from any IP coming from the backbone.
  - —Allow the web server to query the database with SQL.
  - —Allow SMTP connections into the email server and from the email server out, along with DNS.

Set the chassis cluster IDs and node config, and reboot as follows:

```
root@SRX3400-1> set chassis cluster cluster-id 1 node 0 reboot
root@SRX3400-2> set chassis cluster cluster-id 1 node 1 reboot
```

This is an operational mode command. Also, since this is using SRX3600s, you don't need to configure any control ports.

Configure the data links:

```
{primary:node0}[edit]
root@SRX3400-1# set interfaces fab0 fabric-options member-interfaces ge-0/0/9
```

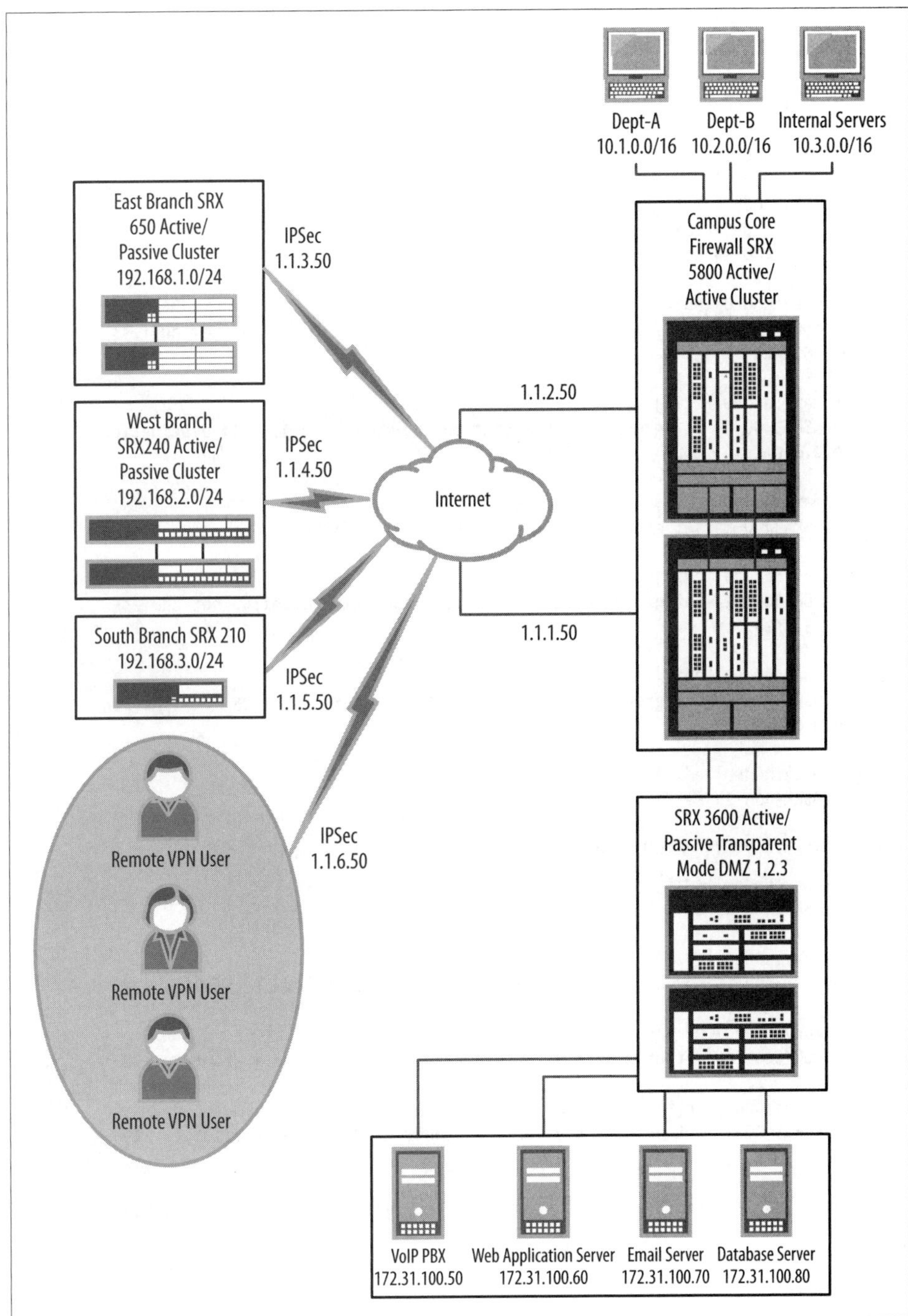

Figure 12-4. Case Study 12-1 network diagram

```
{primary:node0}[edit]
root@SRX3400-1# set interfaces fab1 fabric-options member-interfaces ge-13/0/9
```

Configure the node-specific properties:

```
{primary:node0}[edit]
root@SRX3400-1# set groups node0
{primary:node0}[edit]
root@SRX3400-1# set groups node1
{primary:node0}[edit]
root@SRX3400-1# set groups node0 system host-name SRX3600-1

{primary:node0}[edit]
root@SRX3400-1# set groups node0 interfaces fxp0 unit 0 family inet address
10.3.5.1/24

{primary:node0}[edit]
root@SRX3400-1# set groups node0 system backup-router 10.3.5.254 destination
0.0.0.0/0

{primary:node0}[edit]
root@SRX3400-1# set groups node1 system host-name SRX3600-2

{primary:node0}[edit]
root@SRX3400-1# set groups node1 interfaces fxp0 unit 0 family inet address
10.3.5.2/24

{primary:node0}[edit]
root@SRX3400-1# set groups node1 system backup-router 10.3.5.254 destination
0.0.0.0/0

{primary:node0}[edit]
root@SRX3400-1# set apply-groups ${node}
```

Configure the Reth count and redundancy groups:

```
{primary:node0}[edit]
root@SRX3400-1# set chassis cluster reth-count 5

{primary:node0}[edit]
root@SRX3400-1# set chassis cluster redundancy-group 0 node 0 priority 129

{primary:node0}[edit]
root@SRX3400-1# set chassis cluster redundancy-group 0 node 1 priority 128

{primary:node0}[edit]
root@SRX3400-1# set chassis cluster redundancy-group 1 node 0 priority 129

{primary:node0}[edit]
root@SRX3400-1# set chassis cluster redundancy-group 1 node 1 priority 128
```

Configure the Reth and IRB interfaces:

```
{primary:node0}[edit]
root@SRX3400-1# set interfaces ge-0/0/0 gigether-options redundant-parent reth0

{primary:node0}[edit]
```

```
root@SRX3400-1# set interfaces ge-13/0/0 gigether-options redundant-parent reth0

{primary:node0}[edit]
root@SRX3400-1# set interfaces ge-0/0/1 gigether-options redundant-parent reth1

{primary:node0}[edit]
root@SRX3400-1# set interfaces ge-13/0/1 gigether-options redundant-parent reth1

{primary:node0}[edit]
root@SRX3400-1# set interfaces ge-0/0/2 gigether-options redundant-parent reth2

{primary:node0}[edit]
root@SRX3400-1# set interfaces ge-13/0/2 gigether-options redundant-parent reth2

{primary:node0}[edit]
root@SRX3400-1# set interfaces ge-0/0/3 gigether-options redundant-parent reth3

{primary:node0}[edit]
root@SRX3400-1# set interfaces ge-13/0/3 gigether-options redundant-parent reth3

{primary:node0}[edit]
root@SRX3400-1# set interfaces ge-0/0/4 gigether-options redundant-parent reth4

{primary:node0}[edit]
root@SRX3400-1# set interfaces ge-13/0/4 gigether-options redundant-parent reth4

{primary:node0}[edit]
root@SRX3400-1# set interfaces reth0 redundant-ether-options redundancy-group 1

{primary:node0}[edit]
root@SRX3400-1# set interfaces reth1 redundant-ether-options redundancy-group 1

{primary:node0}[edit]
root@SRX3400-1# set interfaces reth2 redundant-ether-options redundancy-group 1

{primary:node0}[edit]
root@SRX3400-1# set interfaces reth3 redundant-ether-options redundancy-group 1

{primary:node0}[edit]
root@SRX3400-1# set interfaces reth4 redundant-ether-options redundancy-group 1

{primary:node0}[edit]
root@SRX3400-1# set interfaces reth0 vlan-tagging

{primary:node0}[edit]
root@SRX3400-1# set interfaces reth0 unit 100 family bridge interface-mode trunk
vlan-id-list 100

{primary:node0}[edit]
root@SRX3400-1# set interfaces reth0 unit 30 family bridge interface-mode trunk

{primary:node0}[edit]
root@SRX3400-1# set interfaces reth0 unit 30 family bridge vlan-rewrite translate
30 1
```

```
{primary:node0}[edit]
root@SRX3400-1# set interfaces reth1 unit 0 family bridge interface-mode access
vlan-id 100

{primary:node0}[edit]
root@SRX3400-1# set interfaces reth2 unit 0 family bridge interface-mode access
vlan-id 100

{primary:node0}[edit]
root@SRX3400-1# set interfaces reth3 unit 0 family bridge interface-mode access
vlan-id 100

{primary:node0}[edit]
root@SRX3400-1# set interfaces reth4 unit 0 family bridge interface-mode access
vlan-id 100

{primary:node0}[edit]
root@SRX3400-1# set interfaces irb unit 100 family inet address 172.31.100.254/24
```

Configure the bridge domains:

```
{primary:node0}[edit]
root@SRX3400-1# set bridge-domains VLAN1 domain-type bridge vlan-id 1

{primary:node0}[edit]
root@SRX3400-1# set bridge-domains VLAN100 domain-type bridge vlan-id 100
routing-interface irb.100
```

Configure security zones and address objects:

```
{primary:node0}[edit]
root@SRX3400-1# set security zones security-zones Backbone interfaces reth0.100

{primary:node0}[edit]
root@SRX3400-1# set security zones security-zones Backbone interfaces reth0.30

{primary:node0}[edit]
root@SRX3400-1# set security zones security-zones VoIP interfaces reth1

{primary:node0}[edit]
root@SRX3400-1# set security zones security-zones WebApp interfaces reth2

{primary:node0}[edit]
root@SRX3400-1# set security zones security-zones Email-Server interfaces reth3

{primary:node0}[edit]
root@SRX3400-1# set security zones security-zones Database interfaces reth4

{primary:node0}[edit]
root@SRX3400-1# set security zones security-zones Backbone address-book address
Dept-A 10.1.0.0/16

{primary:node0}[edit]
root@SRX3400-1# set security zones security-zones Backbone address-book address
Dept-B 10.2.0.0/16

{primary:node0}[edit]
```

```
root@SRX3400-1# set security zones security-zones VoIP address-book address VoIP-
PBX 172.31.100.50/32

{primary:node0}[edit]
root@SRX3400-1# set security zones security-zones WebApp address-book address
WebApp 172.31.100.60/32

{primary:node0}[edit]
root@SRX3400-1# set security zones security-zones Email-Server address-book
address WebApp 172.31.100.70/32

{primary:node0}[edit]
root@SRX3400-1# set security zones security-zones Database address-book address
172.31.100.80/32
```

Configure the security policies:

```
{primary:node0}[edit security policies]
root@SRX3400-1# set from-zone Backbone to-zone VoIP policy Allow-RTSP match
source-address [ Dept-A Dept-B ] destination-address VoIP-PBX application junos-
rtsp

{primary:node0}[edit security policies]
root@SRX3400-1# set from-zone Backbone to-zone VoIP policy Allow-RTSP then permit

{primary:node0}[edit security policies]
root@SRX3400-1# set from-zone VoIP to-zone Backbone policy Allow-RTSP-Out match
source-address VoIP-PBX destination-address [ Dept-A Dept-B ] application junos-
rtsp

{primary:node0}[edit security policies]
root@SRX3400-1# set from-zone Backbone to-zone VoIP policy Allow-RTSP-Out then
permit

{primary:node0}[edit security policies]
root@SRX3400-1# set from-zone Backbone to-zone WebApp policy Allow-Inbound-Web
match source-address any destination-address WebApp application [ junos-http
junos-https ]

{primary:node0}[edit security policies]
root@SRX3400-1# set from-zone Backbone to-zone WebApp policy Allow-Inbound-Web
then permit

{primary:node0}[edit security policies]
root@SRX3400-1# set from-zone WebApp to-zone Database policy Allow-Web-Queries
match source-address WebApp destination-address Database application
[ junos-sql ]

{primary:node0}[edit security policies]
root@SRX3400-1# set from-zone WebApp to-zone Database policy Allow-Web-Queries
then permit

{primary:node0}[edit security policies]
root@SRX3400-1# set from-zone Backbone to-zone Email-Server policy Allow-Emails-
Inbound match source-address any destination-address Email-Server application
[ junos-smtp ]
```

```
{primary:node0}[edit security policies]
root@SRX3400-1# set from-zone Backbone to-zone Email-Server policy Allow-Emails-
Inbound then permit

{primary:node0}[edit security policies]
root@SRX3400-1# set from-zone Email-Server to-zone Backbone policy Allow-Emails-
Outbound match source-address Email-Server destination-address any application
[ junos-smtp junos-dns-udp ]

{primary:node0}[edit security policies]
root@SRX3400-1# set from-zone Email-Server to-zone Backbone policy Allow-Emails-
Outbound then permit

{primary:node0}[edit security policies]
root@SRX3400-1# set default-policy deny-all
```

Summary

Transparent mode is a very powerful feature that can dramatically ease the deployment of a firewall, while providing advanced support for securing your network. Most of the configuration relating to transparent mode is just like standard Layer 3 routed mode, but there are a few new concepts that you need to be aware of regarding the actual interface and VLAN configurations.

Although transparent mode is typically quite easy to deploy, you do need to be aware of the potential for bridge loops, along with the fact that spanning tree may cause links to go into the blocking state, and therefore not pass traffic properly.

In this chapter, we discussed many tools on the SRX and surrounding devices that can help you to determine the cause of an issue so that you can take appropriate steps to resolve it.

Lastly, there are a few limitations of transparent mode at the time of this writing that you need to be aware of. As time goes on, Juniper will continue to strive to eliminate these limitations and achieve full-feature parity, so monitor the Junos release notes to determine what new features and support have arrived in the latest release. After all, Juniper comes out with new software every three months, so things can be developed quite quickly for the SRX.

Chapter Review Questions

1. Why is transparent mode a popular deployment model for firewall deployments?
2. What is the name of the family used on interfaces in transparent mode?
3. How can a device in transparent mode communicate with other devices on the network if the interfaces do not have any Layer 3 addressing?
4. What is the difference between interfaces in access mode and trunk mode?

5. What is the default method for resolving an unknown MAC address when the SRX has received a packet with an unknown MAC address and needs to forward it?
6. If you have non-IP traffic on your network, how can you have the SRX forward it?
7. With what fields can the SRX perform QoS for transit traffic?
8. What is the purpose of VLAN rewriting?
9. What is the most common issue in transparent mode that prevents traffic from flowing properly through the SRX?
10. How does the SRX inform surrounding networking equipment to recalculate spanning tree in the event of a failure?

Chapter Review Answers

1. Transparent mode allows easy deployment of a firewall because the underlying network structure does not need to change from a Layer 3 perspective, thus making it easy to deploy a firewall in transparent mode. Additionally, since the device does not have to perform any routing, this makes it ideal when being inserted into complex routing topologies, although this isn't so much of an issue with the SRX since the SRX supports Junos.
2. The family bridge is the family used on the interface in transparent mode.
3. In transparent mode, you can use IRB interfaces within VLANs to provide a virtual Layer 3 interface which can send and receive traffic, although it cannot route transit traffic itself at the time of this writing.
4. Access mode interfaces provide a single untagged interface on which traffic may arrive. Access mode interfaces do allow the interface to classify any traffic being received on them as being from a particular VLAN; however, the traffic itself is not tagged. Trunk interfaces allow the interface to accept traffic from multiple VLANs which are distinguished by different tags (a tag or range of tags can be allowed by a particular bridge domain) along with the ability to support a native VLAN which has no tag, but all untagged traffic will be classified as being part of this VLAN on the system.
5. The default method of resolution is to forward the packet out all interfaces in the same VLAN except the one on which it was received. Alternatively, you can configure the SRX to ARP for the destination on behalf of the client, along with sending an ICMP with a TTL of 1 to determine the interface on which the destination MAC address lives.
6. You will need to enable the `set security flow bridge bypass-non-ip-unicast` command to allow all non-IP traffic (except IPv6, which currently will be dropped unless tunneled) through the SRX.

7. The SRX can perform classification and rewriting with the 802.1p bits that are present in 802.1q frames. You cannot use IP precedence or DSCP bits for classification on the SRX in transparent mode; you can only do so in Layer 3 mode.
8. VLAN rewriting, also known as VLAN retagging, allows the SRX to swap the incoming or outgoing VLAN tag with another which the system will use for internal processing. This is useful when you want to translate the VLAN tags on the SRX without using routing to transform the packets.
9. A misconfigured spanning tree can result in surrounding network equipment thinking there is a loop in the network, and therefore putting interfaces in blocking mode that otherwise shouldn't be. This can also impact the failover between chassis cluster members.
10. The SRX will flap the interfaces for the respective secondary redundancy groups which are failing over so that the switches will recalculate spanning tree in favor of the new primary node for the respective redundancy groups.

CHAPTER 13

SRX Management

This chapter discusses some of the ways in which both users and management systems can interact with an SRX device. At this point in the book, you must be familiar with the command-line interface (CLI), which provides a text-based interface between the users and the different subsystems in a device. This is our starting point: the management infrastructure and how the CLI interacts with the different system components.

The Management Infrastructure

Central to the Junos management infrastructure is a daemon that interacts with the different daemons and forwarding elements in a device, called the *MGD* (management daemon). This daemon is in charge of performing multiple common tasks on all management interfaces.

Most management interfaces, such as J-Web and the CLI, communicate with MGD by sending XML-formatted commands (procedure calls) and receiving the results, also in XML format. Each user interface then presents the information back to the user in a human-readable way, as shown in Figure 13-1.

Given its central placement in the system, MGD is the interface between the different system daemons and the management interfaces, so when MGD receives a request, it deals with interfacing to the appropriate daemons. In this sense, MGD abstracts the complexity of the system so that the client applications do not need to keep track of which particular daemon is in charge of which task.

MGD also owns the configuration schema, so it can determine if commands are syntactically correct. However, it is still possible to create configurations with a valid syntax that are logically incorrect—for instance, a configuration with an Ethernet interface configured in switched mode as an access port but associated with two different virtual LANs (VLANs)—could be correct in its syntax, but impossible to configure.

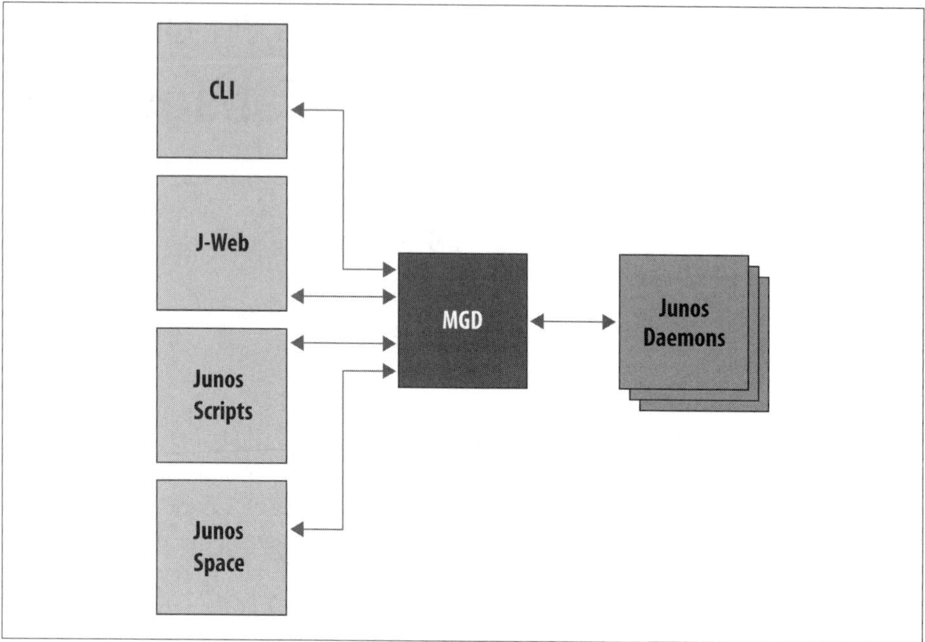

Figure 13-1. The management infrastructure

Since you should already be familiar with the CLI by now (and if not you must have skipped almost the whole book to get here), we will use the CLI to explain some of the concepts that apply to the entire management infrastructure.

When you type a command in the CLI, the command is passed on to MGD. MGD then uses the configuration schema to:

- Perform the command completion.
- Provide a list of options when a "?" character is typed.
- Check the command syntax.

It is in this context that one should try to understand the two very different modes in which the Junos UI operates, either operational or command mode.

Operational Mode

In operational mode, the commands typed by the user are directly translated into commands to the daemons in the system. The results are relayed back to the user and presented in a readable way. Let's see what happens when you submit the `show version` command (the `| display xml rpc` modifier indicates to MGD to echo back the XML Remote Procedure Call [RPC] request that results from typing a given command, that is, instead of executing the request):

```
pato@SRX240-1> show version | display xml rpc
<rpc-reply xmlns:junos="http://xml.juniper.net/junos/10.2I0/junos">
    <rpc>
        <get-software-information>
        </get-software-information>
    </rpc>
    <cli>
        <banner></banner>
    </cli>
</rpc-reply>
```

You can see how the CLI sends a `get-interface-information` RPC to MGD. After a user types this command, MGD queries the appropriate daemon over a socket (or, in some instances, it might execute a shell command directly) and returns the result of the RPC back to the CLI.

The contents of the `banner` tags are used as an indication to the CLI to display a particular banner to the user, and are not germane to this discussion.

Continuing with our example, the result of the `show version` command, as received by the CLI, can be displayed using the `| show xml` command:

```
pato@SRX240-1> show version | display xml
<rpc-reply xmlns:junos="http://xml.juniper.net/junos/10.2I0/junos">
    <software-information>
        <host-name>SRX240-1</host-name>
        <product-model>srx240h-poe</product-model>
        <product-name>srx240h-poe</product-name>
        <jsr/>
        <package-information>
            <name>junos</name>
            <comment>JUNOS Software Release [10.2-20100303.0]</comment>
        </package-information>
    </software-information>
    <cli>
        <banner></banner>
    </cli>
</rpc-reply>
```

The result contains an XML-formatted message that is parsed by the CLI and can be displayed in a more readable way:

```
pato@SRX240-1> show version
Hostname: SRX240-1
Model: srx240h-poe
JUNOS Software Release [10.2-20100303.0]
```

Configuration Mode

In configuration mode, MGD is used to validate and store the configuration changes. In the backend, after a user enters a new configuration statement, MGD validates the statement against the configuration schema and, if it is a valid command, stores the proposed changes in a candidate configuration database. As you already know from this book or other Junos information sources, this operation does not change the system's behavior until the user commits the changes.

There are a few ways a user can edit the candidate configuration database. When entering configuration mode, MGD by default does shared editing of the database, meaning that any other user logged in to the system is able to see all changes as they are being made, even before a commit is committed. Obviously, in this mode, when a user commits the candidate configuration it might be sending along with his own edits configuration changes made by other users with a shared edit of the database.

Here, for example, user `pato` is editing the configuration and looks at the system's host name:

```
[edit]
pato@SRX240-1# show system host-name
host-name SRX240-1;
```

While `pato` is looking at the config, the test user logs in, edits the shared configuration database, and changes the hostname from SRX240-1 to SRX240-NEW:

```
test@SRX240-1> configure
Entering configuration mode
Users currently editing the configuration:
  pato terminal p1 (pid 9956) on since 2010-03-05 00:45:24 PST
      [edit]

[edit]
test@SRX240-1# set system host-name SRX240-NEW
```

User `pato` sees the changes in his session as well, because both users are editing the same candidate configuration database:

```
[edit]
pato@SRX240-1# show system host-name
host-name SRX240-NEW;
```

Users can also do a private edit of the database; each user doing a private edit uses a different candidate configuration database. This has the advantage that the users can make sure nobody changes their edits, but it can create merging problems as different users might be overriding the same sections of the configuration. Again, this concept might be simpler to explain with an example.

Let's have our users, `test` and `pato`, do private configuration edits simultaneously:

```
pato@SRX240-1> configure private
warning: uncommitted changes will be discarded on exit
Entering configuration mode
```

```
[edit]
test@SRX240-1> configure private
warning: uncommitted changes will be discarded on exit
Entering configuration mode
Users currently editing the configuration:
  pato terminal p1 (pid 9956) on since 2010-03-05 01:00:41 PST
      private [edit]

[edit]
```

Note how `test` is notified that a different user (`pato`) is also doing a private configuration edit.

Both `pato` and `test` will change the hostname and commit their changes, but `test` is the last one doing the commit:

```
pato@SRX240-1# set system host-name SRX240-Pato

[edit]
pato@SRX240-1# commit
commit complete
```

When `test` tries to commit his configuration he is notified of the inconsistency: that he has been working with an old configuration database!

```
test@SRX240-1# set system host-name SRX240-Test

[edit]
test@SRX240-1# commit
[edit system host-name]
  'host-name SRX240-Pato'
    statement does not match patch: 'SRX240-Pato' != 'SRX240-1'
```

Our last option, if you want to make sure nobody makes any changes to the configuration while you're working, is to do an *exclusive edit*. In this mode, the candidate configuration is locked and no other user can edit the configuration until the lock is released:

```
pato@SRX210-1> configure exclusive
warning: uncommitted changes will be discarded on exit
Entering configuration mode
```

See what happens after `pato` acquires an exclusive lock, and `test` tries to change the configuration:

```
test@SRX210-1> configure
Entering configuration mode
Users currently editing the configuration:
  pato terminal p1 (pid 10760) on since 2010-03-05 01:22:13 PST
      exclusive [edit]
```

```
[edit]
test@SRX210-1# set system host-name blah
error: configuration database locked by:
  pato terminal p1 (pid 10760) on since 2010-03-05 01:22:13 PST, idle 00:01:13
      exclusive [edit]
```

The different edit modes allow great flexibility in environments when multiple users access the same device simultaneously, as you can simply share the database, or prevent anyone from making any changes, until you're done.

But what happens when you commit changes? As mentioned before, by looking at the configuration schema, MGD can make sure the configuration is syntactically correct, but how can it make sure it is functionally correct? Well, it can't, at least not directly. To make sure the configuration is correct when a commit is initiated, MGD spawns a new copy of the daemons in charge of the configuration segments that have been changed. These new instances can verify if the configuration is correct (they can directly query the configuration database, or, when the configuration for a particular daemon is small, MGD can pass the configuration to the daemon as arguments) and return either an error message or an indication that the configuration is valid. This process is referred to as a *commit check*, and it's possible to just invoke a commit check without applying any changes by issuing the `commit check` command.

If you look at the processes running while a commit check is in progress, you'll find that some processes are running twice (for brevity, the following output has been truncated at the `...`):

```
root@SRX210-1% ps -ax
  PID  TT  STAT       TIME COMMAND
 1082  ??  S      22:18.65 /usr/sbin/chassisd -N
 1083  ??  S       0:38.71 /usr/sbin/alarmd -N
...
 12950  ??  R       0:00.21 /usr/sbin/chassisd -C -X
  860  u0- S       0:00.26 /usr/sbin/usbd -N
...
```

In this particular case, chassisd has been spawned with the `-C` option to check the configuration and return the results to MGD. After the new daemons are done with the check step, they simply exit, so you end up with a single running copy of each (the old copy is unaltered, still running and doing its job, and only the newly spawned copies exit after they are done checking the candidate configuration).

If the commit check process is successful (i.e., no daemon detects any error), MGD makes the candidate configuration the active config, backs up the old configurations, and proceeds to signal all running daemons, for which the configurations have changed, to reload their configs.

If the commit check is not successful, nothing is changed. Daemons are not signaled to reload their configs and the running configuration database is unaltered. In this sense, the commit is an atomic operation. If the commit succeeds, all changes are applied simultaneously; if it fails, none of the modifications get applied.

This overall architecture is common to most of the management interfaces of Junos. The CLI is one of many ways to interact with MGD (and therefore the entire system). Other interfaces present different information and allow users to interact in different ways with the system, but they all leverage the same underlying infrastructure.

J-Web

J-Web, with its web UI, uses a connection to MGD to send and receive configuration and operational information. The underlying protocol used is *NETCONF*, and it's the same protocol the CLI and external management systems use to interact with an SRX.

When editing a configuration, J-Web does a *shared edit* of the configuration database, meaning that if a CLI user has acquired an exclusive lock, J-Web will not be able to do any configuration edits until the lock is released. Two modes are available: single commit and automatic commit.

The default (and recommended) way to use J-Web is to do a single commit, where configuration changes are not automatically applied. The single commit mode mimics the CLI, and a commit button is provided that allows users to apply all pending changes since the last commit. Users can also discard all pending changes or show the difference with the last committed configuration, as shown in the right of the screen capture in Figure 13-2.

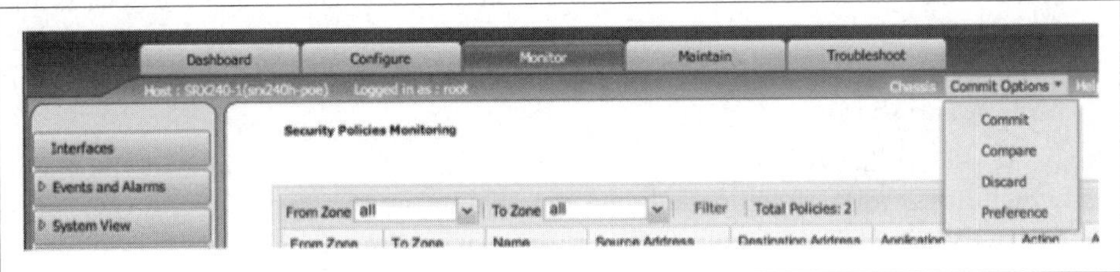

Figure 13-2. J-Web commit options

As an alternative to single commit mode, it is possible to configure J-Web to automatically commit after every change. This option, although sometimes a better alternative because you are always presented with the most up-to-date configuration information, is impractical in small devices where committing a configuration can take more than 10 seconds and making relatively simple configuration changes (when they involve several small steps) can take several minutes.

NSM and Junos Space

Medium to large networks would be difficult to administrate and operate, if every device were to be individually managed. Both the CLI and J-Web provide ways to monitor and configure a single node, but when the number of devices in the network grows, centralized ways to manage the network are needed.

Two central management systems developed by Juniper can be used to control SRX devices: Network and Security Manager (NSM), an evolution of the management system used to configure NetScreen firewalls, and the new Junos Space, a more Junos-centric network manager whose aim is to provide higher-level abstraction of the network.

These two management systems take quite different approaches when dealing with how the network is configured. Here are some of the most salient points:

- NSM approaches the network management problem from the element-management point of view. NSM applies network-wide configurations in a similar way as it does device-specific configurations. That is, device-specific policies and network policies are the same, with the exception that network policies refer to objects (like address lists) that are evaluated differently depending on the device. Junos Space takes a different approach by providing a framework that allows the definition of network-wide policies.
- NSM is menu-driven, while the Security Builder application in Junos Space is topology-driven.
- Junos Space provides a framework for multiple applications to be developed. Applications developed for Junos Space can make use of the different services that Junos Space provides, such as keeping a configuration database of the devices and inventory of the network, managing the communication to the devices, providing a distributed architecture where applications can be load-balanced across multiple servers, and so forth.
- NSM uses a "heavy" client. A large part of the processing is done at the client, which needs to be downloaded and installed in the management console. Junos Space uses an HTTP-based interface instead, where most processing is done at the server and a standard browser is used to access the different applications.
- NSM was designed with the primary goal of configuring security devices and, later on, was extended to other device types such as Ethernet switches. Junos Space took a different line of attack by providing multiple applications to configure different services (such as virtual private LAN service [VPLS] services involving mainly routers, or security services involving all the different devices in the network where security can be enforced).

And the list goes on; as you can probably guess, there are more differences than similarities between the two. That being said, they both have a place depending on the deployment scenario. Because it has been around for a long time, NSM is better suited (at least for the time being) for configuring and monitoring security devices, but in the near future, most of the features available in NSM will be implemented in Junos Space.

In spite of their differences, both network managers use the same protocol to connect to Juniper devices, namely, NETCONF (more on that later). In SRXs, NETCONF is transported over SSH with the TCP session always initiated from the device to the management server. This way, the device IP address does not have to be known in advance by the management server. Since the device's IP might not be known, a unique device identifier is assigned to every node in the network (for those of you who read Chapter 6, this is similar to the role that the local/remote identifier plays in IPsec).

On the device side, the configuration is pretty straightforward, mostly requiring the specification of the IP address of the management system (NSM or Junos Space), the TCP port listening for NETCONF over SSH connections, the device ID, and the shared secret:

```
[edit system services]
outbound-ssh client <client name> {
  <IP address or dns name of the management server> port <port>;
  device-id <device ID as defined in NSM or Space>;
  services netconf;
  secret <shared secret>;
  reconnect-strategy in-order|sticky;
  keep-alive { keep alive parameters };
}
```

The `services netconf` parameter is required, and indicates that the SSH connection is used for the NETCONF protocol (other possible protocols carried over SSH are envisioned, but not yet implemented). The other optional parameters are pretty self-explanatory.

NETCONF

The NETCONF protocol, described in RFC 4741, is central to Junos management. In fact, NETCONF was modeled after the internal protocol used between the different management interfaces (such as J-Web or the CLI) and MGD, which can all obtain configuration information, change the configuration, or get monitoring information from the different daemons in the system. The protocols are not identical, but they are similar enough that, in Junos, NETCONF is implemented by using an adaptation layer that simply translates the NETCONF calls to the format used internally by the devices.

It is not the objective of this section to go through the details of the protocol, but it is instructive to review some of the concepts, as they provide a good introduction and springboard to Junos automation.

NETCONF uses XML-encoded RPCs to exchange information between management systems and devices. In the particular case of devices running Junos, NETCONF can be used from remote device managers, like NSM, but it is also the protocol used between the management daemons in the system. In broad terms, NETCONF follows the same structure as the Junos CLI—there is a separation of configuration and state data and different RPCs are used to access and modify this data.

Messages exchanged between peers follow a request–reply structure. Request messages (normally originating at the management station) are enclosed in `<rpc>` tags, while reply messages (from the device) are enclosed in `<rpc-reply>` tags.

Each device is responsible for defining the different methods that it can process. That is, the NETCONF protocol does not define which methods are available to the management applications (with the exception of a few low-level methods that must be provided), but it does specify the mechanisms to access those methods. In that sense, NETCONF is similar to SNMP, where both deal with how to provide information to management applications. In contrast to SNMP, though, the NETCONF protocol provides a mechanism for management applications to query the schema that defines the different methods that a device implements (which would be similar to providing a way for an SNMP client to query and load the set of MIBs that a particular device implements).

Enough explanation, though, as things are in fact quite simple once you see it working. Let's start by enabling NETCONF over SSH, and establishing an SSH session to the port where NETCONF is configured to listen (don't forget to enable host inbound traffic for any service on the zone connected to the management port; otherwise, the NETCONF traffic will be blocked):

```
set system services netconf ssh connection-limit 2
set system services netconf ssh port 2000

pato$ ssh root@172.19.101.26 -p 2000 -s netconf
root@172.19.101.26's password:
<!-- No zombies were killed during the creation of this user interface -->
<!-- user root, class super-user -->
<hello>
  <capabilities>
    <capability>urn:ietf:params:xml:ns:netconf:base:1.0</capability>
    <capability>urn:ietf:params:xml:ns:netconf:capability:candidate:1.0
</capability>
    <capability>urn:ietf:params:xml:ns:netconf:capability:confirmed-commit:1.0
</capability>
    <capability>urn:ietf:params:xml:ns:netconf:capability:validate:1.0
</capability>
    <capability>urn:ietf:params:xml:ns:netconf:capability:url:1.0?
protocol=http,ftp,file</capability>
    <capability>http://xml.juniper.net/netconf/junos/1.0</capability>
    <capability>http://xml.juniper.net/dmi/system/1.0</capability>
  </capabilities>
  <session-id>10164</session-id>
</hello>
]]>]]>
```

The first thing the NETCONF server (in this case, the SRX) sends back to us is a `<hello>` tag. This tag is used to exchange capabilities between the client and server. For instance, the SRX is stating that it supports the base NETCONF protocol, plus several other capabilities such as commit confirmed, configuration validate, and so on.

Now, let's send a query. Each query is embedded in an `<rpc>` tag; `<rpc>` tags must include a `message-id` attribute (any arbitrary string), used to correlate requests with replies. To figure out the format of a method, you can use the `| display xml rpc` command. For instance, the `show system uptime` command in the CLI generates the following RPC request to MGD:

```
show system uptime | display xml rpc
<rpc-reply xmlns:junos="http://xml.juniper.net/junos/10.2I0/junos">
    <rpc>
        <get-system-uptime-information>
        </get-system-uptime-information>
    </rpc>
    <cli>
        <banner></banner>
    </cli>
</rpc-reply>
```

You can try this out yourself in our NETCONF session:

```
<rpc message-id="1" xmlns="urn:ietf:params:xml:ns:netconf:base:1.0">
        <get-system-uptime-information/>
</rpc>
]]>]]>
```

This results in the following output from the server (the `]]>]]>` characters are used to signal the end of the XML document and are normally added after every request/reply):

```
<rpc-reply xmlns="urn:ietf:params:xml:ns:netconf:base:1.0"
xmlns:junos="http://xml.juniper.net/junos/10.2I0/junos" message-id="1"
xmlns="urn:ietf:params:xml:ns:netconf:base:1.0">
<system-uptime-information xmlns="http://xml.juniper.net/junos/10.2I0/junos">
<current-time>
<date-time junos:seconds="1269376006">2010-03-23 20:26:46 UTC</date-time>
</current-time>
<system-booted-time>
<date-time junos:seconds="1268355347">2010-03-12 00:55:47 UTC</date-time>
<time-length junos:seconds="1020659">1w4d 19:30</time-length>
</system-booted-time>
<protocols-started-time>
<date-time junos:seconds="1268355616">2010-03-12 01:00:16 UTC</date-time>
<time-length junos:seconds="1020390">1w4d 19:26</time-length>
</protocols-started-time>
<last-configured-time>
<date-time junos:seconds="1269319679">2010-03-23 04:47:59 UTC</date-time>
<time-length junos:seconds="56327">15:38:47</time-length>
<user>pato</user>
</last-configured-time>
<uptime-information>
<date-time junos:seconds="1269376006">
8:26PM
</date-time>
<up-time junos:seconds="1020689">
11 days, 19:31
</up-time>
<active-user-count junos:format="1 user">
```

```
1
</active-user-count>
<load-average-1>
11.59
</load-average-1>
<load-average-5>
11.30
</load-average-5>
<load-average-15>
11.21
</load-average-15>
</uptime-information>
</system-uptime-information>
</rpc-reply>
]]>]]>
```

The output is some XML-formatted data that the management application can parse to extract the relevant information. Note how the `message-id` of the `<rpc-response>` matches the one of the request. You are encouraged to try this out using different commands. After a while, you'll get the hang of how the different CLI commands relate to the RPC methods.

To close a NETCONF session, simply use the `<close-session>` tag.

```
<rpc message-id="2" xmlns="urn:ietf:params:xml:ns:netconf:base:1.0">
  <close-session/>
</rpc>

<rpc-reply xmlns="urn:ietf:params:xml:ns:netconf:base:1.0"
xmlns:junos="http://xml.juniper.net/junos/10.2I0/junos" message-id="2"
xmlns="urn:ietf:params:xml:ns:netconf:base:1.0">
  <ok/>
</rpc-reply>
]]>]]>
<!-- session end at 2010-03-23 20:31:16 UTC -->
```

How does this all relate to Junos scripting again? Well, you know the CLI uses XML RPC calls to interact with MGD. Junos scripting allows, via the use of XSLT transformations, to either modify the contents of the configuration before they are applied (they are referred to as *commit scripts*), or simply define subroutines that, using RPC calls, can operate on the system (referred to as *op scripts*).

This is all explained in great detail in the next section. Ready for some management fun?

Scripting and Automation

The Junos infrastructure provides a way for users to extend the system's functionalities. This section explores the different mechanisms supplied, with an emphasis on providing examples of how these mechanisms are commonly used.

Commit Scripts

Perhaps the simplest way to get acquainted with Junos automation is to start by looking at commit scripts.

As previously explained, several operations take place when a commit operation is executed. MGD loads the candidate configuration as shown in Figure 13-3, after which it performs a commit check, and finally, if the commit is successful, it notifies the affected daemons of the new configuration.

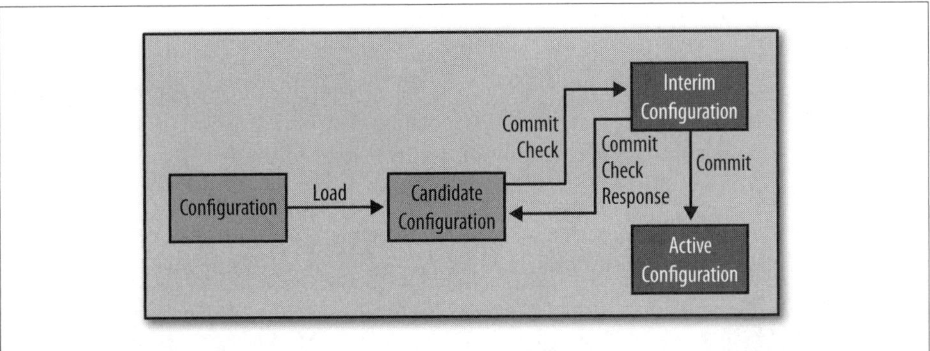

Figure 13-3. Commit model

In fact, this description is incomplete. An intermediate step is performed after the candidate configuration is loaded but before the commit check is performed, as shown in Figure 13-4. In this intermediate step, a set of user-defined XSLT transformations are applied to the configuration that can be used for things such as the following:

- Verify the configuration (e.g., you can create an XSLT template that makes sure that interfaces with an IP address configured are assigned to a security zone, or you could create a template that makes sure the default security policy is not "permit all") and emit a warning, an error, or even a syslog message on certain conditions.
- Modify the configuration. A common and quite useful user-defined transformation is to simplify large configurations that have multiple elements in common. For example, in most cases, the IPsec configuration of a given device with multiple tunnels might require several configuration statements per tunnel, but most of those statements are exactly the same for every tunnel. Using a commit script (Figure 13-3), users can define their own simplified syntax that, when processing the configuration, the script expands into the full configuration required by MGD (i.e., you could create a configuration template with all the common IPsec configurations and only ask operators to enter the remote tunnel IP address, local interface, and preshared key). In large deployments, this would highly simplify the configuration and minimize the risk of configuration errors.

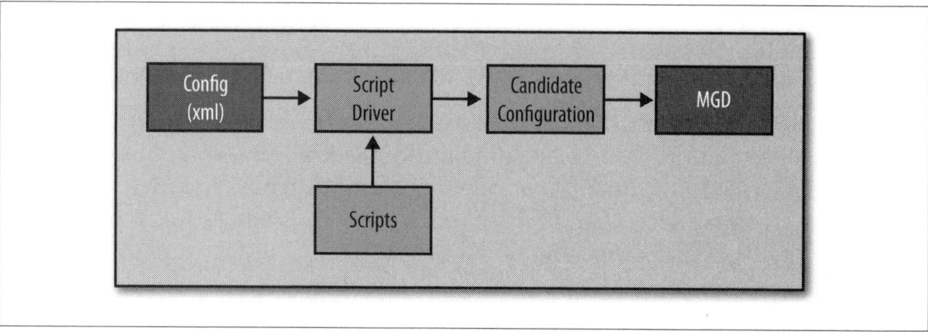

Figure 13-4. Commit scripts

Scripts can be written in XSLT or SLAX. It is not the objective of this chapter to go over either of these languages (in fact, SLAX is nothing more than XSLT with a different syntax), as it would require the whole book to do justice to them.

For more information about Junos automation, see Juniper's Day One booklet series, freely available PDF instruction books, at *http://www.juniper.net/dayone*.

However, let's go over some sample scripts and try to explain their basic operation in an attempt to make you more comfortable with how scripts are written. Anyone interested in Junos scripts should start playing around with some already written scripts—once you are familiar with how to define and configure a script in Junos, you can create some of your own (you will probably want a good book on XSLT).

SLAX may be difficult for some administrators. First, at the time of this writing, there are no extensions to development environments capable of parsing and understanding SLAX, which makes it harder to write large scripts (since you'll have to do all the spellchecking, variable name checking, etc., on your own). Second, there are a lot of good resources on XSLT, but not that many on SLAX (beyond the Day One booklet series on Junos automation). Since this chapter serves as an introduction anyway, it seems appropriate to use a language for which there are many resources available.

Hello World, commit script edition

Our first excursion into a script is to simply print a warning message every time a configuration is committed. This script is also useful as a template as most of our commit scripts have the same structure.

```
<?xml version="1.0" standalone="yes"?>❶
<xsl:stylesheet version="1.0"❷
    xmlns:xsl="http://www.w3.org/1999/XSL/Transform"
```

```
    xmlns:junos="http://xml.juniper.net/junos/*/junos"
    xmlns:xnm="http://xml.juniper.net/xnm/1.1/xnm"
    xmlns:jcs="http://xml.juniper.net/junos/commit-scripts/1.0">

    <xsl:import href="../import/junos.xsl"/>❸

    <xsl:template match="configuration">
        <xnm:warning>
            <message>Hello World!</message>
        </xnm:warning>
    </xsl:template>

</xsl:stylesheet>
```

The first few lines are common to most commit scripts and are used for the following purposes:

❶ The fact that this is an XML formatted document is declared.

❷ The different namespaces used in the document are declared.

❸ Some useful templates and functions that are loaded by default in Junos are imported. (For a complete list of the functions, please check the latest version of the Junos scripting manual, found at *http://www.juniper.net/techpubs*.)

For our purposes, it's enough to know that these lines are needed in every commit script. (Understand that there is a lot more about this than meets the eye, and this is sort of a crash course for you to follow up on.)

When the script is executed (after a user types **commit**), the candidate configuration file is passed to the script driver in XML format, which processes the configuration using the script, as shown in Figure 13-5. The template definition, shown highlighted in the preceding output, defines the operations that are performed to the sections of the configuration that fit the "match" condition in the template definition (in the first line of the highlighted output, matching the `<configuration>` hierarchy).

The result of applying the template to the candidate configuration is to insert a `<warning>` tag. When a candidate configuration includes this tag, MGD continues processing the configuration as normal but returns a message to the CLI, which is then displayed on the user's terminal.

So, what happens when a user commits a configuration with this script? Well, the result would be:

```
pato@SRX650-1# commit check
warning: Hello World!
```

And a useful tool to see the candidate configuration after all commit scripts have been applied is the `| display commit` command:

```
root@J6350-1# show | display commit-scripts | display xml
<rpc-reply xmlns:junos="http://xml.juniper.net/junos/9.5R2/junos">
    <xnm:warning xmlns:xnm="http://xml.juniper.net/xnm/1.1/xnm">
        <message>
```

```
            Hello World!
        </message>
    </xnm:warning>
    <configuration junos:changed-seconds="1269323753" junos:changed-
localtime="2010-03-23  05:55:53 UTC">
...
</rpc-reply>
```

But how do you instruct Junos to use this, or any other script, when processing the configuration file? Read on.

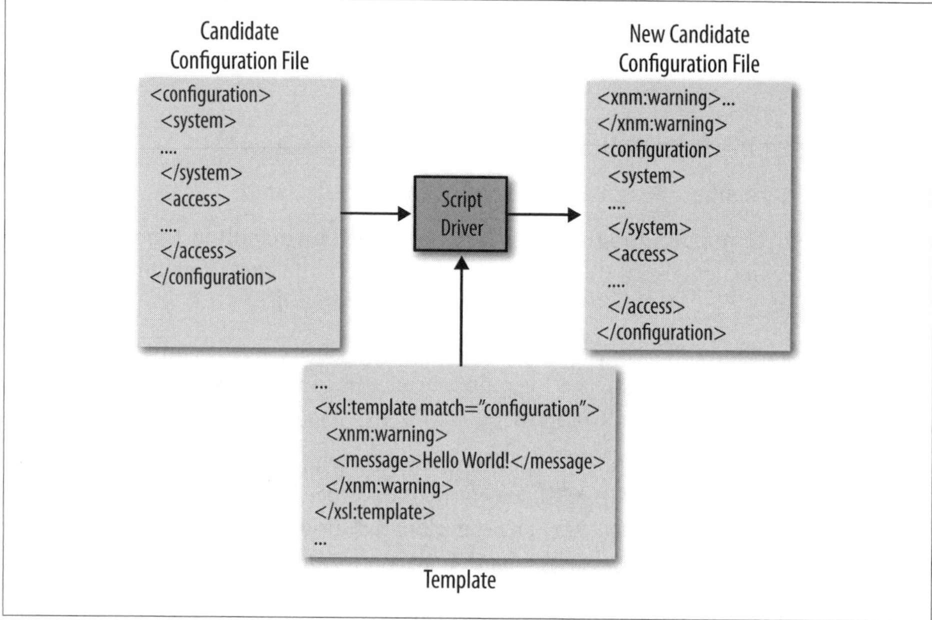

Figure 13-5. Template processing

Adding and enabling commit scripts

Scripts are declared under the `[system scripts commit]` hierarchy. The script must be loaded into the device in the */var/db/scripts/commit* directory, and you can store it there using either FTP or SCP. Alternatively, you can instruct Junos to retrieve the script from a central repository by specifying the URL where it can be downloaded from:

```
system {
  scripts {
    commit {
      file <file name> {
      checksum {...};
      optional;
      refresh;
      refresh-from <URL where the script can be downloaded from>;
      source <URL where the script can be downloaded from>;
```

```
        }
      }
    }
```

If only the filename is specified, the file must be present in the */var/db/scripts/commit* directory. It is also possible to specify a source URL where the file can be fetched. In this case, the `set system scripts commit file <file name> refresh` command triggers the download process.

Several scripts can be specified, in which case they are all applied in the order they have been defined. The candidate configuration is processed using the first script. As a result, a new candidate configuration is created which is then processed with the second script, and so on.

For our Hello World script, a file named *helloworld* with the contents of the script has been uploaded to the */var/db/scripts/commit* directory. The configuration to enable the script looks like this:

```
set system scripts commit file helloworld
```

Special tags for MGD

An `<xnm:warning>` tag was used in our Hello World script as a way to indicate to the CLI to print a warning message. You can use other tags to trigger MGD to perform other useful operations:

- The `<xnm:warning>` tag, as already used, signals MGD to send a message back to the CLI.
- The `<xnm:error>` tag is similar to the `<warning>` tag, but instead of printing a warning, MGD prints an error message, followed by a commit fail.
- The `<xnm:syslog>` tag is used to trigger MGD to generate a syslog message. We can set the message content, facility, and severity.
- The configuration change tags `<change>` and `<transient-change>` can be used to modify the contents. of the configuration and are explained in further detail in "Transient versus persistent changes" on page 776.

Using a script to enforce some condition

You should now be in a position to look at a more useful example (not that it would not be useful to, say, print annoying messages for other users). Our second script, *warn-permit-all.xslt*, checks the configuration and emits a warning message if the `default-permit-all` policy is configured (such a `default-permit-all` policy is useful for debugging purposes, but is not recommended in a production environment if the SRX is used as a security enforcement point):

```
<?xml version="1.0" standalone="yes"?>
<xsl:stylesheet version="1.0" xmlns:xsl=http://www.w3.org/1999/XSL/Transform
    xmlns:junos=http://xml.juniper.net/junos/*/junos
    xmlns:xnm=http://xml.juniper.net/xnm/1.1/xnm
```

```
    xmlns:ext=http://xmlsoft.org/XSLT/namespace
    xmlns:jcs="http://xml.juniper.net/junos/commit-scripts/1.0">

<xsl:import href="../import/junos.xsl"/>

<xsl:template match="configuration/security/policies/default-policy/permit-all">
  <xnm:warning>
    <xsl:call-template name="jcs:edit-path"/>
      <message>All traffic not explicitly dropped will be allowed
      Only use this configuration for debugging!</message>
    </xnm:warning>
  </xsl:template>
</xsl:stylesheet>
```

Our template only matches the configuration if a `<permit-all>` tag is found. XSLT uses a language called XPATH to, among other things, specify different elements in the XML hierarchy. The language is quite powerful, and a book could be written to detail it, but the simplest way to see some of the ways XPATH can be used is to specify a node in the XML hierarchy, similar to how a directory is specified. For instance, say you want to process all interface nodes in the configuration. Let's look at the configuration in XML format to find how the interfaces are defined:

```
<configuration junos:changed-seconds="1269319679"
junos:changed-localtime="2010-03-23  04:47:59 UTC">
  <version>10.2</version>
...
<interfaces>
  <interface>
    <name>ge-0/0/0</name>
      <unit>
       <name>0</name>
       <family>
         <inet>
           <address>
             <name>172.19.101.26/24</name>
           </address>
         </inet>
       </family>
     </unit>
   </interface>
   <interface>
     <name>ge-0/0/3</name>
     <unit>
       <name>0</name>
       <family>
         <inet>
           <dhcp>
           </dhcp>
         </inet>
       </family>
     </unit>
   </interface>
</interfaces>
```

If you wanted to match on any interface (and therefore the template would be applied twice), the abbreviated XPATH expression to use would be something like /configuration/interfaces/interface (this is, in plain English, a way of selecting any <interface> node that is a child of an <interfaces> node that is, in turn, a child of a <configuration> node). If you wanted to only match on a particular interface, you could add the interface name as a further condition. Nodes are matched using a directory-like path, while values such as the text ge-0/0/3 can be matched using *predicates*. Predicates are embedded in brackets and specify matching conditions for the values of a node or its attributes. For example, an XPATH expression to select only the ge-0/0/3 interface could be configuration/interfaces/interface[name='ge-0/0/3'].

Back to our script: the template is only applied if the configuration includes a <permit-all> node, which is a child of a <default-policy> node. Sure enough, if you look at a configuration with a default permit-all policy this is what you'll find:

```
show security policies default-policy | display xml
<rpc-reply xmlns:junos="http://xml.juniper.net/junos/10.2I0/junos">
  <configuration>
    <security>
            <policies>
                <default-policy>
                    <permit-all/>
                </default-policy>
            </policies>
        </security>
  </configuration>
</rpc-reply>
```

So, our script searches for the existence of a <default-policy> node and, if found, prints a warning message:

```
pato@SRX240-1# commit
[edit security policies default-policy permit-all]
  warning: All traffic not explicitly dropped will be allowed
    Only use this configuration for debugging!
```

Missing security zone binding

Of course, you could check for some more complex conditions. For instance, a common mistake is to forget to bind a newly created interface to a security zone. The following script, named *checkzones.xslt*, uses a template that iterates through all interfaces with an IP address assigned (by looking at the configuration for an <address> node). The interface name is extracted and stored in a variable named intfname. If the interface name is not found in any security zone, a warning message is printed.

```
<?xml version="1.0" standalone="yes"?>
<xsl:stylesheet version="1.0"
  xmlns:xsl="http://www.w3.org/1999/XSL/Transform"
  xmlns:junos="http://xml.juniper.net/junos/*/junos"
  xmlns:xnm="http://xml.juniper.net/xnm/1.1/xnm"
  xmlns:jcs="http://xml.juniper.net/junos/commit-scripts/1.0">
  <xsl:import href="../import/junos.xsl"/>
```

```
  <xsl:template match="configuration">

    <xsl:for-each select="./interfaces/interface/unit[family/inet/address]">

      <xsl:variable name="intfname" select="concat(../name,'.',./name)"/>

      <xsl:if test="not(//security/zones/security-zone/interfaces[name=$intfname]
 or //security/zones/functional-zone/management/interfaces[name=$intfname])">

        <xnm:warning>
          <xsl:call-template name="jcs:edit-path">
            <xsl:with-param name="dot" select="."/>
          </xsl:call-template>
          <message>IP address defined but no zone configured.
Add the interface to a security zone.</message>
        </xnm:warning>
      </xsl:if>

    </xsl:for-each>

  </xsl:template>
</xsl:stylesheet>
```

Creating a Configuration Template

Another useful task for a commit script is to generate a configuration template that is used to simplify large configurations. For example, say you want to configure an IPsec tunnel. A common IPsec configuration might require a few lines per tunnel, most of which are the same for every tunnel. Once you know the configuration you want, you can create a commit script that acts as a template. You only need to specify the values that change on a per-tunnel basis (say, the IP address of the remote gateway, preshared key, or local tunnel interface) and the commit script can, using those values, expand the configuration based on the template.

The Junos CLI hierarchy provides a placeholder for information to be passed on to commit scripts, called *macros*. You can add a macro with a set of attributes and values anywhere in the Junos hierarchy. These attributes can be anything you wish.

So, as a follow-up to our previous example, you can use a commit script to specify, under the interface configuration hierarchy, which security zone an interface belongs to. It's quite useful not only because one naturally tends to think of the security zone as an interface-related object, but also because every time an interface is deleted you do not have to remember to remove its binding to a security zone.

The script would then expand a configuration like the following:

```
set interfaces ge-0/0/3 unit 0 apply-macro zone test-zone
set interfaces ge-0/0/3 unit 0 family inet dhcp
```

into this:

```
set interfaces ge-0/0/3 unit 0 apply-macro zone untrust
set interfaces ge-0/0/3 unit 0 family inet dhcp
set security zones security-zone test-zone interface ge-0/0/3.0
```

which is accomplished using *names interface-zone.xslt*:

```
<?xml version="1.0" standalone="yes"?>
<xsl:stylesheet version="1.0" xmlns:xsl=http://www.w3.org/1999/XSL/Transform
  xmlns:junos=http://xml.juniper.net/junos/*/junos
  xmlns:xnm=http://xml.juniper.net/xnm/1.1/xnm
  xmlns:jcs="http://xml.juniper.net/junos/commit-scripts/1.0">

  <xsl:import href="../import/junos.xsl"/>

  <xsl:template match="configuration/interfaces/interface/unit/apply-
macro[name='zone']">

    <xsl:variable name="zone" select="data/name"/>
    <xsl:variable name="ifd" select="../../name"/>
    <xsl:variable name="unit" select="../name"/>
    <xsl:variable name="ifl" select="concat($ifd,'.',$unit)"/>

    <transient-change>
      <security>
        <zones>
          <security-zone>
            <name><xsl:value-of select="$zone"/></name>
            <interfaces>
              <name><xsl:value-of select="$ifl"/></name>
            </interfaces>
          </security-zone>
        </zones>
      </security>
    </transient-change>

  </xsl:template>
</xsl:stylesheet>
```

Here, the script would look for a macro named `zone` defined under the `[interface unit]` hierarchy. The `apply-macro` statement is the one that allows you to add some generic information anywhere in the Junos hierarchy—in this particular script, the security zone name. And multiple macros can be configured, one per logical interface, in which case each logical interface would be bound to a zone.

If you follow the logic in the script, the script looks for an `apply-macro`, and each time it finds one, it emits a `<transient-change>` tag with the configuration (in XML format, of course) to add a binding to the security zone specified in the macro statement.

But what is a transient change? Good question.

Transient versus persistent changes

There are two ways to instruct MGD to modify the configuration via a commit script.

- A `<change>` tag is used to instruct MGD to add a configuration to the configuration database. Any configuration enclosed in this tag is added to the candidate configuration and, once committed, the changes are saved to the current configuration. Using this tag is no different from manually typing the configuration. After the commit script is executed and the configuration database is modified, a `show` command can be used to display the changes (just like with any other configuration).
- A `<transient-change>` tag instructs MGD to add the configuration enclosed in the tag to the candidate configuration without saving the added configuration to the candidate config. A transient configuration then is sent to MGD and applied upon commit, but the configuration changes are not stored.

The transient change option is particularly useful for commit scripts because, when using a `<transient-change>` tag, the commit script does not have to worry about cleaning up the configuration if the macro (or whatever other indication used to create the configuration) is removed. When using transient changes, the commit script always adds the configuration after a commit operation, but if the script or macros are removed, the configuration will not be added, and therefore will not be applied.

Configuration templates part II

Since our commit script emits a `<transient-change>`, how can you make sure it worked? The configuration file will not show any of the changes, but the operational commands from the running configuration will.

Transient changes must be enabled in the Junos configuration; otherwise, the script will result in an error:

```
set system scripts commit allow-transients
set system scripts commit file ifl-zone.xslt
```

With the commit script in the */var/db/script/commit* directory you can test the script. Back to our sample configuration:

```
set interfaces ge-0/0/3 unit 0 apply-macro zone test-zone
set interfaces ge-0/0/3 unit 0 family inet dhcp
```

After the commit operation, you should see that a new zone, the `test-zone`, is created and bound to the `ge-0/0/3.0` interface:

```
pato@SRX650-1# run show security zones test-zone

Security zone: test-zone
  Send reset for non-SYN session TCP packets: Off
  Policy configurable: Yes
  Interfaces bound: 1
  Interfaces:
    ge-0/0/3.0
```

Transient changes will not be reflected in the configuration, but it is still possible to see the candidate configuration after expansion by the commit scripts. The `display commit-scripts` command can be used to see the new candidate configuration, as can be seen from this output:

```
[edit security zones]
pato@SRX650-1# show | display commit-scripts
security-zone test-zone {
    interfaces {
        ge-0/0/3.0;
    }
}
```

Operational Scripts

You have seen how to modify the configuration before it is passed on to the MGD for processing, and you know that it could be a very powerful feature, but due to its nature, it only applies to the configuration.

Another way to use XSLT to interact with MGD is through the use of *operational scripts*. Instead of being executed after a commit, operational scripts are executed by a user, much like any operational mode command (hence their name). They allow you to interact with the MGD in new ways, to do things such as the following:

- Create new commands to extract and correlate information from different sources and present it in a new way (e.g., a script that mimics the ScreenOS `get interface` command, showing a list of interfaces, their IP addresses, and the security zone they belong to).
- Automate a sequence of commands (e.g., you could automate the series of troubleshooting steps required to diagnose a connectivity problem).

The main difference between a commit and an operational script is that, whereas commit scripts receive the configuration file as input and output a modified version of it, operational scripts do not receive any input. They interact directly with MGD by generating RPC calls. By interacting directly with MGD, operational scripts can:

- Print out useful information in the CLI, obtained from the different daemons in the system.
- Modify and commit new configurations.
- Generate log messages.
- Publish generic information in the Utility MIB (this is useful when external SNMP collectors require some information for which no MIBs are defined).

Operational scripts are defined under the `[system scripts op]` hierarchy in the same way as commit scripts are:

```
system {
  scripts {
```

```
        op {
          file <file name> {
          arguments { Optional list of arguments passed to the script };
          checksum {};
          command <Command alias>;
          refresh;
          refresh-from <URL where the script can be downloaded from>;
          source <URL where the script can be downloaded from>;
        }
      }
    }
```

Here you can see two new commands that are present: the *arguments command* which allows users to define a set of arguments passed on to the script upon execution, and the *command alias*, which allows users to change the name of the command.

Let's introduce the concepts with an example. We will redo the Hello World commit script, this time using an op script, named *hello-world-op.xslt*, as shown in the following output. If no arguments are sent to it, it simply prints out "Hello World" and exits.

```
<?xml version="1.0" standalone="yes"?>
<xsl:stylesheet version="1.0" xmlns:xsl=http://www.w3.org/1999/XSL/Transform
  xmlns:junos=http://xml.juniper.net/junos/*/junos
  xmlns:xnm=http://xml.juniper.net/xnm/1.1/xnm
  xmlns:jcs="http://xml.juniper.net/junos/commit-scripts/1.0">

  <xsl:import href="../import/junos.xsl"/>

  <xsl:variable name="arguments">
    <argument>
      <name>message</name>
      <description>Display message</description>
    </argument>
  </xsl:variable>
  <xsl:param name="message"/>

  <xsl:template match="/">
    <op-script-results>
      <output>
        <xsl:choose>
          <xsl:when test="$message">
            <xsl:value-of select="jcs:printf('%s',$message)"/>
          </xsl:when>
          <xsl:otherwise>Hello World!</xsl:otherwise>
        </xsl:choose>
      </output>
    </op-script-results>
  </xsl:template>

</xsl:stylesheet>
```

The first thing to note is that, as opposed to the commit script, the op script is not passed the configuration, but instead is passed a set of parameters. These parameters can be defined in two ways: they can be declared within the script using an XSLT variable named `arguments` or they can be declared within the CLI when the script is defined.

Our script used the first method, defining the parameters it accepts directly in the script. When an operational script is declared, MGD reads the script file looking for the argument's definition that it uses to provide help and command completion, just as it would any other native Junos CLI command. Operational scripts are invoked using the `op` command in operational mode. The op script definition is, therefore, as follows (provided the script is saved in the */var/db/scripts/op* directory):

```
set system scripts op file hello-wolrd.xslt
```

Execute the script by using the `op` command in operational mode.

If you are interested, the script logic is pretty straightforward. If no parameter is provided (i.e., the script is invoked with no arguments) a `<command>` tag is printed with the "Hello World" message. This tag is relayed back to the CLI so that a message is printed out. If an argument is passed instead, the script simply prints out the argument passed and exits.

This code executes the script without an argument:

```
pato@SRX650-1> op hello-world.xslt
Hello World!
```

This code passes a message to display:

```
pato@SRX650-1> op hello-wolrd.xslt message "Houston, we have a problem!"
Houston, we have a problem!
```

Note how the description field is used to provide a help message for each argument. You can see how command completion and help are both available for our newly created script:

```
pato@SRX650-1> op hello-world.xslt ?
Possible completions:
  <[Enter]>             Execute this command
  <name>                Argument name
  detail                Display detailed output
  message               Display message
  |                     Pipe through a command
```

If you decide to declare the attributes in the Junos configuration, you can do so using the `arguments` command. In this case, it's not necessary to declare the `arguments` variable in the script, but you must still define, for each argument, an XSLT parameter with the same name as the name of the argument. The conversion of our script to this different way to pass the parameters yields the following script:

```
<?xml version="1.0" standalone="yes"?>
<xsl:stylesheet version="1.0" xmlns:xsl=http://www.w3.org/1999/XSL/Transform
  xmlns:junos=http://xml.juniper.net/junos/*/junos
  xmlns:xnm=http://xml.juniper.net/xnm/1.1/xnm
  xmlns:jcs="http://xml.juniper.net/junos/commit-scripts/1.0">
```

```
    <xsl:import href="../import/junos.xsl"/>

    <xsl:param name="message"/>

    <xsl:template match="/">
      <op-script-results>
        <output>
          <xsl:choose>
            <xsl:when test="$message">
              <xsl:value-of select="jcs:printf('%s',$message)"/>
            </xsl:when>
            <xsl:otherwise>Hello World!</xsl:otherwise>
          </xsl:choose>
        </output>
      </op-script-results>
    </xsl:template>

  </xsl:stylesheet>
```

The script declaration must then include the arguments that can be passed to the script:

```
set system scripts op file hello-wolrd.xslt
set system scripts op file hello-wolrd.xslt arguments message description
"Display message"
```

You can see how our scripts can receive arguments from the CLI, but how can the script interact with MGD? This is where NETCONF comes in (or a NETCONF-like interface).

You can send RPC requests to MGD and retrieve their output, allowing you to interact with the system in many different ways. Here again the `| display xml rpc` command can show you which RPCs to use to obtain information. For example, if you only wanted to print the list of interfaces with an IP address configured, you can use the `<get-interface-information>` RPC to obtain the list of interfaces, iterate through it, and print only the interfaces with `address family inet` configured.

First, to warm up, let's write a script that only queries MGD and prints out the returned information:

```
<?xml version="1.0" standalone="yes"?>
<xsl:stylesheet version="1.0" xmlns:xsl="http://www.w3.org/1999/XSL/Transform"
  xmlns:junos="http://xml.juniper.net/junos/*/junos"
  xmlns:xnm="http://xml.juniper.net/xnm/1.1/xnm"
  xmlns:jcs="http://xml.juniper.net/junos/commit-scripts/1.0">

  <xsl:import href="../import/junos.xsl"/>

  <!-- This function is used to open a persistent connection to MGD, returning a
handler -->
  <xsl:variable name="connection" select="jcs:open()"/>

  <xsl:template match="/">

    <xsl:variable name="get-int-rpc">
      <rpc>
```

```
        <get-interface-information/>
      </rpc>
    </xsl:variable>

    <!-- Send the request to MGD and store the response -->
    <xsl:variable name="interface-information" select="jcs:execute($connection,
$get-int-rpc)"/>

    <!-- Send the received XML fragment to the CLI -->
    <op-script-results>
      <output>
        <xsl:copy-of select="$interface-information"/>
      </output>
      </op-script-results>

  </xsl:template>

</xsl:stylesheet>
```

The <xsl:copy-of> element creates a copy of all the nodes in the response. In simpler terms, it outputs the returned XML tree. Still, the CLI does not know how to print this information, as evidenced by a sample output:

```
pato@SRX240-1> op all-interfaces-xml
```

A closer look reveals that, in fact, the script is sending out the resultant XML output to the CLI, but not in a format that the CLI can use to display the information (normally the output has to adhere to some very specific XML format for the CLI to display it in a human-readable way). But the output using the `| display xml` modifier shows the data as passed from the script to the CLI:

```
pato@SRX240-1> op all-interfaces-xml | display xml
<rpc-reply xmlns:junos="http://xml.juniper.net/junos/10.2I0/junos">
    <output>
        <interface-information xmlns="http://xml.juniper.net/junos/10.2I0/junos-
interface" junos:style="normal">
            <physical-interface>
                <name>
                    ge-0/0/0
                </name>
                <admin-status junos:format="Enabled">
                    up
                </admin-status>
                <oper-status>
                    up
                </oper-status>
                <local-index>
                    133
                </local-index>
... (Truncated output)
```

Used this way, the <xsl:copy-of> element can become pretty handy in debugging script problems, as it allows us to dump some of the variables in our script.

Back to our goal, to have a variable with the list of all interfaces. Using XPATH it's easy to filter them and only print the ones with family INET configured:

```
<?xml version="1.0" standalone="yes"?>
<xsl:stylesheet version="1.0" xmlns:xsl="http://www.w3.org/1999/XSL/Transform"
  xmlns:junos="http://xml.juniper.net/junos/*/junos"
  xmlns:xnm="http://xml.juniper.net/xnm/1.1/xnm"
  xmlns:jcs="http://xml.juniper.net/junos/commit-scripts/1.0">

  <xsl:import href="../import/junos.xsl"/>

  <!-- This function is used to open a persistent connection to MGD,
returning a handler -->
  <xsl:variable name="connection" select="jcs:open()"/>

  <xsl:template match="/">
    <xsl:variable name="get-int-rpc">
      <rpc>
        <get-interface-information/>
      </rpc>
    </xsl:variable>

    <!-- Send the request to MGD and store the response -->
    <xsl:variable name="interface-information" select="jcs:execute($connection,
$get-int-rpc)"/>

    <!-- Send the received XML fragment to the CLI -->
    <op-script-results>
      <output>
        <xsl:value-of select="jcs:printf('Logical Interfaces with family inet
configured  &#10;')"/>
      <xsl:for-each select="$interface-information//physical-interface/logical-
interface[address-family/address-family-name='inet']">
          <xsl:value-of select="jcs:printf('Name: %s Zone: %s  &#10;',name,
logical-interface-zone-name)"/>
      </xsl:for-each>
    </output>
    </op-script-results>

  </xsl:template>

</xsl:stylesheet>
```

If you are still following all this, there are a few things to mention. The character `
` is the HTML entity code for a newline; a `\n` could have been used, but at the time of this writing, the `printf` extension function supplied as part of the function library did not interpret the `\n` character correctly. The other thing to point out is the XPATH expression in the first line of highlighted code; it selects the `<logical-interface>` nodes in the XML result that have an `<address-family>` child with an `<address-family-name>` with value `inet` configured. The second line of highlighted code uses the `printf` library function to display the values of the `<name>` and `<logical-interface-zone-name>` nodes.

Just like before, save the script (this one is named *ip-interfaces.xslt*) under the */var/db/scripts/op* directory and declare it in the Junos hierarchy:

```
set system scripts op file ip-interfaces.xslt
```

The script will print out a list of interfaces with 'family inet' defined and the security zones assigned to them:

```
pato@SRX650-1> op ip-interfaces.xslt
Logical Interfaces with family inet configured
Name: ge-0/0/0.0 Zone: management
Name: ge-0/0/1.0 Zone: trust
Name: fe-0/0/2.0 Zone: untrust
Name: lo0.16384 Zone: Null
Name: lo0.16385 Zone: Null
```

Event Scripts

Event scripts are plain operational scripts that instead of being executed by a user are executed by the system in response to an event. They provide a great way to automate operations or to automatically react to changing network conditions.

The central concept behind event scripts is the use of event policies. They provide a way to filter and correlate any events generated in the system and, in response, perform one of the following actions:

- Execute a set of CLI commands and store the resultant output in a file (this file could be stored in the local filesystem or, if preferred, it can be uploaded to a central repository).
- Upload the last committed configuration to a central repository.
- Raise a trap.
- Execute an event script.

Event policies follow a similar structure to other policies in the system, such as routing policies. A set of matching conditions define which events, or group of events, trigger a policy—a set of actions that specify the procedures to take in response to the events. Here is a sample:

```
event-options {
  destinations {
    destination-name {
      archive-sites {
        url <password password>;
      }
      transfer-delay seconds;
    }
  }
  policy policy-name {
    attributes-match {
      event.attribute equals event2.attribute;
      event.attribute matches <regexp>;
```

```
            event.attribute starts-with event2.attribute;
          }
          events [ event1 event2 ... ];
          within <seconds> {
            events [ events ];
            not events [ events ];
            trigger (on | after | until) event-count;
          }
          then {
            event-script filename {
              arguments {
                argument-name argument-value;
              }
              destination <destination name> { Destination options }
              output-filename filename;
              output-format (text | xml);
              user-name name;
            }
            execute-commands {
              commands {
                "command";
              }
              destination <destination name> { Destination options }
              output-filename filename;
              output-format (text | xml);
              user-name username;
            }
            ignore;
            raise-trap;
            upload filename (filename | committed) destination destination-name
      { Destination options }
          }
        }
      }
```

The command hierarchy might seem daunting at first, but it is simpler than it appears. Let's forget about the destination options for a moment and just concentrate on how to filter and correlate events.

In its simplest form, a policy will be triggered when any of the events listed in the "events" list is generated. With every Junos release, the *System Log Messages Reference* document is published and it contains an updated list of all the syslog messages generated by Junos (the list can also be downloaded from the Juniper support site). Alternatively, the `help syslog` command provides a list of all the log messages and a description of each log.

```
pato@SRX240-1> help syslog ?
Possible completions:
  <[Enter]>            Execute this command
  <syslog-tag>         System log tag or regular expression
  ACCT_ACCOUNTING_FERROR  LOG_PFE,Error occurred during file processing
  ACCT_ACCOUNTING_FOPEN_ERROR  LOG_PFE,Open operation failed on file
  ACCT_ACCOUNTING_SMALL_FILE_SIZE  LOG_PFE,Maximum file size
is smaller than record size
```

```
  ACCT_BAD_RECORD_FORMAT  LOG_PFE,Record format does not match accounting profile
  ACCT_CU_RTSLIB_ERROR  LOG_PFE,Error occurred obtaining current class usage
statistics
  ACCT_FORK_ERR        LOG_PFE,Could not create child process
... (Truncated output)
```

Anything that generates an event can potentially trigger an action, including executing a script. Event scripts are then commonly used to diagnose problems in a system, such as periodically collecting information, or saving information after an important event such as a daemon crashing or a card crashing.

Following the style of this chapter, a simple (yet useful) example will help illustrate some of these concepts a bit better.

A common issue found when running Intrusion Detection and Prevention (IDP) in a high availability (HA) cluster is that, in some instances, the `fxp0` interfaces are not connected to the Internet. This results in the need to download the security packages from a revenue port in the system (commonly a Reth interface) and it's problematic because the control plane's backup node (i.e., the secondary node of redundancy group 0) has no connectivity other than from the `fxp0` interface. At the expense of digressing for a bit, this is due to the fact that host-inbound traffic is always sent to the control plane's primary node because the primary node is the one in charge of all control plane operations. The forwarding threads always forward all host-inbound traffic to the primary node, and so the secondary node cannot receive any traffic, which is why the `fxp0` interface was created. Traffic received through this port is not handled by the forwarding plane (`flowd`), but sent directly to the device's kernel.

So, back to our example. If the backup node has no connectivity to the rest of the world, how can we make sure the security packages are kept up-to-date in that node?

Well, the primary node has no problems updating its signatures, and when a new security package is installed an event is generated notifying administrators of the results. Enter event scripts—this event could trigger a script that copies the downloaded signatures into the backup node followed by a package install.

The event-policy configuration is pretty simple:

```
set event-options policy idp-update events IDP_SECURITY_INSTALL_RESULT
set event-options policy idp-update attributes-match
idp_security_install_result.status matches successful
set event-options policy idp-update then event-script idp-update.xslt
set event-options event-script file idp-update.xslt
```

The *idp-update.xslt* script, when executed, copies the files and sends an RPC to MGD to install the new security package into the secondary node. Event scripts (including this one, of course) must be downloaded to the */var/db/scripts/event* directory:

```
<?xml version="1.0" standalone="yes"?>
<xsl:stylesheet version="1.0" xmlns:xsl="http://www.w3.org/1999/XSL/Transform"
    xmlns:junos="http://xml.juniper.net/junos/*/junos"
    xmlns:xnm="http://xml.juniper.net/xnm/1.1/xnm"
    xmlns:ext="http://xmlsoft.org/XSLT/namespace"
```

```
xmlns:jcs="http://xml.juniper.net/junos/commit-scripts/1.0">

<xsl:import href="../import/junos.xsl"/>

<!-- Open a connection to MGD-->
<xsl:variable name="connection" select="jcs:open()"/>

<!-- Figure out which node is the secondary -->
<xsl:variable name="cluster-info-rpc">
    <rpc>
        <get-route-engine-information>
            <node>local</node>
        </get-route-engine-information>
    </rpc>
</xsl:variable>
<xsl:variable name="cluster-info"
    select="jcs:execute($connection, $cluster-info-rpc)"/>
<xsl:variable name="local-node"
    select="$cluster-info//multi-routing-engine-item/re-name"/>
<xsl:variable name="remote-node">
    <xsl:choose>
        <xsl:when test="$local-node = 'node0'">node1</xsl:when>
        <xsl:when test="$local-node = 'node1'">node0</xsl:when>
    </xsl:choose>
</xsl:variable>

<xsl:variable name="rg0-master">
    <xsl:call-template name="get-master">
        <xsl:with-param name="redundancy-group">0</xsl:with-param>
    </xsl:call-template>
</xsl:variable>

<xsl:template name="get-master">
    <xsl:param name="redundancy-group">0</xsl:param>

    <xsl:variable name="get-cluster-status">
        <rpc>
            <get-chassis-cluster-status>
                <redundancy-group>
                    <xsl:value-of select="$redundancy-group"/>
                </redundancy-group>
            </get-chassis-cluster-status>
        </rpc>
    </xsl:variable>
    <xsl:variable name="cluster-status-results"
        select="jcs:execute($connection, $get-cluster-status)"/>

    <!-- Determine the master of the chassis cluster-->
    <xsl:variable name="rg-node0-priority"
        select="$cluster-status-results/redundancy-group
            [$redundancy-group+1]/device-stats/redundancy-group-status[1]"/>
    <xsl:variable name="rg-node1-priority"
        select="$cluster-status-results/redundancy-group
            [$redundancy-group+1]/device-stats/redundancy-group-status[2]"/>
    <xsl:choose>
```

```
        <xsl:when test="$rg-node0-priority = 'primary' and $rg-node1-priority
            != 'primary'">
            <!-- Node0 is the primary returning Node0-->
            <text>node0</text>
        </xsl:when>
        <xsl:when test="$rg-node0-priority != 'primary' and $rg-node1-priority
            = 'primary'">
            <!-- Node1 is the primary returning Node1-->
            <text>node1</text>
        </xsl:when>
    </xsl:choose>
</xsl:template>

<xsl:template name="copy-idp-signatures">
    <xsl:param name="from-node"/>
    <xsl:param name="to-node"/>
    <xsl:param name="path">/var/db/idpd/sec-download/</xsl:param>

    <xsl:variable name="ls-rpc">
        <rpc>
            <file-list>
                <path>
                    <xsl:value-of select="$path"/>
                </path>
                <detail/>
            </file-list>
        </rpc>
    </xsl:variable>
    <xsl:variable name="files"
        select="jcs:execute($connection, $ls-rpc)//file-information
            [starts-with(file-permissions/@junos:format,'-')]/file-name"/>

    <!-- Loop through the files and copy every file to the new node -->
    <xsl:for-each select="$files">
        <xsl:variable name="file-copy-rpc">
            <rpc>
                <file-copy>
                    <source>
                        <xsl:value-of select="concat($path, '/', . )"/>
                    </source>
                    <destination>
                        <xsl:value-of
                            select="concat($remote-node, ':/var/db/idpd/
                                sec-download/')"/>
                    </destination>
                </file-copy>
            </rpc>
        </xsl:variable>

        <xsl:value-of select="jcs:execute($connection, $file-copy-rpc)"/>
    </xsl:for-each>

</xsl:template>

<xsl:template name="install-packages">
```

```
    <xsl:param name="node"/>
    <xsl:variable name="regex-result" select="jcs:regex('node([01])', $node)"/>
    <xsl:variable name="node-id" select="$regex-result[2]"/>
    <xsl:variable name="install-package-rpc">
        <rpc>
            <command> request security idp security-package install node
                <xsl:value-of select="$node-id"/>
            </command>
        </rpc>
    </xsl:variable>

    <xsl:value-of select="jcs:execute($connection, $install-package-rpc)"/>

</xsl:template>

<xsl:template match="/">
    <op-script-results>
        <output>
            <xsl:choose>

                <xsl:when test="$local-node = $rg0-master">

                    <!-- Copy the security packages to the backup node -->
                    <xsl:call-template name="copy-idp-signatures">
                        <xsl:with-param name="from-node" select="$local-node"/>
                        <xsl:with-param name="to-node" select="$remote-node"/>
                        <xsl:with-param name="path">/var/db/idpd/sec-download
                            </xsl:with-param>
                    </xsl:call-template>
                    <!-- If the package was installed by nsm the files are stored
                        in a different location -->
                    <xsl:call-template name="copy-idp-signatures">
                        <xsl:with-param name="from-node" select="$local-node"/>
                        <xsl:with-param name="to-node" select="$remote-node"/>
                        <xsl:with-param name="path">/var/db/idpd/nsm-download
                            </xsl:with-param>
                    </xsl:call-template>

                    <!-- Installl the packages-->
                    <xsl:call-template name="install-packages">
                        <xsl:with-param name="node" select="$remote-node"/>
                    </xsl:call-template>

                </xsl:when>
                <xsl:otherwise>
                    <xsl:value-of select="jcs:printf('Local node is not the RG0
                        master. Nothing to do\n')"/>
                </xsl:otherwise>
```

```
                </xsl:choose>
            </output>
        </op-script-results>
    </xsl:template>

</xsl:stylesheet>
```

Of course, there is more to the event policies than this. You can correlate several events, or pass some of the attributes in the received event to the script. For example, say you wanted to reboot a card if you receive some message about a PIM going offline. The log message could include the PIM number, and this number could be passed on to your event script so that it could reboot the appropriate card.

Some of the sample scripts in the case studies at the end of this chapter use more complex policies that correlate several events. In particular, the event policies for Case Study 13-5 are complex enough that a commit script was written to generate them.

For those of you who are interested in digging deeper into scripting, the Configuration and Diagnostic Automation Guide downloadable from the Juniper Networks support site is a good reference that provides some more examples and, more importantly, a detailed list of all the available auxiliary functions and configuration options.

In any case, the case studies at the end of this chapter go through how to use some of the scripts shown here to solve common problems found in SRX deployments. Some of these issues have already been addressed, but the scripts still provide good insight into what can be done with Junos automation. But before you get to do that, and since you are going to be dealing with a bunch of scripts, let's see how to simplify the deployment of scripts on SRX devices.

Keeping Your Scripts Up-to-Date

It is easy to copy the scripts to a single device, but things can get out of control when managing multiple devices, or when you want to make sure the scripts are always kept up-to-date.

Instead of manually downloading the scripts to every single device every time something changes, you can use a repository and instruct the SRXs to periodically retrieve the scripts from the repository, and only the repository needs to be up-to-date.

Your repository can be a simple FTP, TFTP, or HTTP server storing the scripts. The `source` parameter is used to specify the network location of the scripts and it can be done on a per-script basis (i.e., each script could be stored in a different repository).

When user authentication is required (commonly the case with FTP) the format of the URL is *service://user:password@server-address:/path*. Here are a few examples using these URLs:

http://server-address/path/filename
ftp://user:pass@server-address/path/filename
tftp://path/filename

Most of the examples in this chapter have used an HTTP server to store all the scripts. If you have a server that can be used as a central repository, and it is reachable from your devices, the SRXs can download the script directly from the repository using the following configuration:

```
[edit system script]
set system scripts op file int.xslt source http://<address of your repository>/
    <path to the script>/<script filename>
```

Two commands are provided to trigger a download of the script into the appropriate directory—this way, you don't have to remember where to store the scripts; you just need to specify where to download them from and Junos will store them in the right place! You can either set the `refresh` flag in the script's configuration (note how this command must be entered in configuration mode):

```
[edit system script op]
pato@SRX210-1# set file int.xslt refresh
refreshing 'int.xslt' from 'http:///172.19.101.103/op/int.xslt'
/var/home/pato/...transferring.file.........FU100% of 3800  B  629 kBps
```

or use the `request system script` command:

```
pato@SRX650-1> request system scripts refresh-from op url http://
172.19.101.103/op/int.xslt
```

Note that, in these examples, I am using an HTTP server with the 172.19.101.103 address where all the scripts are stored. There is no command to trigger a periodic download, however, so to update the scripts automatically simply schedule a periodic event, which triggers an event policy that executes the update command! Something close to the following should do:

```
set event-options generate-event refresh-script time-interval 14400
set event-options policy load-int-script events refresh-script
set event-options policy load-int-script then execute-commands commands "request
system scripts refresh-from op url http://172.19.101.103/op/int.xslt"
```

Case Studies

By now you should have a basic understanding of the things you can do using Junos scripts. You've been exposed to some examples of how you can use Junos automation to solve some common problems, so now let's drill down into a few case studies.

The focus is *not* on how each script works, but rather how they are *used*.

You can download all scripts from this book's web page at *http://www.oreilly.com/9781449381714*.

Case Study 13-1: Displaying the Interface and Zone Information

The *int.xslt* script shows all the interfaces in the system with an IP address configured (with the exception of a few pseudointerfaces that do not need to be bound to a zone) in a ScreenOS-like format:

```
pato@J6350-1# run op int.xslt
Logical Interface Address         Zone       Routing Instance Status Description
ge-0/0/0.0        172.19.101.37   management Master           Up
pd-0/0/0.32769    Null            Master                      Up
ge-2/0/0.0        10.1.1.5        trust      Master           Up     EX4200-1
ge-3/0/0.0        10.2.1.5        trust      Master           Up     EX4200-1
wx-6/0/0.0        1.1.1.1         wx-zone    Master           Up
lo0.0             10.255.255.255  trust      Master           Up
st0.0             10.10.1.1       vpn        Master           Up
```

The description field is taken from the description in the unit and, if not present, the physical interface description is used. Of course, if neither of those is defined, the description is left blank.

Case Study 13-2: Zone Groups

The *zone-groups.xslt* script simulates a zone group, or a zone that contains multiple zones. When used in a policy, the zone group is expanded so that a new policy is added for each zone in the group (to prevent a zone explosion, a group zone can only be used as the source zone or the destination zone, but not both).

To use it, load the script under */var/db/scripts/commit/* and add the following to the config:

```
set system scripts commit allow-transients
set system scripts commit file zone-groups.xslt
```

To define a zone group, simply define a normal security zone and add a macro statement called `zone-group` with all the zones in the group. For instance, to create a group called `test-zone-group` that includes the Management and Untrust zones, add the following to the config file:

```
set security zones security-zone test-zone-group apply-macro
zone-group management
set security zones security-zone test-zone-group apply-macro
zone-group untrust
```

Then use the zone group as you would use any normal zone:

```
set security policies from-zone trust to-zone test-zone-group policy test match
source-address server-address
```

```
set security policies from-zone trust to-zone test-zone-group policy test match
destination-address any
set security policies from-zone trust to-zone test-zone-group policy test match
application junos-http
set security policies from-zone trust to-zone test-zone-group policy test then
permit
```

The test policy is expanded into two policies (one from zone Trust to zone Management and the other from zone Trust to zone Untrust, both matching source IP `server-address`, destination IP `any`, and application `junos-http`).

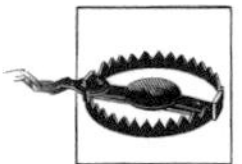

Because address book entries are tied to zones, when using a global zone address book entries defined in that zone will be copied to each member zone, so please be careful not to add too many entries.

Case Study 13-3: Showing the Security Policies in a Compact Format

The *policies.xslt* script displays the list of security policies, each in a single line. The standard format of the `show security policy` command is somewhat verbose and not adequate, at a glance, to view the different policies in a system.

For example, only three security policies are shown here, and the output is, well, verbose. Imagine what the output would be like with a more standard configuration with, say, 20 policies:

```
pato@SRX650-1> show security policies
Default policy: deny-all
From zone: trust, To zone: trust
  Policy: default-permit, State: enabled, Index: 4, Scope Policy: 0, Sequence
number: 1
    Source addresses: any
    Destination addresses: any
    Applications: any
    Action: permit
From zone: trust, To zone: untrust
  Policy: default-permit, State: enabled, Index: 5, Scope Policy: 0, Sequence
number: 1
    Source addresses: any
    Destination addresses: any
    Applications: any
    Action: permit, application services, log
From zone: untrust, To zone: trust
  Policy: default-permit, State: enabled, Index: 6, Scope Policy: 0, Sequence
number: 1
    Source addresses: any
    Destination addresses: any
    Applications: any
    Action: permit, application services
```

Instead, the script shows each policy in a single line (well, multiple lines per policy if it matches across multiple addresses or applications), making it easier (at least for most people) to follow large configurations:

```
pato@SRX650-1# run op policies
From-Zone  To-Zone  Name         Src-Addr Dst-Addr Application Action Comment
trust      trust    def-permit   any      any      any         permit
trust      untrust  allow-out    any      any      any         permit
untrust    trust    Server-A-in  Server-A any      any         permit
```

Optionally, a parameter can be passed to instruct the script to output the policies from the operational information, instead of from the configuration, which is especially useful when the configuration does not reflect all the policies in the system (as is the case when using the group-zone commit script shown in Case Study 13-2):

```
pato@J6350-1# run op policies expand yes
From-Zone   To-Zone Name        Src-Addr       Dst-Addr       Application Action
trust       untrust test-policy addr_10_1_1_1  any            junos-http  deny
trust       trust   match-some  test-1         addr_10_1_1_1  junos-http  permit
                                test-2                        junos-https
trust       trust   reject-all  any            any            any         deny
group-test  trust   match-some  test-1         addr_10_1_1_1  junos-http  permit
                                test-2                        junos-https
group-test  trust   reject-all  any            any            any         deny
management  trust   match-some  test-1         addr_10_1_1_1  junos-http  permit
                                test-2                        junos-https
management  trust   reject-all  any            any            any         deny
```

Case Study 13-4: Track-IP Functionality to Trigger a Cluster Failover

In a cluster, the mastership status of a redundancy group can be influenced by monitoring the status of a server, or a group of servers, by using simple pings. This allows you to failover a cluster when, due to some network condition, the connectivity to a server through a particular node is affected.

High-end SRX devices support this feature natively, but the branch SRX Series devices do not (yet). For devices in which Track-IP is not supported in a chassis cluster, the *track-ip* script can be used to monitor the status of a device and, in a failure, trigger a failover.

The *track-ip* script uses the event system to schedule a `TRACKIP` event every 60 seconds. An event policy triggered by the `TRACKIP` event calls the script, which reads the chassis cluster redundancy group information looking for Track-IP configuration macros. The macros specify the different parameters used to monitor the device (such as the device's IP address, number of pings to send, timeout, etc.):

```
set chassis cluster reth-count 2;
set chassis cluster control-ports fpc 2 port 0;
set chassis cluster control-ports fpc 14 port 0;
set chassis cluster redundancy-group 0 node 0 priority 254;
set chassis cluster redundancy-group 0 node 1 priority 1;
set chassis cluster redundancy-group 1
set chassis cluster redundancy-group 1 apply-macro track-gateway
set chassis cluster redundancy-group 1 apply-macro track-gateway
server 1.1.1.222;
set chassis cluster redundancy-group 1 apply-macro track-gateway weight 255;
```

```
set chassis cluster redundancy-group 1 apply-macro track-gateway count 5; /*
Optional */
set chassis cluster redundancy-group 1 apply-macro track-gateway
routing-instance Test; /* Optional */
set chassis cluster redundancy-group 1 apply-macro track-gateway interval 2; /*
Optional */
set chassis cluster redundancy-group 1 apply-macro track-gateway wait 1; /*
Optional */
```

The macro name must begin with `track-` (i.e., the *track-ip* script will only read the configuration of the macros defined under the `[chassis cluster]` hierarchy whose name starts with the `track-` prefix) and must contain the server IP address and a weight. The script then sends some pings to the server's address; if successful, the script will exit without any changes. If the pings fail, the script will check the configured weight and failover for the redundancy group if the weight is equal to or greater than 255.

Multiple hosts can be listed (using multiple macros, one per host), and when several of them fail, the weights are added and, as in the single host case, checked to see if they are larger than or equal than 255 in order to trigger a failover. This sequence allows for configurations where a single failure does not trigger a failover, but a group of them will.

To trigger the script, we need to configure an event to periodically call our *track-ip* script. The following configuration shows how to do this on a 60-second interval:

```
set event-options generate-event TRACK-IP time-interval 60
set event-options policy TRACK-IP events TRACK-IP then event-script track-ip.xsl
set event-options event-script file track-ip.xsl
```

It's also possible to pass some options to the script through the use of a macro named `monitoring-options` under the `[chassis cluster]` hierarchy. Two options are available for the macro:

- The `clear-failover` option clears the `failover` flag after a failover is triggered. Without this option, the *track-ip* script only fails over once, until the `failover` flag is manually cleared by a user.
- The `full-failover` option triggers a full failover of all redundancy groups, regardless of which redundancy group failed its Track-IP checking. This option is useful to ensure that all redundancy groups are active in the same node:

```
set chassis cluster apply-macro monitoring-options clear-failover
set chassis cluster apply-macro monitoring-options full-failover
```

Case Study 13-5: Track-IP Using RPM Probes

Often a simple mechanism is required to detect when problems occur on the network and to divert traffic accordingly. Routing protocols were designed for this task, but unfortunately, you cannot always assume they are used in every network deployment. In particular, small branch devices connected to the Internet using common DSL or cable links are, most of the time, not able to use dynamic routing protocols with their service provider.

To solve this issue (among others), several different approaches are used in Junos. Bidirectional forwarding detection (BFD) can be used to monitor static routes, or, in the case of chassis clusters, Track-IP uses ICMP messages to trigger redundancy group failovers (or the *track-ip* script in Case Study 13-4). Although BFD is extremely useful, it requires support on the target machine. By using simple ICMP messages, Track-IP is much more likely to be supported (as most devices support ICMP), but it can only be used on chassis cluster configurations and it only measures reliability.

The main idea is to use RPM probes to track a device (or a group of devices) and, based on the results, either change route metrics or enable or disable an interface.

To use the script, first configure standard `rpm probes` monitoring the desired resources:

```
set services rpm probe pato test js-eth1 target address 10.1.1.110;
set services rpm probe pato test js-eth1 probe-count 10;
set services rpm probe pato test js-eth1 probe-interval 1;
set services rpm probe pato test js-eth1 test-interval 1;

set services rpm probe pato test js-eth2 target address 10.2.1.110;
set services rpm probe pato test js-eth2 probe-count 10;
set services rpm probe pato test js-eth2 probe-interval 1;
set services rpm probe pato test js-eth2 test-interval 1;
```

A macro called `rpm-monitor-<name>` configured under each tracked route is used to point to the RPM probe used to track the route. The macro must specify the following:

`test-name`
: This is the name of the RPM test used to track this route.

`test-owner`
: This is the owner of the RPM test.

`weight`
: This is the weight used to increment the route metric after a failover occurs. For instance, if the original metric is 10 and the weight is 100 after a failover occurs, the new metric will be set to 110.

`hold-down` *(optional)*
: This is the minimum time (in seconds) after which the metric is allowed to be reverted back from the time the first probe failure occurred. It is used to prevent flapping and it defaults to 300 seconds (five minutes).

The following configuration shows an example using some of the probes previously configured:

```
set routing-options static route 10.255.255.255/32
set routing-options static route 10.255.255.255/32 qualified-next-hop 10.1.1.110
apply-macro rpm-monitor hold-down 120
set routing-options static route 10.255.255.255/32 qualified-next-hop 10.1.1.110
apply-macro rpm-monitor test-name js-eth1
set routing-options static route 10.255.255.255/32 qualified-next-hop 10.1.1.110
apply-macro rpm-monitor test-owner pato
set routing-options static route 10.255.255.255/32 qualified-next-hop 10.1.1.110
```

```
apply-macro rpm-monitor weight 100
set routing-options static route 10.255.255.255/32 qualified-next-hop 10.1.1.110
metric 150

set routing-options static route 10.255.255.255/32 qualified-next-hop 10.2.1.110
apply-macro rpm-monitor-2 test-name js-eth2;
set routing-options static route 10.255.255.255/32 qualified-next-hop 10.2.1.110
apply-macro rpm-monitor-2 test-owner pato;
set routing-options static route 10.255.255.255/32 qualified-next-hop 10.2.1.110
apply-macro rpm-monitor-2 weight 200;
set routing-options static route 10.255.255.255/32 qualified-next-hop 10.2.1.110
metric 100
```

The script can also be used to bring up a backup interface when a probe fails. In the following configuration, the `ge-0/0/1` interface is connected to a backup link and it is enabled only when the RPM probes (routed through the main link) fail:

```
set interface ge-0/0/1 apply-macro rpm-monitor-ifd test-name js-eth2
set interface ge-0/0/1 apply-macro rpm-monitor-ifd test-owner pato

set interface ge-0/0/1 disable
set interface ge-0/0/1 unit 0 family inet address 10.1.1.90/16
```

The second use case is commonly found when using the external 3G wireless bridge (which can be configured to establish a connection through the 3G network when either the physical Ethernet link is up or, alternatively, a DHCP request is received).

Two scripts are used. A commit script, *rpm-monitor-config.xslt*, takes care of doing some config validation and generates event policies based on the configured probes. These policies are used to trigger an event script, *rpm-monitor.xslt*, which is used to change the metrics (and enforce the hold-down time, among other things).

You can rename the commit script as desired, but the event script must be named *rpm-monitor.xslt* since this is the event script name used in the event policies configuration, as expanded by the commit script:

```
set event-options event-script file rpm-monitor.xslt
set system scripts commit allow-transients
set system scripts commit file rpm-monitor-config.xslt
```

Case Study 13-6: Top Talkers

Given that both branch and high-end SRX devices can locally store session logs (constrained to a max for 1.5k logs/s) it is quite a common request to be able to extract some useful information such as top talkers, top destinations, and so forth.

Logs are saved in ASCII format, making them easy to process by a script. It is trivial to configure a file to store session logs in the */var/log* directory when a device is configured in event mode. For instance, the config shown here creates a file named *sessions* where all the session logs are stored:

```
set system syslog file sessions user info
set system syslog file sessions match RT_FLOW
set system syslog file sessions structured-data brief
```

Each log contains a lot of useful information. It is enough to see a single record to realize that it can be a challenging task to make much sense of all the information, when thousands of logs are stored there, so it's been truncated into a few lines to make it more readable:

```
<14>1 2010-02-15T17:28:30.198-08:00 SRX240-1 RT_FLOW - RT_FLOW_SESSION_CLOSE
[junos@2636.1.1.1.2.39
reason="response received"
source-address="10.1.1.101"
source-port="1"
destination-address="10.2.1.45"
destination-port="12558"
service-name="icmp"
nat-source-address="10.1.1.101" nat-source-port="1"
nat-destination-address="10.2.1.45" nat-destination-port="12558"
src-nat-rule-name="None" dst-nat-rule-name="None"
protocol-id="1"
policy-name="permit-all"
source-zone-name="trust"
destination-zone-name="trust"
session-id-32="59950"
packets-from-client="1" bytes-from-client="84" packets-from-server="1"
bytes-from-server="84"
elapsed-time="3"]
```

Fortunately, Junos scripting can come to the rescue. You can use an op script to parse a file with session logs and aggregate the information by any of the fields present in the log. To that extent, the *top-talkers.xslt* script takes a filename and attribute as an argument and it generates a table with the cumulative traffic stats for that attribute.

For instance, say you want to see the traffic stats grouped by source address. You simply pass the `source-address` attribute and your sessions filename as parameters and the script generates output such as the following:

```
pato@SRX240-1# run op top-talkers filename sessions aggregate source-address
source-address         Packets              Bytes                Sessions
10.1.1.101             290                  170073               12
```

In this case, all the sessions in the session table originate from the 10.1.1.101 address. Let's aggregate the records using a couple of other attributes:

```
pato@SRX240-1# run op top-talkers filename sessions aggregate destination-
address
destination-address  Packets              Bytes            Sessions
10.2.1.45            6                    504              3
157.166.226.26       40                   26850            1
96.17.141.15         21                   10002            1
157.166.255.18       40                   26868            1
200.42.136.212       42                   26598            1
207.58.150.180       48                   36583            1
74.86.132.180        48                   26106            2
```

```
74.125.19.147          22                   11446                 1
72.246.175.148         23                   5116                  1

pato@SRX240-1# run op top-talkers filename sessions aggregate service-name
service-name           Packets              Bytes                 Sessions
icmp                   6                    504                   3
junos-http             261                  164453                8
junos-https            23                   5116                  1

pato@SRX240-1# run op top-talkers filename sessions aggregate policy-name
policy-name            Packets              Bytes                 Sessions
permit-all             6                    504                   3
allow-out              284                  169569                9

pato@SRX240-1# run op top-talkers filename sessions aggregate reason
reason                 Packets              Bytes                 Sessions
response received      6                    504                   3
TCP FIN                191                  116424                6
TCP RST                93                   53145                 3
```

You should get the idea. Of course, for an analysis of large logfiles or more complex correlations, an external collector such as STRM, or Junos Space is the way to go.

Case Study 13-7: Destination NAT on Interfaces with Dynamic IP Addresses

Another common question relates to how to do destination NAT when the IP address of the ingress interface is dynamically assigned.

Consider this simple scenario, where an SRX is connected to the Internet via a DSL line, and the IP address assigned to the Untrust interface is dynamically assigned, and therefore is not known at configuration time (it is only known at runtime).

In this hypothetical network shown in Figure 13-6, an HTTP server is connected to the Trust network and you want to translate all traffic sent to the Internet-facing interface port 80, to the address of the HTTP server in the DMZ zone (and port 80 as well).

If you knew the public address of the SRX at configuration time, all you would have to do is to configure a destination NAT rule-set such as the following:

```
set security nat destination pool http-server-1 address 10.2.1.103/32
set security nat destination pool http-server-1 address port 80
set security nat destination rule-set access-to-DMZ-servers from
interface ge-0/0/0.0
set security nat destination rule-set access-to-DMZ-servers rule http-server-1
match destination-address <Address of the Internet-facing Interface>
set security nat destination rule-set access-to-DMZ-servers rule http-server-1
match destination-port 80
set security nat destination rule-set access-to-DMZ-servers rule http-server-1
then destination-nat pool http-server-1
```

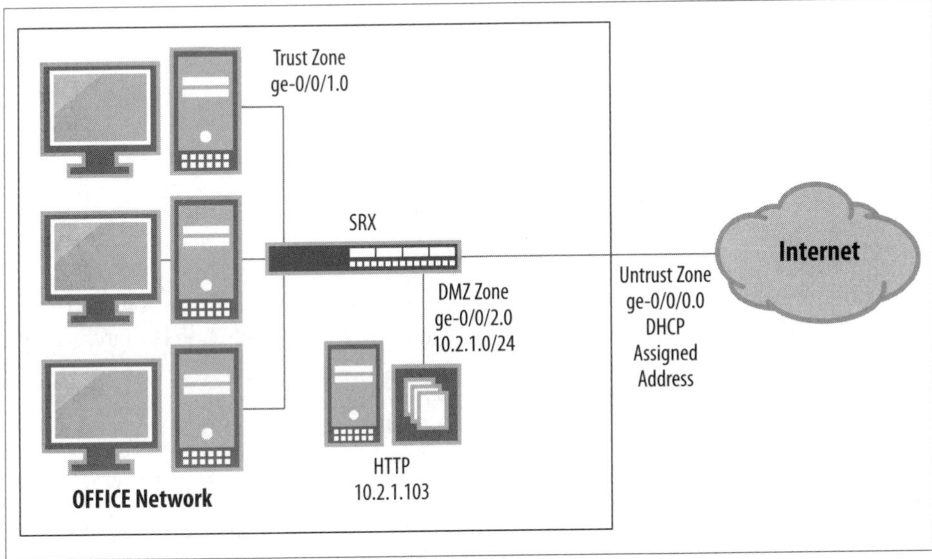

Figure 13-6. Destination NAT on a dynamically assigned interface

Unfortunately, you don't know the address of the Internet-facing interface in advance. However, you do know that if the SRX has no other public addresses assigned to it, the only traffic forwarded to the Untrust interface must be destined to the IP address of that interface (because you assume that there are no other public addresses configured behind the SRX), and therefore you can simply match on *any* destination address:

```
set security nat destination pool http-server-1 address 10.2.1.103/32
set security nat destination pool http-server-1 address port 80
set security nat destination rule-set access-to-DMZ-servers from
interface ge-0/0/0.0
set security nat destination rule-set access-to-DMZ-servers rule http-server-1
match destination-address 0.0.0.0/0
set security nat destination rule-set access-to-DMZ-servers rule http-server-1
match destination-port 80
set security nat destination rule-set access-to-DMZ-servers rule http-server-1
then destination-nat pool http-server-1
```

So far so good, but what if your branch network has a dynamically assigned address and some public range of addresses that are owned by that branch? In that case, the traffic received at the Untrust interface could be destined to the IP address of the interface itself, but it could also be destined to the public subnet (or subnets) behind the SRX. How can you differentiate between the two?

One option is to create a rule matching on the known public subnet with a `no-nat` action, followed by a rule matching on any destination address with an action to NAT the traffic to the address of the HTTP server. You can do that one on your own.

However, a second option is to use a script so that you can match on the address of the Untrust interface. An event script is executed every time the Untrust interface is assigned a new address—the script simply changes the destination NAT rule to match on the newly assigned address. This is a more flexible alternative since you could add and remove new public subnets without having to modify the NAT configuration.

```
set event-options policy ip-renew events SYSTEM
set event-options policy ip-renew attributes-match SYSTEM.message
matches "EVENT Add"
set event-options policy ip-renew then event-script dyn-nat.xslt
arguments message "{$$.message}"
set event-options event-script file dyn-nat.xslt
```

The configuration is identical to the previous one, but this time let's use a macro statement to indicate to the script which interface address a particular rule is matching on:

```
set security nat destination pool http-server-1 address 10.2.1.103/32
set security nat destination pool http-server-1 address port 80
set security nat destination rule-set access-to-DMZ-servers from
interface ge-0/0/0.0
set security nat destination rule-set access-to-DMZ-servers rule http-server-1
match destination-address 0.0.0.0/0
set security nat destination rule-set access-to-DMZ-servers rule http-server-1
match apply-macro match-interface interface ge-0/0/0.0
set security nat destination rule-set access-to-DMZ-servers rule http-server-1
match destination-port 80
set security nat destination rule-set access-to-DMZ-servers rule http-server-1
then destination-nat pool http-server-1
```

Case Study 13-8: High-End SRX Monitor

Let's conclude this chapter with a simple but very useful script written for high-end SRX devices. Due to the device's distributed nature, multiple moving parts are involved in forwarding packets across a system. Monitoring the system's status involves pooling information from the various processors in a device.

Multiple CLI commands display the status of a particular Services Processing Card (SPC), but no single command shows an overview of the status of the various CPUs in the node. The *srx-monitor* script takes care of this by collecting the statistics of the different processors and displaying them in a single table:

```
set system scripts op file srx-monitor.xsl

root@SRX5800-1# run op srx-monitor
Route Engine
Slot Mem Size Mem Used CPU Avg CPU User CPU Bkgd CPU Krnl CPU Intpt CPU Idle
-----------------------------------------------------------------------------
  0    2048        18      11        3        0        7         1        89
SPUs
FPC PIC CPU Mem  Flow Sess Cur   Flow Ses Max  CP Ses Cur  CP Ses Max
---------------------------------------------------------------------
  0   0   0  83              0             0           0    10485760
  0   1   0  67              0       1048576           0           0
  1   0   0  67              0       1048576           0           0
  1   1   0  67              0       1048576           0           0
```

```
2   0   0  67          0         1048576          0          0
2   1   0  67          0         1048576          0          0
3   0   0  67          0         1048576          0          0
3   1   0  67          0         1048576          0          0
```

Summary

Due to the complexity of SRX devices, it is difficult to predict the numerous and creative ways in which people will try to use them to perform the different operations required on any modern network. Instead of trying to solve every possible problem, Juniper Networks has chosen to provide a relatively simple but powerful set of features that allow users to extend the capabilities of the devices in multiple new ways.

The scripting capabilities are not meant to be used in every scenario. Features that require tighter integration—for example, to perform operations on every packet or to implement new control-plane protocols—require a different approach, provided by the Junos SDK. But for relatively simple operations, the scripting infrastructure allows us to extend Junos capabilities without the effort required to write new programs and learn multiple new APIs. To someone who has to find quick solutions to the different problems encountered in new deployments, this trade-off is a real bargain.

Chapter Review Questions

1. What is MGD?
2. When are commit scripts executed?
3. Which languages can be used to write Junos scripts?
4. What is the difference between an operational script and an event script?
5. What are the event policies?
6. How do we pass information to commit scripts?
7. Which are the tags supported by MGD to perform some action?
8. What is the main difference between a transient and a permanent change?
9. In which two ways can we define which parameters can be passed to an operational script?
10. What is the default mode used to edit the Junos configuration database (for a standalone device)?

Chapter Review Answers

1. MGD is a daemon running in the control plane and in charge of interfacing between the different daemons running in the control plane and the forwarding elements in a Junos device, and the management interface such as J-Web or the CLI.

2. Commit scripts are triggered by a commit operation.
3. Junos scripts can be written in XSLT or SLAX. In the backend, all scripts are evaluated by an XSLT interpreter. SLAX has been developed to provide a cleaner and more familiar syntax to people who are used to writing programs in C or other C-like languages.
4. They are identical with the exception of how they are executed. Operation scripts are invoked by the user, while event scripts are executed by an event policy.
5. Event policies are policies used to process and correlate system-generated events.
6. The full configuration file is passed to the commit scripts. If a particular set of parameters is required for a script to perform its function, the parameters can be added to the configuration by using a macro.
7. At the time of this writing, the following tags are the ones executed by MGD:
    - `<xnm:warning>`
    - `<xnm:error>`
    - `<xnm:syslog>`
    - `<transient-change>`
    - `<change>`
8. Although configuration changes done with the `<transient-change>` tag are not saved to the running configuration, changes done with the `<change>` tag are always saved.
9. Arguments passed to operational scripts can be defined in the Junos configuration together with the script configuration, using the `arguments` keyword. Alternatively, the arguments can be defined directly in the script and are read by Junos when the script is declared.
10. By default, the configuration database is edited in shared mode. Other edit modes have to be explicitly invoked with the `configuration <mode>` command.

Index

Symbols

A

We'd like to hear your suggestions for improving our indexes. Send email to *index@oreilly.com*.

B

C

D

E

F

G

H

I

J

K

L

M

Q

R

S

T

U

V

W

X

Z

About the Authors

Rob Cameron is the technical marketing engineering manager for Juniper Networks' Data Center Firewall Group, which oversees the data center SRX and high-end NetScreen platforms. In his 10-plus-year career, he has held positions as a security reseller, service provider engineer, and security consultant. For the past five years, he has worked for Juniper Networks as a systems engineer, a data center architect, and a technical marketing engineer. He is the primary author of the books *Configuring NetScreen Firewalls* and *Configuring NetScreen and SSG Firewalls*, both published by Syngress. He is also a contributing author of *Security Interviews Exposed and the Best Damn Firewall Book Period*, Second Edition (also published by Syngress).

Brad Woodberg (JNCIE-M #356, JNCIS-FWV, JNCIS-SSL, JNCIA-IDP, JNCIA-EX, JNCIA-UAC, CCNP R&S) holds a bachelor's degree in computer engineering from Michigan State University and is a technical marketing engineer for Juniper Networks' High-End Security Systems organization. Before joining Juniper Networks, he spent four and a half years working at a Juniper reseller where he designed, deployed, supported, and managed computer networks worldwide with equipment from a variety of vendors. In addition to being an author of this book, he is a coauthor of *Juniper Networks NetScreen* and *SSG Firewalls and Juniper Networks Secure SSL VPN*, both published by Syngress.

Patricio Giecco holds a bachelor's degree in electrical engineering from the Instituto Tecnologico de Buenos Aires and is currently pursuing a master's degree in electrical engineering at UCLA. In his tenure at Juniper he has worked as a solutions engineer designing best-practice security solutions, and he is currently working as a technical marketing engineer for the Branch Solutions Business Unit. With more than 10 years of networking consulting experience working for both vendors and service providers in Latin America, Europe, Asia, and North America, he specializes in network security architecture, routing, and high availability.

Tim Eberhard is a member of the Tier III Ops/Engineering team for the 4G wireless network at Clearwire. Previously, he was a team lead and subject matter expert at Sprint, supporting Sprint's wireless data network for more than five years. He is CCSP, C|EH, JNCIS-FWV, JNCIS-ER, and JNCIS-M certified. He has written two open source software tools utilized by engineers around the world for supporting production networks: the NSSA firewall session analyzer and the TPCAT packet capture analyzer.

James Quinn (JNCIE-M #117, JNCIE-ER #40, CCIE #8919) is a consulting systems engineer for the Strategic Alliances team at Juniper Networks, where he has worked for more than five years. Most recently he was a technical marketing engineer specialist in mobile security for Juniper's High-End Security Systems organization, and before that he represented Juniper's Advanced Services team for several years as the senior resident engineer stationed at one of the largest wireless carriers in the world. Before Juniper, he was a happily itinerant network geek spending years as a senior engineer for a large public university system. Today he travels the world making friends, speaking, teaching, learning everything he can along the way, and helping brilliant people build some of the magic stuff that is our networking future. His specialties are mobility, security, and, when he gets his druthers, dreaming up all manner of networking wizardry.

Colophon

The animal on the cover of *Junos Security* is a European night heron. This is a local name for the black-crowned night heron (*Nycticorax nycticorax*), which is found on every continent except Australia and Antarctica. The scientific name means "night raven," an apt label for this noisy nocturnal bird. (The black-crowned night heron is also nicknamed "quark," an imitation of the sound of its call.)

These medium-size herons have distinctive black crowns and backs and gray or white bodies. Their necks are short and their bodies stocky. They have red eyes and black bills. Their relatively short legs are usually yellow, but the legs of both sexes turn pink once they form a pair during breeding season.

Black-crowned night herons breed in wetlands, forming nesting colonies in trees or on the ground. These colonies are usually fairly small, but they can include as many as several thousand families. Up to 30 pairs of herons may nest in a single tree. These herons may also form multispecies colonies with other herons or ibis. A clutch consists of three to eight pale blue or green eggs. Black-crowned night herons do not recognize their own chicks and will brood young from other nests.

Black-crowned night herons are crepuscular (active at dawn and dusk) and nocturnal (active at night). They are opportunistic feeders, and they will eat prey as varied as fish, frogs, snakes, lizards, dragonflies, mollusks, small rodents, bats, leeches, and eggs and chicks of other birds. They may vibrate their bills in the water to lure swimming prey. They can be highly disruptive to commercial fish hatcheries, and they may be considered a pest if they nest near humans.

The cover image is from *Johnson's Natural History, Vol. II*. The cover font is Adobe ITC Garamond. The text font is Linotype Birka; the heading font is Adobe Myriad Condensed; and the code font is LucasFont's TheSansMonoCondensed.

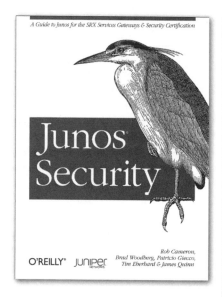